Criminal Justice

Fourth Edition

Jay S. Albanese

Virginia Commonwealth University

PEARSON

Boston New York San Francisco
Mexico City Montreal Toronto London Madrid Munich Paris
Hong Kong Singapore Tokyo Cape Town Sydney

Senior Editor: Dave Repetto
Editorial Assistant: Jack Cashman
Senior Marketing Manager: Kelly May
Production Supervisor: Beth Houston
Photo Research: Kate Cebik
Editorial-Production Service and Electronic Composition: Elm Street Publishing Services, Inc.
Composition/Prepress Buyer: Linda Cox
Manufacturing Buyer: Debbie Rossi
Cover Administrator: Kristina Mose-Libon
Text Design: Glenna Collett

For related titles and support materials, visit our online catalog at www.ablongman.com.

Library of Congress Cataloging-in-Publication Data

Albanese, Jay S.
Criminal justice / Jay S. Albanese.—4th ed.
p. cm.
ISBN 978-0-205-49909-0
1. Crime—United States. 2. Crime—Government policy—United States. 3. Criminal justice, Administration of—United States. I. Title.

HV6789.A366 2008
364.973—dc22 2007016498

ISBN-13: 978-0-205-49909-0
ISBN-10: 0-205-49909-0

Printed in the United States of America
10 9 8 7 6 5 4 3 2 1—RRD-OH—11 10 09 08 07

Photo Credits are found on pages 582–583, which constitutes a continuation of the copyright page.

Dedicated to my Godchildren
who understand that a life of meaning
is made of many little-noticed acts of justice
rather than a few grand deeds

Bridget Anne Lonergan
Jeffrey Samuel Albanese
Kaitlin Mary Lonergan
Ethan Mather Carpenter
Gracie Rae Hunkler

Contents

4 Perpetrators and Victims of Crime 78

5 Criminal Law 97

6 The Criminal Justice System 128

7 Criminal Procedure and the Police 151

8 Origins and Organization of Law Enforcement 178

9 Issues in Law Enforcement and Police Behavior 218

13 Origins and Organization of Jails and Prisons 356

14 Probation and Community Corrections 390

15 Justice and Punishment in the Twenty-First Century 426

18 Comparative Criminal Justice 518

Features

MEDIA AND CRIMINAL JUSTICE

THAT'S A FACT: PERSPECTIVES ON . . .

CRITICAL THINKING EXERCISES

Preface

Crime and justice are compelling subjects. The themes of good and bad behavior, right and wrong, and justice and injustice are timeless. The facts surrounding these issues are often clouded by fiction, emotion, and rare events. Only through systematic examination of these issues can we properly gauge our fear, know which precautionary measures should be taken, and determine whether or not we should support various new laws or policies.

Criminal Justice, Fourth Edition, examines the themes of crime and justice to reveal their significant history, current facts and modern trends, tracing them from the past to the present and into the future. The phrase "criminal justice" refers to the operation and management of police, courts, and corrections agencies. The decision to punish certain behaviors as crimes, the arrest decision, charging decision, jury decision, and sentencing decision are a few of the far-reaching decisions made many times each day in criminal justice. The balance to be struck among public safety, concern for victims, and the protection of the accused is fundamental and is reflected throughout this book.

Surveys have reported for many years that the fear of crime is steadily increasing, especially among the poor and disenfranchised, who often lack the ability to change the nature and condition of their communities. There is also evidence that this fear reduces the mobility of citizens, affects their social interactions (through increased fear of strangers), hurts the commercial sector (especially nighttime shopping), and generally affects the quality of life by which we judge our leaders, our communities, and our country.

This fear is intensified when reports of new crimes, new criminals, police problems, plea bargaining, overcrowded courts, and ineffective prisons leave the individual citizen with the feeling that little is being done to improve existing conditions, and that life is becoming more dangerous. The consequences of these feelings include declining participation in the political process (by continuing drops in the percentage of eligible citizens who vote). People also react unexpectedly, and sometimes violently, to additional stresses placed upon them (as evidenced by sporadic incidents of workplace violence and road rage).

In the pages that follow, the issues of crime and justice that affect us all are clearly presented so that readers, through greater understanding of these problems that have such far-reaching personal and social consequences, will be better able to participate in informed strategies for their amelioration.

Organization of the Book

Perhaps the best feature of this book is that it is written like a book rather than an encyclopedia. The chapters read as a narrative rather than an encyclopedia of facts too numerous for readers to learn, prioritize, or connect. An emphasis is placed on fitting concepts and the criminal justice system together rather than cramming as many facts as possible onto each page. This is extremely important for students taking what is likely their first course in criminal justice. This book is written so students are able to read with understanding and not be lost in an avalanche of facts and figures that serve to confuse rather than inform.

The topics are arranged logically beginning with a comparison of the fear of crime with other dangerous life events in Chapter 1. It explains the influence of media and politics on the fear of crime. Chapter 2 defines crime and its causes and correlates, placing it in historical and political context. This is followed in Chapter 3 with a discussion of the differences among the various types of violent and property crimes, and how measuring crime accurately is more difficult than it might appear. Chapter 4 describes the backgrounds of offenders and victims and the basis for crime profiling. The similarities among these crimes are presented as well as a typology to understand them more clearly. Chapter 5 explains the scope of the criminal law in how we define crime in precise terms, determine liability, and excuse conduct under certain circumstances. Chapter 6 provides an overview of the criminal justice system and criminal procedure, showing in exact terms how an individual case proceeds from arrest through disposition.

Chapters 7, 8, and 9 address the history and organization of law enforcement, together with how police discretion is exercised and the legal limits on police conduct. Police are the gatekeepers of the criminal justice system; thus, an understanding of police is central to the study of criminal justice. Chapter 10 explains how courts are organized in the United States and how they operate in practice. Innovations in dispute resolution are described. Chapter 11 offers a discussion of prosecutors and their role in criminal justice, plea bargaining, and the conflicting pressures placed on the prosecution. The role of defense counsel in criminal cases is also examined, including the important issue of the competing interests between seeking the truth versus winning criminal cases. Chapter 12 explains trials, judges, and sentencing and how the history and philosophy of sentencing has changed over the years. Chapter 13 discusses prisons and their role and purpose in dealing with offenders, including trends in prison populations. Chapter 14 introduces the reader to the concept of authentic versus restorative justice and discusses how alternatives to prison often can serve the dual purposes of deterrence and rehabilitation. Chapter 15 provides a look at innovations in justice and punishment for the 21st century. Chapter 16 explains fundamentals and trends in juvenile crime and justice. Chapter 17 offers a unique look at the sophisticated crimes, including white-collar crime, computer crime, organized crime, and terrorism, and Chapter 18 compares crimes and justice in different nations.

Features of the Book and Changes in the Fourth Edition

There are several important features in this book; each adds to the book's usefulness as a source of information and as a tool for teaching and learning. The

Fourth Edition continues the tradition of the popular Albanese hallmarks and incorporates exciting additions and new content.

- **Critical Thinking Exercises** are included in each chapter. These exercises describe an interesting issue; relate some facts, history, and research about it; and then ask the reader two or three questions that encourage them to *think* about alternatives, rather than merely *recall* facts. The **Critical Thinking Exercises** force readers to think about issues of concern and come up with thoughtful responses rather than rehearsed answers. Examples of critical thinking topics included in the book are binge drinking, carjacking, school shootings, chain gangs, campus law enforcement, violence in entertainment, juries for juveniles, and many other topics.

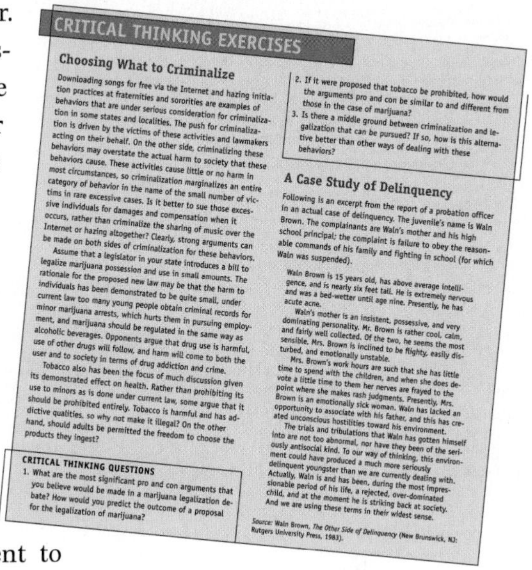

CRITICAL THINKING EXERCISES

Choosing What to Criminalize

Downloading songs for free via the Internet and hazing initiation practices at fraternities and sororities are examples of behaviors that are under serious consideration for criminalization in some states and localities. The push for criminalization is driven by the victims of these activities and lawmakers acting on their behalf. On the other side, criminalizing these behaviors may overstate the actual harm to society that these behaviors cause. These activities cause little or no harm in most circumstances, so criminalization marginalizes an entire category of behavior in the name of the small number of victims in rare excessive cases. Is it better to sue those excessive individuals for damages and compensation when it occurs, rather than criminalize the sharing of music over the Internet or hazing altogether? Clearly, strong arguments can be made on both sides of criminalization for these behaviors.

Assume that a legislator in your state introduces a bill to legalize marijuana possession and use in small amounts. The rationale for the proposed new law may be that the harm to individuals has been demonstrated to be quite small, under current law too many young people obtain criminal records for minor marijuana arrests, which hurts them in pursuing employment, and marijuana should be regulated in the same way as alcoholic beverages. Opponents argue that drug use is harmful, use of other drugs will follow, and harm will come to both the user and to society in terms of drug addiction and crime.

Tobacco also has been the focus of much discussion given its demonstrated effect on health. Rather than prohibiting its use to minors as is done under current law, some argue that it should be prohibited entirely. Tobacco is harmful and has addictive qualities, so why not make it illegal? On the other hand, should adults be permitted the freedom to choose the products they ingest?

CRITICAL THINKING QUESTIONS

1. What are the most significant pro and con arguments that you believe would be made in a marijuana legalization debate? How would you predict the outcome of a proposal for the legalization of marijuana?
2. If it were proposed that tobacco be prohibited, how would the arguments pro and con be similar to and different from those in the case of marijuana?
3. Is there a middle ground between criminalization and legalization that can be pursued? If so, how is this alternative better than other ways of dealing with these behaviors?

A Case Study of Delinquency

Following is an excerpt from the report of a probation officer in an actual case of delinquency. The juvenile's name is Waln Brown. The complainants are Waln's mother and his high school principal; the complaint is failure to obey the reasonable commands of his family and fighting in school (for which Waln was suspended).

Waln Brown is 15 years old, has above average intelligence, and is nearly six feet tall. He is extremely nervous and was a bed-wetter until age nine. Presently, he has acute acne.

Waln's mother is an insistent, possessive, and very dominating personality. Mr. Brown is rather cool, calm, and fairly well collected. Of the two, he seems the most sensible. Mrs. Brown is inclined to be flighty, easily disturbed, and emotionally unstable.

Mrs. Brown's work hours are such that she has little time to spend with the children, and when she does devote a little time to them her nerves are frayed to the point where she makes rash judgments. Presently, Mrs. Brown is an emotionally sick woman. Waln has lacked an opportunity to associate with his father, and this has created unconscious hostilities toward his environment.

The trials and tribulations that Waln has gotten himself into are not too abnormal, nor have they been of the seriously antisocial kind. To our way of thinking, this environment could have produced a much more seriously delinquent youngster than we are currently dealing with. Actually, Waln is and has been, during the most impressionable period of his life, a rejected, over-dominated child, and at the moment he is striking back at society. And we are using these terms in their widest sense.

Source: Waln Brown, *The Other Side of Delinquency* (New Brunswick, NJ: Rutgers University Press, 1983).

- Each chapter has an illustrated **Media and Criminal Justice** feature that highlights examples from film, television, and popular culture that deal with criminal justice issues. Each media feature is followed by questions that require the student to respond thoughtfully rather than give a pre-scripted response. Films in the media feature include both contemporary and classic portrayals of fundamental issues of crime and justice. The Fourth Edition includes some new and revised **Media and Criminal Justice** boxes, such as "Seeking Justice on TV," "Superheroes and Crime Prevention," "Police and Terrorists in Film," "*The Matrix* Made Me Do It," and "Hotel Rwanda."

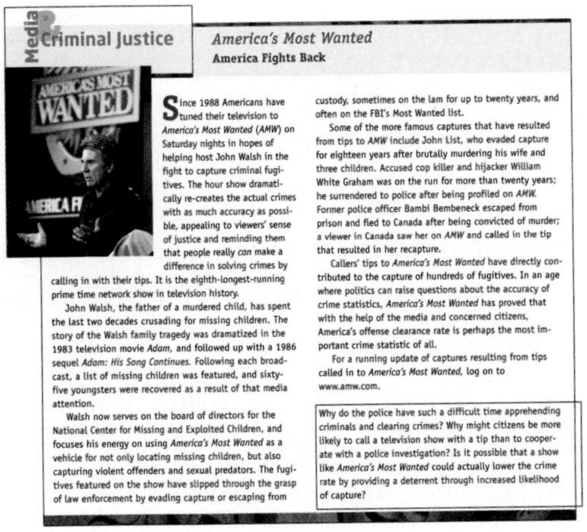

Media & Criminal Justice

America's Most Wanted
America Fights Back

Since 1988 Americans have tuned their television to *America's Most Wanted (AMW)* on Saturday nights in hopes of helping host John Walsh in the fight to capture criminal fugitives. The hour show dramatically re-creates the actual crimes with as much accuracy as possible, appealing to viewers' sense of justice and reminding them that people really *can* make a difference in solving crimes by calling in with their tips. It is the eighth-longest-running prime time network show in television history.

John Walsh, the father of a murdered child, has spent the last two decades crusading for missing children. The story of the Walsh family tragedy was dramatized in the 1983 television movie *Adam*, and followed up with a 1986 sequel *Adam: His Song Continues*. Following each broadcast, a list of missing children was featured, and sixty-five youngsters were recovered as a result of that media attention.

Walsh now serves on the board of directors for the National Center for Missing and Exploited Children, and focuses his energy on using *America's Most Wanted* as a vehicle for not only locating missing children, but also capturing violent offenders and sexual predators. The fugitives featured on the show have slipped through the grasp of law enforcement by evading capture or escaping from custody, sometimes on the lam for up to twenty years, and often on the FBI's Most Wanted list.

Some of the more famous captures that have resulted from tips to *AMW* include John List, who evaded capture for eighteen years after brutally murdering his wife and three children. Accused cop killer and hijacker William White Graham was on the run for more than twenty years; he surrendered to police after being profiled on *AMW*. Former police officer Bambi Bembeneck escaped from prison and fled to Canada after being convicted of murder; a viewer in Canada saw her on *AMW* and called in the tip that resulted in her recapture.

Callers' tips to *America's Most Wanted* have directly contributed to the capture of hundreds of fugitives. In an age where politics can raise questions about the accuracy of crime statistics, *America's Most Wanted* has proved that with the help of the media and concerned citizens, America's offense clearance rate is perhaps the most important crime statistic of all.

For a running update of captures resulting from tips called in to *America's Most Wanted*, log on to www.amw.com.

Why do the police have such a difficult time apprehending criminals and clearing crimes? Why might citizens be more likely to call a television show with a tip than to cooperate with a police investigation? Is it possible that a show like *America's Most Wanted* could actually lower the crime rate by providing a deterrent through increased likelihood of capture?

- This is the only book of its kind with **a separate chapter on political and economic crimes**. It addresses the growth of white-collar crime, organized crime, computer crimes, and terrorism, expanding the scope of criminal justice books from traditional street crimes. As technology advances and the economy changes to reflect that technology, these sophisticated crimes will continue to grow in number and in the severity of outcomes.

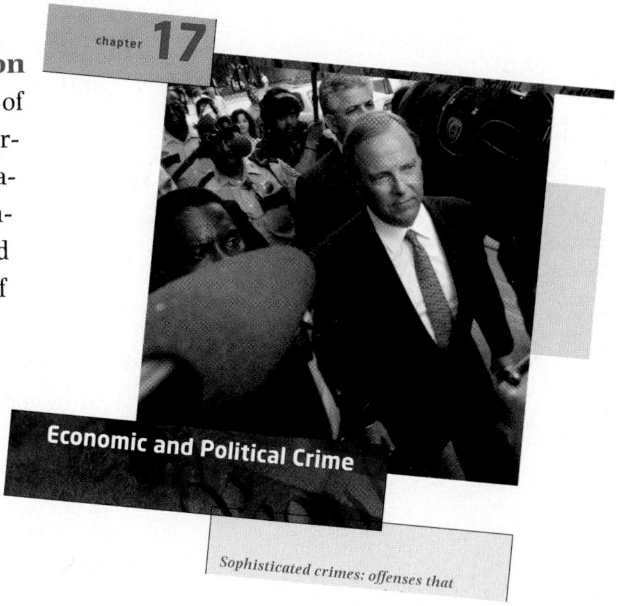

- A special boxed feature, **That's a Fact**, presents a series of charts and graphs for more in-depth study of a key chapter topic. In these concise, thought-provoking, and interactive exercises, students answer critical thinking questions on the basis of these statistical case studies. **That's a Fact** features new and updated in the Fourth Edition include "A New Role

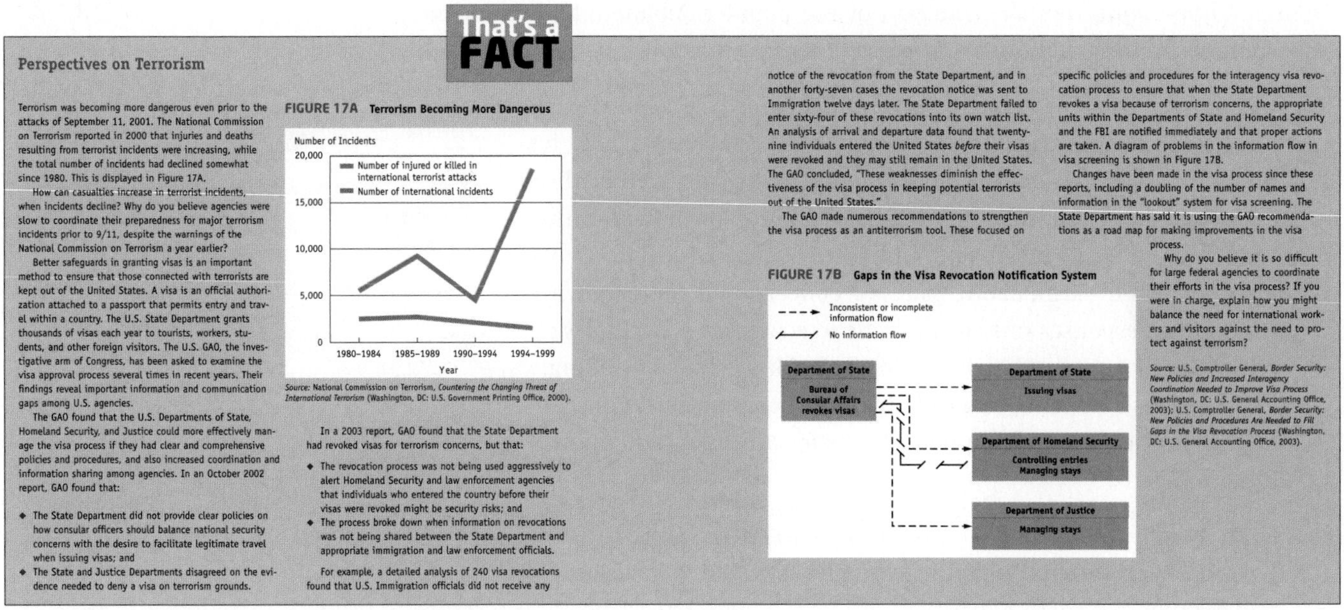
That's a FACT

Perspectives on Terrorism

Terrorism was becoming more dangerous even prior to the attacks of September 11, 2001. The National Commission on Terrorism reported in 2000 that injuries and deaths resulting from terrorist incidents were increasing, while the total number of incidents had declined somewhat since 1980. This is displayed in Figure 17A.

How can casualties increase in terrorist incidents, when incidents decline? Why do you believe agencies were slow to coordinate their preparedness for major terrorism incidents prior to 9/11, despite the warnings of the National Commission on Terrorism a year earlier?

Better safeguards in granting visas is an important method to ensure that those connected with terrorists are kept out of the United States. A visa is an official authorization attached to a passport that permits entry and travel within a country. The U.S. State Department grants thousands of visas each year to tourists, workers, students, and other foreign visitors. The U.S. GAO, the investigative arm of Congress, has been asked to examine the visa approval process several times in recent years. Their findings reveal important information and communication gaps among U.S. agencies.

The GAO found that the U.S. Departments of State, Homeland Security, and Justice could more effectively manage the visa process if they had clear and comprehensive policies and procedures, and also increased coordination and information sharing among agencies. In an October 2002 report, GAO found that:

- The State Department did not provide clear policies on how consular officers should balance national security concerns with the desire to facilitate legitimate travel when issuing visas; and
- The State and Justice Departments disagreed on the evidence needed to deny a visa on terrorism grounds.

FIGURE 17A Terrorism Becoming More Dangerous

Source: National Commission on Terrorism, *Countering the Changing Threat of International Terrorism* (Washington, DC: U.S. Government Printing Office, 2000).

In a 2003 report, GAO found that the State Department had revoked visas for terrorism concerns, but that:

- The revocation process was not being used aggressively to alert Homeland Security and law enforcement agencies that individuals who entered the country before their visas were revoked might be security risks; and
- The process broke down when information on revocations was not being shared between the State Department and appropriate immigration and law enforcement officials.

For example, a detailed analysis of 240 visa revocations found that U.S. Immigration officials did not receive any notice of the revocation from the State Department, and in another forty-seven cases the revocation notice was sent to Immigration twelve days later. The State Department failed to enter sixty-four of these revocations into its own watch list. An analysis of arrival and departure data found that twenty-nine individuals entered the United States *before* their visas were revoked and they may still remain in the United States. The GAO concluded, "These weaknesses diminish the effectiveness of the visa process in keeping potential terrorists out of the United States."

The GAO made numerous recommendations to strengthen the visa process as an antiterrorism tool. These focused on specific policies and procedures for the interagency visa revocation process to ensure that when the State Department revokes a visa because of terrorism concerns, the appropriate units within the Departments of State and Homeland Security and the FBI are notified immediately and that proper actions are taken. A diagram of problems in the information flow in visa screening is shown in Figure 17B.

Changes have been made in the visa process since these reports, including a doubling of the number of names and information in the "lookout" system for visa screening. The State Department has said it is using the GAO recommendations as a road map for making improvements in the visa process.

Why do you believe it is so difficult for large federal agencies to coordinate their efforts in the visa process? If you were in charge, explain how you might balance the need for international workers and visitors against the need to protect against terrorism?

FIGURE 17B Gaps in the Visa Revocation Notification System

Source: U.S. Comptroller General, *Border Security: New Policies and Increased Interagency Coordination Needed to Improve Visa Process* (Washington, DC: U.S. General Accounting Office, 2003); U.S. Comptroller General, *Border Security: New Policies and Procedures Are Needed to Fill Gaps in the Visa Revocation Process* (Washington, DC: U.S. General Accounting Office, 2003).

for Police: Intelligence Gathering," "Police Agencies You Haven't Heard About," "Perspectives on Profiling," and "Juvenile Backgrounds and Crime," among others.

- Classic cases in each chapter-opener grab students' interest at the outset and ask readers to think critically about real-life situations from a variety of points of view.
- Photo captions are specially designed to stimulate learning directly by asking questions. Specific application questions ask students to relate the content of each image to chapter concepts and information.
- An additional pedagogical element, topical headings, helps students learn the chapter material. These topical headings in the margins of each page guide student reading and aid in chapter study and review.
- Dozens of new tables and figures clearly show the latest crime statistics and trends.

The Fourth Edition features new content in the following areas:

- Substantial coverage of criminal justice responses to terrorism and the Patriot Act, and their repercussions (Chs. 4, 8, 9, 17, 18).
- Coverage of technology-related crimes, such as crimes facilitated by computer, crimes occurring on the Internet, and identity theft and fraud, America's number one growing crime. This coverage provides the most current examples of how the criminal justice system must continually evolve in response to society (Chs. 15, 16, 17).
- Coverage of the issues surrounding DNA evidence, the overturning of erroneous convictions, and inmates who are exonerated due to DNA evidence (Chs. 8, 12).

- New information on the changing victimization rates of women and the shift in domestic violence and human trafficking (Chs. 3, 9, 13, 18).
- Dozens of new tables and figures clearly show the latest crime statistics and trends (every chapter).
- Important cases from the headlines in each chapter-opener grab students' interest at the outset and ask readers to think critically about real-life situations from a variety of points of view (every chapter).
- **That's a Fact** features in every chapter are updated and even more concise, more interactive, and thought-provoking, displaying data and information in understandable ways (every chapter).
- The **Media and Criminal Justice** feature in each chapter, a popular Albanese hallmark, has been updated with new examples from television, movies, and popular culture. (One in every chapter.)
- Two **critical thinking exercises** in each chapter (with accompanying questions) challenge students to apply current events to chapter themes.

Supplemental Materials

Instructor Resources

Criminal Justice, Fourth Edition, is accompanied by an expansive package of supplementary materials to facilitate teaching and learning. These materials include:

- INSTRUCTOR'S MANUAL AND TEST BANK Each chapter of this valuable teaching tool includes a chapter summary, annotated chapter outline, learning objectives, key terms, class discussion questions, guest speaker suggestions, projects, and sample test questions. More than 1,000 test questions are included.
- COMPUTERIZED TEST BANK A computerized version of the printed Test Bank is available with our testing system, Pearson MyTest, a powerful assessment generation program that helps instructors easily create and print quizzes and exams. Questions and tests can be authored online, and exported to PDF and MS Word files, allowing instructors ultimate flexibility and the ability to efficiently manage assessments anytime, anywhere!
- POWERPOINT LECTURE PRESENTATIONS This complete set of chapter-by-chapter lecture presentations contains approximately 20 slides per chapter specific to Albanese, *Criminal Justice,* Fourth Edition. The slides reinforce the main ideas of each chapter. Available online at **www.ablongman.com/suppcentral**.
- ALLYN AND BACON VIDEO LIBRARY FOR CRIMINAL JUSTICE Qualified adopters may select from a wide variety of high quality videos from sources such as Films for the Humanities and Sciences. Contact your publisher's representative for more information.

- THE BLOCKBUSTER APPROACH: A GUIDE TO TEACHING CRIMINAL JUSTICE WITH VIDEO, SECOND EDITION This manual lists and describes hundreds of commercially available videos, and shows how they can be incorporated in the classroom. The videos are organized by topic and presented in an order common to most introductory textbooks. A fun and unique supplement for instructors!

Student Resources

- ***MyCrimeLab*—where students dig into criminal justice!**

  Discover *MyCrimeLab,* Allyn & Bacon's new interactive online teaching and learning system. *MyCrimeLab* uses powerful multimedia and technology resources to bring criminal justice to life, making teaching and learning more productive, more satisfying, more exciting! *MyCrimeLab* is easy to use—and at no extra cost with your Allyn & Bacon textbook! *MyCrimeLab* helps students succeed through . . .

  Contextual Learning Icons placed throughout the E-book let students launch multimedia resources—such as an audio glossary, video clips, an Interactive Terrorism TimeLine, PowerPoint™ slides, and activities—right from where the topic is discussed in the text.

  Interactive Learning Material from outside sources, including illustrations and synopses of popular movies, reinforces and expands upon concepts introduced in the text. Students are also able to get the inside details from experts in the field, including police officers, prosecutors, probation officers, and other practitioners, as they analyze the facts and figures of the criminal justice system.

  An Individualized Study Plan *MyCrimeLab* compiles results from structured test and quiz opportunities in each chapter to generate an individual study plan for each student, showing exactly which topics he or she needs to review.

  Research Navigator™ Pearson Education's exclusive database of reliable source material, including the EBSCO Academic Journal and Abstract Database and *The New York Times* Search by Subject Archive, helps students quickly and efficiently make the most of their research time. *Research Navigator*™—**a $15 value**—is FREE to your students with *MyCrimeLab.* Visit **www.researchnavigator.com** to learn more.

MyCrimeLab is a one-stop, time-saving resource for instructors. Designed to accommodate a range of instructor needs, *MyCrimeLab* can be used to enhance a traditional course or as a complete online course solution—the choice is yours. Text content is conveniently pre-loaded, and you can easily find abundant options to customize *MyCrimeLab* to your course needs. For professors, access to the secure Instructor's area is fast and simple. With the click of a mouse, you'll find PowerPoint™ lectures, lecture outlines, test item files, a grade book, and more!

Visit **www.mycrimelab.com** today and discover a powerful new destination for student success!

- RESEARCH NAVIGATOR: CRIMINAL JUSTICE This handy reference guide contains a relevant discussion of Internet basics written for students in language to which they can relate. It includes criminal justice Internet activities; a section on critical evaluation of Internet sources; proper electronic documentation guidelines for both MLA and APA styles; and a multitude of criminal justice–specific URLs. Access to the ContentSelect Research Database of thousands of academic journals and periodic articles is also included within this guide. Visit **www.researchnavigator.com** for more information.
- THEMES OF THE *TIMES* FOR INTRODUCTORY CRIMINAL JUSTICE Thirty current articles from *The New York Times* have been selected for their relevance to topics covered in the introductory criminal justice course and are brought together in this newspaper-like print supplement. Available free in a value package with the text.
- CAREERS IN CRIMINAL JUSTICE, SECOND EDITION This supplement goes beyond the academic career path of the criminal justice major and explores careers in criminology and criminal justice, showing how people entered the field, and how a degree in criminal justice can be preparation for careers in a wide variety of areas.

Acknowledgments

This book is much more than a collection of several hundred thousand words. It took a significant portion of my life to gather the personal and social experience and knowledge that resulted in this manuscript. It began while a senior undergraduate at Niagara University when my sociology professor, Nicholas Caggiano, mentioned in class that Rutgers University was opening a new School of Criminal Justice. I applied there and was admitted to the only graduate school to which I applied. To this day, I do not believe I would have heard about Rutgers if I had cut that class.

After finishing my master's degree at Rutgers and working as a criminal justice planner for a year, I considered attending law school. An emergency appendectomy the night before the law school admission test sidetracked those plans. Instead, I received a call from Don Gottfredson at Rutgers a few weeks later, inviting me to apply to their newly established doctoral program at the School of Criminal Justice. I entered the Ph.D. program that fall. I am indebted to Rutgers for starting the School of Criminal Justice when it did and also for supporting my studies with assistantships and fellowships along the way. I made a number of lifelong friends with faculty and students there. I finished the Ph.D. in 1981, having obtained a variety of work experiences in the process. These experiences included research, consulting, and a great deal of teaching. The opportunity to teach enabled me to discover I enjoyed interacting with students, and that I had a knack for explaining ideas clearly.

I returned to Niagara University in the fall of 1981 and taught there for fifteen years. During that time I had the opportunity to revise the undergraduate curriculum in criminal justice, write the curriculum for a master's program, and teach most of the criminal justice courses at the University at one time or another. I have gained more knowledge through teaching than through any other activity because good teaching requires preparation. The lack of many good books in the field, especially during the early years of my career, forced me to look to primary sources. This instilled an appreciation of the history and philosophy that underlies the field of criminal justice and that is reflected in this book. Teaching is a very important profession, and I am gratified to have the opportunity to do it for a living. I thank my students for providing the forum for me to do so.

I began research for the original manuscript of *Criminal Justice* while serving as president of the Academy of Criminal Justice Sciences and then moved to my current position at Virginia Commonwealth University. These undertakings slowed my progress on this book somewhat, but they made it more interesting in light of a series of major events in criminal justice that have occurred in recent years, including major acts of domestic terrorism, dramatic growth in media coverage of criminal trials, and significant growth in international and sophisticated crimes.

Once again, I would like to thank the reviewers of the earliest drafts of the manuscript, as well as reviewers of the earlier editions. They include: Yaw Ackah, Delaware State University; James Albrecht, St. John's University; Leroy Black, California University of Pennsylvania; Shannon M. Barton, Ferris State University; Lloyd Klein, Macon State University; Eugene E. Bouley, Georgia College & State University; Richard De Lung, Wayland Baptist University; Christopher J. Drew, Montclair State University; Harold A. Frossard, Salt Lake Community College; Arnett Gaston, University of Alabama; Kimberly Greer, Minnesota State University–Mankato; Christopher A. Hertig, York College of Pennsylvania; William E. Kelly, Auburn University; Charles J. Kocher, Cumberland County College; Howard A. Kurtz, Oklahoma City University; Bernard H. Levin, Blue Ridge Community College; Stephen C. Light, SUNY–Plattsburgh; Catherine Montsinger, Johnson C. Smith University; Ted Paul McNeilsmith, Adams State College; Carol Pogue, Century College; Wayne D. Posner, East Los Angeles College; Jo Ann M. Scott, Ohio Northern University; Judith M. Sgarzi, Mount Ida College; Lizabeth A. Wiinamaki, Juniata College; DeVere D. Woods, Jr., Indiana State University; Anthony D. Woolf, Dixie State College of Utah. I would also like to thank those who reviewed the Second Edition and the Brief Edition for the purposes of the Third Edition. They include: Paul Becker, Morehead State University; Matt DeLisi, Iowa State University; David N. Falcone, Illinois State University; Alan Harland, Temple University; Ronald Holmes, University of Louisville; Stacey Nofziger, Kansas State University; Caryl Lynn Segal, University of Texas–Arlington; and Lynn L. Snowden, University of North Carolina–Wilmington. Their comments undoubtedly improved the quality of the final manuscript as did Casey Jordan's work on the media features.

My editors deserve recognition for their help in seeing this project through to publication. Karen Hanson, Editor-in-Chief, thought the idea for this book was a good one and I thank her for her tactful yet persistent attention to details and deadlines. Editor Dave Repetto deserves thanks for always welcoming new ideas and his faith in the project throughout the writing process, and Beth Houston cheerfully kept everything moving in the production process just as authors are prone to slow down. Kelly May did a wonderful job on the marketing plan for the book. The field representatives of Allyn & Bacon I have met have impressed me with their knowledge of both publishing and the field of criminal justice. I am indebted to them.

Like most families, mine wonders why projects like this take as long as they do to complete. Continual changes in the field of criminal justice, updates, and the production process prolonged completion, but the book is better for it. I thank my family for giving up asking me when it would be over. Character-building exploits such as teaching college students during the week, and playing bass in the church band on weekends, provided wonderful possibilities for constructive behavior by day, and welcome relief from the dark side of crime I wrote about at night. Without all these experiences this book would have been quite different and probably not as good.

Jay S. Albanese

About the Author

JAY S. ALBANESE is Professor of Government & Public Policy at Virginia Commonwealth University. He served as Chief of the International Center at the National Institute of Justice, the research arm of the U.S. Department of Justice, from 2002–2006. Jay received his M.A. and Ph.D. from the Rutgers University School of Criminal Justice, where he was the first Ph.D. graduate. Dr. Albanese is author of numerous articles and books that include *Professional Ethics in Criminal Justice: Being Ethical When No One Is Looking* (Allyn & Bacon, 2006), *Organized Crime in Our Times* (4th ed., Lexis/Nexis/Anderson, 2004), and editor of *Transnational Crime* (de Sitter, 2005) and *Combating Piracy: Intellectual Property Theft and Fraud* (Transaction, 2007). Dr. Albanese is recipient of the Elske Smith Distinguished Lecturer Award from Virginia Commonwealth University. He has served as Executive Director of the International Association for the Study of Organized Crime, and is a past president of both the White Collar Crime Research Consortium and the Academy of Criminal Justice Sciences (ACJS).

chapter 1

Perspectives on Criminal Justice

Risk, crime, and the evolution of the justice process: discovering how our fears are formed, what we define as crime, and how they form the foundation of criminal justice.

CHAPTER OUTLINE

LEARNING OBJECTIVES

- Evaluate impacts of mass media on people's perspectives on crime.
- Analyze impacts of political and ideological factors on public responses to crime.
- Evaluate consequences of the fear of crime in relation to risk of victimization.
- Characterize crime using a cross-cultural perspective.
- Identify ways that historical and political factors have shaped definitions of crime in the United States.
- Trace the evolution of due process and early developments in the American criminal justice system.

Three Birmingham, Alabama, college students were charged in a spree of rural church arson fires carried out "as a joke." In upstate New York, a thirteen-year-old girl was shot to death while walking with her father as he argued with another man and a car drove by, spraying them with bullets. In Florida, a teenager was sentenced to twenty-one years in prison for dropping a twenty-two pound piece of concrete from a highway overpass, killing a university professor in his car. In Virginia, a father was convicted of involuntary manslaughter for leaving his two-year-old child strapped in her car seat for seven hours in the stifling heat.[1]

In Michigan, a teenager was sentenced to prison for planning a Columbine-like massacre at his high school, based on threats made on the Internet and a search of his home, which uncovered a stash of weapons and various Nazi books.[2] Two teenagers killed husband-and-wife Dartmouth College professors at random in a robbery scheme to steal a lot of money and run off to Australia. They received life sentences.[3]

These random acts of violence and criminal omission are featured regularly in the news. Reports of homicides, thefts, robberies, and assault typically are lead stories on television and in newspapers. But are shocking incidents like these simply very rare tragedies, or are they typical? How do these media portrayals affect Americans' perceptions of crime?

A Gallup poll in 2006 found that three of the top seven concerns of Americans were related to crime: illegal aliens, political corruption, and terrorism. Regarding street crime, a Gallup survey foreshadowed recent increases in crime, as the poll indicated that the average American was already seeing signs of increasing crime in his or her local area before official statistics appeared. The 2006 survey results showed higher concern about crime than at any point in the last decade.[4]

How concerned about crime *should* we be?

Perspectives on Crime

Media Perspectives on Crime

media portrayals
Public perceptions of crime and its victims are based largely on media images, which focus on atypical sensational incidents.

CRIME TV

Much of what we know about crime is shaped by atypical sensational incidents, because our perceptions of crime and its victims are based largely on **media portrayals.** Most of us lack personal experience with serious crime. Serious crime is relatively rare (as described more fully in Chapter 3), so most people's experience with crime is largely petty thefts and burglary. These experiences do not produce the fear and anxiety that hate crimes, murders, rapes, or other serious crimes create. News reporting has become a round-the-clock enterprise with the advent of CNN, Court TV, and other outlets for crime-related news, as well as Internet news carriers of many kinds. There is competition for viewers, listeners, and readers among these sources, so media outlets tend to spotlight extreme and dramatic cases in order to generate public interest. A study of the contents of crime stories and news production concluded that the focus on sensational incidents has a cyclical effect, that is, "the public is more likely to think they are representative because of the emphasis by the media."[5] These perceptions are reinforced further because people are more likely to recall these sensational incidents when thinking about crime. The result is a sometimes oversensitized public preoccupied with crime and fear of crime. For example, a **Gallup poll on crime** shows how a single event shapes public perceptions. Almost no Americans mentioned terrorism as the nation's most important problem prior to the September 11, 2001, terrorist attacks, but in a Gallup poll the next month, 46 percent of Americans said terrorism was the top problem in America.[6] A similar effect occurs in the case of domestic crimes. As previously mentioned, the 2006 Gallup Poll revealed that Americans' concerns about the crime rate in the United States was at its highest point since the mid-1990s, with 67 percent believing there was more crime in the country—up from 2004, when just 53 percent shared this point of view.[7]

Gallup poll on crime
Survey of a representative sample of the American public which found that crime surpassed education and economic issues as the most pressing local problem.

The adage "if it bleeds, it leads," is well known in television news. The stories featured on network news have been shown to disproportionately focus on violent crimes, something that is attributed to competition for viewers and the public's interest in crime news.[8] This exposure to violent crimes through the news results in public demands for solutions. **Criminologists** Alida Merlo and Peter Benekos believe the solutions sought are often shortsighted due to the shocking nature of the

criminologists
Those who study the causes of crime and the treatment of offenders.

How would you characterize media perspectives on crime? What factors might make those perspectives inaccurate or unfair? What is the Internet's impact on public perceptions of and reactions to crime?

incidents: “The presentation of these crimes and their seeming randomness in society heightens the public's sensitivity to the crime problem, reinforces emotional reactions, and encourages the ‘quick fix’ mentality regarding solutions.”[9]

The Political Perspective on Crime

THERE OUGHTA BE A LAW

When crime is portrayed in terms of dramatic incidents that heighten the public's desire to “fix” the problem, politicians are often quick to oblige. Politicians are elected officials who must appear responsive to the public's wishes, and media images of crime thus shape their actions as well. Individual cases of sensational crimes have led to the passage of laws that are sometimes sweeping in scope, but that are named after specific crime victims as described in Table 1.1. This phenomenon illustrates the relationship among the media's selection and reporting of crimes, public fear of crime, and how this is turned into political action.

Politicians often shape crime news to match their political ideology. For example, a drive-by shooting can alternately be portrayed as the product of drug-selling, idle youth who are disposed to violence, or as the result of poor or absent parental supervision, failure of the educational system, and inattention to effective drug treatment. There usually is some truth to both perspectives, but one side is usually highlighted, so that politicians can distinguish themselves from their political opponents. A quick fix usually involves the passing of a law, which costs nothing. If crime is portrayed as part of a larger social problem (e.g., drug use, educational failure, parental incompetence), solutions require major investments to change. This occurs much less frequently.

As concern about crime has risen dramatically, crime and “law and order” have become national political issues. The 1964 presidential election campaign

Table 1.1 Laws Named after Crime Victims

Amber's Law (Texas)	Enhanced penalties for repeat child sex offenders.
Jenna's Law (New York)	Proposed to end parole for all violent felons.
Joan's Law (New Jersey)	Imposes life-without-parole sentence for murder of a child under fourteen during a sexual assault.
Megan's Law (New Jersey)	Requires states to notify communities when a sex offender moves in.
Stephanie's Law (Kansas)	Allows for commitment of repeat sex offenders to mental hospitals if they are deemed too dangerous to release after prison term ends.

Source: Reprinted from *What's Wrong with the Criminal Justice System: Ideology, Politics, and the Media,* by Alida V. Merlo and Peter J. Benekos. Copyright 2000 Matthew Bender & Company, Inc., a member of the Lexis/Nexis Group. All rights reserved. Used with permission.

LAW AND ORDER

saw Republican Senator Barry Goldwater criticize the Kennedy–Johnson administration for its failure to deal with "crime in the streets."[10] Although Goldwater lost the election, President Lyndon Johnson recognized the public's sensitivity to the issue of "lawlessness." On July 23, 1965, Johnson established the President's Commission on Law Enforcement and Administration of Justice to "deepen our understanding of the causes of crime and how society should respond to the challenge of the present levels of crime."

In addition to the public interest in law and order aroused by Goldwater, other events during this period undoubtedly influenced Johnson's decision to form the Commission. In 1963, an informant, Joseph Valachi, testified in televised Senate hearings that there existed a nationwide criminal conspiracy called the Cosa Nostra, which was responsible for most of the illegal gambling, loan-sharking, and narcotics trade in the United States. In November 1963, President Kennedy was assassinated and the governor of Texas seriously wounded while riding in a motorcade in Dallas. Two days later the suspected assailant, Lee Harvey Oswald, was murdered before he could be brought to trial. In June 1964, the U.S. Supreme Court held in the case of *Escobedo v. Illinois* that crime suspects have the right to legal counsel during certain types of police interrogations. In 1966, the Court held that suspects in custody have the right to an attorney and to remain silent during questioning. These decisions led to widespread belief that the police were being "handcuffed" and could not carry out their duties effectively under such restrictions. All of these events, many of which occurred in the space of little more than two years, help explain the public's responsiveness to Goldwater's "lawlessness" theme and Johnson's willingness to act on the issue.

Megan's Law is named after seven-year-old Megan Kanka, a New Jersey girl who was raped and killed by a known child molester who had moved across the street from the family without their knowledge. How has this and similar tragedies affected the politics that shape the American criminal justice system?

The Commission was the first in a long line of national commissions formed to study various aspects of the crime problem. Table 1.2 presents a chronology of these investigations. Each of these commissions was formed in response to a specific issue or event for

Table 1.2 National Commissions, 1967–2005

1967	President's Commission on Law Enforcement and Administration of Justice
1968	National Advisory Commission on Civil Disorders
1969	National Advisory Commission on the Causes and Prevention of Violence
1970	President's Commission on Campus Unrest
1970	National Commission on Obscenity and Pornography
1972	U.S. Commission on Marijuana and Drug Abuse
1973	National Advisory Commission on Criminal Justice Standards and Goals
1974	U.S. Senate Watergate Report
1975	President's Commission on CIA Activities within the United States
1976	U.S. Senate Select Committee Report on Intelligence Activities
1979	U.S. House of Representatives Final Assassination Report
1982	President's Task Force on Victims of Crime
1986	Attorney General's Commission on Pornography
1987	President's Commission on Organized Crime
1998	National Commission on the Future of DNA Evidence
1999	National Gambling Impact Study Commission
2000	National Commission on Terrorism
2004	The National Commission on Terrorist Attacks Upon the United States

NATIONAL COMMISSIONS

which there was no easy answer. The Commission on Civil Disorders investigated the causes and response to urban riots and civil rights and anti–Vietnam War demonstrations. The other commissions investigated other major problems of crime and justice, including violence, assassinations, obscenity, pornography, drugs, political corruption, misconduct by the Federal Bureau of Investigation (FBI) and Central Intelligence Agency (CIA), and organized crime. A seemingly endless series of political scandals, such as the Iran–Contra affair and the savings and loan scandal, as well as hate crimes, serial and mass murders, acts of domestic terrorism, family violence, and so on, have occurred in recent decades. The underlying message the public receives from such events is that crime and lawlessness are rampant and that American society is being destroyed from within.

Presidential candidates continue to seize on crime and criminal justice issues to propose policy and to attack opponents. During the 2004 election, Senator John Kerry criticized the Bush administration for not handling the threat of terrorism properly, arguing that existing policies in Iraq and government surveillance in the United States have made Americans less safe. In rebuttal, President Bush said that under Kerry's leadership Saddam Hussein would still be in power and that Kerry would be too timid and indecisive to be effective in the war on terrorism. Sixteen years earlier, President Bush's father, President George H.W. Bush, made what is widely seen as the classic use of a single crime to effectively characterize his opponent. Bush used Willie Horton—a Massachusetts offender on furlough from prison—who had raped a woman and stabbed her fiancé—to argue

A protest against capital punishment illustrates how divided public views are often used in politics for proposals that vary dramatically from banning capital punishment, to appointing better qualified defense attorneys, to DNA tests for all death row inmates, to speedier executions of those convicted. What issues do the public feel more strongly about than issues of crime and justice?

against furloughs and parole and to show that his opponent, Massachusetts Governor Michael Dukakis, was "soft" on crime. The Willie Horton case was featured in campaign ads in an effort to suggest it was a typical case. Lost in this debate, however, was the fact that of the more than 76,000 furloughs granted to prisoners in Massachusetts during Dukakis' tenure, less than one-half of 1 percent of the offenders escaped.[11] Whether the crime issue is terrorism today or prison furloughs in 1988, crimes can be used in an effort to attack an opponent based on a single incident.

Crime and Other Life Events

When one compares the actual risk of being victimized by crime to the risk of experiencing other negative events, crime does not appear so rampant. For example, each year about 250 of every 1,000 adults in the United States are hurt in accidents—nearly a 1 in 4 chance of injury in any given year. The odds of being struck by lightning are 1 in 9,100; and those of dying from cancer are 2 in 1,000. These are all far higher than the risk of being victimized by crime. The top thirteen causes of death in the United States are presented in *That's a Fact* on page 8. As shown there, health problems and accidents are far more common causes of death than criminal homicide. A person is forty-five times more likely to die of a heart attack than to die as a homicide victim. Likewise, a person is thirty-seven times more likely to die from cancer and ten times more likely to die from a stroke than to die from homicide. In fact, you are twice as likely to die in a car accident as you are to die from homicide, and seven times more likely to die in any kind of accident than you are to be a homicide victim. When one views homicide in context, therefore, it is clear that other risks, especially poor health and accidents, pose a much greater threat to life.

That's a Fact presents the most common causes of death in the United States; the rankings of the various causes of death have shifted generally downward as public health has improved. Homicide deaths dropped 30 percent over the last decade, when the overall death rate from all causes dropped only slightly over the same period. Thus, the risk of homicide has decreased while concern about its incidence has remained high.

This risk is amplified when one realizes the relative lack of control an individual has over homicide compared with other leading causes of death. Decreases in rates of death from heart disease, cancer, pneumonia and flu, and liver disease are largely due to changes in the lifestyle, exercise habits, and diet of U.S. citizens over the last two decades. Through research findings and public education regarding the links between personal habits and bad health, many people have gained increased awareness and adopted healthier lifestyles. The same is true for accidental deaths. Seat-belt laws, child bicycle helmets and car seats, air bags, and greater regulation of dangerous devices have done much to reduce the rate of deaths caused by accidents. Each of us can exert a certain amount of influence over the causes of bad health and accidents by changing our behavior. In contrast, homicide is thrust upon us by others. It is also sudden and violent, distinguishing it from most other causes of death.

Effects of Fear

Forty years ago, a Gallup poll asked, "What do you think is the most important problem facing this country today?" Forty-six percent of respondents cited international problems (mostly relating to the Cold War); 35 percent cited racial problems; and 6 percent or fewer cited high cost of living, unemployment, or too much government control.[12] When asked the same question in 2006, respondents ranked the country's most pressing problems as the situation in the Middle East/Iraq war (25 percent), immigration/illegal aliens (10 percent), health care (9 percent), political corruption and failed leadership (9 percent), energy prices (9 percent), the economy in general (8 percent), terrorism (7 percent), and poverty and unemployment (4 percent each). The survey results show that Cold War fears have been replaced by concerns about violence in the Middle East, and that the focus on domestic race relations has been replaced with concern over illegal immigration, corruption, terrorism, and economic issues.

The public's general concerns about crime result in apprehension and fear. A Gallup poll found that close to half of Americans (49 percent) described the nation's crime problem as either "extremely" or "very" serious. The percentage perceiving more crime in the country than there was a year earlier increased from 53 percent in 2004 to 67 percent in 2005. And the percentage of Americans who worry about being the victim of crimes is correspondingly high. A significant proportion worry about having their car stolen or broken into, having their home burglarized, and being the victim of terrorism. The results of this poll are presented in *That's a Fact,* Table 1B.

Gallup has tracked the problems of local communities since 1959 and concluded that "crime and education are as high on the list today as ever," while other issues such as the economy and race relations have declined in importance.[13] Crime has been the number 1 or 2 local concern every time Gallup has conducted this poll.

Photos from street video cameras in a growing number of cities illustrate that fear of crime and victimization has outstripped privacy concerns in recent years. Do you think it is a good idea to have 24-hour video cameras linked from all public places to the police department in your town?

That's a **FACT**

Perspectives on Fear of Crime

Study Table 1A. How do the odds of being murdered compare to your chances of dying from heart disease? How do the odds of being murdered compare to your chances of dying in an accident?

How worrisome is crime to Americans? Table 1B shows high levels of concern about crime, especially for car theft, burglary, and terrorism. How might you explain this level of concern? How would you answer these questions?

Figure 1A shows trends in public perceptions of crime compared to what it was a year earlier. What is the reason for the spike upward in the fall of 2002? Why do you believe this level of concern has continued to the present?

Table 1C reports on a Gallup youth survey of teenagers and their problems. Of the eighteen problems identified, five are crime-related. Drugs have led this list since the question was first asked in 1977. Why do you think drug use remains a top-ranked problem of teenagers? What would you rank as the most important problem?

Table 1A Leading Causes of Death in the United States

Causes of Death	*Odds of Occurrence (per 100,000 population)*
1. Heart Disease	223
2. Cancer	187
3. Stroke	51
4. Lung Disease	42
5. All accidents	37
6. Diabetes mellitus	25
7. Alzheimer's disease	22
8. Pneumonia and flu	21
9. Kidney disease	15
10. Blood poisoning	11
11. Suicide	11
12. Liver disease	9
13. Hypertension	8
14. Parkinson's	6
15. Pneumonitis	6
16. Homicide	5

Source: Arialdi M. Minifio, Melonie P. Heron, and Betty L. Smith, "Deaths: Preliminary Data for 2004," *National Vital Statistics Reports,* vol. 54 (June 2006).

Table 1B Concern about Crime: Results of a Gallup Poll

Percentage Worry Frequently/Occasionally About Being a Victim of Each Crime (2005)	*Percent*
Your home being burglarized when you are not there	45
Having your car stolen or broken into	42
Being the victim of terrorism	38
Having a school-aged child physically harmed while attending school	29
Getting mugged	28
Your home being burglarized when you are there	24
Being attacked while driving your car	22
Being sexually assaulted	19
Being a victim of a hate crime	17
Getting murdered	15
Being assaulted/killed by a coworker/employee where you work	6

Source: Lydia Saad, "Public Grows More Pessimistic about U.S. Crime," *Gallup News Service* (October 20, 2005).

FIGURE 1A Crime in the United States versus a Year Ago

Source: Lydia Saad, "Public Grows More Pessimistic about U.S. Crime", *Gallup News Service* (October 20, 2005).

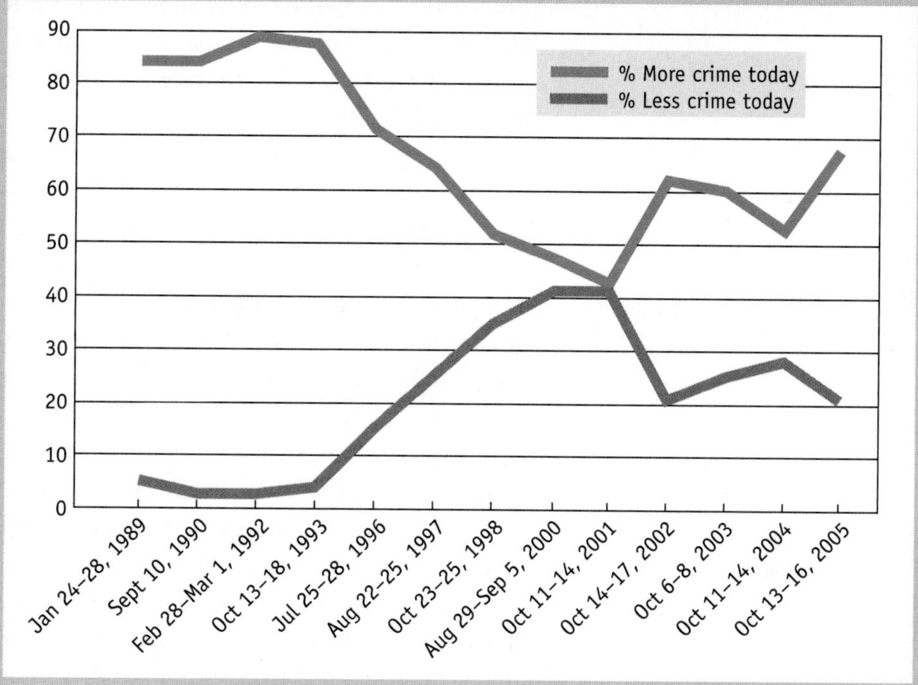

Table 1C The Most Important Problem Facing Teenagers Today

What do you think is the most important problem facing people your age today?	*Percent*
Drugs/smoking/alcohol	31
Peer pressure/fitting in/looks/popularity	17
Sexual issues (teen pregnancy/abortion/STDs)	14
Education	14
Ignorance/lacking of youth caring/getting involved	10
Career/employment/economy/money/future	10
Morals/attitude	8
Lack of respect/treatment from society	7
Violence/gangs	6
World politics	5
Parents	4
Negative effects of media on youth	3
War/draft/terrorism	3
Stress	2
People don't listen to us	2
Health/medical care/coverage	2
Social Security	2
Safety	1
Other	5
No opinion	2

Source: Joseph Carroll, "Drugs, Smoking, Alcohol Most Important Problem Facing Teens," *Gallup News Service* (February 16, 2006).

A high level of fear can produce undesirable changes in behavior as well. A survey undertaken by the Metropolitan Washington, D.C., Council of Governments in the 1960s reflects concerns that continue today in many cities: "65 percent of the city's largely white suburban residents visit the downtown area less than once a month, and 15 percent come downtown less than once a year." When citizens are afraid to go downtown, stores close, restaurants close, and the economy and quality of life suffer.

Fear can also turn otherwise law-abiding citizens into outlaws. Perhaps the definitive example of what high levels of fear can do is the case of Bernard Goetz. In 1984 Goetz, a thirty-seven-year-old white man, was riding on a New York City subway train when one of four boisterous black youths said to him, "How are ya?" Two of them approached Goetz, and one asked him for five dollars. Goetz asked him what he wanted, and he repeated, "Give me five dollars." Goetz proceeded to shoot at the youths five times, emptying his .38 revolver. He wounded each of the youths, paralyzing one of them.[14] The Goetz case illustrates what can happen when a citizen experiences high levels of fear over a prolonged period. Citizens arm themselves (sometimes illegally), focus on events that feed their fears, and sometimes act violently, convinced that they are acting in self-defense. Goetz was found guilty only of criminal possession of a weapon (his revolver), but it is clear that his actions pushed the rules of self-defense to their limit. Since the Goetz case, many states have passed laws making it easier for homeowners and battered spouses to employ force in self-defense, although the new rules apply to very few situations.[15]

The changes in behavior provoked by fear of victimization are not confined to individuals. Businesses also may alter their policies. For example, in an effort to prevent carjackings (in which criminals force their way into occupied vehicles, commandeering the car and sometimes robbing, assaulting, or killing the driver), car rental companies have removed their corporate logos and special license plates from rental cars in order to make it harder for car thieves and robbers to identify tourists. Some are warning their customers *not* to stop when bumped from behind or when told that something is wrong with their car.[16] Similarly, after a series of thefts and violent crimes occurred in South Florida in the wake of Hurricane Andrew, the level of fear and concern about crime led several Miami hotels to block local television news from TV sets in rooms to shield guests from "body-bag journalism."[17] Similarly, newspapers in New York were criticized for highlighting the most sensational details of the disappearance and murder of a college student in New York.

WORKPLACE CRIME

Even places that are usually considered safe, such as the workplace and the home, have been the scenes of serious violence in recent years. More than forty people were killed in post office shootings throughout the United States in the 1980s and 1990s.[18] Nearly 250,000 individuals are victims of violent crimes while at work each year.[19] And homes are not always safe havens. Susan Smith was convicted of murder in the killing of her two children in South Carolina. In Chicago a mother was sentenced to fifty-five years in prison for forcing her eleven-year-old daughter to have sex with a man in exchange for money. A man critically burned his girlfriend's ten-year-old son in an effort to find out who had taken $20 in food stamps. A Wisconsin high school teacher was convicted for hiring three students to kill her estranged husband. In Rochester, New York, four young teenagers were charged with spraying nail polish remover on an eight-year-old boy and setting him on fire.[20] An eighteen-year-old who was being sought in a hatchet and gun attack at a gay bar in Massachusetts later killed a police officer, a companion, and himself in Arkansas, leaving behind a web site with this message: "I'm interested in death, destruction, chaos, filth, and greed." These are just some of the hundreds of shocking, bizarre, and violent crimes that occur throughout the United States. It does not take many such events to produce high levels of fear and resulting behavior changes. A Texas man formed an organization called Dead Serious that offered members $5,000 for legally killing a criminal who attacked them at home.[21] A survey of the residents of New Orleans after Hurricane Katrina, both residents who had returned and residents who were still displaced, found that their number one concern was a low crime rate, followed by good street lighting, no litter, good schools, and other community issues.[22] Throughout many parts of the nation, the perception that the government is not adequately protecting public safety has contributed to the arming of the citizenry. When this occurs, more people take the law into their own hands, and instances of wrongful shooting, **vigilantism,** and lawlessness among otherwise law-abiding citizens increase.

A citizen walks down the street at night in fear. What is the consequence of large numbers of citizens living in fear of crime in their neighborhoods?

VIGILANTES AND SCAPEGOATS

vigilantism
Seeking justice through lawless violence.

scapegoating
Unfairly blaming and punishing a person or group for crimes.

Fear of crime also enhances fear of strangers and promotes stereotyping and **scapegoating.** Attacks against Japanese, Canadian, German, and other tourists, immigrants, and residents offer evidence of this problem.[23] This situation contributes to a self-fulfilling prophecy in which criminal incidents lead to fear, which then leads to more criminal incidents as people react incautiously to perceived threats brought about by fear.

The Universality of Crime

The prevalence of crime in societies throughout the world raises the question of whether crime is actually a "normal" part of modern life that we just have to live with. Crime and punishment are universal components of all societies of all types. There is no society that does not report problems with crime and what to do with offenders. This **universality** makes crime a global phenomenon that transcends both time and place. More than a century ago, the French sociologist Emile Durkheim observed that "Crime is present not only in the majority of societies of one particular species but in all societies of all types. There is no society that is not confronted with the problem of criminality."[24] Writing in 1895, Durkheim made the point that crime is "normal" inasmuch as every society has it; it would be abnormal to experience no crime. Nevertheless, crime is not a desirable phenomenon either. Although we cannot expect a society to have no deviance whatsoever, there is considerable variation among the rates of crime in different societies. As a result, it is not unrealistic to seek significant reductions in crime rates—at least for certain types of crimes.[25] Related to this issue is evidence that concern about crime may be a cyclical phenomenon. A presidential crime commission identified several historical periods in which concern about crime was at high levels: "A

universality of crime
There is no society that has not reported problems with crime and with what to do with offenders, but there is considerable variation among crime rates in different societies.

hundred years ago contemporary accounts of San Francisco told of extensive areas where no decent man was in safety to walk the street after dark; while at all hours, both day and night, his property was jeopardized by incendiarism and burglary." At that time it was widely believed that "crime especially in its more violent forms, and among the young, is increasing steadily and is threatening to bankrupt the Nation."[26]

The fact that concern about crime and violence may be cyclical does not mean, however, that its causes and its level remain the same. The nature and extent of crime differ widely from one time and place to another, and it is not unrealistic to search for ways to reduce current levels of crime and fear.

What Is Crime?

Crime is a natural phenomenon, because people have different levels of attachment, motivation, and virtue. If people are to live in society successfully, however, rules are required to make sure they can live together peacefully with a high degree of order. Of course, there will always be some people who do not obey the rules. Therefore, the rules must carry penalties to serve both as a warning and as an enforcement mechanism. Rules that prohibit certain forms of conduct so as to maintain social order identify a set of behaviors termed **crimes,** which form the basis of the **criminal law.** Violations of the criminal law are considered crimes against society because they break rules designed for the common good. That is to say, the rules elevate the good of the community over the desires of any given individual. Without such a system, anarchy would prevail as individuals competed to fulfill their own wants and needs without regard for those of others.

crimes
Forms of conduct that society prohibits in order to maintain order.

criminal law
A code that categorizes all crimes and punishments by type.

The distinction between serious and nonserious crimes is related to the possible sentences that can be imposed. Serious crimes that are punishable by incarceration for more than one year are called **felonies** in most states. Less serious crimes that are punishable by imprisonment for one year or less are called **misdemeanors.**

felonies
Serious crimes that are punishable by incarceration for more than one year.

misdemeanors
Less serious crimes that are punishable by imprisonment for one year or less.

Historical and Political Contexts of Crime

The history of U.S. criminal law is a history of change. Some acts that were once against the law later became lawful (e.g., profanity, sale of alcoholic beverages after Prohibition). Other acts that were once lawful later became illegal (e.g., possession of slaves, sale of alcoholic beverages during Prohibition). Are such changes random, depending only on the whims of legislators? Or do they reflect true changes in public views of certain acts? Moreover, are there "fundamental" crimes that do not change over time?

GOVERNMENTAL AFFAIRS

As a society grows larger, it becomes less and less feasible for all citizens to participate in the daily operation of government. In a representative government, the people elect representatives to direct governmental affairs on their behalf. These governmental affairs include the defining and punishing of crimes. It has been argued that government "creates" or selectively enforces some crimes without the consent of the public in order to protect the government from perceived threats to its existence. During times of war, conflict, or civil unrest, the government has sometimes used its legislative and enforcement powers to persecute alleged enemies rather than to seek justice.

During the post–World War II era there were instances in which government overzealously identified crimes and criminals, causing several miscarriages of justice. In 1949 the infamous "Tokyo Rose" was convicted of treason for broadcasting propaganda to U.S. troops in the Pacific. She was sentenced to ten years in prison on the basis of dubious evidence.[27] During the 1950s, the era of McCarthyism, many reputations were destroyed through false charges of communist association by U.S. Senator Joseph McCarthy.[28] In 1951 this hysteria resulted in the trial of Julius and Ethel Rosenberg for allegedly giving U.S. nuclear secrets to the Soviet Union. On debatable evidence the Rosenbergs were convicted of espionage and sentenced to death.[29] The Vietnam War produced a similar outcry against perceived anti-American sentiment, with aggressive prosecutions of draft dodgers and antiwar protestors.[30]

criminalization
The legislative decision to make a behavior a crime.

decriminalization
The legislative decision to change a crime into a noncriminal act.

The **criminalization** or **decriminalization** of certain behaviors, and the public's reaction to them, continue to make the application of the law controversial. Thus, when four Los Angeles police officers were acquitted in the beating of black motorist Rodney King, a riot erupted that lasted several days. When Timothy McVeigh was charged in the bombing of the federal office building in Oklahoma City in 1995, many believed that antigovernment militias were unfairly investigated and treated as suspects. In the Rodney King case, the *failure* of the government to treat questionable police behavior as criminal caused the public outcry. In the Oklahoma City case, it was the government's *action* to criminalize the activities of groups opposed to the government that caused division among the public. These debates have not been completely resolved, and the public is likely to remain divided and wary of the role of government in creating and administering the law.

SOCIAL AND POLITICAL HISTORY

Definitions of crime can therefore be viewed as evidence of development in social and political history, because they emerge from the public and political concerns that characterize different historical periods. For example, in 1920 the Eighteenth Amendment to the U.S. Constitution went into effect, banning the manufacture, transportation, or sale of alcoholic beverages to any person of any age. This policy, Prohibition, was enforced by the Volstead Act, passed by Congress in the same year. One can imagine what would happen if such a law were in effect today. Prohibition failed to recognize the demand for liquor, and it is not surprising that millions of people manufactured, sold, and bought alcoholic beverages in violation of the law. In 1933 the Eighteenth Amendment was repealed by the Twenty-first Amendment, which permits the sale of alcoholic beverages under the regulated system that exists today.

What caused the outright prohibition of such a desired commodity? For a brief period in U.S. history, the temperance movement's intolerance of *all* liquor consumption garnered enough political support to bring about the enactment of Prohibition and the Volstead Act.[31] As the history of Prohibition illustrates, however, laws passed without widespread public support are ultimately changed. Therefore, control of the political process results in only temporary changes; it is necessary to have true public support for laws to be effective.

VICTIMLESS CRIMES

Although it may be said that Prohibition did in fact reduce liquor consumption in the United States, there are no reliable estimates of the true extent of the illegal manufacture and sale of alcoholic beverages from 1920 to 1933.[32] The

Media & Criminal Justice

Television Crime Dramas and the Causes of Homicide

Crime-oriented programs are among the most popular forms of entertainment on television. TV newsmagazines, televised trials, "reality" police shows, and crime dramas can be found every night on many different channels. *NYPD Blue, Law & Order,* and *CSI* are popular examples. Crime dramas are fictional and are created to entertain viewers. It is likely that fact-based crime shows also serve primarily to entertain rather than inform, given their propensity to feature the most sensational and violent cases. Many people, however, derive a significant part of what they know about crime from crime dramas; most people do not have personal experience with violent crime.[a]

Most crime dramas focus on homicides. This emphasis runs counter to the fact that homicide is by far the least common serious crime. Television crime dramas also devote very little time to the causes of the criminal behavior depicted, often resorting to "blind passions, crazy plots, and references to magic, if not to clinical madness,"[b] while simultaneously placing great emphasis on careful, scientific gathering and analysis of evidence. These contradictions between media images of crime and its reality have given rise to increasing criticism of the media's role in creating inaccurate public perceptions.

A study analyzed the content of all episodes of regularly scheduled network television crime dramas over a period of six weeks. A total of sixty-nine programs were studied. (Movies, news broadcasts, reruns, magazine shows, "reality" police shows, and comedies that dealt with crime were excluded.) The study found that most programs left viewers "with the impression that homicides were the consequences of idiosyncratic behavior; the result of vague and indeterminate causes, often perpetrated by 'people who were killers'; and generally unconnected to events of the past or present that might otherwise account for the behavior."[c] The programs made virtually no attempt to account for the homicidal behavior in terms of the offender's social background, past experiences, deprivations, or failure to develop moral values; nor did they consider the deterrent influences of the criminal law. In two-thirds of the crime dramas reviewed, the most common plot motives were greed, mental illness, self-protection, murder for hire, vengeance, or being jilted by a friend or lover.

Such a portrayal suggests that homicide stems from individual characteristics and circumstances and that larger social factors are irrelevant. The viewer comes away with the notion that homicide offenders are different from the rest of us. Rarely is an effort made to provide insight into why most people, when placed in similar situations, do not commit (or even consider) homicide. The result over the long term may be to lead us to see law-abiding people as "us" and offenders as "them"—with no thought to the influences and motivations that are common to all of us.

If many people base their views about the causes and prevention of homicide on television crime dramas, what will be the impact of the increasing numbers of these programs that are being broadcast on an increasing number of channels?

NOTES

a. E. Mandel, *Delightful Murder* (Minneapolis: University of Minnesota Press, 1984), p. 43.

b. Ray Surette, *Media, Crime, and Criminal Justice: Images, Realities,* and *Policies,* 3rd ed. (Belmont, CA: Wadsworth, 2007).

c. David Fabianic, "Television Dramas and Homicide Causation," *Journal of Criminal Justice* 25 (1997), p. 200.

criminalization of a desired product may have an impact on when, where, and how one consumes it, but it usually does not affect *whether* one consumes it. The law is remarkably ineffective when it comes to so-called **victimless crimes.**

victimless crimes
Offenses in which the "offender" and the "victim" are the same individual or in which the behavior is consensual.

Though laws without public support are sometimes passed (and invariably changed or left unenforced), such temporary attempts to mold social history rather than to respond to it can exact a high price. Thousands of people were arrested and convicted during Prohibition. In 1924 alone, more than 22,000 cases related to

What factors led to the criminalization of the buying and selling of alcoholic beverages in the 1920s and the decriminalization of these acts in the 1930s? Did Prohibition reduce alcohol abuse? What unintended negative social consequences did Prohibition foster?

liquor were pending in the federal courts.[33] When it became apparent during the late 1920s that Prohibition was not working, the government did what governments often do when a "crime" problem appears out of control: It increased the penalties for violation (through the Jones Act). The result was additional thousands of arrests for liquor law violations.

SHADOW ECONOMIES

An even more pernicious result of unpopular laws is the creation of black markets. Studies have found that Prohibition was responsible for the creation of organized criminal syndicates, some of which still exist today. The influence of Al Capone and Johnny Torrio in Chicago and the beginnings of the Cosa Nostra in New York can be traced to Prohibition.[34] In addition, a great deal of public corruption in Chicago, New York, and other cities was rooted in Prohibition.

The Prohibition experience has been paralleled in many ways by the ebb and flow of laws against gambling, drugs, and prostitution—the other consensual crimes in which the line between offender and victim is not clear or does not exist at all. In different sociocultural contexts these "vices" have alternatively been defined as crimes, highly regulated behaviors, or mere leisure activities. The contemporary difficulties with the prosecution of the "war on drugs" have many similarities to what occurred during the 1920s, when alcohol was the drug of choice.

Origins of the Criminal Justice System

Perhaps the most important thing to remember in learning about the American system of justice is that there is no such thing as the criminal justice "system." No mention of a criminal justice system appears in the Constitution or in any federal or state law. In reality, the criminal justice system is a string of more than 55,000 independent government agencies set up to deal with different aspects of crime and the treatment of offenders.

criminal justice
The management of police, courts, and corrections, and the study of the causes of and treatment for crime.

The agencies of **criminal justice** have no legal obligation to cooperate with one another, and they often do not. The only thing they have in common is the fact that they all deal with the same clientele: crime suspects, people accused of crimes, and offenders. It is because of their relative lack of cooperation that they are sometimes called a "nonsystem" of criminal justice.[35] For example, a city may hire more police officers, who will contribute to an increase in the overall number of arrests. This results in more cases being brought to court, more adjudications of guilt, and more offenders sentenced to probation and prison. The need for more prosecutors, defense lawyers, judges, courtrooms, probation officers, and prison space created by the increase in police and arrests is rarely accounted for. This lack of "systemwide" thinking has hurt both the efficiency and effectiveness of criminal justice in the United States throughout the nation's history.

It is important to keep the idea of a "system" in mind, because we will see that anything done by one criminal justice agency invariably affects the others. Therefore, despite the fact that the various criminal justice agencies were not set up as a system, they must attempt to act together if justice is to be achieved. In fact, many of the problems of criminal justice are caused by the failure of the various criminal justice agencies to act as a system. Throughout this book, therefore, the term *criminal justice system* is used to emphasize the importance of cooperation among criminal justice agencies.

FUNCTIONS OF A CRIMINAL JUSTICE SYSTEM

Over the course of history, societies have been fairly consistent in the way they handle criminal justice. First, the members of societies place authority in the hands of a government to act on their behalf. When some members do not follow the codified rules—that is, the laws—the government often establishes an agency that is responsible for making sure that the laws are obeyed. In American society this enforcement function is performed by the police.

Next, societies often set up agencies to arbitrate in these matters. That is, if a person has an excuse or justification for violating the law, how do we determine whether it is a valid one? In American society this arbitration function is performed by the courts.

Finally, when an assessment of blame or responsibility is made, a penalty or punishment is administered to the offender and compensation is sometimes given to the victim. In American society this is carried out by the corrections system. Thus, it is rather easy to see how a system of justice evolves in a society to resolve disputes. The need for rules and a method to enforce those rules, together with a way to evaluate justifications for rule violations and the administration of penalties, are all necessary to serve the common good. These fundamental components of criminal justice are required to resolve the sometimes conflicting interests of individual citizens in ways that serve the wider public interest.

The agencies of law enforcement, the courts, and corrections comprise what we loosely call the criminal justice system. In the United States there are two levels of criminal justice systems: state and federal. Each state has its own set of criminal justice agencies, and the federal government has a criminal justice system that handles concerns that apply to some or all of the states. Therefore, there are actually fifty-one criminal justice systems in the United States.

Justice in the Colonial Period

Our modern system of criminal justice is a product of evolutionary changes such as those just described. It has evolved as American society has developed mechanisms for establishing rules, enforcing them, determining responsibility for violations, and deciding on appropriate remedies.

Early America was a sparsely populated domain that extended from New Hampshire to Georgia, and was no more than 200 miles wide. Unlike the situation today, in which paid professionals make, enforce, and adjudicate the law and carry out penalties, "colonial justice was a business of amateurs."[36] The first police force was not established until 1845, lawyers often played no role in the justice process, and cases were usually decided by lay magistrates. This made justice "democratic" in that it was communal in nature, protecting the perceived shared rights of the community. This was unlike the system in England, which was dominated by aristocrats enforcing the law against the less privileged.[37]

RELIGION AND SIN

Religion and sin played a significant role in colonial justice, inasmuch as crime and sin were viewed as essentially the same. In many ways religion formed the basis for colonial justice. Colonial criminal codes often defined crime in biblical terms, and blasphemy, profanity, and violations of the Sabbath were seen as serious offenses and punished severely. This religious orientation manifested itself in corrections as well. Rather than punishment or treatment, which typify the modern era, shame and repentance characterized the colonial period. Punishments were used to "lead" a violator toward repentance and to serve as an example to others.[38] Therefore, the stocks, whipping, and the dunking stool were used as methods of shaming rather than as punishment for its own sake.[39] In the modern era we still expect offenders to express remorse for their actions, even though such expressions make little difference in terms of punishment or forgiveness.

As the shared values of a common religious tradition were dissipated by rapid population growth, geographical expansion, and a lessening of the role of religion in the lives of citizens, the law gradually came to be relied on more and more often to enforce a standard of morality that previously had been the province of religion. The result was a dramatic increase in both the number of laws and the number of law violators, a trend that continues today. Simply stated, the more widely shared cultural and religious traditions one finds in a society, the less reliance is placed on the law to maintain the boundaries of acceptable behavior. The police, courts, and corrections are poor substitutes for the internalized controls that are the product of cultural traditions and religious beliefs.

How were crimes identified and defined in colonial times? Do you think those criteria still apply? What are the two chief goals of that system?

The development of the criminal justice system as we know it today resulted from this historical progression from small, religiously and culturally similar communities to larger towns and cities with more diverse populations in which religious tenets were less dominant. As can be seen in the next chapter, the first police departments were established in cities where individual responsibility for security broke down. This invariably occurred when population growth and increasing diversity weakened responsibility among the citizens, resulting in an "everyone for himself or herself" mentality.

This created the need for criminal justice agencies to maintain order and public safety. These agencies appeared in one city after another and gradually expanded to become state and federal agencies.[40]

The Evolution of Due Process

due process
The use of accuracy, fairness, and reliability in criminal procedure to protect individual rights.

The criminal justice process is no longer a simple one run by amateurs. The many legal steps and procedures that have been added are designed to achieve two goals: accuracy and fairness. These are the essential elements of **due process,** a legal protection included in the U.S. Constitution that guarantees all citizens the right to be adjudicated under the law. This protection from arbitrary and unjust treatment became more important as those making, enforcing, and adjudicating laws increasingly became strangers in a more populated and urban nation. As strong religious values weakened, a common moral fiber could no longer be counted on to promote conformity to laws.

ACCURACY AND FAIRNESS

Accuracy is a fundamental goal because confidence in the outcome is pivotal if a criminal justice system is to survive. If the public did not believe that the findings of the criminal justice process were accurate, they would lose confidence in the system, turn to private forms of justice, and eventually look for new forms of government.

Fairness is closely related to accuracy. Fairness in the justice process refers to the balance between the government's interest in apprehending crime suspects and the public's interest in avoiding unnecessary government interference in the lives of individuals. The establishment of thresholds for government intervention, such as probable cause, are designed to achieve a *fair* balance between the sometimes conflicting interests of the government and individual citizens.

Some have held that the criminal justice process has other functions besides accuracy and fairness. It is claimed, for example, that crime control is an important function.[41] However, there is little reliable evidence to suggest that the criminal justice system deters offenders or reforms those who pass through it. It has also been argued that overemphasis on accuracy and fairness interferes with the system's ability to deter or prevent crime.[42] Not only is this a speculative view, but it is impractical as well, since it is unlikely that a nation born only two hundred years ago out of violent revolution would be willing to lower the legal thresholds established to preserve accuracy and fairness in the balance between government and citizen. Indeed, Americans have long been suspicious of government. This suspicion dates back to the Revolution and to the philosophy of John Locke, which holds that government exists not by divine right or by force, but only by the consent of the governed, who may alter or abolish the government if it acts in a manner inconsistent with the natural rights of citizens.[43] It should be remembered that an important cause of the American Revolution was the widespread perception that British government procedures were arbitrary and unfair.[44]

The relative emphasis placed on the goals of accuracy, fairness, or crime control remains relevant today. Contemporary criticisms about police misconduct, unfairness in the judicial system, and sentencing disparities illustrate that neither law enforcement nor criminal justice is a simple concept. They both involve the rights and interests of the innocent, the guilty, those victimized, and those empowered to enforce the law. These competing concerns are highlighted throughout this book.

CRITICAL THINKING EXERCISES

Carjackings in the United States

- A fifty-year-old driver of a Jaguar had her arm broken by a sixteen-year-old carjacker in San Mateo County, California.
- An eighty-year-old woman in Omaha foiled a carjacking attempt when she refused to surrender her car keys and began screaming.
- A cab driver in Ventura County, California, had his taxi stolen at gunpoint.
- A man who test-drove a Lexus in Brooklyn liked the car so much he decided to take it at gun point.[a]

Reports of incidents like these seem to occur with alarming frequency. Are these events new, typical, or rare occurrences?

Carjacking is defined as robbery of a motor vehicle by a stranger. It differs from other kinds of car thefts because the offender threatens force and the victim is present.

A federal study found that about 34,000 carjacking incidents occur each year, and a downward trend has been observed since 1998. Nearly two-thirds of carjacking incidents occurred within 5 miles of the victim's home, and about half of all incidents occurred in open areas, such as on the street.

Fear that some carjackings are designed to kidnap infants led to an analysis of all newspaper accounts over a single year. A total of eight infants (up to age two) were reported kidnapped as part of carjackings. Seven of the eight infants were found soon after the incidents.[b] It appears that most offenders were unaware a baby was in the car (strapped into a car seat in the rear). After realizing an infant was inside, offenders usually left the infant or abandoned the car.[c]

A law permits federal prosecution of carjackers in cases where there is intent to cause serious injury or death.[d] More than 200 carjacking cases are filed in federal court each year, but more than half of these are not prosecuted (and were left to be adjudicated in state courts). This is because most carjacking victims are not injured, although in about half the cases the offender brandished a firearm.

Ninety percent of carjacking incidents involved one person in a car. Victims were predominantly black males in urban area, and carjacking offenders had similar characteristics.

CRITICAL THINKING QUESTIONS

1. Carjacking does not appear to be as widespread a problem as many believe. What influence may the media or politics play in our perceptions about carjacking?
2. Stories of carjackings often are reported when they involve children left in the car. Why does this occur considering that incidents of this type are so rare?

NOTES

a. Mike Claffey, "Test-Drive Turns into Carjacking," *New York Daily News* (May 23, 1999).
b. Patsy Klaus, *Carjackings,* 1993–2002 (Washington, DC: Bureau of Justice Statistics, 2004).
c. Robert Ingrassia, "Relief, Rage After Carjack," *New York Daily News* (February 26, 2000).
d. *Holloway v. United States,* 119 S.Ct. 966 (1999).

Binge Drinking

Despite gains made in reducing alcohol-related traffic fatalities, other drinking behaviors remain a problem. Heavy episodic alcohol use, or binge drinking, has been identified by the Harvard School of Public Health as "the single most serious public health problem confronting American colleges."[a]

In 1993, the Harvard Alcohol Study surveyed a nationally representative sample of college students and found that 44 percent were binge drinkers—the men reporting that they consumed five or more drinks in a row and the women four or more drinks in a row at least once in the two weeks before the survey. Twenty percent of students were found to be frequent binge drinkers, and only 16 percent abstained from drinking alcoholic beverages.[b] A 2001 follow-up survey found the same proportion of binge drinkers (44 percent), and slight *increases* in both abstainers (19 percent) and frequent binge drinkers (23 percent). A major predictor of college binge drinking was found to be students' alcohol use while in high school.

Binge drinkers in both the 1993 and 2001 surveys were at least five times more likely than non–binge drinkers to experience alcohol-related problems such as missing classes, falling behind in their work, forgetting where they were or what they did, getting hurt or injured, damaging property, or driving after drinking. In addition, others experienced secondhand effects of students' binge drinking, including having their study or sleep interrupted (61 percent), having to take care of a drunken student (50 percent), or being insulted or humiliated (29 percent).

Despite a high level of public attention to responsible alcohol consumption, there appears to be little impact thus far on binge drinking by college students. For example, the 2001 Harvard survey found a continuing high rate at which residents of fraternities or sororities binge drink (75 percent).

In addition, research has found that students who consumed more than five drinks at one setting were more likely to believe that other college students also drank. In particular, male college students, on-campus students, and sorority students perceived that other college students drank more than they actually did.[c]

CRITICAL THINKING QUESTIONS

1. Is binge drinking a crime? Why or why not?
2. What are the social, economic, political, and historical contexts of binge drinking?
3. What might be some consequences of criminalizing binge drinking?

NOTES

a. Henry Wechsler, Jae Eun Lee, Meichun Kuo, and Hang Lee, "College Binge Drinking in the 1990s: A Continuing Problem: Results of the Harvard School of Public Health 1999 College Alcohol Study," *Journal of American College Health* 48 (March 2000), pp. 99–210.

b. Henry Wechsler and Bernice Wuethrich *Dying to Drink: Confronting Binge Drinking on College Campuses* (Rodale Press, 2002); Henry Wechsler, George W. Dowdall, B. Moeykens, and S. Castillo, "Health and Behavioral Consequences of Binge Drinking in College: A National Survey of Students at 140 Campuses," *Journal of the American Medical Association* 272 (1994), pp. 1672–77.

c. William M. Miley and Michael Frank, "Binge and Non-Binge College Students' Perceptions of Other Students' Drinking Habits," *College Student Journal*, vol. 40 (June 2006), p. 259.

SUMMARY

PERSPECTIVES ON CRIME

- Public concern about crime has risen dramatically since the 1960s.
- Health problems and accidents are far more common causes of death than criminal homicide.
- Fear of death due to homicide is related to the lack of control an individual has over homicide, compared with other causes of death.
- Polls have found that citizens rank feeling safe from crime ahead of job satisfaction, financial security, and health.
- Fear of crime leads many people to give up activities that they would normally undertake, especially activities at night.
- High levels of fear can turn otherwise law-abiding citizens into outlaws.
- Crime of some type is present in all societies, but its nature and extent differ from one time and place to another.

WHAT IS CRIME?

- As a society becomes larger and more complex, more rules are required to ensure that citizens do not exploit one another.
- The criminal law punishes actions that violate the common good.
- The political nature of crime leads to efforts to criminalize or decriminalize certain behaviors, depending on public sentiment at the time.
- The Prohibition era showed that it is necessary to have true public support for laws if they are to be effective.

ORIGINS OF THE CRIMINAL JUSTICE SYSTEM

- There are more than 55,000 independent criminal justice agencies that sometimes do not cooperate with one another, so the American criminal justice "system" is often called a nonsystem.
- A system of justice evolves in society in order to enforce rules, resolve disputes, and administer punishment. In the United States this occurred in the colonial period as small, religiously and culturally similar communities evolved into large towns and cities with more diverse populations.
- The criminal justice process has two fundamental goals: fairness and accuracy.

KEY TERMS

media portrayals 2
Gallup poll on crime 2
criminologists 2
vigilantism 11
scapegoating 11
universality of crime 11
crimes 12
criminal law 12
felonies 12
misdemeanors 12
criminalization 13
decriminalization 13
victimless crimes 14
criminal justice 16
due process 18

QUESTIONS FOR REVIEW AND DISCUSSION

1. How do mass media influence public perceptions of crime?
2. How is public fear of crime turned into political action?
3. What historical events have heightened people's fear of violent crime?
4. What are the comparative risks of criminal victimization in the United States?
5. What are some negative consequences of the fear of crime?
6. In what sense can crime be said to be "normal"?
7. By what process do societies define crimes?
8. What is the criminal justice system? In what sense is criminal justice a non-system?
9. What are the roots of the American system of criminal justice?
10. How has the American criminal justice system changed since colonial times?

NOTES

1. Carol Robinson and Val Walton, "Three Set Church Fires as Joke, Agents Say," *Birmingham News* (March 9, 2006); Leslie Eaton, "With Killings on the Rise, Upstate Cities Look for Answers," *The New York Times* (December 30, 2002); "Teen Sentenced in Death," *Richmond Times Dispatch* (February 2, 2002); "Father Guilty of Involuntary Manslaughter of Baby in Car," *The New York Times* (November 22, 2002).
2. Edward L. Cardenas, "Teen Gets Prison in Terror Case," *Detroit News* (July 5, 2005).
3. J. M. Hirsch, "Teen Gets Life in Slaying of Two Professors," *USA Today* (April 5, 2002), p. 3.
4. Joseph Carroll, "Gallup Reviews Americans' Attitudes about Crime," *Gallup News Service* (June 16, 2006); "What Do You Think Is the Most Important Problem Facing This Country Today?" *Gallup Poll* (July 6–9, 2006).
5. Steven M. Chermak, "Body Count News: How Crime Is Presented in the News Media," *Justice Quarterly*, vol. 11 (1994), pp. 561–82; Vincent F. Sacco, "Media Constructions of Crime," *The Annals of the American Academy of Political and Social Science*, vol. 539 (1995), pp. 141–54; Dennis T. Lowry, Tarn Ching Josephine Nio, and Dennis W. Leitner, "Setting the Public Fear Agenda: A Longitudinal Analysis of Network TV Crime Reporting, Public Perceptions of Crime and FBI Crime Statistics," *Journal of Communication*, vol. 539 (March 2003); Nick Madigan, "Grisly Murder in New York Makes Perfect Grist for Tabloids," *Baltimore Sun* (March 19, 2006).
6. Frank Newport, "Americans' Mood Drops as Economy and War Dominate Concerns," *Gallup News Service* (February 13, 2003).
7. Joseph Carroll, "Gallup Reviews Americans' Attitudes about Crime," *Gallup News Service* (June 16, 2006).
8. Gary W. Potter and Victor E. Kappeler, *Constructing Crime: Perspectives on Making News and Social Problems* 2d ed. (Prospect Heights, IL: Waveland Press, 2006; Jeremy H. Lipschultz and Michael L. Hilt, *Crime and Local Television News: Dramatic, Breaking, and Live From the Scene* (Mahwah, NJ: LEA, 2002).
9. Alida V. Merlo and Peter J. Benekos, *What's Wrong with the Criminal Justice System: Ideology, Politics, and the Media* (Cincinnati: Anderson, 2000).
10. Jonathan Simon, "Governing Through Crime Metaphors," *Brooklyn Law Review*, vol. 67 (summer, 2002); Nancy E. Marion, *A Primer in the Politics of Criminal Justice* (New York: Harrow and Heston, 1995); James O. Finckenauer, "Crime as a National Political Issue: 1964–76: From Law and Order to Domestic Tranquility," *Crime & Delinquency*, vol. 24 (January 1978).
11. Kathleen Hall Jamieson, *Dirty Politics: Deception, Distraction, and Democracy* (New York: Oxford University Press, 1992); "Cheney Blasts Kerry's Record on National Security," *The Frontrunner* (March 18, 2004).
12. George H. Gallup, *The Gallup Polls: Public Opinion, 1935–1971*, vol. 3 (New York: Random House, 1972), p. 2108.
13. Linda Lyons, "Agnst Aplenty: Top Worries of Young Americans," Gallup Poll (July 15, 2003).
14. George P. Fletcher, *A Crime of Self-Defense: Bernard Goetz and the Law on Trial* (New York: Free Press, 1990).
15. Cynthia Lee, *Murder and the Reasonable Man: Passion and Fear in the Criminal Courtroom* (New York: New York University Press, 2003); Robert F. Schopp, ed., *Justification Defenses and Just Convictions* (New York: Cambridge University Press, 1998).

16. Kennon J. Rice, William R. Smith, "Socioecological Models of Automotive Theft: Integrating Routine Activity and Social Disorganization Approaches," *Journal of Research in Crime and Delinquency*, vol. 39 (August 2002), pp. 304–33; Pierre Tremblay, Yvan Clermont, Maurice Cusson, "Jockeys and Joyriders: Changing Patterns in Car Theft Opportunity Structures," *British Journal of Criminology*, vol. 34 (summer 1994), pp. 307–21.
17. Deborah Sharp, "In Miami Hotels, Checkout Time for TV News of Violence," *USA Today* (June 6, 1994), p. 8; Nick Madigan, "Grisly Murder in New York Makes Perfect Grist for Tabloids," *Baltimore Sun* (March 19, 2006).
18. Jonathan T. Lovitt, "California Postal Worker Held in Boss's Slaying," *USA Today* (July 10, 1995), p. 3; Carrie Dowling and Bruce Frankel, "Former Postal Worker Held in New Jersey Shootings," *USA Today* (March 23, 1995), p. 5; "Postal Feud Ends in Fatal Shootings," *Richmond Times-Dispatch* (December 20, 1997), p. 3.
19. Detis T. Duhart, *Violence in the Workplace* (Washington, DC: Bureau of Justice Statistics, 2001).
20. "Murder for Hire," *USA Today* (May 22, 1995), p. 3; "Boy Burned," *USA Today* (March 27, 1995), p. 3; "Mom Sentenced," *USA Today* (October 25, 1993), p. 3; "Four Teens Charged after 8-Year-Old Is Set on Fire," *Buffalo News* (March 21, 1995), p. 14; Andrew Ryan, "Killers, Victims Post Their Thoughts on Personal Web Pages," *Seattle Post-Intelligencer* (February 16, 2006).
21. Mark Potok, "A Deadly Serious Call to Arms," *USA Today* (February 17, 1995), p. 3.
22. Coleman Warner, "Survey: Crime is Residents' No. 1 Priority," *The Times-Picayune* (July 10, 2006).
23. Les Johnston, "What is Vigilantism?" *British Journal of Criminology*, vol. 36 (spring 1996), pp. 200–36; Richard Price and Jonathan T. Lovitt, "Murder of Two Students Stuns Japan," *USA Today* (March 29, 1994), p. 1; Jeff Leen and Don Van Natta, Jr., "Canada Fears Escalating Crime While Miami Can Barely Keep Up," *Buffalo News* (September 11, 1994), p. 12; "Immigration Issues, Controlling Our Borders Top America's Agenda," *Richmond Times-Dispatch* (March 30, 2006).
24. Emile Durkheim, *The Rules of Sociological Method* (originally published in 1895) (New York: Free Press, 1964), pp. 65–66.
25. Freda Adler, *Nations Not Obsessed with Crime* (Littleton, CO: Fred B. Rothman, 1983); Jay S. Albanese, "Moving towards Utopia: Elements of a Crime-Free Society," in *Justice, Privacy, and Crime Control* (Lanham, MD: University Press of America, 1984), pp. 46–56.
26. President's Crime Commission, *Task Force Report: Crime and Its Impact—an Assessment* (Washington, DC: U.S. Government Printing Office, 1967), p. 19.
27. Stanley I. Kutler, *The American Inquisition: Justice and Injustice in the Cold War* (New York: Hill & Wang, 1982).
28. Melvin I. Urofsky, *A March of Liberty: A Constitutional History of the United States* (New York: McGraw-Hill, 1988), pp. 750ff.
29. Lawrence M. Friedman, *Crime and Punishment in American History* (New York: Basic Books, 1993), p. 372.
30. Steven E. Barkan, *Protectors on Trial: Criminal Justice in the Southern Civil Rights and Vietnam Antiwar Movement* (New Brunswick: Rutgers University Press, 1985).
31. Friedman, p. 341.
32. Mark H. Moore, in "Actually, Prohibition Was a Success," in R. L. Evans and I. M. Berent, eds., *Drug Legalization* (LaSalle, IL: Open Court Press, 1992), argues that Prohibition worked, citing a decline in cirrhosis deaths during the period. The unreliability of the data and reporting methods of the period make both the statistics used and the conclusions drawn suspect.
33. Ibid., p. 266.
34. Jay S. Albanese, *Organized Crime in Our Times* (Cincinnati: Anderson, 2004); Samuel Walker, *Popular Justice: A History of American Criminal Justice* (New York: Oxford University Press, 1980).
35. Daniel L. Skoler, *Governmental Structuring of Criminal Justice Services: Organizing the Non-System* (Washington, DC: U.S. Government Printing Office, 1978).
36. Friedman, p. 27.
37. Ibid., p. 3; Peter Charles Hoffer and William B. Scott, eds., *Criminal Proceedings in Colonial Virginia* (Athens: University of Georgia Press, 1984).
38. Bradley Chapin, *Criminal Justice in Colonial America, 1606–1660* (Athens: University of Georgia Press, 1983).
39. See Herbert A. Johnson and Nancy Travis Wolfe, *History of Criminal Justice*, 3rd ed. (Cincinnati: Anderson Publishing, 2005); Mitchell P. Roth, *Crime and Punishment: A History of the Criminal Justice System* (Belmont, CA: Wadsworth, 2005).
40. Abram Chayes, "How the Constitution Establishes Justice," in R. A. Goldwin and W. A. Schambra, eds., *The Constitution, the Courts, and the Quest for Justice* (Washington, DC: American Enterprise Institute, 1989), pp. 25–39; F. Thornton Miller, *Juries and Judges Versus the Law: Virginia's Provincial Legal Perspective, 1783–1828* (Charlottesville: University Press of Virginia, 1994); Francis A. Allen, *The Habits of Legality: Criminal Justice and the Rule of Law* (New York: Oxford University Press, 1996); Ronald Dworkin, *Freedom's Law: The Moral Reading of the American Constitution* (Cambridge, MA: Harvard University Press, 1996); Stephen B. Presser, *Recapturing the Constitution: Race, Religion, and Abortion Reconsidered* (Washington, DC: Regery, 1994); Cass R. Sunstein, *The Partial Constitution* (Cambridge, MA: Harvard University Press, 1993).
41. Herbert Packer, *The Limits of the Criminal Sanction* (Stanford, CA: Stanford University Press, 1968).
42. Charles L. Gould, "The Criminal Justice System Favors Offenders," in Bonnie Szumski, ed., *Criminal Justice: Opposing Viewpoints* (St. Paul, MN: Greenhaven Press, 1987), pp.∞33–39.
43. John Locke, *Concerning the True Original Extent and End of Civil Government* (Chicago: Encyclopaedia Britannica, 1952).
44. George H. Smith, *The American Revolution* (Nashville, TN: Knowledge Products, 1979).

chapter 2

The Nature and Causes of Crime

Defining deviance: establishing the outer limits of acceptable conduct and what causes the continual violation of those rules.

CHAPTER OUTLINE

LEARNING OBJECTIVES

- Compare and contrast deviance and crime.
- Differentiate the roles of intent and behavior in defining crime.
- Explain the differences between *mala in se* and *mala prohibita* crimes.
- Identify three types of *mala prohibita* crime and describe their roles in the criminalization of behavior.
- Illustrate the issue of overcriminalization as it might apply to alcohol, prostitution, gambling, and narcotics.
- Compare and contrast the four principal explanations of crime (classical school, positivism, ethical view, structural/conflict view).
- Compare and contrast biological, psychological, and sociological perspectives on crime.
- Distinguish among six sociological explanations of criminal behavior.
- Evaluate the roles of guns, alcohol, and drugs as correlates of crime.

The problem began when Shawn Fanning, a nineteen-year-old student at Northeastern University, wrote a computer program and then started a company called Napster. The program allowed users to download and exchange songs in MP3 format. Hundreds of thousands of college students downloaded the free software to obtain copies of favorite songs and CDs. Large recording companies do not allow the recordings of their most popular performers to be released in MP3 format, due to fears that store sales will be affected. Therefore, MP3 songs by popular artists exist only when someone copies a store-bought CD and uploads it to the Internet. It is legal to make copies of your own CDs in other formats for personal use on tape players, computers, and so forth, but when those copies are given (or sold) to others in a way that deprives the artists and the record company of income from their creative work, it is illegal.

The result was a degree of chaos in both the recording industry and among Internet downloaders in knowing what was legal and what was illegal. Beginning in 2003, both the recording industry and the government began suing individuals for downloading illegal copies of songs for free, rather than pursuing only the Internet sites that offered the music. This created confusion among many who could not understand that freely available music on the Internet could be illegal.

Most of these suits, which appeared to be designed to raise public awareness and to deter negligent music downloaders, were settled out of court. It became a case where technology created the capability to accomplish a useful function that was not illegal, but that some believed should be. Customers want to be able to listen to songs in advance and then obtain copies instantly, and Napster made this possible. For its part, the recording industry sued universities, bootleggers, and teenagers who uploaded pirated songs. Napster was also sued.[1] According to the recording industry, "this is not the harmless swapping of music by a couple of friends. This is organized piracy."[2] Even high-profile artists Metallica and Dr. Dre joined in the movement and in the legal action against Napster.[3] Napster supporters argued that it promotes new music by performers who are not yet well known and thereby may increase the consumer market. Users do not make money on the material they download, and even if some users are violating copyright laws, it is argued that Napster should not be held liable for the abuses of its customers in the same way that the telephone company is not liable for illegal business conducted over the telephone. Napster ultimately was ordered by the court to block attempts to download copyrighted songs from its service, and it later re-emerged as a legitimate pay service, together with Apple's iTunes, MusicMatch, RealOne, America Online, and Walmart, among others. Songs are now available for downloading via the Internet for a flat fee of 99 cents or less. But making music downloading easy and cheap has not deterred illegal music downloads, resulting in music industry lawsuits against downloaders. On one hand, the music industry is seeking to protect the investment made by artists and recording companies in their songs and their distribution rights, but many listeners claim the industry has caused its own problem by overpricing CDs and by not effectively preventing freely available music on the web from being available. The lawsuits against individual downloaders have drawn mixed reviews and their long-term impact remains to be seen. Downloading music via the Internet is at the borderline of deviant behavior inasmuch as some music (copyright-free) can be downloaded but other music cannot.[4]

Defining Deviance

The Napster controversy is a modern example of how rules or **norms** develop in society. Norms establish social expectations about what is appropriate behavior under different circumstances. They reflect a society's values about what is considered desirable and proper. Norms against stealing and assault, for example, are well established in society, but the norms for acceptable behavior in sharing music over the Internet are just now developing—as the Napster case makes clear.

norms
Social expectations about what constitutes appropriate behavior under different circumstances.

Deviance is violation of a social norm, and minor examples include rudeness, disobedience, and gossiping about others. Deviance becomes crime when laws are passed or courts apply existing laws that make a social norm into a legal norm allowing the government to sanction the behavior. Sanctions are penalties designed to express disapproval and punish violation of norms. Therefore, as norms

NORMS AND VALUES

deviance
Violation of a social norm.

develop, deviance will occur that violates these norms. Crime results when the deviance is seen as serious enough to warrant the attention of the government for sanctioning.

Thinking versus Acting

All of us have occasionally wished that something bad would happen to another person. You may have cursed out the driver of an automobile you believe cut you off; you may have wished your employer or professor would become ill; you may have said nasty things about a former lover. When do such thoughts or statements become crimes?

COMMISSION AND OMISSION

As a general rule, crimes prohibit only acts or omissions of acts. Therefore, it is a crime to strike or steal from someone without a compelling justification. Omissions that constitute crimes are rare; they include forms of inaction such as *failure to stop* for a stop sign or *failure to file* your income tax return.

There is a middle ground where the line between thinking and acting becomes thin. What if you *think* evil thoughts about someone but do nothing else? Fortunately, that is not a crime (otherwise we would all be in jail). It is also impossible for law enforcement officials to know what a person is really thinking, although they may *infer* thoughts from evidence provided by polygraphs, surveillance, and other methods. But what if you want to punch your boss in the face, and take a swing at him, but miss? What if you want to kill someone, go out and buy a gun, but take no further action? The history of American criminal law is filled with cases like these, in which the distinction between thought and action is at issue. These cases have helped refine our definitions of crimes and the allowable defenses for questionable actions.

The precise behaviors needed (beyond thought) for actions to be considered crimes are explained in Chapter 3 with reference to the more serious violent and property crimes. The elements of conspiracy, or the planning of a criminal act, are detailed in Chapter 17. Suffice it to say here that the criminal law punishes *actions*, not *thoughts*. This is because it is impossible to know with accuracy a person's thoughts, and thoughts alone do not pose a threat to social control (which is the purpose of the criminal law). Only actions can pose a threat to society. Therefore, the criminal law is concerned only with actions.

Mala in Se, Mala Prohibita, and Criminal Harm

mala in se
Acts considered evil in themselves (e.g., assault and theft).

mala prohibita
Acts considered undesirable although not inherently evil (e.g., drug use).

Are there some behaviors that are objectively and inherently criminal, regardless of when and where they occur? It appears that there are. Although the criminal law had its origins among the ancient Greeks and Romans, the primary source of U.S. criminal law is England's common law. Under common law, crimes were seen as being of two types. Acts were considered either as ***mala in se*** (evil in themselves) or as ***mala prohibita*** (simply prohibited by law). *Mala in se* offenses include serious crimes of assault and theft, such as murder, rape, robbery, larceny, and burglary. *Mala prohibita* offenses are the result of legislative decisions to prohibit certain undesirable behaviors, such as alcohol use, drunkenness, drug use, and gambling.

The number of *mala in se* offenses has remained fairly constant over the centuries. That is, acts that are identified as evil nearly always involve crimes against persons or property. In fact, crimes of assault (murder, rape, robbery) and theft (burglary and larceny) are illegal in societies of all types. This universality of certain serious crimes demonstrates that crime is not entirely a subjective phenomenon, nor is it arbitrarily defined by particular nations during particular historical periods. From the earliest years of recorded history, basic acts of assault and theft have been criminalized in most of their forms.

CRIMES THAT TRANSCEND

The reasons for this uniformity are fascinating. For example, if the law against murder were abolished tomorrow, it is unlikely that the murder rate would increase. This is because a strong moral force exists independently of the law. The law against murder merely reinforces a strongly held community sentiment. The same is true of all crimes of assault. It is doubtful that assault would become common if criminal laws against it did not exist. The same is true for crimes of theft, although thefts are perceived as less serious than assaults (which is probably why they are more common). Clearly, then, there exist crimes that transcend the boundaries of time and place.

It is sometimes argued that *no* acts are inherently criminal. For example, abortion is considered murder in Ireland but is not so defined in most other nations. Revenge killings also were permitted in some societies in earlier times.[5] But as governments became more competent and better able to protect citizens, the need for revenge killings disappeared. There is now consensus in most societies that the government's criminal justice system is able to determine justice more objectively and safely than revenge killings. Likewise, scientific knowledge regarding when human life begins in the womb (made possible through technological advances) has complicated the abortion debate, as has the need to balance the competing interests of the mother and child in light of society's long-term interests. So while the cases of abortion and revenge killings may *modify* the scope of the definition of murder, they do not cause it to appear or disappear from the criminal law.

MALA PROHIBITA

On the other hand, the number of *mala prohibita* offenses has grown dramatically in the United States. These offenses can be grouped into three general categories: crimes without victims, political offenses, and regulatory offenses. Crimes without victims are offenses in which the offender and the "victim" engage in the act voluntarily. This category of offenses has been increasing steadily in recent years. Sometimes called **offenses against morality**, these acts include adultery and fornication, prostitution, gambling, the use and selling of drugs, and drunkenness, among others. Another expanding category consists of **political crimes**, which include any act that is viewed as a threat to the government. These activities may involve treason, sedition, espionage, sabotage, and bribery. None of these political crimes are *mala in se* offenses, because they are not necessarily evil. Many of those who engage in these activities believe that they are acting justly against an unjust government. As the history of the United States illustrates, today's revolutionary can sometimes become tomorrow's hero. Therefore, political crimes are acts not necessarily bad in themselves.

offenses against morality
Acts considered undesirable, such as adultery and fornication, prostitution, and gambling.

political crimes
Acts viewed as a threat to the government.

A third type of *mala prohibita* offense that has grown dramatically in recent years is criminality produced through the powers delegated by Congress or state legislatures. These **regulatory offenses** are usually activities of a business or corporate nature that are viewed as a threat to public health, safety, or welfare. These offenses are violations of laws regulating pollution levels, workplace safety, the manufacture of unsafe products, and other aspects of business. They are crimes created by regulatory agencies as part of the agencies' effort to oversee certain activities of business enterprises. Regulatory offenses often change over time as acceptable levels of pollution, acceptable employee exposure to risk, and allowable margins for safety in consumer products evolve. Examples of regulatory agencies include the Federal Trade Commission, the Federal Communications Commission, the Consumer Product Safety Commission, the Food and Drug Administration, and the Environmental Protection Agency.

regulatory offenses
Activities of a business or corporation that are viewed as a threat to public health, safety, or welfare.

The increase in *mala prohibita* offenses has raised concern that the distinction between crime and merely inappropriate or offensive behaviors may be becoming blurred, a phenomenon called **overcriminalization**. Overcriminalization may dilute the moral force of the law if the law comes to be regarded as petty and intrusive rather than as a necessary means of social control.

overcriminalization
Blurring the distinction between crime and merely inappropriate or offensive behaviors.

It can be seen, therefore, that *mala in se* offenses are common to all societies. They differ only in regard to the breadth of their definitions (e.g., inclusion or exclusion of abortion from the definition of murder). *Mala prohibita* offenses vary widely over time, among societies, and sometimes even *within* societies. In the United States, for example, there is great variation in the extent to which gambling and marijuana use are considered crimes. Table 2.1 illustrates the three types of *mala prohibita* offenses and their differences.

VIOLATION OF PRINCIPLES

Mala prohibita and *mala in se* offenses are distinct both in their substance and in the nature of the harm they cause. *Mala prohibita* offenses cause harm that violates moral, business, or political principles. In the case of victimless crimes the offense is usually moral and consensual in nature. Gambling, prostitution, and most drug offenses are of this type. Unfairness in business is the typical harm in regulatory offenses. Price-fixing, bid rigging, and manufacturing shortcuts violate the principles of free markets. Subversion of a government principle is the harm caused by political crimes. Treason and sedition are examples. In each of these cases of *mala prohibita* offenses, *violation of principles* is the focus of concern.

Table 2.1 A Typology of *Mala Prohibita* Offenses

Type of Offense	*Nature of Offense*	*Examples*
Victimless crimes	Offenses against morality involving consensual acts between offender and victim.	Gambling, prostitution, drug offenses.
Political crimes	Acts viewed as threats to the government.	Espionage, bribery, treason.
Regulatory offenses	Acts viewed as threats to public health, safety, and welfare.	Inadequate food and drug labeling or usage warnings, unsafe products.

Is inhaling smoke from an illicit drug a victimless crime? To what extent should the law be used to protect adults from potentially dangerous activity?

For *mala in se* offenses the harm is more personal and direct. All variations of assault, rape, and homicide result in physical harm to the victim in addition to violation of generally accepted moral principles. Burglary and theft involve loss and violation of property in addition to transgression of moral rules. Therefore, the seriousness of *mala in se* offenses is manifested by the physical loss or harm that they cause. *Mala prohibita* offenses involve violation of moral, business, or political principles, but they do not entail *direct physical loss or harm.* It is the harm caused by *mala in se* offenses that results in their central position in discussions of crime and justice.

Criminalization of Behavior

As the case of Prohibition makes clear, the ability to *create* crime through the actions of government is cause for concern. In assessing current events or historical ones, how can we determine the extent to which changes in the law truly reflect social consensus or are merely the fruits of lobbying efforts that try to shape political action? One way to determine this is to examine the enforcement of newly enacted laws. Take the 55-mph speed limit, for example. It was enacted in the 1970s in an effort to promote fuel economy; but it was not enforced, and eventually the speed limit was raised in most states. The point is that it is impossible to enforce a law if it is violated by large numbers of people. Other laws have had similar fates. Still others, however, are actively enforced because the public wants them to be enforced.

In the continuing effort to establish the limits of acceptable behavior, the *mala prohibita* offenses of alcohol consumption, commercialized sex, gambling, and drug use have drawn the most attention over the years. Throughout the nation's history, alcohol consumption has been viewed alternately as a vice, an evil, a

Is prostitution considered a *mala in se* or a *mala prohibita* offense? Why? How could you argue that selling sex is or is not inherently criminal? What other behaviors are categorized today as offenses against morality?

crime, or a leisure activity. In the 1980s the attack on alcohol consumption began anew with the campaign mounted by Mothers Against Drunk Driving (MADD). MADD was founded by a mother whose teenage daughter had been killed in an automobile crash. The accident was caused by a man with two prior drunk driving convictions who was out on bail on a third charge. MADD became a powerful political lobbying group, because it addressed the already widespread belief that drunk driving was not adequately criminalized. The 1980s began an anti–drunk driving era in which some states increased penalties for drunk driving, establishing mandatory prison sentences and suspending the licenses of violators. In 1984 the federal government established rules that forced every state to raise its drinking age from eighteen to twenty-one. Drunk driving awareness programs became common throughout the United States.

ALCOHOL AND PROSTITUTION

The selling of sex for money has existed at least as long as alcohol consumption, gambling, and the other "vices." Historically, prostitution was seen as an undesirable behavior, and that view continues today. The disagreement lies in opinions about whether criminalization is the best way to address it. Since the late 1960s the rise of the women's movement and the work of the National Organization for Women (NOW) have cast prostitution in a new light. NOW condemned the exploitation of women but in 1971 came out in favor of decriminalizing prostitution.[6] Today Nevada licenses prostitution on a county-by-county basis in jurisdictions with fewer than 400,000 residents, but other states have not followed suit. It appears that public sentiment still favors the criminalization of prostitution, although this sentiment may be due to the lack of noncriminal alternatives that do not appear immoral to a large segment of the public.

GAMBLING

Gambling encompasses games of chance, in which the outcome is determined by luck rather than skill. Like prostitution, gambling has existed throughout recorded history. Biblical accounts of the Crucifixion include an anecdote about four soldiers who each wanted Jesus's robe. They resolved the dispute by saying, "Let's not tear it; let's throw dice to see who will get it."[7] Gambling was also popular among the Native Americans: The Onondaga and the Iroquois wagered using dice.[8] The Narragansett and the Chumash often gambled for days in games in which "the worldly goods of entire tribes might change hands."[9]

Lotteries were the most popular form of gambling in the American colonies. The Virginia Company of London was given permission to conduct lottery drawings in England to help fund its plantation in Virginia—yet at the same time it attempted to reduce gambling in Virginia. Reports of "gaming, idleness, and vice" were rampant, and antigambling ordinances became part of Jamestown's first legal code.[10] Nevertheless, gambling remained popular.

This particular dichotomy, in which gambling was encouraged for one purpose (public funding) but viewed as dissolute for another (recreation), provides an early illustration of how attitudes toward gambling have vacillated throughout history. The Puritans of Massachusetts saw gambling as an "appearance of evil" and therefore irreligious.[11] Like Virginia, Massachusetts and other colonies passed laws that attempted to limit or prohibit gambling; but despite these laws gambling (especially card and dice games) continued.[12] During the early 1700s, when funds were needed for public works (e.g., schools and roads), many northeastern colonies started lotteries to raise the required funds. This example shows again how gambling has been viewed as either a vice or a virtue, depending on how the profits are used.

Public sentiment toward gambling has been marked by indifference. Despite periodic scandals and moral crusades, the "now it's legal, now it's not" history of gambling reflects public attention or inattention to the issue, rather than indignation. Today gambling enjoys renewed popularity and legitimacy, largely as a way to boost local economies without raising taxes. Lotteries are legal in most states, and in a majority of the states casino gambling has been approved or is under active review. Like alcohol consumption, gambling is tolerated as a social vice largely because of the government's ability to profit from it (mostly through taxation). It appears that the only difference between legal and illegal gambling is whether or not the state is running the game.

NARCOTICS

Unlike gambling, narcotics distribution and use was generally not a crime until late in the nineteenth century. Although drug use was always considered a vice, during the 1800s the only laws addressing the consumption of drugs were those that criminalized opium use, which was associated largely with Chinese immigrants. Around the turn of the century, several states passed laws against morphine and cocaine use, but these laws were directed largely at pharmacists and physicians.[13]

The situation changed dramatically in the early twentieth century as intolerance for all the vices peaked. In 1914 Congress passed the Harrison Narcotic Drug Act, which added cocaine to the list of drugs whose use was subject to severe restrictions. Prohibition began in 1920, and during the following decade far fewer arrests were made for narcotics use than for violations of the liquor laws. However, evidence of continuing concern with narcotics can be seen in the establishment of the Federal Bureau of Narcotics (FBN) in 1930. The FBN led the crusade to add marijuana to the list of dangerous narcotics, a crusade that ultimately resulted in the Marijuana Tax Act of 1937.[14]

The prohibition of narcotics has continued ever since, highlighted by the formation of the Drug Enforcement Administration in 1973 and the creation in 1989 of the position of "drug czar" to head the Office of National Drug Policy. These initiatives further promoted the criminalization of narcotics, increasing the penalties for violations and emphasizing law enforcement approaches to controlling the problem. It is interesting that despite the moderation of public attitudes toward other vices during the late twentieth century, narcotics use is now criminalized more extensively than at any time in the nation's history (with the exception of marijuana laws in a few states).

The evidence suggests that drug usage decreased among most Americans during the 1990s but remains much worse among the poor and addicted. Figure 2.1 illustrates that in 2004 illicit drug use was highest among 18- to 20-year-olds (21.7 percent), followed most closely by those aged 21 to 25 (17.9 percent) and 16 to 17 (17.3 percent). As in prior years, illicit drug use in 2004 tended to increase with age for young persons, peaking among 18- to 20-year olds and generally declining after that point with increasing age. Among all youths aged 12 to 17 in

FIGURE 2.1 Past Month Illicit Drug Use among Those Aged 12 and Older in 2004.

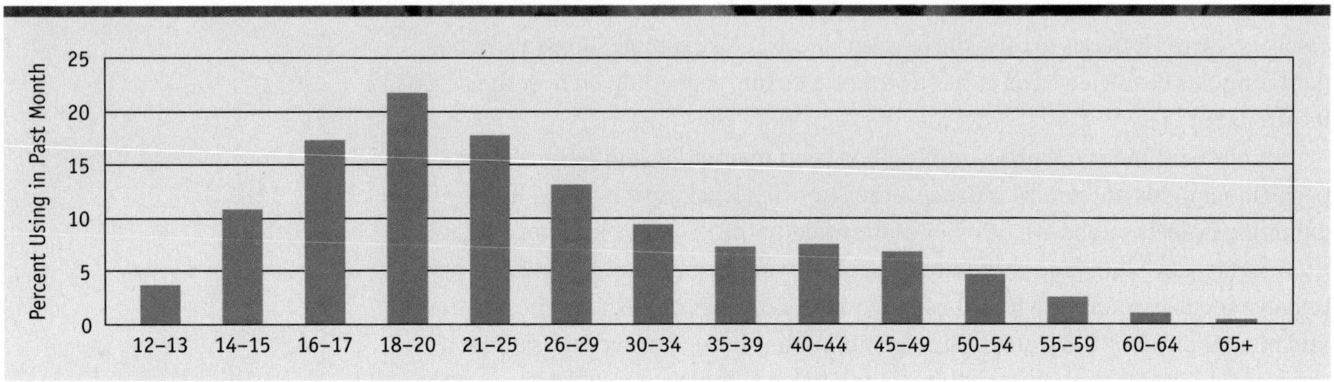

Source: 2004 National Survey on Drug Use and Health, U.S. Department of Health and Human Services, Substance Abuse and Mental Health Services Administration.

2004, 10.6 percent were current illicit drug users: 7.6 percent used marijuana, 3.6 percent used prescription-type drugs nonmedically, 1.2 percent used inhalants, 0.8 percent used hallucinogens, and 0.5 percent used cocaine. The rate of current illicit drug use among youths aged 12 to 17 has gradually declined. The rate was 11.6 percent in 2002, 11.2 percent in 2003, and 10.6 percent in 2004. It is not clear whether the intensive criminalization of narcotics has been responsible for the general decline in drug use or if the decline is due to its growing identification as an unhealthful and harmful activity, similar to alcohol use. Nevertheless, the issue of drugs, smoking, and alcohol is still identified by teenagers as the single most important problem they face.[15]

legalization
Legislative decision to remove a prohibited behavior from the criminal law.

Several prominent conservatives have joined with liberals in advocating the legalization of drugs.[16] **Legalization** is unlikely to occur any time soon, however, because drugs still carry the same degree of stigma that prostitution does. It is difficult to imagine elected representatives voting in favor of any kind of legalization plan as long as they are afraid to give the appearance of supporting drug use. Nevertheless, this stigma has been overcome in the case of gambling, so legalization of drugs may be a matter of time. There is abundant evidence regarding the ineffectiveness of police crackdowns, interdiction efforts, and attempts to eradicate drug production in source countries, as well as of the high economic and social costs of long-term imprisonment.[17] It is interesting to speculate as to whether today's war on drugs will be discussed seventy-five years from now in the same way that we now speak of the Prohibition era.

These activists in the second annual International Millennium Marijuana March in Seattle in 2000 are calling for the legalization of marijuana for personal use. How might these protesters draw parallels between drug laws of the 1930s and prohibition laws of the 1920s? Is it only a matter of time before the use of marijuana will be decriminalized?

How Can Crime Be Explained?

Understanding the motives of criminal offenders is a central question in criminal justice, because all attempts to prevent and control crime are based on assumptions about its causes. Consider these questions, all of which arise from highly publicized actual crimes:[18]

How can a mother kill her own children?

How can children kill their own parents?

How can a sex offender be punished severely, released, and then commit another crime?

How can young people commit brutal assaults without any provocation?

explain crime

Questions such as these make it clear that we have a long way to go in understanding the causes of crime. During the twentieth century growing concern led to systematic study of the causes of crime, but this study has not discovered a uniform explanation. Some have argued that a single explanation should be able to account for all criminality, whereas others believe that different explanations are required for different types of crime and different offenders.[19] At present there are four general types of explanations of crime: classical, positivistic, ethical, and structural.

The **classical school** of thought in criminology sees crime as resulting from the conscious exercise of an individual's free will. Classicists see people as hedonists: They believe that all people pursue pleasure while attempting to minimize pain. Two of the best-known classicists, Cesare Beccaria and Jeremy Bentham, wrote during the eighteenth century.[20]

classical school
A perspective in criminology that sees crime as resulting from the conscious exercise of an individual's free will.

Classical thinking, sometimes called the free will school, dominated criminal codes during the nineteenth century because the law assumed that all people were equal in their capacity to guide their conduct rationally. If the law was violated, the punishment was based on the violation committed rather than on the type of person who committed it. This punishment was designed to deter future misconduct by the offender and by other members of society. Recent exponents of the classical explanation are Michael Gottfredson and Travis Hirschi; these criminologists believe that crime is a course of conduct chosen by individuals who have low self-control and are unable to defer immediate gratification of their desires.[21] Empirical studies continue to test the ability of classical explanations to account for the commission of crimes, but the results are inconsistent.[22]

Dissatisfaction with the classical school first appeared toward the end of the nineteenth century. Crime was seen as a growing problem, and punishment of violators apparently was not deterring others from committing criminal acts—a perception that remains widespread today more than a century later. The late 1800s also witnessed the rise of the scientific method and the beginnings of social science. Charles Darwin developed his theory of evolution through natural selection, publishing it in his famous work *The Origin of Species.*[23] Emile Durkheim observed differences in rates of suicide in different regions of France. He used these observations to develop a theory of social factors in suicide.[24] Both Darwin and Durkheim were pioneers in the use of the scientific method, in which knowledge is advanced through observation rather than by theorizing without first gathering data.

This scientific approach to explanations gave rise to the positivist school of criminology. According to **positivism,** individual human behavior is determined by internal and external influences, which include biological, psychological, and/or social factors. Rather than seeing crime as the product of the rational exercise of free will, as classicists do, positivists see crime as largely determined by a

positivism
The perspective in criminology that sees human behavior as determined by internal and external influences, such as biological, psychological, and/or social factors.

variety of internal and external influences on a person. In many ways the positivist school in criminology emphasizes "nurture" (i.e., factors in the individual's environment), whereas the classical school emphasizes "nature" (i.e., a presupposed "natural" inborn tendency to seek pleasure and avoid pain).

POSITIVISM

Positivists believe that fundamental differences between criminals and noncriminals are based on these internal and external influences, which may include personality imbalances, family role models, and peer group pressure, among many others. From the positivist perspective all people are *not* equal, because the criminal act is seen as a symptom of an underlying problem rather than as the problem itself (the classicists' view). Instead of punishment, therefore, positivists see reform or rehabilitation of the offender as the best way to prevent future crime; they advocate changing the influences on an individual or changing how he or she reacts to those influences.

ethical view
The perspective that sees crime as a moral failure in decision making.

The **ethical view** sees crime as a moral failure in decision making. Simply stated, crime occurs when a person fails to *choose* the proper course of conduct; and this bad choice results from failure to appreciate an act's wrongfulness, rather than from lack of concern about being caught, as the classicists suggest. According to the ethical view, the positivist and classical views are both inadequate. This is because external factors may play a role in influencing some people to engage in crime, but they do not *cause* crime (as positivists suggest). Although freely willed decisions lie at the base of virtually all criminal behavior, there is no hedonistic tendency to engage in crime that is controlled only through the possibility of apprehension (as classicists suggest). Instead, crime is caused by failure to appreciate the wrongfulness of criminal conduct; that is, the failure to appreciate its long-term impact both on the offender and on the community or victim.

A young woman makes a decision to shoplift from a grocery store. Can you surmise what were the influences that might have resulted in this decision to commit crime: positive, classical, structural, or ethical?

In the ethical view, crime results when criminal acts bring pleasure rather than guilt. The key to understanding crime causation, then, lies in discovering *how* people make noncriminal choices. Stated another way, where do people learn to make decisions in accord with legal and ethical principles? Ethicists argue that most people are incapable of thinking through decisions in ethical terms, because ethical principles are rarely included in the educational process.[25] Lacking education or experience in ethical decision making, people often do what comes naturally: They base decisions on self-interest rather than on the greater interest of the community; they are concerned primarily with the short-term consequences of their decisions; and they confuse competing values such as honesty and loyalty. This tendency is shown by individuals who derive pleasure from shortchanging a store clerk, shoplifting, participating in gang crimes, and engaging in vandalism and other crimes, rather than feeling guilt over their wrongful behavior or empathy for their victims. For example, a study of college students and prison inmates found the students were much more likely to feel bad or stressed about committing a crime, whereas the prison inmates were more likely to feel exhilarated or proud.[26] This finding suggests that greater appreciation of the wrongfulness of conduct (the basis for ethics) may be a bulwark against criminal behavior.

A fourth approach to explaining crime, the **structural/conflict view**, focuses less on individual behavior and more on the behavior of law. That is to say, social, political, and economic conditions cause certain behaviors to be defined by the law as criminal. These conditions also cause the law to be applied in certain ways. As a result, those in power define a great deal of "marginal" behavior as criminal as a way to control people who are perceived as "undesirable." Laws against gambling, loan-sharking, and vagrancy are examples of the use of law as a tool of social control rather than as a means of protecting society from harm.

structural/conflict view The perspective that sees the criminal law as reflecting the will of those in power, and behaviors that threaten the interests of the powerful are punished most severely.

According to this structural or conflict view, the crime problem has roots deeper than the immediate environment or the pursuit of pleasure. This perspective sees the criminal law as reflecting the will of those in power, and notes that behaviors that threaten the interests of the powerful are punished most severely.[27] Thus, prisons are filled largely with poor and powerless people rather than with middle- and upper-class wrongdoers. According to conflict theory, there is little consensus within society on basic values, so the interests of the powerful are imposed through the criminal law and the manner in which it is enforced.[28] This explanation of crime clearly has merit in explaining politically or ideologically motivated crimes that are committed to protest some social, economic, or political condition. People who publicly refuse to pay their federal income taxes, or who protest mandated changes in the school curriculum by refusing to send their children to school, provide examples of the conflict view. In both cases it might be said that there is conflict regarding basic values and that the powerful (i.e., those who make the laws) have used their position to impose their values on society. On the other hand, the conflict view has less relevance in explaining murder, rape, robbery, assault, burglary, larceny, and many other crimes, which are rarely committed for ideological reasons.[29]

The tensions among the classical, positivist, ethical, and structural/conflict explanations of crime lie in their respective emphases. These emphases are summarized in Table 2.2. The positivist and structural explanations place most of the responsibility for crime on social factors that influence behavior. The classical and ethical explanations place most of the responsibility on individual decision making. The classicists place more emphasis on how the likelihood of apprehension and

Table 2.2 Four Approaches to Explaining Criminal Behavior

Type of Explanation	*Primary Cause of Crime*	*Prescribed Remedy*
Classical	Free-will decision guided by hedonistic tendency to maximize pleasure and minimize pain	Deterrence through threat of apprehension and punishment
Positivist	Internal or external factors (e.g., biological, psychological, social, economic)	Rehabilitation or reform by changing these internal or external conditions, or changing someone's reaction to them
Ethical	Free-will decision guided by ethical principles in which an individual fails to appreciate an act's wrongfulness and lacks empathy for the victim	Education and reinforcement in ethical decision making from an early age; reduction of external factors that promote unethical decisions
Structural	Political and economic conditions promote a culture of competitive individualism in which individual gain becomes more important than the social good	More equitable distribution of power and wealth in society, so that all individuals have a greater stake in a better society

An armed robbery of an innocent victim reflects a widely-held public fear. What are the factors that would cause a person to make the choice to threaten or use violence against a stranger just to obtain the contents of a purse?

the threat of penalties (i.e., pain) control crime (i.e., the pursuit of pleasure), whereas the ethical view places more emphasis on the fact that crime (i.e., victimizing others) does not bring pleasure to ethical individuals.

Biological Determinism and Psychological Explanations

biological determinism Positivists who see the roots of criminal behavior in biological attributes.

NATURAL-BORN CRIMINALS?

The earliest positivists saw the roots of criminal behavior in biological attributes, an approach known as **biological determinism.** Cesare Lombroso (1836–1909) took body measurements of offenders in Italian prisons and concluded that there were "born criminals" with distinctive body measurements and skull sizes. On the basis of his measurements, Lombroso developed a theory of *atavism* that suggested that "born criminals" were biological throwbacks to an earlier stage of human evolution.[30] In 1913, however, an English physician, Charles Goring, published the results of his measurements of 3,000 English convicts, which he had compared to similar measurements of a group of nonconvicts. Goring found no evidence of a distinct physical criminal type, thereby discrediting Lombroso's theory of atavism.[31]

Biological determinism did not die with Lombroso, however. Studies focusing on the body build of delinquents have been followed by investigations of chromosomal abnormalities, glandular dysfunction, chemical imbalances, and nutritional deficiencies. As measurement methods and techniques for assessing subtle biological differences have improved, interest in biological influences on crime has grown. Some criminologists now see links between certain biological features and a propensity to engage in crime.[32] Studies of twins raised separately, for example, have compared the incidence of their delinquent behavior, and studies of adopted children have compared their criminality to that of their biological parents. These studies suggest that genetic factors play some role in delinquency, but it is not clear that biological factors outweigh environmental factors.[33] A Panel on the Understanding and Control of Violent Behavior of the National Academy of Sciences concluded that biological studies have "produced mixed results, suggesting at most a weak genetic influence on the chance of violent behavior."[34] Nevertheless, there is continuing interest in the interplay between biological predispositions and social influences on behavior. Such a biosocial approach attempts to link factors such as prenatal complications, malnutrition, brain dysfunction, poor attention span, hyperactivity, and low IQ with social "triggers," such as abuse, neglect, poverty, and antisocial role models, that may result in criminal violence.[35]

MALADJUSTED PERSONALITIES?

psychoanalytic theory Freudian theory that sees behavior as resulting from the interaction of the three components of the personality: id, ego, and superego.

Psychological explanations of crime look inside the human psyche (or internalized controls) for the causes of crime. Instead of examining human physiology, psychologists look at how the human mind operates. The oldest and most influential psychological explanation of crime is based on the work of Sigmund Freud (1856–1939). Freud's **psychoanalytic theory** sees behavior as resulting from the interaction of the three components of the personality: id, ego, and superego. The id is defined as the primitive, instinctual drives of aggression and sex that everyone is born with. The superego acts as a person's conscience, reflecting the values one develops in the early years of life through interactions with family members. The ego mediates between the self-centered desires of the id and the learned values of the superego. The id, ego, and superego are theoretical constructs, of course; you cannot open someone's head and find them. Freud hypothesized their existence, attempting to demonstrate their presence through case studies of individuals' behavior.

Most explanations of crime based on Freud's theory see crime as resulting from faulty ego or superego structures that fail to control the id adequately. This results in personality imbalances, which produce deviant behavior. A weak or defective superego, for example, might result in "unsocialized aggressive behavior," in which a person has insufficient control over his or her aggressive or sexual instincts.[36] The conscience, in other words, is not sufficiently developed.

The ego and superego are said to develop by age six, and some psychologists believe it is difficult if not impossible to correct the damage caused when these components of the personality develop inadequately because of poor family relationships or other negative experiences during the early years.[37] Studies of juvenile murderers have found many to be "volatile" and "explosive" and some to be mentally ill as a result of personality problems that began during early childhood.[38] A study of 210 chronic delinquents found that those who committed violent crimes were more than twice as likely as their nondelinquent peers to have been exposed to serious physical abuse and to violence involving weapons between the adults in their household.[39] Prior exposure to violence may trigger psychological reactions that produce greater risk of delinquent behavior in the future.

MALADJUSTED THOUGHTS?

Other psychological theories look to other sources for problems in the human psyche. A **cognitive theory** of crime was developed by Walters and White, who observed that career criminals are irresponsible, self-indulgent, and rule breaking in most every area of their lives. They perennially act as adolescents in their hedonism, short-term thinking, and lack of self-discipline. This thinking pattern is not caused by their social environment, but rather environmental conditions merely limit their choices. Walters and White found that these career criminals perpetuate their behavior by always making choices that favor their own short-term self-interest.[40] A further refinement of this approach claims that persistent offenders define and interpret situations differently from less frequent offenders and non-offenders. A recent study found that aggressive delinquents usually define an ambiguous situation in hostile terms when confronted with it and they act accordingly.[41] For example, staring at a person can be considered inconsequential, flattering, bold, rude, or threatening. Persistent offenders tended to regard it as threatening. Cognition theories, therefore, look to how individuals define situations differently in ways that result in crime.

cognitive theory
View that behavior results from habits of thought and interpretations of reality.

Sociological Explanations

Sociological explanations of crime are more common than any other type. These approaches arose largely in response to the inability of biological and psychological explanations to account for many types of crime that appeared to be "normal" reactions of people raised in dysfunctional families or neighborhoods. Unlike biological or psychological explanations, which look at problems *within* the individual (whether physiological abnormalities or personality conflicts), sociological

Table 2.3 Sociological Explanations of Crime

Type of Explanation	*Primary Cause of Crime*	*Prescribed Remedy*
Differential association	Learned behavior	Early intervention; alter the social environment
Blocked opportunity	Lack of access to legitimate means of achieving goals	Prevention; improve the opportunity structure of society
Labeling theory	Self-fulfilling prophecy	Intervention; improve self-esteem and role expectations
Social bonding	Lack of attachment to family and society	Prevention; strengthen social bonds and educate
Rational choice	Individual motivation and routine opportunity	Prevention; educate people on how to avoid becoming a victim
Gender-based	Economic marginalization and victimization of women	Intervention; e.g., reduce violence against women

explanations look at *environmental* influences that affect the way people behave. Sociological explanations can be grouped into six types: theories based on learning, on blocked opportunity, on labeling, on the social bond to conventional society, on rational choice, and on gender-based explanations (see Table 2.3). A leading theory of each type is summarized here.

Theories Based on Learning An influential sociological theory based on learning was proposed by Edwin Sutherland in 1939. Sutherland felt that delinquent behavior is learned in much the same way that people learn anything else: through observation, role modeling, and so forth. Sutherland called this learning process **differential association** and argued that a person becomes criminal or delinquent when he or she associates more with people who condone violation of the law than with people who do not. These attitudes toward the law are learned from intimate personal groups such as family, friends, and peers. Although everybody is exposed to procriminal and anticriminal attitudes, the *proportions* in which a person is exposed to these kinds of attitudes determine whether or not that individual will acquire those attitudes. Therefore, Sutherland does not speak of association with criminals or noncriminals but rather of association with those holding attitudes favorable to or tolerant of criminal behavior versus those who do not.[42] Subsequent researchers have investigated the link between juvenile associations and delinquency in order to determine how well the theory of differential association explains juvenile crime.[43] A study of chronic delinquents found that violent offenders were more likely to have experienced serious domestic violence and physical abuse. These juveniles were also more likely to believe that aggression has little impact on its victims and that it enhances one's self-image.[44] The results thus are mixed, suggesting that the differential association theory is a better explanation of the spread of delinquency than of its ultimate cause.

differential association
Theory that a person becomes criminal or delinquent when he or she associates more with people who condone violation of the law than with people who do not.

ILLEGITIMATE MEANS

blocked opportunity
Theory that crime results from lack of access to legitimate means for achieving goals.

Theories Based on Blocked Opportunity Sociologists Richard Cloward and Lloyd Ohlin believed that delinquency and crime resulted from lack of access to legitimate means for achieving goals, or **blocked opportunity.** But they also felt

Media & Criminal Justice

Perceptions and the Reality of Crime

We've all heard the statistics. By the time a teenager turns eighteen, he or she has witnessed 40,000 dramatized murders and 200,000 other acts of violence on television and in the movies. So what difference does it make?

Public concern about exposure to violence, even if fictionalized, has resulted in the addition of ratings for movies, video games, and even television shows over the years. But these ratings have not had the desired result, because movies, games, and television programs with violent content often do rather well in attracting their target audience: young people. And the number of these programs has increased in recent years, despite the negative attention.

A federal study documented a number of unsavory practices, such as showing previews for R-rated films to audiences waiting to see a PG-rated movie. Young shoppers and viewers were easily able to buy M-rated video games, gain entrance into R-rated films, and purchase CDs labeled with parental advisories. Efforts to pressure the entertainment industry to limit their marketing campaigns and placement of ads in magazines and programs aimed at younger audiences have had only modest success.[a]

What is the evidence to show that these practices negatively impact children? Anecdotal evidence suggests that some school shootings in recent years and other senseless acts of violence have been committed by young people who were enthralled by violent entertainment and who idolized unsavory characters in movies, often obtaining the same weapons their "heroes" used.[b] Scientific studies attempt to measure exposure to violence and its effects on behavior in a more systematic way. In general they have found that exposure to violence has an impact on people, but its extent is not clear or uniform. For example, studies have found that the more television a viewer watches the more likely he or she is to believe that murder rates are higher than they really are; studies have also shown that greater exposure to depictions of violence often leads to more aggressive behavior and desensitization to violence among young people.[c] It appears that some people are more susceptible to media portrayals of violence than are others, and this is likely the result of individual differences, the mix between *actual* violence in the lives of young persons (at home, in school, in the community), and the presence of nonviolent role models in their lives.

How would you explain the way in which watching media portrayals of violence can change someone's behavior? How might the explanations discussed in this chapter be applied to your explanation? Can you suggest practical ways to limit the impact of media violence?

NOTES

a. Federal Trade Commission, *Marketing Violent Entertainment to Children: A Report to Congress* (Washington, DC: Federal Trade Commission, 2002).

b. Betsey Streisand, "Lawyers, Guns, Money: Hollywood under New Probe May Have a Lot to Hide," *U.S. News & World Report* (June 14, 1999).

c. Donald L. Diefenba and Mark D. West, "Violent Crime and Poisson Regression: A Measure and a Method for Cultivation Analysis," *Journal of Broadcasting & Electronic Media* (summer 2001); American Academy of Pediatrics, "Media Violence," *Pediatrics* (November 2001).

that even illegitimate means are unevenly distributed in society. As a result, some lower-class neighborhoods provide greater opportunity for illegal gain than do others. Cloward and Ohlin did not believe that individuals substitute new goals; instead, they use illegitimate means to achieve accepted goals. Rather than getting a job and earning money to buy new shoes, for example, an individual may steal them. Cloward and Ohlin believed, however, that not all delinquents can attain their goals through illegitimate means, because the opportunities for doing so are not available to everyone—just as there are differences in the opportunities available to individuals to achieve these goals by legitimate means.

criminal subcultures
Different forms of deviance that result when youths cease to adhere to middle-class standards and become part of the adult *criminal, conflict,* or *retreatist* subculture.

Cloward and Ohlin describe three types of **criminal subcultures** that develop when youths cease to adhere to middle-class standards.[45] Youths may become part of the adult *criminal* subculture; they may participate in the *conflict* subculture by forming fighting gangs that emphasize violence and seek status by coercion; or they may become part of the *retreatist* subculture when either no opportunities exist in the criminal subculture or status cannot be obtained in the conflict group. Cloward and Ohlin maintain not only that legitimate opportunities for success are often blocked for lower-class juveniles but that illegitimate opportunities can also be blocked, leading to the creation of one of these types of delinquent subcultures.

labeling theory
View that adjudicating a juvenile as a delinquent encourages future delinquency through a negative public identity or changed self-image.

LABELING DEVIANT BEHAVIOR

Labeling Theory Sociologist Howard Becker popularized **labeling theory** in his 1963 book *The Outsiders.* Originally put forth in 1951 by Edwin Lemert, labeling theory holds that "when society acts negatively to a particular individual (by adjudicating a person through the criminal justice system) by means of the 'label' (delinquent)—we actually encourage future delinquency." For Lemert and Becker the labeling process depends less on the behavior of the delinquent than on how others respond to delinquents' acts.[46] It is society's labeling of the individual (through adjudication of delinquency) that promotes deviant behavior, rather than any action by the juvenile. For example, a juvenile who is suspended from school or adjudicated in court as a delinquent gains a bad reputation. This bad reputation lowers the behavioral expectations of others (e.g., teachers, parents, friends). Also, the juvenile internalizes this reputation and acts in accord with it, resulting in more of the bad behavior everyone expects. According to this view, juveniles who are labeled as delinquents are actually encouraged to commit future acts of delinquency through the lowered expectations of others and their own changed self-image. The more frequent and prolonged the individual's contacts with the juvenile justice system, the more likely it is that he or she will ultimately accept the delinquent label as a personal identity and perhaps enter a life of crime.

Strength of the Social Bond A fourth type of sociological explanation of crime is based on the individual's bond to society. When that bond is weakened or broken, the constraints that society places on the individual are also weakened or broken. As a result, this theory suggests, the person becomes more likely to break the law. A person's **social bond** has four primary elements: attachment to others, commitment to conventional activities, involvement in conventional activities, and belief in widely shared moral values.

social bond
Individual's attachment to society, including attachment to others, commitment to conventional activities, involvement in those activities, and belief in widely shared moral values.

In an attempt to test social bond theory, sociologist Travis Hirschi administered a self-report survey to 4,000 junior and senior high school students in California. He found that strong attachments to parents, commitment to values, involvement in school, and respect for police and law reduced the likelihood of delinquency. Replications of this study in Albany, New York, and elsewhere have generally supported Hirschi's results.[47]

It is clear that sociological explanations of crime far outnumber psychological or biological explanations. This is because a far greater number of social influences can be identified and measured. Also, each person's social environment is different and changes over time, making sociological explanations popular among positivists.

No single explanation of crime accounts for all incidents, as was made clear in an examination of 100 rampage killings that occurred over the last fifty years. These rare but serious cases of violence were studied in an effort to find common features. In 63 of the 100 cases it was found that the killers had made earlier general threats of violence, 55 regularly displayed explosive anger, and 35 had a history of violent behavior and assaults. Warning signs like these were missed either by the mental health system, by families who were unable to face the reality of the problem, or by schools, neighbors, and police, who either failed to take the danger signs seriously or were unable to intervene prior to violence occurring. Very few of the killers were interested in violent video games or violent movies, but "in case after case, family members, teachers and mental health professionals missed or dismissed signs of deterioration."[48] Thus, a combination of psychological problems, combined with ineffective social support from families, schools, and treatment appear to be at the root of these rampage killings. This study demonstrates the need for an integrated social and psychological approach to understanding the causes of criminal behavior.

Take another look at the burglar. Was he destined to commit this crime because of biological or psychological factors, or did environmental factors play a bigger role? What would Edwin Sutherland say caused him to become a criminal? According to Howard Becker, could his criminal behavior be the result of a self-fulfilling prophecy? According to Travis Hirschi, what failures of social bonding could account for his criminal behavior? Which of these sociological explanations, or what combination thereof, makes the most sense to you?

WARNING SIGNS

Rational Choice Explanations

Biological, psychological, and sociological theories have been criticized for placing too much emphasis on how these conditions *cause* criminal behavior. The individual is not given enough credit for defining the situation and making rational decisions—interacting with his or her environment, making judgments, and taking actions. A newer explanation of crime focuses the choices that offenders make and the situational factors that cause them. These **rational choice theories** attempt to explain why offenders commit crimes in some situations and not in others by examining how circumstances affect criminal thinking.[49]

A popular explanation of this type is **routine activities theory** described by Marcus Felson. He observed that three things must exist simultaneously for a criminal event to occur: a motivated offender, a suitable target, and the absence of a capable guardian to intervene.[50] According to this view, routine activities of everyday life bring potential offenders and victims together. Changes in society have led people to work and play farther from home, fewer children have continuous supervision, more homes are empty during the day, and related social trends lead to changes in crime in neighborhoods and cities because motivated offenders, suitable targets, and absence of guardians are occurring together more often. Therefore, crime control becomes a matter of educating potential victims about being targets and avoiding situations without guardians. This explanation does not deal with the important issue of how motivated offenders develop in the first place, but it states that individuals with low self-control exist and will exploit suitable targets that are not well protected.

rational choice theories
Theories that examine how circumstances affect criminal thinking to explain why offenders commit crimes in some situations but not in others.

routine activities theory
The theory that sees criminal events as the result of a combination of a motivated offender, a suitable target, and the absence of a capable guardian to intervene.

Gender-Based Explanations

There are a growing number of explanations that focus on explaining female criminality. Because men dominate arrest statistics and most research historically has been done on male offenders, gender-based explanations seek to focus more attention on female offending. For example, it is interesting to consider that in typical cases of prostitution the female is still the one arrested while the "john" usually is not. This anachronism speaks directly to the point that those who make, enforce, and adjudicate the laws are still overwhelmingly male, and that reasons why women are present or absent in arrest statistics may have little to do with their own behavior.

FEMALE CRIME

Freda Adler wrote an influential book in 1975 titled *Sisters in Crime* in which she proposed the idea that as women's social roles in society change in terms of greater freedoms, education, and employment opportunities, they obtain more assertive roles previously reserved for men. She argued that women would commit more traditionally "male" crimes.[51] This has occurred in the area of white-collar crime, but not for violent crimes. Other explanations of female crime have focused on the economic marginalization of women and its effect on their criminal opportunities.[52] Many women remain unemployed and underemployed despite a general improvement in the status of women in society. The crimes committed by these women reflect their class status, but arrest practices make the true extent of female offending difficult to determine. Closely related to this issue is the status of women within families where women suffer from high rates of domestic violence. Some of these women strike back, and studies show a complex relationship between violent women and women who suffer from violence.[53] Thus, gender-based criminology seeks to bring attention to both the reasons for the behavior of women and also to the behavior of the criminal justice system and society at large in its treatment of women.[54]

Guns, Drugs, and Crime

Regardless of one's perspective on the causes of criminal activity, however, there is agreement that guns and drugs are frequent accompaniments to crime. The disagreement occurs in determining precisely how to counteract these dangerous associations among crime, guns, and drugs.

Guns

Few issues in criminal justice provoke more boisterous debate than the connection between guns and crime. The incidence of crimes involving guns is extremely high, but it is not clear whether the absence of guns would necessarily reduce the rates of violent crime. If all guns disappeared tomorrow, would violent crime disappear? Would it be significantly reduced?

Crime involves a decision by an individual. It is unlikely that a gun determines this decision, but it is possible that the presence of a gun may give a potential offender the "courage" to proceed with a crime he or she might not otherwise commit. This is what much of the **gun control** debate is about. To what extent would better control of guns result in better control of crime?

gun control
Regulation of gun manufacturers, buyers, and sellers in an effort to minimize gun-related crime.

CRIMES WITH HANDGUNS

According to surveys of crime victims, 22 percent of victims or rape, robbery, and assault faced an offender with a weapon. More than a quarter of these weapons (6 percent) were firearms, comprised mostly of handguns. Guns are used most often in robberies (19 percent) and less often in assaults or rapes (5 percent or less). Over the last 10 years, the rate of violent crime committed with firearms has declined from 11 percent of all violent incidents to 6 percent.[55] According to the FBI statistics, two-thirds (66 percent) of murders are committed with firearms, and most of these were handguns. The rate of handgun use in murder appears stable, as Table 2.4 indicates. It also shows that trends in weapon use in murder have changed very little since 2000.[56]

GUN CONTROL?

Despite the relatively low rate of gun use for violent crimes other than murder, efforts to keep guns away from criminals are hotly debated. Proposals to reduce the availability of guns for criminal use most often involve one or more of the following: banning handguns altogether for most citizens; banning assault weapons; banning the carrying of weapons; banning certain kinds of bullets; imposing mandatory sentences for crimes using guns; and performing background checks of gun purchases. The Centers for Disease Control and Prevention reviewed fifty-one separate studies that looked at the impact of different types of gun laws on preventing violent crimes. They found "insufficient evidence" to demonstrate that these laws have been effective.[57] A brief examination of alternative gun proposals illustrates why they have had limited success.

AVAILABILITY OF HANDGUNS

Several cities have banned handguns for nearly all citizens except police officers, but the impact on crimes committed with handguns has been negligible for two reasons.[58] The first is that local gun control laws are unlikely to be effective when guns are readily available in bordering jurisdictions. The classic case is that of John Hinckley, who bought a gun in another jurisdiction, brought it to Washington, and shot President Reagan. The second reason is that there are an estimated 70 million handguns in the United States. Even though most are owned by law-abiding citizens, guns often find their way into the hands of criminals.

Table 2.4 Murder by Weapon Used (Top Five Methods Used)

	2000	*2002*	*2004*
Firearm (all types)	8,661 65%	9,528 67%	9,326 66%
Handgun only	6,778 51%	7,294 51%	7,265 51%
Knives	1,782 13%	1,776 12%	1,866 13%
Hands/Feet	927 7%	954 7%	933 7%
Blunt object	617 5%	681 5%	663 5%
Total murder victims	13,230	14,263	14,121

Source: Federal Bureau of Investigation, *Crime in the United States*, www.fbi/gov/ucr

In the twentieth century more than 220 million guns were manufactured in or imported to the United States. Since 1973 alone, more than 40 million handguns have been produced in the this country.[59] It is not known what percentage of these guns have been lost, seized, stolen, or destroyed, but it is reasonable to believe that most are still in working order. A survey of inmates in state prisons found that 9 percent had stolen a gun and 28 percent had acquired a gun illegally from a fence or drug dealer.[60] Interviews with juvenile and adult inmates in other studies have found that between 10 and 50 percent have stolen a gun at some point in their criminal career.[61] In fact, the FBI's National Crime Information Center listed more than 300,000 *reported* incidents of stolen guns, ammunition, cannons, and grenades in a single year.[62] Of the guns stolen, almost 60 percent were handguns. Thus, other than increasing the black-market price for stolen handguns, attempts to ban handguns will have little impact in the foreseeable future.

ASSAULT WEAPONS

A second proposal is to ban assault weapons. Such a ban is even less likely to lower crime rates, because criminals rarely use these weapons to commit crimes. As noted earlier, 70 percent of murders with guns are committed with handguns, and most of the remainder do not involve assault weapons. A ban on assault weapons would have extremely little impact on gun crimes, even if the assault weapons now in circulation could be effectively monitored, something that is not currently possible. The National Firearms Act requires that all automatic weapons be registered with the Bureau of Alcohol, Tobacco, Firearms, and Explosives, but about 8 percent of legally registered automatic weapons are reported stolen in a given year.[63]

"CARRYING"

A third approach is to restrict severely the unauthorized carrying of a handgun. The idea behind these laws is that handguns are easily carried and concealed. Interviews with convicted offenders show that many purchased a gun for self-defense, left home without intending to commit a crime, but ended up using the gun while committing a crime.[64] Many states have made it illegal to carry a handgun without a special license. The penalty is a mandatory sentence of one year in prison, simply for illegally carrying the weapon. In Massachusetts, gun crimes decreased after the handgun law was enacted, but assaults with other kinds of weapons increased, suggesting a "substitution effect" in weapon choice. Also, murders and robberies with guns decreased in Boston, but over the same period they also decreased in cities without such prohibitions.[65] These findings suggest that guns are an *accompaniment* to crime rather than a causal influence. A controversial claim has been that states which permit citizens to carry concealed handguns have lower rates of violent crime, because potential criminals are deterred by the fear of possible armed resistance by citizens. This research tries to tease out the effects of handgun laws from the many other factors that cause crime rates to vary across states. It is difficult to identify and measure all the factors that might account for variations in these crime rates across states, so such research is necessarily arduous. A number of subsequent analyses have drawn mixed conclusions with some supporting, while others casting doubt on this claim.[66]

BULLET BAN

A fourth proposal is to ban bullets. Such bans have been proposed several times, mostly in relation to armor-piercing bullets that would be dangerous to police. Few criminals have been caught with such dangerous bullets, so it is not clear how common they really are. The problem is that bullets are easily manufactured at home by the enterprising citizen, whether hunter or criminal. Therefore, a ban on bullets "would stimulate a sizable cottage industry" of bullet making.[67]

STRICT SENTENCING

The fifth tactic is to impose mandatory sentences for crimes committed with guns. Many states and cities have passed laws increasing the penalties for these offenses. Evaluations of their impact reveal that these sentencing laws have had little effect, because the criminals involved were already receiving severe sentences.[68] Simply stated, offenders who commit crimes with guns already receive

That's a FACT

Perspectives on Gun Control by Teenagers and Adults

Gun control is one of those crime-related issues that is particularly divisive. Gun control advocates argue that making it more difficult to own a gun would ultimately lead to reduced crime, whereas opponents believe there is a constitutional right to gun ownership and restrictions would not have a significant impact on gun crimes. The evidence that exists to support these arguments is presented in this chapter, and it illustrates why solutions to gun-related crimes are so difficult.

Figure 2A displays the results of Gallup poll surveys from 1993 to 2005. It shows how public views toward restrictions on firearms sales have shifted over time. Overall, more people now believe there should be fewer restrictions on gun sales.

It is interesting to compare the views of teenagers and adults on this issue to see if there are any generational differences of opinion. More than half (54 percent) of 13- to 17-year-old teens believe that laws covering firearm sales should be made more strict, while 34 percent feel these laws should remain unchanged. Only 10 percent of teens feel gun laws should be made less strict. Interestingly, these views are very similar to what the U.S. adult population believes, according to a Gallup poll. Teenage girls are significantly more likely than boys to want stricter firearm sales laws, with 66 percent of girls believing gun laws should be made more strict. This gender difference is similar to that observed among adults.

Forty-two percent of teens report that there are guns in their households, but majorities of teens and adults say they do not have guns in their homes. Teens who do not have guns in their homes are more likely to support stricter firearm legislation. Sixty-five percent of teens who do not have guns in their homes say the laws should be made more strict, versus 39 percent of teens with guns in their home. Furthermore, teens with guns in the home are somewhat more likely to say that firearm sales laws should be kept as they are now, rather than made more strict. A similar trend is found for adults.

How would you explain the similarities in views between teenagers and adults regarding gun laws? Why do you believe that fewer of those having a gun in the home believe gun laws should be made more strict?

Source: Julie Ray, "Growing Up with Guns," *Gallup News Service,* (April 15, 2003); "Guns," *The Gallup Poll Tuesday Briefing* (reporting on a survey of January, 2004).

FIGURE 2A Public Views on the Sale of Firearms

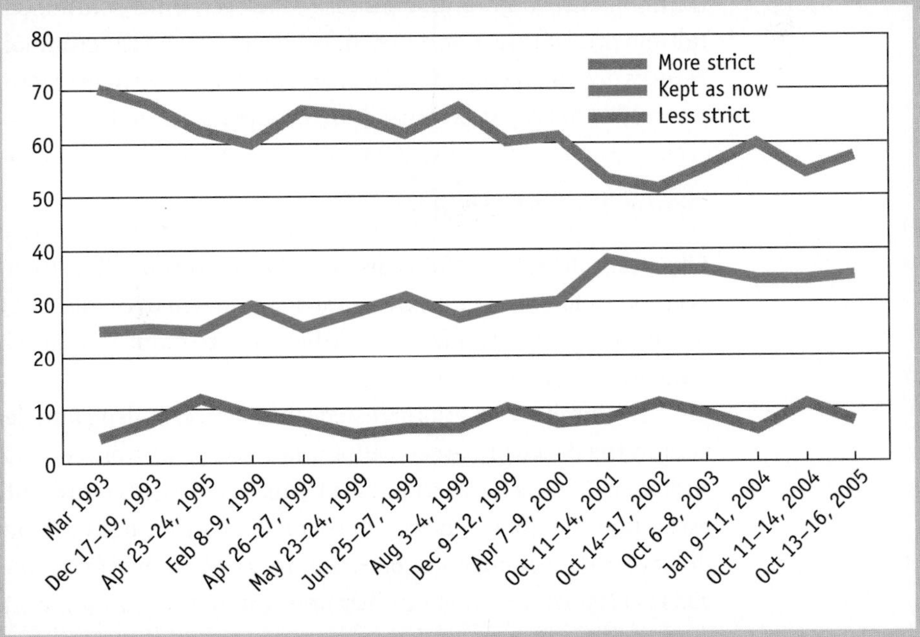

Source: Gallup News Service.

Where did these youths get this weapon? What are the chances that they will commit violent crimes? Who will be their likely victims? Do you think violent crime could be significantly reduced through gun control? Why or why not?

severe sentences (for the robbery, assault, or murder they committed). The impact of a gun law that adds a year or more in prison is insignificant in comparison.

The sixth strategy is to try to keep guns out of the hands of criminals by conducting background checks of prospective buyers. Background checks have been hotly debated by legislatures and pro-gun lobbyists as an infringement on the rights of hunters and target shooters. The 1994 Brady law required a waiting period and background check but was not shown to reduce homicide rates, although gun suicide rates fell.[69] Instant background checks of buyers at gun shows and between private owners do not occur in many states, even though 72 percent of gun purchaser background checks occur within thirty seconds of entering the purchaser's identifying information into the system.[70] Still, about 2 percent (81,000) of the FBI's background checks conducted thus far have resulted in denials, suggesting that a large number of unsuitable persons attempt to buy weapons.

BACKGROUND CHECKS

These six gun control proposals each have flaws and the current debate often does not focus on the central issue: How can we keep guns out of the hands of juveniles, criminals, and the mentally ill? The gun debate focuses heavily on civil and criminal penalties rather than on access to weapons by unsuitable persons. Data obtained from tracing guns used in crimes reveal that less than 2 percent of the nation's licensed dealers sold almost 60 percent of the guns used in crimes, indicating that more needs to be done to keep guns away from criminals.[71]

CIVIL SUITS

Proposals to sue gun manufacturers, require gun insurance, and establish gun-free zones around schools tend to replace more serious discussion of the connection between guns and crime.[72] However, until point-of-sale checks (both retail and private) are monitored more effectively and the criminal and mental health records on which background checks are based are made more accurate, it will be impossible to keep guns away from criminals, juveniles, and the mentally ill.

Drugs and Alcohol

Like guns, drugs are often raised in discussions of what to do about crime. The issue is twofold: To what extent are drugs linked to crimes of violence and crimes against property? And what is the best way to reduce the proportion of criminals who use drugs?

The number of adults arrested for violation of drug laws increased by 24 percent in the decade between 1994 and 2003.[73] The proportion of drug offenders in state prisons is 21 percent of all inmates.[74] These figures illustrate a dramatic escalation in public concern about drug offenses, but in themselves they do not demonstrate a connection between drugs and other forms of criminal conduct. This is because the total number and penalties for drug law violations increased over the same period, and those arrested may have been entrepreneurs catering to the public demand for drugs, rather than drug users.

The National Institute of Justice sponsored a drug testing program in thirty-five cities called ADAM (Arrestee Drug Abuse Monitoring). In each city urine spec-

DRUG USE FORECASTING

imens from a sample of arrestees were taken soon after arrest to determine what proportion of those arrested had already used drugs. More than half of all arrestees (male and female) tested positive for drugs at the time of arrest, regardless of the crime for which they were arrested.[75] Although these figures do not necessarily mean that drugs *caused* the criminal activity in question, it suggests that drugs play a role in the lifestyle of arrestees. Better-controlled studies have found that criminals who use drugs commit robberies and assaults more often than non-drug-using offenders.[76]

It appears that alcohol also plays an important role in crime, particularly violent crime. It has been found, for example, that chronic drinkers are more likely than nondrinkers to have histories of violent behavior. Tests have shown that drinking immediately preceded half of all violent crimes studied by researchers.[77]

An assessment of inmates in jail (either awaiting trial or already convicted of crimes) found that more than two-thirds (68 percent) either abused or were dependent on drugs or alcohol (see Table 2.5). Nearly half (45 percent) of inmates were dependent on alcohol or drugs, while nearly one-fourth abused alcohol or drugs but were not dependent on them. Estimates of substance dependence or abuse were based on accepted clinical criteria. Fifty percent of inmates convicted of crimes said they committed the offense while under the influence of drugs or alcohol. In addition, 16 percent of convicted jail inmates said they committed their crime to get money to buy drugs.[78] The evidence is quite strong, therefore, that use of drugs and alcohol is correlated with criminal behavior.

DRUG PREVENTION

Proposals for reducing the use of drugs are intended to reduce either the supply of drugs or the demand for them. Strategies to reduce the supply of drugs include massive increases in arrests for drug crimes and prevention of the flow of drugs into the United States. Neither of these strategies has had significant long-term impact. So-called police crackdowns or sweeps, in which many arrests are made in a specific geographic area, have been found to have little effect. Although these crackdowns often reduce drug trafficking for short periods in the targeted areas, studies have found that drug markets are simply moved, and customers go elsewhere to purchase the product.[79] Strategies to prevent the import of drugs have been unsuccessful for related reasons. Source countries have little incentive to substitute less profitable crops for drug-producing plants such as coca and poppies, and the immense borders of the United States are difficult to monitor effectively.[80]

Table 2.5 Drug and Alcohol Use by Jail Inmates

	Alcohol	*Drugs*	*Alcohol or Drugs*
Dependent only	23%	36%	45%
Abuse only	24%	18%	23%
Any dependence *or* abuse	47%	53%	68%
No dependence or abuse	53%	47%	32%
Under the influence at the time of the offense	33%	29%	50%

Source: Jennifer C. Karberg and Doris J. James, *Substance Dependence, Abuse, and Treatment of Jail Inmates* (Washington, DC: Bureau of Justice Statistics, 2005).

Demand reduction strategies focus on drug education, treatment, and punishment as methods to reduce the public's appetite for drugs. These efforts have shown sporadic success. In Maricopa County, Arizona, for example, a zero tolerance program was instituted to hold all drug users accountable for their behavior. In two years of operation, a drug task force made 730 arrests, 32 percent of which were for marijuana possession. A large number of cases that previously would have been dismissed were referred for drug treatment, thus "widening the net" of the criminal justice system by including more offenders of all types. The program did succeed in increasing the use of treatment as an alternative to prosecution in some cases, and it fostered a communitywide consensus regarding the seriousness of the drug problem.[81]

DARE

The Drug Abuse Resistance Program (DARE) attempts to reduce drug use through educational programs for students in kindergarten through high school. More than half of the nation's school districts have adopted this program in at least one of their schools. An evaluation of DARE programs found that they had little effect on drug use, attitudes toward drugs, attitudes toward the police, or self-esteem. On the other hand, DARE programs did increase student knowledge about substance abuse.[82] A revised DARE program was begun in 1993, and it appears that more interactive learning strategies in which students play roles and respond to case-based scenarios may prove more effective.

A study of drinking at college parties found that students who did not drink believed the risk of being caught was very high if they committed a crime. Those who drank most heavily condemned crime less strongly and believed the risk of being caught was low. A major implication of this research is that it may be possible to reduce crime by preventing heavy drinking.[83]

DRUG TREATMENT PROGRAMS

Treatment programs to reduce the drug-using population have had mixed results. Such programs are of two types: treatment with medications (i.e., other drugs, such as methadone), and behavioral programs that employ counseling and other techniques to reduce drug dependency. Perhaps the largest study of the impact of drug treatment tracked 10,000 patients receiving methadone maintenance, residential treatment, or outpatient treatment. Regardless of the type of treatment used, it was found that heroin use was reduced even three to five years after the treatment ended. The rate of serious crimes committed by these patients also dropped after treatment. Unfortunately, treatment for at least six months was necessary to overcome heroin addiction. In addition, no treatment program was found to have much success in reducing use of cocaine, which is more addictive than heroin.[84] On the other hand, intensive drug treatment programs for offenders have shown some success when a therapeutic community was established with a strong behavior management emphasis.[85]

It appears that attempts to reduce drug use by reducing either supply or demand will require new ideas if they are to become more effective. Clearly, a reduction in demand would make a reduction in supply unnecessary. Even if the supply were somehow reduced, lingering demand would create new criminal opportunities such as we now find in the domestic manufacture of synthetic drugs through chemical combinations.[86] Despite these roadblocks, efforts are under way to reduce both the demand and the availability of drugs. The central role of the family is made clear by the fact that inmates whose parents abused drugs began using drugs themselves by age thirteen. If the parents did not abuse drugs or alcohol, the child did not use drugs until age sixteen.[87] An examination of community antidrug campaigns in thirteen cities found that efforts with a broader scope (such as community education, family support, and security programs) and those that forged cooperative partnerships with the local police had some impact regardless of the type of neighborhood involved.[88] Much of the hope for reducing drug use in U.S. society is likely to emerge from these community efforts.

CRITICAL THINKING EXERCISES

Choosing What to Criminalize

Downloading songs for free via the Internet and hazing initiation practices at fraternities and sororities are examples of behaviors that are under serious consideration for criminalization in some states and localities. The push for criminalization is driven by the victims of these activities and lawmakers acting on their behalf. On the other side, criminalizing these behaviors may overstate the actual harm to society that these behaviors cause. These activities cause little or no harm in most circumstances, so criminalization marginalizes an entire category of behavior in the name of the small number of victims in rare excessive cases. Is it better to sue those excessive individuals for damages and compensation when it occurs, rather than criminalize the sharing of music over the Internet or hazing altogether? Clearly, strong arguments can be made on both sides of criminalization for these behaviors.

Assume that a legislator in your state introduces a bill to legalize marijuana possession and use in small amounts. The rationale for the proposed new law may be that the harm to individuals has been demonstrated to be quite small, under current law too many young people obtain criminal records for minor marijuana arrests, which hurts them in pursuing employment, and marijuana should be regulated in the same way as alcoholic beverages. Opponents argue that drug use is harmful, use of other drugs will follow, and harm will come to both the user and to society in terms of drug addiction and crime.

Tobacco also has been the focus of much discussion given its demonstrated effect on health. Rather than prohibiting its use to minors as is done under current law, some argue that it should be prohibited entirely. Tobacco is harmful and has addictive qualities, so why not make it illegal? On the other hand, should adults be permitted the freedom to choose the products they ingest?

CRITICAL THINKING QUESTIONS

1. What are the most significant pro and con arguments that you believe would be made in a marijuana legalization debate? How would you predict the outcome of a proposal for the legalization of marijuana?
2. If it were proposed that tobacco be prohibited, how would the arguments pro and con be similar to and different from those in the case of marijuana?
3. Is there a middle ground between criminalization and legalization that can be pursued? If so, how is this alternative better than other ways of dealing with these behaviors?

A Case Study of Delinquency

Following is an excerpt from the report of a probation officer in an actual case of delinquency. The juvenile's name is Waln Brown. The complainants are Waln's mother and his high school principal; the complaint is failure to obey the reasonable commands of his family and fighting in school (for which Waln was suspended).

> Waln Brown is 15 years old, has above average intelligence, and is nearly six feet tall. He is extremely nervous and was a bed-wetter until age nine. Presently, he has acute acne.
>
> Waln's mother is an insistent, possessive, and very dominating personality. Mr. Brown is rather cool, calm, and fairly well collected. Of the two, he seems the most sensible. Mrs. Brown is inclined to be flighty, easily disturbed, and emotionally unstable.
>
> Mrs. Brown's work hours are such that she has little time to spend with the children, and when she does devote a little time to them her nerves are frayed to the point where she makes rash judgments. Presently, Mrs. Brown is an emotionally sick woman. Waln has lacked an opportunity to associate with his father, and this has created unconscious hostilities toward his environment.
>
> The trials and tribulations that Waln has gotten himself into are not too abnormal, nor have they been of the seriously antisocial kind. To our way of thinking, this environment could have produced a much more seriously delinquent youngster than we are currently dealing with. Actually, Waln is and has been, during the most impressionable period of his life, a rejected, over-dominated child, and at the moment he is striking back at society. And we are using these terms in their widest sense.

Source: Waln Brown, *The Other Side of Delinquency* (New Brunswick, NJ: Rutgers University Press, 1983).

CRITICAL THINKING QUESTIONS

1. What important factors are identified in the probation report on Waln that might bear on the likelihood of criminal behavior?
2. Which explanations of crime discussed in this chapter address these factors most directly?

SUMMARY

DEFINING DEVIANCE

- Deviance is violation of a social norm, which becomes crime when laws are passed allowing the government to sanction the behavior.
- As a general rule, crimes prohibit only acts or omissions of acts.
- Criminal behaviors can be *mala in se* (acts bad in themselves) or *mala prohibita* (acts not inherently evil that are deemed undesirable).
- The government's ability to create new categories of criminal conduct by passing new laws can pose problems when there is not consensus about the harmfulness of the conduct, as was seen during Prohibition and in cases of consensual adult behavior involving alcohol, gambling, prostitution, and drugs.

HOW CAN CRIME BE EXPLAINED?

- The classical school of thought in criminology sees crime as resulting from the conscious exercise of an individual's free will that is controlled by the threat of punishment.
- Positivism sees crimes as the result of internal and external influences on an individual.
- Structural explanations of crime focus on the selective formulation and application of the law rather than on the behavior of individuals.
- The ethical view sees crime as a moral failure in decision making.

GUNS, DRUGS, AND CRIME

- The incidence of crime involving guns is high, but it is not clear whether the absence of guns would necessarily reduce the rate of violence.
- There is strong evidence that use of drugs or alcohol is correlative with criminal behavior.

KEY TERMS

norms *25*
deviance *25*
mala in se *26*
mala prohibita *26*
offenses against morality *27*
political crimes *27*
regulatory offenses *28*
overcriminalization *28*
legalization *32*
classical school *33*
positivism *33*
ethical view *34*
structural/conflict view *35*
biological determinism *36*
psychoanalytic theory *36*
cognitive theory *37*
differential association *38*
blocked opportunity *38*
criminal subcultures *40*
labeling theory *40*
social bond *40*
rational choice theories *41*
routine activities theory *41*
gun control *43*

QUESTIONS FOR REVIEW AND DISCUSSION

1. How is deviance defined? What is the difference between criminal and deviant behavior?
2. How do thoughts and deeds enter into the definition of crime?
3. What are the three types of *mala prohibita* offenses and how do they differ from *mala in se* offenses?
4. What are some examples of the possible overcriminalization of behavior?

5. What are the four main views by which crime is explained?
6. What are some arguments for and against biological and psychological determinism as explanations of crime?
7. How is crime explained according to the sociological theories of differential association, blocked opportunity, labeling, and social bonding?
8. How do rational-choice and gender-based theories account for criminal behavior?
9. Why and how are guns, alcohol, and drugs pivotal concerns in the battle against crime?

NOTES

1. Warren Cohen, "Napster Is Rocking the Music Industry," *U.S. News & World Report* (March 6, 2000), p. 41; Fred Vogelstein, "Is It Sharing or Stealing?," *U.S. News & World Report* (June 12, 2000), pp. 38–40; Nick Timiraos, "Colleges Offer Music Downloads, but Students Balk," *The Wall Street Journal* (July 6, 2006).
2. Kenneth Terrell, "A Nation of Pirates," *U.S. News & World Report* (July 14, 2003); Hilary Rosen, "Napster Is 'Organized Piracy,' " *USA Today* (June 23, 2000), p. 16A.
3. Keith L. Alexander, "Lawsuit Targets Music Swap," *USA Today* (April 21, 2000), p. 3B.
4. "Why Block Free Exchange of Records and Movies?," *USA Today* (June 23, 2000), p. 16A; Lia Sestric, "Ohio University Considers Responses to Illegal File Sharing," *University Wire* (January 8, 2004); Cynthia L. Webb, "Down on Downloading," *The Washington Post* (January 5, 2004); Malcolm Venable, "Colleges Try to Discourage Students' Illegal Music Downloading," *Virginian-Pilot* (Norfolk, VA) (October 17, 2005).
5. Lawrence M. Friedman, *Crime and Punishment in American History* (New York: Basic Books, 1993), pp. 6–7.
6. Deborah Rhode, *Justice and Gender* (Cambridge, MA: Harvard University Press, 1989).
7. Mark 15:24; Luke 23:34; John 19:24.
8. Henry Chafetz, *Play the Devil: A History of Gambling in the United States from 1492 to 1955* (New York: Potter, 1960), p. 8.
9. John Rosecrance, *Gambling without Guilt: The Legitimation of an American Pastime* (Belmont, CA: Brooks/Cole, 1988), p. 12.
10. Ibid., pp. 12–13.
11. Gilbert Geis, *Not the Law's Business* (New York: Schocken, 1979), p. 223.
12. Chafetz, p. 17.
13. Friedman, pp. 137–38.
14. David F. Musto, *The American Disease: Origins of Narcotic Control* (New York, 1973).
15. Lyle W. Shannon, Judith L. McKim, and Kathleen R. Anderson, *Alcohol and Drugs, Delinquency, and Crime: Looking Back to the Future* (New York: St. Martin's Press, 1998); Joseph Carroll, "Drugs, Smoking, Alcohol Most Important Problem Facing Teens," *Gallup News Service* (February 16, 2006).
16. Kurt L. Schmoke, "Decriminalizing Drugs: It Just Might Work—and Nothing Else Does," in R. L. Evans and I. M. Berent, eds., *Drug Legalization* (LaSalle, IL: Open Court Press, 1992); Ethan A. Nadelmann, "Drug Prohibition in the United States: Costs, Consequences, and Alternatives," *Science* 245 (September 1989); Jeffery A. Miron, "The Economics of Drug Legalization and Prohibition," *Social Research*, vol. 68 (fall 2001).
17. Lawrence W. Sherman, "Police Crackdowns: Initial and Residual Deterrence," in M. Tonry and N. Morris, eds., *Crime and Justice: An Annual Review of Research* (Chicago: University of Chicago Press, 1990); U.S. Comptroller General, *Drug Control: Interdiction Efforts in Central America Have Had Little Impact on the Flow of Drugs* (Washington, DC: U.S. General Accounting Office, 1994); Samuel Walker, *Sense and Nonsense about Crime and Drugs*, 6th ed. (Belmont, CA: Brooks/Cole, 2006).
18. Mathew Durose, Caroline Harlow, Patrick Langan, Mark Motivans, Romana Ratala, and Erica Smith, *Family Violence Statistics* (Washington, DC: Bureau of Justice Statistics, 2005); Donna M. Vandiver, "A Prospective Analysis of Juvenile Male Sex Offenders: Characteristics and Recidivism Rates as Adults," *Journal of Interpersonal Violence*, vol. 21 (May 2006), p. 673; George B. Palermo. "Murderous Parents: A Study of Parents Who Kill Their Children," *International Journal of Offender Therapy & Comparative Criminology*, vol. 46 (April 2002), p. 123; Noel S. Brady, "Motive Often Remains a Mystery When Kids Murder Their Parents," *King County Journal* (Washington), (May 7, 2006).
19. Compare the conclusions of Don C. Gibbons, "Talking about Crime: Observations on the Prospects for Causal Theory in Criminology," *Criminal Justice Research Bulletin* 7 (1992), pp. 1–10 with Michael R. Gottfredson and Travis Hirschi, *A General Theory of Crime* (Stanford, CA: Stanford University Press, 1990).
20. For excerpts from the writings of Bentham and Beccaria, see Joseph E. Jacoby, *Classics of Criminology*, 3rd ed. (Prospect Heights, IL: Waveland Press, 2004).
21. Gottfredson and Hirschi, pp. 90–91.
22. Michael G. Turner and Alex R. Piquero, "The Stability of Self-Control," *Journal of Criminal Justice*, vol. 30 (Nov–Dec 2002), p. 457;Augustine Brannigan, "Self-control, Social Control, and Evolutionary Psychology: Towards an Integrated Perspective on Crime," *Canadian Journal of Criminology* 39 (October 1997), pp. 403–31; T. David Evans, Francis T. Cullen, Velmer S. Burton Jr., R. Gregory Dunaway, and Michael L. Benson, "The Social Consequences of Self-Control: Testing the General Theory of Crime," *Criminology* 35 (August 1997), pp. 475–501; L. Thomas Winfree, Jr., Terrance J. Taylor, Ni He, and Finn-Aage Esbensen, "Self-control and Variability over Time: Multivariate Results Using a 5-year, Multisite Panel of Youths," *Crime and Delinquency*, vol. 52 (April 2006), p. 253.

23. Charles Darwin, *The Origin of Species* (New York: Modern Library, 1936).
24. Emile Durkheim, *Suicide* (New York: Free Press, 1951).
25. Jay Albanese, *Organized Crime in Our Times*, 4th ed. (Cincinnati: Lexis/Nexis/Anderson, 2004); Catherine A. Sanderson and John M. Darley, "I Am Moral, But You Are Deterred: Differential Attributions about Why People Obey the Law," *Journal of Applied Social Psychology*, vol. 32 (February 2002), p. 375; Jay Albanese, *Professional Ethics in Criminal Justice: Being Ethical When No One is Looking* (Boston: Allyn & Bacon, 2006).
26. Peter B. Wood, "Nonsocial Reinforcement and Habitual Criminal Conduct: An Extension of Learning Theory," *Criminology* 35 (1997), pp. 335–66.
27. Jeffrey Reiman, *The Rich Get Richer and the Poor Get Prison: Ideology, Class, and Criminal Justice*, 7th ed. (Boston: Allyn & Bacon, 2006).
28. Jeffrey Reiman, *. . . And the Poor Get Prison: Economic Bias in American Criminal Justice* (Needham Heights, MA: Allyn & Bacon, 1996).
29. Ronald L. Akers and Christine S. Sellers, *Criminological Theories*, 4th ed. (Los Angeles: Roxbury 2004).
30. Cesare Lombroso and Gina Lombroso-Ferrero, *The Criminal Man* (Montclair, NJ: Patterson Smith, 1972).
31. Charles Goring, *The English Convict* (London: Her Majesty's Stationery Office, 1913).
32. Richard J. Herrnstein, "Criminogenic Traits," and Patricia A. Brennan, Sarnoff A. Mednick, and Jan Voluka, "Biomedical Factors in Crime," in J. Q. Wilson and J. Petersilia, eds., *Crime* (San Francisco: ICS Press, 1995).
33. Marshall B. Jones and Donald R. Jones, "The Contagious Nature of Antisocial Behavior," *Criminology*, vol. 38 (February 2000), pp. 25–47; Janet Katz and William J. Chambliss, "Biology and Crime," in Joseph F. Sheley, ed., *Criminology: Contemporary Handbook* (Belmont, CA: Wadsworth, 1991); Lee Ellis, "Genetics and Criminal Behavior," *Criminology* 20 (1982), pp. 43–66; William Gabrielli and Sarnoff Mednick, "Urban Environment, Genetics, and Crime," *Criminology* 22 (1984), pp. 645–53.
34. Jeffrey A. Roth, "Understanding and Preventing Violence," *National Institute of Justice Research in Brief* (February 1994), p. 8; Albert J. Reiss and Jeffrey A. Roth, eds., *Understanding and Preventing Violence* (Washington, DC: National Academy Press, 1993).
35. For a summary of this research, see Lee Ellis and Anthony Walsh, "Gene-Based Evolutionary Theories in Criminology," *Criminology* 37 (1997), pp. 229–76; Nicole Rafter, "Earnest A. Hooton and the Biological Tradition in American Criminology," *Criminology*, vol. 42 (August 2004), p. 735; Robert Wright, "The Biology of Violence," *The New Yorker* (March 13, 1995), pp. 68–77.
36. Richard Jenkins and Lester F. Hewitt, *Fundamental Patterns of Maladjustment* (Springfield, IL: Thomas, 1947).
37. William McCord and Joan McCord, *Psychopathy and Delinquency* (New York: Grune & Stratton, 1956).
38. James Sorrells, "Kids Who Kill," *Crime and Delinquency* 23 (1977), pp. 312–20; Richard Rosner, Melvin Widerlight, M. Bernice Horner Rosner, and Rita Reis Wieczorek, "Adolescents Accused of Murder and Manslaughter: A Five-Year Descriptive Study," *Bulletin of the American Academy of Psychiatry and the Law* 7 (1979), pp. 342–51.
39. Steven Spaccarelli, Blake Bowden, J. Douglas Coatsworth, and Soni Kim, "Psychosocial Correlates of Male Sexual Aggression in a Chronic Delinquent Sample," *Criminal Justice and Behavior* 24 (March 1997), pp. 71–95.
40. Glenn D. Walters and Thomas W. White, "The Thinking Criminal: A Cognitive Model of Lifestyle Criminality," *Criminal Justice Research Bulletin* vol. 4 (1989), pp. 1–10; Glenn D. Walters, *The Criminal Lifestyle* (Beverly Hills, CA: Sage, 1990).
41. Vera A. Lopez and Edmund T. Emmer, "Adolescent Male Offenders: A Grounded Theory Study of Cognition, Emotion, and Delinquent Crime Contexts," *Criminal Justice and Behavior*, vol. 27 (June 2000), pp. 292–311.
42. Edwin H. Sutherland, *Principles of Criminology* (Philadelphia: Lippincott, 1939).
43. Jack Gibbs, "The State of Criminological Theory," *Criminology* 25 (1987), pp. 821–40; Mark Warr and Mark Stafford, "The Influence of Delinquent Peers: What They Think or What They Do?," *Criminology* 29 (1991), pp. 851–66.
44. Spaccarelli et al., "Psychosocial Correlates," p. 92.
45. Richard A. Cloward and Lloyd E. Ohlin, *Delinquency and Opportunity: A Theory of Delinquent Gangs* (New York: Free Press, 1960).
46. Howard Becker, *The Outsiders: Studies in the Sociology of Deviance* (New York: Free Press, 1963); Edwin M. Lemert, *Social Pathology: A Systematic Approach to the Theory of Sociopathic Behavior* (New York: McGraw-Hill, 1951).
47. Travis Hirschi, *Causes of Delinquency* (Berkeley: University of California Press, 1969); Michael J. Hindelang, "Causes of Delinquency: A Partial Replication and Exposition," *Social Problems* 20 (1973), pp. 470–87; LeGrande Gardiner and Donald Shoemaker, "Social Bonding and Delinquency: A Comparative Analysis," *Sociological Quarterly* 30 (1989), pp. 481–500.
48. Laurie Goodstein and William Glaberson, "The Well-Marked Roads to Homicidal Rage," *New York Times* (April 9, 2000), p. 1; Ford Fessenden, "They Threaten, Seethe and Unhinge, Then Kill in Quantity," *New York Times* (April 8, 2000), p. 1.
49. Derek B. Cornish and Ronald V. G. Clarke, eds. *The Reasoning Criminal: Rational Choice Perspectives on Offending* (New York: Springer Verlag, 1986); M. Lyn Exum, "The Application and Robustness of the Rational Choice Perspective in the Study of Intoxicated and Angry Intentions to Aggress,"*Criminology*, vol. 40 (November 2002), p. 933.
50. Marcus Felson, *Crime & Everyday Life*, 3rd edition (Thousand Oaks, CA: Pine Forge Press, 2002).
51. Freda Adler, *Sisters in Crime* (New York: McGraw-Hill, 1975).
52. Clarice Feinman, *Women in the Criminal Justice System* (New York: Praeger, 1986); Ngaire Naffine, *Gender, Crime and Feminism* (Brookfield, VT: Dartmouth, 1994).
53. Henry H. Brownstein, *The Social Reality of Violence and Violent Crime* (Boston: Allyn & Bacon, 2000).
54. See Frank P. Williams and Marilyn D. McShane, *Criminological Theory*, 4th ed. (Upper Saddle River, NJ: Prentice Hall, 2004); Kathleen Daly, "Different Ways of Conceptualizing Sex/Gender in Feminist Theory and Their Implications for Criminology," *Theoretical Criminology*, vol. 1 (1997), pp. 25–51.
55. Shannon M. Catalano, *Criminal Victimization, 2004* (Washington, DC: Bureau of Justice Statistics, 2005).
56. Federal Bureau of Investigation, *Crime in the United States, 2004* (Washington, DC: U.S. Government Printing Office, 2005).
57. Gary Kleck, *Point Blank: Guns and Violence in America* (New York: 2005); Robert A. Hahn, Oleg O. Bilukha, Alex Crosby, Mindy Thompson Fullilove, Akiva Liberman, Eve K. Moscicki, Susan Snyder, Farris Tuma, and Peter Briss. *First Reports Evaluating the Effectiveness of Strategies for Preventing Violence: Firearms Laws* (Atlanta: Centers for Disease Control and

Prevention, 2003) www.cdc.gov/mmwr/preview/mmwrhtml/rr5214a2.htm.

58. Tomislav V. Kovandzic and Thomas B. Marvell, "Right-to-Carry Concealed Handguns and Violent Crime: Crime Control through Gun Decontrol?," *Criminology & Public Policy*, vol. 2 (July 2003), p. 361; Philip J. Cook and Jens Ludwig, *Gun Violence: The Real Costs* (New York: Oxford University Press, 2000); John R. Lott, Jr. *More Guns, Less Crime: Understanding Crime and Gun Control Laws* (Chicago: University of Chicago Press, 1998).
59. Data from Bureau of Alcohol, Tobacco, Firearms, and Explosives, www.atf.gov.
60. Allen Beck, Darrell Gilliard, and Lawrence Greenfeld, *Survey of State Prison Inmates, 1997* (Washington, DC: Bureau of Justice Statistics, 2000), pp. 18–19.
61. Joseph F. Sheley and James D. Wright, "Gun Acquisition and Possession in Selected Juvenile Samples," *Research in Brief* (Washington, DC: National Institute of Justice, 1993); James D. Wright and Peter H. Rossi, *Armed and Dangerous: A Survey of Felons and Their Firearms* (Hawthorne, NY: Aldine, 1986).
62. www.fas.org/irp/agency/doj/fbi/is/ncic.htm.
63. www.atf.gov.
64. Wright and Rossi, op. cit.
65. Glenn L. Pierce and William J. Bowers, "The Bartley–Fox Gun Law's Short-Term Impact on Crime," *The Annals* 455 (May 1981), pp. 120–37.
66. For a summary of this research, see "'More Guns, Less Crime' Thesis Rests on a Flawed Statistical Design, Scholars Argue," *Chronicle of Higher Education*, Vol. 49 (May 9, 2003).
67. Samuel Walker, *Sense and Nonsense about Crime and Drugs*, 6th ed. (Belmont, CA: Wadsworth, 2006).
68. Colin Loftin and David McDowall, "One with a Gun Gets You Two: Mandatory Sentencing and Firearms Violence in Detroit," *The Annals* 455 (May 1981), pp. 150–67; Alan Lizotte and Marjorie S. Zatz, "The Use and Abuse of Sentence Enhancement for Firearms Offenses in California," *Law and Contemporary Problems* 49 (1986), pp. 199–221; David McDowall, Colin Loftin, and Brian Wiersema, "A Comparative Study of the Preventive Effects of Mandatory Sentencing Laws for Handgun Crimes," *Journal of Criminal Law and Criminology*, vol. 83 (summer 1992), p. 378.
69. Jens Ludwig and Philip J. Cook, "Homicide and Suicide Rates Associated with Implementation of the Brady Handgun Violence Prevention Act," *Journal of the American Medical Association*, vol. 284 (August 2, 2000); Michael Satchell, "Taking Aim at the Brady Law," *U.S. News & World Report* (August 14, 2000), p. 8.
70. U.S. Comptroller General, *Gun Control: Implementation of the National Instant Criminal Background Check System* (Washington, DC: U.S. General Accounting Office, 2000); Michael Bowling and Matthew J. Hickman, *Background Checks for Firearms Transfers, 2004* (Washington, DC: Bureau of Justice Statistics, 2005).
71. Fox Butterfield, "Guns: The Law as a Selling Tool," *New York Times* (August 13, 2000), p. 1.
72. James D. Torr, ed. *Guns and Crime.* (Greenhaven Press, 2004).
73. Federal Bureau of Investigation, Uniform Crime Report—2004 (Washington, DC: U.S. Government Printing Office, 2005).
74. Paige Harrison and Allen J. Beck, *Prisoners in 2004* (Washington, DC: Bureau of Justice Statistics, 2005), p. 13.
75. Annual Report on Drug Use among Adult and Juvenile Arrestees (Washington, DC: National Institute of Justice, 2003).
76. H. R. White and D. W. Gorman, "The Dynamics of the Drug-Crime Relationship," in G. LaFree, ed., *The Nature of Crime: Continuity and Change* (Washington, DC: National Institute of Justice, 2000); J. Q. Wilson, "Drugs and Crime," in M. Tonry and J. Q. Wilson, eds., *Drugs and Crime* (Chicago: University of Chicago Press, 1990).
77. Jeffrey Fagan, "Intoxication and Aggression," in M. Tonry and J. Q. Wilson, eds., *Drugs and Crime* (Chicago: University of Chicago Press, 1990).
78. Jennifer C. Karberg and Doris J. James, *Substance Dependence, Abuse, and Treatment of Jail Inmates* (Washington, DC: Bureau of Justice Statistics, 2005).
79. David M. Kennedy, *Closing the Market: Controlling the Drug Trade in Tampa, Florida* (Washington, DC: National Institute of Justice, 1993); Lawrence W. Sherman, "Police Crackdowns: Initial and Residual Deterrence," in M. Tonry and N. Morris, eds., *Crime and Justice: A Review of Research* (Chicago: University of Chicago Press, 1990).
80. U.S. Comptroller General, *Drug Control: Efforts to Develop Alternatives to Cultivating Illicit Crops in Colombia Have Made Little Progress and Face Serious Obstacles* (Washington, DC: U.S. General Accounting Office, 2002); U.S. Comptroller General, *Drug Control: Long-Standing Problems Hinder U.S. International Efforts* (Washington, DC: U.S. General Accounting Office, 1997).
81. John R. Hepburn, Wayne Johnston, and Scott Rodgers, *Do Drugs, Do Time: An Evaluation of the Maricopa County Demand Reduction Program* (Washington, DC: National Institute of Justice, 1994).
82. Christopher Ringwalt et al., *Past and Future Directions of the D.A.R.E. Program: An Evaluation Review* (Research Triangle Park, NC: Research Triangle Institute, 1994).
83. Lonn Lanza-Kadua, Donna M. Bishop, Lawrence Winna, "Risk Benefit Calculations, Moral Evaluations, and Alcohol Use: Exploring the Alcohol–Crime Connection," *Crime and Delinquency* 43 (1997), pp. 222–39; see also J. J. Thompson, "Plugging the Kegs: Students Benefit When Colleges Limit Excessive Drinking," *U.S. News & World Report* (January 26, 1998), pp. 63–67; Curtis VanderWaal, Lisa Powell, Yvonne Terry-McElrath, Yanjun Bao, and Brian Flay. "Community and School Drug Prevention Strategy Prevalence: Differential Effects by Setting and Substance," *Journal of Primary Prevention*, vol. 26 (July 2005), p. 299.
84. National Treatment Improvement Evaluation Study, *The Persistent Effects of Substance Abuse* (Washington, DC: U.S. Department of Health and Human Services, 1998); R. L. Hubbard, *Drug Abuse Treatment: A National Study of Effectiveness* (Chapel Hill: University of North Carolina Press, 1998).
85. Mary K. Stohr, Craig Hemmens, Diane Baune, Jed Dayley, Mark Gornik, Kirstin Kjaer, and Cindy Noon, *Residential Substance Abuse Treatment for State Prisoners: Breaking the Drug-Crime Cycle among Parole Violators* (Washington, DC: National Institute of Justice, 2003).
86. Domestic Chemical Action Group, *Controlling Chemicals Used to Make Illegal Drugs: The Chemical Action Task Force and the Domestic Chemical Action Group* (Washington, DC: National Institute of Justice, 1998); www.streetdrugs.org.
87. Jennifer C. Karberg and Doris J. James, *Substance Dependence, Abuse, and Treatment of Jail Inmates* (Washington, D.C.: Bureau of Justice Statistics, 2005).
88. Saul N. Weingart, Francis X. Hartmann, and David Osborne, *Case Studies of Community Anti-Drug Efforts* (Washington, DC: National Institute of Justice, 1994); See also www.cadca.org (2000).

chapter 3

Defining and Measuring Crime

Classifying crimes: Revealing the categories of criminal conduct and the methods we use to determine how much crime is actually occurring.

CHAPTER OUTLINE

LEARNING OBJECTIVES

- Identify and exemplify the three general types of crime.
- Distinguish among the violent crimes and property crimes of homicide, sexual assault, assault, robbery, burglary, larceny, and arson.
- Compare and contrast the FBI's Uniform Crime Reports, victimization surveys, and self-report surveys as sources of data about crime in the United States.
- Critically evaluate statistics about crime rates for crimes in the Crime Index.
- Explain the purposes and uses of the National Crime Victimization Survey and the National Incident-Based Reporting System.
- Summarize trends in crime rates in the United States in the last twenty-five years and project future trends.

Seung-Hui Cho, a 23-year-old senior at Virginia Tech University, was a non-communicative loner with a history of mental instability. An English professor said Cho's creative-writing work was so disturbing that he had been referred to on-campus counseling services. Other students, including his roommate, said that Cho hardly spoke even when greeted or asked a question in class. He was admonished twice by police for frightening coeds who complained about his weird, vaguely menacing behavior.

On April 16, 2007 he lashed out unexpectedly, killing two people in a dorm room, then returned to his own dorm room where he re-armed with his two pistols, and went to a classroom building on the other side of campus. There, he fired more than 100 shots, killing 30 more people in four classrooms before shooting himself in the head. He left a rambling note in his dorm room blaming others for his actions, railing against "rich kids" and "debauchery" and "deceitful charlatans" on campus, and at one point states, "You caused me to do this."

Eight years earlier, Eric Harris and Dylan Klebold were typical high school students who reveled in their status as outcasts. The two boys were insulted by some other students at school, and the jocks (student athletes) sometimes called them "fags" to their face. Eric and Dylan wore arm bands that said "I Hate People," and even made a video for class that showed them in school pretending to shoot friends dressed as jocks.

It all took a terrible turn into reality when Eric and Dylan walked into their school, Columbine High School in Littleton, Colorado, with a semi-automatic pistol, a carbine, and two sawed-off shotguns. They laughed as they shot at people at the school, ultimately killing twelve students and a coach. They also planted at least thirty pipe bombs and other explosives, discovered later, around the school.[1]

The shooting tragedies at both Virginia Tech and Columbine occurred in otherwise safe surroundings, and were apparently planned in advance by marginalized perpetrators who outwardly made little effort to interact with their peers or teachers. After both incidents several copycat events occurred—and some were prevented—in the weeks that followed. To what extent do cases like these reflect known crime patterns and trends in the United States?

What Are the Types of Crime?

crimes against persons Violent crimes involving the use of physical force.

crimes against property Crimes in which property is taken unlawfully and misused.

crimes against public order Acts that disrupt the peace in a civil society.

Crimes are of three general types: crimes against persons, crimes against property, and crimes against public order. **Crimes against persons** are called violent crimes, because they involve the use of physical force. These crimes include criminal homicide, rape, assault, and robbery. **Crimes against property** are those in which property is taken unlawfully and misused. Examples include burglary, larceny, arson, and vandalism. **Crimes against public order** are acts that disrupt the peace in a civil society. Examples of these offenses include drug, liquor, and gambling law violations; disorderly conduct; weapons offenses; and loitering and prostitution violations. These three categories of offenses are summarized in Table 3.1.

Table 3.1 Three General Categories of Crime

Crimes Against Persons	*Crimes Against Property*	*Crimes Against Public Order*
Criminal homicide	Burglary	Drug, liquor, and gambling law violations
Rape	Larceny	Disorderly conduct
Assault	Arson	Weapons offenses
Robbery	Vandalism	Loitering and prostitution violations

Although these three categories of crime comprise the vast majority of the more than 14 million arrests made by police each year, there are other kinds of offenses that involve sophisticated fraud and deceit rather than stealth or force. Chapter 17 examines these sophisticated economic crimes. In addition, specific acts of violence are perpetrated to achieve political, racial, ethnic, or religious objectives. These acts constitute terrorism or hate crime, also examined in Chapter 17.

How Are Violent Crimes and Property Crimes Classified?

VIOLENT CRIMES

The violent crimes of homicide, rape, robbery, and assault lie at the heart of the public's fear of crime. Even though these constitute only 12 percent of all serious crimes reported to police, they can involve serious injury or death and are greatly feared. The crimes of rape, robbery, and assault make up nearly 20 percent of all crimes counted by victimization surveys (whether reported or not). Essential information about these crimes includes the specific types of actions they do and do not involve, as well as the nature of the circumstances under which they occur. Crimes against property account for the overwhelming majority (80 to 90 percent) of all serious crimes. It seems that stealing by stealth is more common than any other predatory crime. As a greater proportion of citizens have come to own more property of more kinds, burglary and larceny have come to be regarded as more serious crimes. The three main types of property crimes—burglary, larceny, and arson—are counted nationally each year. This section describes these categories of crime in detail.

CRIMES AGAINST PROPERTY

Homicide

Criminal homicide includes both murder and manslaughter. **Murder** includes all intentional killings, as well as deaths that occur during dangerous felonies. A person who robbed someone on the street who then died from the shock would be held liable for felony murder, that is, for causing a death in the course of a dangerous felony.

criminal homicide
Murder or manslaughter.

murder
All intentional killings, as well as deaths that occur in the course of dangerous felonies.

Likewise, if you aim to shoot a person but miss and kill that person's companion instead, you are liable for murder of the companion even though you had no intention of killing that person. This is because you *intentionally* took a person's life without lawful justification. All the criteria for the definition of murder are fulfilled. The law does not punish you less severely because you are a poor shot.

Manslaughter is a mitigated murder. It involves causing death recklessly, or intentionally under extenuating circumstances. An example of a reckless manslaughter would be killing a pedestrian with your car while drunk or speeding. In law, **recklessness** is conscious disregard of a substantial and unjustifiable risk. In this example, a reasonable person would know that it is difficult to control an automobile properly when one is speeding or drinking. This "reasonableness standard" is used throughout the criminal law to assess the culpability of an individual's conduct. Reckless manslaughter is punished less seriously than murder because of the "lower" state of mind involved (recklessness versus intention).

manslaughter
A mitigated murder: causing a death recklessly, or intentionally under extenuating circumstances.

recklessness
Conscious disregard of a substantial and unjustifiable risk.

Recklessness is distinguished from **negligence,** which is failure to be aware of a substantial and unjustifiable risk. Negligence is not subject to criminal prosecution, although a person can be sued in civil court for damages caused by negligent conduct.

negligence
Failure to be aware of a substantial and unjustifiable risk.

A middle ground between negligence and recklessness is gross negligence. **Gross negligence** is failure to perceive a substantial and unjustifiable risk when such a failure is a "gross deviation" from the standard of care a reasonable person would observe. The charge of gross negligence is usually applied in cases involving fatal car accidents in which conduct is seen as not serious enough to constitute recklessness but more blameworthy than negligence. Gross negligence is the borderland of the criminal state of mind and is the least severely punished form of criminal homicide.

gross negligence
Failure to perceive a substantial and unjustifiable risk when such failure is a gross deviation from the standard of care a reasonable person would observe.

"HEAT OF PASSION" KILLINGS

In two very limited circumstances, intentional killings may be punished as manslaughter rather than as murder: "heat of passion" killings and imperfect self-defense. So-called heat of passion killings are treated as manslaughter rather than murder only when the offender responds to an unlawful act in the sudden heat of passion (without time to cool off). Imperfect self-defense occurs when a person kills another while responding to an unlawful act with excessive or unnecessary force. If a husband walks in on his wife in bed with someone else and shoots her, he has responded to an unlawful act (adultery) with excessive force (death is not the penalty for adultery). "Heat of passion" cases often occur in troubled marital or cohabitation situations.[2] Reduction of a charge from murder to manslaughter only reduces the length of the possible sentence; it does not excuse the conduct.

The incidence of criminal homicide does not fluctuate widely. The *number* of homicides has fluctuated over the years; but after peaking in the early 1990s, the *rate* of homicide (per 100,000 population) has been declining steadily (because of proportional increases in the population). Therefore, a person's risk of being the victim of a criminal homicide is slightly less today than it was in 1980.[3]

More than two-thirds of homicides are committed with guns, and 13 percent with knives. According to the FBI, about 25 percent of all criminal homicides in which the circumstances are known are related to the commission of a felony, as in robbery that results in death. Nearly 45 percent of all homicides result from arguments and romantic triangles, and 13 percent from drug- or alcohol-influenced brawls.[4]

Sexual Assault

rape
Sexual intercourse without effective consent.

sexual assault
Forced sex, whether vaginal, anal, or oral.

Rape is sexual intercourse without effective consent. The term **sexual assault** is often used to accommodate homosexual rape; it includes both rape (forced vaginal intercourse) and sodomy (forced oral or anal sex). Victimization surveys include sodomy, and in the future the Uniform Crime Reports (UCR; discussed later in this chapter) will include it in the definition of rape.

Intercourse is defined as any penetration, however slight. Any kind of physical force, including "terrorizing of the senses," suffices to establish lack of effective consent. Effective consent also is not present if the victim is a minor, mentally ill, mentally retarded, or physically helpless.

statutory rape
Nonforcible sexual intercourse with a minor.

Statutory rape is nonforcible sexual intercourse with a minor, an offense that the law provides as a way of protecting young people from exploitation by older ones. Statutory rape is not included in the UCR or victimization surveys because of its consensual nature.

According to victimization surveys, rapes of males accounted for 3 percent of all rapes. (Victimization surveys are conducted among the general public, so sexual assaults among the prison population are not included in this number.) In two-thirds of rapes of a female, the victim knew the offender; in only 8 percent of all cases did the offender brandish a weapon. Thirty-six percent of rape victims reported the incident to the police. Most female victims who fought back through words or actions believed that their efforts helped the situation rather than aggravated it.[5]

Assault

simple assault
A thrust against another person with the intention of injuring that person.

Simple assault is distinguished from aggravated assault by the nature of the offender's intent. **Simple assault** is a physical thrust against another person intended to injure that person. **Aggravated assault** additionally involves the intention to cause serious bodily harm or death. A "thrust" can be a punch, a gunshot, a threatening action that causes fear and anxiety, or any form of "offensive touching." Assault has been charged in cases of spitting at another person and in cases of fondling an individual without his or her consent. Aggravated assault is a felony; simple assault is punished less severely as a misdemeanor.

aggravated assault
A thrust against another person with the intention to cause serious bodily harm or death.

Victimization surveys include data on simple assaults, accounting for some differences in the rates of assault reported in victim surveys as opposed to the rates indicated in the Uniform Crime Reports. Still, aggravated assault is the most common crime of violence, accounting for nearly 900,000 reports to the police each year and more than 500,000 arrests.[6] More than 14 percent of assaults of all kinds occur at or near the victim's home. Only about 5 percent occur inside a bar, restaurant, or nightclub. Only a quarter of aggravated assaults involve a weapon; blunt objects cause more injury in assaults than any other type of weapon. As in the case of rape, approximately 60 percent of victims who used words or actions in self-defense felt that their efforts helped the situation.[7] Therefore, victims who defend themselves often fare better in their own judgment.

Robbery

Robbery is a combination of two other crimes: larceny (theft) and assault. **Robbery** consists of theft from a person involving threats or force. Threats must be serious enough to fulfill the element of assault and involve *immediate* harm, such that the victim cannot call the police or take other action to prevent the crime. The number of victims in a robbery incident determines the total number of robbery charges that can be brought against a defendant. Robbery is punished according to the amount of force used.

robbery
Theft from a person using threats or force.

After assault, robbery is the most common violent crime. It provokes high levels of fear, because two-thirds of robberies are committed by strangers. Approximately half of all robberies are committed by armed offenders (using guns

A barroom fight in progress. How can you tell if it will be a simple or aggravated assault?

about half the time). Nearly 27 percent of robbery victims are physically injured, although most who resisted the attacker report believing that it helped.[8]

Burglary

burglary
Unlawful entry into a building in order to commit a crime while inside.

Burglary is unlawful entry into a building for the purpose of committing a crime while inside. Entry involves trespass, but breaking or force need not occur. In a case in Buffalo, a man entered a store during regular business hours and hid there when the store closed. After everyone had left, he "shopped" at his leisure in the empty store, leaving his selections in a bin near the loading dock. When the store reopened in the morning, he planned to pose as a new customer and simply leave through the back door. However, a security guard noticed his selections by the loading dock and was waiting for him as he attempted to leave. In this case the person's entry into the store was legal, but he remained behind surreptitiously, making his action criminal trespass.

HOUSEHOLD BURGLARIES

Burglaries of dwellings cause the greatest concern among the public. Most burglaries have theft as their object, but burglaries can also occur for the purpose of assault. As noted earlier, there are about 4 million household burglaries per year, representing about 4 percent of all U.S. households. Therefore, the odds of household burglary are low. Only 30 percent of burglaries result in losses valued at $500 or more. More than 70 percent of burglaries with forced entry are reported to police, whereas only 42 percent of entries without force are reported.[9]

Larceny

larceny
Taking property of another person with the intent of depriving the owner.

Larceny is the most common serious crime in the United States. **Larceny** consists of taking the property of another person with the intent of depriving the owner. If force is used in a case of larceny, it becomes robbery. If deceit or trickery is used, the larceny becomes fraud, forgery, or embezzlement. The intention to deprive the owner is important, because moving companies take people's property all the time, as do valets, dry cleaners, and people who borrow books from libraries. These instances do not constitute larceny, because there is no intention to *deprive* the owner. Instead, the owner hands over the property for a short period, often in exchange for a service. Consent by the owner of the property is an absolute defense against charges of larceny.

"TAKING" UNDER THE LAW

The slightest movement of property may also be defined as "taking" under the law. If a shopper stuffs silk underwear under his jacket but is stopped before leaving the store, he has "taken" the property and can be charged with larceny, even though he never made it out the door.[10] Treating the silk underwear in a manner inconsistent with the buyer's right to inspect merchandise and the store's ownership of the property constitutes larceny in this case.

More than 15 million larcenies occur each year; 8 million of them involve property taken from households. Only about 300,000 involve pickpockets or purse snatchers. Larceny is the offense least likely to be reported to police, according to national victimization surveys. The total loss from larceny each year is approximately $6.1 billion, although most incidents involve losses under $250.[11]

Arson

Arson is burning of property without the lawful consent of the owner. As in the case of larceny, the lawful consent of the owner is an absolute defense against a charge of arson. Consent can be unlawful, however, if the owner is a minor or mentally incompetent, or if the owner gives consent with the intent of defrauding an insurance company.

Accidental fires do not constitute arson, although the law holds people to the reasonableness standard in evaluating their decisions. A competent adult who started a bonfire at a school pep rally only ten feet from the gymnasium could be charged with reckless arson if the gym burned down. This is because a reasonable person would have had a higher standard of care and would have recognized the substantial and unjustifiable risk of starting a large fire next to a building. Reckless arson is punished less severely than intentional arson.

Nearly 70,000 arsons are reported to police each year. Interestingly, only 45 percent of arsons occur in cities. Eighteen percent occur in rural areas; the remainder, in suburban locations. About 30 percent of arsons involve automobiles and 30 percent involve residences. The remainder involve commercial and community properties. The average loss in a typical incident of arson is about $11,000.[12] For arson to be charged, a structure or vehicle must be fire or smoke damaged intentionally or recklessly in some way by fire or explosion.

This is the scene of a crime involving a burglary with intent to commit larceny that turned into a robbery when a resident investigated a disturbance. How are these types of crimes against people and property distinguished? Who are the victims of these types of crimes?

arson
Burning property of another without the lawful consent of the owner.

How Are Crime Rates Determined?

The Federal Bureau of Investigation tallies crimes reported to police and arrests made each year for eight types of offenses; the FBI counts only arrests for nineteen other types of offenses. These tallies are published annually in the FBI's Uniform Crime Reports (UCR). The offenses for which detailed information is collected are criminal homicide, forcible rape, robbery, aggravated assault, burglary, larceny, motor vehicle theft, and arson. The FBI called these eight offenses its *Crime Index* up until June 2004, when it discontinued the terminology. The FBI now publishes separate violent crime totals and property crime totals and will continue to do so until a more viable index is developed. The *Crime Index* was first published in 1960 in the *Uniform Crime Report;* arson was added in 1979. Unfortunately, the *Crime Index* was not a true indicator of criminality because it was driven upward by the single offense with the largest number (larceny, which accounts for about 60 percent of reported crimes), creating an appearance of high crime rates, when more serious crimes, like rape and robbery, might be quite low. Therefore, violent crime totals and property crime totals are now considered separately. The offenses for which only arrests are counted are simple assault; forgery and counterfeiting; fraud; embezzlement; buying, receiving, or possessing

Media & Criminal Justice

America's Most Wanted

America Fights Back

Since 1988 Americans have tuned their television to *America's Most Wanted* (*AMW*) on Saturday nights in hopes of helping host John Walsh in the fight to capture criminal fugitives. The hour show dramatically re-creates the actual crimes with as much accuracy as possible, appealing to viewers' sense of justice and reminding them that people really *can* make a difference in solving crimes by calling in with their tips. It is the eighth-longest-running prime time network show in television history.

John Walsh, the father of a murdered child, has spent the last two decades crusading for missing children. The story of the Walsh family tragedy was dramatized in the 1983 television movie *Adam*, and followed up with a 1986 sequel *Adam: His Song Continues*. Following each broadcast, a list of missing children was featured, and sixty-five youngsters were recovered as a result of that media attention.

Walsh now serves on the board of directors for the National Center for Missing and Exploited Children, and focuses his energy on using *America's Most Wanted* as a vehicle for not only locating missing children, but also capturing violent offenders and sexual predators. The fugitives featured on the show have slipped through the grasp of law enforcement by evading capture or escaping from custody, sometimes on the lam for up to twenty years, and often on the FBI's Most Wanted list.

Some of the more famous captures that have resulted from tips to *AMW* include John List, who evaded capture for eighteen years after brutally murdering his wife and three children. Accused cop killer and hijacker William White Graham was on the run for more than twenty years; he surrendered to police after being profiled on *AMW*. Former police officer Bambi Bembeneck escaped from prison and fled to Canada after being convicted of murder; a viewer in Canada saw her on *AMW* and called in the tip that resulted in her recapture.

Callers' tips to *America's Most Wanted* have directly contributed to the capture of hundreds of fugitives. In an age where politics can raise questions about the accuracy of crime statistics, *America's Most Wanted* has proved that with the help of the media and concerned citizens, America's offense clearance rate is perhaps the most important crime statistic of all.

For a running update of captures resulting from tips called in to *America's Most Wanted*, log on to www.amw.com.

Why do the police have such a difficult time apprehending criminals and clearing crimes? Why might citizens be more likely to call a television show with a tip than to cooperate with a police investigation? Is it possible that a show like *America's Most Wanted* could actually lower the crime rate by providing a deterrent through increased likelihood of capture?

stolen property; vandalism; weapons offenses; prostitution and commercialized vice; other sex offenses; drug law violations; gambling; offenses against the family and children; driving under the influence; liquor law violations; drunkenness; disorderly conduct; vagrancy; violations of curfew and loitering laws; and runaway cases.

Is the crime rate increasing or decreasing? The simplest questions are sometimes the most difficult to answer. To understand the difficulty of this seemingly straightforward question, visualize the sources of information for a typical criminal incident, such as the one illustrated in Figure 3.1.

How many sources of information are there in this incident? Perhaps three parties are involved: the offender, the victim, and the police. Perhaps there also are witnesses present. Police often are involved after the fact, however; and victims and

FIGURE 3.1 Sources of Information about a Crime How many potential sources of information are there about the nature and extent of crime in this incident? In what ways might the information vary depending on the availability and the nature of each source?

witnesses often are not able to provide precise information or to agree on what actually happened. Nevertheless, different surveys attempt to explore each of the three primary sources of information to see how well they capture the true extent of crime. Offenders' views are counted in self-report studies, victims' and witnesses' views are counted in victimization surveys, and police data are counted in the FBI Uniform Crime Reports.

The FBI Uniform Crime Reports

In the United States, national crime statistics have been collected since 1930. Every time a crime is reported to police, a notation of the incident is made. Data on these incidents are recorded by local police and sent to the FBI in Washington, D.C. Each year the FBI compiles these statistics and publishes them in its **Uniform Crime Reports (UCR).** Although this process was initiated in 1930 at the recommendation of the International Association of Chiefs of Police (IACP), it was not until 1958 that participation in this voluntary program by local (especially rural) police departments was sufficient to permit national crime estimates. The UCR system now covers virtually all of the U.S. population.

Uniform Crime Reports (UCR) An annual compilation by the FBI of all crimes reported to the police in the United States.

WAYS TO COUNT CRIME

There are, of course, many ways to count crime—by incident, victimization, arrest, conviction, and so forth. The UCR system collects information only on *offenses known to police.* For many years, detailed information was collected for only seven types of offenses, selected on the basis of their seriousness, frequency of occurrence, and likelihood of being reported to the police: criminal homicide, forcible rape, robbery, aggravated assault, burglary, larceny, and motor vehicle theft. Arson was added to the list in 1979. The four violent crimes (criminal homicide, rape, robbery, aggravated assault) and four property crimes (burglary, larceny, motor vehicle theft, and arson) provide an indication of the level of major crimes against persons and property in the United States. For these crimes, information on the age, sex, and race of suspects is collected.

The UCR system also collects arrest data for nineteen other types of offenses. Because the Uniform Crime Reports collect only arrest information for those offenses (not all the instances reported to the police), the utility of UCR data is limited, in that we know only about offenders who are caught.

NOT ALL CRIMES ARE REPORTED

If the Uniform Crime Reports were our sole source of information about the true extent of crime, it is likely that our picture of the crime rate would be incomplete. For example, many crimes are not reported to the police, but only crimes reported to the police are included in the UCR. Changes in reporting procedures by local police departments also can create artificial increases or decreases in apparent crime rates. In 1998, for example, the FBI announced that it was discarding the crime statistics submitted by the Philadelphia Police Department for the previous two years. The statistics were inaccurate, and Philadelphia agreed to submit corrected figures to the Uniform Crime Reports. Underreporting and fraudulent reporting of crime data by police to the FBI have been discovered in other jurisdictions as well, due to pressures to make it appear that local crime had dropped, or lack of cooperation from local and state police agencies to compile accurate crime statistics.[13] Another disadvantage is that data on the Index crimes provide only partial coverage of all serious crime. Corporate price-fixing, illegal dumping, and the manufacture of unsafe products are examples of crimes that cause harm and loss to a much greater extent than do the Index crimes; yet the impact of these crimes is overlooked by the UCR system. The true extent of crime in the United States thus is a bit more difficult to determine than one might think.

Table 3.2 provides a summary of crimes reported to police in the United States over a twenty-five-year period. This table, taken from the UCR, includes both the number of crimes reported to the police and the crime rate (i.e., number per 1,000 population). In 1980, for example, a total of 654,960 aggravated assaults were reported to police. Twenty-five years later the number had increased to 854,911. The decimal numbers in Table 3.2, appearing under the number of reported offenses, indicate the rates. That is, the 854,911 aggravated assaults reported to police in 2004 meant that there were 2.91 aggravated assaults for every 1,000 people in the country.

crime rates
The number of crimes committed divided by the population at risk. This provides an indication of the risk of victimization per capita.

personal risk
An individual's risk of being a victim of crime; determined through calculation of crime rates in relation to population.

Crime rates are a more reliable way to measure crime than raw numbers of crimes. This is because raw numbers do not account for changes in the population, which can greatly affect the degree of risk faced by an individual. For instance, if there are 100 people in your town and 10 Index crimes were committed last year, your chances of being a victim (on average) will be 1 in 10. However, if your town has 1,000 people living in it and 10 Index crimes are reported, the Uniform Crime Reports will show that the chances of being victimized are only 1 in 100. So even though the number of crimes is the same, each individual's **personal risk** of being the victim varies, depending on the population of potential victims.

Because the population of the United States has been increasing steadily (as displayed in the bottom row of Table 3.2), reports of numbers of crimes can be misleading. An actual example illustrates the point. Table 3.2 indicates that in 1980 there were 82,990 rapes reported to police in the United States—a rate of .368 per

Table 3.2 Serious Crimes Reported to Police in the United States (number and rate per 1,000 population)

Offense	*1980*	*1990*	*2000*	*2004*
Homicide	23,040 .102	23,440 .094	15,586 .055	16,137 .055
Rape	82,990 .368	102,560 .412	90,178 .320	94,635 .322
Robbery	565,840 2.51	639,270 2.57	408,016 1.45	401,326 1.37
Aggravated assault	654,960 2.98	1,054,860 4.24	911,706 3.24	854,911 2.91
Burglary	3,759,200 16.8	3,073,900 12.4	2,050,992 7.29	2,143,456 7.30
Larceny	7,112,700 31.7	7,945,700 31.9	6,971,590 24.7	6,947,685 23.7
Motor vehicle theft	1,114,700 5.02	1,635,900 6.6	1,160,002 4.12	1,237,114 4.2
U.S. population	225.3 million	249 million	281.4 million	293.7 million

Source: Federal Bureau of Investigation, *Crime in the United States* (Washington, DC: U.S. Government Printing Office, published annually).

1,000 people (or about 1 per 3,000). Twenty-five years later this number had grown to 94,635, an increase of more than 11,000. However, 94,635 rapes in 2004 was equal to a rate of .322 per 1,000 people, which actually resulted in a *lower personal risk* of being a victim—because the overall population of the United States was larger. What this means is that although the number of rapes increased, the population grew proportionately faster than the number of rapes taking place. The U.S. population grew from 225.3 million to 293.7 million between 1980 and 2004, a greater rate of growth than the rate of increase in the number of rapes. As a result, there was a slight *reduction* in an individual's personal risk of being a victim of a rape. When comparing changes in the extent of crime, therefore, it is important to rely only on crime *rates*, because they account for changes in the population at risk. Measuring risk, after all, is the purpose of counting crimes.

THE TRUE EXTENT OF CRIME?

Recently, efforts have been made to measure crimes that were not known to the police, because not all crimes are reported. For example, some victims may fear embarrassment, public disclosure, or interrogation by the police. Some victims may know the offender and not want to inform police of his or her identity. For property crimes, a victim may feel that the value of the property taken is not worth the effort to get police involved. Some may think the police cannot do anything about the crime. Further, some people simply fear or mistrust the police. Some are afraid of possible retaliation by the offender. Finally, some victims of crimes are engaging in criminal behavior themselves and therefore are reluctant to have any involvement with police. For all these reasons, police statistics reported in the Uniform Crime Reports provide an incomplete picture of the true extent of crime.

The National Crime Victimization Survey

In 1967 the President's Crime Commission, recognizing the need for more accurate knowledge about the amount and kinds of crime, conducted the first national survey of crime victimization. In a survey of 10,000 households (containing 33,000 people), people were asked whether they had been the victim of a crime during the past year and, if so, whether the crime had been reported to the police.

National Crime Victimization Survey (NCVS)
A representative sample of the U.S. population is surveyed annually to determine the extent of victimization and the extent to which these incidents were reported to police.

Since 1973 the **National Crime Victimization Survey (NCVS)** has interviewed more than 100,000 individuals from 50,000 households throughout the nation each year. People are asked to report anonymously whether they have been the victims of certain crimes during the past year. Participants in the survey are selected through a representative sampling of households across the country; every household therefore has an equal chance of being included in the survey, so estimates of the true extent of crime can be given with a relatively small margin of error.

In each household surveyed, family members at least twelve years of age are interviewed individually. These surveys elicit much more information than is gathered by the Uniform Crime Reports, in that they include not only crime data but also information about each crime victim's age, sex, race, education level, and income; the extent of injury or loss suffered; any relationship with the offender; and whether or not the crime was reported to the police. As a result, victimization surveys have many more potential uses than do police statistics. NCVS data have been used for the following purposes:

PURPOSES OF NCVS DATA

1. To estimate the costs of victim compensation programs and thus help communities determine whether such programs are economically feasible.
2. To determine the kinds of special programs needed for elderly victims of crime. Older citizens' fear of crime remains high, even though victimization rates are low among the elderly.
3. To analyze the circumstance in cases of rape in order to provide better information on ways of preventing this crime.

Victimization surveys thus provide a great deal of information about criminal incidents that can serve as a basis for crime prevention programs.

Victimization surveys also provide a more complete picture of the risk posed by crime than do UCR data, because they count both reported crimes and those not reported to police. For example, the 1967 survey consisted of interviews with 33,000 people and found only 14 rapes, 31 robberies, 71 aggravated assaults, 309 larcenies, and 68 motor vehicle thefts.[14] These numbers showed that crime was relatively rare even when one counted crimes not reported to police. Since 1973 the sample has included more than 100,000 people, and the survey has been conducted twice a year. The larger sample ensures that enough crime is uncovered so that precise estimates can be made. By contrast, most public opinion polls interview a sample of fewer than 2,000 people to determine nationwide opinion on a particular subject. Fortunately, crimes are much less common than opinions.

While the Uniform Crime Reports collect a little information about all crimes known to police, victimization surveys collect extensive information about a representative sample of the population, whether or not the victimization was reported. Like the Uniform Crime Reports, the National Crime Victimization Survey collects information about forcible rape, robbery, assault, burglary, larceny, and motor vehicle theft. (Murder victims, obviously, are not included in victim surveys.) For victimization surveys, forcible rape is defined in the same manner as it is for the Uniform Crime Reports, although the UCR system counts only rapes of females. The NCVS, however, counts both simple (minor) assaults and aggravated assaults, whereas only aggravated assaults are recorded in the UCR.

COMPARING UCR AND NCVS DATA

The crimes of robbery, burglary, larceny, and motor vehicle theft are counted somewhat differently in victimization surveys than they are in the Uniform Crime Reports. The UCR system counts these crimes whether the victim is a private individual or a commercial establishment. The NCVS includes only households, however; so it does not count commercial robberies, burglaries, larcenies, and motor vehicle thefts. Therefore, bank and store robberies, nonresidential burglaries, and larcenies from commercial establishments are omitted from victimization estimates. Further, the UCR definition of motor vehicle theft includes snowmobiles and golf carts, but the NCVS definition does not.

Despite these differences, there is a fairly close correspondence between the definitions used in the UCR and NCVS. As a result, it is possible to gather nationwide crime information from two points of view: that of the victim and that of the police.

Table 3.3 is a summary of nationwide victimization rates over a twenty-five-year period. As in the Uniform Crime Reports, both numbers of crimes and rates of victimization are presented. For example, NCVS estimates that 130,000 forcible rapes and attempts occurred in the United States in 1990. This means that there were approximately 0.6 rapes for every 1,000 residents in the nation (or 6 per 10,000 people). In 2000, the estimated number increased to 147,000 rapes—an increase of about 17,000 over ten years. Nevertheless, the personal risk of rape

VICTIM SURVEYS SHOW MORE CRIME

Table 3.3 Crime Victimization in the United States (number and rate per 1,000 population)

Offenses	*1980*	*1990*	*2000*	*2004*
Rape	174,000 0.9	130,000 0.6	147,000 0.6	108,950 0.4
Robbery	1,209,000 6.6	1,150,000 5.7	732,000 3.2	501,820 2.1
Aggravated assault	1,707,000 9.3	1,601,000 7.9	1,293,000 5.7	1,030,080 4.3
Household burglary	6,973,000 84.3	5,148,000 53.8	3,444,000 31.8	3,427,690 29.6
Larceny from the person	15,300,000 83.0	12,975,000 63.8	14,916,000 137.7	14,211,940 122.8 (all larcenies)
Household larceny	10,490,000 126.5	8,304,000 86.7	— —	Combined with other larcenies beginning 1993
Motor vehicle theft	1,381,000 16.7	1,968,000 20.5	937,000 8.6	1,014,770 8.8

Source: Shannan Catalano, Lisa D. Bastian, Patsy Klaus, Craig Perkins, Callie Marie Rennison, and Cheryl Ringel, *Criminal Victimization* (Washington, DC. Bureau of Justice Statistics, published annually).

That's a FACT

Perspectives on the Crime Index

Perhaps the most significant news regarding crime in recent years has been the large drop in many serious crimes. Figure 3A graphically displays the drop in crime victimization for violent and property crimes from 1973 (when victimization surveys first began) to 2004. Given the information provided in this chapter, what reasons can you offer for such a sub-

FIGURE 3A

Source: Shannan M. Catalano, *Criminal Victimization, 2004* (Washington, DC: Bureau of Justice Statistics, 2005).

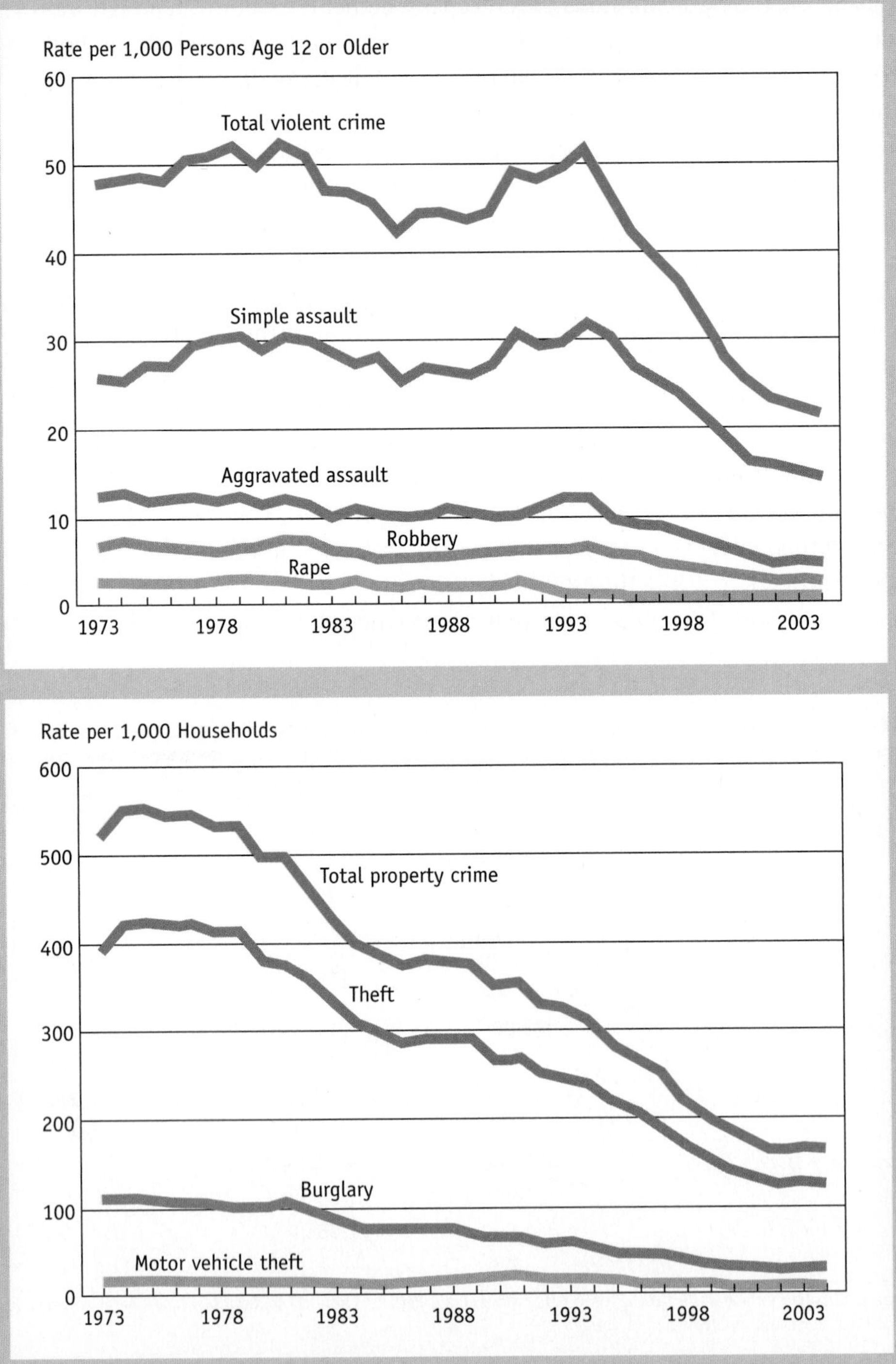

stantial drop in these crimes? Are there reasons to believe that crime will start to climb again?

Figure 3B illustrates the different forms of larceny counted in police crime statistics. Why do you believe thefts from automobiles are so common? Why do you believe pocket-picking and thefts from coin-operated machines are so uncommon? Do you have ideas about what types of theft the "other" category might include?

FIGURE 3B Types of Larceny

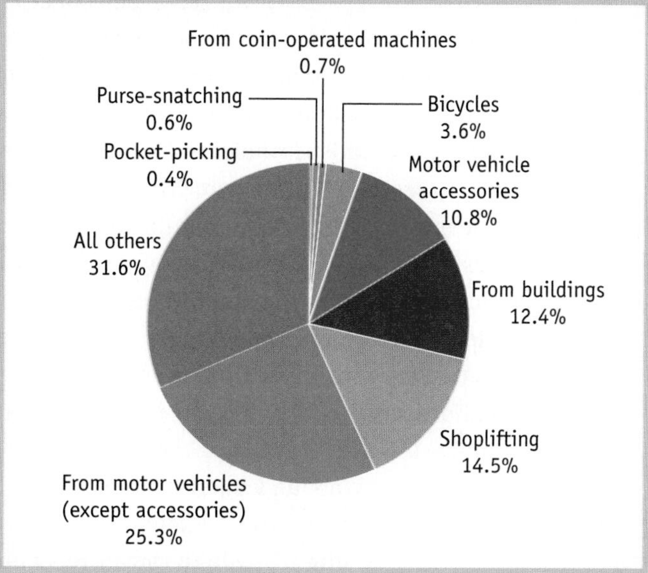

Source: FBI Uniform Crime Reports, 2004.

One of the chief limitations of the Uniform Crime Reports is that the data is based on crimes reported to the police. Why is this a limitation in understanding crime rates? Why might crimes not be reported? The person in this photograph is being interviewed as part of a National Crime Victimization Survey. How is the NCVS different from the UCR as a source of data? How will information from this interview contribute to knowledge about crime in the United States?

victimization *remained the same*, because the population of the United States increased at a higher rate than did the number of rapes. Once again, it can be seen that the use of raw numbers of crimes is misleading, because such numbers provide no indication of changes in degree of personal risk.

A comparison of the extent of crime as reported in police statistics and in victimization surveys reveals significant differences. For instance, the Uniform Crime Reports (Table 3.2) indicate that there were 94,635 reported cases of forcible rape in 2004, whereas victim surveys show 108,950—nearly 15,000 additional rapes! There were 401,326 reported robberies in 2004, but victim surveys uncovered 501,820 robberies: 25 percent greater than the number reported to police. The same is true for all the other crimes counted by both the UCR and NCVS. In every instance, victim surveys show that there is significantly more serious crime than police statistics indicate. Taken as a whole, victim surveys annually uncover two to three times more crime than is reported in the Uniform Crime Reports. This is clearly one of the most significant findings of the NCVS. As Figure 3.2 illustrates, the amount of crime discovered from interviews with the general public is much greater than the amount reported to police.

REASONS FOR NOT REPORTING CRIMES

Table 3.4 provides a major part of the explanation for these differences. Victimization surveys reveal that, overall, 50 percent of all violent crimes and 39 percent of property crimes are reported to police, a percentage that has been generally increasing over the years. Larceny is the crime least likely to be reported (about 32 percent of the time), and motor vehicle theft is the crime most likely to be reported (about 85 percent of the time). The high rate of reporting of auto theft is undoubtedly due to mandatory automobile insurance, which usually requires that a police report be submitted before the owner can make a claim.

FIGURE 3.2 The Level of Serious Crime as Measured by UCR and NCVS

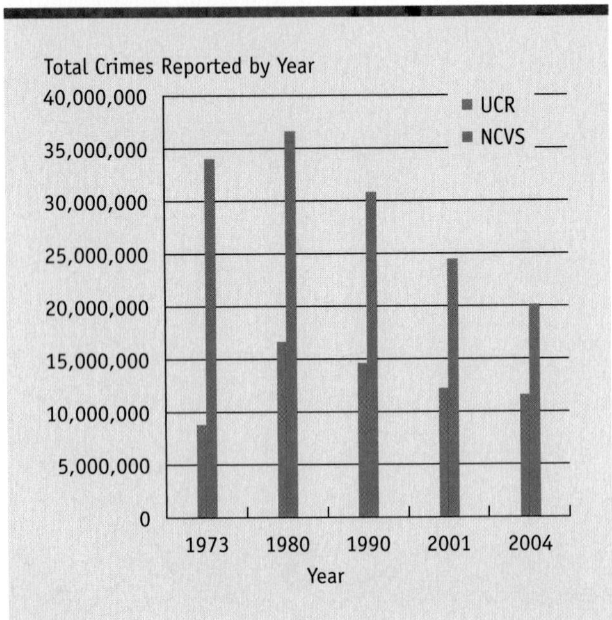

Source: FBI Uniform Crime Report and National Criminal Victimization Survey data published annually by the Federal Bureau of Investigation and Bureau of Justice Statistics.

The reasons for reporting crimes to police have been found to vary according to the nature of the crime. Figure 3.3 presents the reasons given to interviewers in the National Crime Victimization Survey. The most common reasons for reporting violent crimes included the fact that the event was a crime, and that the victims wanted to prevent future crimes against themselves or others. For property crimes, the concerns were similar with the important added desire to recover the property that was taken. The most common reasons for *not* reporting violent crimes are that the victim saw the incident as a private matter or that the offender was not successful in his or her attempt. The most common reasons for not reporting thefts are that the object was recovered, proof was lacking, the offender was unsuccessful, or the incident was reported to someone other than the police.

Table 3.4 Victimizations Reported to the Police

Type of Crime	*Percentage Reported in 1995*	*Percentage Reported in 2004*
Crimes of violence (total)	42%	50%
Rape	31	36
Robbery	56	61
Aggravated assault	54	64
Simple assault	36	45
Crimes of theft (total)	34%	39%
Larceny	35	32
Household burglary	51	53
Motor vehicle theft	76	85

To make crime data more useful for purposes of crime analysis, law enforcement, and the design of prevention programs, the **National Incident-Based Reporting System** (NIBRS) is under development in the U.S. Department of Justice. This program collects data on each criminal incident for twenty-two different categories of offenses. The purpose is to gather more complete information about when and where crimes take place, and about the characteristics of the victims and perpetrators. By 2004, twenty-nine states were certified to submit this more comprehensive information about each criminal incident, and sixteen more states are in various stages of implementation. Once the NIBRS program is implemented on a national basis, we will know a great deal more about every criminal incident, will understand some underlying factors behind crime trends, and can effectively target crime prevention initiatives.

National Incident-Based Reporting System
Data collection program designed to gather information on victims, perpetrators, and circumstances of crime.

CRIMES AGAINST HOUSEHOLDS

Another way to assess crime trends is to look at crimes against households (i.e., apartments and homes). A household touched by crime is one that was victimized by burglary or theft, or in which a household member was robbed, raped, or assaulted or had property stolen (no matter where the crime occurred). Approximately 14 percent of households in the United States are touched by crime, and less than 3 percent of the incidents involve violent crimes. This reflects a steady decline in the risk of victimization since 1975, when these statistics were first gathered. Table 3.5 summarizes these changes.

In 1975 approximately 1 in 3 households were touched by crime (6 percent involving violence). Thirty years later, fewer than 1 in 7 households were victimized.[15] Despite the increase in the total number of households, from 73.1 million in 1975 to 115.8 million in 2004, the risk of both violent and property crimes against household members dropped. In fact, the level of risk in 2004 was at its lowest point since this measure of victimization was first used in 1975. Naturally, individual risk is affected greatly by place of residence, income, and size of household; but for the nation as a whole, the risk of victimization declined following 1975.

FIGURE 3.3 Reasons that Crimes are Reported to Police

Reasons	*Crimes of Violence*	*Property Crimes*
Because it was a crime	20%	23%
Stop or prevent this incident	19	8
Prevent future crimes against victim	18	9
Prevent future crime against anyone	11	6
To punish offender	7	5
To recover property	4	23
To catch or find offender	5	7
Duty to notify police	5	6

Source: Criminal Victimization in the United States, 2004: Statistical Tables (U.S. Bureau of Justice Statistics, 2006). http://www.ojp.usdoj.gov/bjs/pub/pdf/cvus04.pdf.

Table 3.5 Households Victimized by Crime

Offense	1975	1992	2000	2004
Violent crimes (rape, robbery, assault)	5.8%	5.0%	3.9%	3.1%
Burglary	7.7	4.2	2.7	2.5
Theft (from person or household)	26.6	16.9	10.9	9.6
Motor vehicle theft	1.8	2.0	0.8	0.8
Total (any crime above)	32.1%	22.6%	16.2%	14.1%

Source: Michael R. Rand, *Crime and the Nation's Households, 1992* (Washington, DC: Bureau of Justice Statistics, 1993); Patsy A. Klaus, *Crime and the Nation's Households, 2004* (Washington, DC: Bureau of Justice Statistics, 2006).

What Offenders Say

A third possible source of information about the extent of crime is the offenders themselves. Efforts to conduct self-report surveys of offenders date from the 1940s.[16] The first studies attempted to identify differences between offenders who were caught and those who were not apprehended. Many subsequent self-report studies have been undertaken, but most use small samples, rather than representative samples of the entire U.S. population as victimization surveys do.[17]

SELF-REPORT SURVEYS OF OFFENDERS

There have been only two national self-report surveys, and these were limited to young people.[18] These surveys were designed to investigate the causes of delinquency rather than to estimate national crime trends.[19] A **National Longitudinal Survey of Youth** begun in 1997, however, administers self-report surveys to a cohort of 9,000 youths aged twelve to sixteen every two years over an extended period of time.

National Longitudinal Survey of Youth
Self-report study investigating the extent of delinquency among young people.

The early results of the National Longitudinal Survey support the findings of early self-report studies. Information from these studies differs from statistics on

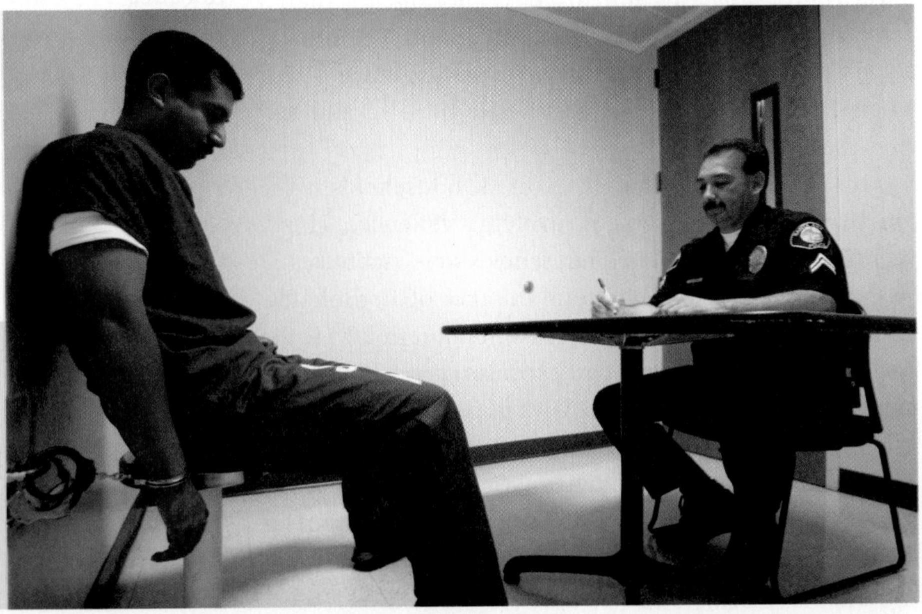

Self-report surveys find that the race and social class of offenders is more evenly distributed in society than police or prison statistics indicate. Why do you think more minorities and poor people find themselves arrested and imprisoned than do middle-class persons and majorities who commit similar crimes?

crimes reported to police. Most important and consistent among the findings of the self-report studies is that virtually all juveniles break the law at one time or another, although only 10 to 20 percent are caught and arrested. Only a small proportion of all youth engage in serious or frequent criminal behavior. Self-report surveys usually do not include questions about many serious crimes, owing to the reluctance of respondents to report their involvement in such crimes. Therefore, they are weighted toward less serious offenses such as alcohol and drug use, truancy, and simple assaults. Also, the administration of self-reports has been confined mostly to schools and communities, environments that exclude some of the most serious and frequent offenders.

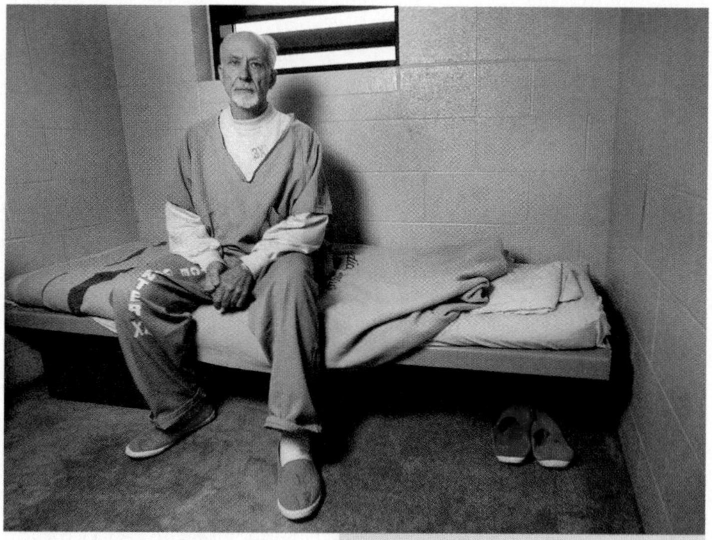

Crime rates have shown a steady decline in many places, yet the best predictors of crime are still age, opportunity, and motivation. How do you think these factors are likely to change in the coming years?

Self-reports have also suggested that offenders are more evenly distributed in terms of race and social class than police statistics indicate. To date, self-reports have dealt primarily with characteristics of offenders. Questions could be added about victim selection, victim description, and offenders' relationship to victims. Answers to these questions would help in the development of crime prevention programs that raise public awareness of the causes of victimization.

The Future of Crime in the United States

Trends in crime rates have shown a steady decline, especially since the early 1990s, which is reflected in both Uniform Crime Reports and the National Crime Victimization Survey. The three best predictors of the perpetration of crime are age, opportunity, and motivation. Most people who commit serious crimes are males who are between the ages of sixteen and twenty-four, poor, and from a central city. And victimization surveys show that most victims have the same characteristics as their offenders.

BEST PREDICTORS OF CRIME?

Age is one of the strongest predictors of serious violent and property crime, because these crimes involve force and/or stealth and hence are more likely to be committed by younger people. Few forty-year-olds rob convenience stores, because to do so you may have to be able to hop over the counter, hop back, and maybe outrun a pursuer. People between the ages of sixteen and twenty-four are strong and agile and therefore are the most crime-prone age group. Victims also tend to be in this age range: They are out more often, for more hours, later at night, and in a greater diversity of neighborhoods and settings. However, this is a shrinking age group in the U.S. population. In 1970 the median age in America was twenty-seven; in 2000 it was thirty-five; and by 2020 it is expected to rise past forty as life expectancy increases and birth and immigration rates remain low.[20] These facts and projections led one criminologist to conclude that "there is no evidence that violent or property crimes will increase dramatically over the next two decades, and all indications would seem to be that the rates will actually undergo an overall decline."[21] This view corresponds with the findings of victimization surveys, which show a general decline in the rates of serious crime in recent years.

This forecast is subject to change, however, especially considering the possible impact of changes in opportunities and motivation for criminal activity in coming years. Opportunities for crime may increase. Serious crimes most often occur in central cities and involve people in poverty. Large pockets of low-income inner-city dwellers, who tend to be undereducated, unskilled, and underemployed, will contribute to serious crimes against persons and property. Twenty percent of all children in the United States are living below the poverty level. Also, 15 percent of young people do not graduate from high school.[22] These facts do not bode well for the future of poverty, a factor closely associated both with serious criminal offenders and with victims.

OPPORTUNITIES FOR CRIME?

Added to economic opportunities for crime are those provided by new technology. The popularity of portable equipment of all types—cellular telephones, computers and handheld computer games, and tape and CD players, among many others—offers opportunities for theft, robbery, and misuse that did not exist even a decade ago. ATM machines, credit cards, and commerce via the computer also have created new opportunities for crime that are technology driven.

MOTIVATION FOR CRIME?

The third important factor, after age and opportunity, is motivation. If people are not motivated to be law-abiding, little can be done to stop them. Police now catch only 20 percent of offenders who commit reported serious crimes, a rate that has declined somewhat over the years. Thus, the odds of apprehension are low, have always been low, and are unlikely to increase any time soon. Law and order depends on the fact that most people choose not to break laws. Decisions to commit or to refrain from crime often are based on values and morals established early in life. Respect for others and their property is what keeps most of us law-abiding, whatever our economic background. We learn these values primarily through family and school role models.

What are the characteristics of youth in custody? How are they different from other juveniles (many of whom also commit crimes but are not incarcerated)?

Surveys of youth in custody have found that 70 percent of all juveniles in custody come from single-parent homes, 52 percent have a family member who has been incarcerated, more than half engage in regular drug or alcohol use, and more than 85 percent have been arrested at least twice before.[23] Surveys of high school youth have found that 4 in 10 have been involved in a physical fight and that 33 percent have had property stolen or vandalized at school; more than half of high school seniors have used illicit drugs.[24] A ten-year study tracked more than 1,000 children from age three to age fifteen. It found that preschool behavior problems were the single best predictor of antisocial behaviors' appearing at age eleven.[25] The best predictor of adult criminality is juvenile delinquency, and the best predictor of juvenile delinquency is behavior problems that date back to early childhood. These significant problems in the behavior and supervision of many juveniles may result in increased crime in the years ahead, despite the shrinking proportion of young people in the U.S. population.

The Columbine High School shooting incident that opened this chapter turned out to be one of 27 shooting incidents that occurred in U.S. schools from 1996 to 2003.[26] The incident at Columbine was the deadliest, but others involved more students and teachers who were wounded but escaped death. High levels of security and fear now grip many schools. In Oregon, for example, more than half the 1,100 stu-

PREDICTING ANTISOCIAL BEHAVIOR

dents at Parkrose High School stayed out of school after graffiti was found on a bathroom wall saying, "If you think Columbine was bad, wait until Dec. 10."[27] Nothing occurred on that date, and it was not determined whether the message was a prank; but it is clear that many schools and communities are taking potential violence seriously. There were seven foiled school shooting and violence plots across the United States in 2006, which apparently arose in response to the seventh anniversary of the Columbine tragedy. A total of seventy-eight nonfatal, school-related shootings occurred in 2006, up from fifty-two the previous year. There were twenty school-associated violent deaths during the 2005–06 school year.[28] Fear of violent crime remains high. Despite falling rates of violent crime nationwide, crime remains a serious problem that is drawing significant attention. That attention increasingly is drawn to the highest-risk group—the young.

CRITICAL THINKING EXERCISES

The Circumstances of Crime

Statistics merely summarize experience, and crime statistics summarize patterns that enable us to take preventive action. Table 3A presents crime data about robbery victims gathered through the National Crime Victimization Survey. On the basis of this information, answer the Critical Thinking Questions that follow.

CRITICAL THINKING QUESTIONS

1. You are involved with developing a robbery prevention program. Given the information in the table, what group of potential victims should you target?
2. Where would be a good place to pilot the program?
3. What points might you make and what issues might you address in your prevention program?
4. How could you assess the effectiveness of your program? What measures of this type of crime would you use? Which information would you favor more: UCR, NCVS, or self-report data? Why?

Table 3A Crime Data about Robbery Victims

Characteristics of Robbery Victims	*Findings from National Crime Victimization Survey*
Household income	Less than $7,500 = 6.5 victims per 1,000 population 12 and older
	$7,500–14,999 = 5.8
	$15,000–24,999 = 3.6
	$25,000–34,999 = 6.9
	$35,000–49,999 = 3.1
	$50,000 or more = 2.9
Marital status	Never married = 8.0/1,000
	Married = 1.3
Region of U.S.	Northeast = 3.2/1,000
	Midwest = 3.8
	South = 3.8
	West = 5.2
Residence	Urban = 6.5/1,000
	Suburban = 3.2
	Rural = 2.6
Relationship with offender	Stranger = 57%
	Friend/acquaintance = 21%
	Intimate = 12%
	Other relative = 8%
Weapon use by offender	None = 49%
	Gun = 21%
	Knife = 10%

Identifying Serious Crimes

Seven felony offenders escaped from prison by overpowering a guard and arming themselves. All the escapees were serving sentences ranging from thirty years to life. They later entered a sporting goods store, tied up the employees, and took guns and $70,000 in cash and clothes. A police officer arrived on the scene as the offenders were leaving, and he was shot and killed. It is believed that members of this group of escapees were responsible for another crime a few days later when employees at a Radio Shack store were held at gunpoint while the perpetrators took police scanners and fled in the store manager's truck, which was later found abandoned.

In addition to escaping from prison (which is a crime in itself), the offenders committed a series of crimes after their escape. Once they were caught, these offenders were charged by police with specific offenses under Texas criminal law. Can you identify the appropriate crimes that correspond to the facts above?

Source: Erin Hayes, Jim Ryan, Sascha Segan, "The Hunt Continues: Texas Fugitives Continue to Evade Police," *ABCNews.com* (January 2, 2000).

CRITICAL THINKING QUESTIONS

1. Identify and explain each crime against property committed by the escapees.
2. Identify and explain each violent crime (crime against persons) committed by the escapees.

SUMMARY

WHAT ARE THE TYPES OF CRIME?

- Crimes are of three general types: crimes against persons (violent crimes), crimes against property, and crimes against public order.

HOW ARE VIOLENT CRIMES AND PROPERTY CRIMES CLASSIFIED?

- Murder includes all intentional killings as well as deaths that occur in the course of felonies; manslaughter involves causing death recklessly, or intentionally under extenuating circumstances.
- Rape is sexual intercourse without effective consent; statutory rape is nonforcible sexual intercourse with a minor.
- Assault is a thrust against another person intended to injure that person.
- Robbery consists of larceny from a person involving threats or force.
- Burglary is unlawful entry into a building for the purpose of committing a crime while inside.
- Larceny consists of taking the property of another person with the intent of depriving the owner.
- Arson is burning of property without the lawful consent of the owner.

HOW ARE CRIME RATES DETERMINED?

- Each year the FBI compiles statistics on crimes reported to the police and publishes them in its Uniform Crime Reports.
- The National Crime Victimization Survey provides information about crimes that are and are not reported to the police.
- Victimization surveys reveal that the amount of serious crime is much higher than police statistics indicate.
- Surveys of offenders show that virtually all juveniles break the law at one time or another.
- Victimization surveys can provide a precise estimate of the risk of crimes against households.
- Crime rates have generally been falling in recent years.

KEY TERMS

crimes against persons *56*
crimes against property *56*
crimes against public order *56*
criminal homicide *57*
murder *57*
manslaughter *57*
recklessness *57*
negligence *57*
gross negligence *57*
rape *58*
sexual assault *58*
statutory rape *58*
simple assault *58*
aggravated assault *59*
robbery *59*
burglary *60*
larceny *60*
arson *61*
Uniform Crime Reports (UCR) *63*
crime rates *64*
personal risk *64*
National Crime Victimization Survey (NCVS) *66*
National Incident-Based Reporting System *71*
National Longitudinal Survey of Youth *72*

QUESTIONS FOR REVIEW AND DISCUSSION

1. What is meant by recklessness? By negligence?
2. In what circumstances are intentional killings punished as manslaughter rather than as murder?
3. How does aggravated assault differ from simple assault?
4. What is the difference between larceny and robbery?
5. Why do the Uniform Crime Reports present an incomplete picture of the true extent of crime?
6. What advantages does the National Crime Victimization Survey have over the UCR?
7. What are the most common types of crime as revealed by victimization surveys?
8. What reasons do people give for not reporting crimes to the police?
9. Why are both offenders and victims likely to be young?

NOTES

1. Angie Cannon, Betsy Streisand, and Dan McGraw, "Why?," *U.S. News & World Report* (May 3, 1999), pp. 16–19; Brendan Koerner, "From Way Cool to Out of Control," *U.S. News & World Report* (May 3, 1999), pp. 20–21; Brooks Brown and Rob Meritt, No *Easy Answers: The Truth Behind Death at Columbine* (New York: Lantern Books, 2003); David Maraniss, "That Was the Desk I Chose to Die Under," *The Washington Post*, (April 19, 2007), 1.
2. See *State v. Ott*, 297 Or. 375 (Supreme Ct. Oregon 1984) and *State v. Gounagais*, 88 Wash. 304 (Supreme Ct. Washington 1915); *Allen v. Ward*, 2006 U.S. App. LEXIS 14340 (U.S. Court of Appeals for Tenth Circuit 2006).
3. James Alan Fox and Marianne W. Zawitz, *Homicide Trends in the United States* (Washington, DC: Bureau of Justice Statistics, 2006), www.ojp.usdoj.gov/bjs.
4. Federal Bureau of Investigation, *Crime in the United States, 2005* (Washington, DC: U.S. Government Printing Office, 2005).
5. Shannan M. Catalano, *Criminal Victimization, 2004* (Washington, DC: Bureau of Justice Statistics, 2005); *Criminal Victimization in the United States: Statistical Tables* (Washington, DC: Bureau of Justice Statistics, 2006).
6. Federal Bureau of Investigation, *Crime in the United States, 2004* (Washington, DC: U.S. Government Printing Office, 2005).
7. *Criminal Victimization in the United States, 2004.*
8. Catalon, p. 9; *Criminal Victimization in the United States, 2004.*
9. *Criminal Victimization in the United States, 2004.*
10. *Berry v. State*, 90 Wis. 2d 316 (Supreme Ct. Wisconsin 1979).
11. *Criminal Victimization in the United States, 2004.*
12. Federal Bureau of Investigation, 2005, p. 58.
13. "Phony Statistics a Big Part of Philadelphia's Anti-Crime Success," *Richmond Times–Dispatch* (December 10, 1998), p. 5; Wanda J. DeMarzo, "Sheriff Shakes Up Top Staff in Crime-Statistics Scandal," *Miami Herald* (January 8, 2005); Jill Leovy, "LAPD Gave Misleading Crime Data," *Los Angeles Times* (August 30, 2005); "State Police Lax on Compiling Data, FBI Says," *Lexington Herald-Leader* (September 15, 2004).
14. James Garofalo and Michael J. Hindelang, *Introduction to the National Crime Survey* (Washington, DC: U.S. Government Printing Office, 1977).
15. Michael R. Rand, *Crime and the Nation's Households, 1992* (Washington, DC: Bureau of Justice Statistics, 1993); Patsy A. Klaus, *Crime and the Nation's Households, 2004* (Washington, DC: Bureau of Justice Statistics, 2006).
16. Austin L. Porterfield, *Youth in Trouble* (Fort Worth: Texas Christian University Press, 1946); J. S. Wallerstein and C. L. Wylie, "Our Law-abiding Law-breakers," *National Probation* (March–April, 1947), pp. 107–12.
17. Jay S. Albanese, *Dealing with Delinquency: The Future of Juvenile Justice*, 2nd ed. (Chicago: Nelson-Hall, 1993), pp. 26–31.
18. Delbert S. Elliott, *The Prevalence and Incidence of Delinquent Behavior, 1976–1980* (Boulder, CO: Behavioral Research Institute, 1983); Martin Gold, *Delinquent Behavior in an American City* (Belmont, CA: Brooks/Cole, 1970); Martin Gold and D. J. Reimer, "Changing Patterns of Delinquent Behavior among Americans 13–16 Years Old: 1967–1972," *Crime and Delinquency Literature* 7 (1975), pp. 483–517.
19. Robert M. O'Brien, *Crime and Victimization Data* (Beverly Hills, CA: Sage, 1985), pp. 63–79.
20. Gregory Spencer, *Projections of the Population of the United States by Age, Sex, and Race: 1988 to 2080*, U.S. Bureau of Census Current Population Reports, Series P-25, No. 1018 (Washington, DC: U.S. Government Printing Office, 1998).
21. Chester L. Britt, "The Nature of Common Crime in the Year 2010," in J. Klofas and S. Stojkovic, eds., *Crime and Justice in the Year 2010* (Belmont, CA: Wadsworth, 1995), p. 99.
22. Neil Bennett, Jiala Li, Younghwan Song, and Keming Yang, *Young Children in Poverty: A Statistical Update* (New York: National Center for Children in Poverty, 1999); Federal Interagency Forum on Child and Family Statistics, *America's Children: Key National Indicators of Well-Being, 2006* (Washington, DC: Office of Juvenile Justice and Delinquency Prevention, 2006).
23. Allen Beck, Susan Kline, Lawrence Greenfield, *Survey of Youth in Custody* (Washington, DC: U.S. Government Printing Office, 1998).
24. Howard N. Snyder and Melissa Sickmund, *Juvenile Offenders and Victims: 2006 National Report* (Washington, DC: Office of Juvenile Justice and Delinquency Prevention, 2006).
25. Jennifer L. White, Terrie E. Moffit, Felton Earles, Lee Robins, and Phil A. Silva, "How Can We Tell?: Predictors of Childhood Conduct Disorder and Adolescent Delinquency," *Criminology* 28 (1990), pp. 507–33.
26. "A Time Line of Recent Worldwide School Shootings," www.infoplease.com/ipa/A0777958.html (2003).
27. "Oregon Students Absent after Threat," *Associated Press Online* (December 11, 1999).
28. "Columbine 7th Anniversary: 7 Foiled School Violence Plots Since March," *Yearbook of Experts* (April 20, 2006); Greg Toppo, "Columbine Remains a Disturbing Benchmark," *USA Today* (June 4, 2006).

chapter 4

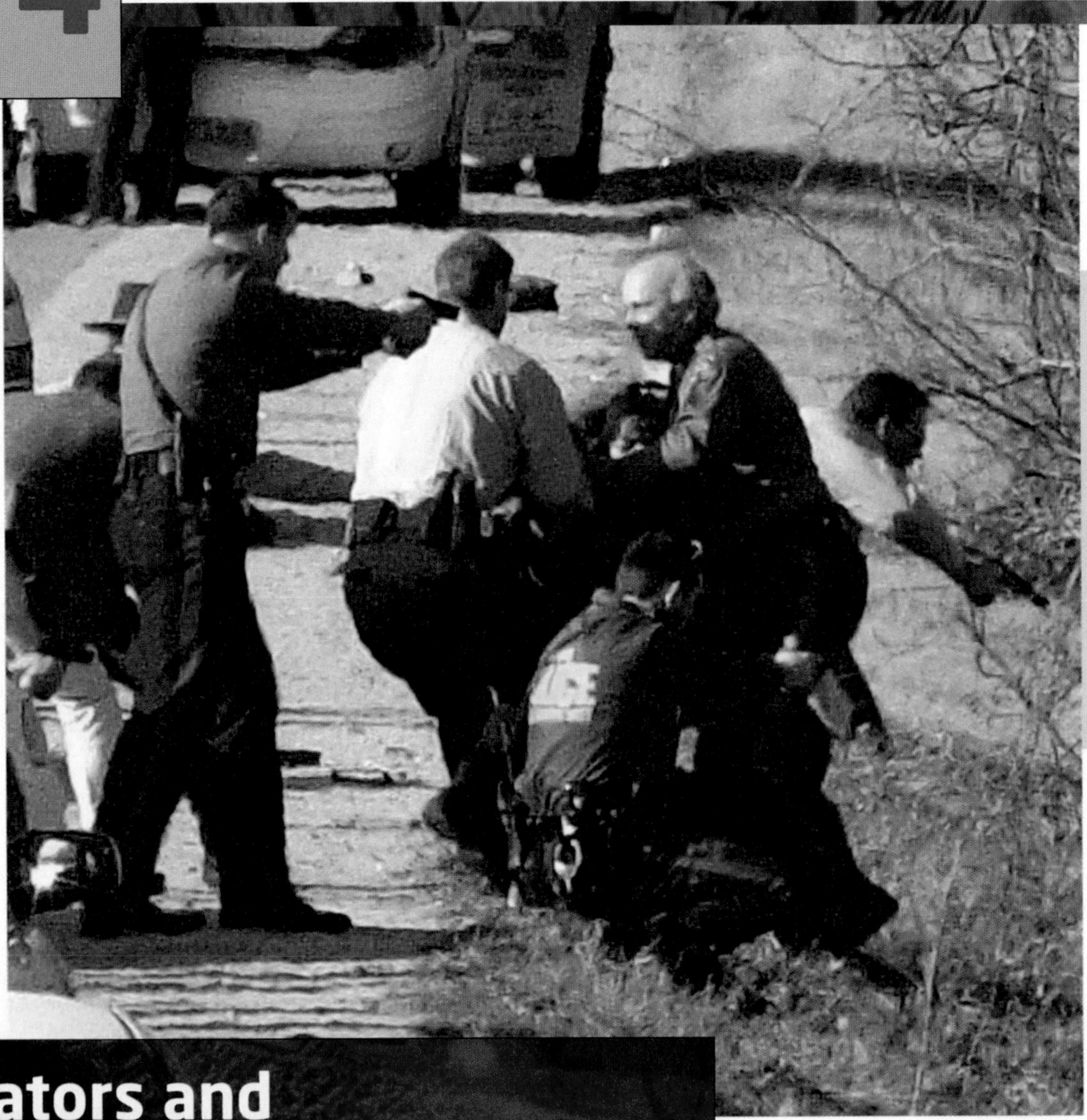

Perpetrators and Victims of Crime

Offenders and victims: understanding and classifying those involved in criminal acts and how we can develop profiles for preventing future crimes.

CHAPTER OUTLINE

LEARNING OBJECTIVES

- Explain how data on demographic factors can help prevent and solve crimes.
- Identify factors of age and gender in offenders and victims of crime.
- Analyze differences between male and female offending and victimization and the role of victim– offender relationships.
- Evaluate factors of race, ethnicity, and socioeconomic status in offending and victimization.
- Define and describe three types of crime profiling and explain their uses.
- Give a specific example of a profile for one of the Index crimes.

Michael W. Kennedy, age eighteen, was crouching between two vehicles in the parking lot of the Sully District station of the Fairfax County Police Department in Virginia when he suddenly opened fire without warning on a police officer who had just parked his car at the end of his shift. The fifty-three-year-old officer was hit five times, but was able to call for help on his police radio. At least four officers returned fire on Kennedy, in a long exchange of gunfire. When the shooting stopped, Detective Vicky Armel was dead, a third officer was wounded, and Kennedy, dressed in camouflage fatigues, lay dead in the parking lot.

"He fired at least seventy rounds," said Major Bob Callahan, commander of the police department's major crimes division. The shots came from a modified AK-47 style assault weapon and a long-barreled, high-powered rifle. Five handguns found on Kennedy's body had not been fired.

Friends who attended high school with Kennedy recalled that he would sometimes talk about attacking police, but no one ever reported those statements to school officials or the authorities. "He started making those jokes about shooting up a police station about a year ago, but we never took him seriously," said a high school classmate. A few months earlier, even close friends began noticing a change in Kennedy. His style of dress changed; he started hoarding weapons and ammunition; and his conversation focused increasingly on talk of fighting zombies and aliens. "He thought he was Jesus," said another acquaintance.

Three weeks before the shootings, Kennedy's parents drove him to the Potomac Ridge Behavioral Health Center in Maryland, where he was voluntarily admitted, apparently to treat psychological problems. Within seven hours, he walked out of an unlocked room in the ninety-seven-bed facility, broke a window, and escaped.

Claiming he had a gun, Kennedy carjacked a sport utility vehicle and drove back to Virginia where he surrendered to Fairfax County police. He was returned to Maryland and charged with armed carjacking and theft. His family posted a $30,000 bond, and he was expected to stand trial within a month. Kennedy never returned to Potomac Ridge, however, and friends said he had been calmer in recent weeks. "He told me he'd been on medication for a while," Baker said. Police were trying to determine what fueled Kennedy's contempt for police officers.[1]

Are incidents like this one common? What kinds of people typically commit serious crimes of violence and crimes against property? A better understanding of the types of persons likely to become involved in these crimes as victims or offenders helps us to evaluate the circumstances of crime and provides clues for prevention.

Who Are the Victims and Perpetrators of Crime?

Information about the nature of criminal incidents comes from the reports of citizens to the National Crime Victimization Survey (NCVS) and from the FBI Uniform Crime Reports, which gather information about persons arrested. The new NIBRS program, described in the previous chapter, will gather more information about the circumstances of crimes known to police once that program becomes nationwide in scope.

FIGURE 4.1 Age Distribution of Crime Victims for Violent Crimes (age twelve and older)

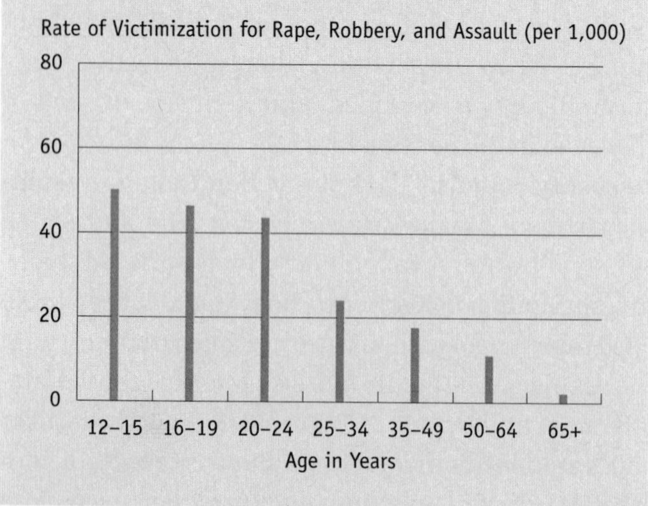

Source: Compiled from Shannan M. Catalano, *Criminal Victimization 2004* (Washington, DC: Bureau of Justice Statistics, 2005).

Age

There is often little relation between an individual's fear of crime and the actual chances that that person will be a victim of a crime. The elderly have been found to be most fearful of crime, yet they are victimized less often than any other age group. Figure 4.1 summarizes the distribution of crime victims by age. The figure indicates that in general, from age twelve onward the younger the person, the greater the likelihood of being victimized by a violent crime (rape, robbery, assault). People age sixty-five or older are victimized by rape, robbery, aggravated assault, and personal larceny at a rate of less than 3 per 1,000. This is nearly twenty-five times lower than the victimization rate for the same crimes for twelve- to nineteen-year-olds, the highest-risk group. It appears that one of the advantages of aging is a reduction in one's likelihood of being a crime victim. The risk is highest during the teenage and young adult years, but it drops dramatically after age twenty-five.

The reasons for these discrepancies by age are not difficult to understand. Young people are more active and mobile and expose themselves to risk more often. They also visit more dangerous places, at later hours, and take fewer security precautions than do older people. In fact, although they own considerably less property than older people, young people expose themselves to risk much more often and hence are victimized more often.

According to the UCR, 16 percent of all persons arrested nationally are under eighteen and 46 percent are under age twenty-five. This age pattern does not vary much by type of crime, with 44 percent of violent crime arrests (including homicide) and 55 percent of property crime arrests involving people under age twenty-five.[2] This finding suggests that the majority of crimes are committed by young people, although not necessarily juveniles. Juveniles represent less than 16 percent of all arrests, a number that has been dropping steadily.

FIGURE 4.2 Five-Year Trends in Arrests of Juveniles (number of arrests by year)

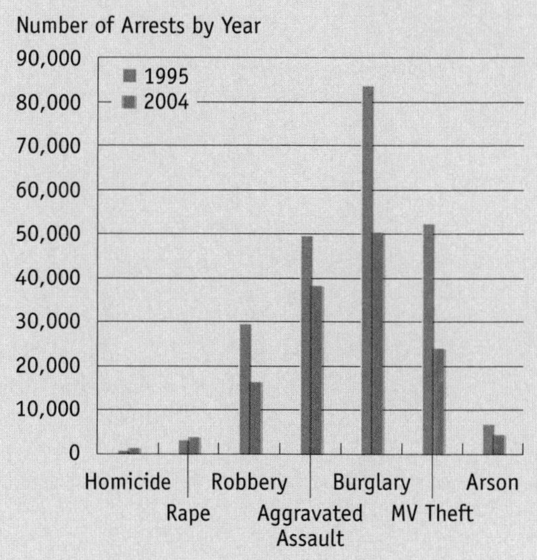

Source: Federal Bureau of Investigation, *Uniform Crime Report* (Washington, DC: U.S. Government Printing Office, published annually).

Figure 4.2 illustrates trends in arrests of those under age eighteen. The graph illustrates that juvenile arrests dropped in every major crime category over the ten years shown, for an overall decline of 27 percent. Nevertheless, those aged eighteen to twenty-four are the most likely to be arrested. Violent and property crimes require some combination of force and/or stealth and therefore are most easily carried out by younger people. Older people disposed to violence or theft are much more likely to be arrested for forgery, fraud, embezzlement, and offenses against the family, crimes in which the victims either are tricked or have little chance of escape.

JUVENILE OFFENDERS

Gender

Women make up 24 percent of all those arrested in the United States. Men make up 82 percent of individuals arrested for violent crimes and 68 percent of those arrested for property crimes. Women are most frequently arrested for larceny, although they account for only 38 percent of all larceny arrests.[3] It is clear that serious crimes are far more likely to be committed by men than by women. Nevertheless, trends in female criminal activity are increasing. For the ten-year period from 1995 to 2004, female arrests rose 9 percent (compared to a 9 percent decrease for males), as shown in Table 4.1. Likewise, female arrests for violent

Table 4.1 Arrest Trends by Sex, 1995–2004

	Males	*Females*
Total arrests	−9%	+9%
Arrests for violent crimes	−20%	+3%
Percentage of total arrests for all crimes	−3% (76% of total)	+3% (24% of total)

Compiled from Federal Bureau of Investigation, *Uniform Crime Report* (published annually).

FIGURE 4.3 Gender and Victimization

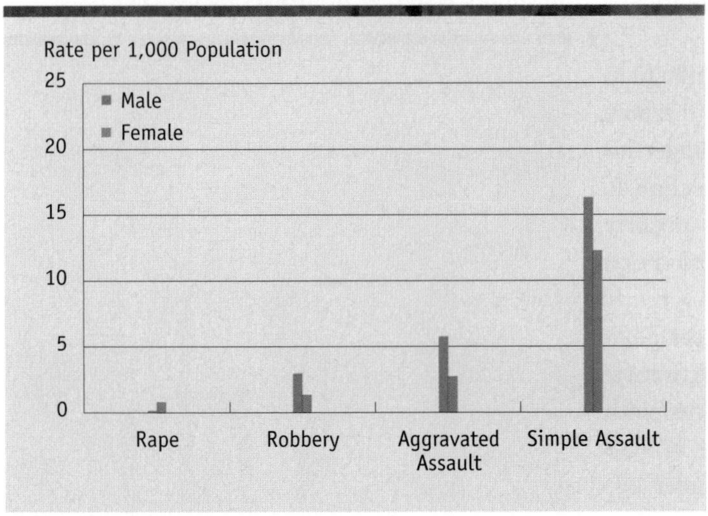

Source: Criminal Victimization 2004: Statistical Tables (Washington, DC: Bureau of Justice Statistics, 2006).

crimes rose by 3 percent during that period, while male arrests for crimes of violence decreased by 20 percent. In general, although female involvement in crime has been increasing in recent years, males still are arrested three times more often than women.

The same is not true for victims, however. Victimization rates for men and women show that property crimes affect women as often as men. The rate of personal theft against men is 0.6 per 1,000 population, virtually the same rate as for women. However, women are victimized by violent crimes at a rate of 21 per 1,000 population, whereas the rate for men is 26 per 1,000.[4] Except for the crime of rape, women are significantly less likely than men to be victims of serious crime. This is illustrated in Figure 4.3, which shows that women suffer the vast majority of sexual assaults. For other types of assaults, however, men are far more likely to be victimized. Overall, women are overrepresented among crime victims in relation to the rates of arrests of females. This suggests that for virtually all serious crimes, men victimize women in disproportionate numbers.

VICTIMIZATION RATES FOR WOMEN

VICTIM-OFFENDER RELATIONSHIPS

A significant factor in these patterns of victimization is the victim–offender relationship. More than half of violent crime victims know the offender. In cases of rape and sexual assault, 72 percent of victims knew the offender: Female victims of sexual assault are most likely to be victimized by friends/acquaintances (47 percent), intimates (22 percent), and relatives (2 percent).

STALKING

Intimate Partner Violence Violence between intimate partners (current or former spouses, boyfriends, or girlfriends) is a growing problem that disproportionately victimizes women. The NCVS estimates that approximately one million violent crimes are committed annually by current or former intimate partners, about 85 percent of which are against women. This represents 22 percent of all violent crime against women, whereas only 3 percent of all violence against men is committed by intimate partners.[5]

What are the characteristics of people who are statistically more likely to become involved in criminal events, either as victims or as perpetrators? What is your risk of criminal victimization?

A **National Violence Against Women (NVAW) Survey** was sponsored by the National Institute of Justice and the Centers for Disease Control and Prevention to obtain more information about the circumstances of offenses against women. The survey consisted of telephone interviews with 8,000 women and 8,000 men in a nationally representative sample. The survey concluded that "intimate partner violence is pervasive in U.S. society," with nearly 25 percent of surveyed women and 8 percent of men reporting they were physically assaulted or raped by a current or former spouse, cohabiting partner, or a date at some point in their lives.[6] During the preceding twelve months 1.5 percent of women and 0.9 percent of men said they had been physically assaulted or raped by a partner. The survey also found that stalking by intimate partners is more prevalent than once thought. Nearly 5 percent of women and 0.6 percent of men reported being stalked by a current or former spouse, date, or intimate partner during their lifetime. Based on these estimates, approximately 500,000 women and 185,000 men are stalked by an intimate partner annually.

National Violence Against Women (NVAW) Survey Interviews a national sample of 16,000 men and women regarding the circumstances of crimes against women.

These findings suggest that crimes by persons known to the victim are both common and serious. Violence by intimates is difficult to detect due to the low visibility of these incidents and the low likelihood of their being reported to police. Crime prevention programs historically have not strongly emphasized crimes within intimate relationships, but greater public education and awareness are needed to encourage reporting of these crimes to authorities and to enable persons in abusive relationships to recognize their situation and take steps to remove themselves from a dangerous situation. Studies have found that the causes of **intimate partner violence** are distinct from the causes of general crime, and that the effectiveness of existing partner abuse interventions have not been evaluated extensively.[7] Therefore, more needs to be learned about the dynamics of how relationships deteriorate and result in criminal violence. On the positive side, the rate of intimate partner violence has fallen from 9.8 to 7.5 per 1,000 women according to the NCVS. Thirty years ago, 3,000 murders involved intimate partners each year. Since that time, the number has been reduced by almost half. Over that thirty-year period, approximately 11 percent of murder victims were determined to have been killed by an intimate.[8] This decrease might be a reflection of the overall drop in crime rates in general in recent years.

intimate partner violence Physical assaults between current or former spouses, boyfriends, or girlfriends.

How do offenses committed by males and females differ? How can gender differences in offending be explained? How are gender, age, and race and ethnicity associated with victimization in the United States?

Characteristics of Female Offenders Female offenders have several distinct characteristics that distinguish their offending patterns from those of males. For example, female-to-female violence occurs in about 75 percent of all cases of violent female offending (rape, robbery, assault). This compares to male-to-male violence, which occurs in 70 percent of male violence. The result is that about 29 percent of violent offenders overall had a victim of a different gender, and nine in ten of these were male offenders with female victims.[9]

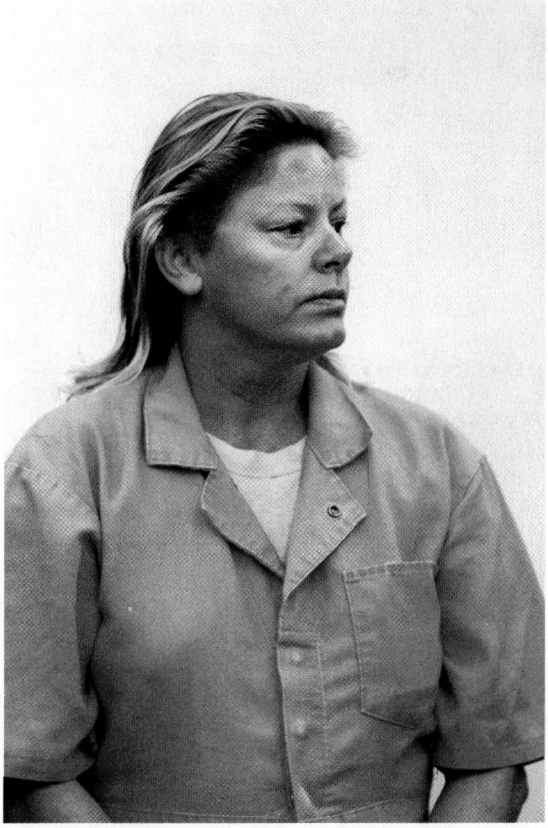

The location of violent offending by women is also different from men. Approximately half of female offenders committed their offense at or near the victim's home or at school. Less than a third of male offenders committed crimes at these locations. This difference reflects the fact that women are more likely to commit crimes against intimates, relatives, or acquaintances than are men. About 60 percent of female violent offenders had a prior relationship with the victim, whereas only 44 percent of male violent offenders knew the victim.[10] Females also use weapons in their crimes about half as often as males, which may be a reflection of the unplanned nature of many of these incidents.

Explaining the differences in female versus male offending is difficult. A research study looked at both property and violent crimes committed by males and females, examining the impact of poverty, income inequality, joblessness, and female-headed households. These factors were found to be equally important to both female and male offending, although they could not explain why males committed crimes at much higher rates than females.[11] The

That's a **FACT**

Perspectives on Partner Violence

Violence between intimate partners (current or former spouses, boyfriends, or girlfriends) constitutes 20 percent of all nonfatal violence against females over age twelve. Three percent of the nonfatal violence against females is the result of intimate partner violence. Examination of trends over time provides insight into the effectiveness of efforts in law enforcement, domestic violence prevention programs, and public awareness. New legislation increasing penalties against domestic violence, civil protection orders to protect victims from further violence, mandatory arrest policies for police departments in responding to calls for domestic violence, and prosecution practices that avoid reducing charges are examples of strategies that have been attempted with varying degrees of success.[a]

Table 4A presents trends in victimization for crimes of violence (rape, sexual assault, robbery, and nonsexual assault) by examining the relationship of the victim to the offender. What trends do you see? Can you explain the reasons behind them?

Of all the incidents of violence between intimate partners, less than 10 percent are rapes or sexual assaults. The vast majority (two-thirds) of the victimizations are simple assaults.

Why do you believe simple assault is the most common form of intimate partner violence? Can you explain why robberies can be a form of intimate partner violence?

Murder victims of an intimate partner reveal dramatic distinctions between male and female victims. One-third of all female murder victims are the result of intimate partner violence, compared to 4 percent of male murder victims. This illustrates the greater threat of this form of violence to women. Trends over time show a general drop in the level of risk. Intimates are defined to include spouses, ex-spouses, boyfriends, and girlfriends. Figure 4A shows that the number

Table 4A Trends in Crimes of Violence and Relationship with Offender

	1996	*2000*	*2004*
Total crimes of violence	9.1 million	6.2 million	5.2 million
Related to offender	9%	10%	11%
Spouse or ex-spouse	4	5	5
Well-known acquaintance	23	25	24
Casual acquaintance	16	15	16
Stranger	48	45	43

Compiled from *Criminal Victimization: Statistical Tables* (Bureau of Justice Statistics, produced annually).

DIFFERENCES IN FEMALE OFFENDING

causes and consequences of female offending are likely to be found only after examining the circumstances and context of individual incidents. Such an analysis will shed light on the relationship between crime and factors that are not easy to measure, such as stress, emotional abuse, and failure to recognize noncriminal alternatives in highly charged situations.

Race and Ethnicity

Whites account for 70 percent of all arrests, while blacks are arrested for 27 percent of all crimes. Whites comprise 60 percent of arrests for violent crimes and 69 percent of arrests for property crimes.[12] These police statistics count only those offenders who are caught, however. The NCVS, on the other hand, asks respondents who see their attacker in cases of rape, robbery, and assault to identify the

FIGURE 4A Homicides of Intimates by Gender of Victim, 1976–2004

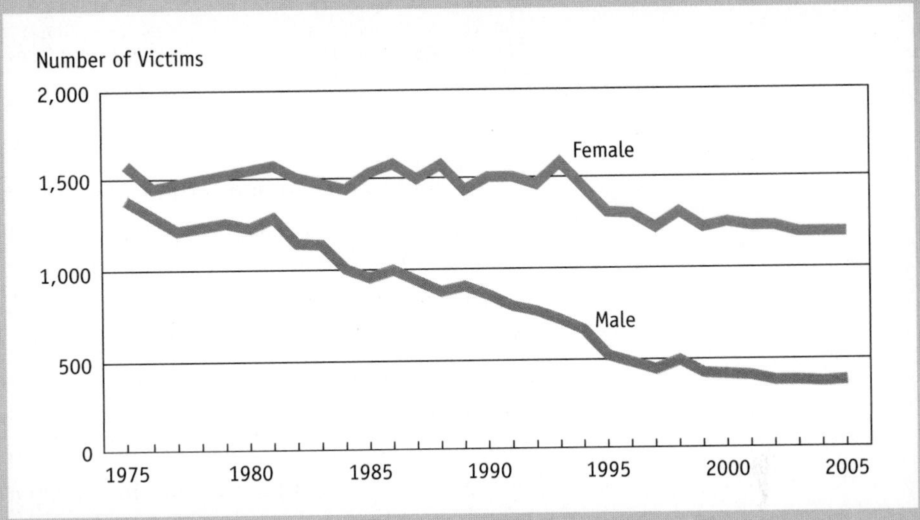

of men murdered by intimates dropped by 71 percent since 1976. The number of women killed by intimates was stable for two decades. After 1993, the number declined and now appears to be leveling off.

How would you explain the wide difference in the risk of men versus women?

NOTES

a. Robert C. Davis, Barbara E. Smith, and Bruce Taylor, "Increasing the Proportion of Domestic Violence Arrests That Are Prosecuted: A Natural Experiment in Milwaukee," *Criminology & Public Policy*, vol. 2 (March 2003); Laura Dugan, "Domestic Violence Legislation: Exploring Its Impact on the Likelihood of Domestic Violence, Police Involvement, and Arrest," *Criminology & Public Policy*, vol. 2 (March 2003); Rebecca E. Dobash, "Domestic Violence: Arrest, Prosecution, and Reducing Violence," *Criminology & Public Policy*, vol. 2 (March 2003); Faith E. Lutze and Megan L. Symons, "The Evolution of Domestic Violence Policy through Masculine Institutions: From Discipline to Protection to Collaborative Empowerment," *Criminology & Public Policy*, vol. 2 (March 2003); Elizabeth Richardson Vigdor and James A. Mercy, "Do Laws Restricting Access to Firearms by Domestic Violence Offenders Prevent Intimate Partner Homicide," *Evaluation Review*, vol. 30 (June 2006), pp. 313–34.

Source: Callie Marie Rennison, *Intimate Partner Violence, 1993–2001* (Washington, DC: Bureau of Justice Statistics, 2003); FBI Supplementary Homicide Reports; *Criminal Victimization in the United States, 2004: Statistical Tables* (U.S. Bureau of Justice Statistics, 2006).

perceived race of the offender. Table 4.2 shows the significant discrepancy in the racial composition of offenders from these two data sources. These differences, which are striking, can be accounted for by the fact that most offenders are not caught, so those arrested may not represent offenders in general. It also is true that victims are sometimes mistaken about the race of the offender, given the circumstances of the crime (e.g., darkness, a very brief look at the offender, or a masked offender), and that there are a significant number of cases where the victim is unsure about the race of the offender.

African Americans Blacks are victims of violent crime at higher rates than any other race. Their victimization rate for rape, robbery, and assault is 26 per 1,000, compared to a victimization rate of 21 per 1,000 for whites. In a similar way, black households are victimized by property crimes (burglary, larceny, and motor

Table 4.2 Race of Offenders in Violent Crimes (rape, robbery, assault)

Race	*Arrested By Police*	*Identified By Victim*
White	60%	46%
Black	37	18
Other or Unknown	3	36

Source: FBI Uniform Crime Report, *Crime in the United States* (Washington, DC: U.S. Government Printing Office, 2006); *Criminal Victimization in the United States, 2004: Statistical Tables* (Washington, DC: Bureau of Justice Statistics, 2006).

vehicle theft) at a rate more than 30 percent higher than that of whites (191 property crimes per 1,000 households versus 157 per 1,000 households for whites).[13] As noted in the previous section, victimization is related to age. The median age for blacks in the United States is 30 years of age, whereas the average age for whites is 37 years. This age difference would be expected to increase the involvement of blacks in crimes. Victimization also is strongly influenced by the opportunity for crime, however. In the case of motor vehicle theft, for example, whites own 189 million vehicles in the United States, whereas blacks own 20 million vehicles. Accounting for this huge difference in the opportunity for theft (i.e., tenfold greater availability of stealing a car owned by a white), the victimization rate for blacks is still twice as high as it is for whites (16 thefts per 1,000 motor vehicles owned for blacks versus 8 thefts per 1,000 for whites).[14] This suggests that opportunity impacts victimization rates for African Americans.

RACE AND OPPORTUNITY

Hispanics Hispanics constitute a small but growing segment of victims of serious crimes. People of Hispanic origin constitute about 12 percent of the U.S. population, and may be of any race. They are immigrants from Spanish-speaking countries such as Mexico (62 percent), Puerto Rico (13 percent), and Central and South America (12 percent). Their rate of victimization by violent crimes is 18 per 1,000 population, 17 percent lower than the rate for other whites and 44 percent lower than that for blacks.

In the case of the property crimes of burglary, larceny, and motor vehicle theft, Hispanic households are victimized at a rate of 204 per 1,000 households, a rate that is 30 percent higher than that of whites, and 7 percent higher than that of blacks.[15]

The good news is that the overall rate of victimizations has been declining for all races and ethnicities. From 1973 to 2004 both property crime and violent crime rates have dropped significantly for all races. The drop in violent crime victimization is illustrated in Figure 4.4. Black, white, and other races experienced about the same rates of rape/sexual assault in 2004, and over the last ten years, the rate of victimization against Hispanics fell 67 percent from 55 to 18 victimizations per 1,000 population.

Native Americans Native Americans constitute about 1.5 percent of the total U.S. population or 4.1 million people. This group consists of Alaska Natives, Aleuts, American Indians, and those combined with one or more other races.

FIGURE 4.4 Violent Crime Rates by Race of Victim Adjusted victimization rate per 1,000 persons age twelve and over

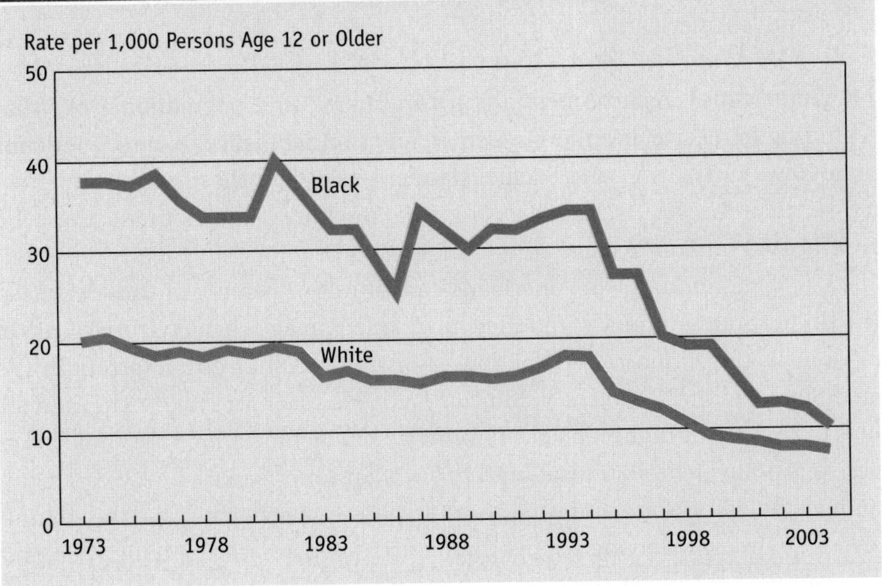

Source: Bureau of Justice Statistics (2006) http://www.ojp.usdoj.gov/bjs/glance/race.htm.

Historically, this group has not received systematic attention from the American criminal justice system. Native Americans comprise one percent of arrests for violent crimes in the United States, and their low median age, twenty-eight years, is the youngest of any population group in the United States. As noted earlier, young adults are much more likely to be involved in Index crimes than are those past age thirty. This is reflected in NCVS data shown in Figure 4.5 that Native Americans experience the highest per capita rate of violence of any group (about 1 violent crime for every 10 persons aged twelve or older). Overall, victimization rates for Native Americans are about twice that of the rest of the U.S. population.[16]

ALCOHOL-RELATED OFFENSES

Issues of particular concern for Native Americans are interracial violence and arrests for alcohol-related offenses. More than 66 percent of violent crime victimizations of Native Americans are committed by persons of other races. This is markedly different from whites, for whom 70 percent of victimizations are white-on-white crimes, and for blacks, from whom 80 percent of victimizations are black-on-black crimes. The high proportion of victimizations of Native Americans by persons of other races suggests that underlying social and racial problems may be at the root of some of this violence. Second, alcohol use was a factor in 48 percent of violent crime victimizations of Native Americans, compared to 34 percent for whites and 26 percent for blacks.[17] Disproportionate levels of alcohol abuse also is suggested by the fact that arrest

FIGURE 4.5 Violent Victimizations by Race

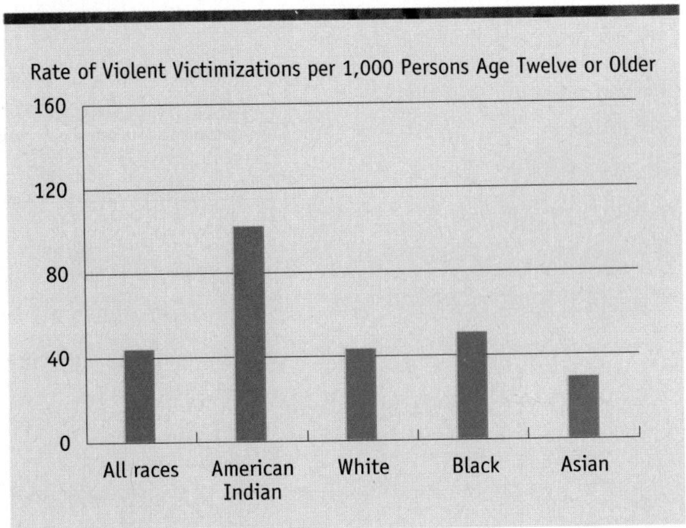

Source: Steven W. Perry, *American Indians and Crime* (Washington, DC: Bureau of Justice Statistics, 2004).

rates of Native Americans for alcohol-related offenses (i.e., driving under the influence, liquor law violations, and public drunkenness) are more than double that for all races. These factors help to explain the high crime and victimization rate for Native Americans.

Asian Americans Asian Americans are another diverse population group that is beginning to receive attention in American criminal justice. Asian Americans include Hawaiian Natives and Pacific Islanders, as well as those whose ancestors came from countries in Asia, such as China, Japan, Korea, and Vietnam. There are currently 10.4 million "Asians" in the United States, comprising nearly 4 percent of the U.S. population. Asian Americans constitute 1.2 percent of those arrested in the United States annually, and they have a median age of thirty-three years of age. Their victimization rate is the lowest of any racial or ethnic group in the United States, with 22 violent victimizations per 1,000 persons.[18] The rate for whites is 70 percent higher; blacks have twice the victimization rate, and Native Americans 4 times the victimization rate of Asian Americans.

RACIAL TENSION AND VICTIMIZATION

Important issues for Asian Americans are interracial violence and the circumstances of murders involving Asians. Similar to Native Americans, a high percentage (about 68 percent) of their violent victimizations involve offenders of other races. This suggests underlying racial tension that may affect victimization rates. Second, Table 4.3 illustrates that although murders involving Asians are far fewer than for most groups, homicide victimizations involving Asians are much less likely to result from violent felonies than is found for any other race. On the other hand, Asian Americans are significantly less likely than any other race to be involved in murders that involve fights under the influence of alcohol or drugs. Clearly, Asian Americans use alcohol and drugs at very low levels, but the incidence of homicides resulting from violent felonies suggests possible problems with gangs, extortion, and other serious social problems.

It should be kept in mind, of course, that race itself does not predispose a person to crime. In the United States, race and ethnicity are closely tied to age, income, and residence in cities (where crime rates are higher). Whites tend to be older and have higher incomes than blacks and Hispanics. Whites are also more likely to live

Table 4.3 Circumstances of Murder by Race

Murders with Known Circumstances	*White*	*Black*	*Native American*	*Asian American*
Violent felony	16%	11%	11%	27%
Other felony	10	11	5	8
Suspected felony	4	3	4	3
Brawl under the influence of alcohol or drugs	6	4	13	2
Arguments	38	50	45	35
Other circumstances	27	21	22	25
Total number	181,043	156,203	2,515	4,545

Source: FBI Supplemental Homicide Reports, 1976–2001.

outside cities. These factors contribute greatly to the differences in rates of victimization by race.

Socioeconomic Status

VICTIMIZATION RATES FOR LOW-INCOME HOUSEHOLDS

The influence of income on the risk of victimization is illustrated by the fact that the risk of household burglary declines as income rises. Households with incomes below $15,000 per year are more likely to be burglarized than those with incomes above $15,000. Middle-income households ($25,000 to $75,000) have the lowest property crime victimization rates, but the rate increases for those households with incomes more than $75,000 per year.[19] Higher property crime rates at the high and low ends of income levels can be explained by several factors. First, victimization rates are significantly higher in cities where most low-income households are located. Second, those with higher incomes own more property, thereby increasing the opportunities for victimization.

For violent crimes, persons with higher incomes have the lowest rate of victimization, and those with the lowest incomes (less than $7,500 annually) experience the highest rate of violence (58 per 1,000 persons). This is accounted for primarily by location of residence (higher income allows for housing in lower crime areas). Also, the fact that those with higher incomes are able to move about in safer (low crime) areas reduces their exposure to victimization risk.

What Is Crime Profiling?

Crime profiling involves analysis of criminal incidents to isolate the precise characteristics of offenders, victims, and situations in order to better understand and prevent crime. Behavioral profiling focuses on the characteristics and conduct of offenders and victims (e.g., demographic characteristics, prior history, and current conduct), while crime scene profiling involves examination of the physical and situational characteristics of criminal incidents (e.g., place, time, and physical evidence). In both cases the objective is to assess numerous incidents of similar kinds in order to develop typologies, or models, to explain and predict how crimes occur. This information is used to help police in surveillance and crime prevention activities and also helps educate the public and policymakers about individuals and situations at high risk for crime.

crime profiling
Analysis of criminal incidents to isolate the precise characteristics of offenders, victims, and situations in order to better understand and prevent crime.

Offender Profiles

Offender profiles are developed by examining a large number of similar crimes to look for common patterns. The offender's physical characteristics, prior history, and method of conduct are all relevant in creating the profile.[20] Information that is commonly used is from the NCVS and UCR, which provide national data on known incidents. More detailed data about offender motivations and specialization is taken from studies conducted by researchers on smaller groups of known offenders.

offender profiles
Examination of offender backgrounds (e.g., physical and social characteristics, prior history, and method of conduct) to look for common patterns.

Media & Criminal Justice

Superheroes and Crime Prevention

It is amazing that comic books have spawned several of the most well-known fictional characters ever developed. Superman, Batman, and Spiderman are perhaps the strongest characters of this genre. They have been developed into television shows, movies, books, video games, and other forms that survive each generation. Why do they last? Are there messages they provide that we want to hear?

The profile of each of these characters is similar: humble backgrounds, family tragedies in early life, and being thrust into their crime-fighting roles by circumstances almost beyond their control. Superman usually works within the boundaries of the law to catch lawbreakers, while Batman and Spiderman sometimes bend or break the rules, but the superhero crime-fighting format is the same: They work to help the oppressed, and their quest for justice is often made difficult because the police or the courts are sometimes corrupt or incompetent. Superman, Batman, and Spiderman are viewed by the criminal justice system, and the public, alternately as dangerous freaks or crime-fighting superheroes. They are not universally loved—although their actions should merit that—leading to their tortured personal lives. In analogous fashion, the criminals they fight are portrayed similarly, as genetically mutant, freakish, insane, or otherwise bad for reasons beyond their control.

Superman first appeared in 1938, Batman in 1939, and Spiderman in 1968. The longevity of these characters in comics that continue to be published today is remarkable, considering the short life of most characters in popular culture. There may be several reasons for their continuing popularity: First, they always encounter obstacles, yet *always* catch the bad guy or right the wrong, reinforcing to us that success is possible although never easy (even with super powers or gadgets). Second, they are all incorruptible, never yielding to temptations for money or power—helping us see an ideal often lost in daily news stories of human greed and corruption. Third, they give us hope that crime can be stopped if everyone had the vigilance and perseverance of these superheroes. Fourth, the line between good and bad is sharply drawn in fiction, while in the real world the lines are often fuzzy at best, making comic book heroes a way to help clearly distinguish between good and evil. Fifth, they succeed despite the odds being stacked against them in the crime-ridden Metropolis, Gotham, and New York depicted in the comics, movies, and games.

Can you think of other reasons why superheroes seem to maintain their popularity through the generations? The idea of an idealistic crime fighter working against the odds of a corrupt environment is appealing. Of these superheroes, only Batman lacks special powers. Are there analogies to him in real life of people who work to prevent crime outside the criminal justice system?

Source: Scott Vollum and Cary D. Adkinson, "The Portrayal of Crime and Justice in the Comic Superhero Mythos," *Journal of Criminal Justice and Popular Culture,* vol. 10 (2003), pp. 96–108; B. W. Wright, *Comic Book Nation: The Transformation of Youth Culture in America* (Baltimore: The Johns Hopkins University Press, 2001). Danny Fingeroth, *Superman on the Couch: What Superheroes Tell Us about Ourselves and Our Society* (New York: Continuum International Publishing, 2004).

STUDY OF BURGLARS

In the case of burglary, for example, UCR arrest statistics reveal that 71 percent of those arrested are white and 27 percent are black, and two-thirds are committed by offenders over eighteen years of age. Nearly 86 percent of burglary arrestees are males. The U.S. Bureau of Justice Statistics tracks felony defendants in large counties, which provides additional detailed information about those formally charged with burglary. Sixty-eight percent have a prior felony arrest, and 64 percent had prior convictions. A total of 40 percent were on probation, parole, or on pretrial release at the time of their arrest.[21] Studies of burglars, based on interviews with known offenders and police, have found that most burglars do not specialize in burglary as a crime. They tend to commit a variety of offenses, but only rarely commit violent crimes. Burglars do not appear to escalate into more serious crimes, although they may specialize in certain types of burglary (e.g., jewelry stores or vacation houses) for short periods.[22] Combining different sources of information like these enables the investigator to develop leads in cases where the suspect is unknown, and to form offender profiles for use in detection and prevention efforts.

Crime mapping has been a new addition to profiling efforts. Geographical areas of concentrated criminal activity (called "hot spots") are analyzed to determine patterns and underlying issues based on specific location (why are certain addresses prone to problems at certain times?), based on repeat victimization (what are the reasons for multiple attacks on the same individuals?), and based on general streets or neighborhoods (why are certain local areas targeted?). Visual displays of mapped crime patterns offer another tool to use in establishing a profile of criminal incidents in space and in time.[23]

Victim Profiles

victim profiles
Examination of a large number of similar criminal incidents to find patterns in the types of persons who are victimized under certain circumstances.

Victim profiles are analogous to offender profiles in looking at a large number of criminal incidents to find patterns of the types of persons who are victimized under certain circumstances. The primary source of data for victim profiles is the NCVS, because it encompasses a large national sample of citizens who are interviewed about their victimization experiences. Continuing with our burglary profile, the NCVS counts only household burglaries, but these are much more common than commercial burglaries. Despite the fact that there are approximately 14.4 million black households in the United States versus 96 million white households, blacks are victimized at a rate of 44 per 1,000 households. The rate for whites is 28 per 1,000 and 23 per 1,000 for households of other races. In cases where the head of the household in 20 to 49 years of age, burglaries occur 20 percent more often than if the head of the household is 50 or older. Households headed by teenagers are burglarized at an even higher rate—more than three times the rate of those 50 and over. Poor households are at the highest risk (a victimization rate ranging between 39 and 59 per 1,000 for incomes under $15,000) versus wealthier households where the victimization rate is 22 per 1,000 (for incomes $50,000 and up). The Northeast has a significantly lower per-capita burglary rate than do other regions of the country, and urban households are significantly more likely than rural or suburban households to be victimized. Likewise, rented dwellings are almost twice as likely to be burglarized as owned homes.[24] Interviews with burglars have found that the extent to which the household can be seen by passersby or neighbors, has good area lighting, shows no obvious displays of wealth, and displays signs of occupancy all lower the risk of victimization.[25] Organizing these common elements, a profile of a typical burglary victim can be constructed to form the basis for crime prevention programs.

HOUSEHOLD VICTIMIZATION

Crime Scene Profiles

crime scene profiles
Examination of the circumstances surrounding criminal incidents in a search for patterns associated with criminal offending.

Crime scene profiles examine the circumstances that surround criminal incidents in a search for patterns associated with criminal offending. One important source of this information is the NCVS, because that survey asks victims about the situation in which they were victimized. A crime scene profile for burglary would include the fact that household burglaries involving unlawful entry without the use of force are by far the most common. Forcible entries and attempted forcible entries occur about half as often. This suggests that unlocked and open doors and windows are a primary entry point for burglars. The NCVS also reveals that the risk of victimization for burglary increases as the number of people living in the household increases. Households with six or more members have a burglary victimization rate twice that of households with only two or three members. In an analogous way, the number of housing units or apartments in the building is related to the risk of victimization. Buildings with between five and nine units have the highest rate of victimization, compared to those with fewer units, or those with ten or more units. The lowest risk of burglary is in single-family homes. The longer a person lives in the same dwelling also lowers the likelihood of burglary.

BURGLARY PROFILE

In 90 percent of burglaries the losses are not recovered, although the typical loss is valued at less than $250. The most common items stolen are personal effects, such as jewelry, clothing, portable electronic gear and cameras, household furnishings, and wallets. Most burglaries occur during the day between 6:00 A.M. and 6:00 P.M.[26] Research studies help to put this data in context. Interviews with burglars show that most engage in the crime due to a need for money. They look for attractive targets (dwellings likely to have money or property that can be sold), no sign of occupants or other guardians present (e.g., dogs, neighbors), and convenience (ease of entry and exit).[27] Therefore, the circumstances around which offenders decide to act can be determined from close scrutiny of past incidents. A

Which of these homes do you think is most likely to be burglarized. Why? According to your text, what is the profile for a burglar? What are some benefits and drawbacks of crime scene profiling? How might you profile the crime or the offender that begins and ends this chapter?

Table 4.4 **Crime Profile for Burglary (high risk factors associated with past incidents)**

Offender	*Victim*	*Crime Scene*
Male	Black household	Unforced entry
White	Headed by teenager or young person (under fifty)	Five to nine units in building
Prior felony arrest(s)	Rented dwelling	Loss under $250
Prior convictions	Household income under $15,000	Occurred during the day
Little crime specialization	Urban location	Attractive target
Violence rare		No occupants or guardians

burglary profile based on the information presented here is summarized in Table 4.4.

The case of the shootings of Fairfax County police officers by Michael Kennedy described at the beginning of this chapter continues. A subsequent police search of his home found additional weapons and writings, and police were seeking a warrant to search Kennedy's cell-phone messages to look for further evidence regarding his background and motives.[28] The Critical Thinking Exercise on homicide illustrates how better knowledge of the circumstances of homicide, combined with profiling techniques, could be used to predict and prevent such tragedies in the future by providing more accurate understanding of the perpetrators and victims of crime.

CRITICAL THINKING EXERCISES

The Characteristics of Homicide

Although the homicide rate appears to be starting to increase again, overall the rate has fallen in recent years to its lowest level in three decades.[a] This good news of low homicide rates, however, is mitigated by the apparent randomness of homicide and our inability to predict and prevent its occurrence. An analysis by the *New York Times* closely examined the circumstances of one hundred rampage murders (sudden killings without apparent motive). It found that "most of the killers spiraled down a long slow slide, mentally and emotionally."[b] This kind of homicide is quite rare, but careful review of these cases shows that red flags existed in most cases, such as the accumulation of weapons, talking openly of committing violence, and sudden dramatic changes in behavior. This suggests that even homicides that appear random and without motive might be preventable if closer attention is paid to the circumstances surrounding criminal incidents.

Consider five important facts about more typical homicides in the United States:

- More the half of all homicides occur in cities with populations over 100,000.
- Blacks are disproportionately involved as both homicide victims and offenders, and 94 percent of black homicide victims are killed by blacks.
- Males are nine times more likely than females to commit homicide, although most homicides by females involve male victims.
- Only 4 percent of homicides involve multiple victims, while 19 percent involve multiple offenders.
- The circumstances of many homicides are unknown, although arguments are still the leading known cause,

followed by deaths caused during the commission of a felony.[c]

CRITICAL THINKING QUESTIONS

1. Given what you've learned in this chapter about the factors associated with crime, offenders, and victims, explain why you believe each of the five facts about homicide listed above is true.
2. How would you attempt to change the disproportionate involvement of blacks in homicides as victims and offenders, given what you know about the factors associated with crime?

NOTES

a. Federal Bureau of Investigation, *Preliminary Annual Uniform Crime Report, 2005* (Washington, DC: U.S. Government Printing Office, 2006).
b. Laurie Goodstein and William Glaberson, "The Well-Marked Roads to Homicidal Rage," *New York Times* (April 9, 2000), p. 1.
c. *Homicide Trends in the U.S.* (Washington, DC: Bureau of Justice Statistics, 2006) www.ojp.usdoj.gov/bjs/homicide.

Preventing School Shootings

The Federal Bureau of Investigation's National Center for the Analysis of Violent Crime invited 160 educators, mental health professionals, and members of the law enforcement community to a symposium on school shootings and threat assessment. Among the attendees was someone who knew the shooter at each of eighteen separate incidents of school shootings in the United States and the investigators who worked on each case.

A report was published based on this symposium that identified a series of "warning signs" involving the student's personality, family dynamics, school dynamics, and social dynamics. The report cautioned that these warning signs should not be considered in isolation from one another, but "if all or most of them" occur together with a threat made by a student, the threat must be taken seriously and acted upon.

1. **Personality**—leakage of violent thoughts or feelings in words or pictures; low tolerance for frustration, poor coping skills; lack of resiliency; failed love relationship; resentment over perceived injustices; signs of depression, narcissism, or alienation; dehumanizings attitudes; lack of empathy, exaggerated sense of entitlement, attitude of superiority, exaggerated or pathological need for attention; externalized blame; masked low self-esteem; anger management problems; intolerance; inappropriate humor; manipulative; lack of trust; closed social group; change of behavior; rigid and opinionated; unusual interest in sensational violence; fascination with violence-filled entertainment; negative role models; behavior relevant to carrying out a threat.
2. **Family dynamics**—turbulent parent-child relationship; acceptance of pathological behavior; access to weapons; lack of intimacy; few limits on the child's conduct; no limits or monitoring of television and Internet.
3. **School dynamics**—student is "detached" from school; school tolerates disrespectful behavior; student perceives inequitable discipline; school culture is inflexible; students have a pecking order; a code of silence; and unsupervised computer access.
4. **Social dynamics**—easy access to media–entertainment–technology with themes of extreme violence; extremist peer group or peers fascinated with violence; use of drugs and alcohol; unusual nature of students' interests outside school; copycat behavior.[a]

CRITICAL THINKING QUESTIONS

1. As a former high school student, what do you see as the pros and cons in applying these criteria to assess threats made in school settings?
2. School shootings occur infrequently despite their dreadfulness, and the more infrequent an event, the more difficult it is to predict. Would it be possible to predict which students are at high risk of such conduct based on these, or other, factors?

NOTE

a. Mary Ellen O'Toole, *The School Shooter: A Threat Assessment Perspective* (Quantico, VA: FBI Academy, 2000).

SUMMARY

WHO ARE THE VICTIMS AND PERPETRATORS OF CRIME?

- Information about the nature of criminal incidents and crime victims comes from the reports of citizens to the National Crime Victimization Survey (NCVS).
- The FBI Uniform Crime Reports gathers information about the characteristics of persons arrested.
- Most property and violent crime offenders are young—between the ages of eighteen and twenty-five.

- Males comprise 82 percent of arrests for violent crime, although the rate of female arrests is rising slowly.
- Women are more likely to commit crimes against intimates, relatives, or acquaintances than are men.
- Whites account for 68 percent of all arrests, while blacks are arrested for 30 percent of all crimes.
- Except for the crime of rape, males are victimized by violent crimes at a rate almost twice that for women.
- Women are the victims of property crimes at a rate similar to that for men.
- Approximately 1 million violent crimes are committed annually by current or former intimate partners, about 85 percent of which are against women.
- Blacks are victims of violent crime at higher rates than any other race.
- Hispanics have crime victimization rates lower than that of whites and blacks.
- Victimization rates for Native Americans are about twice that of the rest of the U.S. population.
- The victimization rate for Asians is the lowest of any racial or ethnic group in the United States.
- For violent crimes, persons with higher incomes have the lowest rate of victimization, and those with the lowest incomes (less than $7,500 annually) experience the highest rate of violence.
- Crime profiling involves analysis of criminal incidents to isolate the precise characteristics of offenders, victims, and situations in order to better understand and prevent crime.
- Behavioral profiling focuses on the characteristics and conduct of offenders and victims (e.g., demographic characteristics, prior history, and current conduct).
- Crime scene profiling involves examination of the physical and situational characteristics of criminal incidents (e.g., place, time, and physical evidence).

KEY TERMS

National Violence Against Women (NVAW) Survey *82*
intimate partner violence *83*
crime profiling *89*
offender profiles *89*
victim profiles *91*
crime scene profiles *92*

QUESTIONS FOR REVIEW AND DISCUSSION

1. Where does information about the nature of criminal incidents come from?
2. How does age affect rates of offending and victimization in the United States?
3. How does gender affect rates of offending and victimization?
4. What does research show about offenders and their victims in instances of violent crime?
5. How common or rare is intimate partner violence in the United States, and who are the victims?
6. How do male and female offenders differ in their crimes?
7. How do rates of offending and victimization vary by race and ethnicity?
8. How common or rare is race-based crime in the United States, and who are the victims?
9. What is the influence of income on the risk of victimization?
10. What kinds of profiling can help in the prevention of crime?

NOTES

1. Derrill Holly, "Teen Who Killed Detective Slain in Exchange of Gunfire," *Associated Press State & Local Wire* (May 9, 2006); Kiran Krishnamurthy, "Guns and Writings Seized from Teen's Home," *Richmond Times Dispatch* (May 11, 2006).
2. Compiled from Federal Bureau of Investigation, *Crime in the United States* (Washington, DC: U.S. Government Printing Office, 2006), p. 296.
3. Ibid.
4. Shannan M. Catalano, *Criminal Victimization, 2004* (Washington, DC: Bureau of Justice Statistics, 2005).
5. Callie Marie Rennison, *Intimate Partner Violence* (Washington, DC: Bureau of Justice Statistics, 2003).
6. Patricia Tjaden and Nancy Thoemnes, *Extent, Nature, and Consequences of Intimate Partner Violence: Findings from the National Violence Against Women Survey* (Washington, DC: National Institute of Justice, 2000).
7. Terrie E. Moffitt, Robert F. Krueger, Avshalom Caspi, and Jeff Fagan, "Partner Abuse and General Crime: How Are They the Same? How Are They Different?," *Criminology*, vol. 38 (February, 2000), pp. 199–232; Rosemary Chalk and

Patricia A. King, *Violence in Families: Assessing Prevention and Treatment Programs* (Washington, DC: National Academy Press, 1998); Douglas L. Yearwood, "Judicial Dispositions of Ex-Parte and Domestic Violence Protection Order Hearings: A Comparative Analysis of Victim Requests and Court Authorized Relief," *Journal of Family Violence*, vol. 20 (June 2005), pp. 161–71.

8. Rennison, p. 2.
9. Lawrence A. Greenfeld and Tracy L. Snell, Women Offenders (Washington, DC: Bureau of Justice Statistics, 1999); *Criminal Victimization in the United States, 2004: Statistical Tables* (U.S. Bureau of Justice Statistics, 2006) http://www.ojp.usdoj.gov/bjs/pub/pdf/cvus04.pdf.
10. Greenfeld and Snell, p. 3.
11. Darrell Steffenmeier and Dana Haynie, "Gender, Structural Disadvantage, and Urban Crime: Do Macrosocial Variables Also Explain Female Offending Rates?," *Criminology*, vol. 38 (May 2000), pp. 403–38; S. C. Moore, R. Harris, C. McDougall, and J. Clarbour, "Male and Female Reasoning Biases and Offending Behavior," *Journal of Criminal Justice*, vol. 31 (November 2003), pp. 497–510.
12. Federal Bureau of Investigation, *Crime in the United States* (Washington, DC: U.S. Government Printing Office, 2006).
13. *Criminal Victimization in the United States, 2004: Statistical Tables* (U.S. Bureau of Justice Statistics, 2006).
14. Ibid.
15. Ibid.
16. Steven W. Perry, *American Indians and Crime* (Washington, DC: Bureau of Justice Statistics, 2004).
17. Perry, p. 10.
18. Ibid, p 12
19. *Criminal Victimization in the United States, 2004: Statistical Tables* (U.S. Bureau of Justice Statistics, 2006).
20. Terance D. Miethe, Richard McCorkle, and Shelley Listwan, *Crime Profiles: The Anatomy of Dangerous Persons, Places, and Situations* 3rd ed. (Los Angeles: Roxbury, 2006).
21. Timothy H. Cohen and Brian A. Reaves, *Felony Defendants in Large Urban Counties, 2002* (Washington, DC: Bureau of Justice Statistics, 2006).
22. Wim Bernasco and Paul Nieuwbeerta, "How do Residential Burglars Select Target Areas?: A New Approach to the Analysis of Criminal Location Choice," *British Journal of Criminology*, vol. 45 (May 2005), pp. 296–316; Melanie Wellsmith and Amy Burrell, "The Influence of Purchase Price and Ownership Levels on Theft Targets: The Example of Domestic Burglary," *British Journal of Criminology*, vol. 45 (Sept 2005), pp. 741–65; Richard Wright and Scott Decker, *Burglars on the Job: Streetlife and Residential Break-ins* (Boston: Northeastern University Press, 1994); R. I. Mawby and Hazell Croall, eds. *Burglary* (Willan Publishing, 2002); Jan M. Chaiken and Marcia R. Chaiken, *Varieties of Criminal Behavior* (Santa Monica, CA: Rand Corporation, 1982).
23. John E. Eck, Spencer Chainey, James G. Cameron, Michael Leitner, and Ronald E. Wilson, *Mapping Crime: Understanding Hot Spots* (Washington, DC: National Institute of Justice, 2005).
24. *Criminal Victimization in the United States, 2004: Statistical Tables* (U.S. Bureau of Justice Statistics, 2006).
25. Paul M. Cromwell and James N. Olson, *Breaking and Entering: Burglars and Burglary* (Wadsworth Publishing, 2004); Darrell J. Steffensmeier and Jeffery T. Ulmer, *Confessions of a Dying Thief: Understanding Criminal Careers and Illegal Enterprise* (New Brunswick, NJ: Transaction Publishing, 2005); Bill Mason and Lee Gruenfeld, *Confessions of a Master Jewel Thief* (New York: Villard Books, 2005); George Rengert and John Wasilchick, *Suburban Burglary: A Time and Place for Everything* (Springfield, IL: Charles C. Thomas, 1985); Neal Shover, *Great Pretenders: Pursuits and Careers of Persistent Thieves* (Westview Press, 1996).
26. *Criminal Victimization in the United States, 2004: Statistical Tables* (Washington, DC: Bureau of Justice Statistics, 2006).
27. Cromwell and Olson, 2004; Mason and Gruenfeld, 2005.
28. "Police Find Guns, Knives Inside Teen Shooter's Home," *Associated Press State & Local Wire* (May 11, 2006); Tom Jackman, "Gunman Made Threats On Police, Warrant Says; Fairfax Teen's Phone Messages Sought," *Washington Post* (May 31, 2006); "Another Needless Death," *Washington Post* (May 18, 2006).

chapter 5

Criminal Law

The limits of law: determining the sources and types of law and how we decide to create new laws; offering insights into the limits of mental illness, the use of force, and borderline behaviors.

CHAPTER OUTLINE

LEARNING OBJECTIVES

- Distinguish between criminal law and civil law and between substantive and procedural law.
- Identify and characterize the four principal sources of criminal law.
- Trace the origins and development of criminal law in the United States.
- Describe the evolution of the concept and practice of due process in the United States.
- Explain and illustrate the three elements of a criminal act.
- List and illustrate the basic types of defenses against criminal charges recognized by law.
- Identify and discuss controversial defenses and issues in the application of criminal law.

Robert Thompson, age thirty-five, was arrested for taking pictures during a high school football game in San Antonio, Texas. Two police officers watched him for about thirty minutes and saw him angle the camera with a 300mm telephoto lens at least once at a group of young girls walking in the stands. The police officers asked to see his camera and looked through more than 250 photos of the game, including shots of women's cleavage and girls on the field. The officers didn't believe they had enough evidence to arrest Thompson, who handed them a business card for a pornographic publication, until he gave them consent to search his car. Inside the car police found photo collages of young girls and pornographic magazines.

Thompson was booked on a little-known state charge called improper photography, one of many new video voyeurism laws passed by states to deal with actual and potential abuses of the photo and video capabilities of easily concealed cell phones, digital cameras, and camcorders. Some say these laws are too vague and subject to wide interpretation, while others believe they are the only way to protect the privacy of individuals from unwarranted intrusion.[1] Is this kind of conduct simply bad judgment, or should it be illegal? What is the proper role of the criminal law in cases like these?

These questions are fundamental to an understanding of criminal justice, because the criminal law defines the outer boundaries of the criminal justice system. Police, courts, and the corrections system can take no action until a behavior has been criminalized under the law. Knowledge of the nature, elements, and sources of criminal law enables us to comprehend how acts become defined as crimes, and how liability is imposed or excused under various circumstances.

What Is Criminal Law?

The law can be divided into two basic categories: civil and criminal. **Civil law** is the set of formal rules that regulate disputes between private parties. Civil laws are concerned primarily with issues of personal injury and compensation. Most law is civil law, reflecting the large number and many types of disputes that can arise between individuals. **Criminal law,** on the other hand, is the set of formal rules for maintaining social order and control. Violations of criminal law are considered crimes against society, because they break rules that have been established for the common good of society. In civil law, in contrast, no general societal interest is at stake. Criminal cases are concerned primarily with issues of societal injury and the appropriate punishment of the offender.

civil law
Formal rules that regulate disputes between private parties.

criminal law
Formal rules designed to maintain social control.

The nature of punishment is one of the basic differences between civil and criminal law. Only the government, which represents society, can use legitimate force against a person. Civil penalties only provide compensation to an injured party. In the case of the voyeuristic photographer, the civil law provides only for compensation to the victim for harm suffered. Many states, however, have decided to make these types of actions a crime, determining that such behavior fulfills the elements of crime by unlawfully causing injury to others. These states have found that secretive photography of this kind serves a specific unlawful purpose; the evidence discovered in the chapter opening case, for example, connected the act to participation in pornographic magazines. Therefore, the photographer can be criminally punished through fines or jail terms. In addition, those photographed unknowingly can also bring civil suits against the photographer to seek compensation for harm caused. The difference between the criminal and civil cases would be in their objectives: punishment in one case and compensation in the other.

The criminal law can be further divided into two types: substantive and procedural. **Substantive criminal law** defines behaviors that are prohibited, and **procedural law** provides the rules for adjudication of cases involving those behaviors. For example, the precise definitions of rape, robbery, burglary, or assault are included in the substantive criminal law. The rules of criminal procedure (discussed in Chapter 6) are specified in procedural law. These procedural rules are designed to ensure fairness in arrests, searches, preliminary hearings, arraignments, trials, and every other stage of the criminal justice process. All states, as well as the federal government, have both substantive and procedural criminal laws, which vary somewhat among jurisdictions. This chapter will focus on substantive criminal law.

substantive criminal law
Law defining the specific behaviors prohibited under the criminal law.

procedural law
The rules for adjudication of individuals suspected of violating the law.

Four Sources of American Criminal Law

Today criminal law in the United States has four main sources. The fundamental principles that guide the enactment of specific laws and the interpretations of courts are found in **constitutions.** The U.S. Constitution guides the formulation of federal law, and each state has a constitution that guides the passage of state law. If a contradiction arises between state and federal law, the U.S. Constitution supersedes any state law or constitution. For example, if Kansas passed a law making it a crime to criticize government officials, that law would be found unconstitutional by the courts. The First Amendment to the U.S. Constitution guarantees freedom of speech, and therefore such a law would be in violation of a constitutional principle and could not stand.

constitutions
The fundamental principles of a society that guide the enactment of specific laws and the application of those laws by courts.

Another source of criminal law is statutes. **Statutes** are the specific laws passed by state legislatures or the U.S. Congress that prohibit or mandate certain acts. **Ordinances** are laws that apply only to a specific county, city, or town. Ordinances relating to crime are often systematically codified and compiled in a single volume called a **criminal code** or **penal code.** Legislatures can pass any law they desire as long as it does not violate a constitutional principle.

statutes
Specific laws passed by legislatures that prohibit or mandate certain acts.

ordinances
Laws that apply to a specific county, city, or town.

criminal (penal) code
A compilation of all the criminal laws of a jurisdiction.

A third source of criminal law consists of court decisions. These decisions, often collectively called **case law,** involve judges' interpreting laws passed by legislatures to determine their applicability in a given case or to clarify their meaning. In the United States, judges are required to follow previous decisions, or **precedents,** in order to maintain consistency regarding what is deemed lawful or unlawful. This precedent rule—formally termed *stare decisis*—is occasionally broken when judges believe that a reversal or modification is necessary because of changing social values. For example, some courts have ruled in favor of "right to die" laws in recent years, reflecting changing social attitudes about the proper treatment of terminally ill patients. Reversals or modifications of earlier rulings are made by appellate courts.

case law
Judicial application and interpretation of law as it applies in a given case.

precedents
Previous court decisions that are followed in current cases to ensure consistency in the application of the law.

Administrative regulations are a fourth source of criminal law. These regulations have the force of criminal law to the extent that they can provide for criminal penalties. They are written by regulatory agencies empowered by legislatures to develop rules governing specific policy areas. For example, many regulatory agencies were established during the second half of the twentieth century to protect public health, safety, and welfare in an increasingly complex marketplace. The Food and Drug Administration was established to screen products to protect consumers. Similarly, the Environmental Protection Agency, the Securities and Exchange Commission, and the Consumer Product Safety Commission were established to promulgate rules to promote safety and consistency in dealing with pollution and waste, stock-market transactions, and potentially dangerous products, respectively. If a regulatory agency wishes to add new rules, it must provide public notice of its intention and hold public hearings before adopting the rules.

administrative regulations
Rules applied to organizations that are designed to protect public health, safety, and welfare in the marketplace.

If you were to collect all fifty-one federal and state constitutions, all fifty-one sets of statutes, all state and federal court decisions, and all state and federal administrative regulations, you would have a complete collection of all the criminal law in the United States. Unfortunately, in addition to covering several football fields, your collection would soon be out of date—because court decisions are made every day, and some of these decisions alter existing law. Changes in statutes occur somewhat less often, and constitutions are changed only rarely.

The criminal law can be said to arise from consensus or conflict. According to the **consensus view,** the criminal law reflects a society's consensus regarding behavior that is harmful enough to warrant government intervention. Emile Durkheim, a founder of sociology, declared in 1893 that an act is criminal "when it offends strong and defined states of the collective conscience."[2] This view suggests that the law reflects the moral sense of the people about what actions ought to be prohibited.

The **conflict view** asserts that an act becomes a crime only when criminalizing it serves the interests of those holding positions of power. In this view, the criminal law is used to protect the property interests of the ruling class. The conflict view has been used to explain laws against vagrancy, loitering, and the vices. This view also attempts to explain the selective enforcement of laws against various racial, ethnic, and economic groups, suggesting that such enforcement protects the interests of the powerful rather than promoting public safety in general.[3]

Examples can be found to support both consensus and conflict views. Criminal laws that have existed for centuries, such as those barring murder, assault, and larceny, clearly reflect wide social consensus regarding their harmfulness. Newer laws, on the other hand, such as those that severely penalize crack cocaine and juvenile offenders, may be directed primarily against the actions of poor or powerless groups in society.

CONSENSUS VERSUS CONFLICT VIEWS

consensus view
The view that law reflects society's consensus regarding behavior that is harmful enough to warrant government intervention.

conflict view
The view that an act becomes a crime only when it serves the interests of those in positions of power.

JURISDICTION

jurisdiction
The authority of a state, county, or city to apply its own laws within its own territory.

Limits on Criminal Law

Debates regarding the proper role of criminal law arise when definitions of crimes are not clear, are applied inconsistently, or appear to infringe on constitutionally protected areas. In a famous case in Jacksonville, Florida, two men and two women riding in a car were detained by police after they stopped near a used car lot that had been broken into several times. They were charged with "prowling by auto."[4] The arrestees challenged this charge, which was part of Jacksonville's vagrancy ordinance. The U.S. Supreme Court held that the law was "void-for-vagueness." This phrase means that the language in the law was so imprecise that a person of "ordinary intelligence" could not tell if his or her acts were prohibited. As a result of this 1972 ruling, criminal laws must be written in very precise fashion, creating difficulties for cities attempting to legislate bans on "cruising" and other vaguely defined behaviors.[5]

Another limit on the criminal law has to do with determining responsibility for applying it. One test of responsibility is **jurisdiction:** An act must have been committed in the state, city, or county where the act is prohibited. Another test of responsibility in applying the law involves the balance of power between legislatures and the courts, and between the national and state governments. The Tenth Amendment to the U.S. Constitution gives states

A state legislature is in session. Do you believe they enact statutes that usually reflect public consensus, or do they protect the interests of the wealthy or powerful? Give an example of a recent law that supports your view.

Should states be permitted to require adult riders of motorcycles to wear helmets, or should it be up to the riders?

the power to pass laws. This "police power" enables a state to carry out its responsibility to protect health, safety, and morality, but there are limits on this power. One view is that the power to punish wrongdoers is vested in the legislature and that courts must stringently apply the law as written. Others argue that liberal, rather than strict, interpretation of statutes by the courts is necessary, because no law can anticipate all the possible circumstances that may arise. Courts must be given enough leeway, therefore, to apply the law to situations unforeseen by the legislature.

WHOM DO THE LAWS PROTECT?

This debate continues today, as legislatures pass broader laws covering more types of behaviors but then complain about how courts apply those laws in specific cases. For example, consider laws that require motorcycle riders to wear helmets or automobile occupants to wear seat belts. Whom do these laws protect? Do they infringe on the right of private citizens to be left alone? Clearly, it is important to protect young people; but what about protecting adults from the consequences of their own actions? Do those consequences affect others who need the protection of the law? These are all valid questions that arise when the law attempts to protect "public health and safety" rather than dealing with a predatory harm (such as assault or larceny) where the distinction between offender and victim is clear.[6] Using the reasoning behind helmet and seat-belt laws, could not legislatures outlaw cigarette smoking or obscene gestures, as alcohol consumption was outlawed during Prohibition (see Chapter 2)?[7]

STATE CRIMINAL CODES

The criminal law is more complicated than it appears because it is difficult to specify clearly all the requirements of the law and assess accurately who deserves and who does not deserve criminal liability. A group of law professors led by Paul Robinson ranked state criminal codes in terms of their comprehensiveness and clarity in content and consistency. Part of their rankings is presented in Table 5.1, which shows that western states generally did better than eastern states. In Mississippi, for example, which ranked last, it was found that you can be jailed for over a year for stealing a chicken but only fined for stealing a stereo.[8] Maryland has a maximum punishment of five years' imprisonment for committing arson on most structures that are not homes, but provides a punishment of up to ten years' imprisonment for *threatening* to commit arson on these structures. These peculiarities result from the fact that new laws are passed every year often in response to sensational events or prevailing public opinion. For example, body piercing in Mississippi was made permissible only if parlors are registered with health officials. In Pennsylvania intentionally distributing a computer virus was attached to a sentence of up to seven years in prison.[9] Rarely do states systematically reassess their criminal codes to ensure that offenses and penalties added at different times are logical and proportionate when compared with each other.

Table 5.1 The Five Best and Five Worst State Criminal Codes (in terms of clarity, comprehensiveness, and proportionality)

Ranking	*State*
1	Texas
2	Colorado
3	Arkansas
4	Alaska
5	Missouri
46	Massachusetts
47	Rhode Island
48	Maryland
49	West Virginia
50	Mississippi

Source: Copyright Paul H. Robinson, www.law.pen.edu/fac/phrobins/code.html#4f

How Did the American System of Law and Justice Develop?

American criminal law is derived from British common law. Even though legal codes have existed for thousands of years in societies of all kinds, the structure of law in the United States today is modeled most closely on the British experience.[10] The **common law** was a body of unrecorded decisions made by judges in England during the Middle Ages. These decisions reflected the social values, customs, and beliefs of the period, and they were used as a basis for decisions in subsequent cases. As time went by, these decisions were recorded and followed more formally, so British legal decisions were guided by case law rather than by rules established by legislatures.

common law
The body of unrecorded decisions made by English judges in the Middle Ages, reflecting the values, customs, and beliefs of the period.

When America was first colonized, British precedents and procedures were followed. As in England, courts often relied upon biblical principles. Nevertheless, living as they did in a wilderness thousands of miles from Europe, the colonists faced certain problems that did not exist in England.[11] As a consequence, Americans came to rely on tighter legal rules created by local and state governments. This move toward regulating behavior by statute, rather than by court decisions, distinguishes American criminal law from its British foundations.

It is interesting that there is no mention of a "criminal justice system" in the U.S. Constitution or in federal or state law. In reality, the **criminal justice system** is a string of more than 55,000 independent government agencies that have been set up to deal with different aspects of crime and the treatment of offenders, including law enforcement, the courts, and corrections. These agencies often have failed to work together effectively because of a lack of systemwide thinking.[12] In fact, many of the problems of criminal justice throughout U.S. history have been caused by the failure of the various criminal justice agencies to act as a system. Yet it is important to keep in mind the idea of a system, because actions of one criminal justice agency invariably affect the others—and because agencies must attempt to act as a system if justice is to be achieved.

criminal justice system
The more than 55,000 government agencies in the United States that deal with aspects of crime, including criminal law enforcement, the courts, and corrections.

Evolution of Lawful Justice

Over the course of history, societies have been fairly consistent in the way they handle criminal justice. First, the members of societies give a government authority to act on their behalf. When some members do not follow a society's codified rules—that is, its laws—the government usually establishes an agency whose responsibility is to make sure that the laws are obeyed. In U.S. society this enforcement function is performed by the police.

Next, societies often set up agencies to arbitrate in these matters. That is, if a person has an excuse or justification for violating the law, how do we determine whether it is a valid one? In U.S. society this arbitration function is performed by the courts.

Finally, when an assessment of blame or responsibility is made, a penalty or punishment is administered to the offender and compensation is sometimes given to the victim. In U.S. society this action is carried out by the corrections system. Thus, a system of justice evolves in a society to resolve disputes. A set of rules, a method to enforce those rules, a way to evaluate justifications for rule violations, and a way to administer penalties are all necessary to serve the common good. These fundamental components of criminal justice are required to resolve the sometimes conflicting or competing interests of individual citizens in ways that serve the wider public interest.

STATE AND FEDERAL SYSTEMS

As stated previously, the United States has two levels of criminal justice systems: state and federal. Each state has its own set of criminal justice agencies, and the federal government has a criminal justice system that handles concerns that apply to some or all of the states. Therefore, there are actually fifty-one criminal justice systems in the United States. Our modern system of criminal justice has evolved as U.S. society has developed mechanisms for establishing rules, enforcing them, determining responsibility for violations, and deciding on appropriate remedies.

BRITISH ROOTS

Revolutionary Justice The contemporary structure of law enforcement, courts, and corrections institutionalizes basic notions of how law should be enforced and adjudicated and how violators should be dealt with. The United States was founded in the aftermath of a revolution against the British government, which was seen as arbitrary, not representative of the people, and far too strong. This experience has guided the establishment of criminal justice agencies, which have been granted the power to intrude into the lives of citizens only under certain specified circumstances. Also, many criminal justice agencies exist on the local level, and local control prevents these agencies from becoming too powerful or abusive.

Why was the justice system less formal in early America than it is today? What does *posse comitatus* mean, and why was it important years ago?

Frontier Justice In early America, most of the country was rural, and large population centers were few. The justice system was less formal than it is today: There were many fewer lawyers and judges and law enforcement officers, and many individuals did not wish to have their disputes formally adjudicated. Sheriffs had the authority, called *posse comitatus*

(power of the county), to summon all males over fifteen years of age to assist them in apprehending a suspected law violator. This was very important in the expansion westward because of the vast open spaces between towns and the small number of sheriffs.

In 1804, Aaron Burr exercised his traditional right to private vengeance and shot and killed Alexander Hamilton in a duel. How did this duel contribute to the evolution of public justice in the United States? What other forms of private justice did the rule of law seek to replace? What are the sources of American criminal law and the concept of due process? What goals and benefits of due process constitute the bedrock of the American criminal justice system?

The custom of dueling, which continued even into the twentieth century in some parts of the United States, was a way to settle disputes outside the formal justice process. Dueling involved two disputing parties who used guns or swords to resolve their disagreement. Dueling was seen as a more direct and honorable way to resolve breeches of trust, property ownership disputes, and offenses against one's family or honor. The famous duel in which Aaron Burr killed Alexander Hamilton in 1804 was an incident that helped ultimately to end dueling and to encourage the use of the public justice system to resolve criminal and civil wrongs. Church ministers of that period used the Hamilton–Burr duel as a prime example of why such private vengeance was wrong: In the words of one sermon, "[Hamilton] was no less a murderer because he was deceived by the wickedness of the law of honor."[13]

Private settlement of disputes continues today in the form of vigilante groups. These groups sometimes attempt to enforce a standard of conduct by taking the law into their own hands. Shooting trespassers, assaulting unpopular members of the community, and using deadly force in cases in which the police should have been summoned are contemporary examples of private settlement of disputes—all of which undermine the effectiveness of the justice system in assessing the proper course of conduct and in determining responsibility for wrongdoing.[14]

Evolution of Due Process

PRIVATE JUSTICE

The criminal justice process is no longer an informal one run by amateurs. Many legal steps and procedures have been added, all with two goals: accuracy and fairness. These are the essential elements of **due process**, a legal protection included in the U.S. Constitution that guarantees all citizens the right to be adjudicated under established law and legal procedures. Both the Fifth and the Fourteenth Amendments prohibit all jurisdictions from depriving any person "of life, liberty, or property, without due process of law." Historically, this protection from arbitrary and unjust treatment became more important as the nation grew and became more urban, and as those making, enforcing, and adjudicating laws increasingly were strangers rather than neighbors. The growing size and diversity of the population also meant that a common core of religious values could no longer be counted on to promote conformity to laws.

due process (constitutional) A legal protection included in the U.S. Constitution that guarantees all citizens the right to be adjudicated under established law and legal procedures.

ACCURACY AND FAIRNESS

In due process accuracy is a fundamental goal, because confidence in the outcome is pivotal if a criminal justice system is to work. If the public did not believe that the findings of the criminal justice process were accurate, people would lose confidence in the system, turn to private forms of justice, and eventually look for new forms of government.

The requirement that agents of the government treat citizens fairly and according to the law was a fundamental principle in the founding of the United States. What were the historical circumstances for this concern?

Fairness is closely related to accuracy. Fairness in the justice process is a matter of the balance between the government's interest in apprehending and punishing crime suspects and the public's interest in avoiding unjust punishments and unnecessary government interference in the lives of individuals. Thresholds for government intervention, such as probable cause, are designed to achieve a *fair* balance between the sometimes conflicting interests of the government and individual citizens.

CRIME CONTROL

Some have held that crime control is an important function of the criminal justice process,[15] despite the fact that there is little reliable evidence to suggest that the criminal justice system deters offenders or reforms those who pass through it. Proponents of the deterrence theory sometimes argue that overemphasis on accuracy and fairness interferes with the system's ability to deter or prevent crime.[16] It is unlikely, however, that a nation born only 225 years ago out of violent revolution would be willing to lower the legal thresholds established to preserve accuracy and fairness in the balance between government and citizen. Indeed, Americans have long been suspicious of government. This suspicion dates back to the Revolution and to the philosophy of John Locke, which holds that government exists not by divine right or by force, but only by the consent of the governed, who may alter or abolish the government if it acts in a manner inconsistent with the natural rights of citizens.[17] An important cause of the American Revolution was the widespread perception that British government procedures were arbitrary and unfair—another reason that the U.S. criminal justice process seeks to achieve impartiality and consistency in the application of the law.[18] Accuracy, fairness, and social control in the justice process would not have the continued support of the public unless applied consistently in an impartial manner.

IMPARTIALITY AND CONSISTENCY

CRIMINAL PROCEDURES

The relative emphasis on these goals of due process remains relevant today. Criminal procedure, in which a citizen becomes a suspect and perhaps a defendant and a convicted offender, is a crucial part of criminal justice. The power of the government is vast compared to the resources of a private citizen, so it is extremely important that criminal procedures safeguard the rights of individuals in the adjudication process. An interesting example is the case of Terry Nichols, who was charged with conspiracy and murder for the planning and execution of the 1995 bombing of the federal office building in Oklahoma City. Nichols was associated with Timothy McVeigh, who was convicted of murder in the bombings. But Nichols was not in Oklahoma City at the time of the bombing.[19] In view of the horror of the most deadly terrorist act in the United States at that time, an objective presentation and evaluation of the evidence against Nichols was difficult but necessary under the law of criminal procedure. Without criminal procedure to guide the inquiry into guilt or innocence, public sentiment and outrage can result in unfair verdicts and gross injustices. In the case of Terry Nichols, the jury considered his role in the crime and convicted him of conspiracy and involuntary manslaughter, clearing him of murder charges. He was sentenced to life in prison.

How Does the Law Define the Elements of a Crime?

When a legislature decides to create a new criminal law, the crime in question must contain several defining elements. Without any one of these elements, a crime does not exist. If these elements are present, however, legislatures can make any undesirable behavior illegal so long as the new law does not violate a constitutional principle. Thus, it is important for citizens to be informed of proposed new laws so they can determine whether the social goal to be accomplished by the new law will justify the possible infringement on individual liberty.

Perhaps the most important element of a crime is the ***mens rea*** or "guilty mind." The *mens rea* is a conscious decision to commit an unlawful act. This element consists of more than just criminal intent; it includes intention to commit *any* act that is illegal. For example, a person who intends to rob me and steal my criminal justice book might erroneously rob another person who happens to look like me. The original intent to rob meets the *mens rea* requirement, because the offender intended to rob someone and did so. Offenders will not be punished less severely merely because they victimize the wrong person, because their mistake does not negate their guilty mind. Thus, *mens rea* connotes a guilty state of mind rather than merely criminal intent.

mens rea
The "guilty mind" or conscious decision to commit a criminal act.

The second element of a crime is the act itself, the ***actus reus,*** the behavior that must be committed to meet the definition of the crime. No murder can occur without a death, for example, and no arson can occur without a fire or explosion. Thus, intent to commit a crime is not sufficient for criminal liability without a specific act taking place. *Actus reus* can take the form of an illegal act or can consist of the *omission* of an act one has a legal duty to perform.

actus reus
The behavior that must be committed to meet the definition of a crime.

ATTENDANT CIRCUMSTANCES

The third defining element of a crime is the attendant circumstances or causal link. That is, in order for a crime to occur, there must be a concurrence between the act and the harm that results. For example, taking the life of another person does not always constitute criminal homicide. Homicide by police officers in the line of duty or by citizens in self-defense is viewed as justifiable. Only the unlawful or unjustifiable taking of the life of another constitutes criminal homicide. Likewise, the harm caused must follow directly from the illegal act. Intervening or superseding causes can remove criminal liability. For example, in an assault that resulted in the victim's being taken away by ambulance, the offender might escape liability for the person's ultimate death if the victim were dropped by the ambulance crew or were left waiting in the emergency room for four hours before treatment was administered. In such a case the court would determine the extent to which the intervening or superseding causes independently resulted in harm apart from the original assault.[20]

In sum, the attendant circumstances or causation, together with the *actus reus* and *mens rea,* are referred to as the *elements of a crime.* Whenever a legislature defines a new form of criminal behavior, all three elements must be present.

Media & Criminal Justice

Murder on TV: *Law & Order, The Practice,* and *NYPD Blue*

There are a number of popular television programs that feature criminal justice themes. *Law & Order, The Practice,* and *NYPD Blue* are considered three of the best programs of this type, and each has won numerous critics awards. Like most crime-oriented programs, murder is featured as a crime far more often than it occurs in real life. But it is interesting to see if the circumstances that surround the murders in these crime dramas are portrayed in accordance with what we know about actual murders.

More than twenty episodes of each program were evaluated, and the results did not fit the general pattern in society that most murders are not planned, but are situationally induced acts of violence. Nearly one-third (32 percent) of the murder incidents presented across the three justice programs were planned (see Table 5A below).

Nearly one-half (45 percent) of the murder incidents on *Law & Order* were planned, and 38 percent of the murder incidents on *The Practice* were planned. Planned murders were less common on *NYPD Blue,* with only three (12 percent) of the murder incidents being planned. Therefore, only *NYPD Blue* fits the reality that murder is typically spontaneous rather than planned.

The spontaneity of murder is often due to the fact that many murders that occur are the result of an argument or dispute. Nearly one-quarter (24 percent) of the murder incidents presented in the three justice programs occurred in the context of an argument.

FBI statistics report that murders are also likely to occur in conjunction with the commission of a felony. Fourteen percent of the murder incidents on *Law & Order* occurred in the context of a felony. Ten percent of the murder incidents on *The Practice* were felony murders, while 20 percent of the murder incidents on *NYPD Blue* were classified as felony murders.

Researcher Danielle Soulliere concludes that "television crime dramas tend to give the impression that most murders are meticulously planned. Indeed, the over-emphasis on planned murders on television masks the spontaneity of real-life murder, which is often the result of an argument or dispute or fuelled by alcohol and/or drugs." It can be seen, therefore, that television crime dramas highlight the dramatic, rather than offer a true reflection of reality.

Why do you believe that television crime dramas disproportionately focus on the crime of murder? Do you believe this emphasis on homicide has any impact in the public's beliefs about the true incidence of murder? Why are planned murders featured more prominently on crime dramas than the more spontaneous killings that better reflect real life?

Table 5A
Context Factors for Murder/Attempted Murder Incidents Presented on Three Prime-Time Crime Dramas

	Law & Order	*The Practice*	*NYPD Blue*	*Total*
Planned	13 (45%)	8 (38%)	3 (12%)	24 (32%)
Argument or Dispute	7 (24%)	4 (19%)	7 (28%)	18 (24%)
Felony	4 (14%)	2 (10%)	5 (20%)	11 (15%)
Other/Unknown	5 (17%)	7 (33%)	10 (40%)	22 (29%)

Note: Percentage totals may not always add up to exactly 100 due to rounding.

Source: From Danielle M. Soulliere, "Prime-Time Murder: Presentations of Murder on Popular Television Justice Programs." *Journal of Criminal Justice and Popular Culture,* 10(1) 2003, pp. 12–38. www.albany.edu/scj/jcjpc/vol10is1/soulliere.html.

For example, a common definition of the crime of burglary is "the unauthorized entry or surreptitious remaining in a building or occupied structure for the purpose of committing a crime therein." The *actus reus* for this crime is entry into or the remaining in a building, while the *mens rea* is "for the purpose of committing a crime therein." The attendant circumstances prescribe that the entry must be "unauthorized" or the remaining "surreptitious." Without these circumstances there can be no burglary. The three elements of a crime, then, tell us the conditions that must exist before a person can be found guilty of a particular crime.

Characteristics of Criminal Acts

prepare & discuss

The three elements of a crime—act, guilty mind, and attendant circumstances—can be more difficult to establish than appears at first glance. For instance, *how much* of an act is necessary for criminal liability? Five characteristics of acts can incur **criminal liability** or punishable responsibility under criminal law: sufficiency, possession, status, voluntariness, and omission.

FIVE CHARACTERISTICS OF A CRIME

criminal liability
Establishing the presence of the elements of a crime in a given case, thereby subjecting the accused person to criminal penalties.

Sufficiency In a Utah case, the defendant fell asleep in his car on the shoulder of the highway. Police stopped, smelled alcohol on his breath, and arrested him for driving while intoxicated. His conviction was reversed by the Utah Supreme Court, because the defendant was not in physical control of the vehicle at the time as required by the law.[21] The case against him failed because he was not violating the law at the time of the arrest and because it was also possible that he could have driven while sober, then have pulled over, drank, and fell asleep. In short, the act observed by the police was not sufficient to confirm the existence of a guilty mind. If the car had been running, or had been parked on the traveled portion of the highway, this would have been sufficient for police to conclude that the defendant was operating the automobile while drunk, even though the police arrived after he had fallen asleep.

Possession Possession alone is sufficient to fulfill the act requirement. In a New Jersey case, the defendant and his brother had marijuana and LSD in a locked box in a closet. Both had access to the box, although both testified that the LSD did not belong to the defendant but to his brother. Should the defendant be held liable for items that were not on his person and did not belong to him? The court affirmed his conviction, holding that the elements of possession were fulfilled: The defendant knew of the existence and illegal nature of the object, and he had the opportunity to exercise control over it.[22] This concept is called **constructive possession.** Although distinguished from **actual possession,** in which a defendant has exclusive control over an object (such as a concealed weapon), constructive possession meets the act requirement.

constructive possession
A condition in which a person has the opportunity to exercise control over an object.

actual possession
A condition in which a person has exclusive control over an object.

Status A particular status does not suffice to meet the act requirement. In a well-known California case, a man was convicted of a misdemeanor for being "addicted to the use of narcotics." His conviction was reversed on grounds that narcotics addiction has been held to be an illness, and people cannot be punished for being ill.[23] In other words, addiction is a status, not an act. A person can be convicted of buying, selling, or possessing narcotics, because these are acts. But the status of being an addict does not suffice for criminal punishment.

Voluntariness A fourth feature of criminal acts is that they must be both voluntary and conscious. Unconscious and involuntary acts are not subject to criminal penalties. Sleepwalking and reflexive or convulsive acts are not voluntary,

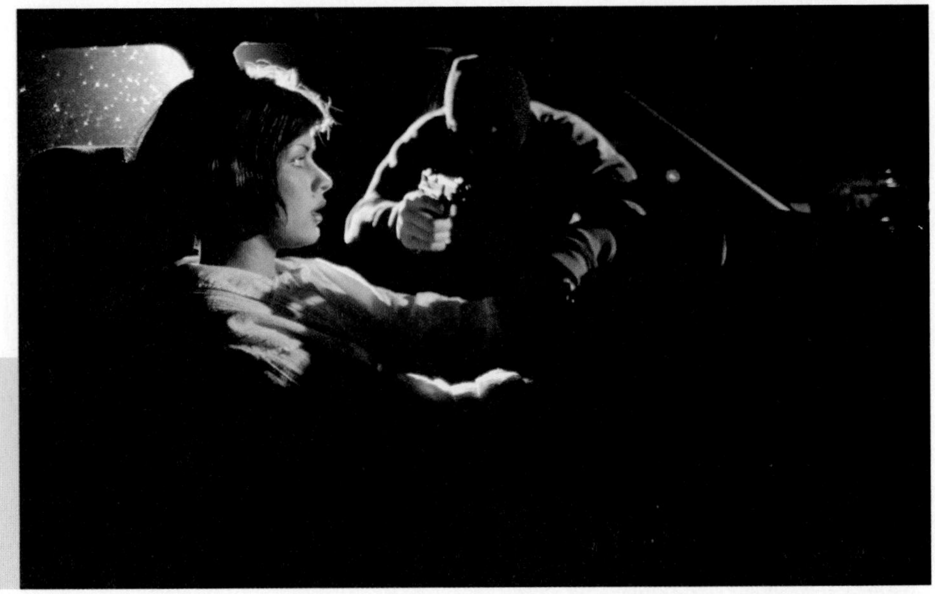

A robbery and assault of the victim, and perhaps also the theft of the car, is suggested in the photo. Point to at least three features of this photo that help you draw conclusions about the offender's criminal intention or guilty state of mind.

because they are not consciously carried out. "Shaken baby syndrome" cases, in which babies die from brain swelling after being shaken or struck, often involve questions of voluntariness. In the case of Louise Woodward in Massachusetts, the judge reduced a murder charge to involuntary manslaughter because he did not believe there was evidence that Woodward deliberately and voluntarily harmed the infant in her care.[24] The key legal challenge in these cases is to establish whether death resulted accidentally from normal activity or whether it was the outcome of malicious action.[25]

Omission A fifth characteristic of a criminal act is that omission of an action meets the act requirement when there is a duty to perform it. In a child abuse case in Pennsylvania, a woman with a five-year-old daughter lived with her boyfriend, who regularly beat the child, ultimately causing the child's death. The court faced the question: Should the mother be held liable for failing to protect her child from the boyfriend's beatings? The court held that as a parent the mother had a legal duty to protect her child, which she had failed to do.[26] Omissions most often incur criminal penalties in situations in which there is a legal or contractual duty to act. Failure to file income tax returns and failure to obey traffic laws are two common examples.

The State of Mind Requirement

The state of mind requirement separates criminal from civil law. Criminal law requires *mens rea*, or a guilty mind, which is not required in civil law. Punishments for violations of criminal law are based on assessment of degrees of *mens rea*. In New York State, for example, there are three degrees of assault. Third-degree assault is causing an injury *recklessly*; second-degree assault is causing *serious* injury recklessly; and first-degree assault is causing serious injury *with intent to cause* that injury. As explained in Chapter 3, *recklessness* connotes conscious disregard for a substantial and unjustifiable risk. It is punished because it fails to meet the standard of conduct of a *reasonable* person. The courts often use the behavior of a hypothetical "reasonable person" to assess whether a defendant's conduct is culpable or excusable. This standard of conduct is referred to as the **reasonableness standard.**

reasonableness standard
A standard under which persons are culpable for their actions if they understand the consequences of those actions. Young children and the mentally ill are generally not held culpable owing to their inability to reason effectively.

intention
Conscious purposiveness in conduct; a factor in the determination of criminal responsibility.

Intention characterizes conduct that is carried out *knowingly* or *purposely;* that is, the defendant either had a conscious intention to commit an act or at least was aware that the act would cause a certain result. In an Ohio case, the defendant was upset when another driver blew his car horn at him. The defendant took it upon himself to follow the other driver home and harass him, despite warnings that the other driver had a heart condition. The other driver had a heart attack and died. The defendant was charged with manslaughter, and his conviction was affirmed. The court held that the death could have been "reasonably anticipated by an ordinary prudent person."[27] The defendant, therefore, had acted recklessly in this case, and his actions were the proximate (immediate) cause of the victim's death.

An individual's state of mind, then, is central to a determination of criminal responsibility. The more an act reflects planning or deviates from the standard of a reasonable person, the more severe the punishment. This state of mind criterion distinguishes criminal law from civil law, in which the objective is to obtain compensation for private injury and the defendant's state of mind is less relevant.

What Defenses against Criminal Charges Does the Law Recognize?

CRIMINAL LIABILITY

In criminal cases, police and prosecutors attempt to establish *criminal liability:* to establish the presence of the elements of the crime that subject the accused person to criminal penalties. Defendants, and defense lawyers working in their behalf, attempt to establish reasons why the act, guilty mind, or attendant circumstances do not apply. In many cases the defense will stipulate that although the act and harm were both caused by the defendant, there is a valid excuse for the defendant's conduct. Acceptable legal defenses are of three general types: defenses related to mental illness, defenses involving force, and defenses involving justification or excuse.

Defenses Related to Mental Illness

Mental illness can play a role in a criminal case in two ways. First, it must be asked whether the defendant is sane enough to be placed on trial. Second, it must be established whether the defendant was sane at the time of the act. Defendants must be mentally competent to stand trial so as to understand the legal proceedings against them. The legal standard for determining competency to stand trial was established back in 1960, when the U.S. Supreme Court held that a person is incompetent to stand trial if he or she lacks the ability to consult with a lawyer with a reasonable degree of understanding *and* lacks a rational and factual understanding of the legal proceedings.[28]

COMPETENCY

A defendant who is found incompetent to stand trial does not go free but rather can be committed to a mental institution and can be tried after recovering competency. Courts have held that a person may be held in a mental institution for "a reasonable period" to achieve competency to stand trial. Some courts have interpreted this period to be no more than the maximum sentence that would be imposed for the crime if the person were convicted of it.[29]

A more controversial application of mental illness to criminal law occurs in the attempt to determine if a defendant was sane at the time of the act. A defense based on the claim that the defendant was not sane at the time of the act is referred to as the **insanity defense.** It is based on the principle that people who are not blameworthy should not be punished. Thus, the law treats young children and mentally ill individuals in the same way. Neither are held criminally liable for their actions, because they do not understand the consequences of those actions—another example of the reasonableness standard. The inability of young children or people with mental illness to reason or rationalize in a competent manner makes criminal punishment of their conduct both ineffective and unreasonable.

insanity defense
A claim that the defendant was not sane under law at the time of the act.

Over the years the courts have adopted several different formulations of the insanity defense. None has been satisfactory, because in each instance the legal system finds itself asking a question that it cannot answer: What was the person's level of mental functioning at the time of the crime, and did that constitute insanity? This is ultimately a question of *mens rea* (or lack of it), and psychiatrists are unable to agree on a standard for determining the presence or absence of *mens rea* in any given case.

THE M'NAGHTEN CASE

The insanity defense originated in England in 1843 in the case of Daniel M'Naghten. M'Naghten suffered from the delusion that the British prime minister, Sir Robert Peel, was going to have him killed. To frustrate this imagined conspiracy against him, M'Naghten went to the prime minister's house in an effort to kill him first. He killed the prime minister's secretary by mistake. After a trial for murder, M'Naghten was found not guilty by reason of insanity. On appeal, England's highest court formulated the M'Naghten rule, which defined legal insanity for the first time. The definition of insanity focused on the *reasoning ability* of the defendant; it asked whether he understood the nature and quality of his act or was incapable of knowing that it was wrong "owing to a disease of the mind."[30]

In 1972 the federal courts adopted the test for legal insanity proposed by the American Law Institute in the Model Penal Code. In this formulation legal insanity exists when a defendant "lacks substantial capacity to appreciate the wrongfulness of his conduct or to conform his conduct to the requirements of the law." The Model Penal Code is now used in all federal courts and in about half the states.

In practice, the application of definitions of legal insanity is quite subjective. Prosecutors always seem able to find mental health experts who will argue that the defendant is mentally competent; experts for the defense always argue the reverse. Juries often are left to their own judgment in the battle of dueling experts in the courtroom.[31] To the public, the insanity defense often looks like a mechanism by which offenders get away with murder. Some have called for abolition of the insanity defense. Aside from the possibility that it may allow dangerous people to go free, the insanity defense also has created some ironic situations. During a trial a prosecutor might argue that the defendant was sane at the time of the act. However, if the defendant were found not guilty by reason of insanity, to obtain a civil commitment to a mental institution the prosecutor would then have to argue the opposite: that the defendant was insane.

John Hinckley was found not guilty by reason of insanity in the attempted murder of President Ronald Reagan. He is indefinitely confined in a mental hospital. How were legal insanity laws changed after this case?

In practice, the insanity defense has been seldom invoked. Studies have found that the insanity plea is used in only 2 percent of cases that go to trial.[32] Moreover, the insanity defense has rarely been successful. Judges and juries issue verdicts of not guilty by reason of insanity in only 2 to 5 percent of the cases in which the defense is attempted.[33] The number of people in mental hospitals who have been found not guilty by reason of insanity constitutes less than 1 percent of the number of inmates in prison who were found guilty of the crime with which they were charged.[34] Interestingly, the debate over the insanity defense may be beside the point, as follow-up studies of insanity cases have found that the length of incarceration in prison of those found guilty was virtually the same as or even shorter than the length of incarceration in mental hospitals of those found not guilty by reason of insanity.[35] Nevertheless, dissatisfaction with the insanity defense has led to its abandonment in four states (Montana, Idaho, Kansas, Utah). In general, however, defendants who are likely to plead insanity have been found incompetent to stand trial. The result is that they are confined indefinitely to the same mental hospitals to which they would have been committed if they had been found not guilty by reason of insanity.[36]

PROBLEMS WITH THE INSANITY DEFENSE

THE HINCKLEY CASE

In 1982 John Hinckley was found not guilty by reason of insanity in the attempted murder of President Reagan. Many believed that Hinckley "got away with murder," although he remains confined indefinitely at St. Elizabeth's Hospital in Washington, D.C. In response to public outrage over that case, seventeen states adopted a new type of verdict, "guilty but mentally ill." This wording means that the defendant was not legally insane at the time of the offense but suffered from a disorder that may have affected the commission of the crime. If found guilty but mentally ill, an offender is sentenced to prison but given psychological treatment. This is a troublesome alternative for two reasons. First, most prisons have no facilities for treating mental illness, and such treatment often is not guaranteed or implemented as directed by the court.[37] Second, "guilty but mentally ill" verdicts appear to constitute punishment without *mens rea* by holding a person criminally responsible for conduct despite finding that they are mentally ill.

Nevertheless, the public remains skeptical of the insanity defense. A number of murder cases have been tried where observable mental illness was deemed not sufficient for a defense of insanity.[38] State laws continue to limit the use of insanity defenses, as was illustrated in the case of Eric Clark, a man who shot a police officer in Arizona believing that "aliens" (some impersonating government agents) were trying to kill him and that bullets were the only way to stop them. A psychiatrist and a number of other individuals all testified that Clark was suffering from paranoid schizophrenia with delusions about "aliens" when he killed the officer, and that Clark had engaged in increasingly bizarre behavior during the preceding year. But Arizona law severely limits the definition of legal insanity, and also limits the type of expert psychiatric testimony that can be introduced at trial, and Clark was convicted. The U.S. Supreme Court upheld Arizona's law (and Clark's conviction) in 2006, holding that the law violates no fundamental principle of justice.[39] Therefore, it is likely that the insanity defense will be used even less in the future as states continue to restrict its use, and as juries remain doubtful in those cases when it is raised.

Defenses Involving Force

SELF-DEFENSE

Defenses involving force are of three types: self-defense, defense of others, and defense of property. A person may use force for self-protection or to protect others, but the extent of that force is limited by law. As a general rule, a person is permitted to use whatever force reasonably seems necessary, short of deadly force, to prevent immediate and unlawful personal harm. Killing in self-defense is permitted only to prevent imminent death or serious injury threatened by the attacker. Although the concept of self-defense is easily understood, problems can arise when the victim's *perception* of potential harm is not reasonable.

In a Louisiana case, a bar patron weighing 215 pounds threatened to kill the bartender, who weighed only 145 pounds, for refusing to serve him drinks after he had become intoxicated. The unarmed patron started to climb over the bar, and the bartender shot and wounded him. Clearly, the extent of force used by the bartender exceeded that used by the patron. However, the court ruled that the shooting was lawful because of the circumstances. The size and age of the parties, the threat of weapons, and the aggressiveness of the assault are all relevant in determining the reasonableness of a defendant's behavior. In this case the court believed that the patron's large size and irrational, aggressive behavior were enough to justify the bartender's belief that his life was in danger.[40]

Under what circumstances is the use of force in self-defense permitted? Is it possible to know from this photo which person is acting in self-defense?

Some states require a person who can safely retreat from danger to do so before using deadly force, on the principle that it is not reasonably necessary to use extreme force if one can avoid danger by running away. Other states see the issue differently, basing their self-defense laws on the belief that a person should not be required to run away from an aggressor. In no state, however, is a person required to retreat from an attack in one's own home. Florida has become the first state to allow citizens to use deadly force against muggers, carjackers, and other attackers in what has been called "Stand Your Ground" laws passed in recent years. These laws generally grant immunity from prosecution and lawsuits to those who use deadly force to counter any attack or unlawful entry; these laws also remove any retreat requirement. This is an expansion of traditional laws of self-defense and has spurred debate about whether the laws better protect citizens or whether they will spur more crime and reckless shootings. As of 2006, fifteen states have passed a version of these laws. It will be interesting to see the impact of these laws on claims of self-defense.[41]

BATTERED WOMAN SYNDROME

The dual conditions of "reasonably necessary force" and "no requirement to retreat" in one's own home often conflict in cases of spouse abuse. In one case the defendant killed her husband by stabbing him with a pair of scissors. She was not in fear of immediate harm at the time of the act, but her husband had a history of assaulting her when he was drunk.[42] In another case a woman set fire to her husband's bed while he was sleeping, because he had beaten her severely and would not allow her to leave.[43] The ordinary rules of self-defense do not apply in these cases because of the absence of an immediate threat of harm. Nevertheless, many courts have permitted defendants in such cases to claim self-defense, on the grounds that an ongoing pattern of severe physical abuse constitutes a continual threat of harm. This pattern has been called the **battered woman syndrome.** Some states have changed their laws to expand the application of self-defense to situations in which women have been the victims of chronic physical abuse. In 1996 brothers Lyle and Erik Menendez received life sentences without possibility of parole for killing their parents.[44] This case was unusual because the brothers claimed that they had been abused by their parents throughout their childhood and that they had killed in retaliation for that abuse. The Menendez brothers were in their mid-twenties at the time of the crime, however, stretching a claim of self-defense to years after the abuse occurred. The trial jury rejected their argument.

battered woman syndrome An ongoing pattern of severe physical abuse that constitutes a continual threat of harm.

Laws permitting the use of force in defense of others are designed to encourage citizens to come to the aid of others. A person may use reasonable force to

Under what circumstances can a person use force to defend property? Can deadly force be used to protect property?

defend another person against unlawful force, but the force used can be no more than what would be justified in self-defense. In one case an inmate in a Massachusetts prison attempted to rescue a fellow inmate from a severe beating by assaulting a corrections officer who was inflicting the beating. In determining that the inmate's intervention was legally justified, the court held that defense of others "does not necessarily stop at the prison gates."[45]

DEADLY FORCE

The right to defend one's property by force is narrowly limited. In general, reasonable force, short of deadly force, can be used to protect property or prevent a crime. Deadly force in defense of property is permitted only in one's own home during a burglary or other dangerous felony, such as rape, kidnapping, or robbery. In a California case, a man had tools stolen from his garage. To prevent further thefts he rigged a pistol that would fire at the door if it was opened slightly. This contraption shot a sixteen-year-old in the face during an attempted theft. The garage owner was convicted of assault, because "deadly mechanical devices are without mercy or discretion."[46] The owner's pistol placed at risk children, firefighters, and others who might have entered the garage for reasons other than theft. Thus, deadly force in defense of property is not permitted unless the victim is in imminent danger of serious bodily harm (in which case the rules for self-defense would apply).

Defenses Involving Justification or Excuse

FIVE JUSTIFICATIONS OR EXCUSES

In certain cases defendants admit to unlawful conduct but claim that an overriding justification or excuse makes their actions lawful. Five defenses involving justification or excuse are duress, necessity, mistake of fact, ignorance of law, and entrapment.

duress
A defense in which a person claims to have engaged in criminal conduct because of a threat of immediate and serious bodily harm by another person.

Duress Three conditions must be met for a claim of **duress** (called *coercion* or *compulsion* in some jurisdictions). For duress to succeed as a defense, the defendant must have engaged in a criminal act because of a threat of serious bodily harm by another person. In addition, the threat must be immediate, and there must be no reasonable possibility for escape. In many jurisdictions the defense of duress is disallowed if the defendant intentionally or recklessly placed himself or herself in a situation subject to duress.

In a Washington, D.C., case, Clifford Bailey and James Cogdell escaped from jail, claiming that there had been "various threats and beatings directed at them." In addition, conditions at the jail were deplorable:

> *Inmates . . . and on occasion the guards . . . set fire to trash, bedding, and other objects thrown from the cells. According to the inmates, the guards simply allowed the fires to burn until they went out. . . . [And] poor ventilation caused the smoke to collect and linger in the cellblock.*[47]

COERCIVE THREATS

The defendants also testified that the guards had subjected them to beatings and death threats and that medical attention was inadequate. In response to the charge of escape, they claimed the defense of duress, citing the horrible conditions they had endured in prison.

The U.S. Supreme Court held that duress was not applicable in this case, because the defendants had made no "bonafide effort to surrender or return to custody as soon as the claimed duress or necessity had lost its coercive force." The defendants had been at large for a month or more. Criminal acts committed while under immediate, serious, and nonreckless duress are excused only while the coercive threats are in force. Once the duress has ended, no further criminal conduct is excused.

Necessity In a classic case from the late 1800s, two men and an eighteen-year-old boy were shipwrecked and adrift at sea in a raft for twenty days. After a week without food or water, and with little hope of rescue, the two men decided to kill the boy and eat him so that they could survive. They reasoned that the boy was more expendable because he had no family responsibilities, whereas they did. The two men were rescued four days later.

Were the men guilty of homicide, or could their behavior be excused? They claimed the defense of **necessity,** which argues that a defendant has engaged in otherwise criminal behavior because of the forces of nature. In this case the men were convicted of homicide and sentenced to death—sentences that were later commuted to six months in prison. The court held that people may not save themselves at the expense of another.[48] The defense of necessity is successful only in cases in which the necessity is great, there is no reasonable alternative, and the harm done is less than the harm avoided. In this case a death was caused to prevent other deaths, so the defense was not applicable.

necessity
A defense in which a person claims to have engaged in otherwise criminal behavior because of the forces of nature.

"CHOICE OF EVILS"

Necessity is called the "choice of evils" in the Model Penal Code. This phrasing conveys the principle that harm is done in these cases and that the defense is allowed only where the correct choice is made between degrees of harm. That choice must always be the lesser evil. In a Colorado case an attorney's claim of necessity in response to a charge of speeding was rejected. He claimed that he was late for a court hearing because of delays in a previous hearing elsewhere, but he "failed to establish that he did not cause the situation or that his injuries [penalties for speeding] would outweigh the consequences of his conduct."[49] Nevertheless, one can imagine a circumstance in which speeding might be excused, such as a medical emergency. Here again, the balance between two evils lies at the heart of the defense of necessity.

Mistake of Fact **Mistake of fact** can serve as a defense if it neutralizes the "guilty mind" required for the commission of a crime. The mistake or ignorance must be both honest and reasonable. If a woman mistakenly picked up a purse very similar to her own and walked off with it, she could claim mistake of fact in response to a charge of larceny. In this case the mistake of fact would be a defense because it would negate the *mens rea* element of the crime of larceny. A court would assess the circumstances to determine whether the mistake was both honest and reasonable.

mistake of fact
A defense in which a person claims that honest ignorance rules out the presence of a "guilty mind."

BIGAMY

An interesting exception is the law against bigamy. Both English common law and rulings in some states in this country have upheld bigamy charges even when the defendant has been shown to have had a reasonable belief that a prior

That's a FACT

Perspectives on Liability for the Death of Others

A growing trend in American criminal law is to bring charges against those deemed responsible for the death of others, although they were not present at the scene of the crime. For example, a carnival ride owner was charged with manslaughter when a fifteen-year-old girl was thrown from a ride into a wall and killed. The lap bar on her seat was not secure. It was the first time a carnival ride company was held criminally responsible for causing a death due to a malfunctioning ride.[a] In years past, cases like this were resolved through civil suits in which the responsible party would pay damages (in the form of money) to the victim and/or the victim's family. Criminal charges are now being added as further punishment to the parties found responsible.

Do you see the addition of criminal charges as a positive or negative development in cases like these? In this case the carnival ride owner was not even present at the time of the death. On what grounds can he be held criminally liable?

THIRD-PARTY INVOLVEMENT

Attention is now being paid to third-party involvement in another setting: their contribution or failure to act in cases of violent crime. About two-thirds of rapes, robberies, and assaults occur under circumstances where a third party is present. See Figure 5A. What is the obligation of that third party?

In a New Jersey case, a woman stood by as her boyfriend fatally beat her infant son in a drug-induced rage. She also admitted to watching the child slowly die over the next twenty-four hours and then let the boyfriend burn the body in the fireplace. The couple fled to Florida and were later caught.[b]

Should the mother share criminal liability with the boyfriend? If so, on what grounds? Does it make a difference if the mother feared the boyfriend would turn on her? Explain.

FIGURE 5A Third Party Involvement in Crimes

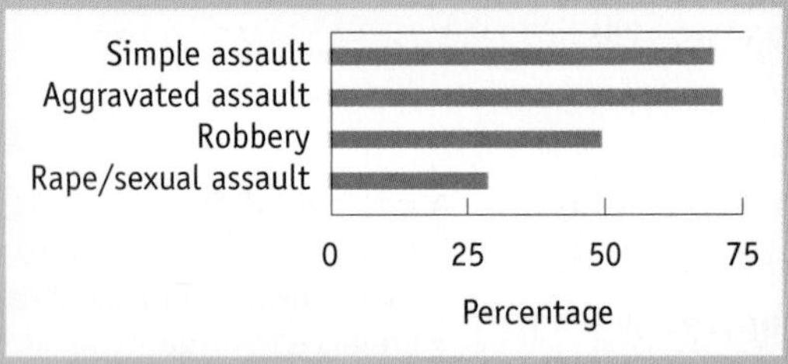

Source: Mike Planty, *Third Party Involvement in Violent Crime* (Washington, DC: Bureau of Justice Statistics, 2002).

CAUSE AND EFFECT

Criminal liability requires a direct link between the act and the harm that results. In most cases this is clear: An offender hits a victim, the victim is injured, and the offender is held criminally responsible for that injury. But in some cases the connection is not so obvious.

In Brooklyn, a man was beaten on the head with a baseball bat by an attacker. The victim, who was five-feet-five-inches tall, was known for his toughness, having earlier gotten the better of his attacker, who was six-feet-three-inches tall and weighed 230 pounds. The bat attack was prompted by the large man's humiliation from the first fight. The man was convicted of aggravated assault and sentenced to five to fifteen years in prison.

The case is interesting because the attack occurred in 1989, but the victim remained in a coma for thirteen years before he ultimately died in 2002.[c] The attacker had served his sentence for aggravated assault and was released from prison years earlier. The district attorney had to decide whether or not to bring new charges.

What possible new charges could the district attorney bring? How can the attacker be criminally liable for a death that occurred from an injury suffered thirteen years earlier?

NOTES

a. "Carnival Ride Owner Guilty in Teen's Death," *apbnews.com* (November 21, 2001).

b. "Mount Holly: Mother Pleads Guilty in Baby's Death," *New York Times* (April 8, 2003).

c. William K. Rashbaum, "In Coma for 13 Years, Beating Victim Dies," *New York Times* (December 26, 2002).

marriage ended in divorce or the death of the previous spouse.[50] This is because bigamy laws often are written as strict liability offenses, in which no *mens rea* is required. Strict liability offenses are exceptions to the guilty mind requirement and therefore are rare.[51] In cases such as bigamy, a person who engages in the criminal conduct, however reasonable the circumstances, still incurs a criminal penalty.

Ignorance or Mistake of Law **Ignorance of law** has rarely been sufficient to excuse criminal conduct. It is permitted as a defense only in situations in which the law is not widely known and a person cannot be expected to be aware of a particular law. These situations are not common; citizens generally are expected to know the law, and a claim of ignorance could be used to excuse virtually any type of illegal conduct. In a California case, Neva Snyder claimed that her conviction for possession of a firearm as a convicted felon should be overturned. She had mistakenly believed that her prior conviction for marijuana sales was only a misdemeanor. The court held that she was "presumed to know" what the law was, so her mistake was not reasonable.[52]

ignorance of law
A defense in which a defendant claims that a law is not widely known and that the person could not have been expected to be aware of it.

In another case an offender failed to register under a local ordinance requiring convicted persons to do so. The U.S. Supreme Court reversed the conviction, stating that ignorance of law could be used as an excuse in this case.[53] Thus, if the ignorance or mistake is reasonable under the circumstances, and if there is no evidence that the defendant should have known of the illegality of the conduct, ignorance or mistake of law can be a defense.[54]

Entrapment The traditional formulation of the defense of **entrapment** was established by the U.S. Supreme Court in 1932. The Court ruled that "entrapment exists if the defendant was not predisposed to commit the crimes in question, and his intent originated with the officials of the government."[55] Because this definition of entrapment focuses on the defendant's frame of mind, it is known as the subjective formulation of the entrapment defense.

entrapment
A defense designed to prevent the government from manufacturing crime by setting traps for unwary citizens.

SUBJECTIVE AND OBJECTIVE FORMULATION

The purpose of the entrapment defense is to prevent government agencies from "manufacturing" crime by setting traps for unwary citizens. The precise activities necessary for entrapment to occur have been the subject of much scrutiny, especially as police undercover tactics have become more common. It should be noted that the entrapment defense is aimed strictly at misconduct on the part of the government. If a private citizen, not associated with the government, entraps another into committing an offense, the entrapment defense is not available.

A second formulation of the entrapment defense, adopted in the Model Penal Code in federal courts and in about half the states, focuses on the conduct of police and its potential to trap innocent persons. This standard is called the *objective formulation* and can be stated as follows: Entrapment occurs when government agents induce or encourage another person to engage in criminal behavior by knowingly making false representations about the lawfulness of the conduct or by employing methods that create a substantial risk that such an offense will be committed by innocent (i.e., unpredisposed) persons. The primary difference between the two formulations is that the objective standard shifts attention from the defendant's frame of mind to the conduct of the police.

THE JACOBSON CASE

The significance of this difference is made clear by an actual case. Keith Jacobson ordered two magazines from a bookstore containing photographs of nude preteen and teenage boys. Finding Jacobson's name on the bookstore's mailing list, the Postal Service and the Customs Service sent mail to him under

A police sting operation is underway where they are working undercover to lure criminals. How do the objective and subjective formulations of entrapment differ in their focus?

the names of five different fictitious organizations and a bogus pen pal. The organizations claimed to represent citizens interested in sexual freedom and opposed to censorship. The proceeds from sales of publications were supposedly used to support lobbying efforts. Jacobson occasionally corresponded with the organizations, expressing his views of censorship and the "hysteria" surrounding child pornography.

The mail sent to Jacobson was designed to elicit a response that would violate the Child Protection Act of 1984, which bars individuals from receiving sexually explicit depictions of children through the mails. After receiving these mailings for more than two years, Jacobson ordered a magazine that depicted young boys engaging in sexual acts; he was arrested under the Child Protection Act. A search of his house revealed no sexually oriented materials except for the magazines and the government agencies' bogus mailings. Jacobson claimed entrapment. He was convicted at trial, but he appealed and had his conviction overturned. The appeal was heard by the U.S. Supreme Court, which based its decision on the subjective formulation of entrapment: The prosecution must prove beyond a reasonable doubt that the defendant was disposed to commit the criminal act *before* being approached by government agents. At the time Jacobson violated the law, he had been the target of twenty-six months of repeated mailings. His earlier bookstore order could not be used to show predisposition, because this act was legal at the time. Moreover, Jacobson's uncontradicted testimony stated that he did not know the magazines would depict minors until they arrived in the mail.

The Supreme Court had previously held that a person's sexual inclinations, tastes, and fantasies are "beyond the reach of the government." In Jacobson's case, the government provoked and aggravated his interest in illegal sexually explicit materials and "exerted substantial pressure" on him to purchase them under the pretense that his purchases would be part of a fight against censorship. Jacobson's conviction was reversed.[56] Government agents "in their zeal to enforce the law . . . may not originate a criminal design" that creates the disposition to commit a criminal act "and then induce commission of the crime so that the government may prosecute."[57] The entrapment defense is designed to prevent this. The split among the states in adopting the objective versus the subjective formulation of the entrapment defense is a primary reason why entrapment, and some police undercover tactics, remain controversial.

What Are Some Concerns about Applying Criminal Law?

The application of the law to actual cases is not always straightforward. Contemporary concerns in criminal law nearly always involve disagreements about how the law ought to be applied to new situations created by major incidents or by advancing technology. This section will examine one example of each type of situation. In each of these contexts the principles of criminal law must be brought to bear to determine the best way to deal with potentially dangerous conduct.

Should breed-specific legislation be permitted against dogs, such as pit bulls? To what extent should laws hold owners liable for the actions of their pets?

Controlling Animals or Owners?

Pit bulls, a breed of dog, were involved in several attacks on humans in recent years. Although accurate statistics do not exist, this type of dog is said to be especially aggressive and has a particularly harmful bite. Some localities have proposed ordinances that single out pit bulls for special licensing, registration, or banning.[58] Others have sought to label them as a "vicious breed," requiring that when on the street or in other public places pit bulls must be muzzled and kept on a six-foot chain with a 300-pound tensile strength. Proposed regulations would require owners of these dogs to carry liability insurance in the amount of $100,000.[59]

Do such ordinances violate the principles of due process set forth in the Constitution, or do they effectively balance the interests of all those involved—pit bull owners and those who might be bitten? It can be seen that the answer is not easy; it requires balancing a responsible owner's interest in possessing a dog against the public's need to be protected from dangerous animals. Questions that have to be answered include: Should the pit bull be singled out? Is it more dangerous than other breeds? Would it make more sense simply to hold owners liable for the actions of all dogs, regardless of breed? If so, under what circumstances should the law apply? What about a fenced or restrained dog that somehow manages to escape? Concerns about the application of the law to achieve due process in a given case are commonplace.

An analogous issue is the trend toward holding parents responsible for the criminal conduct of their children. In South Carolina, for example, a judge ordered a truant daughter and her mother to be tethered by a two-foot rope. Thus far, parental responsibility laws have been created in response to school vandalism and shootings. In some states parents are responsible for up to $300,000 in damages caused by their children. Criminal charges against parents are fewer, because they are difficult to prove. Nevertheless, a father was sentenced to sixty days in jail and paid a fine after his son gave vodka to underage girls in his home while the father was asleep.[60] The boundary between young people's personal responsibility for conduct and the responsibility to be shared by parents is still being debated.

Assisted Suicide or Murder?

Determining the presence of the guilty mind required for criminal liability also can be difficult, as in the case of Dr. Jack Kevorkian. In the 1990s Kevorkian claimed to have provided deadly drugs to 130 terminally ill patients. His work has been alternately called "assisted suicide" and "murder." Many people believe that provision of these drugs allows for "death with dignity." Others believe

Kevorkian is "playing God" and has no right to provide people with the means to hasten their death. The application of the criminal law to this kind of behavior is not uniform, because not all states include these acts in their definition of homicide. The ethics of assisted suicide are still being debated as communities evaluate a patient's right to make the choice and the physician's role in that choice. After a highly publicized televised assisted suicide in 1999, Jack Kevorkian was convicted of second-degree murder in Michigan and sentenced to ten to twenty-five years in prison.[61] Application of the elements of a crime is complicated in these cases, both because the physician plays a passive role (does not administer the drug) and because the patient consents or self-administers a lethal dose. Nevertheless, consent is not a valid defense to the crime of assault or homicide, because the law generally does not permit people to victimize themselves. As a result, the debate has focused on the role of the physician. The state of Oregon passed a law that permits physicians to prescribe lethal medicines to terminally ill patients near the end of their lives. After the first year, only fifteen people had ended their lives with lethal medication; six others obtained the medications but died of their diseases. By 2002, the number of doctor-assisted suicides surged to a five-year high of thirty-eight people.[62] The impact of a law is only one consideration in determining its desirability, of course, as the morality of the action also must be deemed acceptable.

The U.S. Attorney General challenged Oregon's assisted suicide law in court, arguing that physicians who prescribed lethal drug overdoses to terminally ill patients violated federal drug law. In 2006, the U.S. Supreme Court upheld Oregon's controversial assisted suicide law in a 6–3 vote, rejecting a challenge first brought to the Court by then–Attorney General John Ashcroft and continued by his successor Alberto Gonzales. The Court held that the federal Controlled Substances Act does not allow the Attorney General to prohibit doctors from prescribing regulated drugs for use in physician-assisted suicide under a state law permitting the proce-

Dr. Jack Kevorkian claims to have provided deadly drugs to 130 terminally ill patients in cases of "assisted suicide." He was sentenced to prison. How does Oregon law address the role of the physician in cases like these?

dure.[63] Nevertheless, assisted suicide remains a rare procedure that is still unlawful in most states due to continuing questions of consent, physician involvement, and whether a right to die really exists.

CRITICAL THINKING EXERCISES

Justice on the Carolina Frontier (1764)

Before the American Revolution the back country of South Carolina was a lawless place. Because of the remoteness of the region, criminals could operate with impunity. Following is an excerpt from a petition from the Reverend Charles Woodmason to the British government on behalf of the people of his community:

> That for many years past, the back parts of this province have been infested with an infernal gang of villains, who have committed such horrid depredations on our properties and estates, such insults on the persons of many settlers, and perpetrated such shocking outrages throughout the back settlements as is past description.
>
> Our large stocks of cattle are either stolen or destroyed, our cow pens are broken up, and all our valuable horses are carried off. Houses have been burned by these rogues, and families stripped and turned naked into the wood. Stores have been broken open and rifled by them. Private houses have been plundered. . . . Married women have been ravished, virgins deflowered, and other unheard of cruelties committed by these barbarous ruffians, who . . . have hereby reduced numbers of individuals to poverty. . .
>
> No trading persons (or others) with money or goods, no responsible persons and traders dare keep cash or any valuable articles by them. Nor can women stir abroad but with a guard, or in terror. . . . Merchants' stores are obliged to be kept constantly guarded (which enhances the price of goods). And thus we live not as under a British government . . . but as if we were in Hungary or Germany, and in a state of war . . . obliged to be constantly on the watch and on our guard against these intruders and having it not in our power to call what we possess our own, not even for an hour; as being liable daily and hourly to be stripped of our property.
>
> Representations of these grievances and vexations have often been made by us to those in power, but without redress.[a]

CRITICAL THINKING QUESTIONS

1. What characteristics of colonial and frontier justice would you expect to find in South Carolina at the time Woodmason wrote his petition?
2. What ideas from English common law do you expect were already part of criminal law in the colony?
3. How would you respond to this petition to make the community a more just place, knowing that the population was small and could not afford a police force?
4. In the actual petition, Charles Woodmason requested the establishment of a better court system and local jails, a printed criminal code, the requirement that public officials carry out their duty under penalty of law, the founding of public schools, and the establishment of parishes with ministers. How might a printed criminal code and new laws for public officials have been expected to have an impact on the situation in South Carolina?

NOTE

a. Charles Woodmason, "Lawlessness on the South Carolina Frontier" (1764), in *The Annals of America,* vol. 2 (Chicago: Encyclopedia Britannica, 1976), pp. 185–95.

What Are the Crimes of the Century?

At the end of the twentieth century, *U.S. News & World Report* ranked what it found to be cases that at their time in history were considered to be the "crime of the century." One crime was selected for each decade of the century, and they are summarized below. Each crime tells us something about that period in history and the focus of the criminal law and public opinion at that time. From the unemployment, labor unrest, and Prohibition of the early decades of the twentieth century to the shocking serial and mass murders of latter decades, these crimes provide a window for understanding American society and its fascination with crime and criminal law.

1900s—Revenge Killing

Harry Thaw shot Stanford White, the nation's leading architect, in front of dozens of theatergoers watching a musical at Madison Square Garden. White had seduced a woman five years earlier whom Thaw had eventually wed. He was found not guilty by reason of insanity.

1910s—Joe Hill

Joe Hill, a labor union member, was accused of shooting two men in a grocery store. There was question about whether his unpopular union membership was related to his being the prime suspect in the case, and even President Woodrow Wilson asked that Hill be spared, but he was sentenced to death.

1920s—St. Valentine's Day Massacre
It is alleged that some of Al Capone's men dressed as cops and staged a bogus raid in the garage of Bugs Moran's, a Prohibition rival of Al Capone's. Seven men were lined up in the garage and slaughtered with machine guns.

1930s—The Lindbergh Baby
The twenty-month-old son of flying ace Charles Lindbergh was kidnapped from his bedroom. Lindbergh paid a $50,000 ransom, but the baby was found dead two months later. Bruno Hauptmann was arrested two years later and found in possession of the marked ransom money. He was executed.

1940s—The Rosenberg Spy Case
Julius and Ethel Rosenberg, an engineer and his wife in New York City, were Communists accused of spying for the Soviet Union. Their unpopular political affiliation was said by some to be behind the charges. They were both convicted and executed.

1950s—The Lynching of Emmett Till
Emmett Till was a fourteen-year-old black from Chicago visiting relatives in Mississippi. He disappeared and was found brutally murdered. Two white men were charged with the crime, but an all-white, all-male jury acquitted them, after deliberating for only an hour. This case helped to galvanize the civil rights movement.

1960s—Charles Manson
His "family" of followers killed five well-known individuals in a Hollywood home, after beating and stabbing them dozens of times. The next night two other victims were brutally killed in their home in a nearby area. Manson was not at the scene, but later was linked to the crimes. He is serving a life prison term.

1970s—Son of Sam
David Berkowitz terrorized New York City for more than a year, killing six people and wounding seven others with a .44 caliber revolver. He struck randomly at night and often in secluded areas. A parking ticket he received near the scene of one of his crimes ultimately led to his arrest. He pled guilty and was sentenced to twenty-five years to life in prison for each of the six slayings.

1980s—Jeffrey Dahmer
Dahmer was drawn primarily to black and gay young men, whom he took to his apartment and drugged, strangled, and then dismembered. He kept pieces of some of his victims in his refrigerator. He pled guilty and was serving sixteen consecutive life terms when he was beaten to death by other inmates in prison.

1990s—The O.J. Simpson case
Nicole Simpson, the estranged wife of popular former football player O.J. Simpson, and Ron Goldman were slashed to death near Nicole's home in California. There were no witnesses, and a great deal of blood and fiber evidence was handled poorly by police and forensic technicians. After a prolonged televised trial, Simpson was acquitted, but he was later found civilly liable for the deaths and ordered to pay $33.5 million in damages.[a]

CRITICAL THINKING QUESTIONS

1. What criminal laws appear to be in question most often in these "crimes of the century"? How do you explain this fact?
2. How would you explain the changes in the nature of "crimes of the century" over the decades?
3. Can you think of other well-known violations of the criminal law that could be added to this list? Why should they be considered "crimes of the century"?

NOTE

a. Angie Cannon, "Crime Stories of the Century," *U.S. News & World Report* (December 6, 1999), pp. 41–51.

SUMMARY

WHAT IS CRIMINAL LAW?

- In contrast to civil law, the set of formal rules that regulate disputes between private parties, criminal law is the set of formal rules designed to maintain social control.
- Substantive criminal law defines behaviors that are prohibited; procedural law provides the rules for adjudication of cases involving those behaviors.
- The four main sources of criminal law are constitutions, statutes, case law, and administrative regulations.

- Criminal law arises from society's consensus about harmful conduct (consensus view) or is codified to advance the interests of those holding positions of power (conflict view).
- The scope of the criminal law is limited, in that laws must precisely define the behavior that is prohibited and must not contradict constitutional principles.

HOW DID THE AMERICAN SYSTEM OF LAW AND JUSTICE DEVELOP?

- Because there are more than 55,000 independent criminal justice agencies that often do not cooperate with one another, the American criminal justice "system" is often called a nonsystem.
- A system of justice evolves in a society in order to enforce rules, resolve disputes, and administer punishment. In the United States this occurred in the colonial period as small, religiously and culturally similar communities evolved into larger towns and cities with more diverse populations.
- The criminal justice process has two fundamental goals: fairness and accuracy.
- Colonial, revolutionary, and frontier justice was less formal than it is today because of the more sparse and homogenous population in early America.

HOW DOES THE LAW DEFINE THE ELEMENTS OF A CRIME?

- No crime can exist without three elements: *mens rea* ("guilty mind"), *actus reus* (a specific behavior), and attendant circumstances (a specific relationship between the act and the harm that results).
- Five characteristics of acts can invoke criminal sanctions: sufficiency, possession, status, voluntariness, and omission.
- Punishments for violations of criminal law are based on assessment of the offender's state of mind, including degree of recklessness (conscious disregard for a substantial and unjustifiable risk) and intention (whether the act was carried out knowingly or purposely).
- For an act to be considered a crime, the harm suffered must have occurred *because of* the act, and the act must be the proximate or direct cause of the harm.

WHAT DEFENSES AGAINST CRIMINAL CHARGES DOES THE LAW RECOGNIZE?

- A defense based on the claim that the defendant was not sane at the time of the act is referred to as the insanity defense. Although the Model Penal Code proposes a specific test for legal insanity, in practice the determination of insanity is highly subjective. Some states have adopted a finding of "guilty but mentally ill."
- Defenses involving force are of three types: self-defense, defense of others, and defense of property.
- Defenses involving justification or excuse include duress, necessity, mistake of fact, ignorance of law, and entrapment.
- The subjective formulation of the entrapment defense focuses on the defendant's state of mind; the objective formulation focuses on the conduct of police and its potential to cause innocent persons to engage in criminal conduct.

WHAT ARE SOME CONCERNS ABOUT APPLYING CRIMINAL LAW?

- Special concerns arise when the law must be applied to new situations, changing values, and new technologies.

KEY TERMS

civil law *99*
criminal law *99*
substantive criminal law *99*
procedural law *99*
constitutions *100*
statutes *100*
ordinances *100*
criminal (penal) code *100*
case law *100*
precedents *100*
administrative regulations *100*
consensus view *101*
conflict view *101*
jurisdiction *101*
common law *103*
criminal justice system *103*
due process (constitutional) *105*
mens rea *107*
actus reus *107*
criminal liability *109*
constructive possession *109*
actual possession *109*
reasonableness standard *111*
intention *111*
insanity defense *112*
battered woman syndrome *115*
duress *116*
necessity *117*
mistake of fact *117*
ignorance of law *119*
entrapment *119*

QUESTIONS FOR REVIEW AND DISCUSSION

1. Distinguish between civil and criminal law and give an example of each.
2. Name and describe the four main sources of criminal law.
3. What is meant by *mens rea* and *actus reus*?
4. Describe the five characteristics of acts that can be sufficient to invoke criminal sanctions.
5. Define recklessness and intention. How do these terms relate to the determination of *mens rea*?
6. How has the legal definition of insanity changed since the M'Naghten case of 1843?
7. What degree of force is permitted in defense of property in one's own home during a dangerous felony?
8. What conditions must be met for a claim of duress to succeed as a defense?
9. Distinguish between the subjective and objective formulations of the entrapment defense.

NOTES

1. Vianna Davila, "Bleacher Cameraman's Arrest Puts Focus on Voyeurism Law," *San Antonio Express-News* (November 14, 2005).
2. Emile Durkheim, *The Division of Labor in Society* (New York: The Free Press, 1893), p. 80.
3. William J. Chambliss, *Power, Politics, and Crime* (New York: Westview Press, 2001).
4. *Papachristou v. Jacksonville,* 92 S. Ct. 839 (1972). See also *State v. Palendrano,* 120 N.J. Superior 336 (1972).
5. Deborah Sharp, "Cruising Taking a Bruising in Miami Beach," *USA Today* (September 1, 1993), p. 9; *City of Chicago v. Morales,* 119 S.Ct. 1849 (1999).
6. Richard Price, "Helmet Law Jolts Motorcyclists," *USA Today* (December 31, 1991), p. 3; Jeanne DeQuine, "Miami Case Tests Child Car-Seat Laws," *USA Today* (April 29, 1991), p. 3; Fawn Germer, "The Helmet Issue—Again," *U.S. News & World Report* (June 19, 2000), p. 30.
7. Jonathan Schonsheck, *On Criminalization: An Essay in the Philosophy of Criminal Law* (Boston: Kluwer Academic, 1994).
8. Ted Gest, "Cracking the States' Secret Codes," *U.S. News & World Report* (May 22, 2000), p. 83.
9. Robert Tanner, "Wave of New Laws Rolls into States This Weekend," *USA Today* (June 30, 2000), p. 8; "About 440 New Laws Take Effect Tuesday," *Associated Press State & Local Wire* (August 14, 2006).
10. Lawrence M. Friedman, *A History of American Criminal Law* (New York: Simon & Schuster, 1973).
11. Lawrence M. Friedman, *Crime and Punishment in American History* (New York: Basic Books, 1993), pp. 22–23.
12. Daniel L. Skoler, *Governmental Structuring of Criminal Justice Services: Organizing the Non-System* (Washington, DC: U.S. Government Printing Office, 1978).
13. Reverend James B. Britton, "The Practice of Dueling in View of Human and Divine Law," preached before the Congregation of Christ Church, Indianapolis, March 25, 1838. Cited in Susan Jacoby, *Wild Justice: The Evolution of Revenge* (New York: Harper Colophon, 1984).
14. Les Johnson, "What Is Vigilantism?," *British Journal of Criminology* 36 (spring 1996); "No Place for Vigilantism in Our Towns," *Hartford Courant* (May 22, 1998), p. 18; Joshua Getzler, "Use of Force in Protecting Property," *Theoretical Inquiries in Law*, vol. 7 (January 2006), p. 131.
15. Herbert Packer, *The Limits of the Criminal Sanction* (Stanford, CA: Stanford University Press, 1968).
16. Charles L. Gould, "The Criminal Justice System Favors Offenders," in Bonnie Szumski, ed., *Criminal Justice: Opposing Viewpoints* (St. Paul, MN: Greenhaven Press, 1997), pp. 33–39.
17. John Locke, *Concerning the True Original Extent and End of Civil Government* (Chicago: Encyclopedia Britannica, 1952).
18. George H. Smith, *The American Revolution* (Nashville, TN: Knowledge Products, 1989); Leonard W. Levy, *Seasoned Judgments: The American Constitution, Rights, and History* (New Brunswick, NJ: Transaction, 1995).
19. Jonah Blank, "Guilty—but Just How Guilty?," *U.S. News & World Report* (January 12, 1998), p. 21.
20. See Joel Samaha, *Criminal Law,* 8th ed. (St. Paul, MN: West, 2005); Thomas J. Gardner and Terry M. Anderson, *Criminal Law: Principles and Cases,* 9th ed. (St. Paul, MN: West, 2006).
21. *State v. Bugger,* 25 Utah 2d 404, Sup. Ct. of Utah (1971).
22. *State v. McMenamin,* 133 N.J. Superior 521 (1975).
23. *Robinson v. California,* 82 S. Ct. 1417 (1962). See also *Powell v. Texas,* 88 S. Ct. 2145 (1968).
24. *Commonwealth of Massachusetts Middlesex Superior Court Criminal No. 97–0433 v. Memorandum and Order Louise Woodward* (November 10, 1997).
25. Rob Parrish, "The Proof Is in the Details," *Shaken Baby Syndrome* (winter 1998).
26. *Commonwealth v. Howard,* 265 Pa. Superior 535 (1979); *Jones v. United States,* 308 F. 2d 307, D.C. Cir. (1962).
27. *State v. Nosis,* 22 Ohio App. 2d 16, Ct. Appeals of Ohio (1969).
28. *Dusky v. United States,* 80 S. Ct. 788 (1960).
29. See *Jackson v. Indiana,* 92 S. Ct. 1845 (1972); Richard J. Bonnie et al., "Decision-Making in Criminal Defense: An Empirical Study of Insanity Pleas and the Impact of Doubted Client Competence," *Journal of Criminal Law and Criminology* 87 (fall 1996), pp. 48–62.
30. *M'Naghten's Case,* 8 Eng. Rep. 718 (1843).
31. David Rohde, "Insanity Defense Puts Big Burden on Juries," *New York Times* (October 11, 1999), p. 1; Ralph Slovenko, *Psychiatry and Criminal Culpability* (New York: Wiley, 1995).
32. Norval Morris, *Madness and the Criminal Law* (Chicago: University of Chicago Press, 1982).
33. See Henry J. Steadman, *Beating a Rap?* (Chicago: University of Chicago Press, 1979); Henry J. Steadman, Margaret A. McGreevey, Joseph P. Morrissey, and Lisa A. Callahan, *Before and After Hinckley: Evaluating Insanity Defense Reform* (New York: Guilford Press, 1994).

34. Norval Morris, *Insanity Defense* (Washington, DC: National Institute of Justice, 1979); Ralph Slovenko, *Psychiatry and Criminal Culpability* (New York: John Wiley & Sons, 1995).
35. Henry J. Steadman et al., eds. *Before and after Hinckley: Evaluating Insanity Defense Reform* (New York: Guilford Press, 1994); Steadman, *Beating a Rap?*; *Jones v. United States*, 103 S. Ct. 3043 (1983).
36. Gordon Witkin, "What Does It Take to Be Crazy?," *U.S. News & World Report* (January 12, 1998), p. 7.
37. Debra T. Landis, " 'Guilty but Mentally Ill' Statutes: Validity and Construction," *American Law Reports* 702 (1991).
38. Jonathan Turley, "Insanity's Fall from Legal Grace," *USA Today* (May 30, 2006), p. 13A.
39. *Clark v. Arizona*, 126 S. Ct. 2709 (2006).
40. *Mullin v. Pence*, 390 So. 2d 803, Ct. App. La. (1974).
41. Robert Tanner, "States Signing on to Deadly Force Law," *Washington Post* (May 24, 2006); Richard Willing, "States Allow Deadly Self-Defense," *USA Today* (April 1, 2006); Adam Liptak, "15 States Expand Right to Shoot in Self-Defense," *The New York Times* (August 7, 2006).
42. *State v. Kelly*, 97 N. J. 178 (1978).
43. Faith McNulty, *The Burning Bed* (New York: Bantam, 1981).
44. Linda Deutsch, "Menendez Brothers Get Life," *Detroit News* (July 3, 1996). Ron Soble and John H. Johnson, *Bad Blood: The Inside Story of the Menendez Murders* (London: Onyx Books, 1994).
45. *Commonwealth v. Martin*, 369 Mass. 640, Sup. Ct. (1976).
46. *People v. Ceballos*, 12 Cal. 3d 470, Sup. Ct. (1974).
47. *U.S. v. Bailey*, 100 S. Ct. 624 (1980). See *U.S. v. Webb*, 747 F. 2d 278, cert. denied 105 S. Ct. 1222 (1984).
48. *Regina v. Dudley and Stephens*, 14 Q.B.D. 273 (1884).
49. *People v. Dover*, 790 P. 2d 834 (Col. Sup. Ct. 1990).
50. *Crown v. Tolson*, 23 Q.B.D. 168 (1889); *Stuart v. Commonwealth*, 11 Va. App. 216 (1990).
51. Kenneth W. Simons, "When Is Strict Liability Just?," *Journal of Criminal Law and Criminology* 87 (1997), pp. 1075–1137.
52. *People v. Snyder*, 186 Cal. Rptr. 485 (Cal. 1982).
53. *Lambert v. California*, 78 S. Ct. 240 (1957).
54. Douglas Husak and Andrew von Hirsch, "Culpability and Mistake of Law," in S. Shute, J. Gardner, and J. Horder, eds., *Action and Value in Criminal Law* (New York: Oxford University Press, 1993), pp. 157–74.
55. *Sorrells v. United States*, 53 S. Ct. 210 (1932).
56. *Jacobson v. United States*, 112 S. Ct. 1535 (1992).
57. *U.S. v. Russell*, 93 S. Ct. 1637 (1973).
58. Kris Antonelli, "Fearing Attacks, Long Reach Residents Seek Ban on Pit Bulls," *Baltimore Sun* (December 13, 1999), p. 1B; John Castellucci, "Ban on Pit Bulls Gains Support," *Providence Journal-Bulletin* (September 25, 2003), p. D1.
59. David, Plata, "Vicious Dog Law Is Being Opposed," *Sun Newspapers* (March 12, 1998); Amy Klein, "Pit Bulls Kill Woman," *The Bergan Record* (December 11, 2001), p. A1.
60. Joanne M. Schrof, "Who's Guilty?," *U.S. News & World Report* (May 17, 1999), p. 40.
61. Joseph P. Shapiro, "Dr. Death's Last Dance," *U.S. News & World Report* (April 26, 1999), p. 44.
62. Joseph P. Shapiro, "Casting a Cold Eye on 'Death with Dignity,' " *U.S. News & World Report* (March 11, 1999), p. 56; Don Colburn, "Assisted Suicide Numbers Surge," *The Oregonian* (March 6, 2003), p. A.
63. *Gonzales v. Oregon*, 126 S. Ct. 904 (2006).

chapter 6

The Criminal Justice System

The process of justice: our system of justice begins with law and proceeds from crimes to arrest, court procedures, and sentencing—illustrating how fairness and balance are central to the process.

CHAPTER OUTLINE

What Are the Agencies of Criminal Justice?
- Law Enforcement
- Courts
- Corrections

What Is Procedural Law?
- Law, Investigation, and Arrest
- The Fourth Amendment and Probable Cause
- Arrest

What Is Involved in Criminal Court Procedure?
- Initial Appearance and Preliminary Hearing
- Grand Jury, Indictment, Arraignment
- Trial and Conviction
- Sentencing and Appeals

What Are Some Concerns about the Criminal Justice System?
- The Cost of Justice
- Fairness in Adjudication

THAT'S A FACT:
Perspectives on Fairness in the Criminal Justice System

MEDIA AND CRIMINAL JUSTICE:
The Star Chamber

CRITICAL THINKING EXERCISES:
- The Limits of Drug Testing
- Addressing Violence in Entertainment

LEARNING OBJECTIVES

- Identify and distinguish federal, state, and local law enforcement agencies in the United States.
- Identify and distinguish federal, state, and local court systems in the United States.
- Identify and distinguish federal, state, and local correctional facilities in the United States.
- Characterize the criminal justice process as a filter.
- Define procedural law and explain the sources of procedural law in the United States.
- Trace the steps in the criminal justice process leading to an arrest.
- Trace the steps in criminal court procedure leading to an indictment and trial.
- Distinguish four alternatives defendants have in making a plea.
- Trace the steps in criminal court procedure leading to the disposition of a case.
- Discuss the cost of justice and fairness in adjudication as two contemporary concerns about the criminal justice system.

New York and other major cities experienced a remarkable drop in the crime rate during the late 1990s and early 2000s. The drop was attributed in part to more aggressive police tactics against minor offenses that affect the quality of life: drinking in public, playing loud music, urinating in public, jumping subway turnstiles, loitering. It turned out that many of those arrested for these minor crimes were also wanted for more serious crimes. But these aggressive police tactics involved stopping people on the street and requesting identification, conducting drug sweeps of entire neighborhoods, and frisking people. These tactics drew considerable criticism because they created at least temporary infringements on the privacy of many innocent persons.

As one neighborhood organizer said, "In the beginning we all wanted the police to bomb the crack houses, but now it's backfiring at the cost of the community. I think the cops have been given free rein to intimidate people at large."[1] Police were alleged to be pulling people out of cars at gunpoint, roughing up those who didn't speak English, frisking citizens for no clear reason, conducting searches in an abusive manner, selectively harassing minorities, and using force without provocation. These specific complaints against police all resulted from an effort to *reduce* crime in New York City.

Complaints against police grew considerably not only in New York, but in Pittsburgh; Charlotte, North Carolina; Washington, D.C., and elsewhere—in each case alleging overly aggressive police tactics in the effort to reduce crime.[2] These charges are serious, and they reflect a dilemma that lies at the heart of the American criminal justice system: What is the best way to balance the rights of individuals to be left alone against the community's interest in apprehending criminals? This dilemma is most evident in the activities of police, because of their continual interaction with the public.

This balance between individual and community interests also must be struck in the decision to formally charge a person with a crime, in the determination of guilt or innocence at trial, and in sentencing and prison release decisions. The entire criminal justice system is designed to provide a mechanism for achieving this balance in a just manner. This chapter will examine the agencies, laws, and procedures that are devoted to this task—even though they sometimes fall short of achieving their goal.

What Are the Agencies of Criminal Justice?

The contemporary structure of law enforcement, courts, and corrections institutionalizes basic notions of how law should be enforced and adjudicated and how violators should be dealt with. The nation's history as a democracy has guided the establishment of criminal justice agencies, which have been granted the power to intrude into the lives of citizens only under certain circumstances. In addition, many criminal justice agencies exist on the local level, and local control helps prevent these agencies from becoming too powerful or abusive. As a result, the United States has perhaps more criminal justice agencies than any other nation, including more than 19,000 police departments, 17,000 courts, and 6,000 correctional facilities centered largely in local government. These agencies have in common criminal law and criminal procedure, which specify the types of acts over which the system has jurisdiction and the precise way that individual cases are to be handled.

policing
Enforcing the law by apprehending violators and thereby protecting citizens. Crime prevention and social services such as education of the public are more recent emphases in law enforcement.

limited jurisdiction
The jurisdiction of courts that have narrow legal authority over specific types of matters (e.g., surrogate court, tax court).

general jurisdiction
The jurisdiction of courts where most trials for felonies occur, as well as trials in major civil cases.

appellate jurisdiction
The jurisdiction of courts that review specific legal issues raised in trial courts.

Law Enforcement

Law enforcement agencies exist at all levels of government: federal, state, and local. In each case, however, these agencies' duties are the same. We generally expect law enforcement agencies to perform four tasks: protect people and their rights, apprehend those who violate laws, prevent crimes, and provide social services. The first two responsibilities are traditionally associated with the function of **policing;** that is, enforcing the law by apprehending violators and thereby protecting citizens. Crime prevention and social services such as education of the public are more recent emphases in policing.

The only difference between law enforcement agencies at different levels of government is in the types of laws they enforce. Federal law enforcement officers are charged with enforcing federal laws; state police enforce state laws; and local police must enforce both state and local laws. As Figure 6.1 shows, the majority of police agencies and police officers are at the local level of government, which includes towns, cities, metropolitan districts, and counties.

FIGURE 6.1
Law Enforcement in the United States

Federal Law Enforcement
17 major agencies
70,000 officers

State Law Enforcement
49 agencies
60,000 officers

Local Law Enforcement
19,000 agencies
500,000 officers

Courts

In criminal courts, legal responsibility is determined through interpretation of the law in relation to the circumstances of individual cases. More than 17,000 courts and related agencies operate in the United States, mostly at the state and local levels. These courts can be grouped into the federal court system (courts that interpret federal law) and a state court system (courts that interpret state and local laws). Both the state and the federal court systems have three basic types of jurisdiction. Courts of **limited jurisdiction** have narrow legal authority and may arbitrate only in certain types of disputes; these include family courts, municipal courts, and special courts such as tax courts. Courts of **general jurisdiction,** on the other hand, usually are referred to as trial courts. These are the courts in which felonies and civil cases go to trial. General jurisdiction courts across the country may be called county courts, circuit courts, and even supreme courts in some jurisdictions. The highest level of jurisdiction is **appellate jurisdiction.** Appellate courts review specific legal issues raised by cases in courts with general jurisdiction. An appellate court may uphold or reverse a conviction in a criminal case tried in a trial court. Figure 6.2 illustrates the court system structure. The sequence in which a case moves from a trial court to an appellate court occurs in every state and in the federal court system, although the names of the courts vary.

The U.S. Supreme Court is the appellate court of last resort in the United States. It has nine justices who are appointed by the president. The U.S. Supreme Court can hear on appeal any case involving federal law, suits between states, and cases involving interpretations of the U.S. Constitution. The decisions of the U.S.

These are nine current justices of the U.S. Supreme Court. Do you know their names? The Court's caseload has increased steadily to a current total of more than 7,000 cases on the docket per term. Case review, with oral arguments by attorneys, is granted in only about 100 cases per year. Formal written opinions are delivered in about 80 to 90 cases.

FIGURE 6.2 The Court System

Supreme Court cannot be appealed further, and the Supreme Court can also choose *not* to review a case if it so desires. In fact, of the more than 7,000 cases that reach the U.S. Supreme Court each year, more than three-fourths are not heard. When the Supreme Court decides not to review a case, the previous court's ruling stands as the final decision.

Corrections

Like law enforcement, the correctional system exists at all three levels of government: local, state, and federal. There are more than 6,000 correctional facilities in the United States. Of these, nearly 3,400 are **local jails,** of which the vast majority are administered by counties. Usually operated by the county sheriff, a local jail is used to detain adults awaiting trial and offenders serving sentences of one year or less.

When offenders convicted in state courts are sentenced to periods of imprisonment, they usually are sent to the state correctional system. The state system includes prisons and prison farms and camps as well as community-based facilities such as halfway houses, work release centers, and drug and alcohol treatment facilities. About 95 percent of offenders sentenced to state correctional systems are incarcerated in prisons or other locked facilities. Nearly 60 percent of all persons incarcerated in the United States on a given day are held in state facilities.

Many offenders are placed on **probation,** which involves serving a sentence in the community under the supervision of a probation officer. There are more than 4.1 million offenders on probation in the United States today, 750,000 in jail, and 1.5 million in prison.[3] These numbers are at record levels, indicating the extent to which the correctional system is used to deal with offenders.

The criminal justice system includes individuals and agencies that serve as links between law enforcement and the courts, such as prosecutors and defense counsel, and between the courts and corrections, such as parole agencies. These agencies will be considered in later chapters.

local jails
Facilities used to detain adults awaiting trial and offenders serving sentences of one year or less.

probation
A system under which a person convicted of a crime serves a sentence in the community under the supervision of a probation officer.

THE CRIMINAL JUSTICE PROCESS

It is useful to think of the criminal justice process as a *filter.* The law, police, courts, and corrections each capture their share of law violators. The law itself casts the widest filter, reflecting the large number of behaviors that are illegal. The police arrest some law violators, depending on priorities, resources, public policies, and other factors. The courts find some offenders guilty and sentence them, and the corrections system carries out those sentences. As shown in Figure 6.3, decisions at the stages of arrest, preliminary hearing, grand jury, arraignment, trial, and sentencing represent the major decision points in the criminal justice process. Each step acts as a filter, pushing through serious cases that also have sufficient evidence to prove them. When cases are not serious, or when there is insufficient evidence for prosecution, the case is filtered out. Sometimes a serious case makes it a long way through the system, only to end in an acquittal at trial because the evidence was weak. At other times, a nonserious case may go on to a preliminary hearing or grand jury, where a judge or jury may determine that the case is not worthy of further prosecution. Thus, the filters provide multiple opportunities for the system to correct itself as a case moves through it. Because of the many actors involved (politicians, police, prosecutors, judges, and juries), there is room for con-

FIGURE 6.3 **The Criminal Justice Filter**

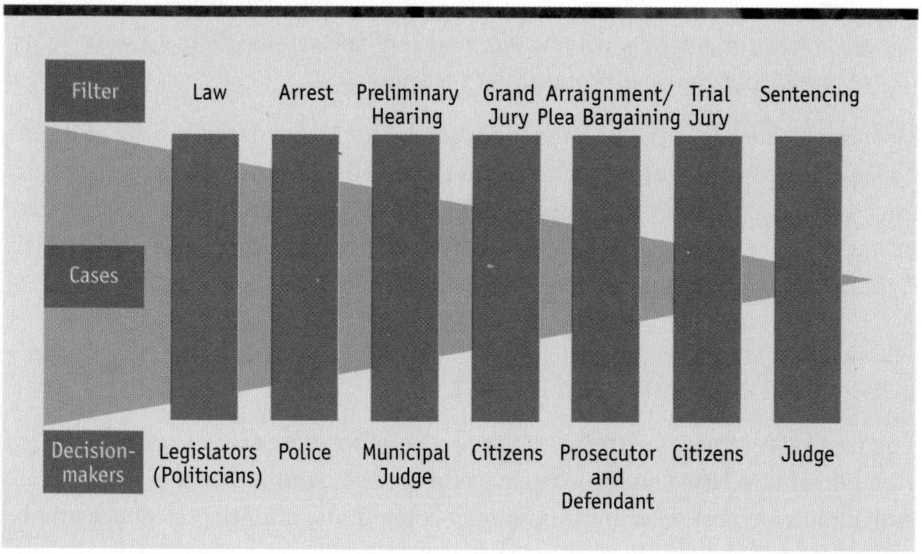

fusion or error in any given case. The rules of criminal procedure provide a way to ensure that *most* offenders whose cases make it all the way through the system are actually guilty.

What Is Procedural Law?

Procedural law is a very important part of the criminal justice process, because it specifies how people accused of crimes will be treated. As in substantive law (see Chapter 5), the provisions of criminal procedure are guided by the principles of the U.S. Constitution. The **Bill of Rights**—the first ten amendments to the Constitution—details many of the requirements for adjudication, such as arrests, warrants, searches, trials, lawyers, punishment, and other important aspects of criminal procedure. The purpose of the Bill of Rights is to protect the individual citizen against arbitrary use of power by the government. Table 6.1 lists the Bill of Rights Amendments that relate directly to procedural law.

THE BILL OF RIGHTS

Bill of Rights
The first ten amendments to the Constitution—details many of the requirements for adjudication, such as arrests, warrants, searches, trials, lawyers, punishment, and other important aspects of criminal procedure.

Table 6.1 **Bill of Rights Provisions Relating to Procedural Law**

Amendment	*Guarantee*
Fourth	Protection against unreasonable searches and seizures.
Fourth	No warrants except upon probable cause.
Fifth	A person shall not be compelled to be a witness against himself or herself.
Fifth and Fourteenth	Life, liberty, and property shall not be taken away without due process of law.
Eighth	Cruel and unusual punishments shall not be inflicted.

Although the Bill of Rights was added to the Constitution more than 200 years ago, it had little impact on the administration of justice until the 1960s. This situation existed because the majority of all criminal law is state law, whereas the Constitution is a federal document. For much of the nation's history the Bill of Rights was interpreted as protecting citizens against mistreatment by the federal government, rather than by state or local governments. After the Civil War, however, the Fourteenth Amendment was added to the Constitution. It states that

> *No State shall make or enforce any law which shall abridge the privileges or immunities of citizens of the United States; nor shall any State deprive any person of life, liberty, or property, without due process of law; nor deny any person within its jurisdiction the equal protection of the laws.*

Most people have read the Fourteenth Amendment to mean that the Bill of Rights applies to the states, but it was not until the 1960s that the U.S. Supreme Court interpreted it in this way. The important phrase in this amendment is "due process of law"; the due process clause means that individuals cannot be denied their rights as citizens without adjudication according to law.

Law, Investigation, and Arrest

The first requirement of the criminal justice process is, of course, a suspected violation of law, based on the existence of a specific criminal law. For example, an individual who possesses marijuana may come to the attention of police and be subject to the criminal justice process. If it is not illegal to possess marijuana, however, the criminal justice system plays no role. Thus, the law makes possible all the subsequent steps in the process by providing the raw material that feeds the criminal justice process. As the number of laws increases, so does the potential number of cases to be handled by the system.

POLICE INVESTIGATION

Breaking the law, however, is no guarantee of becoming subject to the criminal justice process. Not only must lawbreaking occur; it must be made known to the police. If the police do not know of the criminal act, the perpetrator will not be subject to the criminal justice process.

The first action to be taken by the police is an investigation, which may be the most important part of a case once it enters the criminal justice process. Although it seems obvious, the first fact to be ascertained is whether or not a crime has been committed. Naturally, if a police officer hears a gunshot, enters the room, and finds a body on the floor with a person standing over it holding a smoking gun, it is safe to assume that a crime may have been committed. In most instances, however, police respond to calls from citizens *after* a crime has been committed; only rarely do they see a serious crime in progress. As a result, police often must reconstruct an incident from the accounts of victims and witnesses in order to determine whether a crime was actually committed. As it turns out, many of the complaints to which police respond are unfounded: Property reported stolen is actually misplaced or lost, suspicious noises outside are not burglars, and suspicious persons reported to police have committed no crime.

The Fourth Amendment and Probable Cause

Perhaps the most intrusive authority possessed by police is their ability to search citizens and their belongings and to seize people's possessions. When a suspect is arrested, a search usually is conducted. Questions often arise regarding the scope of the police authority to search, its limits, and the circumstances in which a search may or may not be appropriate. When these questions are raised in a par-

What law protects the occupants of this dwelling against unreasonable search and seizure? Under what circumstances could these officers enter the dwelling to conduct a search to gather evidence to make an arrest? Under what circumstances could they search a student at school?

ticular case, they inevitably refer back to a single source: the **Fourth Amendment** to the Constitution. This amendment provides the guidelines and underlying principles for all law and policy regarding search and seizures by police:

> *The right of people to be secure in their persons, houses, papers, and effects, against unreasonable searches and seizures, shall not be violated, and no warrants shall issue but upon probable cause, supported by oath or affirmation, and particularly describing the place to be searched, and the persons or things to be seized.*

Fourth Amendment
Amendment to the Constitution that prohibits searches without probable cause.

Individuals thus are protected against searches and seizures conducted without a warrant specifying "probable cause." This provision goes back to the nation's early years. The ability of British soldiers to enter homes in America and seize property at will played a significant role in the colonists' movement toward independence. Without the protection of the Fourth Amendment, government agents could conduct searches in an arbitrary fashion. The Fourth Amendment created a standard—probable cause—by which the privacy of individuals would be protected.

Probable cause has been interpreted to mean a reasonable link between a specific person and a particular crime, given the "totality of circumstances."[4] It is a lower standard than that required for conviction at trial (proof beyond a reasonable doubt), but it is higher than the standard required for frisking of a suspect (reasonable suspicion). If police have evidence that establishes probable cause, they write it in a sworn statement, a statement supported by "oath or affirmation." When a judge signs this statement, it becomes a **warrant.** Issuance of a warrant indicates that the judge agrees with the officers' assessment of the evidence. It also means that there is little chance that the evidence will be thrown out of court at a later date, because the judge has approved the warrant *before* the search.

probable cause
A reasonable link between a specific person and a particular crime; the legal threshold required before police can arrest or search an individual.

warrant
A sworn statement by police that attests to the existence of probable cause in a given case; it is signed by a judge who agrees with the officers' assessment of the facts.

Arrest

Once it is established that a crime has been committed, evidence is collected to support the case and a search for the offender is begun. If the police do not find a suspect, no arrest is made; the case remains "open" until a suspect is found. Continuing investigations are conducted by police detectives. One of the most serious problems facing police is their low rate of solving (or "clearing") crimes by making arrests. For the criminal justice process to continue, however, a suspect must be found and must be placed under arrest. An **arrest** involves taking a suspected law violator into custody for the purpose of prosecution. To carry out a valid arrest, a police officer must have probable cause to believe that a specific person committed a particular illegal act. This requires a reasonable link between the person and the crime. The police officer must have more than mere suspicion as a basis for linking a person to an act but does not need to be certain beyond a reasonable doubt.

arrest
Process of taking a suspect into custody for the purpose of prosecution.

Following an arrest, the suspect is booked. **Booking** is a procedure in which an official record of the arrest is made. Fingerprints and photographs of the suspect are usually taken at this point. For minor offenses, such as traffic violations, a citation is issued and the suspect is not taken into custody. A **summons** or citation is a written notice to appear in court. It documents the offense charged, the person suspected, and the time and place at which the person must appear in court. After signing the citation, thereby agreeing to appear in court, the person charged is entitled to be released pending the court appearance.

booking
A procedure in which an official record of the arrest is made.

summons
A written notice to appear in court.

What Is Involved in Criminal Court Procedure?

Criminal procedure provides the legal linkage among the agencies of the criminal justice system. It specifies the rules by which individual cases are to be adjudicated. Once arrested, a suspect's liberty is at stake, so criminal court procedure is designed to safeguard the rights of the suspect while also protecting the interests of the community at large.

Initial Appearance and Preliminary Hearing

After an arrest and booking, the suspect must be brought before a judge within a reasonable period of time. In many states the time limit is forty-eight hours, excluding Sundays and holidays. This limit was established in response to past injustices in which arrestees were held in jail for long periods without knowledge of the charges against them and without an opportunity to post bail. At the initial appearance, which usually takes place in municipal court, the arrestees are given formal notice of the charge(s) for which they are being held. The suspects are also informed again of their legal rights, such as the right to legal counsel and the protection against self-incrimination.

THE BAIL SYSTEM

bail
A form of pretrial release where the court holds money or property to ensure that the arrestee will appear for trial.

Bail is set at the initial appearance in order to ensure that the arrestee will appear in court for trial. An arrestee who posts bail remains free pending the court appearance. Bail is posted in the form of cash or its equivalent, which is refunded when the arrestee appears for trial. For instance, if the judge sets bail at $1,000, a person with access to that amount of money or a property owner with equity of $2,000 will go free until trial. Most arrestees do not have sufficient money or property to make bail, however, and must rely on bail posted by a bail bondsman; this is known as a **surety.** For a fee, the bail bondsman will post bail for the arrestee. When the arrestee appears for trial, the court gives the money back to the bondsman, who charges the arrestee 10 percent of the amount for the use of the money.

An initial appearance is where the accused stands before a judge. What happens at an initial appearance? At what point in the criminal justice process does the suspect get the opportunity to present evidence of his innocence?

Sometimes, if the risk of forfeiture appears too great, a bail bondsman will refuse to post bail. In such cases, unless the money can be obtained from other sources, the arrestee will be held in custody until the criminal proceedings have been completed. In some states it is assumed that persons who are charged with serious crimes or who have criminal records will not appear for trial and that they pose a threat to the community. These persons are denied bail, unless a judge can be convinced the person is not likely to disappear or commit crimes while on bail. Because the bail system relies exclusively on cash or its equivalent, it can be said to discriminate against poor people. And in fact, the overwhelming majority of people in jail awaiting trial are poor.

surety
Bail posted by a bondsman on behalf of an arrestee.

Most states allow judges to release suspects *on their own recognizance.* This means that a judge can release a suspect pending trial after receiving the suspect's written promise to appear in court. It is within the judge's discretion, however, later to require bail or to increase the bail amount. In setting bail the judge may consider the seriousness of the crime charged as well as the arrestee's prior criminal record, employment history, family ties, and financial burdens or obligations.

If the crime charged is within the jurisdiction of a municipal court, the arrestee may also be asked to make a **plea,** a statement of innocence or guilt, at the initial appearance. For minor crimes this appearance is sometimes called an **arraignment.** The judge then sets a date for trial in municipal court.

plea
A statement of innocence or guilt.

arraignment
A hearing where the defendant is informed of the charges and of his or her rights and enters a plea.

In the case of a serious crime, the criminal procedure is more extensive and the trial is heard in a higher (general jurisdiction) court. Following the initial appearance, the next step of criminal justice procedure is the preliminary hearing (or "probable cause" hearing): an appearance in court at which a judge determines whether there is probable cause to hold the arrestee for trial. On behalf of the police, the prosecutor presents evidence against the accused person. The arrestee is present and may be represented by an attorney, who has the right to cross-examine witnesses and present evidence showing that the defendant is innocent. If the judge is convinced that there is probable cause to believe that a crime has been committed and that the person charged committed it, the case is bound over for trial. If the judge does not find the evidence convincing enough to establish probable cause, the complaint is dismissed and the defendant is released.

Before trial a defendant must be formally accused based on a determination of probable cause. This formal step occurs in either of two ways: through an

information
A formal accusation of a crime filed by a prosecutor based on the findings of a preliminary hearing.

information, which is a formal accusation filed by a prosecutor based on the findings of a preliminary hearing, or through an indictment, discussed in the next section.

Grand Jury, Indictment, Arraignment

grand jury
A group of citizens who hear the evidence presented by a prosecutor to determine whether probable cause exists to hold a person for trial.

A **grand jury** consists of a group of citizens who hear the evidence presented by a prosecutor to determine whether probable cause exists to hold a person for trial. The grand jury system was originated in England to prevent the holding of accused persons without justification. Following this common law tradition, grand juries in the United States consist of sixteen to twenty-three people, who are usually selected from voter registration rolls in the same way as members of trial juries. Evidence is presented by the prosecutor, and members of the grand jury can question witnesses. The defendant is not permitted to attend grand jury proceedings, and all grand jury hearings are secret.

GRAND JURY ABUSES

The secrecy of grand jury proceedings, together with the absence of defense counsel, can lead to abuses. Grand juries often act as a "rubber stamp" for prosecutors, according to Abraham Blumberg, "since in practice grand juries tend to ratify the charges that are presented to them."[5] The prosecutor's evidence and arguments are unopposed, and questions about a suspect's political beliefs or associations can be used to influence a grand jury.[6] These criticisms were renewed in the grand jury investigation of President Clinton's alleged liaison with a White House intern. The intern's mother and Secret Service agents assigned to the White House were *subpoenaed* (given a written order to appear in court) to testify before the grand jury. Numerous leaks to the media about the content of secret grand jury testimony suggested efforts to attack the president and to intimidate certain individuals rather than to discover the truth.[7]

In a similar way, extensive excerpts from grand jury material in the Michael Jackson child molestation case were leaked and published in the press in 2005, as was grand jury testimony from investigations of alleged use of illegal steroids by baseball player Barry Bonds. Leaked grand jury information taints potential jurors by suggesting facts that have not yet been scrutinized or rebutted by the defense.[8]

Concern about the fairness and integrity of the grand jury process exists for federal prosecutions as well. Although the grand jury was originally designed to protect citizens from excesses by the government, some believe the balance has shifted in favor of the prosecutor to such an extent that "a good prosecutor could get a grand jury to indict a ham sandwich."[9] This suggests that grand jury protections of the suspect are so few that innocent people can be easily indicted. The

COMMISSION TO REFORM

Commission to Reform the Federal Grand Jury reported in 2000 that significant changes were needed in grand jury procedures. These recommendations included guaranteeing the right to counsel for suspects during grand jury proceedings, requiring prosecutors to disclose evidence that would exonerate the suspect, and making it a right for subjects of a grand jury investigation to testify before the grand jury.[10] There has been resistance to enact these recommendations, however, because persons are able to defend themselves fully at a subsequent trial if they are indicted. Reformers argue that the trial occurs only after a person is subjected to loss of reputation and funds in marshaling a defense against the charges made in the government's indictment.

If a majority of the members of a grand jury believe there is probable cause to hold the accused for trial, the grand jury issues a "true bill," or **indictment**, in which the accused is formally charged with the crime. If a majority of the grand jury members believe there is not enough evidence against the accused to establish probable cause, the charges are dismissed. It is possible, however, for a grand jury proceeding to begin before a person has even been arrested. If the grand jury votes to indict, a judge can issue a warrant for the person's arrest based on the grand jury's finding of probable cause. This proceeding, called a *secret indictment*, is carried out when knowledge of a pending investigation would cause a suspect to flee the jurisdiction or to alter his or her conduct.

indictment
A formal accusation of a crime based on the vote of a grand jury.

Grand juries are still used in about half the states, although the Supreme Court has permitted the states to use preliminary hearings in place of grand juries. Until grand jury proceedings attain greater public confidence, visibility, and consistent fairness, they will be seen by some as "serving more as an adjunct of prosecutorial power" than as a buffer between the power of the state and the interests of those suspected of crimes.[11]

After a grand jury votes to indict, or after an information has been drawn up on the basis of a preliminary hearing, the defendant is arraigned. An arraignment takes place before a judge, who reads the information or indictment, formally notifying the suspect, of the charge or charges. The judge again formally announces the defendant's constitutional rights, such as the right to a trial by jury, the right to have legal counsel at trial, and the right to cross-examine witnesses. If relevant to the case, the defendant's competency to stand trial is assessed, and the court appoints legal counsel if the defendant cannot afford to retain a lawyer. Finally, the judge asks the defendant to make a plea.

Defendants generally have four alternatives in making a plea: They can plead guilty, *nolo contendere*, no plea, or not guilty. If a defendant pleads guilty (which rarely occurs without negotiations with the prosecutor), the judge will set a date for sentencing. *Nolo contendere* means "no contest" and is treated as a plea of guilty. In states where *nolo contendere* pleas are permitted, the judge accepts or disallows the plea.

A *nolo* plea may not be used against a defendant in a later civil suit. Former Vice President Spiro Agnew provides a well-known example. Agnew's plea of "no contest" to charges of accepting illegal kickbacks as governor of Maryland protected him from having his plea used against him in civil suits brought by residents of Maryland or other injured parties. Those seeking damages had to offer independent proof that he had accepted kickbacks; they could not rely on his plea alone.[12]

If a defendant chooses to make no plea, the court assumes a "not guilty" plea. "No plea" is sometimes entered when a defendant has not yet had an opportunity to discuss the case with an attorney. Finally, when a defendant pleads "not guilty" (which most accused people do at their arraignment), the judge sets a date for trial. A defendant can change the plea to guilty at any time, however, waiving the right to trial.

Thomas Junta's reaction after being arraigned on the charge of felony manslaughter, to which he ultimately pleaded guilty. Junta is responsible for the beating death of another hockey dad at a hockey practice. What were his other options for a plea? What happens to him next in the criminal justice process? What correctional options did the judge have in his case? What are his chances of winning a mistrial on appeal?

Trial and Conviction

bench trial
A trial in which the judge determines guilt or innocence.

jury trial
A trial in which the jury determines guilt or innocence.

After the arraignment a trial takes place in one of two formats. In a **bench trial** the prosecutor and defense counsel make their arguments to a judge, who determines guilt or innocence. A **jury trial** is similar except that guilt or innocence is determined by a jury. In a jury trial the judge is present only to rule on issues of law or procedure.

BEYOND A REASONABLE DOUBT

Whether a case is heard at a bench trial or a jury trial, the standard of proof is the same. To arrive at a verdict of guilty, a judge or jury must believe "beyond a reasonable doubt" that the defendant committed the crime.[13] This is the highest standard of proof in American jurisprudence. While "beyond a reasonable doubt" is not the same as 100 percent certainty, it is a much higher standard than probable cause. The precise meaning of "beyond a reasonable doubt" has been the subject of much debate. Some jurisdictions define reasonable doubt as "a serious and substantial doubt," whereas others define it as "a doubt based on reason." In *Victor v. Nebraska* the judge used "actual and substantial doubt" to explain the meaning of "beyond a reasonable doubt" to a jury. On appeal, the U.S. Supreme Court agreed that the Nebraska definition was ambiguous but upheld the constitutionality of the judge's explanation.[14] The definition of "reasonable doubt" is critical, because it has a bearing on jurors' comprehension of the burden of proof when a defendant's liberty is at stake. The Supreme Court has been reluctant to prescribe a uniform definition, and the result is wide disparity in terminology and meaning among the states.[15]

acquittal
A finding after trial of not guilty.

conviction
A finding of guilt beyond a reasonable doubt.

Unlike a grand jury, a trial jury most often consists of twelve citizens, who in most states must unanimously agree on a verdict of guilt. That is, if only eleven of the twelve agree that the evidence indicates guilt beyond a reasonable doubt, then the verdict must be "not guilty." A finding of not guilty is an **acquittal,** and acquittal means that no further legal action can be taken against the accused person on the charge in question. Therefore, it is possible for probable cause to exist for an arrest, but in the trial the evidence may be insufficient to establish proof beyond a reasonable doubt. A finding of guilt by a judge or jury is a **conviction.** Only at this point can a defendant be termed an *offender.* An offender can challenge the conviction only by appealing to a higher court, attempting to show that errors have been made in law or procedure in the case. While most appeals are unsuccessful, those that succeed usually result in a new trial.

Sentencing and Appeals

sentencing
A judge's decision as to what is to be the most appropriate punishment, given the type of crime and offender, and within a specified range established by law.

presentence investigation
An investigation by the probation department that seeks information regarding the offender's personal and social background, criminal record, and any other information that may help the judge match the sentence to the offender.

Upon a finding of guilt, the judge sets a date for sentencing. In **sentencing** the judge decides what is to be the most appropriate punishment, given the type of crime and type of offender. The judge's discretion is guided only by the minimum and maximum sentence for the crime as set by law. If the penalty established by law for a certain crime is one to ten years in prison, a judge can sentence a convicted offender to any term between one and ten years. A sentence outside this range would be a violation of law and would require resentencing.

Before deciding on an appropriate sentence, the judge often will ask the probation department to conduct a **presentence investigation** of the offender. This investigation seeks information regarding the offender's personal and social background, criminal record, and any other information that may help the judge match the sentence to the offender. For example, information indicating a history of drug or alcohol abuse or knowledge that an offender has dependents may influence the judge's decision.

At the sentencing hearing, the judge can fine the offender, impose a sentence of incarceration, or place the offender on probation, depending on the type of crime involved. In probation the offender is placed under the supervision of a probation officer employed by the court. Although the use of incarceration has been increasing steadily in recent years, probation remains the most widely utilized sentencing alternative in criminal court. **Incarceration** segregates offenders from the rest of the community in jails or prisons to rehabilitate, incapacitate, or punish them and to deter others from committing similar crimes.

incarceration
Segregation of offenders from the rest of the community in jails or prisons to rehabilitate, incapacitate, or punish them and to deter others from committing similar crimes.

After serving part of a sentence of incarceration, an offender may be placed on **parole.** In this phase of the criminal justice process, an offender is released before completing the sentence and serves the remainder of the term under the supervision of a parole officer in the community. Parole is designed to assist the offender in readjusting to life and work in society after serving time in prison. Parole is not available in all states or to all types of offenders.

parole
A phase of the criminal justice system in which an offender completes the end of a prison sentence under supervision in the community.

Appeals are an often misunderstood part of the criminal justice process. Appellate courts never hear new trials or sentence offenders; once convicted, however, an offender can appeal the conviction to an appellate court. The appeal is a written statement, called a *brief,* which explains the alleged legal errors made during the trial. The appellate court, consisting of a panel of several judges, reviews the brief and the trial transcript. If the court finds that there is no basis for the appeal, the appeal is dismissed. Otherwise, the court holds a hearing in which the defense attorney and the prosecutor present arguments on the issue raised in the brief. This is not a retrial but a hearing on a particular legal issue. For example, the appeal in *Victor v. Nebraska* dealt only with the legal meaning of proof "beyond a reasonable doubt."[16] The evidence presented at trial, the defendant's background,

appeal
A review of lower court decisions by a higher court to look for errors of law or procedure.

THE APPEAL PROCESS

Justices sitting on an appellate court. Appellate courts do not re-try cases. What do they do instead? What are the piles of papers sitting in front of the justices?

the length of the sentence, and all other aspects of the case were not relevant to the appeal and were not argued.

justices
The title of the judges of an appellate court.

Sometime after the hearing, the appellate court **justices** discuss the issue and vote either to affirm the conviction by leaving it undisturbed, or to reverse the conviction by overturning it on the grounds that a significant legal error was made during the trial. Occasionally an appellate court will find "harmless error," meaning that a legal error was made during the trial but was not serious enough to affect the fairness of the trial.[17]

REVERSAL OF CONVICTION AND RETRIAL

Most appeals are unsuccessful. The defendant usually has little recourse but to accept the trial court's verdict, unless a violation of a constitutional right is alleged. In that case the defendant may appeal to the federal courts. Here again, however, appeals usually are unsuccessful. In the rare event that a conviction is reversed, the case usually is retried in the original court of general jurisdiction. For example, if a confession is ruled to be defective on appeal, a new trial may occur, but the confession used in the original trial may not be used in the retrial. Other evidence of guilt, independent of the confession, must be produced. The reversal of the conviction renders the initial trial a **mistrial,** and the retrial is treated as the first trial under law. Thus, a retrial is not considered a violation of the *double jeopardy clause* of the Fifth Amendment, which prohibits a defendant from being tried twice for the same crime.

mistrial
A trial that has been declared invalid because of a substantial error in law or procedure.

What Are Some Concerns about the Criminal Justice System?

The criminal justice system faces continuing challenges to its successful operation. Two of the most pressing concerns involve (1) its cost and (2) the effect of the rules of criminal procedure on efforts to obtain truth and justice in the criminal justice process. The cost of justice is escalating, and the impact of the rules of criminal procedure can be deleterious if the rules are oppressive or obscure the search for truth.

The Cost of Justice

Justice is expensive. Each year, federal, state, and local governments spend $185 billion on civil and criminal justice system agencies (or $638 per capita). States spent the most ($39 billion) for corrections, while local governments spent the most on police ($58 billion). In comparison, the federal expenditure on police was $20 billion. Nearly 2.3 million people are employed in the justice system, including about 1.1 million police employees, 748,000 in corrections, and 494,000 in judicial posts, prosecution, defense, and legal services. As you have seen, most law is on the state and local level, so most expenditures for the criminal justice system also occur there. Local governments funded half of all justice system expenses, and another 33 percent came from the states.[18] All this money, of course, is provided by taxpayers.

WHY SO HIGH?

Why is the cost of justice so high? The primary reason is increased spending on prisons and police. Legislatures appropriate funds to these agencies because the public either actively encourages them or does not object strongly. The high levels of fear of crime, documented in Chapter 2, have put pressure on legislators to "do something" about crime. Spending on police and prisons is a popular way to "do something" because these agencies already exist and have clear legal mandates. Indeed, total national spending on the justice system has increased by 300 percent over the last twenty years (in constant dollars).[19] Spending on more innovative programs, such as delinquency prevention and family intervention initiatives, is less popular because these are not established political institutions.

FIGURE 6.4 Expenditures on Criminal Justice Compared to Other Government Spending (percentages of total government expenditures: federal, state, and local)

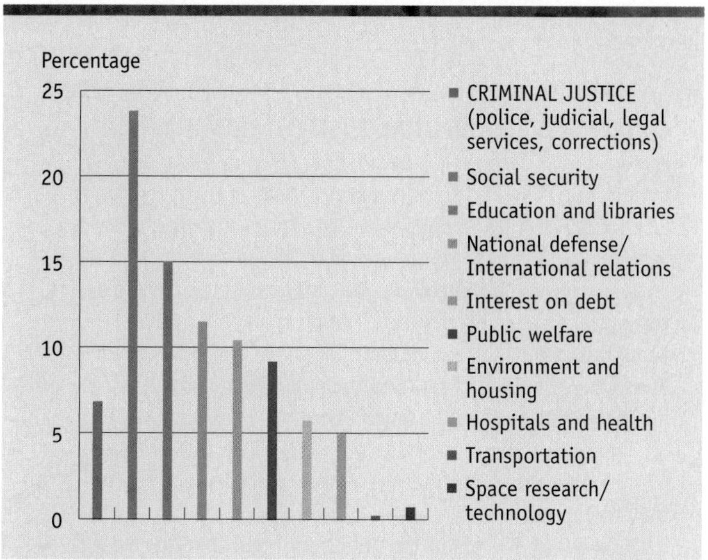

Source: Kristen A. Hughes, *Justice Expenditure and Employment in the United States* (Washington, DC: Bureau of Justice Statistics, 2006).

Despite the apparently high cost of justice, outlays in this area pale in comparison to other expenditures by government. Of the more than 3 trillion spent by governments in this country, only about 8 percent goes to criminal justice. Much higher amounts go toward social security (24.4 percent), education and libraries (15 percent), national defense and international relations (12 percent), interest on government debt (11 percent), public welfare (9 percent), and environment and housing (5.5 percent). As Figure 6.4 shows, then, many other government priorities outpace criminal justice in terms of total expenditures. It is true that the costs of crime in terms of physical harm, the costs of doing business, the need for locks and alarms, and related human costs are difficult to quantify. It is clear, however, that successful crime prevention initiatives might avert the human losses caused by crime and the fear it creates. This, in turn, might ultimately lower the cost of the justice system, because we would turn to it less often. The rising cost of the justice system is not likely to be reduced in the near future, however. Calls for police

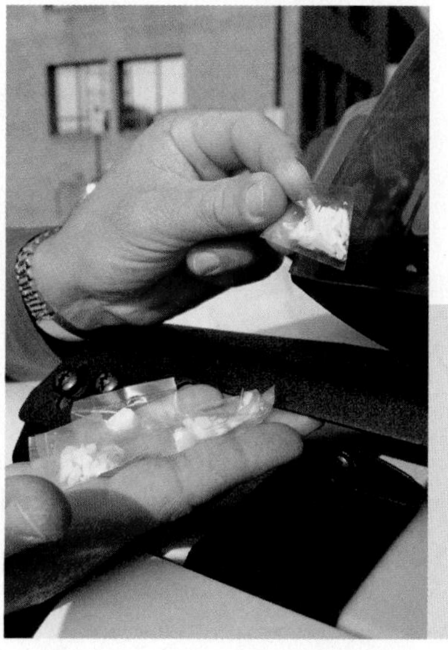

An offender in court receiving a long sentence for drug trafficking. One reason for the high cost of justice is the high percentage of drug offenders who are sentenced to very long prison terms. What would you recommend as a long-term strategy in reducing these costs of incarceration?

That's a FACT

Perspectives on Fairness in the Criminal Justice System

CONFIDENCE IN CRIMINAL JUSTICE INSTITUTIONS

Perceptions of fairness in the criminal justice process are as important as the existence of fairness itself. For without public confidence in the criminal justice system, its decisions will lack public support. This support is crucial to deter potential law violators and to encourage the public to rely on the justice system to resolve conflicts (rather than using private vendettas, violence, and vigilantism, which characterize societies where the rule of law and the public justice system is not respected, trusted, or relied upon).

Figure 6A shows the results of a Gallup poll in which people rated American institutions as to how much confidence they had in each one.

How do the ratings of the police and the U.S. Supreme Court compare to the ratings of Congress and big business? How might you explain these differences? The criminal justice system (as a whole) was rated much lower than the police, which are part of the criminal justice system. How do you explain this discrepancy? Compared to a similar poll three years earlier, confidence in police, the presidency, the U.S. Supreme Court, and the criminal justice system in general have all dropped. Can you think of reasons for these trends?

FIGURE 6A

I am going to read you a list of institutions in American society. Please tell me how much confidence you, yourself, have in each one– a great deal, quite a lot, some, or very little?

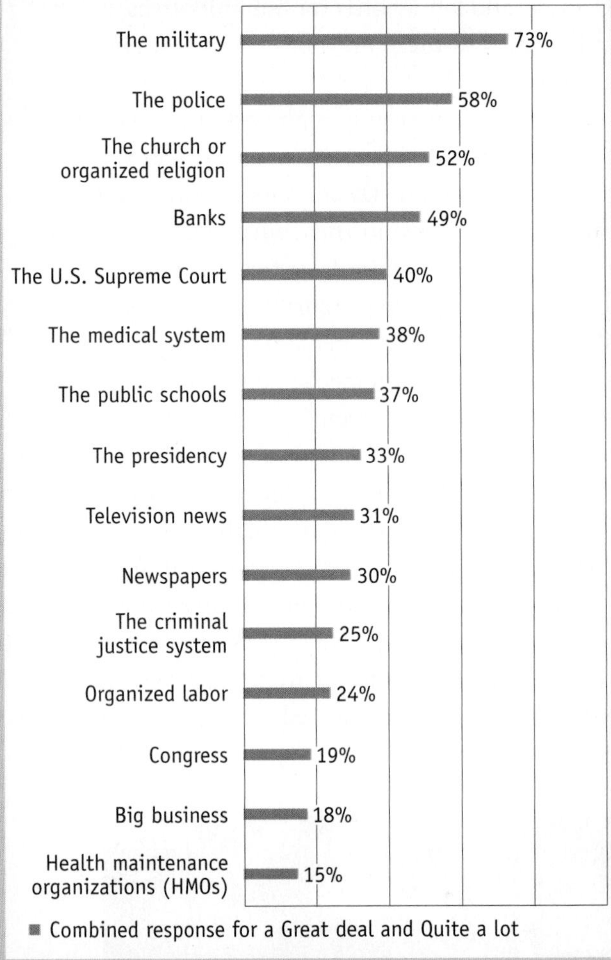

Source: "Confidence in Institutions," *Gallup News Service* (June 2006). ©2006 The Gallup Organization. Reprinted with permission from www.gallup.com.

service have increased; jails are filled beyond their capacity; police departments are increasing staffing; and prosecutors report that they are unable to keep up with caseloads. Prosecutors, public defenders, judges, trial court administrators, and probation, parole, and correctional administrators all believe that the current system is not achieving its goals.[20] At the same time, public confidence in the ability of government agencies to handle state and local problems is declining.[21] The time appears ripe for innovations in crime prevention, policing, adjudication, and

RACIAL DIFFERENCES IN PERSPECTIVE

Although police are rated highly compared to other social institutions, this confidence is not uniform. There is no significant variation in confidence in the police among people living in urban, suburban, or rural settings. Further, those making low salaries (under $20,000) are less likely than those making high salaries (over $75,000) to express a "great deal" of confidence in the police. Of the factors studied, race appears to be the primary reason for significant difference of opinion.

Figure 6B displays the difference of opinion about police by race, community setting, and income. The significant difference by race is apparent.

How might you explain this lack of confidence in police across minorities of all communities and incomes, compared to the significantly higher ratings by whites? What strategies might you suggest to improve confidence in police protection?

FIGURE 6B Confidence in Police Protection

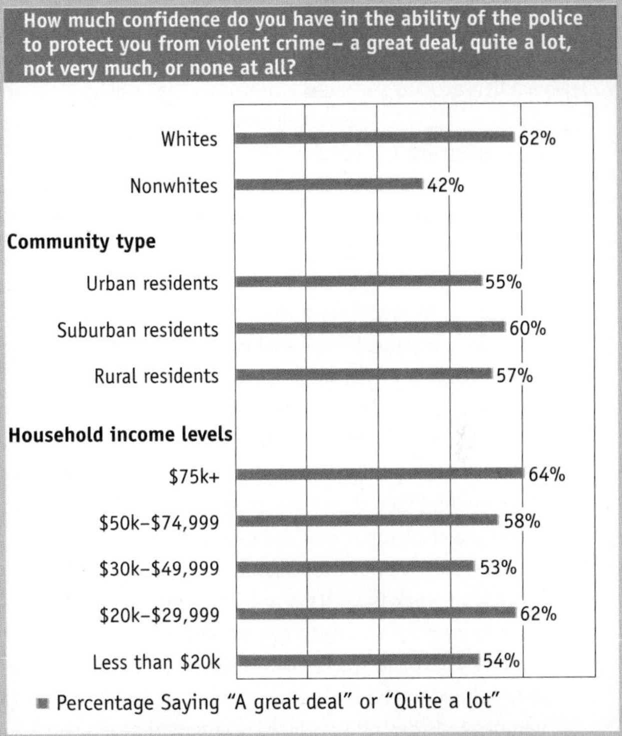

Source: Darren K. Carlson, "Racial Divide: Crime and Police Protection," *Gallup News Service* (October 29, 2002). ©2002 The Gallup Organization. Reprinted with permission from www.gallup.com.

sentencing so that we can be assured that our expenditures are being put to their best possible use.

Fairness in Adjudication

Criminal procedure is designed to ensure accuracy and fairness in the adjudication process. The requirements of probable cause for arrest and the need for

Media & Criminal Justice

The Star Chamber

The name of the classic 1983 film *The Star Chamber* comes from an English court in the fifteenth and sixteenth centuries that was composed primarily of lawyers and judges to supplement the regular common law courts. Popular in its day, the Star Chamber was eventually abolished because in meting out arbitrary justice, it undermined the protections of democracy.

In the film, a modern-day star chamber is established by a group of judges who meet in a secretive backroom court and reevaluate rape and murder cases that they have had to dismiss based on perceived legal "technicalities."

In one case, a perpetrator tosses the gun used in a crime into a garbage can as he flees from the police. The police see the gun go into the trash container but, trained in procedural law, they know that the contents of the container are the property of the owner and are thus protected from a warrantless search and seizure. Luckily, a sanitation truck is on its way up the street; the officers cleverly wait for the trash can to be routinely emptied into the city's garbage truck, then remove the evidence from the garbage in the truck's rear trough. But at the trial the perpetrator's lawyer successfully argues that evidence from the search should be excluded, because the truck's scoop had not been lowered before the removal of the gun. The judge has no choice but to admit that the garbage in the trough had not been mixed with all the other garbage; thus, the police action constituted an illegal search of private property.

In another case, seasoned patrol officers find themselves pulling over a suspicious van, using a radio report of unpaid parking tickets on the license plate as their probable cause. Citing the phantom smell of marijuana smoke as their basis for searching the vehicle they find the bloody sneaker of a recently missing child and immediately arrest the van's occupants for the child's murder. In court it is learned that the defendant's parking tickets were indeed paid on time, but that a backlog in computer data entry caused the dispatcher to relay outdated information on the vehicle to the arresting officers. Once the basis for the pullover is excluded, the consequent fruits of the illegal search also have to be excluded.

These vignettes provide the basis for the movie's panel of judges' creation of their own star chamber. To the judges, the legal system isn't working anymore, and it is up to them to make sure true justice prevails. They collectively rule that the accused they have set free in a court of law are indeed actually guilty, and dispatch professional hit men to serve the interests of justice.

The Star Chamber does not consider the ultimate question: What if the judges of the star chamber are wrong? In the end, the film allows that any system of justice in our complex society has flaws, but that due process is a necessary evil in balancing the costs.

What aspects of criminal court procedure does the judges' star chamber circumvent? What weakness or criticism of the American criminal justice system does this star chamber address? Do you feel a body like the English Star Chamber is the solution to problems of justice?

concurrence of a judge or grand jury hearing at the preliminary hearing or grand jury hearing are examples of the overlapping processes aimed at safeguarding those suspected of crimes from the power of the criminal justice system. These protections defend against innocent persons being caught up in the criminal justice process without objective evidence of a law violation.

UNFAIR TREATMENT?

Despite these procedures, unfairness sometimes occurs. Allegations of racial discrimination by police in traffic stops and arrests, erroneous convictions in court, and disparity among judges in sentencing similar offenders for similar crimes, are examples of how fundamental safeguards such as "probable cause" and "beyond a reasonable doubt" can be inadequate. Investigations have found racial disparities in the treatment of juvenile offenders, and in some arrest decisions, sentencing decisions, and death penalty decisions.[22] Most of these investigations are focused on specific geographic areas and time periods, but they show that without the objective and unbiased application of American criminal procedures, the legal safeguards themselves cannot protect against unfair application of the law. When this occurs, citizens lose confidence in the criminal justice system and in the government it represents. Future chapters will address several specific issues of unfair treatment in the criminal justice system in more detail.

CRITICAL THINKING EXERCISES

The Limits of Drug Testing

A growing number of school districts around the country now require random drug tests. It began with student athletes and then expanded when the U.S. Supreme Court upheld a lower court decision permitting drug testing of all students who enjoy special privileges. In Cave City, Arkansas, for example, pupils must agree to random drug testing in order to attend field trips or the prom. In Indiana, some schools require drug tests of any student who drives a car to school. These requirements are defended by one high school principal who said, "If we can save just one kid from being maimed or killed by drugs, it's worth the infringement on their rights."[a]

Courts have ruled thus far that such random drug tests do not violate any legal rights, but critics charge it's too large an intrusion given the comparatively small number of drug users. In Lewis Center, Ohio, tests of 1,400 middle and high school students over the course of a year produced only three positive results. In addition, urine tests have high error rates. In a Utah case an honor roll student tested positive for marijuana use, but his mother had him immediately re-tested at two clinics, which found negative results. The student was still kicked off the baseball team.[b]

When the treatment of students is compared to other groups, the law has been applied inconsistently. A Georgia law required candidates for state office to take a drug test, but a challenge to the U.S. Supreme Court overturned the law on grounds such testing was "not tied to individualized suspicion of wrongdoing."[c] In another case that landed in the Supreme Court, a public school district in Oklahoma instituted a policy that required all students—such as band members, choir members, academic team members, and athletic team members—who participated in any competitive extracurricular activities to submit to urinalysis drug testing. The samples were collected by a teacher who listened for the sounds of normal urination while the student was in a bathroom stall. Positive results were to be kept confidential, except that such results were to lead to parent notification and drug-counseling recommendation. The U.S. Supreme Court held in 2002 that such mandatory testing did not violate the Fourth Amendment, because the invasion of the students' privacy was not significant—the results (a) were not turned over to any law enforcement authority, (b) did not lead to the imposition of discipline, and (c) did not have any academic consequences.[d]

CRITICAL THINKING QUESTIONS

1. Should probable cause of drug use be the minimum standard to conduct a school drug test? Explain why or why not.
2. What would you argue is acceptable error rate in mandatory drug tests?
3. Explain why mandatory drug tests of state office holders and school students are either consistent or inconsistent with the language of the Fourth Amendment.

NOTES

a. Dana Hawkins, "Trial by Vial," *U.S. News & World Report* (May 31, 1999), pp. 70–71.
b. Ibid; Jacob L. Brooks, "Suspicionless Drug Testing of Students Participating in Non-Athletic Competitive School Activities: Are All Students Next?" *Wyoming Law Review,* vol. 4 (winter 2004), pp. 365–96.
c. *Chandler v. Miller,* 117 S. Ct. 1295 (1997).
d. *Board of Education v. Earls,* 122 S. Ct. 2559 (2002).

Addressing Violence in Entertainment

Following the tragic school shooting in Littleton, Colorado, the president requested that the Federal Trade Commission and Department of Justice conduct a study of whether violent entertainment was being marketed to teenagers and younger children. A report was released in late 2000 revealing that major movie studios have specifically targeted R-rated films to underage audiences. For example, forty-four movies rated "R" for violent content were studied, and 80 percent were targeted to children under seventeen. The marketing plan for one of these films stated the "goal was to find the elusive teen target audience and make sure everyone between the ages of twelve and eighteen was exposed to the film."[a] Similarly, of 118 electronic games with a "Mature" rating for violence, 70 percent were targeted to children under seventeen years of age according to the industry's own advertising plans. Twenty-seven percent of music recordings with labels for "explicit content" specifically identified teenagers as part of their target audience.

The heads of major entertainment companies were asked to explain their actions before a congressional committee. It was revealed that children as young as age nine were asked by studio researchers to help with ideas for the sequel to *I Know What You Did Last Summer,* an R-rated "slasher" movie. Columbia Pictures persisted in trying to buy advertising on the Nickelodeon children's network for the PG-13 film *The Fifth Element,* even after Nickelodeon had rejected the ads. The head of the studio said later, "That was a judgment lapse."[b]

The Motion Picture Association of America has proposed a self-regulation plan for the industry, but there are loopholes. Some studios have pledged not to market R-rated films to audiences in which more than 35 percent of the viewers are under age seventeen, but sports programs, which attract many young male viewers, are excluded. Other studios have agreed not to run ads for R-rated films between 8:00 and 9:00 P.M.—television's "family hour." In a follow-up report in 2004, it was found that movie studios "continue to advertise violent, R-rated films and DVDs on programs with large teen viewership, [and] some studios have conducted promotions for R-rated films in venues to attract significant numbers of young teens." In addition the report found that the music industry's compliance with labeling CDs for explicit content had "improved only slightly."[c]

Congress and a large segment of the American public are unhappy with the way that violent entertainment is marketed, but there is disagreement over how it should be regulated beyond the voluntary labeling procedures that now exist in the movie, recording industry, and electronic game industries.

CRITICAL THINKING QUESTIONS

1. The decision to make a behavior illegal is an important one with significant consequences for the criminal justice system. What are arguments for and against criminalizing the marketing of R-rated films to underage audiences?
2. Why do you believe Congress has been reluctant to regulate the marketing of violent entertainment to children?
3. If marketing of violent entertainment was made illegal, what kinds of evidence should be used to establish proof beyond a reasonable doubt that such marketing was intentional?

NOTES

a. Federal Trade Commission, *Marketing Violent Entertainment to Children: A Review of Self-Regulation and Industry Practices in the Motion Picture, Music Recording, and Electronic Game Industries.* Testimony before the U.S. Senate Committee on Commerce, Science, and Transportation (September 13, 2000). Available at www.ftc.gov/opa/2000/09/youthviol.htm.

b. Betsey Streisand, "Slasher Movies the Family Can Enjoy," *U.S. News & World Report* (October 9, 2000), p. 50.

c. Federal Trade Commission, *Marketing Violent Entertainment to Children: A Fourth Follow-up Review of Industry Practices* (2004). Available at http://www.ftc.gov/os/2004/07/040708kidsviolencerpt.pdf.

SUMMARY

WHAT ARE THE AGENCIES OF CRIMINAL JUSTICE?

- The main types of criminal justice agencies are law enforcement agencies, courts (including trial and appeals courts), and correctional systems. All three types are found at all three levels of government (federal, state, and local).
- The criminal justice process acts like a filter in which the agencies of criminal justice each capture a share of law violators.

WHAT IS PROCEDURAL LAW?

- Many important aspects of criminal procedure are detailed in the Bill of Rights, the first ten amendments to the U.S. Constitution.
- Only since the 1960s have the provisions of the Bill of Rights been applied to the states as well as to the federal government.
- The criminal justice process begins with a violation of the law that is made known to the police. The police

conduct an investigation, which may or may not lead to the arrest and booking of the suspect.

- The Fourth Amendment protects individuals from searches and seizures conducted without a warrant specifying probable cause.

WHAT IS INVOLVED IN CRIMINAL COURT PROCEDURE?

- At the initial appearance formal notice of the charge(s) is given to the arrestee, who is then informed of an arrestee's legal rights; in addition, the judge sets bail. This step is followed by a preliminary hearing to determine whether there is probable cause to believe that a crime has been committed and that the person charged committed it.
- A grand jury consists of a group of citizens who hear the evidence presented by a prosecutor in order to determine whether probable cause exists to hold a person for trial, in which case it will issue a true bill or indictment in which the accused person is formally charged with the crime.
- At an arraignment a judge reads the information or indictment and announces the defendant's constitutional rights. The defendant then makes a plea.
- In a bench trial the prosecutor and defense make their arguments to a judge, who determines guilt or innocence. A jury trial is similar except that guilt or innocence is determined by a trial jury. A finding of not guilty is an acquittal; a finding of guilty is a conviction.
- In the case of a guilty verdict the judge sets a date for sentencing and may ask the probation department to conduct a presentence investigation of the offender. At the sentencing hearing the judge can fine the offender, impose a sentence of incarceration, or place the offender on probation.
- A convicted offender can appeal the conviction to an appellate court consisting of a panel of several justices, who may vote either to affirm the conviction or to reverse it—that is, to overturn it because a significant legal error was made during the trial.

WHAT ARE SOME CONCERNS ABOUT THE CRIMINAL JUSTICE SYSTEM?

- Criminal justice is expensive. A major reason for the cost of justice is a significant increase in spending on prisons and police in recent years.
- There is concern about the adequacy of legal rules to ensure fairness in criminal procedure. Allegations of bias in arrest, conviction, and sentencing decisions indicate that objective application of legal rules is not occurring in all cases.

KEY TERMS

QUESTIONS FOR REVIEW AND DISCUSSION

1. How is the criminal justice system designed to provide a just balance between individual and community interests?
2. What are the four basic tasks that law enforcement agencies at all levels of jurisdiction are expected to perform? How do law enforcement agencies differ by jurisdiction?

3. What are the three basic jurisdictions that state and federal court have? How do state and federal courts differ?
4. How does the correctional system reflect the organization of law enforcement and the courts?
5. Why is it useful to think of the criminal justice system as a filter?
6. What does the Bill of Rights have to do with the criminal justice system? What is meant by due process of the law?
7. How does the criminal justice system operate from the time a suspected violation of a law occurs until the time a suspect is arrested?
8. What legal right does the Fourth Amendment protect? What is meant by probable cause?
9. How does the bail system operate? What is the process by which cases are brought to trial? What kinds of trials are there?
10. What are the four kinds of plea? What are the possible outcomes of a trial?
11. Why is the cost of justice so high? Why are there concerns about fairness in the adjudication process?

NOTES

1. Larry Reibstein, "NYPD Black and Blue," *Newsweek* (June 2, 1997), p. 67; Alexandria Marks, "The Case of Patrick Dorismond: When Civilians Are Casualties of Drug Wars," *Christian Science Monitor* (April 4, 2000), p. 1.
2. Bob Herbert, "Attention Must Be Paid," *New York Times* (September 30, 1999), p. A31.; William K. Rashbaum and Al Baker, "Police Commissioner Closing Controversial Street Crime Unit," *New York Times* (April 10, 2002), p. B1.
3. Lauren E. Glaze and Seri Palla, *Probation and Parole in the United States 2004* (Washington, DC: Bureau of Justice Statistics, 2005); Paige Harrison and Allen J. Beck, *Prisoners in 2004* (Washington, DC: Bureau of Justice Statistics, 2005); Paige Harrison and Allen J. Beck, *Prisoner and Jail Inmates Mid-Year 2005* (Washington, DC: Bureau of Justice Statistics, 2006).
4. *Illinois v. Gates*, 426 U.S. 318 (1982).
5. Abraham S. Blumberg, *Criminal Justice: Issues and Ironies*, 2nd ed. (New York: New Viewpoints, 1979).
6. Marvin E. Frankel and Garry P. Naftalis, *The Grand Jury* (New York: Hill & Wang, 1977); Leslie Berger, Austin Sarat, B. Marvis, *The Grand Jury* (New York: Chelsea House, 1999).
7. Judy Keen and Gary Fields, "Deal Sought on Guards' Testimony," *USA Today* (February 13, 1998), p. 1; Walter Shapiro, "Loneliest Job in the World—Except for All the Lawyers," *USA Today* (February 13, 1998), p. 6.
8. John M. Broder, "From Grand Jury Leaks Comes a Clash of Rights," *New York Times* (January 15, 2005).
9. National Association of Criminal Defense Lawyers—*Federal Grand Jury Reform Report* (Washington, DC: National Association of Criminal Defense Lawyers, 2000), p. 1.
10. Ibid.
11. Blumberg, p. 144.
12. See Spiro T. Agnew, *Go Quietly . . . or Else* (New York: Morrow, 1980).
13. Ronald L. Carlson, *Criminal Justice Procedure*, 7th ed. (Cincinnati: Lexis/Nexus/Anderson, 2005), p. 189.
14. *Victor v. Nebraska*, 114 S. Ct. 1239 (1994).
15. Craig Hemmens, Kathryn E. Scarborough, and Rolando V. Del Carmen, "Grave Doubts about 'Reasonable Doubt': Confusion in State and Federal Courts," *Journal of Criminal Justice* 25 (1997), pp. 231–54; Erik Lillquist, "Recasting Reasonable Doubt: Decision Theory and the Virtues of Variability," *University of California Davis Law Review*, vol. 36 (November 2002), p. 85.
16. *Victor v. Nebraska*, 114 S. Ct. 1239 (1994).
17. Cliff Roberson, Harvey Wallace, Gilbert Stuckey, *Procedures in the Justice System*, 8th ed. (Upper Saddle River, NJ: Prentice Hall, 2007), p. 263; John F. Costello Jr., "Mandamus as a Weapon of Class Warfare in Sixth Amendment Jurisprudence," *John Marshall Law Review*, vol. 36 (spring 2003), p. 733.
18. Kristen A. Hughes, *Justice Expenditure and Employment in the United States* (Washington, DC: Bureau of Justice Statistics, 2006).
19. Ibid.
20. Christian Parenti, *Lockdown America: Police and Prisons in an Age of Crisis* (New York: Verso, 1999); Tom McEwen, *National Assessment Program: 1994 Survey Results* (Washington, DC: National Institute of Justice, 1995).
21. Jeffrey M. Jones, "Issues Facing State, Local Governments Affect Public Trust," *Gallup News Service* (October 14, 2003).
22. Roy L. Austin and Mark D. Allen, "Racial Disparity in Arrest Rates as an Explanation of Racial Disparity in Commitment to Pennsylvania's Prisons," *Journal of Research in Crime & Delinquency*, vol. 37 (May 2000), pp. 200–21; Fox Butterfield, "Racial Disparities Seen as Pervasive in Juvenile Justice: A Snow-balling Effect," *New York Times* (April 26, 2000), p. A1; U.S. Comptroller General, *Racial Profiling* (Washington, DC: U.S. General Accounting Office, 2000); Illya Lichtenberg, "Driving While Black: Examining Race as a Tool in the War on Drugs," *Police Practice & Research*, vol. 7 (March 2006), pp. 49–61.

chapter 7

Criminal Procedure and the Police

Enforcing the law: police are the gatekeepers of the criminal justice system. The rule of law establishes the relationship between the rights of private citizens and the interests of the government in catching crime suspects.

CHAPTER OUTLINE

LEARNING OBJECTIVES

- Explain the role of police in criminal procedure.
- Distinguish a stop from an arrest and a frisk from a search, and define legal search and seizure.
- Explain the purpose of the exclusionary rule and give examples of the exceptions to the exclusionary rule for lawful search and seizure.
- Identify and give examples of five situations in which searches can be made without a warrant.
- Describe the rights protected by the Fifth Amendment and the effects of the Fifth Amendment on police interrogations and confessions.
- Discuss the legal significance of the *Miranda* ruling and describe the exceptions to it.
- Evaluate the effects of the exclusionary rule and the *Miranda* ruling on law enforcement, and the effects of exceptions to these rules on criminal procedure.

An anonymous caller to the Miami–Dade police said there was a young black male wearing a plaid shirt and carrying a gun at a particular bus stop. Officers went to the bus stop and saw three black males, one of whom was wearing a plaid shirt. They observed no suspicious activity and did not see any firearms. One of the officers decided to approach and frisk the one with the plaid shirt, uncovering a concealed firearm. The suspect was fifteen years old and was charged with carrying a weapon without a license and possessing a firearm while under the age of eighteen. Is this a legal search? Was the anonymous information possessed by the police sufficient to justify the intrusion into the privacy of a citizen who was not acting suspiciously in any way?

THRESHOLD OF EVIDENCE

This case was ultimately decided by the U.S. Supreme Court. It hinged on an interpretation of the Fourth Amendment of the U.S. Constitution and the threshold of evidence needed by police before they may stop and search citizens. It is one of many significant cases decided by the U.S. Supreme Court since the 1960s that involved interpretations of the Fourth Amendment and the balance between the right of citizens to be free from unwarranted intrusions by the government (e.g., the police) and the public interest in apprehending criminals.

What Is the Role of Police in Criminal Procedure?

Police play a central role in criminal procedure because they are the gatekeepers of the criminal justice system. They observe behavior and must make judgments about potentially criminal behavior in order to prevent crime and apprehend criminals. Police make crucial decisions about whether individuals should be stopped, frisked, searched, arrested, or interrogated. This is a difficult task guided by the Fourth Amendment to the U.S. Constitution, which offers only general direction using the standard of "probable cause."

Court decisions have been necessary over the years to interpret and apply the general Fourth Amendment standard in a changing world of drug trafficking, automobile travel, and suspicious persons and activities that fall short of the probable cause threshold. In a similar way, the Fifth Amendment, which provides general direction for the conduct of interrogations by police, also has required court interpretation to apply to contemporary situations. This chapter reviews important legal standards and court rulings that illustrate how the constitutional principles written 200 years ago are applied in practice today.

Reasonable Suspicion and Stop and Frisk

For many years the police, the courts, and the public have been uncertain about the scope of a police officer's authority to stop a suspect when there are no grounds for arrest. Although it is common practice for officers to stop and question citizens, it was not clear until the late 1960s whether the police actually had this right—and, if they did, what its limits were. The case that established the legal authority and limits for a "stop and frisk" was *Terry v. Ohio.*[1] The case involved a Cleveland police officer who had been a plainclothes detective for thirty-five years and had patrolled a certain section of the downtown area for shoplifters and pickpockets for nearly thirty years.

TERRY V. OHIO

The officer saw three men repeatedly walk slowly past a store window and suspected that they were casing the store for a robbery. He identified himself as a police officer and proceeded to ask them several questions, to which they "mumbled something" in response. The officer then grabbed one of the men, turned him around, and patted him down. He felt something in the man's left breast pocket and removed it; it was a .38 caliber revolver. He proceeded to pat down the outer garments of the other men and found another pistol on one of them. The men were charged with carrying concealed weapons in violation of the law.

In court, the men claimed that the officer had no probable cause to search them. Therefore, they argued, the search was illegal and the guns should not be admitted as evidence against them. On appeal, the U.S. Supreme Court agreed that the police officer did not have probable cause to conduct a search, but the gun possession charge was allowed to stand.

The Court distinguished between a "stop" and an "arrest" and between a "frisk" and a "search." A **frisk** was defined as a patting down of outer clothing, whereas a **search** is an exploration for evidence. **Seizure** of property occurs when there is some meaningful interference with an individual's possession of

FRISK VERSUS SEARCH

frisk
A patting down of the outer clothing of a suspect based on reasonable suspicion, designed to protect a police officer from attack with a weapon while an inquiry is made.

search
An exploratory inspection of a person or property based on probable cause of law violation.

seizure
Confiscation of property occurring when there is some meaningful interference with the individual's possession of property.

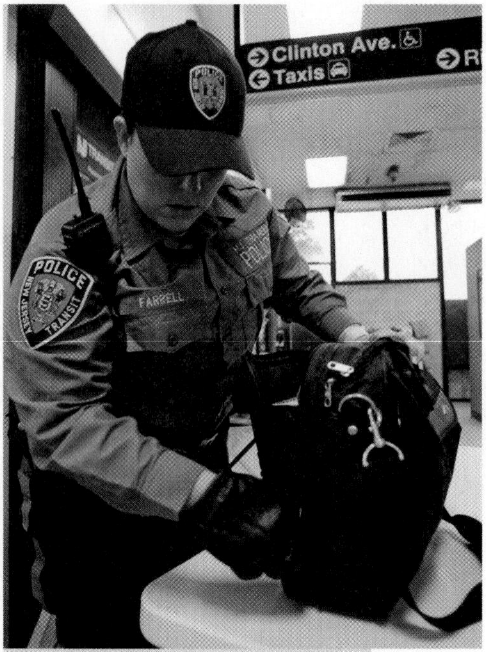

What are the five general types of situations in which searches can reasonably be conducted without a warrant? Why are these situations treated as exceptions to the exclusionary rule, that is, as instances of lawful search and seizure? How do you think these exceptions affect the balance between individual and community interests in the American criminal justice system?

that property.[2] The Court held that a frisk is essential to the proper performance of a police officer's investigative duties, for without it "the answer to the police officer may be a bullet, and a loaded pistol discovered during the frisk is admissible [as evidence]." As a result, the two men were convicted of illegally carrying concealed weapons. The Court concluded that the experienced officer's observations were "enough to make it quite reasonable to fear that they were armed; and nothing in their response to his hailing them, identifying himself as a police officer, and asking their names served to dispel that reasonable belief." The officer's actions were not "the product of a volatile or inventive imagination, or undertaken simply as an act of harassment; the record evidences the tempered act of a policeman who in the course of an investigation had to make a quick decision as to how to protect himself and others from possible danger, and took limited steps to do so."

According to the Supreme Court, frisks are limited to a search for weapons that may pose an immediate threat to the officer's safety. The Court concluded that cases like these must be decided on the basis of their own facts; generally, however, police officers who observe unusual conduct that leads them to conclude that criminal activity may be involved and that the persons may be armed and dangerous are entitled to conduct "a carefully limited search of the outer clothing of such persons in an attempt to discover weapons" that might be used to assault them. Such a frisk was held to be reasonable under the Fourth Amendment, and any weapons seized may be introduced in evidence.

The decision in *Terry v. Ohio* lowered the standard determining when police could take action against a suspect. Before 1968, police could search only if they had probable cause. After *Terry*, police could conduct a frisk of a person's outer clothing to search for weapons if they had only "reasonable suspicion." **Reasonable suspicion** is a lower standard of evidence than probable cause, so the scope of the search permitted is less intrusive.[3]

reasonable suspicion
A situation in which a police officer has good reason to believe that criminal activity may be occurring; this permits a brief investigative inquiry of the suspect.

FLORIDA V. J. L.

The case presented at the opening to this chapter was decided by the U.S. Supreme Court in 2000 in *Florida v. J. L.* The Court had to determine whether the anonymous tip that a person was carrying a gun was sufficient to justify a stop and frisk of that person. In this case the officers' suspicion that the suspect was carrying a weapon was not supported by their own observations. The anonymous tip also provided no additional information to test the informant's credibility (such as having provided good information to the police in the past or more details that predicted the suspect's movements). As a result, the Court held that there was insufficient evidence to establish reasonable suspicion of law violation, so the stop and frisk was unconstitutional under the Fourth Amendment.[4]

In a variation on stop and frisk, the U.S. Supreme Court in 2004 became involved in a case involving an Illinois state trooper who stopped a driver for speeding on a highway. When the trooper radioed the police dispatcher to report the stop, a second trooper, who had a narcotics-detection dog with him, overheard the transmission. While the first trooper was writing a warning ticket, the second trooper walked the dog around the car, although there was no suspicion of drugs at the time of the stop. The dog reacted at the trunk, and the troopers searched it, found marijuana, and arrested the driver. The entire incident lasted less than ten minutes. The Court held that such a nonintrusive "sniff" by the narcotics dog during a lawful traffic stop "generally does not implicate legitimate privacy interests," because it does not change the character of the lawful traffic stop and is executed in a reasonable manner. The Court found this analogous to *Terry v. Ohio*, because in a *Terry*-type investigatory stop, "the officer's action [must be] justified at its inception, and . . . reasonably related in scope to the circumstances which justified the interference in the first place." A majority of the Court had held in earlier cases that a routine traffic stop "is a relatively brief encounter and is more analogous to a so-called *Terry* stop . . . than to a formal arrest."[5]

In another case, the Supreme Court held that a suspect can be compelled by law to give his or her name to police during a *Terry* stop.[6] In a case with a more difficult set of facts, a federal border patrol agent made an investigatory stop of a minivan in a remote area of southeastern Arizona and found marijuana. The circumstances of this case included the following: the van was traveling along a little-traveled route often used by smugglers in an attempt to avoid a border patrol checkpoint thirty miles away; the agent suspected that the driver intended to pass through the area at a time when officers would be away from backroads patrols to change shifts; although a family was in the van, the vehicle turned away from some known recreational areas accessible to the east; the knees of two of the children were elevated, suggesting the existence of concealed cargo in the passenger compartment; and the driver slowed down, stiffened, and failed to acknowledge the border agent after sighting him. Although the U.S. Supreme Court found that each individual factor by itself was "susceptible to innocent explanation," the Court also found that there was reasonable suspicion for the investigatory stop when considering the totality of the circumstances.[7] These cases illustrate the difficulty in applying the threshold of reasonable suspicion in practice.

Stop and frisk is now a common police practice. A recent survey that asked citizens if they had been stopped by the police during the past year found that an estimated 45.3 million residents age sixteen or older—about 21 percent of all persons this age—had at least one face-to-face contact with police during the year. About 59 percent of these contacts were initiated by police, while the remaining contacts were initiated by the individual, a family member, or someone else who summoned the police.[8] The most common reason for a police contact was being stopped while driving a motor vehicle—nearly 9 percent of drivers age sixteen or older are stopped by police each year, representing nearly 17 million of the 193 million drivers in the United States (see Figure 7.1). The majority of these (55 percent) were stopped for speeding. Only about 8 percent of all those stopped by police were stopped because the police were investigating a crime or suspecting them of something. Only 5 percent of the 17 million drivers who were stopped by the police had their cars or persons frisked or searched, and less than 2 percent involved instances where the police threatened or used force. In cases where police suspected the individuals of something, however, more than 20 percent were handcuffed and arrested. The vast majority of those stopped by police (90 percent) believed

FIGURE 7.1 Contacts between the Police and the Public

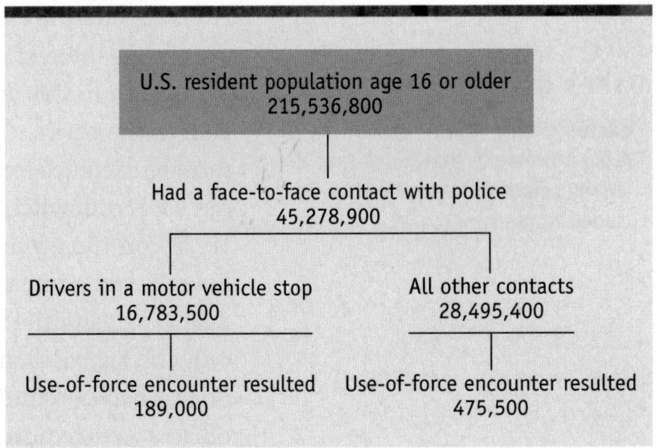

Source: Matthew R. Durose, Erica L. Schmitt, and Patrick A. Langan, *Contacts between the Police and the Public* (Washington, DC: Bureau of Justice Statistics, 2005).

the police acted properly.[9] These data suggest that the role of police in face-to-face contacts is significant, yet the public generally sees it as appropriate.

The Exclusionary Rule

The landmark case that applied the provisions of the Fourth Amendment to searches was decided in 1961. Three Cleveland police officers had arrived at Dolree Mapp's residence in response to information that a person wanted in connection with a recent bombing was hiding there. The officers knocked on the door and demanded entrance. After telephoning her attorney, Mapp refused to admit them without a search warrant. The police left the scene.

Three hours later the police (now numbering at least seven officers) again tried to enter Mapp's house. An officer knocked on the door, and when Mapp did not answer immediately, they forced one of the doors and gained entry. Mapp, who was halfway down the stairs, demanded to see a warrant. One of the officers held up a piece of paper that he claimed was a warrant. Mapp grabbed the paper and stuffed it into her blouse. After a struggle the police recovered the piece of paper and handcuffed Mapp because she had been "belligerent" during their recovery of the "warrant."

Meanwhile Mapp's attorney arrived, but the officers would not let him enter the house or see his client. Mapp was then forcibly taken upstairs to her bedroom, where the police searched a dresser, a closet, and suitcases. They also searched several other rooms, including the basement, where they found a trunk that contained obscene materials. Mapp was arrested for possession of those materials.

At trial it was discovered that the police had never obtained a search warrant for the search of Mapp's residence. Nevertheless, Mapp was convicted of illegal possession of obscene materials. The conviction was appealed, and the case eventually reached the U.S. Supreme Court.

The Supreme Court had ruled in 1914 that illegally seized evidence could not be used in federal prosecutions.[10] In 1949 the Court held that the Fourth Amendment protected individuals from both state and federal actions, but it did not extend the 1914 exclusionary rule to the states.[11] It was not until the Mapp case that the Supreme Court held that because the Fourth Amendment's right of privacy is enforceable in states through the due process clause of the Fourteenth Amendment, the exclusionary rule applies to both state and federal prosecutions. A growing interest in civil rights combined with concern for due process in police actions led to this decision.[12] The *Mapp v. Ohio* decision applied the exclusionary rule to the states.[13] The **exclusionary rule** holds that illegally seized evidence must be excluded from trials. Searches conducted without probable cause (or without a warrant where one is required) are illegal. Mapp's conviction in Ohio was reversed on the ground that her residence had been searched in violation of the Fourth Amendment. The Court explained, "Our holding that the exclusionary rule is an essential part of both the Fourth and Fourteenth Amendments is not only the logical dictate of prior cases, but it also makes very good sense. There is no war between the Constitution and common sense." In the *Mapp* case the police officers were required to possess a warrant in order to search Mapp's house legally. Because they did not have a warrant, their presence in her home was illegal under

MAPP V. OHIO

exclusionary rule
A legal principle that holds that illegally seized evidence must be excluded from use in trials.

the Fourth Amendment. Therefore, any evidence they found was obtained illegally. No matter what the officers found in Mapp's house, it could not be used in court because their presence there was illegal.

The Good Faith Exception

The ruling in *Mapp v. Ohio* remained intact for nearly twenty-five years. During the 1980s, however, a trend toward greater conservatism in U.S. society resulted in a change in the composition of the U.S. Supreme Court through presidential appointments of new justices. The result was a shift in the balance between the individual's interest in privacy and the government's interest in apprehending criminals. Although the exclusionary rule still exists, the number of exceptions to the rule has grown.

The first and most significant exception was created in 1984 in the case of *U.S. v. Leon.*[14] Police in Burbank, California, initiated a drug-trafficking investigation of Alberto Leon on the basis of a tip from a confidential informant. After conducting a surveillance of Leon's activities, the police applied for a warrant to search three residences and Leon's cars for drug-related items. The warrant application was reviewed by several deputy district attorneys, and the warrant was signed by a state court judge. The searches turned up large quantities of illegal drugs, and Leon was indicted for federal drug offenses.

U.S. V. LEON

A problem arose in that the surveillance of Leon had not actually produced the probable cause needed for a warrant or search. The original affidavit was therefore insufficient to establish probable cause, and the warrant application was signed by the judge in error. The case eventually reached the U.S. Supreme Court, which established a **good faith exception** to the exclusionary rule. The Court based the exception on three arguments. First, it held that "the exclusionary rule

good faith exception
A rule stating that evidence seized with a defective warrant, not based on probable cause, is admissible in court if the police acted in good faith in presenting the evidence and the error was made by the judge.

A police officer searches a crime scene. In what circumstances do police not need a warrant in order to conduct a search? Could the good faith exception apply to the situation in the photo?

is designed to deter police misconduct rather than to punish the errors of judges." The rationale was that it did not seem fair to penalize police for the error of the state court judge who acted in good faith in signing the defective warrant. Second, the Court argued that a good faith exception would not defeat the purpose of the exclusionary rule. Police acted reasonably in this case, and the intent of the exclusionary rule is not to deter reasonable police conduct. Finally, the Court said that the exclusionary rule still applies if police act improperly. That is, if police misled a judge by using false information in a warrant application, the exclusionary rule would apply and any evidence seized on the basis of that warrant would be excluded at trial. In addition, the good faith exception would not apply if a judge were found to have "abandoned his detached or neutral role" or if police officers were "dishonest or reckless in preparing their affidavit" or did not reasonably believe that probable cause existed.[15]

OTHER EXCEPTIONS FOR LAWFUL SEARCH AND SEIZURE

Three justices dissented from this decision, and their opinion captures the essence of the ongoing debate over exceptions to the exclusionary rule. The dissent argued that an exception to the exclusionary rule for judicial errors is self-contradictory. How can a search and seizure be "reasonable" (because it was conducted in good faith) but at the same time "unreasonable" (because probable cause did not exist)? The Fourth Amendment does not address the role of intent in police decisions about search and seizure.

In subsequent cases the Court attempted both to refine the limits of the good faith exception and to create new exceptions for searches and seizures under law. For example, the Court held that inmates have no reasonable expectation of privacy in a prison cell and therefore are not protected by the Fourth Amendment:[16] Neither probable cause nor warrants are required for searches of inmates or seizures of their property. In a case involving the search of a high school student's purse, the Court held that the Fourth Amendment applies to school officials but not to students, because of a "substantial need" to maintain order in schools.[17] In a Maryland case, police mistakenly searched the wrong apartment without probable cause and found illegal drugs there; the evidence was allowed at trial, because the police error was an "honest mistake." Once again the Supreme Court relied on the intent of the officers rather than on the presence of probable cause, thereby creating what has been called the "honest mistake" exception.[18]

Knock and Announce

The manner in which a search warrant is executed has also been the subject of court review. The common law principle that law enforcement officers must announce their presence and provide residents with an opportunity to open the door is an ancient one that has been made part of U.S. law.[19] Nevertheless, there are exceptions to the "knock and announce" rule when circumstances indicate a threat of physical violence or reason to believe that evidence will be destroyed if advance notice is given. In 2003, the Supreme Court heard a case in which police obtained a warrant to search for cocaine in an apartment, called out "police search warrant," and knocked on the apartment's front door, receiving no response. They waited fifteen to twenty seconds and then broke open the door with a battering ram. The Court held that this time interval was long enough to satisfy the Fourth Amendment guarantee against unreasonable searches and seizures.[20]

In a 2006 case, police obtained a warrant authorizing a search of a home for drugs and firearms and found both. When the police arrived to execute the warrant, however, they announced their presence but waited only a short time—perhaps "three to five seconds"—before turning the knob of the unlocked front door and entering the home. The Supreme Court found this very short time interval to be acceptable also, arguing that excluding the incriminating evidence entails "the risk of releasing dangerous criminals," and that civil suits and disciplinary actions within police departments will counter any police abuses of "no-knock" searches (see the Critical Thinking exercise at the end of the chapter).[21]

In these and other cases the U.S. Supreme Court has permitted the use of evidence seized by police that would have been excluded under the rule applied in *Mapp v. Ohio.* The Court's reliance on reasonable police activity, rather than on strict application of the probable cause standard of the Fourth Amendment, reflects the recent expansion of the authority of government officials to search citizens.

Searches without Warrants

The ability of police officers to search suspects without a warrant emerged from the need for police to protect themselves and to prevent the destruction of evidence in street encounters. It is not practical, timely, or safe to obtain a warrant to search someone who has just been arrested for a violent crime. As a result, the U.S. Supreme Court has interpreted the Fourth Amendment clause "no warrants shall issue but upon probable cause" to mean that warrants must be based on probable cause, *not* that a warrant is the only way to establish probable cause. The Fourth Amendment as a whole has been interpreted to mean that citizens are protected against "unreasonable searches and seizures." Therefore, police are permitted to search without a warrant under circumstances in which it is "reasonable" to do so.

FIVE SEARCHES WITHOUT WARRANTS

Over the years the Supreme Court has delineated five general types of situations in which searches can reasonably be conducted without a warrant. These exceptions to the warrant requirement include searches incident to a lawful arrest, searches with voluntary consent, searches of evidence in plain view, searches of automobiles and their contents, and searches of open fields and abandoned property.

Police are knocking and announcing their presence before entering an apartment. How long do they have to wait before entering? According to what criteria does the U.S. Supreme Court evaluate police conduct in cases like this?

Searches Incident to a Lawful Arrest

The case that established the authority of police to conduct a warrantless search in a lawful arrest was *Chimel v. California.* Police officers went to Chimel's home with a warrant to arrest him for the burglary of a coin shop. Chimel was not home, but his wife allowed the police to enter and wait for his return. When Chimel arrived, the police showed him the warrant, placing him under arrest, and proceeded to search the house. They found the coins that he was suspected of stealing and used them as evidence to convict him of burglary. On appeal, the U.S. Supreme Court overturned the conviction on the ground that the search of Chimel's entire house was unreasonable under the Fourth Amendment.

> *When an arrest is made, it is reasonable for the arresting officer to search the person arrested in order to remove any weapons the [suspect] might seek to use in order to resist arrest or effect his escape. Otherwise, the officer's safety might well be endangered, and the arrest itself frustrated. In addition, it is entirely reasonable for the arresting officer to search for and seize any evidence on the arrestee's person in order to prevent its concealment or destruction. And the area into which an arrestee might reach in order to grab a weapon or evidentiary items must, of course, be governed by a like rule. A gun on a table or in a drawer in front of one who is arrested can be as dangerous to the arresting officer as one concealed in the clothing of the person arrested. There is ample justification, therefore, for a search of the arrestee's person and the area "within his immediate control"—construing that phrase to mean the area from within which he might gain possession of a weapon or destructible evidence.*[22]

WITHIN IMMEDIATE CONTROL

The Court's finding in *Chimel* allows for a search for only two purposes: to remove weapons and to seize evidence that might be concealed or destroyed. To accomplish these purposes, the police officer is permitted to search the arrestee and the area "within his immediate control." The difficulty of defining the area "within his immediate control" has resulted in a large number of cases that have attempted to delimit this area in different situations. Many of these have involved automobiles. The Supreme Court summarized its current position in *Pennsylvania v. Labron*, stating that when there is probable cause for a belief that a car holds contraband and the car can move, the police have authority to search it without a warrant.[23]

In a 2001 case, *Illinois v. McArthur*, two police officers accompanied a wife, at her request, to a trailer where she lived with her husband. She wanted the officers to keep the peace while she removed her belongings, and the two officers remained outside the home while the wife and husband were inside. When the wife emerged after collecting her possessions, she told the police that her husband had slid "dope" underneath a couch in the home. When the husband refused a police request to search the home, one officer and the wife as witness went to obtain a search warrant. Once the husband exited the home, the remaining officer told him that he could not re-enter unless accompanied by the officer. The husband was thus prevented from entering his home for approximately two hours until the other officer returned with a search warrant. The police executed a search and found under the couch a marijuana pipe, a box for marijuana, and a small amount of marijuana. The U.S. Supreme Court held that given the nature of the intrusion and the law enforcement interest at stake, the brief seizure of the home (keeping the husband outside the home for two hours) was reasonable and therefore lawful under the Fourth Amendment.[24] This holding corresponds to the principles of *Chimel*, where prevention of the destruction of evidence permits a warrantless seizure (in the *McArthur* case, not permitting re-entry into the home).

Searches with Voluntary Consent Another well-established exception to the warrant requirement occurs when a search is made with the consent of the suspect. The primary concern here is the voluntariness of the consent. In the landmark case of *Schneckloth v. Bustamonte*,[25] a police officer in Sunnyvale, California, stopped a car that had only one working headlight. Six men were in the car. The driver could not produce a driver's license. When the officer asked if he could search the car, the owner, who was present as a passenger, gave permission. Under the rear seat the officer found three checks that had previously been reported stolen from a car wash. The checks were used as evidence in a trial in which the owner and an accomplice were convicted of possessing stolen checks. The question on appeal was whether the consent to search was truly voluntary.

VOLUNTARY VERSUS INVOLUNTARY

The distinction between a voluntary and an involuntary search is extremely important in this case, because the police did not have probable cause to conduct a search without consent. The car was stopped because of a burned-out headlight, for which the police could not make a custodial arrest (in which case a search would have been allowed).

The U.S. Supreme Court held that the search was legal and that the evidence discovered was therefore admissible in court. Consent was "voluntarily given, and not the result of duress or coercion, express or implied." The dissenting opinion in this case expressed concern about exploiting the ignorance of suspects who do not know this rule. Subsequent Supreme Court decisions on this issue culminated in the decision in *Ohio v. Robinette* that people stopped for traffic violations do not have to be told they are free to go before their consent to a search can be recognized as voluntary.[26]

A variation of these facts occurred in the case of a bus en route from Florida to Michigan. Three plainclothes police officers were permitted to board the bus during a routine stop, and they displayed their badges and talked individually with passengers regarding their luggage in a "routine" search of illegal weapons and drugs. Passengers were permitted to enter and exit the bus as the officers spoke with passengers. The officers approached two men and asked to search their luggage. Consent was given and nothing was found. The officers then asked, "Do you mind if I check your person?" The two men agreed, and a patting down of their pants found packets that are sometimes used to carry drugs. A subsequent search found that both suspects had duct-taped bags of cocaine to their underwear. They challenged their arrests on drug charges, arguing that their consent to the search was not voluntary. The U.S. Supreme Court held in this case *U.S. v. Drayton* that police officers are not required by the Fourth Amendment "to advise bus passengers of their right not to cooperate and to refuse consent to searches."[27] This finding is consistent with earlier decisions that do not require police notification of suspects of their right to refuse consent.

In a case with an interesting variation on consent searches, a police officer was present at a married couple's house in Georgia after the wife contacted the police concerning a domestic dispute. In the presence of the husband, the wife volunteered to the officer that there was evidence inside the house of the husband's illegal drug use. The husband refused the officer's request for permission for a warrantless search of the house. However, the wife then consented to a search and

Would police need a warrant to seize this pistol lying on the ground? Why or why not? What if the gun was lying on the seat of a car and a police officer saw it during a traffic stop?

led the officer to the evidence. The police seized this evidence and, after subsequently obtaining a search warrant, seized further evidence of drug use. Was this a search with voluntary consent? The Supreme Court ruled in 2006 that because the husband and wife both lived at the home and both were present, the refusal of one to a voluntary search of the premises without a warrant is controlling. Therefore, the search violated the Fourth Amendment, the drug paraphernalia was seized unlawfully, and the husband's conviction on drug charges was overturned.[28]

Plain View Searches The right of police to search without a warrant items that are in "plain view" is another well-established exception to the warrant requirement. This exception was explained in the Supreme Court's decision in *Coolidge v. New Hampshire.*[29] The Court specified two conditions for a plain view search: (1) The police officer's presence where the plain view search is made must be lawful, and (2) the discovery must be inadvertent. That is, if police have probable cause before the search, they must obtain a warrant.

The Court established a third condition for plain view searches in *Texas v. Brown* and other cases.[30] It held that police do not have to be "absolutely certain" that evidence is incriminating before making a plain view search. In this case, during a routine traffic stop a police officer seized an opaque green party balloon (which was knotted) together with several small vials, white powder, and empty balloons that were in the automobile. The Court held that the circumstances established probable cause for arrest for possession of an illegal substance, even though the officer was not certain that the balloon he had seized contained an illicit substance.

Evidence seized in a plain view search must be "open to view."[31] The Court has held, however, that a person has no reasonable expectation of privacy in the visible interior of his or her car, even if the interior is inspected by police with a flashlight from outside the car.[32]

BOND V. UNITED STATES

Although the Court generally has relaxed earlier restrictions and allowed police to search under a wider variety of circumstances, in the 2000 case of *Bond v. United States*, the Court placed limits on random "squeezing" of carry-on luggage. In this case a border patrol agent boarded a bus in Texas to check the immigration status of passengers. On his way off the bus he squeezed the soft luggage passengers had placed in the overhead bins. In one bag, he felt the form of a "brick-like" object, which was ultimately discovered to be a brick of methamphetamine. Although the officer's presence on the bus was lawful, the Court noted that squeezing the bags was "physically invasive," and more intrusive than mere visual inspection. The Court held that bus passengers have a reasonable expectation that their carry-on bags will not be inspected in an "exploratory manner" absent other evidence of unlawful conduct.[33]

THE AUTOMOBILE EXCEPTION

Searches of Automobiles and Their Contents The so-called "automobile exception" to the warrant requirement was established in 1925 in the case of *Carroll v. United States.*[34] The defendants were arrested and convicted of transporting sixty-eight quarts of whiskey and gin in an automobile in violation of the National

The police officer is conducting a thorough search of a car. Under what circumstances is a warrant not required before conducting a search like this?

Prohibition Act. They challenged their convictions on the ground that the search and seizure was conducted in violation of the Fourth Amendment. The defendants claimed that because the search was made without a warrant, the evidence discovered in the search should be excluded. In ruling on the appeal, the Supreme Court clarified a legal point it had made in 1914, stating that once a person has been lawfully arrested, "whatever is found upon his person or in his control which it is unlawful for him to have and which may be used to prove the offense may be seized and held as evidence in the prosecution."[35]

In *New York v. Belton,* the Supreme Court held that when a police officer makes a lawful custodial arrest of an occupant of an automobile, the Fourth Amendment allows the officer to search the vehicle's passenger compartment incident to the arrest.[36] This holding was refined further in a 2004 case in which a city police officer tried to pull over an automobile that had license tags that had been issued for another vehicle. Before the officer could stop the car, however, the driver drove into a parking lot, parked, and left the automobile. The officer then accosted the driver, found marijuana and cocaine in the driver's pocket, and arrested him. Incident to the arrest, the officer searched the automobile and found a handgun under the driver's seat. The Supreme Court held that Belton rule applied even though the officer first made contact with the arrestee *after* the arrestee had left the vehicle. So long as an arrestee was a "recent occupant" of a vehicle, such as the arrestee in the instant case, officers can search the vehicle incident to the arrest.[37]

In the cases of *Chambers v. Maroney*[38] and *Michigan v. Thomas,*[39] the Supreme Court expanded the power of police to search an automobile without a warrant. It held that police do not have to obtain a warrant to search a car that is stopped on a highway and impounded, if they have probable cause. Therefore, a vehicle does not necessarily have to be "moving" or even capable of moving for a warrantless search to be lawful. In recent years the scope of the automobile exception has been expanded further to vehicles that have already been impounded.[40] In *Ross v.*

FIGURE 7.2 Searches Conducted by Police during Traffic Stops

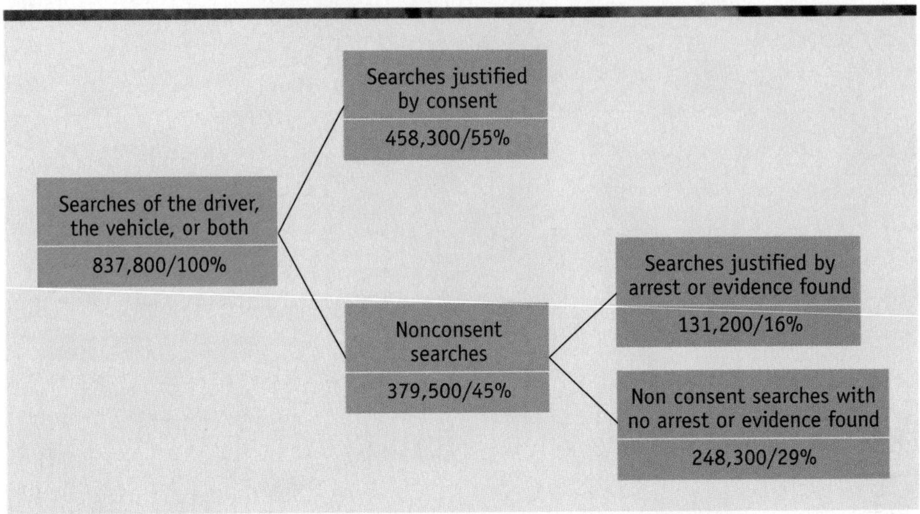

Source: Matthew R. Durose, Erica L. Schmitt, and Patrick A. Langan, *Contacts between the Police and the Public* (Washington, DC: Bureau of Justice Statistics, 2005).

United States the U.S. Supreme Court held that "if probable cause justifies the search of a lawfully stopped vehicle, it justifies the search of every part of the vehicle and its contents that may conceal the object of the search."[41]

Of the estimated 837,800 searches conducted by police in a recent year, more than half (55 percent) were based on the driver's consent (see Figure 7.2). The remaining searches were conducted without consent, with 131,200 of them (16 percent) justified on the basis of an arrest (e.g., for intoxication) or upon probable cause that led to an arrest (e.g., smell of marijuana that led to a seizure). Searches were made incident to a lawful arrest in about two-thirds of the cases.[42]

Why have the courts frequently had to reinterpret the U.S. Constitution on questions of individual rights in criminal investigations by police? What are the criteria for determining if the law enforcement officers in this photo are conducting a legal search? How does this situation represent an exception to the exclusionary rule?

Open Fields and Abandoned Property The fifth exception to the warrant requirement allows for searches of open fields and abandoned property, which have been found not to be protected by the Fourth Amendment. The open fields exception was first recognized in 1924 in the case of *Hester v. United States.*[43] Police officers suspected that liquor was being manufactured illegally at Hester's home. Fleeing from police across an open field, the suspects dropped bottles they were carrying. The bottles contained the evidence that a crime had occurred. Although the officers did not have a search warrant or an arrest warrant, the Supreme Court upheld the men's convictions, holding that "there was no seizure in the sense of the law when the officers examined the contents of each bottle after it had been abandoned."

Since this decision, the meaning of "house" under the Fourth Amendment has been extended to include the grounds and buildings immediately surrounding a home, known as the "curtilage." However, there are no precise guidelines for determining where curtilage ends and open fields begin.[44] In *California v. Ciraolo* police flew an airplane over private property at 1,000 feet in response to an anonymous tip that marijuana was being grown in the yard. A search warrant was obtained on the basis of an aerial photograph in which marijuana plants could be easily identified. The Supreme Court upheld this search and seizure, holding that "the Fourth Amendment simply does not require the police traveling in the public airways at this altitude to obtain a warrant in order to observe what is visible to the naked eye."[45] Like other decisions of federal courts in the 1980s and 1990s this ruling expanded the authority of police to conduct searches without judicial warrants.[46]

Modern technology poses new challenges in delineating where public space ends and private space (protected by the Fourth Amendment) begins. Based on suspicion that marijuana was being grown inside a home, a government agent used a thermal imaging device to scan the building to see whether there was a high level of heat emanating from the home, consistent with the use of high-intensity lamps often used for growing marijuana indoors. The scan was done from the agent's car across the street, and it found that the walls of the home were substantially warmer than neighboring homes. Using this evidence, a search warrant was obtained, and an indoor marijuana growing operation was discovered with more than one hundred plants. The suspect challenged the use of the thermal imaging device, claiming it constituted the equivalent of a search of his home without a warrant. The U.S. Supreme Court held that use of a thermal-imaging device aimed at a private home from a public street constitutes a search within the meaning of the Fourth Amendment. Therefore, the use of the imaging device without a warrant is unlawful under the Fourth Amendment because it involves obtaining and using sense-enhancing technology not in general public use, resulting in information about the interior of a home that could not otherwise have been obtained without physical intrusion into a constitutionally protected area (inside the house).[47] As technology improves, it is clear that there will be more cases attempting to draw the distinction between public space open to surveillance and searches, and private spaces protected by the Fourth Amendment.

The Fifth Amendment and the *Miranda* Warning

After an arrest and search have been carried out, the police have the authority to interrogate the arrested person. Interrogations are not specifically mentioned in the Constitution, but the limits of official interrogations are implied in the **Fifth Amendment:**

> *No person shall be held to answer for a capital, or otherwise infamous crime, unless on a presentment or indictment of a Grand Jury, except in cases arising in the land or naval forces, or in the Militia, when in actual service in time of War or public danger; nor shall any person be subject for the same offense to be twice put in jeopardy of life or limb; nor shall be compelled in any criminal case to be a witness against himself, nor be deprived of life, liberty, or property, without due process of law; nor shall private property be taken for public use, without just compensation.*

Fifth Amendment
The amendment to the Constitution that includes protection against self-incrimination.

FIGURE 7.3 Layout of the Interview Room in the Denver Police Department

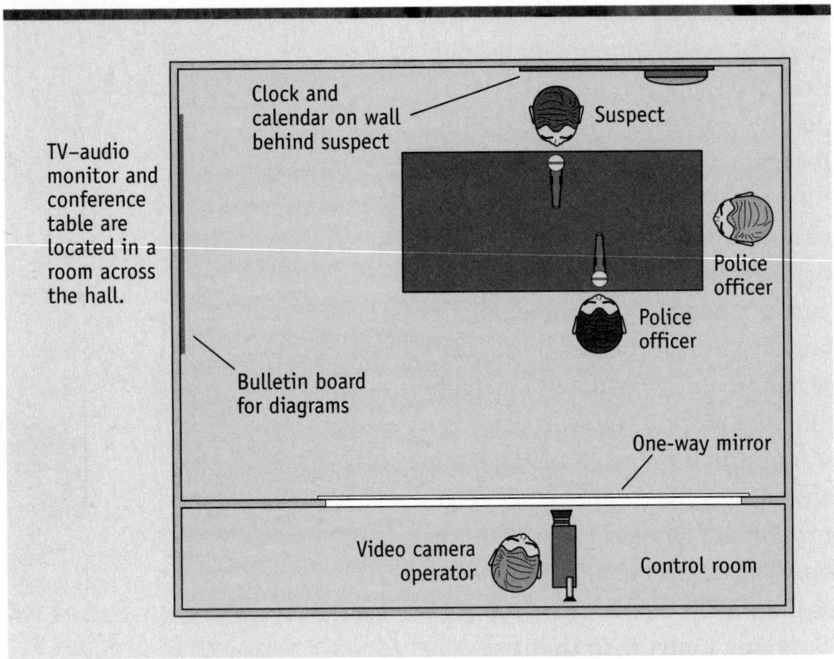

Source: William A. Geller, *Videotaping Interrogations and Confessions* (Washington, DC: National Institute of Justice, 1993), p. 8.

The Fifth Amendment mentions interrogations when it states that no person can be "compelled in any criminal case to be a witness against himself." The inclusion of this phrase in the Fifth Amendment was a reaction to the Court of the Star Chamber, which was established by Henry VII in 1487. Sedition and heresy trials were conducted in this court, which allowed for forced testimony. This inquisitional system resulted in confessions due to torture rather than guilt. It was not until the seventeenth century that England guaranteed individuals protection from forced testimony against themselves. This history of arbitrary and malicious accusatory practices led the framers of the U.S. Constitution to include in the Fifth Amendment specific provisions for protection against self-incrimination.

The Fifth Amendment has had its greatest impact on interrogations and confessions obtained by the police. The landmark case in which the U.S. Supreme Court applied the Fifth Amendment to specific police procedures was *Miranda v. Arizona.*[48] Ernesto Miranda was arrested at his home and taken to the Phoenix police station. A rape victim identified Miranda as her assailant. He was then taken into a police interrogation room and questioned by two officers. (The layout of a typical interrogation room is shown in Figure 7.3.) Two hours later the officers emerged from the room with a written confession signed by Miranda. A typed paragraph at the top of the confession said that it had been made voluntarily "with full knowledge of my legal rights, understanding any statement I make may be used against me."

MIRANDA V. ARIZONA

At his trial, the officers admitted that Miranda had not been told that he had the right to have an attorney present during the interrogation. Nevertheless, the written confession was admitted into evidence. Miranda was found guilty of kidnapping and rape and was sentenced to twenty to thirty years in prison. He appealed his conviction, but the appeal was denied on the ground that he did not specifically request legal counsel at the interrogation. The case was finally appealed to the U.S. Supreme Court.

The Supreme Court took special notice of the typed paragraph at the top of Miranda's signed confession stating that it had been made "with full knowledge of my legal rights." As the Court noted, Miranda was uneducated, indigent, and "a seriously disturbed individual with pronounced sexual fantasies." Moreover, no one other than the police had been present during his interrogation. The Court felt that these circumstances cast doubt on whether the confession was truly voluntary.

> *The current practice of incommunicado interrogation is at odds with one of our nation's most cherished principles—that an individual may not be compelled to incriminate himself. Unless adequate protective devices are employed to dispel the compulsion inherent in custodial surroundings, no statement obtained from the defendant can truly be a product of free choice.*

FIGURE 7.4 The *Miranda* Warning

The Miranda Warning

- The suspect must be warned prior to any questioning that he or she has the right to remain silent.
- Any statements made by the person can be used in a court of law.
- The suspect has the right to the presence of an attorney.
- If the person cannot afford an attorney, one will be appointed prior to any questioning.
- Opportunity to exercise these rights must be afforded to the suspect throughout the interrogation. After such warnings have been given, a person may knowingly and intelligently waive these rights and agree to answer questions or make a statement.

Using this rationale, the Supreme Court overturned Miranda's conviction, stating that the confession was inadmissible as evidence. To ensure protection from self-incrimination in future cases, the Supreme Court said that once a suspect is taken into custody, he or she must receive the five-point warning now known as the ***Miranda* warning** (see Figure 7.4). This warning is required when an individual is taken into custody and is subjected to questioning, because this is when the protection against self-incrimination is jeopardized.

***Miranda* warning**
A five-point warning derived from the case of *Miranda v. Arizona*. Its purpose is to provide fair notice to crime suspects of their basic constitutional rights.

Although the *Miranda* decision set specific guidelines for the conduct of police interrogations, it did not prohibit interrogators in any way. The Court's only objective was to ensure fairness in nonvoluntary interrogations. As the Court observed, "there is no requirement that police stop a person who enters a police station and states that he wishes to confess a crime, or a person who calls the police to offer a confession or any other statement he desires to make. Volunteered statements of any kind are not barred by the Fifth Amendment and their admissibility [as evidence] is not affected by our holding today."

The *Miranda* decision ensures that those who are ignorant of the law will be given the same understanding of their constitutional protections as those who already understand their rights under the law. The decision added specific legal protections beyond the right to an attorney—a right that was guaranteed to a suspect in custody by the Supreme Court's 1964 decision in *Escobedo v. Illinois.*[49] In that case the suspect, Danny Escobedo, was interrogated by police for fifteen hours, released, and rearrested eleven days later. Escobedo's attorney arrived at the police station for the second interrogation, but the police would not allow the attorney to see his client until the police had finished their questioning. It was during this second interrogation that Escobedo made self-incriminating statements. The Supreme Court reversed Escobedo's conviction, holding that Escobedo was in custody as a suspect in a crime, was interrogated by police, had requested to speak with his lawyer, but was denied access. The Supreme Court's decision in *Miranda* two years after the *Escobedo* decision added specific warnings required at police interrogations to deter this kind of police conduct.

ESCOBEDO V. ILLINOIS

The definition of interrogation was the subject of the case *Rhode Island v. Innis*, in which the Supreme Court used police intent to determine if a violation of *Miranda* had occurred. In this case a suspect who indicated that he wanted to speak with a lawyer before talking to police inadvertently incriminated himself during casual conversation with police officers. At issue was whether the officers

RHODE ISLAND V. INNIS

Media & Criminal Justice — *Law & Order*

Since 1990, viewers have been intrigued by NBC's art-imitates-life drama *Law & Order.* It is the longest running crime series in the history of American broadcast television. The show's opening narrative offers a simple explanation for each show: In every criminal justice system there are two major players in the fight against the crime—the police and the prosecutors. "These are their stories," states the narrator, and the viewer is propelled into a one-hour roller-coaster version of a criminal case, from start to finish, with so many plot twists that even die-hard fans often find themselves confused.

Set in downtown Manhattan in New York City, each show begins with a crime that imitates real-life crime covered by the media. For example, the story might include a jogger who is raped and beaten in Central Park, or a famous mystery writer shot by someone in her deviant love triangle, or a man who awakens on a park bench to find that while he's been beaten unconscious, during his coma his kidney was surgically removed!

The magic of the television series lies in the excellent cast of characters who portray the law enforcement officers and prosecutors seeking justice in the tangled web of events. Like pawns on a chessboard, the police officers provide the first line of attack, gathering evidence and cajoling witnesses into offering up the information necessary to make a case. While real-life cases never proceed as smoothly as on *Law & Order,* the dynamics between the beat cops, their female supervisor, the moralistic district attorney, and his own politically astute supervisor truly reflect the complexities of enforcing the law while respecting the parameters of criminal procedure.

The police do make mistakes—and over the years, only one of the police characters has survived the political realities of the system. As in real life, a police officer who perjures himself on the witness stand can compromise a conviction, lose his job, and even land in jail. The conflict between the police officers who try to uphold justice at any price, and the DA who must prosecute the corrupt officer even when it is clear that the cop was only seeking justice, are harsh realities that *Law & Order* refuses to ignore.

In 2000, the success of *Law & Order* resulted in a spin-off drama called *Law & Order: Special Victims Unit,* which introduced a new set of characters to the stage of criminal procedure: victim advocates and special investigators. As in real life, these relatively new practitioners in the criminal justice system have taken on increasing importance in an effort to offer balance between the police, the prosecutors, and the citizens that they have taken an oath to serve.

How realistic is the depiction of the police investigative role in the cases shown on *Law & Order?* Can you identify procedural problems that the police make which could be raised by the defendant in a court of law? Should the police be honest with the DA about their mistakes if it means losing the case, or are minor cover-ups to be expected in the interest of justice? How should a DA handle allegations of police misconduct?

had conducted the functional equivalent of an interrogation, thereby violating the suspect's *Miranda* rights.

WHAT IS "QUESTIONING"?

The Supreme Court found that the suspect's rights has not been violated; but the Court also made it clear that the *Miranda* warnings apply during the "functional equivalent" of questioning, which consists of words or questions by police that are "reasonably likely to elicit an incriminating response from the suspect." The Court concluded that for a violation of *Miranda* to take place, "It must also be established that a suspect's incriminating response was the product of words or actions on the part of the police that they should have known were reasonably likely to elicit an incriminating response."[50] This decision narrows the scope of the *Miranda* warning by applying it only to direct questioning by police or to situations in which police actions are "reasonably likely" to result in self-incrimination.

The Public Safety Exception

In a landmark New York case, a woman approached two police officers on patrol and told them that she had just been raped. She described her assailant and said that he had just entered a nearby supermarket and was carrying a gun. While one of the officers radioed for assistance, the other entered the store and spotted a man named Benjamin Quarles who matched the description of the assailant. The suspect spotted the officer and ran to the rear of the store as the officer pursued him with his gun drawn. The officer momentarily lost sight of the suspect but soon saw him again. He then ordered the suspect to stop and put his hands over his head. He frisked the suspect and discovered that he was wearing an empty shoulder holster. After handcuffing him, the officer asked him where the gun was. The suspect nodded toward some empty cartons and said, "The gun is over there." The officer retrieved the gun, arrested the suspect, and read him his *Miranda* rights.

This man was stopped and frisked on the street and then was arrested. What rules of law did the law enforcement officer observe in making a legal stop and frisk? What procedures did the officer follow in making the legal arrest? What protects suspects from illegal interrogation and self-incrimination?

The case reached the U.S. Supreme Court because the officer's first question to the handcuffed suspect was likely to be incriminating. If the suspect's statement, which gave the location of the gun, was obtained illegally (i.e., without benefit of the *Miranda* warning), it should be excluded from trial, as should the gun that was discovered as a result of the illegally obtained statement. A majority of the justices held that "overriding considerations of public safety justify the officer's failure to provide *Miranda* warnings before he asked questions devoted to locating the abandoned weapon."[51] This decision created the **public safety exception** to the *Miranda* warning. The exception was justified on the ground that it would be allowed only in cases involving "questions reasonably prompted by a concern for public safety."

public safety exception
Police may omit the *Miranda* warning prior to questioning a suspect when public safety is jeopardized.

Interrogations and Confessions

Beginning in the 1980s the Supreme Court decided many cases that provided additional exceptions to the *Miranda* rule. In *South Dakota v. Neville*, the Court held that it is not "fundamentally unfair" to use a defendant's refusal to take a blood-alcohol test as evidence of guilt. In other words, this refusal, if used as evidence, does not violate the protection against self-incrimination.[52] In *Oregon v. Bradshaw*, the Court held that if the accused waives the right to counsel and then initiates further conversation, those statements may be used as evidence.[53] In another case the Court found that a probation officer seeking incriminating evidence is not required to give the *Miranda* warning to a probationer.[54] And roadside questioning of a motorist detained in a routine traffic stop was determined not to constitute a "custodial interrogation" for the purposes of *Miranda*.[55] In still another case, police arrested a man for purchasing stolen firearms but questioned him about a murder. The Supreme Court held that "mere silence by law enforcement officials as to the subject matter of an interrogation is not 'trickery' sufficient to invalidate a suspect's waiver of *Miranda* rights." The constitutionality of the interrogation was upheld.[56]

This juvenile is being charged by police. An officer will read the arrestee her *Miranda* rights. What are the *Miranda* warnings? When is this procedure required, and why? Do you think the *Miranda* impedes police in their work? Do you think the rule protects citizens from unfair police practices?

These cases characterize the direction of U.S. Supreme Court decisions in recent years, which have given police greater latitude to stray from the strict language of the *Miranda* finding.[57]

Congress enacted a law that challenged the *Miranda* ruling claiming that admissibility of statements should be decided solely on whether or not they are voluntary—regardless of whether the *Miranda* warning was given by police. The U.S. Supreme Court ruled in *Dickerson v. United States* that as a constitutional decision of the Court, *Miranda* "may not be in effect overruled by an Act of Congress." Although Congress can modify or eliminate legal rules that are not constitutionally required, it cannot supersede U.S. Supreme Court decisions that apply and interpret the U.S. Constitution. In addition, the Court held that "*Miranda* has become embedded in routine police practice to the point where the warnings have become part of our national culture."[58] The Court appears to be correct in its assessment because both leading police administrators and the public favor the *Miranda* rule.[59] A Gallup poll found that 94 percent of Americans believe the police should be required to inform arrested persons of their constitutional rights.[60]

DICKERSON V. UNITED STATES

The many conditions and exceptions to the *Miranda* rule have created uncertainty in its application. This uncertainty regarding confessions has prompted many police departments to videotape interrogations and confessions. Videotaping provides an objective record of the interrogation that prosecuters can use in responding to challenges from defense attorneys and in proving that confessions are voluntary. One study estimated that more than 60 percent of large police agencies in the United States now videotape interrogations or confessions in at least some types of cases. About 85 percent of police departments surveyed believe that videotaping improves the quality of interrogations.[61] Some states have begun to require viedotaping of interrogations in order to protect against false confessions.[62]

Impacts of Procedural Law on Law Enforcement

Since the U.S. Supreme Court's 1961 decision in *Mapp v. Ohio,* there has been much debate over the desirability of the exclusionary rule. Supporters of the rule maintain that the *Mapp* case illustrates how citizens need the rule if they are to be protected against police misconduct. Without the protection provided by the exclusionary rule, there would be nothing to prevent police from making illegal searches in the hope of finding some kind of incriminating evidence. The potential for harassment of citizens would be great. On the other hand, opponents argue that the exclusionary rule makes it possible for criminals to go free. Just because a search is conducted illegally, all the evidence found is excluded from use at trial. Such a sweeping rule may "handcuff" the police in their efforts to obtain evidence against criminals.

STUDIES ON EFFECTS OF THE EXCLUSIONARY RULE

This debate has prompted empirical investigations aimed at determining the relative merits of the exclusionary rule. Are many suspects released because searches are found to be illegal? Is there any evidence that the exclusionary rule deters police from making illegal searches? Sheldon Krantz and his colleagues examined the effect of the exclusionary rule in 512 drug and gambling cases in Boston. They found that the rule was used to exclude evidence in only 2 percent of those cases.[63] The U.S. General Accounting Office assessed the impact of the exclusionary rule in federal court. A review of 2,804 cases found that the rule had been invoked successfully in only 1.3 percent of the cases.[64]

A National Institute of Justice study examined felony cases over three years and found that once cases reached trial, fewer than one-half of 1 percent (0.4 percent) were dismissed because of the exclusionary rule, although there was some variation by jurisdiction and by type of crime.[65] Thus, as one expert noted, the impact of the exclusionary rule on prosecution of violent crime was "infinitesimal."[66] Nevertheless, the rule appeared to have some effect in drug cases, in which police rarely have a complainant whom they can rely on to establish probable cause for search and arrest.

The debate over the desirability of the exclusionary rule has continued, and the Supreme Court anticipated this controversy in its decision in the *Mapp* case:

> *Because [the Fourth Amendment protection of privacy] is enforceable in the same manner and to like effect as other basic rights secured by the Due Process Clause, we can no longer permit it to be revocable at the whim of any police officer who, in the name of law enforcement itself, chooses to suspend its enjoyment. Our decision, founded on reason and truth, gives to the individual no more than that which the Constitution guarantees him, to the police officer no less than that which honest law enforcement is entitled, and, to the courts, that judicial integrity so necessary in the true administration of justice.*

The Court argued that the exclusionary rule guarantees a constitutional right to individuals and grants to the government only the authority it needs if it is to carry out police functions with integrity. Since the 1980s, however, the composition of the Supreme Court has changed, resulting in a shift in the Court's views regarding the proper balance between the right to privacy and the government's desire to apprehend crime suspects. The Court has moved from adhering to a clear exclusionary rule to creating various exceptions, as noted earlier in this chapter, in which police may conduct searches without a warrant under a variety of circumstances.

Also at issue are laws governing police procedures. Law enforcement officials initially criticized *Miranda v. Arizona* for limiting their ability to obtain evidence through interrogation. Many believed that officers would no longer be able to conduct interrogations of suspects without lawyers present, and that suspects who understood that they had the right to remain silent would always invoke this right and refuse to talk to the police.

STUDIES ON EFFECTS OF THE *MIRANDA* WARNING

What has been the impact of the *Miranda* warning on contemporary police interrogations? One study of this question was carried out in Connecticut by Richard Ayres two years after the *Miranda* decision. Ayres placed ten observers in the New

That's a **FACT**

Perspectives on Profiling

A recent survey assessed public opinion on racial profiling in two ways. First, respondents were asked how widespread they think the practice is in certain situations. Then, respondents were asked whether they think racial profiling is justified in those situations. Respondents were asked about three different situations: motorists stopped on roads and highways, passengers stopped at airport security checkpoints, and shoppers questioned in malls and stores about possible theft.

Results show that a substantial proportion of Americans believe racial profiling is widespread in all three contexts (see Figure 7A). Slightly more than half (53 percent) think the practice of stopping motorists because of their race or ethnicity is widespread. Roughly half (49 percent) think racial profiling is used widely by those attempting to prevent theft in shopping malls and stores, and 42 percent think the practice is widespread at security checkpoints in airports. Perceptions about the prevalence of racial profiling differ by racial and ethnic group—Hispanics and blacks generally believe it is more common than whites.

FIGURE 7A How Widespread is Racial Profiling

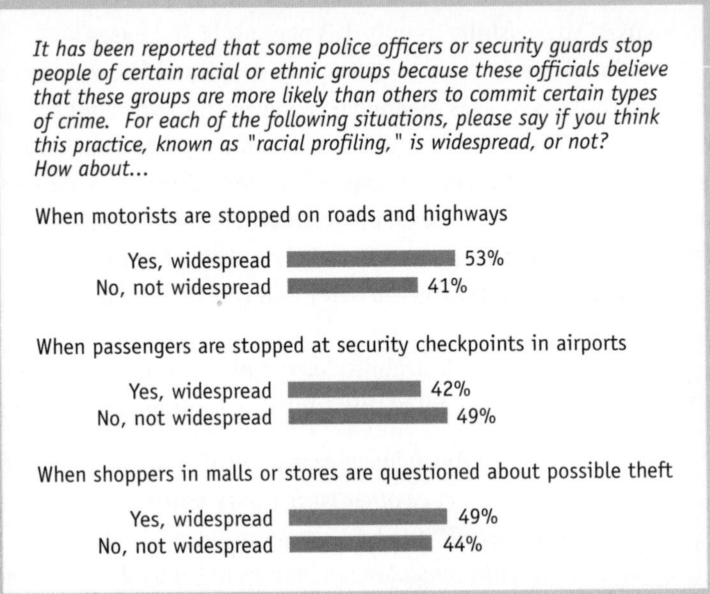
It has been reported that some police officers or security guards stop people of certain racial or ethnic groups because these officials believe that these groups are more likely than others to commit certain types of crime. For each of the following situations, please say if you think this practice, known as "racial profiling," is widespread, or not? How about...
When motorists are stopped on roads and highways
Yes, widespread 53%
No, not widespread 41%
When passengers are stopped at security checkpoints in airports
Yes, widespread 42%
No, not widespread 49%
When shoppers in malls or stores are questioned about possible theft
Yes, widespread 49%
No, not widespread 44%

Haven Police Department for eleven weeks. Working around the clock, they observed all interrogations and interviewed detectives, defense counsel, prosecutors, and suspects after the interrogations. On the basis of these observations and interviews, Ayres concluded that the *Miranda* decision "had virtually no effect on police investigation."[67] Ayres also discovered that detectives often found ways to reduce the effect of the *Miranda* warnings by changing the words in subtle ways: "Whatever you say may be used *for* or against you in a court of law," or "You don't have to say a word, but you ought to get everything cleared up," or "You don't have to say anything, of course, but you can explain how . . ." The U.S. Supreme Court has ruled that the *Miranda* warnings do not have to be stated in their exact form.[68]

Interestingly, suspects rarely reacted to the *Miranda* warnings when they were given. Most suspects chose not to exercise their rights to have counsel present or to remain silent. They appeared not to grasp the importance of the warnings and felt compelled by the circumstances to talk with the police. Subsequent investigations in Oakland, Los Angeles, Washington, D.C., and an unnamed midwestern city have yielded similar results: Police often fail to inform suspects of their rights, and few suspects exercise their rights under *Miranda* when they are informed of them.[69]

A majority of Americans do not believe racial or ethnic profiling is justified, but opinions vary depending on the specific situation. Only a quarter of the public thinks the practice is justified when it comes to questioning shoppers in stores; roughly a third (31 percent) thinks it is justified in the case of stopping motorists. Significantly more Americans (45 percent) feel it is justified at airport security checkpoints (see Figure 7B). Again, the answers to this question differ along racial and ethnic lines. In all three cases, black Americans tend to be least likely to say racial profiling is justified, while in most cases Hispanics hold opinions that are more similar to those of non-Hispanic whites.

Why do you believe public opinion about the justification for profiling differs between questioning shoppers in stores and questioning people at airport security checkpoints? Why do opinions differ along racial lines? Do you have ideas to change these perceptions?

FIGURE 7B Is Racial Profiling Justified?

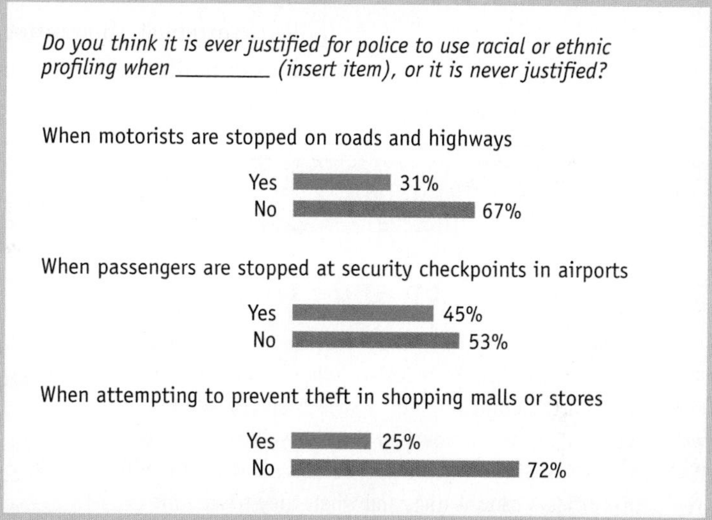

Source: Darren K. Carlson, "Racial Profiling Seen as Pervasive, Unjust," *Gallup News Service* (July 20, 2004).

On the other hand, studies by Paul Cassell in the 1990s concluded that thousands of cases had not been prosecuted because suspects did not make statements after being given the *Miranda* warning. Cassell found that more cases were pled to a lesser charge and that confession rates by suspects also had dropped since *Miranda*.[70] These conflicting findings are difficult to reconcile, although the Supreme Court continues to give wide latitude to police in interrogation settings. In a 2004 case, a seventeen-year-old suspect was questioned at a sheriff's office but was not given the Miranda warning. The issue was whether or not the teenager was effectively in custody. Some facts suggested he was not in custody: Police did not transport him to the station; he was not threatened with arrest; his parents were in the lobby during what they were told was to be a brief interview; the questioning focused more on the alleged accomplice's actions; and police appealed to the suspect's interest in telling the truth. On the other hand, circumstances also weighed in favor of the view that the suspect had been in custody: The interview occurred at the sheriff's station; it lasted two hours; the detective did not tell the suspect that he was free to leave; the suspect was brought to the police station by his parents; and the parents were not permitted to be present during the interview. The Supreme Court held that the teenager's statements were admissible in court, despite not being given the Miranda warnings, because he was not in custody, and that such a finding "was reasonable and fit within the matrix of the Supreme Court's prior decisions."[71]

The importance of confessions to police work may be overstated, however. Police rarely take a suspect into custody without some kind of evidence, and a confession rarely forms the basis for a conviction without other corroborating evidence. Likewise, guilty suspects who are taken into custody usually have a story, excuse, or alibi to sell the police; and innocent suspects are eager to talk with police to establish their innocence. Therefore, remaining silent when in police custody is difficult to do under most circumstances.

CRITICAL THINKING EXERCISES

The Limits of Stop and Frisk

The Supreme Court is still wrestling with the question of limits on frisks of suspects. In the case *Illinois v. Wardlow*, decided in 2000, the Court ruled on a case from Chicago in which four police cars approached the sidewalk where Sam Wardlow was standing. Wardlow turned and ran down an alley. The police officers caught him, and when they frisked his outer garments they found a gun.

The issue in this case was whether the police had the requisite reasonable suspicion that criminal activity was afoot. In a five-to-four vote a divided Supreme Court held that Wardlow's presence in an area known for heavy narcotics trafficking, combined with his unprovoked flight, justified the search.[a] This ruling suggests that a suspect's flight at the mere sight of a police officer can be suspicious enough to justify a stop and frisk for weapons. Critics argued that the ruling encourages racial profiling of suspects based on prejudice rather than on evidence of criminal behavior. Police organizations, on the other hand, saw the decision as important for effective law enforcement.[b]

Other cases decided by the Supreme Court reflect this tension between the need to stop and question suspects and the evidence police must have to do so. For example, the Court has held that an automobile cannot be stopped unless there is a reasonable suspicion that the occupants are violating traffic or criminal law. The Court felt that random automobile stops could lead to arbitrary or discriminatory law enforcement—although the Court did not rule out the use of roadblock stops, because such stops do not permit discriminatory use of police authority.[c] Nevertheless, in a 1995 case the Court upheld a traffic stop based on an erroneous computer readout stating that the person stopped was wanted by the police. A clerical error had caused the false report, and the result was a traffic stop without probable cause.[d] Criminal evidence was found in the vehicle, however. As in *U.S. v. Leon*, the Court held that exclusion of the evidence would penalize police for a clerical (or judge's) error, even though it is the suspect who is penalized in these circumstances.

These cases point to the difference between a stop for purposes of further investigation and a "seizure." In a later case, police moved a bag from the overhead compartment on a bus to the seat to allow a drug-sniffing dog to smell it. This procedure took a short time and did not impair the owner's access to the bag, making the stop reasonable under the Fourth Amendment.[e] The Supreme Court has held that a twenty-minute investigatory stop without unnecessary delay is reasonable under the Fourth Amendment.[f] Therefore, physical movement of property does not constitute a seizure, although keeping it from the owner for an extended period, or destroying it, does.[g]

The U.S. Supreme Court held in *Minnesota v. Dickerson* that a frisk that goes beyond a pat-down search is not permissible, because of the limited purpose and scope of frisking. In this case an officer felt a small lump in a suspect's pocket; the officer then examined the lump with his fingers and determined it to be cocaine wrapped in cellophane. The Court held that once the officer concluded that the lump was not a weapon, the continued examination constituted a search without probable cause. The search was disallowed, because it was unrelated to the purpose of the frisk: to protect an officer's safety.[h]

CRITICAL THINKING QUESTIONS

1. When does the line between a frisk and a search become blurred?
2. What is the difference between a stop and a seizure?
3. How are probable cause and reasonable suspicion different as grounds for search and seizure?

NOTES

a. *Illinois v. Wardlow*, 120 S. Ct. 673 (2000).
b. Linda Greenhouse, "Person's Flight Can Justify Police Stop and Search, Supreme Court Rules," *New York Times* (January 13, 2000).
c. *Delaware v. Prouse*, 99 S. Ct. 1391 (1979).

d. *Arizona v. Evans,* 115 S. Ct. 209 (1995).
e. *U.S. v. Gant,* 112 F. 3d 239 (1997). See also *U.S. v. Hary,* 961 F. 2d 1361 (1992) (cert. denied 113 S. Ct. 238); *Illinois v. Caballes,* 125 S. ct. 834 (2005).
f. *United States v. Sharpe,* 105 S. Ct. 1568 (1985).
g. *Fuller v. Vines,* 36 F. 3d 65 (1994) (cert. denied 115 S. Ct. 1361); *Bills v. Agetine,* 958 F. 2d 697 (1992) (cert. denied 116 S. Ct. 179).
h. *Minnesota v. Dickerson,* 113 S. Ct. 2130 (1993).

Civil Suits against Police

New York City agreed to pay nearly $3 million to settle a lawsuit filed by the family of a man who died after being held in an illegal choke hold by a police officer. The officer was acquitted of negligent homicide but was convicted in federal court of violating the man's civil rights.[a]

Clearly, the consequences of police conduct on both civil and criminal liability can be significant. Police officers and their departments are increasingly being sued for damages. This trend is due in part to a general tendency in the United States to seek compensation through lawsuits. Police are especially susceptible to lawsuits because of their authority over the liberty of others and their ability to use force to ensure compliance with the law under certain circumstances. Most lawsuits against police involve claims of false arrest, negligence, or excessive use of force.

The U.S. Supreme Court has held that a police officer can be sued for false arrest or false imprisonment "when a reasonably well-trained officer, under the same circumstances" would have known that probable cause did not exist for the arrest. This liability holds even if the officer has a warrant signed by a judge, because the judge's incompetence in not recognizing the lack of probable cause cannot excuse the officer's conduct.[b]

Police have been sued for negligence when they have failed to be aware of a substantial and unjustifiable risk posed by their conduct. Many of these lawsuits involve high-speed pursuits for nonserious crimes in which bystanders or suspects have been injured or killed; in other cases a lack of adequate training "amounts to deliberate indifference to the rights of persons" police encounter. The Supreme Court has held that when poor training is the result of a conscious or deliberate choice, police may be held liable for civil damages.[c] The Supreme Court made it clear that only deliberate indifference to obvious consequences can result in a successful civil suit against police.[d]

A study was conducted to investigate what police administrators might do to avoid civil lawsuits against their departments. This survey of 248 police departments discovered three factors that are associated with fewer civil suits lodged against police departments: community policing, minority recruitment, and citizen review. As community-oriented policing programs were adopted, lawsuits declined quite markedly in those departments. Also, stronger interest in minority recruitment of police officers and citizen involvement in handling complaints against police were associated with fewer civil suits. As study author John Worrall concluded, research like this can help police agencies arrive at "preemptive and preventive administrative decisions" that make a difference in the lives of both police and the public.[e]

Improved police training and administration will become increasingly important, because the U.S. Supreme Court in 2006 cited "increasing professionalism of police forces, including a new emphasis on internal police discipline" as a trend "that deters civil-rights violations."[f] The court ruled that the existence of increased professionalism and the threat of lawsuits will prevent police from violating the rights of citizens. Therefore, it was not necessary to exclude seized evidence in court in a case in which Detroit police entered a home in violation of the "knock-and-announce" in a search for drugs and weapons. The Court cited a book by criminologist Samuel Walker that noted "wide-ranging reforms in the education, training, and supervision of police officers."[g] In a subsequent news article, Walker claimed that the Supreme Court misquoted him. Walker says he argued that Supreme Court interventions during the 1960s to place procedural constraints on police played "a pivotal role in stimulating these [police] reforms" and in setting higher standards for police conduct.[h] So whether professionalism of police is a *cause* for Supreme Court intervention, or a *result* of it, it is clear that quality police work is being relied upon more than ever to secure the rights of citizens.

CRITICAL THINKING QUESTIONS

1. Why do you believe lawsuits against police have been increasing in recent years?
2. What kinds of Supreme Court decisions regarding searches and seizures might best protect police from future lawsuits?

NOTES

a. "New York Pays $3 Million to Police Victim Kin," *Associated Press Online* (October 2, 1998).
b. *Malley v. Briggs,* 106 S. Ct. 1092 (1986).
c. *City of Canton, Ohio v. Harris,* 109 S. Ct. 1197 (1989).
d. *Board of the County Commissioners of Bryan County, Oklahoma v. Brown,* 117 S. Ct. 1382 (1997).
e. John L. Worrall, "Administrative Determinants of Civil Liability Lawsuits against Municipal Police Departments: An Exploratory Analysis," *Crime and Delinquency* 44 (April 1998), p. 295; Michael S. Vaugh, Tab W. Cooper, and Rolando V. del Carmen, "Assessing Legal Liabilities in Law Enforcement: Police Chiefs' Views," *Crime & Delinquency,* vol. 47 (January 2001). p. 3.
f. *Hudson v. Michigan,* 126 S. Ct. 2159 (2006).
g. Samuel Walker, *Taming the System: The Control of Discretion in Criminal Justice 1950–1990* (New York: Oxford University Press, 1993), p. 51.
h. Samuel Walker, "Scalia Twisted My Words," *Los Angeles Times* (June 25, 2006).

SUMMARY

WHAT IS THE ROLE OF POLICE IN CRIMINAL PROCEDURE?

- A frisk is a patting down of an individual's outer clothing on the basis of a reasonable suspicion, whereas a search is an exploratory quest for evidence. Frisks are limited to a search for weapons that may pose an immediate threat to the officer's safety. Automobiles may be searched without probable cause if officers possess a reasonable belief that the occupant is armed.
- The exclusionary rule holds that illegally seized evidence must be excluded from trials. The "good faith" exception to this rule occurs when police conduct a search on the basis of a warrant that is later found to be defective.
- Searches may be conducted without a warrant if they are incident to a lawful arrest; are conducted with voluntary consent; or involve evidence in plain view, automobiles and their contents, or open fields and abandoned property.

THE FIFTH AMENDMENT AND THE *MIRANDA* WARNING

- The Fifth Amendment provides for grand juries, protection against double jeopardy, and protection from self-incrimination. It has had its greatest impact on interrogations and confessions obtained by the police.
- To ensure protection against self-incrimination, suspects taken into custody must be read the *Miranda* warning, which states that the suspect has the right to remain silent and to have an attorney present during questioning.
- The Supreme Court has established some exceptions to the *Miranda* rule. These include the public safety exception, in which a suspect may be asked questions prompted by concern for public safety before being read the *Miranda* warning.

IMPACTS OF PROCEDURAL LAW ON LAW ENFORCEMENT

- Debate continues about the benefits of the exclusionary rule and *Miranda* for citizens and for law enforcement, reflecting continuing conflict in the balance to be struck among the interests of government, the public interest, and the rights of private citizens.
- The importance of confessions to police work is limited because most suspects are taken into custody based on other evidence.

KEY TERMS

frisk *153*
search *153*
seizure *153*
reasonable suspicion *154*
exclusionary rule *156*
good faith exception *157*
Fifth Amendment *165*
Miranda warning *169*
public safety exception *169*

QUESTIONS FOR REVIEW AND DISCUSSION

1. What limits does the Fourth Amendment place on searches and seizures by police?
2. What is the difference between a frisk and a search?
3. What is meant by the "reasonable suspicion" standard? How is it different from the "probable cause" standard?
4. What is the exclusionary rule, and what are some exceptions to that rule?
5. In what kinds of situations may a search be conducted without a warrant?
6. What protections are provided by the Fifth Amendment?
7. What is the *Miranda* rule, and what exceptions to the rule have been allowed by the Supreme Court?
8. Why are the impacts of procedural law on law enforcement controversial?

NOTES

1. 88 S. Ct. 1868 (1968); see also the related cases of *Sibron v. New York*, 88 S. Ct. 1902 (1968) and *Peters v. New York*, 88 S. Ct. 1904 (1968).
2. *Saldal v. Cook County*, 113 S. Ct. 538 (1992).
3. *Alabama v. White*, 496 U.S. 325 (1990); see also *Ornelas v. United States*, 116 S. Ct. 1657 (1996).

4. *Florida v. J. L.*, 120 S. Ct. 1462 (2000).
5. *Illinois v. Caballes*, 125 S. Ct. 834 (2005); *Knowles v. Iowa*, 119 S. Ct. 484 (1998).
6. *Hiibel v. Sixth Judicial District Court of Nevada*, 124 S. Ct. 2451 (2004).
7. *United States v. Arvizu*, 122 S. Ct. 744 (2002).
8. Erica L. Schmitt and Mathew R. Durose, *Characteristics of Drivers Stopped by Police* (Washington, DC: Bureau of Justice Statistics, 2006).
9. Matthew R. Durose, Erica L. Schmitt, and Patrick A. Langan, *Contacts between the Police and the Public* (Washington, DC: Bureau of Justice Statistics, 2005).
10. *Weeks v. United States*, 34 S. Ct. 341 (1914).
11. *Wolf v. Colorado*, 338 U.S. 25 (1949); Henry J. Abraham, *Freedom and the Court: Civil Rights and Liberties in the United States* (New York: Oxford University Press, 1977).
12. *Rochin v. California*, 342 U.S. 165 (1952); *Rea v. United States*, 350 U.S. 214 (1956).
13. *Mapp v. Ohio*, 367 U.S. 643 (1961).
14. *U.S. v. Leon*, 104 S. Ct. 3405 (1984) and *Massachusetts v. Sheppard*, 104 S. Ct. 3424 (1984).
15. Robert L. Misner, "Limiting *Leon:* A Mistake of Law Analogy," *Journal of Criminal Law and Criminology* 77 (fall 1986), pp. 507–45.
16. *Hudson v. Palmer*, 104 S. Ct. 3194 (1984).
17. *New Jersey v. T. L. O.*, 105 S. Ct. 733 (1985).
18. *Maryland v. Garrison*, 107 S. Ct. 1013 (1987).
19. 18 U.S.C. §3109; *Wilson v. Arkansas*, 115 S. Ct. 1914 (1995).
20. *United States v. Banks*, 124 S. Ct. 521 (2003).
21. *Hudson v. Michigan*, 126 S. Ct. 2159 (2006).
22. *Chimel v. California* 89 S. Ct. 2034 (1969).
23. 116 S. Ct. 2485 (1996).
24. *Illinois v. McArthur*, 121 S. Ct. 946 (2001).
25. 93 S. Ct. 2041 (1973).
26. *U.S. v. Matlock*, 94 S. Ct. 988 (1974); *U.S. v. Watson*, 96 S. Ct. 820 (1976); *Florida v. Jimeno*, 111 S. Ct. 1801 (1991); *Ohio v. Robinette*, 117 S. Ct. 417 (1996).
27. *U.S. v. Drayton*, 122 S. Ct. 2105 (2002); see Thomas W. Hughes, "Bus Interdiction by the Police: *United States v. Drayton*," *American Journal of Criminal Justice*, vol. 27 (Spring 2003), p. 197.
28. *Georgia v. Randolph*, 126 S. Ct. 1515 (2006).
29. 91 S. Ct. 2022 (1971).
30. 103 S. Ct. 2317.
31. *U.S. v. Roblem*, 37 F. 3d 1260 (1994); *United States v. Jacobson*, 104 S. Ct. 1652 (1984).
32. *Arizona v. Hicks*, 107 S. Ct. 1149 (1987); *Horton v. California*, 496 U.S. 120 (1990); *U.S. v. Hatten*, 68 F. 3d 257 (1995) (cert. denied 116 S. Ct. 1026).
33. *Bond v. United States*, 120 S. Ct. 1462 (2000).
34. 45 S. Ct. 280 (1925).
35. *Weeks v. United States*, 34 S. Ct. 341 (1914).
36. *New York v. Belton*, 101 S. Ct. 2860 (1981).
37. *Thornton v. United States*, 124 S. Ct. 2127 (2004).
38. 90 S. Ct. 1975 (1970).
39. 102 S. Ct. 3079 (1982).
40. *South Dakota v. Opperman*, 96 S. Ct. 3092 (1976); *Pennsylvania v. Mimms*, 98 S. Ct. 330 (1977); *Colorado v. Bertine*, 107 S. Ct. 738 (1987); *California v. Acevedo*, 111 S. Ct. 1982 (1991); *Brown v. United States*, 116 S. Ct. 1769 (1996); *Florida v. Meyers*, 104 S. Ct. 1852 (1985); *United States v. Johns*, 105 S. Ct. 881 (1985).
41. 102 S. Ct. 2157 (1982); see also *Maryland v. Dyson*, 119 S. Ct. 2013 (1999).
42. Matthew R. Durose, Erica L. Schmitt, and Patrick A. Langan, *Contacts between the Police and the Public* (Washington, DC: Bureau of Justice Statistics, 2005).
43. 44 S. Ct. 445 (1924).
44. *Oliver v. United States*, 104 S. Ct. 1735 (1984); *U.S. v. Gorman*, 104 F. 2d 272 (1996); *U.S. v. Van Damme*, 48 F. 3d 461 (1995).
45. 106 S. Ct. 1809 (1986).
46. *U.S. v. Gorman*, 104 F. 3d 272 (1996); *U.S. v. Van Damme*, 48 F. 3d 461 (1995).
47. *Kylio v. United States*, 121 S. Ct. 2038 (2001).
48. 86 S. Ct. 1602 (1966).
49. *Escobedo v. Illinois*, 378 U.S. 478 (1964).
50. *Rhode Island v. Innis*, 100 S. Ct. 1682 (1980).
51. *New York v. Quarles*, 104 S. Ct. 2626 (1984).
52. 103 S. Ct. 916 (1983).
53. 103 S. Ct. 2830 (1983).
54. *Minnesota v. Murphy*, 104 S. Ct. 1136 (1984).
55. *Berkimer v. McCarty*, 104 S. Ct. 3138 (1984).
56. *Colorado v. Spring*, 107 S. Ct. 851 (1987); see also *Clabourne v. Lewis*, 64 F. 3d 1373 (1995).
57. *Oregon v. Elstad*, 105 S. Ct. 1285 (1985); *Moran v. Burbine*, 106 S. Ct. 1135 (1986); *Colorado v. Spring*, 107 S. Ct. 851 (1987); *Illinois v. Perkins*, 111 S. Ct. 1121 (1990).
58. *Dickerson v. United States*, 120 S. Ct. 2326 (2000).
59. William J. Bratton, "Miranda Protects the Public," *APB-news.com* (April 19, 2000).
60. "Supreme Court's Miranda Decision: The Public's Opinion," *Gallup News Service* (June 27, 2000).
61. William A. Geller, *Videotaping Interrogations and Confessions* (Washington, DC: National Institute of Justice, 1993).
62. Steven A. Drizin and Beth A. Colgan, "Let the Cameras Roll: Mandatory Videotaping of Confessions," *Loyola University of Chicago Law Journal*, vol. 32 (winter 2001), p. 337.
63. Sheldon Krantz, Bernard Gilman, Charles G. Benda, Garol Rogoff Hallstrom, and Gail J. Nadworny, *Police Policymaking* (Lexington, MA: Lexington Books, 1979).
64. U.S. Comptroller General, *The Impact of the Exclusionary Rule on Federal Criminal Prosecutions* (Washington, DC: U.S. Government Printing Office, 1979).
65. Robert W. Burkhart, Shirley Melnicoe, Annelsely K. Schmidt, Linda J. McKay, and Cheryl Martorana, *The Effects of the Exclusionary Rule: A Study in California* (Washington, DC: National Institute of Justice, 1982).
66. James J. Fyfe, "The NIJ Study of the Exclusionary Rule," *Criminal Law Bulletin* 19 (May–June 1983), pp. 253–60.
67. Richard Ayres, "Confessions and the Court," *Yale Alumni Magazine* (December 1968), p. 287.
68. *Duckworth v. Eagan*, 492 U.S. 195 (1989).
69. Alan Carlson and Floyd Feeney, "Handling Robbery Arrestees: Some Issues of Fact and Policy," in F. Feeney and A. Weir, eds., *The Prevention and Control of Robbery*, vol. 2. (Davis, CA: University of California Center on Administration of Justice, 1973); R. J. Medalie, L. Zeitz, and P. Alexander, "Custodial Police Interrogations in Our Nation's Capital: The Attempt to Implement *Miranda*," *Michigan Law Review* 66 (May 1968), pp. 1347–1422; David W. Neubauer, *Criminal Justice in Middle America* (Morristown, NJ: General Learning Press, 1974).
70. Paul G. Cassell, "Miranda's Social Costs: An Empirical Reassessment," *Northwestern Law Journal* 387 (1996).
71. *Warden v. Alvardo*, 124 S. Ct. 2140 (2004).

chapter 8

Origins and Organization of Law Enforcement

Police expectations: how we got the policing structure we have and how law enforcement operates in a dynamic environment.

CHAPTER OUTLINE

How Did Policing Evolve?
The Watch and Ward System
The New Police Bobbies
Metropolitan Police in American Cities
Crime Commissions and the Professionalization of Policing
The Law Enforcement Assistance Administration

What Is the Organization of Law Enforcement?
Local Police
State Police
Federal Law Enforcement Agencies
Transnational Law Enforcement

Who Are the Police?
Training and Education
Issues of Gender and Race

What Are Some Concerns about Policing in the United States?
The Dilemma of Jurisdictions and Need for Cooperation
The Impacts of Technology and the Media on Police Work
The Movement toward Private Policing

THAT'S A FACT:
Perspectives on Police Agencies You Haven't Heard About

MEDIA AND CRIMINAL JUSTICE:
Police Dramas on Television

CRITICAL THINKING EXERCISES:
- Campus Law Enforcement and Crime
- The Cyclical Nature of Community Policing

LEARNING OBJECTIVES

- Trace the history of policing from the Middle Ages in England to the 1990s.
- Identify specific contributions that led to the early professionalization of law enforcement.
- Explain the role of crime commissions and legislation in the professionalization of policing.
- Analyze the organization of law enforcement at the federal, state, and local levels.
- Give examples of law enforcement agencies at the state, national, and transnational levels.
- Describe the diversity of people in law enforcement and discuss issues relating to that diversity.
- Identify characteristics of good police work.
- Explain why multijurisdictional crime and the privatization of law enforcement are concerns today.
- Evaluate the impacts of technology and the media on police work.

A woman's frantic 911 emergency call to police said, "Where are you? Where are you? My husband has a gun. He's trying to kill me!" Police officers did not arrive until more than fifteen minutes after the woman's first of four calls to the 911 operator. The woman was shot to death by her estranged husband before the police came. A subsequent lawsuit resulted in a $4.25 million settlement when it was admitted that police officers took far too long to respond to the 911 calls in this incident. Callers to 911 in Washington, D.C., complained for years about getting no answer, a recording, or being put on hold when calling 911. After calls reporting a fatal house fire were bungled, the 911 emergency communication center was ultimately moved out of the police department. On the other hand, the police chief of Norristown, Pennsylvania (just outside Philadelphia), reported that his officers were dispatched to a single residence seventy-eight times in one year because of "a fight every night." As the chief indicated, such problem locations "mean that the officer is not patrolling someplace else." In Maryland, a new law made available emergency protective orders for domestic violence cases twenty-four hours a day. Although intended to give victims better access to legal protection, more than 6,800 calls were received in the first eight months, producing incredible strain on the system.[1]

At the other end of the policing spectrum, some police departments are using computerized analyses of homicide, robbery, and burglary data to analyze local crime trends, and the reasons for these trends, on a daily, weekly, or monthly basis. The analyses are then used to alter police strategies to counteract the identified crime trends and to serve as a crime prevention tool. Innovative uses of more kinds of information have shown success in reducing crime and in understanding the local circumstances that produce crime. In addition, the percentage of local police departments using computers in the field (in their cars) has increased from 5 to 56 percent since 1990.[2]

These examples reflect the disjunction in our images of police—from slow and overwhelmed to highly efficient and effective. This chapter will survey the evolution of law enforcement in the United States as a context for understanding the growing sophistication of police work. This sophistication has backfired in some ways, making the public overreliant on the police for help with a growing array of social and personal problems.

How Did Policing Evolve?

Long before police departments were formally established, less formal measures of self-protection were used by property owners who could afford them. These measures are illustrated by the **mutual pledge system** that was prevalent in Britain during the Middle Ages. Alfred the Great (who ruled from approximately 870–900) established an organized system of community self-responsibility in which everyone in the community was responsible for everyone else. Communities were divided into ten-family groups called "tithings." Cities as we know them did not exist, so each tithing was responsible for maintaining peace within its own boundaries. "It was each citizen's duty to raise the 'hue and cry' when a crime was committed, to collect his neighbors and to pursue a criminal who fled from the district. If such a group failed to apprehend a lawbreaker, all were fined by the Crown."[3] This system of mutual responsibility and shared penalties was designed to ensure that all members of the community made a conscientious effort to control crime.

Every ten tithings, or hundred families, constituted a "hundred" and was headed by a **constable** (who was appointed by a local nobleman to be in charge of weapons and equipment). The hundreds, in turn, were grouped together to form a "shire" (about the equivalent of a county). For each shire the Crown appointed a supervisor called a **shire reeve,** from which the modern term *sheriff* is derived.

mutual pledge system
A system of community self-responsibility that existed in Britain during the Middle Ages, in which residents were held responsible for the conduct of their neighbors.

constable
A citizen in charge of weapons and equipment for one hundred families in his geographic area. In England constables were appointed by a local nobleman beginning around the year 900.

shire reeve
An official appointed by the British Crown who was responsible for overseeing the constables and several hundred families in a given area (called a "shire"). The modern word *sheriff* is derived from this term.

watch and ward system
A system established in England in 1285 to aid constables in their law enforcement efforts. Men from each town were required to take turns standing watch at night. Crime suspects were turned over to the constable.

The Watch and Ward System

The Statute of Winchester, enacted in 1285, established the **watch and ward system** to aid constables in their law enforcement efforts.[4] This system also emphasized community responsibility for crime control. Men from each town were required to take turns standing watch at night. If any criminals were apprehended, they were turned over to the constable for trial the following day. In 1326 Edward II established the position of **justice of the peace.** The justice of the peace assisted the sheriff in enforcing the law. Eventually the role of the justice of the peace shifted to adjudication of cases in court, while the sheriffs retained their local peacekeeping function.

justice of the peace
An office established by Edward II in 1326 to assist the sheriff in enforcing the law. Eventually the role of the justice of the peace shifted to adjudication, while the sheriffs retained their local peacekeeping function.

This system of law enforcement, based on the mutual pledge and supplemented by the watch and ward, was in effect for several hundred years, but gradually it lost community support and declined. This happened because citizens who were required to take their turn at the watch started evading this duty by paying others to do it for them. These substitutes were usually poorly paid and ignorant, and often too old to be effective.[5] In the sixteenth century "bellmen," who watched for fires, relieved the watchmen of that duty, but watchmen still did little to prevent crime. They were generally incompetent, sometimes drank on the job, and eventually came to be ridiculed. Consider the situation as it existed in London at that time:

> *During the 16th and 17th centuries, there was no question in the minds of Londoners that they lived in a dangerous place which was ill-protected by their watchmen. . . . The watchmen generally were considered to be incompetent and cowardly. By the mid-17th century they had acquired the derisive name of "Charlies." It was a common sport of rich young men of the time to taunt and terrorize them, to wreck the watchhouses, and occasionally to murder the watchmen. The large rattles they carried to signal for help were little comfort since they knew their colleagues were not dependable; the watchmen spent a good deal of time discreetly concealed from the public.*[6]

Jonathan Rubinstein describes the citizens' reactions to these circumstances, noting that there was no public outcry to change the watch and ward system. There were no lights in the city, so home owners were required to place a candle on the street in front of their homes at night. This rule was not enforced, however, and as a result the streets were dark and considered dangerous. Those who could afford to do so hired guards and armed themselves. Women never went out on the street unaccompanied. Those who could not afford these self-protective measures were often victimized. Given this situation, in which the rich could buy protection for themselves and the poor were being victimized in unsafe streets, a catalyst was needed—some unanticipated influence or event that would galvanize the poor to act. That catalyst was gin.

PUBLIC SAFETY VERSUS GIN

The catalyst that provoked a more organized effort toward the establishment of public policing was the invention of gin by a Dutch chemist during the seventeenth century. The British government encouraged the manufacture of gin as a way to deal with grain surpluses while also making a profit. Gin was much cheaper than brandy and much more potent than beer, wine, or ale. Sales of gin skyrocketed; by 1725 more than 7,000 gin shops operated in London, and gin was sold as a sideline by many other shopkeepers. Between 1727 and 1743 consumption more than doubled. According to one historian, London became "awash in an orgy of drinking which has probably not been matched in history."[7] For a penny a person could drink all day, and public drunkenness became commonplace. Drunken mobs often roamed through the city. The streets of London became filled with people who engaged in unpredictable and occasionally violent behavior.

In response, the government "got tough" on offenders. Street lighting was improved; more watchmen were hired; and the penalties for many crimes were dramatically increased. Individual citizens also began arming themselves and stayed off the streets at night. In addition, the rich began to move away from areas where poor people lived.

The Gin Act, passed in 1736, attempted to limit the availability of gin by establishing extremely high licensing fees for all gin sellers and manufacturers and providing rewards for information leading to the conviction of unlicensed distillers or retailers. These measures had little positive effect. Constables overlooked violations; informers were beaten or murdered; and although the act was in force for seven years and resulted in 10,000 prosecutions, only three licenses were sold. There was no reduction in the consumption of gin.[8] Consumption fell only when taxes were increased, resulting in higher prices.

The problems associated with gin were alleviated, but fear of crime did not decline correspondingly. Members of Parliament continued to be accompanied by bodyguards, and bulletproof coaches were advertised to thwart the highwaymen (robbers) who victimized travelers on the roads to the city. The Lord Mayor of London was robbed at gunpoint, and the Duke of York and the Prince of Wales were mugged as they walked in the city during the day. During the same period the Great Seal of England was stolen from the house of the Lord Chancellor and melted down for the silver. There was a growing demand for protection from crime, and private police organizations flourished.[9]

THE BOW STREET RUNNERS

In 1748, in response to growing concern, Henry Fielding proposed that the watch and ward system be centralized. He organized a private agency that patrolled the streets rather than staying at the watch boxes. He also organized a mounted patrol, the Bow Street Runners, to guard highways. The Runners quickly established a reputation for their ability to catch criminals.[10] Although this system declined after Fielding's death, he is credited with being the first person to propose the idea of a mobile police force.

Despite the success of the Bow Street Runners, fear of crime continued to increase. The Gordon Riots of 1780 produced serious mob violence in London, but the notion of a centralized police agency still was not widely accepted. There was fear, particularly among the wealthy (who controlled the constables), that a centralized police agency would become too strong and abuse its power.

The New Police Bobbies

preventive police
The first organized police department in London, established in 1829. The popular English name for police officers, "bobbies," comes from Sir Robert Peel, a founder of the Metropolitan Police.

In response to the urging of legal reformer and philosopher Jeremy Bentham and the lobbying of English statesman Sir Robert Peel, the Metropolitan Police of London was established in 1829. The force, also referred to as the New Police or the **preventive police,** was seen as "a civilizing instrument whose effort and example would make possible more harmonious relations among city people."[11] The popular English name for police officers, "bobbies," comes from the name of the founder of the Metropolitan Police, Robert Peel.

The basis of this new police force was very different from that of the watch and ward system. The city was to be patrolled by officers who were assigned specific territories (or beats). The watch and ward system had made it clear that strict supervision was required to ensure that officers would actually perform their duties and not sleep, drink, or loaf on the job. Robert Peel sought to provide inspiration by employing military principles in organizing what had traditionally been a civilian force. Thus, the Metropolitan Police were distinguished by their patrolling of specific areas and by their paramilitary organization, which was designed to maintain discipline.

What historical and social factors forced cities and states to replace the watch and ward system with formal police forces? Why were these "Keystone Cops" (Hollywood's tag for uniformed metropolitan police) objects of ridicule? What events then encouraged the professionalization of policing?

The New Police were not immediately popular according to historical accounts, because they were seen as an unnecessary encroachment into the lives of Londoners. Nevertheless, the early Metropolitan Police were successful in reducing crime and maintaining order so they were gradually accepted by the citizenry, culminating in 1856 when Parliament mandated that English provinces outside London establish police forces.[12] Part of the reason for the success of the Metropolitan Police was Peel's insistence that their mission and principles of conduct be explicitly stated. Peel's nine principles of policing, presented in Figure 8.1, illustrate how public approval and support are necessary for effective police work and that police actions must be carefully restricted to ensure that abuses of authority do not occur.

BRITAIN'S NEW POLICE

The New Police were not without problems, however. Poorly supervised patrol officers often drank or slept on the job, and there was a general lack of discipline. The first police commissioner was Colonel Charles Rowan, a former military officer. In order to maintain discipline, he instituted severe penalties for even minor infractions. For most violations the officer was dismissed from the force. As a result, during the early years of the Metropolitan Police more than a third of the force was discharged each year.[13]

Metropolitan Police in American Cities

Despite the problems experienced in England, the American colonies repeated the British experience. As early as 1636 Boston had night watchmen to protect warehouses and homes. This approach was imitated in other eastern cities. As in England, the night watch was supervised by constables at the local level and by sheriffs at the county level.

Sir Robert Peel

The night watchmen were poorly paid, poorly supervised, and known for drinking and falling asleep on the job. Perhaps the most widespread criticism, however, was the same one that plagued the British watch and ward system: The watchmen did nothing to prevent crime.[14]

After the American Revolution there were no further efforts to establish a full-time police force. Because the British had used their army to enforce their laws in the colonies, most Americans saw a police force as the equivalent of a standing domestic army. This was an important issue at the Constitutional Convention.[15] It was believed that a police force would lead to the same kinds of oppression and abuse that the colonists had come to America to escape.

It was not until 1838 that Boston created a daytime police force to supplement the night watch. This occurred only after major riots in 1834, 1835, and 1837.[16] The day and night police forces were separate agencies, however, and there was intense rivalry between the two Boston forces. New York was the first city to create a unified day and night police force (and to abolish the night watch). The New York City Police Department, established in 1845, was unique in its payment of (low) salaries, its use of uniforms to distinguish police officers from other citizens, and its paramilitary organization. New York's example was soon followed by other cities, including Chicago (1851), New Orleans (1852), Cincinnati (1852), Philadelphia (1855), Newark (1857), and Baltimore (1857). By 1900 nearly every U.S. city of any size had established a full-time police force.

FIGURE 8.1 Sir Robert Peel's Nine Principles

Sir Robert Peel's Nine Principles

- The basic mission for which the police exist is to prevent crime and disorder.
- The ability of the police to perform their duties is dependent upon public approval of police actions.
- Police must secure the willing cooperation of the public in a voluntary observance of the law to be able to secure and maintain the respect of the public.
- The degree of cooperation of the public that can be secured diminishes proportionately to the necessity of the use of physical force.
- Police seek and preserve public favor not by catering to public opinion but by constantly demonstrating absolute impartial service to the law.
- Police use physical force to the extent necessary to secure observance of the law or to restore order only when the exercise of persuasion, advice, and warning is found to be insufficient.
- Police, at all times, should maintain a relationship with the public that gives reality to the historic tradition that the police are the public and the public are the police; the police being only members of the public who are paid to give full-time attention to duties which are incumbent on every citizen in the interests of community welfare and existence.
- Police should always direct their action strictly toward their functions and never appear to usurp the powers of the judiciary.
- The test of police efficiency is the absence of crime and disorder, not the visible evidence of police action in dealing with it.

Source: New Westminster Police Service, 2000. www.newwestpolice.org/peel.htm

UNIFORMED POLICE IN THE UNITED STATES

Most of the new police forces assigned officers to specific territories. At first the officers resisted wearing uniforms, because they felt demeaned by them. There were other, more serious problems as well:

> *These first formal police forces in American cities were faced with many of the problems that police continue to confront today. Police officers became objects of disrespect. The need for larger staffs required the police to compromise personnel standards in order to fill the ranks. And police salaries were among the lowest in local government service, a factor which precluded attracting sufficient numbers of high standard candidates. It is small wonder that the police were not respected, were not notably successful, and were not noted for their visibility and progressiveness.*[17]

These problems of low pay, disrespect, and ineffectiveness existed for a number of reasons. First, the military model of organization was not well suited to police work. Unlike the soldier, the police officer is primarily a solitary worker, and military discipline is most effective for people who work together in a group. Second, police officers have the contradictory tasks of both protecting and arresting their employers—the public. Citizens expect the police to protect them, but they become irate when they are stopped, questioned, or arrested. Third, police forces were often used as a source of political patronage and control, and police work therefore became associated with corrupt politics.[18]

Efforts to improve police efficiency and discipline were impeded by problems of communication. During much of the 1800s there were no police telephones or call boxes, and those that existed could be sabotaged by officers who did not wish to be bothered by their superiors.[19] In fact, it was not until 1929 that the first two-way radio was installed in a patrol car.

Crime Commissions and the Professionalization of Policing

The early decades of the twentieth century saw the beginnings of a movement toward police professionalism. The Progressive Era was marked by renewed concern about crime, because the passage of the Eighteenth Amendment (Prohibition) led to extensive illegal manufacturing and distribution of alcoholic beverages. This period was characterized by criticism of corruption and inefficiency in social institutions, and by recommendations for change that centered on better management and training. Government concern was manifested as early as 1919, which saw the formation of the Chicago Crime Commission; similar commissions were created to investigate crime in twenty-four states. In addition, two national **crime commissions** were established: the National Crime Commission in 1925 and the Wickersham Commission in 1931. These commissions focused on improved operation of the criminal justice system as the best way to reduce crime. They recommended a number of reforms in police operations.

> *The dominant concern of the crime commissions was to find ways to bring criminals to justice more swiftly and certainly. The first agency in the criminal justice system responsible for this task was the police. Professionalization of the police came to be defined in terms of those changes in police organization, administration, and technology that would improve the efficiency of the police in the deterrence and apprehension of criminals. Police officials measured progress toward police professionalism in terms of expansion of police services, development of scientific methods of criminal investigation and identification, police training, communications, transportation, police records, police selection, executive tenure, and police organizational growth.*[20]

In short, the themes of **progressivism** in policing were efficiency, professionalism, and improved technology.

During this period a dedicated effort was made to transform police work from an undesirable job into an attractive career. A leader in the movement to improve police professionalism was August Vollmer, chief of police in Berkeley, California, from 1905 to 1932. Vollmer established the first crime detection laboratory in the United States, and John Larson invented the polygraph (lie detector) while working for him. This period also saw the inauguration of investigative techniques such as fingerprint identification, firearms identification, toxicology, document examination, and other methods that had not been used in policing in the United States before 1900.[21]

Police **professionalization** also included improved selection and training procedures. In 1900 the only criteria used in the selection of police officers

crime commissions
Early twentieth-century crime commissions included the Chicago Crime Commission (1919), the National Crime Commission (1925), and the Wickersham Commission (1931). These commissions focused on the improved operation of the criminal justice system as the best way to reduce crime.

POLICING IN THE PROGRESSIVE ERA

progressivism
Early twentieth-century era in policing that focused on efficiency, professionalism, and improved technology.

professionalization
Those changes in police organization, administration, and technology aimed at improving the efficiency of the police in the deterrence and apprehension of criminals.

August Vollmer established the first crime detection laboratory in the United States. How has forensic science worked hand-in-hand with criminal investigation to modernize police work? What other technological developments have revolutionized police work in the modern era? What developments in law enforcement would you predict for the future?

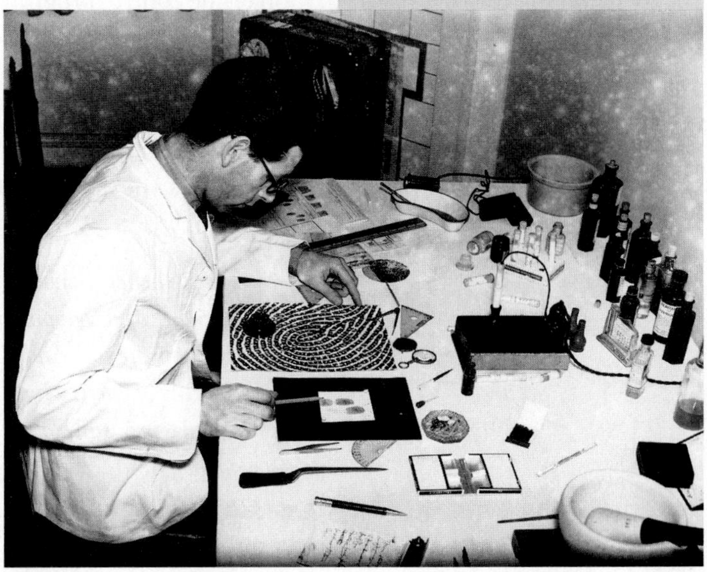

were physical fitness and political influence. After World War I psychological and intelligence tests began to be employed; these "revealed a shockingly low level of intelligence and psychological fitness among police personnel."[22] A 1934 survey estimated that only 20,000 of the 134,000 police officers in the country had participated in any kind of training program. As Vollmer pointed out, however, twenty-five years earlier training programs for police had not existed at all.[23] The problem continues today, as classroom training and written testing of police recruits are chronically under fire. These training and assessment methods turn out not to be good predictors of successful performance on the job. As a result, there is now a move toward "authentic assessment," which consists of rating police candidates' ability to carry out actual job-related tasks.[24] This movement reflects a continuing emphasis on the progressive idea of improved professionalism and training.

Innovations in equipment also contributed to improved police work during the twentieth century. In 1930 there were fewer than 1,000 patrol cars in the entire country. By 1966 there were more than 200,000 radio-equipped cars. The advent of the patrol car, the two-way radio, and the telephone had dramatic effects on policing in the United States.[25] These technological advances enabled police to patrol much larger geographic areas, respond to calls more quickly, and generally increase their accessibility to the public.

The Law Enforcement Assistance Administration

THE POLICE AND URBAN RIOTS

Law Enforcement Assistance Administration (LEAA)
Established in 1968, the LEAA was set up within the U.S. Department of Justice to allocate money to improve the efficiency and effectiveness of the criminal justice system. Between 1968 and 1977 the LEAA spent more than $6 billion on crime control programs and college education for police officers.

The growing reliance on technology, coupled with the increasing demand for police services, began to peak during the 1960s, when concern about crime was also at an all-time high.[26] This concern manifested itself in a series of government investigations. Between 1967 and 1973 there were no fewer than seven national crime commissions. Among their recommendations were improvements in police professionalism, training, and technology. In 1968 the **Law Enforcement Assistance Administration (LEAA)** was set up within the U.S. Department of Justice to allocate money to improve the efficiency and effectiveness of the criminal justice system. Between 1968 and 1977 the LEAA spent more than $6 billion on crime control programs and college education for police officers. Much of the money was spent on weaponry, riot control equipment, helicopters, SWAT (Special Weapons and Tactics) equipment, and other equipment for police. This occurred despite the fact that use of such equipment had resulted in violent outcomes and widespread criticism of the police during the civil rights and antiwar protests of the late 1960s and early 1970s.[27] A 1977 article from the *New York Times* illustrates the problem:

> *The Attorney General has publicly criticized such LEAA-financed activities as the $250,000 development of a shoe to accommodate a pistol that could be shot through the toe. And [the attorney general] was reportedly upset when he learned that the agency, which is financing about 55,000 programs, was planning to spend $2.5 million for a brochure telling local police departments how to apply for agency funds.*[28]

End of LEAA

The expenditure of money on questionable items, coupled with poor or nonexistent evaluations to assess the effectiveness of the programs funded, led to growing criticism of the LEAA. By the late 1970s there was a move to abolish the LEAA and discontinue federal aid to local law enforcement. The LEAA was finally abolished in the early 1980s. Law enforcement now is almost entirely the responsibility of local governments, although the federal government plays a role in the allocation of funds. For example, federal highway and transportation funds are increasingly allocated to states on the basis of their enforcement of laws involving drunk driving, acceptable blood-alcohol levels, and speed limits in keeping with standards imposed by the federal government. In this way the federal government manages to control some aspects of local law enforcement.

How did the Law Enforcement Assistance Administration (LEAA) influence the development of policing in the United States? Why was the LEAA later abolished, and with what consequences for American law enforcement? To what extent or in what ways do you think the federal government should be involved in local law enforcement today?

What Is the Organization of Law Enforcement?

As a result of the fear of a strong central government that existed at the time of the nation's founding, the U.S. Constitution has no provision for a national police force with broad enforcement powers. Most other countries have large, centralized national police forces. The United States, in contrast, has many different agencies at each level of government that specialize in the enforcement of certain types of laws. The result is a patchwork of law enforcement agencies with differing types of jurisdictions in terms of the types of laws they enforce and the level of government they work for.

THREE LEVELS OF POLICE

On the local and state levels, most police are generalists, responsible for the enforcement of most criminal laws. On the federal level there is much more specialization in the types of crimes different agencies handle. These distinctions are illustrated in Table 8.1.

Local Police

The vast majority of police agencies exist at the local level of government. Of the nearly 19,000 police agencies in the United States, more than 17,000 are operated by municipal and other local governments.[29] Most of these are the police departments of municipalities, but local law enforcement also includes county sheriffs and special police agencies such as park, airport, transit, and university police. Local police departments have nearly 581,000 full-time employees, about 80 percent of whom are police officers. The remaining 20 percent are civilian employees of police departments who perform specific tasks, such as communications specialists, evidence technicians, crime analysts, and people involved in victim assistance. Over the years, there has been a steady rise in the total number of sworn local police officers and civilian employees, resulting in an overall increase of about 30 percent in each category since 1987 (see Figure 8.2).[30]

Local police primarily enforce applicable state laws, but they also enforce local ordinances and traffic laws and investigate accidents and suspected crimes. Sheriffs provide police protection and investigate crimes in jurisdictions within

local police
The police departments of municipalities; local law enforcement also includes county sheriffs and special police agencies such as park, airport, transit, and university police.

Table 8.1 Career Opportunities in Law Enforcement

lawenforcementjob.com http://www.lawenforcementjob.com	Free employment information on over 3,500 municipal police, state police and patrol, sheriff, federal, international, corrections, and university and college departments.
Federal Bureau of Investigation (FBI) http://www.fbi.gov/	Largest federal law enforcement agency, responsible for enforcing all federal laws not assigned to other agencies. *Qualifications:* Bachelor's degree; skills in police work, teaching, foreign languages, engineering, accounting, computer sciences, chemistry, or law.
Drug Enforcement Administration (DEA) http://www.usdoj.gov/dea/	Enforces all federal narcotics laws. *Qualifications:* Bachelor's degree; skills in law, accounting, piloting aircraft, and/or foreign languages.
U.S. Marshals Service http://www.usdoj.gov/marshals/	Provides security in U.S. courtrooms, transports federal prisoners, operates the federal witness protection program. *Qualifications:* Bachelor's degree and work experience.
U.S. Immigration and Customs Enforcement http://www.ice.gov/enforcement	Involved with narcotics interdiction and illegal currency violations at the nation's borders; investigates fraud and imports and exports. Investigates illegal immigration and handles deportations from the U.S. *Qualifications:* Bachelor's degree and prior law enforcement experience.
Border patrol http://www.cbp.gov/xp/cgov/enforcement/border-patrol/	Patrols areas between points of entry into the United States from Mexico to guard against illegal immigration. *Qualifications:* Bachelor's degree or work experience and competency in Spanish.
State police http://www.policeemployment.com	In each state, enforces laws on state roads and investigates crimes that cross county lines or cannot be handled by local police. *Qualifications:* Two years of college or more.
Local police Use a search engine for "[*city*] Police Department"	In each city and town, county and municipal police enforce laws. *Qualifications:* Passage of competitive entrance examinations; college preferred.
Regulatory enforcement examples http://www.epa.gov/ http://www.atf.treas.gov/ http://www.osha.gov/	Specialized law enforcement for government regulatory agencies, such as environmental protection; alcohol, tobacco, firearms and explosives; gambling; postal system; forests and parks; wildlife protection; occupational health and safety. *Qualifications:* Bachelor's degree.
Private security http://www.securitymagazine.com/ http://www.asisonline.org	Protects private property for banks, airports, college campuses, insurance companies, hospitals, and corporations; investigates crimes by employees and customers. *Qualifications:* Law enforcement or private security background.

their county that lack their own police forces; they also serve court papers, maintain order in courtrooms, and operate county jail facilities.[31]

The local nature of American policing is further illustrated by the fact that nearly two-thirds of local police and sheriffs' departments employ fewer than ten full-time officers. Of this number, nearly 2,000 departments have only one full-time officer or only part-time officers.[32] The number of officers is related to the size of the population served. In towns with populations of 2,500 or less, the typical police department has three sworn full-time officers. As towns develop into cities, their police departments also grow: Towns with populations of 2,500 to 10,000 have police departments with an average of twelve full-time sworn officers, and the numbers are higher in cities with populations of 100,000 to 250,000, which average 284 full-time sworn officers.[33]

In large metropolitan areas, police agencies sometimes perform law enforcement tasks for both the city and surrounding jurisdictions. The Boston Police Department, for example, is assisted by the Metropolitan District Commission, which patrols public parks, parkways, and related areas. In New York City, the police department has taken over policing public housing projects and subway law enforcement tasks by merging smaller agencies into the NYPD. Other large metropolitan areas have similar arrangements, in which local police tasks have been consolidated into larger police efforts to serve the overlapping needs of surrounding communities with a growing list of law enforcement demands and responsibilities. Table 8.2 shows the sizes of the fifty largest local police departments in the United States. It can be seen that the highest ratio of police officers to residents occurs in Newark, Chicago, New York City, and St. Louis (45 to 48 officers per 10,000 residents), and the lowest ratio exists in Fairfax County (VA), Miami-Dade, Indianapolis, and Prince George's County (MD) (13 to 16 officers per 10,000 residents). The localities with the highest percent of their police force responding to call for service (versus other kinds of duties such as investigation, administration, or other duties) include Louisville (78 percent) Atlanta (76 percent), New Orleans (75 percent), and Miami-Dade (73 percent).

FIGURE 8.2 Full-Time Employment by Local Police Departments, 1987–2003

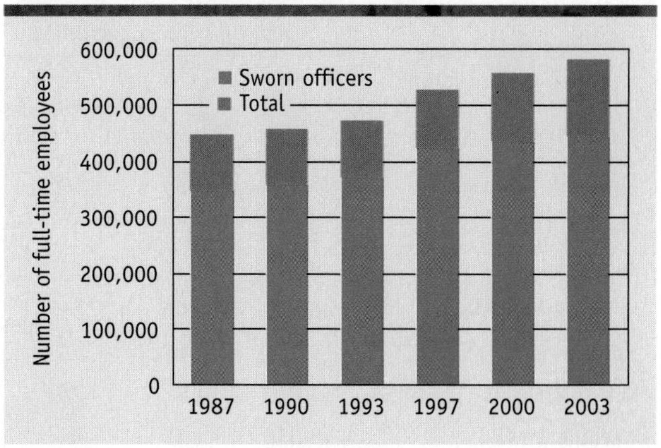

Source: Matthew J. Hickman and Brian A. Reaves, *Local Police Departments* (Washington, DC: Bureau of Justice Statistics, 2006).

Homeland Security Following the terrorist attacks of September 11, 2001, the role of local police took on a new dimension. The tasks of apprehension of terrorists, threat assessment, intelligence gathering, and better coordination with state and federal antiterrorism agencies have been added to the repertoire of local police, which will require new training and organization to accomplish this efficiently.[34] Clearly, the role of local law enforcement in terrorism can be significant. One need only look as far back as 1995, when Oklahoma City bomber Timothy McVeigh was stopped by a state trooper who noticed something wrong. Local police also played the central role in the apprehension of the Washington, D.C., area serial sniper attacks during 2002.

HOMELAND SECURITY

Terrorism can be a nebulous threat, often difficult to pin down. America's early experiences in setting threat levels (the red-orange-yellow-blue-green terror alert system) caused many problems because no one was sure what changes in levels meant and because precise information was lacking to guide actions. Historically, police have been trained to act on specific information using established standards such as probable cause. The threat of terrorism appears to be much less specific, and it will require new skills to gather intelligence effectively in this area. Several large local police departments attempted to gather domestic intelligence on radical groups during the 1960s, and some of these efforts resulted in successful legal challenges for unwarranted surveillance.[35] This experience points to the need for specific guidelines for police actions in this area, which is a problem, given the often nonspecific nature of terrorism and the need for intelligence.

Table 8.2 The 50 largest local police departments by total number of full-time sworn personnel, number of full-time sworn personnel per 10,000 residents, and percent of full-time sworn personnel regularly assigned to respond to calls for service.

	Full-Time Sworn Personnel				Full-Time Sworn Personnel		
Jurisdiction	*Total Number*	*Number per 10,000 Residents*[a]	*Percent Responding to Calls*[b]	*Jurisdiction*	*Total Number*	*Number per 10,000 Residents*[a]	*Percent Responding to Calls*[b]
New York (NY)	35,973	45	57%	New Orleans (LA)	1,622	35	75%
Chicago (IL)	13,469	47	72	St. Louis (MO)	1,507	45	62
Los Angeles (CA)	9,307	24	51	Charlotte-Mecklenberg Co. (NC)	1,499	22	45
Philadelphia (PA)	6,853	46	59	Atlanta (GA)	1,462	35	76
Houston (TX)	5,350	27	70	Denver (CO)	1,429	26	42
Detroit (MI)	3,837	42	26	San Jose (CA)	1,408	16	55
Washington (DC)	3,632	65	44	Newark (NJ)	1,332	48	55
Baltimore (MD)	3,258	52	61	Prince George's Co. (MD)	1,328	16	40
Miami-Dade Co. (FL)	3,178	14	73	Fairfax Co. (VA)	1,317	13	69
Dallas (TX)	2,943	24	63	Nashville (TN)	1,312	24	53
Suffolk Co. (NY)	2,808	19	46	Kansas City (MO)	1,299	29	61
Phoenix (AZ)	2,763	20	36	Fort Worth (TX)	1,249	21	44
Las Vegas-Clark Co. (NV)	2,640	17	49	Seattle (WA)	1,238	22	53
Nassau Co. (NY)	2,497	19	54	Austin (TX)	1,198	18	46
San Francisco (CA)	2,216	30	49	Louisville (KY)	1,195	17	78
Boston (MA)	2,109	36	66	Indianapolis (IN)	1,170	15	49
San Diego (CA)	2,103	17	48	El Paso (TX)	1,137	20	56
San Antonio (TX)	2,056	17	67	Montgomery Co. (MD)	1,089	12	69
Milwaukee (WI)	1,989	34	68	Cincinnati (OH)	1,047	33	48
Memphis (TN)	1,939	30	52	Miami (FL)	1,038	28	53
Honolulu (HI)	1,916	21	59	Pittsburgh (PA)	1,030	32	48
Cleveland (OH)	1,846	40	43	Oklahoma City (OK)	1,007	19	67
Columbus (OH)	1,797	25	57	Portland (OR)	1,005	19	44
Baltimore Co. (MD)	1,788	23	68	Tampa (FL)	962	30	65
Jacksonville-Duval Co. (FL)	1,624	21	61	Tucson (AZ)	960	19	52

Note: Sworn employees are those with general arrest powers. Officers not assigned to respond to calls for service typically were assigned to other areas of duty related to administration, investigations, technical support, jail operations, or court operations.

[a]In some cases populations were adjusted to more accurately reflect the population for which an agency provided law enforcement services.

[b]Includes all full-time sworn personnel with general arrest powers who were uniformed officers with regularly assigned duties that included responding to calls for service.

Source: Matthew J. Hickman and Brian A. Reaves, *Local Police Departments* (Washington, DC: Bureau of Justice Statistics, 2006).

One study found that police and firefighters agreed "they do not know what they need to be protected against, what form of protection is appropriate and where to look for such protection." Another study found that most school resource officers (specially trained police officers assigned to schools) believed that their schools were a "soft target" for terrorists, and that their schools were not protected adequately.[36] This uncertainty points to the need for better information and police training on what are the most significant terrorist threats in the

Table 8.3 Traditional versus Community-Based Policing

	Traditional	*Community Policing*
Philosophy	Probable cause of criminal activity is the basis for most police interventions into the lives of citizens.	Suspicion of criminal activity, identification of neighborhood problems, and disorderly public behavior to prevent more serious conduct and crimes.
Addressing Crime	Focus on responding to violations of the law.	Focus on noncriminal public disorder because it is a precursor of crime.
Role of the Public	The public's primary role is as witnesses and victims.	The public's primary role is to offer information to police that affects public safety and order in the community.
Role of the Private Sector	Police take bulk of responsibility for law enforcement.	Private businesses contribute to crime awareness campaigns and work with police in crime prevention efforts.

powerpoint

United States, what strategies and tactics are likely to be effective against these threats, and how enforcement activities should be prioritized among antiterrorism and more traditional law enforcement tasks. This kind of information is currently being developed at the federal level, and it will be a challenge in the coming years to see that local police are able to take on antiterrorism as a completely new part of their function, given the fact that training and resources will be needed to succeed.

In recent years there has been a trend back toward **community policing.** The central tenet of community policing is a service-oriented style of law enforcement, as opposed to the traditional focus on serious street crimes. Table 8.3 summarizes the major differences between community policing and traditional law enforcement. Community-based policing differs from the traditional approach in at least four distinct ways.[37]

community policing
A service-oriented style of law enforcement that focuses on disorder in the community, crime prevention, and fear reduction (as opposed to the traditional focus on serious street crimes).

As the table shows, community policing focuses more broadly on disorder in the community, crime prevention, and community support in organized prevention and enforcement efforts. Traditional policing, in contrast, focuses primarily on serious crime and the apprehension of offenders; citizens are involved only to the extent that they can help police carry out their law enforcement role. Traditional policing responds to crimes after they occur, whereas community policing attempts to solve underlying problems that ultimately result in crimes. Perhaps most important is the difference in the attitudes of police officers: Officers are detached in the traditional model, but in the community policing model they act in conjunction with citizens in an involved way.

Despite this trend, national surveys have found that police departments continue to embrace the crime control model of enforcement. Many police departments continue to view law enforcement as more important than community service.[38] A survey of police departments employing one hundred or more officers

How would you describe the differences between policing at the local level and policing at the state level? What is "community policing"? What are some other trends in the organization of law enforcement in the United States? What do you think are the advantages and disadvantages of having a number of separate jurisdictions in which police work is conducted?

found that an announced change to a community policing philosophy did not change the departments' organizational structure in any significant way.[39] In addition, it is not clear whether the role of the media will help or hinder community policing, because the media seek up-to-the-minute news and pay less attention to community trends than to immediate crises.[40]

The **Weed and Seed** program is an example of a popular community policing initiative of the 1990s. It is a federal program that provides funds to cities to help prevent and control crime and to improve the quality of life of high-crime neighborhoods.[41] It began in only three cities in 1991 and grew to 315 sites nationwide by 2003. Weed and Seed programs combine enforcement with community services. The "Weed" part of the program concentrates law enforcement by coordinating the efforts of police and prosecutors to identify, arrest, and prosecute violent offenders and drug traffickers in targeted areas. The "Seed" portion coordinates neighborhood revitalization efforts designed to prevent future crime.

Weed and Seed
Federal programs that combine enforcement with community services in an effort to reduce crime in targeted neighborhoods.

Typical Weed and Seed efforts include weekend and after-school activities for youth, adult literacy classes, and parental counseling. Police officers and prosecutors in Weed and Seed cities attempt to gain community and business support for their efforts by involving them in the problem-solving effort. An evaluation of the impact of the Weed and Seed program in eight cities found varied results so far. However, the most effective efforts "were those that relied on bottom-up, participatory decision-making approaches, especially when combined with efforts to build capacity and partnership among local organizations."[42] It appears that following the principles of community policing have produced positive results for the Weed and Seed program.

State Police

Every state except Hawaii has a state police force. These agencies were created in response to the need for law enforcement on roads that pass between municipalities. **State police** are different from local and federal police agencies in that they enforce state laws exclusively. Most states also have specialized law enforcement agencies similar to those at the federal level, such as state departments of environmental protection, alcohol control, and other specialized units.

state police
Enforcement agencies primarily engaged in highway patrol activities. About half of state police agencies also have the authority to conduct investigative work.

HIGHWAY PATROL

In all, state police departments have approximately 82,000 full-time employees, of whom about 70 percent are sworn officers. These departments vary widely in size. The largest state police department is the California Highway Patrol, with 6,700 sworn officers; the smallest is the North Dakota Highway Patrol, with 125 full-time officers.[43]

All state police departments are responsible for traffic law enforcement and accident investigation. Nearly all are engaged primarily in highway patrol activities. Only about half have the authority to conduct investigative work. The focus on patrol work is evidenced by the fact that in the nation as a whole there are ninety-eight police cars (marked and unmarked) for every hundred sworn state police officers.[44]

Approximately 70 percent of all state police are uniformed officers whose primary duty is patrolling roads and responding to calls for service. Eleven percent of state police are investigators, who attempt to solve crimes once they are reported. Other state police personnel have administrative or training tasks. Seventeen states have more than 1,000 state police officers; the largest is the California Highway patrol, with 9,700 employees all told. The smallest state police agency is the North Dakota Highway patrol, with a total of 193 employees.[45]

The U.S. Department of Homeland Security reorganized national and local efforts to address the threat of terrorism. What do you see as the most important role(s) for local police in anti-terrorism efforts?

Federal Law Enforcement Agencies

FEDERAL AGENCIES

There are more than 105,000 federal law enforcement officers in the United States, and 94 percent of these are employed by seventeen different agencies. These officers are authorized to carry firearms and make arrests in investigating violations of federal law. Unlike state police agencies, few federal agencies engage in patrol work; most perform exclusively investigative functions.

federal law enforcement Seventeen different agencies that investigate violations of federal law. Unlike state police agencies, few federal agencies engage in patrol work; most perform exclusively investigative functions.

Federal law enforcement agencies can enforce only laws enacted by Congress. Congress has the power to coin money, for example, and hence has delegated law enforcement authority to the U.S. Treasury Department. The Treasury Department is responsible for the printing of currency and therefore is also responsible for enforcing federal laws against counterfeiting and forgery. This function is performed by the Secret Service (which has the ancillary task of protecting the president). In addition, the Treasury Department is responsible for collecting federal income taxes and regulating the sale and distribution of alcohol, tobacco, and firearms. As a result, the Treasury Department houses the enforcement division of the Internal Revenue Service and the Bureau of Alcohol, Tobacco, Firearms and Explosives.

HOMELAND SECURITY

A significant change occurred in the organization of federal law enforcement with the passage of the Department of Homeland Security Act of 2002. It combined and reorganized federal antiterrorism and related law enforcement efforts into a single agency. Over the course of more than a year, the agencies that became part of the Department of Homeland Security were housed in one of four major directorates: Border and Transportation Security, Emergency Preparedness and Response, Science and Technology, and Information Analysis and Infrastructure Protection. The Border and Transportation Security directorate brought the major border security and transportation operations under one roof, including:

- The U.S. Customs Service (moved from the Treasury Department)
- The Immigration and Naturalization Service (INS) (part) (from the Justice Department)
- The Federal Protective Service (from the General Services Administration)
- The Transportation Security Administration (from the Department of Transportation)

- Federal Law Enforcement Training Center (from the Treasury Department)
- Animal and Plant Health Inspection Service (part) (from the Department of Agriculture)
- Office for Domestic Preparedness (from the Justice Department)

The Emergency Preparedness and Response directorate oversees domestic disaster preparedness training and coordinates government disaster response. It brings together:

- The Federal Emergency Management Agency (FEMA)
- Strategic National Stockpile and the National Disaster Medical System (from the Department of Health and Human Services)
- Nuclear Incident Response Team (from the Department of Energy)
- Domestic Emergency Support Teams (from the Justice Department)
- National Domestic Preparedness Office (from the FBI)

The Science and Technology directorate seeks to utilize all scientific and technological advantages when securing the homeland. This includes:

- CBRN Countermeasures Programs (from the Department of Energy)
- Environmental Measurements Laboratory (from the Department of Energy)
- National BW Defense Analysis Center (from the Department of Defense)
- Plum Island Animal Disease Center (from the Department of Agriculture)

The Information Analysis and Infrastructure Protection directorate analyzes intelligence and information from other agencies (including the CIA, FBI, Defense Intelligence Agency, and National Security Agency) involving threats to homeland security and evaluates vulnerabilities in the nation's infrastructure. It brings together:

- Critical Infrastructure Assurance Office (from the Commerce Department)
- Federal Computer Incident Response Center (from the General Services Administration)
- National Communications System (from the Department of Defense)
- National Infrastructure Protection Center (from the FBI)
- Energy Security and Assurance Program (from the Department of Energy)

The Secret Service and the Coast Guard also were relocated to the Department of Homeland Security, remaining intact and reporting directly to the Secretary. In addition, the INS adjudications and benefits programs report directly to the Deputy Secretary as the new agency U.S. Citizenship and Immigration Services.[46]

This major restructuring of federal law enforcement is significant because U.S. Customs and Border Protection, U.S. Immigration and Customs Enforcement, and the Secret Service are among the top five largest federal law enforcement agencies. Together with the FBI, they constitute about two-thirds of all federal law enforcement officers.

The Federal Bureau of Investigation is responsible for enforcing more than 250 federal laws that are not specifically designated to other federal agencies. The FBI is thus a catchall agency and has the widest jurisdiction of any federal law enforcement agency. Finally, the Federal Bureau of Prisons employs more than

13,500 corrections officers, who maintain security at all U.S. correctional facilities for convicted offenders and for defendants awaiting trial.

The remaining federal law enforcement agencies employ fewer than 4,000 officers each; among the smallest is the U.S. Fish and Wildlife Service, which employs only 888 agents. Table 8.4 presents a summary of all federal law enforcement agencies employing more than 500 full-time officers with authority to carry firearms and make arrests.

Table 8.4 Federal Law Enforcement Agencies

Agency	*Number of Officers*	*Primary Responsibility*
U.S. Customs and Border Protection	27,705	Investigates contraband entering or leaving country.
Federal Bureau of Prisons	15,200	Corrections officers in federal jails and prisons.
Federal Bureau of Investigation	12,200	Enforces 250 federal laws not specifically designated to other agencies.
U.S. Immigration and Customs Enforcement	10,400	Border patrol and investigation of illegal aliens at ports of entry.
U.S. Secret Service	4,800	Investigates counterfeiting and federal computer fraud; provides security for federal officials.
Drug Enforcement Administration	4,400	Investigates federal narcotics crimes.
Administrative Office of U.S. Courts	4,100	Federal probation officers.
U.S. Marshals Service	3,200	Provides security in federal courtrooms; finds fugitives; transports prisoners; manages witness security program and federal forfeitures.
U.S. Postal Inspection Service	3,000	Investigates crimes committed using the mails.
Internal Revenue Service	2,800	Criminal Investigation division investigates tax fraud.
Veterans Health Administration	2,400	Security and police services at VA hospitals.
Bureau of Alcohol, Tobacco, Firearms and Explosives	2,400	Investigates illegal firearm, explosive use; enforces federal alcohol, tobacco regulations.
National Park Service	2,100	Police services for the U.S. park system.
U.S. Capitol Police	1,500	Police services for U.S. Capitol.
Diplomatic Security Service	800	Security for U.S. and foreign diplomats
U.S. Fish and Wildlife Service	700	Enforces federal laws relating to hunting and fishing.
U.S. D.A. Forest Service	600	Protects national forest land, animals, natural resources, and visitors.

Source: Adapted from Brian A. Reaves, *Federal Law Enforcement Officers* (Washington, DC: Bureau of Justice Statistics, 2006).

Because the historical evolution of policing in America began at the local level, and because most federal agencies do not engage in patrol work, the organization of police in the United States is skewed heavily toward local police. For example, the New York Police Department, with more than 36,000 officers, is three times the size of the FBI. Likewise, the Chicago Police Department (13,000 officers), the Los Angeles Police Department (9,000), the Philadelphia Police Department (7,000), the Houston Police Department (5,000), and other large city police departments are larger than most federal law enforcement agencies.

Transnational Law Enforcement

transnational law enforcement International agreements and law enforcement efforts that attempt to serve the interests of all nations in the face of the growth of international travel, the transnational nature of the Internet, and the threat of international organized crime and terrorism.

Interpol The International Criminal Police Organization composed of 177 member nations. It assists member law enforcement agencies requiring information about crimes or criminals of a transnational nature.

Transnational law enforcement is not centrally organized, because individual nations around the world have sovereignty and resent other nations that attempt to enforce their laws outside their own borders. Nevertheless, the growth of international travel, the transnational nature of the Internet, and the threat of international organized crime and terrorism have combined to bring about international agreements and law enforcement efforts that attempt to serve the interests of all nations.

INTERPOL AND EUROPOL

Interpol, the International Criminal Police Organization, was begun in 1923 and took its current name in 1956. Interpol assists the law enforcement agencies of its 177 member nations by providing information about crimes or criminals of a transnational nature.[47] It provides information in four languages: Arabic, English, French, and Spanish. The U.S. National Central Bureau (USNCB) is the point of contact between Interpol and police agencies in the United States. The USNCB is located within the U.S. Department of Justice and is jointly managed with the U.S. Treasury Department. All requests from federal, state, or local police are transmitted to Interpol through the USNCB.[48]

The importance of Interpol will increase as internal and external security concerns merge. As Malcolm Anderson has observed, "State security is now threatened by political violence which falls short of conventional military operations but which arises from complex criminal conspiracies—areas formerly considered squarely in the domain of policing."[49] Organized crime, drug trafficking, corruption, and other traditional concerns of law enforcement are becoming national security concerns in many nations. The demise of the Soviet Union has freed intelligence agencies and the military to focus more on transnational crime than on military threats. Evidence that reliance on Interpol is increasing can be seen in the fact that the USNCB staff has increased steadily. This rise reflects an increase in transnational criminal activity as well as greater attention to international criminal matters on the part of U.S. agencies.[50]

Interpol headquarters in Lyon, France. What is Interpol's primary role? Why is an agency like Interpol necessary?

Another effort to combat transnational crimes is Europol, which was established in 1991 to share information about drug trafficking among member countries of the European Union. Europol emerged out of growing concern over drug trafficking and money laundering, as well as a growing awareness of the need for better coordination among European police agencies and customs officials. The removal of many of the barriers to free trade and economic growth in Europe since the late 1980s has made it easier to communicate and travel among the European nations. This situation also makes it easier for criminals to smuggle stolen property and drugs across borders. Europol was seen as a mechanism for organizing international law enforcement activities.[51]

GLOBALIZATION OF LAW ENFORCEMENT

The need for shared information is paralleled by the need for trained law enforcement personnel. Efforts are being made to professionalize law enforcement agencies around the world. The Federal Bureau of Investigation now trains law enforcement officials from other nations in a program sponsored by the U.S. State Department. These officials come to the United States to be trained in modern law enforcement and prosecution techniques. In addition, the FBI opened an international police training academy in Budapest in 1995, and subsequently opened two others in Botswana and Thailand. As former FBI Director Louis Freeh observed, there is a need for "a centrally located school where we can develop a network of police partners in countries where we do not now have those relationships."[52]

There are now more than 2,000 American law enforcement personnel working overseas. Nearly a third of these are agents with the Drug Enforcement Administration, which has agents in thirty nations. The Departmental Homeland Security and Coast Guard each have law enforcement personnel in more than twenty countries. The FBI; Internal Revenue Service; Secret Service; and Bureau of Alcohol, Tobacco, Firearms and Explosives also have agents assigned overseas.[53] This high level of international law enforcement activity points to the growth in international crime and the need for coordination of law enforcement activities.

Beginning in the 1990s the United Nations has held several conferences on themes of concern to international law enforcement, such as international money laundering, transnational organized crime, and law enforcement cooperation.

Under what circumstances might local and state police be involved in police operations at the federal or transnational levels? What agencies are involved in transnational and overseas police work? What crimes in the global community are their greatest concerns? What do you predict will be the future of international law enforcement?

The purpose of the meetings was to examine existing international standards, legislation, and models for cooperation in dealing with international organized crime. The conferences were attended by representatives from the vast majority of the 192 member countries of the United Nations, reflecting the high level of interest and concern about these problems.[54] Such meetings permit open discussion of the problems posed by international criminal behavior, along with exploration of possible solutions.[55] This is extremely important when so many U.S. law enforcement agencies are working in other countries. Nations can feel threatened when there is not consensus about the seriousness of a problem or about the appropriateness of the measures taken. It is through such efforts that international law enforcement trust, cooperation, and professionalism are improving. International cooperation also is a mechanism for placing pressure on nations that are not diligent in their efforts to thwart transnational crime.

Who Are the Police?

People in law enforcement in the United States are a diverse group totaling more than 1 million sworn officers and civilians. In 1987 the Bureau of Justice Statistics began the Law Enforcement Management and Administrative Statistics (LEMAS) program, which is a nationwide survey of state and local police agencies employing one hundred or more officers that is conducted every three years. According to the most recent survey, local police departments employed an average of 16 officers per 10,000 city residents, but varied from 8 to more than 78 officers per 10,000 residents.[56] This shows that the relative size of police departments varies considerably.

FEMALES IN POLICE WORK

In addition, a growing proportion of these officers are women. Until recent decades, women and those of certain heights, weights, and backgrounds were excluded from police work. The 1972 amendments to Title VII of the Civil Rights Act of 1964 made its provisions applicable to *both* public (e.g., police) and private sector employers. The act prohibits discrimination on the basis of gender, and it also mandates that gender must be shown to be a "bona fide occupational qualification" if women are not hired or promoted on the same basis as men. Therefore, an employer must prove that there is a significant difference in the performance of men versus women if they are not to be hired or assigned in the same manner.

Although the idea of women in police work is more than a century old, it has only been during the last forty years that women have been hired and assigned in the same manner as men. The guidelines of the Equal Employment Opportunity Commission (EEOC) also have helped to eliminate discrimination on the basis of gender. Under these guidelines both public and private employers "must demonstrate that any requirement for employment or promotion is specifically related to some objective measure of job performance."[57] Although there has been criticism of the EEOC for a sluggish enforcement record, the guidelines have helped to eliminate arbitrary police qualifications such as minimum height requirements, unless they can be shown to affect job performance.[58]

MINORITIES IN POLICE WORK

The result of these trends is that police officers are increasingly diverse. Female officers now make up 11 percent of all local police, African Americans nearly 12 percent, and Hispanic Americans more than 9 percent of the total. These figures vary by size of police agency. For example, the percentage of female officers ranged from 4 percent in places with fewer than 2,500 to 16.5 percent in jurisdictions of 500,000 or more. The total of 51,000 female police officers nationwide represents an increase of 9 percent since 2000.[59] Police recruits are increasingly college graduates (as discussed in the next section), and many have had internship experiences within police agencies. In addition, many larger police departments now recruit prospective officers from outside their own jurisdiction, in an attempt to obtain better-qualified recruits and have their department more closely reflect the makeup of their community.[60]

Police officer candidates are trained in a police academy classroom. Why is it important that police officers become more diverse in terms of gender, race, and ethnicity?

A detailed job analysis of the tasks performed by New York City police officers, for example, identified forty-two distinct tasks that police officers carry out. As a result, all police exams, interviews, and other testing must be based on these performance criteria.[61] This requirement ensures that the officers chosen will conform to the qualifications for the job, rather than to stereotypes not based in fact. Nevertheless, job expectations change. The growth of community policing, for example, requires police to work with the noncriminal public more than ever before and makes crime prevention as important a goal as the apprehension of law violators. Police researcher Stephen Mastrofski has identified six characteristics that summarize current expectations of "good service" from police officers:[62]

CHARACTERISTICS OF GOOD POLICE WORK

- Attentiveness—vigilance and accessibility to the public and to their concerns.
- Reliability—predictable and error-free police service when called upon.
- Responsiveness—"client-centered" service that always provides a good faith effort by police.
- Competence—use of police legal authority and discretion in acceptable ways.
- Manners—interaction with the public in a respectful way.
- Fairness—enforcement of the law and treatment of suspects in an evenhanded manner.

These six characteristics reflect the belief that police work requires much more than the application of the law in the community. The quality of police service is increasingly scrutinized, because the manner in which police tasks are carried out is considered as important as the tasks themselves. This situation has placed increased emphasis on the way in which police officers are selected and trained.

Training and Education

Selection processes vary somewhat among police departments, but most agencies require applicants to pass a written test, a physical agility test, a drug test, a medical exam (including visual and hearing tests), an oral interview, a psychological assessment, a polygraph test, and a background investigation. There are questions about the utility of some of these requirements. Research has shown, for

What kind of education and training has this law enforcement officer received for his job in the Border Patrol? How does his job interface with other law enforcement agencies involved in transnational crime? According to research, what are the characteristics of good police work that professional training and education support?

example, that written tests do not always provide a valid indication of who will be a successful police officer. Police departments are looking for better ways to screen recruits; some of these methods include scenario-based testing, which requires physical and verbal responses by an applicant to simulated situations. Also, a report from the National Academy of Sciences concluded that government agencies should not rely on polygraph examinations for screening prospective or current employees to identify spies or other security risks because the test results are too inaccurate, missing both lying persons, as well as mistakenly identifying large numbers of truthful innocent test takers as deceptive. "National security is too important to be left to such a blunt instrument," said Stephen E. Fienberg, chair of the committee that wrote the report.[63] Figure 8.3 illustrates the testing and screening methods used by local police departments in the United States. Polygraphs and personality tests are used least often, while criminal record, driving, and background investigations are nearly universal.

IMPROVEMENTS IN POLICE TRAINING

Police training has improved dramatically over the years. The typical police agency requires more than 800 hours of classroom training for new recruits. This training includes detailed knowledge of diverse subjects, such as criminal law, traffic law, patrol function, criminal investigation, ethics, first aid, and related subjects. In addition, police agencies require an average of more than 400 hours of field training in subjects such as defensive driving, use of firearms, arrest and control of suspects, and general physical fitness. Wide variations in these training requirements continue to exist around the nation. Likewise, the criminal law and rules for its enforcement change continually, as you have seen; yet requirements for in-service training for police vary widely. The average annual in-service training requirement for non-probationary officers was forty-seven hours, including twenty-four hours mandated by state laws.[64]

FIGURE 8.3 Local Police Officers Employed by Departments Using Various Recruit Screening Methods, 2003

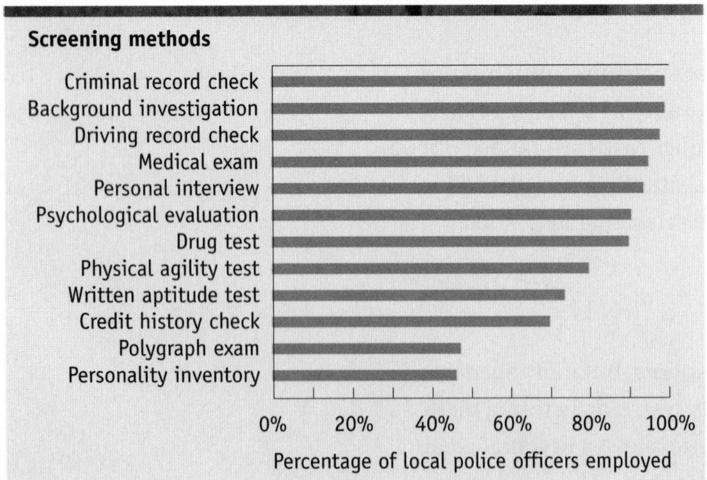

Source: Matthew J. Hickman and Brian A. Reaves, *Local Police Departments* (Washington, DC: Bureau of Justice Statistics, 2006).

The basic education required of most new police officers is a high school diploma, but that is changing. Sixteen percent of state police agencies now require a two-year college degree, and 4 percent require a bachelor's degree. Virtually all federal law enforcement agencies require a bachelor's degree. Similar to the state police, 16 percent of county police departments require either a two-year or four-year degree, followed by 9 percent of large municipal police departments. These percentages have increased in recent years and will continue to do so as higher salaries and benefits make police work a more desirable profession.

Police salaries vary by jurisdiction and are related to the size of the police department and the cost

POLICE SALARIES

of living in different parts of the country. The average starting salary in large municipal police departments (communities with more than 100,000 population) is $36,900, according to the most recent data published, which is slightly more than the average paid by county and state police agencies. Officer salaries increase by an average of 10 percent after one year of experience on the job, and more than half of all police agencies provide educational incentive pay to encourage officers to further their education. Police sergeants in cities with a population of 25,000 or larger earn between $53,000 and $73,000 per year.[65]

Issues of Gender and Race

PERSISTING SEXISM AND RACISM

The human element of police professionalism has not always kept pace with organizational and educational changes. Female officers, minority officers, and new tactical approaches to policing have not always won ready acceptance. A study in a midwestern city found de facto segregation of officers by race, as well as sexual harassment and marginalization of women. Although no single factor was found to cause the lack of integration of women and minorities, entrenched attitudes and organizational policies appeared to be implicated.[66] Studies in other locations also find that female officers often struggle for acceptance and do not receive equal treatment from male officers and superiors.[67] These findings provide context for the cases that come to public attention when lawsuits are filed. In Southborough, Massachusetts, for example, a police dispatcher was awarded $250,000 in settlement for a claim of sexual harassment. A female police sergeant in Florida was awarded $100,000 after a jury found that her chief had used racial slurs when calling her. An Illinois county settled a discrimination suit for $444,000 and agreed to make significant changes in its hiring practices when an investigation found it had not hired a female patrol officer in seventeen years. In similar fashion, the Bureau of Alcohol, Tobacco, Firearms and Explosives agreed to pay $5.9 million in damages and overhaul its hiring and promotion system in response to a suit by African American agents who claimed they had been assigned to lower-ranking positions and lower salaries.[68] In Delaware, a federal court ruled the state had discriminated against African American applicants for entry-level state trooper positions through the use of a particular written examination. The state had to provide $1.4 million to qualified African American applicants who had applied for entry-level state trooper positions.[69]

Discrimination on the basis of gender occurs despite the fact that numerous objective studies have demonstrated that women perform police tasks as well as men. In St. Louis, New York City, and many other jurisdictions, it has been found that female officers perform police tasks as competently as male officers do. No significant difference has been found between men and women in the time it takes to handle an incident, the way threatening situations are handled, the proportion of arrests that result in prosecution, injuries on the job, citizen satisfaction with the way that an incident is handled, or other important aspects of the job.[70] Yet female officers in the United States encounter barriers and "gendered images that establish them as outsiders, sexual objects, targets of men's resentment, and competitors who threaten to change the rules of officer interaction."[71]

That's a FACT

Perspectives on Police Agencies You Haven't Heard About

There are many police agencies that you often don't hear about. These are smaller, specialized agencies that do law enforcement work in particular substantive areas. Look at Table 8A, and you are guaranteed to find some agencies you have not heard of. What do these law enforcement officials do? The Pentagon Force Protection Agency, formerly the Defense Protective Service (DPS), was established in 2004 to expand on the DPS mission of providing basic law enforcement and security against all potential threats to the 280-acre area around the Pentagon in Arlington, Virginia, and for other Department of Defense facilities in the National Capitol region. The U.S. Mint is a bureau in the Department of Treasury. Its officers provide police and patrol services for U.S. Mint facilities to protect the nation's coinage and gold bullion reserves. The Bureau of Indian Affairs in the Department of the Interior provides police services in Indian country. In addition, many tribal governments operate their own police departments.

Look up the missions of the other law enforcement agencies listed in Table 8A. Which police tasks most interest you? Why?

There are fifty-seven federal offices of inspector general (IG) in the United States. IG offices detect and prevent fraud, waste, and abuse in federal programs, operations, and employees. They also investigate criminal violations (see www.ignet.gov). Twenty-seven of the IG offices employ criminal investigators with police powers (see Table 8B). As shown in the table, the Office of the Inspector General in the Department of Health and Human Services was the largest employer of those with police powers, followed by the Treasury Inspector General for Tax Administration.

Why do you think the investigative staffs of these IG offices vary so widely? Which IG offices appear most interesting to you? Why?

Table 8A Federal Agencies with 100 to 500 Enforcement Employees who Carry Firearms and Have Arrest Powers

Agency	*Number*
Pentagon Force Protection Agency	482
U.S. Mint	376
Bureau of Indian Affairs	320
Amtrak	317
Department of Energy*	292
Bureau of Land Management	249
Bureau of Engraving and Printing	234
Environmental Protection Agency	209
Food and Drug Administration	177
Tennessee Valley Authority	168
National Marine Fisheries Service	141
U.S. Supreme Court	125
Library of Congress	116

Note: Table excludes offices of inspector general. Number of employees excludes those in U.S. Territories of foreign countries.

*Office of Secure Transportation

Table 8B **Employees of Offices of Inspector General Authorized to Make Arrests and Carry Firearms**

Office of Inspector General	*Number of Full-Time Officers with Arrest and Firearm Authority*
Total	2,867
Department of Health and Human Services	374
Department of the Treasury, Tax Administration	330
Department of Defense	326
Social Security Administration	279
Department of Housing and Urban Development	213
Department of Agriculture	170
Department of Labor	142
Department of Homeland Security	132
Department of Justice	128
Department of Veterans Affairs	116
Department of Transportation	108
Department of Education	97
Department of the Interior	57
National Aeronautics and Space Administration	54
Environmental Protection Agency	53
General Services Administration	50
Department of Energy	47
Federal Deposit Insurance Corporation	39
Small Business Administration	29
Office of Personnel Management	27
Department of State	18
Department of the Treasury	16
Nuclear Regulatory Commission	15
U.S. Railroad Retirement Board	14
Department of Commerce	13
Agency for International Development	13
Government Printing Office	7

Note: Table excludes employees in U.S. Territories or foreign countries.

Source: Brian A. Reeves, *Federal Law Enforcement Officers* (Washington, DC: Bureau of Justice Statistics, 2006).

What kind of training and amount of education are police officers required or encouraged to have? What are the demographic characteristics of people who tend to choose police work as their profession? What perennial issues of gender and race compromise police professionalism? Would you consider law enforcement as a career? Why or why not?

Despite the satisfactory performance of female officers, these attitudes may be responsible for the slow assimilation of women in policing.

Analogous attitudes may be responsible for lingering instances of racism within police departments. Studies have found that minorities are more likely than whites to have unfavorable attitudes toward police in general, although the race of crime victims or the race of police officers handling a case has been found to make no difference in the degree to which victims feel the police fulfilled their expectations in a given incident.[72] In sum, race and gender images appear not to hold up when one looks at specific cases and makes objective comparisons.

Findings like these have led to growing emphasis on ongoing research within police agencies and promotion of the concept of police departments as "learning organizations" that are more dynamic and better able to respond to both social and technological changes. Researchers examine, for example, changes in the behaviors of both police and society; and they study the impact of those changes to ensure that efforts to improve police professionalism are not subverted by negative attitudes or archaic organizational policies.[73]

What Are Some Concerns about Policing in the United States?

This nation's historical ambivalence about establishing an organized police system and reluctance to centralize it and make it more efficient has hampered the ability of police to apprehend criminals and reduce the fear of crime. On one hand is the need to organize law enforcement efforts more efficiently. On the other hand is society's reluctance to provide the resources, technology, and authority that are required if a system of property protection and personal safety is to be effective. Concerns about policing include jurisdictional cooperation, the impacts of high technologies on police work, and the privatization of policing.

The Dilemma of Jurisdictions and Need for Cooperation

As you have learned, law enforcement is carried out by municipalities. In the United States today, only 1 percent of the 19,000 law enforcement agencies in the nation are state or federal agencies. As the President's Commission stated in 1967, "A fundamental problem confronting law enforcement today is that of fragmented crime repression efforts resulting from the large number of uncoordinated local governments and law enforcement agencies."[74] A 1996 investigation came to a similar conclusion regarding federal police, citing a "need for greater coordination of the numerous agencies involved in federal law enforcement."[75] In the new era of domestic and international terrorism and multijurisdictional and multinational

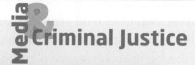

Media & Criminal Justice

Police Dramas on Television

Perhaps there is no more enduring form of television drama than the police show. Currently, there are ten police dramas on the major broadcast networks, and many others in re-reruns on cable channels. Why do police dramas remain so popular?

At this writing, *CSI: Crime Scene Investigation* is the number-1-rated show on television, producing a spin-off, *CSI: Miami,* in the same way that three different versions of *Law & Order* were spun off, and a new version of *Dragnet* has emerged. In addition, production companies are working on new versions of *Kojak, McCloud, Baretta,* and *Miami Vice,* which were hugely popular during the 1970s, 1980s, and 1990s.[a]

Two explanations for the popularity of these shows involve the dimensions of power and human frailty. Police on television shows "seem simultaneously to have their way and to possess the power to keep people from achieving theirs."[b] The interaction between the legal powers and use of force by police against the unlawful use of force by criminals is a compelling premise. Similar to the plots of many popular detective novels, police dramas on television also portray cops fighting a corrupt, inefficient, or unjust system, which offers another opponent to combat legally or illegally—in ways the private citizen (i.e., the viewer) cannot. This constant battle between good and evil often makes for interesting viewing.

A second explanation is the human dimension, made popular in recent years by *NYPD Blue,* where cops are portrayed very much like private citizens, torn by anger, lust, love, alcoholism, and personality problems, but somehow remain on the right side of the law (most of the time).

The portrayal of police on crime dramas impacts public views of real police, so police agencies view the television shows cautiously. For example, the Los Angeles Police Department receives five or six requests a week from producers who wish to use the LAPD as part of either a reality or fictional program. Many of these requests are turned down, when the portrayal is seen as one-sided. As the creator of *Law & Order* states, "It's easy to focus on the bad cops. That makes for lazy drama. What I find more interesting is looking at how a good cop stays human and keeps his sense of duty and hope."[c]

Are there reasons other than those offered above for the enduring popularity of police dramas on television? What do you find most compelling about these shows? Do you believe police dramas should reflect police in a balanced fashion (following the example of real life)?

NOTES

a. Glenn Whipp, "LAPD under Siege from Filmmakers' Request," *The Daily News of Los Angeles* (February 16, 2003), p. 4.
b. Lee Siegel, "Why Cop Shows Are Eternal," *The New Republic* (March 31, 2003), p. 25.
c. Whipp, p. 5.

crime, an organized and systematic police response has become even more critical. The need for coordination has been a problem throughout the history of policing in the United States, even though the amount of resources devoted to the task has increased dramatically in recent years. The growing police presence must be organized efficiently to be fully effective.[76]

MULTIJURISDICTIONAL CRIMES

An example of this problem is the enforcement of drug laws. A person who sells crack cocaine in any city could be under surveillance by, and arrested by, the city police, the state police, the FBI, or the DEA. Other agencies also could be involved if certain other circumstances are present, such as the possession of weapons, terrorist purposes, or affiliation with organized crime. Overlapping jurisdictions sometimes result in several law enforcement agencies investigating the same suspects for the same crimes. Because of the ease with which people, planes, cars, and electronic communications can traverse local boundaries, multijurisdictional crimes are becoming more common. Police agencies tend to respect geographic boundaries, but criminals do not. The creation of **multijurisdictional task forces** allows for different levels of enforcement to pool evidence, personnel, and expertise while reducing unnecessary duplication of effort. A study of eight cities found that each had a combined federal, state, and local law enforcement task force that focused on some combination of drug crimes, weapons, and violent crimes.[77] The Metropolitan Richmond Task Force in Virginia includes detectives from the DEA; the Richmond Police Department; the Virginia State Police; the Henrico, Chesterfield, and Hanover County Police; and the City of Petersburg. Two major task force investigations culminated with the conviction of twenty members of two drug-trafficking organizations. Similarly, the Cold Homicide Task Force involves the FBI, Virginia State Police, and Richmond Police Department. The task force identified an East Coast drug organization as responsible for twelve homicides in New York City and Virginia.[78] Such task forces, although they deal with only a small proportion of all the crimes that occur in an area, often pursue complicated cases requiring resources that no single agency can devote.

multijurisdictional task forces Multiagency efforts to combat multijurisdictional crimes allowing for pooling of evidence, personnel, and expertise and to reduce unnecessary duplication of effort.

Thus, additional resources alone have not improved the efficiency of policing. It will take greater recognition of the limits of political boundaries and jurisdictions to make law enforcement more effective.

The Impacts of Technology and the Media on Police Work

POLICE COMMUNICATIONS

In recent decades improvements in police communications and technology have backfired to a certain extent. Following the lead of police in other countries, police in the United States have made it easier for people to contact them through the introduction of the 911 emergency phone number, nontoll telephones, and remote communications equipment. The public makes use of these innovations so frequently that police efficiency has suffered. As one observer commented in the 1970s,

> *These efforts have been so successful that they threaten to overturn the traditional conceptions of police work and to undermine the efficiency and purpose of street patrols. Since New York City introduced its emergency number in July 1968, the average number of calls each day to the police has risen from 12,000 to 17,000, and it is still climbing. In Philadelphia, a city one-fourth the size of New York, during a 14-hour period of a Friday in June 1971, more than 8,000 emergency calls were received. During peak periods, patrolmen are often unable to handle all of their assignments. They are so busy answering calls that they have no time to patrol these territories.*[79]

During the 1990s this problem became even more serious with the explosion in the number of cell phones. Total phone usage went up dramatically as a push was on to install E911 ("Enhanced 911") nationwide, a system that permits the police dispatcher to determine the location from which a person is calling. E911 is still not yet available nationwide, as implementation costs are high, and technological glitches have occurred, especially with cell phones. It has been estimated that 82 million 911 calls are placed each year by callers using mobile phones alone, so the burden on police is increasing. Some jurisdictions have added a 311 number to report non-emergencies to take the load off of 911 calls, but so far it appears that adding the 311 number has only served to increase the total number of calls for service.[80]

CALLING 911

The problem lies not only in the growing volume of calls to the police. An increasing proportion of 911 calls do not involve emergencies. Also, the growing use of cellular phones has resulted in 18 million additional 911 calls each year from locations that are difficult to trace; and undertrained and poorly paid dispatchers have contributed to several tragedies due to failure to respond.[81] Better training of dispatchers, new fiber-optic systems designed to handle a higher volume of calls, and the use of alternate nonemergency numbers are some recent initiatives designed to address the dramatic increase in emergency calls.

Technology will make some aspects of police work more efficient. The FBI upgraded the National Crime Information Center (NCIC), a system of 39 million computer records that contains criminal histories and lists of missing persons, wanted persons, and stolen property. The new system includes electronic mug shots and a fingerprint of each wanted person. The FBI's goal is for all police agencies to have laptop computers, miniature fingerprint scanners, and video cameras in patrol cars to allow police officers to see photos of wanted or missing persons on computer screens in their cars, and to permit police officers to take fingerprints from suspects at the scene and compare them instantly to the NCIC database. It is expected to cost about $2,000 to equip a patrol car with this equipment, but this system should dramatically improve the ability of police to screen suspects quickly and accurately.[82]

DNA EVIDENCE AND CODIS

The National Commission on the Future of DNA Evidence was created in 1998 in response to concern about wrongful convictions in rape and homicide cases. The Commission found unrealized potential for the use of DNA evidence in crime scene investigations.[83] Historically, DNA has been used in laboratory testing and as courtroom evidence to link suspects with crimes by using their unique DNA "genetic fingerprint" obtained from blood, saliva, semen, or other body tissue found at a crime scene. The FBI's DNA Index System (CODIS) was authorized in 1994, and since then every state has enacted legislation establishing a CODIS database, requiring that DNA profiles be entered into the system for offenders convicted of serious crimes. Currently there are more than 3.5 million DNA profiles in the CODIS system, permitting police who have found body fluids or residue from a crime scene, but no suspects, to compare it to the CODIS database. Thus far, police have had hundreds of "cold hits" in which suspects were identified from the DNA database without other evidence of their involvement in the crime. Police also have been able to include or exclude suspects based on the results of DNA testing.[84] Progress on the national level has been slow, however, and many states currently have large backlogs of untested samples due to limitations of lab size and a shortage of forensic scientists on staff to analyze these samples.[85] As the CODIS database continues to grow, more crimes will be solved by means of DNA evidence.

The president proposed $1 billion over five years to improve the use of DNA in the criminal justice system. These funds are being used to eliminate backlogs in testing unanalyzed DNA samples for violent crimes; improve lab capacity through better equipment, staffing, and training; stimulate research to develop quicker and less costly methods of DNA testing; provide access to post-conviction DNA testing to correct wrongful convictions; and use DNA to identify missing persons. This initiative addresses many of the problems raised in a number of criminal cases about poorly qualified forensic science analysts, poor lab facilities, and questionable evidence being used in court.[86]

COP TV AND LIVE CRIME

The influence of the mass media on police work has been dramatic. The ability of media to access police records (through the Freedom of Information Act) and the use of remote video cameras, automobiles, and even helicopters to film police in action have all contributed to changes in the way police behave. According to police researcher Peter Manning, police demonstrate "reflexivity," in which their choices are influenced by the anticipated responses of others. Those responses, in turn, are shaped by how police decisions are portrayed in the media.[87] For example, news footage of police beating a motorist, as in the Rodney King incident, is repeated and analyzed on television many times, blurring the distinction in people's minds between unusual and everyday police actions. Misrepresentations of this kind can confuse or mislead both the public and policymakers. According to Manning, the police are countering extensive media coverage with media of their own. They are using surveillance videos and video cameras mounted in patrol cars to record actual police conduct, including pursuits and arrests. This police footage sometimes is aired as entertainment on network television. Thus, the boundaries between police and public tend to merge as the mass media (for better or for worse) become partners in police work.

The impact of the media clearly involves more than public image. "Reality" television programs follow police on the job—but feature episodes of violent action and high-speed pursuits as if they were typical. *America's Most Wanted* also features the most gruesome unsolved cases, then advertises for leads from the general public. The result of these media portrayals is public misunderstanding about the true nature of police work, the success of police in solving crimes, and the true level of crime and violence in society. There is an increase in unrealistic expectations of

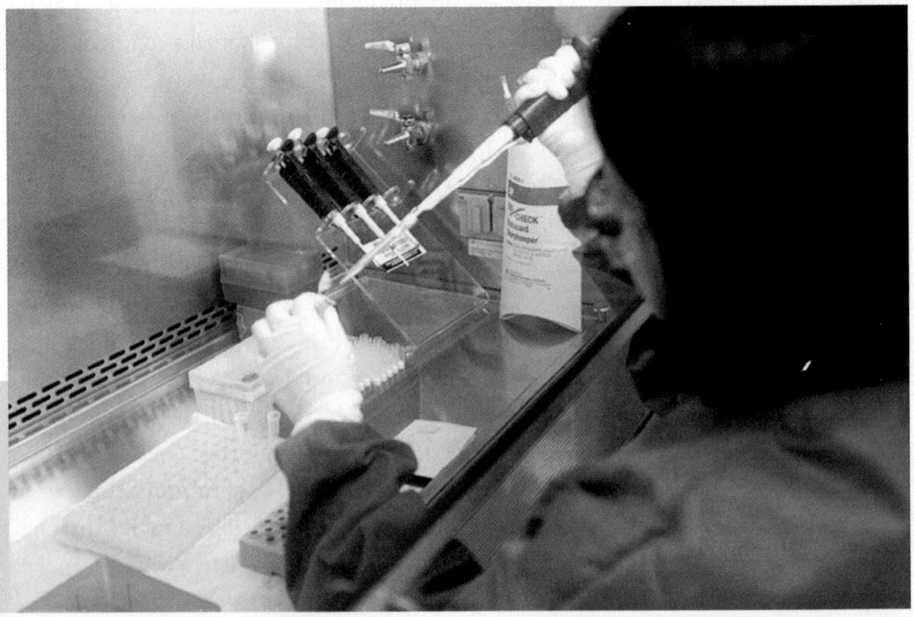

Testing for DNA evidence in a forensic lab. DNA testing has been used to exonerate the innocent, but such testing is expensive and time consuming. Should there be limits on kinds of cases for which DNA testing is used?

police when television alternately portrays them either as a fearsome force that always catches the offender or as an agency hopelessly trying to deal with an extremely violent society—when the true situation is somewhere in between.

FIGURE 8.4 Trends in Private Security and Law Enforcement Employment

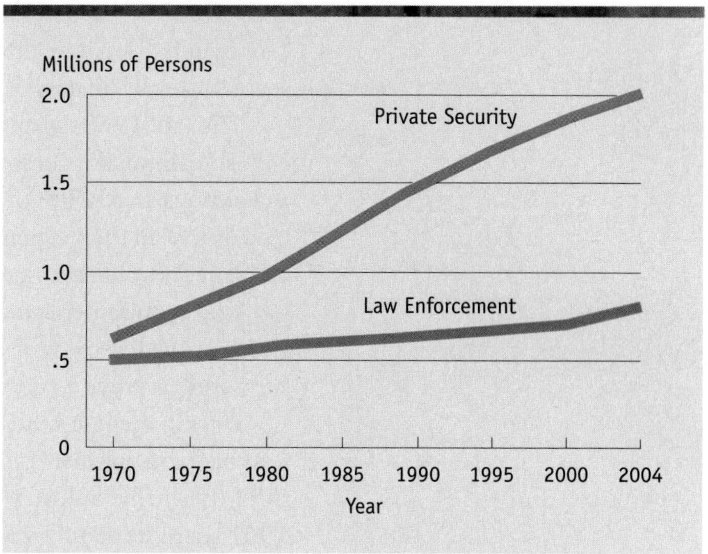

Source: Data from William Cunningham, J. Strauchs, and Clifford W. VanMeter, *The Hallcrest Report II: Private Security Trends 1990–2000* (Boston: Butterworth–Heinemann, 1990); Office of Community Oriented Police Services, *National Policy Summit: Building Private Security-Public Policing Partnership* (2004) Washington, DC: Office of Community Oriented Police Services.

The Movement toward Private Policing

Private security is growing at an incredible rate. There are more than twice as many private security officers as there are police officers in the United States (see Figure 8.4).

private security
Law enforcement agencies that protect private property and are paid by private individuals and corporations.

In an interesting reversal of history, public policing, which arose because of the ineffectiveness of private security measures, is now faced with a movement back toward privatization. Historically, private security has taken on law enforcement tasks when public police forces have not adapted quickly to major social or technological changes. These changes have resulted in new manifestations of crime, spurring private entrepreneurs to offer protective services to those who can afford them. This response has played a significant role in the continuing growth of private security.[88]

PINKERTON'S AND BRINK'S

An early example was the need for multijurisdictional law enforcement. The development of an interstate railroad system during the mid-1800s created new opportunities for theft, robberies, and vandalism that were beyond the capacity of public police agencies to control. Regional policing and regulatory enforcement agencies were not yet developed, and local police agencies were not well equipped to deal with multijurisdictional crimes. In 1855 Allan Pinkerton was hired by six railroads to provide police protection over a five-state region. Within the next few years Pinkerton extended his activities into areas normally the responsibility of municipal police, providing detective services and an evening patrol for businesses in the Chicago area.[89]

In 1844 Samuel Morse invented the telegraph, which not only revolutionized communication but also provided the means to detect burglaries electronically through the use of relays. In 1858 an entrepreneur named Edwin Holmes seized the opportunity to establish the first central office burglar alarm. He later founded Holmes Protection, Inc., a private security agency that is still operating today. In 1874 American District Telegraph (ADT) was established to provide protective services through the use of messengers and telegraph lines.[90] Today private security agencies continue to manage a larger proportion of the central burglar alarm market than do police departments.

The 1850s also saw social changes resulting from an expanding population and increasing distance between population centers. Robberies, thefts, and unreliable delivery of goods led Perry Brink to form a truck and package delivery service in 1859. Brink later expanded into armored car services, delivering his first payroll in 1891; today Brink's is the largest agency of its kind in the United States.[91]

PRIVATIZATION IN BUSINESS AND INDUSTRY

During the 1960s the deterioration of central cities caused many urban residents to move to the suburbs. The resulting changes in public shopping patterns accelerated the development of enclosed shopping malls in suburban locations. This trend, in turn, led to the utilization of private protective services on a large scale. Virtually all enclosed malls now have private security forces.

The late 1960s also witnessed widespread demonstrations and uprisings on college campuses. These protests were not handled adequately by local police. According to a RAND Corporation study, many colleges and universities have doubled or tripled their expenditures on private security since then.[92] The increasing incidence of robberies, assaults, and theft on college campuses, together with new national requirements for reporting of campus crime, have kept campus security forces at the forefront of a growing industry. Campus law enforcement expenditures now average $109 per student.[93]

During the late 1960s and early 1970s there was a dramatic increase in the number of people using air transportation, largely owing to the increasing capacity of the airline industry and the decreasing cost of air travel. Between 1963 and 1967 there were only 4 attempted skyjackings in the United States, but between 1968 to 1972 there were 134 such attempts. In addition, a large number of bomb threats were made against aircraft in the United States and elsewhere. In response to this situation, the Federal Aviation Administration (FAA) began compulsory point-of-departure screening of airline passengers in 1972. This screening for weapons and explosives is the responsibility of the airlines and was carried out primarily by contract security firms until taken over by the new Transportation Security Administration of the federal government as a response to the terrorist attacks of September 11, 2001. Similar procedures have been established in other countries, and many are conducted by private security agencies.[94]

The expanding frontiers of international business have increased the scale and influence of U.S. multinational corporations—and the number of terrorist threats and kidnappings of corporate executives and their families. It is estimated that in the 1990s there were more than 30,000 kidnappings of Americans overseas.[95] As a result, more than 20,000 private security personnel are involved in executive protection. This protection has been extended to computer networks to protect them from acts of sabotage and theft of company secrets.[96]

There is every reason to believe that private security will continue to grow and to assume tasks that were previously the responsibility of public law enforcement. The vast majority of America's infrastructure is protected by private security, so it is positioned to play a major role in crime prevention and anti-terrorism efforts. As the 9/11 Commission report observed, "Because 85 percent of our nation's critical infrastructure is controlled not by the government but by the private sector, private sector civilians are likely to be the first responders in any future catastrophe."[97] Private security defends most power plants, financial centers, computer systems, shopping malls, railroad lines, and other potential targets, so training and operational linkages between private security and public police are needed more than ever. It remains to be seen whether public law enforcement agencies will embrace aspects of privatization that can benefit their communities, and whether private security agencies can perform police tasks in a consistently efficient, effective, and accountable manner.

CRITICAL THINKING EXERCISES

Campus Law Enforcement and Crime

Campus security has grown as an industry as crime on college campuses has become a national concern. This attention has been aroused by highly publicized homicides at universities as well as by the more common problems of binge drinking, rape, and reckless deaths on college campuses. Today, three-fourths of four-year colleges and universities with more than 2,500 students employ sworn police officers who have general arrest powers under state or local law. There are nearly 11,000 full-time sworn officers serving these colleges and universities, plus 9,000 additional full-time campus security personnel who are not sworn officers.

The backgrounds and training requirements of campus security officers vary widely. Most sworn campus police officers are armed, including 95 percent of security personnel serving campuses with 20,000 or more students. One-fourth of campuses contract for private security services, most involving private security companies. Training for new officers ranges from less than 400 to more than 900 hours. Similarly, 30 percent of campus security agencies require that new officers have some college education, but only 2 percent require a four-year degree.

Campus security officers engage in a variety of tasks, from investigation of serious crime to enforcement of parking regulations. Most campus security agencies are responsible for alarm monitoring, building lockup, investigation of serious crimes, personal safety escorts, stadium security, parking, and traffic enforcement. A smaller number handle medical center or nuclear facility security.

The vast majority (85 percent) of campus law enforcement agencies operate general crime prevention programs. These programs are designed to increase awareness of criminal opportunities and reduce the risk of victimization. Two-thirds of campus police agencies have education programs for date rape prevention, for example, and half have programs for prevention of drug and alcohol abuse.[a]

Figure 8A shows that violent crime against college students, and non-students of the same age, has dropped significantly, and that the overall victimization rate of college students is lower than that of non-students. Nevertheless, a survey of violent crimes against college students found male

FIGURE 8A Violent Crime Victimization Rates of College Students versus Non-Students Aged 18–24

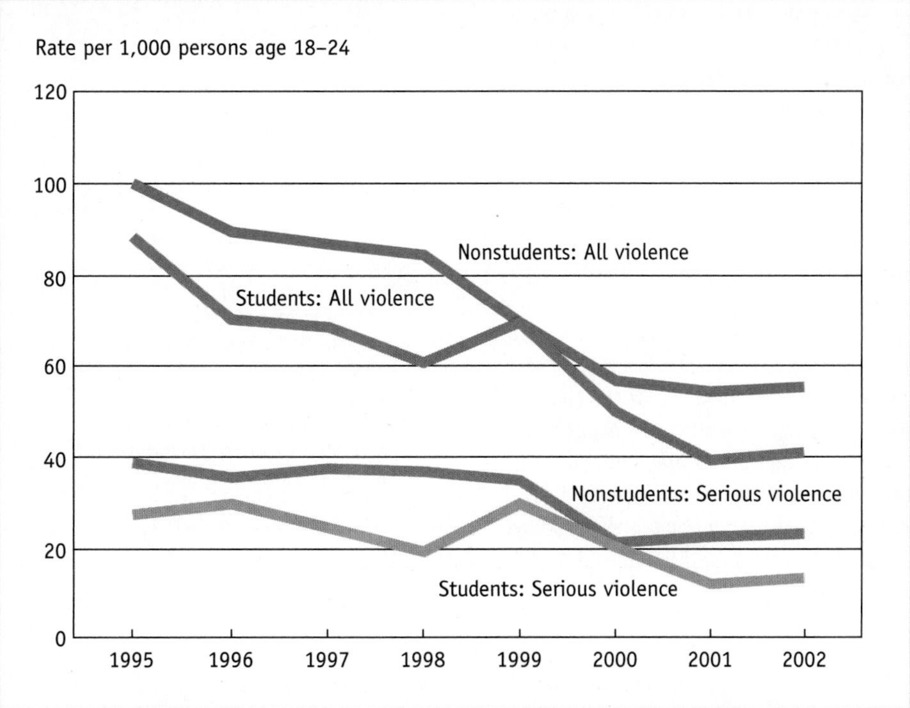

Source: Katrina Baum and Patsy Klaus, *Violent Victimization of College Students, 1995–2002* (Washington, DC: Bureau of Justice Statistics, 2005).

(continued)

college students were twice as likely to be victims than female students (80 versus 43 per 1,000). Fifty-eight percent of the violent crimes were committed by strangers, 41 percent of offenders were perceived to be using alcohol or drugs, and 93 percent of the crime occurred off campus (of which 72 percent occurred at night).

CRITICAL THINKING QUESTIONS

1. What aspects of local law enforcement have come to your attention as a member of your college community? How do you rate your campus security?
2. Given what is known about the backgrounds of college students who are victims of violent crime, what elements would you include in a crime prevention program and to whom would it be targeted?

NOTE

a. Brian A. Reaves, *Campus Law Enforcement* (Washington, DC: Bureau of Justice Statistics, 1996); Verna A. Henson and William E. Stone, "Campus Crime: A Victimization Study," *Journal of Criminal Justice* 27 (July–August 1999); Katrina Baum and Patsy Klaus, *Violent Victimization of College Students* (Washington, DC: Bureau of Justice Statistics, 2005).

The Cyclical Nature of Community Policing

Before the establishment of full-time police in the 1800s, private citizens were largely responsible for protecting their own property. With advances in police professionalism and technology, the public has come to rely on the police for this service. The dramatic growth in calls for police service over the years testifies to this reliance.

Increased calls to police have diminished their effectiveness in solving crimes; fewer than 20 percent of serious crimes are solved by an arrest. Community policing attempts to reintroduce the public as a significant player in crime control. Community policing has been defined as "a collaboration between the police and the community that identifies and solves community problems." Recognizing that crime often plagues poor and disorganized neighborhoods, community policing is designed to incorporate members of the community as "active allies in the effort to enhance the safety and quality of neighborhoods" so that police are "no longer the sole guardians of law and order."[a] It is ironic that in 150 years the United States evolved from a crime prevention system in which private citizens fended for themselves to one in which they are almost totally dependent on police—and that the trend is now being reversed.

The nature of community policing varies in different jurisdictions, but the theme is the same: assigning a neighborhood patrol officer who gets to know the local residents, building trust between police officers and citizens, devoting time to solving problems before they develop into crimes. This approach to law enforcement makes citizens partners with the police in controlling crime rather than passive recipients of police services.

Evaluations of the effectiveness of community policing strategies have found mixed results thus far. On the positive side, citizens in many neighborhoods have reported a more positive view of police and of the crime situation in their area. On the negative side, community policing has had no uniform effects on crime rates; it has proved difficult to involve neighborhood organizations in the programs; and within police departments there appears to be some resistance to community policing strategies.[b]

CRITICAL THINKING QUESTIONS

1. Why do you believe the public's attitude toward police often improves in neighborhoods where community policing is practiced?
2. How might changes in the impacts of the mass media and telecommunications technologies affect community policing?
3. At what point do you think the involvement of private citizens in policing could go too far?

NOTES

a. Bureau of Justice Assistance, *Understanding Community Policing* (Washington, DC: Office of Justice Programs, 1994), p. vii.

b. Gary W. Cordner, "Community Policing: Elements and Effects," *Police Forum* 5 (July 1995), pp. 1–8; Susan Sadd and Randolph M. Grinc, *Implementation Challenges in Community Policing: Innovative Neighborhood-Oriented Policing in Eight Cities* (Washington, DC: National Institute of Justice, 1996); Jerome H. Skolnick, *On Democratic Policing* (Washington, DC: Police Foundation, 1999); David H. Bayley and Clifford D. Shearing, *The New Structure of Policing* (Washington, DC: National Institute of Justice, 2001); David Lilley and Sameer Hinduja, "Officer Evaluation in the Community Policing Context," *Policing: An International Journal of Police Strategies and Management*, vol. 29 (January 2006), pp. 19–38.

SUMMARY

HOW DID POLICING EVOLVE?

- Before police departments were formally established, less formal measures of self-protection were used. In the mutual pledge system, everyone in the community was responsible for everyone else. In the watch and ward system, men from each town were required to take turns standing watch at night.
- The invention of gin was a catalyst for the establishment of public policing. Although the gin craze abated, the fear of crime did not. This led to the creation of the Bow Street Runners, a private agency that patrolled the streets.
- The first police force was established in London in 1829. Police officers patrolled specific areas and were organized in a paramilitary fashion to maintain discipline.
- The first daytime police force in the United States was established in Boston in 1838; New York was the first city to create a unified day and night police force. By 1900 nearly every city of any size had established a full-time police force.
- Urban police forces were plagued by problems of low pay, disrespect, and ineffectiveness. During the Progressive Era there was a movement toward police efficiency, professionalism, and improved technology.
- Police effectiveness was increased through improved investigative techniques and better selection and training procedures.

WHAT IS THE ORGANIZATION OF LAW ENFORCEMENT?

- The vast majority of police agencies are found at the local level of government. Local police enforce applicable state laws, local ordinances, and traffic laws; they also investigate accidents and suspected crimes.
- State police agencies enforce state laws and investigate accidents. They include specialized law enforcement agencies for such purposes as alcohol control.
- There are seventeen different federal law agencies that enforce laws enacted by Congress. The largest federal agencies are the U.S. Customs Service, the Federal Bureau of Investigation, the Federal Bureau of Prisons, and the Immigration and Naturalization Service.
- The growth of international travel, the transnational nature of the Internet, and the threat of international organized crime and terrorism have combined to bring about international agreements and law enforcement efforts that serve the interests of all nations.

WHO ARE THE POLICE?

- Police selection processes vary among police departments, but most agencies require applicants to pass a written test, physical agility test, drug test, medical exam (including visual and hearing test), oral interview, psychological assessment, polygraph test, and background investigation. The typical police agency requires more than 800 hours of classroom training for new recruits.
- Police officers are increasingly female and minorities, although there continue to be cases of harassment and discrimination within some police departments, despite the fact that performance studies and victim interviews show that females and minority officers perform well and are accepted by the public.

WHAT ARE SOME CONCERNS ABOUT POLICING IN THE UNITED STATES?

- Policing faces a dilemma: There is a need to organize law enforcement efforts in a more efficient way. However, there is also reluctance to provide the necessary resources and authority.
- Innovations in equipment have contributed to improved police work. However, the introduction of 911 lines led to unanticipated problems due to an extremely high volume of calls.
- Reliance on technology in policing is increasing with the updated National Crime Information Center, which will allow for police to access criminal histories, wanted person files, and fingerprint comparisons via computers in their patrol cars. DNA banking is enabling police to compare human tissue found at crime scenes with a database of known offenders to solve more crimes.
- Media images of police work often distort the true nature of policing, providing the public with an unrealistic view of the capabilities and performance of police.
- Private security is a burgeoning industry, taking on law enforcement tasks in areas where public police forces do not adapt sufficiently to social and technological changes.

KEY TERMS

mutual pledge system *180*
constable *180*
shire reeve *180*
watch and ward system *180*
justice of the peace *181*
preventive police *182*
crime commissions *185*
progressivism *185*
professionalization *185*
Law Enforcement Assistance Administration (LEAA) *186*
local police *187*
community policing *191*
Weed and Seed *192*
state police *192*
federal law enforcement *193*
transnational law enforcement *196*
Interpol *196*
multijurisdictional task forces *206*
private security *209*

QUESTIONS FOR REVIEW AND DISCUSSION

1. What systems for community protection evolved before the establishment of formal police departments?
2. Why did the invention of gin act as a catalyst for the establishment of public policing?
3. What were some of the problems faced by early police forces?
4. How was police professionalism enhanced in the early decades of the twentieth century?
5. Why is growing reliance on technology a problem for police operations today?
6. Why is law enforcement carried out largely by municipalities in the United States?
7. What are the primary activities of local and state police forces?
8. What are the major federal law enforcement agencies, and what are their responsibilities?
9. What are important issues facing transnational law enforcement?
10. Explain the growing diversity among police officers in recent years.
11. How is the growth of private security related to the police?

NOTES

1. Don Babwin, "Chicago Pays $4.25 Million to Settle Lawsuit over Police Response," *Associated Press State & Local Wire* (June 26, 2006); Petula Dvorak, "Agency Planned to Handle 911 Calls," *Washington Post* (August 14, 2002), p. B1; Keith Herbert, "House Is Giving Police a Handful," *Philadelphia Inquirer* (August 14, 2003); Stephanie Hanes, "Protective Orders Rise with New Law," *The Baltimore Sun* (October 6, 2003).
2. Jennifer Brevorka, "Police Use Computers to Prevent Crime; They Study Trends, Then Plan Strategy," *News & Observer* (Raleigh, NC), (March 2, 2005); Matthew J. Hickman and Brian A. Reaves, *Local Police Departments* (Washington, DC: Bureau of Justice Statistics, 2006); Ken Maguire, "Crime Alert at Your Fingertips in Boston," *Washington Post* (June 20, 2006); John E. Eck, Spencer Chainey, James G. Cameron, Michael Leitner, and Ronald E. Wilson, *Mapping Crime: Understanding Hot Spots* (Washington, DC: National Institute of Justice, 2005).
3. President's Commission on Law Enforcement and Administration of Justice, *Task Force Report: The Police* (Washington, DC: U.S. Government Printing Office, 1967), p. 3.
4. Harold T. Amidon, "Law Enforcement: From 'The Beginning' to the English Bobby," *Journal of Police Science and Administration* 5 (September 1977), pp. 355–67.
5. President's Commission, p. 4.
6. Jonathan Rubinstein, *City Police* (New York: Ballantine, 1974), pp. 4–5.
7. Rubinstein, p. 6.
8. M. Dorothy George, *London Life in the Eighteenth Century* (New York: Capricorn, 1925).
9. Rubinstein, pp. 8–9.
10. Amidon, p. 366.
11. Rubinstein, p. 10.
12. "The Metropolitan Police," Available at ds.dial.pipex.com/mbloy/peel/police.htm (2000).
13. Rubinstein, p. 11.
14. Center for Research on Criminal Justice, *The Iron Fist and the Velvet Glove*, revised ed. (Berkeley, CA: Center for Research on Criminal Justice, 1977), p. 22.
15. George Smith, *The United States Constitution* (Nashville, TN: Knowledge Products, 1987).
16. Roger Lane, *Policing the City: Boston, 1822–1885* (Cambridge, MA: Harvard University Press, 1971); Center for Research on Criminal Justice, *The Iron Fist and the Velvet Glove.*
17. President's Commission, p. 5.
18. Carl B. Klockars, *The Idea of Police* (Beverly Hills, CA: Sage, 1985).
19. Rubinstein, pp. 15–20.

20. Nathan Douthit, "Enforcement and Nonenforcement Roles in Policing: A Historical Inquiry," *Journal of Police Science and Administration* 3 (September 1975), p. 339.
21. Harry Soderman, "Science and Criminal Investigation," *The Annals* 146 (1929), pp. 237–48.
22. Douthit, p. 341.
23. August Vollmer, "Police Progress in the Last Twenty-Five Years," *Journal of Criminal Law, Criminology, and Police Science* 24 (1933), pp. 161–75.
24. Clifford E. Thermer, "Authentic Assessment for Performance-Based Police Training," *Police Forum* 7 (July 1997), pp. 1–5.
25. See Samuel Walker, *A Critical History of Police Reform* (Lexington, MA: Lexington Books, 1977).
26. James O. Finckenauer, "Crime as a National Political Issue: 1964–76, from Law and Order to Domestic Tranquility," *Crime and Delinquency* 24 (January 1978), pp. 1–23.
27. See National Advisory Commission on Civil Disorders (1968) and President's Commission on Campus Unrest (1970).
28. Wendell Rawls, "Justice Department May Seek Special Revenue Sharing to Replace Anti-Crime Grants," *New York Times* (June 30, 1977), p. 30.
29. Matthew J. Hickman and Brian A. Reaves, *Local Police Departments* (Washington, DC: Bureau of Justice Statistics, 2006).
30. Ibid.
31. Ibid.
32. Ibid., p. 9.
33. Ibid., p. 2.
34. Jonathan R. White, *Defending the Homeland: Domestic Intelligence, Law Enforcement, and Security* (Belmont, CA: Thomson Wadsworth, 2004), pp. 38–39.
35. Jerry Berman and Lara Flint, "Intelligence Oversight and Control for the Challenge of Terrorism," *Criminal Justice Ethics*, vol. 22 (winter/spring 2003), p. 57.
36. Philip Shenon, "Two Studies Cite Confusion on Terrorism," *New York Times* (August 21, 2003); Ronald V. Clarke and Graeme R. Newman, *Outsmarting the Terrorists* (New York: Praeger, 2006).
37. George L. Kelling and Catherine M. Coles, *Fixing Broken Windows: Restoring Order and Reducing Crime in Our Communities* (New York: Touchstone, 1997), pp. 240–41; Wesley G. Skogan et al., *Taking Stock: Community Policing in Chicago* (Washington, DC: National Institute of Justice, 2002).
38. Jihong Zhao and Quint C. Thurman, "Community Policing: Where Are We Now?," *Crime and Delinquency* 43 (July 1997), pp. 345–57; J. Kevin Ford, Daniel A. Weissbein, Kevin E. Plamondon, "Distinguishing Organizational from Strategy Commitment: Linking Officers' Commitment to Community Policing to Job Behaviors and Satisfaction," *Justice Quarterly* 20 (2003), pp. 159–85.
39. Edward R. Maguire, "Structural Change in Large Municipal Police Organizations during the Community Policing Era," *Justice Quarterly* 14 (September 1997), pp. 547–76; see also John Murray, "Policing Terrorism: A Threat to Community Policing or Just a Shift in Priorities?" *Police Practice and Research*, vol. 6 (September 2005), pp. 347–62.
40. Joanne Ziembo-Bogl, "Exploring the Function of the Media in Community Policing," *Police Forum* 8 (January 1998), pp. 1–12; Steven Chermak and Alexander Weiss, *Marketing Community Policing in the News: A Missed Opportunity?* (Washington, DC: National Institute of Justice, 2003).
41. U.S. Comptroller General, *More Can Be Done to Improve Weed and Seed Program Management* (Washington, DC: U.S. General Accounting Office, 1999); U.S. Comptroller General, *Despite Efforts to Improve Weed and Seed Program Management, Challenges Remain* (Washington, DC: U.S. General Accountability Office, 2004).
42. Terence Dunworth and Gregory Mills, *National Evaluation of Weed and Seed* (Washington, DC: National Institute of Justice, 1999).
43. Brian A. Reaves and Matthew J. Hickman, *Census of State and Local Law Enforcement Agencies* (Washington, DC: Bureau of Justice Statistics, 2002); Matthew J. Hickman and Brian A. Reaves, *Local Police Departments* (Washington, DC: Bureau of Justice Statistics, 2006).
44. Ibid., p. 11.
45. Ibid.
46. www.dhs.gov; http://csis.gov.
47. Mathieu Deflem, "Bureaucratization and Social Control: Historical Foundations of International Policy Cooperation," *Law & Society Review*, vol. 34 (October 2000), pp. 739–778; Fenton Bresler, *Interpol* (Toronto: Penguin, 1993); Michael Fooner, *Interpol* (New York: Plenum, 1989).
48. www.interpol.int/.
49. Malcolm Anderson, "Interpol and the Developing System of International Police Cooperation," in William F. McDonald, ed., *Crime and Law Enforcement in the Global Village* (Cincinnati: Anderson, 1997), p. 101.
50. Ethan A. Nadelmann, "The Americanization of Global Law Enforcement: The Diffusion of American Tactics and Personnel," in McDonald, ed., *Crime and Law Enforcement in the Global Village*, p. 124.
51. John Benyon, "The Developing System of Police Cooperation in the European Union," in McDonald, ed., *Crime and Law Enforcement in the Global Village*, p. 115.
52. Ordway P. Burden, "Law Enforcement Agencies Working Overseas," *CJ International* 11 (November–December 1995), p. 17; Leslie E. King and Judson M. Ray, "Developing Transnational Law Enforcement Cooperation: The FBI Training Initiatives," *Journal of Contemporary Criminal Justice*, vol.16 (November 2000), pp. 386–408.
53. Ibid.
54. "The World Ministerial Conference on Organized Transnational Crime," *United Nations Crime Prevention and Criminal Justice Newsletter*, nos. 26/27 (November 1995); Kauko Aromaa and Terhi Viljanen, eds. *Enhancing International Law Enforcement Cooperation, including Extradition Measures* (Helsinki: HEUNI, 2005).
55. See Gary T. Marx, "Social Control across Borders," in McDonald, ed., *Crime and Law Enforcement in the Global Village*, pp. 23–39; Guy Stessens, *Money Laundering: A New International Law Enforcement Model* (Cambridge: Cambridge University Press, 2000).
56. Brian A. Reaves and Mathew L. Hickman, *Law Enforcement Management and Administrative Statistics, 2000* (Washington, DC: Bureau of Justice Statistics, 2002).
57. Theresa M. Melchionne, "The Changing Role of Policewomen," *The Police Journal* 47 (October 1974), pp. 340–58.
58. Nancy E. McGlen and Karen O'Connor, *Women's Rights* (New York: Praeger, 1983); Janis Appier, *Policing Women: The Sexual Politics of Law Enforcement and the LAPD* (Philadelphia: Temple University Press, 1997); Mangia Natarajan, "Women

Police in a Traditional Society: Test of a Western Model of Integration," *International Journal of Comparative Society"* (February–May 2001), p. 211.
59. Hickman and Reaves, 2006.
60. Kevin W. Dale, "College Internship Program: Prospective Recruits Get Hands-On Experience," *The FBI Law Enforcement Bulletin* 65 (September 1996), p. 21; Michele McNeil, "Fighting for Recruits," *Indianapolis Star* (December 5, 2005).
61. *Guardians Association of New York City Police Department v. Civil Service Commission of New York*, 23 FEP 909 (1980).
62. Stephen D. Mastrofski, *Policing for People* (Washington, DC: Police Foundation, 1999).
63. Larry K. Gaines and Steven Falkenberg, "An Evaluation of the Written Selection Test: Effectiveness and Alternatives," *Journal of Criminal Justice* 26 (May–June 1998), p. 175; National Research Council, *The Polygraph and Lie Detection* (Washington, DC: National Academies Press, 2003).
64. Hickman and Reaves, 2006.
65. Ibid.
66. Robin N. Haarr, "Patterns of Interaction in a Police Patrol Bureau: Race and Gender Barriers to Integration," *Justice Quarterly* 14 (March 1997), pp. 53–85.
67. Jihong Zhao, Leigh Herbst, and Nicholas Lovrich, "Race, Ethnicity and the Female Cop: Differential Patterns of Representation," *Journal of Urban Affairs* (summer–fall 2001), p. 243; James Daum and Cindy Johns, "Police Work from a Woman's Perspective," *Police Chief* 61 (1994), pp. 46–49; Mary Brown, "The Plight of the Female Officer: A Survey," *Police Chief* 61 (1994), pp. 50–53.
68. "The High Cost of Discrimination," *Law Enforcement News* (December 31, 1996), p. 19.
69. "Justice Department Settles Lawsuit Regarding Delaware State Police Hiring Practices," *State News Service* (August 2, 2005); see also Jim Edwards, "Thirty Years and Counting: The Oldest Federal Litigation in New Jersey Is a Decades-Long Dispute over Bias in Police and Firefighter Hiring, and It's Still Going Strong," *New Jersey Law Journal*, vol. 172 (April 14, 2003), p. 1.
70. Susan Ehrlich Martin and Nancy C. Jurik, *Doing Justice, Doing Gender: Women in Law Enforcement Occupations* (Thousand Oaks, CA: Sage, 1996), p. 73; Lewis J. Sherman, "An Evaluation of Policewomen on Patrol in a Suburban Police Department," *Journal of Police Science and Administration* 3 (December 1975), pp. 434–38; Joyce L. Sichel, Lucy N. Friedman, Janet C. Quint, and Michael E. Smith, *Women on Patrol: A Pilot Study of Police Performance in New York City* (Washington, DC: U.S. Department of Justice, 1978).
71. Anthony V. Bouza, "Women in Policing," *FBI Law Enforcement Bulletin* 44 (1975), pp. 2–7; Susan Ehrlich Martin, *Breaking and Entering: Policewomen on Patrol* (Berkeley: University of California Press, 1980); Bernadette Jones Palombo, "Attitudes, Training, Performance and Retention of Female and Minority Police Officers," in G. T. Felkenes and P. C. Unsinger, eds., *Diversity, Affirmative Action and Law Enforcement* (Springfield, IL: Thomas, 1992), pp. 76–79; Donna C. Hale and Stacey M. Myland, "Dragons and Dinosaurs: The Plight of Patrol Women," *Police Forum* 3 (April 1993); Daniel Bell, "Policewomen: Myths and Reality," *Journal of Police Science and Administration* 10 (March 1982), pp. 112–20; Peter Horne, *Women in Law Enforcement*, 2nd ed. (Springfield, IL: Thomas, 1980); Sean A. Grennan, "Findings on the Roles of Officer Gender in Violent Encounters with Citizens," *Journal of Police Science and Administration* 15 (1987); Kerry Segrave, *Policewomen: A History* (Jefferson, NC: McFarland, 1995); Susan Ehrlich Martin, "Women on the Move?: A Report on the Status of Women in Policing," *Women and Criminal Justice* 1 (1989), pp. 21–40; Tim R. Sass and Jennifer L. Troyer, "Affirmative Action, Political Representation, Unions, and Female Police Employment," *Journal of Labor Research*, vol. 20 (fall 1999), p. 571.
72. Ronald Weitzer and Steven A. Tuch, "Race, Class, and Perceptions of Discrimination by the Police," *Crime and Delinquency* 45 (October 1999), pp. 494–507; Meghan Stroshine Chandek, "Race, Expectations and Evaluations of Police Performance," *Policing: An International Journal of Police Strategies and Management* 22 (1999), pp. 675–95.
73. William A. Geller, "Suppose We Were Really Serious about Police Departments Becoming 'Learning Organizations'?," *National Institute of Justice Journal* 234 (December 1997), pp. 2–8; John J. Donohue III and Steven D. Levitt, "The Impact of Race on Policing and Arrests," *Journal of Law and Economics*, vol. 44 (October 2001), pp. 367–94.
74. President's Commission, p. 68.
75. U.S. Comptroller General, *Federal Law Enforcement* (Washington, DC: U.S. General Accounting Office, 1996), p. 8.
76. Mahesh K. Nalla, Michael J. Lynch, and Michael J. Leiber, "Determinants of Police Growth in Phoenix, 1950–1988," *Justice Quarterly* 14 (March 1997), pp. 115–43; William Wechsler, "Law and Order: Reconstructing U.S. National Security," *Current*, vol. 446 (October 2002), p. 9; David H. Bayley, *Changing the Guard: Developing Democratic Police Abroad* (New York: Oxford University Press, 2006).
77. Pamela K. Lattimore, K. Jack Riley, James Trudeau, Jordan Leiter, and Steven Edwards, *Homicide in Eight U.S. Cities: Trends, Context, and Policy Implications* (Washington, DC: National Institute of Justice, 1997).
78. Lattimore et al., pp. 125–29; Jim Adams, "Gang Strike Force Was Key in Murder Case," *Star Tribune* (June 24, 2003) p. 5B.
79. Rubinstein, p. 22.
80. Gordon Witkin with Monika Guttman, "This is 911 . . . Please Hold," *U.S. News & World Report* (June 17, 1996), pp. 31–38; U.S. Comptroller General, *States' Collection and Use of Funds for Wireless Enhanced 911 Services* (Washington, DC: U.S. General Accountability Office, 2006); "911 Calls: More Trouble Ahead?," *Consumer Reports* (February 2004); Lorraine Mazerolle, Dennis Rogan, James Frank, Christine Famega, and John E. Eck, *Managing Calls to the Police with 911/311 Systems* (Washington, D.C.: National Institute of Justice, 2005).
81. Ibid.
82. Gary Fields, "Upgraded Database to Aid Patrol Officers," *USA Today* (July 12, 1999), p. 3A.
83. See Victor Walter Weedon and John W. Hicks, *The Unrealized Potential of DNA Testing* (Washington, DC: National Institute of Justice, 1998).
84. Christopher H. Asplen, "Forensic DNA Evidence: National Commission Explores Its Future," *National Institute of Justice Journal* (January 1999), pp. 17–24.
85. Richard Willing, "Victims: Use DNA to Nab More Criminals," *USA Today* (May 5, 2000), p. 7.
86. *Advancing Justice through CAN Technology* (Washington, DC: Office of the President, 2003); Roma Khana and Steve McVicker, "Private DNA Lab Can't Replicate Houston Police Department Results," *Houston Chronicle* (September 5, 2003); Robert Tanner, "Scandals and Probes Put Crime Labs on

Trial," *The Associated Press* (July 11, 2003); Leslie A. Pappas, "Focus Sharpens on Crime Labs' Work," *Philadelphia Inquirer* (June 23, 2003).

87. Peter K. Manning, "Policing and Reflection," *Police Forum* 6 (October 1996), pp. 1–5; Alan D. Gold, "Media Hype, Racial Profiling, and Good Science," *Canadian Journal of Criminology and Criminal Justice*, vol. 45 (July 2003).
88. Jay S. Albanese, "The Future of Policing: A Private Concern?," *Police Studies: The International Review of Police Development* 8 (1986), pp. 86–91.
89. Samuel Walker, *A Critical History of Police Reform* (Lexington, MA: Lexington Books, 1977), p. 30.
90. National Advisory Committee on Criminal Justice Standards and Goals, *Report of the Task Force on Private Security* (Cincinnati: Anderson, 1977).
91. James S. Kakalik and Sorrel Wildhorn, *The Private Police: Security and Danger* (New York: Crane Russak, 1977), p. 75.
92. Kakalik and Wildhorn; Brian Foest and Peter K. Manning, *The Privatization of Policing: Two Views* (Washington, DC: Georgetown University Press, 1999).
93. Brian A. Reaves, *Campus Law Enforcement Agencies* (Washington, DC: Bureau of Justice Statistics, 1996), p. 2.
94. Hilary Draper, *Private Police* (Atlantic Highlands, NJ: Humanities Press, 1978), pp. 85–89; www.tsa.gov.
95. Tom Carter and Jasminka Sktlec, "Americans Easy Targets for Greedy Kidnappers," *Insight on the News* (April 26, 1999), p. 42.
96. William C. Cunningham and Todd H. Taylor, *Crime and Protection in America: A Study of Private Security and Law Enforcement Resources and Relationships* (Washington, DC: U.S. Government Printing Office, 1985), p. 7; Steve Rigney, "Thinking about Security," *PC Magazine* (January 4, 2000), p. 191; Jim Kerstetter, "Hackers Stake Out New Turf," *PC Week* (January 10, 2000), p. 1.
97. John T. Krimmel, "The Northern York County Police Consolidation Experience: An Analysis of Consolidation of Police Services in Eight Pennsylvania Rural Communities," *Policing: An International Journal of Police Strategies and Management* 20 (1997), pp. 497–507; Bruce Swanton, *Police and Private Security: Possible Directions* (Australian Institute of Criminology, 1993); Mahesh K. Nalla and Cedrick G. Heraux, "Assessing Goals and Functions of Private Police," *Journal of Criminal Justice*, vol. 31 (May–June 2003) p. 237; National Commission on Terrorist Attacks Upon the United States, *Final Report* (U.S. Government Printing Office, 2004); Dennis Wagner, "Private Security Guards Play Key Roles Post 9/11," *Arizona Republic* (January 2, 2006).

chapter 9

Issues in Law Enforcement and Police Behavior

Pressures on police: how officers make decisions that affect the liberty of private citizens. How police deal with the pressures of performance and the use of deadly force, and how they face the issues of corruption and brutality.

CHAPTER OUTLINE

LEARNING OBJECTIVES

- Evaluate stereotypes about police.
- Describe three common styles of policing.
- Discuss the conflicts and challenges police face in their work and some outcomes of those conflicts and challenges.
- Summarize research on police attitudes toward their jobs and the public they serve.
- Analyze standards of police performance, taking a stand on the best way to measure police performance.
- Identify and define forms of police corruption.
- Evaluate explanations for police corruption and strategies for preventing it.
- Explain the issues surrounding the legitimate and illegitimate use of deadly force by police.

More than 100 police officers lost the right to wear a badge in Colorado, following a new law that added forty-four misdemeanors involving crimes of moral turpitude in addition to felony convictions for revocation of police certification. Four Memphis police officers were sentenced to prison for planning crimes that included taking bribes, protecting drug dealers, and planning burglaries. Three Los Angeles police officers were convicted of fabricating evidence in order to obtain false confessions.[1]

At the same time seven officers in New York were honored for extraordinary bravery for overcoming a suspect who opened fire on them with two dozen weapons when they responded to a call at his home. Five of the officers were shot in the incident. Twelve Long Island police officers were cited for heroism and bravery in making 154 drug arrests in one year as part of an undercover operation that targeted drug dealers. A thirty-member police SWAT team in Georgia was honored for obtaining the surrender of a quadruple murder suspect during a hostage situation.[2] Incidents of corruption are featured more prominently in the media, yet instances of bravery occur often. Is it surprising how public perceptions of the police are shaped? This chapter presents both the incidents and research studies that provide an objective understanding of law enforcement and police behavior.

Is There Such a Thing as a Police Personality?

Police must impose themselves into the lives of citizens in order to do their job. They make traffic stops, question loiterers, stop suspicious persons, help those in need of assistance, and apprehend suspected criminals. As one police chief asserts, police must address crime and disorder "respectfully but aggressively"—a paradoxical assignment that is not always easy to accomplish.[3] The need to be helpful to the public, yet always on the lookout for law violators, requires an evenhanded approach and an objective attitude in all interactions with citizens.

Police officers are sometimes accused of cynicism or of having a "bad attitude" toward the public they serve. These attitudes are thought to influence police stop and arrest decisions and to contribute to poor community relations, corruption, and brutality. To what extent do police officers acquire personality characteristics that are unique to their job? Are police different from the general public? And, most important, do certain personality characteristics affect a police officer's discretion and performance on the job?

Myths and Stereotypes about Police

PROPER POLICE ROLE?

The police are the focus of a wide range of public opinion. Many people have strong views about what police ought to be doing and openly express their praise or criticism of police officers and police work. Everyone agrees that police should attempt to prevent crime and apprehend offenders, for example; but few enjoy being stopped, questioned, or ticketed by police. This debate about the proper role of police is reflected in state legislatures, where lawmakers debate such questions as whether police should be permitted to stop a driver for nothing more than failure to wear a seat belt.[4]

racial profiling
Alleged practice whereby police stop and search minorities for minor violations significantly more often than whites.

There also is concern about underlying attitudes that contribute to apparent **racial profiling** in some jurisdictions, where police are alleged to stop and search minorities for suspected minor violations significantly more often than they stop and search whites.[5] Specific incidents of racial profiling have been discovered that reflect police misconduct, but it is not clear that these incidents characterize police in general or merely the attitudes, practices, or personalities of a small group of officers or departments. An analysis by the U.S. General Accountability Office (the investigative arm of Congress) found that there are studies in only a few jurisdictions about the extent of racial profiling.[6] Although these studies tend to show that minorities were more likely than whites to be subjected to traffic stops, controlled studies are needed that compare traffic stops to the profile of drivers, travelers, and law violators in general, as well as the reasons for the stops and other legitimate factors that play a role in these police decisions. Many studies thus far have not shown conclusive evidence of racial profiling by police.[7]

A related problem is trying to determine in the face of public pressure and preconceptions about police behavior whether racial profiling has in fact occurred. For example, when the St. Louis Police Department responded to the problems caused by teenagers "cruising" around town in cars by treating the teens' behavior as a form of loitering, critics argued that black teenagers were selectively targeted. Although it was not established that targeting of minorities actually occurred, there was a community perception that racial bias motivated the police.[8]

Black police officers arresting a white suspect. What criteria should be used to assess fairness in the way that police carry out their duty?

A study by the Bureau of Justice Statistics found that nearly 9 percent of drivers age sixteen or older were stopped by police, which translates to about 17 million of the 193 million drivers in the United States. More than half (55 percent) of these stops were for speeding. Males (61 percent) were more likely than females (39 percent) to be stopped by police, and the likelihood of being pulled over did not differ among whites, blacks, and Hispanics (about 9 percent for all). Nevertheless, younger drivers (age sixteen to twenty-four) were more likely to be stopped than drivers age twenty-five or older. Figure 9.1 summarizes these differences and also shows that driver opinions varied significantly. About 84 percent of all drivers stopped by police felt they were pulled over for a legitimate reason, but young male drivers (79 percent), particularly black male drivers (58 percent), were less likely than others to believe the stop was legitimate. These figures reinforce the fact that from the public's point of view, perceptions of police conduct are as important as the conduct itself.

COMMUNITY PERCEPTIONS

Perceptions of the police and their attitudes are extremely important, because they affect the level of citizen cooperation with police, the reporting of crimes, and people's willingness to share responsibility for crime prevention in the community. The news and entertainment media play a role in forming attitudes toward the police by portraying various police actions. Media portrayals have a significant impact, because most citizens have little direct contact with police and form their attitudes about police through incidents they experience vicariously through the media.

FIGURE 9.1 **Drivers Stopped by Police**

	Drivers Stopped by Police	*Driver opinion that stop was legitimate*	*Black drivers believing stop was legitimate*
Males age 16 to 24	18%	79%	58%
Males age 25+	9	84	70
Females 16 to 24	12	85	79
Females age 25+	6	86	79
Total (all drivers)	9%	84%	73%

Compiled from: Erica L. Schmitt and Matthew R. Durose, *Characteristics of Drivers Stopped by Police, 2002* (Washington, DC: Bureau of Justice Statistics, 2006).

Police are taking a more proactive role in developing public attitudes by working with communities in crime prevention programs. In Hampton, Virginia, for example, the local police department developed the KEEPS program (Knowledge, Enforcement, and Enhancement for Public Safety) to establish police–community action committees. These committees design and carry out strategies to improve the quality of life in specific neighborhoods.[9] Police agencies also use mass media and the Internet to encourage positive views. The U.S. Department of Justice has an Internet site designed to inform children about police work, drugs, and safety.[10] These efforts indicate the importance of public image in police work and illustrate how the police are working to improve that image.

KEEPS PROGRAM

Three Styles of Policing

Management of police decision making is a major concern of police supervisors. It is difficult to balance the competing goals of protecting the community and avoiding undue interference in the lives of citizens. Three "styles" of policing have been identified that characterize different approaches to the management of police discretion: the watchman style, the legalistic style, and the service style.[11]

WATCHMAN STYLE

The watchman style of policing emphasizes the maintenance of order. Order is threatened by both serious crimes and nonserious but disruptive offenses. Therefore, police may use both formal methods (arrest) and informal methods (warnings or threats) to maintain order. The watchman style is characteristic in lower-class neighborhoods, where police intervention is seen as necessary to control behavior. The Christopher Commission, which investigated the Los Angeles Police Department after the beating of Rodney King by police officers, observed that the police in Los Angeles emphasized crime control over crime prevention, thereby distancing themselves from the community they served.[12]

LEGALISTIC STYLE

The legalistic style of policing focuses more strictly on law violations than on the maintenance of order. This more limited approach to policing is largely reactive. The police respond to calls for service, act only if there is probable cause to suspect serious law violation, and generally avoid intervention in problems that do not constitute violations. This approach to policing is becoming rare as police take on responsibilities for tasks other than law enforcement.

SERVICE STYLE

The service style of policing approaches law enforcement from a broad problem-solving perspective. Police seek to correct problems that are correlated with crime, such as loitering, public intoxication, delinquency, and domestic arguments. Police departments address these social problems both through direct intervention and through referrals to other social agencies.[13] This style of policing is found most often in middle- and upper-class neighborhoods; it avoids legal processing of minor offenses as much as possible.

To reflect their different emphases, the three styles also have been termed the *neighbor* (watchman), *soldier* (legalistic), and *teacher* (service) styles.[14] The style of policing employed by a department depends largely on the chief's preferences and, in larger cities, on those of the precinct commander, as well as on the responsiveness of the neighborhood. The nature of the public's reaction to local police often corresponds to the style of policing employed.[15] Public hostility is more common in watchman-style police departments, for example, because of their emphasis on order rather than service. Nevertheless, the personalities of the officers involved also play a significant role in the use of discretion, regardless of the style of policing characteristic of the department.

The officer is warning residents about a rape that occurred in their neighborhood. What style of policing seems most relevant to the situation? According to research, what are some common attitudes and values of people who are attracted to and do well in police work? How do you think the officer's performance in this encounter should be evaluated?

Prince George County in suburban Maryland provides an example of how different approaches to policing can make a significant difference in how police carry out their tasks. A police officer tailed a black Jeep from there through Washington, D.C. and into a Virginia neighborhood. After a confrontation, the officer killed the driver of the Jeep and was indicted for manslaughter. The Jeep driver was one of twelve persons shot by police in Prince George County in a period of thirteen months. Although this case, and others like it in Boise, Idaho, and Riverside, California, have focused on alleged racial profiling, the issue is fundamentally one of the style of policing in a jurisdiction.[16] When should suspects be pursued? When should force be used? When should jurisdictional boundaries be crossed? How should police respond to minor incidents to avoid escalation into more serious incidents? These are all questions that address a department's style or philosophy of policing. Is the department's mission primarily to provide service and problem solving? If so, its policies and the actions of its officers will likely be different from a department that sees its mission as fundamentally legalistic in responding primarily to violations of the law. In an era of community policing, when police are expected to perform a growing variety of tasks, legal criteria alone for police action "are but one standard and perhaps not the most compelling in many cases," so police must balance a greater diversity of interests.[17] Different departments will employ different styles, which affects the way they approach the task of public safety.

POLICING PHILOSOPHY

Current Research on Police Attitudes toward Their Jobs

"POLICE PERSONALITY"

In a classic study Jerome Skolnick examined police attitudes and discretion in a medium-sized city that he called Westville. Skolnick believed that the police officer's "working personality" grows out of social environment rather than being a product of preexisting personality traits. Skolnick maintained that the "police personality" emerges from several aspects of police work—in particular, danger, isolation, and authority. He felt that danger causes police officers to become more wary of people in general. They grow more suspicious and tend to isolate themselves from others. Skolnick recognized that police have authority to direct and restrain citizens, but noted that this authority often is challenged. This questioning of legitimate authority by some members of the public reinforces officers' perception of danger and further isolates them from the rest of society.

DANGER AND ISOLATION

According to Skolnick, this link between danger and suspicion, coupled with constant challenges to their authority, can lead police officers to overreact to "vague indications of danger suggested by appearance." These perceptions are reinforced by the police system, which encourages sensitivity to danger. Skolnick found that confining and routine jobs were considered least desirable by police officers, whereas the potentially most dangerous jobs were preferred. He concluded that officers "may well enjoy the possibility of danger, especially its associated excitement, while fearing it at the same time."[18] A similar observation was made in a survey of officers from five different police departments, which found that "even though the officers surveyed did not perceive physical injury as an everyday happening . . . nearly four-fifths of the sample believed that they worked at a dangerous job"—despite the fact that they had not faced dangerous situations themselves.[19]

Skolnick found that police officers believe that their biggest problems are relations with the public and racial issues, and that the public generally has negative, or at least nonsupportive, views of them. This feeling of isolation may increase solidarity among police officers, making them more likely to associate with one another than with people in other occupations. Isolation increases as police officers are called upon to direct ordinary citizens or restrain their freedom of action (as in traffic stops or in the questioning of citizens). The average citizen resents this intrusion and thinks or says something like "Why are the police bothering me? They should be catching crooks."[20]

Despite this conflicting and difficult task of trying to protect the public via intrusions and restraint, studies have found that commitment to the job remains high for police officers, even after the idealism of the early years in the profession has passed.[21] At the same time it has been shown that police officers who become alienated from the public because of personal experiences of antipolice sentiment feel less confident in their decision making and show declining motivation.[22] Despite the effects of lack of citizen support, however, police dedication to the job remains high.

police stress
Emotional pressure that is produced by the nature of police work such as public apathy, exposure to criminals, and injury to fellow officers.

Police stress is another outcome of the conflicts faced by police. The nature of police work and department practices are the two primary sources of police stress. Public apathy, exposure to the criminal element, and injury to fellow officers are examples of stress emanating from the nature of the job. Rotating shift work, perceived nonsupport from department leadership, and political interference in departmental affairs are examples of how police organizations can produce stress.[23]

OUTCOMES OF STRESS

Police stress can produce several types of deleterious effects: psychological problems, alcohol or drug abuse, and family problems. Prolonged exposure to stress can result in posttraumatic stress disorder, which has been linked to cases of police brutality.[24] Domestic violence by police officers also has been linked to stress and the issue formed the basis for a conference at the FBI Academy in an effort to identify, prevent, and intervene in these situations.[25]

Current Research on Police Attitudes toward the Public They Serve

NIEDERHOFFER'S STUDY

cynicism
A belief that human conduct is motivated entirely by self-interest. A cynical person attributes all actions to selfish motives and has a pessimistic outlook on human behavior.

Police officers often are viewed as cynical; that is, as believing that human conduct is motivated entirely by self-interest. A cynical person attributes all actions to selfish motives and has a pessimistic outlook on human behavior. The pioneering study of police **cynicism** was conducted by Arthur Niederhoffer, a twenty-year New York City police officer who earned a Ph.D. in sociology and began a teach-

Police officers are chasing suspects who are fleeing after being told to stop. Put yourself in the place of the officers. How far should you chase the suspects before giving up? Should you threaten or use force? Should you be concerned about bystanders? Do you feel the stress of the situation?

ing career. He was the first researcher to attempt to quantify police cynicism and explain its origins and variations among police officers.

According to Niederhoffer, cynicism is a by-product of "anomie" in the social structure. The term **anomie** was coined by sociologist Emile Durkheim in the late 1800s to describe a "normlessness" or lack of attachment felt by some people toward their society. As Niederhoffer explained,

anomie
A "normlessness" or lack of attachment felt by some people toward their society.

> *As the cynic becomes increasingly pessimistic and misanthropic, he finds it easier to reduce his commitment to the social system and its values. If the patrolman remains a "loner," his isolation may lead to psychological anomie and even to suicide.*[26]

Niederhoffer supported his view by pointing out that suicide rates are 50 percent higher among police officers than in the general population.

According to Niederhoffer, all police officers enter a law enforcement career with an attitude of professionalism and commitment, but all soon experience failure and/or frustration on the job. The resulting disenchantment leads to cynicism for some but renewed commitment for others. Niederhoffer believed the degree of cynicism experienced by an officer increases with age and length of experience on the job.

Niederhoffer developed a questionnaire to assess levels of cynicism and administered it to 220 male officers in the New York Police Department at various stages of their careers. The lowest possible score one could receive was 20, while the highest (i.e., most cynical) was 100. As Table 9.1 indicates, the most cynical group consisted of patrol officers with seven to ten years of experience (a score of 69.1). The least cynical group consisted of officers on their first day on the job; even a small amount of experience seemed to increase cynicism. As Table 9.1 suggests, however, cynicism is not strictly a function

Table 9.1 Cynicism and Police Experience

Experience	*Cynicism Score*
Controls on first day	42.6
Recruits 2–3 months on job	60.3
Patrolmen 2–6 years on job	64.1
Patrolmen 7–10 years	69.1
Patrolmen 11–14 years	62.9
Patrolmen 15–19 years	62.5

Source: From *Behind the Shield: Police in Urban Society,* by Arthur Niederhoffer. Copyright © 1967 by Arthur Niederhoffer.

of experience on the job. Superiors were less cynical than patrolmen; also, college-educated patrolmen were more cynical than other patrolmen, and officers approaching retirement became less cynical.

Niederhoffer's cynicism scale was a pioneering effort—the first attempt to quantify police cynicism. Subsequent efforts in Detroit, Washington State, Idaho, and elsewhere have both validated and challenged his model. The mixed results suggest that cynicism is a multidimensional attitude caused not only by police work but also by other factors.[27]

THE SOCIALIZATION MODEL

socialization model
The view that holds that police officers learn their attitudes and values from socializing experiences such as education and experience on the job.

predispositional model
The view that the attitudes and values of police officers are developed prior to entry into the law enforcement profession.

Police attitudes can come from one of two sources. One group of investigators, including Niederhoffer and Skolnick, base their work on the **socialization model:** They view the police personality as a product of learning—of education and of experience with the demands of police work. An alternative explanation, the **predispositional model,** holds that the police personality is a product of the values of individual officers.[28]

To assess the validity of the predispositional model, Richard Bennett and Theodore Greenstein administered a survey asking people to assign priorities to the values that served as guiding principles in their lives.[29] The list included choices such as a comfortable life, an exciting life, a sense of accomplishment, equality, freedom, and happiness. The respondents, all students at a state university, were divided into three groups: police officers, police science majors, and non–police science majors. Bennett and Greenstein expected that the police officers and the police science majors, who were seriously contemplating careers in law enforcement, would have similar value orientations. Interestingly, however, the opposite was the case. They found that the police science majors had value systems that were "nearly identical" to those of students majoring in other subjects but markedly different from those of experienced police officers.[30] Therefore, the researchers rejected the idea that individuals are predisposed to (enter the job with) a police personality.

These findings gained further support in a study conducted in England that compared three groups: male constables with more than two years of experience, new recruits with less than seven days on the job, and working-class male civilians. The researchers found that "police recruits have similar values to those of the population from which they are recruited, whereas there are more differences between the values of experienced policemen and the community."[31] As in the earlier study, the researchers found no empirical support for the predispositional model.

PSYCHOLOGICAL TESTING

It appears from these and other studies that police officers acquire their attitudes from their work environment and that people who choose a police career do not differ from the general population in personality characteristics.[32] Despite these findings, most police departments continue to use psychological tests and interviews as part of their recruitment process.[33] Popular screening tests, such as the Minnesota Multiphasic Personality Inventory (MMPI) and the California Psychological Inventory (CPI), generally have been unable to predict the on-the-job success of police applicants.[34] Similarly, other personality screening devices have been unable to identify the reasons that some people become police officers or to explain why some are successful and some are not.[35]

Many investigators have tried to identify influences that prevent the development of cynical or suspicious attitudes. The most commonly recommended strategy for reducing undesirable police attitudes is college education.[36] Alexander Smith, Bernard Locke, and William Walker conducted a series of studies on the influence of education on attitudes at John Jay College of Criminal Justice in New York City. They looked specifically at the effect of college education on **authoritarianism.** An authoritarian person is one prone to blind obedience to authority and strong reliance on authority—characterized by statements such as "You should listen to me because I tell you to." The researchers compared the attitudes of officers who were college graduates with the attitudes of police who had not attended college and with those of students who were not police officers. College education made a significant difference.[37] Police officers attending college were less authoritarian than students who were not police at the same educational level, and police officers graduating with a bachelor's degree were less authoritarian than officers of similar age and experience lacking a college education.

A police officer shouting a command. What causes a police officer to make good tactical decisions in handling individuals, groups, or large crowds? Does having a college education affect a police officer's attitudes or performance?

authoritarianism
A tendency to favor blind obedience to authority.

THE ROLE OF EDUCATION

dogmatism
An attitude characterized by tenacious adherence to one's opinions even though they may be unwarranted and based on insufficiently examined premises.

Dogmatism is closely associated with authoritarianism. Dogmatic persons are positive about their opinions even though the opinions may be unwarranted. A dogmatic viewpoint is often based on insufficiently examined premises. An important study examined officers' level of education, score on a dogmatism scale, and job performance as measured by ratings on a standard police evaluation form. The researchers considered twenty factors ranging from attendance to effectiveness on the job. The results showed that officers with higher levels of education had more open belief systems and performed in a more satisfactory manner than did those with less education. Another study that examined a cohort of eighty-four officers over ten years found the same result: improved performance by officers with college education.[38] Age, length of experience, and college major did not affect this relationship.

This finding is extremely important, because it reveals the links among education, attitudes, and performance and shows how a college education plays a direct role in this relationship. The more college education officers had attained, the less dogmatic their attitudes were and the higher their job performance was rated by their supervisors. Numerous studies have corroborated the relationship between attitudes and performance. Most have focused on successful performance in the police training academy or in the early years on the job and have shown that higher educational levels are associated with better performance.[39] This finding is consistent with the socialization model: Education serves to change attitudes and values that form the police personality in a way that results in better performance on the job.

How Should Police Performance Be Evaluated?

Most people agree that the primary job of police is law enforcement, but police have other tasks as well. If police performance is to be evaluated, what should be the criteria? Police are expected to question citizens and make decisions about stops, frisks, and arrests both quickly and accurately. Clearly, mistakes sometimes will be made, given that police often must make quick and important decisions in a small

POOR PERFORMANCE?

amount of time and with incomplete facts at their disposal. To what extent should these errors be classified as poor performance? Should we hold police responsible for increases in the crime rate, or for decreases in total arrests? Should conviction rates and community service be considered? These are all significant issues if the job of policing is to be evaluated fairly and consistently, and if public expectations of police are to be realistic.

Police Discretion and Police Misconduct

For many people, the police are the closest contact they ever have with the criminal justice system. It is not surprising, therefore, that when the system is examined or criticized, police take a central role. The primary task of police is law enforcement, but that job description is not as clear as it may seem. Should police give a ticket to anyone who does not make a full stop at a stop sign? What about people who drive at 35 mph in a 30 mph zone? Should teenagers hanging out in a mall be arrested for loitering? What soon becomes evident is that although the laws in the criminal code are quite specific, it is far less clear how the police should act in practice in concrete situations.

More than forty years ago, Joseph Goldstein recognized that a police officer's decision to place a suspect under arrest "largely determines the outer limits of law enforcement."[40] Today, renewed interest in this claim is based on the observation that police have greater latitude in deciding whether to make an arrest than was once believed. Although police officers are sworn to enforce the law, they choose to take official action only part of the time. This is the essence of **police discretion:** the ability to choose between arrest and nonarrest solely on the basis of one's own judgment as a police officer. In many instances an officer warns, reprimands, or releases a person rather than making an arrest. Traffic violations, gambling offenses, prostitution, violations of liquor laws, and minor assaults are examples of crimes about which police often exercise discretion.

police discretion
The ability to choose between arrest and nonarrest solely on the basis of the officer's judgment.

Police discretion upsets some people, who feel that the police are not performing their job as they should. Other people believe that full enforcement of the laws is not desired by the public (who would feel harassed), the courts (which are already overloaded), the police (who would be bogged down by court appearances), or the nation's legislatures (which may not have intended certain laws to be enforced fully). In addition, police do not have the resources that they would need in order to process each case, even if an arrest were made every time one was possible. As a result, police engage in an unofficial policy of **selective enforcement,** meaning that not all laws are fully enforced.

selective enforcement
An unwritten policy in which police are not required to fully enforce all laws as written.

The idea that the enforcement of the law is selective is reflected in data gathered on police traffic stops. As shown in Table 9.2, police issue warnings in about 25 percent of all traffic stops and tickets more than half the time (59 percent). Searches of the driver or vehicle, handcuffing, and arrest occur much less frequently (although it should be kept in mind that more than half of these stops were for speeding). It should also be noted that there are differences by gender, race, and age. These differences, however, cannot be construed as age, gender, or racial profiling without data showing that these subgroups are no more likely to violate traffic laws than the general population and that police pull them over at higher rates than other groups. It is clear from these figures, however, that police do not ticket

Table 9.2 Police Discretion at Traffic Stops

Drivers Stopped by Police	*Issued a Warning*	*Ticketed the Driver*	*Searched Driver or Vehicle*	*Handcuffed Driver*	*Arrested Driver*
Male	24%	60%	7%	4%	4%
Female	27	57	2	1	1
White	27	56	4	2	2
Black	18	58	10	6	6
Hispanic	18	72	11	6	5
Age 16–19	31	59	9	3	3
Age 20–29	25	64	7	4	4
Total all drivers	25%	59%	5%	3%	3%

Source: Compiled from Matthew R. Durose, Erica L. Schmitt, and Patrick A. Langan, *Contacts between Police and the Public: Findings from the 2002 National Survey* (Washington, DC: Bureau of Justice Statistics, 2005).

in every instance where they can under law, illustrating the broad discretion given to police in these circumstances.

As Goldstein pointed out, "the mandate of full enforcement, under circumstances which compel selective enforcement, has placed the municipal police in an intolerable position" in which some laws are enforced and some are not, depending on the police officer involved, the situation, the offense, and other, possibly arbitrary, factors.[41] Whenever discretion is exercised in important matters—such as the denial of a person's liberty through arrest—without clear or consistent objectives, there is the possibility of unfairness and discrimination.

RESEARCH ON POLICE DISCRETION

Since the issue of discretion came to prominence, researchers have focused largely on the range and appropriateness of factors that influence a police officer's decision to arrest. For example, Nathan Goldman examined 1,083 contacts between police and juveniles in four Pennsylvania cities and found that most resulted in no legal action, although arrest rates varied widely among the cities.[42] Irving Piliavin and Scott Briar found that the demeanor of juveniles—their attitude and conduct toward the officer—was the most important factor in a police officer's decision as to whether to take them into custody.[43] In Washington, DC, Donald Black and Albert Reiss found that the complainant's preference—whether the complainant was insistent on or indifferent to arrest of the suspect—was the most important factor.[44] This study was replicated in an unnamed large midwestern city with the same results.[45] More recent studies find conflicting results regarding the impact of a suspect's demeanor in arrest situations, but the complainant's preference is clearly influential.[46] Studies assessing the type of offense and the age, education, experience, race, and gender of the officer, as well as similar attributes of the offender, have yielded inconsistent results.[47]

A police officer can choose to warn, issue a citation, or sometimes make an arrest during a traffic stop. What factors are appropriate in choosing among these alternatives?

Although these studies help us understand the nature and scope of police discretion, they do not explain how or why discretion is used in some situations and not in others. There are several reasons for this:

REASONS FOR INCONCLUSIVE FINDINGS

- Most studies examine only a few factors that may influence police decision making and do not attempt to explain it comprehensively.
- Most do not cover a wide enough range of offenses to account adequately for discretion in serious versus nonserious crimes.
- Findings on factors influencing police decisions in one city may not hold true for police decisions in other cities.
- Many studies rely on responses to hypothetical scenarios rather than actual observations of police work.
- Even factors found to be important in police discretion do not accurately predict behavior more than 25 percent of the time.

> **Citizen Respect for Police**
>
> Since the 1960s, the Gallup Poll has periodically surveyed the public regarding their respect for the police in their local area. Fifty-six percent of Americans say they have a great deal of respect for the police in their area (see Figure 9.2). The last time Gallup asked this question, in 2000, 60 percent said they respected the police in their area a great deal. During the 1960s, more than seven in ten Americans had a great deal of respect for their local police.
>
> Can you offer reasons for this decline? Do you believe specific, publicized events play a role in these perceptions?

The Task Force on Police of the 1965 President's Commission noted that the arrest decision "continues to be informal, and, as a consequence, may very well serve to complicate rather than solve important social problems."[48] The commission recommended that police departments "should develop and enunciate policies that give police personnel specific guidance for the common situations requiring police discretion."[49]

In 1973 the National Advisory Commission on Criminal Justice Standards and Goals also called for specific guidelines, recommending "comprehensive policy statements that publicly establish the limits of discretion, that provide guidelines for its exercise within those limits, and that eliminate discriminatory enforcement of the law."[50] In 1974 the American Bar Association and the International Association of Chiefs of Police (ABA–IACP) jointly published standards for policing in urban areas. Their report stated that police administrators should "give the highest priority to the formulation of administrative rules governing the exercise of discretion, particularly in the areas of selective enforcement, investigative techniques, and enforcement methods."[51] According to President's Commission, the advantages of systematically drafting policy in this manner "would remove from individual [officers] some of the burden of having to make important decisions ad hoc, in a matter of seconds":

STANDARDS FOR POLICING

> *It would create a body of standards that would help make the supervision and evaluation of the work of the individual [police officer] consistent. It would help courts understand the issues at stake when police procedures are challenged and lessen the likelihood of inappropriate judicial restriction being placed on police work.*[52]

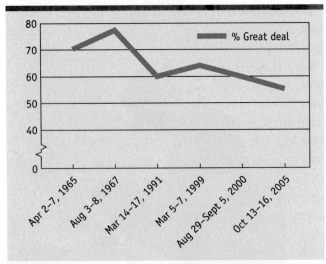

FIGURE 9.2 How Much Respect Do You Have for the Police in Your Area—a Great Deal, Some, or Hardly Any?

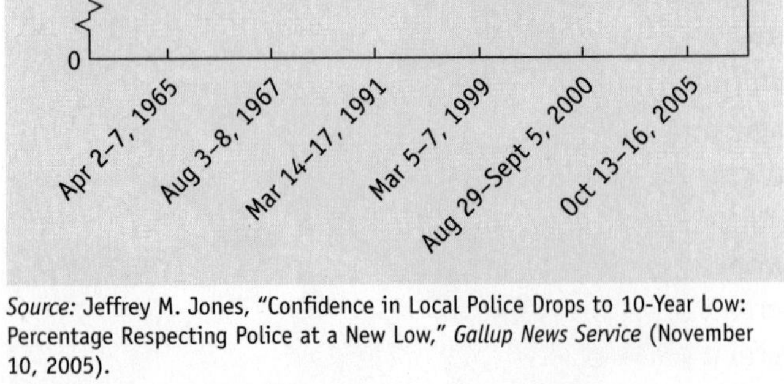

Source: Jeffrey M. Jones, "Confidence in Local Police Drops to 10-Year Low: Percentage Respecting Police at a New Low," *Gallup News Service* (November 10, 2005).

Criticisms of police arrest decisions are common. Researcher David Klinger argues that police discretion is tied to local crime rates; as crime increases, deviant acts must be more serious to result in formal action by police.[53] Thus, decision-making guidelines or policy should be developed on the basis of current practice. This idea is not new. Corresponding efforts have been made in parole decision making and in sentencing policy.[54] Although police decision making often requires spontaneous judgments, a properly developed policy based on an understanding of current practice, together with guidelines on factors that departments believe police also should consider, promotes consistent and defensible police decisions.

Police Pursuits

Police traditionally have had considerable discretion in the decision to pursue a suspect. This discretion has come under increasing scrutiny in recent years, however, because of incidents in which police chases resulted in accidents and the deaths of suspects, police, and innocent bystanders. For example, the Los Angeles Police Department led the nation in chases with 781 pursuits that resulted in 283 crashes. The U.S. Supreme Court supported police discretion in pursuits by deciding in *Sacramento v. Lewis* that police officers can be held liable only for activities that "shock the conscience."[55] In this case a motorcyclist fled after ignoring a police order to stop. In a chase that lasted less than two minutes but reached speeds of 100 mph, the motorcycle skidded and fell. The pursuing officer was unable to stop his car in time, hitting and killing the motorcyclist. The police department was sued for the wrongful death of the motorcyclist. The U.S. Supreme Court held that the cyclist's "outrageous behavior" caused the accident and that imposing liability on the police would fail to take into account the need for split-second decision making.

SACRAMENTO V. LEWIS

It is still not clear, however, when police officers should undertake a pursuit, what the best pursuit strategies are, or when a pursuit should be terminated. An investigation of pursuits in six jurisdictions, shown in Table 9.3, found that most incidents do not involve fleeing or pursuits and that the nature of pursuits varies. A review of the circumstances of **police pursuits** found that many are unnecessary. In Miami–Dade County, a review of all 488 police pursuits occurring over five years found that only 35 percent involved suspected felonies. Forty-five percent of the pursuits were initiated for traffic violations.[56] The findings in other cities were similar: In Omaha, only 40 percent of pursuits involved suspected felonies; in Aiken County, South Carolina, 43 percent were felony pursuits.

police pursuits
Police chases of suspects immediately after a crime has been committed.

The average time devoted to driving training at police academies is less than fourteen hours, and in-service training adds three hours per year. This training,

Table 9.3 Suspect Flight and Police Pursuits (six jurisdictions)

Type of Flight by Suspect	*Percentage of Arrests (N = 7,512)*	*Type of Pursuit by Police*	*Percentage of Arrests (N = 7,512)*
No flight	93.5	No pursuit	94.4
Flee on foot	4.7	Pursue on foot	3.0
Flee in car	1.7	Pursue in car	2.4
Other	0	Pursue in helicopter	0.3

Source: Joel H. Garner and Christopher D. Maxwell, "Measuring the Amount of Force Used by and against Police in Six Jurisdictions," *Use of Force by Police* (Washington, DC: National Institute of Justice, 1999).

When should police officers undertake a pursuit? When should a pursuit be terminated? Why do you think police discretion is so difficult to define and regulate?

however, focuses on the mechanics of police pursuit and defensive driving, not on the decision to engage in a pursuit. As police expert Geoffrey Alpert has observed, "It is shameful for our law enforcement agencies to expect their officers to make proper and appropriate decisions with minimal or no training."[57]

Although nearly all police departments have written policies governing pursuits, few have collected pursuit statistics to assess the effectiveness of their policy.[58] A Pursuit Management Task Force (PMTF) was created in 1996 by the National Institute of Justice to help define police practices and to see if technology might be used to protect police officers and citizens in pursuit situations. A public opinion survey has found strong support for "reasonable pursuits," but reasonableness can be difficult to define, especially in cases where pursuits continue for a long period.[59] Currently, a variety of technological alternatives are being developed and tested in an effort to both reduce and shorten police pursuits. These include helicopter support, electrical devices that stall a suspect's vehicle, and other mechanisms that hamper the ability of a suspect in a car to flee.[60]

PURSUIT MANAGEMENT TASK FORCE

Crime Response and Clearance Rates

One common indicator of police performance is the crime rate. If the crime rate is going up in a town, residents may claim that the police are not controlling crime effectively. Is the crime rate a fair indicator of police performance?

Police are primarily a *reactive* force. In the vast majority of cases, police are informed of an incident *after* it occurs by a complaining victim, a witness, or an alarm. (A study of police response time found that only about 6 percent of callers reported crimes while they were in progress.[61]) In addition, the National Crime Victimization Survey (NCVS) reveals that only about a third of serious crime is reported to police. It is difficult to hold police responsible for increases in the crime rate when they are not called for most crimes or are called after the incident has ended. Several other factors may cause the crime rate to rise, such as an increase in the proportion of young people in the population, higher rates of long-term unemployment, and the criminalization of drug use. Police have no control over these conditions. Thus, the crime rate is really not a useful indictor of police effectiveness.

MEASURES OF POLICE EFFECTIVENESS

The number of officers in a jurisdiction also is inadequate as an indicator. Police forces in the United States range in strength from 1 to 55 officers per 1,000 residents. In cities with populations of 250,000 or more, police departments vary in size from 1.7 to 7 officers per 1,000 citizens. For example, San Diego has 1.7 officers per 1,000 residents, yet has a much lower crime rate than Baltimore, with 4.7 officers per 1,000, or Newark, with 5.4 officers per 1,000 residents.[62] There is no evidence that the mere presence of more officers has any effect on the crime rate in a city.

Another common measure of police performance is the proportion of crimes cleared by arrest—that is, the proportion of "open" cases that are "closed" or solved by an arrest. This proportion is called the **clearance rate.** It could be argued that because we know the number of crimes reported, we should be able to determine how well the police perform by looking at the number of cases they clear. But clearance rates, too, have drawbacks as an indicator of police performance. Low clearance rates may be due to factors other than poor police work. For example, some crimes remain "open" because police cannot spend an unlimited amount of time on an unsolved case. New crimes occur every day, and the police are forced to move on. Moreover, note that clearance rates are lowest for property offenses. Because burglary, larceny, motor vehicle theft, and arson generally occur without the knowledge or presence of the owner, a significant lag occurs between the crime and the time police are informed of it. Analyses of police investigations have found that the older the crime, the lower its chances of being solved.[63]

clearance rate
The proportion of open crime cases that are solved through the arrest of a suspect by police.

IMPROVING CLEARANCE RATES

A multicity study of homicide clearance rates identified factors associated with cases that were solved. For example, homicides were more likely to be solved when the first officer on the scene promptly notified the homicide unit, medical examiner, and crime lab. Also, when detectives arrived at the scene in less than thirty minutes and three or more detectives were assigned to the case (versus only one detective), the case was more likely to be solved. Other important factors included interviews with family and acquaintances of the victim, computer checks on the weapon and suspect, and any witnesses and forensic specimen collection by the medical examiner.[64] The study also found, however, that some kinds of homicides were simply more difficult to solve regardless of the police approach taken. For example, drug-related killings, homicides that occur on the street, and a lack of eyewitnesses make homicides difficult to solve, and these factors are outside police control. Nevertheless, this research makes clear that there are some actions police can take to improve clearance rates in certain kinds of cases.

Arrest and Conviction Rates

If clearance rates are not a good measure of police performance, why not use arrests as an indicator of effectiveness in controlling crime? In a given year there are more than 14 million arrests in the United States. But if there are one hundred arrests in your town in a year, what does that tell you? It could be that one hundred people were arrested once, or it could be that one person was arrested one hundred times. Moreover, arrests provide no indication of how many cases were dismissed in court because of insufficient evidence, illegal searches, or other problems. Thus, arrests alone do not offer a good measure of police performance.

Even the number of arrests resulting in convictions is not a good indicator. In a typical year about 80 percent of all arrests are prosecuted. Of these, about 25 percent are acquitted or dismissed, and approximately 68 percent are convicted on the same or a lesser charge.[65] The reasons for acquittals, dismissals, or reduced charges may have nothing to do with police work, however. They may involve reluctant victims or witnesses, incompetent counsel, errors in court procedure, or any number of circumstances that are beyond police control.

ARRESTS RESULTING IN PROSECUTIONS

A superior indicator of police performance is *arrests resulting in prosecutions.* Prosecutors will not bring a case to court unless it involves a meaningful charge resulting from a legal arrest and is based on sufficient evidence. Beyond this, further criminal justice processing is the responsibility of the prosecutor. Therefore,

That's a FACT

Perspectives on a New Role for Police: Intelligence Gathering

The role of police as principals in antiterrorism efforts is a new one. Before September 11, 2001, antiterrorism efforts in the United States were the responsibility of the intelligence community. Parts of the Central Intelligence Agency, National Security Agency, Defense Intelligence Agency, and Federal Bureau of Investigation were primarily responsible for gathering "intelligence" or information that might be important in protecting American national security. This interest in intelligence gathering has now reached the local level, as we have realized that local police can play a crucial role in gathering information at the neighborhood level about suspicious or unusual activity that is suggestive of criminal or terrorist motives.

In some ways, this move toward "intelligence-led" policing is an outgrowth of the community policing movement, which asks police to be "problem solvers" as well as crime fighters, seeking to identify circumstances that are precursors to crime instead of responding only to crimes that have already occurred.[a] Intelligence gathering is a difficult task, however, because it takes a great deal of skill and experience to distinguish disjointed information from true intelligence. For mere information to become intelligence it must be linked to particular individuals, locations, known groups, methods of operation, patterns of past conduct, or communications that raise the level of suspicion. Still, most intelligence leads to deadends, making it time-consuming and sometimes frustrating work. This is characteristic of criminal investigative work of all kinds.

In the effort to develop information into intelligence, police are subject to criticism. They have been accused of "profiling" racial or ethnic groups by singling them out for scrutiny, unnecessary surveillance of suspects, of following false terrorism tips that disrupt the lives of the subjects, and of gathering intelligence without proper oversight. These criticisms are not to be taken lightly, but they are common any time police take on a new role. For example, when civil disorder and riots occurred in the 1960s and 1970s, police were forced to respond to a new kind of investigative task, and abuses occurred.[b] With significant financial and training resources being put into the antiterrorism effort, it is hoped that fewer mistakes will be made. An obstacle, of course, is the elusive nature of terrorism and terrorist threats, which often are committed by small, unconnected groups that are difficult to identify in advance.

The change to terrorism-related intelligence gathering has also widened on the federal level. Now more than twenty federal agencies do investigative work leading to terrorism-related prosecutions. In 2001, for example, the FBI was the lead investigative agency for 73 percent of cases prosecuted for terrorism or internal security matters. By 2002, however, the FBI was the lead agency for only 31 percent of the prosecutions.

Some of the increase in terrorism cases immediately after 9/11 reflects the expanded definition of terrorism, when the U.S. Justice Department added to its list of what would be tracked as a terrorism matter. An analogous development has occurred on the state and local levels as they passed new terrorism-related laws that focused on intrastate matters.

In the twelve months immediately after 9/11, the prosecution of individuals classified as international terrorists by the government surged sharply higher than in the previous year. But five years later, the total number of these prosecutions returned to roughly what they were just before the attacks

using arrests resulting in prosecutions as a measure of police performance overcomes the limitations of using number of arrests or number of arrests resulting in convictions. In sum, the evaluation of police performance is an important concern and should be based only on valid, reliable, and representative indicators of police efforts to control crime.

Community Service

Evaluation of overall police performance by arrests that result in prosecutions assumes that the police spend most of their time making arrests. This is not the case, however. Examinations of calls for police service in cities as varied as Tampa, Rochester, and St. Louis have found that the vast majority of police time is devoted

(see Figure 9A). Given the widely accepted belief that the threat of terrorism in all parts of the world is much larger today than it was a few years ago, the decline in prosecutions is unexpected. Can you think of any reasons why?

Some have argued that local police should not be part of the antiterrorism investigative effort. What grounds would argue for their inclusion? One of the largest categories of terrorism-related offenses is identity theft. How might that offense be related to terrorism?

NOTES

a. Rachel Boba, *Problem Analysis in Policing* (Washington, DC: Police Foundation 2003); Jerry H. Ratcliffe, *Intelligence-Led Policing* (Canberra: Australian Institute of Criminology, 2003).

b. Irene Jung Fiala, "Anything New? The Racial Profiling of Terrorists," *Criminal Justice Studies,* vol. 16 (2003), p. 53; Jerry Berman and Lara Flint, "Intelligence Oversight and Control for the Challenge of Terrorism," *Criminal Justice Ethics,* vol. 22 (winter/spring 2003), p. 2.

FIGURE 9A Federal Criminal Prosecutions under Justice Department Program of International Terrorism

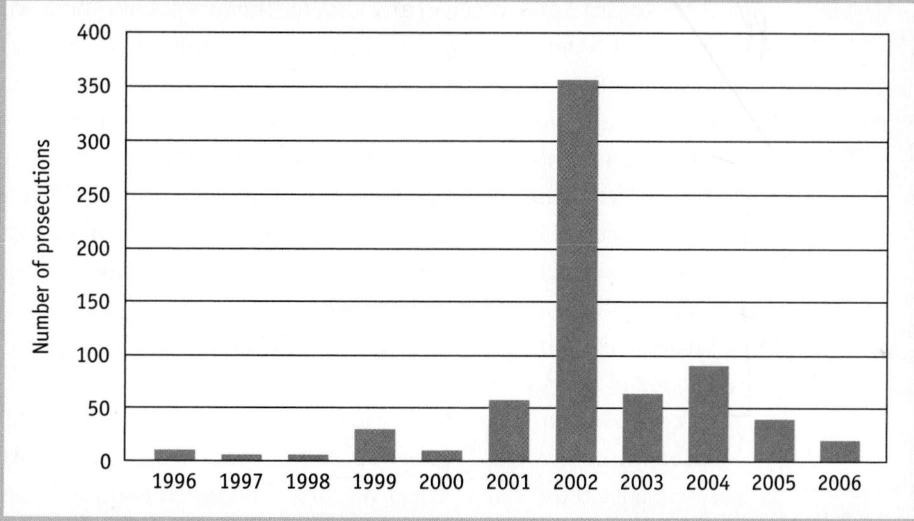

Source: TRAC Reports, Inc.

to noncriminal matters. It is not unusual for police to spend more than three-fourths of their working day responding to calls that have nothing to do with crime.[66]

NONCRIME WORK

There are two major reasons for this heavy preponderance of noncrime work: (1) Often police are the only social service agency available twenty-four hours a day, and (2) the police will deal with the social problems of the poor and disadvantaged, groups that may be underserved by other agencies. As a result, police devote the majority of their time to social service tasks. This role has expanded as problem-oriented or community policing has become popular as a means of addressing underlying problems that lead to criminal incidents.[67] For example, a concentration of burglaries, larcenies, loiterers, or vandalism in a particular neighborhood may relate to poor lighting, a local school problem, or community difficulties that can be remedied with proper analysis of the problem.[68] Public satisfaction with the police in their community service role is an important part of a valid evaluation of police performance.

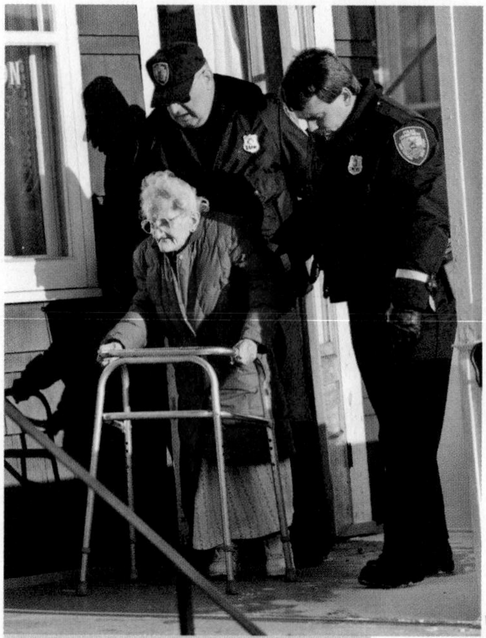

Police officers performing helpful or heroic tasks appear in the news much less often than do cases of police corruption. Knowing that police corruption involves a small percentage of all police officers and police actions, why do you believe corruption gets so much attention?

What Are Some Forms of Police Corruption?

Forty-two police officers from northern Ohio were arrested on cocaine distribution charges—the largest number of officers ever arrested in a single day in U.S. history. In the late 1990s more than 500 convictions resulted from federal investigations of police corruption in only five years. Two former police detectives in New York were sentenced to life in prison for their participation in eight gangland murders while being paid by a mafia crime family.[69] How common is police corruption, and why does it occur?

Police corruption consists of illegal acts or omissions by police officers in the line of duty who, by virtue of their official position, receive (or intend to receive) any gain for themselves or others. The important elements of this definition are the illegal acts or omissions, the fact that they occur while the officer is on duty, and the intent to receive a reward for these acts. Fundamentally, police corruption is misuse of authority for personal gain.

Every encounter between a police officer and citizen involves a decision. As discussed earlier, if the behavior is serious enough, the officer will arrest the offender. In the majority of cases, however, the officer has considerable discretion in choosing a course of action. Sometimes police are offered money or other inducements to take no official action or to release a suspect. A police officer who accepts money or favors in exchange for performing or omitting a specific legal duty has committed an act of corruption.

police corruption
Illegal acts or omissions of acts by police officers who, by virtue of their official position, receive (or intend to receive) any gain for themselves or others.

nonfeasance
A form of police corruption involving failure to perform a legal duty.

misfeasance
A form of police corruption involving failure to perform a legal duty in a proper manner.

malfeasance
A form of police corruption involving commission of an illegal act.

Corruption can take three forms: nonfeasance, misfeasance, and malfeasance. **Nonfeasance** involves failure to perform a legal duty; **misfeasance** is failure to perform a legal duty in a proper manner; and **malfeasance** is commission of an illegal act. For example, an officer who sees a car swerving down the road can legitimately pull it over. If the driver hands the officer his license with a $50 bill clipped to it and the officer takes the money, does not write out a ticket, and then proceeds to search the driver by tearing off his clothes, the officer is guilty of nonfeasance (in failing to write a ticket), misfeasance (in conducting a search improperly), and malfeasance (in accepting a bribe).

You can see that corruption is always malfeasance, whereas nonfeasance and misfeasance do not always involve corruption. For example, many police departments set enforcement priorities and ignore petty offenses in favor of serious crimes. Under these circumstances nonfeasance in certain situations represents department policy rather than an individual failure to perform a legal duty. Likewise, misfeasance is not always considered corruption. An officer's search in violation of legal rules may reflect improper understanding of the law rather than a willful attempt to circumvent it. A general definition of police corruption thus should reflect the possibility of various types of official wrongdoing.

Explanations of Corruption

Sergeant Edward Ortiz at a Los Angeles Police Department, Rampart division corruption trial in 2000. Ortiz and others were accused of conspiracy to frame innocent people, writing false reports and perjury. The Rampart scandal brought seventy LAPD officers under suspicion and led to more than one hundred tainted criminal convictions being overturned.

Several investigators have offered useful explanations of the existence of police corruption. Some explanations focus on individual officers, some on departmental problems, and others on problems external to the department.[70]

Explanations focusing on individuals see the particular officer as the primary problem. Supporters of this view claim that if a few "rotten apples" were eliminated, police corruption would disappear. For example, some officers are seen as having "low moral caliber." If they feel underpaid, unjustly maligned by the public, or unrecognized for good work, this moral weakness may make them corruptible. Another type of corrupt officer may misuse authority for selfish ends, thinking, "I might as well make the most of the situation," actively seeking opportunities for illicit payoffs, and justifying this activity with a rationalization such as low pay or lack of recognition.[71] The case of Michael Dowd of the New York Police Department is an example of a "bad apple." Dowd was found to be organizing raids on the apartments of drug dealers to steal cash and narcotics.[72] His behavior was featured in the Mollen Commission's investigation of corruption in New York City during the mid-1990s.

"ROTTEN APPLES"

Although explanations that focus on the individual officer are popular, most experts reject the "rotten apple" theory of corruption. It fails to explain how individual officers become corrupt or why police corruption is so widespread. Nor does it explain differences between departments or within a particular department over time. As one investigator notes, if corruption is to be explained in terms of a few "bad" people, then some departments must have attracted a disproportionately high number of rotten apples over long periods.[73] Michael Dowd was one of nearly fifty officers who were arrested in New York City on charges of brutality, drug trafficking, extortion, and civil rights violations.[74] Another drawback to the rotten apple theory, noted by the Knapp Commission in its investigation of corruption in the New York Police Department during the 1970s, is that the theory can become an excuse for command officers to deny that a serious problem exists.[75] This kind of thinking delayed FBI self-policing initiatives. In 1998 the FBI disciplined 301 employees and fired 32 of them for sexual harassment, unprofessional conduct, misuse of their position, or theft of government property. And of those punished, 44 percent had previous recorded rule violations.[76]

"BAD BARREL"

deviant police subculture hypothesis
The view that some police departments have groups of officers who place loyalty to each other above obedience to the law.

A second type of explanation of police corruption is the "departmental" explanation. If corruption cannot be explained in terms of a few bad apples, then the barrel itself must be examined. An example of this approach is the **deviant police subculture hypothesis.** According to this view, small groups of officers within a department have a similar outlook regarding their commitment to the job and the support they receive from superiors. If these officers feel uncommitted and unsupported, their outlook and values are reinforced by others in the group and may lead to cynicism, opening the door to corruption.[77] In New Orleans, for example, more than fifty police officers were charged with offenses including rape, assault, drug trafficking, and murder committed during the 1990s.[78] Group corruption in that instance suggests the existence of an organized subculture within the department that condoned illegal behavior.

Another version of the "bad barrel" explanation focuses on loyalty and secrecy within the department. A questionnaire administered by William Westley revealed that three-quarters of the officers surveyed said they would not report on partners who engaged in a corrupt activity. Moreover, officers would perjure themselves rather than testify against their partners. When Westley asked respondents for their reasons, he found that an officer who violated the unwritten code of secrecy within the police organization was regarded as a "stool pigeon," "rat," or "outcast," even if the behavior reported was illegal.[79]

POLICE INTEGRITY

A recent effort to measure police integrity involved eleven hypothetical scenarios that were part of a survey of 3,235 police officers from thirty different police departments. The scenarios are presented in Table 9.4, and they reflect a range of questionable behaviors from routinely accepting free meals to stealing from a burglary scene. Each officer was asked to rank the seriousness of each scenario, what they believed should be the appropriate penalty for engaging in the behavior (from none to dismissal from the police force), and whether or not they would report a fellow officer who engaged in the behavior. There was general agreement regarding the appropriate and expected penalties, but scenarios describing behaviors regarded as less serious were much more likely to be tolerated. The survey found "substantial differences in the environments of integrity in U.S. police agencies," meaning that there was wide variation in the responses of the officers surveyed and among departments.[80] Most officers said they would not report a fellow officer who engaged in conduct such as accepting free gifts, meals, discounts, or having a minor accident while driving under the influence of alcohol. On the other hand, most police officers said they would report a colleague who stole from a burglary scene, accepted a bribe, or used excessive force.

Departmental explanations have been investigated in several studies, which have shown that certain conditions within a department can be conducive to corruption.[81] As the Pennsylvania Crime Commission found in its investigation of corruption in the Philadelphia Police Department, "Systematic corruption does not occur in a vacuum. Officers succumb to pressures within the department" such as illegal conduct by fellow officers and failure by superiors to take action against "open and widespread violations" of the law and of department policy.[82] The Mollen Commission in New York City found that beyond merely overlooking the illicit behavior of other officers, groups of officers were acting as criminal gangs.[83] A federal study of drug-related police corruption found a pattern of "small groups of officers who protected and assisted each other in criminal activities."[84] A major police corruption scandal in the Los Angeles Police Department resulted in reversals of numerous criminal convictions because of planted evidence and false testimony. It resulted in the appointment of an external federal monitor, which a federal judge extended until 2009, because the city still needed to enact reforms to prevent ongoing occurrences of police corruption and brutality.[85]

OUTSIDE FACTORS

A third explanation of corruption focuses on factors external to the department, especially government actions that make honest policing more difficult. For example, laws prohibiting such behaviors as gambling, personal drug use, and

Table 9.4 Case Scenarios to Measure Police Integrity

Case 1.	A police officer runs his own private business in which he sells and installs security devices, such as alarms, special locks, etc. He does this work during his off-duty hours.
Case 2.	A police officer routinely accepts free meals, cigarettes, and other items of small value from merchants on his beat. He does not solicit these gifts and is careful not to abuse the generosity of those who give gifts to him.
Case 3.	A police officer stops a motorist for speeding. The officer agrees to accept a personal gift of half of the amount of the fine in exchange for not issuing a citation.
Case 4.	A police officer is widely liked in the community, and on holidays local merchants and restaurant and bar owners show their appreciation for his attention by giving him gifts of food and liquor.
Case 5.	A police officer discovers a burglary of a jewelry shop. The display cases are smashed, and it is obvious that many items have been taken. While searching the shop, he takes a watch, worth about two days' pay for that officer. He reports that the watch had been stolen during the burglary.
Case 6.	A police officer has a private arrangement with a local auto body shop to refer the owners of cars damaged in accidents to the shop. In exchange for each referral, he receives payment of 5 percent of the repair bill from the shop owner.
Case 7.	A police officer, who happens to be a very good auto mechanic, is scheduled to work during coming holidays. A supervisor offers to give him these days off, if he agrees to tune up his supervisor's personal car. Evaluate the *supervisor's* behavior.
Case 8.	At 2:00 A.M., a police officer, who is on duty, is driving his patrol car on a deserted road. He sees a vehicle that has been driven off the road and is stuck in a ditch. He approaches the vehicle and observes that the driver is not hurt but is obviously intoxicated. He also finds that the driver is a police officer. Instead of reporting this accident and offense, he transports the driver to his home.
Case 9.	A police officer finds a bar on his beat that is still serving drinks a half-hour past its legal closing time. Instead of reporting this violation, the police officer agrees to accept a couple of free drinks from the owner.
Case 10.	Two police officers on foot patrol surprise a man who is attempting to break into an automobile. The man flees. They chase him for about two blocks before apprehending him by tackling him and wrestling him to the ground. After he is under control, both officers punch him a couple of times in the stomach as punishment for fleeing and resisting.
Case 11.	A police officer finds a wallet in a parking lot. It contains an amount of money equivalent to a full day's pay for that officer. He reports the wallet as lost property but keeps the money for himself.

Source: Carl B. Klockars, Sanja Kutnjak Ivkovich, and Maria R. Haberfeld, *Enhancing Police Integrity* (Washington, DC: National Institute of Justice, 2005).

prostitution are difficult to enforce, because there is no complainant except the government (represented by the police). As a result, police are mandated to enforce laws that neither the offender nor the "victim" wish to have enforced. In the words of one book on the subject, "the law enforcement system is placed in the middle of two conflicting demands. On the one hand, it is their job to enforce the law, albeit with discretion; on the other hand, there is considerable disagreement as to whether or not certain particular activities should be declared criminal."[86] In this situation police may "look the other way"—or be paid to do so. Also, when arrests are made in gambling, drug, or prostitution cases and the offenders are treated leniently in the courts, it is easier for police to be drawn into corruption, because neither the public nor the criminal justice system appears to be serious about enforcing the law.

BAD GOVERNMENT

A second category of externally caused corruption stems from weak or ineffectual local government. When government is unwilling or unable to oversee or manage its police force, the operation of the department becomes haphazard, and corruption often results. In addition, corruption in the local government can spread to the police department through calls for the "protection" of illegal activities. A study of police corruption in three cities found that corruption was made possible by informal systems allowing politicians to influence personnel decisions within the police department. "Determining who will occupy key positions of power within a department, and by making as many members of the . . . department as possible obligated to the politicians, political leaders can impose their own goals on the department—including protection of vice for the financial benefit of the political party in power or of the party leaders themselves."[87]

POLITICAL CLIMATE

Other investigators have found that corruption can result from the "political climate" of the city.[88] An example is the case of Chicago. In 1998, when a new police chief was appointed, the Chicago Police Department faced accusations that police brutality was endemic. The previous chief had been forced to resign after it was discovered that he had maintained a close friendship with a convicted felon. In addition, officers had been charged with taking bribes and selling drugs. When this pervasive culture of corruption came to light, the police union blamed local politicians for placing political interests above the law.[89] In a similar vein, the City of Philadelphia also appointed a new police chief in 1998 to "improve the performance of a 7,000-officer force that has been troubled over the years by numerous accusations of brutality, graft and . . . ineptitude." In 2003, the U.S. Justice Department appointed a federal monitor to oversee the Detroit Police Department following a probe of excessive force by police there.[90] These cities had a long history of political interference in department affairs and higher-than-average incidences of police brutality against citizens and corruption involving the vices.

Preventing Corruption

The most effective strategies for preventing police corruption are those based on carefully identified causes. If corruption in a particular department involves only a few officers, several control strategies may be appropriate. Examples include closely monitoring complaints against the police, making all police hirings and dismissals more visible to serve as examples and deterrents, and making sure police officers do not get into debt. Other, longer-term strategies include more exhaustive background checks of recruits; periodic retraining of all police; and measures aimed at enhancing professionalism, such as leaves for study or specialized training. These longer-term strategies are designed to improve the commitment of individual officers to the ideals and values of a law enforcement career.

If corruption is found to be due to problems in the department itself, a different set of control strategies will be appropriate. For example, establishing civilian review boards to hear complaints against the department and enhancing career

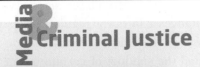

Media & Criminal Justice

Police and Terrorists in Film

The police/criminal investigation genre in books, television, and film is one of the most enduring. In recent years, however, a growing number of movies depict police fighting terrorists. Among the more popular is Bruce Willis in the *Die Hard* series of movies where he plays a rogue cop fighting against supercriminals usually with terrorist motives. In fact, virtually every action movie star, including Clint Eastwood, Harrison Ford, Sylvester Stallone, Arnold Schwarzenegger, and Sean Connery, among others, has made one or more movies of this type.

The attraction to danger that police have been shown to possess (documented by Jerome Skolnick—see discussion in this chapter) is not unlike that found in other professions, including firefighters, the military, and even journalists who report from dangerous places.[a] In all these cases, public service is an important motivation to those holding jobs in these fields, but the willingness to do it at personal risk separates these professions from other public service occupations.[b]

Depicting high-risk activity lies at the foundation of an action movie, so it is not surprising that so many movies use police work as a means to develop an action story. The use of terrorists as the antagonist probably reflects current events, as well as the need to develop larger-than-life supercriminals to match up against increasingly larger-than-life fictional police, capable of unbelievable infiltration, fighting skills, and escapes.

Action movies are designed for escapist entertainment, but the question can be raised whether these films raise unrealistic expectations for police. Greater use of movies to portray or reenact successful police investigations of actual cases adds a dose of realism for the public. The success experienced by television series on the A&E channel with programs such as *American Justice* suggests there is also a public appetite to see how police work really occurs.

Can you identify other occupations in which danger can be part of the job? Have they been depicted in action films? Do you believe the general public clearly distinguishes between the actions of fictional police in the movies and their expectations of actual police? How do you know?

NOTES

a. Sebastian Junger, "Addicted to Danger," *Vanity Fair* (February 1999), p. 88.

b. John M. MacDonald, Robert J. Kaminski, Geoffrey P. Alpert, and Abraham N. Tennenbaum, "The Temporal Relationship between Police Killings of Civilians and Criminal Homicide: A Refined Version of the Danger-Perception Theory," *Crime & Delinquency*, vol. 47 (April 2001), p. 155.

mobility within the department may help prevent hidden corruption. Likewise, procedures to ensure the fair and confidential hearing of personnel matters within the department and to guarantee that promotions are based on qualifications, rather than on patronage, can help prevent political considerations from inhibiting honest police work.

When corruption is due to external, governmental factors, the most fruitful strategies involve both supervision of police and legislative decision making. A jurisdiction can improve supervision of officers by making sure that only qualified police and government officials are given supervisory responsibilities. Political reform through legislation may be needed to eliminate government interference with police department operations. Similarly, decriminalization of minor undesirable behaviors can eliminate opportunities for corruption by removing "victimless" crimes from police jurisdiction.

THE KNAPP COMMISSION

In its New York City investigation, the Knapp Commission found that the most important source of police corruption was control of the city's illegal gambling, narcotics, loan-sharking, and sex-related enterprises. The next most important source was "legitimate business seeking to ease its way through the maze of City ordinances and regulations."[91] In this case changes in laws and regulations could have a substantial impact on police corruption. As the Knapp Commission noted, "The laws against gambling, prostitution, and the conduct of certain business activities on the Sabbath all contribute to the prevalence of police corruption."[92] One expert has concluded that without "a public commitment . . . to realistic vice laws . . . the elimination of police corruption will not occur."[93]

What Is Legitimate Use of Deadly Force?

deadly force
The use of lethal force by police against a suspect.

There is growing controversy about the legitimate use of **deadly force** by police against citizens. When is the shooting of a suspect by police reasonable? When should the use of lethal force be prohibited? Do police discriminate in their use of force? In this section we will examine the extent of police shootings, the nature of the victims, and the constitutionality of deadly force laws.

The legal justification for police use of deadly force stems from English common law. Under common law an arresting officer could use deadly force to prevent the escape of a fleeing felon, but *not* to prevent the escape of a fleeing suspect who had committed a misdemeanor. The reason for this distinction was that in the fifteenth century most felonies were punishable by death. Death sentences could be imposed for the crimes of arson, murder, manslaughter, rape, robbery, burglary, sodomy, escape from prison, and larceny, among other offenses.

THE "FLEEING FELON" RULE

"fleeing felon" rule
The now obsolete common-law rule that police can use deadly force against any felon who flees the scene of a crime.

This common-law **"fleeing felon" rule** was adopted in the early years of the United States. Since then, however, the number of crimes defined as felonies has risen dramatically, whereas the use of capital punishment has dropped significantly. As a result, by the late nineteenth century the historical justification for the "fleeing felon" rule had disappeared. Also, for many offenses, the distinction between misdemeanor and felony is no longer obvious. The difference between felony larceny and misdemeanor larceny, for instance, is the value of the property taken. A police officer operating under the "fleeing felon" rule cannot readily determine whether a larceny suspect has stolen enough property to be a fleeing felon rather than a fleeing misdemeanant.

Victims of Violent Crime Control

The National Center for Health Statistics collects information on "deaths by legal intervention"; that is, on civilian fatalities caused by police. During the 1950s there were 240 homicides by police in the nation as a whole. Between 1968 and 1976 this number was 342.[94] In the 1990s a survey of city police departments found that citizens were shot and killed at a rate of nearly 1 person for every 1,000 sworn officers.[95] Homicides by police may be underreported by 25 to 50 percent, however, because medical authorities may inaccurately determine the cause of death or omit mention of police involvement. Upon examination of death records from the California Department of Health over a seven-year period, Lawrence Sherman and Robert Langworthy found official records of 257 homicides by police. To check this number, they asked the police departments themselves for the number of police homicides that had occurred in each jurisdiction. This yielded a total of 544 homicides for the same period. As a result, the actual number of civilian deaths caused by police shootings may be significantly higher than "official" statistics indicate.[96]

The Violent Crime Control and Law Enforcement Act of 1994 requires the U.S. attorney general to obtain data on the use of excessive force by law enforcement officers. To gather this information, the Justice Department conducted a national survey of citizens ages twelve and older. This survey made it possible for the first time to estimate the prevalence of the use of force in police–citizen encounters. Of the more than 215 million U.S. residents age sixteen or older, 21 percent have a face-to-face contact with police during a given year. These contacts involve traffic stops and all other kinds of police–citizen encounters. Approximately 1.5 percent of these resulted in police use of force—force that ranged from being held at gunpoint to being pushed or grabbed by police (see Figure 9.3). About three-quarters of the 664,500 persons against whom forced was used characterized the force as "excessive."[97] Future surveys will study the trends in police use of force over time.

If these officers were to use deadly force in the course of their investigation, by what standards would their actions be judged? What if they encounter a felon who attempts to flee from the scene? What if they see a suspect they think might have a gun to use against them?

VIOLENT CRIME CONTROL ACT

A primary objection to use of deadly force by police is that police appear to shoot blacks significantly more often than whites, leading to charges of racial discrimination. Investigations in different cities have found that blacks are shot by police two to four times more often than one would expect, given their proportion of each city's population.[98] Arnold Binder and Peter Scharf suggest that a better indicator of discrimination in police shootings would be the rate of police shootings of blacks in relation to blacks' arrest rate for violent felonies (compared to the same rates for whites). Binder and Scharf argue that "police as a general rule do not shoot college professors [white or black], physicians [white or black], infants [white or black], shopkeepers [white or black], and so on." Police do, however, shoot at felons, white or black. Binder and Scharf examined arrest rates for violent crimes and found that the proportion of black suspects shot by police closely mirrored the proportion of people arrested for serious crimes who were black.[99] More recent studies have found that race of officers and suspects "played no role" in predicting police use of force.[100]

RACIAL DISCRIMINATION

Another way to determine possible racial discrimination is to examine the situational factors present in police shootings of all types. Studies have found no situational differences between white and black shooting victims in Atlanta, Kansas City, or New York City.[101] On the other hand, studies in Los Angeles, Chicago, and Memphis found police more likely to shoot blacks than whites under similar circumstances.[102] As Blumberg has noted, this variation in findings among cities "underscores the need to examine this issue on a city-by-city basis."[103] Potential discrimination in police shooting decisions remains an important issue for study and policy. These efforts will be assisted by further national surveys of police–citizen encounters conducted under the mandate of the Violent Crime Control and Law Enforcement Act of 1994.

In response to threats that police face which are serious, but not lethal, there has been a growing interest in less-than-lethal weapons that can immediately

FIGURE 9.3 Police Contacts with Public Resulting in Use of Force

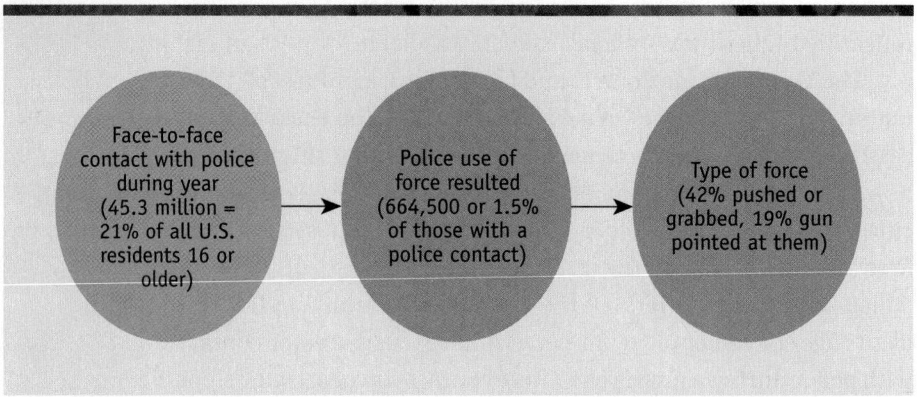

Source: Matthew R. Durose, Erica L. Schmitt, and Patrick A. Langan, *Contacts between Police and the Public: Findings from the 2002 National Survey* (Washington, DC: Bureau of Justice Statistics, 2005).

disable a suspect without causing death. The Taser, the most popular of these weapons, uses electric shock to disable a suspect. Tasers are now used in nearly half of U.S. police agencies. A review by the U.S. General Accountability Office found that the police departments they reviewed had separate policies for the use of Taser, and their growing use shows the need for training and clear policies for usage. Amnesty International reports that 156 U.S. deaths were caused by Tasers from 2001 to 2005, so there is growing concern that although Tasers are less lethal than guns, they should be used according to the same rules as guns, due to their ability to cause death under certain circumstances.[104]

"Fleeing Felon" and "Prowler Inside" Laws

For many years a significant element in the controversy over police use of deadly force was the lack of a uniform national standard governing the use of force by police. In 1980 a review of state laws found that eight states allowed deadly force only in defense of life or when the suspect threatened deadly force or showed a substantial likelihood of doing so. Ten states permitted deadly force by police only against individuals suspected of violent crimes. Thirty-two states, however, allowed police to shoot any "fleeing felon," including unarmed suspects fleeing from nonviolent felonies.[105]

The primary rationale given by supporters of the "fleeing felon" rule is deterrence. It is argued that the authority of police to shoot unarmed, nonviolent suspects will deter future felonies. Researchers have tested this belief by comparing crime rates in cities with differing rates of police shootings. A review of these investigations concluded that "nothing in the research to date suggests that a high frequency of police shooting reduces crime rates in any way."[106] A further justification for the "fleeing felon" rule is that it increases the rate of apprehension of nonviolent felony suspects who might otherwise escape. But shootings are extremely rare in nonviolent circumstances. Given the large number of nonviolent felonies, one investigator estimated that in order to apprehend by shooting even 1 percent of nonviolent felony suspects in a year, police would have to "increase the rate at which they shot people during that year by fifty-fold."[107]

TENNESSEE V. GARNER

The debate over the use of deadly force changed dramatically in 1985 with the ruling of the U.S. Supreme Court in *Tennessee v. Garner.* Responding to a "prowler inside call," two Memphis police officers saw a woman standing on her porch and gesturing toward an adjacent house. She told them that she had heard glass breaking and that "they" or "someone" was breaking in next door. While one officer radioed the police station, the other went behind the house. The officer heard a door slam and saw someone run across the backyard. The fleeing suspect, Edward Garner, stopped at a six-foot-high chain-link fence at the edge of the yard. The officer was able to see Garner's face and hands with his flashlight. He saw no sign of a weapon and was "reasonably sure" that Garner was unarmed. While Garner crouched at the base of the fence, the officer called out "police, halt!" and took a few steps toward him. Garner then began to climb over the fence. Convinced that Garner would escape if he made it over the fence, the officer shot him. The bullet hit Garner in the back of the head and killed him. Ten dollars and a purse taken from the house were found on his body.

The Supreme Court held in *Tennessee v. Garner* that the use of deadly force is subject to the Fourth Amendment, because such a use of force "restrains the freedom of a person to walk away," and that person is therefore "seized." Using the rationale employed in all search and seizure cases, the Court attempted to evaluate the constitutionality of the officer's action by balancing the extent of the intrusion (deadly force) against the government's interest in apprehending people suspected of crimes. The Court found the "fleeing felon" law to be unconstitutional.

NO IMMEDIATE THREAT?

> *The use of deadly force to prevent the escape of all felony suspects, whatever the circumstances, is constitutionally unreasonable. It is not better that all felony suspects die than that they escape. Where the suspect poses no immediate threat to the officer and no threat to others, the harm resulting from failing to apprehend*

A crime scene at a bank in which the suspect was shot and killed. These situations evolve quickly, and police are often forced to make rapid decisions. Assume you were the police officer who shot the suspect. Would it matter if the weapon the suspect pointed at you turned out to be a toy gun? What if the suspect threatened to shoot but displayed no weapon? On what legal standard must you rely?

him does not justify the use of deadly force to do so. . . . A police officer may not seize an unarmed, nondangerous suspect by shooting him dead.[108]

when ok to use deadly force

This decision struck down all "fleeing felon" laws in the United States. Police are constitutionally justified in using deadly force to stop a fleeing suspect only "if the suspect threatens the officer with a weapon or there is probable cause to believe that he has committed a crime involving the infliction or threatened infliction of serious physical harm," the Court said. In the latter instance, police may use deadly force to prevent the suspect from escaping after some warning has been given "where feasible."

The Supreme Court admitted that there are practical difficulties in assessing the suspect's dangerousness, but pointed out that "similarly difficult judgments must be made by the police in equally uncertain circumstances [such as stop and frisk]." The justices also found evidence showing that during the previous ten years "only 3.8 percent of all burglaries involved violent crime." As a result, they felt that burglars cannot be presumed to be dangerous and therefore be subjected to deadly force unless additional aggravating conditions are present.

Today the use of deadly force by police has been greatly reduced. Many police departments have enacted policies that restrict the use of force according to *Tennessee v. Garner* and define "dangerousness" in specific terms to guide the decisions of police officers. The frequency with which deadly force is used now appears to be related to the extent to which departments help their officers by limiting use of force to specifically defined circumstances.[109]

Police Brutality

The case of the Haitian immigrant in New York City who was sodomized and tortured while in police custody produced a new public outcry about police brutality in the United States. Earlier, the videotaping of the 1991 Rodney King beating had done more to focus public attention on police use of force against an individual than had any previous incident. King, a twenty-five-year-old black man, was stopped by Los Angeles police for alleged violation of motor vehicle laws. He was subjected to a beating that lasted several minutes, in which he was shocked twice with stun guns and struck numerous times with nightsticks and fists by four officers while twenty-one others watched. King suffered multiple skull fractures, a crushed cheekbone, lost teeth, and a broken ankle. What made this incident vivid was the fact that a private citizen had captured it on a home video camera. The video footage was replayed numerous times on news broadcasts.

police brutality
Use of excessive physical force by police in carrying out their duties.

In an era of growing police professionalism, this incident looked like a step backward and a clear instance of police brutality. **Police brutality** occurs when police use excessive physical force in carrying out their duties. Many observers, including some police officials, saw the Rodney King beating as a case of excessive and intolerable behavior on the part of police.[110] Other sensational cases have resulted in heightened public concern about excessive force by police. In 2000 four New York City police officers were put on trial for killing an unarmed African immigrant, using forty-one bullets.[111] These highly publicized cases have far-reaching consequences. In the Rodney King case, the first trial ended in acquittal of the police officers, but the announcement of this verdict was followed by sev-

A prosecutor reconstructing a scene involving police use of force. In court, the events are recounted in slow-motion, whereas in practice, the actual event unfolded very quickly. How can police protect themselves from allegations of excessive force under law?

eral days of rioting in Los Angeles. The New York City cases resulted in protests and ill will that will take years to overcome.[112]

In practice, however, the use of force by police in making arrests is relatively low. A national study of large state and local police agencies (encompassing 59 percent of all officers) found a total of 26,556 citizen complaints about police use of force during 2002. This is a rate of 6.6 force complaints per 100 full-time sworn officers. Differences among types of police agencies are illustrated in Figure 9.4, which shows that municipal police departments have the highest rate of complaints. Table 9.5 illustrates the disposition of these complaints. About a third of all force complaints were not sustained, 25 percent were unfounded, officers were exonerated in 23 percent of cases, and 8 percent of complaints were sustained. About 20 percent of large municipal police departments have a civilian complaint review board (CCRB), and these departments had a rate of force complaints nearly twice that of other departments. If sustained excessive force complaints are used as an indicator, there are an estimated 2,000 incidents of police use of excessive force, which is a rate of about one incident per 200 officers annually.

Another study in six large metropolitan areas found that of 7,512 adult arrests, fewer than 1 in 5 involved police use of physical force in any form (use of weapon, weaponless force, or use of severe restraints).[113] The study also found that when police use force, they rarely use deadly force, although the level of force usually is related to the amount of resistance offered by the suspect. One study has found that officers are more likely to be injured when they use less force than that of a resisting suspect.[114] Nevertheless, widely publicized incidents of excessive force command the attention of both the public and policymakers.

FIGURE 9.4 Citizen Complaints about Police Use of Force

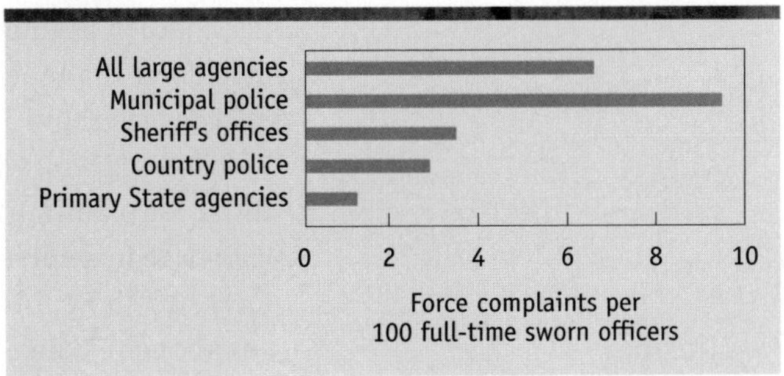

Source: Matthew J. Hickman, *Citizen Complaints about Police Use of Force* (Washington, DC: Bureau of Justice Statistics, 2006).

Table 9.5 Dispositions of Citizen Complaints of Police Use of Force (by type of agency, 2002)

		Complaint Dispositions				
Type of Agency	*Total with Disposition*	*Not Sustained*	*Unfounded*	*Exonerated*	*Sustained*	*Other Disposition*
All large agencies	94%	34%	25%	23%	8%	9%
Local agencies	94%	35%	26%	23%	8%	9%
Municipal police	94	37	25	21	8	9
Sheriffs' offices	95	20	30	32	12	6
County police	93	25	17	35	6	17
Primary State agencies	95%	16%	19%	52%	9%	4%

Source: Matthew J. Hickman, *Citizen Complaints about Police Use of Force* (Washington, DC: Bureau of Justice Statistics, 2006).

GRAHAM V. CONNOR

In all cases of this kind the question is the same: What should be the limits on the use of force by police in arresting and subduing citizens? The U.S. Supreme Court addressed this issue in the 1989 case *Graham v. Connor.* It held that police officers may be held liable under the Fourth Amendment when they use excessive force.[115] In this case police handcuffed a suspect, refusing to allow him to explain that he had passed out because he was diabetic. While he was in their custody, the officers attacked him and inflicted injuries, including cut wrists, ear damage, and a broken foot. This use of force was held to be excessive according to an "objective reasonableness" standard: the perspective of a hypothetical reasonable officer on the scene. In the Rodney King case, many citizens found it difficult to accept explanations by police that the officers' use of force was "reasonable" and necessary to subdue the suspect, because the videotape appeared to speak for itself. In a second trial, two Los Angeles police officers were ultimately convicted for violating King's constitutional rights. The following year, the City of Los Angeles settled a civil suit for damages suffered by King, who was awarded $3.8 million.

The Supreme Court's decision in *Graham* sets forth four kinds of factors that police must consider in evaluating the reasonableness of use of force: the immediacy of the threat to the officer, the severity of the crime alleged, whether the suspect is resisting arrest, and whether the suspect is attempting to escape from custody. When applied objectively, these standards protect a reasonable police officer from harm while also protecting suspects from unreasonable use of force by police.

CODE OF SILENCE

A survey of nearly 1,000 police officers confirmed that extreme cases of police abuse of authority are rare, and that most officers find it unacceptable to use more force than the law allows. However, it also was found that an unspoken code of silence in some departments inhibits some officers from reporting misconduct by fellow officers, and that 85 percent of officers believed strong positions against the abuse of authority by first-line supervisors and police chiefs can play a significant role in deterring such conduct.[116] Therefore efforts made by police departments to show intolerance of excessive use of force can both encourage and enforce compliance with existing legal standards.

CRITICAL THINKING EXERCISES

Responding to Spouse Abuse

One of the important lessons of the O. J. Simpson trial was the need for improved police response to domestic violence. Yet at the time of the Simpson case, many experts believed that the police response to these incidents had already been greatly improved.

The watershed was an incident that resulted in the 1985 judgment in *Thurman v. The City of Torrington, Connecticut.*[a] In this case a woman had been repeatedly and severely abused and threatened by her former husband, who was no longer living with her. The Torrington Police Department failed to enforce a court order prohibiting the husband from harassing her. After an attack in which her husband nearly killed her, Ms. Thurman sued the police department for negligence and for violation of her civil rights. She won the case and was awarded a settlement of $2 million.

But the question remained: How *should* police handle domestic violence cases?

The Torrington case dramatically changed the way police exercised discretion in cases of domestic violence. Police departments, and their insurers, realized that their potential legal accountability made a new policy mandatory. But the question remained: How *should* police handle domestic violence cases? As one former police chief remarked, "The chief's responsibility is to take whatever legal measures he believes wisest, based on something other than seat-of-the-pants feelings."[b]

Today 93 percent of large local police agencies and more than three-fourths of sheriffs' departments have written policies concerning domestic disputes. Nearly half of these agencies also have special units to deal with domestic violence.[c]

The precise actions taken by police vary by state, and sometimes even by locality. Fourteen states have laws requiring that arrests be made in domestic violence situations. These laws were passed in response to a study in Milwaukee that found that when police made arrests there was a reduction in the number of subsequent complaints. This finding is controversial, however, because it has not been found to hold in other locations; the decline in subsequent complaints may have been due to intimidation by the arrested spouse rather than to the deterrent impact of an arrest.[d]

Victims report that police respond to more than three-fourths of domestic incidents by coming to the scene, although they appear to respond more quickly to victimizations by strangers than to victimizations by intimates.[e] This fact points to a problem in current police policies. Even in jurisdictions where police are required to arrest the offender when responding to episodes of domestic violence, they often do not do so. Some officers feel that they will place the victim in more danger by making an arrest. In other cases police departments may give these types of situations low priority or may assume that the victim will not follow through with a complaint.[f] Therefore, many cases of domestic violence continue to be handled informally.

It has been observed that police are aware of households that are at high risk of a serious domestic assault (owing to a history of complaints), but that their focus on case-by-case responses prevents effective police action *prior* to such an assault.[g] It appears that paying greater attention to problem *households,* rather than just responding to assaultive *incidents,* may hold the best prospects for long-term prevention.

CRITICAL THINKING QUESTIONS

1. How do you explain the different results found in various studies of the impact of arrests in domestic violence cases?
2. How do you explain the fact that 90 percent of all domestic violence cases involve men assaulting women? Why is the proportion not closer to 50 percent?
3. Why do you think society is reluctant to target problem households rather than simply having police respond to specific incidents of domestic assault?

NOTES

a. 595 F. Supp. 1521 (1985).
b. Anthony Bouza, "Responding to Domestic Violence," in M. Steinman, ed., *Woman Battering: Policy Responses* (Cincinnati: Anderson, 1991), p. 201.
c. Callie Marie Rennision, *Intimate Partner Violence* (Washington, DC: Bureau of Justice Statistics, 2003).
d. Jannell D. Schmidt and Lawrence W. Sherman, "Does Arrest Deter Domestic Violence?," in Eve S. Buzawa and Carl G. Buzawa, *Do Arrests and Restraining Orders Work?* (Thousand Oaks, CA: Sage, 1996), pp. 43–53; Jeffrey Fagan, *The Criminalization of Domestic Violence: Promises and Limits* (Washington, DC: National Institute of Justice, 1996); Loretta J. Stalans and Arthur J. Lurigio, "Responding to Violence against Women," *Crime and Delinquency* 41 (October 1995), pp. 387–98; Christopher D. Maxwell, Joel H. Garner, and Jeffrey A. Fagan, *The Effects of Arrest on Intimate Partner Violence* (Washington, DC: National Institute of Justice, 2001).
e. Zawitz, *Violence between Intimates,* p. 5.
f. See Eve S. Buzawa, Thomas L. Austin, and Carl G. Buzawa, "The Role of Arrest in Domestic versus Stranger Assault: Is There a Difference?," in Buzawa and Buzawa, *Do Arrests and Restraining Orders Work?,* p. 152.
g. Lawrence W. Sherman, Jannell D. Schmidt, and Daniel P. Rogan, *Policing Domestic Violence: Experiments and Dilemmas* (New York: Free Press, 1992); Shelly Feuer Domash, "Putting the Cuffs on Domestic Abusers," *Police* (January 1998), pp. 46–47; Laura Dugan and Marybeth J. Mattingly, *Family and Employment*

Consequences of Intimate Partner Violence: A Longitudinal Analysis (Washington, DC: National Institute of Justice, 2005).

An Appropriate Remedy for Police Misconduct?

Much of the controversy over improper police searches, interrogations, and use of force focuses on the question of appropriate remedies. Should police be criminally punished, be civilly sued, have their cases thrown out of court, or suffer some other consequence if they are found to have engaged in misconduct?

Some argue that police officers should be punished as individuals for engaging in improper conduct in the course of their duties. In view of the extensive screening of police applicants, their training requirements, and the authority they hold over the liberty of other citizens, police should be held to a high standard of conduct. On the other hand, police are often asked to make quick decisions without knowing all the facts. Is it fair to punish them for decisions that seem reasonable at the time but are incorrect?

Over the years court decisions have attempted to reach a middle ground. It has been held that government officials (including police) enjoy "qualified immunity" when performing discretionary functions on the job. This means that they are shielded from liability "if their conduct does not violate clearly established statutory or constitutional rights of which a reasonable person should have known."[a]

It has also been argued that the exclusionary rule (see Chapter 7) is too permissive, because it can allow a guilty person to go free, as in the *Miranda* case. Should police misconduct benefit the suspect? One alternative is to fine or suspend a police officer who makes improper decisions that a "reasonable" officer would not make under the same circumstances. This leads to the question of whether fines or suspensions are appropriate or sufficient punishment for improper conduct.

In most states, police officers who abuse their powers may be subject to "decertification proceedings" that strip them of the ability to work as police unless they are recertified at a later date.[b] Decertification might serve as a deterrent to future police misconduct, but it does not directly address the effects of past misconduct.

CRITICAL THINKING QUESTIONS

1. Do you think the exclusionary rule should be abolished in favor of punishing the officer for an illegal search?
2. If police officers were fined, suspended, or decertified for making certain kinds of improper decisions, how would such punishments serve the interests of justice?
3. What do you think should be done with police officers who make reasonable but incorrect decisions?

NOTES

a. *Harlow v. Fitzgerald*, 457 U.S. 800 (1982); Donald Dripps, "The Case for the Contingent Exclusionary Rule," *American Criminal Law Review*, vol. 38 (winter 2001), p. 1.

b. Roger Goldman and Steven Puro, "Decertification of Police: An Alternative to Traditional Remedies for Police Misconduct," *Hastings Constitutional Law Quarterly* 15 (1987), pp. 45–80; Steven Puro, Roger Goldman, and William C. Smith, "Police Decertification: Changing Patterns among the States, 1985–1995," *Policing: An International Journal of Police Strategies and Management* 20 (1997), pp. 481–96; Raymond A. Franklin, *2005 Survey of POST Agencies Regarding Certification Practices* (Washington, DC: Bureau of Justice Assistance, 2005).

SUMMARY

IS THERE SUCH A THING AS A POLICE PERSONALITY?

- Many myths and stereotypes about police develop because most people have comparatively little contact with police and tend to generalize from media images of incidents that are not typical.
- There are three styles of policing: the watchman, legalistic, and service styles.
- Current research on police attitudes toward their jobs shows that police develop these attitudes through job experiences rather than through preexisting personality traits.
- Authoritarian attitudes are more likely to be found in officers without a college education who have been on the job a long time. Officers with less education have also been found to be more dogmatic than those with higher levels of education.
- Current research on police attitudes toward the public indicates that police are affected by citizens' negative sentiment toward them but that they remain dedicated to the job.

HOW SHOULD POLICE PERFORMANCE BE EVALUATED?

- Various measures of police response to crime have been used, but most have problems stemming from the fact that the police are primarily reactive and cannot spend unlimited time on unsolved cases.

- The number of arrests resulting in prosecutions is, however, a useful indicator of police performance.
- Police spend a great deal of time on noncriminal matters, and their community service function should be taken into account in evaluations of their performance.

WHAT ARE SOME FORMS OF POLICE CORRUPTION?

- Police corruption takes three forms: nonfeasance (failure to perform a legal duty), misfeasance (failure to perform a legal duty in a proper manner), and malfeasance (commission of an illegal act).
- Some explanations of police corruption focus on individual "rotten apples," whereas others focus on the "barrel"—the whole department. Most experts reject individual explanations and suggest that there is a deviant police subculture or that corruption results from secrecy within departments.
- Still other explanations look to external factors such as laws that are difficult to enforce or a weak local government.
- Prevention of corruption depends on careful identification of its causes.

WHAT IS LEGITIMATE USE OF DEADLY FORCE?

- Research on civilian fatalities due to police shootings has found that such incidents are underreported.
- The Supreme Court has ruled that police may use deadly force to stop a suspect only if the suspect threatens the officer with a weapon or there is probable cause to believe that the suspect is dangerous.
- Police brutality occurs when police use excessive physical force in carrying out their duties.
- Police officers may be held liable under the Fourth Amendment when they use excessive force.

KEY TERMS

racial profiling *220*
police stress *224*
cynicism *224*
anomie *225*
socialization model *226*
predispositional model *226*
authoritarianism *227*
dogmatism *227*
police discretion *228*
selective enforcement *228*
police pursuits *231*
clearance rate *233*
police corruption *236*
nonfeasance *236*
misfeasance *236*
malfeasance *236*
deviant police subculture hypothesis *237*
deadly force *242*
"fleeing felon" rule *242*
police brutality *246*

QUESTIONS FOR REVIEW AND DISCUSSION

1. What is meant by selective enforcement?
2. Why is it difficult to formulate a clear policy to guide police decision making?
3. What are the key findings of research on police cynicism?
4. What factors were identified by Skolnick as leading to the development of police attitudes?
5. Why has the predisposition hypothesis been discredited as an explanation of the formation of the police personality?
6. In what way does college education influence authoritarianism in police officers?
7. How do police officers' attitudes affect their performance?
8. What are the three forms of police corruption? Give an example of each.
9. What are the three main types of explanations of police corruption?
10. What can be done to prevent police corruption?
11. What numerical measure is the best indicator of police performance in crime control?
12. What can be done to relieve police of noncriminal tasks so that they can devote more time to crime control?
13. What justification is there for the use of deadly force by police?
14. What actions have police departments taken to prevent incidents of police brutality?

NOTES

1. "Fourth Defendant Sentenced in Memphis Police Corruption Case," *Associated Press State & Local Wire* (March 28, 2006); Brian D. Crecente, "2001 Law Pushing Bad Cops Out Door," *Rocky Mountain News* (December 30, 2005); Matt Lait and Tina Daunt, "The Rampart Verdicts: L.A. Will Feel Ripple Effect of Corruption for Years," *Los Angeles Times* (November 16, 2000), p. 1.
2. Greg Wilson, "Heroic Cops Are Honored: Wounded Hunting Gunman," *New York Daily News* (November 22, 2000), p. 3; Robert Gearty, "Gulotta Cites 12 Officers for Heroism," *New York Daily News* (January 12, 2000), p. 9 ; Lateff Mungin, "Kudos Keep Coming for SWAT Team; Gwinnett Police to Be Honored for Arrest of Shooting Suspect," *Atlanta Journal-Constitution* (March 24, 2005).
3. Jerry Oliver, "Police Target Most Likely Criminals of All Races," *Richmond Times–Dispatch* (January 30, 2000), p. C5.
4. Michael Hardy and Pamela Stallsmith, "House Kills Stricter Law on Car Belts," *Richmond Times–Dispatch* (February 10, 2000), p. 1.
5. "A New Flap over Racial Profiling," *U.S. News & World Report* (May 3, 1999), p. 10; Tammerlin Drummond, "It's Not Just in New Jersey," *Time* (June 14, 1999), p. 61; Curt Anderson, "Federal Agencies Get Racial Profiling Ban," *The Associated Press* (June 18, 2003); Maria Glod, "Virginia to Train Police against Profiling," *Washington Post* (August 21, 2003), p. B1.
6. U.S. Comptroller, General, *Racial Profiling: Limited Data Available on Motorist Stops* (Washington, DC: U.S. General Accountability Office, 2000).
7. Tom R. Tyler and Cheryl J. Wakslak, "Profiling and Police Legitimacy: Procedural Justice, Attributions of Motive, and Acceptance of Police Authority," *Criminology*, vol. 42 (May 2004), pp. 253–82; Patrick McGreevy, "Question of Race Profiling Unanswered," *Los Angeles Times* (July 12, 2006).
8. Charles L. Klotzer, "Perception—Not Intent—Is What Counts," *St. Louis Journalism Review* 30 (October 1999), p. 4; John M. Glionna, "Cops Are behind Fast Teens," *Los Angeles Times* (June 6, 2003) ; see also Robin Shepard Engel, "Citizens' Perceptions of Distributive and Procedural Injustice During Traffic Stops with Police," *Journal of Research in Crime and Delinquency*, vol. 42 (November 2005), pp. 445–82.
9. Pat G. Minetti and Jacqueline Stephan, "Playing for Keeps: The Importance of Strong Citizen–Police Relationships," *The Police Chief* 66 (October 1999), p. 133; Michael D. Reisig and Roger B. Parks, *Satisfaction with Police: What Matters?* (Washington, DC: National Institute of Justice, 2002).
10. The URL is http://www.usdoj.gov/kidspage/
11. James Q. Wilson, *Varieties of Police Behavior* (Cambridge, MA: Harvard University Press, 1968).
12. Independent Commission on the Los Angeles Police Department, *Report of the Independent Commission on the Los Angeles Police Department* (1991).
13. Robert C. Davis and Bruce G. Taylor, "A Proactive Response to Family Violence: The Results of a Randomized Experiment," *Criminology* 35 (May 1997), pp. 307–33 ; Lorraine Mazerolle, Dennis Rogan, James Frank, Christine Famega, and John E. Eck, *Managing Calls to the Police with 911/311 Systems* (Washington, DC: National Institute of Justice, 2005).
14. Roy R. Roberg, Jack Kuykendall, and Kenneth Novak, *Police Management*, 3rd ed. (Los Angeles: Roxbury Publishing, 2002).
15. Douglas W. Perez, *The Paradoxes of Police Work* (Incline Village, NV: Copperhouse, 1997); Robin Shepard Engel, *How Police Supervisory Styles Influence Patrol Officer Behavior* (Washington, DC: National Institute of Justice, 2003).
16. Angie Cannon, "Cop-Shop Woes in the 'Burbs," *U.S. News & World Report* (September 25, 2000), p. 26.
17. Stephen D. Mastrofski, Jeffrey B. Snipes, Roger B. Parks, and Christopher D. Maxwell, "The Helping Hand of the Law: Police Control of Citizens on Request," *Criminology*, vol. 38 (May 2000), pp. 307–42.
18. Jerome H. Skolnick, *Justice without Trial: Law Enforcement in Democratic Society*, 3rd ed. (New York: Macmillan, 1994), p. 46.
19. Francis T. Cullen, Bruce G. Link, Lawrence F. Travis, and Terrence Lemming, "Paradox in Policing: A Note on Perceptions of Danger," *Journal of Police Science and Administration* 11 (December 1983), pp. 457–62.
20. Skolnick, *Justice without Trial*, p. 54.
21. James C. McElroy, Paula C. Morrow, and Thomas R. Wardlow, "A Career Stage Analysis of Police Officer Work Commitment," *Journal of Criminal Justice* 27 (1999), pp. 507–16; B. Metcalfe and G. Dick. "Is the Force Still with You? Measuring Police Commitment," *Journal of Managerial Psychology*, vol. 15 (November 2000): 812–33; B. Metcalfe and G. Dick. "Is the Force Still with Her? Gender and Commitment in the Police," *Women in Management Review*, vol. 17 (November 2002), pp. 392–404.
22. Robert C. Ankony and Thomas M. Kelley, "The Impact of Perceived Alienation on Police Officers' Sense of Mastery and Subsequent Motivation for Proactive Enforcement," *Policing: An International Journal of Police Strategies and Management* 22 (1999), pp. 120–32.
23. Roy R. Roberg, Kenneth Novak, and Gary Cordner, *Police & Society*, 3rd ed. (Los Angeles: Roxbury Publishing, 2005).
24. H. M. Robinson, M. R. Sigman, and J. R. Wilson, "Duty-Related Stressors and PTSD Symptoms in Suburban Police Officers," *Psychological Reports*, vol. 81 (1997), pp. 835–45; Leanor Boulin Johnson, Michael Todd, and Ganga Subramanian, "Violence in Police Families: Work–Family Spillover," *Journal of Family Violence*, vol. 20 (February 2005), pp. 3–13; Andrea Kohan and Dwight Mazmanian, "Police Work, Burnout, and Pro-Organizational Behavior: A Consideration of Daily Work Experiences," *Criminal Justice and Behavior*, vol. 30 (October 2003), pp. 559–84.
25. Donald C. Sheehan, ed. *Domestic Violence by Police Officers* (Washington, DC: U.S. Government Printing Office, 2000).
26. Arthur Niederhoffer, *Behind the Shield: The Police in Urban Society* (Garden City, NY: Anchor, 1967), p. 101.
27. G. Marie Wilt and James D. Bannon, "Cynicism or Realism: A Critique of Niederhoffer's Research into Police Attitudes," *Journal of Police Science and Administration* 4 (March 1976), p. 40; Robert M. Regoli, Eric D. Poole, and John D. Hewitt, "Refining Police Cynicism Theory: An Empirical Assessment, Evaluation, and Implications," in D. M. Peterson, ed., *Police Work: Strategies and Outcomes in Law Enforcement* (Beverly Hills, CA: Sage, 1979), pp. 59–68; John P. Crank, Robert G. Culbertson, Eric D. Poole, and Robert M. Regoli, "The Measurement of Cynicism among Police Chiefs," *Journal of Criminal Justice* 15 (1987), pp. 37–48; Robert H. Langworthy, "Police Cynicism: What We Know from the Niederhoffer Scale," *Journal of Criminal Justice* 15 (1987), pp. 17–35.

28. Richard S. Bennett and Theodore Greenstein, "The Police Personality: A Test of the Predispositional Model," *Journal of Police Science and Administration* 3 (1975), pp. 439–45.
29. Milton Rokeach, *The Nature of Human Values* (New York: Free Press, 1973).
30. Bennett and Greenstein, p. 444.
31. Raymond Cochrane and Anthony J. P. Butler, "The Values of Police Officers, Recruits, and Civilians in England," *Journal of Police Science and Administration* 8 (June 1980), pp. 205–11.
32. S. J. Saxe and M. Reiser, "A Comparison of Three Police Applicant Groups Using the MMPI," *Journal of Police Science and Administration* 4 (December 1976), pp. 419–25; L. S. Schoenfeld, J. C. Kobos, and I. R. Phinney, "Screening Police Applicants: A Study of Reliability with the MMPI," *Psychological Reports* 47 (1980), pp. 419–25; Edward E. Johnson, "Psychological Tests Used in Assessing a Sample of Police and Firefighter Candidates," *Journal of Police Science and Administration* 11 (December 1983), pp. 430–33; Jack Aylward, "Psychological Testing and Police Selection," *Journal of Police Science and Administration* 13 (spring 1975), pp. 201–10; Bruce W. Topp and Frederic A. Powell, "A Short-Form Dogmatism Scale for Use in Field Studies," *Social Forces* 44 (December 1965), pp. 211–14; George Pugh, "The California Psychological Inventory and Police Selection," *Journal of Police Science and Administration* 15 (June 1985), pp. 172–77.
33. Beth Sanders, Thomas Hughes, and Robert Langworthy, "Police Office Recruitment and Selection: A Survey of Major Police Departments in the U.S.," *Police Forum* 5 (October 1995), pp. 1–4; Philip Ash, Karen B. Slora, and Cynthia F. Britton, "Police Agency Selection Practices," *Journal of Police Science and Administration* 17 (1990), pp. 258–69.
34. Bruce N. Carpenter and Susan M. Raza, "Personality Characteristics of Police Applicants: Comparisons across Subgroups and with Other Populations," *Journal of Police Science and Administration* 15 (March 1987), pp. 10–17; Joseph Putti, Samuel Aryee, and Tan Seck Kang, "Personal Values of Recruits and Officers in a Law Enforcement Agency: An Exploratory Study," *Journal of Police Science and Administration* 16 (1988), pp. 249–54; Stephen B. Perrott and Donald M. Taylor, "Attitudinal Differences between Police Constables and Their Supervisors," *Criminal Justice and Behavior* 22 (September 1995), pp. 326–39; Jennifer M. Brown and Elizabeth A. Campbell, *Stress and Policing* (New York: Wiley, 1994); Jorge G. Varela, Marcus T. Boccaccini, Forrest Scogin, Jamie Stump, and Alicia Caputo, "Personality Testing in Law Enforcement Employment Settings: A Meta-analytic Review," *Criminal Justice and Behavior*, vol. 31 (December 2004), pp. 649–76.
35. David Lester, "Why Do People Become Police Officers?: A Study of Reasons and Their Predictions of Success," *Journal of Police Science and Administration* 11 (June 1983), pp. 170–74; Deirdre Hiatt and George E. Hargrave, "Predicting Job Performance Problems with Psychological Screening," *Journal of Police Science and Administration* 16 (1988), pp. 122–25; Joyce I. McQuilkin, Vickey L. Russell, Alan G. Frost, and Wayne R. Faust, "Psychological Test Validity for Selecting Law Enforcement Officers," *Journal of Police Science and Administration* 17 (1990), pp. 289–94.
36. Matt L. Rodriguez, "Increasing Importance of Higher Education in Police Human Resource Development Programs," *Criminal Justice: The Americas* 8 (April–May, 1995), pp. 1–9.
37. Richard K. Wortley, "Measuring Police Attitudes toward Discretion," *Criminal Justice and Behavior*, vol. 30 (October 2003), p. 538; Alexander B. Smith, Bernard Locke, and William F. Walker, "Authoritarianism in College and Non–College Oriented Police," *Journal of Criminal Law, Criminology, and Police Science* 58 (spring 1967), pp. 128–32; Alexander B. Smith, Bernard Locke, and William F. Walker, "Authoritarianism in Police College Students and Non-Police College Students," *Journal of Criminal Law, Criminology, and Police Science* 59 (fall 1968), pp. 440–43; Alexander B. Smith, Bernard Locke, and Abe Fenster, "Authoritarianism in Policemen Who Are College Graduates and Non-College Police," *Journal of Criminal Law, Criminology, and Police Science* 61 (summer 1969), pp. 313–15; A. F. Dalley, "University vs. Non-University Graduated Policemen: A Study of Police Attitudes," *Journal of Police Science and Administration* 3 (December 1985), pp. 458–68.
38. Roy R. Roberg, "An Analysis of the Relationship among Higher Education, Belief Systems, and Job Performance of Patrol Officers," *Journal of Police Science and Administration* 6 (September 1978), pp. 336–44; Milton Rokeach, *The Open and Closed Mind* (New York: Basic Books, 1960); Donald M. Truxillo, Suzanne R. Bennett, and Michelle L. Collins, "College Education and Police Job Performance: A Ten-year Study," *Public Personnel Management*, vol. 27 (summer 1998), pp. 269–81; Teresa C. LaGrange, "The Role of Police Education in Handling Cases of Mental Disorder," *Criminal Justice Review*, vol. 28 (spring 2003), pp. 88–113.
39. S. M. Smith and M. G. Aamodt, "The Relationship between Education, Experience, and Police Performance," *Journal of Police and Criminal Psychology*, vol. 12 (1997), pp. 7–14; Thomas S. Whetstone, "Getting Stripes: Educational Achievement and Study Strategies Used by Sergeant Promotional Candidates," *American Journal of Criminal Justice*, vol. 24 (spring 2000), pp. 247–57; Elizabeth J. Shusman, Robin E. Inwald, and Hilary Knatz, "A Cross-Validation Study of Police Recruit Performance as Predicted by the IPI and MMPI," *Journal of Police Science and Administration* 15 (June 1987), pp. 162–68; Gerald Gruber, "The Police Applicant Test: A Predictive Validity Study," *Journal of Police Science and Administration* 14 (June 1986), pp. 121–29; George E. Hargrave and Deirdre Hiatt, "Law Enforcement Selection with the Interview, MMPI, and CPI: A Study of Reliability and Validity," *Journal of Police Science and Administration* 15 (June 1987), pp. 110–17; Anthony R. Moriarty and Mark W. Field, *Police Officer Selection* (Springfield, IL: Thomas, 1994).
40. Joseph Goldstein, "Police Discretion Not to Invoke the Criminal Process: Low-Visibility Decisions in the Administration of Justice," *Yale Law Journal* 69 (1960), p. 543.
41. Ibid., p. 580.
42. Nathan Goldman, *The Differential Selection of Juvenile Offenders for Court Appearance* (Hackensack, NJ: National Council on Crime and Delinquency, 1963).
43. Irving Piliavin and Scott Briar, "Police Encounters with Juveniles," *American Sociological Review* 70 (September 1964), pp. 206–14.
44. Donald J. Black and Albert J. Reiss, "Police Control of Juveniles," *American Sociological Review* 35 (1970), pp. 63–77.
45. Richard J. Lundman, Richard E. Sykes, and John P. Clark, "Police Control of Juveniles: A Replication," *Journal of Research in Crime and Delinquency* 15 (1978), pp. 74–91.
46. Robin S. Engel, James J. Sobol, and Robert E. Warden, "Further Exploration of the Demeanor Hypothesis: The Interaction Effects of Suspects' Characteristics and

Demeanor on Police Behavior," *Justice Quarterly*, vol. 17 (June 2000), pp. 235–58; David A. Klinger, "More on Demeanor and Arrest in Dade County," *Criminology* 34 (February 1996), pp. 61–82; Robert E. Worden and Robin L. Shephard, "Demeanor, Crime, and Police Behavior: A Reexamination of the Police Services Study Data," *Criminology* 34 (February 1996), pp. 83–105; Richard E. Sykes, James E. Fox, and John P. Clark, "A Socio-Legal Theory of Police Discretion," in Arthur Niederhoffer and Abraham Blumberg, eds., *The Ambivalent Force*, 2nd ed. (Hinsdale, IL: Dryden, 1976), pp. 171–83.

47. James O. Finckenauer, "Higher Education and Police Discretion," *Journal of Police Science and Administration* 3 (1975), pp. 450–65; Wayne R. LaFave, *Arrest: The Decision to Take a Suspect into Custody* (Boston: Little, Brown, 1965); James O. Finckenauer, "Some Factors in Police Discretion and Decisionmaking," *Journal of Criminal Justice* 4 (1976), pp. 29–46; Imogene L. Moyer, "Demeanor, Sex, and Race in Police Processing," *Journal of Criminal Justice* 9 (1981), pp. 235–46; Dennis D. Powell, "A Study of Police Discretion in Six Southern Cities," *Journal of Police Science and Administration* 17 (1990), pp. 1–7; Stephen D. Mastrofski, Robert E. Worden, and Jeffrey B. Snipes, "Law Enforcement in a Time of Community Policing," *Criminology* 33 (1995), pp. 539–63; David A. Klinger, "Demeanor or Crime?: Why 'Hostile' Citizens Are More Likely to Be Arrested," *Criminology* 32 (1994), pp. 475–93; Richard J. Lundman, "Demeanor or Crime?: The Midwest Police–Citizen Encounters Study," *Criminology* 32 (1994), pp. 631–56; Brad W. Smith, Kenneth J. Novak, James Frank, and Christopher Lowenkamp. "Explaining Police Officer Discretionary Activity," *Criminal Justice Review*, vol. 30 (December 2005), pp. 325–47; Claudia Mendias and E. James Kehoe, "Engagement of Policing Ideals and Their Relationship to the Exercise of Discretionary Powers," *Criminal Justice and Behavior*, vol. 33 (February 2006), pp. 70–93.
48. President's Commission on Law Enforcement and Administration of Justice, *Task Force Report on Police* (Washington, DC: U.S. Government Printing Office, 1967), p. 22.
49. President's Commission on Law Enforcement and Administration of Justice, *The Challenge of Crime in a Free Society* (Washington, DC: U.S. Government Printing Office, 1967), p. 103.
50. National Advisory Commission on Criminal Justice Standards and Goals, *Report on Police* (Washington, DC: U.S. Government Printing Office, 1973), p. 21.
51. American Bar Association, *The Urban Police Function* (Gaithersburg, MD: International Association of Chiefs of Police, 1974), p. 8.
52. President's Commission on Law Enforcement and Administration of Justice, *The Challenge of Crime in a Free Society*, p. 271; Lorne C. Kramer and Mora L. Fiedler, "Beyond the Numbers: How Law Enforcement Agencies Can Create Learning Environments and Measurement Systems," *The Police Chief*, vol. 69 (April 2002), p. 164.
53. David A. Klinger, "Negotiating Order in Patrol Work: An Ecological Theory of Police Response to Deviance," *Criminology* 35 (May 1997), pp. 277–306.
54. Don M. Gottfredson, Leslie T. Wilkins, and Peter B. Hoffman, *Guidelines for Parole and Sentencing Policy: A Policy Control Method* (Lexington, MA: Lexington Books, 1978).
55. *Sacramento v. Lewis*, 118 S. Ct. 1708 (1998); Nick Madigan, "Police Chases Scrutinized in Los Angeles after Death," *New York Times* (December 18, 2002).
56. Geoffrey P. Alpert, "Pursuit Driving: Planning Policies and Action from Agency, Officer, and Public Information," *Police Forum* (January 1997), pp. 1–12.
57. Alpert, "Pursuit Driving," p. 3; Caroline L. Curry, "Stop or I'll Sue! Police Chases and the Price Cities May Pay," *Arkansas Law Review*, vol. 55 (spring 2002), pp. 425–460.
58. Geoffrey P. Alpert, "Analyzing Police Pursuit," *Criminal Law Bulletin* 27 (July–August 1991), pp. 358–67.
59. *Pursuit Management Task Force* (Washington, DC: National Institute of Justice, 1998).
60. Geoffrey P. Alpert, *Helicopters in Pursuit Operations* (Washington, DC: National Institute of Justice, 1998).
61. Marianne W. Zawitz, ed., *Report to the Nation on Crime and Justice*, 2nd ed. (Washington, DC: Bureau of Justice Statistics, 1998).
62. Brian A. Reaves and Matthew J. Hickman, *Census of State and Local Law Enforcement Agencies* (Washington, DC: Bureau of Justice Statistics, 2002).
63. Peter Greenwood, Jan M. Chaiken, and Joan Petersilia, *The Criminal Investigation Process* (Lexington, MA: Lexington Books, 1977); John E. Eck, *Solving Crimes: The Investigation of Burglary and Robbery* (Washington, DC: Police Executive Research Forum, 1983).
64. Charles Wellford and James Cronin, "Homicide: What Police Can Do to Improve Clearance Rates," *National Institute of Justice Journal* (April 2000), pp. 2–7.
65. Thomas H. Cohen and Brian A. Reaves, *Felon Defendants in Large Urban Counties* (Washington, DC: Bureau of Justice Statistics, 2006). New York.
66. George Autunes and Eric J. Scott, "Calling the Cops: Police Telephone Operators and Citizen Calls for Service," *Journal of Criminal Justice* 9 (1981); David H. Bayley, *Police for the Future* (New York: Oxford University Press, 1994), ch. 2; Elaine Cumming, Ian Cumming, and Laura Edell, "Policemen as Philosopher, Guide and Friend," *Social Problems* 12 (1965).
67. William Spelman and John E. Eck, *Problem-Oriented Policing* (Washington, DC: National Institute of Justice, 1987); Michael D. Reisig and Roger B. Parks, *Satisfaction with Police: What Matters?* (Washington, DC: National Institute of Justice 2002); Rachel Boba, *Problem Analysis in Policing* (Washington, DC: Police Foundation, 2003).
68. Lorraine Green Mazerolle and William Terrill, "Problem-Oriented Policing in Public Housing: Identifying the Distribution of Problem Places," *Policing: An International Journal of Police Strategies and Management* 20 (1997), pp. 235–55; Richard H. Ward, "On the Cutting Edge: Policing Research Shows Changes," *Criminal Justice: The Americas* 1 (August–September, 1988), p. 1.
69. Warren Cohen, "The Feds Make a Cop Drug Bust," *U.S. News & World Report* (February 2, 1998), p. 36; Kevin Johnson, "42 Law Officers Arrested in Sting," *USA Today* (January 22, 1998), p. 3; Sanja Kutnjak Ivkovic, "To Serve and Collect: Measuring Police Corruption," *Journal of Criminal Law and Criminology*, vol. 93 (winter–spring 2003), p. 593; John Marzulli, "Mafia Cops Will Die Behind Bars," *New York Daily News* (June 6, 2006).
70. Mark Pogrebin and Burton Atkins, "Probable Causes for Police Corruption: Some Theories," *Journal of Criminal Justice* 4 (1976), pp. 9–16; Samuel Walker, *The Police in America* (New York: McGraw-Hill, 1983).

71. Herman Goldstein, *Policing in a Free Society* (Cambridge, MA: Ballinger, 1977); Virgil Peterson, "The Chicago Police Scandals," *Atlantic* (October 1960), pp. 58–64; Howard S. Cohen and Michael Feldberg, *Power and Restraint: The Moral Dimension of Police Work* (New York: Praeger, 1991); Edwin J. Delattre, *Character and Cops: Ethics in Policing*, 2nd ed. (Washington, DC: AEI Press, 1994); Steve Herbert, "Morality in Law Enforcement: Chasing 'Bad Guys' with the Los Angeles Police Department," *Law and Society Review* 30 (1996), pp. 799–817.
72. Gordon Witkin, "When the Bad Guys Are Cops," *Newsweek* (September 11, 1995), pp. 20–22; Mike McAlary, *Good Cop Bad Cop* (New York: Pocket Books, 1994).
73. Walker, *The Police in America*, p. 181.
74. Witkin, "When the Bad Guys are Cops," pp. 20–22; Tom Morganthau, "Why Good Cops Go Bad," *Newsweek* (December 19, 1994), p. 34.
75. Knapp Commission, *Report on Police Corruption* (New York: Braziller, 1972), p. 6.
76. Michael Hedges, "Lawbreakers among Law Enforcers," *Richmond Times–Dispatch* (August 10, 1999), p. 3.
77. John Kleinig, *The Ethics of Policing* (New York: Cambridge University Press, 1996).
78. Witkin, p. 22; Andrew Blankstein, "Deputies Code of Silence Targeted," *Los Angeles Times* (October 30, 2003).
79. William A. Westley, *Violence and the Police* (Cambridge, MA: MIT Press, 1970).
80. Carl B. Klockars, Sanja Kutnjak Ivkovich, William E. Harver, and Maria R. Haberfeld, *The Measurement of Police Integrity* (Washington, DC: National Institute of Justice, 2000), p. 9.
81. Albert J. Reiss, *Police and the Public* (New Haven: Yale University Press, 1971); J. Roebuck and T. Barker, "A Typology of Police Corruption," *Social Problems* 21 (1974), pp. 423–27; E. Stoddard, "The Informal Code of Police Deviancy: Group Approach to Blue Coat Crime," *Journal of Criminal Law, Criminology, and Police Science* 59 (1968), pp. 201–13.
82. Pennsylvania Crime Commission, *Report on Police Corruption and the Quality of Law Enforcement in Philadelphia* (St. Davids: Pennsylvania Crime Commission, 1974).
83. Morganthau, "Why Good Cops Go Bad," p. 34.
84. U.S. Comptroller General, *Information on Drug-Related Police Corruption* (Washington, DC: U.S. General Accounting Office, 1998).
85. James Sterngold, "Police Corruption Inquiry Expands in Los Angeles," *New York Times* (February 11, 2000), p. A16; "L. A. Mayor: Use Tobacco Funds to Pay Police Suits," *USA Today* (February 18, 2000), p. 3; Patrick McGreevy, "LAPD Faces 3 More Years of Scrutiny," *Los Angeles Times* (May 16, 2006).
86. William Chambliss and R. Seidman, *Law, Order and Power* (Reading, MA: Addison-Wesley, 1971), p. 490.
87. Lawrence W. Sherman, *Scandal and Reform: Controlling Police Corruption* (Berkeley: University of California Press, 1978), p. 35.
88. John A. Gardiner, *The Politics of Corruption: Organized Crime in an American City* (New York: Russell Sage, 1970); Chambliss and Seidman, *Law, Order, and Power;* Knapp Commission, *Report on Police Corruption.*
89. Dirk Johnson, "Popular Detective Will Head Chicago Police," *New York Times* (February 19, 1998), p. 2.
90. B. Drummond Ayres, Jr., "Former New York Official to Lead Philadelphia Police," *New York Times* (February 19, 1998), p. 16; M. L. Elrick and Ben Schmitt, "U.S. Plans to Oversee Detroit Cops," *Detroit Free Press* (June 11, 2003).
91. Knapp Commission, *Report on Police Corruption*, p. 68.
92. Ibid., p. 18.
93. Edward A. Malloy, *The Ethics of Law Enforcement and Criminal Punishment* (Lanham, MD: University Press of America, 1982), p. 45.
94. Gerald D. Robin, "Justifiable Homicide by Police Officers," *Journal of Criminal Law, Criminology, and Police Science* (June 1963), pp. 225–31; Arthur L. Kobler, "Police Homicide in a Democracy," *Journal of Social Issues* 31 (1975), pp. 163–91; Cynthia G. Sulton and Phillip Cooper, "Summary of Research on the Police Use of Deadly Force," in Robert N. Brenner and Marjorie Kravitz, eds., *A Community Concern: Police Use of Deadly Force* (Washington, DC: U.S. Government Printing Office, 1979).
95. Anthony M. Pate and Lorie A. Fridell, *Police Use of Force: Official Reports, Citizens Complaints, and Legal Consequences* (Washington, DC: Police Foundation, 1993).
96. Lawrence W. Sherman and Robert H. Langworthy, "Measuring Homicide by Police Officers," *Journal of Criminal Law and Criminology* (winter 1979), pp. 546–60; Tom McEwen, *National Data Collection on Police Use of Force* (Washington, DC: Bureau of Justice Statistics, 1996); Roger Roy, "Killings by Police Under-reported," *Orlando Sentinel* (May 24, 2004).
97. Lawrence A. Greenfield, Matthew R. Durose, Erica L. Schmitt, and Patrick A. Langan, *Contacts between Police and the Public: Findings from the 2002 National Survey* (Washington, DC: Bureau of Justice Statistics, 2005).
98. James J. Fyfe, *Shots Fired: An Examination of New York City Police Firearms Discharges* (Albany: State University of New York at Albany Ph.D. Dissertation, 1978); Richard W. Harding and Richard P. Fahey, "Killings by Chicago Police," *Southern California Law Review* (March 1973), pp. 284–315; Marshall W. Meyer, "Police Shooting at Minorities: The Case of Los Angeles," *The Annals* (November 1980), pp. 98–110; C. H. Milton, J. W. Hallack, J. Lardner, and G. L. Abrecht, *Police Use of Deadly Force* (Washington, DC: Police Foundation, 1977); Robin, "Justifiable Homicide."
99. Arnold Binder and Peter Scharf, "Deadly Force in Law Enforcement," *Crime and Delinquency* 28 (January 1982), pp. 1–23.
100. Kenneth Adams, "What We Know about Police Use of Force," in *Use of Force by Police* (Washington, DC: National Institute of Justice, 1999); Joel Garner, John Buchanan, Tom Schade, and John Hepburn, *Understanding the Use of Force by and against Police* (Washington, DC: National Institute of Justice, 1996); Geoffrey P. Alpert and Roger G. Dunham, *Understanding Police Use of Force: Officers, Suspects, and Reciprocity* (New York: Cambridge University Press, 2004).
101. Mark Blumberg, "Race and Police Shootings: An Analysis in Two Cities," in James J. Fyfe, ed., *Contemporary Issues in Law Enforcement* (Beverly Hills, CA: Sage, 1981); James J. Fyfe, "Blind Justice: Police Shootings in Memphis," *Journal of Criminal Law and Criminology* 83 (summer 1982).
102. Jerome H. Skolnick and James J. Fyfe, *Above the Law: Police and the Excessive Use of Force* (New York: Free Press, 1993); William A. Geller and Hans Toch, eds., *And Justice for All: Understanding and Controlling Police Abuse of Force* (Washington, DC: Police Executive Research Forum, 1995); Geoffrey P. Alpert and Lorie A. Fridell, *Police Vehicles and Firearms: Instruments of Deadly Force* (Prospect Heights, IL: Waveland Press, 1992).

103. Mark Blumberg, "Research on Police Use of Deadly Force: The State of the Art," in Abraham Blumberg and Elaine Niederhoffer, eds., *The Ambivalent Force: Perspectives on the Police*, 3rd ed. (New York: Holt, Rinehart, and Winston, 1985), p. 344.
104. U.S. Comptroller General, *Taser Weapons: Use of Tasers by Selected Law Enforcement Agencies* (Washington, DC: U.S. General Accountability Office, 2005); Mark Sherman, "Amnesty International U.S. Taser Deaths Up," *Washington Post* (March 28, 2006).
105. Lawrence W. Sherman, "Execution without Trial: Police Homicide and the Constitution," *Vanderbilt Law Review* (January 1980), pp. 71–100; Geoffrey P. Alpert and Roger G. Dunham, *Understanding Police Use of Force: Officers, Suspects, and Reciprocity* (New York: Cambridge University Press, 2004).
106. James J. Fyfe, "Observations on Police Deadly Force," *Crime and Delinquency* 27 (July 1981), pp. 376–89; Brenner and Kravitz, eds., *A Community Concern.*
107. Fyfe, 1981, p. 381.
108. *Tennessee v. Garner,* 105 S. Ct. 1694 (1985).
109. Skolnick and Fyfe, *Above the Law;* James J. Fyfe, "Police Use of Deadly Force: Research and Reform," *Justice Quarterly* 5 (June 1988), pp. 165–205; U.S. Comptroller General, *Use of Force* (Washington, DC: U.S. General Accounting Office, 1996).
110. Lance Morrow, "Rough Justice," *Time* (April 1, 1991), pp. 16–17; Richard Lacayo, "Law and Disorder," *Time* (April 1, 1991), pp. 18–21.
111. Kit R. Roane, "Are Police Going Too Far?," *U.S. News & World Report* (February 7, 2000), p. 25.
112. Ibid.; Nicholas Stix, "Liberal Community Activists Attack Aggressive, 'Racist' Police as the Enemy in Crime-Ridden Cities," *Insight on the News* (April 26, 1999), p. 29; John O'Sullivan, "Black and Blue: New York Erupts over a Race-Tinged Killing—Again," *National Review* (April 19, 1999), p. 33; David Dante Troutt, "Screws, Koon, and Routine Aberrations: The Use of Fictional Narratives in Federal Police Brutality Prosecutions," *New York University Law Review* 74 (April 1999), pp. 18–122.
113. Joel H. Garner and Christopher D. Maxwell, "Measuring the Amount of Force Used by and against the Police in Six Jurisdictions," in *Use of Force by Police* (Washington, DC: National Institute of Justice, 1999).
114. Geoffrey P. Alpert and Roger G. Dunham, "The Force Factor: Measuring and Assessing Police Use of Force and Suspect Resistance," in *Use of Force by Police* (Washington, DC: National Institute of Justice, 1999).
115. *Graham v. Connor,* 490 U.S. 396 (1989).
116. David Weisburd and Rosann Greenspan with Edwin E. Hamilton, Hubert Williams, and Kellie A. Bryant, *Police Attitudes toward Abuse of Authority: Findings from a National Study* (Washington, DC: National Institute of Justice, 2000); David C. Anderson, *Managed Force* (Ford Foundation, 2003).

chapter 10

Origins and Organization of the Courts

Adjudicating offenders: the structure and process by which we determine whether suspects are offenders and what should be done with them.

CHAPTER OUTLINE

LEARNING OBJECTIVES

- Trace significant trends in the development of criminal courts in the United States.
- Explain the origins and political contexts of the state and federal court systems.
- Compare and contrast the types of federal and state courts and their jurisdictions.
- Differentiate the role of the U.S. Supreme Court in the American court system.
- Describe the participants in the judicial process and their roles in criminal court.
- Identify and discuss issues in the roles of prosecuting attorneys and defense counsel.
- Explain how judges are selected and their role in criminal court.
- Identify and discuss issues in the roles of victims and witnesses in the criminal justice process.
- Analyze the roles of juries and courtroom work groups in the criminal justice process.
- Define and describe some alternatives to the criminal court system.
- Evaluate the appropriateness and effectiveness of specialized courts and community-based adjudication.

Timothy McVeigh was convicted for bombing the Oklahoma City federal office building, a crime that killed 168 people. This shocking case of domestic terrorism, the worst in U.S. history at that time, provoked nationwide grief and anger—as well as fear that it was part of a larger criminal conspiracy. The Washington, D.C.–area snipers held the entire region in fear for two months during 2002 while innocent victims were shot at random in a motiveless murder spree. The trial of former Enron executives in 2006 involved one of the biggest business scandals in U.S. history, as the nation's seventh-largest company was driven into bankruptcy due to corrupt mismanagement by the company's leadership. These cases were a challenge to the U.S. court system, which is mandated to prosecute, defend, and adjudicate objectively cases that were on the front page of newspapers and in countless television reports for weeks. How do U.S. courts come to fair and impartial decisions in sensational cases such as these?

How Were Criminal Courts Similar and Different in the Past?

Of the more than 14 million arrests made in the United States each year, far fewer than 1 percent are for murder. The overwhelming majority of court cases involve misdemeanors, because those are the offenses that are most often committed and for which suspects are most often arrested. If we examine the historical record of both misdemeanor and felony trials and compare it to contemporary court proceedings, we find both striking similarities and significant differences.

THE SIMPSON AND RING TRIALS

For example, compare the O.J. Simpson case with one that occurred two centuries ago. In 1995 O.J. Simpson, a successful and popular former football player, was charged with brutally killing his estranged wife and another man with a knife. There was circumstantial evidence, such as shoe prints and blood, that tended to incriminate him. On the other hand, there were no eyewitnesses; no murder weapon was recovered; there was no apparent motive; and questions were raised about whether the physical evidence had been tampered with. The O.J. Simpson case was unique in many ways. Most notably, it is rare for such a popular celebrity to be a defendant in a murder trial. It is also rare to have so little conclusive physical evidence linking a particular person with a murder of this nature.

In the year 1800 the body of Gulielma Sands was found in a well. Her cousin, Catherine Ring, was suspected of the crime because she lived with Sands. A coroner had concluded that the death was due to willful murder, and there were no other suspects. Ring was indicted for the crime, but she had an alibi and the assistance of a "dream team" of defense attorneys that included Alexander Hamilton and Aaron Burr, who were among the most well-known Americans at that time. It was a long trial involving seventy-five witnesses. The trial procedure was similar to today's procedure, though less cumbersome; and, in a striking similarity to the Simpson case, the jury returned a verdict of acquittal in five minutes.[1] The historical record shows that both the Ring and Simpson trials are atypical, because murders are uncommon, murder trials are rare, and long, celebrated murder cases are rarer still.

INFORMAL ADJUDICATION

A major difference between trials today and trials in earlier centuries is the absence of lawyers in most trials in times past, even in felony trials. Defense attorneys were not required in most types of cases until 1963, when the U.S. Supreme Court ruled in *Gideon v. Wainwright* that indigent defendants charged with felonies were guaranteed the right to an attorney at trial—a right that has since been expanded to most other stages of criminal procedure. It took the Supreme Court nearly 200 years to interpret the Sixth Amendment "right to counsel" as applying to all defendants, even poor ones. Most earlier trials, for both felonies and misdemeanors, took place without the accused being represented by a lawyer.

Misdemeanor cases historically have tended to be handled in an "amateur" or nonprofessional fashion. As in today's TV *People's Court* and *Judge Judy* series, individuals, often neighbors, brought small claims against one another without benefit of legal counsel on either side. Minor criminal cases were treated the same way until the late twentieth century. A century ago many cities had local aldermen or justices of the peace who would hear and decide cases for a fee. Their role was similar to that of today's local judges, except that aldermen were untrained in the law and were not paid a salary. As one historian has written, "In some ways a [minor] criminal case was not much more than a civil suit with a government subsidy." And although there was no such penalty as banishment, the historical record has frequent references to local alderman and magistrates telling minor offenders to "get out of town."[2]

The nature of justice was indeed informal in cases involving minor crimes; and in many ways this is still true, although the presence of legal counsel in these cases has expanded dramatically since the 1960s. In typical felony cases (robbery, burglary, larceny, and assault), however, the court system has always been more formal and the criminal procedure more elaborate. The United States initially modeled its grand jury system on England's, which required that a group of citizens find probable cause before a felony case could go to trial. This rule resulted in greater deliberation on the merits of a case. Since then, the U.S. Supreme Court has granted states the right to determine probable cause using other procedures, such as preliminary hearings.[3] Thus, the right to a trial by jury is guaranteed in the Bill of Rights but until recently was reserved for serious cases.

THE MERITS OF A CASE

Historically, juries consisted of white males. Even after the Civil War, some states excluded blacks from juries until the U.S. Supreme Court specifically ruled against this practice in 1879.[4] In the past, as today, people generally were reluctant to serve on juries. Historical records reveal that people have routinely attempted to evade jury service despite believing that a jury system is fundamental to fair trial.[5]

THE ROLE OF DEFENDANTS

Another change is the role of the defendant in criminal cases. Until the late 1800s defendants had no say in their own cases. Defendants could not act as witnesses or take the stand in their own defense. Beginning just over a century ago, both the states and the federal government permitted defendants to testify under oath. This made the role of defendants and defense counsel more significant, because a defendant could take an active role rather than being limited to reacting indirectly to prosecution's allegations. Today, defendants are expected to testify and those who do not are often seen as having something to hide.

How Did the State and Federal Court Systems Develop?

Before the nation's founding, each colony had its own court system. Under the Constitution the states retained significant powers, including the powers to create, enforce, and apply laws. During the colonial period punishments generally were more severe, and the death penalty was permitted for virtually all felonies, including crimes such as stealing crops, sacrilege, sodomy, and trading with Indians.[6] The severity of punishment may have stemmed both from the uncertainty and dangerousness of frontier life and from the association of crime with sin. Civil laws often were used to enforce moral and religious behavior. Fines and imprisonment also were used to punish blasphemy, failure to attend church, and violation of accepted religious practices.

LEGITIMACY OF A LAW

During the American Revolution the courts increasingly were used as a forum to dispute "unjust" laws imposed by England, such as laws that taxed the colonies for paper, tea, various other imports, and trade with non-English nations. Because of shortages of desired goods and the high prices people had to pay when these goods were obtained by legitimate means, smuggling became common. Customs officials often were harassed, threatened, and beaten, but few juries were willing to convict alleged assailants. It was argued in court that taxation on the colonies without representation in the British Parliament was unjust. Unlike juries today, juries at that time were permitted to address the legitimacy of a law rather than the illegal act alone.[7] The establishment of the United States in the late eighteenth century, the rapid growth of a population that included immigrants from many nations, and rapid urbanization created a need for more courts with specialized tasks. Differing legal and social cultures often clashed, requiring court systems to decide disputes neutrally.

POLITICAL PATRONAGE

Although courts were designed as a means to obtain neutral and nonpolitical judgments on the application of the law in practice, this has not always been the case. Political influence in judicial appointments and the long terms of many judges have permitted them to have personal impact on how the law is applied. Unlike legislators, who attempt to effect change slowly by developing consensus among a large body of colleagues, judges with long terms "have the time and opportunity to address many issues and evolve a coherent and distinctive point of view."[8] For example, the U.S. Supreme Court in a 1999 case granted broad discretion to all federal judges to exclude from trial any "expert witnesses" they believe are not relevant or whose testimony does not depend on a reliable foundation.[9] An **expert witness** is a person called to testify because of his or her special expertise in an area at issue in the case. This court decision arose from a case involving testimony of a "tire failure expert" whose opinions about the connections between tire design flaws and a fatal accident was questioned. Although this decision aims to keep "junk science" out of the courtroom, it places a technical or scientific judgment in the hands of a judge to determine its relevance and reliability.[10] This potential influence on the types of evidence that can be heard in court and on trial outcomes has resulted in growing political interest in the views of judicial nominees prior to their appointment in an attempt to predict how they might decide on legal issues they will face. Therefore, courts increasingly are seen as "mechanisms of power, personnel, patronage and public image," where rulings are seen in personal, social, and political context instead of being viewed as objective rulings on legal issues.[11]

expert witness
A person called to testify because of his or her special expertise in an area at issue in a legal proceeding.

State Court Systems

The majority of criminal cases are heard in state courts, because most felonies are defined by state laws. For example, murder generally is a violation of state law—unless one kills the President of the United States. Robbery also is a violation of state law, unless it is a robbery of a federally insured bank. In these cases, the murder or robbery would be adjudicated in a federal court as a violation of federal law. As you read in Chapter 3, the definitions of murder, robbery, and other crimes are quite similar among the states, but often there are significant differences as

FIGURE 10.1 Virginia Court Structure

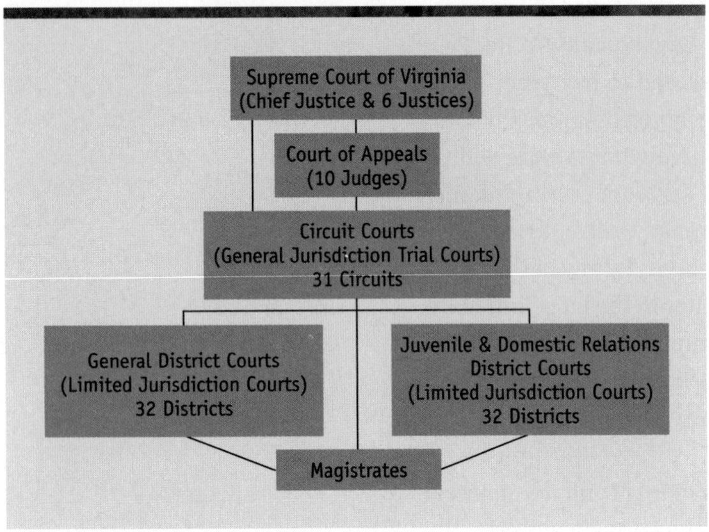

Source: http://www.courts.state.va.us/cib/cib.htm

well: in the variations and degrees of these crimes, in aggravating or mitigating circumstances, and in the penalties that may be imposed. These differences are permitted under the Tenth Amendment to the Constitution, which grants police power to the states.

STATE COURTS INTERPRET STATE LAW

State courts interpret only state law. Courts in all states are organized in a similar manner, with three levels of jurisdiction: limited, general, and appellate. Each state determines how its system is organized, however, so the names of the state courts and their precise jurisdictions vary.

As an example, Figure 10.1 diagrams the court system in the Commonwealth of Virginia. Cases flow from the lower courts (at the bottom of the diagram) up through the court of last resort. General district courts and juvenile and domestic relations courts have restricted jurisdiction over a specific range of matters; circuit courts are the general trial courts; and the court of appeals and Supreme Court of Virginia are the two appellate courts in the state.

MUNICIPAL COURTS

Limited and General Jurisdictions In all states, the lowest (i.e., most restricted) courts are the courts of limited jurisdiction, such as municipal courts. Their legal authority is restricted to certain specific types of cases. For example, small claims courts hear only civil cases involving amounts less than $10,000. Surrogate courts hear cases involving probate of wills and administration of estates. Family courts hear matters involving children and the family, such as cases of juvenile delinquency, child protection, status offenders, foster care placement, paternity suits, family offenses, support of dependent relatives, and adoptions. Municipal courts include all city, town, village, and district courts. These courts handle trials for minor criminal and civil cases, traffic and motor vehicle violations, and ordinance violations, and conduct probable cause hearings for felonies. Each type of limited jurisdiction court is permitted to hear only a narrow range of alleged offenses involving mostly civil cases.

TRIAL COURTS

Courts of general jurisdiction often are referred to as trial courts. Most felony trials are held at this level. In sixteen states general jurisdiction courts are called circuit courts. Fifteen states call them district courts, twelve call them superior courts, and the balance use a combination of names or other names. Each county usually has one felony court, making a nationwide total of more than 3,200.[12] General jurisdiction courts hear felony trials and civil suits involving amounts that are too large to be handled in small claims court. There are more than 9,000 full-time judges serving in general jurisdiction courts.

TWO TYPES OF APPELLATE COURTS

Appellate Courts At the highest level of state court systems are appellate courts, which hear appeals from courts of general jurisdiction. Appellate courts usually have a panel of three to ten judges (justices) who hear arguments in cases that are referred to them from lower courts. There are two types of appellate courts: courts of last resort and intermediate appellate courts. Courts of last resort, usually called supreme courts, have final jurisdiction over appeals and are usually provided for in a state's constitution. Intermediate appellate courts were developed over the last hundred years to relieve the burden of so many appeals to the courts of last resort. Thirty-four states have one intermediate court of appeal, five have two courts of this kind, while eleven states have no intermediate court of appeal. Appellate courts hear arguments on specific legal issues that arise in trial courts. If a significant error was made in law or procedure, the trial court finding is set aside, and the case often is sent back to the trial court for reconsideration. People convicted of crimes have a right to appeal and some appeals are mandatory (such as in death penalty cases). For example, in the *Miranda* case the appellate courts heard arguments about whether or not the defendant's confession was obtained voluntarily. Other aspects of the case that were part of the trial were not reconsidered, because they were not a basis for the appeal. If the justices of an appellate court believe an error was made in law or procedure in a court of general jurisdiction, they refer the case back to that court for retrial.

The Federal Court System

EXAMPLES OF FEDERAL COURTS

The federal court system parallels the state court systems. Federal courts exist at three levels of jurisdiction, but they hear only cases involving alleged violations of federal laws. In most cases federal laws are designed to adjudicate misconduct that occurs in more than one state. Interstate transportation of stolen property, kidnapping across state lines, and some forms of drug trafficking are examples. Figure 10.2 diagrams the federal court system in the United States. As in state courts, there is a case flow from courts of limited jurisdiction to courts of general jurisdiction to appellate courts.

FIGURE 10.2 The Federal Court System

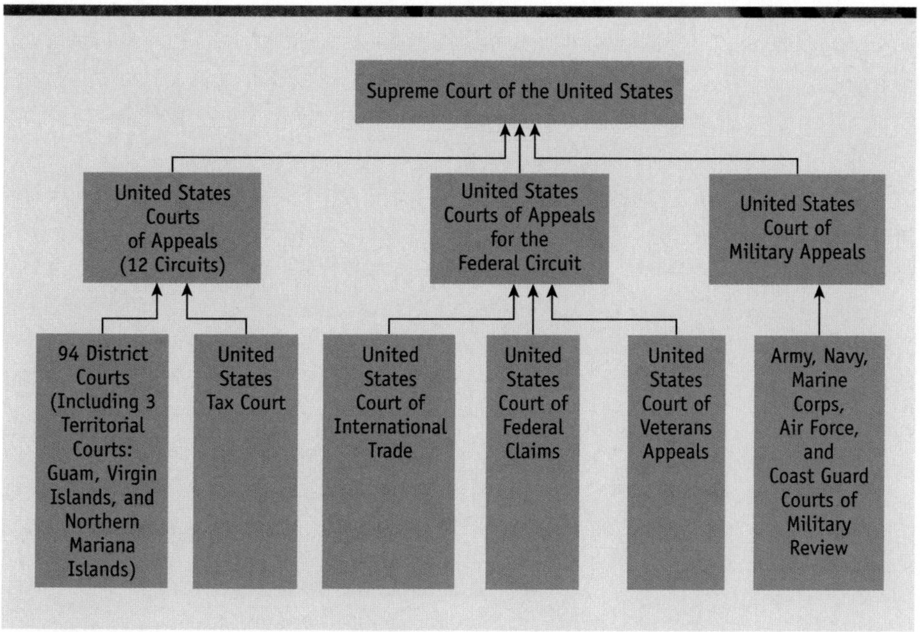

Source: http://www.uscourts.gov/understanding_courts/gifs/figure1.gif

The U.S. Court of Claims and the U.S. Tax Court are examples of federal courts. The titles of these courts indicate their limited jurisdictions. Many of these courts were created by Congress and are therefore called legislative courts. Congress has greater control over courts it has created than over courts created by the Constitution. The jurisdiction of legislative courts and the terms of office for judges can be changed by an act of Congress. In constitutional courts, in contrast, the authority of the courts does not rely on legislative acts.

U.S. district courts Federal trial courts of general jurisdiction.

District Courts and Courts of Appeals The federal courts of general jurisdiction are the **U.S. district courts.** These courts have unlimited jurisdiction in both civil and criminal matters, and most federal trials are conducted in them. The trials in the Oklahoma City bombing case occurred in a U.S. district court, because the bombing was an attack on a federal building and resulted in the death of federal agents. In addition, district courts also hear appeals from the courts of limited jurisdiction. There are ninety-four U.S. district courts in the United States, with at least one in each state. They can hear cases involving alleged violations of federal law wherever they may occur. Larger states may have several federal district courts.

U.S. courts of appeals Intermediate federal appellate courts.

Above the courts of general jurisdiction are the appellate courts. In the federal system, as in many states, there are two levels of appellate courts. The first level is the intermediate appellate court, which reviews judgments handed down in the federal trial courts. These intermediate appellate courts are the **U.S. courts of appeals.** There are thirteen of these courts, located in federal judicial districts throughout the United States. Figure 10.3 illustrates the composition of the fed-

FIGURE 10.3 The Number and Composition of Federal Judicial Circuits

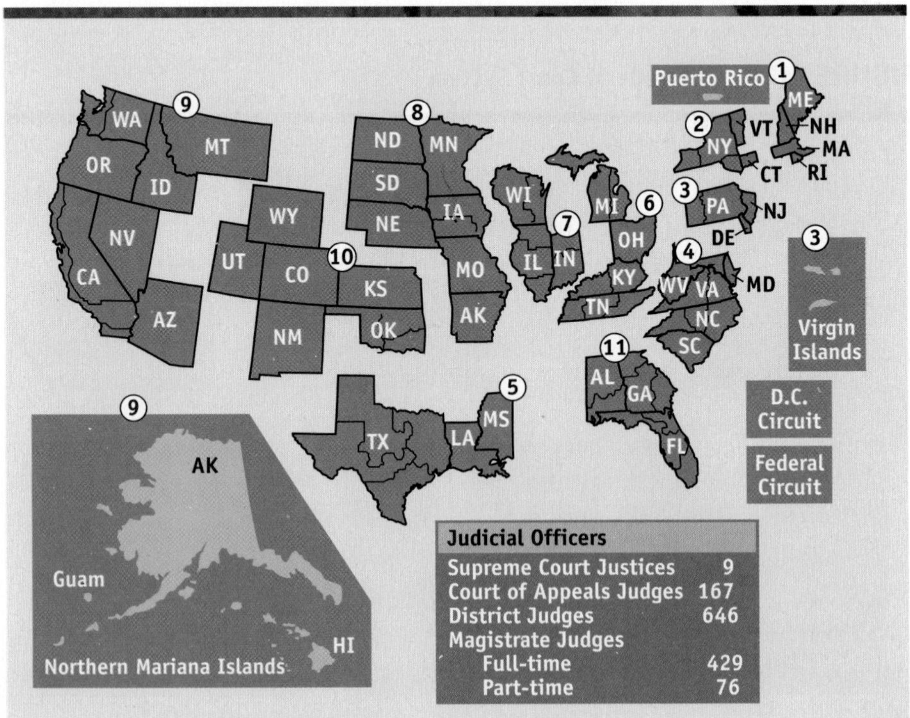

Source: http://www.uscourts.gov/understanding_courts/gifs/map.gif

eral judicial districts or circuits. Each district groups three or more states, and all federal appeals from those states are directed to the court of appeals in that circuit. The courts of appeals were created in 1891 to take some of the burden off the nation's court of last resort, the U.S. Supreme Court.

The U.S. Supreme Court The **U.S. Supreme Court** can hear on appeal any case involving federal law, suits between states, and cases involving interpretations of the U.S. Constitution. This judicial power comes from Article III of the U.S. Constitution, which itemizes the types of cases in which the U.S. Supreme Court has original jurisdiction (e.g., suits in which states are parties) and appellate jurisdiction (e.g., most other kinds of cases arising from law violations).The decisions of the U.S. Supreme Court cannot be appealed further, and the Supreme Court also can choose *not* to review a case if it so desires. In fact, of the more than 5,000 cases that reach the U.S. Supreme Court each year, more than three-fourths are not heard. When this happens, the previous court's ruling stands as the final decision.

U.S. Supreme Court
The highest court in the United States, which hears final appeals in cases involving federal law, suits between states, and interpretations of the U.S. Constitution.

ARTICLE III

There are four types of cases in which the U.S. Supreme Court *must* render an opinion, and all involve interpretations of the U.S. Constitution:

FOUR TYPES OF CONSTITUTIONAL CASES

1. When an act of Congress has been found unconstitutional in a lower federal court
2. When a state supreme court has found a federal law unconstitutional
3. When a U.S. court of appeals has found a state law unconstitutional
4. When a constitutional challenge of a state law has been upheld by a state supreme court

The U.S. Supreme Court's ability to choose which cases it will hear is known as certiorari. This term is derived from the **writ of certiorari,** which is a legal order from the U.S. Supreme Court stating that a lower court must "forward the record" of a particular case for review. Such a writ is issued when four or more justices on the U.S. Supreme Court believe that the legal issues presented in the case merit review.

writ of certiorari
A legal order from the U.S. Supreme Court stating that a lower court must forward the record of a particular case for review.

The decisions of the Supreme Court are made by a majority vote of the nine justices, who are appointed for life by the president with the consent of the Senate. The far-reaching powers of the Supreme Court were not included in Article III of the U.S. Constitution, which created the Court. The powers were established in the 1803 case of *Marbury v. Madison,* in which the Court claimed the authority to review the constitutionality of acts of Congress.[13] After Thomas Jefferson defeated incumbent John Adams in the presidential election of 1800, the Congress and President Adams created many new federal judgeships, appointed new judges, and reduced the number of U.S. Supreme Court justices. This partisan strategy limited Jefferson's ability to appoint judges of his own choosing when he took office. Chief Justice John Marshall led the U.S. Supreme Court in ruling that Congress had exceeded its power, however, and had acted unconstitutionally. This case established the principle known as **judicial review** of legislative acts. The *Marbury* ruling is considered one of the most significant court decisions in U.S. history, for it specifies how the balance of powers operates and clarifies the extent of the Supreme Court's authority.

MARBURY V. MADISON

judicial review
The U.S. Supreme Court's authority to review the constitutionality of acts of Congress.

Who Are the Participants in the Judicial Process?

The court system lies at the heart of the American system of justice. It is through the judicial process and the courts that police, prosecutors, and victims square off against defendants and defense counsel to determine liability for crimes. Before a case comes to trial, only allegations and suspected crimes exist. The only proof required to initiate a trial is probable cause. The probable cause requirement is set forth in the Fourth Amendment to the Constitution, which was added to protect the privacy of citizens from warrantless searches. To convict a defendant at trial, however, prosecution must meet a higher standard of proof, usually requiring the concurrence of a jury. The purpose of this higher standard is to ensure that only those who in fact *are* guilty are punished, not those who we believe *might be* guilty. A higher standard of proof also maintains public confidence in the accuracy and fairness of the system and of the government it represents.

PARTICIPANTS IN THE JUDICIAL PROCESS

Five main groups of participants in the judicial process are prosecutors, defense counsel and defendants, judges, victims and witnesses, and juries. The roles of these participants and their interactions determine the nature and quality of the justice that results from the adjudication process. It is important, therefore, to understand how these participants can and should convict the guilty, exonerate the innocent, and protect the community.

Prosecutors

prosecutors
Elected or appointed officials who represent the community in bringing charges against an accused person.

Prosecutors also are called district, county, state, commonwealth, or U.S. attorneys, depending on the jurisdiction. Whatever the title, the task of prosecutors is the same: to represent the community in bringing charges against an accused person. The job of the prosecutor is constrained by political factors, caseloads, and relationships with other actors in the adjudication process.

CONSTRAINTS ON PROSECUTORS

First, most prosecutors are elected (although some are appointed by the governor), so it is in their interests to make "popular" prosecution decisions—and in some cases these may run counter to the ideals of justice. For example, prosecution "to the full extent of the law" of a college student caught possessing a small amount of marijuana may be unwarranted, but failure to prosecute may be used by political opponents as evidence that the prosecutor is "soft on crime." Likewise, a prosecutor may not believe that a first offender deserves the maximum penalty for a robbery or assault, but uninformed public or political pressure may encourage the prosecutor to pursue the maximum sentence anyway. Thus, a prosecutor must be able to deal effectively with demands for action that may not be in the best interests of justice. As the standards of the American Bar Association state, the "duty of the prosecutor is to seek justice, not merely convict."[14]

A second constraint on the job of prosecutor is caseload pressures, which often force prosecutors to make decisions based on expediency rather than justice. A prosecutor in a jurisdiction where many serious crimes occur may have to choose which cases to prosecute to the full extent of the law and which ones to plea-bargain (as discussed in Chapter 11). There may not be enough prosecutors

A prosecutor argues a case to a jury. Who does the prosecutor represent? Is it the prosecutor's role to portray the facts in a certain way, win the case, or do justice?

to handle all the cases being filed in criminal court. Therefore, priorities must be set, meaning that some cases will be given superficial attention in order to free prosecutors to focus more fully on others. The result is that violent crimes, which are relatively rare, usually receive full attention, whereas the more common crimes against property are handled outside the courtroom in plea bargains. Caseload problems can lead to accusations of "assembly-line justice," in which cases often end in reduced sentences.

GOOD RELATIONSHIPS

Third, prosecutors must maintain good relationships with the other participants in the adjudication process: police, judges, juries, defense attorneys, victims, and witnesses. Cases typically are brought to prosecutors by the police, and police officers usually serve as witnesses. Prosecutors need the police to provide valid evidence and to serve as reliable witnesses. Cases in which the evidence is weak ultimately result in dismissal or acquittal, so prosecutors must work closely with police to ensure that time and effort is not wasted by either party. Prosecutors also need judges to rule on the admissibility of evidence, to decide guilt or innocence in nonjury trials, and to follow their recommendations in sentencing decisions. Prosecutors must maintain good relationships with defense counsel, because most cases end in plea bargains and both sides must be willing to reach an agreement. Prosecutors also must communicate well with juries, victims, and witnesses. Victims and witnesses provide evidence that may be crucial in determining guilt or innocence; so it is important that they understand the judicial process, are forewarned about what they may face in court, and receive support throughout the process.

The Prosecutor's Role The prosecutor is the only actor in the criminal justice system who is involved in all aspects of criminal justice processing from arrest through disposition. Prosecutors make decisions that greatly affect the outcome of a case. The scope of prosecutors' discretion is rarely defined by statute, but it dramatically affects the operation of the criminal justice system.

PROSECUTORS REPRESENT THE PUBLIC

Whether they work at the federal, state, or county level, prosecutors represent the public in their actions. Because violations of the criminal law are crimes against society, prosecutors represent their jurisdictions, not the victims or other individuals. Federal prosecutors are called U.S. attorneys; state prosecutors are called state, district, or commonwealth attorneys; and local prosecutors are called **district attorneys** or county prosecutors. Most prosecutions are conducted at the state or county level. Of the more than one million felony convictions each year in the United States, only about 6 percent occur in federal courts.[15]

district attorneys
The name for city and county prosecutors in many jurisdictions.

FIGURE 10.4 Total Staff in Prosecutors' Offices

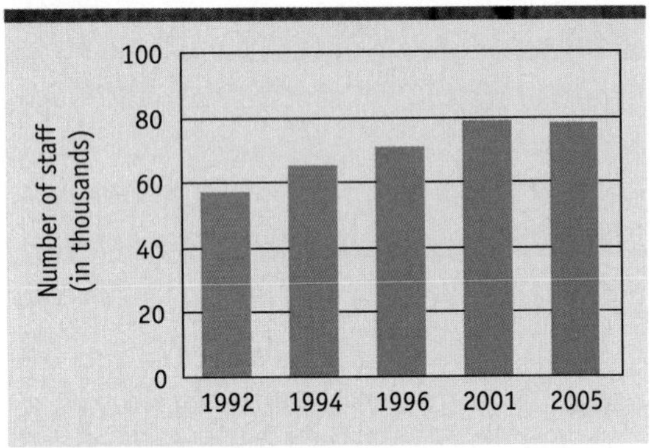

Source: Steven W. Perry, *Prosecutors in State Courts* (Washington, DC: Bureau of Justice Statistics, 2006).

Selection of Prosecutors The nearly 2,400 state, county, and local prosecutors' offices in the United States handle felony cases in state trial courts, and most also have jurisdiction for misdemeanor cases and traffic violations.[16] Most prosecutors are county-level officials, and approximately three-quarters of chief prosecutors hold full-time salaried positions. The typical prosecutor's office has three assistant prosecuting attorneys in addition to the chief prosecutor, although this number varies widely according to the size of the jurisdiction. Large cities with populations of 1 million or more average 141 assistant prosecutors, whereas smaller cities with populations of 250,000 to 999,999 average 34 assistant prosecutors.

Nationwide, prosecutors' offices had a total workforce of approximately 78,000 full-time and part-time staff, including assistant prosecutors, supervisory attorneys, investigators, victim advocates, and support staff. This total represents an increase from the 57,000 staff in 1992, but the increase leveled off after 2001 (see Figure 10.4). Together, assistant prosecutors (31 percent) and support staff (33 percent) represent about two-thirds of all prosecutors' office personnel.[17]

APPOINTMENT VERSUS ELECTION OF PROSECUTORS

In all but four states, prosecutors are elected. Supporters of *appointed* prosecutors point out that appointment reduces the possibility of overzealous or lackluster prosecutions of unpopular or controversial cases for election-related reasons. According to this argument, for example, prosecutors may pursue more cases involving high-profile defendants during election years.[18] Or they may try to match public expectations of being the "toughest" prosecutor. The best prosecutors, however, do their best to see that justice and fairness are sought in every case, which may have little to do with being "tough."

Supporters of *elected* prosecutors believe that elections provide regular opportunities for the public to express their approval or disapproval of a prosecutor's policies—and that appointments to the position of prosecutor may be based on political considerations. According to this line of thought, political patronism can result in appointments of individuals who may not have the background or experience to be effective prosecutors on behalf of a jurisdiction.

SPECIAL PROSECUTORS

In some states special prosecutors can be appointed to investigate extraordinary crimes. Special prosecutors are appointed by the governor to investigate multijurisdictional crimes that involve a potential conflict of interest on the part of the state attorney general (who is part of the state government). In these cases the offense usually involves allegations of misconduct on the part of a government official or a government agency. Therefore, an outside special prosecutor is appointed to conduct an independent objective evaluation of the evidence.

Defense Counsel and Defendants

Defense attorneys represent the legal rights of accused persons in criminal proceedings. Unlike the image that has emerged from some notorious cases, the reality is that defense attorneys' task is not to get the best deal for their client but to ensure that their client's legal rights are protected. Defense attorneys provide this protection by examining the evidence used to establish probable cause and questioning whether the evidence proves guilt beyond a reasonable doubt. This role sometimes brings defense counsel into conflict with police and prosecutors, and with victims and witnesses who may believe they are being "attacked" by the defense. An effective defense attorney, however, skillfully examines the reliability and validity of the evidence produced by police, prosecutors, victims, and witnesses; the attorney does not attack anyone *as an individual.* Attaining this neutrality is difficult, however. Strong advocacy of the legal rights of a defendant can become blurred with the desire to win at all costs. Nevertheless, the role of a defense attorney is crucial, because it increases certainty about outcomes of the adjudication process. Without high levels of certainty in court findings of guilt or innocence, the public might lose faith in the justice system and in the government it represents.

defense attorneys
Attorneys who represent the legal rights of the accused in criminal or civil proceedings.

CRIMINAL LAWYERS

A defense lawyer represents a client in a criminal case. How does a defense attorney justify representing someone he or she believes is guilty? Why do we guarantee a defense attorney in court to defendants, even when evidence of guilt is very strong?

The majority of lawyers are not criminal lawyers. Of the more than 1 million lawyers in the United States (with an additional 40,000 graduating from law school each year), only about 3 percent work in legal services or are public defenders.[19] The reasons that most defense attorneys are not involved in criminal law are many. As defense attorney Seymour Wishman reports, "You spend most of your time with monsters," "you're in and out of depressing places like prisons all day long," "the pay isn't extraordinary," and "you're looked down upon."[20] Some defense lawyers dislike visiting police stations, jails, and prisons; and because most defendants are poor, comparatively little money is made defending crime suspects. In addition, the public sometimes views defense attorneys as trying to subvert justice by successfully defending guilty people.[21] Public opinion polls show little confidence in lawyers, especially defense lawyers.[22] As a result, lawyers who choose careers as criminal attorneys, especially as public defenders, are in a distinct minority. Dramatic increases in the number of attorneys graduating from law schools in recent years may change this situation.

Because most defendants in criminal cases are poor, three-fourths of prison inmates were represented by court-appointed attorneys.[23] The case that most increased the availability of defense counsel to the poor was *Gideon v. Wainwright* in 1963. The Supreme Court ruled that indigent persons who are charged with felonies but cannot afford counsel must be appointed counsel at trial. In 1972, in *Argersinger v. Hamlin*, the Court extended the right to counsel to indigent defendants charged with misdemeanors for which imprisonment can be the penalty.[24] Other decisions have further extended the right to counsel to most stages of the criminal justice process. To meet the representation requirement, most states provide assigned counsel, contract attorney programs, or public defender services to indigent individuals charged with crimes. **Assigned counsel** is a private attorney appointed by the court on a case-by-case basis from a list of available attorneys. In **contract attorney programs,** private attorneys, firms, or local bar associations—professional associations of lawyers—provide legal representation to indigent defendants for a specific period under a contract with the county. Over the last fifteen years contract systems have been used increasingly. In some jurisdictions they have replaced assigned counsel. This growth results largely from an increase in the percentage of indigent defendants in criminal cases and the search for a way to reduce caseloads at public defender offices. There has been concern about the quality of representation obtained under contract systems, however, because of caseload pressures, low pay per case, and use of inexperienced attorneys.[25] **Public defender** programs are usually public nonprofit arrangements in which salaried attorneys are paid by the government to represent indigent defendants. About half of all counties in the United States have assigned counsel systems, and contract programs are found in about 11 percent of counties. Public defenders exist in 37 percent of all counties, including most of the largest jurisdictions, serving two-thirds of the U.S. population.[26] Eighty-one percent of all felony defendants receive appointed counsel, either public defenders or assigned counsel. Only 18 percent can afford to hire their own lawyer.

assigned counsel
A private attorney appointed by the court on a case-by-case basis from a list of available attorneys.

contract attorney programs
Programs in which private attorneys, firms, or local bar associations provide legal representation to indigent defendants for a specific period contracted with the county.

public defenders
Salaried attorneys paid by the government to represent indigents charged with crimes.

CONTRACT SYSTEMS

Judges

Judges play a pivotal role in the criminal justice process in upholding the rights of the accused and arbitrating between the prosecution and the defense in criminal cases. From the initial appearance through sentencing, the task of the **judge** is to objectively assess the strength of a case, rule on issues of law and procedure, and sometimes determine the ultimate disposition of a case.

judge
A person who objectively assesses the strength of a case, rules on issues of law and procedure, and in many cases determines the disposition of a case.

METHODS OF SELECTING JUDGES

Judges, sometimes called magistrates in courts of limited jurisdiction, are selected in one of four ways, depending on the state. Most magistrates are popularly elected. In eighteen states judges in trial courts are appointed by the governor, usually with the consent of the state legislature; this method is similar to the selection process for federal judges, who are appointed by the president with the approval of the U.S. Senate. In three states general jurisdiction trial judges are selected by the state legislature alone. Nonpartisan elections (in which candidates are not affiliated with any political party) are held in eighteen states, and eleven other states elect judges in partisan elections. In ten states gubernatorial judicial appointments are part of a merit selection process.[27]

Strengths and weaknesses are associated with each method of selection, and the diversity of methods indicates a lack of consensus on which method is best. Selection of judges by election gives the political party or the public direct input in the selection process, but it may pressure a judge seeking election or reelection to make "popular" decisions rather than ones based on principles of justice. Political appointment by the governor or the legislature sometimes results in the selection of a judge who is well connected politically but lacks some of the credentials one might wish to see in a judge.

A judge explains the legal situation to a defendant. Who do judges represent in the justice process? If we expect judges to be neutral arbiters of the facts, what measures are taken in their selection process to insure objectivity?

MISSOURI PLAN

merit selection
A method for selecting judges that involves a combination of appointment and election.

Merit selection was designed to overcome the drawbacks of both election and appointment of judges. The Missouri **merit selection** plan was initiated in 1940. When a judicial vacancy occurs, a nominating commission composed of citizens and attorneys recommends three candidates to the governor. The governor must appoint one of the three candidates. After the appointed judge has served on the bench for a year, a public referendum is held in which the voters are asked, "Shall Judge Z remain in office?" If a majority vote "yes," the judge completes his or her term of office; a "no" vote starts the process all over again. The merit selection system was designed to remove judicial candidates from the political arena while allowing the public to confirm or unseat a judge after one year. Although it is not a foolproof system, the procedure has been approved by both the American Bar Association and the American Judicature Society. Only sixteen states employ the merit selection system, but thirty-seven states now use some form of judicial nominating commission to guide gubernatorial appointments or to screen candidates for election.[28]

Whatever selection method is used, judges play a significant role in the adjudication process. They are asked to serve as an informed, neutral party, ruling on issues of fact and law throughout the court process. Even in cases in which the evidence of guilt appears overwhelming, the judge must ensure that the defendant's legal rights have been adequately safeguarded by the defense and that the community's interests have been effectively represented by the prosecution.

JUDICIAL REFORMS

In recent decades two important reform movements, state court unification and the establishment of U.S. magistrates, have increased the quality of the judicial system. Courts had been criticized for the use of nonlawyers in judicial roles, especially in local "justice of the peace" courts in small jurisdictions. Local court procedures were idiosyncratic, giving unfair advantages to local attorneys practicing in those courts. Local courts also were found to be more interested in generating revenue by imposing fines than in seeking justice.[29] During the 1960s and 1970s several national commissions recommended the abolition of many local courts and the creation of unified lower courts of limited and general jurisdiction. Uniform procedures for these courts were developed to reduce confusion about legal rules; additional recommendations mandated legal training for judges, provided for the rotation of judges among courts, and specified other reforms.[30] Many states have streamlined their court systems to some extent, but few have completely unified their courts. Texas, for example, still has more than 2,000 courts of limited jurisdiction. Nevertheless, the court unification movement has helped standardize court jurisdiction, procedure, and personnel qualifications in many states.

U.S. magistrates
Judges appointed by U.S. district court judges to conduct pretrial hearings and trials for minor civil and criminal offenses in federal court.

The second important reform movement was the establishment of **U.S. magistrates** by Congress in 1968. These magistrates are appointed by U.S. district court judges; they hold pretrial hearings as well as trials for minor civil and criminal offenses. They replaced U.S. commissioners, who were not required to be trained lawyers (and in many cases were not). Like the court unification movement in the state courts, the establishment of legally trained magistrates served to enhance and standardize the quality of justice in the lower federal courts.

FEDERAL JUDICIAL CENTER

Judges are better qualified now than at any time in the nation's history. Virtually all are required to hold law degrees, and legal education is more standardized today than in the past. The Federal Judicial Center, established in 1967, is responsible for judicial education and research in the federal courts, but not all states have a similar organized system of regular judicial training.[31] Standardized judicial training is important for maintaining high levels of competence and for fostering public confidence in the adjudication process.

Victims and Witnesses

"FORGOTTEN PLAYERS"

Victims and witnesses have sometimes been called the "forgotten players" in the criminal justice process, because no one specifically represents them. The police and prosecutor represent the community at large, the defense counsel represents the accused, and the judge is a neutral third party. The adjudication process is designed in this manner because violations of criminal law are viewed as violations of the rules of social order. It is society at large, not just the victim, that is harmed by an assault or robbery. Therefore, the prosecutor represents the entire jurisdiction and not just the victims or witnesses in a particular case.

Recent years have seen efforts to give victims and witnesses a greater role in the criminal justice process, usually at sentencing and at parole hearings, where they are permitted to voice their concerns. However, the criminal justice process is not designed to settle private disputes between victims and offenders; that is the purpose of civil law. Greater input by victims and witnesses in criminal proceedings should not blur the distinction between criminal and civil proceedings.

Nevertheless, victims and witnesses sometimes are not appropriately informed of the progress of criminal proceedings or of the pending release of offenders from prison. Also, until recently the impact of crime on victims has received little recognition.[32] In gang-dominated neighborhoods, for example, there are high levels of victim and witness intimidation.[33] Intimidation occurs most often in connection with violent crimes and often involves people with some previous connection with the defendant; many such people are young, and many are illegal immigrants. Explicit threats, physical violence, and property damage have been reported in these cases.

In response, prosecutors have requested high bail and initiated aggressive prosecution of reported attempts at intimidation. In recent years new strategies have been developed, such as emergency relocation and support of victims and witnesses, more extensive pretrial and courtroom security measures, and coordination with other agencies that provide support services. These measures are part of what has been called the "victims' rights movement," which is a grassroots ef-

THE VICTIMS' RIGHTS MOVEMENT

Which of the many participants in the criminal judicial process are evident in this photograph? What are the roles of victims and witnesses? How would the scene change in a community court for resolving disputes? Do you think community dispute resolution is an appropriate and effective way to ease overcrowding in the courts? Why or why not?

fort to make the criminal justice system more responsive to the perspective and suffering of crime victims. More than 10,000 organizations now provide counseling, transportation to court, temporary housing, and advocacy services for victims.[34] To the extent that the victims' rights movement has helped keep victims informed, aware, and protected in the adjudication process, it has accomplished a useful public service.

The criticism that victims are not adequately represented in the criminal justice process peaked during the 1980s, when a presidential Task Force on Victims of Crime recommended a more formal role for crime victims in criminal proceedings.[35] In 1991 the U.S. Supreme Court permitted judges and juries to consider **victim impact statements** in arriving at sentencing decisions. Before that time statements made by victims after the trial were considered inflammatory and prejudicial and were not considered in sentencing hearings. A majority of states have now made victim impact statements a mandatory part of criminal procedure.

victim impact statements
Statements by victims to the judge before sentencing about how the crime has harmed them.

The effect of victim impact statements on actual sentences is not clear. Several studies have found these statements to have little influence.[36] Other analyses indicate that victim impact statements foster sentencing based on perceptions of the victim's worth rather than on the seriousness of the crime.[37] The inclusion of these statements is relatively new, however, and changes in sentencing laws to accommodate the requests of victims are still occurring. It is too early, therefore, to determine the full effect of victim impact statements.

In addition to this trend toward providing a greater voice and more services to victims, there is a national push for a constitutional amendment to protect victims' rights during criminal proceedings.[38] Sometimes crime victims and families are excluded from trials where they may be called as witnesses, and there is a perception that defendants' rights are given more attention than the concerns of

Victim's Bill of Rights
Legal changes that formally recognize the role and rights of victims in the justice process.

victims. More than half the states have enacted some form of a **Victims' Bill of Rights,** giving formal legal recognition to the role of victims in the justice process in state courts. And a proposed amendment to the U.S. Constitution would guarantee victims nationwide the right to restitution and the right to be heard during plea bargaining, at trial, at sentencing, and at parole hearings.

A CONSTITUTIONAL AMENDMENT?

One version of the proposed constitutional amendment is presented in Figure 10.5. This version would give victims legal authority to object to plea bargaining, would guarantee a speedy trial, would require full restitution by the offender, and would provide for "reasonable measures" to protect the victim where necessary. Some prosecutors fear that this amendment, if passed, would give victims "veto power" over their decisions. Others have expressed concern about victims being present during trials in which they later appear as witnesses. They might then be able to shape their testimony according to the version of events presented by earlier witnesses.[39] The proposed constitutional amendment has languished in Congress for years but has not reached a vote, because many lawmakers believe that crime victim rights can be achieved through new federal laws that do not require a constitutional amendment.[40] Such a new federal law was enacted in the Justice for All Act of 2004, which included many of the objectives of the proposed constitutional amendment. The Act amends the federal criminal code to grant victims new rights, such as the right to be reasonably heard at any public proceeding involving release, plea, or sentencing. The Act also requires prosecutors to advise victims that they can seek the advice of an attorney with respect to the rights established by the Act. It allows victims to file motions to reopen a plea or a sentence in certain circumstances.[41] A summary of these new rights is presented in Figure 10.6. A comparison of the proposed constitutional amendment and the Justice for All Act (Figures 10.5 and 10.6) shows they incorporate a number of the same ideas.

FIGURE 10.5 Proposed Constitutional Amendment to Guarantee Victims' Rights

As a matter of fundamental rights to liberty, justice and due process, the victim shall have the following rights:

to be informed of and given the opportunity to be present at every proceeding in which those rights are extended to the accused or convicted offender; to be heard at any proceeding involving sentencing, including the right to object to a previously negotiated plea, or a release from custody; to be informed of any release or escape; and to a speedy trial, a final conclusion free from unreasonable delay, full restitution from the offender, reasonable measures to protect the victim from violence or intimidation by the accused or convicted offender, and notice of the victim's rights.

(Proposed by U.S. Senators John Kyl, R-Arizona and Dianne Feinstein, D-California)

FIGURE 10.6 Major Provisions of the Justice for All Act of 2004

(The Act amends the federal criminal code to grant crime victims specified rights.)

1. The right to be reasonably protected from the accused.
2. The right to reasonable, accurate, and timely notice of any public court proceeding or any parole proceeding involving the crime, or of any release or escape of the accused.
3. The right not to be excluded from any such public court proceeding, unless the court, after receiving clear and convincing evidence, determines that testimony by the victim would be materially altered if the victim heard other testimony at that proceeding.
4. The right to be reasonably heard at any public proceeding in the district court involving release, plea, sentencing, or any parole proceeding.
5. The reasonable right to confer with the attorney for the Government in the case.
6. The right to full and timely restitution as provided in law.
7. The right to proceedings free from unreasonable delay.
8. The right to be treated with fairness and with respect for the vitim's dignity and privacy.

Juries

When a trial takes place, it begins with the selection of a jury. The right to a jury dates from the signing of the Magna Carta in 1215, and it is incorporated into both Article III of the Constitution and the Sixth Amendment—which states that "in all criminal prosecutions, the accused shall enjoy the right to a speedy and public trial by an impartial jury." The jury pool typically is selected from voter registration records, property tax rolls, or motor vehicle records. This selection process has been widely criticized, because it excludes from the jury pool those who do not vote, own property, or drive cars.[42] Nevertheless, experiments with other methods of sampling have not found a completely effective way to choose a jury pool representative of the entire community.[43]

The U.S. Supreme Court has held that it is not necessary for every jury to contain a representative cross-section of the community by race, gender, religion, economic status, or other attributes. Instead, the Court has held that jurors may not be *excluded* on the basis of these characteristics and has overturned convictions in cases where blacks or males were purposely excluded from juries.[44] In a paternity suit in which the mother was suing the purported father, nine of the prosecutor's ten "peremptory challenges" (challenges without a reason required) were used to strike males from the jury panel, thus biasing the jury toward the plaintiff. The Supreme Court held that this use of peremptory challenges was unconstitutional, because it attempted to exclude an entire class of potential jurors.[45]

PEREMPTORY CHALLENGES

In a Texas case, a defendant was charged with capital murder and, when the jury was being selected, the prosecution used peremptory challenges to exclude ten of eleven (91 percent) of the eligible African American members of the jury pool. The accused was convicted of capital murder and sentenced to death. The U.S. Supreme Court held on appeal that a fair interpretation of the record revealed that the prosecutors had designed their questions for potential jurors to give responses that would justify the removal of African Americans from consideration. This suggests unfairness and bias that requires judicial review.[46]

In order to increase the number of available jurors, New York State added a million formerly exempt individuals to jury eligibility: physicians, lawyers, nurses, and other professionals. After three years, the results were not as expected. These better-educated jurors have been found to play a leading role in deliberations and ask good questions, but they do not influence the opinions of less-educated jurors. According to court records, there also has been no change in the proportion of convictions, acquittals, or damages awarded in civil court. As a result, New York now has much greater diversity in its jury pools without suffering any negative effects. As one observer stated, "You don't want twelve Ph.D.'s and you don't want twelve high school dropouts" on a jury, "you want a cross-section."[47]

A strategy lawyers use to assist juries in their decision making is to call an expert witness, as discussed earlier. A common expert witness in criminal trials is the coroner or medical examiner. Coroners are appointed or elected officials who investigate the causes of suspicious deaths in the jurisdiction. Over the years the position of coroner came to be filled politically by laypersons who were not competent at the job. The office of medical examiner has now been established in many jurisdictions, taking the place of the coroner. Medical examiners must be physicians with training in pathology, the study of the causes of death. The role of the medical examiner and of forensic science in solving criminal cases of all types has grown dramatically since the 1990s. This growth has been largely the result of the invention and increasing sophistication of DNA testing, which allows very small samples of body tissue or fluids from evidence to be matched against those of a suspect. Similarities or differences in the genetic coding of the samples can implicate or exclude suspects in cases. Similar advances have been made in drug testing in recent years, helping juries sort through sometimes conflicting testimony of victims and witnesses at trial.

ROLE OF FORENSIC SCIENCE

In 1997 the Office of the Inspector General in the U.S. Department of Justice released a five-hundred-page report charging the FBI forensic lab with errors in its forensic testing. It was widely believed that thousands of convictions might be overturned, but only twenty defendants tried to overturn their convictions. This inaction was due in part to the lack of legal counsel to enable prisoners to challenge their convictions and to the fact that federal law permitted a prisoner only one year to file a petition challenging a conviction after new evidence is discovered.[48] On the other hand, FBI and other forensic lab procedures have improved greatly with the assistance of a laboratory accreditation program of the American Society of Crime Lab Directors, which imposes minimum standards on laboratory equipment, conditions, and staffing. Nevertheless, major scandals in state forensic science labs regarding improper, false, or incompetent analysis of evidence indicates that greater oversight is needed of forensic laboratory procedures and personnel.[49]

The Courtroom Work Group

courtroom work group
The prosecutors, defense counsel, judges, and other courtroom personnel who represent distinct interests but share the goal of shepherding large numbers of cases through the adjudication process.

In many ways, prosecutors, defense counsel, and judges form a **courtroom work group.** They represent distinct interests but share the goal of shepherding large numbers of cases through the adjudication process. As one observer put it, "The client, then, is a secondary figure in the court system . . . a means to other ends of the organization's incumbents."[50] A defense attorney who is perceived as pushing too hard in a case may be informally sanctioned by inconvenient scheduling or contrary rulings from judges or by reluctance on the part of prosecutors to share reports or to plea-bargain in good faith.[51] Defense attorneys also need to maintain good relations with all other court personnel in order to maintain and build their law practice.[52] Thus, the actors in the courtroom work group must "get along," even if cooperation places some defendants at a disadvantage. Interviews with participants in courtroom work groups have revealed that certain laws (such as "three strikes" laws, which mandate severe penalties for repeat offenders) create tension among prosecutors, defense attorneys, and judges in their expectations from one another, and that they seek alternatives to preserve the working relationships and their perceptions of justice rather than enforcing the letter of the law.[53]

COOPERATE AT ALL COSTS?

In addition to prosecutors, defense attorneys, and judges, the courtroom work group includes sheriffs, court clerks, stenographers, and witnesses. *Sheriffs* or *bailiffs* are responsible for maintaining order in the courtroom. They most often track and ensure the appearance of defendants, and they sometimes also handle general court security tasks and handle witnesses. The *court clerk* keeps track of the

Media & Criminal Justice

Seeking Justice in Court and on TV

There's a cable channel for just about everyone, including Court TV. The television channel claims to be one of the most watched stations, especially when it shows a live, televised case from a location where cameras are permitted in the courtroom. Beginning in 2002, Court TV started making its own original films that documented actual cases. The first film, *Guilt by Association,* focused on the issue of mandatory minimum sentences for drug crimes by focusing on a specific case. It is clear there is some educational value in televising actual cases and dramatizing cases with interesting issues.

On the other hand, Court TV rounds out its lineup with reruns from network fictional crime shows, which take many more liberties with the realities of courts and the criminal justice system. Therefore, Court TV attempts to combine some educational television with more traditional dramas.

Some questions arise in the depiction of the courts and criminal justice system on television, however, that are worthy of discussion:

1. When a jury reaches a verdict in a popular case (e.g., the murder trials of O. J. Simpson or former football player Rae Carruth), many viewers develop strong opinions (and sometimes incorrect notions) about guilt or innocence because they have seen excerpts on television. Excerpts form the basis for this opinion because no one other than the jury generally expends the time or patience necessary to sit through an entire trial, and it is rare for all parts of a trial to be televised. Therefore, televised trials offer more information than traditional news sources, but less than that known by the actual participants in the case. Does this situation result in misguided public opinion, or does the increased coverage and information value of how the system works outweigh any negative effects?
2. Courts increasingly reject motions to have cases televised. Part of the reasoning is to avoid arousing public opinion, which might become known to the jury during the trial during evening off-hours and unduly influence jury decision making. Another reason is that people may act differently when they know they are on television. Do you believe that being on television during a trial changes the behaviors or actions of the participants in a criminal case?
3. The images the public receives of courts create a mixed bag. Fictional trial dramas with popular actors, coverage of actual cases from Court TV, and films that dramatize actual cases combine to present a partial view of how courts operate and how evidence is gathered. This "CSI" or "Court TV" effect leads potential jurors to believe that most cases are solved by conclusive scientific evidence, when this is not the reality.[a] Should television shows use more typical cases so as not to mislead the public about actual criminal justice, or should it stick to the most compelling stories and drama?

NOTES

a. Melissa Dribben, "Jurors Influenced by TV Shows Demanding Prime-time-style Evidence," *Philadelphia Inquirer* (February 19, 2006); Allison Klein, "Art Trips Up Life: TV Crime Shows Influence Jurors," *Baltimore Sun* (July 25, 2004).

cases pending before the court. The clerk does this by preparing the court's calendar of cases, calling each case as scheduled, and maintaining court records of case status and judicial rulings. Many court clerks are lawyers. A *court stenographer* or *court reporter* makes a transcript of each court appearance. *Witnesses* are also an important part of the courtroom work group, because they are involved in every case. Most witnesses are police officers. Laypersons who are crime victims or witnesses rely on guidance from the attorneys, court clerk, and sheriff's officers to understand the proceedings. The ability of defense attorneys to work successfully with all these players can improve the treatment of their clients in court and in jail.

How Are Specialized and Alternative Courts Changing the Court System?

The court system lies at the center of the justice system, for it is here that justice is most clearly carried out. Police and prosecutors work to assemble evidence of guilt. Defense attorneys closely scrutinize this evidence on behalf of the accused. Only in court, with a judge serving as referee and a jury sitting in judgment, does an objective assessment of the facts and law occur. Without neutral and detached courts and judges, there would be no forum in which the rights of the community could be balanced against the rights of the accused. The future of the court system will reflect improved judicial quality, discussed above; it will also reflect the development of specialized courts and alternatives to the courtroom for certain kinds of cases, which we will consider in this section.

Felony Drug Courts

felony drug courts
Courts that handle only drug offenses and attempt to correct underlying causes of the illegal conduct.

Specialized courts have emerged as a way for society to deal more effectively with the problem of drug-related crime. The drug court movement began during the late 1980s in response to the dramatic growth in drug-related cases. The most frequently charged felonies in the nation's seventy-five largest counties are drug offenses, accounting for more than a third of all defendants. The purpose of **felony drug courts** is to hold the defendant or offender "personally and publicly accountable for treatment progress."[54] Drug courts began in Miami and are now found in nearly 330 jurisdictions. Each drug court is coordinated by the judge, who works with the prosecutor, defense counsel, and drug treatment personnel. Members of this team select an appropriate treatment; address issues of housing, employment, or other barriers to progress; and monitor the offender's progress.[55] The two different models of drug courts are treatment after adjudication and treatment while prosecution is deferred. See Figure 10.7 for a summary of key components of drug courts.

EVALUATING DRUG COURTS

An evaluation of Miami's felony drug court found that fewer defendants were incarcerated but also that fewer drug cases were dropped during adjudication and offenders were rearrested less frequently.[56] Remaining challenges include obtaining accurate information about defendants, ensuring proper screening of drug offenders, and providing different treatments for different kinds of drug abuse. In 1994, Congress passed the Violent Crime Control and Law Enforcement Act to support specialized local and state drug courts.

NIGHT COURT

The drug court movement has built on the experiences of night courts and expedited case processing for drug cases in selected cities. Through night courts and expedited case processing, various jurisdictions responded to expanding drug caseloads by increasing hours of operation and handling these cases more efficiently.[57] Drug courts concentrate cases and expertise in a single courtroom, thereby reducing the time from arrest to disposition while relieving the caseload in general felony courts.[58] Goals are consistency in the handling of drug cases, timeliness in adjudication, and reduction of offender recidivism through treatment of underlying drug addictions. There are now more than 1,500 drug courts operating in the United States and more are planned. Research thus far indicates that drug

FIGURE 10.7 Ten Key Components of Drug Courts

- Integration of substance abuse treatment with justice system case processing.
- Use of a non-adversarial approach, in which prosecution and defense promote public safety while protecting the right of the accused to due process.
- Early identification and prompt placement of eligible participants.
- Access to a continuum of treatment, rehabiliation, and related services.
- Frequent testing for alcohol and illicit drugs.
- A coordinated strategy among the judge, prosecution, defense, and treatment providers to govern offender compliance.
- Ongoing judicial interaction with each participant.
- Monitoring and evaluation to measure achievement of program goals and gauge effectiveness.
- Continuing interdisciplinary education to promote effective planning, implementation, and operation.
- Partnerships with public agencies and community-based organizations to generate local support and enhance drug court effectiveness.

Source: Drug Courts: The Second Decade (Washington, DC: National Institute of Justice 2006).

courts can reduce recidivism as well as court costs, but that more sophisticated treatment services are needed to achieve more consistent results. It is essential that more offenders complete drug treatment and that treatment teams follow through with service delivery, because these are strongly related to a decrease in the likelihood of offender recidivism.[59]

Dispute Resolution and Community Courts

The use of alternatives to the formal adjudication process is a growing trend. Mediation and pretrial intervention programs have been instituted partly in response to high caseloads, but they also reflect a change in philosophy from "adjudication at any cost" to "justice at lower cost." Through these alternatives courts permit defendants to complete programs of restitution or rehabilitation in exchange for holding their cases in abeyance. After the restitution or rehabilitation is completed, the charges are dropped. In other programs, the victim and the accused mutually agree on an appropriate remedy outside of court.[60]

RESOLVING CONFLICT CREATIVELY PROGRAMS

Taking this trend one step further are efforts to prevent disputes from arising in the first place. The Resolving Conflict Creatively Program (RCCP) in New York City is a school-based program designed to teach young people how to resolve conflicts peacefully. The goal is to reduce violence, delinquency, and court appearances by young people by equipping youth with the skills they need in order to make more rational decisions in dealing with conflict. Workshops teach young people about cooperating, appreciating diversity, and being aware of bias, and provide specific skills for avoiding and de-escalating conflicts.[61] An evaluation found that most students in the program "learn the key concepts and are able to apply them when responding to hypothetical conflicts." In addition, the students report fewer fights and less name-calling behavior compared to a matched group of nonparticipants. Finally, teachers in the program have been found to be "more willing to let students take responsibility for solving their own conflicts."[62] Efforts like RCCP may

That's a FACT

Perspectives on the Deluge of Criminal Cases

State trial courts averaged about one incoming civil, domestic relations, criminal, juvenile, or traffic case for every three citizens in the United States in 2003. This represents more than one million new cases, an 11 percent increase over a decade ago. About 55 percent of these cases were traffic violations of various kinds; criminal court cases were the second highest, with more than 20 million new cases or 21 percent of the total caseload. These figures are displayed in Table 10A.

Trends in new cases over the last decade are interesting to observe. As Figure 10A illustrates, every type of case, except traffic, increased over the last decade in courts of general jurisdiction. The increase is even more dramatic in courts of limited jurisdiction, where all cases (including traffic) have increased (not shown). Can you offer reasons for these trends? What measures would you propose to reduce the number of new case filings?

Table 10A Total Incoming Cases in State Courts by Case Type, 2003

Case Type	*Millions*
Traffic	54.7
Criminal	20.6
Civil	17.1
Domestic	5.6
Juvenile	2.1
Total	**100.1**

FIGURE 10A Incoming Caseloads in Unified and General Jurisdiction Courts, by Case Type, 1994–2003

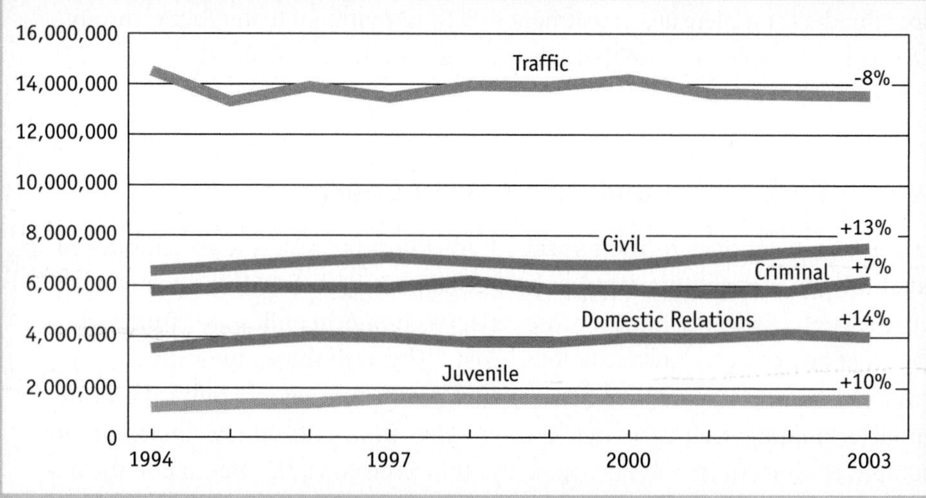

Source: Richard Y. Schauffler, Robert C. LaFountain, Neal B. Kauder, and Shanna M. Strickland, *Examining the Work of State Courts* (Williamsburg, VA: National Center for State Courts, 2005).

offer a long-term solution to crowded courts by disseminating the skills people require for avoiding conflicts or resolving them *before* civil or criminal misconduct occurs.

dispute resolution
A method of handling complaints outside the judicial process through a mediator appointed by the court.

A predictable response to increasing court caseloads has been to resolve more disputes outside the courtroom. Historically, this has meant reliance on plea bargaining; but this approach still involves the full adjudication process, from prosecution and defense representation to sentencing. **Dispute resolution,** in contrast, involves handling complaints outside the judicial process entirely. The goal of this practice is to get both sides to agree to a settlement facilitated by a mediator or arbiter who is appointed by the court. The incentives for dispute resolution are three: A dispute is resolved more quickly, less expensively, and often with a settlement more mutually agreeable than one likely to emerge from the normal adjudication process. For example, a teenager who spray-paints his name on the walls of a school gymnasium can be charged with vandalism, taken to court, and placed on probation or perhaps incarcerated. Alternatively, a dispute resolution procedure might involve a "teen court" made up of students from the teenager's school who would suggest penalties proportional to the offense. Or a dispute resolution procedure could involve an advisory committee of local citizens who would impose a sentence, such as cleaning up the paint, attending counseling, or other remedies. The purpose is to permit the community to address its problems in ways it sees as fair, proportional, and locally controlled.[63]

According to your text, what specific skills are involved in dispute resolution and conflict management? How effectively do you think this program might prevent crime? Why are alternatives to the court system needed? Do you think justice can still be served?

Dispute resolution works most effectively for first and minor offenders who commit "disorderly" offenses—offenses that are nonviolent yet disruptive and sometimes threatening to the community, such as loitering, vandalism, thefts, and public nuisance offenses. In Hawaii, for example, it was found that different cultural, ethnic, and neighborhood groups sometimes have different views regarding appropriate responses to these types of misconduct.[64] Dispute resolution gives neighborhoods a greater voice in dealing with misconduct that occurs in their own communities.

THREE INCENTIVES FOR RESOLUTION

A variation on dispute resolution is **community prosecution,** which has been used on an experimental basis in several counties around the nation. Responding to the demands of community groups, assistant district attorneys (ADAs) are assigned to specific neighborhoods, where they intervene in disorderly behavior (vandalism, prostitution, drug sales, loitering, etc.). The ADAs work to bring affected parties together to negotiate solutions, to make it easier for property owners to arrest trespassers and use civil eviction to remove undesirable tenants, and to close properties that are found to violate local ordinances.[65] Community prosecution efforts force prosecutors to work on a neighborhood level, acting as problem solvers rather than only as processors of criminal cases. These efforts have helped local communities respond more effectively to crimes that erode the quality of life in the neighborhood.

community prosecution
A program in which prosecutors intervene in all disorderly behavior that affects the quality of life in a neighborhood.

A parallel development is **community courts,** decentralized courts that respond directly to neighborhood concerns rather than waiting for serious crimes to occur. Community courts are being instituted in localities around the country. Many have "satellite" courtrooms in problem neighborhoods, facilities designed to forge a stronger connection between unruly conduct and the adjudication process. Many courts have formed citizens' advisory committees; use citizen volunteers; and have established teen courts, school outreach programs, and other programs that involve the community more closely in the adjudication process.[66]

community courts
Decentralized courts that respond to neighborhood conditions using citizen advisory committees, volunteers, and teen courts.

"SATELLITE" COURTS

Dispute resolution, community prosecution, and community courts are related ideas that attempt to accomplish three key objectives: address more quickly nonserious crimes that affect community order, permit organized community input into the adjudication and sentencing processes, and establish a court presence and understanding at the neighborhood level. These initiatives, if widely adopted, will increase confidence in the judicial process and its outcomes by reflecting the values of the local community.

CRITICAL THINKING EXERCISES

Independent Counsel and Prosecutorial Misconduct

In the early 1980s Congress passed legislation creating the Office of the Independent Counsel. This federal office was formed in response to allegations of misconduct by officials in the executive branch of the federal government. Several officials within the Reagan administration were convicted of lying to Congress through the efforts of independent counsel Lawrence Walsh, who spent $35 million in the Iran–Contra investigation.[a] Since then, numerous independent counsel investigations have been authorized. The most well known is that headed by Kenneth Starr, whose investigation of President Clinton's real estate dealings as governor of Arkansas expanded into an investigation of alleged sexual misconduct in the White House. Concern about the scope of the broad authority of the independent counsel grew when Starr had the friend of a targeted White House intern wear a concealed microphone to surreptitiously tape conversations, then subpoenaed the intern's mother to testify before a grand jury about her conversations with her daughter. The independent counsel was seeking evidence of presidential involvement in obstructing justice or in encouraging perjury, but these intrusive tactics were widely criticized.[b] It has been suggested that the strong-arm tactics prosecutors used in this case would have resulted in disciplinary proceedings if they had been used by a private attorney representing a client.[c] The law that created the independent counsel mandates that any evidence gathered is given to Congress, but no guidance is provided about when evidence should be provided or in what form.[d] Starr was criticized for an investigation that lasted more than five years and cost more than $40 million. Ultimately, Congress chose in 1999 not to reauthorize the independent counsel statute.

Across the nation, the conduct of prosecutors in handling criminal cases has been a growing concern. In one well-known murder case a prosecutor concealed from the jury the fact that red stains on the defendant's clothing were paint, not blood.[e] In some instances prosecutors have attempted to sway juries by appeals to inadmissible evidence, appeals to prejudice, or inflammatory statements.[f] In other cases prosecutors retried defendants after the case had been earlier dropped or dismissed. In a Louisiana case a man was tried five times for a murder.[g] Nevertheless, the U.S. Supreme Court has granted prosecutors absolute immunity from being sued for misconduct in the courtroom, even if the misconduct is intentional. The Court made this ruling in a case in which a prosecutor was sued for knowingly using perjured testimony that resulted in an innocent person's being convicted and incarcerated for nine years.[h] The Supreme Court held that without absolute immunity prosecutors risked "harassment by unfounded litigation" that would make it difficult for them to carry out their duties effectively.

Nevertheless, prosecutors have only limited immunity from being sued for actions taken outside the courtroom. For example, when one prosecutor was sued for deciding to authorize a warrantless wiretap, he was not granted absolute immunity.[i] In another case a prosecutor was found to have fabricated evidence by shopping around for a favorable expert witness and to have made false statements to the press. Here again, the prosecutor was not granted absolute immunity.[j] The pattern in these cases shows that prosecutors enjoy absolute immunity in courtroom actions but only qualified immunity for investigative actions (such as advice and direction to the police).[k] One former prosecutor has recommended imposing civil penalties on prosecutors for professional misconduct and has encouraged appellate courts to discipline prosecutors as they do defense attorneys to curb unethical actions.[l] It is unethical for a prosecutor to bring a case to trial knowing that the defendant is innocent. Closer scrutiny and enforcement of ethical standards can serve as a way to control prosecutorial misconduct.

CRITICAL THINKING QUESTIONS

1. Whom did the federal independent counsel represent? Why did Congress create and then abolish this role?
2. How can the role and duties of a prosecutor lead to misconduct or abuse of power?
3. Why did the U.S. Supreme Court grant prosecutors absolute immunity? What are the limits on that immunity?
4. How do you think ethical standards should apply to the other players in the U.S. court system?

NOTES

a. Constance Johnson, "High Crimes and Special Prosecutors," *U.S. News & World Report* (November 8, 1993), p. 47.
b. Mortimer B. Zuckerman, "Has Mr. Starr No Shame?," *U.S. News & World Report* (April 6, 1998), p. 74; Barry A. Bohrer, "President Clinton Is No Mafia Chieftain," *National Law Journal* 20 (March 2, 1998), p. 23; Paul Glastris, "'False Statements': The Flubber of All Laws," *U.S. News & World Report* (March 30, 1998), pp. 25–26.
c. Harvey Silvergate, "Prosecutors Tread Where Defenders Daren't Go," *National Law Journal* 20 (February 16, 1998), p. 21.
d. Douglas Stanglin, "Starr Weighs His Options," *U.S. News & World Report* (May 4, 1998), p. 9.
e. *Miller v. Pate,* 386 U.S. 1 (1967).
f. See Alschuler, "Courtroom Misconduct by Prosecutors and Trial Judges," *Texas Law Review* 50 (1972), pp. 627–35.
g. Pamela Coyle, "Tried and Tried Again: Defense Lawyers Say the D.A. Went Too Far Prosecuting a Louisiana Man Five Times for Murder," *ABA Journal* 84 (April, 1998), p. 38.
h. *Imbler v. Pachtman,* 424 U.S. 409 (1976).
i. *Mitchell v. Forsyth,* 472 U.S. 511 (1985); 515 U.S. 304 (1995).
j. *Buckley v. Fitzsimmons,* 509 U.S. 259 (1993).
k. Erwin Chemerinsky, "Prosecutorial Immunity: The Interpretation Continues," *Trial* 34 (March, 1998), p. 80.
l. Bennett L. Gershman, "Why Prosecutors Misbehave," in P. F. Cromwell and R. G. Dunham, eds., *Crime and Justice in America: Present Realities and Future Prospects* (Upper Saddle River, NJ: Prentice Hall, 1997), pp. 192–200.

Limiting Criminal Appeals

The adjudication process is undermined when there are long delays between the commission of the crime and imposition of a sentence. Growth in the number of appeals filed by convicted offenders may be seen as an example. An appeal simply argues that an error of law or procedure was made and that a new trial is warranted. Although 80 percent of appeals are unsuccessful, appeals delay punishment while they are heard by an appellate court.[a] A common kind of appeal is a writ of habeas corpus, which requires that a prisoner be brought before a judge and that the judge determine whether he or she is incarcerated lawfully (i.e., whether no legal error has been made). The number of habeas corpus petitions filed has increased dramatically over the years, even though few result in a new trial or the release of an offender. This large volume of appeals from criminal trials adds to already mushrooming caseloads.

During the 1990s the U.S. Supreme Court made rulings that limit an offender's right to appeal. The Court has held that an offender is entitled to federal appeal from a state court finding only when bias or unfairness would result from a failure to appeal or "when a fundamental miscarriage of justice would result" without a review of the case.[b] This ruling limits the circumstances in which an offender can have a state case reviewed in federal court for legal errors.

In 1993 the Court held that an offender sentenced to death for murder is not necessarily entitled to a federal order for a new state trial if new evidence emerges, because new evidence is not automatic grounds for a new trial.[c] This holding also makes it more difficult for an offender to have a state court conviction reviewed by a federal court.[d] The outcome in practice has been fewer appeals accepted for review. In death penalty cases, in which numerous appeals are common, the ruling has resulted in more executions.

CRITICAL THINKING QUESTIONS

1. What are the positive and negative consequences of limiting the number of appeals made by convicted offenders?
2. How would you evaluate the relative strengths of the positive and negative consequences of limiting criminal appeals?
3. Why do you believe the Supreme Court ruled that new evidence is not always sufficient grounds for a new trial of a person sentenced to death?
4. Do you think rights to appeal should be further limited or abolished? Why or why not?

NOTES

a. Dwight Aarons, "Getting Out of This Mess: Steps toward Addressing and Avoiding Inordinate Delay in Capital Cases," *Journal of Criminal Law and Criminology* 89 (fall 1998); Joy A. Chaper and Roger A. Hanson, *Understanding Reversible Error in Criminal Appeals* (Williamsburg, VA: National Center for State Courts, 1989).
b. *Kenney v. Tamayo-Reyes,* 504 U.S. 1 (1992).
c. *Herrera v. Collins,* 113 S. Ct. 853 (1993).
d. Arleen Anderson, "Responding to the Challenge of Actual Innocence Claims after *Herrera v. Collins,*" *Temple Law Review* 71 (fall 1998); Robert D. Pursley, "The Federal Habeas Corpus Process: Unraveling the Issues," *Criminal Justice Policy Review* 7 (1995), pp. 115–41.

SUMMARY

HOW WERE CRIMINAL COURTS SIMILAR AND DIFFERENT IN THE PAST?

- Although celebrated cases have occurred on occasion in the past, in many cases lawyers were absent from the trial. Misdemeanor cases were handled in a nonprofessional fashion; the processing of felonies tended to be more formal, as it is today.
- Until the late 1800s defendants could not act as witnesses or take the stand in their own defense. Today defendants are permitted to testify under oath.

HOW DID THE STATE AND FEDERAL COURT SYSTEMS DEVELOP?

- The vast majority of criminal cases are heard in state courts, because most felonies are defined by state laws.
- There are three levels of jurisdiction: limited, general, and appellate. These are found in all state court systems, but each state determines how its system is organized.
- The legal authority of courts of limited jurisdiction is restricted to certain specific types of cases. Courts of general jurisdiction are often referred to as trial courts, and most felony trials are held at this level. Appellate courts hear appeals from courts of general jurisdiction.
- The federal court system parallels the state court systems. There are courts of limited jurisdiction such as the U.S. Court of Claims. There are also courts of general jurisdiction, the U.S. district courts; these are located throughout the country and hear cases involving alleged violations of federal law.
- There are two levels of federal appellate courts. The intermediate level consists of U.S. courts of appeals. The highest level is the U.S. Supreme Court.
- The U.S. Supreme Court can hear on appeal any case involving federal law, suits between states and cases involving interpretations of the U.S. Constitution. The Court can choose which cases it will hear through a procedure termed *certiorari;* a writ of certiorari is issued when four or more justices believe that the legal issues presented in a case merit review.
- The decisions of the Supreme Court are made by a majority vote of the nine justices, who are appointed for life by the president with the consent of the Senate.

WHO ARE THE PARTICIPANTS IN THE JUDICIAL PROCESS?

- Prosecutors represent the community in bringing charges against an accused person. Most prosecutors are elected officials and therefore may feel pressure to make "popular" prosecution decisions. Other influences on prosecutors' decisions include caseload pressures and the need to maintain good relations with other actors in the adjudication process.
- Defense attorneys represent the legal rights of the accused in criminal proceedings. They examine the evidence used to establish probable cause and assess the strength of the evidence to be used to prove guilt.
- The duties of judges are to objectively assess the strength of a case, to rule on issues of law and procedure, and sometimes to determine the ultimate disposition of a case. Judges are selected in a variety of ways, including appointment, nonpartisan election, and merit selection.
- Two recent reform movements—state court unification and the establishment of U.S. magistrates—have increased the quality of the judicial system.
- Victims and witnesses are not represented by specific actors in the adjudication process. In recent years there have been efforts to give victims a greater role in the process, usually at sentencing and at parole hearings.
- A proposed constitutional amendment would give victims legal authority to object to plea bargaining, guarantee a speedy trial, require full restitution by the offender, and provide protection of victims where necessary.
- The right to a jury trial is stated in the Constitution, but historically it has been difficult to obtain a jury that represents the community. Expert witnesses are used to help a jury understand technical issues.
- Prosecutors, defense counsel, and judges can be viewed as a courtroom work group. Although they represent distinct interests, these actors share the goal of moving large numbers of cases through the adjudication process.

HOW ARE SPECIALIZED AND ALTERNATIVE COURTS CHANGING THE COURT SYSTEM?

- Improved judicial quality, specialized courts such as felony drug courts, and alternatives to the courtroom are good news for the future of the court system.
- Dispute resolution, community prosecution, and community courts are three alternatives to formal adjudication in criminal court; all three of these approaches attempt to achieve dispositions that match the offense and will prevent crimes in the future.

KEY TERMS

expert witness *261*
U.S. district courts *264*
U.S. courts of appeals *264*
U.S. Supreme Court *265*
writ of certiorari *265*
judicial review *265*
prosecutors *266*
district attorneys *268*
defense attorneys *269*

assigned counsel *270*
contract attorney programs *270*
public defenders *270*
judge *270*
merit selection *271*
U.S. magistrates *272*
victim impact statements *273*
Victim's Bill of Rights *274*
courtroom work group *276*
felony drug courts *278*
dispute resolution *280*
community prosecution *281*
community courts *281*

QUESTIONS FOR REVIEW AND DISCUSSION

1. What are some of the most important differences between the way trials were conducted in the past and the way they are conducted today?
2. How are state court systems organized?
3. What are U.S. district courts?
4. What kinds of cases are heard by the U.S. Supreme Court?
5. Describe the five main groups of participants in the judicial process.
6. What are some of the ways in which judges are selected in different states?
7. What is meant by state court unification?
8. What initiatives have been taken to give victims and witnesses a greater role in the criminal justice process?
9. What are the major challenges facing the justice system in the future?

NOTES

1. Julius Goebel, Jr., ed., *The Law and Practice of Alexander Hamilton: Documents and Commentary* (New York: Columbia University Press 1964).
2. Lawrence M. Friedman, *Crime and Punishment in American History* (New York: Basic Books, 1993), p. 239.
3. *Hurtado v. California*, 110 U.S. 516 (1884).
4. *Strauder v. West Virginia* (1879).
5. Friedman, pp. 245–50.
6. Herbert A. Johnson and Nancy Travis Wolfe, *History of Criminal Justice*, 2nd ed. (Cincinnati: Anderson, 1996), pp. 81, 112.
7. Peter Hoffer, *Law and People in Colonial America* (Baltimore, MD: Johns Hopkins University Press, 1992).
8. Thomas Morawetz, "The Paradox of Charismatic Judging," *Connecticut Law Review*, vol. 32 (summer 2000), p. 1705.
9. *Kumho Tire Company v. Carmichael*, 119 S. Ct. 1167 (1999).
10. Tony Mauro, "Judges Can Bar 'Junk Science' Testimony," *USA Today* (March 24, 1999), p. 1.
11. Clarissa Campbell Orr, "Court History," *History Today* (September 1999), p. 34; Nan Aron, "Power Shift Down—The Lower Courts Count," *Nation* (October 9, 2000), p. 16.
12. David B. Rottman and Shauna M. Strickland, *State Court Organization* (Washington, DC: Bureau of Justice Statistics, 2006), p. 15.
13. *Marbury v. Madison*, 1 Cr. 138 (1803).
14. American Bar Association, *ABA Standards for Criminal Justice* (Washington, DC: American Bar Association, 1992), Standard 3-1.
15. Matthew R. Durose, *Felony Sentences in State Courts* (Washington, DC: Bureau of Justice Statistics, 2004).
16. Steven W. Perry, *Prosecutors in State Courts* (Washington, DC: Bureau of Justice Statistics, 2006).
17. Ibid., p. 3.
18. Comments of several defense attorneys appearing on *Rivera Live* on CNBC television, May 29, 1997, in reference to the sexual harassment case of Paula Jones against President Clinton and the prosecution of sportscaster Marv Albert.
19. Ronit Dinovitzer, Bryant G. Garth, Richard Sander, Joyce Sterling, and Gita Z. Wilder, *After the JD: First Results of a National Study of Legal Careers* (Chicago: The NALP Foundation and the American Bar Association, 2004).
20. Seymour Wishman, *Confessions of a Criminal Lawyer* (New York: Penguin, 1982), p. 231.
21. Charles M. Sevilla, "Criminal Defense Lawyers and the Search for Truth," *Harvard Journal of Law and Public Policy* 20 (winter 1997), pp. 519–28; American Bar Association, *Perceptions of the U.S. Justice System Opinion Confidence in Institutions/Professions*. http://www.abanet.org/media/perception/perception32.html (accessed September 5, 2006).
22. Stephen Budiansky with Ted Gest, "How Lawyers Abuse the Law," *U.S. News & World Report* (January 30, 1995), pp. 50–56.
23. Carol J. DeFrances, *State-Funded Indigent Defense* (Washington, DC: Bureau of Justice Statistics, 2001).
24. *Argersinger v. Hamlin*, 92 S. Ct. 2006 (1972).
25. The Spangenberg Group, *Contracting for Indigent Defense Services: A Special Report* (Washington, DC: Bureau of Justice Assistance, 2000).
26. DeFrances, *State-Funded Indigent Defense*, p. 2.
27. Rottman and Strickland, pp. 25–28.
28. Rottman and Strickland, p 20.
29. Thomas Henderson and Cornelius Kerwin, *Structuring Justice: The Implications of Court Unification Reforms* (Washington, DC: National Institute of Justice, 1984).
30. American Bar Association, *ABA Standards Relating to Court Organization* (Chicago: American Bar Association, 1990).
31. U.S. Comptroller General, *The Federal Judiciary: Observations on Selected Issues* (Washington, DC: U.S. General Accounting Office, 1995).

32. Ted R. Miller, Mark A. Cohen, and Brian Wiersema, *Victim Costs and Consequences: A New Look* (Washington, DC: National Institute of Justice, 1996).
33. Kerry Murphy Healey, *Victim and Witness Intimidation: New Developments and Emerging Responses* (Washington, DC: National Institute of Justice, 1995).
34. Office for Victims of Crime, *What Is the Office for Victims of Crime?* (Washington, DC: U.S. Department of Justice, 2002).
35. President's Task Force on Victims of Crime, *Final Report* (Washington, DC: U.S. Government Printing Office, 1982).
36. Robert C. Davis and Barbara E. Smith, "The Effects of Victim Impact Statements on Sentencing Decisions: A Test in an Urban Setting," *Justice Quarterly* 11 (September 1994), pp. 453–69; Edna Erez and Pamela Tontodonato, "The Effect of Victim Participation in Sentencing on Sentence Outcome," *Criminology* 28 (1990), pp. 451–74; Edna Erez and Kathy Laster, "Neutralizing Victim Reform: Legal Professionals' Perspectives on Victims and Impact Statements," *Crime & Delinquency*, vol. 45 (October 1999), p. 530.
37. Wayne A. Logan, "Through the Past Darkly: A Survey of the Uses and Abuses of Victim Impact Evidence in Capital Trials," *Arizona Law Review* 41 (spring 1999); Amy K. Phillips, "Thou Shalt Not Kill Any Nice People: The Problem of Victim Impact Statements in Capital Sentencing," *American Criminal Law Review* 35 (fall 1997), pp. 93–118.
38. Tony Mauro and Bill Nichols, "Obligation of a Fair Trial vs. Victims' Rights," *USA Today* (June 26, 1996), p. 8; Rachelle K. Hong, "Nothing to Fear: Establishing an Equality of Rights for Crime Victims through the Victims Rights Amendment," *Notre Dame Journal of Legal Ethics & Public Policy*, vol. 16 (2002), p. 207.
39. Ibid.
40. Marlene A. Young and Roger Pilon, "Should We Amend the Constitution to Protect Victims' Rights?," *Insight on the News* (August 31, 1998), p. 24; "Senate Panel Approves 'Victims' Rights' Amendment," *CongressDaily/A.M.* (October 1,1999).
41. Justice for All Act of 2004 (H.R. 5107, Public Law 108–405).
42. James P. Levine, *Juries and Politics* (Pacific Grove, CA: Brooks/Cole, 1992); Charles J. Ogletree, "Just Say No! A Proposal to Eliminate Racially Discriminatory Uses of Peremptory Challenges," *American Criminal Law Review* 31 (1994), pp. 1099–1151; "Racial Exclusion in Jury Pool Composition," *Harvard Law Review*, vol. 116 (June 2003), p. 2678.
43. Hiroshi Fukurai, Edgar W. Butler, and Richard Krooth, "Cross-Sectional Jury Representation or Systematic Jury Representation? Simple Random and Cluster Sampling Strategies in Jury Selection," *Journal of Criminal Justice* 19 (1991), pp. 31–48; Mary R. Rose, "The Jury in Practice: A Voir Dire of Voir Dire," *Chicago-Kent Law Review*, vol. 78 (2003), p. 1061.
44. *Thiel v. Southern Pacific Company*, 328 U.S. 217 (1945); *Batson v. Kentucky*, 106 S. Ct. 1712 (1986); Audrey M. Fried, "Fulfilling the Promise of Batson: Protecting Jurors from the Use of Race-Based Peremptory Challenges by Defense Counsel," *University of Chicago Law Review 64* (fall 1997), pp. 1311–36.
45. *J. E. B. v. Alabama ex rel. T. B.*, 55 CrL. 2003 (1994).
46. *Miller-El v. Cockrell*, 123 S. Ct. 1029 (2003).
47. David Rohde, "Do Diplomas Make Jurors Any Better? Maybe Not," *New York Times* (April 10, 2000), p. 1.
48. David E. Rovella, "Predictions of Big Effects from Ills in FBI Lab Prove False," *Fulton County Daily Report* (April 23, 1998), pp. 1–5.
49. Maurice Possley, Steve Mills, and Flynn Roberts, "Scandal Touches Even Elite Labs: Flawed Work, Resistance to Scrutiny Seen Across U.S.," *Chicago Tribune* (October 21, 2004); Richard Willing, "Errors Prompt States to Watch Over Crime Labs," *USA Today* (April 1, 2006); Steve McVicker and Roma Khanna, "More Problems Found in Houston Police Department Crime Lab Cases," *Houston Chronicle* (May 11, 2006); Roma Khanna and Steve McVicker, "Police Lab Tailored Tests to Theories, Report Says," *Houston Chronicle* (May 12, 2006).
50. Abraham S. Blumberg, "The Practice of Law as a Confidence Game," in George S. Bridges, Joseph G. Weis, and Robert D. Crutchfield, eds., *Criminal Justice* (Thousand Oaks, CA: Pine Forge Press, 1996), p. 269.
51. James Eisenstein, Roy Fleming, and Peter Nardulli, *The Contours of Justice: Communities and Their Courts* (Boston: Little, Brown, 1988).
52. Blumberg, "The Practice of Law as a Confidence Game," p. 269.
53. John C. Harris and Paul Jesilow, "It's Not the Old Ball Game: Three Strikes and the Courtroom Workgroup," *Justice Quarterly* vol. 17 (March, 2000), pp. 185–203.
54. *The Drug Court Movement* (Washington, DC: National Institute of Justice, 1995).
55. U.S. Comptroller General, *Drug Courts: Overview of Growth, Characteristics, and Results* (Washington, DC: U.S. General Accounting Office, 1997); Rottman and Strickland, 2006.
56. James L. Nolan, ed. *Drug Courts in Theory and Practice* (Hawthorne, NY: Aldyne de Gruyter, 2002); Duren Banks and Denise C. Gottfredson, "The Effects of Drug Treatment and Supervision on Time to Rearrest among Drug Treatment Court Participants," *Journal of Drug Issues*, vol. 33 (spring 2003), p. 385; John S. Goldkamp and Doris Weiland, *Assessing the Impact of Dade County's Felony Drug Court* (Washington, DC: National Institute of Justice, 1993).
57. American Bar Association, *Drug Night Courts: The Cook County Experience* (Washington, DC: Bureau of Justice Assistance, 1994); Douglas B. Marlowe, "Are Judicial Status Hearings a Key Component of Drug Court?: During-Treatment Data from a Randomized Trial," *Criminal Justice & Behavior*, vol. 33 (April 2003), p. 141.
58. John S. Goldkamp, "The Drug Court Response: Issues and Implications for Justice Change," *Albany Law Review*, vol. 63 (2000), p. 923; Steven Belenko and Tamara Dumankovsky, *Special Drug Courts* (Washington, DC: Bureau of Justice Assistance, 1993).
59. *Drug Courts: The Second Decade* (Washington, DC: National Institute of Justice 2006).
60. David Rottman and Pamela Casey, "Therapeutic Jurisprudence and the Emergence of Problem-Solving Courts," *National Institute of Justice Journal* (July 1999), pp. 11–19.
61. William DeJong, *Building the Peace: The Resolving Conflict Creatively Program* (Washington, DC: National Institute of Justice, 1996); Donna Crawford and Richard Bodine, *Conflict Resolution Education* (Washington, DC: Office of Juvenile Justice and Delinquency Prevention, 1996); Stephen C. Aldrich, "Both Sides Now," *Juvenile and Family Court Journal*, vol. 51 (spring 2000), p. 35.
62. DeJong, *Building the Peace*, p. 11.
63. Daniel McGillis, *Resolving Community Conflict: The Dispute Settlement Center of Durham, North Carolina* (Washington, DC: National Institute of Justice, 1998).
64. Sharon Rodgers, "The Future of Cultural Forms of Dispute Resolution in the Formal Legal System," *Futures Research*

Quarterly 9 (winter 1993), pp. 41–49; Marianne L. Bell and David R. Forde, "A Factorial Survey of Interpersonal Conflict Resolution," *The Journal of Social Psychology*, vol. 139 (June 1999), p. 369.

65. Barbara Boland, "What Is Community Prosecution?," *National Institute of Justice Journal* (August 1996), pp. 35–40; Richard A. Devine, "Chicago's Approach to Community Prosecution," *Prosecutor, Journal of the National District Attorneys Association*, vol. 36 (January–February 2002), p. 35; Devin J. Doolan, Jr., "Community Prosecution: A Revolution in Crime Fighting," *Catholic University Law Review*, vol. 51 (winter 2002), pp. 547–82.

66. David B. Rottman, "Community Courts: Prospects and Limits," *National Institute of Justice Journal* (August 1996), pp. 46–51; Yael Scahchev, "Red Hook Center to Be Model Community Court," *New York Law Journal* (June 2, 2000), p. 1; Elaine Nugent and Gerard A. Rainville, "The State of Community Prosecution: Results of a National Survey," *Prosecutor, Journal of the National District Attorneys Association*, vol. 35 (March–April 2001), p. 26; Richard B. Hoffman, "Community Courts: The Viable Alternative; A New Approach to Meting Out Justice Is Using Local Resources to Reduce Recidivism," *Washington Lawyer*, vol. 19 (October 2004), pp. 34–40.

chapter 11

Trial Defense and Prosecution

The state versus the accused: assessing the strengths and weaknesses of current practice in the prosecution and defense of those charged with crimes.

CHAPTER OUTLINE

What Are the Rights of the Accused?
Right to Counsel
Right to *Effective* Counsel

How Are Cases Settled without Trial?
Prosecutorial Discretion
Diversion of Cases
Plea Bargaining

What Are Some Problems of the Court System?
Caseloads
Case Mortality
Adjudicate the Offender or the Act?
Crime Control or Due Process?

THAT'S A FACT:
Perspectives on Adjudication

MEDIA AND CRIMINAL JUSTICE:
The Matrix Made Me Do It

CRITICAL THINKING EXERCISES:
- Selective Prosecution of High-Rate Offenders
- Should a Lawyer Defend a Guilty Person?

LEARNING OBJECTIVES

- Explain how the Sixth Amendment bears on rights of the accused.
- Summarize the main case law precedents establishing the right to counsel.
- Trace the development of extensions of the right to counsel and to effective counsel.
- Evaluate the effectiveness of indigent defense.
- Explain the prosecutor's powers and discuss issues relating to prosecutorial discretion.
- Describe the means by which cases are settled without going to trial.
- Assess the advantages and disadvantages of plea bargaining from different points of view.
- Discuss plea bargaining and caseloads as problems of the criminal justice system.
- Summarize research findings on reasons and solutions for high case mortality.
- Analyze the effects of extended and new criminal defenses on the justice system.
- Explain why balance is needed between a crime control model and a due process model.

Darrell Harris was placed on trial for killing three people and seriously wounding a fourth at a Brooklyn social club. Harris was charged with robbing the victims of $200 and then killing them because he wanted no witnesses. His defense attorney claimed that Harris "lost control and snapped" during this incident because he suffered from posttraumatic stress disorder, having endured "combatlike" work conditions in jails when he worked as a corrections officer.[1] In addition, Harris's attorney argued that Harris's mental health was affected by a chaotic and abusive childhood, spinal meningitis that caused brain damage, cocaine and alcohol abuse, and failure to hold a job. Harris had resigned from his job as a corrections officer several years earlier after failing a drug test. Two days before the homicides occurred, Harris had been fired from his job as a security guard. He also had discovered his car had been towed.

Most of these claims bore little relationship to the charges filed, and such arguments feed the perception that defense attorneys focus less on seeking truth than on exoneration of their client at any cost. Cases such as this one raise other questions as well: What is the proper role of a defense attorney? What is the scope of a defendant's right to have counsel? And what are the limits of proper representation?

What Are the Rights of the Accused?

The Sixth Amendment to the U.S. Constitution deals specifically with the rights of people accused of crimes. It states:

THE SIXTH AMENDMENT

In all criminal prosecutions, the accused shall enjoy the right to a speedy and public trial, by an impartial jury of the State and district wherein the crime shall have been committed, which district shall have been previously ascertained by law, and to be informed of the nature and cause of the accusation; to be confronted with the witnesses against him; to have compulsory process for obtaining witnesses in his favor, and to have the Assistance of Counsel for his defense.

The right "to have the assistance of counsel" has drawn a great deal of attention over the years. Do all defendants have this right? Does it apply to all crimes? At what stage of criminal procedure does this right become effective? What kind of counsel does it guarantee?

The Sixth Amendment also guarantees the rights to "a speedy and public trial" and to "an impartial jury." The definition of "speedy" has been the subject of much debate. For example, a prisoner on death row asked the court for a speedy execution but was denied until, finally, his appeals were exhausted.[2] Jury trials date back in history nearly 800 years, but the scope of a defendant's right to choose a jury trial has been subject to U.S. Supreme Court interpretation of the Sixth Amendment.[3]

Right to Counsel

right to counsel
A Sixth Amendment protection that guarantees suspects the right to representation by an attorney when their liberty is in jeopardy.

POWELL V. ALABAMA

The scope of the **right to counsel** has been defined by the U.S. Supreme Court in a series of cases involving the interpretation and application of the Sixth Amendment. The Supreme Court applied the right to counsel narrowly at first but has expanded it significantly over the years. In 1931 the Court held in *Powell v. Alabama* that legal counsel is guaranteed to defendants who are charged with a capital crime, are indigent, or are unable to represent themselves due to ignorance, illiteracy, or low intelligence.[4] The case involved nine young black men accused of raping two white women. The Supreme Court reversed their convictions, although they were retried with the assistance of counsel and four of the nine defendants were convicted (even though one of the victims recanted the charges of rape). Six years after the *Powell* decision, in *Johnson v. Zerbst*, the Supreme Court extended the right to counsel to *all* indigent felony defendants in *federal* cases, but did not extend the right to state cases (where most felony trials take place).[5] The Court justified this position in the 1942 case *Betts v. Brady*, stating that the right to counsel "is not a fundamental right" in noncapital cases unless special circumstances such as lack of education or mental illness are present.[6] Many states did not follow the guidelines of *Betts*, however, and often failed to provide attorneys even in cases that warranted provision of defense counsel. In 1963 this situation culminated in the case *Gideon v. Wainwright*, one of the Supreme Court's most significant decisions.

Gideon v. Wainwright Clarence Earl Gideon was charged with breaking into a poolroom in Panama City, Florida. A witness claimed to have seen Gideon through the broken poolroom window at 5:30 A.M. A cigarette machine and jukebox were broken into and coins were taken. A "small amount of beer and some wine" were also taken.[7] This offense was a felony under Florida law. Appearing in court without funds and without a lawyer, Gideon asked the court to appoint counsel for him, whereupon the following exchange took place:

Why did Clarence Earl Gideon petition the government to protest his conviction and sentence to prison? What did the U.S. Supreme Court decide? To what other situations was the *Gideon* decision later extended?

> The Court: *Mr. Gideon, I am sorry, but I cannot appoint counsel to represent you in this case. Under the laws of the State of Florida, the only time the Court can appoint Counsel to represent a Defendant is when that person is charged with a capital offense. I am sorry, but I will have to deny your request to appoint Counsel to defend you in this case.*
>
> The Defendant: *The United States Supreme Court says I am entitled to be represented by Counsel.*

GIDEON'S COMPLAINT

Gideon was forced to conduct his own defense at trial. As the Supreme Court later said, he performed "about as well as could be expected from a layman. He made an opening statement to the jury, cross-examined the State's witnesses, presented witnesses in his own defense, declined to testify himself, and made a short argument emphasizing his innocence to the charge."

Nevertheless, the jury returned a verdict of guilty, and Gideon was sentenced to five years in state prison. From prison Gideon filed a handwritten habeas corpus petition challenging his conviction and sentence on the ground that the trial court's refusal to appoint counsel for him denied him rights "guaranteed by the Constitution and the Bill of Rights of the United States Government."

In considering the petition, the Supreme Court noted that the government spends large amounts of money on lawyers to prosecute defendants and that defendants who have money hire the best lawyers they can find to represent them. The Court concluded:

> *That government hires lawyers to prosecute and defendants who have money hire lawyers to defend are the strongest indications of the widespread belief that lawyers in criminal courts are necessities, not luxuries. The right of one charged with crime to counsel may not be deemed fundamental and essential to fair trials in some countries, but it is in ours. From the very beginning, our state and national constitutions and laws have laid great emphasis on procedural and substantive safeguards designed to assure fair trials before impartial tribunals in which every defendant stands equal before the law. This noble ideal cannot be realized if the poor man charged with crime has to face his accusers without a lawyer to assist him.*[8]

The Court went on to quote Justice Sutherland's opinion from the 1932 *Powell v. Alabama* case. That opinion held that the right to be heard in court would be "of little value if it did not comprehend the right to be heard by counsel":

> *Even the intelligent and educated layman has small and sometimes no skill in the science of law. If charged with crime, he is incapable, generally, of determining*

COUNSEL'S GUIDING HAND

> *for himself whether the indictment is good or bad. He is unfamiliar with the rules of evidence. Left without the aid of counsel he may be put on trial without a proper charge, and convicted upon incompetent evidence, or evidence irrelevant to the issue or otherwise inadmissible. He lacks both the skill and knowledge adequately to prepare his defense, even though he have a perfect one. He requires the guiding hand of counsel at every step in the proceedings against him. Without it, though he be not guilty, he faces the danger of conviction because he does not know how to establish his innocence.*[9]

Following this line of argument, the Court made the right to counsel during felony trials binding on all the states. The case of *Gideon v. Wainwright* proved to be a precedent-setting case in establishing the scope of the right to counsel.

Extensions of the Right to Counsel After the *Gideon* decision, questions remained regarding its scope. Would it extend to misdemeanor cases? What about nontrial proceedings? Beginning in 1963, the same year as the *Gideon* decision, the Court extended the right to counsel to other stages of the criminal justice process to ensure fair and impartial treatment of those accused of crimes. The Sixth Amendment right to counsel now extends to crime suspects questioned while in police custody[10] or during preliminary hearings,[11] to first appeal after conviction,[12] to police lineups,[13] to juvenile delinquency proceedings,[14] and to those charged with misdemeanors when imprisonment may result.[15] As described in Chapter 10, the decision in *Argersinger v. Hamlin* held that in situations in which a person can be deprived of liberty, the right to counsel exists, even when imprisonment for only one day can result.[16]

The impact of these legal decisions on practice illustrates their importance. Table 11.1 summarizes the findings of a survey of jail inmates awaiting trial in the United States. As Table 11.1 indicates, of those who hired their own legal counsel, 60 percent first spoke with their attorney either within 24 hours of arrest or during the first week in jail. Of those for whom counsel was provided by the government, only 38 percent spoke with a lawyer that early in the process. The timing of access to legal counsel can be critical, because interrogations and statements often are made early in the process and can influence the outcome of a case. This survey of jail inmates also shows the significance of the Supreme Court decisions

Table 11.1 Contact with Defense Counsel (from a survey of state inmates)

Contact with Counsel	*Public or Appointed Counsel*	*Private Attorney*
Within 24 hours of arrest	9%	26%
Within a week of arrest	28	34
More than a week before trial	33	30
Within a week of trial	13	5
At trial	14	4
Did not talk with counsel	4	2

Source: Caroline Wolf Harlow, *Defense Counsel in Criminal Cases* (Washington, DC: Bureau of Justice Statistics, 2000).

guaranteeing legal counsel to indigent defendants. More than 80 percent of all state inmates received appointed counsel, illustrating the large proportion of defendants who are poor.

IMPACTS ON PRACTICE

Right to *Effective* Counsel

A defendant is entitled not only to legal counsel, but to **effective counsel.** In 1970 the Supreme Court ruled that defendants are entitled "to the effective assistance of competent counsel."[17] But litigation is still alleging that effective assistance of counsel is often lacking—because of an inadequate supply of experienced lawyers in some jurisdictions, poor court supervision of the conduct of defense counsel, and jurisdictions' lack of funds to pay good lawyers.[18] The fundamental question in many instances is whether the legal advice given to a defendant is defective to such a degree that a defendant's case is hampered.

effective counsel
Competent representation by an attorney. It is ineffective assistance of counsel when unprofessional errors would have changed the outcome of the case.

reasons for ineffective counsel

STRICKLAND V. WASHINGTON

An actual case, *Strickland v. Washington*, illustrates the issue. Over a ten-day period David Leroy Washington committed a series of crimes, including theft, kidnapping, assaults, torture, and three brutal stabbing murders. After his two accomplices were arrested, Washington surrendered to police and gave a lengthy statement in which he confessed to one of the criminal incidents. The State of Florida indicted Washington for kidnapping and murder and appointed an experienced criminal lawyer to represent him.

Washington's appointed counsel subsequently learned that, against his advice, Washington had confessed to another of the murders. Washington waived his right to a jury trial, again acting against his counsel's advice, and pleaded guilty to all charges, including three capital murder charges.

When entering his plea Washington told the judge that he had no significant prior criminal record and that at the time of the crime spree he was under extreme stress caused by his inability to support his family. He also stated that he accepted responsibility for the crimes. The judge told Washington that he had "a great deal of respect for people who are willing to step forward and admit their responsibility," but he postponed sentencing.

In preparing for the sentencing hearing, Washington's lawyer spoke with his client about his background; he also spoke on the telephone with Washington's wife and mother, but did not seek any other character witnesses for him. The lawyer did not request a psychiatric examination, as his conversations with Washington gave no indications of psychological problems. He successfully excluded Washington's criminal record from consideration in sentencing by not requesting a presentence report. Such a report would have found that Washington did indeed have a significant criminal history.

At the sentencing hearing, the defense counsel argued that Washington's surrender, confession, offer to testify against a codefendant, and remorse and acceptance of responsibility justified sparing him from the death penalty. He characterized Washington as "fundamentally a good person who had briefly gone badly wrong in extremely stressful circumstances."[19] In determining whether the death sentence was appropriate, the judge found that all three murders had been cruel, involving repeated stabbings; all had been committed during the course of robberies; and all had been committed to avoid detection and arrest. The judge held that Washington was not suffering from extreme mental or emotional disturbance, and that his participation in the crimes was significant and not dominated by an accomplice. Washington was sentenced to death.

THE REASONABLENESS STANDARD

On appeal, Washington argued that he had received ineffective assistance of counsel in violation of the Sixth Amendment. He argued that his attorney's failure to request a psychiatric report, present character witnesses, or seek a presentence report had adversely affected his chances of receiving a less severe sentence. The Supreme Court ruled that when ineffective assistance of counsel is claimed, "the defendant must show that counsel's representation fell below an objective standard of reasonableness." In addition, the defendant must show "that there is a reasonable probability that, but for counsel's unprofessional errors, the result of the proceeding would have been different." In reviewing the facts of Washington's case, the Court determined that his lawyer's conduct was reasonable. Moreover, it held that even if his attorney's conduct was unreasonable, the case was not affected to the extent that would warrant setting aside his death sentence.[20]

In sum, under current law crime suspects and defendants are permitted to consult attorneys at most stages of the criminal justice process. The level of assistance provided must be "objectively reasonable, considering all the circumstances"; and for an appeal to be sustained, it must be shown that without counsel's errors the outcome of the trial would probably have been different. Different outcomes are difficult to prove, and grave errors of legal counsel are insufficient to prove that counsel's assistance was ineffective.[21]

STUDIES OF DEFENSE QUALITY

Several studies have attempted to assess objectively the quality of defense counsel. Each study has focused on whether someone who retains counsel receives better legal representation than someone represented by assigned counsel or a public defender. A few facts are clear: Caseloads are high, funding for indigent defense is low, and there are no national data that compare funding of prosecution to funding of defense in criminal cases. More than $1.3 billion is spent on indigent defense services annually in nearly 5 million cases, although the average expenditure per case is less than $300.[22] This low cost of case preparation has led to criticism of how indigent defense works in practice. Critics believe that government reimbursement for assigned counsel is too low, leading to poor-quality representation and inadequate investigations by defense lawyers of the charges against their clients.[23] Even the extent of contact with defense counsel varies significantly between defendants who have hired private attorneys and defendants with appointed counsel or public defenders. This difference in contact with counsel is shown in Table 11.2. Defense for indigents also suffers from lack of access to technology to assist in legal research, case preparation, and case tracking. A government report found that "resources for acquiring technology and providing training to staff are not available to many offices" of public defenders, suggesting that more efficient use can be made of time and energies devoted to indigent defense.[24]

INDIGENT DEFENSE

States vary in how they pay for indigent defense. In twenty states the state government funds the defense of indigent persons; in ten states the county does; and in twenty jurisdictions funding is shared by the county and state. Most counties (75 percent) require the defendant to repay a portion of his or her defense costs, but this money is difficult to collect, because of the indigent status of most defen-

Table 11.2 Number of Times Defendant Talked with Defense Counsel (from a survey of state inmates)

Number of Times Spoke with Defense Counsel	*Public or Appointed Counsel*	*Private Attorney*
0	5%	2%
1	25	10
2–3	44	31
4–5	13	21
6 or more times	13	37

Source: Caroline Wolf Harlow, *Defense Counsel in Criminal Cases* (Washington, DC: Bureau of Justice Statistics, 2000).

dants. Overall spending is much higher for prosecutors' offices than for public defenders' offices, and it is likely that expenditures per case (on investigations, witness interviews, expert opinions, and legal research) are also significantly higher. Mississippi, for example, leaves indigent criminal defense funding to the individual counties, a fact that has caused concern about uniformity in the funding and quality of legal representation.[25] A study of legal representation in Chicago found that public defenders obtained more guilty pleas than did private or assigned counsel.[26] However, a subsequent study discovered that this difference may have been due to the types of cases that public defenders handle. Ninety percent of the public defender caseloads in one city consisted of burglary, forgery, robbery, and theft cases, but only 66 percent of defendants with private counsel were charged with these crimes.[27] Because criminality is strongly related to opportunities to commit crime, it is not surprising that indigent offenders commit different types of offenses than do middle-class offenders. On the basis of the available information, therefore, no definite conclusions can be drawn from this debate—except that perhaps we cannot gauge the quality of defense lawyers by looking at the proportion of guilty pleas they obtain.[28]

A related issue in evaluations of the effectiveness of indigent defense is the nature of attorney–client relations. Defendants usually cannot choose their lawyers, and the feeling that "you get what you pay for" often leads to suspicion, lack of cooperation, and guarded exchanges of information.[29]

These circumstances may have a significant but unmeasured impact on the quality of legal representation and may account for continuing suits by defendants claiming they received ineffective assistance of counsel under the Sixth Amendment.[30]

How Are Cases Settled without Trial?

Police are called to the scene and find an inebriated husband assaulting his wife. They arrest the man and charge him with assault, possession of narcotics, and possession of a weapon. After they complete the arrest report, it is forwarded to the

Media & Criminal Justice

The Matrix Made Me Do It

The Matrix is a futuristic science fiction action movie trilogy about a band of hackers who rebel against their mechanized overlords. According to his defense attorney, a man in an actual Virginia case, charged with killing his parents, "harbored a bona fide belief that he was living in the virtual reality of 'The Matrix.'" A man in San Francisco chopped up his landlord and claimed he had been "sucked into 'The Matrix.'" Even one of the Washington, D.C.–area snipers was said to have written jailhouse sketches that said "Free Yourself of the Matrix."[a]

Of course, these "defenses" are simply modern adaptations of the insanity defense, which juries usually reject. *The Matrix* is not about justifying murder, but it does contain many violent scenes and violence is portrayed as a "solution" to various situations in the film. Therefore, it is possible a disturbed or easily influenced person could internalize the strategy of a fictional movie story and twist it to apply to his own life on the street (usually with disastrous results).

John Hinckley, shooter of President Reagan in 1981, was the first in recent history to blame the movies for his behavior. Hinckley claimed that actress Jodie Foster was the target of his affection and he acted violently in the way that actor Robert DeNiro did in the film *Taxi Driver.* Hinckley's insanity defense was successful, leading to a major change in insanity defense laws in the United States, as described in Chapter 6. It is unlikely that Hinckley's defense would have been successful under current law.

Likewise, other films that depict violence or alternate "realities" seem to find their way into courtrooms as explanations for criminal conduct. The violent film *Natural Born Killers* is another example of a movie referred to in several cases as the cause of "copycat" crimes.[b] Jacqueline Helfgott, a professor, states that these movies can unduly influence those who are affected by mental disorder. "For people already confused between fantasy and reality, [the movie] gives them a framework to articulate it. People who are already on the edge, it can be argued, can be set off by these types of movies."[c]

Why do you think that juries are generally quite skeptical of defenses based on applications of plots or scenes from movies? To what extent, if any, should film makers be held responsible for violence that is said to be provoked by their movies?

NOTES

a. Matt Bean, "'Matrix' Strategy Makes Its Way into Courtrooms," *CNN.com* (May 28, 2003).

b. Bruce Orwall, "Court Dismisses Suit on Movie, Violence," *The Wall Street Journal* (March 13, 2001), p. B10.

c. Quoted in Matt Bean, "'Matrix' Strategy Makes Its Way into Courtrooms."

prosecutor for evaluation. The prosecutor may decide to prosecute on all the arrest charges, drop some of them, reduce the charges, or not prosecute the case at all. A decision not to prosecute may be based on errors in the conduct of the police in the case or on a high volume of felony cases in the area where the offense took place, an overload that forces the prosecutor to set priorities in deciding which cases will be adjudicated to the full extent of the law. If the prosecutor decides not to prosecute a case, the judge and jury cannot serve any function and the arrest is meaningless.

The scope of a prosecutor's discretion is broad. The prosecutor's ability to select the charge on which a case will be prosecuted, or whether the case will be adjudicated at all, can have dramatic effects on the suspect, on the community, and on the criminal justice system. In recent years this role has expanded further, as half the states now permit prosecutors to select a trial by jury even if the defendant prefers a bench trial.[31]

Prosecutorial Discretion

Prosecutors have few limits on how they carry out their role. Consider a Manhattan district attorney in New York City who has established a narcotics eviction program. In response to complaints of tenants in poor neighborhoods, the DA asks landlords to begin eviction proceedings against tenants who are using drugs or allowing others to use their apartment to sell drugs. If the landlord does not act, the DA initiates eviction proceedings under New York's real estate law, which prohibits the use of any premises for the conduct of illegal activity. Police searches of the premises produce evidence that supports allegations of illegal use. In one case a sixty-eight-year-old woman was living with two daughters who were selling drugs. The judge allowed the mother to remain in the apartment but barred the daughters from returning there. In six years the program removed more than 2,000 drug users and dealers from both residential and commercial buildings.[32] This example illustrates the broad powers of prosecutors.

PROSECUTORIAL POWERS

Prosecutors are granted considerable discretion in the manner in which they enforce the law.[33] They can set priorities, concentrate on certain types of cases, and avoid other cases entirely. A good way to assess the extent of prosecutorial discretion is to trace the effects of a prosecutor's decision on a single case as it proceeds through the system. Assume that police have arrested a suspect on a charge of armed robbery. They turn the case over to the prosecutor, who decides (1) whether the case will be prosecuted and (2) what charges will be pressed. In the case of armed robbery, for example, assault, larceny, and weapons charges could be filed in addition to the robbery charge. These additional charges are called **necessarily included offenses** (or "lesser" included offenses) because they are, by definition, included as part of the other (more serious) offense.

necessarily included offenses ("Lesser" included offenses); offenses that are, by definition, included in a charge as part of another (more serious) offense.

After charges have been filed, the prosecutor can decide not to press the charges any further or to reduce the charge in exchange for a guilty plea. When the charge is not pressed further, it is called **nolle prosequi** (or nol. pros.). Such a decision is entirely within the prosecutor's discretion. Exchanging a reduced charge for a guilty plea is a form of plea bargaining (discussed below). After a defendant has pleaded guilty or been convicted in court, the prosecutor usually recommends a particular sentence to the judge. Thus, the prosecutor has considerable discretion at virtually all important decision points in the criminal justice process: determining whether the police decision to arrest was appropriate, determining the charge, recommending bail, playing a role in whether or not a defendant goes to trial, and influencing the judge's sentencing decision.

nolle prosequi A decision by a prosecutor not to press charges; also known as nol. pros.

EXPANDING DISCRETIONARY POWERS

The scope of a prosecutor's discretion continues to expand as the adoption of mandatory minimum sentence laws and truth-in-sentencing laws (discussed later in this chapter) has reduced judges' flexibility in decisions about sentencing. For example, many states have gun-carrying laws that attach mandatory sentences of one year or more for persons who possess a handgun without a proper permit. A prosecutor may choose to prosecute a first offender for a lesser crime, such as disorderly conduct or trespass, that does not carry a mandatory sentence. Alternatively, the prosecutor may wish to charge the first offender with the greater offense—whether for deterrence or for political leverage in a campaign. This shifting of sentencing authority away from judges and toward the prosecutors has been criticized for placing too much power in the hands of individuals, providing prosecutors with too much opportunity to misuse their broad discretionary authority.[34]

Diversion of Cases

diversion programs
Alternatives to the formal criminal justice process that are implemented after charging but prior to adjudication; they attempt to achieve a noncriminal disposition of the case.

pretrial intervention (PTI)
A type of diversion program in which a prosecutor suspends prosecution of a case pending the fulfillment of special conditions by the defendant. If these conditions are met, the case is dismissed.

Another important decision made by prosecutors is to divert some offenders out of the adjudication process. **Diversion programs** are alternatives to the formal criminal justice process, implemented after a suspect has been charged but prior to adjudication. These programs attempt to achieve a noncriminal disposition of the case. Sixty-three percent of all prosecutors' offices in the United States have a diversion program for first-time offenders.[35]

A common type of diversion program is **pretrial intervention (PTI).** Where PTI programs exist, any offender can apply to the prosecutor for admission to the program. If the nature of the offense and the offender's background are such that little risk will be posed to the community, the prosecutor suspends prosecution of the case for one year. During this time the prosecutor can require the offender, for example, to make restitution to the victim, attend a drug or alcohol treatment program, or participate in voluntary service to the community. After one year, if the offender has not gotten into further legal trouble, the prosecutor will move to dismiss the case. If the offender fails to live up to the prosecutor's expectations, the case is resumed and passes through the normal adjudication process. Pretrial intervention gives first-time offenders, property offenders, and people who have committed misdemeanors an opportunity to show that they should not be prosecuted. Such programs increase the possibility that an offender will be rehabilitated. They also reduce court costs and caseloads.

CRITICS OF DIVERSION PROGRAMS

Some critics of diversion programs believe that offenders do not deserve a break and that PTI programs weaken the deterrence effect of the law. Other critics feel that diversion programs do not go far enough and that prosecutors, in

A prosecutor and defense counsel discuss a possible plea bargain with a defendant. What does the prosecutor gain from a plea bargain? What does the defense gain? Do you believe plea-bargaining serves the public interest?

FIGURE 11.1 Adjudication of Felony Arrests in the Seventy-Five Largest Counties in the United States

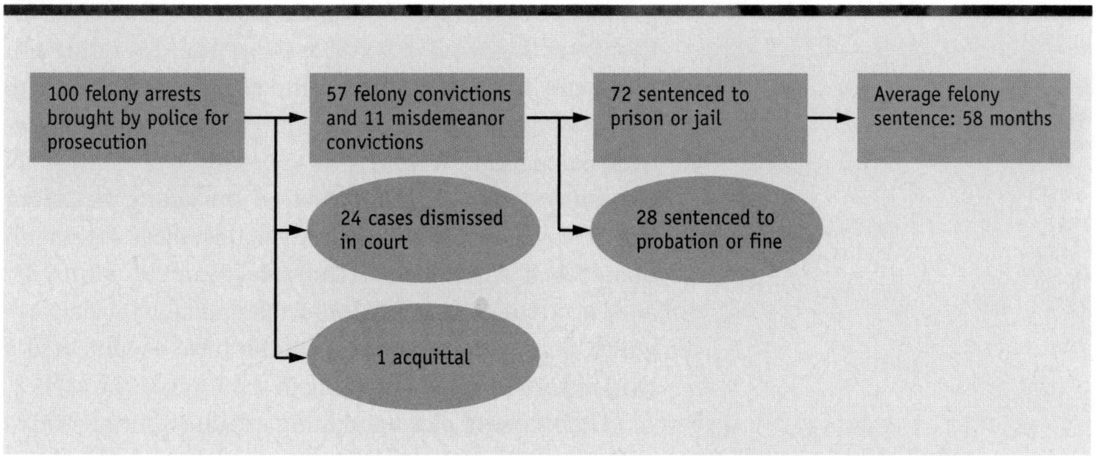

Source: Compiled from Thomas H. Cohen and Brian A. Reaves, *Felony Defendants in Large Urban Counties* (Washington, DC: Bureau of Justice Statistics, 2006).

order to compile a good record of success for their office, may recommend diversion only to the offenders with the greatest chance of completing the program successfully. As a result, people who could benefit from the treatment may be denied access to PTI. Also, prosecutors may be tempted to encourage participation in diversion programs when the case is weak or when they otherwise would not have prosecuted the case. In this sense, diversion may *increase* rather than decrease the number of people who are subjected to the criminal justice process.[36]

INTERMEDIATE SANCTIONS

Diversion also takes the form of conditional sentences. Most prosecutors now recommend a wide range of "intermediate sanctions" that involve neither incarceration nor probation. More than three-fourths of prosecutors' offices nationwide report resolving some cases by recommending alcohol or drug rehabilitation, community service, counseling, or restitution.[37] These kinds of dispositions are designed to deter future misconduct more effectively by addressing the underlying causes of the unlawful behavior.

Evidence indicates, however, that most felony cases result in prosecution. An analysis of prosecutions in the seventy-five largest counties in the United States found that for every 100 persons arrested for a felony, 24 went to court but were dismissed; only 57 were convicted of a felony. Of these, 72 received jail or prison sentences with an average sentence of 58 months.[38] This case shrinkage is illustrated in Figure 11.1. What is not clear is why some of the cases were not prosecuted and why so many suspects escaped conviction and prison sentences.

Plea Bargaining

Plea bargaining occurs when a prosecutor agrees to press a less serious charge, drop some charges, or recommend a less severe sentence if the defendant agrees to plead guilty. Prosecutors often claim that plea bargaining is a necessary evil that enables them to deal with large caseloads. Others claim that it is merely an administrative convenience. To understand this debate, it is important to know the history, nature, and extent of plea bargaining.

plea bargaining
An agreement by a prosecutor to press a less serious charge, drop some charges, or recommend a less severe sentence if the defendant agrees to plead guilty.

FIGURE 11.2 Trial Rates for Felony Defendants
(Seventy-five largest U.S. counties)

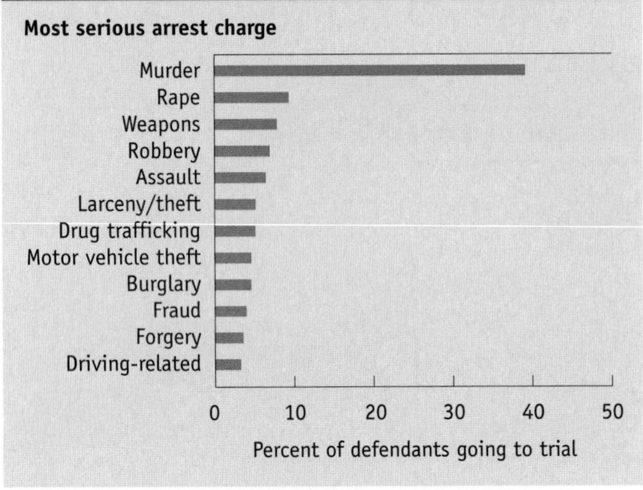

Source: Thomas H. Cohen and Brian A. Reaves, *Felony Defendants in Large Urban Counties* (Washington, DC: Bureau of Justice Statistics, 2006).

THE HEUMANN STUDY

Milton Heumann conducted a classic study to determine how recently plea bargaining became a common practice in the United States. He looked at trial rates for felonies in Connecticut Superior Court from 1880 through 1954 and found that the percentage of cases that went to trial averaged about 9 percent throughout this seventy-five-year period.[39] That is to say, only 9 percent of all dispositions were the result of a trial—meaning that about 9 in 10 cases were resolved through guilty pleas. Heumann then looked at Connecticut trial rates from 1966 to 1973, and found the same low rate of trials and high incidence of guilty pleas. Other historical studies have documented a long history of plea bargaining in the United States.[40]

High rates of plea bargaining also have been found in other studies of plea-bargaining practices in other locations. Abraham Blumberg examined trial rates in a metropolitan court over a period of twenty-five years. Blumberg found no significant variation in the frequency of trials over the years, and never did the trial rate exceed 10 percent.[41] Another study looked at fourteen different counties and found that pleas outnumbered trials by eleven to one.[42] Similarly, studies of felony defendants in the seventy-five largest U.S. counties found that more than 90 percent of those convicted pleaded guilty and did not go to trial.[43] Recent national surveys of prosecutors' offices in the United States found that the proportion of guilty pleas changed little in the period studied, averaging 90 percent of all felony convictions.[44] It appears, therefore, that plea bargaining is not a recent phenomenon and that it is widely used to resolve cases in jurisdictions of all types. Figure 11.2 illustrates that the proportion of pleas to trials does not fluctuate widely by type of offense. These data from the seventy-five largest U.S. counties found that trial rates are 9 percent or less for all offenses except murder, for which 44 percent of cases are tried.

PLEA BARGAINS AND CASELOADS

Contrary to what you might expect, courts with low caseloads have been found to have higher plea rates than courts with high caseloads.[45] In an analogous way, counties with high rates of plea bargaining often were found to have lower caseloads than counties with low rates of plea bargaining. To try to explain this, Heumann interviewed prosecutors, judges, and defendants. He discovered that most cases have no substantial legal or factual issues, and that the risks entailed in going to trial (and possibly losing) are quite high. Therefore, many prosecutors, defense counsel, and suspects feel that a guilty plea is a more advantageous path than going to trial. Thus, plea bargaining appears to result from factors other than high caseloads.

What Are Some Problems of the Court System?

Courts face problems that arise from increasing arrests and higher caseloads, a more litigious society, and overreliance on pleas. These problems have created delays in the adjudication process, growing backlogs of cases to be heard, and claims of unfairness in the way cases are handled.

Courts adjudicate a large volume of cases each year, and the number is growing. This increased volume reflects the growth of the U.S. population, increases in arrests, and increases in the use of lawsuits to resolve disputes. The dramatic growth in caseloads has placed tremendous strain on many courts. The situation was aggravated in 1974 when Congress passed the **Speedy Trial Act.** This act requires that all criminal cases be brought to trial within one hundred days; if they are not, they will be dismissed.

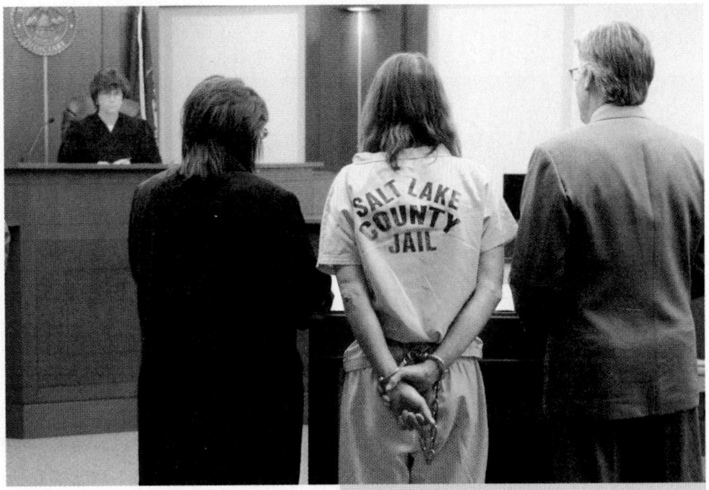

Brian David Mitchell, dressed in prison clothing, appears with his lawyers in court in Salt Lake City, Utah. Mitchell was charged with the alleged abduction of Elizabeth Smart. Under what circumstances could this case be settled without a trial? What are the advantages and disadvantages of a plea versus a trial?

The rationale for the Speedy Trial Act is that the Sixth Amendment requires "a speedy and public trial" and that delays in court often work against the interests of the accused, who may be in jail awaiting adjudication of the case. The result of the act has been an increase in the speed with which criminal cases are brought to trial, but a dramatic slowing in the processing of civil cases, which are not covered by the act. This is why it often takes several years for a civil case to reach the trial stage. In addition, criminal cases take up a great deal of court time. Every criminal case requires an initial appearance, a preliminary hearing or grand jury, arraignment, and possibly a trial and an appeal. Courts must be highly organized to handle so many court appearances and to determine the need for and availability of judges, courtrooms, court clerks, stenographers, sheriff's deputies, and other participants in the adjudication process.

Speedy Trial Act
Legislation requiring that all criminal cases be brought to trial within one hundred days.

The typical felony is now adjudicated in 98 days, although it varies considerably by offense, from 186 days in rape cases to 50 days in cases of motor vehicle theft. Murder cases usually take considerably longer, because of the time it takes to analyze physical evidence and obtain expert witnesses, which are used often in cases of homicide. Cases are permitted to exceed the 100-day limit only when the court agrees that the defense needs additional time to prepare its case.

Caseloads

The problem of rising **caseloads** is serious in federal courts; the volume of cases in federal district courts has nearly tripled since 1980. In 1991 the average federal trial judge handled 401 cases. In 1997 the number was 470. Part of the problem arises because of judicial vacancies: More than 100 positions for federal judges remain unfilled because of disagreement between the president and the Senate (controlled by the opposing political party) about suitable candidates. In 1994 101 new federal judges were approved; in 1996 and 1997 combined, only 53 were confirmed. Another contributing factor to high federal caseloads is the "federalizing" of crimes previously handled by the states.[46] Since 1980 Congress has dramatically increased the number of federal crimes, especially drug and gun offenses. Therefore, crimes once handled exclusively in state courts are increasingly being tried as violations of federal law. There has been a dramatic increase in criminal cases filed in U.S. district courts. In twenty years, the number has more than doubled.

caseloads
The large numbers of cases to be adjudicated in the courts.

Both new criminal charges and appeals from adjudicated cases have increased tenfold in recent decades, and there is no end in sight. In state courts,

That's a FACT

Perspectives on Adjudication

The use of America's courts to solve problems continues at a high rate. Figure 11A illustrates that incoming caseloads have increased in every category over the last decade. Not shown in this graph are traffic court cases, which hover around 15 million cases each year. Can you offer reasons for the continuing increasing in court cases over the years?

Examining the criminal caseload more carefully, the types of cases being prosecuted suggest the nature of some underlying problems. Figure 11B groups the most serious arrest charges in felony cases in the nation's seventy-five largest counties. Drug-related offenses clearly dominate the caseload, followed by assault, larceny, robbery, and burglary.

FIGURE 11A Incoming Caseloads in Unified and General Jurisdiction Courts, by Case Type, 1994–2003

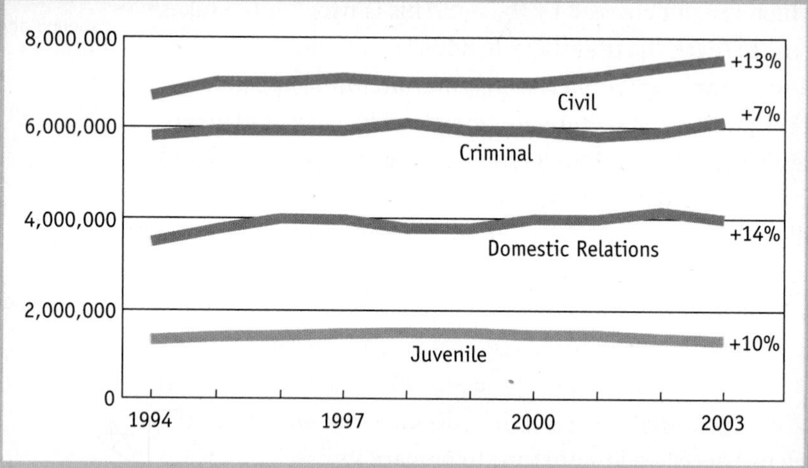

Source: Examining the Work of State Courts (Williamsburg, VA: National Center for State Courts, 2005).

REASONS FOR HIGHER CASELOADS

which handle more than 95 percent of the total volume of cases, nearly 100 million new cases are filed each year. These incoming cases include criminal cases (21 million), juvenile cases (2 million), domestic relations cases (6 million), and traffic (55 million).[47] Despite a growing trend toward the use of mediation and pretrial intervention programs, new cases far outstrip the capacity of these programs to deal with them.

As the U.S. population grows, it is reasonable to expect the numbers of arrests and cases filed to increase as well. One of the largest sources of higher caseloads is drug cases. The increase in laws and law enforcement in this area in recent decades has led to thousands of arrests and prosecutions throughout the nation. As noted in Chapter 10, specialized drug courts have been created in some areas, but it is clear that more judges and more courtrooms and courtroom personnel will be needed for the foreseeable future. Table 11.3 outlines some growing career opportunities in adjudication.

FIGURE 11B Most Frequently Charged Felony Offenses Seventy-Five Largest U.S. Counties

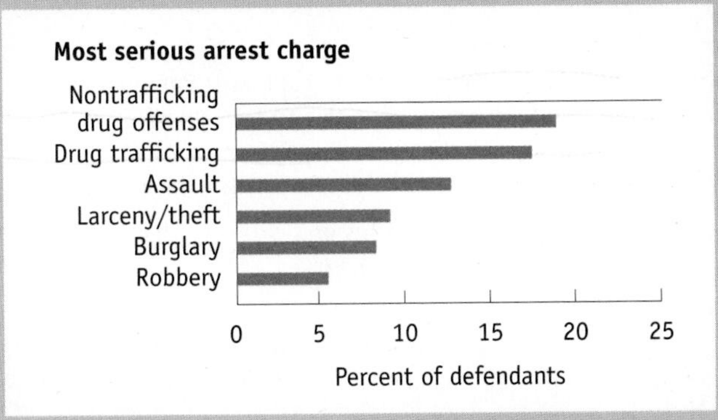

Do you think the drug offenses might be related to these other crimes? Explain why you believe drug offenses are so common in felony court caseloads.

The backgrounds of those charged with felonies also provide some insight into court caseload problems. More than three-quarters of all felony defendants have a prior arrest history for a felony or a misdemeanor. Of those defendants with an arrest record, about seven in eight have more than one prior arrest charge, and a majority have at least five. Figure 11C shows the percentage of defendants who were on probation at the time of their arrest, numbers that exclude those who were on parole or were out on bail on an earlier charge. Why do you believe there are so many repeat arrestees in the felony court caseload?

FIGURE 11C Felony Defendants on Probation at the Time of Their Arrest Seventy-Five Largest U.S. Counties

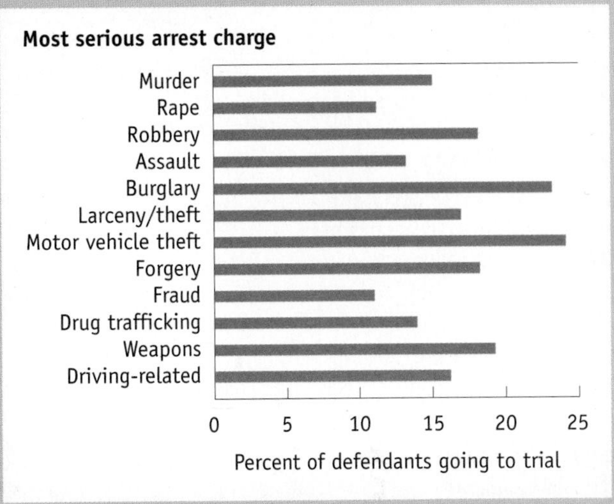

Source: Thomas H. Cohen and Brian A. Reaves, *Felony Defendants in Large Urban Counties* (Washington, DC: Bureau of Justice Statistics, 2006).

Case Mortality

In a controversial case, prosecutors in Ontario, Canada, offered a plea bargain to the wife of Paul Bernado, who was charged with the abduction, rape, torture, and murder of two teenage girls inside the couple's home. Despite evidence that the wife participated in the killings, and despite the fact that a judge found the plea bargain "distasteful," the plea was accepted as possibly the only way to make a case against the husband.[48] Sixteen months after the plea bargain was struck, however, videotapes were discovered that depicted the wife's active participation in the brutal rape and torture of the victims. More than 300,000 citizens signed petitions protesting the plea-bargain agreement, but it could not be changed after the fact. The wife received a twelve-year sentence and Paul Bernado received a life term.[49] Plea bargaining can backfire if prosecutors carry it out before conducting a thorough investigation; and sensational cases, although rare, inflame the public belief

PLEA BARGAINS CAN BACKFIRE

Table 11.3 Career Opportunities in Adjudication

Prosecuting attorney http://www.abanet.org/lsd/jobopp.html http://www.ndaa-apri.org/	Represents a jurisdiction (district or commonwealth) in bringing charges against accused persons arrested by the police. *Qualifications:* Law school graduation and passage of the bar examination.
Legal assistant http://www.paralegals.org http://www.nala.org/	Paralegal employed by prosecutors, defense attorneys, and law firms to assist in the preparation of civil and criminal cases. *Qualifications:* Completion of ten or more college-level courses at a certified school.
Defense attorney http://www.abanet.org/lsd/jobopp.html http://www.law.indiana.edu/law/v-lib/criminal.html http://www.uscourts.gov/	Represents accused persons in court proceedings. Public defenders are salaried attorneys who work on behalf of indigent defendants. Attorneys in private practice also represent clients accused of crimes. *Qualifications:* Law school graduation and passage of the bar examination.
Victim and witness assistant http://www.ilj.org/programs.html http://www.ojp.usdoj.gov/ovc/	Coordinates and provides services to victims and witnesses by providing information, counseling, or other support services. *Qualifications:* Bachelor's degree minimum.
Forensic scientist http://www.cl.state.ut.us/ http://www.ganet.org/gbi/labsci.html http://dpa.state.ky.us/~rwheeler/evidence.htm	Studies and reports on criminal evidence used in adjudication (DNA, drugs, blood, hair, fingerprints, fibers, documents, residue from bullets and explosives). *Qualifications:* Master's degree preferred; background in chemistry and biology lab work.
Judge or magistrate http://www.ajs.org/ http://www.fjc.gov/ http://www.ncsc.dni.us/ http://www.ncjfcj.unr.edu	Upholds rights of the accused, arbitrates between the prosecution and the defense in a criminal case. Instructs juries, rules on issues of law and procedure, may decide on a sentence. *Qualifications:* Attorneys are elected or appointed to the office.

that offenders are getting a "deal" and that prosecutors are not representing the interests of the community effectively.

Few people are satisfied with plea bargaining, and many examples justify this skepticism. Author Stephen King was hit by a car as a pedestrian and was seriously injured. The driver plea-bargained to receive a suspended six-month jail sentence for dangerous driving. Stephen King publicly expressed his dissatisfaction that the driver was able keep his driver's license.[50] Critics have called plea bargaining "injustice for all."[51]

Public officials often have claimed that if prosecutors had smaller caseloads, the number of trials relative to pleas would increase. However, a survey by the U.S. Bureau of Justice Statistics found that only about 1 percent of all felony cases were decided by a jury trial regardless of the size of the prosecutor's office or the jurisdiction. An even smaller number of felony defendants had a bench trial, while all the other defendants pleaded guilty. Prosecutors' offices in jurisdictions with populations of 1 million or more handle an average of nearly 40,000 cases per year. In jurisdictions of less than 250,000, an average of 1,400 cases are prosecuted per year, yet the trial rate remains the same.[52] A study of federal prosecutions found that 93 percent of those convicted pleaded guilty, while 7 percent were convicted at trial.[53]

STUDIES OF CRIMINAL CASE PROCESSING

case mortality
Case attrition, in which arrests do not result in convictions for various reasons.

Studies of criminal case processing have found high levels of **case mortality,** or attrition. An investigation by Boland, Brady, Tyson, and Bassler examined felony arrests in fourteen counties across the country. They found that 50 percent of all cases were either dismissed or rejected by the prosecutor because of lack of sufficient evidence or for other reasons. Forty-five percent ended in guilty pleas, and only 5 percent went to trial.[54] On average, the likelihood that a case will go to trial is between 4 and 8 percent, and 38 percent of violent crimes and 27 percent of property crimes are either rejected by the prosecutor or dismissed by the judge before trial. In federal cases the numbers are similar: Thirty-seven percent of violent crimes and 49 percent of property crimes are prosecuted.[55] The question that remains is: Why are so many cases lost along the way?

VERA INSTITUTE OF JUSTICE STUDY

One of the first studies to address the reasons for case mortality was conducted by the Vera Institute of Justice. In this study, randomly selected case files of felony arrests in New York City were followed to their ultimate disposition. For a small subsample of those cases, participants were interviewed. Of the 53 robbery cases examined in detail, only 1 went to trial, and only 15 resulted in felony sentences.[56] Although it might appear at first glance that justice was not carried out in these cases, a closer look reveals that 23 of the 53 robberies (36 percent) involved a prior relationship between the victim and the defendant—a situation that reduces the possibility of a conviction at trial. In cases involving prior relationships, juries tend to suspect victims of using the court to seek revenge against a former spouse or lover. Of the 30 robberies that remained, 26 (88 percent) resulted in convictions and 20 (77 percent) in a jail or prison sentence. Offenders who managed to avoid felony sentences by pleading guilty to a lesser charge did so primarily because of lack of interest on the part of the victim or because the victim had a criminal record or was engaging in criminal conduct (such as prostitution or drug dealing). In a national survey of prosecutors' offices, the most frequent reasons given for case dismissals were search and seizure problems (52 percent) and unavailability of witnesses (44 percent). In a large proportion of these cases, prosecutors declined to prosecute because of reluctance on the part of the victim (74 percent) or of a witness (58 percent).[57]

In cases that were prosecuted, 98 percent of offenders with a criminal record were sentenced to jail, despite the fact that serious injury occurred in only seven of the fifty-three cases and only six offenders had threatened their victims with guns. These findings were confirmed in studies of different counties, which also found a high incidence of cases involving prior relationships between defendant and victim (45 percent); again, the primary factors preventing prosecution were evidence- and witness-related problems.[58]

The Vera Institute study also found that court congestion caused pretrial delays that induced some defendants to plead guilty who probably would have been acquitted if they had gone to trial, because of weak evidence in the case. Subsequent studies in different cities have uncovered similar findings.[59] Judges tend to equalize the impact of lesser pleas by imposing a relatively longer sentence on the reduced charge, raising the question of whether plea bargaining benefits the defendant. Likewise, some courts have permitted longer sentences in plea bargains by taking dismissed charges into consideration.[60]

"FAKE" PLEA BARGAINS

Overreliance on Plea Bargaining Overreliance on plea bargaining can result in its abuse. A prosecutor in Ulster County, New York, authorized a "fake" plea bargain with a kidnapping defendant in which the prosecutor asked the defendant to lead them to the kidnapped girl, who was found dead. The prosecutor claimed that because the girl had been killed during the kidnapping, the plea bargain was voided. The ethics and constitutionality of rescinding a plea bargain have been questioned.[61] Similarly, some courts have allowed defendants who plea-bargained to be reindicted if their sentence is subsequently overturned on other grounds. These courts view the plea bargain as an obligation to serve the full sentence rather than an obligation to plead guilty.[62] Thus, you can see that the contractual nature of plea bargains is called into question when the plea deal changes after the agreement has been made.

REASONS FOR PLEA BARGAINING

In sum, a growing body of evidence suggests that plea bargaining is not due to overcrowded courts or overburdened prosecutors, and that it usually does not result in lenient sentences. In reality, plea bargaining appears to result from two overriding factors: (1) Most cases have few issues of fact or law to be established at trial, because the evidence against the defendant is or is not present. And (2) the risks of going to trial are high for both sides; at trial even an "open-and-shut" case can be lost because of victims and witnesses who may be poor witnesses, and at trial even a case with weak evidence can be decided in favor of the prosecution. Therefore, plea bargaining occurs so often because it assists both prosecution and defense in obtaining a predictable outcome in an otherwise uncertain process.[63]

ELIMINATE PLEA BARGAINING?

Plea bargaining has many undesirable features, however. Plea negotiations are conducted in private; the rights of the accused and the interests of the community are not visibly balanced (as occurs in trials); and the public may believe that justice is not achieved. In 1973 these features led the National Advisory Commission on Criminal Justice Standards and Goals to recommend that "as soon as possible, but not later than 1978, negotiations between defendants and prosecutors concerning concessions to be made in return for guilty pleas be abolished."[64] This recommendation formed the basis for several ill-fated efforts to eliminate plea bargaining entirely. Perhaps the best-evaluated effort involved New York State's drug laws. Under these laws the possession or sale of heroin or other narcotics was punished by mandatory minimum prison sentences of one to fifteen years, with maximums ranging up to life imprisonment. If released, offenders were placed on parole for the rest of their lives, and pleas to lesser charges were not permitted.

In the 1970s the New York City Bar Association conducted an evaluation of the impact of this law on drug offenders. Researchers compared arrests, indictments, and convictions a year before the law was passed and several years after it had taken effect. Surprisingly, arrests decreased, indictments fell, the proportion of arrests leading to indictments fell, and the number of convictions fell by almost one-half, indicating that the law has had the opposite of its intended effect.[65] Knowing that arrests, indictments, and convictions can lead to very severe penalties, police officers, grand juries, and trial juries are more reluctant to arrest, indict, or convict offenders who they believe do not deserve such harsh penalties.

In this negotiating session, the prosecuting attorney offered to press a less serious charge or drop some charges, or to recommend leniency in sentencing, in exchange for the defendant's guilty plea. The defense attorney is advising her client to take the deal. This kind of arrangement is common in the American court system: What are its advantages and disadvantages for the operation of the courts? for defendants? for justice?

Nevertheless, the New York experience has been repeated elsewhere, and for crimes other than drug possession or sale. Studies have evaluated the effects of establishing mandatory penalties for drunk driving and gun law violations.[66] The results are remarkably consistent. When discretion is removed from one part of the system, it is replaced by greater use of discretion in other parts.

Impact of Mandatory Sentences on Plea Bargaining Mandatory sentences are designed to require a certain penalty upon conviction in order to guarantee that offenders do not escape punishment. When combined with policies forbidding plea bargaining, however, mandatory sentencing appears simply to shift discretion to other parts of the criminal justice system. As Arthur Rosset and Donald Cressey have observed, "efforts to eliminate discretionary decisions or to limit them substantially seem bound to fail because there must be a place in the courthouse both for the rule of law and for discretion."[67]

Perhaps the best-known examples of mandatory sentence laws are the **"three strikes" laws** in which conviction for a third felony results in a life sentence. These laws have increased prison populations, but they incarcerate many nonviolent offenders. In New York State, for example, nearly 80 percent of drug offenders who receive prison sentences have never been convicted of a violent crime.[68] In California and elsewhere the "three strikes" law has not reduced the crime rate.[69] In Michigan, former Republican Governor William Milliken called the "650 Lifer Law" his biggest mistake. The law mandated life terms for offenders possessing 650 grams of heroin or cocaine. As a result, 86 percent of the offenders prosecuted under this law received life sentences when they had never been to prison before.[70]

"three strikes" laws
Laws under which conviction for a third felony results in an extended sentence, up to life imprisonment.

CONSEQUENCES OF NO-PLEA-BARGAINING RULES

Given the consistent findings about the effects of mandatory sentences and policies prohibiting plea bargaining, some general conclusions can be drawn. First, a restrictive plea-bargaining policy usually leads to a restrictive case-screening policy, so fewer cases—the stronger ones—are prosecuted. Second, when sentences are mandatory, the bargaining focuses on the charges against the accused. Third, a combination of no-plea-bargaining policies *and* mandatory sentences leads to fewer arrests, fewer indictments, fewer convictions, and more dismissals, trials (versus pleas), and appeals. Fourth, researchers have not found that harsh penalties have a deterrent effect on the commission of the offenses covered by these policies. Nevertheless, calls for the abolition of plea bargaining continue. These proposals, in turn, are leading to proposals to change the way negotiations are conducted.[71]

Changing Plea Negotiations The difficulty of eliminating plea bargaining has provoked efforts to find ways of reducing unfairness in existing plea-bargaining practices. Various ways to eliminate the undesirable aspects of plea bargaining have been suggested, among them public negotiations, time limitations, better case-screening procedures, and reviews of plea agreements by judges and victims. The National Advisory Commission called for a time limit on all plea negotiations; after a certain period, only pleas to the original charge filed would be permitted. In the commission's view, such a procedure would prevent unnecessary delays, which sometimes result in unwise pleas by defendants in jail awaiting trial. Felony cases typically are concluded in four to seven months, which can be a long time for a defendant serving that period in jail.[72]

What problems of the criminal justice system have been blamed on high caseloads and overburdened prosecutors? What are some consequences of these problems? What recent developments in the criminal justice system are working against plea bargaining, and with what effects?

pretrial settlement conference
A meeting of the prosecutor, defendant, counsel, and judge to discuss a plea before a trial is held. No plea negotiations can take place outside this setting.

Several cities use a **pretrial settlement conference,** in which the prosecutor, the defendant, the defendant's counsel, and the judge meet before a trial to discuss a plea. The arresting officer and the victim are invited to attend these sessions. No plea negotiations can take place outside this setting; and no plea negotiations are admissible as evidence if a trial eventually results, so as not to prejudice a judge or jury. Therefore, trials are reserved for the few cases in which no pretrial settlement can be reached. This procedure makes the plea-bargaining process more visible, and a neutral party (the judge) is present to ensure that the rights of the defendant and the need to protect the community are properly balanced. Experimentation with this procedure has produced encouraging results.[73]

EFFECTIVE SCREENING

Another proposal is that prosecutors adopt more effective screening procedures to eliminate cases unlikely to be prosecuted successfully. A national survey of prosecutors found that inadequate evidence gathering by police and poor preparation of crime reports caused case dismissals, which proper screening might have prevented.[74] Better case screening is becoming mandatory as court caseloads include more drug offenders. Throughout the nation more than 30 percent of the felony court caseload consists of cases involving drug traffickers (19 percent) and possessors (13 percent).[75] Screening can help prosecutors distinguish between major and minor drug cases so as to use criminal justice resources more effectively.

Adjudicate the Offender or the Act?

Sensational cases in recent years have drawn attention to the defendant rather than to the crime. Although the adjudication process is designed to assess responsibility for the criminal act, media portrayals and the tactics of some defense attorneys have shifted the focus to the criminal. Defendant Colin Ferguson, for example, asked to represent himself at his trial. He was accused of engaging in a shooting rampage on a Long Island Railroad train car in which six people were killed and nineteen others wounded. Legal and psychiatric experts argued that Ferguson was paranoid and delusional, but the judge ruled that he was competent to represent himself in court. Ferguson later appealed his conviction, arguing that he was mentally incompetent to stand trial in the first place.[76] This series of events reflects confusion between granting defendants the legal right to represent themselves and the need to maintain the integrity of court proceedings by focusing on the act.

Colin Ferguson went on a shooting rampage on the Long Island Railroad, killing six people. Although his mental competency was questioned, he was permitted to represent himself in court. Adjudication assesses responsibility for the criminal act. To what extent should defendants be permitted to portray themselves as victims?

In the Menendez case and others of a similar nature, the defense has argued that the defendants should be excused because of abuse they suffered as children.[77] Although some observers consider this argument outrageous, several states have extended the excuse of self-defense to battered women who kill their husbands out of fear after a history of physical abuse, even though the husband might be sleeping at the time of the murder.[78] It can be argued that the Menendez "child abuse" defense is simply an extension of the "battered woman syndrome" defense created in the 1980s. Both attempt to employ the principle of self-defense in situations that fall outside the traditional scope of this principle.[79] On one hand, self-defense is being expanded well beyond its logical limits when the defendant is successfully portrayed as a "victim." On the other hand, less sympathetic defendants, such as those convicted of assault and manslaughter for shooting trespassers, are treated according to the traditional rules of self-defense. Again, the focus shifts from the crime to the criminal.

OFFENDERS AS VICTIMS

The same trend can be seen in the "urban survival defense," in which defendants who take lives unlawfully are portrayed as victims.[80] Timothy McVeigh's argument that the Oklahoma City bombing was necessary as "retaliation" against the government for its actions at Waco, Texas, was an effort to stretch "self-defense" to new dimensions. Applying the logic of self-defense in these cases is a slippery slope, yet defendants and their attorneys increasingly are doing so.

After the media onslaught that surrounded the O.J. Simpson trial, courts in Los Angeles proposed new rules to ban hallway interviews during trials.[81] Attorneys in that case often held impromptu news conferences after each day's proceedings in an effort to shape public opinion about the case. Such posturing can indirectly influence the jury, which may learn of the lawyers' statements through the media. Similarly, guidelines have been proposed for lawyers who appear on television as legal commentators during subsequent civil cases, as in O.J. Simpson's civil trial. In these appearances attorneys can accidentally broadcast client confidences or distort information because of their prior involvement in a related criminal case.[82] Here again, it appears that defense attorneys focus on building the image of the defendant rather than on responding to the crimes charged. In a shocking example of this phenomenon, former assistant district attorney Steven Pagones was accused of raping Tawana Brawley. The accusation was made by three prominent individuals from the New York City area, including the Reverend Al Sharpton. Mr. Pagones was ultimately cleared of the charge, and he then successfully sued his accusers on charges of defamation of character. This civil suit was tried in a case marred by name-calling, contempt citations, and other disorderly behavior in the courtroom. A defense lawyer served a night in jail for contempt in refusing to obey a judge's order.[83] Although atypical, misbehavior on the part of defense attorneys fuels the perception that they abuse the process in order to draw attention away from the facts of the case.

Crime Control or Due Process?

Among the most compelling questions for criminal defense in the future is, What do we want the criminal justice system to accomplish? The answer to this question is not straightforward and can involve quite different perspectives on the justice process.

Criminologist Herbert Packer described two ideal models of criminal justice operations that are useful when we try to evaluate the system and its operations. According to the **crime control model,** repression of criminal conduct is the most important function of the criminal justice system. To accomplish this, the system must achieve maximum speed, efficiency, and finality in criminal justice processing. Proponents of this model argue that deterrence of crime is achieved when the penalty is imposed quickly and with certainty. Quick and certain punishment cannot occur when a prolonged series of pretrial hearings, continuances and other delays, and appeals distance the connection between the crime and the punishment. In contrast, the **due process model** treats the preservation of individual liberties as the most important function of the criminal justice system. Therefore, according to this view, accuracy, fairness, and reliability in criminal procedure are keys to a properly functioning system.[84] Proponents of the due process model believe that careful attention to the rights of individuals—when individuals are prosecuted by a much more powerful government—is essential to ensure that only the guilty are convicted and that the public has a high level of confidence in the system. This attention cannot be given when so many cases are plea bargained, defendants are encouraged to waive their constitutional rights, and the outcomes of cases are determined by invisible negotiating behind closed doors rather than in court.

crime control model
The perspective that views the repression of criminal conduct as the most important function to be performed by the criminal justice system, through speed, efficiency, and finality in criminal justice processing.

due process model
The perspective that considers preservation of individual liberties to be the most important function of the criminal justice system, through accuracy, fairness, and reliability in criminal procedure.

These two ideal models allow us to clarify the assumptions we make about criminal justice operations. For example, someone who claims that the largest problem in criminal justice is legal restrictions on the police in stopping, questioning, and searching suspicious individuals probably believes that extensive police powers are necessary to control crime. This person probably subscribes to the crime control model and believes that repression of crime is the criminal justice system's most important function. On the other hand, someone who argues that widespread use of plea bargaining results in unfairness in the adjudication and sentencing process probably sees accuracy and fairness as the primary objectives of the criminal justice system—and believes that the due process model best describes the ideals of criminal justice.

ACHIEVING A BALANCE

Achieving a balance in practice between crime control and due process is not always easy. For example, the federal government spent several million dollars on the defense of Timothy McVeigh in the Oklahoma City bombing case. This amount was criticized as excessive by some observers. The underlying question, however, is: Is speed and finality more important or is accuracy and reliability more important in this case? The question is not about money, therefore, but about which model of justice should be paramount. Most people want both speed and accuracy, but these goals are difficult to achieve simultaneously. Given the constraints imposed by limited resources, the emphasis placed on one or the other of these goals will depend on the philosophy of justice that dominates in a particular case or jurisdiction.

The balance between crime control and due process is complicated also by perceptions. Public perceptions include widespread beliefs to the effect that due process protections frustrate justice rather than advance it. Two examples are the belief that defense lawyers lie to exculpate their clients and the belief that lawyers use legal technicalities to free defendants.[85] The facts generally do not support these beliefs; but the perception is reinforced when a prominent defense attorney shockingly states that "the vast majority of criminal defendants are in fact guilty of the crimes with which they are charged. Almost all of my own clients have been guilty."[86] What is the relevance of the due process model when defendants are admittedly guilty?

From a due process perspective, however, the guilt or innocence of the defendant is secondary to ensuring that the process is carried out with fairness and accuracy to reduce the *possibility* that an innocent person will be convicted unjustly. Thus, a primary difference between the two models lies in where errors are made. From the crime control perspective, the potential for wrongful conviction of a small number of innocent persons is offset by the deterrent impact of more swift and certain punishment of offenders in general. From the due process perspective, it is more egregious to punish an innocent person than it is to let a small number of the guilty go free.

CRITICAL THINKING EXERCISES

Selective Prosecution of High-Rate Offenders

Many of the most serious offenders are also repeat offenders. Often these persons are habitual, high-rate, and/or dangerous offenders who commit a larger proportion of crimes than their numbers would warrant. Selective prosecution of repeat offenders ensures that their cases receive special attention, charges are not reduced, and long sentences are recommended in order to incapacitate problem defendants.

In a growing number of jurisdictions, prosecutors have established formal or informal guidelines under which these offenders are prosecuted on an individualized basis. The TARGET program in Ocean County, California, for example, is a collaborative effort of the district attorney's office, the police department, and the probation department. The program targets the most dangerous gangs and their leadership, using an assessment of gang members' past conduct to predict which one is most likely to offend next. Police place this person under surveillance in an effort to catch him committing even a nonserious crime. The district attorney then aggressively prosecutes the gang member and seeks a long sentence in order to incapacitate the offender and disrupt the gang. In two-thirds of all prosecutors' offices nationwide, a system known as *vertical prosecution* is employed for specialized prosecutions like these. For at least certain kinds of cases (such as sexual assault, gun, or drug cases), a prosecutor stays with the same case through sentencing in order to develop expertise about the offenders involved and legal developments in the area.[a]

A national survey found that a significant proportion of prosecutors' offices deal with serious cases involving repeat offenders, including cases of domestic violence (88 percent repeat offenses), stalking (68 percent), elder abuse (41 percent), hate crime (29 percent), or environmental pollution (26 percent).[b] A problem arises, however, when prosecutors attempt to determine which offenders are "dangerous" or "high-rate" early in their criminal careers. An examination of selective prosecution efforts in several counties found that written criteria defining what constitutes a "career criminal" serve to "promote consistency" in prosecutors' judgments about which cases to handle differently.[c]

Some factors that are commonly believed to be associated with high-rate offending actually are not. Display of a weapon, alcoholism, prior arrests for drug offenses, prior probation or parole revocation, and previous incarceration have been found not to be associated with high-rate offending.[d] On the other hand, some defendants arrested for less serious offenses (such as larceny or burglary of an empty building) have prior records indicating a high rate of violent offenses. These defendants cannot be selectively prosecuted, because the most recent offense does not carry a severe penalty.

To be effective, then, selective prosecution must overcome at least two major hurdles: obtaining accurate knowledge of which factors are in fact associated with repeat and violent offenses, and arresting the repeat offender as early as possible in his or her career for a serious offense that warrants selective prosecution. There exist many repeat offenders: Two-thirds of felony defendants have a felony arrest record, and more than a third are on bail, probation, or parole at the time that they are charged with a new crime.[e] Nearly 20 percent of felony offenders are sentenced for convictions for two or more felonies arising from a single case, indicating that there exists a significant proportion of serious offenders.[f] Multiple felonies in a single case might include a robbery and murder; kidnapping and assault; burglary, theft, and assault; or some other combination of crimes that occur as part of a single incident. In addition, more than 96 percent of all prosecutors' officers use a defendant's criminal history during the course of pretrial negotiations and at sentencing.[g]

Continuing research into criminal offending patterns is needed to ensure that typologies of career criminals are based on factual data and not on inaccurate or outdated "folk wisdom." Also, there must be safeguards to ensure that individuals who are predicted to be high-rate offenders are not handled differently without proof that they have committed prior offenses. The criminal justice system permits punishment only for crimes committed in the past, not for crimes contemplated in the future. Yet, if they are armed with reliable information about past patterns of criminal activity, prosecutors have a strong argument for enhanced sentencing based on the offender's past and on the behavior of other criminals with similar backgrounds.

CRITICAL THINKING QUESTIONS

1. Given the broad scope of prosecutors' discretion, what safeguards exist to make sure that they do not fail to prosecute career criminals to the full extent of the law?
2. How might plea bargaining work against selective prosecution of high-rate offenders?
3. How can defense attorneys ensure that clients are not unjustifiably prosecuted as suspected or predicted career criminals?

NOTES

a. Heike P. Gramckow and Elena Tompkins, *Enabling Prosecutors to Address Drug, Gang, and Youth Violence* (Washington, DC: Office of Juvenile Justice and Delinquency Prevention, 1999).
b. Steven W. Perry, *Prosecutors in State Courts* (Washington, DC: Bureau of Justice Statistics, 2006).
c. Marcia R. Chaiken and Jan M. Chaiken, *Priority Prosecution of High-Rate Dangerous Offenders* (Washington, DC: National Institute of Justice, 1991), p. 4.
d. Ibid., p. 6.
e. Thomas N. Cohen and Brian A. Reaves, *Felony Defendants in Large Urban Counties* (Washington, DC: Bureau of Justice Statistics, 2006).
f. Matthew R. Durose and Patrick A. Langan, *Felony Sentences in State Courts* (Washington, DC: Bureau of Justice Statistics, 2004), p. 6.
g. Perry, p. 6.

Should a Lawyer Defend a Guilty Person?

Many college students wish to go on to law school but do not want to become defense attorneys. Many argue that they do not want to represent guilty people. According to one account, "What many people want to know is how defense attorneys can live with themselves after they help a guilty person escape punishment."[a] This view overlooks the fact that defense attorneys represent only the legal rights of defendants; not their past, their personality, or their guilt or innocence. In fact, it is "not [defense counsel's] job to decide who is guilty and not. Instead, it is the public defender's job to judge the quality of the case that the state has against the defendant."[b] According to the standards of the American Bar Association, "the defense lawyer is the professional representative of the accused, not the accused's alter ego."[c]

In a murder case that was appealed to the U.S. Supreme Court, *Nix v. Whiteside,* a defense attorney did not permit his client to testify falsely about whether he had seen a gun in the hand of the victim. The defendant claimed that he was deprived of effective assistance of counsel because of the lawyer's refusal to permit him to perjure himself. The Supreme Court disagreed and held that the defense lawyer's duty "is limited to legitimate, lawful conduct compatible with the very nature of a trial as a search for truth." As a result, "counsel is precluded from taking steps or in any way assisting the client in presenting false evidence or otherwise violating the law."[d] The proper role of a defense attorney is to represent a defendant in an honest way that seeks the truth in the case.

Nevertheless, there are those who claim that defense attorneys do not act honestly. It has been argued that the defense attorney "is a person who is more concerned with appearance and perceptions than with underlying facts; who puts greater reliance in 'personality' than in knowledge." Although the Code of Professional Responsibility prohibits false statements of fact or law in court, it is said that there is much "fiction weaving that customarily passes for argument to a jury."[e] As a result, there may be a gap between the principles and the actual practice of criminal defense.

CRITICAL THINKING QUESTIONS

1. What is a defense lawyer's role if not to represent "guilty people"?
2. Why do many people disapprove of defense attorneys or belittle their importance in criminal cases? Do you think this criticism is justified or not?
3. Give an example of a specific action or statement made by a defense attorney in a well-known case that leads you to believe that the attorney was acting inappropriately. In what sense was the behavior inappropriate?
4. What pressures do you think defense attorneys face that may lead them to act irresponsibly?

NOTES

a. Lisa J. McIntyre, *The Public Defender: The Practice of Law in the Shadows of Repute* (Chicago: University of Chicago Press, 1987), p. 139.
b. Ibid., p.145; Abbe Smith, "The Difference in Criminal Defense and the Difference It Makes," *Washington University Journal of Law & Policy*, vol. 11 (2003), p. 83.
c. American Bar Association, *Standards for Criminal Justice*, Number 4-1.1.
d. *Nix v. Whiteside*, 475 U.S. 157 (1986).
e. H. Richard Uviller, *Virtual Justice: The Flawed Prosecution of Crime in America* (New Haven: Yale University Press, 1996), pp. 153, 155.

SUMMARY

WHAT ARE THE RIGHTS OF THE ACCUSED?

- The Sixth Amendment to the U.S. Constitution guarantees the right of accused persons to have the assistance of counsel.
- The scope of the right to counsel has been expanded in a series of important Supreme Court cases, beginning with *Gideon v. Wainwright* in 1963.
- In 1970 the Supreme Court ruled that defendants are entitled to *effective* assistance of counsel, but it is difficult to demonstrate that the outcome of a case would have been different without counsel's errors.

HOW ARE CASES SETTLED WITHOUT TRIAL?

- Prosecutors have a great deal of discretion in deciding whether a case will be prosecuted and what charges will be pressed.
- Prosecutors sometimes divert offenders to diversion programs, alternatives to the formal criminal justice process that attempt to achieve noncriminal disposition of cases.
- Plea bargaining occurs when a prosecutor agrees to press a less serious charge, drop some charges, or recommend a less severe sentence if the defendant agrees to plead guilty.
- Historical records show that plea bargaining has long been used in jurisdictions of all types.

WHAT ARE SOME PROBLEMS OF THE COURT SYSTEM?

- A growing court caseload, combined with high case mortality, reveals that most cases end in guilty pleas.
- Critics of plea bargaining point out that it takes place in private; the rights of the accused and the interests of the community are not adequately protected; and the public may believe that justice is not achieved. However, efforts to eliminate the practice have been unsuccessful.
- Proposals to eliminate undesirable aspects of plea bargaining include time limits, more public negotiations, better case-screening procedures, and reviews of plea agreements by panels of judges.
- A major issue for criminal defense is the tendency to focus on the offender rather than on the criminal act. This has led to the creation of new defenses that attempt to stretch the boundaries of concepts such as self-defense.
- Another issue is whether the crime control model (which emphasizes the repression of criminal conduct) or the due process model (which emphasizes the preservation of individual liberties) will dominate the justice process in a particular case or jurisdiction.

KEY TERMS

right to counsel *290*
effective counsel *293*
necessarily included offenses *297*
nolle prosequi *297*
diversion programs *298*
pretrial intervention (PTI) *298*
plea bargaining *299*
Speedy Trial Act *301*
caseloads *301*
case mortality *304*
"three strikes" laws *307*
pretrial settlement conference *308*
crime control model *310*
due process model *310*

QUESTIONS FOR REVIEW AND DISCUSSION

1. What degree of discretion do prosecutors have in the disposition of cases? Explain.
2. What are diversion programs? Give an example of such a program.
3. What is plea bargaining? How long has it been used in the United States?
4. What are some undesirable features of plea bargaining?
5. What happens when mandatory sentences are combined with policies forbidding plea bargaining?
6. What are some proposed alternatives to plea bargaining?
7. What problems are caused by increasing court caseloads?
8. In what ways do the crime control and due process models conflict?

NOTES

1. Patricia Hurtado, "Lost Control and Snapped: Defense Cites Stress in Social-Club Killings," *Newsday* (May 5, 1998), p. 7.
2. David Kocieniewski, "Appeal Is Denied for Death Row Inmate Who Had Asked for Speedy Execution," *New York Times* (July 28, 1999), p. B5.
3. Harry Charles, *The Palladium of Justice: Origins of Trial by Jury* (New York: Reed, 1999); Nancy Jean King, "The American Criminal Jury," *Law and Contemporary Problems* 62 (spring 1999), pp. 41–67; Jason Colin Cyrulnik, "Overlooking a Sixth Amendment Framework, *Yale Law Journal*, vol. 114 (January 2005), pp. 905–13.
4. *Powell v. Alabama*, 287 U.S. 45 (1932).
5. *Johnson v. Zerbst*, 304 U.S. 458 (1938).
6. *Betts v. Brady*, 316 U.S. 455 (1942).
7. Anthony Lewis, *Gideon's Trumpet* (New York: Vintage, 1966), p. 59.
8. *Gideon v. Wainwright*, 83 S. Ct. 1340 (1963).
9. *Powell v. Alabama*, 287 U.S. 45 (1932).
10. *Escobedo v. Illinois*, 378 U.S. 478 (1963); *Miranda v. Arizona*, 384 U.S. 694 (1966).
11. *Coleman v. Alabama*, 399 U.S. 1 (1970).
12. *Douglas v. California*, 372 U.S. (1963).
13. *Gilbert v. California*, 388 U.S. (1967).
14. *In re Gault*, 38 U.S. 1 (1967).
15. See Rolando del Carmen, *Criminal Procedure: Law and Practice* (Belmont, CA: Wadsworth, 2000).
16. *Argersinger v. Hamlin*, 407 U.S. 25 (1972).
17. *McMann v. Richardson*, 397 U.S. 765 (1970).
18. Laurie S. Levenson, "Criminal Law; Effective Assistance," *The National Law Journal* 21 (February 22, 1999), p. B9; Meredith J. Duncan, "The (So-Called) Liability of Criminal Defense Attorneys: A System in Need of Reform," *Brigham Young University Law Review*, vol. 2002 (2002), p. 1.
19. *Strickland v. Washington*, 104 S. Ct. 2052 (1984).
20. *Strickland v. Washington*, 104 S. Ct. 2060 (1984).
21. See *Yarborough v. Gentry*, 124 S. Ct. 1 (2003).
22. Caroline Wolf Harlow, *Defense Counsel in Criminal Cases* (Washington, DC: Bureau of Justice Statistics, 2000).
23. Robert R. Rigg, "The Constitution, Compensation, and Competence: A Case Study," *American Journal of Criminal Law*, vol. 27 (fall 1999), p. 1; Richard Klein, "The Emperor *Gideon* Has No Clothes: The Empty Promise of the Constitutional Right to Effective Assistance of Counsel," *Hastings Constitutional Law Quarterly* 13 (1986), pp. 625–93.
24. The Spangenberg Group, *Indigent Defense and Technology: A Progress Report* (Washington, DC: Bureau of Justice Assistance, 1999), p. 16.
25. David E. Rovella, "Unclogging Gideon's Trumpet; Mississippi Suits Are the Latest to Attack State Defense Funding," *The National Law Journal* 22 (January 10, 2000), p. A1.
26. Dallin H. Oaks and Warren Lehman, *A Criminal Justice System and the Indigent* (Chicago: University of Chicago Press, 1968).
27. Caroline Wolf Harlow, *Defense Counsel in Criminal Cases;* David W. Neubauer, *Criminal Justice in Middle America* (Morristown, NJ: General Learning Press, 1974).
28. Dean J. Champion, "Private Counsel and Public Defenders: A Look at Weak Cases, Prior Records, and Leniency in Plea-Bargaining," *Journal of Criminal Justice* 17 (1989), pp. 253–63; Tony Fabelo, "What Policymakers Need to Know to Improve Public Defense Systems," *Papers from the Executive Session on Public Defense, Harvard University* (December 2001).
29. Roy B. Fleming, "Client Games: Defense Attorneys' Perspectives on Their Relations with Criminal Clients," in George S. Bridges, Joseph G. Weis, and Robert D. Crutchfield, eds., *Criminal Justice* (Thousand Oaks, CA: Pine Forge Press, 1996), pp. 276–82; Lynn Mather, "Ethics Symposium: What

Do Clients Want? What Do Lawyers Do?," *Emery Law Journal*, vol. 52 (2003), p. 1065.
30. Meredith J. Duncan, "Criminal Malpractice: A Lawyer's Holiday," *Georgia Law Review*, vol. 37 (summer 2003), p. 1251; Laurie S. Levenson, "Criminal Law; Effective Assistance," *The National Law Journal* 21 (February 22, 1999), p. B9; *Yarborough v. Gentry*, 124 S. Ct. 1 (2003).
31. "Empowering Prosecutors: Movement to Allow Equal Right to Jury Trial Has Judges Fearing Overload," *ABA Journal* 85 (March, 1999), p. 28.
32. Peter Finn, *The Manhattan District Attorney's Narcotics Eviction Program* (Washington, DC: National Institute of Justice, 1995).
33. Richard Bloom, "Prosecutorial Discretion," *Georgetown Law Journal* 87 (1999); Carolyn B. Ramsey, "The Discretionary Power of 'Public' Prosecutors in Historical Perspective," *American Criminal Law Review*, vol. 39 (fall 2002), p. 1309.
34. Steven R. Donziger, ed., *The Real War on Crime: Report of the National Criminal Justice Commission* (New York: Harper Perennial, 1996), pp. 183–84; Peter J. Henning, "Prosecutorial Misconduct and Constitutional Remedies," *Washington University Law Quarterly* 77 (fall 1999).
35. Steven W. Perry, *Prosecutors in State Courts* (Washington, DC: Bureau of Justice Statistics, 2006).
36. Katherine Beckett and Theodore Sasson, *The Politics of Injustice* (Thousand Oaks, CA: Pine Forge Press, 2000); Daniel Glaser, *Profitable Penalties* (Thousand Oaks, CA: Pine Forge Press, 1997).
37. Perry, *Prosecutors in State Courts*, p. 4.
38. Thomas N. Cohen, and Brian A. Reaves, *Felony Defendants in Large Urban Counties* (Washington, DC: Bureau of Justice Statistics, 2006).
39. Milton Heumann, "A Note of Plea-Bargaining and Case Pressure," *Law and Society Review* 9 (spring 1975).
40. George Fishe, "Plea Bargaining's Triumph," *Yale Law Journal*, vol. 109 (March 2000), p. 855.
41. Abraham S. Blumberg, *Criminal Justice: Issues and Ironies* (New York: New Viewpoints, 1979).
42. Barbara Boland and Brian Forst, *The Prevalence of Guilty Pleas* (Washington, DC: U.S. Bureau of Justice Statistics, 1984).
43. Thomas N. Cohen and Brian A. Reaves, *Felony Defendants in Large Urban Counties* (Washington, DC: Bureau of Justice Statistics, 2006).
44. Matthew Durose and Patrick A. Langan, *Felony Sentences in State Courts* (Washington, DC: Bureau of Justice Statistics, 2004), p. 7.
45. Heumann, p. 55; Boland and Forst.
46. Ted Gest, "Making a Case for Judges," *U.S. News & World Report* (January 12, 1998), p. 29.
47. National Center for State Courts, *Examining Work of State Courts* (Washington, DC: National Center for State Courts, 2005).
48. "Clearing the Homolka Deal," *Maclean's* 109 (April 1, 1996), p. 27.
49. "Questioning Homolka's Deal," *Maclean's* 110 (April 28, 1997), p. 21.
50. "Beyond Misery," *People Weekly* (January 24, 2000), p. 125.
51. George B. Palermo, Maxine Aldridge White, Lew A. Wasserman, and William Hanrahan, "Plea Bargaining: Injustice for All?," *International Journal of Offender Therapy and Comparative Criminology* 42 (June 1998), p. 111.
52. Perry, *Prosecutors in State Courts*.
53. Steven K. Smith and John Scalia, Jr., *Compendium of Federal Justice Statistics* (Washington, DC: Bureau of Justice Statistics, 2002).
54. Barbara Boland, E. Brady, H. Tyson, and J. Bassler, *The Prosecution of Felony Arrests* (Washington, DC: Bureau of Justice Statistics, 2002).
55. Smith and Scalia, *Compendium of Federal Justice Statistics*.
56. Vera Institute of Justice, *Felony Arrests*, revised ed. (New York: Longman, 1981).
57. Perry, *Prosecutors in State Courts*.
58. Boland et al., *The Prosecution of Felony Arrests*.
59. See Nancy Jean King, "Priceless Process: Nonnegotiable Features of Criminal Litigation," *UCLA Law Review* 47 (October 1999); J. Shin, "Do Lesser Pleas Pay?: Accommodations in the Sentencing and Parole Process," *Journal of Criminal Justice* 1 (1973); T. Dungsworth, *Plea-Bargaining: Who Gains? Who Loses?* (Washington, DC: Institute for Law and Social Research, 1978).
60. Eric R. Komitee, "Bargains without Benefits: Do the Sentencing Guidelines Permit Upward Departures to Redress the Dismissal of Charges Pursuant to Plea Bargains?," *New York University Law Review* 70 (April 1995), pp. 166–95.
61. David E. Rovella, "Fake Plea Bargain in Death Case Raises Concerns," *The National Law Journal* 18 (October 9, 1995), p. 13.
62. Ty Alper, "The Danger of Winning: Contract Law Ramifications of Successful Bailey Challenges for Plea-Convicted Defendants," *New York University Law Review* 72 (October 1997), pp. 841–81.
63. Richard Birke, "Reconciling Loss Aversion and Guilty Pleas," *Utah Law Review* (1999), p. 205; Michael Gorr, "The Morality of Plea Bargaining," *Social Theory and Practice*, vol. 26 (spring 2000), p. 129.
64. National Advisory Committee on Criminal Justice Standards and Goals, *A National Strategy to Reduce Crime* (New York: Avon, 1975).
65. Association of the Bar of the City of New York, *The Nation's Toughest Drug Law: Evaluating the New York Experience* (Washington, DC: Drug Abuse Council, 1977).
66. H. Lawrence Ross, "The Neutralization of Severe Penalties: Some Traffic Studies," *Law and Society Review* 10 (1976); David Rossman, Paul Froyd, Glen L. Pierce, John McDevitt, and William J. Bowers, "Massachusetts Mandatory Minimum Sentence Gun Law: Enforcement, Prosecution, and Defense Impact," *Criminal Law Bulletin* 16 (March–April 1980); Colin Loftin, Milton Heumann, and David McDowall, "Mandatory Sentencing and Firearms Violence: Evaluating an Alternative to Gun Control," *Law and Society Review* 17 (1983); Michael L. Rubinstein, Steven H. Clarke, and Theresa J. White, *Alaska Bans Plea Bargaining* (Washington, DC: U.S. Government Printing Office, 1980).
67. Arthur Rosset and Donald R. Cressey, *Justice by Consent: Plea-Bargains in the American Courthouse* (Philadelphia: Lippincott, 1976), p. 161.
68. "New York Governor Offers Limited Revision of Mandatory Sentencing Laws," *Alcoholism and Drug Abuse Weekly* (May 17, 1999), p. 1.
69. Lisa Stolzenberg and Stewart J. D'Alessio, " 'Three Strikes and You're Out': The Impact of California's New Mandatory Sentencing Law on Serious Crime Rates," *Crime and Delinquency* 43 (October 1997), pp. 457–69; Tomislav Kovandzic, John Sloan, and Lynne Vieraitis, "'Striking out' as Crime Reduction Policy: The Impact of "Three Strikes" Laws on Crime Rates in U.S. cities," *Justice Quarterly*, vol. 21 (June 2004), pp. 207–40.
70. John Cloud, "A Get-Tough Policy That Failed: Mandatory Sentencing Was Once America's Law-and-Order Panacea," *Time* (February 1, 1999), p. 48.

71. Tina M. Olson, "Strike One, Ready for More? The Consequences of Plea Bargaining, 'First Strike' Offender under California's 'Three Strikes' Law," *California Western Law Research*, vol. 36 (spring 2000), p. 545; Marcus Dirk Dubber, "American Plea Bargains, German Lay Judges, and the Crisis of Criminal Procedure," *Stanford Law Review* 49 (February 1997), pp. 547–605; Ken Jones, "Affirmation of the Three Strikes Law: Judicial Discretion or Cruel and Unusual Punishment?," *Southern University Law Review*, vol. 33 (fall 2005), pp. 215–26.
72. Barbara Boland, *Felony Case-Processing Time* (Washington, DC: Bureau of Justice Statistics, 1986); Rainville and Reeves, *Felony Defendants in Large Urban Counties.*
73. Wayne A. Kerstetter and Anne M. Heinz, *Pre-Trial Settlement Conference: An Evaluation* (Washington, DC: U.S. Government Printing office, 1979); Debra S. Emmelman, "Trial by Plea Bargain: Case Settlement as a Product of Recursive Decisionmaking," *Law and Society Review* 30 (June 1996), pp. 335–60.
74. Perry, *Prosecutors in State Courts*, p. 5.
75. Durose and Langan, *Felony Sentences in State Courts.*
76. Kevin Johnson, "Train Gunman to Appeal, Use Incompetence Defense," *USA Today* (February 20, 1995), p. 2; Bruce Frankel, "New York Shooting Victims on the Stand: 'You' Did This," *USA Today* (February 9, 1995), p. 3.
77. Tony Mauro, "Child Abuse Becoming a Defense Trend," *USA Today* (September 24, 1993), p. 2.
78. See Faith McNulty, *The Burning Bed* (New York: Dell, 1980).
79. Susan Estrich, *Getting Away with Murder* (Cambridge, MA: Harvard University Press, 1998), pp. 119–30; Robert Schwaneberg, "The Legal Risks of 'Self-Defense'," *Atlantic City Press* (March 15, 1981), p. 1.
80. Steve Timko, "Murder Acquittal in 'Urban Fear' Trial," *USA Today* (April 12, 1995), p. 3; William I. Torry, "Culture and Individual Responsibility: Touchstones of the Culture Defense," *Human Organization*, vol. 59 (spring 2000), p. 58.
81. M. L. Stein, "L. A. Courts Restrict Press: Proposed Courthouse Rules Force Reporters to Wear Passes and Ban Hallway Interviews," *Editor & Publisher* 130 (November 8, 1997), p. 11.
82. Christian Berthelsen, "Guidelines for Lawyers in Court of Television," *New York Times* (April 20, 1998), p. 7.
83. William Glaberson, "Calm Returns to Brawley Case, but Punished Lawyer Doesn't," *New York Times* (May 1, 1998), p. 5.
84. Herbert L. Packer, *The Limits of the Criminal Sanction* (Stanford, CA: Stanford University Press, 1968).
85. Charles M. Sevilla, "Criminal Defense Lawyers and the Search for Truth," *Harvard Journal of Law and Public Policy* 20 (winter 1997), pp. 519–28.
86. Alan M. Dershowitz, *The Best Defense* (New York: Vintage, 1983), p. xiv; Richard D. Friedman, "A Presumption of Innocence, Not of Even Odds," *Standard Law Review*, vol. 52 (April 2000) p. 873.

chapter 12

Trials and Sentencing

Sentencing and death: criminal trials, the purposes and outcomes of criminal sentences, and the imposition of the death penalty.

CHAPTER OUTLINE

LEARNING OBJECTIVES

- Trace steps in the process of adjudication before, during, and after a trial.
- Summarize the principal strategies of prosecution and defense at trial.
- Analyze sentencing in relation to the goals of punishment.
- Analyze the diverse factors that affect sentencing decisions.
- Define the types of sentences in the continuum of sentencing decisions.
- Explain how sentencing options may differ and may have different consequences for the goals of uniformity and proportionality.
- Explain how the Eighth Amendment to the U.S. Constitution may restrict sentencing.
- Analyze arguments for and against the constitutionality, effectiveness, and fairness of the death penalty.

Dr. Robert Bierenbaum, a plastic surgeon, was placed on trial in New York City, accused of killing his wife fifteen years earlier and disposing of her body without a trace. He pleaded not guilty, and prosecutors tried the case with "no body, no forensics, no murder weapon, no bloody clothes, no fingerprints, no brain matter, no body parts."[1] Prosecuting any criminal case requires **corpus delicti** (or proving the crime), which consists of proof of the act and that the act resulted from the illegal actions of the defendant. In a murder case it must be proved that a death occurred, and this is most often accomplished by producing a corpse. In rare murder cases where a body has not been found, the prosecution must prove to a judge or jury that there is no other explanation of a person's disappearance. In the Bierenbaum case the prosecution used friends and relatives of the victim who testified that Dr. Bierenbaum had threatened to kill her and had acted violently toward her, and that his alibi was questionable. It can be seen that careful evaluation of the evidence in a criminal trial is important to determine whether or not the crime occurred and the defendant's responsibility for it.

corpus delicti
Proof of an act and that the act resulted from the illegal actions of the defendant; also called proving the crime.

The swearing in of a witness at trial is a solemn moment that symbolizes the integrity of the criminal justice process. The inner workings of a trial are less visible but equally important to ensuring that justice occurs in the courtroom. The prosecution, defense, and judge represent the interests of the community, the defendant, and the law in a process that is designed to achieve justice in every case—although this goal sometimes is difficult to achieve in practice.

What Happens at Trial?

The trial is the centerpiece of the adjudication process; and this is true even though, as you have seen, most cases are decided without one. Trials serve an educational purpose, helping both jurors and the public understand how the balance is struck between protection of the community and protection of the rights of the individual. The detailed procedures of a criminal trial are designed to ensure that this balance is reached in every case.[2]

DELAYS IN ADJUDICATION

The system of criminal adjudication in the United States has often been criticized for the time it sometimes takes to proceed from arrest to disposition. Delays in the adjudication procedure cause the process to take even longer. Most felony cases are completed within three months of arrest, although cases involving trials take twice as long.[3] The total elapsed time from arrest through sentencing is about seven months nationwide.[4]

continuance
A court-authorized postponement of a case to allow the prosecution or defense more time to prepare its case.

An example of a delay is a **continuance**—a court-authorized postponement of a case to allow the prosecution or defense more time to prepare its case. Judges have the discretion to grant continuances to allow the defense to locate a witness, prepare motions, or obtain medical reports, or for other reasons. Continuances ensure that the most complete information is available for a criminal proceeding. Prosecutors also can obtain continuances, but most states constitutionally require them to be ready for trial within six months. Exceptions are permitted only when the delays are caused by the defense for valid reasons. Most continuances are requested by, and granted to, the defense. By the time of indictment the prosecution already has prepared much of its case, but the defense has not begun to examine the evidence. Delays usually benefit the defendant more than the prosecution, because the memory and recall of witnesses often fade as time passes. Delays also may frustrate or disillusion victims and witnesses, or they may help to calm community sentiment in well-publicized cases. On the other hand, delays cause suffering for defendants who cannot make bail and must await trial in jail. Another cause of delays is a process called **discovery**, which entitles a suspect to see certain information gathered by the prosecutor. For example, suspects have the right to see the results of blood tests or transcripts of interrogations conducted by the police or the prosecutor in preparation for trial. In its examination of the prosecutor's evidence, the defense may find *exculpatory evidence* suggesting the defendant's innocence. For example, exculpatory evidence may consist of statements taken by police from victims or witnesses that show uncertainty about the identity of the offender. With this information defense counsel can assess the strength of the prosecution's case and decide

discovery
The process that entitles a suspect to review certain information gathered by the prosecutor.

FIGURE 12.1 Progression of a Case through Trial

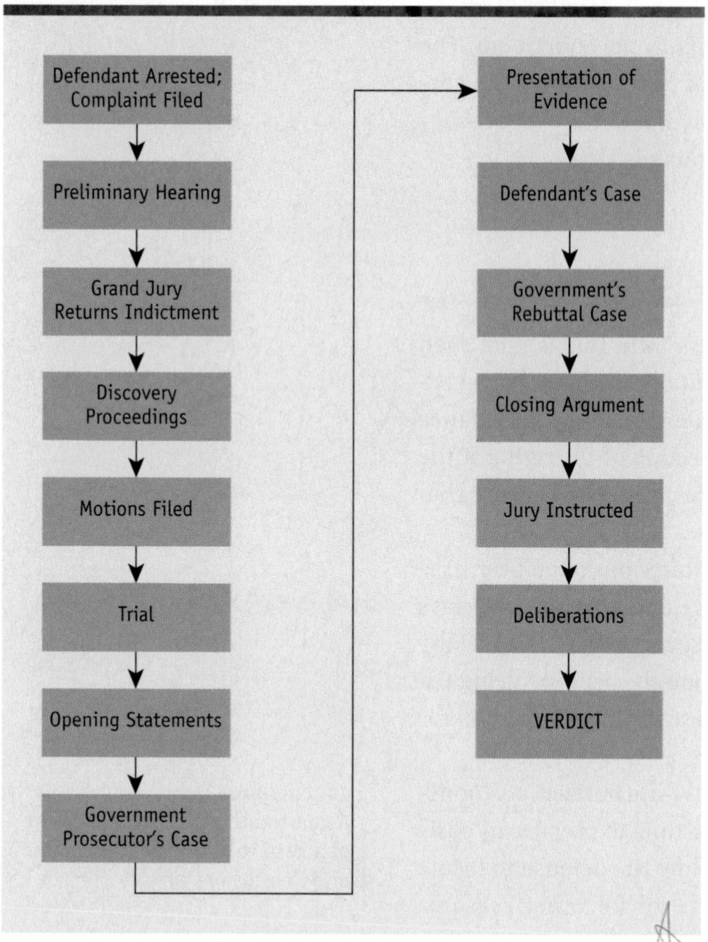

Source: www.uscourts.gov/understanding_courts

whether the defendant will benefit more from going to trial or from pleading guilty. The steps in a criminal case are presented in Figure 12.1.

Jury Selection

When a trial takes place, it begins with the selection of a jury. The right to a **trial jury** dates from the signing of the Magna Carta in 1215 and is incorporated into both Article III of the Constitution and the Sixth Amendment, which states that "in all criminal prosecutions, the accused shall enjoy the right to a speedy and public trial by an impartial jury."[5] The jury pool is typically selected from voter registration records, tax rolls, or motor vehicle records.

trial jury
A group of citizens (usually twelve) who decide on the guilt or innocence of a defendant.

VOIR DIRE

After the jury pool is selected, the process of *voir dire* occurs, in which the judge, prosecution, and defense screen potential jurors by asking them questions. To prevent the inclusion of biased jurors, both the prosecution and the defense can challenge the selection of a certain number of jurors. These challenges, called *challenges for cause,* are used to disqualify jurors whose background or statements may be seen as prejudicial to the prosecution or the defense. In addition, both prosecution and defense have a specific number of *peremptory challenges,* which permit them to remove prospective jurors from consideration without cause. Although peremptory challenges have their origin in British common law, recent high-profile trials have featured the use of jury selection "consultants." These experts examine nonverbal cues such as body language, eye contact, and dress to predict whether a particular juror may be sympathetic to the prosecution or defense. Consultants' methods of juror selection have not been proved valid, but stereotypes persist regarding age, gender, religion, and other juror attributes and their likely impact on jurors' attitudes.[6] Critics of the practice of using jury consultants have proposed barring non-lawyers from giving jury selection advice to the prosecution or defense.[7]

JURY SIZE

The size of juries varies by state. All states require twelve-member juries in death penalty cases, although six states allow for juries of less than twelve jurors in other felony trials. Although the U.S. Supreme Court has left the size of juries up to the state, it has held that a five-member jury is unconstitutional.[8] Thus, states have juries that range in size from six to twelve members.

In rare circumstances the jury is *sequestered:* Jurors are housed in a hotel for the duration of the trial, and their access to newspapers, television, and other media is closely monitored. Sequestration is expensive and occurs only in cases in which public opinion is very strong or divisive or in which the security of jurors is in question (for example, when there are concerns about threats or bribes aimed at influencing jurors' votes).

After a jury has been selected, the prosecution makes an opening statement outlining its case against the defendant. At this time the state summarizes the evidence it will use to show the defendant's guilt. Next, the defense counsel makes an opening argument stating why the defendant should be exonerated of the crime. The evidence to be used to support this position will be summarized.

These individuals are being considered for membership on a jury in a criminal trial. On what grounds could the prosecutor exclude or disqualify a person from serving on the jury? On what grounds could the defense counsel do so? What instructions will the judge give to the jury at the beginning and end of the trial?

Witness Testimony and Evidence

STEPS OF A TRIAL

The body of the trial consists of the presentation of the prosecutor's evidence and the statements of witnesses, followed by the presentation of the case for the defense. Because the state is prosecuting an individual in a criminal case, the burden of proof is on the prosecution to prove guilt beyond a reasonable doubt.

The steps of a trial are elaborate, because accuracy and the determination of the truth have been found to result most often when both sides have fair opportunity to present their views. Witnesses and physical evidence form the substance of all criminal cases. Witnesses are always sworn in by a court officer, usually a sheriff's deputy. *Swearing in* obliges the witness to be truthful; false statements about issues material to the case can result in a charge of perjury. The first round of questions the prosecutor asks prosecution witnesses in a criminal case is called the *direct examination.* Likewise, questions the defense counsel asks defense witnesses also are called direct examination. The types of witnesses and physical evidence that can be used are explicitly defined in the rules of evidence of each state. *Circumstantial evidence* is a form of indirect evidence often used in criminal trials that permits a jury to draw a conclusion by making a reasonable inference. For example, a witness who saw a person walking down the street with two sticks of dynamite just before an explosion offers circumstantial evidence that the person may have been involved in the incident. This form of evidence is very important when direct eyewitness evidence is lacking.

After the prosecution has conducted a direct examination of each of its witnesses, the defense may *cross-examine* those witnesses for inconsistencies, contradictions, or uncertainty. The prosecution may follow the defense cross-examination with a *redirect examination* to clarify issues that have been brought into doubt. Next, the defense may follow once again with a *recross-examination.* This procedure continues for each of the prosecution's witnesses.

The defense then calls its witnesses, and the process continues with prosecution cross-examination followed by redirect questioning by the defense and recross-examination by the prosecutor. At several points throughout the trial, the prosecution or the defense may raise *objections* to questions posed by the other side that seem to violate the rules of evidence. The judge rules on these objections according to the laws of the state. If the objection is *sustained,* the questioner must withdraw the question and the jury must disregard both the question and any response made by the witness. If the objection is *overruled*, the question is deemed proper and the questioning continues.

Defense Strategies

general defenses
Justifications or excuses for criminal conduct that are applicable to all criminal offenses.

justification defenses
Defenses that admit to the criminal conduct, but claim it was justified by overwhelming circumstances, such as self-defense.

excuse defenses
Defenses that claim that criminal conduct should be excused because the defendant cannot be held responsible for it. Insanity and duress are examples.

Certain **general defenses** are applicable to all criminal offenses. The two types of general defenses are justification and excuse. As you read in Chapter 5, **justification defenses** claim that the act was justified by overwhelming circumstances, such as self-defense. **Excuse defenses** argue the act should be excused because the defendant cannot be held responsible for it. Insanity and duress are examples of excuse defenses. The key distinction between justification and excuse defenses is that the former look to justify the offender's *conduct*, whereas the latter seek to excuse the *offender* as an individual.

As Chapter 5 described, there has been a trend toward attempting to create new types of justifications or excuses. In a Texas case, a man had shot two unarmed black men in the head. His lawyers argued that the defendant suffered from "a rational fear of other blacks in violent urban neighborhoods."[9] In another case, sleep apnea was said to have caused a man to kill his wife.[10] Bad chromosomes and multiple personalities (one of which committed a rape) have been put forth as excuses.[11] As defense attorney Alan Dershowitz has remarked, "If you can make it sound like an illness, people are much more sympathetic."[12]

Sometimes lawyers themselves can become defendants, and their claims of excuse are similar. Defense lawyer Gary Kleitman was sentenced to three to six years in prison for stealing more than $366,000 from his clients. He argued that his sentence was excessive because of the various physical disorders he must cope with and the fact that his wife was scheduled to undergo cancer surgery. These medical problems created "crushing financial problems" that Kleitman could not handle and resulted in his stealing money from his own clients.[13]

INDIVIDUAL RESPONSIBILITY

These attempts to create new justifications and excuses for criminal conduct violate a fundamental assumption of criminal law: individual responsibility. If individuals cannot be held responsible for their conduct but instead are victims of their circumstances, the punitive and deterrent purposes of the criminal law are undermined. Individual volition and personal accountability for one's actions must exist if punishment is to be meaningful. Historically, juveniles and people who are mentally ill have been treated as exceptions under the criminal law, because it cannot be assumed that such persons have enough rationality to understand the consequences of their actions. Apart from these exceptions, all people are held to a "reasonableness" standard in their conduct. Very few justifications and excuses for criminal conduct are recognized under law. Even so, cases involving these general defenses are growing in number and have generated a great deal of attention, although they are usually unsuccessful when presented to a trial jury.

Another common defense strategy is to attack the government's case. This strategy was accomplished most famously in the criminal trial of O.J. Simpson, in which the defense placed the conduct of the police at the center of its case rather than focusing on the alibi of the defendant. In some instances the government's case may also be vulnerable to attack because of the background of its informants.

Juries are understandably reluctant to convict a defendant on the testimony of someone with a questionable history.[14] Several acquittals in the mob trials of the 1980s and 1990s occurred because juries disregarded the testimony of informants. During its deliberations in the trial of the alleged "godfather" John Gotti, the jury asked to reexamine a chart produced by the defense that displayed the backgrounds of seven prosecution witnesses. The chart listed sixty-nine crimes, including murder and kidnapping.[15] The jury acquitted Gotti, showing that close scrutiny of the government's case can be used successfully as a defense.

A defense lawyer represents his client's legal rights in court. Why are very few justifications and excuses for criminal conduct recognized under law?

Arguments and Outcomes

When all the evidence has been presented, the prosecution and defense make their final arguments to the jury, summarizing the evidence. Then the judge instructs the jury, explaining the elements of the alleged crime and the degree of proof required—that is, proof beyond a reasonable doubt. The jury then deliberates until it has agreed on a verdict. In order for a defendant to be found guilty, the jury must agree that guilt has been proved beyond a reasonable doubt. In nearly all states unanimous jury verdicts are required in criminal cases.

THE VERDICT

In rare cases (fewer than 6 percent) the jury is not able to agree on a decision of guilt or innocence.[16] This situation, called a *hung jury,* means that the defendant can be tried again before a different jury. In recent years **jury nullification** has occurred in some cases; that is, defendants have been acquitted despite facts that show guilt.[17] Some people believed that the jury that acquitted O.J. Simpson in his criminal trial engaged in jury nullification, but sloppy police evidence gathering and lies told by witnesses led some jurors to conclude that Simpson was not guilty beyond a reasonable doubt.

jury nullification
Acquittal of a defendant despite facts that show guilt.

When a jury reaches a verdict of guilty, the defendant stands convicted of the crime alleged. The defendant then is sentenced within the limits established by law. Commonly both the prosecutor and defense counsel make recommendations to the judge regarding an appropriate sentence.

How Do Judges Decide on a Sentence?

Sentencing is subject to much criticism: Sentences often are seen as either too lenient or too severe. A sentence rarely is viewed as appropriate in a given case. However, judges do not decide on sentences in an arbitrary fashion. The degree of latitude given to judges is established by law. In most states, for example, a petty larceny (a misdemeanor) is punishable by up to one year in jail. In other words, a judge can choose any sentence from a fine (up to $1,000 in this kind of case) to probation or as much as a year in jail. The judge cannot sentence an offender to two years in jail or a fine of $10,000, for these sentences would fall outside the

This judge has just sentenced a convicted "three-strikes" felon to incarceration in a state prison for a maximum period of twenty-five years for purposes of incapacitation. How did the judge arrive at this sentence? What choices among purposes and sentencing options were involved?

allowable range established by the legislature. This leeway is provided to allow judges to individualize sentences on the basis of the nature of the offender and the circumstances of the offense.

In South Carolina, a young mother, Susan Smith, killed her two children by leaving them in a car that she rolled into a lake. Smith could have been convicted of involuntary manslaughter or murder and could have received a death sentence, or she could have been found guilty but mentally ill. In the trial the defense pointed out that she came from a troubled background. Her parents had divorced, and her father had committed suicide when she was six. She had been molested by her stepfather at age fifteen and later, even after she was married. The molestation was covered up by her mother. After her divorce Smith had been rejected by her new boyfriend because she had two children. She had a long history of depression. The defense also noted that she had confessed to her crime and showed deep remorse.[18]

WHAT SHOULD A JURY CONSIDER?

Which of these factors should a jury consider in deciding on a sentence? And how should an appropriate sentence be determined? In the actual case, Smith was convicted of murder and sentenced to thirty years in prison. It is easy to see that other sentencing choices were available to the judge, and that other sentences could have been imposed and defended rationally. This case illustrates why it is important to understand the underlying rationale or philosophy of sentencing.

Retribution and Incapacitation

When judges decide on a sentence, they first consider what the sentence should accomplish. The purposes of a sentence always consist of one or more of the following objectives: retribution, incapacitation, deterrence, and/or rehabilitation.

retribution
Punishment applied simply in proportion to the seriousness of the offense.

When a judge sentences for purposes of **retribution,** punishment is applied simply in proportion to the seriousness of the offense. The "eye for an eye" system of justice described in the Old Testament is an early form of retribution.[19] According to this concept, the more serious the crime, the more serious the punishment should be. What is the goal of retribution? As an objective of sentencing, retribution makes no effort to change the offender and provides nothing for society except a form of revenge. Nevertheless, as states have abandoned social reform as a purpose of sentencing in recent years, the use of retribution as a justification for punishment has become more popular. In the *just deserts* approach to retribution, using the sentencing process as a way to reform an offender or deter other offenders is seen as inappropriate, for it moves attention away from culpability for the past crime for which the offender was convicted.[20]

JUST DESERTS

Sentences based on the concept of **incapacitation** are intended to prevent further criminal behavior by physically restraining the offender from engaging in future misconduct. The primary method of incapacitation in the United States is incarceration, although other methods also are used, such as suspension of the offender's license to practice law or medicine in cases of crimes committed by lawyers or physicians. In a few countries amputation is still used as punishment for robbery and theft.[21] Unfortunately, the use of incapacitation as a justification for punishment provides no clue as to how long it is necessary to incarcerate someone before the person poses no further threat to society. It is not economical to lock up large numbers of offenders for long periods, because the burden on society is increased rather than lessened. Higher prison costs, the need to support families on welfare, and the inability to predict future criminal behavior make incapacitation both expensive and uncertain over the long term. Moreover, the incapacitation rationale can be used to justify incarceration for both trivial and serious offenses. A petty thief who steals many times could conceivably be incarcerated for as long as a one-time rapist.

incapacitation
Prevention of further criminal behavior by physically restraining the offender from engaging in future misconduct (usually through incarceration).

REPEAT OFFENDERS

It has been claimed that if repeat offenders could be identified and incarcerated for long periods, there would be a noticeable drop in crime rates. A major problem with this idea is that some individuals might be identified as probable high-rate offenders who were not.[22] Thus, there is a risk of violating due process by punishing offenders for *predicted* future behavior rather than for criminal acts they have actually committed.[23] In addition, such a policy, termed **selective incapacitation,** would greatly increase prison populations.

selective incapacitation
Identification of potential high-rate offenders for incarceration for longer periods as a means of reducing crime.

Many states have **habitual offender laws** based on the notion of incapacitation. These laws can be applied to certain offenders who have committed two or more offenses within a certain period (usually ten years). Multiple offenders are subject to periods of incarceration ranging up to life imprisonment on the theory that these persons must be physically separated from society if crime is to be prevented. Under California's "three strikes" law, Jerry Williams faced a prison term of twenty-five years to life when he was tried for taking pizza from children at a beach. Williams's two prior robbery convictions made him a habitual offender and therefore subject to an extended sentence on grounds of incapacitation.[24] The rationale behind laws such as "three strikes" is that multiple offenders, who apparently have not been deterred or reformed by past convictions or incarceration, cannot be trusted to refrain from violating the law and must be separated from society. The popularity of incapacitation as a purpose of sentencing, despite the high costs of incarceration, remains high.

habitual offender laws
Laws that subject multiple offenders to periods of incarceration ranging up to life imprisonment, on the grounds that they must be physically separated from society in order to protect society from their criminal conduct.

Habitual offenders are sentenced to longer prison terms than other offenders who commit the same crimes. What is the justification for this difference? Should there be limits on the severity of crimes committed and sentence-lengths imposed on habitual offenders?

deterrence
Prevention of crime through the example of offenders being punished.

DETERRENCE IS INEFFECTIVE

rehabilitation
The view that sees criminal behavior as stemming from social or psychological shortcomings; the purpose of sentencing is to correct or treat these shortcomings in order to prevent future crimes.

SENTENCING DISPARITY

Deterrence and Rehabilitation

Deterrence as a purpose of sentencing aims to prevent crime through the example of offenders' being punished. *General deterrence* is directed at preventing crime among the general population, while *special deterrence* is aimed at preventing future crimes by a particular offender. Unfortunately, the objectives of general and special deterrence are not always compatible. For example, a drunk driver who hits and kills a pedestrian may best be deterred from future drunk driving through participation in an alcohol treatment program. Such a disposition may not serve the purposes of general deterrence, however, if the penalty fails to deter other people from drunk driving. Another problem with the use of deterrence as a justification for punishment is the difficulty of proving its effectiveness; that is, only those who are *not* deterred come to the attention of the criminal justice system. To date, virtually no reliable evidence exists to suggest that penal sanctions can deter crime.[25]

One reason that deterrence is ineffective is that it relies on certainty and speed of punishment.[26] If penalties are high but the chances of being caught are low, it is doubtful that potential offenders will be deterred. The very low clearance rates for serious crimes illustrate the low probability that offenders will be caught. Nevertheless, if in the mind of the would-be offender the perceived *risk of apprehension* is high, it is possible to achieve a deterrent effect.[27] For example, one study proved that mailing warning letters to illegal cable users deterred cable tampering.[28]

The **rehabilitation** or "reformation" approach sees criminal behavior as a consequence of social or psychological shortcomings. The purpose of the sentence, then, is to correct or treat these shortcomings in order to prevent future crimes. This approach assumes that we can identify and treat these shortcomings effectively. Also, it presumes that it is proper to sentence an offender based on the likelihood of reform in the future rather than on criminal conduct already committed. The results of rehabilitation efforts to date have been discouraging, with failures outnumbering successes. Nevertheless, some rehabilitation programs have been shown to work when treatment strategies and offender needs are matched effectively.[29] Successes have been documented in cases in which offender needs have been screened carefully and treatments have been chosen to respond directly to those needs.[30]

The lack of empirical evidence to support the four basic purposes of sentencing has contributed to concern about disparity in sentences. Disparity occurs when offenders with similar histories commit similar crimes but receive widely different sentences. For example, a study of federal courts found offenders in some jurisdictions much more likely to be ordered to pay a fine or restitution than offenders who committed the same type of crime in other jurisdictions.[31] Disparity must be expected, of course, when there is little agreement regarding what a sentence should accomplish. A result of disparity has been a trend toward mandatory and fixed sentences. This move toward uniformity in sentencing can be attributed to the widespread adoption of retribution and incapacitation as guiding sentencing philosophies in most jurisdictions.

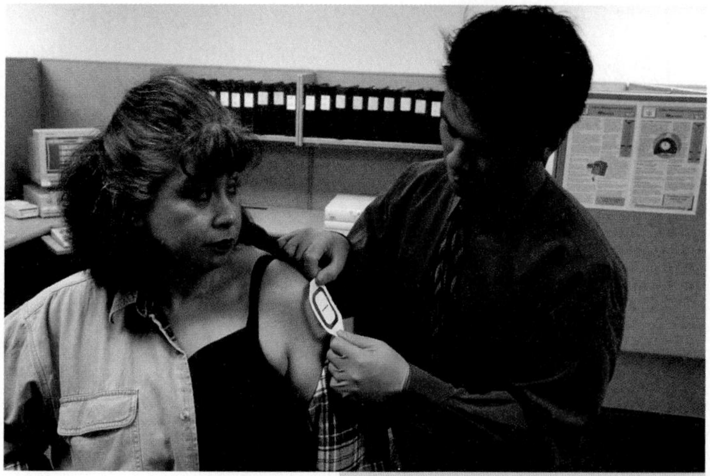

Probation permits offenders to serve their sentence under community supervision. Should there be limits on how far this supervision can extend? Should monitoring be permitted at work, at home, on vacation?

Probation, Restitution, and Incarceration

In addition to considering the various possible purposes of the sentence, the judge usually may choose among a number of sentencing options. As noted earlier, depending on the range of alternatives provided by law, a judge usually can fine an offender or impose a sentence of probation, incarceration, or restitution.

PAYMENT OF FINES

Fines can be used as punishment upon conviction for any offense. Statutes usually provide a maximum fine but allow the judge to impose any fine up to the maximum. Fines also are provided by law for serious crimes as an adjunct to a sentence of probation or incarceration. Fines obviously place a greater burden on the poor than on the wealthy, and in 1970 the U.S. Supreme Court ruled in *Williams v. Illinois* that offenders cannot be held in jail beyond the maximum sentence allowed by law merely because they are unable to pay the fine.[32] In 1971 the Court ruled in *Tate v. Short* that it is unconstitutional to imprison an offender who cannot pay a fine while not imprisoning offenders with the means to pay fines.[33] Several jurisdictions are now experimenting with *day fines*, or fines established according to the daily income of the offender. This system is designed to make the imposition of fines more equitable.

A probation sentence allows the offender to remain in the community under the supervision of the court. Probation is the most widely used form of criminal sentence, because most crimes are not violent and most offenders are not dangerous. Also, probation is much less expensive than incarceration; and probation does not permit the offender to associate with more serious offenders, as often occurs in prison.

Sometimes a judge orders an offender to make restitution as a condition of probation. This means that the offender must make compensation to the victim for any losses caused by the offense. Many states have laws that encourage restitution, but this approach is not utilized on a large scale. Most offenders are never caught, and those who are caught and convicted are often poor; restitution therefore is not feasible in many cases. This problem has led many states, as well as the federal government, to establish victim compensation programs in which the government reimburses victims for the costs of certain types of loss or injury due to crime.

VICTIM COMPENSATION

Although the concept of victim compensation is popular, in many states the programs are underfunded and have imposed burdensome paperwork requirements that discourage legitimate claims.

An offender sentenced to incarceration is physically separated from the community in a jail or a prison. Sentences of up to one year are served in county jails; those of one year or more are served in state or federal prisons. Occasionally a judge delays—or suspends—the execution of a prison sentence and requires the offender to participate in an alcohol, drug, or gambling treatment program, or to pay restitution. This approach is called a **suspended sentence.** If an offender fails to fulfill the prescribed conditions, the court can impose incarceration immediately by applying the suspended sentence. An offender who satisfactorily fulfills the conditions, however, avoids incarceration.

suspended sentence
A delayed imposition of a prison sentence that requires the offender to fulfill special conditions such as alcohol, drug, or gambling treatment or payment of restitution.

The Presentence Report

presentence report
A report conducted by a probation officer into an offender's background to assist the judge in determining an appropriate sentence.

PROBATION OFFICER'S ROLE

The **presentence report** is designed to help the judge decide on an appropriate sentence within the limits established by law. This report is written by a probation officer after an investigation of the offender's background (see Figure 12.2). A presentence investigation is carried out in virtually all felony cases and in some misdemeanor cases, because the sentence will have a significant impact on the offender. If there is any doubt about facts contained in the presentence report, the U.S. Supreme Court has ruled that offenders must be given an opportunity to refute or explain information contained in the report, because their sentences will be based in part on that information.[34]

The probation officer's independent role at sentencing sometimes is impeded when prosecution or defense do not share important information about the circumstances of the offense or the offender. It is crucial that the probation officer obtain objective information to enable an appropriate sentencing decision to be made.[35] Studies have found a high correspondence between the probation officers' recommendations contained in presentence reports and the actual sentences imposed by judges.[36]

FIGURE 12.2 Information in a Presentence Report

A typical presentence report includes the following information:

1. Personal information about the offender and his or her background
2. Detailed description of the offense and its circumstances
3. A description of the offender's criminal record
4. Family information and current family status
5. Education history
6. Employment and military history
7. Health history and status (including drug history)
8. Financial status
9. Mental health status
10. Sentencing recommendation made by the probation officer

How Do Sentencing Options Differ?

Two categories of sentencing are indeterminate and determinate. Indeterminate sentencing systems are based on the philosophy that a wide sentencing range gives an offender an incentive to reform and allows a parole board to determine whether the offender is ready for release prior to serving the maximum sentence. Determinate sentencing systems impose "fixed" sentences that provide little or no flexibility. This approach to sentencing rejects the notion of rehabilitation in favor of the philosophy of retribution, focusing on the seriousness of the crime and basing the sentence on the nature of the offense and the offender's prior record.

Indeterminate Sentencing

indeterminate sentencing
A system of sentencing that empowers the judge to set a maximum sentence (up to the limit set by the legislature), and sometimes a minimum sentence, for the offender to serve in prison.

Indeterminate sentencing systems empower the judge to set a maximum amount of time (up to the limit set by the legislature), and sometimes a minimum amount as well, for the offender to serve in prison. During the sentence a parole board reviews the offender's progress toward rehabilitation to determine whether early release is justified. Therefore, the actual time to be served is set by the parole board. Indeterminate sentencing systems existed in most states until the 1970s, when growing criticism of criminal sentences became widespread. Consider the following points:

REASONS FOR DETERMINATE SENTENCING

- Prison uprisings were found to result in part from disparity in sentences; offenders from similar backgrounds who had committed similar offenses received widely different sentences.
- There were few serious rehabilitation efforts or programs in prisons. Reform of offenders took a back seat to concerns of custody and security.
- Parole boards could not tell whether an offender had actually been rehabilitated. They had to rely on the offender's word, which sometimes did not correspond with the person's actual behavior when released back into the community.
- In several widely publicized cases, offenders who had been released early from prison assaulted or killed again.

This series of incidents and events led to a dramatic shift in the philosophy of sentencing. Beginning in 1975, states began to change from indeterminate to determinate sentencing.

Determinate Sentencing

Determinate sentencing systems permit the judge to impose fixed sentences that cannot be altered by a parole board. In fourteen states parole board release has been abolished. In addition, allowable sentence ranges have been narrowed considerably, giving judges little room for discretion.[37] This has had the effect of treating offenders similarly, as long as the offense is similar. The needs, problems, and backgrounds of offenders are much less important in a determinate sentencing system, because the focus is on the crime that was committed rather than on the type of offender who committed it.

determinate sentencing
A sentencing system that permits judges to impose fixed sentences that cannot be altered by a parole board.

EFFECTS OF DETERMINATE SENTENCING

In practice, determinate sentencing has had a significant impact on sentence lengths and on the proportion of the sentence that is actually served in prison. In 1977, for example, 72 percent of offenders released from a state prison had served an indeterminate sentence and were released by a parole board. By 1997, fewer than 30 percent of prison releases were determined by a parole board.[38] In addition, the proportion of each sentence served in prison before release is increasing. Prisoners convicted of violent crimes and released from prison in 1996 had been sentenced to an average of seven years and had served about half of that time, but newly sentenced violent offenders today are receiving average prison sentences of more than eight-and-a-half years and are expected to serve 85 percent of that time in most states.[39] This percentage may continue to rise with the escalation of political and public concern regarding truth in sentencing.[40]

Truth in Sentencing **Truth in sentencing** refers to the establishment of a closer relationship between the sentence imposed and the actual time served in prison prior to release. The Violent Crime Control and Law Enforcement Act of

truth in sentencing
A sentencing provision that requires offenders to serve the bulk of their sentence (usually 85 percent) before they can be released.

Table 12.1 Truth-in-Sentencing Laws by State

Meet Federal 85% Requirement		*50% Requirement*	*100% of Minimum Requirement*	*Other Requirements*
Alaska	Missouri	Indiana	Idaho	Arkansas[c]
Arizona	New Jersey	Maryland	Nevada	Colorado[d]
California	New York	Nebraska	New Hampshire	Massachusetts[e]
Connecticut	North Carolina	Texas		Wisconsin[f]
Delaware	North Dakota			
District of Col.	Ohio			
Florida	Oklahoma[b]			
Georgia	Oregon			
Illinois[a]	Pennsylvania			
Iowa	South Carolina			
Kansas	Tennessee			
Kentucky	Utah			
Louisiana	Virginia			
Maine	Washington			
Michigan				
Minnesota				
Mississippi				

[a] Qualified for federal funding in 1996 only.

[b] Two-part sentence structure (2/3 in prison; 1/3 on parole); 100% of prison term required.

[c] Mandatory 70% of sentence for certain violent offenses and manufacture of methamphetamine.

[d] Violent offenders with 2 prior violent convictions serve 75%; 1 prior violent conviction, 56.25%.

[e] Requires 75% of a minimum prison sentence.

[f] Two-part sentence: Offenders serve 100% of the prison term and a sentence of extended supervision at 25% of the prison sentence.

Source: Paula M. Ditton and Doris James Wilson, *Truth in Sentencing in State Prisons* (Washington, DC: Bureau of Justice Statistics, 1999).

1994 requires states that wish to qualify for federal financial aid to change their laws so that offenders serve at least 85 percent of their sentences. The federal government offered large grants to states that adopted truth-in-sentencing laws. By 1998 twenty-nine states had truth-in-sentencing laws that met the federal government's guidelines. Another thirteen states adopted their own versions of truth-in-sentencing laws calling for offenders to serve a specific percentage of their sentence. The sentencing status of individual states is presented in Table 12.1. The states that met the federal 85 percent requirement had received more than $400 million in federal grants, a significant factor in a majority of the states that passed these laws.[41]

PROBLEMS WITH TRUTH IN SENTENCING

There are three major concerns associated with truth-in-sentencing laws and the federal government's push to have them implemented. These include the cost of truth in sentencing, the extension of these sentencing provisions to nonviolent crimes, and federal involvement in the states' rights to set sentences. The cost of implementing truth in sentencing is extremely high, because states must build new prisons to house offenders for longer periods. For example, the plan in Virginia to abolish parole and implement truth in sentencing called for construction of twenty-five new prisons at a cost of $2 billion.[42] Indeed, most of the states that have not adopted truth in sentencing cite the high cost of prison construction, even with the available federal grant money. Given severe state budget cuts caused by an economic decline beginning in 2002, a number of states have been forced to release some offenders early in order to create prison space and save on incarceration costs.[43] The practical need to balance the government's budget forced many states to soften their stance on sentencing policy.

A second concern is the extension of truth in sentencing beyond violent crimes. In some states these new sentencing provisions do not exclude property or drug offenders. In Virginia the governor's truth-in-sentencing plan projected that almost four times more nonviolent offenders than violent offenders would be incarcerated. This trend greatly increases the length of sentences and the costs of imprisonment without any offsetting benefit in protecting the public from violent offenders.

The third concern is the federal government's role in state lawmaking. Historically, states have set criminal penalties for most crimes. The intervention of the federal government in rewarding or penalizing states for adopting particular sentencing policies has been criticized. This federal involvement in the sentences to be served by violators of state law represents, one critic argued, "a significant shift in the traditional balance between the state and federal governments and a significant federalization of a traditionally local issue."[44] On the other hand, the federal government uses monetary incentives to encourage states to implement truth-in-sentencing laws that are seen as an improvement over current practice.

Increases in Prison Populations The impact of the trend toward determinacy and longer sentences is apparent when you examine data on correctional populations. As Table 12.2 shows, the number of persons in custody in federal and state prisons and local jails increased 35 percent over 10 years. The fastest-growing segment of the prison population consists of drug offenders, who are sentenced to state prisons each year in greater numbers than are people convicted of violent crimes.[45]

Table 12.2 Persons in Custody and Rate per 100,000 (federal, state, and local jail inmates)

	1995	*2000*	*2002*	*2004*	*10-year change*
Total inmates in custody	1,585,586	1,937,482	2,033,022	2,135,901	+35%
Incarceration rate (per 100,000 U.S. residents)	601	684	701	725	+21%

Source: Compiled from Paige Harrison and Allen Beck, *Prisoners in 2004* (Washington, DC: Bureau of Justice Statistics, 2005).

Table 12.3 Trends in Numbers of Adults under Correctional Supervision (in jail or prison or on probation or parole)

Year	*Total Adults in Jail or Prison*	*Incarceration Rate per 100,000 U.S. Population*	*Total under Correctional Supervision*	*Adult Population under Supervision (per 100,000 adult)*
1985	0.74 million	312	3.01 million	1,719
1990	1.15 million	460	4.35 million	2,348
1995	1.58 million	598	5.37 million	2,751
2000	1.94 million	684	5.7 million	3,072
2004	2.14 million	725	7.0 million	3,175

Source: Compiled from Paige Harrison and Allen Beck, *Prisoners in 2004* (Washington, DC: Bureau of Justice Statistics, 2004).

These increases in prison populations outpace increases in the general U.S. population. As Table 12.3 indicates, the twenty-year incarceration rate more than doubled as the number of adults in prison or jail mushroomed to over 2 million, a rate of 725 per 100,000 population. If you add to the total those on probation or parole, the number of adults under correctional supervision in the United States is 7 million, or 3,175 per 100,000 of the U.S. adult population, nearly double the rate of twenty years earlier.

The rise in the sentenced population in the United States is displayed graphically in Figure 12.3, which shows that the number of persons sentenced to probation, parole, prison, and jail has risen to record levels. The increase in prison populations is a direct result of an increase in the likelihood of offenders' being sent to prison; also, new incarcerations are occurring faster than releases from prison. The rate of admissions into state prisons (per one hundred prisoners) was 55 per-

FIGURE 12.3 Number of Persons under Correctional Supervision, by Type of Supervision, 1990–2004

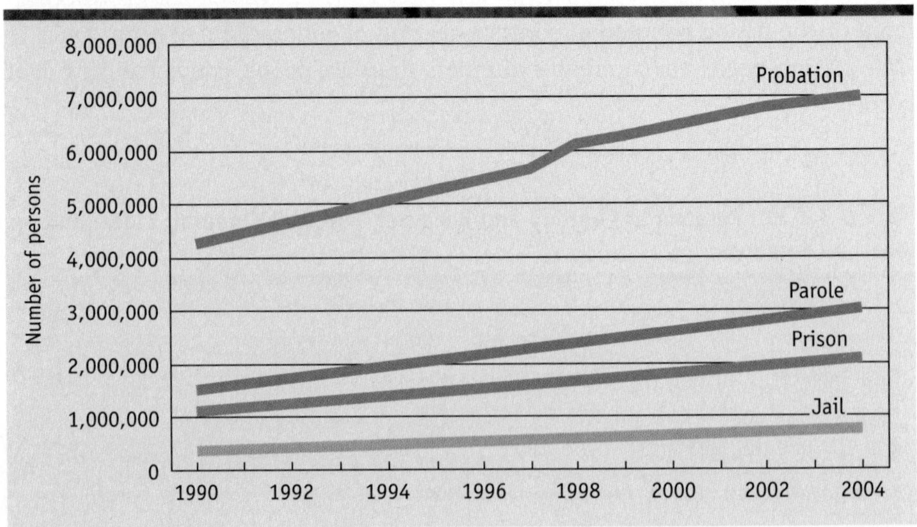

Source: Lauren E. Glaze and Seri Palla, *Probation and Parole in the United States* (Washington, DC: Bureau of Justice Statistics, 2005).

cent; the release rate was 31 percent.[46] This difference of nearly 25 percent is a major cause of prison overcrowding and new prison construction in many jurisdictions. Prison crowding also reflects the decline of indeterminate sentencing and the shrinking power of parole boards in setting actual sentence lengths, and the corresponding rise in determinate sentencing and truth-in-sentencing laws.

Mandatory Sentencing **Mandatory sentences** are a form of determinate sentencing in which fixed sentences are imposed on individuals convicted of certain types of crimes. Most crimes subject to mandatory sentences are gun-related crimes, drug offenses, and drunk-driving offenses. Mandatory sentences for certain crimes have been adopted in every state and by the federal government on the basis of their presumed deterrent and incapacitating effects. As noted in Chapter 11, mandatory sentences often shift decision-making discretion to the police and the prosecutor rather than eliminating discretion altogether. Mandatory sentencing disregards the fact that not all offenders are alike, even though they may commit the same crimes.[47] For example, a study of drug offenders sentenced to mandatory prison terms in Massachusetts found that nearly half of them had no prior record of violent crimes.[48] In New York State the governor reduced the sentences of three drug offenders because he believed their mandatory sentences were too long for the commission of nonviolent crimes, and the state legislature voted in 2004 to reduce steep mandatory drug sentences for current and future offenders. These mandatory sentences were enacted as part of the Rockefeller drugs laws of the 1970s.[49] In California several efforts have been made to limit the application of mandatory sentences to violent crimes.[50]

mandatory sentences
fixed sentences for offenders convicted of certain types of crimes such as gun-related crimes, drug offenses, and drunk-driving offenses.

PROBLEMS WITH MANDATORY SENTENCING

Moving discretion from sentencing to earlier stages of criminal procedure can be seen as an attempt to "correct" injustices that may arise when the system applies the same sentence to offenders from widely different backgrounds and to crimes of differing seriousness.[51] At the same time mandatory sentences reduce the visibility of discretionary decisions at the sentencing stage by shifting discretion to the arrest and charging stages of criminal procedure. Nevertheless, mandatory sentences remain popular as a mechanism to achieve "truth in sentencing," although at a high cost. These policies increase the number of inmates serving longer sentences and slow prison population turnover.[52] Extremely long mandatory sentences can be counterproductive because they incarcerate offenders for long periods (at great expense), well beyond their late teens and early twenties, the ages when most violent crimes are committed.[53]

"Three strikes and you're out" laws, as mentioned earlier, are a form of mandatory sentencing, imposing mandatory minimum sentences of periods up to life in prison for repeat offenders. In a case ultimately decided by the U.S. Supreme Court, a homeless person, Michael Riggs, stole a bottle of vitamin pills from a supermarket. This petty theft was a misdemeanor, but under California law it was elevated to a felony because Riggs had at least two prior felony convictions. This placed him under the California three strikes law that imposed a mandatory minimum of twenty-five years to life imprisonment. Riggs appealed, arguing that such a long sentence was both disproportionate and excessive, violating the Eighth Amendment. The U.S. Supreme Court denied a review of his sentence.[54] Yet a

This parole board is meeting to consider applications for parole from a state prison. How will the board know if a prisoner has been sufficiently reformed or rehabilitated to be released on parole? How do determinate sentencing and mandatory sentencing reduce the discretionary power of parole boards?

study of the three strikes law in California found that it did not reduce crime rates below preexisting levels and "was of no consequence in nine of the ten cities examined."[55] Nevertheless, concern over a perceived decline in morality in society appears to underlie strong public support for these laws.[56]

Frustration with mandatory sentences reached a new threshold when two U.S. Supreme Court justices, Stephen Breyer and Anthony Kennedy, criticized mandatory minimum sentences in separate speeches to the American Bar Association in 2003. Breyer stated that Congress has passed a number of mandatory minimum statutes that "is not a helpful thing to do . . . it's going to set back the cause of fairness in sentencing." Kennedy argued, "Our resources are misspent, our punishments too severe, our sentences too long."[57] It will be interesting to see whether a shift in sentencing policy occurs in the coming years that emanates either from economic concerns or from dissatisfaction with the long-term results of longer prison sentences for offenders.

Sentencing Guidelines

guideline sentences
Sentences developed by examining the averages of past sentences imposed on various combinations of offenders and offenses and designed to achieve proportionality and uniformity without mandating specific sentences for certain crimes or offenders.

Sentencing guidelines are a middle ground between indeterminate and determinate sentencing. They reduce disparity in sentencing by recommending **guideline sentences** that take into account the seriousness of crimes and the offenders' prior records. The guidelines are developed by commissions that examine averages of past sentences for various combinations of offenders and offenses. Guideline sentences achieve the goals of proportionality and uniformity without mandating specific sentences for certain crimes or offenders. Judges may deviate from the guideline sentence for a given offense only if they provide written reasons for doing so. For example, if a sentence of five to seven years is typical for past robbery offenders, judges may sentence outside this range only if they state their reasons for doing so. These reasons might include a particularly serious prior record or severe injury to the victim.

ROLE OF SENTENCING COMMISSIONS

The U.S. Sentencing Commission was created in 1984 to implement changes in the federal sentencing system. The primary thrust was to emphasize the offense, rather than the offender, in criminal sentencing. In 1987 the commission implemented federal sentencing guidelines that apply to all federal offenses. By 1996 ten states also had adopted sentencing guidelines, and seven additional states had established voluntary sentencing guidelines.[58] Voluntary sentencing guidelines, created by a panel of judges, provide no mechanism for dealing with judges who ignore the guidelines. Nonvoluntary or presumptive sentencing guidelines are developed by sentencing commissions created by legislatures. These commissions often *prescribe* a sentencing policy, rather than merely summarizing past practice as is done with voluntary guidelines. It is presumptive guidelines that require the judge to hold a hearing and to provide written reasons for any departure from the sentencing guidelines.

Table 12.4 Advantages and Disadvantages of Sentencing Guidelines

Advantages	*Disadvantages*
1. Guidelines promote uniformity and proportionality in sentencing without the problems of mandatory sentences.	1. Sentence uniformity appears to deteriorate after a few years' experience with sentencing guidelines.
2. Guidelines allow for accurate projection and control of prison populations through the nature and length of the guideline sentences.	2. The purpose of sentencing should revolve around considerations of justice, not managing the prison population.
3. Prescribed sentences allow for departures from guidelines where necessary.	3. Guidelines violate constitutional separation of powers by permitting legislatures to set sentences, which is a judicial prerogative.

Sentencing guidelines have several advantages and disadvantages, as summarized in Table 12.4. The primary advantage of sentencing guidelines is that they reduce disparity in sentencing while allowing greater flexibility than exists in mandatory sentencing schemes. Disparity is unwarranted when differences in sentences cannot be accounted for by the nature of crime or the background of the offender. A major concern, on the other hand, is that sentencing guidelines established by legislatures give the legislative branch of government control over a judicial function (sentencing). Perceived errors in judgment may result.[59] For example, sentence guidelines established for federal drug offenses are so high that some federal judges have refused to impose them; about fifty judges have refused to take new drug cases. As one federal judge observed, "we're building prisons faster than we're building classrooms. . . . The whole thing doesn't seem to be very effective."[60]

In addition, guideline sentences that punish crack cocaine much more severely than powdered cocaine have been found to punish black offenders disproportionately over whites. First-time offenders caught with 5 grams of crack cocaine receive a mandatory minimum term of five years in prison, whereas a first-time powder cocaine offender must possess 500 grams of the drug to receive the same sentence. This 100 to 1 ratio has been called excessive and discriminatory, in light of the fact that the cheaper crack cocaine is used more often by blacks, whereas powdered cocaine is used more often by whites.[61] Nevertheless, sentencing guidelines generally have been shown to reduce discrimination on the basis of race or gender.[62]

UNIFORMITY IN SENTENCING

Although sentencing guidelines have been found to increase uniformity in sentencing in many jurisdictions, this is not the case everywhere. After the first few years, uniformity tends to deteriorate.[63] Another argument for sentencing guidelines is that they make possible more accurate predictions of prison populations, and that jurisdictions can control prison populations by modifying the guidelines.[64] It can be argued that the size of prison populations should not be a factor in sentencing guidelines, because it is unrelated to any particular crime. Nevertheless, the public's fear of crime and willingness to support longer prison sentences has resulted in high prison expenses and new construction at a time when there also is pressure to reduce government spending. Sentencing guidelines may help to limit the use of incarceration so that available prison capacity can be restricted to serious offenders and habitual offenders, rather than being used for nonserious offenses.[65]

The debate over the desirability of sentencing guidelines, together with strong views about judicial discretion in sentencing, have resulted in legal changes. The PROTECT Act of 2003, signed into law by President Bush, severely limited the ability of federal judges to sentence offenders below the recommended guideline sentence, although sentences more severe than the guidelines were still permitted. The U.S. Supreme Court then weighed in on the debate on sentencing guidelines in two cases. In a 2004 case involving state criminal statutes, the court held that under the Sixth Amendment right to a jury trial, any aspect of a case that increases the penalty for a crime beyond the prescribed statutory maximum must be submitted to a jury and proved beyond a reasonable doubt; the increase cannot simply be demanded by sentencing guidelines. In a 2005 case the Supreme Court ruled that the federal sentencing guidelines are unconstitutional; the Court stipulated, however, that the sentencing guidelines can be preserved as long as judges treat them as advisory rather than mandatory (the guidelines had been mandatory since 1984). So judges now have more discretion in sentencing with advisory guidelines, and sentences will be watched carefully to assess excessive severity, leniency, and disparity in sentencing decisions, the very excesses that the sentencing guidelines were designed to prevent.[66]

How Does the Eighth Amendment Restrict Sentencing?

The Eighth Amendment to the U.S. Constitution deals largely with the final stages of the criminal justice process. It is also one of the shortest amendments. It reads as follows: "Excessive bail shall not be required, nor excessive fines imposed, nor cruel and unusual punishment inflicted." As explained in Chapter 6, the purpose of bail is to ensure that a defendant will appear for trial. If the suspect cannot afford bail, he or she must stay in jail until the trial. It is important to note that the Eighth Amendment does not require bail; it only states that the amount cannot be excessive. In many states release on bail is not permitted in capital cases (i.e., those for which the death penalty applies). Otherwise, there are few restrictions on the amount of bail a judge may require. In a controversial 1987 decision, the U.S. Supreme Court held in *U.S. v. Salerno* that preventive detention without bail on grounds of predicted future dangerousness does not violate the Eighth Amendment. The Court did not consider such detention to be "punishment without trial."[67] This decision reflected the popular view that potentially dangerous criminals should be confined—even though our ability to predict future criminality accurately is poor, a fact that raises the question whether offenders are being held for crimes they *might* commit in the future, rather than on the basis of the current charge.

U.S. v. SALERNO

The Eighth Amendment also states that fines cannot be excessive. The Supreme Court has not specified an amount that would constitute an excessive fine, but it has ruled that prison sentences imposed when offenders cannot pay fines discriminate against the poor and therefore are unconstitutional.[68] Other than this restriction, few conditions are placed on the imposition of fines. Maximum fines are, of course, fixed by the legislature and vary according to the seriousness of the crime.

The portion of the Eighth Amendment that has been most rigorously scrutinized is the prohibition of **cruel and unusual punishment.** A punishment is considered cruel and unusual if, in the words of the Supreme Court, it violates "evolving standards of decency that mark the progress of a maturing society."[69] Thus, torture is cruel and unusual punishment under the Eighth Amendment. Courts have sometimes held extreme cases of solitary confinement, corporal punishment, mechanical restraints, and poor medical or sanitary conditions for prisoners to be cruel and unusual.[70]

cruel and unusual punishment A portion of the Eighth Amendment prohibiting criminal penalties that violate "evolving standards of decency that mark the progress of a maturing society."

What Is the Answer to the Death Penalty Debate?

No penalty has received more attention than capital punishment—that is, the death penalty. The penalty of death for commission of murder is controversial, yet it is used with increasing frequency. Proponents argue that death serves as just retribution for murder, prevents future murders, and costs less than life imprisonment. Opponents argue the opposite: that capital punishment does not serve as retribution, does not deter murders, and costs more than life in prison. These are empirical arguments that can be resolved with the use of objective evidence. To what extent has the death penalty been used as retribution in the past? What impact does it have on homicide rates? How expensive are executions compared to life imprisonment? It is important that we answer these questions correctly, because a record number of prisoners await execution on death row, and the appeals process is being shortened, which will increase the pace of executions in the future.

Under what circumstances could a death row inmate appeal his conviction? Under what circumstances could a death row inmate win a stay of execution?

The Legal Status of the Death Penalty

In 1977 the U.S. Supreme Court ruled that for the crime of rape the death penalty is excessive and disproportionate and therefore unconstitutional.[71] Since then, capital punishment has been applied primarily to murder cases. During the 1930s there were nearly two hundred executions in the United States each year. By the 1960s the number of offenders receiving the death penalty dropped to less than fifty per year. Because of growing uncertainty about the constitutionality of capital punishment, there was a virtual halt to executions in the mid-1960s. In two key decisions during the 1970s, however, the U.S. Supreme Court clarified the constitutionality of death sentences.

Furman v. Georgia* and *Gregg v. Georgia In 1972 the Court ruled in *Furman v. Georgia* that the administration of the death penalty in Georgia constituted cruel and unusual punishment. It was argued to the Court that death sentences were imposed in an

Media & Criminal Justice — *Dead Man Walking*

Perhaps no other sentencing issue is as controversial as the death penalty. Many Americans favor capital punishment for convicted murderers. Opponents continue to point out that executions have not been proved to have a deterrent effect on crime. But many supporters of capital punishment counter that if nothing else, executions provide closure for the surviving families of the murder victims.

The 1995 film *Dead Man Walking* embraced all of these controversies in its story of a death row inmate who elicits the help of a nun as he faces the ultimate penalty for murder. Sister Helen Prejean assists this inmate, Matthew Poncelet, in filing a last-minute appeal that might bring him a reprieve. As Sister Prejean and Matthew discuss his plight in light of the impending execution, however, she becomes a spiritual counselor who is troubled by Matthew's lack of remorse for his crimes. She does not believe that Matthew should die for the brutal rapes and murders that he surely committed, but she hopes that the threat of death will cause him to take responsibility for his actions.

The value of *Dead Man Walking* is that it takes no position on the death penalty. Sister Prejean hopes to save Matthew from execution, but she also seeks to understand the ramifications of his crimes. She visits the families of Matthew's murder victims and is faced with the unrelenting heartache of each parent. They remind her that grief is compounded in knowing that their children, young people with such promising futures, suffered horribly in their final moments before death. The families insist that the depth of their tragedy is insulted by Matthew's very existence: It is unfair that the innocent victims are dead and that the murderer continues to live. Sister Prejean's understanding of their loss is made more acute by a visit with Matthew's family; his mother clearly doesn't see the sense in the state's taking another life by executing her son. Do two wrongs make a right?

Dead Man Walking is a careful examination of the emotions and arguments claimed by all sides. The most important message of the movie is dramatized when Matthew, guided to the truth by Sister Prejean, actually breaks down and faces the ramifications of his murderous behavior. His remorse is painful and very genuine, but it comes too late. As he is strapped down for execution, the illogic and wastefulness in executing a truly remorseful person is made evident. Yet even as the lethal injection begins, the poignant scene of execution is interspersed with shocking scenes of the actual rapes and murders of Matthew's innocent victims. The viewer is not allowed to forget the senseless, heinous crimes for which Matthew is dying. Retribution, not mere revenge or incapacitation, is communicated in his final moments.

The film brings a great deal of integrity to the discussion of the death penalty, but it does not attempt to convince the viewer of any particular stance. The theme of *Dead Man Walking* is one of careful contemplation, ensuring that both advocates and opponents of capital punishment understand each other's position.

Why was Matthew executed in *Dead Man Walking?* Which arguments and emotions concerning his death penalty do you find most compelling? In murder cases are there ways to recognize the victim's loss and hold the offender accountable without killing the offender?

arbitrary and discriminatory manner. In this case, Furman had been convicted of a murder that occurred during the course of a burglary attempt. It was left entirely up to the jury to decide, without any guidance in making that decision, whether Furman would receive a sentence of life imprisonment or death.

CONSTITUTIONALITY OF DEATH PENALTY

The Supreme Court's lack of consensus on the death penalty was apparent when each of the nine justices wrote a separate opinion in this case. The majority agreed, however, that Georgia's death penalty law provided for execution "without guidance or direction" as to whether life imprisonment, the death penalty, or other punishment was most appropriate in a given case of murder. The Supreme Court found the Georgia law to be unconstitutional, because offenders who receive the death penalty

> *are among a capriciously selected handful upon whom the sentence of death has in fact been imposed. . . . The Eighth and Fourteenth Amendments cannot tolerate the infliction of a sentence of death under legal systems that permit this unique penalty to be so wantonly and freakishly imposed.*[72]

The lack of guidance to judges and juries charged with determining when the death penalty should be imposed allowed for it to be imposed arbitrarily, and often selectively, against minorities. Under these circumstances the death penalty constituted cruel and unusual punishment and could not stand. The effect of this decision was to invalidate the death penalty laws of thirty-nine states.

By 1976, however, thirty-four states had enacted new death penalty statutes designed to meet the requirements of the *Furman* decision. These laws took one of two forms. Either they removed all judicial discretion by mandating capital punishment upon conviction for certain offenses, or they established specific guidelines for judges to use in deciding whether death was an appropriate sentence in a given case.

The Supreme Court assessed the validity of the new laws in 1976 in the case of *Gregg v. Georgia.* Two hitchhikers, Troy Gregg and Floyd Allen, had been picked up in Florida by Fred Simmons and Bob Moore. A third hitchhiker, Dennis Weaver, rode with them to Atlanta, where he got out of the car about 11:00 P.M. The four men remaining in the car later stopped to rest beside the highway. After Simmons and Moore left the car, Gregg told Allen that he was going to rob them. As Simmons and Moore came back toward the car, Gregg fired three shots at them and they fell to the ground. He then fired a shot into the head of each man at close range. He then robbed them and drove away with Allen. The bodies of Simmons and Moore were discovered the next morning.

Upon reading about the shootings in an Atlanta newspaper, Weaver (the third hitchhiker) contacted the police and described his journey with the victims, including a description of the car. The next afternoon Gregg and Allen (still in Simmons's car) were arrested in Asheville, North Carolina. In the search incident to the arrest a .25-caliber pistol, later shown to be that used to kill Simmons and Moore, was found in Gregg's pocket. After receiving the warnings required by *Miranda v. Arizona* and signing a written waiver of his rights, Gregg signed a statement in which he admitted that he had shot and robbed Simmons and Moore but claimed that he had done so in self-defense. The next day, while being transferred to Lawrenceville, Georgia, Gregg and Allen were taken to the scene of the shootings, where Allen recounted the circumstances surrounding the killings.

The jury found Gregg guilty of two counts of armed robbery and two counts of murder. The judge instructed the jury that it could recommend either a death sentence or a life prison sentence on each count. The jury was free to consider any mitigating or aggravating facts and circumstances in recommending whether a death sentence or life imprisonment was most appropriate. The jury called for the death penalty on each count. The Supreme Court of Georgia affirmed the convictions and the death sentences, but the U.S. Supreme Court decided to hear Gregg's arguments to the effect that the new Georgia death penalty statute still constituted "cruel and unusual punishment" in violation of the Eighth Amendment.

This time, however, the Supreme Court upheld the Georgia law as constitutional, because the new statute requires the jury (which also has sentencing responsibility in some states) to focus

> *on the particularized nature of the crime and the particularized characteristics of the individual defendant. While the jury is permitted to consider any aggravating or mitigating circumstances, it must find and identify at least one statutory aggravating factor before it may impose a penalty of death. In this way the jury's discretion is channeled. No longer can a jury wantonly and freakishly impose a death sentence; it is always circumscribed by the legislative guidelines.*[73]

As a result, Gregg's death sentence was upheld. Nevertheless, this decision, together with two other death penalty cases decided the same day, struck down some state statutes, because they provided for mandatory death sentences in certain cases.[74] The Court felt that the standard of adequately guided discretion was not met when no discretion whatsoever was permitted. In addition, the Court held for the first time that as a form of punishment the death penalty is not inherently cruel and unusual.

JUDICIAL DISCRETION IN DEATH PENALTY

The Supreme Court further refined its decision two years later when it struck down the Ohio death penalty statute, which did not permit a judge to consider mitigating factors such as a defendant's age, absence of prior record, or role in the crime. The Supreme Court concluded:

> *The Eighth and Fourteenth Amendments require that the sentencer, in all but the rarest kind of capital case, not be precluded from considering as a mitigating factor, any aspect of a defendant's character or record and any of the circumstances of the offense that the defendant proffers as a basis for a sentence less than death. . . . The considerations that account for the wide acceptance of individualization of sentences in noncapital cases surely cannot be thought less important in capital cases.*[75]

Therefore, courts must consider both aggravating *and* mitigating factors in determining the appropriateness of a particular sentence.

McCleskey v. Kemp The death penalty was again called into question in 1987. The case of *McCleskey v. Kemp.*[76] made it clear that claims of alleged discrimination in the application of the death penalty had not been resolved. Warren McCleskey, a black man, was charged with armed robbery and murder for killing a white police officer who was answering a silent alarm during a store robbery in Georgia. After consideration of both aggravating and mitigating circumstances, McCleskey was convicted and sentenced to death. He appealed the sentence on the grounds that it was imposed in a racially discriminatory manner, presenting as evidence the findings of a statistical study that had examined more than 2,000 murder cases in Georgia during the 1970s. The investigators had looked at 230 factors that might have accounted for differences in sentences imposed in these cases. They had found that black defendants who killed white victims were much more likely to receive the death sentence than any other racial combination. The

Supreme Court denied McCleskey's appeal on two grounds. First, the majority held that "to prevail under the equal protection clause [of the Fourteenth Amendment], McCleskey must prove that the decision makers in his case acted with discriminatory purpose." On this basis, the statistical study was "insufficient" to prove discrimination in McCleskey's particular case.

RACIAL DISCREPANCY

Second, the majority held that McCleskey's treatment did not violate the Eighth Amendment prohibition of cruel and unusual punishment. It held that the statistical study "indicates a discrepancy that appears to correlate with race" but that this discrepancy is "a far cry from the major systemic defects identified in *Furman.*" The majority found that despite the imperfections identified by the study, "our consistent rule has been that constitutional guarantees are met when the mode for determining guilt or punishment has been surrounded with safeguards to make it as fair as possible."[77]

In a sharply worded dissent, four justices argued that proving discrimination in a particular case is irrelevant, because the Court "since *Furman* has been concerned with the risk of the imposition of an arbitrary sentence, rather than the proven fact of one." The dissent believed the Court's decision should address reducing the risk of arbitrary sentences and not await unfair results before intervening. The statistical study "produced striking evidence that the odds of being sentenced to death are significantly greater than average if a defendant is black and his or her victim is white." According to the dissent, such evidence calls into question the effectiveness of the legal standards established in *Furman* and *Gregg.*[78]

To sum up, under current law, the death penalty can be imposed so long as both aggravating and mitigating circumstances are considered by the judge or jury in a nonarbitrary manner.[79] In a 2000 case, *Weeks v. Angelone,* the Supreme Court held that when a jury is confused about sentencing instructions in a capital case, a judge need not explain explicitly that the jury might impose a life prison sentence rather than the death penalty. Clearly, it is difficult to establish whether or not a sentence was imposed fairly in any given case, although evidence suggests that sentences can be unfairly influenced by factors such as conduct of the prosecutor or defense attorney, juror comprehension, and race.[80]

Application of the Death Penalty

By 2003 a total of thirty-eight states, as well as the federal government, had enacted capital punishment laws in accordance with the guidelines set forth by the U.S. Supreme Court. A record 3,314 people are now under sentence of death and awaiting execution. This reflects an upward trend that began in 1977 after the Supreme Court's ruling in *Gregg v. Georgia,* which specifically stated that capital punishment was not inherently cruel and unusual. Figure 12A in *That's a Fact* graphically illustrates the rise in the number of persons sentenced to death. There are more people awaiting execution than at any time since 1930, when national statistics were first collected. Nearly half of the prisoners on death row are in only four states: California, Texas, Florida, and Pennsylvania.[81]

Support for the death penalty remains high, although public support has dropped to 65 percent, the lowest level in twenty years.[82] There also is some reluctance to carry out executions once a sentence of death has been pronounced.[83]

More than 940 official executions have taken place since 1976. Since 1930, more than 5,000 executions have been carried out.[84]

METHODS OF EXECUTION

The most common methods used to carry out executions are lethal injection (thirty-seven states) and electrocution (nine states). Four states carry out death sentences with lethal gas; three by hanging (Delaware, New Hampshire, Washington); and three by firing squad (Idaho, Oklahoma, Utah). Sixteen states authorize the use of more than one method (lethal injection and an alternative method).[85] Federal offenders are executed by means of the method authorized in the state in which the execution takes place. Several states have provided an alternative to lethal injection because of concern that injection may be found unconstitutional in a court challenge (i.e., does it constitute cruel and unusual punishment in the manner in which it causes death?). There also has been controversy over whether electrocution is cruel and unusual punishment, but the U.S. Supreme Court has not yet ruled on this issue.[86]

Arguments for and against Capital Punishment

Those who support the death penalty usually base their argument on one of four grounds: (1) The death penalty is a necessary punishment as retribution for the life unlawfully taken; (2) the death penalty will deter others from committing murder; (3) the death penalty is less expensive to administer than life imprisonment; and (4) errors in executing innocent persons are rare. Let us examine the evidence that exists to support these claims.

Capital Punishment as Retribution The retributionist argument is perhaps the oldest of all justifications for punishment. It can be traced at least as far back as the Old Testament. The books of Exodus (21:12–25), Leviticus (24:17–21), Numbers (35:30–31), and Deuteronomy (19:11–12), all warn that

> *in case a man strikes any soul of mankind fatally, he should be put to death without fail. . . . And in case a man should cause a defect in his associate, then just as he has done, so it should be done to him. Fracture for fracture, eye for eye, tooth for tooth; the same sort of defect he may cause in the man that is what should be caused in him. And the fatal striker of a heart should make compensation for it, but the fatal striker of a man should be put to death.*

Although modern Israel, established in 1948, quickly abandoned the Mosaic law of "life for life" (except in cases of wartime treason or Nazi collaboration), many people continue to apply this notion of retribution in support of the death penalty. In fact, Christians sometimes use this justification for capital punishment despite Christ's teachings to the contrary. For example, the Gospel according to Matthew (5:38–39) recounts Jesus' stating, "You heard that it was said, 'Eye for eye and tooth for tooth.' However, I say to you: Do not resist him that is wicked; but whoever slaps you on the right cheek, turn the other also to him." Such teachings prompted the disciples of early Christianity to oppose capital punishment. Adherence to this principle wavered, however, when non-Christians came to be seen as heretics and deserving of death. This change of heart relied heavily on Paul's declaration to the Romans (13:1–2):

That's a FACT

Perspectives on the Death Penalty

Figure 12A shows trends in the number of persons receiving the death penalty in the United States over a fifty-year period. Specifically, which court cases discussed in this chapter might account for the rapid increase in death sentences after the 1970s? What social and political factors do you think contributed to those decisions?

Describe the trends in actual executions of persons sentenced to death, shown in Figure 12B. According to your text, why are so few homicide offenders sentenced to death ever executed?

FIGURE 12A Persons under a Sentence of Death, 1954–2004

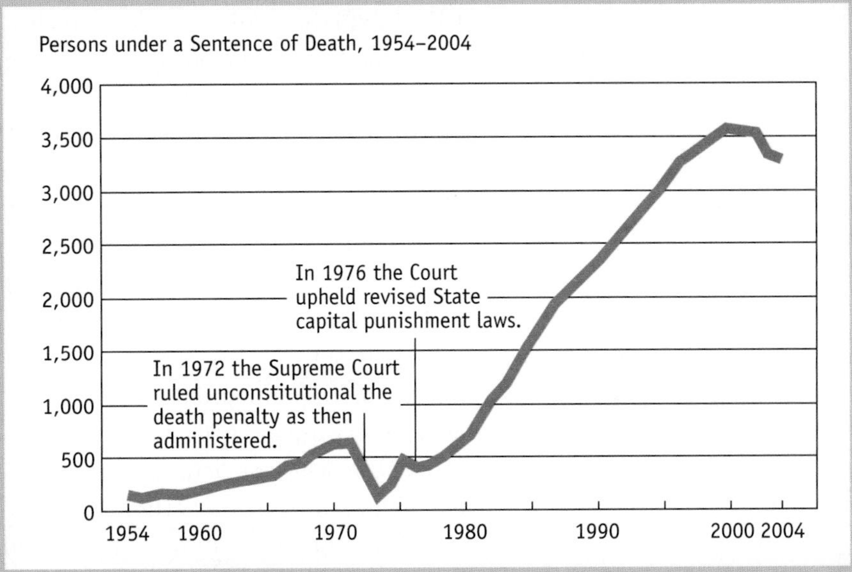

FIGURE 12B Persons Executed, 1930–2004

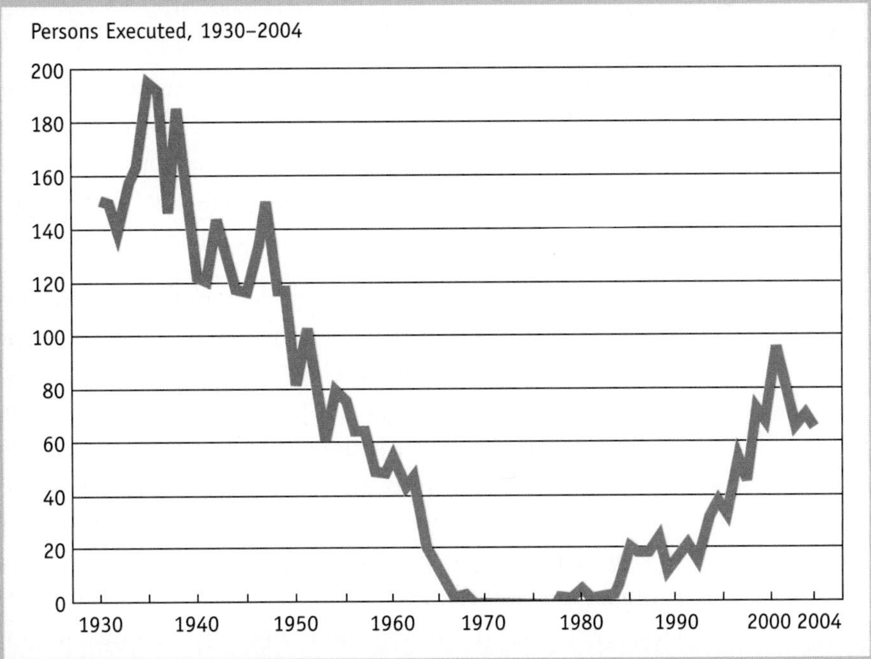

Source: Thomas P. Bonczar and Tracy L. Snell, *Capital Punishment in the United States* (Washington, DC: Bureau of Justice Statistics, 2005).

Let every soul be in subjection to the superior authorities, for there is no authority except by God; the existing authorities stand placed in their relative positions by God. Therefore he who opposes the authority has taken a stand against the arrangement of God.

Some believed that Paul's statements meant that if the state permitted capital punishment, capital punishment must be God's will, because government exists only by God's will. This line of reasoning continues to be employed today by those who defend the death penalty on the basis of Biblical interpretation.

RETRIBUTION IS INEFFECTIVE

Regardless of the basis of the argument, there is little evidence that capital punishment has been effective as a form of retribution. Examinations of willful homicides in the United States have shown that fewer than half are murders involving premeditation or homicides committed during the course of a felony. Further, fewer than 25 percent of homicides are prosecuted as capital cases. In these capital cases males and blacks have been executed much more often than have females and whites convicted of the same crimes. Even when a person is prosecuted for murder, the defendant's odds of actually receiving retribution are extremely small.[87] For example, in Massachusetts between 1931 and 1950, a murder defendant faced a 29 percent chance of being convicted and a 4 percent chance of being put to death. In California between 1950 and 1975, only 29 percent of homicide convictions were capital cases; 6 percent of defendants were sentenced to death, and fewer than 2 percent were executed. In fact, the death penalty has been imposed on only a small minority of offenders convicted of homicide. During its greatest usage in the 1930s, death sentences were handed down in only 1 of 50 homicide convictions. And as criminologist Thorsten Sellin has pointed out, these examples actually *overestimate* the use of the death penalty as retribution:

Considering that these adjudicated murderers were only a part of a group that included the never-discovered offenders and those arrested but not prosecuted or convicted for lack of sufficient evidence, it is obvious that if retribution by death could be measured in relation to the number of actual murders, its failure would be even more evident.[88]

Although in recent years supporters of retribution have succeeded in passing death penalty laws, it can be seen that only a small proportion of criminal homicides are actually subject to the death penalty. Moreover, the penalty is rarely imposed even in cases in which it is applicable. When it is applied, males and blacks receive a disproportionate share of the death sentences imposed.

It appears, therefore, that the goal of the retributionists has yet to be achieved. Even if the number of executions were to rise dramatically, it is unlikely that more than 2 percent of all homicide offenders sentenced would ever be executed. After all, the rate was 2 percent during the 1930s, when executions numbered more than two hundred per year. Limits on appellate review of sentences in death penalty cases have resulted in more executions in recent years, but the numbers are quite small compared to those in the 1930s. Trends in the number of people executed in the United States from 1930 to 2004 are illustrated in Figure 12B in *That's a Fact*. It is clear that the increase in executions during the 1990s is dwarfed by the number of executions that took place each year from 1930 to 1950.

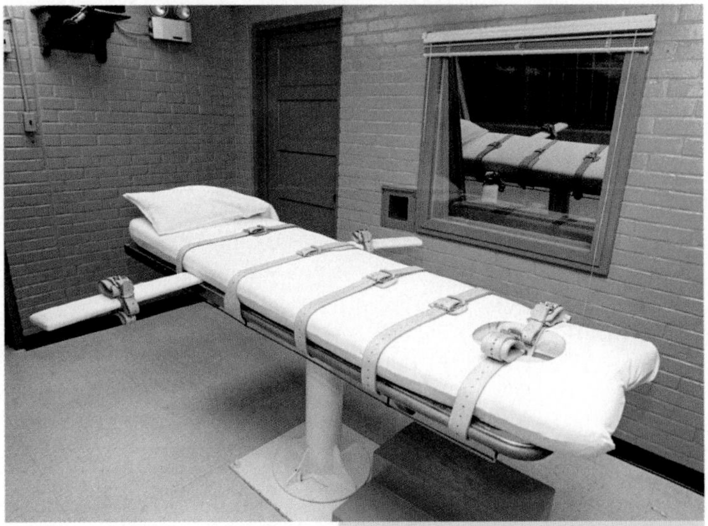

Death by lethal injection is now the most common form of capital punishment in the United States. Why do you believe electrocution and hanging are being phased out? Do you believe that public executions would deter potential homicide offenders?

The Death Penalty as Deterrence The belief that the death penalty will prevent crime by deterring future murders is another common argument in support of capital punishment.[89] One aspect of this argument suggests that police officers in states without the death penalty are more likely to be killed than officers in states that provide for capital punishment for murder (or at least for murder of police officers). Studies consistently have found, however, that the numbers of police officers killed do not differ in death penalty and non–death penalty states.[90]

The deterrence argument also holds that capital punishment prevents the offender from committing another murder if released on parole. In the four-year period from 1969 to 1973, when no death sentences were carried out, 6,835 male offenders serving sentences for murder were released on parole from state prisons. Fewer than 5 percent of those released were returned to prison for additional crimes. Fewer than one-half of 1 percent committed willful homicides. From 1930 to 1962, when executions were more frequent, only 63 offenders convicted of first-degree murder in New York State were released on parole; of these, one person was returned to prison for committing an additional crime (a burglary). Other follow-up studies have had similar results.[91] It is clear that murderers are very rarely released on parole and that when they are, it is extremely uncommon for them to be involved in another homicide.

STUDIES ON DETERRENT EFFECTS

Another way to assess the deterrent effect of capital punishment is to determine whether homicide rates increase when states abolish capital punishment, or to examine the homicide rates in neighboring states, one of which has a death penalty while the other does not. Obviously, if capital punishment prevents murders, states without a death penalty law should have higher homicide rates than neighboring states that employ the death penalty. A comparison of homicide rates and use of the death penalty in Maryland, Delaware, and New Jersey from 1920 through 1974 found no difference in homicide rates, even though each of these states retained, abolished, and sometimes reinstituted capital punishment during this fifty-five-year period. The number of executions in these states varied from none to a high of twenty-six per year, but in no case was a higher number of executions accompanied by a lower homicide rate. Comparable findings were uncovered in tristate comparisons of Arizona, California, and New Mexico and of Indiana, Ohio, and Michigan, as well as of other states.[92] As Brian Forst concluded, "it is erroneous to view capital punishment as a means of reducing the homicide rate."[93] A study using FBI data found that ten of twelve states without capital punishment have homicide rates below the national average. It concluded that "during the last twenty years, the homicide rate in states with the death penalty has been 48 to 101 percent higher than in states without the death penalty."[94] These findings mirror the conclusions of other criminologists.[95]

Studies that appear to show a deterrent effect have been repudiated on methodological grounds.[96] In fact, there is evidence from two studies that there may be a slight *increase* in the number of homicides following a legal execution. These studies found a few more homicides after executions than one would normally expect to occur. It has been suggested that a legal execution may "provoke" homicides by conveying the message that vengeance by means of killing is justified.[97]

There are several important reasons that the death penalty is not a deterrent to criminal homicide. Most significant is that the offenders must consider the consequences of their actions if deterrence is to take place. If a person does not consider the possibility of being penalized for pursuing criminal actions, no penalty, however severe, will act as a deterrent. The crime of murder is rarely carried out in such a rational fashion. First, those who commit murder rarely set out to do it. Most homicides occur as an unplanned act during the commission of a robbery or other felony. Thus, the death penalty is not considered as a possible outcome because murder was not an anticipated part of the crime. Second, offenders rarely believe that they will be caught. Because police solve only a small percentage of all serious crimes, the likelihood of punishment is very low. Certainty of punishment is extremely important if deterrence is to work. The lower the chances of being caught, the lower the deterrent effect of any penalty. Third, when criminal homicides occur, they usually are committed during a moment of intense anger or emotion in which reason is distorted. Police estimate that about half of all homicides occur during arguments between an offender and a victim who know each other. Also, it is not unusual for the offender to be under the influence of alcohol or a drug, which certainly affects rational thinking. All these circumstances work against the exercise of rational behavior, which is pivotal to the notion of deterrence.

THE COST OF CAPITAL PUNISHMENT

Economics and Capital Punishment Some claim that the death penalty is more economical than housing an offender in prison for life. A study conducted in New York State during the 1980s found that it would cost a total of $648,560 to incarcerate a thirty-year-old murderer if he lived to age seventy. On the other hand, at that time the costs of the trials and multiple appeals involved in capital cases amounted to more than $1.8 million.[98] Currently, it costs $20,100 per year to imprison the average inmate, but the cost is usually higher on death row because of segregation practices for those awaiting execution.[99] The average inmate on death row is now twenty-eight years old, suggesting that living thirty or more years in prison is quite possible.[100] A study found that the cost of defending a federal death penalty case through trial was $269,139, plus the cost of subsequent appeals.[101] In Florida, each execution costs the state $3.2 million—six times the cost of life imprisonment.[102] The high cost of capital punishment cases arises from the fact that virtually all death penalty states provide for automatic appellate review of death sentences. To guard against the possibility of a mistake, states usually conduct this review regardless of the offender's wishes. Because of this time-consuming process, the average time between sentencing and execution of offenders executed since 1977 has been more than eight years.[103] Limitations on the right to appeal, enacted in 1996, will reduce the time between sentencing and execution; but it remains to be seen whether the difference will be significant.[104]

EXECUTION IS NOT CHEAPER

The economic argument for the use of the death penalty thus does not hold up under scrutiny. It also overlooks the fact that the proportion of offenders who ever face the death penalty is extremely small. As the New York State report concluded, "a criminal justice system with the death penalty is inordinately more expensive than a criminal justice system without the death penalty."[105]

Errors in Applying the Death Penalty A major criticism of capital punishment is its finality. Proponents of the death penalty argue that errors are rare; but in a criminal justice system based on inexact legal standards such as "probable cause" and "proof beyond a reasonable doubt," there is always room for error.[106] There have been cases in which offenders who were executed have later been found to be innocent. In Illinois, for example, at least thirteen offenders who were convicted of murder and sentenced to death later were found to be innocent.[107] A systematic nationwide study found 400 erroneous convictions in death penalty cases.[108] In 1999 and 2000, both Nebraska and Illinois put a hold on executions because of errors, and possible prosecution misconduct, that put innocent suspects on death row.[109] The 1996 Antiterrorism and Effective Death Penalty Act places restrictions on the appeals available to offenders sentenced to death. Some fear that these new limits will result in additional erroneous convictions in murder cases.[110]

DNA EVIDENCE

Advances in testing for deoxyribonucleic acid (DNA) have been instrumental both in convicting and in exonerating suspects linked to serious crimes. Reliable DNA testing emerged during the late 1980s, and although testing procedures are still improving, DNA tests now are generally accepted as evidence in court.[111] DNA evidence has revealed that eyewitness testimony is sometimes mistaken, that jailhouse informants can be unreliable, and that those with criminal records often become suspects in criminal cases without strong evidence of their involvement in the crime. In one case a rape victim identified her assailant, but DNA evidence later showed she was mistaken. In another case a man was wrongly convicted in the rape of an eleven-year-old girl, even though eleven witnesses had testified he was 300 miles away at the time of the rape.[112] Errors like these are troubling, because they reveal that weak evidence sometimes results in erroneous criminal convictions, and hundreds have been reported around the country. DNA samples taken from hair or body fluids from the victim or crime scene have revealed these errors to the shock of many, resulting in attempts to halt executions in eleven states in order to study the reasons for these errors.[113]

Larry Fuller (center) was exonerated in Texas after serving more than 25 years in prison for a rape he did not commit. DNA evidence was used to prove his innocence. Should all incarcerated offenders be permitted to challenge their convictions based on DNA evidence?

From 1977, the year after the U.S. Supreme Court reinstated the death penalty in *Gregg v. Georgia*, through 2002, a total of 6,532 offenders were sentenced to death. Of these, 820 were executed, but 2,535 were removed from death row by appellate court review, sentence reductions, or death. In 2002 alone, eighty-three inmates in twenty-six states had their death sentences vacated or their convictions overturned.[114] A study of executive clemency by governors revealed that reductions in sentences and pardons of death row inmates were significantly more likely to occur during non-election years, and that executions occurred significantly more often during election years, suggesting political considerations in the imposition of capital punishment.[115] A study of more than 4,500 death penalty appeals filed over a period of twenty-three years found a large number of significant mistakes in death penalty trials, leading to reversals in sixty-eight of the cases. The mistakes primarily involved incompetent defense attorneys who overlooked important evidence in capital cases, as well as overzealous prosecutors who suppressed exculpatory evidence.[116] The large number of prisoners whose sentences are reduced or overturned, often because errors are discovered, has caused many to question the use of so final a penalty as capital punishment in so uncertain a process as the American criminal justice system.

ERRORS DO HAPPEN

CRITICAL THINKING EXERCISES

Victim's Race and Death Penalty Decisions

It has long been debated whether the death penalty can be imposed justly and also blindly with regard to race. Of the more than 3,500 prisoners under a sentence of death in the United States, 44 percent are black. Of the 820 persons executed since the U.S. Supreme Court approved the death penalty in 1976, 36 percent have been black.[a] In both cases, the percentage of blacks is far above their proportion in the general population; this imbalance has led to much speculation that black defendants are discriminated against in death penalty cases.

Less attention has been given to the impact of the race of the victim in murder cases. But in 1990 the U.S. General Accounting Office (GAO), the investigative arm of Congress, undertook an examination of the role of race in death penalty decisions. The researchers identified twenty-eight studies of the death penalty that included race as a variable, and they analyzed each study to determine whether race was a significant factor in death penalty cases.

The GAO's findings were remarkable, showing "a pattern of evidence indicating racial disparities in the charging, sentencing, and imposition of the death penalty."[b] In twenty-three of the twenty-eight studies, the race of the *victim* was associated with the decision to charge the offender with murder or to impose the death penalty. Legally relevant factors such as the offender's prior criminal record did not fully account for the racial disparities.

Interestingly, there was mixed evidence regarding the impact of the *defendant's* race. A slight majority of the studies found the race of the defendant significant, but in some studies white defendants were more likely to be sentenced to death; in others it depended on urban–rural differences or on other factors.[c] The GAO researchers concluded, "The results show a strong race-of-victim influence: the death penalty sentence was more likely to be sought and imposed for an offender if the victim was white."[d] In contrast, the impact of the race of the defendant was not clear or uniform across the studies considered.

CRITICAL THINKING QUESTIONS

1. The typical offender on death row was arrested at age twenty-six, has a prior criminal record, and is from a southern state. How might you explain these findings?
2. What factors surrounding murder cases and trials might help explain the influence of the victim's race in death penalty decisions?
3. Why do you think the victim's race was more significant than the offender's race in cases in which the death penalty was imposed?

NOTES

a. Thomas P. Bonczar and Tracy L. Snell, *Capital Punishment* (Washington, DC: U.S. Bureau of Justice Statistics, 2003).

b. Lowell Dodge, Testimony before the Subcommittee on Civil and Constitutional Rights Committee on the Judiciary, U.S. House of Representatives, May 3, 1990, p. 4.

c. U.S. Comptroller General, *Death Penalty Sentencing: Research Indicates Pattern of Racial Disparity* (Washington, DC: U.S. General Accounting Office, 1990). See also, David C. Baldus and George Woodworth, "Race Discrimination in the Administration of the Death Penalty: An Overview of the Empirical Evidence," *Criminal Law Bulletin*, vol. 39 (March–April 2003), p. 194.

d. Dodge, Testimony, p. 6. See also, David C. Baldus and George Woodworth, "Race Discrimination in the Administration of the Death Penalty: An Overview of the Empirical Evidence," *Criminal Law Bulletin*, vol. 39 (March–April 2003) p. 194.

Is Life Imprisonment a More Severe Punishment Than the Death Penalty?

During the 1960s a majority of people in the United States opposed the death penalty, but today public opinion polls show widespread support for capital punishment. This support is manifested in the existence of death penalty laws in thirty-eight states and the federal government. The current support continues despite concerns about the deterrent effect of capital punishment and despite the fact that most other nations have abolished it. Even South Africa, which had used capital punishment for 350 years, abolished it in 1995.[a] This left the United States among the few developed nations that still carry out death sentences.

In death penalty cases a judge or jury usually may choose between the death penalty and life imprisonment. Supporters of capital punishment often argue that life imprisonment is a less severe penalty than death. An argument can be made, however, that life imprisonment is actually a *more* severe sentence than the death penalty. This argument was made most persuasively by Cesare Beccaria in his 1764 *Essay on Crimes and Punishments*. Beccaria argued that "it is not the terrible yet momentary spectacle of the death of a wretch, but the long and painful example of a man deprived of liberty . . . which is the strongest curb against crimes." He believed that the impression left by an execution is mitigated by a tendency to forget the event because of its brevity. In addition, some offenders may desire death because they are vain or fanatic, or because they wish to escape their misery. Beccaria goes on to argue that life imprisonment is a better deterrent to crime than the death penalty. An execution provides only a single deterrent example, whereas "the penalty of a lifetime of servitude for a single crime supplies frequent and lasting examples" to others. "Adding up all the moments of unhappiness and servitude," Beccaria concludes, life imprisonment "may well be even more cruel; [it is] drawn out over an entire lifetime, while the pain of death exerts its whole force in a moment."

Beccaria also states that the death penalty is not useful "because of the example of barbarity it gives men." He notes, "It seems to me absurd that the laws, which are an expression of the public will, which detest and punish homicide, should themselves commit it, and that to deter citizens from murder, they order a public one."[b]

Former New York State Governor Mario Cuomo opposed capital punishment on grounds similar to those set forth by Beccaria. His opposition to the death penalty was seen by many as a major cause of his failure to win reelection in 1994. During the previous year Cuomo had refused to send an inmate serving a life sentence from New York State to Oklahoma, where the inmate faced the death penalty, despite the inmate's stated wish to die. In 1994 the new governor sent the inmate to Oklahoma to be executed. Ironically, before his execution the inmate wrote a statement that said, "Let there be no mistake, Mario Cuomo is wright [sic]. . . . All jurors should remember this. Attica and Oklahoma State Penitentiary are living hells." Cuomo later remarked about the inmate, "He admitted that being allowed to die was an act of clemency for a double murderer, relieving him of the relentless confinement he dreaded more than death."[c]

CRITICAL THINKING QUESTIONS

1. Do you agree or disagree with Beccaria's argument about the severity of life imprisonment versus the death penalty? What are your reasons for doing so?
2. How would you respond to Beccaria's comment that it appears absurd for the state and its laws to express condemnation of homicide by committing it?

NOTES

a. Chris Eramus, "Death Penalty Is Abolished in South Africa," *USA Today* (June 7, 1995), p. 4.
b. Cesare Beccaria, *Essay on Crimes and Punishments* (1764) (Indianapolis: Bobbs-Merrill, 1984), ch. 16.
c. Doug Ferguson, "Grasso, Just Before Dying, Says Cuomo Is Right: Life in Prison Would Be Worse," *Buffalo News* (March 21, 1995), p. 14.

SUMMARY

WHAT HAPPENS AT TRIAL?

- More than 90 percent of criminal cases are resolved through guilty pleas.
- When a trial takes place, it begins with the selection of a jury, usually consisting of twelve members.
- After a jury has been selected, the prosecution and defense counsel make opening statements. The body of the trial consists of the presentation of the prosecutor's evidence and the statements of witnesses, followed by the presentation of the case for the defense.
- A major issue in criminal defense is the new tendency to focus on the offender rather than on the criminal act. This has led to the creation of new defenses that attempt to go beyond the traditional boundaries of concepts such as self-defense.

- When all the evidence has been presented, the prosecution and defense make their final arguments to the jury. This stage is followed by the judge's instruction to the jury.
- In order for a defendant to be found guilty, the jury must agree unanimously that guilt has been proved beyond a reasonable doubt.

HOW DO JUDGES DECIDE ON A SENTENCE?

- In order to individualize sentences on the basis of the nature of the offender and the circumstances of the offense, judges may choose sentences within a range established by law.
- When a judge sentences for purposes of retribution, punishment is applied simply in proportion to the seriousness of the offense.
- Sentences based on the concept of incapacitation are intended to prevent further criminal behavior by the offender.
- Habitual offender laws such as "three strikes" statutes apply to offenders who have committed two or more offenses within a certain period.
- Deterrence aims to prevent crime through the example of offenders' being punished.
- The rehabilitation approach sees criminal behavior as stemming from social or psychological shortcomings. The purpose of a sentence aimed at rehabilitation is to correct or treat these shortcomings.
- Depending on the range of alternatives provided by law, a judge usually can fine an offender or impose a sentence of probation, incarceration, or restitution.
- Occasionally a judge suspends (delays) a prison sentence on condition that the offender participate in an alcohol, drug, or gambling treatment program or pay restitution.
- A presentence report is written by a probation officer after an investigation of the offender's background; the report is designed to help the judge decide on an appropriate sentence.

HOW DO SENTENCING OPTIONS DIFFER?

- Indeterminate sentencing systems empower the judge to set a maximum sentence; throughout the sentence a parole board reviews the offender's progress in order to determine whether early release is justified.
- Determinate sentencing systems permit the judge to impose fixed sentences that cannot be altered by a parole board.
- The trend toward determinate sentencing has produced significant increases in prison populations.
- Mandatory sentences are fixed sentences imposed on individuals convicted of certain types of crimes.
- Truth-in-sentencing laws endeavor to establish a closer relationship between sentence imposed and actual time served.
- Sentencing guidelines recommend a "guideline sentence" based on past average sentences and taking into account the seriousness of the crime and the offender's prior record.

HOW DOES THE EIGHTH AMENDMENT RESTRICT SENTENCING?

- The Eighth Amendment bars excessive bail, excessive fines, and cruel and unusual punishment.
- The Supreme Court has ruled that the death penalty is cruel and unusual punishment except in cases of murder.

WHAT IS THE ANSWER TO THE DEATH PENALTY DEBATE?

- There has been considerable controversy over how the death penalty is applied, with some critics claiming that it is imposed arbitrarily against minorities.
- Recent Supreme Court rulings require that courts consider both aggravating and mitigating factors in determining the appropriateness of a particular sentence, including the death sentence.
- Some supporters of the death penalty believe that it is a necessary punishment as retribution for the life unlawfully taken. There is little evidence that the death sentence has been effective as a form of retribution.
- Another common argument in support of capital punishment is that the death penalty will prevent crime by deterring future murders. Studies have found that there is no difference in homicide rates in states that have retained, abolished, and reinstituted capital punishment.
- Some death penalty proponents argue that execution is less costly to the state than life imprisonment, but studies show that this is not the case.
- Supporters of capital punishment contend that innocent persons are rarely executed, but studies have found numerous cases of erroneous convictions in death penalty cases. Analysis of DNA evidence has proved that suspects are convicted in error more often than was previously imagined.

KEY TERMS

corpus delicti *318*
continuance *319*
discovery *319*
trial jury *320*
general defenses *322*
justification defenses *322*
excuse defenses *322*
jury nullification *323*
retribution *324*
incapacitation *325*
selective incapacitation *325*
habitual offender laws *325*
deterrence *326*
rehabilitation *326*
suspended sentence *328*
presentence report *328*
indeterminate sentencing *328*
determinate sentencing *329*
truth in sentencing *329*
mandatory sentences *333*
guideline sentences *334*
cruel and unusual punishment *337*

QUESTIONS FOR REVIEW AND DISCUSSION

1. List the sequence of events in a typical criminal trial.
2. What is required if a jury is to reach a verdict of guilty?
3. What are some arguments for and against considering factors other than the crime in deciding on an appropriate sentence for a convicted offender?
4. Name and describe the four main purposes of sentencing.
5. What is a suspended sentence?
6. Distinguish between indeterminate and determinate sentencing systems.
7. What is meant by "truth in sentencing"?
8. What are sentencing guidelines? What effect have they had in the states where they have been adopted?
9. What protections are provided by the Eighth Amendment to the U.S. Constitution?
10. What is the current legal status of the death penalty?
11. Describe the main arguments in support of the death penalty.
12. How has DNA testing changed the way in which convicted criminals are viewed?

NOTES

1. Katherine E. Finkelstein, "No Corpse, but Plenty of Precedent," *New York Times* (October 13, 2000), p. 1.
2. Michael E. Tigar, "Trials Teach Lessons of Rights and Responsibilities," *The National Law Journal* 19 (November 18, 1996), p. 19.
3. Thomas N. Cohen and Brian A. Reaves, *Felony Defendants in Large Urban Counties* (Washington, DC: Bureau of Justice Statistics, 2006).
4. Matthew R. Durose and Patrick A. Langan, *Felony Sentences in State Courts* (Washington, DC: Bureau of Justice Statistics, 2006).
5. Leonard W. Levy, *The Palladium of Justice: Origins of Trial by Jury* (New York: Reed, 1999).
6. Nancy S. Marder, "Juries, Justice, and Multiculturalism," *University of Southern California Law Review*, vol. 75 (March 2002), p. 659.
7. Neil J. Kressel and Dorit F. Kressel. *Stack and Sway: The New Science of Jury Consulting* (Boulder, CO: Westview Press, 2002).
8. *Ballew v. Georgia*, 435 U.S. 223 (1978).
9. Susan Estrich, *Getting Away with Murder* (Cambridge, MA: Harvard University Press, 1998); Robert Davis, "We Live in an Age of Exotic Defenses," *USA Today* (November 22, 1994), p. 2.
10. Davis, pp. 1–2.
11. Alan Dershowitz, *The Abuse Excuse* (New York: Random House, 1994).
12. Davis, p. 2.
13. Margaret Gibbons, "Kleitman Granted Second Chance to Ask for Freedom," *The Legal Intelligencer* (May 6, 1998), p. 5.
14. Ellen Yaroshefsky, "Symposium: The Cooperating Witness Conundrum: Is Justice Obtainable?," *Cardozo Law Review*, vol. 23 (February 2002), p. 747.
15. Jay S. Albanese, *Organized Crime in Our Times* (Cincinnati: Lexis Nexis Anderson, 2004); Leonard Buder, "Gotti Is Acquitted in Conspiracy Case Involving the Mob," *New York Times* (March 14, 1987), p. 1.
16. Melvyn B. Zerman, *Beyond a Reasonable Doubt: Inside the American Jury System* (New York: Crowell, 1981).
17. Nancy S. Marder, "The Interplay of Race and False Claims of Jury Nullification," *University of Michigan Law Review* 32 (winter 1999); Nancy Jean King, "The American Criminal Jury," *Law and Contemporary Problems* 62 (spring 1999), pp. 41–67.
18. Susan Estrich, "A Just Sentence for Susan Smith," *USA Today* (August 3, 1995), p. 11.
19. Exodus 21:12–25; Leviticus 24:17–21; Numbers 35:30–31; Deuteronomy 19:11–12.

20. Andrew von Hirsch, *Doing Justice: The Choice of Punishments* (New York: Hill & Wang, 1976); Andrew von Hirsch, *Past or Future Crimes: Deservedness and Dangerousness in the Sentencing of Criminals* (New Brunswick, NJ: Rutgers University Press, 1985).
21. "Government Has Resumed Amputation as Punishment," *Africa News Service* (April 3, 2000), p. 1.
22. Reuel Shinnar and Shlomo Shinnar, "The Effects of the Criminal Justice System on the Control of Crime: A Quantitative Analysis," *Law and Society Review* 9 (1975), pp. 581–611; Peter W. Greenwood, *Selective Incapacitation* (Santa Monica, CA: Rand Corporation, 1978).
23. Kathleen Auerhahn, "Selective Incapacitation and the Problem of Prediction," *Criminology* 37 (November, 1999), p. 703; Stephen D. Gottfredson and Don M. Gottfredson, "Selective Incapacitation?," *Annals* 478 (1985), pp. 135–49; Andrew von Hirsch, "Selective Incapacitation Reexamined," *Criminal Justice Ethics* 7 (1988), pp. 19–35.
24. "Costly Pizza," *USA Today* (August 4, 1994), p. 3.
25. See Alfred Blumstein, Jacqueline Cohen, and Daniel Nagin, eds., *Deterrence and Incapacitation: Estimating the Effects of Criminal Sanctions on Crime Rates* (Washington, DC: National Academy of Sciences, 1978); Michael L. Radelet and Ronald L. Akers, "Deterrence and the Death Penalty: The Views of the Experts," *Journal of Criminal Law and Criminology* 87 (fall 1996), pp. 1–16; Neal Kumar Katyal, "Deterrence's Difficulty," *Michigan Law Review* 95 (August 1997), pp. 2385–476; Richard S. Frase, "Punishment Purposes," *Stanford Law Review*, vol. 58 (October 2005), pp. 67–84.
26. Scott H. Decker and Carol W. Kohlfeld, "Certainty, Severity, and the Probability of Crime," *Policy Studies Journal* 19 (1990), pp. 2–21; James J. Hennessy, Vincent P. Rao, Jennice S. Vilhauer, and Joyce N. Fensterstock, "Crime and Punishment: Infrequently Imposed Sanctions May Reinforce Criminal Behavior," *Journal of Offender Rehabilitation* 29 (March–April 1999), p. 65.
27. David Grosvenor, Traci L. Toomey, and Alexander C. Wagenaar, "Deterrence and the Adolescent Drinking Driver," *Journal of Safety Research* 30 (fall 1999), p. 187; Daniel S. Nagin and Raymond Paternoster, "The Preventive Effects of the Perceived Risk of Arrest," *Criminology* 29 (1991), pp. 561–85.
28. Gary S. Green, "General Deterrence and Television Cable Crime," *Criminology* 23 (1985), pp. 629–45.
29. D. A. Andrews, Ivan Zinger, Robert D. Hoge, James Bonta, Paul Gendreau, and Francis T. Cullen, "Does Correctional Treatment Work?," *Criminology* 28 (1990), pp. 393–404; Daniele M. Polizzi, Doris Layton MacKenzie, and Laura J. Hickman, "What Works in Adult Sex Offender Treatment? A Review of Prison- and Non-Prison-Based Treatment Programs," *International Journal of Offender Therapy and Comparative Criminology* 43 (September, 1999), p. 357.
30. Gerald G. Gaes, Timothy J. Flanagan, Lawrence L. Motiuk, and Lynn Stewart, "Adult Correctional Treatment," *Crime and Justice* 26 (fall 1999), p. 361; Lee Sechrest, Susan O. White, and Elizabeth D. Brown, eds., *The Rehabilitation of Criminal Offenders* (Washington, DC: National Academy of Sciences, 1979); Anthony Petrosino, "From Martinson to Meta-analysis: Research Reviews and the US Offender Treatment Debate," *Evidence & Policy: A Journal of Research, Debate and Practice*, vol. 1 (May 2005), pp. 149–63.
31. U.S. Comptroller General, *Federal Courts: Differences Exist in Ordering Fines and Restitution* (Washington, DC: U.S. General Accounting Office, 1999).
32. *Williams v. Illinois*, 399 U.S. 235 (1970).
33. *Tate v. Short*, 401 U.S. 395 (1971).
34. *Gardner v. Florida*, 430 U.S. 349 (1977).
35. Catharine M. Goodwin, "The Independent Role of the Probation Officer at Sentencing and in Applying *Koon v. United States*," *Federal Probation* 60 (September 1996), pp. 71–79; S. Scott MacDonald and Cynthia Baroody-Hart, "Communication between Probation Officers and Judges: An Innovative Model," *Federal Probation* 63 (June 1999), p. 42.
36. Barbara Sims and Mark Jones, "Predicting Success or Failure on Probation: Factors Associated with Felony Probation Outcomes," *Crime and Delinquency*, vol. 43 (July 1997), p. 314; Robert M. Carter and Leslie T. Wilkins, "Some Factors in Sentencing Policy," *Journal of Criminal Law, Criminology, and Police Science*, vol. 58 (1967), pp. 503–14; Curtis Campbell, Candace McCoy, and Chimezie Osigweh, "The Influence of Probation Recommendations on Sentencing Decisions and Their Predictive Accuracy," *Federal Probation* 54 (1990), pp. 13–21.
37. *National Survey of State Sentencing Structures* (Washington, DC: Bureau of Justice Assistance, 1998).
38. Paula M. Ditton and Doris James Wilson, *Truth in Sentencing in State Prisons* (Washington, DC: Bureau of Justice Statistics, 1999); Lawrence A. Greenfeld, *Prison Sentences and Time Served for Violence* (Washington, DC: U.S. Bureau of Justice Statistics, 1995).
39. Ditton and Wilson; Greenfeld.
40. Pamela L. Griset, "Determinate Sentencing and Agenda Building: A Case Study of the Failure of a Reform," *Journal of Criminal Justice* 23 (July–August 1995), pp. 349–62; Pamala L. Griset, "New Sentencing Laws Follow Old Patterns: A Florida Case Study," *Journal of Criminal Justice*, vol. 30 (July–August 2002), p. 287.
41. U.S. Comptroller General, *Truth in Sentencing: Availability of Federal Grants Influenced Laws in Some States* (Washington, DC: U.S. General Accounting Office, 1998).
42. Virginia House Appropriations Committee Staff Report, *Analysis of Potential Costs under the Governor's Sentencing Reform Plan* (Richmond: Office of the Governor, 1994); Marc Mauer, "The Truth about Truth in Sentencing," *Corrections Today* 58 (February 1996), pp. 1–9.
43. U.S. Comptroller General, pp. 7–8; Lisa Stansky, "Breaking Up Prison Gridlock," *ABA Journal* 82 (May 1996), p. 70–76; Saasha Abramsky, "No resources, No results," *The American Prospect* (December 2003), p. 51; Susan Haigh, "Auditors Say More Alternative Incarceration Needed," *Associated Press* (September 26, 2003); Ray Carter, "Oklahoma Lawmakers Try to Balance Corrections Cuts with Safety Concerns," *Oklahoma City (OK) Journal Record Legislative Report* (September 29, 2003).
44. Steven R. Donziger, ed., *The Real War on Crime: The Report of the National Criminal Justice Commission* (New York: Harper Perennial, 1996), p. 24; Marc Mauer and Meda Chesney-Lind, *Invisible Punishment: The Collateral Consequences of Mass Imprisonment* (New York: New Press, 2002).
45. Paige Harrison and Allen Beck, *Prisoners in 2004* (Washington, DC: Bureau of Justice Statistics, 2005).

46. Allen J. Beck, *Correctional Populations in the United States* (Washington, DC: Bureau of Justice Statistics, 2002).
47. Paul Simon and Dave Kopel, "Restore Flexibility to U.S. Sentences," *The National Law Journal* 19 (December 16, 1996), p. 15; Ian Weinstein, "Fifteen Years after the Federal Sentencing Revolution: How Mandatory Minimums Have Undermined Effective and Just Narcotics Sentencing," *American Criminal Law Review*, vol. 40 (winter 2003), p. 87.
48. Carey Goldberg, "Study Casts Doubt on Wisdom of Mandatory Terms for Drugs," *New York Times* (November 25, 1997), p. 11.
49. Raymond Hernandez, "Governor Commutes Sentences of 3 Convicted on Drug Charges: Clemencies Are Seen as Protest to Sentencing Laws," *New York Times* (December 25, 1997), p. B1; Michael Cooper, "New York State Votes to Reduce Drug Sentences," *New York Times* (December 8, 2004).
50. Mariel Garza, "Strikeout Reform," *Reason* (April 2000), pp. 12–13; Joe Domanick, "They Changed Their Minds on Three Strikes: Can They Change the Voters?" *Los Angeles Times* (September 19, 2004).
51. Michael Tonry, *Sentencing Reform Impacts* (Washington, DC: National Institute of Justice, 1987).
52. Ditton and Wilson, *Truth in Sentencing in State Prisons;* John Wooldredge, "Research Notes: A State-Level Analysis of Sentencing Policies and Inmate Crowding in State Prisons," *Crime and Delinquency* 42 (July 1996), pp. 456–66.
53. Dale Parent, Terence Dunworth, Douglas McDonald, and William Rhodes, *Mandatory Sentencing* (Washington, DC: National Institute of Justice, 1997).
54. *Riggs v. California*, 1999 U.S. LEXIS 743; John Cloud, "A Get-Tough Policy That Failed," *Time* (February 1, 1999), p. 48; see also *Ewing v. California*, 123 S. Ct. 1179 (2003).
55. Lisa Stolzenberg and Stewart J. D'Alessio, " 'Three Strikes and You're Out': The Impact of California's New Mandatory Sentencing Law on Serious Crime Rates," *Crime and Delinquency* 43 (October 1997), pp. 457–69; James Austin, John Clark, Patricia Hardyman, and D. Alan Henry, *Three Strikes and You're Out. The Implementation and Impact of Strike Laws* (Washington, DC: National Institute of Justice, 1999).
56. Tom R. Tyler and Robert J. Boeckmann, "Three Strikes and You're Out, but Why?: The Psychology of Public Support for Punishing Rule Breakers," *Law and Society Review* 31 (June 1997), pp. 237–65; David Shichor, "Three Strikes as a Public Policy: The Convergence of the New Penology and the McDonaldization of Punishment," *Crime and Delinquency* 43 (October 1997), pp. 470–93; Daniel D. Ntanda Nsereko, "Minimum Sentences and Their Effect on Judicial Discretion," *Crime, Law and Social Change* 31 (June 1999), p. 363.
57. Martin Finucane, "Justice Breyer Decries Minimum Sentences," *Associated Press* (September 22, 2003); "Justice Criticizes Sentencing Guidelines," *Washington Post* (August 10, 2003), p. A8.
58. Richard P. Conaboy, "The United States Sentencing Commission: A New Component in the Federal Criminal Justice System," *Federal Probation* 61 (March 1997), pp. 58–62; *National Survey of Sentencing Structures* (Washington, DC: Bureau of Justice Assistance, 1998).
59. Michael Tonry, *Reconsidering Indeterminate and Structured Sentencing* (Washington, DC: National Institute of Justice, 1999).
60. "Sentencing Reform Gone Awry," *New Jersey Law Journal*, vol. 172 (May 19, 2003), p. 26; Bruce Frankel and Dennis Cauchon, "Judicial Revolt over Sentencing Picks Up Steam," *USA Today* (May 3, 1993), p. 9; "Hands Tied," *The National Law Journal* 18 (January 15, 1996), p. 18.
61. Dorothy K. Hatsukami and Marian W. Fischman, "Crack Cocaine and Cocaine Hydrochloride: Are the Differences Myth or Reality?," *Journal of the American Medical Association* 276 (1996), p. 1580; Kelly McMurry, "Researchers Criticize Cocaine Sentencing Guidelines," *Trial* 33 (April 1997), p. 17; Jeffrey L. Fisher, "When Discretion Leads to Distortion: Recognizing Pre-Arrest Sentence-Manipulation Claims under the Federal Sentencing Guidelines," *Michigan Law Review* 94 (June 1996), pp. 2385–421.
62. Dale Parent, Terence Dunworth, Douglas McDonald, and William Rhodes, *The Impact of Sentencing Guidelines* (Washington, DC: National Institute of Justice, 1996).
63. Michael Tonry, *Sentencing Matters* (New York: Oxford University Press, 1996); David Weisburd, "Sentencing Disparity and the Guidelines: Taking a Closer Look," *Federal Sentencing Reporter* 5 (1992), pp. 149–52; T. D. Miethe and C. A. Moore, "Socioeconomic Disparities under Determinate Sentencing Systems: A Comparison of Preguideline and Postguideline Practices in Minnesota," *Criminology* 23 (1985), pp. 337–63.
64. Don M. Gottfredson, *Effects of Judges' Sentencing Decisions on Criminal Careers* (Washington, DC: National Institute of Justice, 1999); Jeffrey Y. Ulmer and John H. Kramer, "The Use and Transformation of Formal Decision-Making Criteria: Sentencing Guidelines, Organizational Contexts, and Case Processing Strategies," *Social Problems* 45 (May 1998), p. 248.
65. Parent et al., *The Impact of Sentencing Guidelines*, p. 5.
66. *United States v. Booker*, 125 S. Ct. 738 (2005); *Blakely v. Washington*, 124 S. Ct. 2531 (2004).
67. *U.S. v. Salerno*, 107 S. Ct. 2095 (1987).
68. *Tate v. Short*, 91 S. Ct. 668 (1971).
69. *Thompson v. Oklahoma*, 108 S. Ct. 2687 (1988).
70. See *French v. Owens*, 777 F. 2d 1250 (7th Cir. 1985).
71. *Coker v. Georgia*, 97 S. Ct. 2861 (1977).
72. *Furman v. Georgia*, 92 S. Ct. 2726 (1972).
73. *Gregg v. Georgia*, 96 S. Ct. 2909 (1976).
74. *Roberts v. Louisiana* and *Woodson v. North Carolina*, 96 S. Ct. 3207 (1976).
75. *Lockett v. Ohio*, 98 S. Ct. 2954 (1978).
76. *McCleskey v. Kemp*, 107 S. Ct. 1756 (1987).
77. Id. at 1765.
78. Id. at 1770.
79. Jordan M. Steker, "The Limits of Legal Language: Decisionmaking in Capital Cases," *Michigan Law Review* 94 (August 1996), pp. 2590–624.
80. *Weeks v. Angelone*, 120 S. Ct. 727 (2000); Benjamin P. Cooper, "Truth in Sentencing: The Prospective and Retroactive Application of *Simmons v. South Carolina*," *University of Chicago Law Review* 63 (fall 1996), pp. 1573–605; Ted Gest, "A House without a Blueprint: After 20 Years, the Death Penalty Is Still Being Meted Out Unevenly," *U.S. News & World Report* (July 8, 1996), pp. 41–45; Marvin D. Free Jr., "The Impact of Federal Sentencing Reforms on African Americans," *Journal of Black Studies* 28 (November 1997), pp. 268–86; Linda A.

Foley, Afesa M. Adams, and James L. Goodson Jr., "The Effect of Race on Decisions by Judges and Other Officers of the Court," *Journal of Applied Social Psychology* 26 (July 1996), pp. 1190–2113; Scott Burgins, "Jurors Ignore, Misunderstand Instructions," *ABA Journal* 81 (May 1995), pp. 30–32; Leigh B. Bienen, "The Proportionality Review of Capital Cases by State High Courts after *Gregg:* Only 'The Appearance of Justice,' " *Journal of Criminal Law and Criminology* 87 (fall 1996), pp. 230–314.

81. Thomas P. Bonczar and Tracy L. Snell, *Capital Punishment 2004* (Washington, DC: U.S. Bureau of Justice Statistics, 2005), p. 5.
82. Jeffrey M. Jones, "Support for the Death Penalty 30 Years After the Supreme Court Ruling," *Gallup News Service* (June 30, 2006). Available at www.gallup.com/poll.
83. Marian J. Borg, "The Southern Subculture of Punitiveness?: Regional Variation in Support for Capital Punishment," *Journal of Research in Crime and Delinquency* 34 (February 1997), pp. 25–46; David A. Kaplan, "Life and Death Decisions," *Newsweek* (June 16, 1997), pp. 28–30.
84. Bonczar and Snell, p. 16.
85. Ibid., p. 4.
86. *Bryan v. Moore,* 120 S. Ct. 1003 (2000).
87. David A. Kaplan, "Life and Death Decisions," pp. 28–31.
88. Thorsten Sellin, *The Penalty of Death* (Beverly Hills, CA: Sage, 1980), p. 72.
89. "Death Penalty Debates Continue," *America* 176 (May 10, 1997), p. 3; George E. Pataki, "Death Penalty Is a Deterrent," *USA Today Magazine* (March 1997), pp. 52–54.
90. William C. Bailey, "Capital Punishment and Lethal Assaults against Police," *Criminology* 19 (February 1992).
91. Craig J. Albert, "Challenging Deterrence: New Insights on Capital Punishment Derived from Panel Data," *University of Pittsburgh Law Review* 60 (winter 1999); Sellin, *The Penalty of Death;* Brian Forst, "The Deterrent Effect of Capital Punishment: A Cross-State Analysis of the 1960s," *Minnesota Law Review* 61 (1977); Richard Lempert, "The Effect of Executions on Homicides: A New Look in an Old Light," *Crime and Delinquency* 29 (January 1983); Hans Zeisel, "The Deterrent Effect of the Death Penalty: Facts v. Faith," in P. B. Kirkland, ed., *The Supreme Court Review, 1976* (Chicago: University of Chicago Press, 1977).
92. See Charles L. Black Jr., *Capital Punishment: The Inevitability of Caprice and Mistake,* 2nd ed. (New York: Norton, 1981); Hugo A. Bedau, ed., *Capital Punishment in the United States,* 3rd ed. (New York: Oxford University Press, 1982); Sellin, *The Penalty of Death;* Dane Archer, Rosemary Gartner, and Marc Beittel, "Homicide and the Death Penalty: A Cross-National Test of a Deterrence Hypothesis," *Journal of Criminal Law and Criminology* 74 (1983), pp. 991–1013.
93. Forst, "The Deterrent Effect of Capital Punishment"; Scott H. Decker and Carol W. Kohlfeld, "Capital Punishment and Executions in the Lone Star State: A Deterrence Study," *Criminal Justice Research Bulletin* 3 (1988).
94. Raymond Bonner and Ford Fessenden, "States with No Death Penalty Share Lower Homicide Rates," *New York Times* (September 22, 2000), p. 1.
95. James M. Galliher and John F. Galliher, "A 'Commonsense' Theory of Deterrence and the 'Ideology' of Science: The New York State Death Penalty Debate," *Journal of Criminal Law and Criminology* (fall 2001), p. 307; Michael L. Radelet and Ronald L. Akers, "Deterrence and the Death Penalty: The Views of the Experts," *Journal of Criminal Law and Criminology* 87 (fall 1996), pp. 1–16.
96. Craig, J. Albert, "Challenging Deterrence: New Insights on Capital Punishment Derived from Panel Data," *University of Pittsburgh Law Review,* vol. 60 (winter 1999), p. 321; Decker and Kohlfeld, "Capital Punishment and Executions in the Lone Star State"; Samuel Walker, *Sense and Nonsense about Crime,* 3rd ed. (Pacific Grove, CA: Wadsworth, 1993).
97. William J. Bowers and Glenn L. Pierce, "Deterrence or Brutalization: What Is the Effect of Executions?," *Crime and Delinquency* 26 (October 1980); Brian Forst, "Capital Punishment and Deterrence: Conflicting Evidence?," *Journal of Criminal Law and Criminology* 74 (fall 1983).
98. New York State Defender's Association, *Capital Losses: The Price of the Death Penalty for New York State* (Albany, NY: The Association, 1982).
99. James J. Stephan, *State Prison Expenditures* (Washington, DC: Bureau of Justice Statistics, 1999).
100. Bonczar and Snell, *Capital Punishment.*
101. Subcommittee on Federal Death Penalty Cases Committee on Defender Services, *Federal Death Penalty Cases: Recommendations Concerning the Cost and Quality of Defense Representation* (Washington, DC: Judicial Conference of the United States, 1998).
102. Eric M. Freedman, "The Case against the Death Penalty," *USA Today Magazine* (March 1997), pp. 48–50.
103. Bonczar and Snell, *Capital Punishment,* p. 10
104. Marcia Coyle, "Innocent Dead Men Walking?," *The National Law Journal* 18 (May 20, 1996), p. 1.
105. New York State Defender's Association, p. 50.
106. David Stout, "Conviction for Child Abuse Overturned 10 Years Later," *New York Times* (September 30, 1997), p. B3.
107. Joseph P. Shapiro, "Rethinking Executions," *U.S. News & World Report* (February 14, 2000), p. 30.
108. Hugo A. Bedau and Michael L. Radelet, *Conviction of the Innocent* (Boston: Northeastern University Press, 1992); David E. Rovella, "Danger of Executing the Innocent on the Rise," *The National Law Journal* 19 (August 4, 1997), p. 7.
109. Joseph P. Shapiro, "Rethinking Executions," p. 30; Warren Cohen, "Putting a Hold on Executions," *U.S. News & World Report* (May 31, 1999), p. 29; Richard Willing, "Illinois Prosecutors Accused of Framing an Innocent Man," *USA Today* (March 24, 1999), p. 9.
110. Marcia Coyle, "Innocent Dead Men Walking?" p. 1.
111. Lori Urs, "*Commonwealth v. Joseph O'Dell:* Truth and Justice or Confuse the Courts?: The DNA Controversy," *New England Journal on Criminal and Civil Confinement* 25 (winter 1999).

112. Barry Scheck, Peter Neufield, and Jim Dwyer, *Actual Innocence* (New York: Doubleday, 2000); Sharon Cohen, "Hard Work, DNA Advances Are Clearing Death Row Inmates," Associated Press (September 25, 1999).
113. Henry Weinstein, "Moratorium on Executions is Urged," *Los Angeles Times* (January 10, 2006); Steve Mills, "State to Free 18th Person on Death Row," *Chicago Tribune* (May 27, 2004); Abby Goodnough and Terry Aguayo, "DNA Test Comes to Prisoner's Defense," *New York Times* (August 3, 2005); Tresa Baldas, "Exoneration as a Cottage Industry," *National Law Journal* (October 4, 2004).
114. Bonczar and Snell, *Capital Punishment*, p. 9.
115. William Alex Pridemore, "An Empirical Examination of Commutations and Executions in Post-*Furman* Capital Cases," *Justice Quarterly*, vol. 17 (March 2000), pp. 159–83.
116. James S. Liebman, Jeffrey Fagan, and Valerie West, "A Broken System: Error Rates in Capital Cases, 1973–1995," *Columbia Law School* (June 12, 2000) available at URL www.law.columbia.edu/instructional services/liebman; Toni Locy, "Lawyers, Life, and Death: Inept Defense Taints Many Capital Cases," *U.S. News & World Report* (June 19, 2000), p. 26.

chapter 13

Origins and Organization of Jails and Prisons

Incarcerating offenders: confinement as punishment for offenders, who they are, and what goes on inside.

CHAPTER OUTLINE

LEARNING OBJECTIVES

- Trace the historical development of jails and prisons and the different levels of custody.
- Identify the types of correctional institutions at the state and federal levels.
- Describe some problems of jails and prisons and their operation.
- Analyze the concept, conditions, and effectiveness of imprisonment as punishment for crime.
- Characterize incarcerated inmates in terms of family background, race and ethnicity, age, and gender.
- Describe inmate life, prison programs, and risks to the health and safety of incarcerated offenders.
- Discuss issues of prisoners' rights and responsibilities and the roles of corrections officers.

The Virginia State Penitentiary was built in the shape of a horseshoe three stories high and housed men, women, and children. It opened in the year 1800. The cells had no heat, no light, and no plumbing. Solid oak doors made it impossible to see what was going on inside the cells. Sewage runoff ended in a ditch next to the James River, where a fierce odor lingered except when rain gave temporary relief. For the first thirty-eight years of the prison's existence, it was required by law that from 8 percent to 50 percent of a prisoner's sentence be served in solitary confinement. To meet this requirement, each prisoner was placed in a basement cell that was damp, unheated, and dark both day and night.[1]

In 1876 a Virginia State Penitentiary report listed an inmate's death as resulting from a fall into a tub of boiling coffee. The inmate was ten years old. An 1880 report listed 116 prisoners eleven to seventeen years of age.[2] The prison was refurbished several times during the twentieth century before being closed in 1990.

The purpose of prisons and their operating conditions have drawn concern from the very beginning. What is the purpose of prisons, who belongs there, and what should prison life consist of? These are fundamental questions that have been asked as long as prisons have existed. This chapter will take a closer look at U.S. jails and prisons and their inmates.

How Are Correctional Institutions in the United States Organized?

Although many aspects of American criminal justice originated in England, the use of prisons as a method of dealing with law violators is largely an American invention. During the Middle Ages confinement of criminals was considered wasteful, so corporal punishment of criminals was common. In Europe during the sixteenth century, workhouses were established in an effort to instill a work ethic into the poor, who were considered lazy.[3] Workhouse inmates made furniture and other items; and although workhouses were never used to house criminal offenders, they were a precursor of prisons.

BEFORE PRISONS

Interestingly, prisons were established in response to concern for the humanitarian treatment of criminals. Before the invention of the prison, corporal punishment in the form of whipping and mutilation was the primary method of punishing criminals. Fines evolved as an alternative to corporal punishment, but poor offenders (the majority of criminals) could not afford to pay them. In colonial America labor was scarce, so minor offenders often were sentenced to work for their victims for a specified period. Also, government structure and funding were weak, making long-term custody of offenders impractical. Jails were used for debtors and for those awaiting trial, as they were in Europe. Despite the obvious fact that jailed debtors were unable to earn money to repay their debts, it was not until the 1840s that imprisonment for debt was abolished in the United States.[4]

Incarceration became the primary form of sentence for poor offenders who could not afford to pay fines but whose offenses were not serious enough to deserve corporal punishment. Indeed, incarceration was seen as a humane alternative to corporal punishment. Physical punishment was associated with the Puritans, who believed that the doctrine of predestination made any attempt to rehabilitate offenders useless. The philosophers of the Enlightenment, however, advanced a more optimistic view. As stated in the Declaration of Independence, "We hold these truths to be self-evident, that all men are created equal, that they are endowed by their Creator with certain unalienable rights, that among these are life, liberty, and the pursuit of happiness." Rather than simply being part of human nature, crime and deviance came to be seen as a result of negative environmental influences. As a consequence, many humanitarian groups called for reform of the penal system.

The Invention of the Prison

The first of these humanitarian groups was the Philadelphia Society for Alleviating the Miseries of Public Prisons, formed in 1787 by Dr. Benjamin Rush. Rush urged that capital punishment and corporal punishment be replaced with incarceration. The Philadelphia Society, made up mostly of Quakers, believed that criminals could be reformed if they were placed in solitary confinement, where they could reflect on their deviant acts and repent. This is where the term *penitentiary* originated.

The Walnut Street Jail in Philadelphia (1790). What was the purpose of confinement during that period? How is it different from today?

WALNUT STREET JAIL

In 1790 the Pennsylvania legislature was persuaded to convert the Walnut Street Jail in Philadelphia into an institution for the solitary confinement of "hardened and atrocious offenders." Each cell was small and dark, with a small high window so that the offender "could perceive neither heaven nor earth." No communication with the offender was allowed. Later, additional institutions were built, beginning with the Eastern Penitentiary in 1829. This system of incarceration became known as the **Pennsylvania system.** According to its promoters, the Pennsylvania system promoted repentance through solitary confinement, was economical because it did not require long periods of confinement, and prevented offenders from being corrupted by mixing with other offenders. These principles soon fell prey to political and pragmatic considerations, however. The institutions quickly became overcrowded, and offenders were incarcerated for longer periods. As the French writers Gustave de Beaumont and Alexis de Tocqueville remarked in 1833, after visiting several U.S. penitentiaries:

Pennsylvania system
A philosophy of imprisonment that promoted repentance through solitary confinement and prevented offenders from being corrupted by mixing with other offenders.

> *Nowhere was this system of imprisonment crowned with the hoped-for success. In general it was ruinous to the public treasury; it never effected the reformation of prisoners. Every year the legislature of each state voted considerable funds toward the support of the penitentiaries, and the continued return of the same individuals into the prisons, proved the inefficiency of the system to which they were submitted.*[5]

In addition, most of these early prisons were "impersonal institutions marked by brutality and neglect," which defeated the underlying purpose of the confinement.[6] Beaumont and Tocqueville noted that in New York State twenty-six inmates in solitary confinement were pardoned by the governor, but that fourteen of them were returned to prison a short time later for new offenses.[7]

In 1819 a somewhat different system of incarceration was initiated in New York State. The **Auburn system** anticipated the Industrial Revolution with its emphasis on labor and meditation. Offenders worked in groups every day, but they did so in complete silence. The Auburn system spread throughout the country and was seen as a significant advance in the treatment of offenders.

Auburn system
A philosophy of imprisonment that emphasized labor and meditation. Offenders worked every day, but they did so in complete silence.

During the second half of the nineteenth century, there was disillusionment with both the Auburn and Pennsylvania systems. Neither system effectively reformed prisoners, and neither appeared to have a deterrent effect on crime. As Beaumont and Tocqueville had observed in 1833, the silence and isolation of prisoners resulted in depression and death among both inmates and guards.

How did the prison system develop in the United States? Where did the term *penitentiary* come from, and what does it mean? What are prisons really for anyway?

In 1877, believing that education was the key to rehabilitation, Zebulon Brockway developed a new approach to incarceration at the Elmira Reformatory in New York State. Brockway changed the purpose of incarceration from custody to education. The Elmira Reformatory attempted to promote a school-like atmosphere in which inmates could progress at their own pace. The New York State legislature demonstrated its support for the program when it passed an indeterminate sentencing law that allowed for offenders to be released on parole when they showed signs of progress in the reformatory programs. By 1900 the **reformatory movement** had spread to many states.[8]

reformatory movement
Late nineteenth-century trend toward use of incarceration to reform through education.

ELMIRA REFORMATORY

Disenchantment also arose with these education-based systems, however. Many prison administrators were reluctant to adopt the reform strategies and continued to emphasize discipline and control. Educational efforts often took a back seat to the more custodial demands of incarceration as punishment. Moreover, it was more difficult than expected to distinguish truly reformed prisoners from those who pretended to have changed. As a result, parole policies often were based on superficial indications of reform. Also working against prisoner rehabilitation were overcrowding and poor management of prisons.[9]

Today prisons lack a clear philosophical purpose. Most try to do a little of everything: punishment, work, and education. The results are equally mixed. The expectations of prisons and prisoners vary widely from one institution to another, leaving few people satisfied with the outcome. Meditation, labor, and education have not proved effective in stopping or deterring criminal behavior, causing some critics to argue that prisons should exist solely for purposes of punishment and should not make any effort to reform.[10] This view overlooks, however, the fact that the majority of inmates will someday return to society and that prisons can serve an important function in preparing inmates for release.

Levels of Custody

One of the newer prisons in the United States is the ultra–maximum security federal prison in Florence, Colorado. It holds more than four hundred prisoners and cost $60 million to build. Dangerous inmates are confined in their cells twenty-three hours a day. This prison has held some of the nation's most notorious criminals, including Ted Kaczynski (the Unabomber), Timothy McVeigh (the Oklahoma City bomber), and Ramzi Yousef (the World Trade Center attacker). When outside their cells, prisoners wear leg irons and handcuffs and are accompanied by guards.[11] The Florence prison has been called the "Alcatraz of the Rockies," after the prison on the island of Alcatraz in San Francisco Bay. Considered the toughest prison when it opened in the 1930s, Alcatraz was closed in 1963 because of the high cost of maintaining an island prison and a national shift toward rehabilitation as a model of punishment. The federal prison in Marion, Illinois, became the toughest prison in the mid-1980s, when it placed its violent inmates on permanent

THE FLORENCE PRISON

lockdown status after several assaults and deaths of staff and inmates.[12] The Colorado prison, designed exclusively for violent inmates, opened in 1994. Its inmates, all men, are serving sentences that average forty years; most will die in prison. The Florence prison also has its version of solitary confinement, a unit that holds 184 prisoners who never come into physical contact with another human being.[13]

"Ultrasecure" prisons are reserved for the most violent inmates, especially those who have committed assaults while in other prisons or have records of escape or extreme violence or murder. Other types of prisons are distinguished by level of custody. **Maximum security** prisons often have a wall (eighteen to twenty-five feet high) surrounding the entire facility and house dangerous felons who have committed violent crimes or who have a history of escape attempts. About one-fourth of all inmates are incarcerated in such institutions. **Medium security** prisons often have some facilities outside the main enclosure. Usually there are two rows of chain-link fence, topped with barbed wire, around the main enclosure. Medium security prisons hold felony offenders who have not committed violent crimes or whose prior record and institutional conduct do not require a maximum security setting. About half of all inmates are serving time in these institutions. **Minimum security** prison facilities usually have no fences but have locking outside doors and electronic surveillance devices around the perimeter of the institution. Inmates in these facilities are serving short sentences for nonviolent crimes or are near the end of longer sentences and at low risk for escape. About one-fourth of all inmates are in minimum security institutions.

maximum security
Prisons that house dangerous felons and that usually have a wall surrounding the entire facility (about 26 percent of all inmates are incarcerated in such institutions).

medium security
Prisons that have some facilities outside the main enclosure and are surrounded by two rows of chain-link fence, topped with barbed wire (half of all inmates are serving time in these institutions).

minimum security
Prison facilities that usually have no fences but have locking outside doors and electronic surveillance devices around the perimeter of the institution (about 23 percent of all inmates are in these institutions).

State and Federal Correctional Systems

State and federal prisons differ in number, size, and capacity. Table 13.1 summarizes some important differences between the numbers and populations of the state and federal systems. There are approximately 1,668 state, federal, and privately operated prisons in the United States, a number that is increasing as new prisons are being built.The number of adult prisons increased 14 percent from 1995 to 2000. State, federal, and private prisons now have a combined capacity

Table 13.1 State and Federal Prisons

Prison Characteristic	*State*	*Federal*	*Private*
Number of prisons	1,320	84	264
Rated capacity	1,033,408	109,498	98,901
Percent capacity occupied	115%	140%	100%
Maximum security prisons	317	11	4
Medium security prisons	428	29	65
Minimum security prisons	575	44	195

Sources: Paige M. Harrison and Allen J. Beck, *Prisoners in 2004* (Washington, DC: Bureau of Justice Statistics, 2005); James J. Stephan and Jennifer C. Karberg. *Census of State and Federal Correctional Facilities, 2000* (Washington, DC: Bureau of Justice Statistics, 2003).

of less than 1.3 million but hold nearly 1.5 million inmates, for an occupancy rate of approximately 100 to 140 percent.[14] These figures show that despite new prison construction, inmate populations still exceed prison capacity.

The federal correctional system is similar to the state systems, but it houses only federal offenders whose cases have been tried in federal courts. Private prisons are run by corporations, which are paid by states or the federal government to house offenders (see the *Critical Thinking* exercise, "Private Prisons and Liability at the end of the chapter). Maximum security federal institutions are called **penitentiaries;** medium security federal facilities are **correctional institutions;** and federal facilities for pretrial detention and for those serving short sentences are called **metropolitan correctional centers** or **detention centers.** The federal corrections system also includes prison camps and community treatment centers.

penitentiaries
Maximum security federal correctional institutions.

correctional institutions
Medium security federal correctional institutions.

metropolitan correctional centers (detention centers)
Federal jail facilities for pretrial detention and for those serving short sentences.

VIOLENT OFFENDERS

An offender's assignment to a particular level of custody depends largely on whether the conviction was for a violent crime. For example, 62 percent of inmates in maximum security prisons were sentenced for a violent crime, compared to 45 percent of those in medium security and 34 percent of those in minimum security institutions. Conversely, there are more property and drug offenders in medium security prisons (47 percent of inmates) and minimum security prisons (60 percent of inmates) than in maximum security prisons (33 percent of inmates). Approximately 80 percent of all state prison inmates have a prior conviction and a record of probation or incarceration, but those with both a prior record and current conviction for a violent crime are most likely to be assigned to maximum security prisons.[15] The number of criminals incarcerated two or more times has been increasing steadily—rising, for example, from 18 percent of prison admissions in 1980 to 35 percent in 2000. This trend suggests that prisons are ineffective and may be losing their deterrent force.[16] As criminal justice researcher Al Blumstein has concluded, "we have now locked up so many people that we have lost the stigmatizing effect" of imprisonments.[17]

Problems with Jails

A black Mississippi teenager was discovered hanging by his shoelace in the Simpson County jail. This youth's death was one of forty-two apparent suicides in Mississippi jails in a period of only five years during the 1990s. The U.S. Civil Rights Commission requested a federal investigation into this situation, raising questions not only about why there were so many suicides, but also about whether some inmates had been murdered and then hanged so their deaths would look like suicide.[18] In 2000 there were 198 jail and prison inmate suicides in the United States.[19]

Although prisons attract more attention from the media and policymakers than jails do, the deplorable conditions in many jails have been highlighted in cases like these. **Jails** are operated by counties and municipalities. They hold two main categories of inmates: those awaiting trial and those serving sentences of one year or less. Jails also perform other functions, such as holding probation and parole violators and bail absconders. They also may hold mentally ill persons on a temporary basis. Jails often serve as transfer points between prisons and may also hold offenders who cannot be admitted to state or federal prisons because of over-

jails
Facilities operated by counties and municipalities to hold two main categories of inmates: those awaiting trial and those serving sentences of one year or less.

crowding. Such a mixed bag of suspects, defendants, and offenders makes for a crowded and sometimes confusing jail environment.

The number of jail inmates more than doubled since the 1990s. The total number of jails remained about the same at 3,300, but jail space nearly doubled through new construction and renovation. Five states account for about half the total jail population of more than 600,000 inmates. Six states incarcerate more than half of all local jail inmates: California, Texas, Florida, New York, Georgia, and Louisiana. The two jurisdictions with the most inmates, Los Angeles and New York City, together hold nearly 40,000 inmates, or 7 percent of the national total.[20] Figure 13.1 illustrates the proportion of inmates held in jails versus those held in state and federal prisons. It is shown that since 1995 the total number of inmates increased by more than 30 percent.

Table 13.2 describes some career opportunities in corrections and related fields—areas in which demand for new candidates will grow in the first part of the twenty-first century.

JAIL POPULATIONS

FIGURE 13.1 Prison and Jail Inmates, 1995–2004

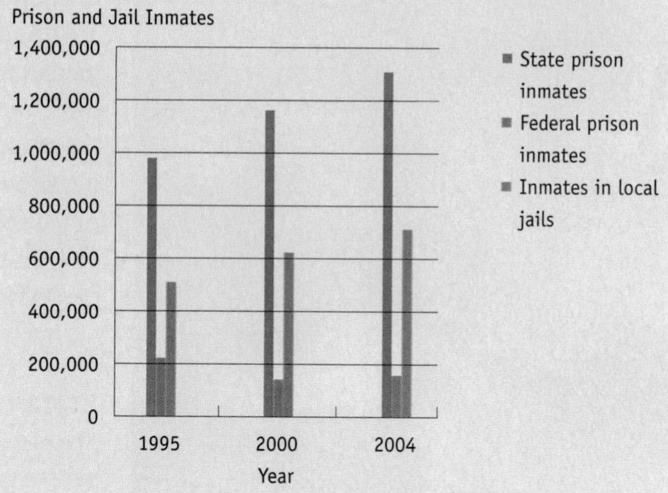

Source: Paige M. Harrison and Allen J. Beck, *Prisoners in 2004* (Washington, DC: Bureau of Justice Statistics, 2005).

Table 13.2 Career Opportunities in Corrections and Related Fields

Probation officer http://www.communitycourts.org/ http://www.nyspoa.com/us.htm	Works for the courts of a particular county or city; conducts investigations to assist the judge in sentencing; supervises and monitors juvenile and adult offenders in the community. *Qualifications:* Bachelor's degree and relevant work experience.
Parole officer http://www.appa-net.org/ http://ajjdp.ncjrs.org/	State employee, often with police powers, responsible for supervising offenders after they are released from prison. *Qualifications:* Bachelor's degree and relevant experience.
Corrections officer http://www.wco.com/~aerick/links.htm http://database.corrections.com/career/index.asp http://www.corrections.com/cjca/ http://www.sun.soci.niu.edu/!critcrim/prisons/prisons.html http://www.nicic.org/inst/nicocjtp.htm	State employee, sometimes with police powers; enforces laws in jails and prisons and transports prisoners. *Qualifications:* Competitive civil service examination; bachelor's degree preferred.
Counselor http://ssw.che.umn.edu/ctr4rjm/ http://www.darien.lib.ct.us/reentry/	Provides counseling and supervision in treatment programs for juvenile, adult, and family offenders, often in a detention center, shelter, reception or diagnostic center, training facility, treatment center, halfway house, or group home; helps offenders reintegrate into their communities and overcome problems that led to their arrest or incarceration. *Qualifications:* Master's degree in criminal justice, social work, or psychology preferred.
Criminologist http://www.jmu.edu/psyc/spcp/ http://www.ncjrs.org	Studies crime, criminals, and criminal behavior; conducts, analyzes, reports, and applies research on crime and social policies relating to crime; teaches courses in college; provides investigative or forensic or prison support services (e.g., research and evaluation). *Qualifications:* Master's degree or Ph.D. in, e.g., criminal justice, sociology, or psychology.

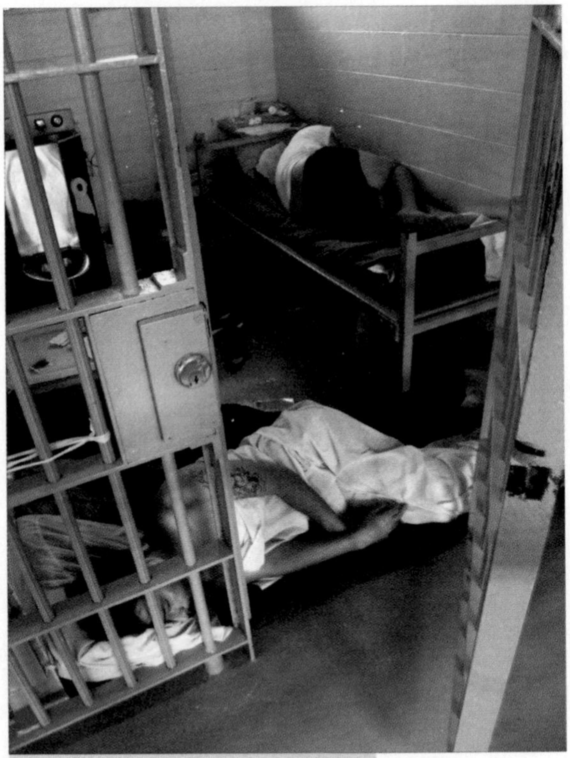

What problem of prisons today does this photograph suggest? What are some other problems of prisons? What prison reforms would you give top priority, and why?

A study of jail inmates revealed that most were not new to the criminal justice system. More than half were on probation, on parole, or out on bail at the time of their arrest. More than 70 percent had a criminal history that included a prior probation or incarceration sentence, and more than 40 percent had served three or more prior sentences. In addition, about 18 percent of jail inmates were regular drug users, and 50 percent of these had never been in a substance abuse treatment program.[21] Twenty-nine percent of inmates were unemployed at the time of their arrest. Thus, jail inmates have drug and employment problems that contribute to their criminal histories.

How Do Correctional Institutions Operate?

Correctional institutions have a difficult task. They must hold criminal offenders securely, in order to protect the public; at the same time, these institutions are supposed to promote behavior and attitude changes in inmates so that they become productive citizens upon release. Offenders' backgrounds often include long histories of criminal offending, drug and alcohol use, failure in school, and physical abuse. The difficulty of overcoming these problems has led to a debate over what correctional institutions should try to accomplish. This debate has centered on the degree to which punishment or reform should be at the center of correctional philosophy and operations.

Punishment

It is generally agreed that the purpose of imprisonment is to serve as punishment for a crime. There is less agreement as to what should occur *inside* prisons. The prevailing legal view is that deprivation of liberty through imprisonment *is* the punishment and that prison should not inflict additional punishment on offenders. For example, a prisoner in the Southern Ohio Correctional Facility sued the state, arguing that double-celling (housing two inmates in a single cell) violates the Eighth Amendment prohibition against cruel and unusual punishment. Studies recommended approximately six by nine feet of space for each inmate in a cell, but the Southern Ohio double-celling cut that space by 40 percent. Lower courts ruled in favor of the inmates, but the U.S. Supreme Court reversed the decision in *Rhodes v. Chapman,* holding that double-celling is not in itself cruel and unusual punishment. The Court stated that "such conditions are restrictive and even harsh, [but] they are part of the penalty that criminal offenders pay for offenses against society."[22] Therefore, "restrictive and even harsh" conditions in prison are permissible, although the Court indicated that deprivation of essential food, medical care, or sanitation is not permissible.

"RESTRICTIVE AND HARSH"

CONDITIONS OF CONFINEMENT

Numerous other challenges have been made to the conditions of confinement. Each case involved interpretation of the Eighth Amendment prohibition against cruel and unusual punishment. Under what conditions does punishment become cruel and unusual? In a landmark case, *Estelle v. Gamble*, the Supreme Court held that "deliberate indifference to serious medical needs of prisoners" violates the Eighth Amendment, because it permits "unnecessary and wanton infliction of pain" and offends "evolving standards of decency."[23] These phrases have become benchmarks in determining whether specific prison conditions, though harsh, exceed the limits imposed by the Constitution.

In the case *Wilson v. Seiter*, an inmate at the Hocking Correctional Facility in Ohio filed suit, claiming that the conditions of his confinement violated the Eighth Amendment. Those conditions included excessive noise, overcrowding, inadequate heating and cooling, improper ventilation, unclean restrooms, unsanitary food preparation, and housing of healthy inmates among people who were mentally and physically ill. As in previous cases, the U.S. Supreme Court agreed that prison officials had shown "deliberate indifference," but the Court also held that inmates must show that prison officials had "intent" or a "culpable state of mind" in allowing these conditions to exist.[24] Simply demonstrating the existence of deplorable conditions, therefore, is not enough. It must be demonstrated that prison officials know about the conditions but fail to act. This burden of proof makes it difficult for claims regarding conditions of confinement to stand up in court. In a 2003 case, *Overton v. Buzzetta*, the U.S. Supreme Court held that regulations limiting visitors to prisoners did not violate the Eighth Amendment because "the regulations bear a rational relation to legitimate penological interests," relating to internal prison security. Restrictions on visits by minor children, child visits, visits by former prisoners, and elimination of most visits to inmates who commit two substance abuse violations were therefore upheld because they had a "valid, rational connection" to a legitimate governmental interest in operating the prison securely.[25]

Custody and Deterrence

Many people agree that prisons should not only punish offenders but also control crime. Some believe that incarceration controls crime merely through custody—by keeping the offender off the streets for a specified period. Others hope that prison will have a deterrent or reformative effect on the offender. The unpleasant experience of imprisonment might deter new criminal activity upon release, or offenders might come to see the error of their ways during imprisonment and make a genuine effort to reform. Statistical evidence shows, however, that the experience of imprisonment does not deter **recidivism**—reoffending—upon release. The majority of inmates in state prisons have been incarcerated before, and more than 90 percent have been under some form of correctional supervision, counting probation, before their current incarceration. Criminal justice researcher Don Gottfredson concluded that incarceration policies are ineffective, do not contribute to public safety, and add to the burden shouldered by taxpayers.[26]

recidivism
Repeat offenses by an offender.

Rehabilitation and Reform

The average felony prison sentence is about five years; thus, the majority of offenders ultimately will be released. Efforts to rehabilitate or reform inmates while they serve their sentences could reduce recidivism and make prison more effective as a

In some modern jails and prisons inmates are granted more privileges and freedom inside the prison based on their perceived level of dangerousness and cooperation. Is this a good idea, or should all inmates be treated alike?

penal sanction. To succeed, rehabilitation and reform efforts do not necessarily require formal programs but do require an attitude change on the part of the offender. For example, some argue that family visitation and conjugal visits for inmates effectively reduce emotional stress on inmates and their families, resulting in more positive attitudes and behavior. Others believe that visits increase frustration and pose safety problems.[27] Studies of treatment programs for sex offenders, addicts, and victims of childhood sexual abuse reveal that rehabilitation programs can be effective in changing behavior.[28]

Models of Prison Administration

control model
Prison management approach characterized by strict enforcement of prison rules and few privileges for prisoners.

responsibility model
Prison management approach that gives inmates more autonomy; staff guides prisoners' decision making rather than making all decisions for them.

consensual model
Prison management approach that maintains order by agreement between inmates and staff on the validity of rules.

Prison administrators attempt to manage inmates in a way that will create the fewest problems for staff and other inmates during their term. Three major prison managerial approaches identified by John DiIulio are the control model, the responsibility model, and the consensus model.[29] The **control model** is characterized by strict enforcement of prison rules and few privileges for prisoners. This approach produces large numbers of rule violations and can increase the level of tension within a prison. Studies have suggested that formal management for control is not the most effective way to prevent prison disorder.[30] The **responsibility model** gives inmates more autonomy; staff guide prisoners' decision making rather than making all decisions for them. This approach employs minimal restraint except in cases requiring restraint for protection of staff or other inmates. The idea of the **consensual model** is to maintain order by getting inmates and staff to agree on the validity of rules, placing inmates in a position of participating in the operation of the prison—although DiIulio believes that this model is not effective, because inmates' self-interest leads them to attempt to manipulate the system. Debate continues over the optimum model of prison administration in terms of impacts on inmate conduct.[31] Nevertheless, each model could be applied in a prison environment, depending on the security level of the institution, the types of offenders involved, and the willingness of staff to support the management model employed.

NATIONAL SURVEY OF PRISON WARDENS

A national survey of prison wardens and state corrections administrators identified three significant problems these officials face: prison overcrowding, gang-affiliated inmates, and understaffed treatment programs. The majority of survey respondents reported that their prisons were at or over capacity, making it difficult for them to maintain inmate and staff security and appropriate conditions of confinement. As with jail administrators, more than 70 percent of prison officials indicated that improvement is needed in the identification of gang-affiliated inmates and in training programs designed to help staff control gang activities. Three-fourths of the wardens indicated a need for more staff to provide treatment for alcohol and substance abuse, mental health, parenting, and vocational education.[32] These problems suggest that even motivated inmates may find it difficult to obtain access to education or treatment to address their problems.

The bipartisan, independent Commission on Safety and Abuse in America's Prisons reported in 2006 on the conditions of confinement and oversight and accountability in prisons. The Commission found that the capabilities and tools currently exist to prevent violence in prison, to provide decent health care to inmates, to limit segregation, to change the subculture of the corrections profession, and to strengthen the accountability and oversight of prison management. The problem lies in the commitment to reform the system and in the investment of resources needed to spur change.[33]

Who Is in Prison?

RELEASE RATES

Many people believe that the sentences offenders currently receive are more lenient than ever before, but nothing could be further from the truth. In fact, the number of offenders in state or federal prisons increased by one-third from 1995 to 2005, and the incarceration rate per 100,000 population increased more than 18 percent over this period. There are now nearly 2.2 million inmates in state and federal institutions and local jails, more than at any other time in the nation's history.[34] The reason for this increase is simple: More people are being sent to prison than are being released. The rate of release also has dropped, reflecting a general increase in the length of time served. This trend is merely an extension of the overall trend since 1925. Despite some fluctuations during the Great Depression (up), World War II (down), and the early 1960s (up), the rate of incarceration has been increasing steadily.

There is growing diversity by age, race, and ethnicity of prison inmates. Should an offender's age influence the type of prison to which an offender is sent?

Correlates of Incarceration

The backgrounds of inmates reveal many factors found to be correlated with crime, especially educational level, family background, age and race, and drug use. Most people who commit felonies and are sentenced to state prisons are not highly educated.

Two-thirds of state prison inmates did not graduate from high school. Of those in jail awaiting trial or serving short sentences, nearly 50 percent did not graduate from high school.[35]

INMATE FAMILY BACKGROUND

The family backgrounds of adult inmates also are revealing. A large proportion of inmates (43 percent) were raised in a single-parent household, and 17 percent lived in a foster home or other institution at some time. Thirty percent of inmates report that their parents abused either alcohol or drugs, and 50 percent of inmates were under the influence of alcohol or drugs at the time of their current offense. A striking 57 percent of female inmates and 16 percent of males report that they were physically or sexually abused in the past.[36] Thirty-nine percent of prisoners have an immediate family member who has been incarcerated, and 94 percent have been convicted for a violent crime *and/or* have a prior record of probation or incarceration.[37] The high incidence of troubled backgrounds far exceeds national averages.

The prospects for children of incarcerated parents is a growing concern, given that 56 percent of state and federal prisoners have a child under the age of eighteen. Forty-three percent of incarcerated women and a third of incarcerated men have two or more children under age eighteen. Nearly half (46 percent) of the parents report that they were living with their children prior to incarceration. As a result, there are 336,300 U.S. households with minor children directly impacted by the imprisonment of a parent who lived there. A growing body of research suggests that fathers play a crucial role in child rearing that has been downplayed in the past. In addition, 6 percent of women inmates are pregnant when they enter prison, and one-third of inmates sentenced for violent crimes victimized a relative, intimate, or person whom they knew well.[38] Victims often include children, who also are likely to become juvenile delinquents due to the absence of adequate parental supervision.

DISPROPORTIONATE MINORITY CONFINEMENT

Two-thirds of inmates in state prison are under age thirty-five, although the prison population is aging. The proportion of inmates between the ages of thirty-five and forty-four rose from 23 to 30 percent. This aging reflects longer average prison sentences, truth-in-sentencing provisions, and a decrease in parole release. Approximately 34 percent of inmates are white, 45 percent are black, and 18 percent are Hispanic. Stated in another way, about 10 percent of black males in their late twenties are in prison, compared to 2.4 percent of Hispanic males and about 1.2 percent of white males. Racial disparity has resulted in criticism of the rate at which minorities are confined.[39] Disproportionate minority confinement occurs when a racial group is incarcerated at rates far above its proportion in the population, a pattern that raises questions of institutional discrimination by the criminal justice system.

Drug offenders are a significant proportion of the prison population. Approximately 250,000 inmates are in prison for drug offenses, and they constitute 21 percent of the total prison population. Seventy percent of all jail inmates had committed a drug offense or were using drugs or alcohol at the time of the offense.[40] These statistics suggest a strong association between drug use and drug-related offenses.

The combination of family violence, substance abuse, lack of education, long criminal history, and incarcerated parents tends to perpetuate the cycle that places

That's a FACT

Perspectives on Prisoner Trends

The number of offenders sentenced to prison has risen dramatically over the years, but so has the U.S. general population. Figure 13A compares the prison population group to the U.S. resident population to establish a *rate* of imprisonment. The graph shows that the prison population is rising at a faster rate than the general population.

FIGURE 13A State, Federal, and Local Prisoners in the United States

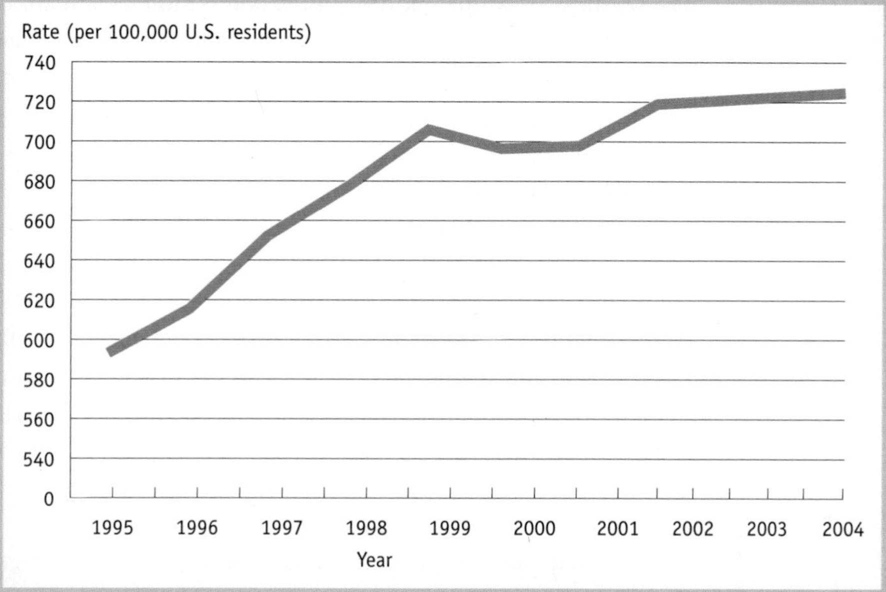

Source: Paige N. Harrison and Allen J. Beck, *Prisoners in 2004* (Washington, DC: Bureau of Justice Statistics, 2005).

A recidivism study examined the rearrest, reconviction, and reincarceration of former inmates for three years after their release from prison. A total of 272,111 were studied from 15 states, representing two-thirds of all those released from prison in a single year. Within three years of their release more than two-thirds of offenders were rearrested (usually for a felony), 50 percent were convicted, and 25 percent were reincarcerated. In addition, 52 percent of the former inmates were back in prison for technical violations of their parole (e.g., failing a drug test). Figure 13B illustrates the results of this study.

Provide reasons why the prison population has increased faster than the U.S. general population for a period of years now. Provide reasons for the recidivism rate of about 67 percent for offenders released from prison. The highest recidivism rates for released prisoners were for property crimes (e.g., robbery, burglary, theft, stolen property)—a rearrest rate of 70 to 80 percent within three years of being released. On the other hand, those incarcerated for violent crimes (e.g., homicide, rape, assault) had the lowest recidivism rates (40 to 50 percent). How would you explain this difference?

FIGURE 13B Offenders Returned to Prison within Three Years, by Type of Crime Committed

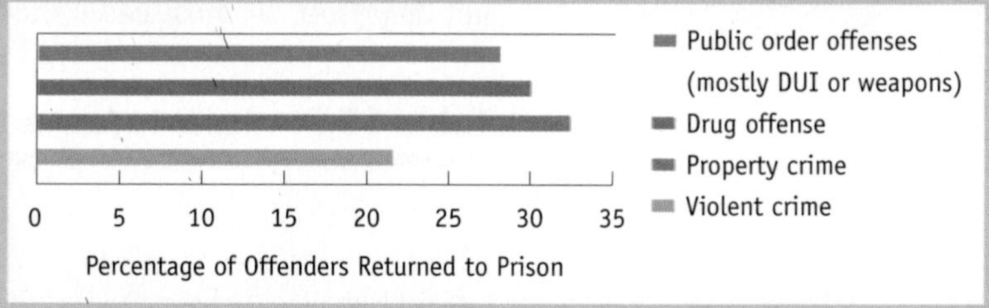

Source: Patrick A. Langan and David A. Levin, *Recidivism of Prisoners Released in 1994* (Washington, DC: U.S. Bureau of Justice Statistics, 2002).

persons at risk of engaging in crime and becoming incarcerated. Even if effective measures could be implemented to improve education, provide substance abuse treatment, and restore family integrity, an entire generation of parents are now in prison and are unlikely to provide effective supervision for their children—who themselves are destined to become at risk for offending.

Incarceration of Women

The number of women incarcerated in state or federal prisons or local jails in the United States has increased significantly. The rate of incarceration in prison increased from 47 per 100,000 women in 1995 to 64 per 100,000 in 2005. Men still outnumber women in the inmate population by a factor of about 14 to 1, but the gap is narrowing—from 17 to 1 a decade ago. Women constituted only 4 percent of the total prison and jail population in the United States in 1980 but 7 percent in 2005. The proportion of women in the local jail population has increased to nearly 13 percent of total inmates, as shown in Table 13.3. This trend is due to increasing criminal activity by women, resulting in more arrests of women and an increase in the number of female defendants convicted of felonies; females' rate of conviction has grown at twice the rate of that of male defendants.[41]

The growing number of women inmates poses society with some unique challenges: dealing with the victims of women's crimes, their family histories, and child care issues. Women serving a sentence for a violent crime are twice as likely as men to have committed the crime against an intimate or relative. Half of all victims of male offenders were strangers, whereas only 35 percent of victims of females were strangers. These differences call for different approaches to treatment and custody of female inmates.[42]

INMATE MOTHERS

Like male inmates, female inmates often grew up in single-parent homes (42 percent) or lived in a foster home or institution (17 percent). Women, however, are more likely to have a family member who has been incarcerated (47 percent versus 37 percent for men) and to have a parent or guardian who abused alcohol or drugs (34 percent versus 26 percent for men). Most significantly, 57 percent of women inmates were physically or sexually abused in the past (compared to 16 percent of men). For 37 percent of the women inmates this abuse took place before age eighteen, often committed by a family member.

Approximately three-quarters of women in prison have at least one child, and two-thirds of female prisoners' children are under eighteen. These figures translate into nearly 200,000 children under age eighteen with mothers in prison or jail.[43] In addition, 6 percent of convicted women are pregnant upon admission to jail or prison. In most cases the child is taken from the mother at birth and is

Table 13.3 Trends in Female Incarceration

	1995	*2000*	*2005*
Females in jail (percent of total)	10.2%	11.4%	12.7%
Females in state and federal prison (rate per 100,000)	47	59	64

Source: Paige M. Harrison and Allen J. Beck, *Prison and Jail Inmates at Midyear 2005* (Washington, DC: Bureau of Justice Statistics, 2006).

placed in custody of relatives or state welfare agencies until the mother is released from prison. Efforts to help maintain family contact and supervision of children of inmates might include pre- and postnatal training and care for the mothers. Travel to prison could be arranged for inmates' children, and more prisons could allow very young children to stay with their mothers for a specified period to encourage greater emotional bonding and parental responsibility.[44]

What patterns and trends can be seen in the incarceration of minorities and women in the United States during the past decade? What factors might account for those patterns and trends? For what types of crimes are women incarcerated most often?

Prison Overcrowding

As you have read, the explosion in the prison population has led to overcrowding and new construction. Most state correctional facilities are operating at or over capacity. Thousands of prisoners are being held in local jails because of lack of available prison space. Several hundred state correctional facilities are under court order to reduce overcrowding or correct conditions that violate the law, usually conditions involving health or safety. New construction has increased total prison capacity by 40 percent since 1990, but the number of inmates has increased faster.

POLITICS OF PRISON OVERCROWDING

Prison overcrowding is a difficult political issue, because the public demands protection from criminals yet generally is reluctant to approve government spending. Nevertheless, public spending on prisons increased dramatically during the 1990s. The nationwide average annual cost to house each state prison inmate is $20,100, which includes facility construction and renovation, repair, wages of corrections employees, food service, medical care, transportation, and programs. Total state prison expenditures were $12 billion in 1990, and have doubled since then. Critics allege that this money is not well spent; too many nonviolent offenders are sent to prison, and prisons are a "revolving door" for violent criminals who often recidivate.[45] Overcrowding must be addressed, as it leads to prison unrest, creating a dangerous situation for both corrections officers and inmates.

PAROLE VIOLATORS

As noted earlier, offenders nationwide are serving longer average sentences, and parole eligibility is limited under truth-in-sentencing laws to offenders who have served at least 85 percent of their sentences. Assistance to new parolees in obtaining employment, training, housing, and other necessities is often minimal or absent. This has led to calls for a new focus on better managing the reentry of offenders into society so that prisons do not become warehouses that continuously recycle the same offenders.[46] An example of such an effort is Washington State's "Corrections Clearinghouse," which is a multiagency effort that provides job readiness courses, job search assistance, substance abuse treatment, and related services for ex-offenders in an effort to reduce recidivism.[47]

What Is Inmate Life Like?

Although opinions differ as to whether inmates should be treated harshly or humanely, no one argues that inmates should be idle or bored. Nevertheless, idleness and boredom are perhaps the conditions most typical of inmates in jails and prisons today. Inmates spend most of the day and night in their cells; depending on security level, they may leave the cell to eat (although most jail inmates eat in their cells) and to exercise. Most inmates are allowed to exercise outside their cells for several hours per day, usually walking, lifting weights, or playing basketball. Most prisoners are assigned a job to do each day, but in most cases the job is menial and lasts for only a few hours. Typical jobs include sweeping and polishing floors, washing dishes, and preparing food. Prisons usually have small libraries, but many prisoners cannot read. Prisoners seeking education or drug or alcohol treatment usually do not have access to programs or must wait for long periods before being admitted. Often the progress inmates make in these programs is quickly undone. For example, education in conflict resolution skills is undermined when the inmate returns to a general inmate population in which threats and violence are common or in which inmate or staff support for educational efforts is lacking. Major issues of inmate life can be grouped into five categories: prison work, drugs and treatment, AIDS, prison gangs, and violence.

Prison Work

In a speech more than two decades ago, Supreme Court Chief Justice Warren Burger asked corrections agencies to establish "factories with fences" to provide inmates with the job skills they would need upon release.[48] This proposal was similar to the Auburn system described earlier in this chapter, in which prisoners worked in a workshop during the day and slept alone at night. The primary difference is that the Auburn system forbade any conversation among inmates for the duration of their sentence.[49]

INMATE WORK

Nearly all observers have viewed inmate work favorably. Work can help inmates learn discipline, accountability, and job skills, and can sometimes enable them to earn money to pay compensation to victims. Nevertheless, starting in the 1930s and 1940s, prison-made products were banned from the open market in response to protests by businesses and labor unions, which feared unfair competition from low-wage inmate labor. In 1979 legislation was passed to restore the relationship between outside businesses and prison labor. Since then, a large number of successful inmate work programs have been created. In Kansas, for example, female inmates from the Topeka Correctional Facility perform housing renovation work in low-income homes. Operation Outward Reach is a nonprofit organization that contracts with five Pennsylvania prisons to provide vocational training in carpentry and masonry. Inmates also perform low-cost construction work for senior citizens and the poor. The Wisconsin Department of Corrections is engaged in the Recycled Mobile Home Project, which rehabilitates homes for the rural homeless and low-income families.[50] There are many other examples of prison and jail work programs that reduce the cost of operating correctional facilities and produce useful products or services.[51]

POLITICS OF PRISON LABOR

Nearly 70 percent of all inmates perform work in prison, but most tasks performed by inmates involve maintenance of the correctional facility itself. These tasks produce savings for the state, because it does not have to contract with outside firms for services. Only about two-thirds of inmates are paid for their work; the

Media & Criminal Justice

The Shawshank Redemption

Dozens of films have plots in which a truly innocent person is wrongfully accused of a crime, but the 1994 Oscar winner for best picture is different from the rest. *The Shawshank Redemption,* unlike other movies about wrongfully convicted inmates in prison, is not really about the circumstances that land the innocent Andy Dufresne in prison for murdering his wife. The story suggests that some details of the crime don't add up, but it accepts the sentence for what it is; its focus is not on the questionable conviction but on the heart-wrenching realities of prison life in the 1940s.

The story is narrated by Red, a longtime prison inmate who has worked his way up to chief proprietor of the prison's smuggled contraband. As the inmates watch new prisoners unload from the bus, Red bets that the fragile-looking banker Andy will be the first to cry. When Andy proves himself to be far more determined and stronger than anyone imagined, he and Red become trusted friends, but not before Red smirks at his story: "You're going to fit right in . . . you know that everybody in here's innocent."

Andy is a character study in survival. He refuses to kiss butt or back down, and he uses his formidable intelligence and confidence instead of violence. He gains the respect of all when he uses his accounting knowledge to barter with the recently audited warden in order to procure some cold beers for his fellow inmates during a roofing job.

The movie has no deep plot beyond the incredibly slow passage of time, as experienced by the inmates. Red measures time in terms of decades, for at the end of ten years (soon twenty, then thirty) he goes before the parole board, where he is asked if he has been rehabilitated. Each time he answers with a heartfelt "Oh, yes, surely!" But when he is never released, hope slowly fades away.

This process of succumbing to prison life as normal, even desirable for its stability and predictability, is referred to as *institutionalization*. Unlike the corrupt warden, disgusting conditions, or cruel predators of the prison, it is institutionalization that is the real enemy. As Red notes at one point, "These walls are funny. First you hate them. Then you get used to them. After time passes, you get so's you depend on them."

One of the most important facets of the movie involves Brooks, the elderly prison librarian who has been incarcerated for so long he has no real memory of life before prison. The highlight of his life as an inmate is domesticating an injured bird, which he keeps hidden in his pocket, feeding it the maggots found in his mashed potatoes. When he is finally paroled after more than fifty years in prison, Brooks finds himself at a loss as to how to deal with the loneliness of a rented room or cope with his non-intellectual job as a grocery bagger at a local store. He even ponders a way to get back into prison, saying "Maybe I should rob the Food Way so they'll send me home. I could shoot the manager while I'm at it, kind of like a bonus." Institutionalized to the extreme, Brooks eventually commits suicide, unable to handle life as a free man.

The Shawshank Redemption is indeed about redemption, as explored in the everyday existence of the lifers at Shawshank Penitentiary. Ironically, the oppressive gothic fortress that serves as the movie's setting was actually Ohio's Mansfield Reformatory, which was later closed down as unsuitable for today's prisoners. As an allegory about the personal worth of prisoners, the movie points out that life—even in prison—is what you make it. Whether prison's purpose is retribution, incapacitation, or reform, Andy sums up the prisoner's life in one simple philosophy: "Get busy living, or get busy dying."

Assuming that the depiction of prison life in *Shawshank* is accurate for the 1940s, discuss how prison life is the same or different today. Do you think that reform is possible in a prison setting that doesn't offer rehabilitative services? What can be done to combat the threat of institutionalization among inmates? And do you believe that the institutionalized mentality is a root cause of recidivism?

average wage is 56 cents per hour. Work involving farming, roadwork, or manufacturing accounts for only a small percentage of inmate work assignments. There are many more inmates than there are meaningful work opportunities.

There is resistance to putting inmates to work in prison. Why? Should inmates receive work skills in prison to help them obtain jobs when released?

Some businesspeople continue to fear that cheap prison labor will drive down prices and force them out of business. A Connecticut manufacturer of draperies complained that his sales to the government dropped by 50 percent because of competition from Federal Prison Industries.[52] Federal Prison Industries may bid on any government contract it can fulfill, and it can fulfill contracts more cheaply than most private companies because inmate labor is cheaper. As a result, labor unions, too, strongly oppose inmate labor. In recent years some prisons have used inmates to do data entry work or telemarketing work, usually for government agencies. Concerns that inmates might gain access to sensitive personal information via the telephone or the Internet prompted a study by the U.S. General Accountability Office, the investigative arm of Congress. The GAO found that 1,100 inmates nationwide had access to names, dates of birth, or social security numbers through the work they performed in prison. About 5,500 inmates had access to names and addresses or telephone numbers only. Information was safeguarded by means of close supervision of inmates, selective hiring, and security checks at exits from work areas. Nevertheless, there were nine documented incidents, summarized in Table 13.4, in which inmates misused this personal information. In five of the incidents the work programs were discontinued, even though poor supervision of the inmates was a primary factor. Work programs are viewed as privileges; even single incidents of inmate misconduct can cause entire programs to be terminated.

PRISON CONTRABAND

Most states permit inmate industries to supply only government agencies, so they do not compete against other businesses in the open market. Prison industry produces office furniture, clothing, textiles, bedding, electronic equipment, gloves, and optics.[53] Federal inmates employed in joint ventures with private firms have paid nearly $2 million in victim compensation, $2 million in family support payments, more than $3 million in taxes, and $5 million toward payment of the cost of their incarceration.[54] Nevertheless, an appropriate balance among the goals of preparing inmates for release, offsetting the costs of incarceration through inmate labor, and competing fairly with the private sector has yet to be achieved.

Drug Use and Treatment Programs

There is considerable evidence that drug use is rampant in prisons and jails. An inmate at the Marcy Correctional Facility in New York State, for example, relied on visitors to supply him with drugs. Some visitors smuggled drugs into prison in the heels of sneakers. Female friends passed small balloons filled with heroin from their mouths to his when they kissed in the visiting room. He then swallowed the balloons or hid them on his body. And sometimes corrupt prison employees would provide drugs. Since 1990, twenty-six corrections officers have been charged with smuggling drugs into Rikers Island jail in New York City. A convicted murderer was found dead of a cocaine overdose in his cell at Great Meadow Correctional Facility

Table 13.4 Incidents of Misuse of Personal Information by Inmates

State	*Incident Description*	*How Safeguards Failed*	*Program Continued After Incident?*
California	An inmate on parole used credit card numbers previously obtained in a prison telemarketing program (1991).	Unknown.	Yes, but discontinued in 1998
New Mexico	Inmate wrote a letter to a Medicare patient identified from information obtained in a data entry work program (1995).	Inmate was not searched when leaving work area.	No
New York	An inmate wrote a letter to a person whose name and address were provided by an inmate in a work program (1995).	Inmate left the premises with the information.	Yes
Oklahoma	An inmate wrote a letter to a person based on information obtained from a data entry program dealing with medical expenses (1990).	Inmate memorized the address.	Yes
Oklahoma	Two inmates attempted to smuggle copies of birth certificates obtained through a work program via U.S. mail (1995).	Papers removed despite secured work area.	Yes
South Carolina	Inmate continued to call a person identified through a work program that telemarketed local newspaper subscriptions (1995).	Inmate was not monitored while making calls.	No
South Dakota	An inmate used a credit card number obtained from a program that made motel reservations (1991).	Unknown.	No
Texas	Inmate wrote a letter to an individual identified through a data entry work program, including personal information (1992).	Unknown.	No
Washington	An inmate sent a Christmas card to a person identified through a 1-800 information line on state parks that inmates staffed (1997).	Lack of supervision.	No

Source: U.S. Comptroller General, *Prison Work Programs: Inmates' Access to Personal Information* (Washington, DC: U.S. General Accountability Office, 1999) and *Prisoner Releases* (Washington, DC: U.S.: General Accountability Office, 2001).

in New York, a hypodermic needle in his hand. Reports from Mississippi, the District of Columbia, Georgia, and other jurisdictions have found significant drug use in prisons, although such use is clearly prohibited.[55]

DRUG USE IN PRISON

Most state departments of corrections deny that drugs are readily available in prison but admit that drugs are present. A review by the U.S. Justice Department's Office of the Inspector General (OIG) examined inmate drug tests, inmate overdoses, drug discoveries inside federal institutions, and other information sources, and concluded that illegal drugs are present in almost all institutions operated by the Federal Bureau of Prisons.[56] As one corrections official explains, "Unless you searched everyone going in and out, kept all packages out and locked all inmates in their cells for twenty-four hours a day, you're going to have contraband."[57]

The effort to prevent drug use in prison has been called a cat-and-mouse game. Corrections officers resort to strip searches and unannounced cell searches, while prisoners become more inventive at smuggling drugs and use sophisticated techniques such as obtaining liquified LSD painted on the back of postage stamps. To combat the problem most state and federal prisons now use random urine testing of inmates. Those found using drugs have privileges taken away or are placed in solitary confinement. Because of overcrowding, however, most inmates are tested less than once a year, so little deterrent effect is achieved. Yet prison officials point to their drug testing findings to show that fewer than 10 percent of all inmates test positive for drugs. However, because of its limited scope, this testing probably misses a great deal of drug usage.

High demand for drugs among prisoners has always existed. In fact, there are anecdotes of prisoners' making a form of wine from fruit juice and other substances long before drugs became widely popular. The increase in very long sentences adds to inmates' feelings of hopelessness and fear of forced sex and unprovoked fights in a population of desperate, angry, and frustrated prisoners. These feelings increase the tendency to seek a kind of temporary escape or relief from the prison environment through drug use.

A large number of inmates also exhibit high levels of anger, fear, and frustration *before* their crime and incarceration, which may account for the high rates of drug use among offenders. A majority of inmates report regular use of drugs in the month before their crime, and a majority committed their offense while under the influence of drugs or alcohol. In fact, about 20 percent of state prison inmates committed their offense in order to obtain money to buy drugs.[58]

EFFECTIVE DRUG TREATMENT

Effective drug treatment would reduce the demand for drugs among both inmates and released prisoners and would have a long-term impact on prison drug smuggling and rates of reoffending. But few efforts to accomplish this goal have been effective. A review of a small number of successful prison-based drug treatment programs found that they shared several features. Each program had a special source of funds dedicated exclusively to drug treatment, which prevented the continual starting and discontinuing of programs that is typical in prison settings. All the successful programs were "guests" of the correctional institution and were not operated by the institution itself. Therefore, providers could focus on the program and not be concerned with custodial issues. In Delaware, a self-contained treatment environment was established inside a men's maximum security prison for drug-involved offenders. This **therapeutic community model** was based on the notion that a person's attitudes, values, and self-esteem must change together with the targeted drug use behavior if lasting change is to occur. The self-contained therapeutic community separated the inmates in the program from the drugs and violence that existed elsewhere in the prison. An evaluation of this program found that inmates who completed it were nearly 50 percent more likely to remain drug-free and arrest-free after six months than a comparison group of nonparticipating offenders.[59] Other characteristics of successful programs included using a variety of treatment strategies, employing trained social workers and counselors rather than correctional officers, providing training in life skills, and contacting participants after the program ended.

therapeutic community model Prison drug treatment approach based on the notion that a person's attitudes, values, and self-esteem must change together with the targeted drug use behavior in order to create lasting change.

AIDS in Prison

Approximately 2 percent (about 24,000) of inmates in state and federal prisons are known to be infected with HIV, the virus that causes AIDS. Of those HIV-positive inmates, about 25 percent have confirmed AIDS. The rate of confirmed AIDS among prison inmates is four times higher than in the general U.S. population.[60] And these figures understate the severity of the problem, because testing policies vary in different jurisdictions. The Federal Bureau of Prisons and twenty states test all inmates for HIV upon admission or release. In most jurisdictions, however, inmates are tested only if they exhibit HIV-related symptoms or request a test. Requests are uncommon, because inmates who test positive for HIV often face discrimination. In Georgia, for example, a thirty-four-year-old inmate was placed in isolation in a city jail. He wanted to mop floors so that his six-month sentence for drunk driving would be reduced one day for each day of work, but he was denied this opportunity because he had HIV. As a result he was required to serve two extra months in jail. In Mississippi and Alabama, inmates with HIV are separated from all other prisoners and are denied equal access to prison jobs, early release, education, the chapel, and the library. As one inmate stated, "the stress, the depression, the boredom, the hopelessness—it's overwhelming."[61]

One result of inmates receiving longer prison sentences is many older inmates are more prone to illness. What should be done with elderly or seriously ill inmates who require expensive medical attention?

Several hundred prisoners die of AIDS-related diseases each year, which together with suicide accounts for most unnatural prison deaths. Many inmates and staff are afraid of contracting HIV through fights, sexual contact, or other involuntary exposure to blood or body fluids. The segregation of inmates with HIV reduces these fears. Nevertheless, prison administrators continue to fear that the disease will spread throughout a captive population, especially because the widespread sharing of hypodermic needles and other unsanitary practices promote the spread of HIV.[62] Table 13.5 illustrates that cases of confirmed AIDS are more than three times more common in prisons than among the general U.S. population.

AIDS DEATHS

Inmates have a right to medical treatment for AIDS-related illnesses. Treatment is expensive, however, and lawsuits have been filed by inmates claiming inadequate treatment of their medical conditions. The extent of treatment that prisons must provide in these cases remains unclear. Special custodial restrictions on inmates with HIV do sometimes interfere with medical treatment, but courts have generally upheld these restrictions when they are based on legitimate health, safety, and security considerations.

Prison Gangs

As mentioned earlier, surveys of jail and prison administrators have found that identifying gang members and training staff in how to handle gangs are pressing concerns. This issue of gangs in prisons first arose during the late 1980s, when cocaine and crack use became widespread and gangs formed to engage in narcotics trafficking. Twenty percent of all male inmates are believed to be gang members. More than half of adult state correctional facilities report that racial conflicts are a problem and that these conflicts are aggravated by gang affiliations. Institutions with a high level of racial disturbances have been found to have a high rate of gang-related disturbances as well.[63]

Table 13.5 Prisoners with AIDS

	Percent of population with confirmed AIDS	
Year	*U.S. general population*	*State and Federal prisoners*
1998	0.11%	0.53%
1999	0.12	0.60
2000	0.13	0.53
2001	0.14	0.52
2002	0.14	0.48
2003	0.15	0.51

Source: Laura M. Maruschak, *HIV in Prisons 2003* (Washington, DC: Bureau of Justice Statistics, 2005).

DEALING WITH PRISON GANGS

Prison officials have identified a large number of gangs. In California, for example, for example, five gangs are said to be dominant in prisons there: the Mexican Mafia, Nuestra Familia (Latin American), Black Guerrilla Family, Aryan Brotherhood, and Nazi Low Riders.[64] In Florida, seven gangs were identified, adding two additional gangs to this list: Neta (Puerto Rican group) and the Texas Syndicate.[65] Gang membership and influence vary around the country. Hundreds of gangs exist, but only a small number dominate in prisons. Nevertheless, this influence can be pervasive and can affect inmate life, prison violence, and recidivism of offenders.

Current methods for dealing with prison gangs include formal staff training, but this training is not very extensive. A majority of jails and prisons have rules that prohibit gang recruitment; but, as noted earlier, it is difficult to identify gang members upon admission to prison. Many state prisons do not take gang membership into account as part of their inmate classification system, although some states have enacted policies that segregate known gang members in high-security "supermax" prisons. These high-security prisons are generally reserved for those who have committed a serious assault while confined. Placement in a supermax facility based on the status of gang affiliation rather than because of violent behavior has been criticized on grounds of unfairness.[66]

Most wardens do not believe that solitary confinement or segregation effectively controls gang members, except possibly in a central federal facility. Both anger management training and mediation between gangs and racial groups in prison have been recommended as ways to change gang attitudes and behavior.[67] Currently wardens rely on transfers of gang members within the state prison system in an attempt to control the proliferation of gangs behind bars. Most troubling is the fact that 80 percent of prison administrators report that "gang members generally have a stronger affiliation with their gang after serving time."[68] The reason for the strengthening of gang ties in prison, in addition to the shared experience and mutual help, is that inmates have more opportunities to meet gang leaders and advance in the gang hierarchy in prison than on the street, where there is more competition. It appears that so long as drug trafficking is controlled by gangs, imprisoning gang members disrupts but does not end gang activity.

Violence in Prison

The number of violent incidents in prisons has increased in recent years. The Atlanta Federal Penitentiary, for example, had five inmate murders in sixteen months during the mid-1990s. The number of assaults on federal corrections officers also has increased throughout the prison system. Officials place some blame on mandatory sentences, which leave inmates with the feeling they have nothing to lose by being violent because their sentences are so long to begin with. Another factor is overcrowding: Prisons are susceptible to uprisings because inmates outnumber staff by three to one. In addition, many prisons are old, and inmates often move throughout the prison during the day, so locking an entire cellblock of inmates away from staff is not always feasible when trouble arises.

A survey of sexual violence in prison found 885 substantiated incidents (a rate of 0.4 per 1,000 inmates) during 2005. As Table 13.6 indicates, the vast majority of these incidents occurred in state prisons and local jails. Half of the incidents involving inmate-on-inmate sexual violence involved physical force or threat, while two-thirds of staff misconduct had romantic motives. Prison staff were arrested or prosecuted in 45 percent of the substantiated incidents of staff sexual misconduct, and they were discharged, fired, or resigned in 82 percent of the incidents.[69]

Table 13.6 Sexual Violence in Prisons

	Number of Substantiated Incidents of Sexual Violence	
Facility Type	*National Estimate*	*Rate per 1,000 Inmates*
Total	885	0.40
Prisons		
Public—Federal	41	0.26
Public—State	458	0.39
Private	24	0.24
Local jails		
Public	336	0.45
Private	13	0.78
Other adult facilities		
Indian country jails*	10	^
Military-operated	2	0.77
ICE-operated	1	0.15

*Excludes facilities housing juveniles only.

^Too few cases to provide a reliable rate.

Source: Allen J. Beck and Paige M. Harrison, *Sexual Violence Reported by Correctional Authorities* (Washington, DC: Bureau of Justice Statistics, 2006).

At Kirkland Correctional Institution in South Carolina, inmates seized control of the unit holding the most violent inmates. They climbed the fence around it and used construction tools left on the grounds to release seven hundred inmates. A riot squad responded and was able to end the disturbance in six hours. The Atlanta Federal Penitentiary had an uprising that lasted eleven days and involved more than a hundred hostages. That disturbance, which began when the government announced that 2,500 Cubans being held there would be sent back to Cuba, was resolved through extensive negotiations. A study sponsored by the National Institute of Justice analyzed eight prison riots and made recommendations for prison riot plans and prevention strategies. The most important elements in plans for responding to an actual riot situation include clearly defined lines of authority in the command structure, clear guidelines on the use of force, interagency cooperation, and adequate staff training. Long-term prevention strategies include supervision by experienced staff, sound security practices, good intelligence, appropriate tactics (i.e., negotiation versus force), and follow-up on staff morale after a riot has occurred.[70] Other studies have found that the personal characteristics of inmates and situational factors within prisons combine to form an organizational climate that can be conducive to prison violence.[71]

PRISON RIOTS

The frequency of prison riots is disturbing. There were riots during the 1990s in three federal prisons over the crack cocaine law that imposed mandatory ten-year, no-parole sentences for possession of only 50 grams of crack. Prison uprisings in Alabama, Illinois, Pennsylvania, and Tennessee left twelve corrections officers injured and millions of dollars in damage.[72] In a riot at Pelican Bay State Prison in California in 2000, corrections officers shot sixteen prisoners, and another thirty-two prisoners were stabbed or slashed by fellow inmates. This event followed nine inmate deaths stemming from earlier fights with fellow inmates.[73] The need for greater preparedness and appropriate responses to prison riots is apparent. The U.S. Supreme Court has held that shooting a prisoner without warning in an effort to suppress a prison riot is not cruel and unusual punishment.[74] Riot situations that are handled badly, such as the 1971 Attica uprising that resulted in the deaths of ten corrections officers and twenty-nine convicts, usually involve immediate forceful intervention. A twenty-five-year-old lawsuit against New York State brought on behalf of 1,281 inmates involved in the Attica uprising was finally settled in 2000 for $8 million.[75] Most prison disturbances today are

ATTICA

Prison gangs are a growing problem both in managing prison security and in recruiting other inmates to join. What might you do to avoid gang-related violence inside prison?

handled with more patience, because the inmates remain locked inside and there is no need for a quick resolution. Negotiations defuse anger over a period of hours and days, with the result that inmates and staff are less likely to engage in further violence. Also, violent responses to inmate uprisings lead to recriminations and lawsuits that last for many years after the incident, making it difficult to implement new prison procedures.[76]

What Are Prisoners' Rights and Responsibilities?

An inmate in a Texas prison was a Buddhist, but he was not permitted to use the prison chapel or to correspond with his Buddhist religious advisor. When he shared Buddhist religious material with other inmates, he was placed in solitary confinement on a diet of bread and water for two weeks for violating prison rules. The inmate alleged that his First Amendment right to freedom of religion had been violated.

The scope of prisoners' legal rights has been carved out by the courts in a large number of cases. Most of these cases involve alleged violations of the Eighth Amendment prohibition against cruel and unusual punishment. In this section we will consider important rights and responsibilities of prisoners under the First and Fourth Amendments. In every case the issues are the same: What rights does a prisoner surrender as a condition of confinement, and what rights do all individuals have regardless of whether or not they are incarcerated?

Constitutional Rights

In the case of the Buddhist inmate, the Texas Department of Corrections argued that inmates with unconventional religious beliefs should not be guaranteed the right to practice their religion in prison. The U.S. Supreme Court disagreed, noting that although Buddhism may be unconventional in the United States, it was established in 600 B.C., long before Christianity. The Court held that Texas had violated the inmate's First Amendment protection of free exercise of religion.[77] The prison system provided chaplains for the Jewish and Christian faiths, as well as Bibles. By refusing to allow the inmate to practice Buddhism, the Texas Department of Corrections discriminated unfairly against the inmate and violated his First Amendment guarantee of freedom of religion.

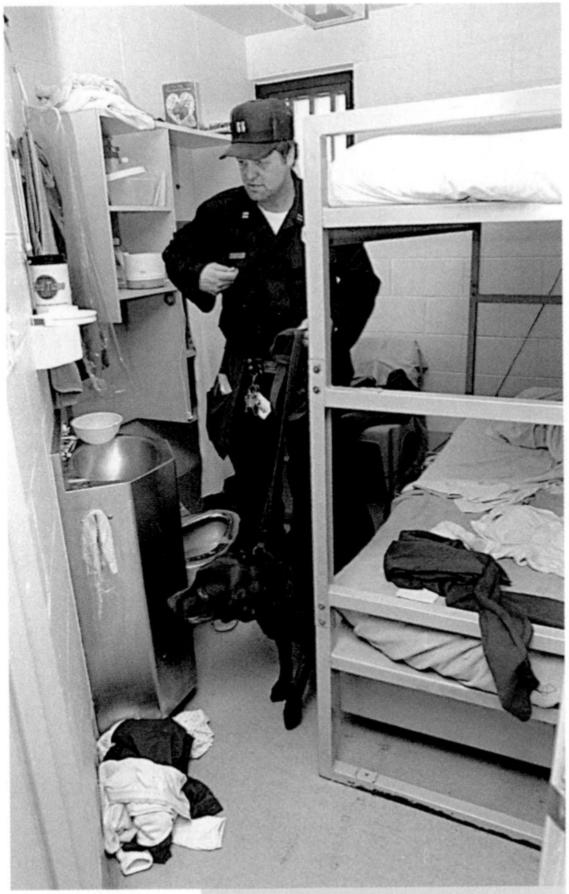

Prisoners forfeit many legal rights upon incarceration. Are there any legal protections inmates should retain while inside prison?

ISLAMIC INMATES

In a subsequent case, however, the Court made it clear that there are limits on the freedom to practice religion in prison. Islamic inmates in a New Jersey prison were not permitted to attend a religious service on Friday afternoons. The prison did not permit inmates to attend services or meetings in buildings outside their housing unit unless they had "minimum" security status. Also, inmates who worked outside the prison were not allowed to return to prison buildings during the day for security reasons. The U.S. Supreme Court ruled against the inmates, stating that because there was a "rational connection to the legitimate governmental interest in institutional order and security," the decision by prison officials was reasonable and did not violate the First Amendment.[78] These cases are typical of court holdings in this area, recognizing the inmate's right to express religious belief within the limits imposed by a prison setting.[79]

The Fourth Amendment protects individuals from intrusions by the government in the absence of probable cause linking them to a crime. The extent to which inmates continue to enjoy the right to privacy was not clear or uniform until the 1980s. A landmark case began at Bland Correctional Center in Virginia, where two corrections officers conducted a warrantless search of an inmate's cell. The officers discovered a ripped pillow case in the trash basket and charged the inmate with destroying state property. The inmate filed suit, contending that the search of his cell violated the Fourth Amendment and had no purpose other than harassment.

HUDSON V. PALMER

The Supreme Court held in *Hudson v. Palmer* that "society is not prepared to recognize any subjective expectation of privacy that a prisoner might have in his prison cell . . . and the Fourth Amendment . . . does not apply within the confines of the prison cell." If inmates had such constitutional protection in their cells, it would contradict "the concept of incarceration and the needs and objectives of penal institutions" in maintaining custody and security.[80] This ruling makes clear that inmates have no reasonable expectation of privacy in their cells. Therefore, no warrant or probable cause is required for searches.

These cases illustrate how the Supreme Court has weighed constitutional rights against the demands of running a prison in two important legal areas. It can be seen that the Court is sensitive to the requirements for operating a secure prison, while also attempting to address the appropriate scope of individual protections in the prison environment.

Prison Rules

A national survey of state prisons found that 53 percent of inmates had been charged with violating prison rules at least once. Examples of prison rules include regulations on maintaining a neat cell and rules governing dress, noise, foul language, littering, and responding appropriately to commands, among many others. The rate of rule violations in prison does not appear to change significantly over time, translating into an average of 1.5 rule violations per year per inmate, according to a national survey.[81]

This rate of violations has led some to question the appropriateness of some prison rules for their supposed function of maintaining order and security. Prison administrators point to the fact that inmates outnumber corrections staff three to one and that numerous assaults on corrections officers have occurred.[82] Rules prohibiting extortion and assault also are needed to protect inmates from one another. Inmates complain, however, that some prison rules are petty or not widely known and are misused to harass inmates. Rules prohibiting horseplay and certain sanitary regulations are examples.

DUE PROCESS IN PRISON

The Supreme Court has held that inmates are entitled to due process (i.e., a hearing) and that some evidence of rule violation must be presented in cases in which penalties, such as solitary confinement, are possible.[83] However, inmates do not have the right to counsel or to cross-examination of witnesses against them in prison disciplinary hearings.[84] More than 90 percent of inmates charged with prison rule violations are found guilty.

Disciplinary procedures vary from one state to another. Penalties range from a notation of the violation in the inmate's file to a disciplinary hearing. The warden usually serves as the final avenue of appeal. If a serious rule violation is also a crime, the offense may be referred for prosecution. More than 30 percent of prison rule violators are placed in solitary confinement or otherwise separated from other prisoners. A second common penalty is loss of "good time," or credit toward early release for good behavior; this is followed by loss of recreational privileges or confinement to the cell for some period of time.

Most rule violations are committed by inmates who have been in prison one to two years. Inmates who have served five years or more generally have the lowest incidence of violations. Younger inmates with a long criminal history and a history of drug use are most likely to violate prison rules. Rule violations are likely to increase, therefore, as increasing numbers of young drug offenders are sentenced to long prison terms in overcrowded prisons with little possibility for early release.

CORRECTIONS OFFICERS

Corrections officers are charged with enforcing prison rules and managing prison facilities. They have a difficult task in that a small force of officers must run a prison that sometimes holds thousands of prisoners. The job is often stressful, and low job satisfaction and poor communication and support have been found to be major factors in high turnover among corrections officers.[85] In addition, corrections officers receive negative media attention when things go wrong but are ignored when things are done well.[86] In an effort to change this negative environment, the Missouri Department of Corrections developed a new prison

PARALLEL UNIVERSE

management strategy called "Parallel Universe," based on the notion that life inside the prison should resemble life outside the prison to the extent possible. Like most states, Missouri found that 97 percent of its prisoners will return to the street one day, and wanted to involve both prisoners and staff in preparing offenders for their ultimate release.

Traditionally, most prisons are managed by controlling inmates and not allowing them to make any meaningful decisions. The "Parallel Universe" strategy creates expectations for inmates that are monitored and supported by staff. For example, offenders who earn a GED receive a pay increase at work, the GED is also a prerequisite for enrolling in certain job training programs and for getting certain prison jobs. Similarly, offenders must participate in victim impact or offender–victim mediation to better understand the impact of their behavior on others. Citizenship is taught as a requirement in an effort to develop racial, religious, and ethnic tolerance among offenders. Treatment is mandatory for certain types of offenders and compliance is monitored closely.[87] The objective of the "Parallel Universe" strategy is to operate the prison more like a community than a total institution, thereby improving the prison environment, reducing the likelihood of offender recidivism, and reducing job stress and dissatisfaction among corrections staff.

These correctional officers are working in a "parallel universe." What is meant by this model of prison management? How is this model different from older, more traditional, models for enforcing prison rules and managing prison facilities? In what ways is the parallel universe model supposed to reduce inmate violence and corrections officers' job stress?

CRITICAL THINKING EXERCISES

Private Prisons and Liability

The failure of correctional institutions to deter offenders from committing further crimes has plagued the system throughout its history. During the 1980s this failure, combined with efforts to reduce the size of government, led to proposals that entire prisons be operated by private contractors. Today, more than 100,000 adult prisoners are held in private correctional facilities. Most are medium or minimum security facilities, and the majority are located in three states—Texas, Florida, and California, which also are the three states with the largest inmate populations.

Corrections Corporation of America is the largest private contractor in this field, followed by Wackenhut. These corporations bid on contracts to build or remodel prisons and to manage and operate them. Proponents of privatization contend that private contractors can operate prisons less expensively than the government while maintaining the same level of custody and quality of service. Opponents argue both that it is improper for private contractors to supervise offenders sentenced by the state and that costs cannot be reduced significantly over the long term.[a]

Despite this debate, many states are currently under court order to reduce overcrowding or to improve conditions inside prisons. States are building new prisons to handle the exploding prison population and seeking ways to pay for them without raising taxes. Private contractors offer construction and supervision costs that initially appear lower than those the state has borne in the past.

The investigative arm of Congress, the U.S. General Accountability Office (GAO), reviewed a series of studies that compared public and private correctional facilities in terms of cost of operation and quality of service. The studies' results were mixed: Some found that private facilities were cheaper and provided similar levels of service; one found private facilities more costly; others found no difference. The GAO concluded that the studies provided little guidance for jurisdictions seeking to reduce costs.[b] Privatization of prisons is likely to continue in the foreseeable future, however, because it relieves states of the immediate burden of financing prisons on their own, which can cost $75,000 per bed. The long-term outlook is less clear.[c]

Operating even a minimum security prison is difficult. A corporation that runs a prison must be able to establish an entirely self-sufficient community and maintain security for the staff, inmates, and surrounding community. A private prison in Youngstown, Ohio, has been accused of staffing the institution with inexperienced guards, ignoring complaints of abuses against prisoners, and maintaining an unsafe prison environment.[d] A private prison in New Mexico experienced four inmate deaths and the killing of a guard within nine months, leading to doubts that private companies can handle high-risk inmates.[e]

The U.S. Supreme Court has ruled that private prison guards are not immune from allegations of civil rights violations. In the case in question, an inmate alleged that corrections officers at South Central Correctional Center in Tennessee, operated privately by Corrections Corporation of America, violated his Eighth Amendment rights by placing restraints on him that were too tight and caused injury serious enough to require hospitalization. The Supreme Court held the privately employed corrections officers responsible, stating that "mere performance of a governmental function does not support immunity for a private person, especially one who performs a job without government supervision or direction."[f] It will be interesting to see how the growth of private prisons is affected by the liability issues the industry has just begun to face.

CRITICAL THINKING QUESTIONS

1. How does disagreement over the purposes of incarceration complicate the privatization of prisons?
2. Why might a private company be expected to run a prison less expensively than the government?
3. Are there certain types of offenders that might be more amenable to handling by a private prison?
4. What do you think are the potential advantages and disadvantages of prison privatization for states? For inmates? For criminal justice?

NOTES

a. Matt Bai, "On the Block," *Newsweek* (August 4, 1997), pp. 60–61; Norman Seabrook and Katherine Lapp, "Should Corporations Run the Jails?," *The Daily News* (August 23, 1995), p. 7.

b. U.S. Comptroller General, *Private and Public Prisons* (Washington, DC: U.S. General Accounting Office, 1996), p. 3; Travis C. Dina and Pratt Perone, "Comparing the Quality of Confinement and Cost-Effectiveness of Public versus Private Prison," *Prison Journal*, vol. 83 (September 2003), p. 301.

c. Robbin S. Ogle, "Prison Privatization: An Environmental Catch-22," *Justice Quarterly* 16 (September 1999), pp. 579–600; Alexander Tabarrok, ed. *Changing the Guard: Private Prisons and the Control of Crime*. (Oakland, CA: Independent Institute, 2003); Sharon Dolovich, "State Punishment and Private Prisons," *Duke Law Journal*, vol. 55 (December 2005), pp. 437–47.

d. Eric Bates, "CCA, the Sequel: The Largest Private Prison Firm Continues Its Pattern of Abuse and Profit," *The Nation* (June 7, 1999), p. 22; Anthony Lepore, "Prison Privatization Proposal Questioned," *Providence Business News* (June 21, 1999), p. 31.

e. Ted Gest, "Private Prisons Suffer a Blow," *U.S. News & World Report* (September 13, 1999), p. 10; Janice Francis-Smith, "After 10 Years, Jury Still Out on Department of Corrections' Contracting with Privately Run Prisons," *Journal Record Legislative Report* (Oklahoma City) (July 25, 2005).

f. Richardson *v.* *McKnight*, 117 S. Ct. 2100 (1997); *Correctional Services Corporation v. Malesko*, 122 S. Ct. 515 (2001).

The Elderly Inmate

Ollie Coleman had been in prison in Columbia, South Carolina, for nearly fifty-two years for killing his wife. At eighty-four years of age, he had heart problems and high blood pressure. A reporter for *USA Today* who interviewed Coleman was his first visitor in thirty years. There are more than 67,000 prisoners age fifty-five or older in the United States, a number that has increased sharply as a result of changes in sentencing and release policies.[a]

The percentage of their sentences served by inmates before release has increased steadily in recent years as states and the federal government have shifted to determinate sentencing systems, the abolition of parole release, and truth-in-sentencing laws.[b] If current trends continue, most inmates could be age fifty or older within the next twenty years because of longer prison sentences and fewer releases.

As the inmate population ages, there is concern about the higher health care costs that older people incur. Virginia announced an entire prison solely for older and disabled inmates who need help with walking, dressing, bathing, and everyday routines.[c] Some have suggested releasing elderly offenders early, but victims and their families oppose early release; moreover, long-term elderly inmates often have nowhere to go upon release. They have no family members who would be willing to take care of them, and they are too old to compete in the workforce. In essence, they have aged out of their crime-prone years, passed middle age, and entered their retirement years, yet are still in prison. Prisons are having difficulty finding private care facilities that will take these inmates when they are eligible for parole. The result is a large number of elderly inmates who have been in prison for much of their lives, whose sentences are ending, but who have no place to go.

CRITICAL THINKING QUESTIONS

1. A person is incarcerated for twenty or thirty years and paroled at age sixty-five. The inmate has no money and no one to take him or her in. If you were a corrections administrator, what would you do?
2. Who should pay for medical care for inmates who require heart surgery, expensive medication, or help with physical or mental disabilities during their prison terms?
3. What are some possible long-term solutions to these problems?

NOTES

a. Tom Watson, "Prisons' Graying Inmates Exact a Price," *USA Today* (March 17, 1995), p. 12; Dana DiFilippo, "Growing Old Behind Bars," *Philadelphia Daily News* (May 8, 2006).

b. Paula M. Ditton and Doris James Wilson, *Truth in Sentencing in State Prisons* (Washington, DC: Bureau of Justice Statistics, 1999).

c. "Capron: A State Prison," *USA Today* (June 29, 1999), p. 13; Seena Fazel, Tony Hope, Ian O'Donnell, Mary Pipes, and Robin Jacoby, "Health of Elderly Male Prisoners: Worse Than the General Population, Worse Than Younger Prisoners," *Age and Ageing*, vol. 30 (September 2001), p. 403; Adam Liptak, "To More Inmates, Life Term Means Dying Behind Bars," *New York Times* (October 5, 2005).

SUMMARY

HOW ARE CORRECTIONAL INSTITUTIONS IN THE UNITED STATES ORGANIZED?

- Before the invention of the prison, corporal punishment was the primary method of punishment of criminals.
- Incarceration was used for poor offenders who could not afford to pay fines but whose offenses were not serious enough to deserve corporal punishment.
- The Pennsylvania system of incarceration aimed to promote repentance through solitary confinement.
- The Auburn system emphasized labor and meditation.
- Various attempts to encourage education within prisons have been unsuccessful, and today prisons lack a clear philosophical purpose.
- Prisons are classified according to level of custody: maximum security, medium security, and minimum security.
- The assignment of an offender to an institution at a particular level of custody depends largely on whether the conviction was for a violent crime.
- Jails are operated by counties and municipalities. They hold inmates awaiting trial and those serving sentences of one year or less.

HOW DO CORRECTIONAL INSTITUTIONS OPERATE?

- Although many people believe that prisons should not only punish offenders but also deter crime, the evidence shows that imprisonment does not prevent offenders from committing further crimes upon release.
- Rehabilitation and reform are other objectives of imprisonment, but they often are superseded by concerns for custody and security.
- Three major managerial approaches in operating prisons are the control model, the responsibility model, and the consensus model.

WHO IS IN PRISON?

- The number of people in prisons has grown dramatically in recent decades, resulting in overcrowding.
- The proportion of prisoners who are women is growing rapidly.
- Prisoners tend to be poorly educated and to come from single-parent households where alcohol or drugs were used. Many were physically or sexually abused and have family members who have been incarcerated.

WHAT IS INMATE LIFE LIKE?

- Nearly all observers have viewed inmate work favorably, but business people and labor organizations fear competition from cheap prison labor.
- Drug use is prohibited in prisons, yet is widespread.
- Many offenders who use drugs in prison were convicted of drug law violations or used drugs before being convicted on some other charge.
- Drug treatment programs in prisons have had little success.
- The growing number of women in prison poses challenges related to the nature of the women's crimes, their family histories, and child care issues.
- All federal and some state inmates are tested for HIV. Those who test positive are often discriminated against.

- Twenty percent of all male inmates are believed to be gang members. However, it is difficult to identify gang members upon admission to prison.
- The number of violent incidents in prison has increased sharply in recent years.
- The National Institute of Justice has made several recommendations regarding prison riot plans and prevention strategies. They include clearly defined lines of authority in the command structure, clear guidelines on the use of force, interagency cooperation, and training programs.

WHAT ARE PRISONERS' RIGHTS AND RESPONSIBILITIES?

- The Supreme Court has heard cases involving prisoners' rights in the areas of free exercise of religion and the right to privacy.
- The Supreme Court has held that inmates are entitled to due process in cases of violation of prison rules.
- Most rule violations are committed by younger inmates who have been in prison one to two years, have a history of drug use, and have a long criminal history.

KEY TERMS

Pennsylvania system *359*
Auburn system *359*
reformatory movement *360*
maximum security *361*
medium security *361*
minimum security *361*
penitentiaries *362*
correctional institutions *362*
metropolitan correctional centers (detention centers) *362*
jails *362*
recidivism *365*
control model *366*
responsibility model *366*
consensual model *366*
therapeutic community model *376*

QUESTIONS FOR REVIEW AND DISCUSSION

1. What were the origins of the concept of incarceration?
2. What are the three main classifications of prisons?
3. What functions are performed by jails?
4. What is the debate between punishment or reform as the focus of correctional philosophy and operations?
5. What are the most typical characteristics of prison inmates?
6. What are the unique challenges associated with the growing numbers of women in prison?
7. What are the advantages and disadvantages of prison labor?
8. Why is drug use pervasive in prisons, and what factors interfere with efforts to prevent it?
9. What issues are raised by the presence of HIV and AIDS in prisons?
10. What are the implications of the presence of gang members in prisons?
11. What actions could be taken to prevent prison riots?
12. How has the Supreme Court ruled in major cases involving prisoners' rights?

NOTES

1. Paul W. Keve, "Old Story," *Richmond Times–Dispatch* (July 6, 1986), pp. F1–2.
2. Ibid.
3. Luke Owen Pike, *A History of Crime in England* (Montclair, NJ: Patterson Smith, 1968); Harry Elmer Barnes, *The Story of Punishment* (Montclair, NJ: Patterson Smith, 1972).
4. Herbert A. Johnson and Nancy Travis Wolfe, *History of Criminal Justice*, 3rd ed. (Cincinnati: Anderson, 2003), p. 137.
5. Gustave de Beaumont and Alexis de Tocqueville, *On the Penitentiary System in the United States and Its Application in France* (1833) (Carbondale, IL: Southern Illinois University Press, 1979), pp. 39–40.
6. Robert Johnson, *Hard Time: Understanding and Reforming the Prison*, 2nd ed. (Belmont, CA: Wadsworth, 1996), p. 29.
7. Ibid., p. 41.
8. Lawrence M. Friedman, *Crime and Punishment in American History* (New York: Basic Books, 1993), pp. 160–61.

9. David J. Rothman, *The Discovery of the Asylum* (Boston: Little, Brown, 1971).
10. Ernest van den Haag, *Punishing Criminals* (New York: Basic Books, 1975).
11. Howard Chua-Eoan, "The Bomber Next Door: What Are the Most Dangerous Men in America Talking About at the Supermax Prison in Colorado?," *Time* (March 22, 1999), p. 55.
12. Gregory L. Hershberger, "To the Max: Supermax Facilities Provide Prison Administrators with More Security Options," *Corrections Today* 60 (February 1998), pp. 54–58.
13. Dennis Cauchon, "The Alcatraz of the Rockies," *USA Today* (November 16, 1994), p. 6; "Supermax Prison is a Terrorist Enclave," *Denver Post* (July 7, 2005); Richard A. Serrano, "The Slow Rot at Supermax," *Los Angeles Times* (May 5, 2006).
14. Paige M. Harrison and James J. Stephan, *Census of State and Federal Correctional Facilities 2000* (Washington, DC: Bureau of Justice Statistics, 2003); Paige M. Harrison and Allen J. Beck, *Prisoners in 2004* (Washington, DC: Bureau of Justice Statistics, 2005).
15. Ibid.
16. Fox Butterfield, "Punitive Damages: Crime Keeps on Falling, but Prisons Keep on Filling," *New York Times* (September 28, 1997) p. 1.
17. Ibid.
18. Mark Mayfield and Tom Watson, "Jail Deaths Spark Call for Probe," *USA Today* (February 19, 1993), p. 3.
19. Harrison and Stephan, *Census of State and Federal Correctional Facilities, 2000.*
20. Paige M. Harrison and Allen J. Beck, *Prison and Jail Inmates at Midyear 2005* (Washington, DC: Bureau of Justice Statistics, 2006).
21. Doris J. James, *Profile of Jail Inmates* (Washington, DC: Bureau of Justice Statistics, 2004).
22. *Rhodes v. Chapman,* 452 U.S. 337 (1981).
23. *Estelle v. Gamble,* 429 U.S. 97 (1976).
24. *Wilson v. Seiter,* 59 U.S. 4671 (1991).
25. *Overton v. Buzzetta,* 123 S. Ct. 2162 (2003). See also *Turner v. Safley,* 107 S. Ct. 2254 (1987).
26. Don M. Gottfredson, "Prison Is Not Enough," *Corrections Today* 57 (August 1995), pp. 16–20.
27. Jill Gordon and Elizabeth H. McConnell, "Are Conjugal Visits and Familial Visitations Effective Rehabilitative Concepts?," *Prison Journal* 79 (March 1999).
28. Danielle M. Polizzi, Doris Layton MacKenzie, and Laura J. Hickman, "What Works in Adult Sex Offender Treatment?: A Review of Prison- and Non-Prison-Based Treatment Programs," *International Journal of Offender Therapy and Comparative Criminology* 43 (September 1999); Serge Brochu, Louise Guyon, and Lynne Desjardins, "Comparative Profiles of Addicted Adult Populations in Rehabilitation and Correctional Services," *Journal of Substance Abuse Treatment* 16 (March 1999); Karen M. Fondacaro, John C. Holt, and Thomas A. Powell, "Psychological Impact of Childhood Sexual Abuse on Male Inmates: The Importance of Perception," *Child Abuse and Neglect* 23 (April 1999); Michael P. Hagan and Karyn L. Bust-Brey, "A Ten-Year Longitudinal Study of Adolescent Rapists upon Return to the Community," *International Journal of Offender Therapy and Comparative Criminology* 43 (December 1999); H. K. Wexler, "The Promise of Prison-based Treatment for Dually Diagnosed Inmates," *Journal of Substance Abuse Treatment*, vol. 25 (October 2003), pp. 223–32.
29. John DiIulio, *Governing Prisons: A Comparative Study of Correctional Management* (New York: Free Press, 1987).
30. Michael D. Reisig, "Rates of Disorder in Higher-Custody State Prisons: A Comparative Analysis of Managerial Practices," *Crime and Delinquency* 44 (April 1998), pp. 229–45.
31. Mark Colvin, *The Penitentiary in Crisis: From Accommodation to Riot in New Mexico* (Albany, NY: SUNY Press, 1992).
32. Tom McEwen, *National Assessment Program: Wardens and State Commissioners of Corrections* (Washington, DC: National Institute of Justice, 1995).
33. Commission on Safety and Abuse in America's Prisons, *Confronting Confinement* (New York: Vera Institute of Justice, 2006).
34. Harrison and Beck, *Prisoners in 2005.*
35. James, *Profile of Jail Inmates.* Caroline Wolf Harlow, *Education and Correctional Populations* (Washington, DC: Bureau of Justice Statistics, 2003).
36. Caroline Wolf Harlow, *Prior Abuse Reported by Inmates and Probationers* (Washington, DC: Bureau of Justice Statistics, 1999).
37. Harrison and Stephan, *Census of State and Federal Correctional Facilities, 2000.*
38. Ibid., p. 16; Christopher J. Mumola, *Incarcerated Parents and Their Children* (Washington, DC: Bureau of Justice Statistics, 2000); Felton Earls, "Men and Fathers in the Community," *Perspectives of Crime and Justice* (Washington, DC: National Institute of Justice, 1999).
39. Heidi M. Hsia and Donna Hamparian, *Disproportionate Minority Confinement* (Washington, DC: Office of Juvenile Justice and Delinquency Prevention, 1998).
40. Doris James Wilson, *Drug Use, Testing, and Treatment in Jails* (Washington, DC: Bureau of Justice Statistics, 2000).
41. Harrison and Beck, *Prisoners in 2004*; Lawrence A. Greenfield and Tracy L. Snell, *Women Offenders* (Washington, DC: Bureau of Justice Statistics, 1999).
42. Barbara A. Koons, John D. Burrow, Merry Morash, and Tim Bynum, "Expert and Offender Perceptions of Program Elements Linked to Successful Outcomes for Incarcerated Women," *Crime and Delinquency* 43 (October 1997), pp. 512–42; Karen Ramoutar and David Farrington. "Are the Same Factors Related to Participation and Frequency of Offending by Male and Female prisoners?," *Psychology, Crime and Law*, vol. 12 (October 2006), pp. 557–69.
43. Toni Locy, "Like Mother, Like Daughter: Why More Young Women Follow Their Moms into Lives of Crime," *U.S. News & World Report* (October 4, 1999), pp. 18–21; Amy C. Conley, "Renny Golden, War on the Family: Mothers in Prison and the Families They Leave Behind," (book review) *Journal of Sociology & Social Welfare*, vol. 33 (September 2006), pp. 192–94.
44. Catherine Conly, *The Women's Prison Association: Supporting Women Offenders and Their Families* (Washington, DC: National Institute of Justice, 1998); Meda Chesney-Lind, "Women in Prison: From Partial Justice to Vengeful Equity," *Corrections Today* 60 (December 1998).
45. John Cloud, "A Get-Tough Policy That Failed," *Time* (February 1, 1999), p. 48.
46. Jeremy Travis, *But They All Come Back: Rethinking Prisoner Reentry* (Washington, DC: National Institute of Justice, 2000); U.S. Comptroller General, *Prisoner Releases: Trends and Information and Reintegration Programs* (Washington, DC: U.S. General Accountability Office, 2001).
47. Peter Finn, *Washington State's Corrections Clearinghouse: A Comprehensive Approach to Offender Employment* (Washington, DC: National Institute of Justice, 1999).

48. Warren E. Burger, "More Warehouses or Factories with Fences?," *New England Journal of Prison Law* 8 (winter 1982), pp. 111–20.
49. Rothman, *The Discovery of the Asylum*, p. 82.
50. Lee Roy Black, "Exemplary Programs Make All Participants Winners," *Corrections Today* (August 1996), pp. 84–87.
51. George E. Sexton, *Work in American Prisons: Joint Ventures with the Private Sector* (Washington, DC: National Institute of Justice, 1995); Rod Miller, George E. Sexton, and Victor J. Jacobsen, *Making Jails Productive* (Washington, DC: National Institute of Justice, 1991); Rod Miller and Joseph Trevathan, "Productive Jails Benefit Many," *Corrections Today*, vol. 65 (April 2003), pp. 96–99.
52. Harry Maier, "Some Businesses Fear Prison Labor," *USA Today* (January 10, 1991), p. 12B.
53. Aaron Epstein, "Study Shows Benefits of Prison Work Programs," *Buffalo News* (December 26, 1991), p. 8.
54. Sexton, *Work in American Prisons*, p. 13.
55. Matthew Purdy, "Bars Don't Stop Flow of Drugs into the Prisons," *New York Times* (July 2, 1995), p. 1.
56. U.S. Department of Justice, *Federal Bureau of Prisons' Drug Interdiction Activities* (Washington, DC: Office of the Inspector General, 2003).
57. Ibid., p. 28.
58. Christopher J. Mumola, *Substance Abuse and Treatment, State and Federal Prisoners* (Washington, DC: Bureau of Justice Statistics, 1999).
59. James A. Inciardi, *A Corrections-Based Continuum of Effective Drug Abuse Treatment* (Washington, DC: National Institute of Justice, 1996); George DeLeon, *Therapeutic Community: Theory, Model, and Method* (New York: Springer, 2000).
60. Laura M. Maruschak, *HIV in Prisons 2003* (Washington, DC: Bureau of Justice Statistics, 2005).
61. Dennis Cauchon, "AIDS in Prison: Locked Up and Locked Out," *USA Today* (March 31, 1995), p. 6.
62. James W. Marquart, Victorio E. Brewer, Janet Mullings, and Ben Crouch, "The Implications of Crime Control Policy on HIV/AIDS-Related Risk among Women Prisoners," *Crime and Delinquency* 45 (January 1999).
63. Gerald G. Gaes, Susan Wallace, Evan Gilman, Jody Klein-Saffran, and Sharon Suppa, "The Influence of Prison Gang Affiliation on Violence and Other Prison Misconduct," *Prison Journal*, vol. 82 (September 2002), p. 359.
64. Bill Wallace, "Five Gangs Dominate California's Prison System," *San Francisco Chronicle* (February 24, 2005).
65. Florida Department of Corrections, "Gang and Security Threat Group Awareness," http://www.dc.state.fl.us/pub/gangs/prison.html (accessed October 1, 2006).
66. Scott N. Tachiki, "Indeterminate Sentences in Supermax Prisons Based upon Gang Affiliations," *California Law Review* 83 (July 1995), pp. 1115–49.
67. Eric Tischler, "Can Tolerance Be Taught?," *Corrections Today* 61 (August 1999); Marie L. Griffin and John R. Hepburn, "The Effect of Gang Affiliation on Violent Misconduct among Inmates During the Early Years of Confinement," *Criminal Justice and Behavior*, vol. 33 (August 2006), pp. 419–49.
68. Ibid., p. 37; Beverly D. Rivera, Ernest L. Cowles, and Laura G. Dorman, "An Exploratory Study of Institutional Change: Personal Control and Environmental Satisfaction in a Gang-Free Prison," *Prison Journal*, vol. 83 (June 2003), p. 149; Chad R. Trulson, James W. Marquart, and Soraya K. Kawucha, "Gang Suppression & Institutional Control," *Corrections Today*, vol. 68 (April 2006), pp. 26–31.
69. Allen J. Beck and Paige M. Harrison, *Sexual Violence Reported by Correctional Authorities* (Washington, DC: Bureau of Justice Statistics, 2006).
70. Bert Useem, Camille Graham Camp, George M. Camp, and Renie Dugan, *Resolution of Prison Riots* (Washington, DC: National Institute of Justice, 1995).
71. Glenn D. Walters, "Time Series and Correlational Analyses of Inmate-Initiated Assaultive Incidents in a Large Correctional System," *International Journal of Offender Therapy and Comparative Criminology* 42 (June 1998); Paul Gendreau, Claire Goggin, and Moira A. Law, "Predicting Prison Misconduct," *Criminal Justice and Behavior* 24 (December 1997).
72. "Texas Prison Riot Kills 1," *New York Times* (April 27, 2000), p. A19; Steve Marshall, "Nine Guards Injured in Ohio Prison Riot," *USA Today* (April 12, 1993), p. 10; Paul Leavitt, "Five Montana Inmates Killed in Uprising," *USA Today* (September 23, 1991), p. 3; Dianne Barth and Roger Neumann, "New York Inmates Hold Three Hostages," *USA Today* (May 29, 1991), p. 3; Kevin Johnson, "Rioting Inmates Locked Away," *USA Today* (October 23, 1995), p. 2.
73. "Racial Violence: Fact of Life Inside Prisons," *USA Today* (February 26, 2000).
74. *Whitley v. Albers*, 106 S. Ct. 1078 (1986).
75. Kit R. Roane, "Attica: The Last Chapter," *U.S. News & World Report* (January 17, 2000), p. 29.
76. Bruce Porter, "Terror on an Eight-Hour Shift," *New York Times Magazine* (November 26, 1995), p. 42; Bruce Frankel, "Attica Inmates' Suit to Begin," *USA Today* (September 9, 1991), p. 3.
77. *Cruz v. Beto*, 405 U.S. 319 (1972).
78. *O'Lone v. Estate of Shabazz*, 107 S. Ct. 2400 (1987); *Turner v. Safley*, 107 S. Ct. 2254 (1987); *Overton v. Buzzetta*, 123 S. Ct. 2162 (2003).
79. See *Howard v. Smith*, 365 F. 2d 28 (4th Cir. 1966); *Hill v. Blackwell*, 774 F. 2d 338 (8th Cir. 1985).
80. *Hudson v. Palmer*, 468 U.S. 517 (1984).
81. James Stephan, *Prison Rule Violators* (Washington, DC: Bureau of Justice Statistics, 1989); J. D. Senese, J. Wilson, A. O. Evans, R. Aguirre, and D. B. Kalinich, "Evaluating Jail Reform: Inmate Infractions and Disciplinary Response in a Traditional and a Podular/Direct Supervision Jail," *American Jails* (September/October 1992), pp. 14–23.

82. Frank Green, "Guards Say Reform Endangers Lives," *Richmond Times–Dispatch* (March 27, 1997), p. 1.
83. *Wolff v. McDonnell,* 418 U.S. 539 (1974); *Superintendent, Massachusetts Correctional Institution, Walpole v. Hill,* 37 Cr. L. 3107 (1985).
84. *Baxter v. Palmigiano,* 425 U.S. 308 (1976).
85. Ojmarrh Mitchell, Fdoris Layton MacKenzie, Gaylene J. Styve, and Angela Grover, "The Impact of Individual, Organizational, and Environmental Attributes on Voluntary Turnover among Juvenile Correctional Staff Members," *Justice Quarterly,* vol. 17 (June 2000), pp. 333–56; Robert M. Freeman, "Social Distance and Discretionary Rule Enforcement in a Women's Prison, *Prison Journal,* vol. 83 (June 2003), p. 191.
86. U.S. Comptroller General, *Women in Prison: Sexual Misconduct by Correctional Staff* (Washington, DC: U.S. General Accounting Office, 1999); Allen J. Beck and Paige M. Harrison, *Sexual Violence Reported by Correctional Authorities* (Washington, DC: Bureau of Justice Statistics, 2006).
87. Dora Schiro, *Correcting Corrections: Missouri's Parallel Universe* (Washington, DC: National Institute of Justice, 2000).

chapter 14

Probation and Community Corrections

Alternatives to incarceration: the supervision of offenders in the community and the distinction between authentic and restorative justice.

CHAPTER OUTLINE

LEARNING OBJECTIVES

- Define community corrections and the two main types of sanctions it provides.
- Identify and describe four alternatives to incarceration.
- Trace the development of fines and probation from colonial times.
- Explain the factors involved in placing offenders on probation and assess the effectiveness of probation compared to incarceration.
- Describe intensive supervision and other forms of intermediate sanctions, and evaluate the effectiveness of electronic monitoring.
- Identify and describe alternative means by which ex-offenders return to communities after prison.
- Define parole and explain the factors involved in releasing prisoners to their communities.
- Identify and describe six forms of authentic and restorative justice.
- Evaluate the effectiveness of mediation, boot camp, corporal punishment, and public humiliation as forms of authentic justice.
- Discuss issues relating to the treatment of sex offenders, and argue for or against the use of sex-offender registries.
- Discuss the issue of asset forfeiture in light of recent events.

Bryon Fritz had a long history of impersonating a police officer. For many years, he pulled over cars at phony traffic stops, dressed like a police officer, and flashed a badge to others, even though he never was a sworn officer of any kind. Fritz even drove a large car, similar to a police patrol vehicle. After several convictions for impersonating a police officer, court-ordered counseling, probation, and prohibitions from owning police-related badges or uniforms, Fritz still engaged in repeated police impersonations. Finally a judge in Virginia Beach required Fritz to wear a sandwich board while marching back and forth in front of the probation and parole office. The sign says, "Warning: Do not violate your suspended sentence or probation or you may end up doing this."[1]

The judge's frustration in this case points to a larger question about what should be done with nonviolent offenders for whom traditional sentences either do not work or do not appear to be appropriate. Vandalism, public drunkenness, disorderly conduct, and all the other lesser crimes against public order and property certainly deserve attention, but *how much* attention should they be given by the criminal justice system? Should the punishment be jail time? A fine? Something else?

These questions are not new. In 1841 a Boston bootmaker named John Augustus raised the same issues. A public drunk was sentenced to jail, but Augustus intervened by posting the man's bail on the promise he would stop drinking. From that point on, Augustus acted as a "private angel and guardian of men convicted of crime." By the time of his death in 1859 he had posted bail for 2,000 convicts.[2] His idea that a middle ground should exist between jail and freedom formed the basis for the invention of probation in the late 1800s. Today this idea seems little more than common sense and has been adopted by every state.

TWO TYPES OF SANCTIONS

community corrections
Sanctions that are *alternatives to incarceration* in jail or prison (such as monetary penalties, probation, intensive supervision, and home confinement with electronic monitoring), or supervision in the community *after a sentence of incarceration* has been served (such as parole, work release, furloughs, and halfway houses).

sanctions
Ways to punish or place restrictions on offenders.

This middle ground, known as **community corrections,** has since grown to encompass two different types of **sanctions,** or ways to punish or place restrictions on offenders:

1. Sanctions that are *alternatives to incarceration* in jail or prison, such as monetary penalties, probation, intensive supervision, and home confinement with electronic monitoring.
2. Supervision in the community *after a sentence of incarceration* has been served. Here the goal is to promote a smooth transition from confinement to freedom. Parole, work release, furloughs, and halfway houses fall into this category.

This chapter examines each of these forms of community corrections from the perspective of the offender, the potential victims, and the goals of the criminal justice system.

What Are the Alternatives to Incarceration?

It is sometimes argued that the phrase *community corrections* is a contradiction in terms. The argument goes like this: The two primary purposes of corrections are to punish offenders and to protect the public. Allowing offenders to serve their sentences in the community violates both of these purposes, because nonprison sentences do not provide "enough" punishment and also create the risk of further offenses by criminals who are not incarcerated. Responses to this argument focus on either economics or rehabilitation:

ARGUMENTS FOR COMMUNITY CORRECTIONS

1. Imprisonment is the most severe and expensive type of criminal sanction, so it should be reserved for offenders who commit the most serious crimes.
2. The vast majority of offenders commit nonviolent crimes and will eventually be released from prison. Imprisonment tends to change offenders for the worse; in the long run public protection is best ensured when criminals reform. Community-based alternatives to imprisonment are the best way to accomplish this.

Both of these arguments are correct—but they are not generally accepted by the public, which believes that imprisonment is necessary if the public is to be protected.[3] The dramatic growth in community corrections in recent years, therefore, has not been due to a change of heart on the part of the public. Public views on crime, criminals, and punishment generally have hardened. Instead, the rapid growth in arrests and prison populations, combined with the soaring costs of building new prisons and operating them, has led to more careful consideration

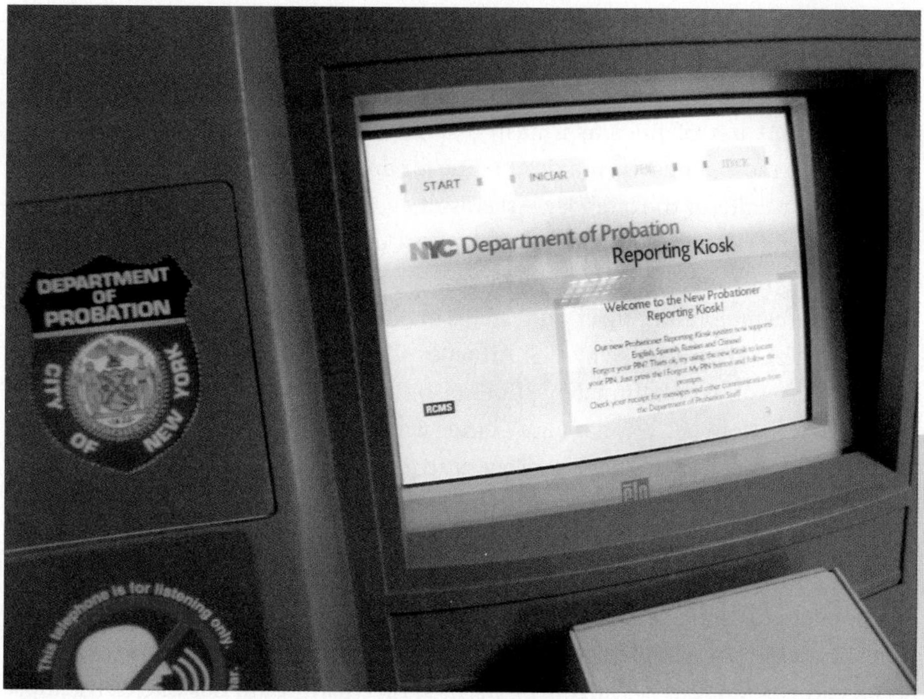

A probation kiosk in New York City which automates the monitoring of offenders serving probation sentences in the community. Why do you believe automated devices like this have become popular? Do you believe they are effective at monitoring offenders?

of community corrections.[4] One survey asked several hundred residents how they would sentence twenty convicted offenders, and virtually all thought prison was appropriate. But after the costs of incarceration and available alternatives to prison were explained, the respondents "resentenced" many offenders to community sanctions.[5]

Alternatives to incarceration take several forms. Among these are monetary penalties, probation, intensive supervision, and home confinement and electronic monitoring.

Fines as a Form of Criminal Sanction

COLONIAL SANCTIONS

Fines and whippings were the two most common penalties during the eighteenth century. In Massachusetts in 1736, a thief was to be fined or whipped upon a first conviction. The next time he would pay triple damages, sit for an hour on the gallows platform with a noose around his neck, and then be taken to the whipping post for thirty lashes. A third conviction resulted in death by hanging. Likewise, a burglar would first be branded with the letter B on his forehead. If convicted a second time, he would sit on the gallows platform with a noose around his neck for an hour and then be whipped. Upon a third conviction, he was deemed "incorrigible" and hanged. The rationale of the colonists was apparent: "Anyone impervious to the fine and the whip, who did not mend his ways after an hour with a noose about him, was uncontrollable and therefore had to be executed."[6] Jail was reserved for suspects awaiting trial and for debtors. Fines were effective when the offender had some wealth, whereas whipping could be applied more generally. There was no clear-cut division by type of crime that distinguished offenders who were fined from those who were whipped. The choice of punishment depended on the circumstances of the offender rather than on those of the offense.[7]

PROBLEMS WITH FINES

Fines continue to be the most common form of criminal sanction in the United States, although they are used primarily in cases involving minor crimes or as an adjunct to incarceration for more serious offenses. There are at least two problems in the current use of fines as a form of criminal sanction: *proportionality* and *collection*. In most states the maximum fine for an offense is set by law without regard for the wealth of the offender. As a result, fines often lack meaning for wealthy offenders, whereas poor offenders (the largest offender group) often cannot pay even a moderate fine. Second, many fines go uncollected because of the lack of effective enforcement and collection systems in many states. The Justice Department keeps track of fines received by U.S. Attorneys' offices, but fines are also collected through courts by probation departments, or in the form of payments to the victim.[8] The U.S. Courts National Fine Center was established to centralize and better organize the fine-collection process in the federal courts and to improve coordination among agencies, but there is no analogous agency at the state or local level.[9]

The collection of fines remains a problem, as is the collection of fees imposed on offenders to reduce the costs of the criminal justice system. More than fifteen states charge application fees to people seeking court-appointed lawyers (requested because the defendant is indigent). The state of Washington has one of the most extensive fee systems; offenders must pay into a 'drug enforcement fund,' in addition to paying a victim assessment fee, court costs, and related fees. An interest rate of 12 percent is charged, and the state of Washington denies the right to vote, to people who have not paid such debts because they have not completed all the terms of their sentence. The result is many unpaid fees and fines by persons simply unable to pay them.[10]

DAY FINES

Day fines, which are commonly used in Europe, offer a solution to the problem of proportionality. They are called "day fines" because the amount of the fine is based on some percentage of an offender's daily earnings. The court attaches a "unit value" to the seriousness of the offense (usually between 5 and 120 units), then calculates the fine by multiplying these units of seriousness by a percentage of the offender's daily income. An offender who takes home $40 per day, for example, is able to keep 40 percent ($16) for housing, 20 percent ($8) for food and clothing, and up to 40 percent of the remainder ($6.40) to support dependents. In this case the fine (gauged to the seriousness of the offense) could range up to nearly $10 per day, or 25 percent of the offender's daily income. Therefore, the amount of the fine is proportional both to the offense and to the offender's ability to pay.

A test of day fines in Staten Island, New York, found that average fine amounts were higher under the day fine system but that collection rates were not affected. Significantly, fewer arrest warrants were issued for offenders' failure to appear at postsentencing hearings, suggesting a higher compliance rate. Also, judges were more comfortable imposing monetary penalties under such an income-based system. Day fine programs have now been implemented in other states.[11] Despite their advantages, day fine systems are still rare in the United States, where traditional offense-based fines are still used in most jurisdictions. There is some concern that day fines are unconstitutional in that they allow for different fines for the same offense, thus violating the Fourteenth Amendment guarantee of equal protection of the laws; but there have not yet been court challenges to day fines.

Probation

JOHN AUGUSTUS

Probation is a criminal sentence of community supervision of the offender that is conducted by a probation officer. The term *probation* was first used by John Augustus to describe his efforts to bail offenders out of jail and allow them to live under supervision in the community. Augustus worked without pay, and he often placed those he bailed out of jail in his own home. He was careful in whom he selected, taking into account "the previous character of the person, his age and the influences by which in the future he would likely be surrounded."[12] Augustus helped offenders of all kinds, and he reported only ten absconders among the 2,000 cases he handled. He worked as a volunteer for eighteen years. Massachusetts did not use paid probation officers until 1878, when it enacted the first probation statute. Other states soon copied Massachusetts's system for providing probation officers to investigate cases and recommend sentences. This growth in probation was aided by the invention of the juvenile court at the turn of the century. This step formally recognized that juveniles should be handled differently than adults, and probation supervision seemed appropriate in a large number of juvenile cases. The first directory of probation officers, published in 1907, identified 795 probation officers, who worked primarily in juvenile courts. By 1920 every state had adopted probation for juveniles, and thirty-three states had provisions for adult probation.[13]

PROBATION TODAY

Today probation is administered in a variety of ways. In thirty-four states adult probation is part of the executive branch of government; in sixteen others it is part of the judicial branch at the state or local level. In half the states a central probation system operates throughout the state; in others probation is operated by the county government, and in the remainder it is administered by the municipality. This variation is similar to that among police agencies, which also exist at all levels of government. There is debate over whether probation is best administered at the state or local level and whether it is best administered by the executive or judicial branch of government. A national commission concluded that probation is administered best at the state level by the executive branch of government, and there appears to be a trend in this direction, as several states have changed the way they administer probation in recent years.[14]

Classification of Offenders Most jurisdictions classify offenders to predict the likelihood of offenders' success on probation and the amount of supervision they will require. Classification or "risk prediction" scales summarize the outcomes in similar past cases and can be compared with a current case. These classification techniques have been used successfully to distinguish among high-, medium-, and low-risk offenders.[15] For example, offenders with substance abuse problems and prior felony records are much more likely than others to violate the conditions of probation and reoffend. Classification systems identify these and other risk factors so that high-risk offenders will receive more intensive supervision in order to reduce the risk of probation violations.

CLASSIFICATION SYSTEMS

Probation is the most widely used form of correctional supervision in the United States. As *That's a Fact* illustrates, of the 7 million adults under correctional supervision in the United States in 2004 (3.2 percent of the adult population), 4 million were on probation. Ten years earlier, 5.3 million adult offenders were

A probation officer holds a monthly meeting with a probationer in Austin, Texas. What questions should the probation officer ask? How does he know if he is being told the truth?

under some form of correctional supervision, including 3.1 million on probation, reflecting a 30 percent increase. Of offenders serving probation sentences, 49 percent were convicted for felonies, 50 percent committed misdemeanors, and 15 percent were convicted for driving under the influence of alcohol.[16]

Conditions of Probation Offenders who are sentenced to probation usually have conditions attached to their sentences. These conditions are designed to control the offender's present behavior and to change it in the future. Conditions of control might include the following: no association with known criminals, no possession of weapons, no use of alcohol or drugs, and no leaving the jurisdiction. The conditions of control are designed to reduce the risk to the community while the offender is under supervision.

CONDITIONS TO CHANGE BEHAVIORS

Conditions designed to change behavior include mandatory drug/alcohol testing or treatment, education or employment requirements, community service, payment of fines, and/or restitution to the victim. The conditions seeking change are designed to produce conforming behavior once the probation sentence has ended. These changes are expected to result from treatment of addiction, steady employment, and greater understanding of the consequences of criminal behavior.

EFFECTIVENESS OF PROBATION

Supervision of Offenders Supervision of offenders in the community poses a risk that prisons do not: People under correctional supervision might commit further crimes. This is the primary reason for negative public attitudes toward probation. Although probation is less expensive than incarceration, huge prison construction programs in many states provide evidence that the public is willing to spend tax dollars in order to guarantee public safety.

The majority of probationers complete their sentence in the community without incident. Probationers completing federal sentences show a success rate of 80 percent. Only six percent of federal probationers commit new crimes. Three percent test positive for drugs, and 2 percent become fugitives.[17] It has been found that misdemeanor offenders are much more likely than felons to complete probation successfully. Also, 21 percent of adult felons on probation were *not* recommended to the judge in the presentence report for placement on probation. These offenders were nearly twice as likely to have their sentence revoked as those recommended for probation.[18] This finding suggests that success rates on probation would be considerably higher if sentencing recommendations were more closely followed.

The impact of probation versus incarceration on the subsequent criminal careers of offenders has been debated for many years. Some believe that probation provides more opportunity for rehabilitation, whereas others believe incarceration has a greater deterrent effect. A twenty-year follow-up of nearly 1,000 felony sentences in New Jersey compared rearrests of offenders sentenced to confinement to rearrests of those sentenced to probation. Controlling for the age and criminal

That's a FACT

Perspectives on Probation and Parole

Probation is the most popular form of correctional supervision, accounting for nearly 60 percent of all adults incarcerated or under community supervision. Figure 14A shows trends in adults under correctional supervision since 1990.

Forty-nine percent of all probationers were convicted of a felony, 26 percent were convicted of a drug law violation, and 15 percent for driving while intoxicated. How might you explain the fact that more than half of the total growth of the correctional population since 1990 has been probationers (new prison inmates account for 27 percent and jail inmates 12 percent)?

FIGURE 14A Adults under Correctional Supervision (in millions)

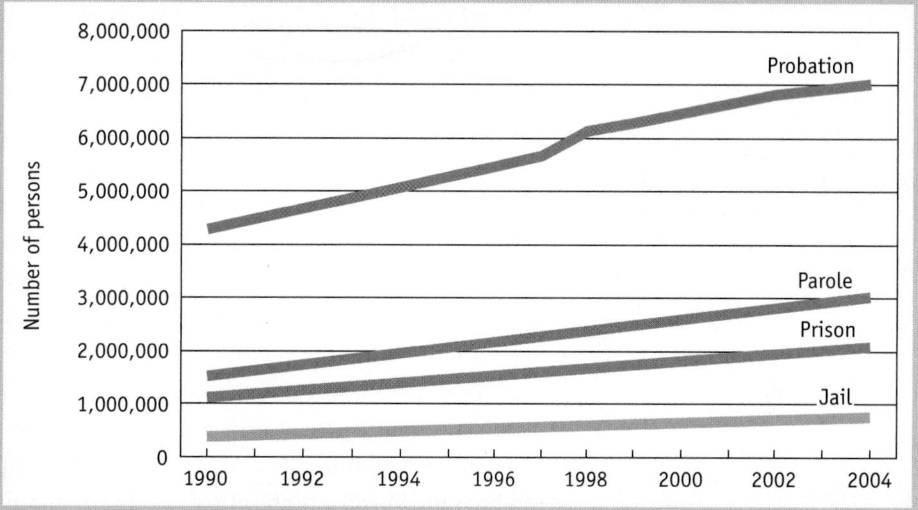

Source: Lauren E. Glaze and Seri Palla, *Probation and Parole in the United States* (Washington, DC: Bureau of Justice Statistics, 2005).

After a more than a decade of dramatic growth during the 1980s into the 1990s, the number of adults under parole supervision is stabilizing. Greater restrictions on parole release is a primary reason for this trend. During the last decade, the number of discretionary releases from prison to parole (by parole boards) has dropped, while the number of mandatory releases from prison of inmates at the end of their sentences has increased correspondingly. This trend away from parole reflects changes in state and federal laws and a distrust of parole supervision as a way to effectively monitor former inmates. These trends are illustrated in Figure 14B.

Why do you believe there is distrust of parole as a way to supervise former inmates near the end of their sentences? Are there other practical ways to reintegrate offenders into society?

FIGURE 14B Annual State Parole Population and Entries to State Parole, 1990–2004

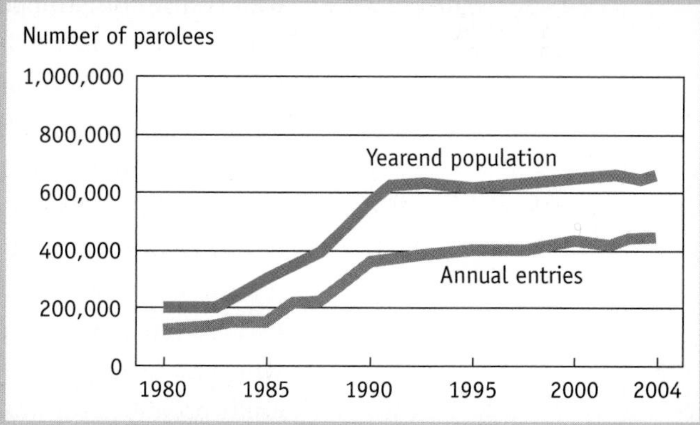

Source: Lauren E. Glaze and Seri Palla, *Probation and Parole in the United States* (Washington, DC: Bureau of Justice Statistics, 2005).

backgrounds of the offenders and the amount of time probationers spent in the community, the study found no difference in the proportion of offenders rearrested.[19] Approximately 55 percent of both groups had at least one new arrest after five years. This finding suggests that the impact of probation deteriorates after the end of the sentence and that the exclusive focus on felony offenders may mask the efficacy of probation for misdemeanor offenders.

Intensive Supervision

intermediate sanctions
Sentences designed to provide more rigorous supervision than normal probation, yet something less expensive than incarceration.

Dissatisfaction with probation, combined with the need to use prison space more efficiently, has produced a movement toward **intermediate sanctions:** sentences designed to provide more rigorous supervision than normal probation, yet something less expensive than incarceration. These sanctions attempt to result in more punishment at less cost, but they raise three questions: (1) Are costs actually reduced? (2) Are these sanctions effective in controlling the growth of prison populations? And (3) do they protect the community?[20]

intensive supervision
Probation or parole for which jurisdictions maintain small caseloads, make frequent contact with offenders under supervision, and require special conditions such as random drug tests, curfews, restitution to victims, electronic monitoring, or house arrest.

The oldest and most common form of intermediate sanction is intensive supervision programs for probationers and parolees. Jurisdictions achieve **intensive supervision** by maintaining small caseloads; making frequent contact with offenders under supervision; and requiring special conditions such as random drug tests, curfews, restitution to victims, electronic monitoring, or house arrest. Georgia was the first state to evaluate its intensive supervision program. It reported both reduced costs and lower recidivism.[21] Between 1980 and 1990 some form of intensive supervision was adopted in every state. Today about 3 percent of of probationers are in an intensive supervision program.[22]

Evaluations of intensive supervision programs have shown mixed results. An evaluation of fourteen programs in nine states found that they provided effective surveillance of offenders but were costly and failed to reduce recidivism.[23] A study in England found a high rate of recidivism for offenders on intensive probation, but the rate was no higher than for offenders serving prison sentences.[24]

STUDIES OF DAY REPORTING

It has been suggested that greater emphasis on treatment would lead to behavioral changes and result in lower recidivism. In California and Texas, offenders under intensive supervision who received substance abuse counseling, held jobs, paid restitution, and performed community service reoffended at a rate 10 to 20 percent lower than that of offenders who did not receive such treatment.[25] However, an evaluation concluded that there is little evidence that intensive supervision programs either rehabilitated offenders or deterred offenders from committing additional crimes more effectively than the sentencing options they replaced.[26] A study of day reporting in North Carolina, a program in which offenders are required to report daily in order to participate in treatment or employment programs, found the success rate to be low and questioned whether the program was cost-effective, given that most of those terminated returned to prison.[27] Thus, while intensive supervision programs have an intuitive appeal, they have not generally produced the anticipated outcomes. There are at least two reasons that may explain this lack of success: (1) The offenders chosen for intensive supervision are inappropriate, or (2) intensive supervision discovers more criminal activity. First, it is possible that a higher success rate could be achieved if offenders were more carefully screened before being assigned to intensive supervision programs. Substance abuse counseling, for example, works best for those motivated to kick the habit. Offenders not motivated in this way may be poor risks regardless of the level of supervision imposed. Second, it may be that closer supervision of offenders in the community is simply resulting in more discovery of recidivism. Offenders on intensive supervision may not be committing any more crimes than they did in the past, but probation officers may now be more aware of crimes because of more frequent contact with the offenders.

Confinement and Monitoring

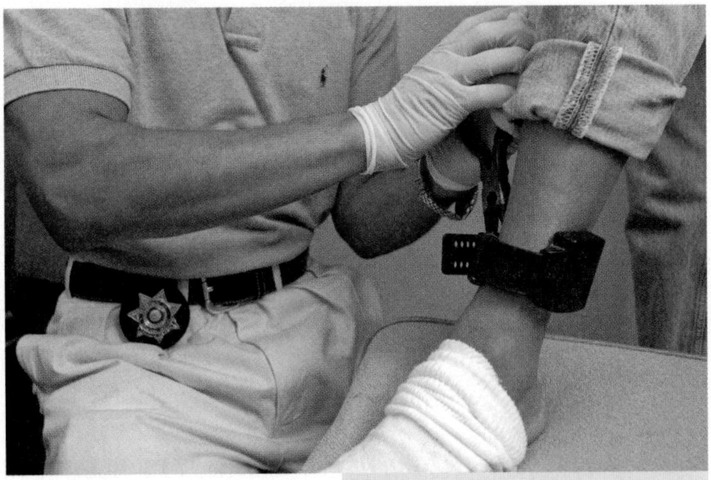

This offender is wearing an electronic monitoring device. What is the purpose of electronic surveillance? According to research, how effective is electronic monitoring as a deterrent against repeat offending in the short term? in the long term?

Offenders under home confinement are not permitted to leave their residences for purposes other than work, school, treatment, or other approved reasons. This form of punishment, sometimes called **house arrest,** can be a condition of probation or parole and is employed to varying degrees in every state.

A primary issue in home confinement is ensuring compliance. Increasingly this is being accomplished through **electronic monitoring,** in which offenders are monitored in the community by means of electronic devices such as radio and telephone transmitters. Such monitoring takes one of two forms: programmed or continuous contact. In programmed contact, offenders are called at home at random intervals and are required to verify their presence by voice or a code, or electronically through a device strapped to their wrists. In continuous contact, the offender wears an ankle bracelet that cannot be removed without setting off an electronic alarm. The supervision office is notified electronically of any movement out of range of a receiver located in the offender's telephone. In recent years house arrest has become synonymous with electronic monitoring, because manual monitoring requires more direct checks of offenders' whereabouts. The lower cost of electronic monitoring, combined with its more efficient surveillance of offenders in the community, has led to its widespread adoption.

The primary cost savings offered by home confinement are reduced jail or prison costs. If an offender can be supervised effectively in the community, the state does not have to pay for room, board, and round-the-clock supervision in jail or prison. A Virginia study reported a total cost per day of $5.67 for an offender on home confinement with electronic monitoring, compared to an average jail cost of $47 per day.[28] On the other hand, if offenders under house arrest would normally have been placed on simple or intensive probation, costs are increased, because more resources are being devoted to surveillance of offenders in the community. This phenomenon is called **net widening.** This term refers to the process whereby more and more offenders end up being placed under supervision of the criminal justice system even though the intent of a program was to divert offenders out of the system.

The effectiveness of home confinement is not clear-cut; evidence from a growing number of jurisdictions has shown that it has both strengths and weaknesses as an intermediate sanction. Florida's home confinement program, the Community Control Program, placed more than 50,000 offenders under house arrest, mostly with manual monitoring. Each offender had a minimum of twenty-eight contacts a month with probation or parole officers. An evaluation found that about half of the offenders sentenced to house arrest would otherwise have been placed on probation, suggesting a net-widening effect.[29] But the other half would otherwise have been sentenced to prison; house arrest for these offenders may have had a positive effect on prison overcrowding. A follow-up study compared two groups of offenders matched by age, gender, type and severity of offense, and prior felony convictions, and found that reconviction rates for new offenses were slightly

house arrest
A condition of probation or parole in which offenders are not permitted to leave their residences for purposes other than work, school, treatment, or other approved reasons.

electronic monitoring
Surveillance of offenders in the community by means of electronic devices such as radio and telephone transmitters.

net widening
Process by which more offenders end up being placed under supervision of the criminal justice system even though the intent of a program was to divert offenders out of the system.

EFFECTIVENESS OF HOME CONFINEMENT

lower for those under house arrest (20 percent) than for those who had been sentenced to prison and then released (24 percent).

In many jurisdictions house arrest lasts no more than three months and is followed by regular probation. A seven-year study of offenders convicted of drunk driving or driving with a suspended license found that 97 percent successfully completed the electronic monitoring phase of their house arrest sentence. A third of these offenders, however, committed a new offense or technical violation while on regular probation.[30] This suggests that electronic monitoring may have only a temporary effect. An evaluation of three Canadian electronic monitoring programs concluded that "their effectiveness as a true alternative to incarceration and reducing recidivism has yet to be demonstrated."[31] House arrest may be effective for offenders with family members who do not mind the inconvenience of a homebound person who receives telephone monitoring calls or signals at all hours. But offenders can become bored and frustrated by their inability to engage in most behaviors, from doing the laundry to going for a walk. As a result, offenders view electronic monitoring as punitive, although better than jail,[32] and house arrest as more punitive than rehabilitative in nature. The building frustration with the limitations of life under house arrest may ultimately lead to violations of the supervision. Over the course of a single year in Marion County, Indiana, for example, nearly half of the suspects placed on home detention while awaiting trial cut off their ankle monitoring bracelets or broke other rules. This points to the need for active and continuous monitoring of those being supervised electronically.[33]

PROBLEMS WITH ELECTRONIC MONITORING

Another significant problem with electronic monitoring has to do with the imperfect technology of surveillance. Radio interference with electronic transmitters and receivers, mountainous terrain, and even cast-iron bathtubs have caused false alarms and alarm failures.[34] In one case a convict under house arrest was able to sell heroin from his apartment.[35] In another an offender was able to remove his bracelet and commit a homicide, causing New Jersey to drop its use of electronic monitoring for early parolees for three years.[36] Incidents like these give rise to concern over adequate protection of the community. Electronics vendors are marketing new, improved electronic monitoring equipment that overcomes some of the flaws of earlier versions and improves the capabilities of probation and parole agencies to respond to violations.[37]

Monitoring systems based on the technology of Global Positioning Satellites (GPS) use a satellite-based navigation system to monitor offenders. These systems have three parts: a tracking unit that looks like a cell phone and is worn on the belt; an ankle bracelet that acts as a transmitter; and a base station at the offender's home that downloads the tracking information and sends it over a phone line to probation officials. The wearer must place the tracking unit into the base unit within five minutes of arriving home each day. Failure to do so sends an electronic page to the probation officer. The device uses mapping software to designate zones where an offender cannot go depending on the court order (e.g., schools, liquor stores, victim's home). If the offender enters a prohibited area, an alert is sent out and both the offender and the probation officer are called immediately.[38] It can be seen, therefore, that effective electronic monitoring requires continuous oversight and immediate response by probation officials.

How Can Ex-offenders Return to the Community after Prison?

Offenders convicted of murder and violent crimes receive the longest average sentences, but fewer than 2 percent of all felony convictions are for murder, and fewer than 19 percent are for violent crimes.[39] Most offenders commit property crimes, and all but the most serious offenders eventually are released. Various kinds of programs have been developed to foster successful entry of offenders back into the community. These programs endeavor both to ensure that public safety is maintained and to improve the offenders' chances for rehabilitation.

Some claim that unsuitable candidates have been released from prison and placed on parole; such releases reduce the effectiveness of parole and affect public safety. Parole guidelines have been adopted in many states and have contributed to more appropriate and consistent parole decisions.[40] These guidelines attempt to help jurisdictions make parole release decisions more uniform by employing standardized criteria. Nevertheless, public confidence in parole continues to erode, and fourteen states have abolished parole release altogether. Work/study release programs, furloughs, and halfway houses are examples of more restrictive forms of temporary release designed to promote successful transition from prison to freedom.

A parole officer looking for a parolee who has violated the conditions of his parole. Why is the work of parole officers often more dangerous than that of probation officers?

PAROLE GUIDELINES

Parole

Parole is perhaps the least popular component of the criminal justice system. It consists of supervision in the community of offenders who were dangerous enough to have been sent to prison but are near the end of their sentences. Parole officers supervise the highest-risk offenders, and these offenders sometimes commit new crimes. The public is outraged when crimes are committed by parolees and cannot understand why dangerous offenders are allowed to go back into the community in the first place.

The logic behind parole is simple: Its goal is to provide a way for inmates to serve the last part of their sentence in the community under supervision in order to make a successful readjustment to freedom. Parole is one of three ways in which inmates are released. A second method is based on the accumulation of **good-time credits,** which are small reductions in the time to be served awarded to inmates for each day on which they obey prison rules. The third type of release is called **maxing out.** This occurs when the offender has served the entire sentence and has not been granted parole or accumulated enough good-time credits to justify early release. Parole is generally available only to prison inmates; jail inmates must serve their entire sentences, even though jail inmates are less serious offenders and presumably would be better candidates for parole.

good-time credits
Small reductions in the time to be served, awarded to inmates for each day on which they obey prison rules.

maxing out
Release from incarceration after the offender has served the entire sentence without ever being granted parole or accumulating enough good-time credits to justify early release.

Media & Criminal Justice — *25th Hour*

The 2003 Spike Lee movie *25th Hour* tells the story of businessman Monty Brogan and his last day of freedom before surrendering and starting a seven-year prison sentence for selling drugs. As Monty says goodbye to his girlfriend, his father, and his two best friends, he comes across as a thoughtful person with some very bad associates. Monty has no remorse for the crime, however, and probably would still be selling drugs if he had not been caught. He does regret his greed, which led him to stay in the drug business too long, and he worries about the violence of prison life.

Monty's friends believe his life is over. He can now become a fugitive, kill himself, or do the prison time, knowing his life will never be the same. Both Monty's father and girlfriend have benefited from the money he obtained in the illicit drug business, and they knew where the money came from. Based on a novel by David Benioff, the film vividly shows Monty's regret, his blame expressed toward others, and ultimately his despising of himself and his situation.

The movie has no plot payoff but rather reveals details of Monty's life choices over the course of a single day. It raises thoughtful questions about the choices people make in life in order to get what they want at whatever price, the regret one feels when caught taking illegal shortcuts, and the new set of choices to be made—to either face the consequences or to once again look for a shortcut way out.

What do you think about the sentence imposed on Monty? Is it too long or short, given that he was a businessman? Can you imagine the thought processes of offenders on electronic surveillance, or offenders like Monty, who think about taking a shortcut to escape from their confinement? Why do you believe more offenders do not try to escape?

Parole Release Decisions In the United States parole is associated with indeterminate sentencing. Back in the 1870s Zebulon Brockway first included indeterminate sentencing and parole in his innovative program for youthful offenders. He persuaded the New York State legislature to adopt indeterminate sentencing and to shift the authority for prisoner release from the courts to corrections officials.[41] **Parole release** is decided by a parole board consisting of corrections officials and/or political appointees who evaluate the inmate's record and behavior inside the prison. Using their discretion, they may release the inmate to serve the remainder of the sentence under community supervision. Parole thus is designed to provide supervised transition from prison to life in the community.

parole release
Prisoner release decided by a parole board consisting of corrections officials and/or political appointees who evaluate the inmate's record and his or her behavior in prison to determine whether the inmate will be released to serve the remainder of the sentence under community supervision.

Offenders who are not released by the parole board can be granted supervised mandatory release if they accumulate enough good-time credits. These offenders are also supervised by parole officers. Inmates who max out and complete their sentences in prison are released, but because their sentence has ended they are not supervised in the community.

HIGH-RISK OFFENDERS

Managing High-Risk Offenders Managing high-risk offenders in the community is a difficult task under the best of circumstances. High caseloads, few resources for helping offenders make the transition into the community, and in some states poorly trained and educated parole officers are major issues. In many jurisdictions the caseloads of parole officers are too high to enable the officers to exercise meaningful supervision, a situation that suggests a lack of commitment to parole as a correctional strategy. Moreover, parole officers are not uniformly educated or trained. In some states a bachelor's degree and minimum training are required; in others there is no such standard. As a result, the quality of parole officers varies greatly. In many jurisdictions parole officers often lack the tools or resources necessary to help offenders adjust to life in the community. Parole officers need to be able to offer job training opportunities, job placement, training in basic skills, substance abuse treatment, and other resources if they are to intervene successfully in the lives of parolees. Despite all these shortcomings, however, approximately 55 percent of state prison parolees successfully complete their supervision. About half of those who do return are sent back for technical violations (e.g., drug test failure, curfew violations, or nonparticipation in required programs) rather than for new crimes.[42] A study of federal offenders found that only 16 percent of 215,000 offenders released from prison returned to prison within three years of their release. Thirty percent of those who returned to prison committed new crimes and the remaining returned because of technical violations. If more were done to make parole meaningful and effective for offenders and for the general public, rates of recidivism could be reduced further with better supervision and support, reducing the fear in the knowledge that virtually all offenders will one day be released.[43]

Work/Study Release and Furloughs

Prolonged incarceration can lead to a serious decline in inmates' capacity to function outside of prison. This decline is seen in several areas, including vocational and social skills, independence and self-esteem, and family support. Temporary release programs are designed to reduce these effects by permitting inmates to enter the community on certain days for work, study, treatment programs, or family visitation. Given the increase in average sentence lengths in recent years, it is likely that temporary release will become even more important in the future.

Work release began as a way to encourage inmates' discipline and work ethic and as a response to complaints that offenders in prison were idle while free citizens had to work to support themselves. Today the reverse argument is employed: Paid employment for inmates is criticized at times when there is not enough work available for law-abiding citizens.[44] Depending on one's view, therefore, work release can be seen as a punitive consequence of incarceration or as a rehabilitative benefit.

work release
Program that permits eligible inmates to work during the day at regular jobs in the outside world, returning to the jail or prison at night.

Work release programs permit eligible inmates to work during the day at regular jobs outside the jail or prison, returning to the prison at night. Work release is generally not available in maximum security institutions; and even for inmates in medium or minimum security institutions, the ability to work is often affected by the location of the prison. Many prisons are located in rural areas where there are relatively few opportunities for employment.

PURPOSES OF WORK RELEASE

The work release experience is designed to instill discipline, a routine, and work habits that closely resemble those found outside of prison. Inmates are paid the prevailing wage, although they are required to submit their earnings to the corrections authorities, who deduct 5 or 10 percent for room and board in the prison and payment of welfare agencies that may be supporting the inmate's family. The remainder of the inmate's earnings is placed in forced savings until the inmate is released. Approximately 65,000 inmates, fewer than 5 percent of the total inmate population, are involved in work release programs.

study release
A program similar to work release, in which an inmate attends school by day and returns to jail or prison at night.

Study release is similar to work release, except that the inmate attends school by day and returns to the jail or prison at night. The study might consist of high school equivalency courses, vocational training, or college education. The inmate must meet the same entrance requirements as any other student, apply for admission, be accepted, and obtain permission from correctional authorities to attend the educational institution. Like work release, study release is feasible only for inmates in correctional facilities near educational institutions, which most prisons are not.

Two factors are most responsible for the limited use of study release: funding and public pressure. Unlike work release, study release costs money. Therefore, like any other student, an inmate must apply for financial aid to cover the cost of education. Funding is not always available, so most prison education is limited to that which takes place within prison walls. Public pressure also limits the use of study release. Concerns over public safety, along with complaints about inmates' being allowed to attend schools that many free citizens cannot afford, deter many corrections officials from allowing inmates to participate in study release. As a result, few inmates participate in study release programs. With the increasingly wide availability of distance education opportunities offered via the Internet, inmates do not have to go off-site to obtain educational opportunities; public opposition and funding constraints, however, prevent wider use of these opportunities.

furloughs
Unsupervised leaves from prison that are granted for only a few hours to permit an eligible inmate to be present at a relative's funeral, visit loved ones, go to a job interview, or otherwise attend to personal or family matters.

Furloughs are unsupervised leaves from prison that are granted for only a few hours. The purpose of a furlough is to permit an eligible inmate to be present at a relative's funeral, visit loved ones, go to a job interview in preparation for release, or otherwise attend to personal or family matters. As with work release and study release, furloughs are designed to help the inmate prepare for a successful transition into free society.

THE CASE OF WILLIE HORTON

This goal must be balanced, however, against the risk that the inmate might commit new crimes. The most infamous case of a furlough violation is that of Willie Horton. Horton was convicted of murder in Massachusetts and sentenced to life imprisonment. He was released on a furlough and did not return. He then kidnapped and raped a Maryland woman and assaulted her fiancé, and was arrested and tried for his new crimes. This case became widely publicized and politicized and undoubtedly had an impact on the use of furloughs around the United States.

Why was the concept of chain gangs reintroduced during the 1990s? Why is this practice controversial? In what sense could you say that chained work gangs are related to community-based corrections?

The available data suggest that furloughs are uncommon; fewer than 3 percent of all inmates are granted furloughs annually. The rate at which offenders on furlough either return late or abscond is similarly low—generally in the 2 percent range.[45] Nevertheless, one sensational crime or violation can produce enough public and political outrage to kill a program, regardless of its merits.

Halfway Houses

halfway houses
Residential centers for ex-offenders in the community. Most halfway house residents are parolees or similar inmates near the end of their sentence.

Halfway houses are residential centers for ex-offenders in the community. They originated with private efforts to help the homeless; houses established by the Quakers, the Salvation Army, and other religious and civic organizations to help the destitute and homeless emerged during the 1800s, and many of them are still in operation today.[46] Residents of halfway houses may be categorized as either halfway in or halfway out. Those who are "halfway in" have been sentenced to probation or diverted from the criminal justice system and are serving time in a halfway house as an alternative to incarceration. Those who are "halfway out" are near the end of their prison sentences or are on parole. Most halfway house residents are parolees or similar inmates near the end of their sentence, although some jurisdictions use halfway houses to hold suspects awaiting trial because of overcrowding in local jails.[47]

There are nearly 500 halfway houses in the United States, with an average of twenty-five residents each. These facilities are located in multiple-family homes or apartment buildings, and residents spend from eight to sixteen weeks there. About 15,000 inmates, or about 2 percent of the total on parole, are living in halfway houses.[48] Halfway houses are considered a form of minimum custody correctional facility, and only offenders with that security status are eligible. The financial distinction between a halfway house and a minimum security prison is significant. A minimum security prison bed costs an average of $32,000 to build, whereas a maximum security bed costs $80,000. Although there is no reliable estimate of the cost of halfway houses, they are considerably less expensive than prisons because of their lower security requirements. For example, in Texas the state pays $30 per day to house an offender in a halfway house.[49] More than 90 percent of halfway houses are operated by private agencies that contract with the government to provide services for inmates.

PURPOSES OF HALFWAY HOUSES

Halfway houses refer residents for counseling, treatment, and employment services, and some provide these services themselves. Thus, halfway houses provide extra custody and services for offenders on probation, or less secure custody and services for offenders after prison. Offenders serving time in halfway houses often have no residence of their own and no family members who are willing to take them in. The halfway house provides food and shelter for a short period, enabling the offender to obtain a stable job and enough income to become self-sufficient.

There are no national data on the effectiveness of halfway houses, but individual reports have shown that they provide a useful, relatively low-cost transition for inmates returning to the community.[50] Their impact on recidivism has not been studied systematically, although it appears that recidivism rates for halfway house residents are comparable to those for offenders on parole.[51] This finding is significant, given that offenders in halfway houses are probably at higher basic risk of reoffending because of their lack of supportive family ties.

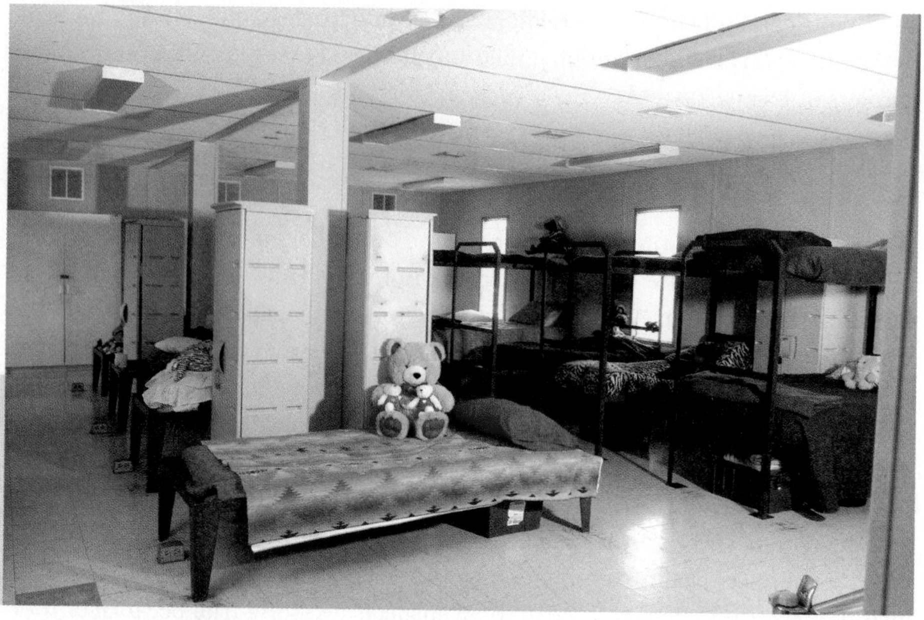

A halfway house for parolees making the transition from prison back into society. What types of offenders should be placed in halfway houses? Should all offenders get the opportunity to live in a halfway house near the end of their prison term?

PUBLIC ACCEPTANCE?

A continuing problem with halfway houses is public acceptance. Most people are reluctant to have ex-offenders living in their neighborhoods. Media accounts of offenders escaping from halfway houses exacerbate the problem, although it is not clear how often this occurs.[52] Communities are more receptive, however, when they are given a voice in the usage and operation of the halfway house, when some space in the halfway house is available to community organizations, and when efforts are made to show how the residents might make a positive contribution to the neighborhood.[53] For example, halfway houses can help to stabilize a deteriorating neighborhood by establishing a visible presence of residents in a well-kept building that is open for community use.

Pardons and Commutations

pardon
A reprieve from a governor or from the president that excuses a convicted offender and allows release from prison without any supervision.

A **pardon** is not actually a form of sentence, but it does allow a convicted offender to be released from prison without any supervision. Historically, pardons have been used as a form of parole to reward "reformed" offenders or those who in hindsight were deemed to have been given too severe a sentence. From the late 1700s to the late 1800s, for example, England sent its prisoners to Australia. The governor there could release convicts from their sentences by granting an *absolute pardon*, which restored all rights, including the right to return to England. A *conditional pardon* gave the convict Australian citizenship but not the right to return to England. A *ticket of leave* freed convicts from their obligation to work for the government or for a master and allowed them to work elsewhere.[54] The power to pardon resided in the king or queen. When the United States Constitution was drafted, the president was given the power to pardon. Article II states that the president "shall have power to grant reprieves and pardons for offenses against the United States, except in cases of impeachment."

TICKET OF LEAVE

There is considerable evidence that pardons were once used as a form of parole. During the mid-1800s more than 40 percent of offenders released from prisons were pardoned. In Ohio, pardons were granted to inmates to make room for new prisoners. Similar circumstances existed in other states until parole was adopted to make the release process more standardized and objective.[55]

CLEMENCY

Today pardons are acts of clemency rather than a kind of parole. They are entrusted to the chief executive: the governor in the case of state offenses, the president in the case of federal crimes. For example, in 2000 President Clinton pardoned a black man who had been a fugitive since 1961, after he fled after being sentenced to eighteen months in prison for draft evasion. The man refused to respond to an all-white draft board that would address him only by his first name after it learned he was black.[56] The pardon enabled the man, now sixty-three, to return to the United States without fear of arrest. A pardon excuses the offender from criminal penalties. Pardons are rare, and in most cases they are granted in order to remedy a miscarriage of justice. In many cases people serving prison sentences for murder have been pardoned when it was discovered that someone else committed the crime. On a less dramatic level, first offenders' criminal records are expunged if they complete special conditions and are not rearrested within a specified period; technically, this constitutes a pardon.

Pardon is distinguished from **commutation,** which modifies or reduces a sentence imposed on an offender. Commutations of death sentences to life imprisonment occur occasionally, especially during the holiday season. It is common for a governor to commute the sentence of a death row inmate as a sign of humane concern; this gesture is often made at the end of the governor's term and therefore cannot harm him or her politically.

commutation
A modification or reduction of a sentence imposed on an offender.

What Are Forms of Authentic and Restorative Justice?

In California an eighteen-year-old boy pleaded guilty to burning a cross on the lawn of a black family's home. No one was hurt, but a crime was committed. What would have been an appropriate sentence? Jail? Probation? A fine? The judge ordered the offender to read *The Diary of Anne Frank,* the journal of a young girl in hiding during the Nazi Holocaust. The offender had to submit a book report to the court.[57]

In a Maryland case, a teenager convicted of a drive-by shooting was required to read *The Ox-Bow Incident* and write a report on it while serving his jail sentence. The book describes people who take the law into their own hands and end up injuring the innocent.[58]

In Jacksonville, Florida, a seventeen-year-old girl pleaded guilty to manslaughter after she suffocated her newborn child and left it in a trash can. In addition to two years in prison, the judge imposed ten years on the contraceptive pill as part of the plea agreement.[59]

In each of these cases the judge, believing that no existing sanction was appropriate, invented an alternative sentence that fit the nature of the crime and the offender. The invention of new criminal sanctions became more common in the late twentieth century and has interesting implications both for society and for the criminal justice system.

restorative justice
Criminal justice process that focuses on sanctions directed primarily at repairing the injury to the victim rather than focusing on the adversarial relationship between the government and the offender.

authentic justice
Approach to criminal justice holding that sanctions should be more closely related to crime and that offenders should be punished in ways that neutralize their gain.

retributive model of justice
Traditional approach to criminal justice that emphasizes the role of adversarial proceedings and the government in punishing offenders for their past acts as retribution and deterrence.

Alternative sentences are of two general types: those that center on justice for the victim ("restorative") and those that attempt to punish the offender in accordance with the nature of the offense ("authentic"). In **restorative justice** the criminal justice process focuses primarily on "making the victim whole," or repairing the injury to the victim, rather than on the adversarial relationship between the government and the offender. **Authentic justice** is based on the idea that sanctions should be more closely related to crimes and that offenders should be punished in ways that neutralize their gain.

RESTORATION VERSUS RETRIBUTION

Table 14.1 illustrates the differences between the elements of the restorative justice model and the traditional **retributive model of justice.** The role of the community, the accountability of the offender, and the centrality of victims in the resolution of a case distinguish the restorative model. Programs based on restorative justice principles proliferated during the 1990s; at the same time, "get tough" sentences based on the retributive model also flourished.[60] These simultaneous movements reflect the ambivalence of the public in desiring punishment and protection from criminals on one hand, while also recognizing that repairing the damage caused by crime in a community requires community action, reconciliation, and reparation. Traditionally, the role of government, the adversarial relationship between the government and the offender, and punishment are featured in the retributive model, which still underlies much of contemporary criminal justice.

Authentic justice attempts to link the nature of the penalty with the nature of the offense in a more explicit way than has traditionally been the case. Courts usually accomplish this by having the penalty mimic the crime to the extent possible. Examples of authentic justice, as this section will discuss, include shock

Table 14.1 Characteristics of the Retributive and Restorative Models of Justice

Retributive Justice	*Restorative Justice*
Crimes are acts against the state.	Crimes are acts against another individual or the community.
Crime is controlled by the criminal justice system.	Crime control comes from the community.
Punishment holds offenders accountable.	Assuming responsibility and taking action to remedy harm results in accountability.
Victims are part of the community protected by the criminal justice system.	Victims are harmed by crime and are central in determining accountability.
Justice is pursued through the adversarial system.	Justice is pursued using dialogue and reconciliation, negotiation, and reparation.
The focus is on punishing the crime that occurred in the past.	The focus is on the consequences of the crime and on how to make the victim and community whole again in the future.
Punishment changes behavior through retribution and deterrence.	Punishment alone is not effective, because it disrupts possibilities for harmony within the community.

incarceration, corporal punishment, public humiliation, and medical interventions for sex offenders.

Restitution and Repair

In the most common form of restorative justice, the offender provides **restitution** to the victim. Making restitution usually means paying money, but it can also include returning property or performing services for the victim. For example, an offender may be required to remove graffiti from a building or to earn money to replace stolen or damaged property. In such cases the offender compensates the victim for the loss either directly or indirectly. Restitution serves both as a way to restore the victim to his or her previous condition and as a way to punish the offender. Although there is widespread support for the concept of restitution, this approach is used infrequently in the criminal justice process. Most offenders are poor and have spent or lost any gain they received from the crime. They often possess few job skills and little education, disadvantages that reduce their access to money for restitution.

Community service makes offenders accountable for their harm to the community when direct restitution is not possible. How are these juvenile offenders providing restorative justice? What other types of authentic justice might be applied in their case?

Community service is a way that offenders can be held accountable when direct restitution is not possible. As a condition of release, an offender can be required to work without pay for a civic, nonprofit, or government organization. Restoration of the grounds of public buildings and schools, conservation projects, and maintenance are among the community service tasks that have been performed by offenders. This form of restitution offers offenders the opportunity to make amends with dignity while providing needed services to the community.[61]

restitution
A form of restorative justice that usually takes the form of money, but it can also include returning property or performing services for the victim.

COMMUNITY SERVICE

Although restitution most often takes the form of monetary compensation, the harm caused to victims is very often physical, psychological, and/or emotional in nature. Also, many crimes have indirect victims such as the victim's family, which suffers from the victim's injury or loss of property. In an Alabama case a pregnant woman was killed, but her baby survived. The focus of the criminal case was exclusively on the culpability of the accused person.[62] Very little attention was given to the orphaned infant and the long-term impact of custody decisions. Similarly, there is a growing trend for police to make arrests in domestic violence cases, but less effort has been devoted to supporting the victims of such violence. In Georgia, for example, as many as half the women and children who seek shelter from abusive family members are turned away because of lack of space.[63] The restorative approach seeks to shift the focus of the justice process more toward repairing the harm done to the victim.[64] This is accomplished by direct involvement of victims and the community at large and by a justice process that relies on dialogue, negotiation, accountability, and reparation in achieving justice.

Mediation

After a crime has been committed, it is rare for the offender and the victim ever to speak to each other again. They may not even see each other, except in court. The prosecutor speaks on behalf of the jurisdiction (which includes the victim), and the defense attorney speaks for the accused person. This arrangement further distances the offender from the victim and promotes an adversarial relationship.

mediation
A process providing a forum in which the offender and the victim meet in a neutral setting where they can ask questions, communicate feelings of anger or remorse, and discuss ways in which the balance of justice can be restored in a fair and equitable manner; this may involve an apology, restitution, community service, or other alternative.

Mediation programs provide a forum in which the offender and the victim meet in a neutral setting in an "atmosphere of structured informality."[65] At these meetings both the victim and the offender relate their versions of what happened and how it affected them. They can ask questions, communicate feelings of anger or remorse, and discuss ways in which the balance of justice can be restored in a fair and equitable manner. This may involve an apology, restitution, community service, or other alternative. An agreement is put in writing and the victim and offender discuss a restitution schedule, monitoring of the agreement, and follow-up procedures.[66]

FOUR BENEFITS OF MEDIATION

Four benefits of mediation programs have been identified. First, mediation gives victims direct input into the justice process and lets them help determine an appropriate disposition. Second, mediation enables victims and offenders to communicate on a personal level, rather than through attorneys or not at all. Third, it allows victims to obtain closure on the trauma caused by the criminal event by exercising some control over its ultimate outcome. Fourth, mediation forces offenders to see victims as human beings with hopes, fears, and dreams similar to theirs. It thus leads offenders to understand and feel empathy for others. Studies have found that some victim–offender mediation programs do have these results. Victims are more likely to feel that justice has been done in mediated cases; in addition, higher rates of successful restitution and lower recidivism rates have been reported.[67]

There are nearly three hundred mediation programs in the United States in which victims and offenders meet voluntarily with trained professionals.[68] The outcomes of these meetings often result in innovative dispositions, including help in refurbishing parks, installation of exterior lights, repair or demolition of deteriorated buildings, and community block watch patrols. When offenders participate in constructive efforts to make victims and neighborhoods safer, the goals of both restorative and authentic justice are served.

Shock Incarceration

CHARACTERISTICS OF BOOT CAMPS

At a boot camp for inmates in Florida, the regimen is not easy. One report summed it up: "Heads shaved. No phone calls for forty-four days, then just to family. No TV, no recreation room. Marching in cadence. Obstacle courses. Spartan barracks. Psychological and substance abuse counseling. Five hours of classes. Homework. And a parade of victims, who tell the boys what it feels like on the other side of a gun."[69] This routine is much more severe and demanding than that experienced by most prisoners.

shock incarceration
Short-term military-style "boot camps" designed primarily for nonviolent young offenders and featuring a military atmosphere and strict discipline.

Many such **shock incarceration** programs were developed during the 1980s. They are short-term (three to six months) military-style boot camps designed primarily for nonviolent offenders. Although there is some variation in how boot camp programs are run, they all maintain a military atmosphere and strict discipline, and all are populated by young offenders for short terms. The extent of the camps' military atmosphere is manifested by the fact that the U.S. Army and Marine Corps train corrections officers to serve as drill sergeants in boot camps.[70]

These youthful offenders are undergoing shock incarceration in a military-style boot camp where they will learn to change the lifestyles that contributed to their criminal behavior. What makes this a form of authentic justice? What is the purpose of authentic justice?

Shock incarceration programs are examples of "authentic" justice because they attempt to mirror the nature of the crimes committed more closely than traditional incarceration does. That is, they try to recreate the shock of being victimized through a complete change in routine, attitude, behavior, and discipline. Boot camps are considered a better alternative than long-term imprisonment, where inmates are generally inactive. Shock incarceration forces inmates to engage in physical activity, drills, work, education, and counseling in order to change their attitudes and behavior patterns.

Because of the rigorous physical activity they require, shock incarceration programs are designed for younger offenders. Most programs are designed for inmates who are serving sentences of less than five years or are in the second half of a longer sentence and have good records. Although originally designed for first offenders, a growing number of boot camp programs accept offenders with prior records of incarceration and convictions for violent crimes.

Usually offenders volunteer to participate in boot camps rather than serving a longer sentence in a traditional prison. An underlying premise is that prisons have not been successful in deterring further crimes by offenders after release. The "shock" portion of shock incarceration, like basic training in the military, is designed to alter the offender's attitude, self-control, and lifestyle. Many inmates are not well prepared for shock incarceration. It is difficult to change a lifestyle that has developed over a period of years and is characterized by poor school attendance, drug use, lack of employment, and low levels of physical activity. Nevertheless, shock incarceration attempts to address these lifestyle issues; traditional incarceration, in contrast, tends to reinforce lethargic, unproductive behaviors, which often continue after release.

EVALUATION OF BOOT CAMPS

Evaluations of the impact of shock incarceration programs have revealed mixed results. These programs generally have not reduced recidivism compared to traditional incarceration. At the same time, offenders report that shock incarceration was a constructive experience.[71] In contrast, inmates who serve their sentences in prison do not view their experience as constructive. Part of the reason why boot camps have not had a stronger impact on recidivism is variation in the amount of time devoted to rehabilitative activities such as education; there is also a frequent lack of supervision or follow-up in the community after release. A national survey of fifty-two boot camp programs found that only thirteen had aftercare programs targeted at boot camp "graduates."[72] Therefore, most offenders completing boot camp programs are released to traditional probation or parole supervision, and the behaviors instilled in the boot camp program are not reinforced after release. Thus, offenders are, in essence, starting over when they reach the community. Boot camp graduates who are placed on intensive probation or parole supervision are under greater surveillance than traditional probationers and parolees, but more intensive services such as employment assistance and family counseling are often not provided.

Corporal Punishment and Public Humiliation

An Ohio teenager, Michael Fay, committed acts of vandalism while visiting Singapore. Along with some friends, he spray-painted and threw eggs and bricks at eighteen cars over a ten-day period. Singapore police also found stolen flags and signs in Fay's Singapore apartment. Fay was sentenced to four months in prison, a $2,320 fine, and six lashes with a wet rattan cane. This kind of caning, administered by an expert in martial arts, breaks the skin and leaves permanent scars on the buttocks.[73] The sentence caused an uproar in the United States, with some people defending it and others vehemently opposing it.

corporal punishment Physical punishment short of the death penalty.

Corporal punishment is defined as physical punishment short of the death penalty. It has often been associated with torture and mutilation, and most forms of corporal punishment are illegal in the United States under the Eighth Amendment's prohibition against cruel and unusual punishment. In 1990, however, legislation was introduced in Texas that would have resulted in amputation of a finger for each conviction a drug dealer received.[74] This bill was an effort to imitate the penalty for theft in some Islamic countries, which is amputation of the offender's right hand.[75] Although such a penalty would seem to constitute a violation of the Eighth Amendment, it would be up to the courts to decide whether it was within the "limits of civilized standards" or "totally without penological justification."[76]

FLOGGING

The U.S. State Department protested Michael Fay's punishment in Singapore, claiming that it was too severe. This reaction is interesting in view of the long history of whipping as a form of punishment in America and elsewhere. Whipping was used as a form of punishment as far back as ancient Egypt, where Hebrew slaves were whipped by their Egyptian masters if they failed to produce enough bricks.[77] The Romans, and later the English, used whipping to punish slaves and vagrants. During the early 1800s England prohibited the whipping of women, but it was not until 1948 that whipping was abolished altogether as a form of punishment.[78] Whipping was employed for more offenses in the American colonies than it was in England. Lying, swearing, failure to attend church services, stealing, selling rum to Indians, adultery (for women), and drunkenness were among the crimes for which people could be whipped. After the American Revolution, incarceration came into use as an alternative to whipping. By 1900 all states except Maryland and Delaware had abolished whipping. The last known floggings occurred around 1950 in those two states, and the Delaware law was not repealed until 1972.[79]

Despite the American protests of the whipping in Singapore, the penalty is still used in many countries. A bill to permit whipping of drug dealers was introduced in the Delaware legislature in 1990 but was not passed. Legislation permitting whipping of vandals was introduced in California and in the cities of St. Louis and Sacramento in the early 1990s.[80] Amnesty International has reported that whipping is still legal in at least thirteen countries, including countries in the Middle East, Africa, the Caribbean, and the Far East.[81]

Singapore responded to criticism of its use of corporal punishment by stating that "it is because of our tough laws against antisocial crime . . . that we do not have a situation like, say, New York, where even police cars are not spared by vandals."[82] This leads to the question of whether whipping is effective as a deterrent to crime. An evaluation of the impact of whipping on subsequent criminal behavior of convicted offenders in the United States found that 62 percent of offenders who were whipped were later convicted of another offense. Further, 65 percent of those who were whipped twice were convicted a third time.[83] Despite the failure of flogging as a deterrent, whipping and other forms of corporal punishment, such as paddling of schoolchildren, continue to attract attention from the public and some policy makers.[84] There are two reasons for this: Corporal punishment more directly imitates the pain suffered by the victim, and it is of short duration and therefore much less expensive to administer than traditional incarceration.

SHAMING

Another ancient form of "authentic justice," public humiliation, also is newly popular. A judge in Pensacola, Florida, has given people convicted of minor crimes a choice: Serve jail time or buy an ad in the local newspaper that shows their photo and details of the crime.[85] A judge in Albany, New York, ordered a six-time drunken driving offender to place a fluorescent sticker saying "Convicted DWI" on his license plates.[86]

"Sentencing by public humiliation" has taken many different forms over its long history. In ancient Greece, deserters from the army were displayed in public wearing women's clothes. In England, public drunkards were walked through the streets wearing only a barrel.[87] Bridles were used on certain offenders in England and colonial America. These devices looked like cages that fit over the head with a metal plate that fit into the mouth. Any movement of the tongue was painful. Bridles were used primarily on "scolds," women who habitually lied or found fault with others.[88] Use of stocks, pillories, and the ducking stool continued in England, France, and America until the early 1800s. These devices held the offender in public view in extremely uncomfortable positions for the purpose of ridicule and punishment. Although the punishment itself was not painful, it was humiliating and exposed the offender to abusive remarks and to objects thrown by passersby. Offenders were sometimes seriously injured or killed when exposed in this manner.[89]

BRANDING

Branding of offenders through permanent scarring dates back to the beginnings of Western civilization. It was used in ancient Greece, and in fourth-century England offenders were branded on their thumbs (e.g., M for murderer) so that a judge could determine whether a person had a prior record. Branding was employed in the United States until the 1800s, and offenders were usually banished from the country.[90] Nathaniel Hawthorne's classic book, *The Scarlet Letter,* written in 1850, described the seventeenth-century practice of forcing offenders to sew letters on their clothing to represent the crimes they had committed. The letters (and sometimes complete descriptions of offenses, worn around the neck) were often used in the American colonies as punishments for blasphemy and public drunkenness.[91]

These sentences have been mimicked in recent years, although not duplicated. Some judges have required men caught soliciting prostitutes and those convicted of other minor crimes to pay to have their names and photos and descriptions of their crimes printed in local newspaper. A judge in Tennessee gives convicted shoplifters who appear before him two choices: serve ten days in jail or stand in front of the store and wear a sign announcing they stole from it. Regency Cruises agreed to pay a $250,000 fine for dumping twenty plastic bags of garbage into the Gulf of Mexico, and the company was forced to run full-page ads in area newspapers stating that it had been convicted of the offense.[92] Are these authentic sanctions, or does public humiliation accomplish no purpose other than shaming? It has been argued that shaming is a useful form of sentencing, because it goes beyond mere punishment and instills feelings of guilt.[93] John Braithwaite claims that the criminal law is "too clumsy and costly a device to be a front-line assault weapon" for sanctioning and preventing crime.[94] He argues that consumer and professional groups, along with self-regulation, are better ways to deter corporate crime; and Braithwaite's argument may hold for the crimes of individuals as well. Just as media exposure of misdeeds and the resulting consumer distrust can do much to prevent repeat offenses by corporations, exposure of individual misdeeds to the media and to neighbors may have a similar impact outside the traditional sentencing process. In this way, public humiliation may exert a deterrent and preventive effect that traditional prison and probation criminal sentences have been unable to achieve with any consistency.

Public humiliation sentences often are linked to reduced sentences or to no jail time, so they are rarely challenged in court. When they have been challenged, they have been found to be constitutional under most circumstances.[95] Public humiliation sentences are still rare, however, and no evaluation of their impact has been conducted. It will be interesting to see if public shaming has any greater effect than other forms of sentencing. Nevertheless, the line must be carefully drawn between sanctions that attempt to be more authentic in relation to the crime committed and those that are simply cruel or vindictive.

Forced Birth Control and Chemical Castration

FORCED BIRTH CONTROL

Darlene Johnson, the mother of four children and pregnant with a fifth, was convicted of three counts of child abuse. The Visalia, California, judge sentenced her to a year in jail, to be followed by implantation of a birth-control device that would prevent her from conceiving any more children. According to the judge, "It is not safe for her to have children."[96] Is such a sentence cruel and unusual, or is it authentic justice?

The contraceptive Norplant was approved for public use by the U.S. Food and Drug Administration in 1990. Norplant prevents conception when six small rods containing hormones are placed under the skin in a woman's arm. The rods can be implanted for a period up to five years.[97] The question for criminal justice is whether such a device can or should be used as a condition of sentencing in cases involving mistreatment of children. From the perspective of restorative justice, use of Norplant may prevent abuse of new victims, but it does not address the current or future harm done to present victims. Those who advocate authentic justice believe that use of Norplant is justified because it forces the offender to suffer the consequences of misconduct in the parental role and prevents the offender from continuing in that role in the future. Once again, however, *existing* victims are not protected, only *future* victims.

Norplant has been made available in school clinics in Baltimore in response to the city's high teenage pregnancy rate. A similar program was initiated in Washington, D.C., where teenage mothers accounted for 18 percent of all births.[98] Although this use of Norplant outside the criminal justice system points to growing acceptance of this form of contraception, the coercion inherent in criminal sentencing poses important legal and social issues. Is forced birth control a weak technological attempt to solve a problem that is educational, social, and cultural in nature? Does the use of Norplant discriminate against women, inasmuch as it holds them entirely responsible for parenting and abuse, even though males also play a significant role in this process? Is this contraceptive used in discriminatory fashion against minorities and the poor? Can the use of Norplant be extended beyond the length of a normal jail or probation sentence? These questions have yet to be addressed by the criminal justice system as it looks for sentences that more directly mirror the nature of the harm inflicted by offenders.

CHEMICAL CASTRATION

Frustration over the difficulty of preventing sex offenses also has led to proposals for the use of hormones in sentencing. It has been estimated that rapists commit an average of seven rapes and that a child molester abuses an average of seventy-five children.[99] The state of Washington required male sex offenders to be given the option of castration in return for a 75 percent reduction in prison time.[100] California enacted a law that requires "chemical castration" (by hormones) of parolees with more than one conviction for child molestation.[101] More common, however, are efforts to treat sex offenders with drugs that merely reduce their sex drive.

The compulsion of some sex offenders to seek out victims repeatedly, despite prior punishment for sex crimes, has led researchers to examine possible biological factors in this type of crime. Some researchers have concluded that there are rapists who suffer from an abnormally high level of the male sex hormone testosterone. As a result, these offenders have an "uncontrollable" urge to seek physical "release." Consider the case of Alcides Quiles, who escaped from a Connecticut prison while serving time for raping a six-year-old boy, only to be caught after raping a two-year-old girl.[102] Crimes such as these have led to the use of the drug Depo-Provera, which causes impotence. Sometimes referred to as "chemical castration," medication with Depo-Provera relieves the biological urge in sex offenders.[103] It does this through its active ingredient, a synthetic hormone similar to progesterone. (Depo-Provera is also used as a contraceptive, as one injection protects a woman against pregnancy for three months.)

Such drug treatments remain controversial. Richard Seeley, director of Minnesota's Intensive Treatment Program for Sexual Aggressiveness, argues that "what's wrong with a sex offender is what's between his ears, not his legs." Seeley claims that it is the rapist's thinking that is dysfunctional, not his sexuality. "Rapists are who they learn to be—it's not a product of their hormones."[104] Rape is often the result of anger and rage in which the offender seeks domination or control over the victim. This anger is not affected by Depo-Provera, leading to speculation that assaultive behavior will continue. This debate continues today. A Texas judge offered a sex offender the opportunity for physical castration (removal of the

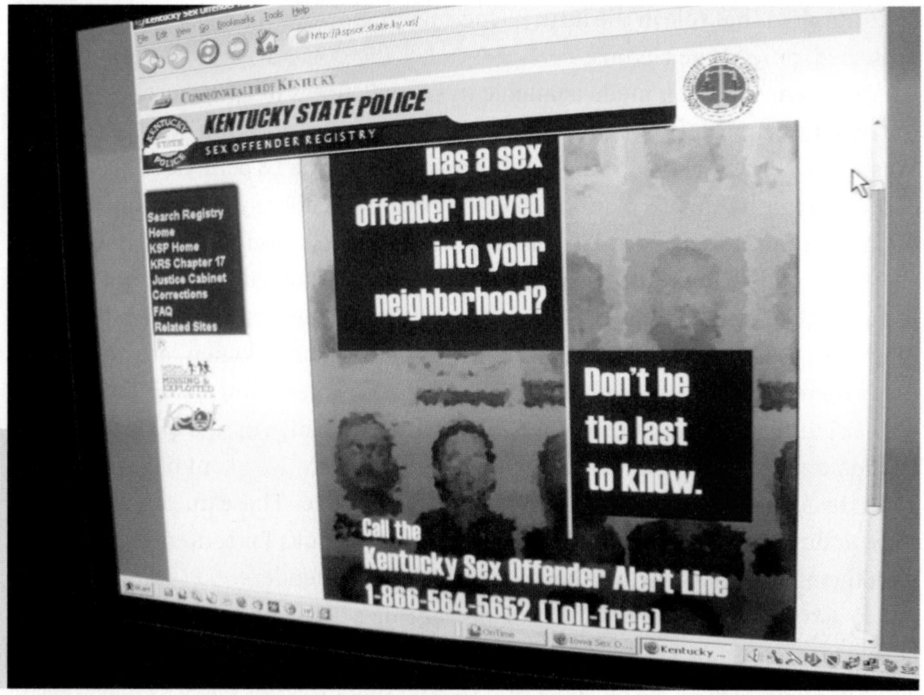

Some states require that convicted rapists and child molesters be registered with police and that the community be warned of their presence. What is the purpose of the sex offender registry? How do you think notification laws affect an ex-convict's reintegration into society?

testicles) in exchange for his freedom. The possibility was abandoned when no physician would come forward to perform the procedure. But this will not always be the case. A Texas gubernatorial candidate supported chemical castration for sex offenders seeking parole.[105]

As with Norplant, the use of Depo-Provera as a sentencing option is an outgrowth of frustration over the ineffectiveness of traditional sentencing alternatives. The social and legal issues posed by Depo-Provera mirror those posed by Norplant, with the added concern that physical castration is a permanent condition. (Chemical castration can be reversed, however, by discontinuation of the drug. This occurred in a Virginia case where a rapist reoffended a few years after he had stopped using the drug.[106]) Chemical castration through Depo-Provera has drawn support not because it is likely to be more effective than traditional sentencing—it is unclear what proportion of rapes have hormonal versus social causes—but because such a sentence more authentically reflects the nature of the crime committed.

Forfeitures and Fees

The "war on drugs" strives to reduce drug abuse and drug-related crime, but long prison sentences for drug offenders have not had a major impact on the drug trade given continued high rates of offending for drug law violations. An alternative to prison sentences is emphasis on a more authentic and restorative sanction: taking the profit out of the highly profitable drug market. The Organized Crime Drug Enforcement Task Force (OCDETF) program, established in 1983 to prosecute high-level drug traffickers, responds to the perception that drug offenders often consider prison sentences merely as a price to be paid for conducting their business. Consisting of members from the major federal law enforcement agencies, OCDETF attempts to seize the illicit assets of drug traffickers. Seizure involves a civil or criminal forfeiture of property if the government can prove that the property was acquired or used illegally. A criminal forfeiture occurs when property is seized after the owner has been convicted of certain crimes, such as drug trafficking or racketeering. A civil forfeiture requires only that the government show probable cause that the property was involved in criminal activity. The burden shifts to the property owner, who must show that such probable cause does not exist.[107] For example, when organized crime boss John Gotti was convicted of racketeering, the government filed a civil forfeiture suit against seven buildings and three businesses that it believed were involved in Gotti's illegal activities. These businesses included a social club, a bar and restaurant, and a clothing manufacturer.[108] Similarly, in a North Carolina case drug traffickers used their illicit profits to buy property within the state; they then sold that property and bought property in Florida. Using asset forfeiture, the government was able to seize the Florida property as "derivative proceeds" of crime.[109]

PURPOSES OF CIVIL FORFEITURE

Cash, cars, boats, planes, jewelry, and weapons constitute 95 percent of all seized assets, although real estate has higher monetary value. Seized property is appraised, and each month the government lists forfeited property in *USA Today* to notify anyone who may hold a claim or lien on the property that the property will be put up for auction. Some jurisdictions allow law enforcement agencies to employ the seized property in combating crime by using seized cars as surveillance vehicles and cash for undercover drug purchases. Seizure of the proceeds of crime, especially the proceeds of high-profit drug crimes, can wipe out any financial gain achieved through illicit activities.

A drug dealer who is found to have packaged drugs in his house, transported them in his car, and held drug-related telephone conversations from his boat can have his house, car, and boat seized under forfeiture provisions in addition to any criminal penalties he may face. In 1997 the Supreme Court ruled that civil forfeitures that occur together with criminal punishment do not violate the constitutional protection against double jeopardy.[110] Therefore, it is not considered double punishment for an offender to be convicted of a crime and incarcerated and then have the government pursue a civil forfeiture. Several instances in which innocent persons lost property and were injured in civil seizures based on false informant tips have resulted in closer scrutiny of the forfeiture process.[111] Congress passed the Civil Asset Forfeiture Reform Act of 2000 in response to these abuses, shifting the burden of proof to the government in showing that a seized item is connected to a crime. This change makes it more difficult to ensnare innocent persons in forfeiture proceedings. Nevertheless, asset forfeiture is an alternative sanction that attempts to address the motives behind profit-driven crimes and restore the balance of justice.

This car, now used by police, was seized by the government because it was used in a crime or was originally purchased with money obtained from crimes. Is it fair to take the property of offenders, if it is being used by family members not part of the original crime?

OFFENDER FEE PROGRAMS

The rising cost of corrections has led many jurisdictions to impose offender fees. These fees are assessed to help pay for the cost of probation, parole, prison, or other forms of correctional supervision. Offender fees are now imposed in forty states, although not all states impose fees on all offenders. Some states restrict fees to probationers or jail inmates, or base the fee on the type of offense, the type of offender, or the offender's ability to pay.

Offender fee programs are based on the recognition that most offenders under community supervision are employed and can afford reasonable fees—and that the costs of operating state and local corrections systems are skyrocketing as correctional populations grow. In Texas, half of the total cost of probation supervision is paid by offender fees, although many offenders are indigent and cannot pay the fees.[112]

Offender fee programs can be seen as a way to hold offenders accountable for their conduct and its long-term consequences. The fees offset the impact the offender has on the criminal justice system by providing compensation to the state. They attempt to reestablish the balance of justice in the community by helping to return the justice system to its previous status before the crime was committed. This is a central tenet of restorative justice.

CRITICAL THINKING EXERCISES

The Return of Chain Gangs

In 1995, Alabama and Florida became the first states to reintroduce chain gangs as a correctional technique. Chain gangs are groups of offenders, sometimes chained together at the ankle, who are taken out of prison to perform roadside cleanup tasks under the supervision of an armed guard. The inmates are returned to the prison at dusk.

On one hand, it can be argued that chain gangs are a part of community corrections. Inmates are on a form of "work release" (albeit under strict supervision) on which they are forced to perform work and returned to prison at the end of the day. Prison officials point out that one corrections officer can supervise up to forty chained prisoners, making chain gangs a cost-effective form of supervision. In addition, chain gangs, unlike inmates in prisons out of public view, serve as a visible deterrent to passersby. The wearing of leg irons has also been said to instill discipline and shame.[a]

On the other hand, chaining criminals together is a throwback to the past; one politician has called it "a return to slavery." Chain gangs were used to control African Americans in the South after the Civil War, and some believe they symbolize a legacy of racial injustice. Chain gangs are humiliating and can make an inmate "feel like an animal." The resulting anger may cause greater frustration and possibly more violence or vengefulness when offenders are released. Furthermore, there is no empirical evidence showing that chain gangs deter future criminal activity.[b]

Nevertheless, certain types of offenders, such as DUI (driving under the influence) offenders, have not responded well to existing forms of punishment. Since 1990 the number of DUI offenders under correctional supervision (jail, prison, probation, parole) has doubled, but a third of DUI offenders on probation and two-thirds of those in jail or prison had prior DUI sentences. Of DUI offenders in jail, more than half were out on probation, parole, or bail at the time of their new offense.[c] Even though many of these offenders were assessed fines or fees or were placed in alcohol or drug treatment programs, the high rate of recidivism has led to support for alternative sentences. Chain gains endeavor to change these offenders through shaming and supervision as well as to repair the harm caused.

CRITICAL THINKING QUESTIONS

1. In what ways are chain gangs similar to and different from work release and intensive supervision?
2. If jail and probation have not deterred repeat DUI offenders, why do you believe work on a chain gang would be any different?
3. How can it be argued that work on a chain gang is dehumanizing? Does this correctional technique violate the Eighth Amendment?

NOTES

a. "Florida Reintroduces Chain Gangs," *Harvard Law Review* 109 (February 1996), pp. 876–81; Tessa M. Gorman, "Back on the Chain Gang: Why the Eighth Amendment and the History of Slavery Proscribe the Resurgence of Chain Gangs," *California Law Review* 85 (March 1997), pp. 441–78; Adam Cohen, "Back on the Chain Gang," *Time* (May 15, 1995), p. 26.

b. Marylee N. Reynolds, "Back on the Chain Gang," *Corrections Today* 58 (April 1996), pp. 108–15; Emily S. Sanford, "The Propriety and Constitutionality of Chain Gangs," *Georgia State University Law Review* 13 (July 1997), pp. 1155–86; Lori Sharn, "Chain Gangs Back in Alabama," *USA Today* (May 4, 1995), p. 3; James F. Anderson, Laronistine Dysun, and Willie Brooks, "Alabama Chain Gangs: Reverting to Archaic Punishment to Reduce Crime and Discipline Offenders," *The Western Journal of Black Studies*, vol. 24 (spring 2000), p. 9.

c. Laura M. Maruschak, *DWI Offenders under Correctional Supervision* (Washington, DC: Bureau of Justice Statistics, 1999); "Chain Gang Revived by Butler County Sheriff (Ohio)," *Associated Press State & Local Wire* (May 15, 2005).

Registering Former Sex Offenders

The public has grave doubts about the ability of community corrections to control the conduct of ex-offenders. Nowhere is this more evident than in the case of sex offenders. Public concern reached a crescendo when a seven-year-old New Jersey girl, Megan Kanka, was raped and murdered by a twice-convicted sex offender who was living across the street. Within six months of the incident, New Jersey passed "Megan's Law," a statute requiring former sex offenders on probation, parole, or furlough to register with police and for communities to be warned when such an offender was living there. The law also requires offenders to notify police of their location every ninety days and calls for penalties of seven months in jail and a fine if they do not comply.

Despite legal challenges, most states have followed New Jersey's lead. Once a sex offender has served his or her sentence, critics argue, the punishment has ended. Registration and notification laws allow a criminal sentence to continue as long as the offender lives, thereby punishing the offender again and again. The Supreme Court ruled in 1995, however, that it is constitutional to notify a community when a former sex offender lives there or moves into the area. The Court has rejected other challenges to New Jersey's Megan's Law, and the provisions of that law have now been adopted by most states.[a] In most states there are publicly accessible Internet sites that contain information on individual sex offenders, and a national database is under construction.[b]

The availability of this information to the public has led to vigilante behavior. Four days after one paroled child molester's name was listed, his car was fire-bombed; the crime was allegedly carried out by his neighbors. A New Jersey man was attacked and beaten up by his son and two other men, who mistakenly believed that he was a child molester. Five bullets were shot through the front window of the house of a former sex offender, after police circulated fliers in the area identifying him by name, address, and photograph. Two registered sex offenders were murdered in Washington.[c] Notification of the community regarding the release of sex offenders appears to produce panic rather than providing useful information, a problem compounded by out-of-date address information in state databases. The notification itself implies that the state has some belief that the freed sex offender may still be dangerous, so it is not surprising that there have been some extreme reactions.

Even though a small percent of all offenders are sex offenders, these cases are highly publicized, and public concern is quite high.[d]

Despite recidivism rates that are not high, even a single instance of reoffending engenders great public apprehension. This public apprehension, combined with increasingly restrictive sex offender reporting laws, might be driving sex offenders underground so their addresses are not known. It is important that public notification offers support and not simply fear. Otherwise, sex offenders will run in fear of the law and of the public; the public will live in fear of former sex offenders who may or may not be dangerous; and former offenders will be deprived of any chance to re-enter society.

CRITICAL THINKING QUESTIONS

1. How is sex offender registration similar to house arrest or electronic monitoring of offenders?
2. Why do you believe sex offenders have been singled out for attention, rather than offenders who have committed murder, aggravated assault, or other serious crimes?
3. In what ways do you believe community notification is helpful or alarming to the public?

NOTES

a. Steve Marshall, "Megan's Law Upheld," *USA Today* (July 26, 1995), p. 2; *Connecticut v. Doe,* 123 501 1160 (2003); "New Jersey's Megan's Law on Sex Offenders Left Intact by Nation's Highest Court," *Buffalo News* (February 23, 1998), p. 4.; *Smith v. Doe,* 123 S.Ct. 1140 (2003).

b. Devon B. Adams, *Summary of State Sex Offender Registries* (Washington, DC: Bureau of Justice Statistics, 2002); "Remarks by President Bush in Signing of H.R. 4472, the Adam Walsh Child Protection and Safety Act of 2006," *PR Newswire* (July 27, 2006).

c. Arlyn Tobias Gajilan and Beth Glenn, "Sex-Crime Database," *Newsweek* (August 11, 1997), p. 12; Paul Leavitt, "Sexual Predators," *USA Today* (August 28, 1993), p. 3; Robert Hanley, "Shots Fired at House of Rapist," *New York Times* (June 17, 1998), p. B1; Tomas Alex Tizon, "Two Registered Sex Offenders are Slain," *Los Angeles Times* (September 4, 2005).

d. Peter Finn, *Sex Offender Community Notification* (Washington, DC: National Institute of Justice, 1997); Robert E. Freeman-Longo, *Revisiting Megan's Law and Sex Offender Registration: Prevention or Problem* (Lexington, KY: American Probation and Parole Association, 2001).

SUMMARY

WHAT ARE THE ALTERNATIVES TO INCARCERATION?

- Monetary fines are the most common form of criminal sanction in the United States. Fines are used primarily in cases involving minor crimes or as an adjunct to incarceration for more serious offenses.
- Fines have problems of proportionality and collection, which can be overcome to some extent by the use of "day fines" based on offenders' daily earnings.
- Probation is a system in which offenders are allowed to live in the community under supervision. Offenders who are sentenced to probation usually have conditions attached to their sentences.
- Supervision of offenders in the community poses the risk that these offenders may commit further crimes.
- Dissatisfaction with probation, combined with the need to use prison space more efficiently, has produced a movement toward intermediate sanctions, which provide more rigorous supervision than normal probation yet are less expensive than incarceration.
- Jurisdictions achieve intensive supervision by maintaining small caseloads, making frequent contact with offenders under supervision, and imposing special conditions such as random drug tests.
- An offender under home confinement or house arrest may leave his or her residence only for approved reasons. Compliance is increasingly ensured through electronic monitoring.

HOW CAN EX-OFFENDERS RETURN TO THE COMMUNITY AFTER PRISON?

- The purpose of parole is to allow inmates to serve the last part of their sentence in the community under supervision in order to readjust to freedom.
- Parole is associated with indeterminate sentencing. Parole release is decided by a parole board consisting of corrections officers.
- Offenders who are not released by a parole board can be granted supervised mandatory release if they accumulate enough good-time credits.
- Because prolonged incarceration can reduce inmates' capacity to function outside of prison, some states have temporary release programs that allow inmates to enter the community for work, study, or other purposes.
- Work or study release programs permit eligible inmates to work or take courses outside the prison during the day and return to the prison at night. Furloughs are unsupervised leaves from prison for specific purposes and are granted for only a few hours.
- Halfway houses are residential centers for ex-offenders in the community. These facilities refer residents for counseling, treatment, and employment services.
- A pardon allows a convicted offender to be released from prison without any supervision. A pardon excuses the offender from criminal penalties—unlike a commutation, which modifies or reduces a sentence.

WHAT ARE FORMS OF AUTHENTIC AND RESTORATIVE JUSTICE?

- Advocates of restorative justice believe that who wins the case is less important than "making the victim whole."
- In the most common form of restorative justice, the offender provides restitution to the victim.
- Mediation programs provide a neutral setting in which offenders and victims can ask each other questions and communicate their feelings about the offense.
- Some forms of restorative justice are designed to repair the physical or psychological harm done to the victim.
- Authentic justice seeks to link the nature of the penalty with the nature of the offense in a direct, tangible way.
- Shock incarceration creates a military-style boot camp atmosphere in which inmates are forced to engage in physical activity, drills, work, education, and counseling. Usually offenders volunteer to participate in boot camps rather than serving a longer sentence in a traditional prison.
- Corporal punishment is physical punishment short of the death penalty. It has a long history in the United States, and it is supported by some advocates of authentic justice because it imitates the pain suffered by the victim.
- Public humiliation also has a long history and can take many different forms. Although there is renewed interest in this approach, public humiliation sentences are still rare.
- Forced birth control has been used as a punishment in cases involving child abuse.

- Some jurisdictions have attempted to treat sex offenders with drugs that reduce their sex drive. These treatments are controversial, because some experts believe that the behavior of sex offenders is psychologically rather than biologically motivated.
- Forfeiture of assets is increasingly being used in cases involving drug trafficking.
- Some jurisdictions impose offender fees on offenders under community supervision who are employed and can afford reasonable fees.

KEY TERMS

community corrections *392*
sanctions *392*
intermediate sanctions *398*
intensive supervision *398*
house arrest *399*
electronic monitoring *399*
net widening *399*
good-time credits *401*
maxing out *401*
parole release *402*
work release *403*
study release *404*
furloughs *404*
halfway houses *405*
pardon *406*
commutation *407*
restorative justice *408*
authentic justice *408*
retributive model of justice *408*
restitution *409*
mediation *410*
shock incarceration *410*
corporal punishment *412*

QUESTIONS FOR REVIEW AND DISCUSSION

1. Why could it be said that the phrase *community corrections* is a contradiction in terms?
2. What do we mean when we say that there is a problem of proportionality in the use of fines as a criminal sanction?
3. What kinds of conditions are usually attached to the sentences of offenders on probation?
4. In what circumstances does probation appear to work best?
5. What are the advantages and disadvantages of house arrest?
6. What is parole, and why is it unpopular with the public?
7. Why are inmates sometimes permitted to participate in work release programs?
8. What is a halfway house?
9. What is the difference between a pardon and a commutation?
10. What legal issues are associated with probation and parole?
11. What is the philosophy underlying restorative justice?
12. What are the major forms of restorative justice?
13. What is meant by authentic justice?
14. What are the main features of shock incarceration, and what is their purpose?
15. What are some drawbacks of boot camp programs?
16. Briefly describe the history of corporal punishment in the United States.
17. Give an example of public humiliation as a criminal sanction.
18. What are some arguments against the use of forced birth control for child abusers?
19. Why is the use of drug treatments for sex offenders controversial?
20. What is the purpose of forfeiture of assets in drug trafficking cases?
21. What are offender fees?

NOTES

1. Associated Press, "Fake Cop Gets Unique Punishment," *Richmond Times–Dispatch* (August 4, 2000), p. B7.
2. Lawrence M. Friedman, *A History of American Law,* 2nd ed. (New York: Basic Books, 1985), p. 596.
3. Michael N. Castle, *Alternative Sentencing: Selling It to the Public* (Washington, DC: National Institute of Justice, 1991), p. 1; Dan M. Kahan, "What Do Alternative Sanctions Mean?," *University of Chicago Law Review* 63 (spring 1996),

pp. 591–653; Heather Mason Kiefer, "Public on Justice System, Fair But Still Too Soft," *Gallup Poll* (February 3, 2004).

4. Leena Kurki, *Incorporating Restorative and Community Justice into American Sentencing and Corrections* (Washington, DC: National Institute of Justice, 1999); "If Not Jail, What?," *The Economist* 337 (December 9, 1995), p. 26; Paul von Zielbauer, "Rethinking the Key Thrown Away," *New York Times* (September 29, 2003).
5. Cited in Castle, *Alternative Sentencing*, p. 2; Laura A. Winterfield and Sally T. Hillsman, *The Staten Island Day-Fine Project* (Washington, DC: National Institute of Justice, 1993), p. 1; Julian V. Roberts and Mike Hough, eds., *Changing Attitudes to Punishment: Public Opinion, Crime and Justice* (Portland, OR: Willan, 2002).
6. David J. Rothman, *The Discovery of the Asylum* (Boston: Little, Brown, 1971), p. 52.
7. Ibid., pp. 48–49.
8. U.S. Comptroller General, *National Fine Center* (Washington, DC: U.S. General Accounting Office, 1993).
9. U.S. Comptroller General, *National Fine Center: Progress Made, But Challenges Remain for Criminal Debt System* (Washington, DC: U.S. Government Accountability Office, 1995).
10. Adam Liptak, "Debt to Society Is Least of Costs for Ex-Convicts," *New York Times* (February 23, 2006); U.S. Government Accountability Office, *Criminal Debt* (Washington, DC: GAO, 2005).
11. Winterfield and Hillsman, *The Staten Island Day-Fine Project;* Vera Institute of Justice, *How to Use Structured Fines (Day Fines) as an Intermediate Sanction* (Washington, DC: Bureau of Justice Assistance, 1996).
12. John Augustus, *John Augustus, First Probation Officer* (Montclair, NJ: Patterson Smith, 1972), p. 34.
13. David Rothman, *Conscience and Convenience: The Asylum and Its Alternatives in Progressive America* (Boston: Little, Brown, 1980), p. 44.
14. National Institute of Corrections, *State and Local Probation Systems in the United States* (Washington, DC: U.S. Department of Justice, 1993); National Advisory Commission on Criminal Justice Standards and Goals, *Corrections* (Washington, DC: U.S. Government Printing Office, 1973), p. 316.
15. Jay S. Albanese, Bernadette A. Fiore, Jerie H. Powell, and Janet R. Storti, *Is Probation Working?: A Guide for Managers and Methodologists* (Lanham, MD: University Press of America, 1981); Sandy Jung and Edward P. Rawana, "Risk and Need Assessment of Juvenile Offenders," *Criminal Justice and Behavior*, vol. 26 (1999), p. 69.
16. Lauren E. Glaze and Seri Palla, *Probation and Parole in the United States* (Washington, DC: Bureau of Justice Statistics, 2005).
17. Steven K. Smith and Marika Litras, *Compendium of Federal Justice Statistics* (Washington, DC: Bureau of Justice Statistics, 2002).
18. Patrick A. Langan and Mark A. Cuniff, *Recidivism of Felons on Probation* (Washington, DC: Bureau of Justice Statistics, 1992); Thomas P. Bonczar, *Characteristics of Adults on Probation* (Washington, DC: Bureau of Justice Statistics, 1997).
19. Don M. Gottfredson, *Effects of Judges' Sentencing Decisions on Criminal Careers* (Washington, DC: National Institute of Justice, 1999).
20. Todd R. Clear and Patricia Hardyman, "The New Intensive Supervision Movement," *Crime and Delinquency* 36 (1990), pp. 42–60; Rebecca D. Petersen and Dennis J. Palumbo, "The Social Construction of Intermediate Punishments," *Prison Journal* 77 (March 1997), pp. 77–92; Gail Caputo, *Intermediate Sanctions in Corrections* (Denton, TX: North Texas Crime and Criminal Justice Series, 2004).
21. Billie S. Irwin and Lawrence A. Bennett, *New Dimensions in Probation: Georgia's Experience with Intensive Probation Supervision* (Washington, DC: National Institute of Justice, 1987); Billie S. Irwin, "Turning Up the Heat on Probationers in Georgia," *Federal Probation* 50 (1986), p. 2; Philip L. Reichel and Billie D. Sudbrack, "Differences among Eligibles: Who Gets an ISP sentence? (Intensive Supervision Probation)," *Federal Probation*, vol. 58 (December 1994), pp. 51–58.
22. Allen J. Beck, *Correctional Populations in the United States* (Washington, DC: Bureau of Justice Statistics, 2002).
23. Joan Petersilia and Susan Turner, *Evaluating Intensive Supervision Probation/Parole: Results of a Nationwide Experiment* (Washington, DC: National Institute of Justice, 1993).
24. Ian D. Brownlee, "Intensive Probation with Young Adult Offenders: A Short Reconviction Study," *British Journal of Criminology* 35 (autumn 1995), pp. 599–612.
25. Petersilia and Turner, *Evaluating Intensive Supervision Probation/Parole*, p. 9.
26. Dale Parent, Terence Dunworth, Douglas McDonald, and William Rhodes, *Intermediate Sanctions* (Washington, DC: National Institute of Justice, 1997), p. 4.
27. Liz Marie Marciniak, "The Use of Day Reporting as an Intermediate Sanction: A Study of Offender Targeting and Program Termination," *The Prison Journal* 79 (June 1999), pp. 205–25; Liz Marie Marciniak, "The Addition of Day Reporting to Intensive Supervision Probation: A Comparison of Recidivism Rates (Statistical Data Included)," *Federal Probation*, vol. 64 (June 2000), p. 34.
28. Virginia State Crime Commission, *The Use of Home Electronic Incarceration in Virginia* (Richmond: Commonwealth of Virginia, 1998).
29. Dennis Wagner and Christopher Baird, *Evaluation of the Florida Community Control Program* (Washington, DC: National Institute of Justice, 1993).
30. J. Robert Lilly, Richard A. Ball, David Curry, and John McMullen, "Electronic Monitoring of the Drunk Driver: A Seven-Year Study of the Home Confinement Alternative," *Crime and Delinquency* 39 (1993), pp. 462–84.
31. James Bonta, Suzanne Wallace-Capretta, and Jennifer Rooney, "Can Electronic Monitoring Make a Difference? An Evaluation of Three Canadian Programs," *Crime and Delinquency* 46 (January 2000), pp. 61–75.
32. Randy R. Gainey and Brian K. Payne, "Understanding the Experience of House Arrest with Electronic Monitoring: An Analysis of Quantitative and Qualitative Data," *International Journal of Offender Therapy and Comparative Criminology* 44 (2000), pp. 84–96; Terry L. Baumer and Robert I. Mendelsohn, "Electronically Monitored Home Confinement: Does It Work?," in James M. Byrne, Arthur J. Lurigio, and Joan Petersilia, eds., *Smart Sentencing: The Emergence of Intermediate Sanctions* (Newbury Park, CA: Sage, 1995), pp. 54–67.
33. Brendan O'Shaughnessy, "Many Suspects Violate Home Detention," *Indianapolis Star* (March 24, 2006).
34. Baumer and Mendelsohn, "Electronically Monitored Home Confinement."
35. "Paterson," *USA Today* (June 1, 1992), p. 8.

36. "Trenton," *USA Today* (October 9, 1992), p. 10; "Newark," *USA Today* (January 16, 1995), p. 6.
37. Tony Fabelo, *"Technocorrections": The Promises, the Uncertain Threats* (Washington, DC: National Institute of Justice, 2000).
38. David A. Leib, "States Move Toward Lifetime GPS Tracking of Sex Offenders," *InformationWeek* (August 1, 2005): Susan Welch, "GPS Helps Keep Offenders in Line," *St. Louis Post-Dispatch* (March 12, 2006).
39. Matthew R. Derose and Patrick A. Langan, *Felony Sentences in State Courts* (Washington, DC: Bureau of Justice Statistics, 2004).
40. Don M. Gottfredson, Leslie T. Wilkins, and Peter B. Hoffman, *Guidelines for Parole and Sentencing* (Lexington, MA: Lexington Books, 1978).
41. Belinda Rodgers McCarthy and Bernard J. McCarthy Jr., *Community-Based Corrections,* 4th ed. (Belmont, CA: Wadsworth, 2003), p. 270.
42. Lauren E. Glaze and Seri Palla, *Probation and Parole in the United States* (Washington, DC: Bureau of Justice Statistics, 2005).
43. William J. Sabol, William P. Adams, Barbara Parthasarathy, and Yan Yuan, *Offenders Returning to Prison, 1986–97* (Washington, DC: Bureau of Justice Statistics, 2000); Joan Petersilia, "Parole and Prisoner Reentry in the United States," in *Crime and Justice: A Review of Research,* vol. 26 (Chicago: University of Chicago Press, 1999). pp. 479–529.
44. Linda Smith, "Intermediate Sanctions: Getting Tough in the Community," in Ira J. Silverman and Manuel Vega, eds., *Corrections: A Comprehensive View* (St. Paul, MN: West, 1996), p. 520; Nicholas Stein, "Business Behind Bars: Put prisoners to Work," *Fortune,* vol. 148 (September 15, 2003), p. 161.
45. Christy A. Visher and Jeremy Travis, "Transitions from Prison to Community: Understanding Individual Pathways," *Annual Review of Sociology,* vol. 29 (August 2003), pp. 89–113; *The Corrections Yearbook* (Middletown, CT: Criminal Justice Institute, 2002).
46. Oliver J. Keller and Benedict S. Alper, *Halfway Houses: Community-Centered Correction and Treatment* (Lexington, MA: Lexington Books, 1970); Donald J. Thalheimer, *Halfway Houses* (Washington, DC: U.S. Government Printing Office, 1975); Gail Caputo, *Intermediate Sanctions in Corrections* (Denton, TX: North Texas Crime and Criminal Justice Series, 2004).
47. Marissa Ballinger, Katherine Kravetz, Eric Lotke, Theresa Rowland, Vincent Schiraldi, and Jason Zeidenberg, *Half Truths: The Complicated Story of D.C.'s Halfway House Escapes* (Washington, DC: The Justice Policy Institute, 1999).
48. *The Corrections Yearbook, 2002.*
49. Kelley Shannon, "State-Run Halfway Houses Possible for Some Felons," *Dallas Morning News* (July 14, 2000), p. 1.
50. John Hopkins, "Halfway Houses are a Small Safety Net," *Virginian–Pilot* (August 13, 2000), p. 1; Edward Latessa and Harry Allen, "Halfway Houses and Parole: A National Assessment," *Journal of Criminal Justice* 10 (1982), p. 161.
51. P. G. Connelly and B. R. Forschner, "Predictors of Success in a Co-Correctional Halfway House: A Discriminant Analysis," in T. Ellsworth, ed., *Contemporary Community Corrections* (Prospect Heights, IL: Waveland Press, 1992).
52. Cheryl W. Thompson, "Hundred Escaping from Halfway Houses," *Washington Post* (January 2, 1999), p. A1; Ballinger et al., *Half Truths: The Complicated Story of D.C.'s Halfway House Escapes.*
53. Margot C. Lindsay, *A Matter of Principle: Public Involvement in Residential Community Corrections* (Washington, DC: National Institute of Corrections, 1990).
54. Richard Hughes, *The Fatal Shore* (New York: Knopf, 1987).
55. Christopher Hibbert, *The Roots of Evil: A Social History of Crime and Punishment* (Boston: Little, Brown, 1968).
56. "Ex-Georgian Returns after Pardon," United Press International (February 23, 2000); "Homecoming King: After 39 Years, Preston King Gets a Presidential Pardon That Puts an End to His Exile," *People Weekly* (March 13, 2000), p. 89.
57. Cited in Marilyn D. McShane and Wesley Krause, *Community Corrections* (New York: Macmillan, 1993), p. 4.
58. "Judge Throws Book at Shooter," *Buffalo News* (April 14, 1995), p. 3.
59. Paul Leavitt, "Birth Control Sentence," *USA Today* (November 15, 1990), p. 3.
60. Kurki, *Incorporating Restorative and Community Justice into American Sentencing and Corrections.*
61. Richard J. Maher and Cheryl Holmes, "Community Service: A Way for Offenders to Make Amends," *Federal Probation* 61 (March 1997), pp. 26–28.
62. Etta F. Morgan and Ida M. Johnson, "Kidnapping and Murder for Motherhood," paper presented at the Annual Meeting of Southern Criminal Justice Association, Richmond, Virginia, 1997.
63. Elizabeth H. McConnell, "Issues in Family Violence in Georgia," paper presented at the Annual Meeting of the Southern Criminal Justice Association, Richmond, Virginia, 1997.
64. Sharon Levrant, Francis T. Cullen, Betsy Fulton, and John F. Wozniak, "Reconsidering Restorative Justice: The Corruption of Benevolence Revisited?," *Crime and Delinquency* 45 (January 1999); Gerry Johnstone, ed. *Restorative Justice: Key Readings* (Devon, UK: Willan Publishing, 2003).
65. Martin Wright and Burt Galway, eds., *Mediation and Criminal Justice: Victims, Offenders, and Community* (Newbury Park, CA: Sage, 1989), p. 2; Allison Morris, ed. *Restorative Justice for Juveniles: Conferencing, Mediation and Circles* (Oxford, UK: Hart Publishing, 2001).
66. Robert Coates and John Gehm, "An Empirical Assessment," in Wright and Galway, eds., *Mediation and Criminal Justice,* pp. 251–56.
67. Mark S. Umbreit, "Victim–Offender Mediation in Canada: The Impact of an Emerging Social Work Intervention," *International Social Work* 42 (April 1999); Mark Umbreit et al., *Victim Meets Offender: The Impact of Restorative Justice and Mediation* (Monsey, NY: Criminal Justice Press, 1994); Mark S. Umbreit and Mike Niemeyer, "Victim–Offender Mediation: From the Margins toward the Mainstream," *Perspectives* (summer 1996), p. 28.
68. Catherine Edwards, "Paying for What They've Wrought," *Insight on the News,* (July 26, 1999), p. 46.
69. Deborah Sharp, "Boot Camps Try for Rehabilitation," *USA Today* (November 9, 1993), p. 3.
70. Doris Layton MacKenzie, "Boot Camp Programs Grow in Number and Scope," *NIJ Reports* (November– December, 1990), pp. 6–8; Jon R. Sorensen, "Shock Camps Get High Marks Despite Violent Incidents," *Buffalo News* (April 15, 1996), p. 8; James Austin, Michael Jones, and Melissa Bolyard, *The Growing Use of Jail Boot Camps: The Current State of the Art* (Washington, DC: National Institute of Justice, 1993).

71. Angela R. Gover, Doris Layton MacKenzie, and Gaylene J. Styve, "Boot Camps and Traditional Correctional Facilities for Juveniles: A Comparison of the Participants, Daily Activities, and Environments," *Journal of Criminal Justice*, vol. 28 (January 2000), p. 53; Michael Peters, David Thomas, and Christopher Zamberlan, *Boot Camps for Juvenile Offenders* (Washington, DC: Office of Juvenile Justice and Delinquency Prevention, 1997).
72. Blair B. Bourque, Mei Han, and Sarah M. Hill, *A National Survey of Aftercare Provisions for Boot Camp Graduates* (Washington, DC: National Institute of Justice, 1996); Doris Layton MacKenzie, Angela R. Gover, Gaylene Styve Armstrong, and Ojmarrh Mitchell, *A National Study Comparing the Environments of Boot Camps with Traditional Facilities for Juvenile Offenders* (Washington, DC: National Institute of Justice, 2001); Dale G. Parent, *Correctional Boot Camps: Lessons from a Decade of Research* (Washington, DC: National Institute of Justice, 2003).
73. Andrea Stone, "Whipping Penalty Judged Too Harsh—by Some," *USA Today* (March 10, 1994), p. 3.
74. Tom Squitieri, "Proposals Seek More Drastic Punishments," *USA Today* (February 14, 1990), p. 3.
75. Sam S. Souryal and Dennis W. Potts, "The Penalty of Hand Amputation for Theft in Islamic Justice," *Journal of Criminal Justice* 22 (1994), pp. 249–65.
76. *Trop v. Dulles*, 356 U.S. 86 (1958); *Rhodes v. Chapman*, 452 U.S. 337 (1981).
77. W. M. Cooper, *A History of the Rod in all Countries* (London: John Camden Hotten, 1870).
78. L. A. Parry, *The History of Torture in England* (Montclair, NJ: Patterson Smith, 1934); Graham Newman, *The Punishment Response* (New York: Lippincott, 1978).
79. S. Rubin, *The Law of Criminal Correction* (St. Paul, MN: West, 1973).
80. Paul Leavitt, "Calls for Caning Keep on Coming," *USA Today* (May 25, 1994), p. 3.
81. Amnesty International, *2000 Report* (New York: Amnesty International, 2000).
82. Cited in Stone, "Whipping Penalty Judged Too Harsh—by Some."
83. R. G. Caldwell, *Criminology*, 2nd ed. (New York: Ronald Press, 1965).
84. Tamara Henry, "Groups Seek to Lay Down Law on Corporal Discipline," *USA Today* (March 8, 1994), p. 6D; Newman, *The Punishment Response.*
85. "Pensacola," *USA Today* (August 5, 1993), p. 9.
86. "Albany," *USA Today* (June 14, 1995), p. 11.
87. G. Ives, *A History of Penal Methods* (Montclair, NJ: Patterson Smith, 1914).
88. Newman, *The Punishment Response;* William Andrews, *Bygone Punishments* (London: William Andrews, 1899).
89. A. M. Earle, *Curious Punishments of Bygone Days* (Montclair, NJ: Patterson Smith, 1896).
90. H. Oppenheimer, *The Rationale of Punishment* (Montclair, NJ: Patterson Smith, 1913); Parry, *The History of Torture in England.*
91. Earle, *Curious Punishments of Bygone Days.*
92. Tony Mauro, "Judge Orders 'Humiliation' Ads: Papers Uneasy," *USA Today* (December 15, 1990), p. 3; "Albany," *USA Today* (June 14, 1995), p. 11; "Pensacola," *USA Today* (August 5, 1993), p. 9; "Tampa," *USA Today* (December 9, 1994), p. 6; "Brand Shoplifters with a Scarlet Letter?," *Chain Store Age*, vol. 82 (January 2006), p. 17.
93. James Q. Whitman, "What Is Wrong with Inflicting Shame Sanctions?," *Yale Law Journal* 107 (January 1998), pp. 1055–92; Kelly McMurry, "For Shame," *Trial* 33 (May 1997), pp. 12–15.
94. John Braithwaite, "Restorative Justice: Assessing Optimistic and Pessimistic Accounts," *Crime and Justice* 25 (spring 1999); John Braithwaite, *Corporate Crime and the Pharmaceutical Industry* (London: Routledge & Kegan Paul, 1984); John Braithwaite, "Transnational Regulation of the Pharmaceutical Industry," *The Annals* 525 (January 1993).
95. Henry J. Reske, "Scarlet Letter Sentences," *ABA Journal* 82 (January 1996), pp. 16–18; Darryl van Duch, "State High Court Rejects Ridicule as Unreasonable," *The National Law Journal* 19 (May 5, 1997), p. 6.
96. Paul Leavitt, "Birth Control Sentence," *USA Today* (January 7, 1991), p. 3.
97. Kim Painter, "Norplant Gets a Shot in the Arm," *USA Today* (August, 22, 1995), p. 4D.
98. Paul Leavitt, "Baltimore Schools Offer Teens Norplant," *USA Today* (December 4, 1992), p. 3.
99. "Debate: Give Sex Offenders Longer Prison Terms," *USA Today* (March 7, 1990), p. 10; Richard Lacayo, "Sentences Inscribed on Flesh," *Time*, vol. 139 (March 23, 1992), p. 54–55; Larry Helm Spalding, "Florida's 1997 Chemical Castration Law: A Return to the Dark Ages," *Florida State University Law Review*, vol. 25 (winter 1998), pp. 117–39.
100. "Castration Bill," *USA Today* (February 13, 1990), p. 3.
101. Kay-Frances Brody, "A Constitutional Analysis of California's Chemical Castration Statute," *Temple Political and Civil Rights Law Review* 7 (fall 1997), pp. 141–70; David Van Biema, "A Cheap Shot at Pedophilia? California Mandates Chemical Castration for Repeat Child Molesters," *Time*, vol. 148 (September 9, 1996), p. 60.
102. "Tot Killing," *USA Today* (October 20, 1990), p. 3.
103. David Gelman, "The Mind of the Rapist," *Newsweek* (July 23, 1990), pp. 46–53.
104. Dori Stehlin, "Depo-Provera: The Quarterly Contraceptive," *FDA Consumer* (March 1993), p. 47; Owen D. Jones, "Sex, Culture, and the Biology of Rape: Toward Explanation and Prevention," *California Law Review*, vol. 87 (July 1999), p. 827.
105. Tom Squitieri, "Proposals Seek More Drastic Punishments"; Craig Turk, "Kinder Cut: A Limited Defense of Chemical Castration (of Habitual Sex Offenders)," *New Republic*, vol. 217 (August 25, 1997), pp. 12–13.
106. Associated Press, "Chemically Castrated Man Sentenced," *New York Times* (February 3, 1999), p. 25.
107. George N. Aylesworth, *Forfeiture of Real Property: An Overview* (Washington, DC: Bureau of Justice Assistance, 1991).
108. Joseph P. Fried, "Government Sues to Seize Gotti's Ill-Gotten Assets," *New York Times* (January 15, 1993), p. B1.
109. *United States v. One Parcel of Real Estate*, 675 F. Supp. 645 (D. Fla. 1987).
110. *Austin v. United States*, 116 S. Ct. 994 (1996); Jerome Spencer, "Auspices of Austin: Examining Excessiveness of Civil Forfeitures under the Eighth Amendment," *American Criminal Law Review* 35 (fall 1997), pp. 163–89; Matthew Costigan, "Go Directly to Jail, Do Not Pass Go, Do Not Keep House," *Journal of Criminal Law and Criminology* 87 (spring 1997), pp. 719–50; *U.S. v. Ursery*, 117 S. Ct. (1997); Gregory M. Vecchi and Robert T. Sigler, *Assets Forfeiture: A*

Study of Policy and Its Practice (Durham: Carolina Academic Press, 2001).

111. Robert E. Bauman, "Take It Away," *National Review* 47 (February 20, 1995), pp. 34–38; David E. Rovella, "Defenders Argue Arrest Bill Is Too Mild," *The National Law Journal*, vol. 22 (April 24, 2000), p. A1; Kelly P. O'Meara, "When Feds Say Seize and Desist,"*Insight* (August 7, 2000), pp. 20–23.

112. Peter Finn and Dale Parent, *Making the Offender Foot the Bill: A Texas Program* (Washington, DC: National Institute of Justice, 1992); Dale Parent, *Recovering Correctional Costs through Offender Fees* (Washington, DC: National Institute of Justice, 1990); Richard L. Lippke, "Making Offenders Pay—For the Costs of Their Punishment," *Social Theory and Practice*, vol. 25 (spring 1999), p. 61; U.S. Government Accountability Office, *Criminal Debt* (Washington, DC: GAO, 2005); Adam Liptak, "Debt to Society Is Least of Costs for Ex-Convicts," *New York Times* (February 23, 2006).

chapter 15

Justice and Punishment in the Twenty-First Century

Emerging issues in punishment: the search for meaningful penalties beyond prison walls.

CHAPTER OUTLINE

LEARNING OBJECTIVES

- Identify technology-driven innovations in the administration of justice and explain their significance for the criminal justice system.
- Describe new ways of dealing with offenders, such as treatment and intervention programs and alternatives to prison.
- Explain how the correctional system addresses problems in dealing with offenders with mental illness and sex offenders.
- Evaluate problems of women in prison and changing correctional approaches to gender issues in the offender population.
- Identify and describe five major trends that are shaping the future of corrections.
- Analyze the roles of accountability, professionalization, intensive surveillance, treatment, and prevention as current trends in the development of corrections in the United States.

Blane Nordahl may be the most celebrated cat burglar ever. He committed more than 150 burglaries in ten states, stealing a total of $3 million worth of silver from homes. He was a throwback in some ways to the romanticized burglars of detective novels. Nordahl was never armed, never violent, and always avoided confrontations by creeping in at night and never entering bedrooms. He usually stole silver tea sets, bowls, and flatware from homes in upscale neighborhoods. He was ultimately caught by tracing his footprint left at a crime scene.

What is an appropriate sentence for an offender like this? On one hand he is a career criminal, admitting that life as a cat burglar "is like a natural high."[1] On the other hand he is not violent and has never even carried a weapon. Should he be sent to jail or prison even though he is not violent, or is there another sentence that is more fitting to the crime and the offender? This chapter focuses on new and emerging alternatives to more effectively achieve the ends of justice, punishment, and crime prevention in the twenty-first century.

What Are New Ways of Administering Justice and Punishment?

Technological advances, and the realization that virtually all offenders in prison will return to the community one day after serving their sentences, have spurred the creation of new strategies to deal with offenders. The average prison sentence in the United States is approximately five years, and most offenders in prison were sentenced for drug offenses, robbery, burglary, and other crimes for which release from prison is inevitable. Can prisons do more to prepare these offenders for a noncriminal life upon release, and are there more effective and less expensive alternatives to prison for nonviolent offenders?

Technocorrections

technocorrections
The use of technology to monitor offenders and to prevent future crimes.

"PROBATION KIOSKS"

Closely monitoring offenders electronically without locking them up, pharmacological treatments, and genetic risk assessments are examples of what has been called **technocorrections**—the use of technology to monitor offenders and prevent future crimes.[2] Electronic tracking and location systems were described in Chapter 14. The most popular form of this technology is electronic "bracelets" placed around the ankles of probationers to monitor their whereabouts. A more advanced form of this technology is "probation kiosks," which have been used in New York City. These kiosks are similar to automatic teller machines and are scattered around the city. They identify probationers using a scan of the geometry of the hand on the device and allow the probationer to respond to questions and to schedule meetings with probation officers. These kiosks are designed as a way to monitor low-risk, nonviolent offenders, thereby permitting probation officers to devote closer supervision to higher-risk offenders.[3]

Miniaturization of technology will allow for similar experiments with tiny cameras that could be placed in offenders' homes or in high-risk places (such as known drug areas or the residence of a battered spouse). Other technologies are being developed that would be more difficult for offenders to disable and that would permit certain behaviors or movements by offenders to trigger alarms.[4]

RX FOR CRIME

Pharmacological advances have occurred in the form of new drugs to control violent behavior, mental illness, and drug abuse. Based on studies suggesting that low levels of the neurotransmitter serotonin may reduce impulsive and violent behavior, experiments are being conducted with drugs that affect these brain neurotransmitters.[5]

genetic risk assessment
Technique that builds upon the discoveries in the area of DNA and genetic mapping, where genetic predispositions toward certain behaviors can be anticipated and prevented.

Genetic risk assessment builds upon the discoveries in the area of DNA and genetic mapping. For example, some studies of twins have shown behaviors that may be attributable to a genetic effect.[6] Genetic predispositions toward certain kinds of behaviors could be profiled and behavioral or pharmacological strategies employed to suppress undesirable behaviors such as violence or sexual deviance. The U.S. Supreme Court already has upheld preventive detention in jail of suspects determined to be dangerous, and the use of new knowledge about genetic links to behavior will be used to try to improve the accuracy of these predictions.[7]

Risk-Based Treatment

ROAD RAGE

Violence between spouses, road rage killings, and repeated offenses are examples of dangerous behavior that has been difficult to predict in advance. As a result, the public is exasperated at the apparent inability of the criminal justice system to deal effectively with dangerous offenders. In Alabama, Shirley Henson was sentenced to thirteen years in prison for tailgating another woman on an Interstate highway for several miles and then shooting her at close range on an exit ramp.[8] Henson's lawyers said she was addicted to a prescription painkiller, which may have contributed to her behavior. The defense also attempted to shift blame to the victim, claiming that she drove erratically and acted in a threatening way toward Henson. Was this crime preventable? Are there characteristics of the incident or the offender and victim that allow a risk assessment that can prevent future incidents like this?

risk assessment
Classifying and evaluating offenders based on their characteristics, crimes, and backgrounds to determine the likelihood of reoffending.

Risk assessment involves classifying and evaluating offenders based on their characteristics, crimes, and backgrounds to determine the likelihood of reoffending. Classifying and evaluating offenders has become more sophisticated and accurate over the last two decades. Studies have had at least three important findings involving variation, reliability, and statistics. First, there is tremendous variation among offenders and there is no "one size fits all" in trying to isolate the characteristics of an offender.[9] Offender characteristics such as mental health and substance abuse are important considerations, as are situational characteristics that trigger offender predispositions. Second, offenders change over time, so it is necessary for periodic reevaluations in order for risk assessments to be reliable. Third, "gut feelings" about criminal propensities have given way to statistical assessments, which compare the behaviors of groups of offenders in the past to similar offenders under current evaluation. This form of statistical assessment, or statistical profiling, has been shown to be superior to clinical assessments by psychologists. For example, a study of female prisoners showed that many had acquired sexually transmitted diseases and had engaged in high-risk sexual behavior and drug use. These offenders require enhanced supervision in the community because of the public health risk they pose.[10]

Risk assessments will be become even more important in the future because the threshold for violence may be lower now than in times past. In another road rage case, a middle-aged man in Minnesota noticed a car in front of him moving erratically. As he passed the car, the driver swerved to hit him and made an obscene gesture. He returned the gesture. Later, after he arrived home, there was a knock on the door. The man opened the door, and the other driver threw battery acid on him, causing burns to his face.[11] Although these bizarre incidents appear unique, they are now occurring with increasing frequency, permitting the establishment of statistical profiles that will probably be used in the future at trial and in providing treatment to those offenders whose anger results in criminal violence.

Will this encounter escalate into violence leading to criminal liability? How could statistical profiling and risk assessment help in preventing crimes such as road rage assaults and killings?

Early Life Interventions

A fifteen-year-old boy was sentenced to twenty years in prison for participating in a gang rape of a fourteen-year-old girl. It was his first offense.[12] How does someone choose such a serious offense as a first crime? In most cases there is a progression of behaviors from nonserious to serious crime. It is likely that the offender in this case had committed previous, lesser crimes, but had not been caught. Recognition of this progression from nonserious to serious crimes has been the basis for early childhood intervention in preventing later juvenile delinquency.

The High/Scope Perry Preschool Project
A developmental program emphasizing intellectual and social development through active learning designed for children of low socioeconomic status and low IQ who are at high risk for failure in school.

The High/Scope Perry Preschool Project has been operating for more than forty years; it emphasizes intellectual and social development through active learning. The program is designed for children of low socioeconomic status and low IQ scores who are at high risk for failure in school. Children ages three and four attend the preschool program weekdays for 2.5 hours each day, followed by teacher visits to the child's family for 1.5 hours each week. There are also monthly parent meetings.[13] An evaluation of this program followed up annually with the children until age twenty-seven provides a fascinating longitudinal assessment of the long-term impact of this preschool program. The children participating in the program were about half as likely to be arrested or land in court as juveniles or adults, compared to a matched group of nonparticipating children from identical backgrounds. Participating children also were significantly more likely to have children only after marriage, to have close family ties and friendships, to experience academic success, to be employed, and to earn higher wages.[14] These positive findings translate to savings for the welfare system, special education, the criminal justice system, and crime victims; and program participants were more likely to have greater earnings to generate general tax revenue.

EARLY LIFE INTERVENTIONS

Early life interventions are important because studies have identified childhood risk factors for later delinquency. These include poor language skills, poor attachment to parents and caregivers, poor parenting skills, and multiple stresses on the family.[15] These risk factors lead to failure in school, which is significantly related to delinquency. The Prenatal and Early Childhood Nurse Home Visitation Program is another program that is directed to reduce these identified risk factors that contribute to delinquency.[16] This program builds parenting skills and family unity as it impacts on child rearing. The Boys and Girls Clubs of America is a national network of more than 2,500 clubs that involve more than three million school-age boys and girls in constructive youth development activities, educational support, and adult supervision.[17] A group of researchers convened by the U.S. Office of Juvenile Justice and Delinquency Prevention agreed that "implementing family, school, and community interventions is the best way to prevent children from developing into serious violent juvenile offenders."[18] Although none of the programs described in this section is primarily a crime prevention program, they all

Early life intervention programs such as the one these children are attending are important because studies have identified childhood risk factors associated with delinquency. What are those risk factors? What outcomes identify a successful early intervention program?

have direct implications for the prevention of crime and the involvement of the criminal justice system in the future.

Virtual Prison

Despite the best efforts at crime prevention, there always will be offenders who require close supervision. Those who are not dangerous may not require imprisonment, yet something more than probation supervision or an electronic bracelet may be desired. A potential middle ground for close supervision that is less than prison might be "**virtual prison.**" A private company has introduced the Satellite Monitoring and Remote Tracking System (SMART), which is billed as "a virtual prison with an orbiting warden."[19] The offender wears an ankle bracelet and a wireless tracking device that is monitored using Global Positioning Satellites (GPS) and the cellular network. In this way the offender is continuously monitored. The offender can also be signalled instantly when entering a prohibited area, which might be a spouse's neighborhood, school, or drug-trafficking area. The president of the company that developed the device is a former governor of Florida and head of the White House Office on National Drug Control Policy. Several states are evaluating the system's cost-effectiveness as an alternative to prison.

virtual prison
An offender monitoring system in which the offender wears an ankle bracelet and a wireless tracking device that is monitored using Global Positioning Satellites (GPS) and the cellular network.

SMART

Injected or surgical implants have been proposed as an alternative to electronic bracelets because they cannot be tampered with or defeated effectively. These implants can also be monitored via Global Positioning Satellites.[20] Questions have been raised about the potential for misuse of such Big Brother technology, but it is unlikely that offenders will oppose a technology that offers more freedom than prison. It is also unlikely that this technology would be used by anyone but offenders, although there is concern about the impact on spouses or other potential victims of these offenders and whether monitoring might eventually include "undesirables" other than offenders.[21]

injected or surgical implants
An alternative to electronic bracelets that cannot be tampered with or defeated effectively, and that can be monitored via Global Positioning Satellites (GPS).

BIG BROTHER?

How Can Offenders with Mental Health and Drug Problems Be Handled in the Criminal Justice System?

A seventy-year-old woman admitted to smothering eight of her babies beginning in 1949. At her sentencing for these homicides the judge said, "It's important for the medical community and the legal community that she admit these murders and . . . something good will come out of the analysis."[22] The judge agreed to an unusual sentence of twenty years probation, the first five of which must be under home confinement. In addition she must undergo sessions with a psychiatrist to determine the causes of her repeated infanticides. She avoided a prison sentence due to her age and the age of her crimes, and the fact that numerous medical officials had said that a medical study of her would be valuable because so little is known about why mothers kill their own babies. This unique sentence illustrates how mental health problems underlie some kinds of law violations, although it is

INFANTICIDE

Table 15.1 Characteristics of Inmates in State Prisons with Mental Health Problems

	State Prison	
Selected Characteristics	*With Mental Problem*	*Without*
Criminal record		
Current or past violent offense	61%	56%
3 or more prior incarcerations	25	19
Substance dependence or abuse	74%	56%
Drug use in month before arrest	63%	49%
Family background		
Homelessness in year before arrest	13%	6%
Past physical or sexual abuse	27	10
Parents abused alcohol or drugs	39	25
Charged with violating facility rules	58%	43%
Physical or verbal assault	24	14
Injured in a fight since admission	20%	10%

Source: Doris J. James and Lauren E. Glaze, *Mental Health Problems of Prison and Jail Inmates* (Washington, DC: Bureau of Justice Statistics, 2006).

difficult to know their true extent. Drug use aggravates many mental conditions, so the combination of drug use and mental conditions often leads to involvement of the criminal justice system.

Mental Health of Offenders

A study of inmates in U.S. prisons found that more than half had a mental health problem. Of these, 61 percent had a current or prior record for a violent crime; a fourth had three or more prior incarcerations; and these inmates were more likely than other inmates to have problems of substance abuse, family abuse, and prison adjustment problems. As displayed in Table 15.1, **prisoners with mental health problems** had a much higher incidence of family, drug, and criminal problems than other inmates.

It should be noted that approximately 11 percent of U.S. adults (eighteen years and over) have symptoms of mental disorder, whereas more than half of inmates in prisons and jails show these symptoms.[23] Therefore, there appears to be some overlap between mental illness and criminality. Table 15.2 shows the proportion of state prison inmates who had a recent history and symptoms of mental illness. The table shows that nearly a quarter (24.3 percent) showed evidence of a recent mental health problem, and that half (49.2 percent) showed actual symptoms within the last year.

prisoners with mental health problems
Half of offenders in prisons were identified as mentally ill.

ALCOHOL DEPENDENCE

Intervening effectively to prevent mental problems from developing into crime problems is a thorny issue. This is because very few mentally ill people violate the law and most law violators are not mentally ill. Nevertheless, there are enough offenders with mental health problems to suggest that reasonable interventions are needed. For example, a third of mentally ill offenders in prison or on probation have a history of alcohol dependence. Nearly half of mentally ill inmates and probationers report drinking as much as a fifth of liquor in a day (or twenty drinks), three six-packs of beer, or three bottles of wine. About 45 percent report that they have gotten into a physical fight while drinking.[24] These data suggest a link among drinking, fighting, mental illness, and law violation, which has ramifications for the criminal justice system because mentally ill inmates serve an average of fifteen months longer in prison than do other inmates, and they are more likely to be involved in fights in prisons than are other inmates. Studies have found an increase in the numbers of schizophrenics convicted of crimes over the last twenty years and substance abuse has been linked to many of these offenders.[25]

Table 15.2 History and Symptoms of State Prison Inmates during Previous Year

Mental Health Problem	*State Prison*
Any mental health problem	56.2%
Recent history of mental health problem[a]	24.3%
Told had disorder by mental health professional	9.4
Had overnight hospital stay	5.4
Used prescribed medications	18.0
Had professional mental health therapy	15.1
Symptoms of mental health disorders[b]	49.2%
Major depressive disorder	23.5
Mania disorder	43.2
Psychotic disorder	15.4

[a]In the year before arrest or since admission.
[b]In the 12 months prior to the interview.

Source: Doris J. James and Lauren E. Glaze, *Mental Health Problems of Prison and Jail Inmates* (Washington, DC: Bureau of Justice Statistics, 2006).

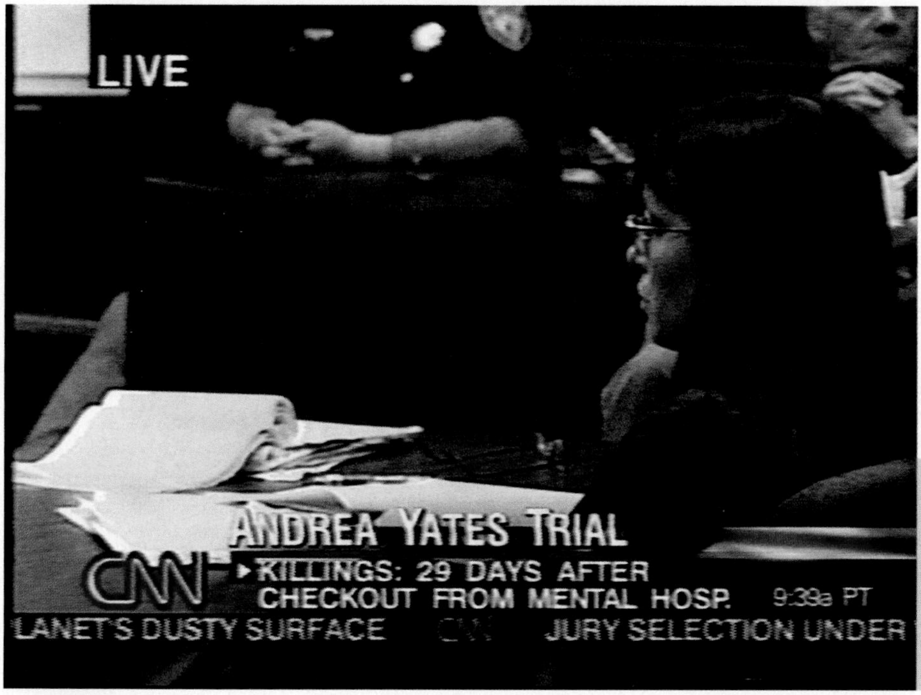

Late in 2000 Congress approved the creation of mental health courts as an alternative form of community corrections. What are the goals of these courts? How are the backgrounds of mentally ill inmates different from those of other inmates?

For these reasons, inmates with mental problems pose significantly greater management issues for prisons.

Federal legislation passed in late 2000 created one hundred **mental health courts** to focus on treatment and rehabilitation of mentally ill offenders who land in the criminal justice system.[26] Combined with effective substance abuse treatment as envisioned by drug courts, mental health problems might be addressed in ways to keep the mentally ill out of the criminal justice system.

mental health courts Specialized courts that focus on treatment and rehabilitation of mentally ill offenders who land in the criminal justice system.

Is There Effective Treatment for Sex Offenders?

Sex offenders are perhaps the most feared and reviled type of criminal offender. Those who victimize children are particularly hated for their abuse of the young and defenseless. Bill, age forty-four, is a sexual felon in Arizona who molested his stepdaughter for three years beginning when she was nine years old. He was sentenced to a year in jail, and then released to lifetime probation. He must pass regular polygraph tests about his behavior and sexual fantasies, attend court-ordered therapy, and "surveillance officers" can stop by his home at any time unannounced. He is not permitted to be around young girls and he must pass periodic tests of a device attached to his penis, which measures the appropriateness of physical responses to audiotapes that describe different kinds of sexual activity.[27] Although this sentence of "lifetime probation" exceeds the usual maximum allowed by law for felons, the U.S. Supreme Court has upheld similarly intrusive programs, even permitting sex offenders to be incarcerated after they have served their sentences if they are predicted to be too dangerous to release into the community.[28] Offenders who have served their entire sentences can be committed to an institution under civil law if it can be shown that they are dangerous.

LIFETIME PROBATION

That's a FACT

Perspectives on Criminal Justice and Mental Illness

It has been shown that mental illness is not strongly related to criminal behavior, but those who do violate the law are much more likely to have significant mental health problems. Table 15A tries to uncover some of the factors associated with inmates known to have mental health problems and how they compare to other inmates.

Given the information in Table 15A, can you offer reasons for the differences in the backgrounds of these two groups of inmates, and how mental illness might account for some of these differences? If you were placed in charge of reducing the proportion of inmates in prison who have mental health problems, explain where you would begin.

Table 15A Backgrounds of Inmates with Mental Health Problems (compared to other inmates)

Background Factors	*Inmates with Mental Health Problems*	*Inmates without Mental Health Problems*
Lived mostly with 2 parents while growing up	42%	48%
Ever lived in foster home	19	10
Sexually abuse history prior to imprisonment	12	4
Ever received public assistance	42	31
Current drug or alcohol dependence	74	56
Income from illegal sources prior to imprisonment	28	21
Member of immediately incarcerated	52	41

Source: Compiled from Doris J. James and Lauren E. Glaze, *Mental Health Problems of Prison and Jail Inmates* (Washington, DC: Bureau of Justice Statistics, 2006).

The premise of Arizona's law, and the laws that punish sex offenders in a growing number of states, is that sex offenders cannot be rehabilitated, so they must be incapacitated to the extent possible by imprisonment, treatment, and close surveillance. A study of 272,000 prisoners released from prisons in fifteen states included nearly 10,000 sex offenders. In their first three years after release, 5 percent of the sex offenders were rearrested for a new sex crime. This recidivism rate is quite low, especially when compared to arrests of non–sex offenders released from prison (for all crimes), which was 68 percent after three years. For the sex offenders, the overall rearrest rate (for all crimes) was lower (43 percent), but the fact that 5 percent of these arrests were for sex crimes inspires public fear and political intolerance.[29] The Federal Violent Crime Control and Law Enforcement Act of 1994 requires all 50 states to establish sex offender registries to track sex offenders upon their release from prison. Although many states already had such registries, the act elevated the failure of a sex offender to register properly to a felony.[30] Most states now publish the known addresses of known sex offenders on the Internet.

SEX OFFENDER REGISTRIES

On the other hand, there is growing evidence that sex offenders can be classified by type and background, and that valid predictions can be made of their likelihood for reoffending and their amenability for treatment. For example, men who were physically or sexually abused as children are nearly three times more likely to be serving a sentence for sexual assault themselves than men not so abused. Studies have also shown that employment history, treatment history, and other factors can reduce or increase the likelihood of reoffending.[31] This perspective sees sex offenses as a treatable predisposition that can be controlled effectively in the same way that alcoholics can be persuaded to avoid alcohol.

Gender Issues

A surge in the number of women arrested and incarcerated over the last decade has raised concern about whether difference in gender should result in difference in treatment by the criminal justice system. **Gender issues** center on the fact that women offenders have different problems in different proportions than men. For example, nearly half of women inmates have been sexually abused in the past versus only 12 percent of men. Women are significantly more likely to kill or assault a spouse or friend than are men. More than two-thirds of women in prison have minor children. Although due process requires that women and men be adjudicated under the same laws and in the same manner, dissimilar treatment of women after adjudication may be warranted. Provisions to permit women inmates to maintain close contact with their young children, and the lower risk shown by women in committing new violent crimes compared to men, may justify differences in how they are treated in the corrections system. For example, 85 percent of women ending federal probation supervision committed no violation and less than 5 percent committed a new crime while on probation. Men were more likely to commit new crimes and to violate conditions of their probation.[32]

gender issues
Issues that center on the fact that women offenders have different problems and in different proportions than men. For example, nearly half of women inmates have been sexually abused in the past versus only 12 percent of men.

Why are the problems of women in prison a major issue today? How are the problems of female prisoners different from those of male prisoners? What new programs have been developed specifically for women offenders in the twenty-first century?

The special circumstances of women offenders are not yet being addressed. A national survey of wardens revealed that in seventeen states no innovative alternative to incarceration for women could be identified. In seventeen others "limited" innovation was occurring.[33] Other studies have found that over one million women in the community are involved in the criminal justice system, (such as probation or parole supervision) and that many challenges face women before their release from prison, including housing, family support, physical abuse, and other significant issues. Another report found that "lack of gender-responsive programs and services results in a 'cycle of incarceration' for women offenders and a 'double jeopardy' for incarcerated mothers," in which families become further disrupted, resulting in additional long-term costs to government once the female offender is released.[34] Because men outnumber women in the prison system by a wide margin, it is common for women and women's prisons to be overlooked when new programs are proposed. The National Institute of Corrections, a government agency within the Federal Bureau of Prisons, has developed programs that specifically address women offenders. These include

PROGRAMS FOR WOMEN OFFENDERS

- a thirty-hour training program for criminal justice officials on the subject of managing female offenders;
- technical assistance to help agencies develop and implement policies that increase the rate of success for female offenders under community supervision; and
- publication of a comprehensive directory of supervision approaches and programs throughout the United States that are designed specifically to address the circumstances of female offenders.[35]

Successful programs of this kind have already been identified, and they include psychological, parenting, work, education, and life-skills programs. Key elements needed for success are a dedicated staff, the recognition of the multiple needs of female offenders, an awareness of the role of peer influence, the commitment to improve skill levels of offenders, and the willingness to establish partnerships with agencies outside the criminal justice system.[36]

Balancing Just Punishment with Public Safety

balance between just punishment and public safety The proper consideration of necessary punishment of the offender to express public disapproval of law violation, and corrective treatment necessary to prevent repeated offenses.

Treatment and correction of offenders' problems must be considered together with the need to punish law violation and to protect public safety. The **balance between just punishment and public safety** is not always easy to accomplish. The public is wary of offenders in the community and treatment has not always been successful, resulting in concern over whether punishment and public safety are being overlooked in the search to "correct" law violators. Public safety is often seen as synonymous with less crime, more arrests, and more criminals in prison. On the other hand, fewer reported crimes can sometimes reflect a fear or lack of confidence in police, more arrests can be a sign of more criminals, and more inmates can be an indication of more serious offenders in society. Instead, public safety is a condition "in which people and property are not at risk of attack or theft and are not perceived to be at risk."[37] Characteristics of public safety include consensus about what is illegal, an understanding that violators will be punished, and efforts made to prevent crime before it occurs and to prevent its reoccurrence.

PUBLIC SAFETY

Punishment of the offender is necessary to express public disapproval of law violation. At the same time corrective treatment is necessary to prevent repeated offenses. This is where the various treatments discussed in this chapter are essential to ensure public safety in the future. Without such treatment efforts, public safety occurs only during the period of imprisonment and it ends once offenders are released into the community with the same problems they had when they entered. The punishment–treatment balance is difficult to achieve in practice. For example, the mayor of New York City announced that the homeless must be willing to work in order to receive free shelter from the city.[38] This form of "workfare" aims to make the nearly 5,000 families and 7,000 single adults in New York City shelters more self-sufficient. Many of these people have drug and alcohol problems, mental health problems, or criminal records, and few have employable skills. Critics have called such a plan impractical, but at the same time it is an effort to reduce the number of those chronically dependent on society. In an analogous way, preventive treatment of law violators attempts to accomplish the same thing—correcting problems that ultimately will lead to a return to crime and jail.

What Is the Future of Corrections?

The future needs of corrections can be anticipated based on current trends. One of the best predictors of criminality by adults is a juvenile criminal record, so it makes sense to focus on trends in offending behavior by young people in anticipating the future. The number of offenders under age eighteen admitted to state prisons more than doubled since 1985. The proportion of juveniles convicted of a violent crime increased from 52 to 61 percent of all juveniles sent to prison, even though the arrest rate for violent crimes overall has been dropping since the mid-1990s. The likelihood of incarceration for this group has nearly doubled for those arrested since 1985, and the minimum time served has also increased.[39] It is clear from these figures that young people are being handled more punitively in recent years. Trends for adults are similar, with a greater proportion of offenders sentenced to prison as opposed to probation, and they are serving longer average sentences.[40] What impact will this have on corrections and on crime in the future?

Offender Accountability

The trend toward **offender accountability** has begun and it is likely to continue. This approach to illegal behavior makes offenders aware of the damage, loss, or injury they cause and of their responsibility for it. It also holds the offender responsible for repairing the damage to the extent possible. Accountability is based on the assumption that a continuum of sanctions are needed to reflect varying degrees of harm and responsibility, suggesting that the penalty should be based as much on the offender's background as it is on the nature of the offense. Jessica G. was a seventeen-year-old in Buffalo who was arrested for vandalism. Upon investigation it was found that she had an underlying drug problem rooted in domestic violence. "I was very depressed and bored," she said. "That's why I turned to drugs. There was nothing to do. . . . I dropped out of high school in my junior year." She ultimately was in and out of jail eight times and kicked out of several residential drug treatment programs—all stemming from the same original charge. A program called "First Time/Last Time" ultimately caused her to take responsibility for her behavior and she is now working on a GED diploma, attending group counseling twice a week, and working at a store.[41]

offender accountability
An approach to illegal behavior that makes offenders aware of the damage, loss, or injury they cause and their responsibility for it.

CONTINUUM OF SANCTIONS

The idea of offender accountability focuses on getting offenders to take responsibility for their actions, which requires a sober and thoughtful look at one's life direction and the consequences of behavior. For this reason drug treatment and counseling are often part of accountability programs to help offenders think clearly and rationally about their behavior and its impact on others. Nearly half the states have amended their juvenile justice system in recent years to establish offender accountability as a central purpose beyond treatment, rehabilitation, or punishment.[42]

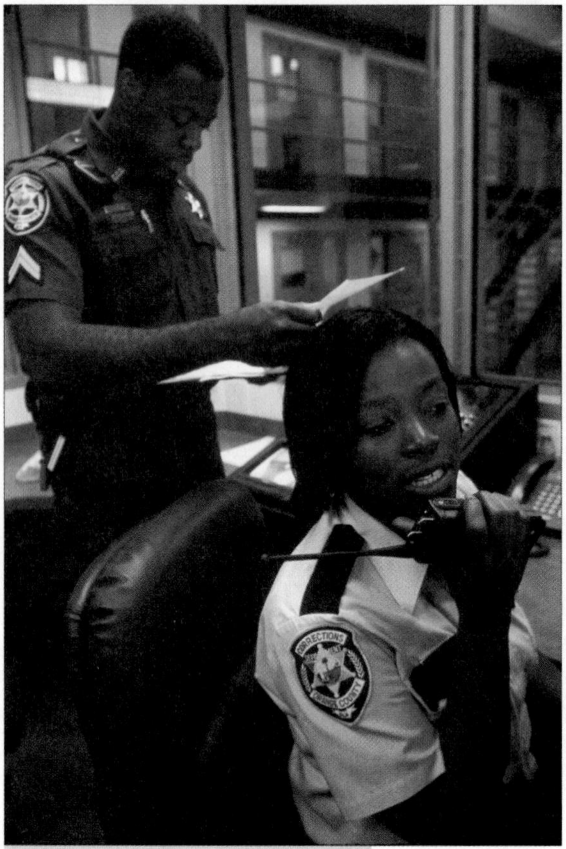

Corrections officers on the job managing a prison holding hundreds of inmates. What kinds of skills do you believe are most important for a corrections officer to possess?

Professionalization of the Corrections Profession

The corrections profession has improved in important ways and this trend is likely to continue. There are more than 45,000 probation and parole officers in the United States and thousands more in community corrections programs of various kinds. These community corrections professionals are an essential part of the criminal justice system because they have the precarious tasks of both supervising offenders in the community and also helping prevent the commission of new crimes through the treatment of offenders. As we have seen, supervision is becoming more scientific with the wide application of risk-assessment instruments, which enable community corrections professionals to focus their efforts on those offenders who pose the highest risk of committing new offenses. The increasing use of technology in community supervision requires professionals in the field to understand and be responsible for complicated computer-based monitoring systems.

COMMUNITY CORRECTIONS PROFESSIONALS

ACCREDITATION

Effective treatment is needed to help reduce the risk of recidivism, and this increasingly takes the form of counseling, drug treatment, and coordination of other agencies in the community to facilitate this process. Community corrections professionals must be resourceful, with an ability to organize available treatments, education, and support agencies to serve the needs of their clients. The American Correctional Association accredits probation, parole, and community corrections agencies to ensure that minimum standards are met in the training of these professionals and in the conditions of the agencies in terms of staff size, treatment offered, funding levels, and so on.[43] This accreditation is now voluntary, but it is an important avenue for community corrections to grow as a profession, in the same way that law and medicine have earned prestige in the society through accreditation.

Compared to prisons, community corrections suffers from lack of funding. Approximately ten cents is spent on probation for every dollar spent on prison, yet community supervision plays a more crucial role in actively working to prevent recidivism.[44] The result of the inadequate funding is high caseloads and officer burnout. In addition, offenders increasingly have multiple problems that include drugs, alcohol, mental illness, family dysfunction, lack of education and employment skills, and related issues. This has made the task of community supervision more difficult because more problems must be addressed in order to place the offender in a position to lead a law-abiding life.

Punishment and Control by Distance

punishment and control by distance
A corrections approach that includes electronic monitoring, probation kiosks, and camera and satellite surveillance to partially restrict offenders' freedom of movement and to deprive them of some portion of their liberty.

Corrections is administered primarily by custody in prison or supervision in the community. This will change in the future with the technological advances noted earlier in this chapter. Electronic monitoring, probation kiosks, and camera and satellite surveillance will allow for **punishment and control by distance** by depriving the offenders of some portion of their liberty and control over their move-

Media & Criminal Justice — *American Me*

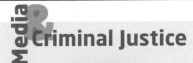

A number of noteworthy films have depicted the realities of prison life throughout history, with a surprising degree of accuracy. *The Concrete Jungle* (1962), *Short Eyes* (1978), *Brubaker* (1980), *Bad Boys* (1985), *Bound by Honor* (1993), *Murder in the First* (1995), *The Green Mile* (1999), and the HBO series *Oz* offer a striking collage of the past century in which policies of incapacitation and retribution have prevailed.

Perhaps the most important film of this genre is *American Me* (1992), because it encompasses a thirty-year span of Chicano gang life in eastern Los Angeles. The film dispels any myth that prison incapacitates gang-related crime; in *American Me,* the gang activity simply continues in the prison as a satellite enterprise to their outside world.

The plot revolves around a young man named Santana, who as a teenager becomes involved in a street gang. A first break-in results in an arrest that lands him in reform school, where he gets into trouble again and is sent directly to Folsom Prison.

The movie covers Santana's eighteen years in prison, sparing no detail of the horrific realities of life behind bars. Santana soon finds himself the leader of the Latino gang, a position that enables him to run a drug operation in the outside world from *inside* the prison. The specific methods of the smuggling operation are graphically presented, as are the gang rapes and other violent necessities of prison survival, such as burning prisoners alive or strangling relatives. The scenes are rife with the wretched desperation of rational criminals who have nothing to lose by committing crime while serving their long sentences.

Santana creates a gang culture that is predictably at war with other groups such as the Italian Mafia and the black street gangs. He is a "big man" in the prison, well-known and respected by Latinos on the outside, yet burdened by his realization of the cyclical nature of Chicano gang activity. Santana sees that an entire Latino generation is being lost to drugs, guns, and crime, but believes this is a result of a crumbling society, and not just the racism that everyone tries to blame.

During Santana's long prison term, prison killings that were once carefully planned retaliations soon become mundane murders for the sake of a senseless thrill. As older gang members perish in prison as a result of such gang violence, new Chicano youth are constantly being incarcerated, leaving Santana to wonder at the worth of it all.

Upon release, Santana finds that life on the outside is so foreign that the viewer wonders if society will allow him to live a reformed life. He returns to the barrio to find his younger brother and neighbor's sons being destroyed by the same gang culture he helped to create. Based on true events, *American Me* is a stomach-wrenching depiction of prison life and gang violence.

What can be done to stop gang activity in prisons? Why would a correctional officer ignore violence and drug activity among inmates? Considering that most inmates will be released to the same neighborhood and friends that contributed to their criminality in the first place, would efforts at rehabilitation work? If rehabilitation won't work, then should violent offenders and drug lords *ever* be released?

ments with limited physical contact. Such remote control will have the advantages of lower cost than imprisonment and closer surveillance than traditional probation or parole can provide.

REMOTE CONTROL

A potential problem of punishment and control by distance will be **expanding the net** by subjecting offenders, who heretofore would be dealt with less severely through traditional probation or other sanctions, to these more stringent forms of surveillance.[45] In this scenario the cost of criminal justice would increase because of the expanded pool of offenders subjected to punishment by distance. Young offenders often lack adequate supervision at home and there might be a propensity to use punishment and control by distance as a way to monitor the

expanding the net
A potential result of punishment and control by distance, subjecting more offenders to stringent forms of surveillance who previously were dealt with less severely through traditional probation or other sanctions.

behavior of the offender in place of improving the competence of the family through counseling or other treatment strategies. Technology can make supervision more effective, but it does not address the underlying causes and motivations of offenders, which must be handled by treatment programs that address these sources of criminal behavior.

Preparing Offenders for Release

In an address to the American Bar Association, the U.S. Attorney General stated, "it makes no sense to send somebody to prison for an armed robbery and have them come out in four years . . . without the problem being addressed." The justice system needs to be given "what it takes to solve the human problems that bring the cases before [it]."[46] This statement illustrates that those who work in the criminal justice system recognize that the system addresses primarily symptoms (i.e., crimes) of deeper underlying problems. Although these crimes must be punished in a fair way, a more substantial effort is needed to address the underlying problems if any long-term impact is to be made.

ADDRESSING UNDERLYING PROBLEMS

Missouri's parallel universe
An effort by Missouri corrections to prepare inmates for release by engaging them in full-time work activities that imitate the outside world.

In Missouri an effort has been made to prepare inmates for release by engaging them in full-time activities that parallel the outside world, called the **parallel universe.** They must make decisions about their life in prison and they are held accountable for them in an effort to cultivate conforming life skills for offenders, many of whom previously led undisciplined lives. During the day inmates must attend school in the prison at least part time, an important task because a majority of offenders entering prison there are functionally illiterate. In prison in Missouri a 40-hour work week is mandatory. Most of this work is maintenance or kitchen tasks within the prison, but prisoners are interviewed for the jobs and must follow directions in order to keep them. Some form of ongoing treatment is also required based on the inmate's offense and background—drug, alcohol, and sex-offender counseling and testing are the most common.

REHABILITATION

In a further effort to ready inmates for the outside world, inmates select charities to which they will donate a portion of their wages during the year. Victim impact classes, reparation projects, and other community-oriented efforts are designed to develop conscience about obligations to the larger community. Recreation activities are permitted only during the evening and weekends after all other tasks are completed, in order to mimic the life of a working person on the outside. When inmates perform responsibly at school, work, and treatment, they earn privileges, including better work assignments, additional visits, and the ability to acquire consumable items in prison. More than 98 percent of the inmates in Missouri are now engaged in some combination of school, work, and treatment on a full-time basis.[47] This innovative approach to socializing inmates illustrates that keeping an offender in prison does not necessarily have to work against rehabilitative goals, and that preparation for success upon release is a fundamental goal of effective corrections.

Corrections as Prevention

Sheila M. is a sixteen-year-old charged with vandalism for breaking a pipe in a bathroom at a children's shelter after she was locked in there for punishment. Her father was arrested for beating her mother, who died of a heart attack during a family quarrel. Sheila has been transferred more than sixty-five times between children's shelters, group homes, psychiatric hospitals, and juvenile jails.[48] The criminal justice system gets this case as a charge of vandalism for which she could receive a sentence of up to three years, but there is clearly much more to it than that. Increasingly, the corrections system receives offenders like this, with multiple problems that preceded involvement in crime. As this chapter has shown, corrections can be more effective only when greater attention is paid to family, drug, alcohol, school, and mental health problems by society at large *before* a person violates the law.

ADDRESSING MULTIPLE PROBLEMS

But there are hopeful signs for the future. The **Incredible Years training series** uses group discussion, videotape modeling, and rehearsing intervention techniques to assist parents and teachers living and working with children ages two to ten. The series is designed to address and intervene in the behavior problems of children and to increase their ability to act appropriately in groups. The specific skills targeted are presented in Table 15.3, which shows how improvement in parenting, academics, and interpersonal skills can help reduce undesirable and ultimately criminal behavior on the part of youth. Effective corrections programs contain many of these targeted skills, which are much more difficult to inculcate later in life.

Incredible Years training series
A program offering behavior intervention techniques to assist parents and teachers living and working with children ages two to ten.

There is a growing body of knowledge based on evaluation research, which is being used to inform efforts to prevent crime.[49] An effective corrections system ultimately prevents crime by dealing with offenders in ways that not only punish but also *correct*. The Intensive Community-Based Aftercare Program for high-risk young parolees is now underway in Las Vegas, Denver, Newark, and Norfolk. It is designed to reduce recidivism among these offenders by preparing them for progressively increased responsibility and freedom, facilitating community interaction, addressing and treating known problems, and monitoring and testing the parolee in the community.[50] Many of the elements of this recidivism prevention program could be used to prevent crime among nonoffenders as well. To achieve **community justice,** where the justice system enhances community life, it will be necessary for communities to partner more effectively with the

RECIDIVISM REDUCTION

community justice
Corrections integrated with prevention efforts, wherein the justice system enhances community life, and communities partner effectively with the criminal justice system to share responsibility for social control.

The Incredible Years training program targets parents, children, and teachers. The child training program focuses on developing social skills, problem-solving skills, and proper classroom behavior. What other skills are important for children to develop to become successful?

Table 15.3 Summary of the Incredible Years Parent, Teacher, and Child Training Programs

Interventions	*Skills Targeted*	*Person Trained*	*Settings Targeted*
Incredible Years BASIC Parent Training Program	Parenting skills • Play/Involvement • Praise/Rewards • Limit setting • Discipline	Parent	Home
Incredible Years ADVANCE Parent Training Program	Interpersonal skills • Problem solving • Anger management • Communication • Depression control • Giving and getting support	Parent	Home, work, and community
Incredible Years EDUCATION Parent Training Program (also known as Supporting Your Child's Education)	Academic skills • Academic stimulation • Learning routine after school • Homework support • Reading • Limit setting • Involvement at school • Teacher conferences	Parent	Home–school connection
Incredible Years Teacher Training Program	Classroom management skills • Encouragement/Praise • Incentives • Proactive teaching • Discipline • Positive relationships • Social skills training • Problem-solving training • Promoting parent involvement	Teacher	School
Incredible Years Child Training Program (also known as Dina Dinosaur Social Skills and Problem-Solving Curriculum)	Social skills • Friendship • Teamwork • Cooperation/Helping • Communication • Understanding feelings/Feeling language • Rules Problem solving • Anger management • Steps of problem solving Classroom behavior • Quiet hand up • Compliance • Listening • Stop-look-think-check • Concentrating	Child	Home and school

Source: Carolyn Webster-Stratton, *The Incredible Years Training Series* (Washington, DC: Office of Juvenile Justice and Delinquency Prevention, 2000).

criminal justice system to share responsibility for social control.[51] Corrections will be able to prevent crime more effectively when it becomes better integrated with prevention efforts that occur outside the criminal justice system *before* a person with problems becomes an offender.

CRITICAL THINKING EXERCISES

Illicit Drug Use in Movies and Music

In a study that was the first of its kind, the White House Office of National Drug Control Policy (WHONDCP) analyzed the content of the two hundred most popular movie rentals and songs over a two-year period. The findings revealed that 98 percent of the movies depicted substance use (drugs, alcohol, or tobacco). Illicit drugs appeared in 22 percent of the movies. Of one thousand popular songs 27 percent contained a clear reference to alcohol, tobacco, or drugs. These findings are summarized in Figure 15A. The Director of the WHONDCP concluded that the entertainment industry can play a key role in protecting youth by "portraying illicit drugs and all substance abuse, as unglamorous, dangerous and socially unacceptable." The head of the Substance Abuse and Health Services Administration laid responsibility on parents, who should be actively involved in selecting entertainment activities for youth and should serve as role models.

Most troubling was the fact that fewer than 15 percent of young characters in films who smoked marijuana or cigarettes experienced any consequences from their use. In addition, 26 percent of movies portrayed illicit drug use in a humorous context. Film ratings did not appear to distinguish films that portrayed substance use. More than 75 percent of all G, PG, PG-13, and R-rated films portrayed tobacco or alcohol use. Illicit drug use was portrayed in 17 percent of PG-13 movies and 20 percent of R-rated movies. These findings are summarized in Figure 15B. In analyzing songs, references to illicit drugs occurred in 63 percent of rap songs, but only about 10 percent of other songs. Similar findings were discovered in reference to alcohol use. The study did not infer that drug messages in movies or songs cause drug use by themselves, but media portrayals were said to influence the perceptions of young people in terms of what is "normal" or "acceptable" or harmful. For example, illicit drugs were associated with wealth or luxury in 15 percent of movies and 20 percent of songs. Sexual activity was associated with illicit drugs in 6 percent of movies and 30 percent of songs. Crime and violence occurred in association with illicit drugs in about 30 percent of movies and 20 percent of songs. Anti-use statements occurred much less often—in 15 percent of movies and 6 percent of songs.

The intent of the study was to open a dialogue with the entertainment industry regarding the content and potential influence of their products, and also to encourage parental involvement in the entertainment choices of their children. The pervasive use of drug and alcohol references in movies and

FIGURE 15A Substance Appearance in Popular Movies and Songs

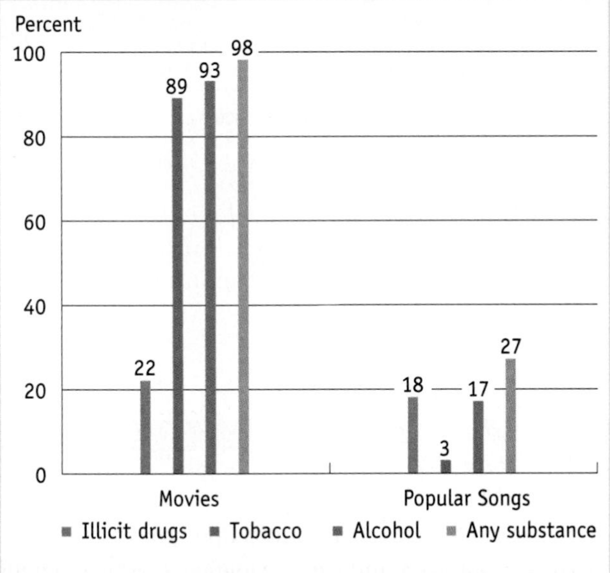

Source: Donald F. Roberts, Lisa Henriksen, and Peter G. Christenson, *Substance Use in Popular Movies and Music,* available at www.mediacampaign.org/publications/movies/movie_partI.html (1999).

FIGURE 15B Substance Use in G or PG, PG-13, and R-rated Movies

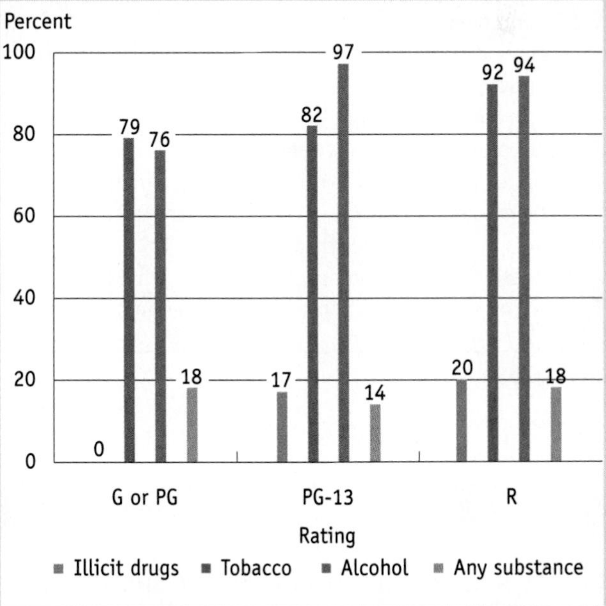

Source: Donald F. Roberts, Lisa Henriksen, and Peter G. Christenson, *Substance Use in Popular Movies and Music,* available at www.mediacampaign.org/publications/movies/movie_partI.html (1999).

(continued)

music aimed primarily at young people raises issues about the scope of interventions that might be employed.

CRITICAL THINKING QUESTIONS

1. If you were an entertainment industry executive, how might you defend the portrayals of substance use in movies and songs? Are there any changes you would be willing to make?
2. If media depictions of substance use do not cause people to use them, why are people so concerned about it?
3. What would be the arguments for and against restricting by law the content of movies and music in portraying illegal substance use?

Source: Donald F. Roberts, Lisa Henriksen, and Peter G. Christenson, *Substance Use in Popular Movies and Music,* available at www.mediacampaign.org/publications/movies/movie_partI.html (1999).

Ecstasy: Crime Problem, Health Problem, or Recreation?

Ecstasy is a synthetic, psychoactive drug, which acts in ways similar to amphetamines and hallucinogenic drugs. Ecstasy is sometimes called "Adam," "XTC," or "MDMA," and it produces a "feel good" high. It was invented nearly one hundred years ago as an appetite suppressant, but it never became popular. In 1986, the government classified it as a Schedule One illicit drug with no medical benefit. Under federal law, possession of about 1,000 tablets can result in a prison sentence of up to five years. Many states have their own laws that supplement the federal prohibition.

Ecstasy users do not see harm in its use. The drug is used at large parties, called "raves," characterized by loud, pulsating music and dancing, and the parties are often alcohol-free. The drug causes involuntary clenching of the jaw and teeth grinding, so partygoers often suck lollipop pacifiers to lubricate their mouths. Users often claim no aftereffects of the drug and believe it is safer than alcohol.

According to some medical researchers, however, Ecstasy suppresses or kills part of the nerve in the brain that releases serotonin, the chemical that controls several bodily functions, including sleep and memory. One study compared the brain scans of fourteen Ecstasy users to non-users and found nerve damage that persists for seven years or more. Skeptics believe that public health officials are exaggerating the long-term risks of Ecstasy, and several studies are under way to obtain more information about its long-term effects.

In the midst of this debate over the effects of Ecstasy, its prohibition has resulted in the emergence of organized crime groups that control its manufacture and distribution. Much of the drug is imported from the Netherlands and Belgium, and distribution has been dominated thus far by Israeli crime groups. Because the pills are small, they are easy to smuggle. U.S. Customs has trained dogs to sniff out Ecstasy at the borders, and the Drug Enforcement Administration hosted its first Ecstasy conference in 2000 to highlight its concerns to law enforcement officials in the United States and internationally. Tightening of international smuggling avenues is likely to produce clandestine labs within the United States to create an alternative supply, one of which was discovered in San Antonio, Texas.

CRITICAL THINKING QUESTIONS

1. If the evidence about the long-term effects of Ecstasy is uncertain, why has it been prohibited by law?
2. How can we balance the goals of preventing use of an undesirable substance with obedience to law?
3. How should we determine whether use of a substance like Ecstasy should be treated as a health problem, crime problem, or recreation?

Sources: National Institute of Drug Abuse, Ecstasy, www.drugabuse.gov (2000); Donna Leinwand and Gary Fields, "Feds Crack Down on Ecstasy," *USA Today* (April 19, 2000), p. 1; "Ecstasy Flow Said Becoming Epidemic," *Associated Press* (April 3, 2000); Donna Leinwand, "New Designer Drug Blamed for Deaths," *USA Today* (October 5, 2000), p. 1; "Increasing MDMA Use among College Students: Results of a National Survey," *Journal of the American Academy of Child and Adolescent Psychiatry,* vol. 41 (October 2002), p. 1215.

SUMMARY

WHAT ARE NEW WAYS OF ADMINISTERING JUSTICE AND PUNISHMENT?

- Technocorrection is the use of technology to monitor offenders and prevent future crimes.
- Genetic risk assessment builds upon the discoveries in the area of DNA and genetic mapping, where genetic predispositions toward certain kinds of behaviors could be profiled and behavioral or pharmacological

strategies employed to suppress violence or sexual deviance.

- Risk assessment involves classifying and evaluating offenders based on their characteristics, crimes, and backgrounds to determine their likelihood of reoffending.
- The High/Scope Perry Preschool Project is a program designed for children of low socioeconomic status and low IQ scores who are at high risk for failure in school, emphasizing intellectual and social development through active learning.
- Virtual prison is an offender monitoring system in which the offender wears an ankle bracelet and a wireless tracking device that is monitored using Global Positioning Satellites and the cellular network so that the offender is continuously monitored.
- Injected or surgical implants have been proposed as an alternative to electronic bracelets because they cannot be tampered with or defeated effectively. These implants can also be monitored via Global Positioning Satellites.

HOW CAN OFFENDERS WITH MENTAL HEALTH AND DRUG PROBLEMS BE HANDLED IN THE CRIMINAL JUSTICE SYSTEM?

- A study of inmates in U.S. prisons found that more than half had a mental health problem.
- Federal legislation passed in late 2000 created one hundred mental health courts to focus on treatment and rehabilitation of mentally ill offenders who land in the criminal justice system.
- Women offenders have different problems and in different proportions than men. For example, nearly half of women inmates have been sexually abused in the past versus only 12 percent of men. Women are significantly more likely to kill or assault a spouse or friend than men. More than two-thirds of women in prison have minor children.
- The balance between just punishment and public safety is not always easy to accomplish. Punishment of the offender is necessary to express public disapproval of law violation. At the same time corrective treatment is necessary to prevent repeated offenses.

WHAT IS THE FUTURE OF CORRECTIONS?

- Offender accountability has begun and it is likely to continue. This approach to illegal behavior makes offenders aware of the damage, loss, or injury they cause and their responsibility for it.
- Punishment and control by distance includes electronic monitoring, probation kiosks, and camera and satellite surveillance that allow for depriving the offenders of some portion of their liberty and control over their movements with limited physical contact.
- Expanding the net involves subjecting more offenders to stringent forms of surveillance who previously would be dealt with less severely through traditional probation or other sanctions.
- Missouri's parallel universe is an effort to prepare inmates for release by engaging them in full-time activities that parallel the outside world. Inmates must make decisions about their life in prison, and they are held accountable for them in an effort to cultivate conforming life skills for offenders.
- The Incredible Years training series is a program offering intervention techniques to assist parents and teachers living and working with children ages two to ten. The series is designed to address and intervene in behavior problems by children and to increase their ability to act appropriately in groups.
- Community justice occurs where the justice system enhances community life and where communities partner effectively with the criminal justice system to share responsibility for social control.

KEY TERMS

technocorrections *428*
genetic risk assessment *428*
risk assessment *429*
the High/Scope Perry Preschool Project *430*
virtual prison *431*
injected or surgical implants *431*
prisoners with mental health problems *432*
mental health courts *433*
gender issues *435*
balance between just punishment and public safety *436*
offender accountability *437*
punishment and control by distance *438*
expanding the net *439*
Missouri's parallel universe *440*
Incredible Years training series *441*
community justice *441*

QUESTIONS FOR REVIEW AND DISCUSSION

1. What recent events and developments have spurred innovation in the correctional system? What forms do those innovations take?
2. What are some examples of technocorrections and risk-based treatment?
3. What features can make early life intervention effective in preventing delinquency?
4. What is meant by a virtual prison? What are some issues involved in this alternative to incarceration?
5. Why is it important to address the mental health of offenders? How are mentally ill inmates different from other inmates?
6. What are some options in the treatment of sex offenders and the prevention of sex offenses?
7. What innovations in corrections address the problems of women offenders?
8. Why and how should a balance be achieved between just punishment and public safety?
9. How do offender accountability and the professionalization of community corrections contribute to effective alternatives to incarceration?
10. What roles will prerelease offender preparation and preventive corrections play in the twenty-first century?

NOTES

1. Lynn Rosellini, "The High Life of Crime," *U.S. News & World Report* (November 20, 2000), pp. 76–77.
2. Tony Fabelo, *"Technocorrections": The Promises, the Uncertain Threats* (Washington, DC: National Institute of Justice, 2000).
3. Isabelle de Pommereau, "NYC Probation Officers to Get High-Tech Helper," *Christian Science Monitor* (February 8, 1997); Martiga Lohn, "Probation Officers Feel the Pinch of Reduced State Aid," *Associated Press State & Local Wire* (May 5, 2005).
4. "Microchip Implants Closer to Reality," *Futurist*, vol. 33 (October 1999), p. 9; Vicki Smith, "West Virginia a Testing Ground for High-tech Crime Fighting Tools," *Associated Press State & Local Wire* (September 23, 2006).
5. Alan I. Leshner, "We Can Conquer Drug Addiction," *Futurist*, vol. 33 (November 1999), pp. 22–25; Debra Niehoff, *The Biology of Violence: How Understanding the Brain, Behavior, and Environment Can Break the Vicious Circle of Aggression* (New York: The Free Press, 1999).
6. G. Carey and D. Goldman, "The Genetics of Antisocial Behavior," in D. M. Stoff, ed., *Handbook of Antisocial Behavior* (New York: Wiley, 1997); Daniel M. Blonigen, Brian M. Hicks, Robert F. Krueger, Christopher J. Patrick, and William G. Iacono, "Continuity and Change in Psychopathic Traits as Measured via Normal-range Personality: A Longitudinal-biometric Study," *Journal of Abnormal Psychology*, vol.115 (February 2006), pp. 85–96.
7. *U.S. v. Salerno*, 107 S. Ct. 2095 (1987).
8. "Woman Gets 13 Years for 'Road Rage' Slaying," *APBnews.com* (December 14, 2000).
9. Edward J. Latessa, "Classifying and Assessing Offenders: Understanding the Criminal Mind," *Corrections Today*, vol. 61 (February 1999), p. 8; Kevin S. Douglas and P. Randall Kropp, "A Prevention-Based Paradigm for Violence Risk Assessment: Clinical and Research Applications," *Criminal Justice and Behavior*, vol. 29 (October 2002), p. 617.
10. James W. Marquart, Victoria E. Brewer, Janet L. Mullings, and Ben M. Crouch, "Health Risk as an Emerging Field Within the New Penology," *Journal of Criminal Justice*, vol. 27 (March–April 1999), p. 143; Zoe N. Hilton, Grant T. Harris, and Marnie E. Rice. "Sixty-six Years of Research on the Clinical versus Actuarial Prediction of Violence," *Counseling Psychologist*, vol. 34 (May 2006), pp. 400–10.
11. "Man Hit with Acid in Road Rage Incident," *APBnews.com* (August 10, 2000).
12. Lisa Teachey, "Three Sentenced in Gang Rape of 14-Year-Old," *Houston Chronicle* (November 21, 2000), p. 19A.
13. Greg Parks, *The High/Scope Perry Preschool Project* (Washington, DC: Office of Juvenile Justice and Delinquency Prevention, 2000).
14. L. J. Schweinhart and D. P. Weikart. "The High/Scope Perry Preschool Study Through Age 27," in R. R. Ross, D. H. Antonowicz, and G. K. Dhaliwal, eds. *Going Straight: Effective Delinquency Prevention and Offender Rehabilitation* (Ottawa, Canada: Air Training and Publications, 1998).
15. D. S. Shaw, E. B. Winslow, E. B. Owens, and N. Hood, "Young Children's Adjustment to Chronic Family Adversity: A Longitudinal Study of Low-Income Families," *Journal of the American Academy of Child and Adolescent Psychiatry*, vol. 37 (1998), pp. 545–53; J. D. Hawkins, T. Herrenkol, D. P. Farrington, D. Brewer, R. F. Catalano, and T. W. Harachi, "A Review of Predictors of Youth Violence," in R. Loeber and D. F. Farrington, eds., *Serious and Violent Juvenile Offenders: Risk Factors and Successful Interventions* (Thousand Oaks, CA: Sage 1998).
16. D. Olds, P. Hill, and E. Rumsey, *Prenatal and Early Childhood Nurse Home Visitation* (Washington, DC: Office of Juvenile Justice and Delinquency Prevention, 1998); Stephen J. Bavolek, *The Nurturing Parenting Programs* (Washington, DC: Office of Juvenile Justice and Delinquency Prevention, 2000).
17. *Boys & Girls Clubs of America* (Washington, DC: Bureau of Justice Assistance, 2000).
18. Richard F. Catalano, Rolf Loeber, and Kay C. McKinney, *School and Community Interventions to Prevent Serious and Violent Offending* (Washington, DC: Office of Juvenile Justice and Delinquency Prevention, 1999).
19. Bob Witnak, "Virtual Prison—Orbiting Warden," www.ptm.com (2006); Tom Sharp, "State to Try GPS Tracking of Paroled Sex Offenders," *Associated Press* (May 31, 2004); Wendy Koch, "More Sex Offenders Tracked by Satellite," *USA Today* (June 6, 2006).
20. Brent Davis, "Hi-Tech Plans for Tomorrow's Prisons: Implants Being Introduced to Monitor Released Offenders," *Kingston Whig–Standard* (March 19, 1998), p. 5; Britain May

Use Chips to Track Pedophiles," *United Press International* (July 31, 2006).
21. Gene Stephens, "Technology Against Crime?," www.mediamente.rai.it (1998).
22. Jennifer Brown, "Woman Admits to Infanticides: Light Sentence Gives Access for Medical Study," *USA Today* (June 29, 1999), p. 3.
23. Doris J. James and Lauren E. Glaze, *Mental Health Problems of Prison and Jail Inmates* (Washington, DC: Bureau of Justice Statistics, 2006).
24. Ibid.
25. Paul E. Mullen, Philip Burgess, Cameron Wallace, Simon Palmer, David Ruschena, "Community Care and Criminal Offending in Schizophrenia," *Lancet*, vol. 355 (February 19, 2000), p. 614.
26. James Gordon Meek, "Congress OKs Mental Health Courts," *APBnews.com* (October 25, 2000); Risdon N. Slate, "From the Jailhouse to Capitol Hill: Impacting Mental Health Court Legislation and Defining What Constitutes a Mental Health Court," *Crime and Delinquency*, vol. 49 (January 2003), p. 6.
27. Mike Tharp, "Tracking Sexual Impulses," *U.S. News & World Report* (July 7, 1997), pp. 30–32; Tanya Caldwell, "Appeals Court Rejects Arousal Test for Sex Offender," *Los Angeles Times* (June 21, 2006).
28. *Kansas v. Hendricks*, 117 S. Ct. 2072 (1997); Steve C. Lee, "How Little Control? Volition and the Civil Confinement of Sexually Violent Predators," *Harvard Journal of Law and Public Policy*, vol. 26 (winter 2003), p. 385; Mark K. Matthews, "Molesters Confined Even After Jail Time is Up," *Stateline.org*, (February 4, 2006).
29. Patrick A. Langan, Erica L. Schmitt, and Matthew Durose, *Recidivism of Sex Offenders Released from Prison* (Washington, DC: Bureau of Justice Statistics, 2003).
30. Bernard C. Parks and Diane Webb, "Sex Offender Registration Enforcement: A Proactive Stance to Monitoring Convicted Sex Offenders," *FBI Law Enforcement Bulletin*, vol. 69 (October 2000), p. 6; Devon B. Adams, *Summary of State Sex Offender Registry Dissemination Procedures* (Washington, DC: Bureau of Justice Statistics, 1999).
31. Candace Kruttschnitt, Christopher Uggen, and Kelly Shelton, "Predictors of Desistance among Sex Offenders: The Interaction of Formal and Informal Social Controls," *Justice Quarterly*, vol. 17 (March 2000), p. 61; James R. Worling and Tracey Curwen, "Adolescent Sexual Offender Recidivism: Success of Specialized Treatment and Implications for Risk Prediction," *Child Abuse and Neglect*, vol. 24 (July 2000), p. 965; Mark J. Hanlon, Stephen Larson, and Sandy Zacher, "The Minnesota SOST and Sexual Reoffending in North Dakota: A Retrospective Study," *International Journal of Offender Therapy and Comparative Criminology*, vol. 43 (March 1999), p. 71; Mario J. Scalora and Calvin Garbin, "A Multivariate Analysis of Sex Offender Recidivism," *International Journal of Offender Therapy and Comparative Criminology*, vol. 47 (June 2003), p. 309.
32. Steven K. Smith and John Scalia, Jr., *Compendium of Federal Justice Statistics, 2000* (Washington, DC: Bureau of Justice Statistics, 2003).
33. Merry Morash, Timothy S. Bynum, and Barbara A. Koons, *Women Offenders: Programming Needs and Promising Alternatives* (Washington, DC: National Institute of Justice, 1998).
34. New Hampshire Commission on the Status of Women, *Double Jeopardy: A Report on Training and Educational Programs for New Hampshire's Female Offenders* (Concord, NH: Commission on the Status of Women, 2005); Women's Prison Association and Home, *Barriers to Re-entry* (New York: The Criminal Justice Initiative, 2003).
35. Phyllis Modley, "NIC Assists Corrections with Managing Female Offenders in the Community," *Corrections Today*, vol. 62 (July 2000), p. 152.
36. Morash, Bynum, and Koons, *Women Offenders: Programming Needs and Promising Alternatives*, pp. 7–8.
37. Michael E. Smith and Walter J. Dickey, *Reforming Sentencing and Corrections for Just Punishment and Public Safety* (Washington, DC: National Institute of Justice, 1999).
38. David Whitman, "New York Says: Work for a Bed," *U.S. News & World Report* (November 8, 1999), p. 22; "From Welfare to Workfare: Helping the Poor," *Economist*, vol. 380 (July 29, 2006), p. 27.
39. Kevin J. Strom, *Profile of State Prisoners under Age 18, 1985–97* (Washington, DC: Bureau of Justice Statistics, 2000).
40. Thomas Bonczar, *Prevalence of Imprisonment in the U.S. Population, 1974–2001* (Washington, DC: Bureau of Justice Statistics, 2003).
41. Lou Michel, "A Pre-emptive Strike on Crime," *Buffalo News* (December 10, 2000), p. 1B.
42. Patrick Griffin, *Developing and Administering Accountability-Based Sanctions for Juveniles* (Washington, DC: Office of Juvenile Justice and Delinquency Prevention, 1999).
43. Kathy Waters, "Accreditation for Probation and Parole/Community Corrections," *Corrections Today*, vol. 61 (July 1999), p. 128.
44. Donald G. Evans, "Broken Windows: Fixing Probation," *Corrections Today*, vol. 61 (December 1999), p. 30; Megan Kurlychek and Cynthia Kempinen, "Beyond Boot Camp: The Impact of Aftercare on Offender Reentry," *Criminology and Public Policy*, vol. 5 (2006), pp. 363–88; James P. Lynch, "Prisoner Reentry: Beyond Program Evaluation," *Criminology and Public Policy*, vol. 5 (2006), pp. 401–12.
45. Fabelo, *"Technocorrections": The Promises, the Uncertain Threats.*
46. "Spend More to Prevent Recidivism," *APBnews.com* (August 10, 1999).
47. Dora Schriro, *Correcting Corrections: Missouri's Parallel Universe* (Washington, DC: National Institute of Justice, 2000).
48. Fox Butterfield, "Concern Rising Over Use of Juvenile Prisons to 'Warehouse' the Mentally Ill," *New York Times* (December 5, 2000), p. 1.
49. Patricia Van Voorhis and Kimberly Spencer, "When Programs 'Don't Work' with Everyone: Planning for Differences Among Correctional Clients," *Corrections Today*, vol. 61 (February 1999), p. 38; Lawrence W. Sherman, Denise C. Gottfredson, Doris L. MacKenzie, John Eck, Peter Reuter, and Shawn Bushway, *Preventing Crime: What Works, What Doesn't, What's Promising* (Washington, DC: National Institute of Justice, 1998); Doris Layton MacKenzie, *What Works in Corrections?* (New York: Cambridge University Press, 2006).
50. Robert G. Weibush, Betsie McNulty, and Thao Le, *Implementation of the Intensive Community-Based Aftercare Program* (Washington, DC: Office of Juvenile Justice and Delinquency Prevention, 2000).
51. Todd R. Clear and David R. Karp, "Toward the Ideal of Community Justice," *National Institute of Justice Journal* (October 2000), pp. 20–28; Steve Jansen and Ellen Dague, "Working with a Neighborhood Community Prosecutor," *Police Chief*, vol. 73 (July 2006), pp. 40–45.

chapter 16

Juvenile Justice

Dealing with delinquency: young offenders and crime trends, legal protections for juveniles, youth in custody, and the future of juvenile justice.

CHAPTER OUTLINE

LEARNING OBJECTIVES

- Distinguish between juvenile justice and criminal justice.
- Describe the nature and extent of juvenile delinquency in the United States today and in the past.
- Evaluate the adequacy of sources of information about juvenile delinquency.
- Trace the foundations of juvenile justice in the nineteenth and early twentieth centuries.
- Explain basic changes in the juvenile justice system since the 1960s.
- Identify and describe significant court cases in the development of due process for juveniles.
- Analyze juvenile law and procedure relating to the Fourth, Fifth, and Eighth Amendments.
- Trace steps in the procedure and disposition of juveniles in custody.
- Predict and explain trends in the future of juvenile justice.

A seventh-grade student in Florida received a suspension on the last day of class for having a water fight and was sent home. He returned later that day with a gun and shot in the face a teacher who would not let him return to class.[1] The teacher was killed and the thirteen-year-old shooter was tried as an adult.

Lionel Tate was twelve years old when his mother left him alone with his six-year-old sister, Tiffany. Lionel stomped his sister badly, severing her liver, and causing her death. His mother never looked in on them, only yelling down the stairs, "Tiffany, stop making that noise or I'm going to spank your butt." At age thirteen, Lionel Tate became the youngest person ever convicted of first-degree murder. His case prompted a public outcry because, under Florida law, he had to be sent to prison for life. His conviction was later overturned by an appellate court, however, citing his young age and immaturity (he had a below-average IQ and the maturity of a nine or ten year old). Tate then pled guilty to second degree murder and was released from prison in 2004 on his seventeenth birthday.[2] He was sentenced to an additional year of house arrest, ten years' probation, 1,000 hours of community service, and regular counseling.

These are examples of headlines made by juveniles around the country, from the unspeakably violent to the ridiculous. Which of these events are typical, or are they rare? What should be done with young people who commit crimes like these? The answers to these questions form the basis for the juvenile justice system. This chapter examines the nature and extent of delinquency and the workings of juvenile justice in dealing with young offenders.

delinquency
A criminal act committed by a person under the age of majority.

In the eyes of the law, the only difference between a juvenile delinquent and an adult criminal is age. If a criminal act is committed by a person under the age of majority, the act is considered **delinquency.** If the illegal act is committed by someone who has reached the age of majority, that person has committed a crime. Depending on the state, a person becomes an adult in the eyes of the law at some point between age sixteen (in three states) or seventeen (seven states) and age nineteen (in one state). In thirty-nine states a person becomes an adult at age eighteen. In addition, an individual under a certain age (seven years old in many states) cannot be held legally responsible for an illegal act. This is because small children are not seen as being old enough to fully understand the consequences of their actions. They cannot be adjudicated in either criminal or juvenile court. Juvenile delinquency is generally concerned, therefore, with the misdeeds of young people between the ages of seven and eighteen.

status offenses
Undesirable behaviors that are unlawful only for juveniles, including habitual truancy, curfew violations, repeated running away, and ungovernability or incorrigibility in failing to respond to the reasonable requests of parents.

Besides delinquency, there are acts for which juveniles can be forced to appear in juvenile court. These acts are called **status offenses** and do not involve violations of the criminal law. In fact, they are merely undesirable behaviors that are unlawful only for juveniles. They are designed to thwart predelinquent behavior that is not serious in itself but that can lead to juvenile delinquency in the future. Examples of status offenses include habitual truancy, curfew violations, repeated running away, and ungovernability or incorrigibility in failing to respond to the reasonable requests of parents.

STATUS OFFENSE BEHAVIORS

The range of behaviors that are considered status offenses varies greatly among the states. Some states view the use of alcohol, tobacco, or marijuana; profanity; or having delinquent associates as status offenses. Also, different states use differing terminology in referring to status offenders. In New York State, for example, they are called PINS (persons in need of supervision); in New Jersey, JINS (juveniles in need of supervision); and in Washington, D.C., CHINS (children in need of supervision). Juveniles can be taken into custody, adjudicated, and incarcerated for the commission of status offenses, as well as for delinquency. Therefore, the juvenile justice system deals with two distinct types of juvenile behaviors: delinquency and status offenses. The system also hears cases involving neglect or abuse of children, but these cases result from adult rather than juvenile misbehavior.

Juvenile Justice versus Criminal Justice

Because of their age, juveniles are treated separately from adults in the justice process. Police departments often have officers who deal exclusively with juveniles. Every state has a separate juvenile court system that deals exclusively with youths.

In addition, every state has separate facilities for the incarceration of juvenile offenders. The legal status of juveniles in this justice process also differs significantly from that of adults in the criminal justice system. For example, cases involving motor vehicle theft are handled quite differently depending on the age of the offender. For an adult the official charge would be motor vehicle theft, but in the case of a juvenile the charge would be simply delinquency. In a criminal case the defendant's name, the court proceedings, and the trial transcripts would all be matters of public record. In juvenile court, however, all of this information would be confidential. Finally, upon a finding of guilty the adult would be convicted of motor vehicle theft, whereas the juvenile would be adjudicated a delinquent.

STATUS OF MINORS

The differences in treatment of juveniles and adults in the justice process are largely a function of historical views of juvenile conduct. At the turn of the century, it was argued that equal treatment of juveniles and adults in the eyes of the law violated American ideals. According to this view, minors who broke the law were actually victims of improper care and treatment at home. When juveniles violated the law, it was a sign that their parents could not or would not take care of them adequately, and it was up to the state to step in and act in the best interests of the child and thus prevent future misbehavior. This view is called **parens patriae** (the state acts as a parent).

parens patriae
(the state acts as a parent) The view that juvenile law violations are a sign that parents cannot or will not take care of their child adequately and that it is up to the state to step in and act in his or her best interests, thus preventing future misbehavior.

The philosophy of parens patriae meant that the state should not punish children for their criminal behavior but instead should try to help them control themselves and prevent future criminality. As a result, it made no sense to convict children of such crimes as motor vehicle theft, burglary, or robbery because they would be labeled as criminals and their chances of reform would be reduced. Instead, the label of delinquency was used to indicate that the child needed the care and treatment of the state. It was on the basis of this notion of parens patriae that the first juvenile court was established in the United States in 1899.

In recent years, however, considerable controversy has arisen over the legal treatment of juveniles. The effectiveness of the state in acting as a surrogate parent has been questioned, as has the adequacy of the legal protections for juveniles in court. The question of whether the philosophy of parens patriae should be abandoned (in favor of the treatment of juveniles as adults) has been considered. A similar controversy has arisen in the handling of status offenders in the juvenile justice process. It is claimed that some status offenders are incarcerated for nonserious behavior and that the definitions of some status offenses are vague. Some critics question whether status offenders and delinquents should be adjudicated separately, whether juvenile justice processing makes status offenders better or worse, and whether status offenses should be abolished altogether. Each of these arguments makes fundamental assumptions about the philosophy and purpose of juvenile justice. It is important to be aware of these assumptions because they determine whether juveniles are treated like adults in an adversarial process or as children in a treatment process.

As Table 16.1 indicates, the juvenile justice system uses more neutral terminology than does the

Table 16.1 Adult and Juvenile Justice System Terminology

Procedure	*Juvenile*	*Adult*
Act	Delinquency	Crime
Apprehension	Custody Petition	Arrest Indictment
Preadjudication	Detention Agree to finding Deny the petition	Jail Plead guilty Plead not guilty
Adjudication	Adjudicatory hearing Adjudicated Delinquent	Trial Convicted Criminal
Corrections	Disposition Commitment	Sentence Incarceration

adult adversarial system, with its formal accusations and convictions. This illustrates the philosophical basis of juvenile justice.

The establishment of juvenile courts corresponded with the rise of a philosophy known as positivism, which saw crimes as the product of external influences rather than free will. The purpose of juvenile justice, therefore, is to correct the way young people respond to those influences, rather than to punish them. However, prevailing views regarding the treatment of juveniles have shifted over the years. Currently there is much disagreement over the proper goals of the juvenile justice system.[3]

The Nature and Extent of Delinquency

Establishing the true extent of delinquency helps citizens assess their actual risk of becoming victims. It also helps public officials determine the degree of urgency that should be attached to delinquency prevention efforts. Unfortunately, the precise level and types of delinquent acts are difficult to establish.

The FBI's annual *Uniform Crime Reports* (UCR) records all crimes known to the police. However, this compilation is of little use in assessing juvenile delinquency because it is impossible to know whether the crimes were committed by juveniles or adults, and victimization surveys reveal that less than 40 percent of all serious crime is actually reported to the police. As a result, one must rely on alternative measures of the extent of delinquency.

Arrest Figures

The most commonly used indicator of delinquency is the rate of juvenile arrests. Arrest figures provide information about the age of suspects, and make it possible to see whether juveniles are engaging in more or less criminal behavior compared to adults. Table 16.2 summarizes the proportion of arrests during the last thirty-five years that involved juveniles. The crimes listed in the table are among the offenses considered in the Federal Bureau of Investigation's annual compilation of arrest data. Criminal homicide, forcible rape, robbery, and aggravated assault are considered violent crimes (i.e., crimes against persons), whereas burglary, larceny, motor vehicle theft, and arson are treated as property crimes (i.e., property is the victim).

JUVENILE ARREST RATES

As is indicated in Table 16.2, a total of 14.1 million arrests were made in the United States in 2005. Of these, 15.3 percent involved juveniles (those under age eighteen). Thirty-five years earlier, however, more than 25 percent of all those arrested were under age eighteen. Table 16.2 makes it clear that a drop occurred in the proportion of juveniles arrested from 1970 to 2005. This is a remarkable finding, given the amount of attention devoted to the "delinquency problem" in recent years. If arrests are used as an indicator of criminal involvement, juveniles are arrested significantly less often now than they were more than two decades ago. This has occurred despite the fact that nearly 8 million more people were arrested in 2005 than in 1970.

Table 16.2 indicates that 20.8 percent of all those arrested for forcible rape in 1970 were juveniles. Thirty-five years later, the proportion of juveniles ar-

Table 16.2 **Offenses of Persons under Eighteen Years of Age That Result in Arrests (percent of total arrests)**

Offense	*1970*	*1980*	*1990*	*2000*	*2005*
Criminal homicide	10.5	9.3	14.0	9.3	9.0
Forcible rape	20.8	14.8	14.9	16.4	15.4
Robbery	33.4	30.1	24.2	25.3	25.2
Aggravated assault	16.5	14.7	13.6	13.9	13.6
Burglary	52.0	44.9	33.0	33.0	26.1
Larceny	50.7	37.5	30.0	31.2	25.7
Motor vehicle theft	56.1	45.3	43.3	34.3	25.5
Arson	59.5	44.2	43.8	52.8	48.6
Total violent crime	22.6	19.3	16.2	15.9	15.8
Total property crime	51.7	40.2	31.9	32.0	26.0
Simple assault	18.2	17.9	14.9	18.0	19.0
Forgery/counterfeiting	10.6	13.0	9.1	5.9	3.5
Fraud	4.0	2.8	3.4	3.1	2.1
Embezzlement	4.3	11.3	7.2	10.3	6.1
Stolen property	30.2	29.9	25.9	23.4	16.6
Vandalism	72.2	49.4	40.4	40.6	37.2
Weapons offenses	16.6	15.3	18.2	23.6	23.1
Prostitution	2.3	3.6	1.4	1.5	1.9
Other sex offenses	21.1	17.5	15.9	18.6	18.2
Drug offenses	22.4	18.9	7.41	12.9	10.4
Gambling	1.9	3.7	5.2	14.0	18.1
Offenses against family	1.5	4.1	4.0	6.4	4.2
DWI	1.1	2.3	1.1	1.4	1.3
Liquor laws	33.8	33.1	22.1	23.3	21.1
Drunkenness	2.7	4.1	2.7	3.4	2.9
Disorderly conduct	21.0	16.5	16.6	25.9	29.7
Vagrancy	12.2	13.7	8.1	9.3	14.0
Suspicion	27.5	17.6	17.0	11.2	14.6
Other (not traffic)	29.6	21.6	9.7	21.1	9.4
Curfew and loitering violations	100	100	100	100	100
Runaways	100	100	100	100	100
Total % juvenile arrests	25.3	20.9	15.6	17.1	15.3
Total no. of arrests (in millions)	6.6	9.7	11.3	14.0	14.1

Source: Federal Bureau of Investigation, *Uniform Crime Reports* (Washington, DC: U.S. Government Printing Office, published annually).

rested for this crime was 15.4 percent. Similarly, 52 percent of those arrested for burglary in 1970 were juveniles. By 2005, this number had dropped to 26.1 percent. The same is true for most of the other offenses listed. Simply stated, the proportion of juvenile arrests has decreased significantly in most crime categories since 1970.

Table 16.3 Offenses for which Juveniles Are Most Often Arrested (other than status offenses) (arrests of persons under eighteen, percent of total arrests)

Offense	*1970*	*2005*	*Change*
Arson	59.5	48.6	−11%
Motor vehicle theft	56.1	25.5	−31
Vandalism	72.2	37.2	−35
Burglary	52.0	26.1	−26
Larceny	50.7	25.7	−25
Liquor laws	33.8	23.3	−10
Robbery	33.4	25.3	−8

Source: Compiled from Federal Bureau of Investigation, *Uniform Crime Reports* (Washington, DC: U.S. Government Printing Office, published annually).

There are exceptions to these trends, however. Arrests of juveniles for weapons offenses increased from 16.6 percent to 23.1 percent over the thirty-five year period, and arrests for disorderly conduct similarly increased from 21 to 29.7 percent of all arrests. These are important trends and imply a potential connection between increases in juvenile weapons use and disorderly conduct. Some have argued that these trends result from the crack cocaine and methamphetamine epidemic that increased the level of violence in the drug trade in some areas. Others see random violence at schools to be the result of increasing depictions of violence in entertainment and the lack of proper supervision from adult role models.[4] Overall, however, total arrests of juveniles for all violent crimes have shown a consistent decline, dropping from 22.6 percent to 15.8 percent of all arrests from 1970 to 2005.

Given the information in Table 16.2, we can identify the crimes for which juveniles are most often arrested. First, it can be seen that every person arrested for curfew and loitering violations, as well as runaways, was a juvenile. This is because these are status offenses that apply only to juveniles. The eight crimes for which juveniles are most often arrested, other than status offenses, are presented in Table 16.3.

JUVENILE PROPERTY CRIMES

The property crimes of vandalism, arson, motor vehicle theft, burglary and larceny, and stolen property accounted for the highest proportion of juvenile arrests in 1970, a trend that continues thirty-five years later. As Table 16.3 indicates, however, the proportion of juveniles arrested for these crimes has decreased steadily. Juveniles thus appear to be responsible for a shrinking proportion of the crime problem. In 1970, they accounted for more than half of all arrests for vandalism, arson, burglary, motor vehicle theft, and larceny. Now, they do not comprise the majority of arrests in *any* crime category counted by the FBI.

Table 16.4 Total Arrests, by Age (percent of total arrests)

Age	*1970*	*1980*	*1990*	*2005*
Under 10	1.2	0.6	0.4	0.1
10–12	2.0	1.4	1.3	1.0
13–14	6.0	4.2	3.6	3.5
15	4.9	3.9	2.9	3.1
16	5.7	5.1	3.5	3.6
17	5.4	5.7	4.0	4.0
Total under age 15	9.2	6.2	5.3	4.6
Total under age 18	25.3	20.9	15.6	15.3
Total ages 18 and over	74.7	79.1	84.4	84.7

Source: Compiled from Federal Bureau of Investigation, *Uniform Crime Reports* (Washington, DC: U.S. Government Printing Office, published annually).

Arrests by Age It is widely believed that *younger* juveniles are engaging in more criminal acts now than was the case years ago. However, this claim is not supported by the facts. Table 16.4 summarizes total arrests in the United States by age over thirty-five years.

It is evident from the data that younger juveniles are arrested significantly less often than older juveniles, a fact that was true in 1970 and remains true now. Juveniles under age fifteen accounted for 9.2 percent of all arrests in 1970 and for 4.6 percent of all arrests in 2005. In addition, adults age eighteen and older account for the overwhelming majority (84.7 percent) of all arrests.

Juveniles commit many more property crimes than violent crimes. Vandalism remains one of the most common offenses for which juveniles are arrested. What do juvenile arrest rates show about trends in juvenile crime?

Arrests by Sex Another frequently heard claim is that girls are becoming increasingly involved in criminal activity, especially delinquency. Table 16.5 summarizes total arrests of persons under age eighteen, by sex.

The data in Table 16.5 indicate that far more boys than girls are arrested for delinquency, although their numbers are declining slowly. Seventy percent of all juveniles arrested are male, a proportion that has fallen by 9 percent over the years. Correspondingly, arrests of girls have risen by 9 percent, to 30 percent of all arrests, over the same period. Eighty-two percent of those arrested for violent crimes (homicide, rape, robbery, and serious assaults) are male. The number of arrests of girls for violent crimes has doubled (from 9 to 18 percent) during the last thirty-five years. These figures reveal a slow but steady increase in female involvement in juvenile delinquency.

Table 16.5 Arrests of Persons under Age Eighteen, by Sex (percent)

Sex	*1970*	*1980*	*1990*	*2005*
All crimes				
Male	79	79	77	70
Female	21	21	23	30
Violent crimes only				
Male	91	90	88	82
Female	9	10	12	18

Source: Compiled from Federal Bureau of Investigation, *Uniform Crime Reports* (Washington, DC: U.S. Government Printing Office, published annually).

Self-Reports

One problem with these figures is that arrests are not an accurate indicator of actual crime rates. As indicated in earlier chapters, arrests are a better measure of police activity than of criminal activity. Moreover, juveniles are overrepresented in arrest statistics because they often commit less sophisticated crimes (such as vandalism and larceny) and are less mobile than adults. Therefore, they are less likely to escape detection.

Self-reports are an alternative way to measure the extent of delinquency. In self-report studies, a sample of juveniles are asked to indicate the types and numbers of crimes they have committed in the past (whether or not they were caught);

the information is kept confidential. Self-reports were first attempted to see if there are differences between juveniles who have been caught and those who have not. As sociologist Albert Cohen recognized nearly fifty years ago, "The defect of these [official] data, of course, is not that they represent too small a sample but that we cannot tell what sorts of delinquency may be over represented or under represented."[5]

WHO GOT CAUGHT?

In 1946, Austin Porterfield conducted the first self-report study ever attempted. He asked 200 precollege men, 130 precollege women, and 100 college men to report delinquent acts on a confidential questionnaire. The precollege men admitted to an average of eighteen offenses each, the women admitted to an average of five offenses, and the college men admitted to an average of eleven offenses. Significantly, every respondent admitted having committed at least one criminal act or status offense.[6] Similar findings were reported in subsequent studies of adults, high school students, and inmates in a juvenile correctional facility.[7]

In addition to showing how common delinquency really is, self-report studies provide an indication of what percentage of juvenile offenders are caught. Martin Gold administered a self-report questionnaire to a random sample of teenagers in Flint, Michigan. Of those admitting to crimes, only 16 percent had been caught.[8] Maynard Erickson and LaMar Empey administered a self-report to a group of fifteen- to seventeen-year-old boys. Fifty of the boys had never been to court, thirty had been adjudicated only once, fifty were recidivists (repeat offenders), and fifty were currently incarcerated in a juvenile institution. Nearly every boy admitted to some offenses surveyed and over 95 percent of their delinquent acts were undetected.[9]

DELINQUENCY PROFILING

Comparisons of self-report surveys and official statistics also provide information about the *types* of juveniles who engage in delinquency. Although official statistics indicate that males engage in delinquency at a rate of four to eight times that of females, self-reports have shown the actual rate of male offenses to be only about twice the female rate (depending on the crime). A national self-report survey found that females engage in petty larceny and use of drugs, and run away from home, as often as males do. Males were found to engage in such offenses as joyriding, alcohol use, and truancy only twice as often as females.[10]

Official statistics also indicate that delinquency is much more common among poor and working-class juveniles than among middle-class juveniles (by about five to one). Self-report surveys, however, suggest that juvenile offenders from middle-class families are just as common as juvenile offenders from lower-class families. In addition, official statistics indicate that most delinquents are nonwhite, but self-reports show rates of delinquency by white and black youths to be very similar.[11]

Perhaps the most significant contribution of self-reports to our knowledge of delinquency is that they reveal that nearly all juveniles break the law at one time or another. Only a small proportion, however, engage in persistent or serious criminal behavior. Official statistics include a greater proportion of the most serious and frequent delinquents. Finally, in contrast to official statistics, self-reports have shown that delinquents are not limited to a particular sex, race, or social class.

DELINQUENCY IS UNIVERSAL

The accuracy of self-reports has been questioned on methodological grounds. Questions have been raised about their validity (was the act really a crime?) and their reliability (are many offenses concealed or exaggerated?). Self-report studies have been administered in different ways to try to reduce these problems and retests have been conducted to check their accuracy.[12] They have been found to provide a generally accurate measure of undetected juvenile crimes. Perhaps the strongest evidence for the validity and reliability of self-reports is the similarity in findings among all studies that have been done. All studies find that delinquency is a nearly universal experience.

What crime(s) does this photo suggest? Why do you believe it is commonly committed by juveniles? Why do you believe this kind of car was targeted?

Victimization Surveys

As was shown in Chapter 3, efforts have been made to estimate the true extent of crime victimization through surveys of a representative sample of the U.S. population. A primary advantage of victim surveys is that they record all victimizations, whether or not they were reported to the police. In addition, they provide much more information about criminal incidents than is included in official statistics.

Victimization surveys have not been very useful in the study of juvenile delinquency. This is because most delinquent acts are victimless crimes, as is evident in Table 16.2. Self-report studies have shown that juveniles most often commit crimes that involve voluntary participation by the victim and the offender, such as drug use, fornication, gambling, alcohol use, and prostitution. These crimes are not included in victimization surveys. In the case of property crimes, it is often impossible to determine the age of offenders. Moreover, in the crimes of burglary, larceny, and motor vehicle theft the "victim" is property; therefore, it is not possible to determine through victimization surveys who the offenders are. In the case of violent crimes, few victims can be positive about the age of the offender. Rape, robbery, and assault all involve personal confrontations, yet it is often difficult for victims to know whether the offender was fifteen, eighteen, or twenty-one years old.

JUVENILES AS VICTIMS

One interesting finding of victimization surveys is that young people are ten times more likely than older citizens to be victims of violence. Likewise, young people are six times more likely to be victims of theft than are older persons. These findings contradict the common belief that the elderly are particularly prone to criminal victimization. Studies by the Bureau of Justice Statistics have found that most teenage offenders victimize other teenagers whom they know. Stranger attacks are less common, probably because more than a third of violent crimes against young teenagers occur on school grounds.[13]

Foundations of Juvenile Justice

The way we deal with juveniles in criminal matters reflects the way that we treat juveniles in other areas of life. As was noted earlier, the establishment of the first juvenile court in 1899 corresponded with the rise of positivism, which saw the social environment as an important cause of behavior. The 1800s also witnessed the

HOUSES OF REFUGE

establishment of "houses of refuge," which were set up to protect wayward youths by reforming them in a family-like atmosphere.[14] Such developments were a manifestation of the philosophy of parens patriae, in which the state took the right of parental control over juveniles from parents who were unwilling or unable to take proper care of the child.[15]

JUVENILE COURT

The juvenile court was a significant innovation in that the concept of juvenile justice was altered from adjudication of guilt to diagnosis of a condition. The emphasis of the justice process was changed from deterrence and incapacitation to rehabilitation, in order to assist, rather than punish, the juvenile. Behavior patterns were seen as more important than specific acts because the acts were considered to be symptoms of some underlying problem. Also, juvenile court proceedings were civil rather than criminal proceedings, on the assumption that the interests of the child were best served through informal adjudication involving no stigma of criminality.[16] By 1920, every state in the country had established a juvenile court based on these principles of positivism and rehabilitation.

Although the idea of the juvenile court spread quickly, it was not carried out in a uniform or standardized manner. As the President's Commission on Law Enforcement and Administration of Justice pointed out in 1967,

> *The mere passage of a juvenile court statute does not automatically establish a tribunal of the sort the reformers contemplated. A U.S. Children's Bureau survey in 1920 found that only 16 percent of all so-called juvenile courts in fact had separate hearings for children and an officially authorized probation service and recorded social information on children brought to court. A similar survey conducted . . . in 1966 revealed significant gaps still existing between ideal and actual court structures, practices, and personnel. Indeed, it has been observed that "there is nothing uniform" in the operation of children's courts.*[17]

Although consensus may have been reached about how the juvenile court should operate, the implementation of this model was not consistent.[18] This inconsistency continues today as states strive "to do something" more effective with juveniles in view of public perceptions of escalating violent juvenile crime.[19]

Objections to Parens Patriae

The juvenile court concept, though widely accepted, was also subjected to criticism. One of the leading critics was Paul Tappan, who wrote during the 1940s.

LACK OF DUE PROCESS

Tappan argued that juveniles were deprived of the due process protections afforded to adults; for example, youthful offenders lacked legal counsel and were charged with over-broad status offenses.[20] Tappan also charged that the juvenile court must measure up to the promise of scientific and humane treatment.

Tappan's allegations were not far off the mark. Many state institutions that were supposed to look after the best interests of children sometimes did not do so. Juvenile reform schools were often harsh, the treatment cruel, and rehabilitation forgotten as juveniles were warehoused like prison inmates.[21] These abuses added strength to Tappan's claims that the rehabilitative juvenile court denied the legal rights of juveniles in exchange for hypothetical benefits of dubious value.

Tappan's arguments received more and more support during the 1950s, while support for the juvenile court concept waned. Because of abuses and the failure of the state to reform delinquents, emphasis shifted to issues such as legal fairness, unjustified detention, and the inability of the juvenile court to deliver on its promise to protect and reform juveniles.[22] These criticisms ultimately led to changes in the juvenile court structure.

When were juvenile courts established? What was the original philosophy behind juvenile courts? How did that philosophy change beginning in the 1960s?

CALLS FOR REFORM

California and New York were the first states to reflect this changing outlook. California, for example, had had a typical juvenile court system since 1915. A juvenile could be taken to court for any one of fourteen violations, including begging, habitually visiting a poolroom or saloon, habitual truancy, refusal to obey parents, being feebleminded or insane, or being afflicted with syphilis or gonorrhea. There was no clear right to legal counsel, adjudication was based on a preponderance of the evidence (unlike "beyond a reasonable doubt" for adults), and the court's jurisdiction extended up to age twenty-one. In 1957, the governor of California appointed a commission to investigate the operation of the juvenile courts. In its reports the commission confirmed many of Tappan's allegations:

> *While supporting the fundamental protective and rehabilitative ideology of the socialized court, the Commission reported a number of serious deficiencies: (a) an absence of well-defined standards and norms to guide juvenile court work meant that dispositions were more often dependent upon the community where a child got into legal trouble than on the intrinsic merits of the case or the needs of the child; (b) basic legal rights of the child were neither uniformly nor adequately protected; (c) the quality of rehabilitative services was questionable and decisions about treatment plans often seemed based on consideration of expediency and administrative convenience rather than on consideration of the needs of the child; and (d) there was excessive and unwarranted detention of children.*[23]

Modifications of the Juvenile Justice System

The commission made numerous recommendations, which led to major modifications in the California juvenile court system. The juvenile court's jurisdiction was divided into three categories: dependent, neglected, and abused children; status offenses; and delinquency (criminal violations). Legal counsel became mandatory for serious (felony) cases, and a pretrial diversion process (six months of "informal probation") was established to remove nonserious cases from formal adjudication. Finally, a two-stage trial process was established, consisting of an adjudication (fact-finding) hearing and a disposition (sentencing) hearing, similar to the procedure for adults.

FAMILY COURT

New York State followed California's lead in 1962, when it abolished its juvenile court and replaced it with a broader "family court." The revisions in New York's system were similar to those in California's, but the due process protection was extended even further. For example, the use of legal counsel was expanded through the establishment of "law guardians," defense lawyers who were paid by the state to represent juveniles exclusively. This innovation rapidly escalated the role of defense counsel in juvenile courts. By 1967, 96 percent of juveniles appearing in family court in New York City were represented by counsel.

The emphasis on due process continued when the U.S. Supreme Court heard its first cases involving juvenile courts in 1966 and 1967. These cases involved the application to juveniles of constitutional protections and procedures that had previously been reserved for adults. They marked a trend toward making adjudication more "adult-like," which carried over into the 1970s. This trend eventually led to still another change in philosophy. From the mid-1970s to the present, further changes in law, policy, and court interpretation have resulted in a virtual abandonment of the parens patriae philosophy in favor of treating juvenile offenders as adults.

The Law and Procedure of Juvenile Justice

As a result of a series of U.S. Supreme Court cases that began during the mid-1960s, the operation of juvenile justice became more uniform and the trend toward due process in juvenile court proceedings solidified. The first of those cases was *Kent v. United States.*[24] Morris Kent, age sixteen, was on probation for several housebreakings and an attempted purse snatching. Two years into his probation, an intruder entered the apartment of a woman in the District of Columbia, raped her, and took her wallet. The police found latent fingerprints in the apartment that matched Kent's fingerprints. Kent was taken into custody by police. He subsequently was convicted of burglary and robbery and was found not guilty by reason of insanity on the rape charge. He was sentenced to thirty to ninety years in prison.

KENT V. UNITED STATES

Kent's conviction was appealed on several alleged violations of due process. Although the Supreme Court agreed that each of these contentions was a matter of substantial concern, it ruled only on the judge's decision to transfer Kent's case to criminal court. This was held to be a violation of due process because no hearing was held, no reasons were given, no findings were made by the juvenile court, and his counsel was denied access to his social-service file. The Court ruled that the juvenile court should have "considerable latitude" to determine whether or not a juvenile's case should be transferred to criminal court. It went on to state that the "special concern" society shows for children does not allow for such treatment.

> *We do not consider whether, on the merits, Kent should have been transferred; but there is no place in our system of law for reaching a result of such tremendous consequences without ceremony—without hearing, without effective assistance of counsel, without a statement of reasons. It is inconceivable that a court of justice dealing with adults, with respect to a similar issue, would proceed in this manner. It would be extraordinary if society's special concern for children, as reflected in the District of Columbia's Juvenile Court Act, permitted this procedure. We hold that it does not.*

In rejecting the way Kent's case was handled by the juvenile court judge, the Supreme Court noted that the judge's decision was "potentially as important to

Kent as the difference between five years confinement [the maximum in juvenile court] and a death sentence [the maximum for rape at that time in criminal court]." The Court concluded that

> *as a condition to a valid waiver order, petitioner was entitled to a hearing, including access by his counsel to the social records and probation or similar reports which presumably are considered by the court, and to a statement of reasons for the Juvenile Court's decision. We believe that this result is required by the statute read in the context of constitutional principles relating to due process and the assistance of counsel.*

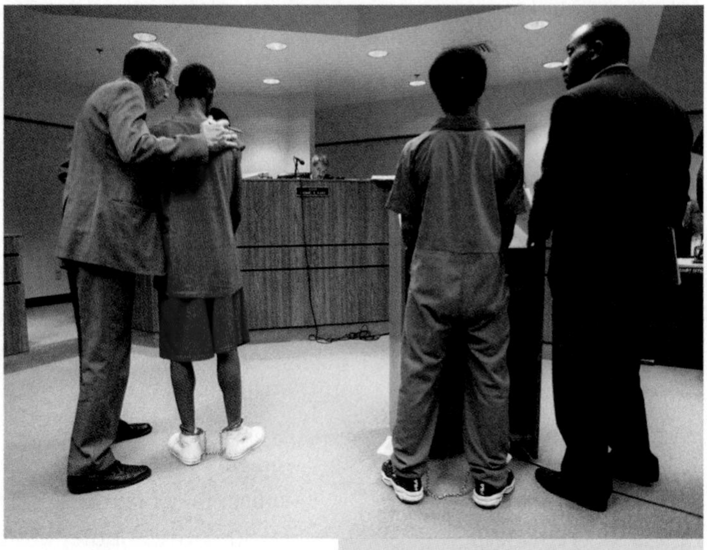

Defense attorney talks with his client, age 16, during a court appearance, while another defense attorney represents another juvenile client in the same case. Do you believe that juveniles should have all the legal rights of adult defendants in court, or should juveniles be treated differently in some ways?

As a result of this case, in all future referrals of juveniles to criminal court, the juvenile must receive a hearing, effective assistance of counsel, and a statement of reasons for the juvenile court's decision.

The *Kent* case is significant because it was the first time the U.S. Supreme Court examined juvenile court procedure, and it found that the procedure in question (referral to criminal court) must measure up to basic standards of due process and fair treatment. Therefore, it can be seen that the due process trend begun in California and New York was continued. As the Supreme Court suggested in *Kent*, the failure of juvenile courts to live up to their promise of scientific and humane treatment was probably the largest factor in the shift toward due process. It concluded that "there is evidence, in fact, that there may be grounds for concern that the child receives the worst of both worlds: that he gets neither the protections accorded to adults nor the solicitous care and regenerative treatment postulated for children."

HEARINGS AND COUNSEL

Lawyers and Self-Incrimination

The Supreme Court made perhaps its most far-reaching decision involving the juvenile court in 1967 in a case that involved several Fifth and Sixth Amendment guarantees. It was an unusual case in that the Court ruled on several issues at once, rather than following its usual pattern of addressing only one legal issue per case.

On June 8, 1964, Gerald Francis Gault and his friend, Ronald Lewis, were taken into custody by the sheriff of Gila County, Arizona. The action followed a verbal complaint by a neighbor of the boys, Mrs. Cook, about a telephone call to her in which the caller or callers made lewd or indecent remarks. The remarks were of the "irritatingly offensive, adolescent, sex variety." The actual remarks made were in the form of three questions: "Do you give any?" "Are your cherries ripe today?" "Do you have big bombers?"

At the time that Gault was picked up by police, his parents were both at work. No notice that he was taken into custody was left at the home, and no other steps were taken to advise them that their son had, in effect, been arrested. Gault was taken to the Children's Detention Home. When his mother arrived home at 6:00 P.M., Gault was not there. His older brother was sent to look for him at the home of the Lewis family. He apparently learned then that Gault was in custody. He and his mother then went to the detention home. Deputy Probation Officer Flagg, who was also superintendent of the Detention Home, told Mrs. Gault "why Jerry was here" and said that a hearing would be held in juvenile court at 3:00 P.M. the following day.

On the next day Gault, his mother, his older brother, and probation officers Flagg and Henderson appeared before the juvenile court judge. (Gault's father was out of town on business.) Mrs. Cook, the complainant, was not present. No one was sworn in at this hearing, no transcript or recording was made. There were conflicting accounts of what Gault said. His mother recalled that he said only that he had dialed Mrs. Cook's number and then handed the telephone to his friend, Ronald. Officer Flagg recalled that Gault admitted making the lewd remarks. Judge McGhee testified that Gault "admitted making one of these [lewd] statements." At the conclusion of the hearing, the judge said he would "think about it."

LEWD STATEMENTS

Gault was taken back to the detention home rather than being sent to his own home with his parents. After being in detention for three or four days, he was released and driven home. There was no explanation as to why he was kept in the detention home or why he was released.

On the next day the Gaults received an informal note from Officer Flagg telling them that a further hearing on their son's delinquency would be held. Witnesses at this proceeding differed in their recollections of his testimony. Mr. and Mrs. Gault recalled that he again testified that he had only dialed the number and that the other boy had made the remarks. Officer Flagg agreed that at this hearing Gault did not admit making the lewd remarks. Judge McGhee recalled, however, that "there was some admission again of some of the lewd statements. He didn't admit any of the more serious lewd statements." Again the complainant, Mrs. Cook, was not present. Mrs. Gault asked that Cook be present "so she could see which boy had done the talking, the dirty talking over the phone." The juvenile court judge said that she was not required to be present. In fact, the judge did not speak to Cook or communicate with her at any time, and Officer Flagg had talked to her only once, by telephone. At the conclusion of the hearing the judge committed Gault to the State Industrial School "for the period of his minority [that is, until age twenty-one], unless sooner discharged by due process of law." The court's order stated that "after full hearing and due deliberation the Court finds that said minor is a delinquent child, and that said minor is of the age of 15 years." Thus, because Gault was fifteen years old and was sentenced to the juvenile institution until he was twenty-one, he effectively received a sentence of six years. The maximum penalty for an adult on the same charge was two months in jail and a fifty-dollar fine.

A juvenile is led away by police after being taken into custody. What is the likelihood that this juvenile will be brought to court for adjudication rather than being warned and released?

Gault's case eventually reached the U.S. Supreme Court on seven separate grounds. Gault charged that the juvenile court procedure in Arizona was unconstitutional because it failed to provide adequate notice of the charges against him, he was not advised of his right to counsel, his protection against self-incrimination was not observed, he was denied the right to confront and cross-examine witnesses against him, he had no right to appeal the juvenile court's holding in Arizona, no transcript was made of the proceedings, and the judge gave no reasons for his finding.

IN RE GAULT

In *In re Gault* the Supreme Court examined each of these issues and their application to juvenile court.[25] The Court agreed with Gault's contention that both a juvenile and the juvenile's parents must be notified of the charges early and in writing. The Court reasoned that due process of law does not allow a hearing to take place in which a youth's freedom and his parents' right to custody are at stake without giving them advance notice of the specific charges alleged. The Court also upheld Gault's claim that juveniles must be notified of their right to counsel, or to appointed counsel if they are indigent, in cases in which commitment to an institution could result. Because a delinquency proceeding is comparable to a serious felony prosecution, the Court supported the right to counsel in delinquency cases.

NOTIFICATION

The Supreme Court also held that juveniles, like adults, have the right of protection against self-incrimination and the right to cross-examine witnesses against them:

CROSS-EXAMINATION

> *We conclude that the constitutional privilege against self-incrimination is applicable in the case of juveniles as it is with respect to adults. We appreciate that special problems may arise with respect to waiver of the privilege by or on behalf of children, and that there may well be some differences in technique—but not in principle—depending upon the age of the child and the presence and competence of parents. The participation of counsel will, of course, assist the police, Juvenile Courts, and appellate tribunals in administering the privilege. If counsel was not present for some permissible reason when an admission was obtained, the greatest care must be taken to assure that the admission was voluntary, in the sense not only that it was not the product of ignorance of rights or of adolescent fantasy, fright, or despair.*

APPEAL

In order to prevent untrustworthy confessions the Court ruled that there are no grounds for a distinction between adults and juveniles in these areas.

The Supreme Court did not hold that juveniles had a right to appeal, to have transcripts of proceedings, or to learn a judge's reasons for his or her adjudication decision. It did address their desirability, however, in its ruling in *Kent*.

In sum, the Court's decision in *Gault* applied to juveniles many of the due process protections that had previously been reserved for adults. Justice Stewart dissented, however, arguing that the decision was "wholly unsound," given the original purpose of the juvenile court:

This juvenile and his parents received advance notice of this hearing. What legal precedent established the right to notification? What have been the long-term positive and negative effects on the juvenile justice system of extending due process rights to juveniles?

> *Juvenile proceedings are not criminal trials. They are not civil trials. They are simply not adversary proceedings. Whether dealing with a delinquent child, neglected child, a defective child, or a dependent child, a juvenile proceeding's whole purpose and mission is the very opposite of the mission and purpose of a prosecution in criminal court. The object of one is the correction of a condition. The object of the other is conviction and punishment for a criminal act. . . .*
>
> *The inflexible restrictions that the Constitution so wisely made applicable to adversary criminal trials have no inevitable place in the proceedings of those public social agencies known as juvenile or family courts. And to impose the Court's long catalog of requirements upon juvenile proceedings in every area of the country is to invite a long step backwards into the nineteenth century.*

Justice Stewart expressed his belief that the Court's ruling in *Gault* would have the effect of replacing the rehabilitative model with an adult, criminal trial. Future Supreme Court decisions would confirm the trend he feared.

The Burden of Proof

For a person to be found guilty of a crime in criminal court, guilt must be proved beyond a reasonable doubt. From its inception, however, the juvenile court has been viewed as a civil proceeding. In civil cases liability is determined by a preponderance of the evidence, which is a somewhat lower standard than beyond a reasonable doubt. This distinction was the central issue in another Supreme Court case dealing with the juvenile court and the Fourteenth Amendment.

Winship was a twelve-year-old boy in New York State who was taken into custody for entering a locker and taking $112 from a woman's pocketbook. In juvenile court the judge acknowledged that the evidence might not constitute proof beyond a reasonable doubt, but he denied Winship's contention that such proof was required by the Fourteenth Amendment to the U.S. Constitution (which guarantees the due process protection of all citizens). The judge claimed that a preponderance of the evidence is all that is required in juvenile court.

PROOF BY PREPONDERANCE

Proof beyond a reasonable doubt means that after consideration of all the evidence the judge believes that there is a moral certainty of the truth in the criminal charge against the defendant. Proof by a preponderance of evidence is a lower standard of proof in which a decision of responsibility is made based on the most impressive or convincing evidence offered in court. Traditionally, proof beyond a reasonable doubt is required in criminal cases, whereas proof by a preponderance of the evidence is the standard of proof in civil cases.

Winship was adjudicated delinquent and placed in a training school for boys for an initial period of eighteen months, subject to annual extensions until he reached the age of eighteen. Because he was twelve at the time that the crime was committed, Winship effectively received a six-year sentence.

Winship's appeal reached the U.S. Supreme Court on the grounds that his due process protections had been violated. The question before the Court was whether proof beyond a reasonable doubt was essential to the fair treatment of a juvenile charged with an act that would be a crime if committed by an adult.

The Court agreed with Winship that such a standard of proof is required during the adjudicatory stage of a delinquency proceeding. "Where a 12-year-old child is charged with an act of stealing which renders him liable to confinement for as long as six years, then, as a matter of due process . . . the case against him must be proved beyond a reasonable doubt." The Court stated that the moral force of the criminal law would be diluted if a weaker standard of proof was used "that leaves people in doubt whether innocent men are being condemned." In one of its most famous statements, it held that "it is far worse to convict an innocent man than to let a guilty man go free."[26] As a result of this ruling, proof beyond a reasonable doubt is now required during the adjudicatory stage of any delinquency proceeding.

IN RE WINSHIP

The Supreme Court's decision in the *In re Winship* case was not unanimous, however, because of differing views regarding the philosophy and purpose of the juvenile court. Justice Harlan, for example, hoped that the higher burden of proof would not impede the rehabilitative functions of the juvenile court. He hoped that procedural constraints in juvenile court hearings would not "(1) interfere with the worthy goal of rehabilitating the juvenile, (2) make any significant difference in the extent to which a youth is stigmatized as a 'criminal' because he has been found to be a delinquent, or (3) burden the juvenile courts with a procedural requirement that will make juvenile adjudications significantly more time consuming, or rigid." He believed that the decision in Winship's case "simply requires a juvenile court judge to be more confident in his belief that the youth did the act with which he has been charged."

On the other hand, Justices Burger and Stewart dissented on grounds that the rehabilitative model had, in effect, been negated in favor of treating juveniles as adult criminals. They hoped that the *Winship* decision "will not spell the end of a generously conceived program of compassionate treatment intended to mitigate the rigors and trauma of exposing youthful offenders to a traditional criminal court." They believed that "each step we take turns the clock back to the pre-juvenile-court era." These justices believed that juvenile court was becoming too much like criminal courts, given the growing similarity in court procedures and due process concerns.

Juries in Juvenile Court

MCKEIVER V. PENNSYLVANIA

The Supreme Court continued its examination of juvenile court procedures in the 1971 case of *McKeiver v. Pennsylvania.*[27] Joseph McKeiver, who was sixteen years old, was a member of a group of twenty to thirty youths who pursued three other juveniles and took twenty-five cents from them. McKeiver had an attorney present at his adjudication hearing. He also asked for a jury trial but was denied it. He was adjudicated delinquent.

The Supreme Court combined McKeiver's case with three others to consider whether or not juveniles had the right to a trial by jury under the Sixth Amendment. McKeiver argued that the Sixth Amendment is applicable to juveniles because juvenile court proceedings are similar to criminal trials. He also claimed that juvenile detention and incarceration are substantially the same as jail and

A juvenile is being adjudicated in court by a jury of his peers. If you were a juvenile, would you want to be adjudicated by a jury of teenagers? Why or why not?

prison for adults. Moreover, the procedures are the same, and the stigma of delinquency is the same as that of an adult conviction. Finally, it was argued that a jury would not deny any of the supposed benefits of the juvenile justice process, such as wide discretion in sentencing.

The Supreme Court did not agree with this rationale and held that "trial by jury in the juvenile court's adjudicatory stage is not a constitutional requirement." This decision was based on several concerns. First, the Court did not believe that juries are a necessary part of a fair and equitable proceeding. Second, there was concern with the possibility that juries would make juvenile proceedings a fully adversarial process. Third, juries would not add to the fact-finding function of juvenile court. It should be noted, however, that although the Court did not require juries in juvenile proceedings, it did not prohibit them either. State juvenile court systems and individual juvenile court judges were free to experiment with juries. The Court merely said that the use of juries in juvenile court is not a constitutional requirement. The *McKeiver* decision, therefore, temporarily halted the growing trend toward providing juveniles with due process protections that were previously held only by adults.

Double Jeopardy

In a case that eventually reached the Supreme Court, a juvenile court petition was filed against a seventeen-year-old Los Angeles boy, Allen Breed, alleging that he had committed an armed robbery. A detention hearing took place, and Breed was placed in detention. At the adjudication hearing, the court took testimony from Breed and two witnesses. The judge found that the allegation of armed robbery was supported by the evidence, and he adjudicated the juvenile delinquent. The judge then ordered the youth detained pending a disposition hearing.

At the disposition hearing the judge said that he found the juvenile "not amenable to the care, treatment and training program available through the facilities of the juvenile court." Breed's counsel immediately asked for a continuance "on the ground of surprise." The disposition hearing was rescheduled for the following week.

BREED V. JONES

A week later the judge, after considering the report of the probation officer, declared Breed "unfit for treatment as a juvenile" and ordered that he be prosecuted as an adult. The juvenile was subsequently tried in criminal court and convicted of armed robbery; he was committed to the California Youth Authority.

This case attracted the attention of the Supreme Court when it was alleged that Breed's Fifth Amendment protection against being "twice put in jeopardy of life and limb" for the same offense had been violated. This constitutional provision means that a person cannot be criminally prosecuted twice for the same offense; it is commonly known as protection against **double jeopardy.**

double jeopardy
A constitutional provision that a person cannot be criminally prosecuted twice for the same offense.

In its decision in *Breed v. Jones,*[28] the Court considered the argument that the protection against double jeopardy had not been violated because the procedure in the case was analogous to retrial after reversal of a conviction on appeal. The Supreme Court did not agree with this view.

> *The Court has granted the Government the right to retry a defendant after a mistrial only where "there is a manifest necessity for the act, or the ends of public justice would otherwise be defeated." [Breed] was subjected to the burden of two trials for the same offense; he was twice put to the task of marshaling his resources against those of the State, twice subjected to the "heavy personal strain" which such an experience represents.*

The Court held that adequate constitutional protections for the juvenile were lacking, given the facts in the case. This decision continued the trend toward applying due process protections in juvenile court proceedings that had emerged from the *Kent, Gault,* and *Winship* rulings. As a result of this series of decisions, the distinction between juvenile and adult proceedings rapidly diminished, beginning in the mid-1960s and continuing through the mid-1970s.

Preventive Detention

During the 1980s, the Supreme Court made several rulings that produced a further shift toward the treatment of juveniles as adults. One case involved a challenge to the New York State Family Court Act, which authorized the use of pretrial detention for juveniles who pose a "serious risk" of committing a crime before their court appearance.

Gregory Martin was arrested after he and two companions allegedly hit a youth on the head with a loaded gun and stole his jacket and sneakers. Martin was fourteen years old and had possession of the gun when he was arrested. The incident occurred at 11:30 at night, and Martin lied to the police about where and with whom he lived. He was detained overnight. The day after his arrest Martin appeared in Family Court accompanied by his grandmother. Citing possession of the loaded weapon, the false address given to the police, and the lateness of the

A juvenile in a detention facility. Do you believe juvenile offenders are more effectively reformed by punishment in custody or through rehabilitative treatment? Explain your view.

hour as evidence of lack of supervision, the judge ordered Martin placed in detention. A probable cause hearing was held five days later, and probable cause was found to exist for all the crimes charged.

At the fact-finding hearing held the following week, Martin was found guilty of robbery and criminal possession of a weapon. He was adjudicated a delinquent and placed on two years' probation. Between the initial appearance and the completion of the fact-finding hearing he had been in detention for a total of fifteen days.

SCHALL V. MARTIN

This case of *Schall v. Martin*[29] became a class-action suit involving a large number of juveniles who, like Martin, had been detained for one to two weeks and then either released or placed on probation. The Supreme Court assessed the balance between the needs of the juvenile and the need for protection of the community. It stated that the "legitimate and compelling state interest" in "protecting the community from crime cannot be doubted," nor can the "juvenile's countervailing interest in freedom" from incarceration before trial, "even for the brief time involved here." The Court held, however, that "juveniles, unlike adults, are always in some form of custody." It went on to explain that because children do not take care of themselves, they are subject to the control of their parents, and to the state (via parens patriae), if the parents do not adequately control the child. As a result, the juvenile's liberty may, in appropriate circumstances, be subordinate to the state's interest in controlling the child. Preventive detention "serves the legitimate state objective . . . of protecting both the juvenile and society from the hazards of pretrial crime."

The Court's reasoning in this case went beyond mere due process concerns to those of community protection, in accordance with the crime control model for juvenile justice. By placing the protection of the community above the needs of the child, the Court showed its preference for crime control and community protection over rehabilitation and treatment of the juvenile.

Three justices dissented in this case, recognizing the apparent trend toward treating juveniles as adults. They attempted to show that neither the goal of due process nor crime control is achieved through preventive detention of juveniles:

PREVENTIVE DETENTION

> *The majority's arguments do not survive scrutiny. Its characterization of preventive detention as merely a transfer of custody from a parent or guardian to the State is difficult to take seriously. Surely there is a qualitative difference between imprisonment and the condition of being subject to the supervision and control of an adult who has one's best interests at heart [under the rehabilitative model].*

REHABILITATIVE MODEL?

The dissenting justices also noted that other courts have concluded that "only occasionally and accidentally does pretrial detention of a juvenile under [New York's law] prevent the commission of a crime." This is because the judges in juvenile court "are incapable of determining which of the juveniles who appear before them would commit offenses before their trials if left at large and which would not." On the basis of its own review, the District Court found that "no diagnostic

Media & Criminal Justice

Scared Straight

In 1978 a film called *Scared Straight* not only won the Academy Award for best documentary; it also received such acclaim from policymakers and juvenile justice professionals that it was shown on television as a public service. This was highly controversial, because the film is rife with gratuitous profanity and graphic depictions of prison life. When the battle to show *Scared Straight* on public television was finally won in the late 1970s, the film could be shown only after 11:00 P.M., when children were presumably sleeping.

The documentary is a no-holds-barred look at the Lifer's Program at Rahway State Prison in New Jersey. This program, initiated and designed by prisoners serving life sentences for their crimes, involves having juvenile delinquents brought to Rahway for a full tour of the facility. Participants are not just guided through cells but they are locked in the cages and forced to experience the closed-in reality of a hard cot, filthy toilet, and pornographic graffiti. The cacophony of cell doors clanking shut and bells ringing is outdone only by the jeering and taunts of the inmates, who literally hurl spit and sexually explicit insults at the juveniles.

As the 1978 documentary shows, following the facility tour the teenage delinquents are locked in a prison room with a dozen lifers, who spend the next several hours enlightening them on the reality of prison life through plain talk, role-playing demonstrations, and direct threats. The prisoners steal the participants' shoes, to remind them of how the victims of their larcenies feel. One young man is challenged to attack an inmate to show how tough he is; when he chooses not to, that inmate suddenly "owns" the boy, then "sells" him to another inmate for a cigarette to show what happens to those who can't defend themselves. One double lifer threatens with genuine animosity to rip out the tearful eye of a young man "and squish it in front of your other good eye, so you can see what's happening to you as I do it."

The controversy surrounding the original *Scared Straight* revolved around its graphic nature and extreme profanity, but the point made by the documentary was that of the seventeen juvenile delinquents who went through the program that day, only one girl was arrested again in the following six months. The idea was that the Lifer's Program served as a tremendous deterrent to juvenile crime by focusing on still impressionable teens and literally "scaring them straight."

Critics would later argue that the *Scared Straight* documentary was premature in its claims of success, pointing out that long-term tracking of the Lifer's Program participants indicated a much higher rate of recidivism over time. To address this criticism, the producers of the original documentary did their own longitudinal study, contacting the youths from the 1978 film ten years later, in 1988, and again ten years after that. The filmmakers presented the true evidence in their 1998 made-for-television documentary *Scared Straight: 20 Years Later.*

The 1998 follow-up film provided qualitative data on how and why each youth came to be either a law-abiding citizen, a reformed criminal, or a chronic offender. The results were mixed. Quadir, who in 1978 had said that he planned to go to security school to learn how to dismantle locks and alarms in order to be a professional thief, was indeed incarcerated in 1998. The one girl who had reoffended within six months of her 1978 visit was now a working mother of three. One participant had died of an AIDS-related illness linked to his drug use; others had overcome drug addiction and alcoholism to become productive members of society.

What factors do you think are involved in recidivism? Do you think the Lifer's Program should be continued? Why or why not?

tools have as yet been devised which enable even the most highly trained criminologists to predict reliably which juveniles will engage in violent crime."

Similar laws in other states have been challenged on these grounds as well, but this Supreme Court decision ended the litigation. It is clear that the original rehabilitative purpose of the juvenile court has been replaced by an emphasis on due process, beginning in the 1960s with the findings in *Kent* and *Winship*. The *Schall v. Martin* case suggests a further shift toward the crime control model, beginning in the 1980s.

Searches and the Fourth Amendment

Most cases requiring court interpretation of the Fourth Amendment deal with police searches. The only U.S. Supreme Court case of this kind that addressed juvenile justice involved a different type of government agent.

A teacher at Piscataway High School in Middlesex County, New Jersey, discovered two girls smoking in a lavatory in violation of a school rule. One of the girls was T. L. O., a fourteen-year-old ninth-grader. The teacher took the girls to the principal's office, where they met with the assistant vice principal, Mr. Choplick. T. L. O.'s companion admitted to violating the school rule, but T. L. O. denied smoking in the lavatory and denied that she smoked at all.

Choplick asked T. L. O. to come into his office and demanded to see her purse. In the purse he found a pack of cigarettes and a package of cigarette rolling papers, which are associated with marijuana use. Upon finding these items, the vice principal searched the purse more thoroughly. He found a small amount of marijuana, a pipe, empty plastic bags, a large amount of money in one-dollar bills, an index card that appeared to be a list of students who owed T. L. O. money, and two letters that implicated T. L. O. in marijuana dealing.

Choplick notified T. L. O.'s mother and turned the evidence over to the police. At the police station, T. L. O. confessed that she had been selling marijuana at school. On the basis of the evidence seized by Choplick, delinquency charges were filed against T. L. O. She was adjudicated delinquent and sentenced to one year on probation.

T. L. O. appealed her sentence on the ground that the incriminating evidence (i.e., the contents of her purse) had been seized in violation of the Fourth Amendment's prohibition against unreasonable searches and seizures. That is to say, her purse had been searched without probable cause. The vice principal had no reason to believe that T. L. O. was guilty of marijuana possession or sale *before* his search of the purse. Moreover, nothing he found in the purse could shed light on the original charge against her, smoking in the lavatory. Therefore, T. L. O. argued, Choplick's search of the purse was both unnecessary and in violation of the Fourth Amendment.

NEW JERSEY V. T. L. O.

In *New Jersey v. T. L. O.* the U.S. Supreme Court affirmed T. L. O.'s delinquency adjudication on three grounds.[30] First, the Court agreed with T. L. O. that the Fourth Amendment is designed to protect citizens from agents of the government. It further agreed that the Fourth Amendment applies to public school teachers as representatives of the state (in addition to the police). Second, the Court held that students have a legitimate expectation of privacy that must be balanced against "the school's equally legitimate need to maintain a [learning] environment." As a result, the school setting was found to require "some easing of restrictions" on searches by public officials. Third, the Court found that the probable cause standard need not be followed for school searches. Rather, "the legality of a search of a student should depend simply on the reasonableness, under all the circum-

Why did the Supreme Court hold that authorities must have "reasonable grounds" that a student has violated a law or school rule in order to conduct a legal search of that student at school? How is "reasonable grounds" different from "probable cause"?

stances, of the search." Therefore, searches of students in public schools are justified when there are "reasonable grounds" that evidence will be found of violations of law *or* school rules. Probable cause is not needed.

"REASONABLENESS" STANDARD

Three Justices dissented in this case, arguing that this new "reasonableness" standard, unlike the probable cause standard stated in the Fourth Amendment, is "unclear, unprecedented, and unnecessary" and "carves out a broad exception" to existing standards of permissible searches and seizures. The new "reasonableness" standard, they declared, "will likely spawn increased litigation and greater uncertainty among teachers and administrators." The dissenters also expressed concern that the new "reasonableness" standard "will permit teachers and school administrators to search students when they suspect that the search will reveal evidence of even the most trivial school regulation." They added that the Court's decision makes no distinction between searches for haircurlers or sunglasses and searches for drugs or weapons. To allow school officials to search for mere violation of school rules (rather than only for law violations), they argued "displays a shocking lack of all sense of proportion."

It is clear from this decision that protection of the community (the school in this case) was given priority over either the rights or the possible needs of the student. As a result, this case follows the philosophy in *Schall v. Martin*, applying the crime control model to juvenile justice.

Punishment and the Eighth Amendment

Most forms of punishment other than torture have been found to be constitutional, and in 1976 the U.S. Supreme Court stated specifically that the death penalty does not constitute cruel and unusual punishment.[31] Current death penalty cases heard by the Court challenge only the *manner in which they are carried out.*

THOMPSON V. OKLAHOMA

The U.S. Supreme Court did not rule on the possibility of the death penalty for juveniles until 1988, in the case of *Thompson v. Oklahoma.*[32] In that case the Court overturned the death sentence for William Thompson, a fifteen-year-old convicted of murder, explaining that the applicability of the Eighth Amendment depends on "evolving standards of decency that mark the progress of a maturing society." The Court noted that few states permitted the execution of young juveniles. The following year the Supreme Court ruled by a five-to-four margin that it is unconstitutional to execute a fifteen-year-old offender, but a sixteen- or seventeen-year-old offender may be executed.[33] In 2002, the United States Supreme Court held in *Atkins v. Virginia* that the execution of offenders who are mentally retarded also constitutes cruel and unusual punishment in violation of the Eighth Amendment.[34]

The use of the death penalty for juveniles was clarified in 2005 when the Supreme Court held that the Eighth Amendment prohibits imposition of the death penalty for crimes committed when offenders are under eighteen years of age. This ruling mirrored a national consensus against the death penalty for juveniles. The Federal Death Penalty Act, enacted by Congress in 1994, for example, determined that the death penalty should not extend to juveniles. Reasons included a consensus that there are maturity-related differences between juveniles under eighteen and adults, and the fact that the United States was the only country in the world that continued to give official sanction to the juvenile death penalty.[35] Therefore, juveniles under age eighteen are no longer eligible for capital punishment in the United States.

Juveniles in the System: Police, Courts, Corrections

Police Disposition of Juveniles Taken into Custody

Once police take a juvenile into custody, they have several options in deciding how to handle the case. Most small police departments make one officer responsible for handling juvenile matters for the entire department. An officer on patrol encountering a juvenile crime suspect will often refer the case to the juvenile officer, or to a juvenile unit or division in larger departments. The National Advisory Committee on Criminal Justice's Task Force on Juvenile Justice and Delinquency Prevention recommended that every police department with more than seventy-five sworn officers establish a separate juvenile unit or division.[36] Today, nearly every department has either juvenile officers or a formal juvenile division. These officers are usually able to use their own discretion in dealing with juveniles, using five alternatives: (1) warn and release, (2) refer to juvenile court, (3) refer to a social welfare agency, (4) refer to another police department (often juveniles are sent back to the town where they live if the offense was committed elsewhere), or (5) refer to criminal court for prosecution as an adult.

FIVE ALTERNATIVES

Table 16.6 Police Disposition of Juveniles Taken into Custody (percent)

Decision Made	*1970*	*1980*	*1990*	*2005*
Released	45.1	33.8	28.3	20.2
Sent to welfare agency	1.6	1.6	1.6	0.4
Sent to other police department	2.2	1.7	1.6	1.4
Sent to juvenile court	50.3	58.1	64.5	70.7
Sent to criminal court	0.8	4.8	4.5	7.4
Total juvenile encounters (in millions)	1.27	1.47	1.11	0.661

Source: Compiled from Federal Bureau of Investigation, *Uniform Crime Reports* (Washington, DC: U.S. Government Printing Office, published annually).

Table 16.6 indicates how police utilize these five alternatives once a juvenile is taken into custody. It can be seen that in 1970 a total of 1.27 million juveniles were taken into custody. This number rose during the 1970s but decreased to 661,000 by 2005, reflecting the general decrease in the proportion of juveniles being arrested.

Despite the overall decline in the number of juveniles taken into custody, an increasing proportion of juvenile suspects are being handled more severely. In 1970, 50 percent of juveniles were sent to juvenile court, while 45 percent were warned and released. Thirty-five years later, 70.7 percent were sent to juvenile court, while only 20.2 percent were released. It is clear that fewer juveniles are released and more are being sent to court. Table 16.6 also makes clear that in 1970 fewer than 1 percent of all juveniles were referred to criminal court to be tried as adults, but that thirty-five years later the proportion was 7.4 percent. This trend is occurring despite the fact that juveniles account for fewer arrests than ever before, and despite the fact that the most common offenses for which juveniles are arrested have remained virtually unchanged. The increasing numbers of referrals to juvenile court and criminal court (now accounting for nearly 80 percent of all police dispositions of juveniles) indicate greater willingness to adjudicate juveniles as delinquents or criminals. This trend among police agencies corresponds with the more punitive philosophy of the U.S. Supreme Court regarding juvenile justice in recent years.

Juvenile Court Outcomes

The adjudication process for juveniles is a bit more complicated than it is for adults because a juvenile can be dealt with in many more ways than can an adult. Figure 16.1 indicates that 1.6 million cases are processed in juvenile court each year. Fifty-eight percent of these were referred on a petition requesting that the court hold a formal hearing. The others were handled informally without a petition or formal hearing. A juvenile court judge or a probation officer makes the decision on how to handle a particular case. This screening or "intake" decision can result in one of several outcomes. For cases handled informally, the charge is not usually serious. If the juvenile admits to committing the offense, the case can be

FIGURE 16.1 Juvenile Court Processing of Delinquency Cases

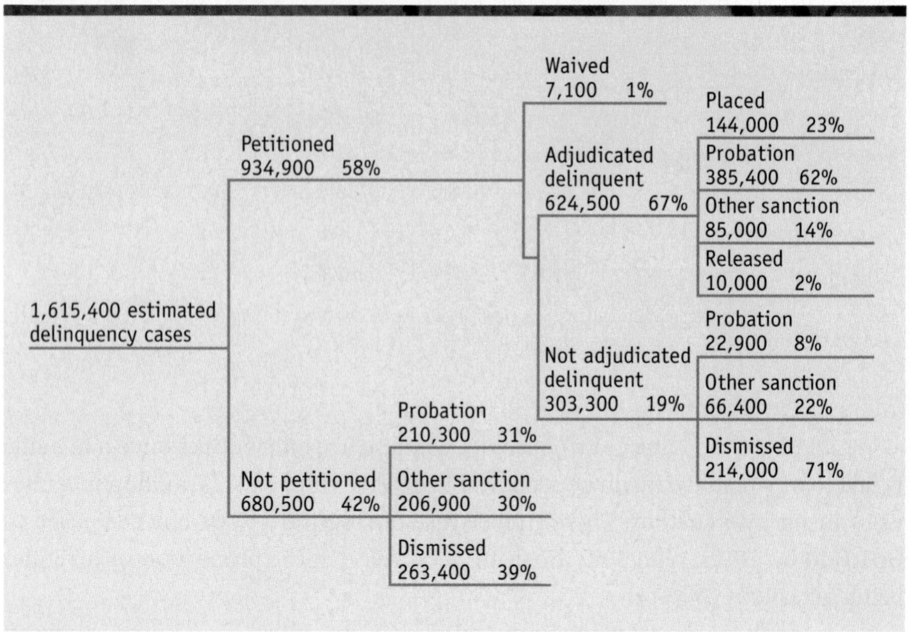

Source: Howard N. Snyder and Melissa Sickmund, *Juvenile Offenders and Victims: 2006* (Washington, DC: Office of Juvenile Justice and Delinquency Prevention, 2006).

closed without further action or the juvenile can be required to make restitution, undergo psychological counseling, or obtain social assistance. No further official action is taken as long as the juvenile fulfills these conditions and stays out of further legal trouble for a certain period of time. If the juvenile denies the charge alleged, there is an automatic referral to juvenile court for adjudication. In some jurisdictions, a case can be referred to a juvenile conference committee (JCC). The JCC is a group of citizens appointed by the juvenile court to recommend a disposition for the juvenile in nonserious cases. Its purpose is to involve the community in the justice process. Normally, only first-time and minor offenders are referred to the juvenile conference committee.

INFORMAL VERSUS FORMAL ADJUDICATION

If the case is handled formally, it is sent to juvenile court, where the judge can choose to handle it through an adjudication hearing, or without such a hearing if the juvenile admits to committing the offense. The adjudication hearing in juvenile court is the equivalent of an adult trial, involving a hearing on the petition against the juvenile where the facts of the case are established. If it is shown that the juvenile did not commit the acts alleged, the petition will be dismissed, as an indictment would be for an adult. If it is found that the juvenile committed the delinquent act, adjudication will follow, as either a delinquent or a status offender, depending on the precise behavior alleged. Once a juvenile is adjudicated a delinquent or a status offender, the juvenile court judge usually adjourns the case and sets a date for a disposition hearing. In the meantime, a probation officer completes a background investigation of the juvenile to help the judge in deciding on a disposition.

The disposition hearing in juvenile court is analogous to a sentencing hearing in criminal court. It is here that the judge determines the best way to resolve

That's a FACT

Perspectives on Juvenile Backgrounds and Crime

Each year since 1997 the Federal Interagency Forum on Child and Family Statistics (Forum) has published *America's Children: Key National Indicators of Well-Being,* a report that includes detailed information on the well-being of children and families in the United States. The Forum updates all data annually on its web site (http://childstats.gov). The report analyzes various background measures and twenty-six key indicators, all chosen due to substantial research connecting them to child well-being and delinquency.

The first section, titled *Population and Family Characteristics,* describes the context in which children live (including aspects such as changes in children's family settings and living arrangements); the sections that follow highlight indicators of child well-being in four key areas: *Economic Security, Health, Behavior and Social Environment, and Education.*

Recent data show that adolescent birth rates continue to decline to the lowest level ever recorded; immunization rates are at record highs; more young children are being read to daily by a family member; the average mathematics scores of fourth- and eighth-graders have reached an all-time high; and teen smoking is at the lowest rate since data collection began. However, the proportion of births to unmarried women continues to rise; the rate of infants born with low or very low birth-weight continues to increase; the number of children classified as overweight is also rising; and the percentage of children living in families with incomes below the poverty thresholds remains at 17 percent. Some important statistics are presented in Table 16A.

Given these indicators of child and family well-being, can you make any predictions regarding their impact on future trends in juvenile delinquency?

Table 16A **Trends in the Background and Characteristics of Young People in America**

Indicator	*Rate*	*Trend*
Births to unmarried women	46 per 1,000	Increase
Inadequate or unstable housing situation with children under age 18	37 percent	Slight increase
Children ages 6–17 who are overweight	18 percent	Slight increase
Low birth-weight children	8.1 percent	Slight increase
Infant mortality (ages 1–4)	32 per 100,000	Slight increase
Adolescent mortality	66 per 100,000	No change
Births to adolescent girls (age 15–17)	22.1 per 100,000	Decrease
12th grade drinking and drug use	23–28 percent	No change
Children age 3–5 read to by family member daily	60 percent	Slight increase
Youth ages 16–19 not in school or working	8 percent	No change

Source: Federal Interagency Forum on Child and Family Statistics, *America's Children in Brief: Key National Indicators of Well-Being 2006,* www.childstats.gov.

the case. As the figure indicates, the juvenile court judge has a number of options in choosing a disposition. The judge can dismiss the case on the condition that the juvenile does not get into further legal trouble within the next year. Other conditions may be added such as requiring the juvenile to undergo diagnostic or therapeutic services or else to make restitution to the victim, observe a curfew, or perform community service. The completion of these obligations would have

Juveniles in a holding cell waiting for their court appearance. A much larger percentage of juveniles are sent to court now than in the past, and fewer are being released. How do you explain this trend?

JUVENILE PROBATION

to take place within a certain period of time (usually one to six months) in order for the case to be terminated. The judge may resentence the juvenile if the conditions are not met.

A juvenile court judge can also choose to place a juvenile on probation. The juvenile normally would be supervised by a probation officer on a weekly or monthly basis for one, two, or three years, similar to the adult system. The third option for a disposition is placement in a juvenile facility or institution. Juveniles involved in serious delinquent behavior may be committed to a secure facility, which would be analogous to an adult prison. Nonsecure facilities would include training schools and camps for delinquent children. Community-based programs include youth development centers, foster care, and independent living arrangements.

Juvenile court judges have a great deal of discretion in deciding upon an appropriate disposition for a juvenile. From outright dismissal to commitment to an institution, a juvenile may be sentenced in any number of ways that can involve many different conditions.[37]

Juvenile Dispositions

Until the 1800s, juveniles were confined together with adult offenders in prisons. Neglected and abused children, as well as delinquents, were incarcerated. The horrible conditions in prisons led to the development of houses of refuge and reform schools specifically for juveniles, culminating in the invention of the juvenile court in 1899 and the development of a separate juvenile justice system.[38] Since then, juveniles and adults have been adjudicated separately for the most part. Today juveniles are held in six different types of facilities:

detention center
A short-term secure facility that holds juveniles awaiting adjudication, disposition, or placement in an institution.

shelter
A short-term nonsecure facility that operates like a detention center but within a physically unrestricted environment.

reception/diagnostic center
A short-term facility that screens sentenced juveniles for assignment to an appropriate level of custody.

training school
A long-term secure facility for adjudicated juveniles.

ranch, forestry camp, or farm
A long-term nonsecure setting for adjudicated juveniles.

group home
Long-term nonsecure facilities that allow juveniles to attend school and employment in the community.

1. **Detention center:** A short-term secure facility that holds juveniles awaiting adjudication, disposition, or placement in an institution.
2. **Shelter:** A short-term nonsecure facility that operates like a detention center but within a physically unrestricted environment.
3. **Reception/diagnostic center:** A short-term facility that screens sentenced juveniles for assignment to an appropriate level of custody.
4. **Training school:** A long-term secure facility for adjudicated juveniles.
5. **Ranch, forestry camp, or farm:** A long-term nonsecure setting for adjudicated juveniles.
6. **Group home:** A long-term nonsecure facility that permits juveniles to participate in schools, employment, and other community agencies.

It can be seen that there are two basic levels of custody. Secure facilities are characterized by locks, bars, and fences, and the movement of juveniles within the institution is monitored closely. Nonsecure facilities are not restricted by "hardware restraints" and permit greater freedom of movement within, and sometimes outside, the facility.[39]

Juvenile corrections is also characterized by the widespread use of private facilities in addition to public institutions. Private facilities are operated by nongovernmental agencies under contract with the government. They are often smaller than public institutions and hold fewer juveniles, and only 12 percent of them are secure facilities. Public facilities are operated directly by a state or local government agency and staffed by government employees. About 70 percent of public institutions for juveniles are secure facilities.

Another way to gauge trends in juvenile justice philosophy is to examine the handling of juvenile delinquency cases by the juvenile court. As Figure 16.2 indicates, between 1991 and 2003 the detained delinquency population (those with their adjudication or disposition pending) in public and private facilities increased by 38 percent. The number of committed (adjudicated) delinquents was 28 percent greater in 2003 than in 1991. The trend toward confining these juveniles appears to have peaked during the late 1990s and has dropped off somewhat since then. This decline may be due to studies that showed no benefit in terms of improved recidivism rates for those juveniles who are tried as adults.[40]

FIGURE 16.2 Juveniles Held in Secure Facilities

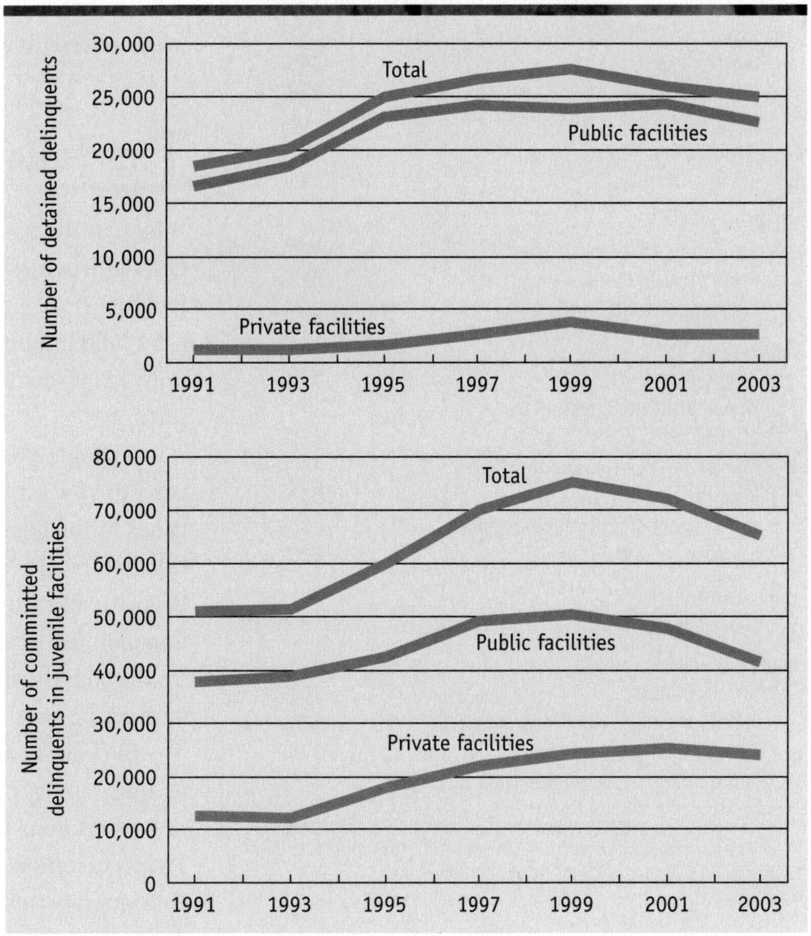

Source: Howard N. Snyder and Melissa Sickmund, *Juvenile Offenders and Victims: 2006* (Washington, DC: Office of Juvenile Justice and Delinquency Prevention, 2006).

Trends in Legislation

A national assessment of legislative changes regarding jurisdiction, sentencing, corrections programming, information sharing, and the role of victims found that forty-seven states and the District of Columbia made "substantive changes" in juvenile justice during the 1990s. Changes of this nature and extent have occurred only three times before: at the turn of the century, when the juvenile court was established; after the U.S. Supreme Court decision in *Gault;* and after the enactment of the Juvenile Justice and Delinquency Prevention Act of 1974.[41] These changes reflect a "fundamental shift in juvenile justice philosophy. Traditional notions of individualized dispositions based on the interests of juveniles are being diminished by interests in punishing criminal behavior."[42] Since 1992, forty states have made it easier to try juveniles as adults, for more types of offenses, and at younger ages in most cases. Thirteen states have enacted mandatory minimum sentences for juveniles convicted of certain serious crimes. These legislative trends reflect the national trend toward punitive treatment of juveniles in a manner similar to the

Table 16.7 Background of Youths in Custody

Offense	
Violent crime	35%
Property crime	29%
Drug offenses	9%
Public order	10%
Status offenses	4%
Prior record	
3 or more arrests	72%
Prior probation	82%
Prior incarceration	58%
Substance use	
Regular drug use	63%
Under drug influence at time of offense	39%
Age at onset of major drug use	14 years
Regular alcohol use	57%
Under alcohol influence at time of offense	32%
Education level	
Median education	8 years
Home situation	
Single parent	70%
Family member ever incarcerated?	52%
Friends involved in crime?	31%
In company of others at time of crime?	62%

Source: Howard N. Snyder and Melissa Schmund, *Juvenile Offenders and Victims A National Report* (Washington, DC: Office of Juvenile Justice and Delinquency Prevention, 2006).

treatment of adults. In fact, we may be closer to treating juveniles as adults under law than at any time since the establishment of the juvenile court.[43]

The Outlook for Juvenile Justice

A look at the backgrounds of juveniles serving time in state facilities provides clues to future prevention strategies. Public facilities hold more serious delinquents: 80 percent of the juveniles held in public facilities are in secure institutions, whereas only 15 percent of those held in private facilities are in secure settings.[44]

As Table 16.7 shows, the typical juvenile delinquent is serving time for a property crime, has been arrested at least three times in the past, and has been on probation and in an institution before. He or she is a regular user of drugs and alcohol and began using major drugs (cocaine, heroin, PCP, LSD) at age fourteen. He or she has not finished the ninth grade, and comes from a single-parent home. A family member has been incarcerated in the past.

In order to reduce the number of serious delinquents such as these (most of whom end up in secure institutions), action must be taken to address the conditions in which they live. These juveniles have problems that began long before their delinquency that involved bad family situations, and school and drug problems. Most juvenile delinquents are at high risk for committing crimes for years before the crimes actually occur.[45] Relatives, neighbors, teachers, churches, and social service agencies are aware of which juveniles and which families are not acting properly, but action often is not taken until the juvenile commits a serious crime. By then it is often too late. Continued inattention to these problems helps to perpetuate the problem of juvenile delinquency. The outlook for juvenile delinquency in the future will depend on the amount of attention given to these underlying problems associated with delinquency.

CRITICAL THINKING EXERCISES

Abolish the Age of Majority?

A problem arises when juveniles commit "adult" crimes. That is, sometimes juveniles commit extremely serious crimes with little reflection, remorse, or fear. The brutal nature of some of these crimes results in demands for punishment as an adult, despite the age of the juvenile. "Treatment" as a juvenile simply is not an adequate punishment for the act and is not a sufficient deterrent to the juvenile or to others. Although rehabilitation is hoped for, it is clearly secondary to the desire for punishment.

In recent years many states have passed laws that make it easier to hold violent juvenile offenders responsible as adults. In these states, juveniles who are charged with certain serious crimes, such as murder, rape, and aggravated assault, are *presumed* to be responsible as adults. These defendants are tried and punished as adults in criminal court unless it can be shown that the juvenile deserves treatment according to the philosophy of rehabilitative juvenile justice.

"Waivers" from juvenile to adult court are often based entirely on the nature of the crime charged. If the crime is serious enough, juveniles are very likely to be tried and punished as adults. The juvenile's actual age or background matters relatively little in these decisions.

The underlying issue is that the age of majority is arbitrary. There is no magic that occurs at age eighteen that makes one a responsible adult. In fact, everyone knows some young people who are mature and responsible at age fifteen, and some who are still immature at age twenty-one. Perhaps arbitrary age distinctions should be eliminated so as to avoid the problem of adjudicating young people as adults or juveniles solely on the basis of their age or the nature of the charges they face. Neither of these factors is a reliable indicator of whether punishment or treatment is most appropriate.

An alternative is to abolish the age of majority, whether it be sixteen, eighteen, or nineteen. Instead, all crime suspects, regardless of age, would be tried at a fact-finding hearing, the sole purpose of which would be to determine whether the suspect did indeed commit the crime alleged. If evidence beyond a reasonable doubt is established, the offender would face a dispositional hearing at which a judge would impose some combination of punishment or treatment, or both, after a complete investigation had been made of the suspect's background. This punishment and/or treatment would be based on the offender's needs, maturity, and skill level and the safety of the community, not on the offender's age.

The juvenile court system is based on an unrealistic assumption: that age is an appropriate indicator of adult behavior. Instead, investigations by the court should replace the current practice of deciding whether to try juveniles as adults before the charges have been proven. This would have a significant impact on outcomes. In the present system, a juvenile who has been waived to criminal court is unlikely to be viewed as a candidate for treatment (versus punishment), regardless of which alternative would best protect the community in the short term and result in responsible behavior by the offender in the long term. Under the proposed system, a broader and more meaningful range of outcomes would be possible.

CRITICAL THINKING QUESTIONS

1. What is your opinion regarding the proposal to abolish the age of majority? How do you defend it?
2. Explain how you would change the sentencing system, given your answer to the preceding question.

Juries for Juveniles?

Why did the U.S. Supreme Court change its position on due process in *McKeiver v. Pennsylvania?* Beginning with *Kent, Gault,* and *Winship,* and continuing in *Breed,* the Court supported due process protections for juveniles in all its cases from 1966 through 1975. *McKeiver* is the only case during this period in which the Court believed such protection was not a "necessary component of accurate fact finding."

In explaining its decision the Court argued that juries in juvenile court could make these proceedings a fully adversarial process, like criminal court for adults, and that the rehabilitative goals of juvenile justice would not be met. It might be argued, instead, that the Court was afraid of how juries in juvenile court might work as a practical matter and that in this decision the Court actually made it more difficult to achieve rehabilitation.

If juries were available in juvenile court, could a juvenile demand a hearing by a jury of juveniles, since they are the true peers of a juvenile charged with a crime? If so, how would juvenile jurors be obtained? Would a school release program be necessary for jurors? How could one ensure that juvenile jurors would take their task seriously? All these questions were effectively avoided through the Supreme Court's denial of the right to a jury for juveniles, even though it is guaranteed in the Sixth Amendment as a right of the accused.

If one reads the Court's decision in *McKeiver v. Pennsylvania* carefully, it can be seen that the Court took pains to avoid making juries available to juveniles. The Court found it "of more than passing interest" that twenty-eight states denied the right to a trial by jury in similar cases. Of course, ten states specifically *permitted* juries in juvenile court. Rather than look for ways to make juries available, the Court actively sought reasons to deny this Sixth Amendment right to juveniles. It quoted the President's Crime Commission, the Uniform Juvenile Court Act, and the Standard Juvenile Court Act, which all stopped short of recommending jury trials in juvenile court. The Court believed that such juries would bring to the juvenile justice system "the traditional delay, the formality, and the clamor of the adversary system and, possibly, the public trial."

The three Justices who dissented in the *McKeiver* case went back to the Magna Carta to demonstrate that the right to a trial by jury has historically been seen as fundamental to due process. They noted that in states where juvenile court juries are available, few jury trials are ever requested by the accused. Interestingly, they also observed that the phrase "judgment of his peers" is taken from the Magna Carta and that the only restriction on juries is that there be "no systematic exclusion" of eligible potential jurors. "Thus, it is quite possible that we will have teenage jurors sitting in judgment of their so-called 'peers,'" they concluded.

The use of advisory juries was not prohibited in *McKeiver*. Therefore, individual states and juvenile court judges are free to use juries if they wish. In Duluth, Minnesota, for example, juvenile juries made up of volunteers from junior and senior high schools have sat in judgment of accused first offenders in their peer group. According to a court administrator there, "The main advantage of the program is that it helps keep administrative costs down and helps keep the time for processing down to under ten days."[a] The presiding judge believed that the primary value of the youth jury is "the education it gives to the jurors and their peers." This education includes a better understanding of how the system works, experience in making difficult decisions that affect the lives of others, and the recognition of the consequences of violation of the law. Experimentation with "teen," "youth," or "peer" courts has grown dramatically in recent years, and there are now 250 teen court programs in thirty states.[b] The guiding principles of these teen court programs are accountability for behavior, knowledge about the law, and assistance in resolving the problems of peers.[c] Inculcation of these principles on a national level would go a long way toward integrating young people into society and its institutions as participants, rather than only as defendants.

CRITICAL THINKING QUESTIONS

1. What are potential disadvantages of peer juries in juvenile court?
2. What is preventing the establishment of a peer jury in the juvenile court in your own jurisdiction? If one exists, what was the primary force behind its establishment?

NOTES

a. Nathaniel Sheppard, "For Teenagers in Duluth, Teenage Juries," *New York Times* (March 31, 1980), p. 6.

b. Tracy M. Godwin, *Peer Justice and Youth Empowerment* (Washington, DC: Office of Juvenile Justice and Delinquency Prevention, 1996); Michelle E. Heward, "The Organization and Operation of Teen Courts in the U.S.: A Comparative Analysis of Legislation," *Juvenile and Family Law Journal*, vol. 20 (2003).

c. Jeffrey A. Butts and Janeen Buck, *Teen Courts: A Focus on Research* (Washington, DC: Office of Juvenile Justice and Delinquency Prevention, 2000); Paige Harrison, James R. Maupin, and G. Larry Mays, "Teen Court: An Examination of Processes and Outcomes," *Crime and Delinquency*, vol. 47 (April 2001), p. 243.

SUMMARY

JUVENILE JUSTICE VERSUS CRIMINAL JUSTICE

- The philosophy that the state should act in the best interests of children who receive improper care and treatment at home is known as parens patriae.
- In recent years controversy has arisen over the legal treatment of juveniles, and there is much disagreement over the proper goals of the juvenile justice system.

THE NATURE AND EXTENT OF DELINQUENCY

- The most commonly used indicator of delinquency is the rate of juvenile arrests. Most of these arrests are for property crimes, although the proportion of juveniles arrested for those crimes has decreased in the last two decades.
- Younger juveniles are arrested significantly less often than older juveniles, and the majority of those arrested are male.
- Self-reports show that delinquency is extremely common and that relatively few delinquents are caught. They also reveal that offense rates do not differ greatly by race or social class.

FOUNDATIONS OF JUVENILE JUSTICE

- When the first juvenile court was established in 1899, the emphasis of the juvenile justice process changed from deterrence and incapacitation to rehabilitation.
- Objections to the parens patriae philosophy centered on the lack of legal counsel and basic due process protections, as well as the failure of the state to reform delinquents.
- In the 1960s, these concerns were addressed through various modifications of the juvenile justice system.

THE LAW AND PROCEDURE OF JUVENILE JUSTICE

- In *Kent v. United States*, the Supreme Court ruled that a juvenile must receive a hearing before being referred to criminal court for trial as an adult.
- The Supreme Court has ruled that juvenile offenders and their parents must be notified of the charges early

and in writing and that juveniles have a right to counsel and the right of protection against self-incrimination.

- During the adjudicatory stage of a delinquency proceeding the charges must be proved beyond a reasonable doubt.
- The Supreme Court has ruled that juveniles have the same protection against double jeopardy as adults.
- In ruling on preventive detention, the Court has placed the protection of the community above the needs of the child.
- Searches of students in public schools are justified when there are "reasonable grounds" that evidence will be found of violations of law or school rules.
- A 2005 Supreme Court decision now prohibits imposition of the death penalty for crimes committed when offenders are under the age of eighteen.

JUVENILES IN THE SYSTEM: POLICE, COURTS, CORRECTIONS

- Police generally have five alternatives in deciding how to handle a juvenile: (1) warn and release, (2) refer to juvenile court, (3) refer to a social welfare agency, (4) refer to another police department, or (5) refer to criminal court for prosecution as an adult.
- Recent statistics show that fewer juveniles are released and more are being sent to court; an increasing number are being tried as adults.
- An increasing number of delinquents are being placed in institutions or other residential facilities for juveniles.
- Recent legislation reflects the national trend toward punitive treatment of juveniles in a manner similar to the treatment of adults.

THE OUTLOOK FOR JUVENILE JUSTICE

- The typical juvenile delinquent is a male serving time for a property crime, is a regular user of drugs and alcohol, has not finished the ninth grade, and comes from a single-parent home.
- To reduce the number of serious delinquents, action must be taken to address the conditions in which they live.

KEY TERMS

delinquency *450*
status offenses *450*
parens patriae *451*
double jeopardy *467*
detention center *476*
shelter *476*
reception/diagnostic center *476*
training school *476*
ranch, forestry camp, farm *476*
group home *476*

QUESTIONS FOR REVIEW AND DISCUSSION

1. What is meant by parens patriae?
2. What information sources are used to establish the nature and extent of delinquency?
3. What do arrest statistics reveal about the age and gender of juvenile delinquents?
4. How do the findings of self-report studies differ from official statistics on the types of juveniles who engage in delinquency?
5. How has the juvenile justice system evolved over the course of the twentieth century?
6. What is the significance of the Supreme Court's decision in *Kent v. United States?*
7. What principles have been established by the Supreme Court with respect to the right to counsel for juveniles?
8. What standard has the Supreme Court established with respect to the burden of proof in juvenile proceedings?
9. Are juries required in juvenile proceedings?
10. How has the Supreme Court ruled with respect to preventive detention of juveniles?
11. How has the Supreme Court ruled with respect to searches of juveniles?
12. Are juveniles subject to capital punishment?
13. What trends can be seen in police disposition of juveniles taken into custody, juvenile court dispositions, and legislation related to juvenile justice?

NOTES

1. David Green, Gail Epstein Nieves, and Wanda DeMarzo, "Suspect's Attitude a Puzzle," *Miami Herald* (May 28, 2000), p. 1.
2. Jill Barton, "Despite Boy's Release, Harsh Punishments for Juveniles Stand," *Associated Press State & Local Wire* (January 30, 2004).
3. Patricia Torbet, Richard Gable, Hunter Hurst IV, Imogene Montgomery, *State Responses to Serious and Violent Juvenile Crime* (Washington, DC: Office of Juvenile Justice and Delinquency Prevention, 1996); Douglas C. Dodge, *Due Process Advocacy* (Washington, DC: Office of Juvenile Justice and Delinquency Prevention, 1997); Fox Butterfield, "Few Options or Safeguards in a City's Juvenile Courts," *New York Times* (July 27, 1997), p. 1; Christine Todd Whitman, "Bringing Balance to the Criminal Justice System," *Crime & Delinquency*, vol. 44 (January 1998), pp. 70–75; Marcy Rasmussen Podkopacz and Barry C. Feld, "The Back-Door to Prison: Waiver Reform, 'Blended Sentencing,' and the Law of Unintended Consequences," *Journal of Criminal Law and Criminology*, vol. 91 (summer 2001), p. 997; Michael A. Corriero, *Judging Children as Children: A Proposal for a Juvenile Justice System* (Philadelphia: Temple University Press, 2006).
4. Jonathan Alter, "Harnessing the Hysteria," *Newsweek* (April 6, 1998), p. 27; Richard Lacayo, "Toward the Root of the Evil: Schoolboy Massacres May Be an Aberration, but the Question Remains: Why Do Kids Kill?," *Time* (April 6, 1998), pp. 38–40; Anthony N. Doob and Jane B. Sprott, "Is the 'Quality' of Youth Violence Becoming More Serious?," *Canadian Journal of Criminology*, vol. 40 (April 1998), pp. 185–94; R. Rita Dorsey, "Reducing Juvenile Violence through Prevention, Intervention, and Law Enforcement Practices," *Police Chief*, vol. 71 (June 2004) pp. 71–74; James Garbarino, *See Jane Hit: Why Girls Are Growing More Violent and What We Can Do About It* (New York: Penguin, 2005).
5. Albert K. Cohen, *Delinquent Boys: The Culture of the Gang* (1955 reprint) (New York: Free Press, 1971), p. 170.
6. Austin L. Porterfield, *Youth in Trouble* (Fort Worth: Texas Christian University Press, 1946).
7. J. S. Wallerstein and C. L. Wylie, "Our Law-Abiding Lawbreakers," *National Probation* (March–April 1947), pp. 107–12; James F. Short and Ivan F. Nye, "Extent of Unrecorded Juvenile Delinquency," *Journal of Criminal Law, Criminology, and Police Science*, vol. 49 (1958), pp. 296–302; Jerald Bachman, Lloyd Johnston, and Patrick O'Malley, *Monitoring the Future: Questionnaire Responses from the Nation's High School Seniors* (Ann Arbor, MI: Institute for Social Research, 1987).
8. Martin Gold, "Undetected Delinquent Behavior," *Journal of Research in Crime & Delinquency*, vol. 3 (1966), pp. 27–46.
9. Maynard L. Erickson and LaMar T. Empey, "Court Records, Undetected Delinquency and Decision Making," *Journal of Criminal Law, Criminology, and Police Science*, vol. 54 (1963), pp. 465–69; see also Franklyn Dunford and Delbert Elliott, "Identifying Career Offenders Using Self-Reported Data," *Journal of Research in Crime & Delinquency*, vol. 21 (1984), pp. 57–86.
10. Charles M. Puzzanchera, *Self-Reported Delinquency by 12-Year-Olds, 1997* (Washington, DC: Office of Juvenile Justice and Delinquency Prevention, 2000); Suzanne S. Ageton and Delbert S. Elliott, *The Incidence of Delinquent Behavior in a National Probability Sample* (Boulder, CO: Behavioral Research Institute, 1978).
11. Delbert S. Elliott and Suzanne S. Ageton, "Reconciling Race and Class Differences in Self-Reported and Official Estimates of Delinquency," *American Sociological Review*, vol. 45 (February 1980), pp. 95–100; Michael J. Hindelang, Travis Hirschi, and Joseph G. Weis, *Measuring Delinquency* (Beverly Hills, CA: Sage, 1981); David Huizinga and Delbert S. Elliott, "Juvenile Offenders: Prevalence, Offender Incidence, and Arrests by Race," *Crime & Delinquency*, vol. 33 (April 1987), pp. 206–23.
12. John P. Clark and Larry L. Tift, "Polygraph and Interview Validation of Self-Reported Deviant Behavior," *Journal of Criminal Law, Criminology, and Police Science*, vol. 58 (1967), pp. 80–86; Gold, pp. 27–46; Mary Louise Cashel, "Validity of Self-Reports of Delinquency and Socio-emotional Functioning among Youth on Probation," *Journal of Offender Rehabilitation*, vol. 37 (July 2003), p. 11.
13. Howard N. Snyder and Melissa Sickmund, *Juvenile Offenders and Victims: 1999 National Report* (Washington, DC: Office of Juvenile Justice and Delinquency Prevention, 1999).
14. Jane Addams, *Twenty Years at Hull House* (New York: Signet Classic, 1961).
15. Ira M. Schwartz, *(In)justice for Juveniles: Rethinking the Best Interests of the Child* (Lexington, MA: Lexington Books, 1989), p. 150; Benjamin Fine, *1,000,000 Delinquents* (New York: Signet, 1957), p. 207.
16. Julian W. Mack, "The Juvenile Court," *Harvard Law Review*, vol. 23 (1909), p. 104.
17. President's Commission on Law Enforcement and Administration of Justice, *Task Force Report: Juvenile Delinquency and Youth Crime* (Washington, DC: U.S. Government Printing Office, 1967).
18. Steven L. Schlossman, *Love and the American Delinquent: The Theory and Practice of "Progressive" Juvenile Justice, 1825–1920* (Chicago: University of Chicago Press, 1977).
19. Torbet et al., *State Responses to Serious and Juvenile Crime*, p. 61.
20. Paul W. Tappan, "Treatment without Trial," *Social Forces*, vol. 24 (1946), p. 306.
21. Alexander W. Pisciotta, "Saving the Children: The Promise and Practice of Parens Patriae, 1838–89," *Crime & Delinquency*, vol. 28 (July 1982), p. 425.
22. Patrick T. Murphy, *Our Kindly Parent—the State* (New York: Penguin Books, 1977).
23. Paul J. Brantingham, "Juvenile Justice Reform in California and New York in the Early 1960s," in F. L. Faust and P. J. Brantingham, eds., *Juvenile Justice Philosophy*, 2nd ed. (St. Paul, MN: West, 1979), p. 263.
24. 383 U.S. 451 (1966).
25. 387 U.S. 1 (1967).
26. *In re Winship*, 397 U.S. 358 (1970).
27. 403 U.S. 528 (1971).
28. 421 U.S. 519 (1975).
29. 104 S. Ct. 2403 (1984).
30. 105 S. Ct. 733 (1985).
31. *Gregg v. Georgia*, 96 S. Ct. 2909 (1976).
32. 108 S. Ct. 2687 (1988).
33. *Stanford v. Kentucky* and *Wilkins v. Missouri*, 109 S. Ct. 2969 (1989).

34. *Atkins v. Virginia*, 122 S. Ct. 2242 (2002).
35. *Roper v. Simmons*, 125 S. Ct. 1183 (2005).
36. National Advisory Committee on Criminal Justice Standards and Goals, *Report of the Task Force on Juvenile Justice and Delinquency Prevention* (Washington, DC: U.S. Government Printing Office, 1976).
37. Joseph B. Sanborn, Jr., "Factors Perceived to Affect Delinquent Dispositions in Juvenile Court: Putting the Sentencing Decision into Context," *Crime & Delinquency*, vol. 42 (January 1996), pp. 99–113; Aaron Kupchik, "Prosecuting Adolescents in Criminal Courts: Criminal or Juvenile Justice?," *Social Problems*, vol. 50 (August 2003), p. 439.
38. J. Hawes, *Children in Urban Society: Juvenile Delinquency in Nineteenth Century America* (New York: Oxford University Press, 1971).
39. Melissa Sickmund, *State Custody Rates, 1997* (Washington, DC: Office of Juvenile Justice and Delinquency Prevention, 2000).
40. Dale Parent, Terence Dunworth, Douglas McDonald, and William Rhodes, *Transferring Serious Juvenile Offenders to Adult Courts* (Washington, DC: National Institute of Justice, 1997); Gerard A. Rainville and Steven K. Smith, *Juvenile Felony Defendants in Criminal Courts* (Washington, DC: Bureau of Justice Statistics, 2003); Howard N. Snyder, Melissa Sickmund, and Eileen Poe-Yamagata, *Juvenile Transfer to Criminal Court in the 1990's: Lessons Learned from Four Studies* (Washington, DC: Office of Juvenile Justice and Delinquency Prevention, 2000).
41. Torbet et al., p. 59.
42. Ibid., p. xi; see Stephen W. Baron and Timothy F. Hartnagel, "Lock 'em Up: Attitudes Toward Punishing Juvenile Offenders," *Canadian Journal of Criminology*, vol. 38 (April 1996), pp. 191–212; Simon M. Fass and Chung-Ron Pi, "Getting Tough on Juvenile Crime: An Analysis of Costs and Benefits," *Journal of Research in Crime and Delinquency*, vol. 39 (November 2002), p. 363.
43. Ibid., p. 59; Patrick T. McCormick, "Fit to Be Tried? Legislators Have Been Making It Easier to Punish Juveniles as Adults," *America*, vol. 186 (February 11, 2002), p. 15.
44. Howard N. Snyder and Melissa Sickmund, *Juvenile Offenders and Victims: A National Report* (Washington, DC: Office of Juvenile Justice and Delinquency Prevention, 2006).
45. J. David Hawkins et al., *Predictors of Youth Violence* (Washington, DC: Office of Juvenile Justice and Delinquency Prevention, 2000); David Huizinga, Rolf Loeber, Terence P. Thornberry, and Lynn Cothern, *Co-occurrence of Delinquency and Other Problem Behaviors* (Washington, DC: Office of Juvenile Justice and Delinquency Prevention, 2000); Rolf Loeber and David P. Farrington, eds., *Serious and Violent Juvenile Offenders: Risk Factors and Successful Interventions* (Thousand Oaks, CA: Sage, 1998); Gail A. Wasserman, Kate Keenan, Richard E. Tremblay, John D. Coie, Todd I. Herrenkohl, Rolf Loeber, and David Petechuk, *Risk and Protective Factors of Child Delinquency* (Washington, DC: Office of Juvenile Justice and Delinquency Prevention, 2003).

chapter 17

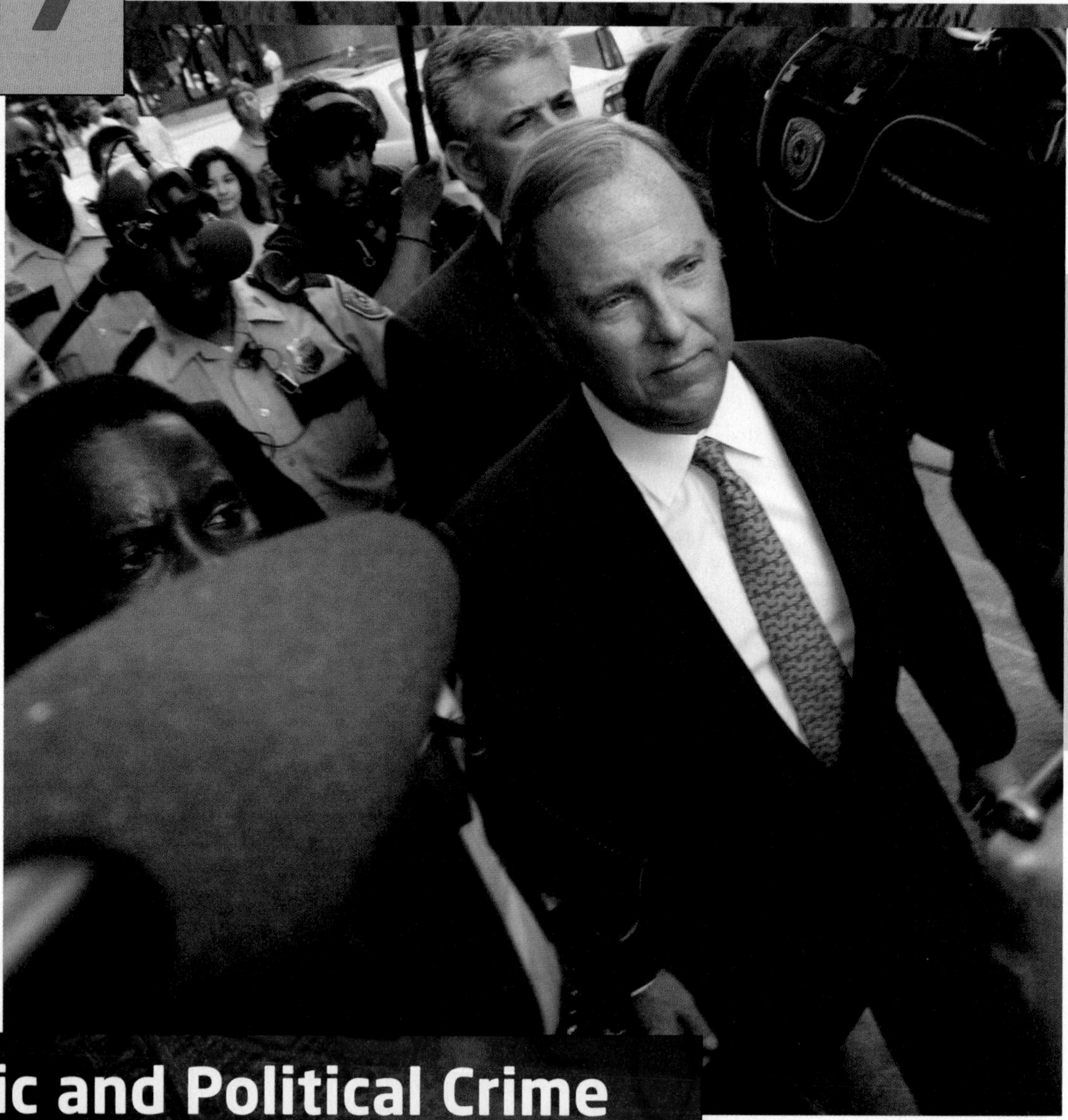

Economic and Political Crime

Sophisticated crimes: offenses that require organization and planning—white collar crime, organized crime, computer crime, and terrorism.

CHAPTER OUTLINE

LEARNING OBJECTIVES

- Identify and define categories of economic and political crime.
- Explain the differences among types of white-collar crimes and their main characteristics.
- Describe patterns and trace trends in economic and political crimes.
- Analyze types of computer crime and their impacts on society today.
- Compare and contrast forms of organized crime and their perpetrators.
- Give examples of challenges in transnational crime prevention and law enforcement.
- Explain the concepts of terrorism and hate crime and their interrelationship.

Speculation was growing that Enron, one of the world's largest companies, was facing serious financial troubles in its cable and energy businesses. Its stock price had plunged by $20 per share. But CEO Jeffrey Skilling told securities analysts in 2001 he was "highly confident" about the company's condition. "I know this is a bad stock market, but Enron's in good shape," he said. Three years later criminal charges were brought against Skilling. The indictment alleged that Skilling knew that Enron was failing and that jobs were going to be cut, that he lied about it, and that Enron failed to meet its budget targets and was able to appear successful only through fraud. Skilling was charged with widespread financial scheming and trading stock on non-public "insider" information, allegedly pocketing $200 million from insider stock sales. Skilling unexpectedly resigned as Enron CEO in 2001, but sold 500,000 company shares of stock a month later for a $15.6 million gain. Skilling was the highest level executive of Enron to be charged in a scandal that ended in his conviction in 2006. It was proven that fraudulent accounting tactics took place to hide Enron's weak financial condition, so that executives could benefit personally before driving the company into bankruptcy, costing employees their jobs and investors their money.

In another Wall Street case, home decorating queen and highly successful businesswoman Martha Stewart went on trial in 2004 on criminal charges she sold 4,000 shares of the biotechnology company ImClone Systems, which was run by her friend Samuel Waksal. The sale came one day before ImClone announced that health regulators had rejected a key new drug application it had developed, sending its stock price plunging. Waksal is serving a seven-year prison term after pleading guilty to securities fraud over his family's sale of the ImClone shares. Stewart was convicted of making false statements to investigators about the sale.

Consider also the case of Royal Caribbean Cruises, the second-largest passenger cruise line in the world. The company had promoted itself as an environmentally responsible company, but pled guilty to twenty-one felony charges for dumping waste oil and hazardous chemicals at sea and then lying about it to the U.S. Coast Guard. Royal Caribbean admitted it routinely dumped oil from its ships a year earlier, but continued the conduct while under court supervision. The investigation found that some of the company's ships had no oil-contaminated wastewater, when these ships produce 100,000 gallons of wastewater annually, suggesting that the wastewater had been dumped at sea. Hazardous chemicals from photo-processing equipment, dry cleaning shops, and printing presses also were dumped at sea, in ports, and in environmentally sensitive areas. The company was fined a record $18 million in addition to $9 million in fines it was assessed a year earlier. Federal investigators said Royal Caribbean crew members wore buttons declaring "Save the Waves" at the same time the company was engaged in illegal dumping.[1]

Consider the similarities between the Wall Street and Royal Caribbean cases and another crime that occurred more than a half century earlier. The famous gangster Al Capone was widely believed to be involved in illegal gambling and bootlegging, but no one was able to prove it. Then the IRS examined his bank accounts and spending habits in Miami and Chicago and found that Capone had spent $7,000 for suits, $1,500 per week for hotel bills, $40,000 for a house on Palm Island, $39,000 on telephone calls, and $20,000 for silverware. This spending pattern suggested that he earned $165,000 per year. The IRS asked Capone to show how he lawfully earned this amount of money. Capone could not do so and was tried and convicted for failure to pay income taxes on $1 million of illegal income.[2]

In these cases it can be seen that planning and organization were central to the commission of the crimes charged, and that the crimes can be ongoing in nature. Sophisticated economic and political crimes are characterized by such planning.

CRIMES OF THE FUTURE

These crimes will reach new levels in the coming years. An aging population no longer suited to committing street crimes, more service industry jobs with access to cash and personal information, computers in most homes and workplaces, the ease of international travel and trade, and Internet communication for terrorists and hate groups—this combination of circumstances will promote new forms of white-collar, organized, and computer crime and will promote terrorism and hate crimes. Those who will exploit the opportunities and technologies of the era will be clever.

Economic and political crimes are the most serious crimes occurring today, and they are the subject of this chapter. The following sections highlight several types of sophisticated crimes and their impact on our lives.

What Is Meant by Economic and Political Crimes?

Economic and political crimes include white-collar crime, organized crime, computer crime, international and domestic terrorism, and some forms of hate crimes. The common behaviors that underlie these crimes link them together. The criminal law punishes the kind of criminal planning that underlies sophisticated crimes such as **conspiracy.** Conspiracy takes place when two or more persons agree to commit a crime or to carry out a legal act in an illegal manner. Conspiracy, then, is essentially *preparation* or planning to commit a crime. The importance of making conspiracy a crime can be seen in virtually every case of white-collar, computer, and organized crime, in which authorities can punish the *planning* activities of sophisticated criminals, thereby thwarting their criminal designs.

CONSPIRACY

conspiracy
Agreement between two or more persons to commit a crime or to carry out a legal act in an illegal manner.

White-collar crimes are crimes that are usually carried out during the course of a legitimate occupation. In place of the force or stealth that is inherent in violent and property crimes, white-collar crimes employ deceit in an effort to trick an unsuspecting victim. White-collar crimes are of three types: crimes of fraud, crimes against public administration, and regulatory offenses.[3] **Crimes of fraud** have money as their object and include embezzlement, extortion, forgery, and fraud. **Crimes against public administration** attempt to impede government processes. These include bribery, obstruction of justice, official misconduct, and perjury. **Regulatory offenses** are violations that circumvent measures designed to protect public health, safety, or welfare in business, industry, and government. It can be seen that *white-collar crime* is a generic term that encompasses several specific types of crimes.

white-collar crimes
Crimes of fraud, crimes against public administration, and regulatory offenses that are usually carried out during the course of a legitimate occupation.

crimes of fraud
Embezzlement, extortion, forgery, and fraud.

crimes against public administration
Attempts to impede government processes through bribery, obstruction of justice, official misconduct, or perjury.

regulatory offenses
Attempts to circumvent regulations designed to ensure fairness and safety in the conduct of business; include administrative, environmental, labor, and manufacturing violations as well as unfair trade practices.

How Can White-Collar Crimes Be Defined?

WHITE-COLLAR CRIME

White-collar crime goes beyond the crimes committed by business and professional people who often wear jackets, ties, and white shirts to work. It is easy to distinguish a mugging from an embezzlement, but what about the difference between simple theft and fraud? Or between assault and an injury caused by a defective product? The distinctions between white-collar and traditional street crimes are not always clear. These two categories of offenses are not distinguishable by the amount of harm they cause, because frauds or unsafe products can cause much more injury and harm than any number of street crimes. Nor are they distinguishable by the level of violence involved. Many street crimes, such as larceny and burglary, involve no personal confrontation, but conspiracy, extortion, or food and drug manufacturing violations can involve threats, injury, and even death.

It is increasingly common to see a defendant in a white-collar crime case being led to court in handcuffs while wearing a business suit. Why do you think prosecutors allow this to occur in full view of the public and media?

The distinctions between white-collar crime and more traditional forms of crime therefore do not lie in the nature of the victim, or in the amount of violence, or in the extent of injury. Instead, white-collar crime is distinguishable by the manner in which it is carried out, given available opportunities. The opportunity to commit such crimes is often determined by one's position in society. One cannot embezzle funds without first holding a position of financial trust, nor can one commit regulatory offenses without holding a particular position in business or industry. Thus, *access* to financial or governmental or institutional resources provides the *opportunity* to commit white-collar offenses.

ROLE OF PLANNING AND DECEIT

Street crimes are characterized by the use of *force or stealth,* which is required for homicide, rape, robbery, assault, burglary, larceny, or arson. In contrast, white-collar crimes are characterized by planning and deceit. *Planning and deceit* are required for successful conspiracy, fraud, extortion, embezzlement, forgery, or regulatory offenses. Thus, white-collar crimes can be defined as:

> *planned illegal acts of deception committed by an individual or organization, usually during the course of legitimate occupational activity by persons of high or respectable social status, for personal or organizational gain that violates fiduciary responsibility or public trust.*[4]

This definition highlights several facts about white-collar crime:

- It can be committed by an individual or by an organization or group of individuals.
- Deception, trickery, or fraud lies at the heart of white-collar crime.
- Most white-collar crimes emanate from otherwise legitimate occupational activity in which access to money or information makes possible the misuse of one or both of these resources.
- White-collar offenses sometimes lie on the border between illegal and unethical behavior, where what a company does may cause harm or even death without actually violating the criminal law. Many unethical offenses are adjudicated in civil proceedings that determine compensation, rather than in criminal court, which determines guilt.

Types of White-Collar Theft

embezzlement
The purposeful misappropriation of property entrusted to one's care, custody, or control to which one is not entitled.

Table 17.1 shows a typology of white-collar crimes. As the table illustrates, white-collar crimes can be divided into three groups: theft, offenses against public administration, and regulatory offenses. White-collar thefts include embezzlement, extortion, forgery, and fraud. **Embezzlement** is the purposeful misappropriation of property entrusted to one's care, custody, or control to which one is not entitled. In some states this crime is called "misapplication of property" and is included under theft as a type of larceny. The essential element of embezzlement is viola-

Table 17.1 **A Typology of White-Collar Crime**

Crimes of Theft	*Crimes against Public Administration*	*Regulatory Offenses*
Embezzlement	Bribery	Administrative violations
Extortion	Obstruction of justice	Environmental violations
Forgery	Official misconduct	Labor violations
Fraud	Perjury	Manufacturing violations
		Unfair trade practices

Source: Albanese, Jay S., *White Collar Crime in America,* 1st Edition, ©1995. Adapted by permission of Pearson Education, Inc., Upper Saddle River, NJ.

EMBEZZLEMENT AND EXTORTION

tion of fiduciary (or financial) trust. An example is seen in the case of the former chief financial officer of Day-Lee Foods in California, who was convicted of stealing $100 million in company funds by manipulating company accounts over a period of seven years.[5] Embezzlement is usually punished on the basis of how much money or property is misappropriated.

extortion
Purposely obtaining property from another person without consent through wrongful use of force or fear or under the guise of official authority.

Extortion also involves theft, but it is accomplished in a different manner. It consists of purposely obtaining property from another person with that person's consent, when that consent is induced through wrongful use of force or threat of force or under the guise of official authority. Many states classify extortion as a type of larceny or theft. Extortion is sometimes called blackmail, as in the case of Sol Wachtler, chief judge of the New York State Court of Appeals, who was charged with telling his former lover that he would sell sexually explicit photos of her and her new boyfriend if she did not give him money.[6] The word *blackmail* is derived from European terms for money or payment (e.g., French *maille,* Gaelic *mal,* German *Mahl*). The "black" is believed to reflect the illegal nature of the payments and also may refer to the metal in which the payment historically was made. Copper or other base metal was usually used, rather than silver (a "white" metal). With the advent of paper currency, metal coins are now infrequently used as a form of payment, but the term *blackmail* continues to be used today.

FORGERY

forgery
Falsely making or altering an official document with the intent to defraud.

A person who falsely makes or alters an official document with intent to defraud commits the crime of **forgery.** The penalty for forgery is often based on the type of document that is forged. For example, forging passports or currency usually carries a higher penalty. Forgery also includes other offenses that are sometimes defined separately under state law. Counterfeiting money, criminal possession of forged documents, and falsifying business records are all variations of the crime of forgery. Federal officials began an investigation in 2000 when counterfeit law enforcement credentials were found to be available for purchase on the Internet. Undercover investigators were able to enter secure areas of airports and government buildings with the false identification.[7]

FRAUD

fraud
Purposely obtaining the property of another person through deception.

Another type of white-collar theft is **fraud,** or purposely obtaining the property of another person through deception. Fraud is at the heart of the concept of white-collar crime. Together with conspiracy, it forms the basis for many organized illegal acts. In many states bankruptcy fraud, false advertising, issuing a bad check, criminal impersonation, and theft of services are regarded as specific types of

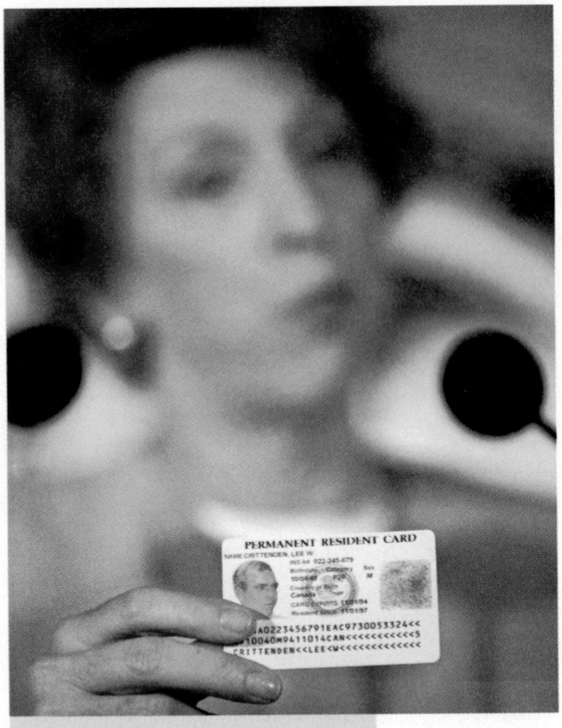

Forgery is the alteration of an official document with intent to defraud, and knowingly buying or selling forged documents also are criminal acts. What "documents" typically are found in forgery cases? What characteristics of forgery make it a white-collar crime? What are some other types of white-collar theft?

fraud. Fraud thus involves larceny by trickery or deceit. A common form of fraud is telemarketing scams. In a typical case, a New Jersey company used a 900 number to charge people up to $28 per call for responding to mail announcing that they had won a prize—which turned out to be worthless jewelry.[8] In a well-known case, American Family Publishers agreed to pay $1.25 million to thirty-two states over allegations of deceptive sales practices. This company sent more than 200 million mailings annually, using the names of well-known celebrities Ed McMahon and Dick Clark, to tell each recipient that he or she was one of a very small number of winners. The mailings suggested that if recipients ordered magazine subscriptions, their chances of winning a multimillion-dollar prize would be enhanced. The company agreed to make it clearer in future mailings that no purchase was necessary to enter or win the sweepstakes prize. This settlement was similar to one reached between Publishers Clearing House and fourteen states a few years earlier.[9] Although money is not obtained by theft in these cases, deceptive practices can trick a person into believing they are buying a chance at a million dollars through a magazine order. Obtaining money through deception is the essence of fraud.

Crimes against Public Administration

Crimes against public administration involve misconduct by government officials and by individuals attempting to disrupt or corrupt government processes. The crimes in this category include bribery, obstruction of justice, official misconduct, and perjury. **Bribery** involves the voluntary giving or receiving of anything of value with the intent to influence the action of a public official. The more important the official act to be performed is, the more serious the penalty. For example, bribery of a judge in a criminal case carries a significant penalty. Bribery law works two ways: One can be convicted of bribery for offering the corrupt payment as well as for receiving it. In South Carolina, for example, fifteen legislators and six lobbyists were among those convicted after the FBI videotaped legislators taking cash from lobbyists in exchange for their votes.[10] Seven Arizona legislators were charged in a similar bribery scandal.[11]

BRIBERY

bribery
Voluntary giving or receiving anything of value with the intent of influencing the action of a public official.

Intentionally preventing a public servant from lawfully performing an official function is **obstruction of justice.** In the infamous cover-up of the 1972 burglary of the Democratic party headquarters in the Watergate complex, for example, members of the White House staff refused to cooperate with investigations of alleged wrongdoing, and some were ultimately convicted of purposely concealing relevant information, which is obstruction of justice.[12] In 1993 three New York State troopers confessed to falsifying fingerprints in more than thirty criminal cases over a period of nine years in order to "solve" cases with adulterated evidence.[13] Lying about this evidence in court was obstruction of justice.

OBSTRUCTION

obstruction of justice
Intentionally preventing a public servant from lawfully performing an official function.

Official misconduct is a public official's unauthorized exercise of an official function with intent to benefit or injure another. Also, a person who uses an

MISCONDUCT

official misconduct
The unauthorized exercise of an official function by a public official with intent to benefit or injure another.

elected office for personal gain is guilty of official misconduct. Such misconduct can result from an act of omission (failure to perform legal duties) or commission (exercising powers in an unauthorized manner). People who use their public office to "fix" tickets, obtain permits without payment, or solicit sex are committing official misconduct. In 2000 a municipal judge in Cleveland was accused of soliciting payments from defendants to influence his decisions, which is a form of official misconduct.[14]

PERJURY

When someone makes a false statement under oath in an official proceeding, he or she is guilty of **perjury** or false swearing. The punishment for perjury is usually based on the nature of the proceeding. Perjury during a trial or grand jury proceeding is considered more serious than false swearing on an affidavit. John Poindexter, former national security advisor to President Reagan, was convicted of perjury when he was shown to have lied to Congress as part of the cover-up in the Iran–Contra affair.[15] Inside information provided by a former officer in the Los Angeles Police Department resulted in the dismissal of several cases due to confirmed instances of false testimony and planted evidence.[16]

perjury
Making a false statement under oath in an official proceeding.

Corporate Crimes

The third category of white-collar crimes is **corporate crimes,** also called regulatory offenses. The laws governing these offenses are designed to ensure fairness and safety in the conduct of business so that the desire for profits does not lead to dangerous or unjust actions. There are hundreds of types of regulatory offenses, but they can be grouped into five different categories: administrative, environmental, labor, and manufacturing violations, and unfair trade practices.

corporate crimes
Dangerous or unjust actions in the conduct of business prompted by the desire for profits. Same as *regulatory offenses.*

ADMINISTRATIVE OFFENSES

Administrative offenses involve the failure to comply with court orders or agency requirements. Failures to keep adequate records, submit compliance reports, acquire a valid permit, and the like are against the law where these procedures are required. For example, Equifax, a leading credit-reporting agency, settled a case brought by eighteen states alleging that it was issuing inaccurate credit reports. The company agreed to make credit reports easier to read, to explain to consumers how a credit rating is derived, and to resolve disputed reports within thirty days. Another credit-reporting agency, TRW, settled a similar case brought by nineteen states.[17] Bayer agreed to pay $1 million over an inaccurate claim that nearly all adults could prevent heart attacks with aspirin.[18] In 2003, the first conviction occurred in the Enron scandal, which involved massive fraud and misrepresentation in an energy-trading company.[19]

ENVIRONMENTAL VIOLATIONS

Environmental violations include emissions or dumping in violation of legal standards. Discharges of harmful substances into the air or water without a permit, failure to treat waste adequately before disposal, and deposit of hazardous waste in a landfill are examples of environmental violations. A Michigan man was sentenced to three years in prison and to pay restitution for his role in abandoning seventy drums of hazardous waste in an empty field.[20]

LABOR VIOLATIONS

Labor violations can take several forms, including discriminatory hiring practices, exposure of employees to harm in the workplace environment, and unfair treatment of employees. Examples of unfair treatment include firing without

In this photograph, what type of regulatory offense has been committed by a corporation? What other types of regulatory offenses are involved in corporate crimes? Do you think corporate crimes are potentially as harmful as violent and property crimes? Why or why not? What accounts for continuing increases in white-collar crime in the United States?

cause, refusing employment, and ignoring complaints of sexual harassment. Imperial Food Products officials were charged with twenty-five counts of involuntary manslaughter for locked exits and other safety violations that resulted in the deaths of twenty-five workers in a fire at Imperial's chicken-processing plant in Hamlet, North Carolina.[21] A Boston contractor was fined by the Occupational Safety and Health Administration for repeated safety violations after a worker fell fifteen feet into a pit and was killed.[22]

The manufacture of unsafe products is the essence of the manufacturing violations category. Electric shock hazards, fire hazards, and lack of adequate labeling or directions on products are examples of such violations. In one of the largest product liability cases in U.S. history the manufacturer of the diet drugs Redux and Pondimin agreed to pay $3.75 billion to thousands of people who suffered, or might suffer in the future, from heart valve damage linked to the drugs. Two members of the Pilgrim family of Mississippi received prison sentences for selling syrup and honey products that were labeled as pure but were not made from pure ingredients.[23]

UNFAIR TRADE PRACTICES

Unfair trade practices prevent fair competition in the marketplace. Monopolization, price discrimination, price-fixing, and bid rigging are examples of unfair trade practices. In one case the state of Florida filed a lawsuit against three manufacturers of infant formula, claiming that they had conspired to raise the price of baby formula. The state pointed out that formula prices had risen 155 percent, whereas the price of milk, the primary ingredient, had risen only 36 percent over the same period.[24] Toys R Us and two other toy makers agreed to pay $50 million to settle a multistate lawsuit claiming that they prevented other toy makers from selling popular toys to discount stores. The case arose from a complaint by the FTC that Toys R Us illegally used its size and domination of the toy market to force toy makers to supply toys to them and not to discount stores. In this way, Toys R Us was alleged to have unfairly reduced its competition in the toy market and to have artificially raised prices.[25]

As the offense categories for corporate crimes illustrate, regulations are designed to protect the public from unscrupulous or dangerous business practices. This type of white-collar crime is based on deviations from legitimate business activity. Penalties for violating regulations sometimes involve criminal sanctions; thus, regulatory offenses are part of the criminal law.

Trends in White-Collar Crime

An important question is whether white-collar crime is increasing or decreasing. An answer is not readily available, because there are no regularly collected data for white-collar crimes as there are for street crimes. Victimization surveys count only rape, robbery, assault, burglary, larceny, and motor vehicle theft. The Uniform Crime Reports, however, include forgery/ counterfeiting, fraud, and embezzlement in their tallies of arrests (which represent only offenders who are caught). As

Media & Criminal Justice
A Civil Action

In the 1999 hit movie *A Civil Action,* the viewer is presented with a familiar stereotype of the civil lawyer: the arrogant, money-hungry, egotistical ambulance chaser. For the dynamic Jan Schlichtmann, winning a case is only about making money , not about procuring justice. The viewer is surprised, then, when Schlichtmann travels to Woburn, Massachusetts, to visit a group of parents who have lost children to leukemia. As the Woburn residents begin to recognize the extraordinarily high rate of cancer in their community, significant toxic pollutants are found in two of the town's water wells.

Based on the book *A Civil Action* by Jonathan Harr, the film provides an excellent account of the real 1970s civil case against Beatrice Foods and W. R. Grace. In the movie we see a tannery foreman explaining that the process by which animal hides are cured involves pouring chemicals over the leather. Questions remain as to whether the chemical spillage from the process is responsible for the toxins in the wells and to what extent the pollutants were spread knowingly or intentionally. Because the alleged environmental violations have been blamed for the illness and deaths of many Woburn residents, Schlichtmann has the responsibility of proving specific cause and effect in relation to the damages he is claiming.

Perhaps the most interesting aspect of the story is how the case humanizes the showboat lawyer Schlichtmann. He is clearly out for profit when he takes the case, but as he is faced with the suffering of the parents of Woburn's leukemia victims, his motive becomes more about justice than money. It is a position that will cost him the case: In his search for truth and justice, he turns down a $20 million offer from Grace and a $4 million offer from Beatrice. (The jury later would award $8 million from Grace, allocated almost exclusively for toxic cleanup, and would absolve Beatrice of liability.) For the parents the civil action was obviously never about the money; but for Schlichtmann, the eye-opening experience leaves his prestigious law firm bankrupt.

Is it possible that corporations are aware of their regulatory crimes but determine that it is more financially advantageous to pay damages than to fix the problem? Should there be a cap on how much injured parties can recover from regulatory crimes? Who ultimately pays for the damages that corporations must remit if they lose in a civil action brought against them?

Table 17.2 indicates, arrest rates for all these offenses have risen dramatically since 1970, even if we control for population growth (rate per 100,000 population). Both the number and the rate of arrests for fraud are higher than those for embezzlement and forgery, although arrest rates for the latter crimes have increased as well.

INCREASES IN WHITE-COLLAR CRIME

Increases in white-collar crime reflect employment trends. The proportion of the U.S. population employed in jobs that provide access to information and financial accounts is increasing, and as a result more people have access to criminal opportunities involving misuse of authority and funds.[26] As Americans move further away from agriculture and manufacturing to jobs in service industries, high technology, and related professions, access to cash and account numbers by more employees will increase the opportunities for fraud.

Increases in white-collar crime also will reflect demographic trends. The average age of the U.S. population is rising. In 1970 the median age was twenty-seven, in 2000 it was thirty-five, and by 2025 it will be about forty.[27] The aging of the U.S. population is due to a low birthrate combined with the fact that people are

Table 17.2 Arrests for White-Collar Crimes (Number and Rate per 100,000 Population)

Offenses	*1970*	*1980*	*1995*	*2005*	*Percent Change in Rate*
Forgery/counterfeiting	43,833 28.9	72,643 34.9	91,991 46.8	87,346 40.1	+39%
Fraud	76,861 50.7	261,787 125.7	320,046 162.9	231,721 106.4	+110%
Embezzlement	8,172 5.4	7,885 3.8	11,605 5.9	14,097 6.5	+20%

Source: Data compiled from Federal Bureau of Investigation, *Crime in the United States* (Washington, DC: U.S. Government Printing Office, published annually).

living longer than earlier generations did. The net result is more people in the age group most prone to white-collar crime—the majority of those arrested for forgery, embezzlement, and fraud are over the age of twenty-five.

Why Is Computer Crime a Growing Threat?

The United States and much of the rest of the world has become completely dependent on computers and electronic telecommunications. Most U.S. households now have computers, as do the vast majority of governments, businesses, and schools. In the very near future, computers will become as central to our lives at home as they already are at work for most people. The opportunities for misuse of information systems and communication technologies grow daily.

The spread of the automobile early in the twentieth century nearly doubled the number of offenses named in the criminal codes of the United States, and the dominance of the computer is likely to have the same impact in the twenty-first century. Automobiles provided opportunities for illegal activity ranging from substandard manufacturing and repair frauds to auto theft. Computers will have a similar impact as computer viruses and cybertheft threaten people's property and the public order. Legal codes are being modified to eliminate opportunities for crime or misuse, much as changes were needed when automobiles became commonplace.

Types of Computer Crimes

COMPUTERS AS INSTRUMENTS OF CRIME

computer crime
Crimes in which computers are used as the *instrument* of the offense, and crimes in which computers are the *object* of the offense.

Computers are most often used to steal, but they can be used to commit other crimes as well. Different types of **computer crime** can be grouped into two basic categories: crimes in which computers are used as the *instrument* of the offense, and crimes in which computers are the *object* of the offense. Computers are used as an instrument in crimes of theft such as embezzlement, fraud, or larceny by computer. For example, the controller at Halifax Technology Services admitted embezzling $15 million by generating corporate checks to herself over a period of three years. She was sentenced to six and a half years in prison, and she must make repayment at a rate of no less than $500 per month until the debt is repaid.[28]

Computers can also be instruments of crime when they are used for purposes of extortion or harassment. The spread of computer viruses, hidden programs that annoy a user or threaten to alter a user's computer files, is an example. Thousands of Internet users received unsolicited e-mails stating that their orders had been processed and their credit card would be charged $300, but these people had not ordered anything. They were advised to call a phone number with a 767 area code if they had questions. The phone number turned out to be a phone sex line that incurred an automatic charge when connected. The number was located in the West Indies. The conspirators received their money from the phone companies who charged the customers for their connection to the phone sex line. The FTC obtained a court order to freeze the funds collected by phone companies for calls to the phone sex number.[29] This scheme illustrates the fact that criminal behavior in the new millennium will involve more sophisticated ways to steal and that the response of the criminal justice system will have to be more sophisticated as well.

A computer is being hacked by a criminal. What is the difference between computers as objects of crime and computers as instruments of crime?

Computers can be the object of a crime when the intention is to cause damage to computer hardware (machines) or software (programs). Data destruction and theft or vandalism of computers or programs are examples of such crimes. Likewise, computers can be the object of crime when the intention is to alter data stored in them. Attempts to alter financial statements, credit histories, or college grades are examples of this type of computer crime. In other cases, privileged or confidential information, such as software or company secrets, can be altered for purposes of sabotage or copied and sold for illicit profit. Table 17.3 illustrates the variations within the two general categories of computer crime.

COMPUTERS AS OBJECTS OF CRIME

Consequences of Computer Crime

The most common form of computer crime is theft by computer. The computer manager at King Soopers stores in Colorado was charged with stealing $2 million by manipulating computer records at the stores while he was supposed to be fixing "bugs" in the system.[30] Increasingly, computers and high-quality color printers are used to counterfeit U.S. currency. Of the $40 million in counterfeited money

Table 17.3 Types of Computer Crime

Computer as Instrument	*Computer as Object*
Theft by computer (using a computer as a tool to steal)	Damage to software/hardware (physical or electronic damage to computers or computer programs)
Harassment/extortion (using a computer as a means for intimidation or threats)	Data alteration (changing information for undue advantage or revenge)

Source: Albanese, Jay S., Pursley, Robert D., *Crime in America: Some Existing and Emerging Issues,* 1st Edition, ©1993. Adapted by permission of Pearson Education, Inc., Upper Saddle River, NJ.

seized annually, about half is computer generated.[31] In these cases computers are used as an instrument to carry out thefts in the form of embezzlement and fraud. This type of computer-assisted theft is sometimes called "identity theft," where personal information is taken to accomplish some kind of fraud involving credit cards, thefts from existing accounts, or misuse of personal information. Interviews with a representative sample of 40,000 U.S. residents found that in one out of every thirty-three households (3 percent), there had been at least one type of identity theft during the previous six months. Credit card theft was found to be the most common type of identity theft. Individuals in households headed by persons aged eighteen to twenty-four and those with incomes of $75,000 or more were the most likely to be victimized.[32]

Growing use of the Internet to make purchases has resulted in frauds where buyers and sellers fail to live up to their computer-based agreement. Bidding on products via e-mail auctions has become an extremely popular form of Internet purchasing, but about 80 to 90 percent of the complaints received by the Federal Trade Commission involve instances where a buyer pays for an item but never receives it from the seller. The FTC reports that complaints about Internet bidding fraud have increased dramatically. The average loss per consumer is estimated at approximately $300.[33]

CYBERTHEFT

Examples of computer crimes abound. Kevin Mitnick was charged with four counts of fraud for using a friend's office computer to break into the computer system at Digital Equipment Corporation. Mitnick copied software that had cost Digital $1 million to develop. He was also charged with electronically entering the Leeds University computer system in England and transferring his telephone charges to a nonexistent MCI long-distance account. Mitnick pled guilty to charges of penetrating business computer systems and causing millions of dollars in damage.[34] In another case, computer hackers apparently stole $12 million in telephone charges from NASA over two years, using long-distance credit card numbers.[35] These are examples of a trend toward using computers as a "burglar's tool" to conduct theft.

HACKER HARASSMENT

Another type of computer crime is the use of a computer to harass or extort a victim. Perhaps the most notorious case of this type is that of Donald Burleson, who inserted a virus (a program that continuously duplicates itself, interfering with the normal operation of computers) into the computer system at a brokerage firm from which he had been fired. The virus erased 168,000 sales commission records.[36] Robert Morris, a twenty-three-year-old graduate student, released a macrovirus that brought more than 6,000 university, research, and military computers to a standstill, although no information was taken or lost. A computer "worm" outbreak in 2003 prompted calls for better regulation of the Internet.[37] Many other viruses have been planted in computer programs. Some are relatively innocuous, flashing "Peace" or other messages on thousands of computer screens; others can be extremely harmful. The potential for damage has intensified efforts to improve security technology.

CYBERTERRORISM

A twenty-one-year-old college student in New Jersey was charged when he sent 24,000 e-mail messages to two administrators, who promptly revoked his computer privileges.[38] Nine regional Internet service providers were infiltrated by hackers—individuals with sophisticated knowledge who go to great lengths to infiltrate computer systems.[39] In each of these cases the computer was used as an instrument to harass, invade privacy, or extort a victim. Hackers were detected in U.S. military computers more than 2,000 times during the 1990s, usually attempting to steal software or data or to leave viruses.[40] Although classified information has not been accessed, the potential threat is clear.

SOFTWARE PIRATING

Another type of computer crime involves damage to hardware or software. The damage can be physical or can exist in terms of competitive value. For example, Microsoft Corporation, working with U.S. marshals, seized more than $1 million in counterfeit software in Los Angeles that had been produced by ten illicit businesses.[41] Pirated software has been smuggled to Hong Kong and elsewhere, where copies of programs such as Windows are sold for only 5 dollars.[42] Printed matter and photographic images also are pirated in acts of copyright infringement.

In some computer crimes the object is acquisition or alteration of data for an unlawful purpose. During the 1980s a computer systems manager at Lawrence Berkeley Laboratory in California realized that an unauthorized user was looking at his computer files, so he set up a phony "Star Wars" computer file that the hacker could not resist. The suspect was eventually tracked to Hanover, West Germany, where three people were charged with selling secrets to the Soviet Union.[43] The FBI's Computer Intrusion Squad found that 30 percent of large corporations and government agencies it surveyed admitted that their computer systems had been penetrated by outsiders during the previous year; 55 percent reported unauthorized access by insiders.[44]

Rates of computer crimes of all types are increasing, posing problems for law enforcement. An FBI survey of 2,000 businesses in 2005 found that 20 percent had been victimized by computer crime.[45] Employees account for nearly two-thirds of suspected cases of computer crime, and some estimates place the number as high as 90 percent. In addition, many huge losses likely go unreported because companies wish to avoid bad publicity and embarrassment, especially if the value of their stock is likely to decrease as a result.

IDENTITY FRAUD

The impact of cybertheft on consumers is evident. In one year two members of a computer hacking group stole 1,749 credit card numbers.[46] This type of activity has resulted in growing numbers of instances of **identity fraud,** in which false identification and credit cards are manufactured based on personal information stolen without the victim's knowledge. The criminal then uses the fake cards to spend lavishly, ruining in the process the victim's financial standing and credit rating. Although credit card insurance often covers much of the financial loss, victims of identity fraud must reestablish their credit ratings and personal reputation, a process that can take several years. Based on its survey of 40,000 U.S. residents, the Bureau of Justice Statistics estimates the annual loss from identity fraud to be $3.2 billion.[47]

identity fraud
Manufacture and use of false identification and credit cards based on personal information stolen without the victim's knowledge.

CAUSES OF COMPUTER CRIME

The causes of computer crime have not been studied extensively, but a survey of 600 university students found that 34 percent had pirated software and 16 percent had gained illegal access to a computer system. The study found that in many cases these behaviors were learned from others or imitated.[48] A complication in understanding the nature and scope of computer crime is the fact that businesses seldom want to admit to vulnerability and therefore tend to underreport breaches of computer security. In 1996 the Department of Justice established its Computer

A press conference in 2006 announcing the Treasury Department's DVD release on ways to reduce vulnerability to identity theft. In most cases, the objective of the criminal is not to steal your identity, but to do what with it?

Crime and Intellectual Property Section to investigate and prosecute computer-related crimes. The biggest challenge has been convincing businesses to report these offenses.[49]

THE NATIONAL COMPUTER CRIME SQUAD

Despite these problems, there have been some notable successes in efforts to combat computer crime. Many of these cases have resulted from work of the FBI's National Computer Crime Squad, which commenced operations in 1992. Undercover sting operations and the sharing of businesses' information about suspected computer hacking are the two most common methods of investigation. For example, seventy-eight people were convicted for trading child pornography over the Internet in an FBI sting operation.[50] A thirty-seven-year-old computer repairman was found to have infiltrated Internet service providers and collected 100,000 credit card numbers. He was ready to sell a CD-ROM with these stolen numbers on it for $260,000 at San Francisco Airport but walked into an FBI sting operation.[51] Two raids on suspected Internet gambling operations in the Northeast found proceeds estimated at $56 million. In sum, it appears that computers are being used to commit both white-collar and organized crimes and that improved law enforcement sophistication is needed to combat them.

How Does Organized Crime Operate?

organized crime
A continuing criminal enterprise that rationally works to profit from illicit activities that are often in great public demand. Its continuing existence is maintained through the use of force, threats, monopoly control, and/or the corruption of public officials.

Organized crime has always fascinated people as a form of criminal behavior, yet its definition and true scope often are unclear. The President's Commission on Law Enforcement in the mid-1960s concluded that "our knowledge of the structure which makes 'organized crime' organized is somewhat comparable to the knowledge of Standard Oil which could be gleaned from interviews with gasoline station attendants."[52] A similar commission appointed by Ronald Reagan, reporting in 1987, also did not offer any clear definition of organized crime. One definition of **organized crime**, based on the work of researchers in the field, reads as follows:

Organized crime is a continuing criminal enterprise that rationally works to profit from illicit activities that are often in great public demand. Its continuing existence is maintained through the use of force, threats, monopoly control, and/or the corruption of public officials.[53]

Even this definition is incomplete, however. For example, how does an otherwise legitimate corporation that collects toxic waste but dumps some of it illegally fit into this definition? Is a motorcycle gang that sells drugs as a sideline part of organized crime? What about a licensed massage parlor that offers some customers sex for money? The National Advisory Committee on Criminal Justice Standards and Goals has recognized that there are more similarities than differences between organized crime and so-called white-collar crime: "The perpetrators of organized crime may include corrupt business executives, members of the professions, public officials, or members of any other occupational group, in addition to the conventional racketeer element."[54]

ORGANIZED VERSUS WHITE-COLLAR CRIME?

At the same time, important differences exist between organized and white-collar crime. Perhaps the most significant distinction is the fact that white-collar crimes generally occur as a deviation from legitimate business activity. Organized crime, on the other hand, takes place through a continuing criminal enterprise that exists to *profit primarily from crime.*

It is important to keep in mind the fact that organized crime is not restricted to the activities of criminal syndicates. As Henry Pontell and Kitty Calavita concluded in their study of the savings and loan scandal of the 1980s, if we apply the term *organized crime* to continuing conspiracies that include the corruption of government officials, "then much of the savings and loan scandal involved organized crime."[55] In interviews with the Federal Bureau of Investigation, the Secret Service, and regulatory agencies, Pontell and Calavita found a "recurring theme" of conspiracies between savings and loan officials ("insiders") and accountants, lawyers, and real estate developers ("outsiders") that operated as a continuing criminal enterprise. If we compare these kinds of corrupt relationships with more traditional organized crime techniques such as no-show jobs at construction sites or payoffs for "protection," we find that they are more similar than different. Examples such as this illustrate that much of the crime committed by private corporations, politicians, and government agencies is as serious and harmful as the organized crimes of criminal enterprises.[56]

A Typology of Organized Crime

What types of illegal acts are we referring to when we speak of organized crime? Organized crime falls into three basic categories: provision of illicit services, provision of illicit goods, and infiltration of legitimate business. Within each of these categories are specific crimes that often come to the attention of the criminal justice system.

PROVISION OF ILLICIT SERVICES

Provision of illicit services involves attempts to satisfy the public's demand for certain services that may not be offered by legitimate society. Specific crimes in this category include loan-sharking, prostitution, and certain forms of gambling. Loan-sharking is the lending of money at an interest rate above that permitted by law.

Organized prostitution offers sex for pay on a systematic basis. Numbers gambling is a type of lottery that operates without the approval of the state.

PROVISION OF ILLICIT GOODS

Provision of illicit goods involves offering particular products that a segment of the public desires but cannot obtain through legitimate channels. The sale and distribution of drugs and the fencing and distribution of stolen property are examples of crimes in this category. There is a great demand for drugs, such as marijuana, cocaine, valium, and heroin, that are either illegal or distributed under very strict regulations imposed by government. In a similar way, many people desire to buy products at the lowest possible price, regardless of how the seller originally obtained them. In response to this demand, organized criminals fence stolen merchandise, buying stolen property and then selling it to customers who do not care where it came from.

INFILTRATION OF LEGITIMATE BUSINESS

racketeering
An ongoing criminal enterprise that is maintained through a pattern of criminal activity.

The third category of organized crime is infiltration of legitimate business. This is often characterized by **racketeering,** which involves an ongoing criminal enterprise that is maintained through a pattern of criminal activity. Labor racketeering and the takeover of waste disposal companies are examples of this type of crime. Labor racketeering involves the use of force or threats to employers or employees that if money is not paid, violence, strikes, and/or vandalism will result. In a similar way, organized crime syndicates have taken over waste disposal companies by coercing the legitimate owners to sell the business or have it operated by an outsider. Having the use of a legitimate business allows an organized crime figure to engage in **money laundering.** This is a method of "washing" illegally obtained money (e.g., money from drug sales or gambling proceeds) by making it appear that the money was earned legally as part of the legitimate business.

money laundering
A method of "washing" illegally obtained money (e.g., from drugs or gambling proceeds) by making it appear as if the money were earned legally as part of a legitimate business.

Table 17.4 illustrates this typology of organized crime. Provision of illicit goods and services is distinguished from infiltration of legitimate business by its consensual nature and by the lack of direct or inherent violence. That is, organized crime figures who offer illegal betting, loan-sharking, or drugs rely on the public's unsatisfied demand for these services. They also rely heavily on return business, so they want the illicit transaction to go well. It is very unusual for criminal syndicates to *solicit* business. Instead, those interested in illicit goods and services seek out the providers. But although violence plays no inherent role in the activities themselves, bad debts cannot be collected through the courts, as they can for loans and sales in the legitimate market. Therefore, violence or threats occur when one party to the transaction feels cheated or shortchanged and has no legal alternative for resolving the dispute. Violence also can occur when an organization attempts to control or monopolize an illicit market. If a group wishes to corner the market on illicit gambling in a particular area, for example, it may threaten or intimidate its illicit competitors. These threats are an enforcement mechanism rather than a part of the activity of providing illicit goods and services.

John Gotti, Jr., son of the infamous New York crime boss John Gotti, being brought to court on racketeering charges. Why do you think the son of a convicted mobster who was imprisoned for life would continue in the same illegal activity that his father did?

The infiltration of legitimate business is more predatory than the provision of illicit goods and services. In this case organized crime groups attempt to

Table 17.4 A Typology of Organized Crime

Type of Activity	*Nature of Activity*	*Harm*
Provision of illicit goods and services	Gambling, loan-sharking, prostitution, distributing narcotics and stolen property	• Consensual activities • No inherent violence • Economic harm
Infiltration of legitimate business	Coercive use of legal businesses for purposes of exploitation	• Nonconsensual activities • Threats, violence, extortion • Economic harm

Source: Reprinted from *Organized Crime in Our Times,* 4th Ed., by Jay S. Albanese. Copyright 2004. Matthew Bender & Company, Inc., a member of the Lexis/Nexis Group. All rights reserved. Used with permission.

create demand for their services rather than exploiting an existing market. Demands for "protection" money or demands that employers provide no-show jobs in return for avoidance of property damage, work stoppages, or violence illustrate the predatory nature of this type of crime. In legal terms, organized crime uses coercion or extortion in the infiltration of legitimate business. "Protection" of prostitutes from robbery and assault in return for coerced payments to pimps is another example of the predatory nature of organized crime.

Organized Crime Offenders

CRIME "FAMILIES"

Ethnicity is a common basis for categorizing organized crime, but this is misleading. A growing body of evidence shows that organized crime is not limited to the activities of a single, or even a few, ethnic groups. The President's Commission on Organized Crime in the 1980s described "organized crime today" as being carried out by eleven different groups:

- La Cosa Nostra (Italian)
- Outlaw motorcycle gangs
- Prison gangs
- Triads and Tongs (Chinese)
- Vietnamese gangs
- Yakuza (Japanese)
- Marielitos (Cuban)
- Colombian cocaine rings (drug cartels)
- Irish organized crime
- Soviet organized crime (the "Russian Mafia")
- Canadian organized crime.[57]

This curious mixture includes groups defined by their ethnic or national origin, by the nature of their activity (cocaine rings), by their geographic location (prison gangs), and by their means of transportation (motorcycle gangs). While such attributes may help describe a group, they are not very useful as explanations of behavior. Moreover, there is evidence that these and other organized crime groups sometimes work together.[58]

ETHNICITY AND ORGANIZED CRIME

Ethnicity, therefore, is not a very powerful explanation for the existence or the causes of organized crime. This conclusion is supported by several studies of ethnically based organized crime. These studies show not only that no single ethnic group or combination of groups accounts for most organized crime, but also that as an explanation for organized crime, ethnicity is secondary to local opportunities for crime. A study by historian Alan Block of the illicit cocaine trade in New York City in the early twentieth century identified Jews as major players but also found evidence of considerable interethnic cooperation among New York's criminals. There was evidence of involvement by Italians, Greeks, Irish, and blacks, who did not always work within their own ethnic groups. Block described these criminals as "entrepreneurs" who were not part of one particular organization but were involved in a "web of small but efficient organizations."[59]

A study of the underground drug market in one community by Patricia Adler found that the market was largely competitive. Participants "entered the market, transacted their deals, [and] shifted from one type of activity to another" in response to the demands of the market rather than the dictates of any ethnically based organization.[60]

Similarly, in a study of illegal gambling and loan-sharking in New York, Peter Reuter found that economic considerations dictated entry into and exit from the illicit marketplace. Reuter concluded that these criminal enterprises were "not monopolies in the classic sense or subject to control by some external organization."[61] Instead, local market forces shaped criminal behavior—more so than ethnic ties or other characteristics of the criminal groups.

CRIME SYNDICATES

In a classic ethnographic study, Francis Ianni became a participant–observer of an organized crime group for two years; he also made observations of two other criminal groups. He found these groups to "have no structure apart from their functioning; nor do they have structure independent of their current 'personnel.'"[62] Joseph Albini's pioneering study of criminal groups in the United States and Italy reached a similar conclusion. Rather than belonging to an organization, those involved in organized crime formed relationships based on the particular activity they were engaged in at any given time. A **crime syndicate,** Albini concluded, is "a system of loosely structured relationships functioning primarily because each participant is interested in furthering his own welfare."[63] These studies suggest that the structure of organized crime groups is derived from the activities they are engaged in, rather than from preexisting ethnic ties.

crime syndicate
A system of loosely structured relationships among groups and individuals involved in organized crime.

National and International Aspects of Organized Crime

The true extent of organized crime is unknown. Typical organized crimes such as conspiracy, racketeering, and extortion are not counted in any systematic way. Other offenses are known only when they result in arrests. The problems with relying on arrests as a measure of criminal activity are apparent: Much crime is undetected, some that is detected is not reported to police, and arrest rates go up or down depending on police activity and do not necessarily reflect levels of criminal activity. However, arrest data are the only available statistics, and they provide some indication of the amount of organized crime committed each year.

ARRESTS FOR ORGANIZED CRIME

The Federal Bureau of Investigation tabulates arrests for several offenses that are characteristic of organized crime. Trends in these arrests from 1970 to 2005 are presented in Table 17.5. As can be seen, arrests for three of the four categories

Table 17.5 Arrests for Crimes Related to Organized Crime

Offense	*1970*	*1980*	*1990*	*2005*	*35-Year Change*
Drug abuse violations	265,734	351,955	785,536	1,846,351	7 times higher
Gambling	75,325	37,805	13,357	11,180	7 times lower
Prostitution and commercialized vice	45,803	67,920	80,888	84,891	2 times higher
Stolen property (buy, receive, possess)	46,427	76,429	119,102	133,856	3 times higher

Source: Data compiled from the Federal Bureau of Investigation, *Uniform Crime Report* (Washington, DC: U.S. Government Printing Office, published annually).

of offenses increased markedly over the thirty-five years shown, whereas arrests for gambling dropped dramatically. These increases and decreases can be attributed to two primary factors: changes in law enforcement priorities and changes in the overall population and in the numbers of police. Both the U.S. population and the number of sworn police officers in the United States have grown significantly since 1970. Therefore, one would expect a "natural" increase in numbers of arrests, simply because there are more potential offenders and victims in the population, as well as more police looking for them.

At the same time, the public mood has shifted, especially with regard to gambling and drugs. Gambling in many forms has been legalized in a majority of the states in response to a shift from the perception of gambling as a vice to its perception as a form of recreation.[64] Conversely, public concern about drugs increased over the same period. The large increases in drug arrests (seven times higher in 2005 than in 1970) are matched only by the huge decline in gambling arrests (seven times lower over the same period). These changes clearly indicate shifting public—and hence law enforcement—views regarding the seriousness of these forms of criminal behavior.

It is possible that the rates of these offenses have also changed over the years, but we cannot determine this from arrest statistics. The fact that prostitution and commercialized vice arrests increased over thirty-five years, and that arrests for stolen property nearly tripled from the 1970 level, suggests that more police, greater enforcement efforts, and increases in the numbers of cases combined to produce these large increases in arrests.

TRENDS IN ORGANIZED CRIME

In the future, organized crime is likely to pose even greater problems than it has in the past. Technological change and economic globalization are likely to contribute to growth in organized crime. Organized crime groups increasingly are making use of stolen and forged credit cards, airline tickets, cell phones, and currency.[65] New Visa check cards and MasterMoney cards require only a signature and no personal identification number to withdraw funds, making it easy for forgers to withdraw large amounts of money quickly.[66] With each advance in technology, new criminal opportunities emerge. Gambling and pornography on the Internet and banking by telephone and by personal computer are examples of new opportunities for both organized crime and white-collar crime to grow in the future.

Why do you believe there is a high illegal demand overseas for stolen cars from the United States? Can you name two ways to reduce the illegal smuggling of stolen automobiles?

Just as advances in technology and the fall of Communism have made worldwide communication and travel much easier in recent years, they have also made the commission of crime much easier. Passenger miles flown on international commercial flights have increased by twenty times since 1970, to more than 600 billion miles per year. Global imports have increased by a factor of ten to $3,500 billion over the same period.[67] International smuggling, drug distribution, alien smuggling, hijacking, and political crimes have grown in proportion to the growth of international communication and movement among countries. As criminal justice researcher Jonathan Winer has observed, "The very networks that legitimate businesses use to move goods so cheaply are the same networks that criminals use to move illicit goods just as easily."[68]

International Stolen Vehicle Trade One manifestation of **transnational crime** is the growing international trade in stolen vehicles. Of the 1.5 million vehicles stolen each year in the United States, approximately 200,000 are shipped overseas for resale. As recently as the mid-1980s, that international market barely existed.[69] To hide stolen cars from investigators, thieves often conceal them behind false container walls or in large steel containers bound for overseas shipping. A single ship holds as many as 4,000 steel containers, each as large as a semitrailer. Ten million containers leave the Los Angeles–Long Beach seaport alone each year, and the United States has 130 seaports. Criminals pay thieves to steal desired cars off the street; or criminals buy or rent the cars by using false identification and making a cash deposit, then drive away never to return. On the foreign end, buying and registering stolen vehicles is not very difficult. Some countries have no central registry of vehicles. In others, aspiring car owners can bypass registration requirements with cash payoffs. In some countries crimes of violence and political unrest are the focus of police attention, so police are not overly concerned with imports of stolen cars.

transnational crime
Organized crime that takes place across two or more countries.

U.S. CUSTOMS

The U.S. Customs Service reports that nearly one million vehicles are presented for export from the United States annually. Customs identifies and seizes nearly 7,000 of these as stolen vehicles with a total value of over $100 million. The National Insurance Crime Bureau estimates that 200,000 stolen vehicles are exported each year, so clearly the vast majority of illegal exports are undetected.[70]

Major reasons why people in many countries do not simply buy the cars legitimately are lack of availability and huge import duties. A $50,000 Lexus, for example, was found selling in a Thailand showroom for $180,000.[71] The total cost of international vehicle smuggling is estimated at $1 to $4 billion annually. As a representative of the National Insurance Crime Bureau remarked, "It's getting to be of epidemic proportion."[72] In response to this situation Interpol, the International Criminal Police Organization (see Chapter 8), has developed the Automated Search Facility-Stolen Motor Vehicle (ASF-SMV) database to support police in member countries in the fight against international vehicle theft and trafficking. At the end of 2005, the database held more than 3 million records of reported stolen motor vehicles (see Figure 17.1). Of the 125 countries using the database regularly, more than 95 countries share their national stolen vehicle database records with Interpol. Close to 18,000 motor vehicles were discovered worldwide in 2005 through the ASF-SMV database.[73]

FIGURE 17.1 Automobile Thefts Reported to Interpol

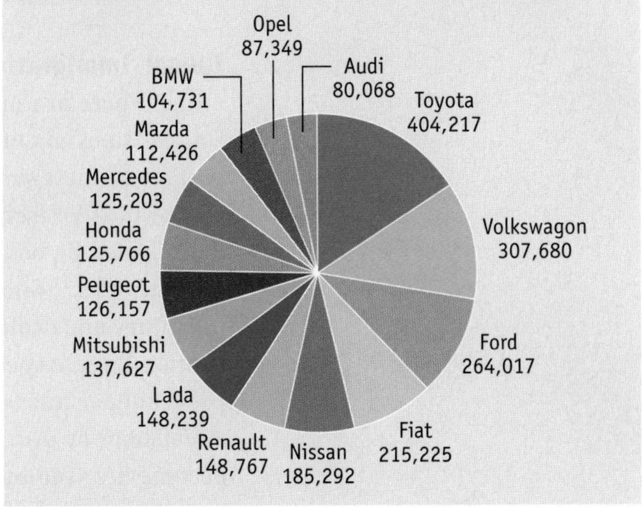

Source: "Vehicle Crime," www.interpol.int (October 16, 2006).

Drug Smuggling The problem of international automobile smuggling is mirrored in international drug smuggling. Drug smuggling begins at a source country where coca or opium is grown, usually in Central or South America or Asia. Next, the raw plant must be processed. This can be done in the source country or in a nation where smuggling is relatively easy. Once the substance has been transformed into a consumable product, it must be smuggled to the consumer drug market; North America and Europe are the largest markets. After the drug has been sold to the consumer, money must be laundered through a legitimate business and transferred overseas; or else large amounts of cash must be physically smuggled by couriers back to the manufacturing and source countries. As discussed earlier, the laundering consists of reporting the drug money as part of the income from a legitimate business, such as a restaurant or other business that has a large number of cash transactions, making the money look as if it were lawfully earned as part of the legitimate business.

HOW THE DRUG TRADE WORKS

Here is an example of how the international drug trade works in practice. Nigerian heroin smugglers recruited non-Nigerian residents of Dallas to serve as couriers, smuggling heroin into the United States. The recruiters provided airline tickets and expense money for the couriers, in addition to a salary of $5,000 to $10,000 per trip. For each batch the first courier was sent to Thailand, the heroin source, and took the heroin from there to an intermediate nonsource nation (such as the Philippines, Kenya, Poland, or western Europe), where it was delivered to a second courier. The second courier concealed the heroin in a suitcase or strapped it to his or her body, and smuggled it into the United States. The strategy was designed to deceive U.S. authorities, who would not suspect a courier who had not come from the source country.[74] This scheme capitalizes on multiethnic cooperation among criminals—and points to the need for international cooperation and surveillance by law enforcement agencies.

In what ways can organized crime often involve international, or transnational, crime? According to statistics on international crime, what three kinds of contraband are most likely to be found on a vessel such as the one shown in the photo?

The two primary opportunities for preventing drug smuggling occur at the courier stages, when the finished product is being smuggled to the market or when the illicit cash is being returned from the consuming country. In the United States, profiles have been established for drug couriers and for "high-risk" and "source" nations and airports that lack effective controls on drug manufacturing or

TARGETING COURIERS

contraband. The profiles are descriptions of travelers who appear likely to be carrying drugs or cash, such as persons who are making short international trips, carry little luggage, appear in a hurry, and pay for their tickets in cash.[75]

Illegal Immigration Illegal immigration is a third example of transnational crime. There are many people throughout the world who wish to come to the United States and other developed countries but have little chance of lawful immigration. Chinese smuggling rings have transported illegal immigrants to New York City by boat for a charge of $30,000 or more per person. Sometimes the "cargo" is smuggled by boat to Canada or Mexico and then transported by land to the United States.[76] Sometimes smugglers ship this human cargo in containers, causing injury and death.[77] The huge smuggling fee often turns the new arrivals into virtual slaves to their transporters. Because they are illegal aliens, it is difficult for these immigrants to obtain legitimate employment, so they often are exploited in sweatshops by unscrupulous employers, become prostitutes or drug couriers, or become involved in criminal activity to raise the money to pay their smuggling fee.[78] The impacts are felt by the U.S. criminal justice system as well as by the illegal immigrants themselves. Nearly half of the non–U.S. citizens prosecuted in federal court are living in the United States illegally. Most have been charged with drug or immigration offenses.[79]

There is also concern about illegal immigrants from terrorist countries who enter Canada and then slip into the United States. Ahmed Ressam, an Algerian immigrant to Montreal, is awaiting trial in the United States on charges he tried to smuggle explosives into the United States. Canada's immigration laws are more lax than those in the United States, and Canadian police agencies are aware of 350 suspects in Canada who are linked to 50 different radical groups. Canada is debating stronger immigration and surveillance measures to prevent it from becoming a "Club Med for terrorists" who might target Canada or the United States.[80]

TRAFFICKING IN PERSONS

Immigrants continue to be victimized by their smugglers in what is called trafficking in persons. Many are brought to the United States using false promises, fraudulent contracts, or outright coercion. Once they arrive, they are forced to work as slaves for their captors, often in forced labor and prostitution. The largest case to date involved Kil Soo Lee who headed a group that trafficked 200 Vietnamese and Chinese women to American Samoa as sewing machine operators in a garment factory. They were forced to work there for up to two years under extreme food deprivation, beatings, and physical restraint. The victims were held in a barracks and guarded at all times to prevent their escape. Virtually all the money they made went to their captors.[81] As William McDonald has remarked, "The problems of organized crime involved in the fraud, corruption, smuggling, and victimization associated with illegal immigration represent a growing area of need for transnational police cooperation which threatens to eclipse international drug trafficking as a social problem in the global village."[82]

Illegal aliens crossing the Rio Grande River along the Mexico–Texas border. Why does this illegal migration and smuggling continue, despite increased security along the U.S. border? What might reduce the incentive to engage in this activity?

U.S. authorities are able to identify only a small percentage of the vessels carrying illegal immigrants. Given the vast extent of the nation's borders and the inability of any nation to search every person, car, boat, and plane that crosses its borders, there is a clear need for international cooperation and coordination of law enforcement efforts.

What Are the Impacts of Terrorism and Hate Crimes?

Terrorism and hate crimes are criminal acts committed for political or social purposes. They are distinguished from most other forms of crime in that these offenders usually have no personal financial motive. Instead, they attempt to make a "point" that goes beyond their own self-interest. Their purpose may be the overthrow of the government, or they may wish to publicize an unpopular opinion. Hate crimes always involve prejudice in some form—usually racial or ethnic in nature. Terrorism sometimes entails prejudice, but more often it stems from political motives or causes. The FBI defines **terrorism** as

> *the unlawful use of force or violence against persons or property to intimidate or coerce a government, the civilian population, or any segment thereof, in furtherance of political or social objectives.*[83]

terrorism
Offenses designed to intimidate or coerce a government or civilians in furtherance of political or social objectives.

hate crimes
Offenses motivated by prejudice, usually against a particular race, religion, or sexual orientation.

Hate crimes can also be defined in this way. The primary difference is the target: In the case of terrorism, the government is usually the target; in the case of hate crimes, a particular minority group is usually the target. Hate arises from prejudice against people's race, ethnicity, religious affiliation, or sexual orientation. In a particularly gruesome case, Aaron McKinney was convicted for the torture killing of gay college student Matthew Shepard in Wyoming.[84]

Both terrorism and hate crimes are new and growing concerns for the U.S. criminal justice system. Before the 1980s major acts of terrorism occurred almost exclusively in foreign countries, and hate crimes had not been defined as such and were not counted in any systematic way. This changed in 1993 with the bombing of the World Trade Center in New York City, which killed six people. The offenders were convicted and the mastermind was sentenced to 240 years in solitary confinement.[85] Subsequent terrorist events in the United States included the 1995 Oklahoma City bombing, which killed 168 people, followed by the September 11, 2001, attacks on the World Trade Center and Pentagon, killing 3,047 people. Acts of terrorism and hate crimes now occur regularly in the United States as well as in other parts of the world. Aircraft bombings, plots against government agents, church burnings, periodic random killings of minorities, and actions by hate groups founded on a premise of racial inequality illustrate the extent of the problem in the United States.[86]

Terrorism and Hate Crime Trends

The number of terrorist incidents in the United States has declined since the 1980s, but the crimes committed are becoming more deadly. Fears of Y2K-related

That's a FACT

Perspectives on Terrorism

Terrorism was becoming more dangerous even prior to the attacks of September 11, 2001. The National Commission on Terrorism reported in 2000 that injuries and deaths resulting from terrorist incidents were increasing, while the total number of incidents had declined somewhat since 1980. This is displayed in Figure 17A.

How can casualties increase in terrorist incidents, when incidents decline? Why do you believe agencies were slow to coordinate their preparedness for major terrorism incidents prior to 9/11, despite the warnings of the National Commission on Terrorism a year earlier?

Better safeguards in granting visas is an important method to ensure that those connected with terrorists are kept out of the United States. A visa is an official authorization attached to a passport that permits entry and travel within a country. The U.S. State Department grants thousands of visas each year to tourists, workers, students, and other foreign visitors. The U.S. GAO, the investigative arm of Congress, has been asked to examine the visa approval process several times in recent years. Their findings reveal important information and communication gaps among U.S. agencies.

FIGURE 17A Terrorism Becoming More Dangerous

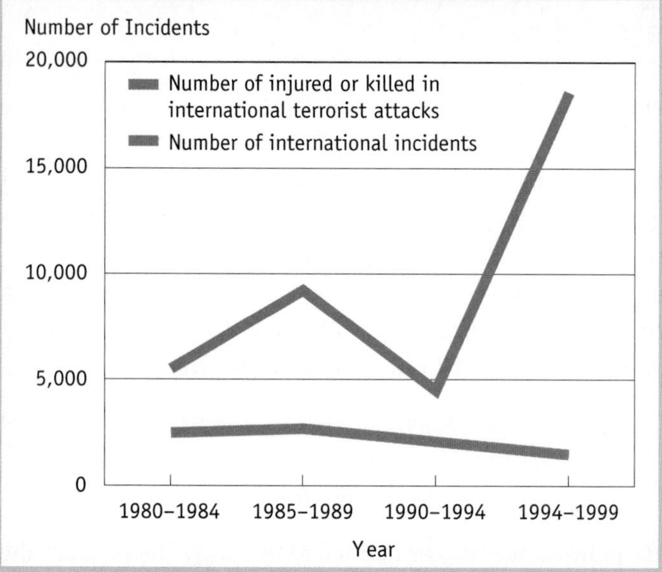

Source: National Commission on Terrorism, *Countering the Changing Threat of International Terrorism* (Washington, DC: U.S. Government Printing Office, 2000).

The GAO found that the U.S. Departments of State, Homeland Security, and Justice could more effectively manage the visa process if they had clear and comprehensive policies and procedures, and also increased coordination and information sharing among agencies. In an October 2002 report, GAO found that:

- ◆ The State Department did not provide clear policies on how consular officers should balance national security concerns with the desire to facilitate legitimate travel when issuing visas; and
- ◆ The State and Justice Departments disagreed on the evidence needed to deny a visa on terrorism grounds.

In a 2003 report, GAO found that the State Department had revoked visas for terrorism concerns, but that:

- ◆ The revocation process was not being used aggressively to alert Homeland Security and law enforcement agencies that individuals who entered the country before their visas were revoked might be security risks; and
- ◆ The process broke down when information on revocations was not being shared between the State Department and appropriate immigration and law enforcement officials.

For example, a detailed analysis of 240 visa revocations found that U.S. Immigration officials did not receive any

sabotage resulted in heightened security around the world, and surveillance efforts resulted in several arrests of persons suspected of terrorist plots.[87] Law enforcement authorities are giving higher priority to terrorism investigations, with emphasis on the *prevention* of terrorist acts. Trends in the prevention of terrorism in the United States are illustrated in *That's a Fact.* A significant number of terrorist acts have been prevented or interrupted in recent years, and these preventions are increasing (Figure 17A). This trend points to the importance of improved intelli-

notice of the revocation from the State Department, and in another forty-seven cases the revocation notice was sent to Immigration twelve days later. The State Department failed to enter sixty-four of these revocations into its own watch list. An analysis of arrival and departure data found that twenty-nine individuals entered the United States *before* their visas were revoked and they may still remain in the United States. The GAO concluded, "These weaknesses diminish the effectiveness of the visa process in keeping potential terrorists out of the United States."

The GAO made numerous recommendations to strengthen the visa process as an antiterrorism tool. These focused on specific policies and procedures for the interagency visa revocation process to ensure that when the State Department revokes a visa because of terrorism concerns, the appropriate units within the Departments of State and Homeland Security and the FBI are notified immediately and that proper actions are taken. A diagram of problems in the information flow in visa screening is shown in Figure 17B.

Changes have been made in the visa process since these reports, including a doubling of the number of names and information in the "lookout" system for visa screening. The State Department has said it is using the GAO recommendations as a road map for making improvements in the visa process.

Why do you believe it is so difficult for large federal agencies to coordinate their efforts in the visa process? If you were in charge, explain how you might balance the need for international workers and visitors against the need to protect against terrorism?

FIGURE 17B Gaps in the Visa Revocation Notification System

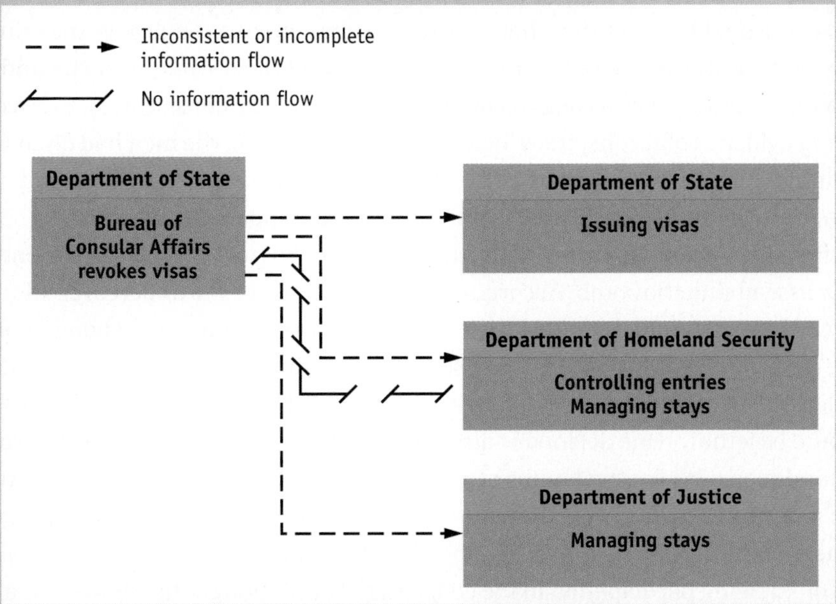

Source: U.S. Comptroller General, *Border Security: New Policies and Increased Interagency Coordination Needed to Improve Visa Process* (Washington, DC: U.S. General Accounting Office, 2003); U.S. Comptroller General, *Border Security: New Policies and Procedures Are Needed to Fill Gaps in the Visa Revocation Process* (Washington, DC: U.S. General Accounting Office, 2003).

gence gathering on terrorist activities, which can anticipate and interrupt planned terrorist activity before it results in damage or death.

HATE CRIME STATISTICS

Statistics for hate crimes were not collected before the 1990s. In 1991 there were 4,755 reported incidents of hate crimes in the United States. By 2005 the number had risen to 7,163, an increase of 50 percent. More than 66 percent of these incidents are racial or ethnic in nature, and two-thirds of these involve anti-black motives. Nearly 18 percent of all reported incidents are religious in nature;

57 percent of these are anti-Semitic (anti-Jewish). More than 14 percent of all incidents involve sexual orientation; of these, two-thirds target homosexual males.[88] It is clear that minority groups are most likely to be the targets of hate crimes, and that prejudice against a particular race, religion, or sexual orientation motivates these offenders.

How Terrorism and Hate Crimes Merge

ARYAN NATIONS

The following case illustrates how the problems of hate crime and terrorism merge. Two men belonging to an organization known as the Aryan Nations traveled from Idaho to Seattle, Washington, with the intent of exploding a bomb inside a gay bar. They were arrested after transporting the parts required for the bomb, but before they had assembled it. The arrest was based on evidence gathered by an undercover informant who had penetrated the Aryan Nations organization and had accompanied the two men on their trip to Seattle. The men were convicted of conspiracy involving interstate travel to kill or hurt human beings in violation of federal law.

The two men appealed their convictions, arguing that there was insufficient evidence of a conspiracy. They claimed that the government had failed to prove beyond a reasonable doubt that there existed an agreement to engage in the crimes charged.[89] However, the U.S. Court of Appeals found the testimony of the undercover informant, as well as tape-recorded statements of the conspirators, to be convincing evidence of a conspiracy. Before leaving for Seattle, the men had discussed obtaining a bomb from someone else. When that person could not be found, the defendants "actively participated in purchasing the components necessary to build another pipe bomb." Once in Seattle, they sought to borrow a drill from a friend to use in assembling the bomb. According to the testimony of the undercover informant, the two men had discussed the effect an explosion from a pipe bomb would have on a room full of people. In discussing the number of homosexuals that would be killed by such a bomb, they concluded that "the gravel and nails inside it would be lethal." One defendant also told the other that it would be best "to buy pipe and pipe caps for the bombs at various stores."[90] The court concluded that once a conspiracy has been shown to exist, evidence establishing a defendant's connection with it beyond a reasonable doubt "is sufficient to convict the defendant of knowing participation in the conspiracy," even though the connection may be slight.[91] This case demonstrates that the concerns about criminal organization and conspiracy that arise in hate crimes are nearly identical to concerns posed by terrorism. The planned and conspiratorial nature of the acts, and the political motives behind them, make terrorism and hate crimes serious threats to public safety and to law enforcement.

UNABOMBER

An infamous case of domestic terrorism is that of Theodore Kaczynski. Called the "Unabomber," Kaczynski pleaded guilty in 1998 to killing three people and injuring two others in five mail bombs. He also admitted to sending an additional eleven bombs that injured twenty-one other people. Kaczynski was a fifty-five-year-old mathematician who believed he was waging a struggle for individual autonomy against the forces of technology. He lived alone in a remote cabin in the woods for twenty-five years. His targets were university professors and others he believed represented the growth of technology. Kaczynski's motives can be viewed both as domestic terrorism and as hate crimes. He had a political agenda, and his choice of victims was based on a strong prejudice against people who advocated technological advancement. Kaczynski ultimately pleaded guilty and was sentenced to life in prison with no chance of parole.[92]

In place of the radicals of the earlier twentieth century, right-wing extremist groups have attracted supporters in recent years. These groups often adhere to an antigovernment or racist ideology. The FBI has found that recruits to these groups feel displaced by rapid cultural and economic changes and in some cases are "seeking some form of personal affirmation." As U.S. society continues to change, the FBI predicts that the potential for hate crimes by extremist right-wing groups will increase.[93]

Prior to September 11, 2001, antiterrorism efforts were splintered among different agencies.[94] To improve their preparedness to respond to terrorist incidents, federal agencies conducted more than 200 exercises, about a third of which include state and local participants. Agreement on an interagency terrorist response program was slow to develop due to problems in securing appropriate levels of agency participation and in transferring command and control responsibilities in multiagency efforts.[95] The National Commission on Terrorism, created by Congress after the bombings of U.S. embassies in East Africa, issued a report in 2000 recommending even more aggressive steps to prevent terrorism. These included making the U.S. military the agency to lead the government's response to terrorist attacks, rather than law enforcement agencies. It was also recommended that foreign students in the United States be monitored and that sanctions be taken against nations that fail to cooperate fully with terrorism investigations.[96] These recommendations sparked some controversy, but they point to flaws in the readiness of the United States in preventing or responding to acts of terrorism.

These warnings and preparations were not sufficient to prevent the attacks of September 11, 2001, which resulted in a new level of fear and concern in the United States about terrorism, and also new legislation designed to accomplish the objectives of the earlier efforts which had fallen short. The USA Patriot Act was passed weeks after the September 11 attacks, and provides a series of provisions to enhance the government's ability to gather information that may be related to terrorism, including expanded authority to monitor communications among citizens.[97] The extended legal power for surveillance of citizens has been criticized in recent years for eroding civil liberties without any corresponding benefit to public safety. The National Commission on Terrorist Attacks Upon the United States (also known as the 9-11 Commission), an independent, bipartisan commission created by congressional legislation in 2002, was assigned to prepare a full and complete account of the circumstances surrounding the September 11, 2001, terrorist attacks, including preparedness for and the immediate response to the attacks. The Commission was also mandated to provide recommendations designed to guard against future attacks. Reporting in 2004, it proposed a strategy with three dimensions: (1) attack terrorists and their organizations, (2) prevent the continued growth of Islamist terrorism, and (3) protect against and prepare for terrorist attacks. This report proposed a major overhaul of the U.S. anti-terrorism effort within the United States and overseas.[98] The coming years will determine the extent to which needed changes are implemented in practice.

The release of the 9/11 Commission Report by former governor Thomas Kean in 2004. Officially titled the National Commission on Terrorist Attacks upon the United States, the Commission was an independent group which prepared a complete account of the circumstances of the September 11, 2001, terrorist attacks and the preparedness of the United States. What did the 9/11 Commission recommend?

CRITICAL THINKING EXERCISES

Is the Internet an Avenue for Terrorists?

A twenty-year-old former computer science student pleaded guilty in Boston for a hacking spree against targets that included the military and NASA.[a] An "urgent" e-mail purportedly from a government agency claimed that bananas from Costa Rica carry a "flesh-eating" bacteria that can eat "2 to 3 centimeters of flesh an hour" resulting in amputation or death. This claim was denied by the U.S. Centers for Disease Control, but a panic was feared. The banana industry called this "just another case of Internet terrorism like the recent hacker attacks on popular web sites."[b] These are examples of a growing number of incidents where both government and business Internet sites have been vandalized and sometimes offensive or subversive material posted.

The Internet has come under increasing fire for posting information that is inaccurate, inflammatory, and/or dangerous. A "police brutality" webpage admits to not verifying the facts posted. The publisher of the webpage said, "I don't think twice about badmouthing presidents, newspaper reporters, or other public officials."[c] The Supreme Court struck down a law barring the posting of "indecent" material on the Internet because that term was too vague. Nevertheless, the government retains the right to prosecute individuals who post obscene material or child pornography on the Internet; these materials are more clearly defined in law.[d]

At the same time, the FBI has stated that some Internet sources "are repositories for inflammatory rhetoric which can influence extremists. Databases on the Internet contain recipes for bombs, dispense information on unconventional weapons, or offer computer viruses for download."[e] There are chat rooms for those who hold extremist, racist, sexist, and separatist views. Sometimes these people gather in person to engage in deviant activities. Occasionally these activities are unlawful. There is hate speech on the Internet as well as antigovernment postings, sites that advocate rape and violence, and many other sites that can be considered offensive. Those who spend time surfing the Internet can find a wealth of useful information posted there. But some of that information can also be used for destructive or illegal purposes.

CRITICAL THINKING QUESTIONS

1. Distinguishing harmless speech from harmful action is difficult. Should bomb recipes be barred from publication on the Internet? Why or why not?
2. Should inflammatory rhetoric that incites racial, ethnic, or government hatred be prohibited on the Internet? Why or why not?
3. Does a person have a right to post whatever he or she wants on the Internet, or should there be a standard for Internet content?

NOTES

a. John Bacon, "Former Student Admits Hacking NASA," *USA Today* (June 30, 2000), p. 3.
b. David Noack, "Banana Rumor Called 'Internet Terrorism,'" *APBnews.com* (February 25, 2000).
c. Mark Johnson, "Lawsuits Spur New Rules for Internet," *Richmond Times–Dispatch* (September 9, 1997), p. 12.
d. *Reno, Attorney General of the United States v. American Civil Liberties Union,* 117 S.Ct. 2329 (1997).
e. Federal Bureau of Investigation, *Terrorism in the United States* (Washington, DC: U.S. Government Printing Office, 2000).

Should There Be a Crackdown on Internet Gambling?

Eleven people were charged in a U.S. crackdown on a multi-billion-dollar Internet sports betting web site with operations in Britain and the Caribbean. The indictment charged the operators, British-incorporated BetOnSports, with illegally taking bets from U.S. residents and failing to pay taxes on $3.3 billion in wagers. The case highlights efforts in the United States to enforce a ban on Internet gambling even though most sites are offshore and not subject to U.S. law. Analysts were divided over the implications of this case for other Internet gambling companies that have U.S. customers. Some felt the language of the indictment amounted to a warning to the wider industry, but others said it appeared to be a company-specific issue relating to BetOnSports's American founder and former owner, Gary Kaplan, one of the key persons indicted. According to some reports, Americans place more than half of all online bets. The American Gaming Association has estimated that U.S. residents bet more than $4 billion offshore each year, and more than 2,000 gambling web sites have been identified. The clampdown has strained trade relations with the Caribbean state of Antigua and Barbuda, a hub for Internet gambling, which has brought the matter to the World Trade Organization.[a]

In 2006, Congress passed a ban on Internet gambling, a ban supported by the religious community, family groups, major sports organizations, and the U.S. President. Because the United States has no authority over gambling sites based in foreign locations, the law makes it illegal for banks and credit card companies to process online gaming payments from the United States. Therefore, it is the banks and credit card companies who will be forced to identify and deny efforts to purchase gambling services from Internet sites. Some believe it will be very difficult in technical terms for banks to accurately identify gambling service providers seeking electronic payments, and that this effort to ban Internet gambling might move the Internet gambling market underground, resulting in more unscrupulous operators and organized crime.[b]

CRITICAL THINKING QUESTIONS

1. Do you believe that Internet gambling should be made illegal? Explain your reasons.
2. Prohibitions and bans often drive an activity underground, resulting in more criminal operators. Is there a way to prevent this from happening?

NOTES

a. "11 charged as U.S. Takes on Net Bets," *Australian* (July 20, 2006).
b. Tony Batt, "Internet Gambling Debate May Not End with Ban," *Las Vegas Review-Journal* (October 3, 2006); Mike Brunker, "Ban Unlikely to End Web Gambling," *MSNBC.com* (October 14, 2006).

Gambling via the Internet is an international problem because the host sites are usually not in the United States, and it is difficult to keep juveniles from playing or those where gambling is illegal. Is there a way to reduce on-line gambling where it is illegal, or by those who are minors?

SUMMARY

WHAT IS MEANT BY POLITICAL AND ECONOMIC CRIMES?

- Sophisticated crimes are characterized by planning and organization. Criminal law punishes criminal planning as the crime of conspiracy.
- Conspiracy takes place when two or more persons agree to commit a crime, or to carry out a legal act in an illegal manner.

HOW CAN WHITE-COLLAR CRIMES BE DEFINED?

- White-collar crimes are distinguished by the manner in which they are carried out. Whereas street crimes are characterized by the use of force or stealth, white-collar crimes are characterized by planning and deceit.
- White-collar thefts include embezzlement (purposeful misappropriation of property entrusted to one's control, to which one is not entitled); extortion (purposely obtaining property from another person with that person's consent, when that consent is induced through wrongful use of force or official authority); forgery (falsely making or altering an official document with intent to defraud); and fraud (purposely obtaining the property of another person through deception).
- Offenses against public administration include bribery (the voluntary giving or receiving of anything of value with the intent of influencing a public official), obstruction of justice (intentional prevention of a public servant from performing an official function), official misconduct (unauthorized exercise of an official function with intent to benefit or injure another), and perjury (false swearing).
- Regulatory offenses, or corporate crimes, include administrative offenses (failure to comply with court orders or agency requirements), environmental violations (emissions or dumping in violation of legal standards), labor violations, manufacturing violations, and unfair trade practices.
- Arrest trends and demographic factors suggest that white-collar crime will increase in the future.

WHY IS COMPUTER CRIME A GROWING THREAT?

- Computers are the instrument in several types of crime. The most common of these is theft by computer.
- Other types of instrumental computer crime include use of a computer for harassment or extortion.
- Crimes in which computers are the object of the criminal act include causing damage to hardware or software, stealing trade secrets, and altering data for an unlawful purpose.
- As computers proliferate and computer literacy increases, rates of computer crime can be expected to increase as well.

HOW DOES ORGANIZED CRIME OPERATE?

- Organized crime is a continuing criminal enterprise that rationally works to profit from illicit activities that are often in great public demand. Its continuing existence is maintained through the use of force, threats, monopoly control, and/or the corruption of public officials.
- In contrast to white-collar crimes, which generally occur as a deviation from legitimate business activity, organized crime takes place through a continuing criminal enterprise that exists to profit primarily from crime.
- The main types of organized crime are provision of illicit services (loan-sharking, prostitution, gambling), provision of illicit goods (drug dealing, fencing of stolen property), and infiltration of legitimate business (demands for "protection" money or no-show jobs).
- Research findings show that organized crime is not structured according to ethnic groups; rather, organized crime groups evolve around specific illicit activities.
- The true extent of organized crime is unknown, although there have been large increases in arrests for certain types of crime.
- Greater ease of travel and communication has made the commission of organized and transnational crime much easier.
- Among the most significant types of international crime are importation of stolen vehicles, drug smuggling, and illegal immigration.

WHAT ARE THE IMPACTS OF TERRORISM AND HATE CRIMES?

- Terrorism is the unlawful use of force or violence against persons or property to intimidate or coerce a government, the civilian population, or any segment thereof, in furtherance of political or social objectives.
- Hate crimes are similar to terrorist acts except that a particular minority group (defined by race, ethnicity, nationality, or sexual orientation) is usually the target.
- There has been a general decline in the number of terrorist incidents since the 1980s, but those that are still being committed are becoming more deadly.

KEY TERMS

conspiracy *487*
white-collar crimes *487*
crimes of fraud *487*
crimes against public administration *487*
regulatory offenses *487*
embezzlement *488*
extortion *489*
forgery *489*
fraud *489*
bribery *490*
obstruction of justice *490*
official misconduct *490*
perjury *491*
corporate crimes *491*
computer crime *494*
identity fraud *497*
organized crime *498*
racketeering *500*
money laundering *500*
crime syndicate *502*
transnational crime *504*
terrorism *507*
hate crimes *507*

QUESTIONS FOR REVIEW AND DISCUSSION

1. What characteristics are common to all types of sophisticated crimes?
2. What factors must be present for conspiracy to be established?
3. What are the three main types of white-collar crime? Give an example of each.
4. Why is there reason to believe that white-collar crime will increase in the future?
5. In what kinds of crimes are computers the instrument? In what kinds are computers the object?
6. What is organized crime?
7. Give examples of each of the three basic types of organized crime.
8. What connection, if any, is there between organized crime and ethnicity?
9. What are some major types of international crime?
10. How is transnational drug smuggling carried out?
11. What is the distinction between terrorism and hate crimes?

NOTES

1. Edward Iwata and Elliot Blair Smith, "Skilling's Fall from Grace Comes to This," *USA Today* (February 20, 2004), p. 1B; "Senior Enron Figure Admits Insider Trading," *Facts on File World Digest* (October 30, 2003); "Waksal Gets 7-Plus Years," *CNN.com* (June 10, 2003); "Closing Arguments Underway," *CNN.com* (March 1, 2004); Paula Dobbyn, "Royal Caribbean to Pay Alaska $3.5 Million in Dumping Charges" *Knight Ridder/ Tribune Business News* (January 17, 2000); Reuters, "Royal Caribbean to Plead Guilty on Dumping Charges," *New York Times* (July 21, 1999), p. 1; Thomas S. Mulligan, "The Enron Verdict: Enron's Top Executives Are Convicted of Fraud," *Los Angeles Times* (May 26, 2006).
2. James D. Calder, "Al Capone and the Internal Revenue Service: State-Sanctioned Criminology of Organized Crime," *Crime, Law and Social Change* 17 (1992), pp. 1–23; Laurence Bergreen, *Capone: The Man and the Era* (New York: Simon & Schuster, 1994).
3. Jay S. Albanese, *White-Collar Crime in America* (Englewood Cliffs, NJ: Prentice Hall, 1995).
4. Adapted from *Proceedings of the Academic Workshop* (Morgantown, WV: National White Collar Crime Center, 1996).
5. Andrew Murr, "Living High on the Hog," *Newsweek* (October 27, 1997), p. 48.
6. John M. Caher, *King of the Mountain: The Rise, Fall, and Redemption of Chief Judge Sol Wachtler* (Buffalo: Prometheus Books, 1998); Bethany Kandel, "Top N. Y. Judge Faces Charges," *USA Today* (November 9, 1992), p. 2.
7. Kevin Johnson, "Probe Focuses on Online Sales of Fake Federal Ids," *USA Today* (May 26, 2000), p. 3A.
8. "Mount Pleasant Suit," *USA Today* (February 28, 1992), p. 8; "Porn Site, 900-Number Purveyors Settle FTC Fraud Charges," *Newsbytes* (January 31, 2002).
9. Tom Lowry, "American Family to Settle," *USA Today* (March 13, 1998), p. 1B; Tom Lowry, "Settlement Won't End American Family Woes," *USA Today* (March 20, 1998), p. 1B.
10. Joseph Stedino with Dary Matera, *What's in It for Me?* (New York: HarperCollins, 1993); Mark Mayfield, "S. Carolina Bribery Scandal Widens," *USA Today* (March 21, 1991), p. 4.
11. "Bribery Plea," *USA Today* (February 20, 1991), p. 5.
12. Albanese, *White-Collar Crime in America*, pp. 47–51.
13. Jacques Steinberg, "Scars in a Proud Police Force," *New York Times* (October 12, 1993), p. B1.
14. Associated Press, "Cleveland Judge Accused of Bribes," *New York Times* (March 2, 2000), p. 1.
15. Aaron Epstein, "Poindexter Guilty on All Counts," *Buffalo News* (April 8, 1990), p. 1.
16. "Cop Scandal May Affect 3,000 Cases," *New York Times* (December 15, 1999).
17. "Equifax Settlement," *USA Today* (July 1, 1992), p. 1B.
18. "Bayer to Pay $1 Million over Advertising Claim," *New York Times* (January 12, 2000) p. A21.
19. Lorraine Woellert "Finally, an Enron Conviction," *Business Week* (September 11, 2003).

20. "Ypsilanti Man Gets 3 Years for Dumping Chemicals," *Associated Press* (February 12, 2004).
21. "Chicken Plant Executives Charged in Deadly Fire," *USA Today* (March 10, 1992), p. 3.
22. "Big Contractor Cited for Safety Violation," *Providence Business News* 14 (October 18, 1999), p. 16.
23. Stacey Schultz, "A Big Fat Settlement," *U.S. News & World Report* (October 18, 1999), p. 74; Paula Kurtzweil, "Sticking Public with Impure Products Puts Syrup Makers in Prison," *FDA Consumer* 31 (April 1997), p. 30.
24. "Baby Food Companies Fixed Price, Florida Says," *USA Today* (January 4, 1991), p. 3.
25. "Toys R Us, 2 Toy Makers to Pay $50 Million in Cash, Toys in Suit," *Richmond Times–Dispatch* (May 26, 1999), p. C1.
26. Edward Cornish, "92 Ways Our Lives Will Change by the Year 2025," *The Futurist* (January–February 1996), pp. 1–15; David E. Bloom and Adi Brender, "Labor and the Emerging World Economy," *Population Bulletin* 48 (October 1993), pp. 2–39.
27. U.S. Bureau of the Census, *Statistical Abstract of the United States*, 116th ed. (Washington, DC: U.S. Government Printing Office, 1998), p. 14.
28. Tom Campbell, "6½ years, $15 Million Payback Ordered in Theft," *Richmond Times–Dispatch* (April 6, 1999), p. 1.
29. Margaret Mannix, "Spammed and Scammed," *U.S. News & World Report* (May 31, 1999), p. 79; Leslie Brooks Suzukamo, "Computer Viruses Threaten to Become More Dangerous," *Pioneer Press* (St. Paul, Minnesota), (February 6, 2005).
30. Kim S. Nash, "PC Manager at Center of $2 Million Grocery Scam: Inside Job Spotlights Critical Security Threat," *Computerworld* (March 30, 1998), p. 1.
31. Fred Bayles, "Computers Aid Amateur Counterfeiters," *USA Today* (May 11, 1999), p. 3.
32. Katrina Baum, *Identity Theft* (Washington, DC: Bureau of Justice Statistics, 2006).
33. Deborah Kong, "Internet Auction Fraud Increases," *USA Today* (June 23, 2000), p. 3B.
34. "Man on Most Wanted List Pleads Guilty to Hacking," *Richmond Times–Dispatch* (March 28, 1999), p. 2; Kathy Rebello, " 'Sensitive Kid' Faces Fraud Trial," *USA Today* (February 28, 1989) p. 1B.
35. "Computer Security a Mess, Report Says," *USA Today* (December 6, 1990), p. 3; see also "Arrest in Hacking at NASA," *New York Times* (March 19, 1998), p. 19.
36. Mark Lewyn, "Computer Verdict Sets 'Precedent'," *USA Today* (September 21, 1988), p. 1.
37. Kathy Rebello and Leslie Werstein, "Brilliance Has Its Roots in Family Life," *USA Today* (November 10, 1988), p. 1B; Ted Eisenberg et al., "The Cornell Commission on Morris and the Worm," *Communications of the ACM* 32, no. 6 (June 1989), pp. 706–9; William Kates, "Cornell Student Convicted in Computer Case," *Buffalo News* (January 23, 1990), p. 3; Amy Harmon, "As Digital Vandals Disrupt the Internet, a Call for Oversight," *New York Times* (September 1, 2003), p. A1.
38. "Computer 'Bomb,'" *USA Today* (November 27, 1995), p. 3; "Man Arrested at Library for Extortion," *Library Journal* (Sept 15, 2000), p. 11.
39. Hoag Levins, "Hackers Devastate Texas Newspapers' Servers," *Editor & Publisher* (June 28, 1997), p. 45.
40. "Cyberwars," *USA Today* (April 24, 1998), p. 8.
41. "Bogus Software," *USA Today* (August 30, 1991), p. 1D.
42. Carroll Bogert, "Windows 95, 5 Bucks," *Newsweek* (May 26, 1997), p. 82.
43. Clifford Stoll, *The Cuckoo's Egg: Inside the World of Computer Espionage* (New York: Doubleday, 1989).
44. Brendan Koerner, "Can Hackers be Stopped?," *U.S. News & World Report* (June 14, 1999), pp. 46–52.
45. Lisa Hoffman, "Feds Trying to Further Scope Out Extent of Cyber-crime," *Scripps Howard News Service* (February 23, 2006).
46. Koerner, "Can Hackers be Stopped?," pp. 46–52.
47. Katrina Baum, *Identity Theft* (Washington, DC: Bureau of Justice Statistics, 2006).
48. William F. Skinner and Anne M. Fream, "A Social Learning Analysis of Computer Crime among College Students," *Journal of Research in Crime and Delinquency* 34 (November 1997), pp. 495–519.
49. Wendy R. Leibowitz, "Low-Profile Feds Fashion Laws to Fight Cybercrime," *National Law Journal* (February 2, 1998), p. 1.
50. Laura DiDio, "Special FBI Unit Targets Online Fraud, Gambling," *Computerworld* (April 27, 1998), p. 47.
51. Carol Levin, "Internet Capers," *PC Magazine* (October 21, 1997), p. 29.
52. President's Commission on Law Enforcement and Administration of Justice, *Task Force Report: Organized Crime* (Washington, DC: U.S. Government Printing Office, 1967), p. 33.
53. Jay S. Albanese, *Organized Crime in Our Times* (Lexis/Nexis/Anderson, 2004), p. 3.
54. National Advisory Committee on Criminal Justice Standards and Goals, *Report of the Task Force on Organized Crime* (Washington, DC: U.S. Government Printing Office, 1976), p. 213.
55. Henry N. Pontell and Kitty Calavita, "White-Collar Crime in the Savings and Loan Scandal," *The Annals* 525 (January 1993), p. 39.
56. See Albanese, *White-Collar Crime in America.*
57. President's Commission on Organized Crime, *The Impact: Organized Crime Today* (Washington, DC: U.S. Government Printing Office, 1987), pp. 33–128.
58. Alan A. Block, "The Snowman Cometh: Coke in Progressive New York," *Criminology* 17 (May 1979), pp. 75–99; President's Commission on Organized Crime, pp. 64, 81, 91.
59. Block, p. 95.
60. Patricia A. Adler, *Wheeling and Dealing: An Ethnography of an Upper-Level Drug Dealing and Smuggling Community* (New York: Columbia University Press, 1985), p. 80.
61. Peter Reuter, *Disorganized Crime: The Economics of the Visible Hand* (Cambridge, MA: MIT Press, 1983), p. 175–76.
62. Francis A. J. Ianni with Elizabeth Reuss-Ianni, *A Family Business: Kinship and Social Control in Organized Crime* (New York: New American Library, 1973), p. 20.
63. Joseph L. Albini, *The American Mafia: Genesis of a Legend* (New York: Irvington, 1971), p. 288.
64. See Jay S. Albanese, "Casino Gambling and Organized Crime: More Than Reshuffling the Deck," in Jay S. Albanese, ed., *Contemporary Issues in Organized Crime* (Monsey, NY: Willow Tree Press, 1995).
65. Kevin Johnson, "Cell Phone 'Cloners' Pushing the Law's Buttons," *USA Today* (June 21, 1996), p. 3.
66. Margaret Mannix, "Keeping a Check on Debit Card Liability," *U.S. News & World Report* (September 8, 1997), p. 7.
67. Richard Barnet and John Cavanagh, *Global Dreams* (New York: Simon & Schuster, 1995); Warren Jestin, "Trading Places," *Global Outlook* (July 2006).
68. Jonathan M. Winer, "International Crime in the New Geopolitics: A Core Threat of Democracy," in William F. McDonald, ed., *Crime and Law Enforcement in the Global Village* (Cincinnati: Anderson, 1997), p. 41; see Moises Naim, *Illicit* (New York: Doubleday, 2005).

69. Carol J. Castaneda, "Car Thieves Wheeling and Dealing Overseas," *USA Today* (March 4, 1996), p. 3.
70. U.S. Comptroller General, *Efforts to Curtail the Exportation of Stolen Vehicles* (Washington, DC: U.S. General Accounting Office, 1999); Cherise Miles, "Detroit Special Agent Wrecks International Car Theft Ring," *U.S. Customs Today* (June 2001).
71. Ibid.
72. www.nicb.org (2003).
73. "Organized Crime and International Terrorism," *International Criminal Police Review,* vol. 472 (1998).
74. "Worldwide Nigerian Heroin Smuggling Ring Smashed," *Organized Crime Digest* (May 27, 1992), p. 3; "New Breed of Smugglers," *USA Today* (September 23, 1991), p. 3; "Nigerian Man Arrested for Heroin Smuggling," *Jakarta Post* (January 11, 2002).
75. U.S. Comptroller General, *Drug Control: Interdiction Efforts in Central America Have Had Little Impact on the Flow of Drugs* (Washington, DC: U.S. General Accounting Office, 2000).
76. Ko-lin Chin, *Smuggled Chinese: Clandestine Immigration into the United States* (Philadelphia: Temple University Press, 2000).
77. Sam Howe Verhovek, "Wretched Masses, Smuggled," *New York Times* (January 16, 2000), p. 2.
78. William F. McDonald, "Illegal Immigration: Crime, Ramifications, and Control (The American Experience)," in William F. McDonald, ed., *Crime and Law Enforcement in the Global Village* (Cincinnati: Anderson, 1997), pp. 65–88.
79. Norman J. Rabkin, *Criminal Aliens: INS' Efforts to Identify and Remove Imprisoned Aliens Need to be Improved* (Washington, DC: U.S. General Accounting Office, 1997); U.S. Government Accountability Office, *Immigration Enforcement: Weaknesses Hinder Employment Verification and Worksite Enforcement Efforts* (June 2006).
80. Kit R. Roane, "North of the Border, Terror's 'club Med'," *U.S. News & World Report* (August 7, 2000), p. 46.
81. U.S. Department of Justice. *Assessment of U.S., Activities to Combat Trafficking in Persons* http://www.usdoj.gov/crt/crim/wetf/us_assessment.pdf (2003).
82. William F. McDonald, "Illegal Immigration," p. 83.
83. Federal Bureau of Investigation, *Terrorism in the United States, 1999* (Washington, DC: U.S. Government Printing Office, 2001), p. 2.
84. Michael Janofsky, "Man Is Convicted in Killing of Gay Student," *New York Times* (November 4, 1999), p. A14.
85. Benjamin Weiser, " 'Mastermind' and Driver Found Guilty in 1993 Plot to Blow Up Trade Center," *New York Times* (November 13, 1997), p. 1; Gary Fields, "Yousef Sentenced to 240 Years in Solitary," *USA Today* (January 1, 1998), p. 4.
86. David E. Kaplan and Mike Tharp, "Terrorism Threats at Home: Two Years after Oklahoma City, Violent Sects Still Abound," *U.S. News & World Report* (January 5, 1998), pp. 22–27.
87. Warren P. Strobel, Kit R. Roane, Chitra Ragavan, "The Case of the Strange Conspiracy," *U.S. News & World Report* (January 17, 2000), p. 27.
88. Federal Bureau of Investigation, *Hate Crime Statistics* (Washington, DC: U.S. Government Printing Office, published annually).
89. *U.S. v. Winslow, Nelson, and Baker,* 962 F. 2d 845 (9th Cir. 1992) at 849.
90. Ibid.
91. Ibid., and also *United States v. Stauffer,* 922 F. 2d 508 (9th Cir. 1990) at 514–15.
92. Gordon Witkin and Ilan Greenberg, "End of the Line for the Unabomber," *U.S. News & World Report* (February 2, 1998), p. 34; Ted Gest, "End of the Line," *U.S. News & World Report* (May 18, 1998), p. 37.
93. Gest, p. 11; Brent L. Smith, *Terrorism in America: Pipe Bombs and Pipe Dreams* (Albany, NY: State University of New York Press, 1994), p. 198–99.
94. "The Real Battle," *U.S. News & World Report* (April 27, 1998), p. 7; U.S. Comptroller General, *Combating Terrorism: Federal Agencies' Efforts to Implement National Policy and Strategy* (Washington, DC: U.S. General Accounting Office, 1997); U.S. Comptroller General, *Terrorism and Drug Trafficking: Responsibilities for Developing Explosives and Narcotics Detection Technologies* (Washington, DC: U.S. General Accounting Office, 1997).
95. U.S. Comptroller General, *Combating Terrorism: Issues to be Resolved to Improve Counterterrorism Operations* (Washington, DC: U.S. General Accounting Office, 1999); U.S. Comptroller General, *Combating Terrorism: Federal Response Teams Provide Varied Capabilities* (Washington DC: U.S. General Accounting Office, 2002).
96. National Commission on Terrorism, *Countering the Changing Threat of International Terrorism* (Washington, DC: U.S. Government Printing Office, 2000).
97. Jonathan R. White, *Defending the Homeland* (Belmont, CA: Wadsworth, 2004).
98. National Commission on Terrorist Attacks upon the United States (9/11 Commission), *Final Report* (New York: Norton, 2004) http://www.9-11commission.gov/report/index.htm.

chapter 18

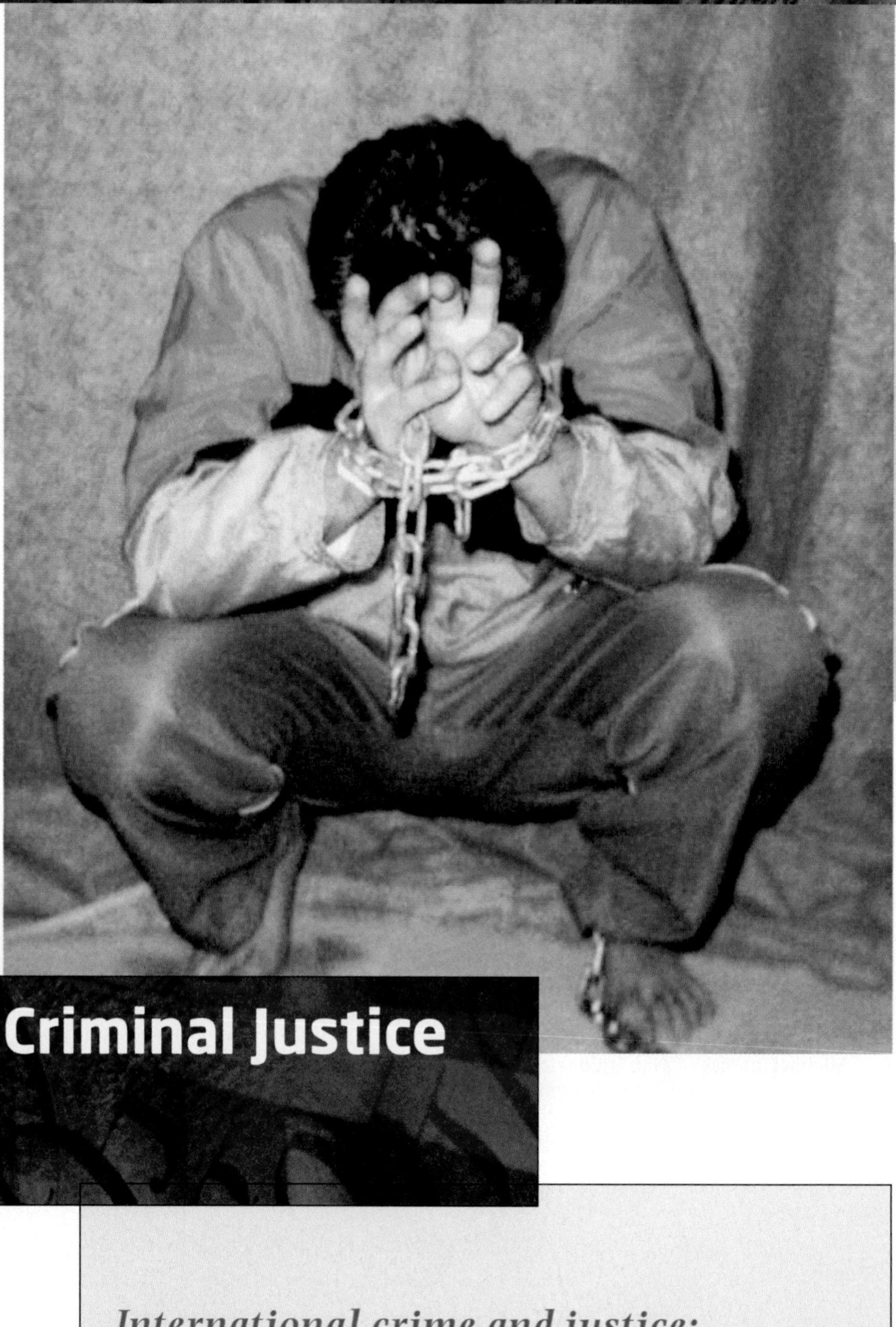

Comparative Criminal Justice

International crime and justice: world crime trends, transnational crimes, and the problems of multinational law enforcement.

CHAPTER OUTLINE

The Risk of Crime around the World
Incidence of Major Crimes
Victimization
Why Study Comparative Criminal Justice?

Transnational Crimes
Hijacking
Trafficking in Humans
Corruption
War Crimes

Transnational Law Enforcement
International Justice
International Corrections
Legal, Ethical, and Practical Problems

THAT'S A FACT:
Perspectives on International Victimization

MEDIA AND CRIMINAL JUSTICE:
Hotel Rwanda

CRITICAL THINKING EXERCISES:
- War Crime Suspects Hiding in the United States?
- Commercial Sexual Exploitation of Children

LEARNING OBJECTIVES

- Analyze the risk of crime around the world in relation to crime rates, types of crime, and victimization surveys.
- Explain the universality of crime and give examples of cross-national similarities and differences in characteristics of crime.
- Argue for the importance of the study of comparative criminal justice.
- Identify and describe four principal types of transnational crimes.
- Describe the agencies of transnational law enforcement and the ways they interact to combat transnational crime.
- Discuss the issues surrounding the concepts of international justice, courts, and corrections.

Daniel Pearl was a reporter for *The Wall Street Journal* who vanished in 2002, four months after the 9/11 terror attacks in America, while researching a story on Islamic extremism in Pakistan. Several weeks later, it was discovered he had been kidnapped by Islamic militants, and he was subsequently executed by them. While cutting his throat, they taped the execution for posting on the Internet. His execution by Khalid Shaikh Mohammed, alleged mastermind of the 9/11 attacks, was shown on a grisly videotape acquired by investigators. Daniel Pearl was the South Asia bureau chief of *The Wall Street Journal* at the time, and he was survived by his new wife, pregnant with their first child. In subsequent books, his wife, Mariane Pearl, blamed a new breed of uneducated but computer-literate terrorists. Bernard-Henri Levy argues that radical Islam is a career choice for the cosmopolitan and well educated, a source of wealth and power.[1] In either case, the death of Daniel Pearl was a galvanizing moment illustrating the sheer brutality that underlies acts of terrorism and its impact on the innocent and blameless. This chapter examines the extent of crime around the world, how that crime is becoming international in nature, and trends toward an international system of adjudication.

The Risk of Crime around the World

The United States is not the only nation with a crime problem. In Mexico a former governor was shot and killed at a busy intersection in broad daylight. The assailant wanted to steal his watch. Armed robberies in Mexico City occur with frightening boldness and regularity. Business, government, and media travelers report thefts, robberies, rapes, and kidnappings. In one case a CNN camera crew was robbed at gunpoint while leaving the parking lot of Mexico's Foreign Secretariat, even though officers were close by.[2] *Wall Street Journal* reporter Daniel Pearl was kidnapped in Pakistan while doing research for a story. In Rio de Janeiro, Brazil, a city of 11 million inhabitants, there are 6,000 murders committed annually and more than 45,000 cars stolen.[3] Similar problems in a number of countries in South America, Africa, Asia, and eastern Europe have resulted in regular travel warnings posted by the U.S. State Department. Twenty-nine country-warnings were added to this list in 2006 alone.[4] These warnings resulted from documented instances of pervasive crime, government instability, terrorist threats, and concern that the government will not respond effectively to instances of wrongdoing. Acts of violence occur with alarming frequency all over the globe. Since the terror attacks of September 11, 2001, and the U.S. military presence in Afghanistan and Iraq, crime and violence resulting from terrorist motives has caused great concern. Consider the following "Worldwide Caution" issued by the U.S. State Department to all U.S. citizens in 2006, which extended into 2007:

TRAVEL WARNINGS

> *The Department of State remains concerned about the continued threat of terrorist attacks, demonstrations and other violent actions against, U.S. citizens and interests overseas. Current information suggests that al-Qa'ida and affiliated*

The U.S. State Department provides travel warnings on its web site to warn American tourists of areas around the world where it may be dangerous to travel due to civil unrest, war, crime, or disease. The photo depicts a situation in central Africa in which Americans were warned to stay away. Studies show that rates of violent crime are much higher in the United States than in other developed countries. Are there any reasons to question these data?

organizations continue to plan terrorist attacks against U.S. interests in multiple regions, including Europe, Asia, Africa and the Middle East. These attacks may employ a wide variety of tactics to include assassinations, kidnappings, hijackings and bombings.

Ongoing events in Iraq and elsewhere in the Middle East have resulted in demonstrations and associated violence in several countries. Americans are reminded that demonstrations and rioting can occur with little or no warning . . .

In the wake of the August 2006 plot against aircraft in London, numerous terrorist attacks on trains in India in 2006, the July 2005 London Underground bombings, and the March 2004 train attacks in Madrid, Americans are reminded of the potential for terrorists to attack public transportation systems. In addition, extremists may also select aviation and maritime services as possible targets.

U.S. citizens are strongly encouraged to maintain a high level of vigilance, be aware of local events, and take the appropriate steps to bolster their personal security. . . . U.S. Government facilities worldwide remain at a heightened state of alert.[5]

This government warning to U.S. citizens illustrates how the threat of terrorism has produced serious concerns about terrorist-motivated crime, including hijackings, bombings, and kidnappings. Do these crimes accurately reflect the overall crime situation in many countries? How does the United States compare in its handling of crime and violence?

As is discussed in Chapter 3, in the United States major violent and property crimes are counted annually. The Uniform Crime Reports count eight serious crimes known to the police, and the national victimization survey counts six of those crimes (excluding murder and arson) to determine the level of crime that actually occurs, whether or not it is reported to police. Unfortunately, there is no international analogy to the Uniform Crime Reports or victimization surveys. Different nations use different methods to count crimes, and some approach the task more diligently than others. Some countries regard crime as a blot on their national image, and others do not see the significance of documenting it in statistical terms.

DISCREPANCIES IN DATA

A major problem in comparing crime rates in different nations is the way crimes are counted. In some nations, rape is rarely reported to the police because victims do not believe it will be taken seriously by police officials. In other nations, crimes are not reported because citizens fear the police. In still other countries, record keeping is not uniform, and therefore not all crimes brought to the attention of police are included in official figures. The result of these methodological problems is that the number of crimes reported to the police is generally lower than the level of crime that is actually occurring. In the United States, victimization surveys have revealed that more than a third of all crime is not reported to police, and it is likely that this figure is higher in other nations.

Incidence of Major Crimes

Despite these problems, several efforts have been made to obtain some kind of international comparison of the incidence of major crimes. There are two reasons

Students honoring the slain victim after a gunman killed a student and wounded 20 others before killing himself at Dawson College in Montreal in 2006. Why do you believe rates of violent crime differ widely around the world?

for these efforts: (1) Without periodically collected baseline data about the incidence of crime, it is impossible to distinguish long-term trends from year-to-year fluctuations, and (2) a comparison of crime rates in different nations might provide clues as to why some nations are more successful than others in controlling crime rates.

The two major multinational efforts to measure the extent of crime in different countries are Interpol and the United Nations crime surveys. Interpol is the International Police Organization, headquartered in Lyons, France. It provides a resource for crime data and intelligence information to member police agencies around the world. Every two years Interpol requests crime reports from each member nation for seven offense categories (murder, sex offenses, serious assault, theft, fraud, counterfeit currency, and drug offenses). Some of these offenses are difficult to compare; for example, the United States counts only rape in the category "sexual offenses," whereas most other nations count sex crimes of all types. Likewise, the nature of drug offenses varies widely by country, making cross-national comparisons problematic. Even murders can sometimes be counted incorrectly, because accidents, suicides, attempted homicides, and "questionable" deaths are either included or erroneously excluded in some countries. Therefore, it is important to be wary of crime "rankings" among nations when using crimes reported to police. Definitional and reporting problems make such rankings suspect.[6]

EFFORTS TO MEASURE CRIME

A comparison of homicides as reported to Interpol, the United Nations, and the World Health Organization reveals differences within the same countries in the same years. Despite such anomalies, however, the homicide figures reported by most nations are more consistent than those for other offenses because of the presence of a deceased victim and the more intensive investigation that occurs in these cases.

The United Nations undertook its first world crime survey in 1978, and has conducted five additional surveys since then. These surveys have continually increased in scope, but participation has not been uniform. A quarter of the countries responding to the first U.N. survey did not respond to the second, and 30 percent of those who responded to the second did not respond to the first. In addition, many questions were asked in later surveys that were not asked in the first survey.[7]

SIMILARITIES AND DIFFERENCES

Nevertheless, the surveys made several important findings. First, theft is the most commonly committed crime in all nations, and its rate goes up in industrialized nations (where there apparently is more to steal). Property crimes were ten times higher in Western developed countries (and in the Caribbean) than elsewhere. Second, assault is the most common crime of violence, although it occurs between four and ten times less often than do crimes of theft. The United States, Latin America, and the Caribbean regions experience the highest rates of homicide, assault, and robbery. Third, men commit reported crimes at a rate that is ten times higher than that of women.[8]

Major findings from these surveys of world crime statistics show that crime is universal in that some crime is found in every country. As noted theft is the most common crime worldwide, followed by burglary. Although violent crime comprises only about 10 to 15 percent of the crime problem, it varies dramatically around the world. For example, the robbery rate in the United States is approximately 240 per 100,000 population as compared to 71 per 100,000 in Germany and 2.2 per 100,000 in Japan.[9] Rates of crime are strongly related to economic deprivation, especially among young people, suggesting that crime rates are related to a lack of opportunities for legitimate earnings. These major findings are summarized in Table 18A in *That's a Fact.*

Victimization

Victimization surveys have been conducted on the national or city level in a growing number of countries, including Canada, England, Finland, Germany, Israel, Mexico, and the Netherlands.[10] In a significant move forward, fourteen nations participated in a standardized victimization survey. Overall victimization rates were found to be highest in the United States (28.8 percent of the population), followed by Canada and Australia. The lowest incidence of crime victimization was reported in Northern Ireland, Switzerland, and Finland (about 15 percent of the population).

The survey found that theft is closely related to opportunities: Nations with the highest rates of car ownership had the highest rates of automobile thefts; those with the highest rates of bicycle ownership had the highest rates of bicycle thefts. Similarly, the methods used to commit robberies closely resembled the tools available to offenders. In the United States, for example, 28 percent of robbers used a gun, a figure that mirrors the percent of Americans who own guns (29 percent). Conversely, only about 8 percent of robbers in other nations used guns, a proportion that reflects rates of gun ownership in other countries (6 percent).[11]

Rates of assaults and threats were much higher in the United States (5.4 percent), followed by Australia (5.2 percent) and Canada (4.0 percent), than they were in Europe, where the average was 2.5 percent (ranging from 0.5 percent in Switzerland to 3.4 percent in the Netherlands). The ability of some cultures to resolve disputes without resorting to assaultive behavior is an area that needs further cross-national study.

Victimization surveys in various countries have produced two common findings: (1) Crime is not often reported to police, and (2) victims and offenders share many of the same characteristics.[12] These findings are consistent with those of victimization surveys in the United States, and they suggest that criminals generally victimize people in the same socioeconomic class as themselves and that the number of crimes reported to police is significantly lower than the number actually committed.

In an effort to explain why low-crime countries avoid criminal behavior with greater success than other nations, Freda Adler examined ten countries that have

That's a FACT

Perspectives on International Victimization

Table 18A summarizes the findings of the *Global Report on Crime and Justice* of the United Nations. Which of the four general findings surprises you the most, and why?

Figure 18A illustrates the extent of adults victimized by burglaries and "contact crimes" (assaults and robberies) over a five-year period. Taken from international crime victim surveys, these data indicate that victimization is twice as high in Latin America and Africa than it is in Europe and Asia. (The "New World" combines the United States, Canada, Australia, and New Zealand.)

In developing countries the victimization surveys are administered only in the largest cities, so it is difficult to obtain a true national estimate. But even among the developed nations there exists significant variation. Of course, there are differences in the quality of data produced in each of these country surveys, but large differences are not likely to be due to chance variations.

How might you explain the differences between the victimization rates in Latin America and Africa compared to Europe and Asia?

Table 18A Crime in International Perspective

General Finding	*Explanation*
Crime exists in every country.	Rates vary greatly by country and region. Arab states report very low crime rates, Latin America and (Sub-Saharan) Africa report the highest crime rates.
The most common crime worldwide is theft.	Rates of theft are higher in industrialized than in nonindustrialized countries.
Violent crime (homicide, assault, robbery) accounts for 10 to 15% of all reported crime.	Violent crime rates vary greatly. They are highest in the United States, Latin America, and the Caribbean region.
Crime rates are related to poverty levels among young people in all regions.	Crime rates are higher when there is more economic deprivation.

Source: Compiled from Graeme Newman, ed., *United Nations Office for Drug Control and Crime Prevention, Global Report on Crime and Justice* (New York: Oxford University Press, 1999).

FIGURE 18A Percentage of Adults Victimized (previous 5 years)

Source: Data from Irvin Waller, *Crime Victims: Doing Justice to Their Support and Protection* (Helsinki: European Institute for Crime Prevention and Control, 2003); John van Kesteren, Pat Mayhew, and Paul Nieuwheerta, *Criminal Victimization in 17 Industrialized Countries: Key Findings from the 2000 International Crime Victims Survey* (The Hague: Ministry of Justice, 2000).

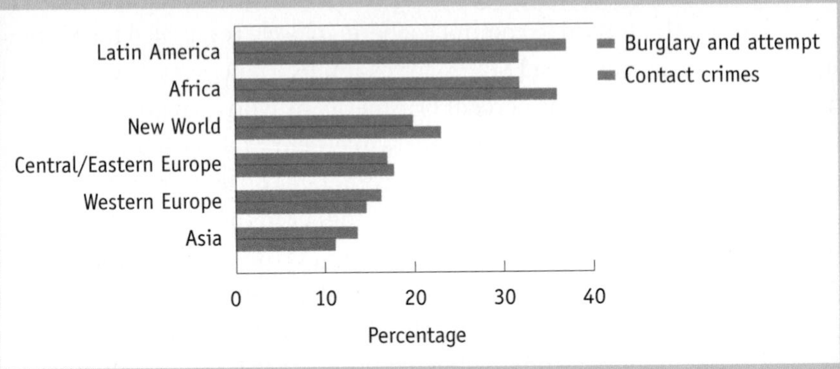

CROSS-NATIONAL STUDIES

low crime rates as measured by the U.N. world crime surveys: Switzerland, Ireland, Bulgaria, Germany, Costa Rica, Peru, Algeria, Saudi Arabia, Japan, and Nepal. She studied forty-seven different socioeconomic and cultural factors ranging from birthrates to literacy, and found that they explained little of the variation in crime rates in these nations. Also, in no country did the agencies of criminal justice appear to prevent crime (i.e., with different policies, laws, practices, and penalties). Adler concluded that all ten low-crime countries "appear to have developed some form of strong social control, outside and apart from the criminal justice system."[13]

Two key characteristics of low-crime nations are solid family systems and strong religious tradition, practice, and belief. This suggests that crime may be an outgrowth of instability within families or religious communities, regardless of cultural differences in countries' location, history, or economics. Adler coined the term **synnomie** to indicate the sharing of values to the point of harmonious accommodation of divergent views. This is the opposite of **anomie,** a term that is often used to indicate the disharmony that is created by social disorganization and that pushes people toward deviant behaviors. As Adler observed, "The sharing of activities 'for the common good' accounts for apparently strong social solidarity" and low crime in these nations.[14] Investigations such as Adler's, together with efforts to measure crime rates in different cultures more accurately, represent the beginnings of a "global criminology" that will take the study of crime and criminal justice beyond individual cultures and countries to the world as a whole.[15] This will become increasingly important with the growing ease of international travel and the rise in international criminal activity.

The Swiss population enjoys the comparative security of living in a low-crime country. What characteristics of a low-crime country do cross-national studies, and this photograph, suggest?

synnomie
The sharing of values to the point of harmonious accommodation of divergent views.

anomie
A "normlessness," or lack of attachment felt by some people toward their society.

Why Study Comparative Criminal Justice?

There is no way to know whether the experience of crime and justice in the United States is typical, acceptable, or intolerable without a comparison with other nations. Indeed, a comparison of the known with the unknown is a fundamental principle in advancing knowledge. In the twenty-first century such comparisons become increasingly important with the globalization of the economy, improved international communications, and more open borders around the world than ever before allowing for international travel and immigration. As criminologist James Finckenauer has remarked, "Ignoring the transnationalization of crime would be akin to adopting a 'head in the sand' strategy."[16] Ignorance of the experiences with crime, police, courts, and corrections in other parts of the world results in a failure to anticipate crime trends first experienced elsewhere and to a lack of awareness of successful innovations tried in other countries, leading to the repeat of mistakes in policy.

Transnational Crimes

More than one hundred celebrities were subpoenaed by the U.S. government in an investigation of *shahtoosh* wool shawls and scarves costing between $2,000 and $3,000, which are popular among the wealthy as status symbols.[17] A zoologist exposed the link between the *shahtoosh* shawls and the wool from skinned Tibetan antelopes, an endangered species. Dealers claimed that the wool came from wild goats, but it was found that Tibetan antelopes were killed illegally, clothing was fashioned illegally from animals hides, and that clothing was sold illegally in the United States. Because crimes were committed in at least three countries, the overarching offense is transnational in nature. This is the essence of **transnational crime**—offenses in which the planning and execution of the crime involve more than one country. This chapter addresses four specific types of transnational crime: hijacking, trafficking in humans, corruption, and war crimes.

transnational crime
Offenses in which the planning and execution of the crime involve more than one country.

Just as advances in technology and the fall of communism have made worldwide communication and travel much simpler in recent years, they have also made the commission of crime much easier. Passenger miles flown on international commercial flights have increased by twenty times over the last three decades, to more than 6 hundred billion miles per year. Global imports have increased by a factor of ten over the same period. International smuggling, drug distribution, alien smuggling, hijacking, and political crimes have grown in proportion to the growth of international communication and movement among countries. As criminal justice researcher Jonathan Winer has observed, "The very networks that legitimate businesses use to move goods so cheaply are the same networks that criminals use to move illicit goods just as easily."[18]

Hijacking

A man told a flight attendant on a Southwest Airlines flight from San Diego to San Jose, California, to "tell the captain that he should take the plane to Hollywood or else he was going to start killing people."[19] The flight attendant convinced the man to allow the plane to land in Burbank because there is no airport in Hollywood, and the man was taken into custody there after a brief struggle. None of the seventy-four passengers or flight crew was injured, although not all incidents of this kind end so well. The suspect in this case was indicted for **hijacking,** which is the unauthorized seizure of a land vehicle, aircraft, or other conveyance while it is in transit. The term *hijacking* originated during the 1920s and referred to thefts of truckloads or boatloads of liquor illegally manufactured in the Prohibition era.

hijacking
The unauthorized seizure of a land vehicle, aircraft, or other conveyance while it is in transit.

The hijacking of an airplane is sometimes called skyjacking. The first incident of skyjacking occurred in the United States in 1961, when a man forced a plane bound for Florida to go to Cuba. This began a rash of hijacking attempts in the United States, usually carried out to gain political asylum or to obtain ransom for releasing passengers. The United States responded by beginning mandatory point-of-departure screening and searches of all airline passengers in the early 1970s and for a time placed federal agents on certain flights. During the last thirty years skyjacking has dropped in the United States but has increased in the Middle East and Europe, where political dissidents use hijacking as a means for releasing political prisoners in foreign countries or obtaining ransom money to support

SKYJACKING

This image from *United 93* shows how airplane hijacking re-emerged as a serious public concern after September 11, 2001. Why did fears of airplane hijacking subside prior to 2001?

their political cause. In the late 1970s a group of Western democracies and the European Economic Community agreed to boycott the airlines of any nation that protected hijackers and to isolate those nations through economic sanctions. Hijacking continues today, but it has shifted back to truck and boat hijackings of legal products for sale as stolen merchandise, and to the hijacking of illegal goods, such as drugs or guns, among organized crime groups.[20]

After the terrorist attacks of September 11, 2001, in which skyjacking was used to turn the plane into a suicide/homicide bomb, security at airports around the world has been reexamined. The Transportation Security Administration (TSA) was tasked with securing all modes of transportation, including the screening of airline passengers. TSA deployed more than 50,000 federal screeners at 440 commercial airports nationwide. Needless to say, the task of training, applying intelligence information in a timely manner, and accurately screening millions of airline passengers each year is daunting.[21]

Human beings are still being bought and sold in some regions of the world. What is human trafficking? How is it different from slavery? What are the primary driving forces behind it?

Trafficking in Humans

Trafficking in humans, primarily women and children, from their home countries is a serious problem in many developing countries. The purpose of this trafficking is primarily sexual exploitation. Some estimates place the total number of women and children trafficked at 1 million per year.[22] Sometimes this illicit transport occurs with the knowledge of the victim, but most often it occurs under the ruse of work abroad as a housekeeper or nanny. When the victims arrive as illegal immigrants, they do not understand the language, often work for very low wages, and sometimes are forced to pay back exorbitant transit fees. Those who have passports often have them taken away, forcing them to work as slaves for the trafficker.

trafficking in humans
The smuggling of women and children from their home countries, usually for purposes of sexual exploitation.

SLAVERY TODAY

Human trafficking is driven by the demand for inexpensive labor and sexual services in developed countries combined with high unemployment and poor economic opportunity for women in many developing countries. For example, the Bangladesh National Women Lawyers Association identified 250 villages as recruiting and collection centers from which more than 7,000 women and children are sent to Pakistan and India each year.[23] The Internet has facilitated trafficking by allowing for direct communication between potential suppliers and consumers. Human trafficking is attractive to organized crime groups because the odds of apprehension are low since more than one country is generally involved and because human victims can be victimized multiple times, unlike illegal drug trafficking, in which a new supply is continually needed.[24] The discovery of fifty-eight smuggled immigrants who suffocated to death in a sealed truck ferried to England and a similar case at the U.S.–Mexican border drew international attention to the problem of human trafficking, but it remains to be seen if coordinated international action will follow.[25]

Corruption

corruption
A term referring to bribery or extortion, through misuse of official position, either for personal gain or through threats of harm or legal action to force payment.

GOVERNMENT CORRUPTION

Political and law enforcement corruption in nations around the world are the largest impediment to effective action against transnational crime. **Corruption** occurs in the form of bribery or extortion, where an official position is misused for personal gain, or where threats of harm or legal action are used to force payment. In both cases it is the misuse of an elected or appointed government position that lies at the heart of corruption. Interviews with police officers in Mexico City reveal that most officers take or solicit bribes in a system that requires them in turn to make payments to higher government officials.[26] In Rio de Janeiro, Brazil, and South Africa police killed 371 and 550 civilians, respectively, in a single year.[27] This situation has led to charges that police in some nations operate as outlaws, using their government authority to enrich themselves rather than protect public safety. In recent years police corruption scandals in Nigeria, China, and Japan have been seen as symptomatic of larger political corruption at higher levels.[28] The result is cities and nations where the government victimizes the people instead of working to improve their lives.

The problem of transnational crime is worsened when corrupt government agencies use their power to exploit their citizens further. Improvements in this situation will occur when changes that were made in the United States starting in the 1930s are made internationally. When policing is professionalized through better training and higher pay, loyalty to the job is enhanced and corruption is less likely to succeed. This change in law enforcement can only be successful, however, in democracies where power is balanced to prevent its abuse for personal gain. At this point in history the world has a large number of new democracies. The future of transnational crime and corruption will depend to a significant degree on the ability of these nations to develop into stable governments that strive to advance the interests of their citizens. A United Nations Convention on Corruption was open for ratification in late 2003. When ratified, it will place binding legal requirements on countries to take specific measures to address corruption.[29]

War Crimes

In July, 2000, an International War Crime Tribunal in the former Yugoslavia upheld a ten-year prison sentence of a Bosnian Croat paramilitary commander convicted of rape and torture. The commander failed to stop a sexual assault by a soldier under his command. Earlier the same year the tribunal found five Bosnian Croats guilty in the murders of 116 Muslim men, women, and children in an attack during the Bosnian war.[30] War crimes were first punished on an international basis after World War II when the United Nations established a commission to investigate them. **War crimes** are violations of law committed in excess of the brutality of the war itself. They include atrocities against civilians, slave labor, looting, the maltreatment or murder of prisoners, and genocide. **Genocide** is intentionally destroying an ethnic, racial, national, or religious group in a systematic manner. War crimes tribunals after the war in Bosnia and Rwanda show international intolerance for unlawful excesses during wartime. The current Bosnian and

war crimes
Violations of law committed in excess of the brutality of the war itself.

genocide
Intentionally destroying an ethnic, racial, national, or religious group in a systematic manner.

Rwandan tribunals are in some ways more expansive than the famous Nuremberg and Tokyo war tribunals following World War II. The current tribunals have successfully prosecuted rape cases as war crimes when they are used as attacks against an entire ethnic group.[31] These prosecutions show that international consensus exists regarding human rights even during a war, which may serve as a warning for future potential aggressors.

The genocide in Rwanda occurred in 1994 when Hutu extremists killed more than 500,000 people, mostly the minority Tutsi group. The scope of war crimes was expanded further when George Ruggiu was convicted as a non-Rwandan for inciting genocide. He hosted a French-language program on the radio that fomented ethnic violence against the Tutsis and helped the Hutu cause by using the radio to inform them of where Tutsis were hiding. Ruggiu was sentenced to twelve years in prison for broadcasts that "incited massacres."[32] Therefore, speech that incites genocidal violence can be prosecuted as a war crime.

A Rwandan survivor of the genocide that occurred there in 1995 prays at a mass grave. More than 500,000 people were slaughtered in the ethnic killings. How do you think genocide can still occur in modern-day Rwanda, Bosnia, and elsewhere after the Holocaust of World War II?

GENOCIDE

Transnational Law Enforcement

The International Criminal Police Organization (Interpol) was begun in 1923 and took its current name in 1956. It is composed of 177 member nations. Interpol assists member law enforcement agencies that require information of a transnational nature about crimes or criminals.[33] It provides information in four languages: Arabic, English, French, and Spanish. The U.S. National Central Bureau (USNCB) is the point of contact between Interpol and police agencies in the United States. It is located within the U.S. Department of Justice and is jointly managed with the U.S. Department of Treasury. All requests from federal, state, or local police are transmitted to Interpol through the USNCB.[34]

U.S. NATIONAL CENTRAL BUREAU

The importance of Interpol will increase as internal and external security concerns merge. As Malcolm Anderson has observed,

INTERPOL

> *The blurring of the distinction between internal and external security, resulting from the disintegration of the Soviet empire and the removal of the immediate threat of a military confrontation between the super-powers has altered the context in which police cooperation takes place. State security is now threatened by political violence which falls short of conventional military operations but which arises from complex criminal conspiracies—areas formerly considered squarely in the domain of policing.*[35]

Organized crime, drug trafficking, corruption, and other traditional concerns of law enforcement are becoming national security concerns in many nations. The demise of the Soviet Union has freed intelligence agencies and the military to focus on transnational crime rather than on military threats. This reflects an increase in transnational criminal activity as well as greater attention to international criminal matters on the part of U.S. agencies.[36]

Europol headquarters in the Netherlands. Europol is the European Union law enforcement organization that handles criminal intelligence. Why is a multinational intelligence agency needed in Europe?

EUROPOL

Another effort to combat transnational crimes is Europol, which was established in 1991 to share information about drug trafficking among member countries of the European Union. Europol emerged out of growing concern over drug trafficking and money laundering, as well as the need for better coordination among European police agencies and customs officials. The removal of many of the barriers to free trade and economic growth in Europe since the late 1980s has made it easier to communicate and travel among the European nations. This situation also makes it easier for criminals to smuggle stolen property and drugs across borders. Europol is seen as a mechanism for organizing international law enforcement activities.[37]

The need for shared information is paralleled by the need for trained law enforcement personnel. Efforts are being made to professionalize law enforcement agencies around the world. The Federal Bureau of Investigation now trains law enforcement officials from other nations in a program sponsored by the U.S. State Department. These officials come to the United States to be trained in modern law enforcement and prosecution techniques. In addition, the FBI opened an international police training academy in Budapest in 1995, and subsequently two others in Thailand and Botswana. By 2000 it trained more than 7,000 police officers and supervisors from around the world.[38] As FBI Director Louis Freeh observed, there is a need for "a centrally located school where we can develop a network of police partners in countries where we do not now have those relationships."[39]

AMERICAN POLICING OVERSEAS

More than 2,000 American law enforcement personnel are now working overseas. Nearly a third of these are agents with the Drug Enforcement Administration (DEA), which has agents in thirty nations. The U.S. Immigration and Naturalization Service, Customs Service, and Coast Guard each have law enforcement personnel in more than twenty countries. The FBI, Internal Revenue Service, Secret Service, and Bureau of Alcohol, Tobacco, and Firearms also have agents assigned overseas. This high level of international law enforcement activity points to the growth in international crime and the need for coordination of law enforcement activities.[40]

In June 1994, the United Nations held a conference on international money laundering in which forty-five countries participated.[41] A second U.N. gathering, the World Ministerial Conference on Organized Transnational Crime, was held in Naples. The purpose of the meeting was to examine existing international standards, legislation, and models for cooperation in dealing with international organized crime. The conference was attended by representatives from 142 countries.[42] The high level of interest and concern about these problems is clear from the level of participation. These meetings permit open discussion of the problems posed by international criminal behavior, along with possible solutions.[43] This is extremely important when so many U.S. law enforcement agencies are working in other countries. Nations can feel threatened when consensus has not been reached about the seriousness of the problem and the appropriateness of the measures taken. It is through such efforts that international law enforcement trust, cooperation, and professionalism are improving. It also is a mechanism for placing pressure on nations that are not diligent in their efforts to thwart transnational crime.

International Justice

THE WORLD COURT

The idea of an international criminal court to prosecute genocide, crimes against humanity, and war crimes was first considered when the United Nations was established after World War II. Differences of opinion among nations stalled the process until 1992, when the General Assembly called for a draft statute for an international criminal court. Renewed interest was largely the result of alleged war crimes and genocide in Yugoslavia and Rwanda.[44] As noted earlier, the United Nations Security Council established an ad hoc International Criminal Tribunal to investigate these incidents. Since that time, the precise composition and jurisdiction of the proposed international court, process for appeals and reviews, and enforcement issues have been negotiated.

One reason for the delay in the establishment of an international court has been opposition by the United States, which fears that such a court would act as a barrier to the use of diplomatic pressure and diplomatic solutions to international problems.[45] Nevertheless, the ability of such a court to convict criminals for international crimes could do much to enhance the moral and political force against war crimes and other international offenses. The likelihood that such a court could succeed is suggested by the fact that more than eighty indictments have been handed down and twenty suspects are in custody in the war crimes tribunal investigating incidents in the former Yugoslavia. Rwanda's former prime minister and defense minister are in custody, and three trials are under way in that tribunal. All this has been accomplished through a melding of different legal systems, rules of evidence, and even witness-protection programs, without any help from police or military officials.[46]

Nevertheless, resistance continues from powerful nations reluctant to accept rulings of the world court in specific cases. In 2000, for example, the U.S. Ambassador to the United Nations made a plea to bring rebel leaders in Sierra Leone's civil war to trial for war crimes, while other U.S. negotiators were trying to win an exemption from prosecution for U.S. military leaders at a planned international criminal court. The United States fears its military leaders could become targets for politically motivated prosecutions, but the United States was one of only seven countries that voted against creating the new court in 1998.[47] Negotiations continue on the rules, procedures, and jurisdiction for a permanent international court, but such a court must have full authority in order to be able to enforce its ruling.

LACK OF CONSENSUS

Consensus for an international court has been difficult to achieve for legal reasons as well as political ones. Legal traditions vary considerably among nations, and this can result in opinion derived from quite different sources. Legal systems can be grouped into four major types: civil law, common law, Islamic law, and socialist law.[48] Civil law systems, as are found throughout most of Europe, are the

Table 18.1 Justice in International Perspective

General Finding	*Explanation*
Civil law legal systems exist in more than half of all countries.	The common law tradition is the second most common, followed by Islamic, socialist, and hybrid forms.
Components of the criminal justice system are similar in all countries.	All countries have police, courts, and corrections systems, but their names differ widely.
Prison is the most common sentence for serious crimes in all countries.	There are wide variations in rates of imprisonment and length of sentences among countries.
Fines are the most common sentence overall in most countries.	Africa, Latin America, and Asia use sentences that do not involve physical custody less often.

Source: Data from Graeme Newman, ed., United Nations Office for Drug Control and Crime Prevention, *Global Report on Crime and Justice, 1999* (New York: Oxford University Press, 1999).

most common type and are based on legal rules or codes that are written to cover all possibilities of behavior. Common law systems, the basis for both English and American law, are based on legal precedents established by both law and court decisions, so laws are continually refined by courts on a case-by-case basis. Socialist systems such as China use law as a means to create a socialist system rather than to simply settle disputes. Socialist law systems control the distribution of property and power in a society in addition to addressing individual legal problems. Islamic law systems, found in many Middle Eastern countries, are based in the Muslim religion, so they address both acts against God and acts against individuals. Individual behavior such as dress, food, etiquette, and consensual sexual conduct are included in Islamic law and violations are judged harshly compared to other legal traditions. These differences in legal traditions make it difficult for nations to agree on the nature of violations, court jurisdiction and procedure, and appropriate punishment for crimes. Table 18.1 summarizes important similarities and differences among different national legal systems.

International Corrections

WORLD PRISON?

There is no proposal for a "world prison" similar to the proposed world court. Individuals who are adjudicated in the world court will be sent to their own country or exiled to agreed-upon locations. The penalties to be imposed on those who commit international crimes might be difficult to establish because of wide variations in the punitiveness of sentences in different nations. Table 18.2 compares incarceration rates in different nations. As the table shows, the United States's per capita prison population is higher than that of any other country. In addition, the United States has more offenders in prison than any other nation, by a wide margin. This has been a source of criticism in the United States, given the fact that its rate of violent crime is also among the world's highest. It cannot be said that the nation's incarceration policy has any direct impact on its crime rate.

HUMAN RIGHTS

The scope and limits of criminal punishment vary widely from one culture to another. Most nations, including all the Western industrialized countries, prohibit the death penalty or simply do not implement it. Nations that keep death penalty laws on the books usually reserve them for war crimes or cases of genocide.[49] There are exceptions, however, primarily in developing countries such as China, where it is alleged that more than 1,000 offenders are executed each year and their body organs harvested.[50] Nevertheless, despite these exceptions, the worldwide trend is away from use of the death penalty. In similar fashion, the use of corporal punishment has diminished. Instances of whipping, branding, maiming, and similar forms of punishment have declined steadily around the world except in Islamic countries.[51]

Although international differences in the punishment of criminals are to be expected, there are "human rights" or baseline standards of humane treatment that should apply everywhere. In an effort to specify the precise nature and scope of human rights in criminal justice, the United Nations established the *Standard Minimum Rules for the Treatment of Prisoners.* These rules were adopted at the first United Nations Congress on the Prevention of Crime and Treatment of Offenders, held in 1955. They represent a worldwide consensus on major issues such as torture, interrogation, and the living conditions of prisoners. These standards continue to be used in the training of law enforcement officers, corrections officers, and peacekeepers throughout the world.

Since 1955, the United Nations has held Congresses on the Prevention of Crime and the Treatment of Offenders every five years. The 2005 Congress was attended by a record 2,370 participants from 170 countries, fifteen intergovernmental organizations, and 167 nongovernmental organizations. This represents an overwhelming majority of the world's nations. The United Nations has since adopted a *Code of Conduct for Law Enforcement Officers, Declaration of Basic Principles of Justice for Victims of Crime and Abuse of Power,* and *Basic Principles on the Independence of the Judiciary.*[52] The multinational analysis and discussion of these important issues help promote consensus regarding the appropriate limits of the law and criminal justice. The level of dialogue among nations on issues of crime and justice has continued to expand, as has the range of topics discussed.

Table 18.2 International Incarceration Rates
(top 30 countries ranked by incarceration rate and having more than 20,000 inmates)

Country	*Number of Inmates*	*Rate per 100,000 Population*
USA	2,085,620	714
Russia	763,054	532
Belarus	52,500	532
Turkmenistan	22,000	489
Cuba	55,000	487
Ukraine	198,386	416
South Africa	186,000	413
Kazakhstan	58,300	386
Thailand	168,264	264
Tunisia	23,165	252
Chile	33,098	212
Poland	79,087	209
Iran	133,658	194
Uzbekistan	48,000	184
Brazil	330,642	183
Romania	39,015	180
Malaysia	43,424	174
Mexico	191,890	158
Zimbabwe	20,000	155
England & Wales	75,340	142
Spain	59,899	140
Cameroon	25,000	125
Netherlands	20,000	123
Korea	57,902	121
Myanmar	60,000	120
Australia	23,362	117
China	1,548,498	118
Peru	32,129	114
Saudi Arabia	23,720	110
Sri Lanka	20,975	110

Source: Roy Walmsley, *World Prison Population List,* www.kcl.ac.uk (2005).

INTERNATIONAL CODE OF CONDUCT

Legal, Ethical, and Practical Problems

During the 1980s, a narcotics cartel was responsible for transporting drugs from Mexico to the United States. The U.S. Drug Enforcement Administration was having some success in interrupting the drug flow with large seizures of drugs and cash. The cartel retaliated against DEA agents stationed in Mexico, killing DEA

Media & Criminal Justice *Hotel Rwanda*

Genocide occurred in Rwanda during a period of one hundred days in 1994, and the world did not take notice. More than 500,000 members of the Tutsi tribe were massacred by members of the Hutu tribe in a tragic case of ethnic rivalry and hatred. The movie *Hotel Rwanda,* released in 2005, focuses not on the massacre but instead tells the story of a hotel manager who saved the lives of 1,200 people during the genocide. The manager, Paul, is a Hutu married to a Tutsi, bringing the tension to the personal level.

Rwanda was earlier ruled by Belgium. During that period Tutsis ruled and the Hutus were oppressed, and many were killed. The Hutus are now in control, and the genocide consisted of armed troops prowling for and slaughtering Tutsis. The movie shows how the United Nations and the international community ignored the pending massacre and failed to intervene while it was occurring. A colonel, representing the United Nations as a peacekeeper, is shown in the film reporting the situation to his superiors and being ignored. Paul, the hotel manager, also informs his corporate headquarters of what is going on, but his hotel location is not a priority for them. These two men then act on their own to save as many lives as possible.

Rather than a film about a million deaths, it is a film about how two people respond to tragedy when no one else does. Even though the situation seemed impossible, the movie shows how these two men used finesse and guile to battle genocide, saving many lives in the process. Like other films that depict actual situations of gross injustice, such as *Midnight Express* (1978) and *In the Name of the Father* (1993), *Hotel Rwanda* raises important questions about human strength and weakness in the face of persecution.

Why do you believe such a large massacre could have happened without outside intervention? Could it happen again today?

agent Enrique Camarena, various informants, and others mistakenly believed to be associated with the DEA.[53] The United States had a strong interest in apprehending those responsible and bringing them to trial. Because Mexican authorities seemed unable to bring the suspects to justice, U.S. agents forcibly abducted a suspect from Mexico for trial in the United States. Is such an action ethical or legal?

ISSUES OF SOVEREIGNTY

The forcible abduction of a fugitive from one country to be brought to justice in another can be seen as a violation of international law. This is because nations are generally bound to respect the laws of other nations when operating inside their territory. The DEA case just described was unusual, and it went all the way to the U.S. Supreme Court. The Court held that even the forcible abduction of a suspect from a foreign country does not preclude prosecution in the United States.[54] This ruling was made despite the fact that the abduction was illegal under Mexican law.

Situations such as these occur only rarely, usually in very serious cases such as mass murders, treason, or the killing of a public official. Nevertheless, such actions violate the national sovereignty of the foreign country. They can result in public protest and unrest, acts of retaliation, unrelated sanctions (e.g., economic), and tension in diplomatic relations that can last for years.

EXTRADITION

In a similar way, fugitives from justice are sometimes "lured" from nations without *extradition agreements,* or from nations that wish to protect their citizens from the justice systems of other nations. Extradition agreements are treaties between the United States and other countries that provide for the surrender of any fugitives accused or convicted of a crime in one country to be tried or punished, or both, in the home country. These fugitives are usually tricked by means of false drug deals or conspiratorial meetings in other countries. When such "lures" are discovered, the target nation is usually outraged by the presence of undercover operatives working within their nation without their knowledge. Sometimes even a telephone call to a fugitive living in their country is seen as objectionable.[55] As with the forcible abduction of fugitives from foreign countries, the luring of fugitives by means of deception raises both ethical and legal questions that, to date, are not guided by generally accepted principles of ethics or international law.

The International Criminal Court in The Hague, Netherlands. Are there universal, transnational civil rights that such a court can protect? Why has the United States opposed the idea of a world court?

A third example of this problem has to do with *extraterritorial subpoenas.* For example, Swiss banks are known for their protection of the privacy of depositors. U.S. prosecutors have served extraterritorial subpoenas on U.S. branches of banks operating in nations with strong secrecy laws, such as Switzerland. If the banks do not produce the records requested, they may be fined. The problem is that foreign governments view this practice as an invasion of their national sovereignty.[56] Extraterritorial subpoenas have been resisted in court and through diplomatic channels, although U.S. courts have upheld the use of evidence obtained in this fashion.[57] Here again, the interest of the United States in obtaining evidence for a criminal prosecution is pitted against concerns for the legal rights and sovereignty of other nations. As international concerns regarding money laundering increase, it is likely that tensions will continue to rise until binding international agreements can be established.

DIPLOMACY

There are practical considerations as well to enforcing the law outside a nation's borders. It is often simply not possible to enter another country to pursue a suspect without posing real danger to the pursuing investigator, especially in nations characterized by corruption. Political pressure through diplomacy and economic incentives is a longer-term strategy that can also produce results.

CRITICAL THINKING EXERCISES

War Crime Suspects Hiding in the United States?

The U.S. Immigration and Naturalization Service concluded "Operation Home Run" when they arrested fourteen illegal immigrants in South Florida who were attempting to escape justice in their home country. Some were former secret police from Haiti wanted for human rights violations.

Former military and government leaders wanted for crimes in their homeland sometimes end up in the United States leading normal lives. These individuals are wanted for human rights violations often involving torture and murder that occurred during conflicts in countries that include Somalia, Haiti, Serbia, Peru, and other nations.

Finding these people is not easy. Some are undocumented aliens or live under false identities that are carefully established. It is expensive and time-consuming to locate them, and many blend into ethnic communities in the United States. When they are found, proving their actual identity and deporting them can be complicated. Under American law, war criminals other than Nazis are permitted to reside in the United States. America has a long history of protecting those who are fleeing persecution in other nations, but in the process some of the alleged persecutors land in America as well. Legislation has been proposed to change this law, but some of the individuals in question are not clearly war criminals, because some have not been charged with war crimes and others committed acts that are heinous but not necessarily war crimes. Nevertheless, human rights groups believe there are thousands of immigrants in the United States who were persecutors in their native countries.

CRITICAL THINKING QUESTIONS

1. What are some of the obstacles in the United States and internationally that the Immigration and Naturalization Service might face in trying to apprehend suspected war criminals more effectively?
2. Why might a foreign country not want to inform U.S. authorities about their knowledge of a suspected war criminal living in the United States?
3. What are the ways in which law or foreign policy could be used to reduce the incidence of suspected war criminals in the United States?

Sources: James Gordon Meek, "INS Targets Human Rights Abusers," *APBnews.com* (November 17, 2000); Chitra Ragavan, "A Safe Haven, but for Whom?" *U.S. News & World Report* (November 15, 1999), pp. 22–24; Aryeh Neier, "Bringing War Criminals to Justice: A Brief History," *Social Research*, vol. 69 (winter 2002), p. 1085.

Commercial Sexual Exploitation of Children

The commercial sexual exploitation of children—sexual abuse of a minor for economic gain—encompasses physical abuse, pornography, prostitution, and the smuggling of children for unlawful purposes. Although there have been efforts in recent years to better define the commercial exploitation of children (CSEC), more needs to be done to publicize the existence of this crime and develop strategies to reduce its incidence.

The number of known cases of CSEC is growing. Children are being kidnapped and sold into forced labor in the illegal sex industry. Some impoverished families are selling their children to traffickers in the hope of giving them a better life. There are documented reports of children being held in basements and in other slave-like conditions with beatings, malnutrition, and threats to them and their families while they are sexually exploited.

As technology and communication become more advanced and as global travel becomes easier, the effort to prevent CSEC must become more sophisticated. In addition to existing efforts to improve legislation, enforcement, and cooperative investigations, there are five directions that must also be pursued to more effectively prevent CSEC.

These are:

- Keeping pace with technology.
- Educating potential victims.
- Deterring demand.
- Increasing parental supervision.
- Improving the role of women and children in society.

It is estimated that 10 to 15 percent of homeless and street children in the United States are trafficked for sexual purposes within national and international trafficking networks. Victims include both U.S. residents trafficked within and outside the country, as well as children from other countries.

Participants in organized trafficking include:

- Arrangers/investors who provide money for trafficking operations and oversee the criminal enterprise.
- Recruiters, usually based in countries of origin, who find children and collect fees for them.
- Transporters who move the children through the origin, transit, and destination countries.
- Corrupt public officials who receive bribes to provide identity documents and negotiate illegal passage and entry between countries.
- Debt collectors, based in destination countries, who collect trafficking fees (which can run to $30,000 or more per person).

Although many foreign children trafficked into the United States work in "sweatshops" under coercive and sometimes slave-like circumstances, others become victims of commercial sexual exploitation. The trail for most of these children is strewn with false promises of legitimate work, fraudulent documentation, and false destinations, all within a web of smuggling and intimidation. Traffickers' recruitment efforts attempt to convince families—sometimes through "success" stories—that their children will be safer, better taken care of, and taught a useful skill or trade. Cash may be advanced to families, to be repaid through their child's earnings. Sometimes conditions are stipulated by a "contract," which makes children debt-bonded and provides leverage to force them into prostitution. Traffickers are skilled in providing false documents with false names and ages. Sometimes an easily acquired tourist visa suffices. Some traffickers tell children that if they escape or cooperate with law enforcement,

The Wall of Shame in the Exploited Child Unit of the National Center for Missing and Exploited Children depicting those arrested and convicted for these crimes. What measures can be taken to protect children more effectively from commercial sexual exploitation via the Internet?

previous cash advances to their families and other money owed will be collected from their parents, who may also be physically harmed.[a]

Child prostitution for sex tourists—including Americans who travel to destinations in or outside of the United States—is common in some locales. In Tijuana, Mexico, sex tourism is a daily occurrence as Americans cross the border every day for the purpose of having a sexual exchange with minors. Sex tourists usually frequent relatively poor countries that have well-developed commercial sex industries, although the travel pattern is also reversed, with sex tourists coming from poorer countries (for example, Argentina, India, and Mexico) to such affluent sex-tourist destinations as Amsterdam, Las Vegas, and New York.[b]

Most countries have laws—with substantial penalties—prohibiting the sexual exploitation of children, including the kidnapping, smuggling, and, more recently, trafficking in human beings. Nonetheless, the globalization of crime, dramatically increased access to the Internet, and ease of travel have brought new challenges to the prevention of the commercial sexual exploitation of children.

One way to meet these challenges is through binding international agreements and treaties. The United Nations Convention on Transnational Organized Crime has a protocol aimed at combating human trafficking, focusing on women and children, protecting and assisting victims, and promoting greater international cooperation. Law enforcement agencies in countries that ratify the protocol are required to cooperate in the identification of offenders and trafficked persons, share information about the methods of offenders, and train investigators and victim support personnel. As of summer 2006, 101 counties had ratified the protocol and another sixteen had signed but not yet ratified. These signatory countries are required to implement security and border controls and develop standards for passports, visas, and other travel documents. The protocol also calls for measures to prevent re-victimization, in which victims are returned to their countries of origin only to be trafficked out again.

CRITICAL THINKING QUESTIONS

1. If child exploitation is driven by demand, what are ways to reduce that demand?
2. Are there other ways to remove the influence of organized crime in the trafficking of children?

NOTES

a. U.S. Department of State, *Trafficking in Persons Report June 2003* (Washington, DC: U.S. Department of State, 2003); Laura A. Barnitz, *Commercial Sexual Exploitation of Children: Youth Involved in Prostitution, Pornography, and Sex Trafficking* (Washington, DC: Youth Advocate Program International, 2000); The Protection Project, *Trafficking in Persons, Especially Women and Children in the Countries of the Americas* (Washington, DC: Johns Hopkins University School of Advanced International Studies, 2000).

b. Eva J. Klain, *Prostitution of Children and Child-Sex Tourism: An Analysis of Domestic and International Responses* (Washington, DC: National Center for Missing and Exploited Children, 2000); Kevin Bales, *Understanding Global Slavery* (Berkeley: University of California Press, 2005).

SUMMARY

THE RISK OF CRIME AROUND THE WORLD

- It is difficult to compare crime rates in different nations because of various methodological problems.
- The world crime surveys conducted by the United Nations have found that theft is the most common crime. Assault is the most frequently committed violent crime.
- Victimization surveys have found that crime is not often reported to police and that victims and offenders share many of the same characteristics.
- Countries with low crime rates appear to have developed strong social control through family systems and religious tradition, practice, and belief.

TRANSNATIONAL CRIMES

- Greater ease of travel and communication has made the commission of crime much easier.
- Among the most significant types of international crime are hijacking, trafficking in humans, corruption, and war crimes.

TRANSNATIONAL LAW ENFORCEMENT

- The International Criminal Police Organization (Interpol) assists member law enforcement agencies requiring information about crimes or criminals of a transnational nature.
- Europol shares information about drug trafficking among member countries of the European Union.
- Efforts are being made to professionalize law enforcement agencies around the world.
- Efforts to establish an international criminal court have been hampered by differences of opinion among nations.
- There are four families of law: civil, common, Islamic, and socialist.
- Although there are international differences in the punishment of criminals, basic standards of treatment should apply everywhere. These have been codified by the United Nations in the *Standard Minimum Rules for the Treatment of Prisoners.*
- The forcible abduction of a fugitive from one country to be brought to justice in another raises legal and ethical problems. Similar problems arise when fugitives are lured to other countries.

KEY TERMS

synnomie *525*
anomie *525*
transnational crime *526*
hijacking *526*
trafficking in humans *527*
corruption *528*
war crimes *528*
genocide *528*

QUESTIONS FOR REVIEW AND DISCUSSION

1. What are some of the methodological problems faced in efforts to compare crime rates in different nations?
2. What factors appear to account for different rates of theft in different countries?
3. What characteristics did Adler identify in her study of countries with low crime rates?
4. What are some major types of international crime?
5. What is Interpol?
6. Why has the proposed international criminal court not been established?
7. What are some of the resolutions adopted by the 1995 U.N. Congress on the Prevention of Crime and Treatment of Offenders?
8. What problems are raised by the forcible abduction of a fugitive from one country to be brought to justice in another?

NOTES

1. Mariane Pearl with Sarah Crichton, *A Mighty Heart* (New York: Scribner, 2003); Bernard-Henri Levy, *Who Killed Daniel Pearl?* (Melville House Publishing, 2003); Anwar Iqbal, "Retracing Daniel Pearl's Steps, *United Press International* (February 16, 2004).
2. Chris Woodyard, "Business Travelers Face Dangers on Road," *USA Today* (October 6, 2000), p. 1D; Linda Robinson, "Mexican Mayhem," *U.S. News & World Report* (July 19, 1999), p. 39.
3. Debra Daugherty, "Police Tactics Questioned as Brazil Confronts Rising Tide of Crime," *CNN.com* (April 18, 2000); "Brazil Murder Rate Similar to War Zone, Data Shows," *Reuters* (September 25, 2006).
4. U.S. State Department, *Current Travel Warnings*, http://travel.state.gov/warnings_list.html (2006); see Robert Young Peltion, *The World's Most Dangerous Places*, 5th ed. (New York: Collins, 2003).
5. U.S. State Department, *Public Announcement: Worldwide Caution* (October 11, 2006). http://travel.state.gov/travel.
6. Harry Dammer, Erica Fairchild, and Jay Albanese, *Comparative Criminal Justice Systems*, 3rd ed. (Belmont, CA: Wadsworth, 2006).
7. Graeme Newman and Bruce DiCristina, "Data Set of the First and Second United Nations World Crime Surveys," *United Nations Crime and Justice Information Network* (Vienna, Austria: United Nations Crime Prevention and Criminal Justice Branch, 1994).
8. Graeme Newman, ed., United Nations Office for Drug Control and Crime Prevention, *Global Report on Crime and Justice* (New York: Oxford University Press, 1999).
9. Interpol, *International Crime Statistics* (Lyons, France: Interpol, 2001).
10. See Ton Eijken, "Surveys Provide Insight into Crime," *CJ Europe*, vol. 5 (March–April 1995), pp. 1, 8–11; Anna Alvazzi del Frate and J. N. Van Kesteren, *Criminal Victimisation in Urban Europe: Key Findings of the 2000 International Crime Victims Survey* (Turin, Italy: UNICRI, 2004).
11. Jan van Dijk, Peter Mayhew, and Martin Killias, *Experiences of Crime across the World* (Boston: Kluwer, 1990); Irvin Waller, *Crime Victims: Doing Justice to Their Support and Protection* (Helsinki: European Institute for Crime Prevention and Control, 2003).
12. van Dijk, Mayhew, and Killias, *Experiences of Crime across the World;* Wesley Skogan, "Reporting Crimes to the Police: The Status of World Research," *Journal of Research in Crime & Delinquency*, vol. 21 (1984), pp. 113–37; John van Kesteren, Pat Mayhew, and Paul Nieuwheerta, *Criminal Victimization in 17 Industrialized Countries: Key Findings from the 2000 International Crime Victims Survey* (The Hague: Ministry of Justice, 2000).
13. Freda Adler, *Nations Not Obsessed with Crime* (Littleton, CO: Fred B. Rothman, 1983), p. 130.
14. Ibid., p. 132.
15. William F. McDonald, "Crime and Justice in the Global Village: Towards Global Criminology," in W. F. McDonald, ed., *Crime and Law Enforcement in the Global Village* (Cincinnati: Anderson, 1997), pp. 3–21.
16. James O. Finckenauer, "Meeting the Challenge of Transnational Crime," *National Institute of Justice Journal* (July 2000), p. 4.
17. Jonathan M. Winer, "International Crime in the New Geo-politics: A Core Threat of Democracy," in McDonald, p. 41.
18. David Whitman, "Better Burn That Shawl," *U.S. News & World Report* (October 18, 1999), p. 74.
19. "Man Who Threatened Airline Crew Indicted," *USA Today* (October 6, 2000), p. 3.
20. Jack A. Gottschalk, Brian P. Flanagan, Lawrence J. Kahn, *Jolly Roger with an Uzi: The Rise and Threat of Modern Piracy* (Annapolis, MD: Naval Institute Press, 2000).
21. U.S. Comptroller General, *Airport Passenger Screening: Preliminary Observations on Progress Made and Challenges Remaining* (Washington, DC: U.S. General Accounting Office, 2003).
22. Sally Stoecker, "The Rise in Human Trafficking and the Role of Organized Crime," *Demokratizatsiya*, vol. 8 (winter 2000), p. 129.
23. "Human Trafficking Rampant in Bangladesh," *United Press International* (October 6, 2000).
24. Jay Albanese, "A Network Approach to Understanding and Measuring Trafficking in Human Beings." Presentation at United Nations International Scientific and Professional Advisory Council," Courmayeur, Italy (November 2005).
25. Nic Robertson, "Britain, EU Launch Major Investigation After Deaths of Smuggled Immigrants," *CNN.com* (June 19, 2000); Andrea Marie Bertone, "Sexual Trafficking in Women: International Political Economy and the Politics of Sex," *Gender Issues*, vol. 18 (winter 2000), p. 4; Lynn Brezosky, "Two More Arrests Made in Texas Human Smuggling Case," *Associated Press* (May 22, 2003); Kevin Bales, *Understanding Global Slavery* (Berkeley: University of California Press, 2005).
26. Alan Zarembo, "The Worst Job in the World," *Newsweek International* (December 4, 2000), p. 36.
27. "Democracies and Their Police," *New York Times* (May 1, 2000); Debra Daugherty, "Police Tactics Questioned as Brazil Confronts Rising Tide of Crime," *CNN.com* (April 28, 2000).
28. "Policeman Fired for Corruption," *Africa News Service*, (November 21, 2000); Erik Eckholm, "Chinese Find Power Abuse Isn't Limited to the Cities," *New York Times* (December 3, 2000), p. 5; Peter Hadfield, "Japanese Shocked by Police Misdeeds," *U.S. News & World Report* (July 10, 2000), p. 32; David Bayley, *Changing the Guard: Developing Democratic Police Abroad* (New York: Oxford University Press, 2006).
29. Diego Cevallas, "Corruption: First UN Treaty to Fight a Global Vice," Inter Press Service (December 11, 2003).
30. "War Crimes Appeals Court Upholds Bosnian Commander's Rape Sentence," *CNN.com* (July 21, 2000); Patricia Kelly, "International Court Convicts 5 in Bosnian Massacre," *CNN.com* (January, 14, 2000).
31. Kevin Whitelaw, "Rape as a War Crime," *U.S. News & World Report* (April 3, 2000), p. 32.
32. Thomas Omestad, "The Voice of Hate Radio," *U.S. News & World Report* (June 12, 2000), p. 34.
33. Fenton Bresler, *Interpol* (Toronto: Penguin Books, 1993); Michael Fooner, *Interpol* (New York: Plenum, 1989).
34. Interpol webpage.
35. Malcolm Anderson, "Interpol and the Developing System of International Police Cooperation," in McDonald, p. 101.
36. Ethan A. Nadelmann, "The Americanization of Global Law Enforcement: The Diffusion of American Tactics and Personnel," in McDonald, p. 124.

37. John Benyon, "The Developing System of Police Cooperation in the European Union," in McDonald, p. 115.
38. Leslie E. King and Judson M. Ray, "Developing Transnational Law Enforcement Cooperation," *Journal of Contemporary Criminal Justice*, vol. 16 (November 2000), pp. 386–408.
39. Ordway P. Burden, "Law Enforcement Agencies Working Overseas," *CJ International*, vol. 11 (November–December 1995), p. 17.
40. U.S. Department of State Office of International Criminal Justice, *Transnational Organized Crime*, www.ncjrs.org/intloicj.htm (2000).
41. "International Conference on Preventing and Controlling Money-Laundering and the Use of the Proceeds of Crime: A Global Approach," *United Nations Crime Prevention and Criminal Justice Newsletter*, nos. 24/25 (January 1995).
42. "The World Ministerial Conference on Organized Transnational Crime," *United Nations Crime Prevention and Criminal Justice Newsletter*, nos. 26/27 (November 1995).
43. See Gary T. Marx, "Social Control Across Borders," in McDonald, pp. 23–39.
44. "Preparatory Committee on Establishment of International Criminal Court to Meet at Headquarters," *United Nations Press Release*, August 1, 1997.
45. Gerhard O. W. Mueller, "Enforcing International Criminal Justice," in McDonald, pp. 139–50.
46. Thomas Omestad, "The Brief for a World Court," *U.S. News & World Report* (October 6, 1997), pp. 52–54; "Rwandan to Go to War Crimes Tribunal," *USA Today* (January 14, 2000), p. 3.
47. Kevin Whitelaw, "On a Matter of Justice," *U.S. News & World Report* (July 10, 2000), p. 33.
48. Harry Dammer, Erica Fairchild, and Jay Albanese, *Comparative Criminal Justice Systems*, 3rd ed. (Belmont, CA: Wadsworth, 2006).
49. Franklin Zimring and Gordon Hawkins, *Capital Punishment and the American Agenda* (New York: Cambridge University Press, 1986).
50. Harry Wu Hongda, "A Grim Organ Harvest in China's Prisons," *World Press Review* (June 1995), pp. 22–23.
51. Harry Dammer, Erica Fairchild, and Jay Albanese, *Comparative Criminal Justice Systems*, 3rd ed. (Belmont, CA: Wadsworth, 2006).
52. "Third and Fourth Sessions of the Commission on Crime Prevention and Criminal Justice," *United Nations Crime Prevention and Criminal Justice Newsletter*, nos. 30/31 (December 1995).
53. *United States v. Vasquez-Velaso*, 15 F. 3d 833 (9th Cir. 1994); *United States v. Lopez-Alvarez*, 970 F. 2d 583 (9th Cir.) *cert. denied* 113 S. Ct. 504 (1992).
54. *United States v. Alvarez-Machain*, 112 S. Ct. 857 (1992).
55. Thomas G. Snow, "Competing National and Ethical Interests in the Fight Against Transnational Crime: A U.S. Practitioner's Perspective," in McDonald, pp. 169–86.
56. Ibid., p. 173.
57. *In re Grand Jury Subpoena Directed to Marc Rich and Co.*, 707 F. 2d 663 (2nd Cir., 1983); Kauko Aromaa and Terhi Viljanen, eds. *Enhancing International Law Enforcement Co-operation, including Extradition Measures* (Helsinki: HEUNI, 2005).

Appendix

The Constitution of the United States of America

We the People of the United States, in Order to form a more perfect Union, establish Justice, insure domestic Tranquility, provide for the common defence, promote the general Welfare, and secure the Blessings of Liberty to ourselves and our Posterity, do ordain and establish this Constitution for the United States of America.

ARTICLE I

SECTION 1 All legislative Powers herein granted shall be vested in a Congress of the United States, which shall consist of a Senate and House of Representatives.

SECTION 2 The House of Representatives shall be composed of Members chosen every second Year by the People of the several States, and the Electors in each State shall have the Qualifications requisite for Electors of the most numerous Branch of the State Legislature.

No person shall be a Representative who shall not have attained to the Age of twenty five Years, and been seven Years a Citizen of the United States, and who shall not, when elected, be an Inhabitant of that State in which he shall be chosen.

Representatives and direct Taxes shall be apportioned among the several States which may be included within this Union, according to their respective Numbers which shall be determined by adding to the whole Number of free Persons, including those bound to Service for a Term of Years, and excluding Indians not taxed, three fifths of all other Persons. The actual Enumeration shall be made within three Years after the first Meeting of the Congress of the United States, and within every subsequent Term ten Years, in such Manner as they shall by Law direct. The Number of Representatives shall not exceed one for every thirty Thousand, but each State shall have at Least one Representative; and until such enumeration shall be made, the State of New Hampshire shall be entitled to chuse three, Massachusetts eight, Rhode-Island and Providence Plantations one, Connecticut five, New York six, New Jersey four, Pennsylvania eight, Delaware one, Maryland six, Virginia ten, North Carolina five, South Carolina five, and Georgia three.

When vacancies happen in the Representation from any State, the Executive Authority thereof shall issue Writs of Election to fill such Vacancies.

The House of Representatives shall chuse their speaker and other Officers; and shall have the sole Power of Impeachment.

SECTION 3 The Senate of the United States shall be composed of two Senators from each State chosen by the Legislature thereof, for six Years; and each Senator shall have one Vote.

Immediately after they shall be assembled in Consequence of the first Election, they shall be divided as equally as may be into three Classes. The Seats of the Senators of the first Class shall be vacated at the Expiration of the second year, of the second Class at the Expiration of the fourth Year, and of the third Class at the Expiration of the sixth Year, so that one third may be chosen every second Year and if Vacancies happen by Resignation, or otherwise, during the Recess of the Legislature of any State, the Executive thereof may make temporary Appointments until the next Meeting of the Legislature, which shall then fill such Vacancies.

No Person shall be a Senator who shall not have attained to the Age of thirty Years, and been nine Years a Citizen of the United States, and who shall not, when elected, be an Inhabitant of that State for which he shall be chosen.

The Vice President of the United States shall be President of the Senate, but shall have no Vote, unless they be equally divided.

The Senate shall chuse their other Officers, and also a President pro tempore, in the Absence of the Vice President, or when he shall exercise the Office of President of the United States.

The Senate shall have the sole Power to try all Impeachments. When sitting for that Purpose, they shall be on Oath or Affirmation. When the President of the United States is tried, the Chief Justice shall preside: And no Person shall be convicted without the Concurrence of two thirds of the Members present.

Judgment in Cases of Impeachment shall not extend further than to removal from Office, and disqualification to hold and enjoy any Office of honor, Trust or Profit under the United States; but the Party convicted shall nevertheless be liable and subject to Indictment, Trial, Judgment and Punishment, according to Law.

SECTION 4 The Times, Places and Manner of holding Elections for Senators and Representatives, shall be prescribed in each State by the Legislature thereof; but the Congress may at any time by law make or alter such Regulations, except as to the Places of chusing Senators.

The Congress shall assemble at least once in every Year, and such Meeting shall be on the first Monday in December, unless they shall by Law appoint a different Day.

SECTION 5 Each House shall be the Judge of the Elections, Returns and Qualifications of its own Members, and a Majority of each shall constitute a Quorum to do Business; but a smaller Number may adjourn from day to day, and may be authorized to compel the Attendance of absent Members, in such Manner, and under such Penalties as each House may provide.

Each House may determine the Rules of its Proceedings, punish its Members for disorderly Behaviour, and with the Concurrence of two thirds, expel a Member.

Each House shall keep a journal of its Proceedings, and from time to time publish the same, excepting such Parts as may in their judgment require Secrecy; and the Yeas and Nays of the Members of either House on any question shall, at the Desire of one fifth of those present, be entered on the Journal.

Neither House, during the Session of Congress, shall, without the Consent of the other, adjourn for more than three days, nor to any other Place than that in which the two Houses shall be sitting.

SECTION 6 The Senators and Representatives shall receive a Compensation for their Services, to be ascertained by Law, and paid out of the Treasury of the United States. They shall in all Cases, except Treason, Felony and Breach of the Peace, be privileged from Arrest during their Attendance at the Session of their respective Houses, and in going to and returning from the same; and for any Speech or Debate in either House, they shall not be questioned in any other Place.

No Senator or Representative shall, during the Time for which he was elected, be appointed to any civil Office under the Authority of the United States, which shall have been created, or the Emoluments whereof shall have been encreased during such time; and no Person holding any Office under the United States, shall be a Member of either House during his Continuance in Office.

SECTION 7 All Bills for raising Revenue shall originate in the House of Representatives; but the Senate may propose or concur with Amendments as on other Bills.

Every Bill which shall have passed the House of Representatives and the Senate, shall, before it become a Law, be presented to the President of the United States; If he approves he shall sign it, but if not he shall return it, with his Objections to that House in which it shall have originated, who shall enter the Objections at large on their journal, and proceed to reconsider it. If after such Reconsideration two thirds of that House shall agree to pass the Bill, it shall be sent, together with the Objections, to the other House, by which it shall likewise be reconsidered, and if approved by two thirds of that House, it shall become a Law. But in all such Cases the Votes of both Houses shall be determined by Yeas and Nays, and the Names of the Persons voting for and against the Bill shall be entered on the Journal of each House respectively. If any Bill shall not be returned by the President within ten Days (Sundays excepted) after it shall have been presented to him, the Same shall be a Law, in like Manner as if he had signed it, unless the Congress by their Adjournment prevent its Return, in which Case it shall not be a Law.

Every Order, Resolution, or Vote to which the Concurrence of the Senate and House of Representatives may be necessary (except on a question of Adjournment) shall be presented to the President of the United States; and before the Same shall take Effect, shall be approved by him, or being disapproved by him, shall be repassed by two thirds of the Senate and House of Representatives, according to the Rules and Limitations prescribed in the Case of a Bill.

SECTION 8 The Congress shall have Power To lay and collect Taxes, Duties, Imposts and Excises, to pay the Debts and provide for the common Defence and general Welfare of the United States; but all Duties, Imposts and Excises shall be uniform throughout the United States;

To borrow Money on the credit of the United States;

To regulate Commerce with foreign Nations, and among the several States, and with the Indian Tribes;

To establish a uniform Rule of Naturalization, and uniform Laws on the subject of Bankruptcies throughout the United States;

To coin Money, regulate the Value thereof, and of foreign Coin, and fix the Standard of Weights and Measures;

To provide for the Punishment of counterfeiting the Securities and current Coin of the United States;

To establish Post Offices and post Roads;

To promote the Progress of Science and useful Arts, by securing for limited Times to Authors and Inventors the exclusive Right to their respective Writings and Discoveries;

To constitute Tribunals inferior to the supreme Court;

To define and punish Piracies and Felonies committed on the high Seas, and Offences against the Law of Nations;

To declare War, grant Letters of Marque and Reprisal, and make Rules concerning Captures on Land and Water;

To raise and support Armies, but no Appropriation of Money to that Use shall be for a longer Term than two Years;

To provide and maintain a Navy;

To make Rules for the Government and Regulation of the land and naval Forces;

To provide for calling forth the Militia to execute the Laws of the Union, suppress Insurrections and repel Invasions;

To provide for organizing, arming, and disciplining, the Militia, and for governing such Part of them as may be employed in the Service of the United States, reserving to the States respectively, the Appointment of the Officers, and the Authority of training the Militia according to the discipline prescribed by Congress;

To exercise exclusive Legislation in all Cases whatsoever, over such District (not exceeding ten Miles square) as may, by Cession of particular States, and the Acceptance of Congress, become the Seat of the Government of the United States, and to exercise like Authority over all Places purchased by the Consent of the Legislature of the State in which the Same shall be for the Erection of Forts, Magazines, Arsenals, dock-Yards, and other needful Buildings;—And

To make all Laws which shall be necessary and proper for carrying into Execution the foregoing Powers, and all other Powers vested by this Constitution in the Government of the United States, or in any Department or Officer thereof.

SECTION 9 The Migration or Importation of such Persons as any of the States now existing shall think proper to admit, shall not be prohibited by the Congress prior to the Year one thousand eight hundred and eight, but a Tax or duty may be imposed on such Importation, not exceeding ten dollars for each Person.

The Privilege of the Writ of Habeas Corpus shall not be suspended, unless when in Cases of Rebellion or Invasion the public Safety may require it.

No Bill of Attainder or ex post facto Law shall be passed.

No Capitation, or other direct, Tax shall be laid, unless in Proportion to the Census or Enumeration herein before directed to be taken.

No Tax or Duty shall be laid on Articles exported from any State.

No Preference shall be given by any Regulation of Commerce or Revenue to the Ports of one State over those of another; nor shall Vessels bound to, or from, one State, be obliged to enter, clear, or pay Duties in another.

No Money shall be drawn from the Treasury, but in Consequence of Appropriations made by Law; and a regular Statement and Account of the Receipts and Expenditures of all public Money shall be published from time to time.

No Title of Nobility shall be granted by the United States: And no Person holding any Office of Profit or Trust under them, shall, without the Consent of the Congress, accept of any present, Emolument, Office, or Title, of any kind whatever, from any King, Prince, or foreign State.

SECTION 10 No state shall enter into any Treaty, Alliance, or Confederation; grant Letters of Marque and Reprisal; coin Money; emit Bills of Credit; make any Thing but gold and silver Coin a Tender in Payment of Debts; pass any Bill of Attainder, ex post facto Law, or Law impairing the Obligation of Contracts, or grant any Title of Nobility.

No State shall, without the Consent of the Congress, lay any Imposts or Duties on Imports or Exports, except what may be absolutely necessary for executing its inspection Laws: and the net Produce of all Duties and Imposts, laid by any State on Imports or Exports, shall be for the Use of the Treasury of the United States, and all such Laws shall be subject to the Revision and Controul of the Congress.

No State shall, without the Consent of Congress, lay any Duty of Tonnage, keep Troops, or Ships of War in time of Peace, enter into any Agreement or Compact with another State, or with a foreign Power, or engage in War, unless actually invaded, or in such imminent Danger as will not admit of delay.

ARTICLE II

SECTION 1 The executive Power shall be vested in a President of the United States of America. He shall hold his Office during the Term of four Years, and, together with the Vice President, chosen for the same Term, be elected as follows.

Each State shall appoint, in such Manner as the Legislature thereof may direct, a Number of Electors, equal to the whole Number of Senators and Representatives to which the State may be entitled in the Congress; but no Senator or Representative, or Person holding an Office of Trust of Profit under the United States, shall be appointed an Elector.

The Electors shall meet in their respective States, and vote by Ballot for two Persons, of whom one at least shall not be an Inhabitant of the same State with themselves. And they shall make a List of all the Persons voted for, and, of the Number of Votes for each; which List they shall sign and certify, and transmit sealed to the Seat of the Government of the United States, directed to the President of the Senate. The President of the Senate shall, in the Presence of the Senate and House of Representatives, open all the Certificates, and the Votes shall then be counted. The Person having the greatest Number of Votes shall be the President, if such Number be a Majority of the whole Number of Electors appointed; and if there be more than one who have such Majority, and have an equal Number of Votes, then the House of Representatives shall immediately chuse by Ballot one of them for President; and if no Person have a Majority, then from the five highest on the List the said House shall in like Manner chuse the President. But in chusing the President, the Votes shall be taken by States, the Representation from each State having one Vote; A quorum for this Purpose shall consist of a Member or Members from two thirds of the States, and a Majority of all the States shall be necessary to a

Choice. In every Case, after the Choice of the President, the Person having the greatest Number of Votes of the Electors shall be the Vice President. But if there should remain two or more who have equal Votes, the Senate shall chuse from them by Ballot the Vice President.

The Congress may determine the Time of chusing the Electors, and the Day on which they shall give their Votes; which Day shall be the same throughout the United States.

No Person except a natural born Citizen, or a Citizen of the United States, at the time of the Adoption of this Constitution, shall be eligible to the Office of President; neither shall any Person be eligible to that Office who shall not have attained to the Age of thirty five Years, and been fourteen Years a Resident within the United States.

In Case of the Removal of the President from Office, or of his Death, Resignation, or Inability to discharge the Powers and Duties of the said Office, the Same shall devolve on the Vice President, and the Congress may by Law provide for the Case of Removal, Death, Resignation or Inability, both of the President and Vice President, declaring what Officer shall then act as President, and such Officer shall act accordingly, until the Disability be removed, or a President shall be elected.

The President shall, at stated Times, receive for his Services, a Compensation, which shall neither be encreased nor diminished during the Period for which he shall have been elected, and he shall not receive within that Period any other Emolument from the United States, or any of them.

Before he enter on the Execution of his Office, he shall take the following Oath or Affirmation—"I do solemnly swear (or affirm) that I will faithfully execute the Office of President of the United States, and will to the best of my Ability, preserve, protect and defend the Constitution of the United States."

SECTION 2 The President shall be Commander in Chief of the Army, and Navy of the United States, and of the Militia of the several States, when called into the actual Service of the United States; he may require the Opinion, in writing, of the principal Officer in each of the executive Departments, upon any Subject relating to the Duties of their respective Offices, and he shall have Power to grant Reprieves and Pardons for Offences against the United States, except in Cases of Impeachment.

He shall have Power, by and with the Advice and Consent of the Senate, to make Treaties, provided two thirds of the Senators present concur; and he shall nominate, and by and with the Advice and Consent of the Senate, shall appoint Ambassadors, other public Ministers and Consuls, Judges of the supreme Court, and all other Officers of the United States, whose Appointments are not herein otherwise provided for, and which shall be established by Law: but the Congress may by Law vest the Appointment of such inferior Officers, as they think proper, in the President alone, in the Courts of Law, or in the Heads of Departments.

The President shall have Power to fill up all Vacancies that may happen during the Recess of the Senate, by granting Commissions which shall expire at the end of their next Session.

SECTION 3 He shall from time to time give to the Congress Information of the State of the Union, and recommend to their Consideration such Measures as he shall judge necessary and expedient; he may, on extraordinary Occasions, convene both Houses, or either of them, and in Case of Disagreement between them, with Respect to the Time of Adjournment, he may adjourn them to such Time as he shall think proper; he shall receive Ambassadors and other public Ministers; he shall take Care that the Laws be faithfully executed, and shall Commission all the Officers of the United States.

SECTION 4 The President, Vice President and all civil Officers of the United States, shall be removed from Office on Impeachment for, and Conviction of, Treason, Bribery, or other high Crimes and Misdemeanors.

ARTICLE III

SECTION 1 The judicial Power of the United States, shall be vested in one supreme Court, and in such inferior Courts as the Congress may from time to time ordain and establish. The Judges, both of the supreme and inferior Courts, shall hold their Offices during good Behaviour, and shall, at stated Times, receive for their Services, a Compensation, which shall not be diminished during their Continuance in Office.

SECTION 2 The judicial Power shall extend to all Cases, in Law and Equity, arising under this Constitution, the Laws of the United States, and Treaties made, or which shall be made, under their Authority;—to all Cases affecting Ambassadors, other public Ministers and Consuls;—to all Cases of admiralty and maritime Jurisdiction;—to Controversies to which the United States shall be a Party;—to Controversies between two or more States;—between a State and Citizens of another State;—between Citizens of different States,—between Citizens of the same State claiming Lands under Grants of different States,—and between a State, or the Citizens thereof, and foreign States, Citizens of Subjects.

In all Cases affecting Ambassadors, other public Ministers and Consuls, and those in which a State shall be Party, the supreme Court shall have original Jurisdiction. In all the other Cases before mentioned, the supreme Court shall have appellate Jurisdiction, both as to Law and Fact, with such Exceptions, and under such Regulations as the Congress shall make.

The Trial of all Crimes, except in Cases of Impeachment, shall be by Jury; and such Trial shall be held in the State where the said Crimes shall have been committed; but when not committed within any State, the Trial shall be at such Place or Places as the Congress may by Law have directed.

SECTION 3 Treason against the United States, shall consist only in levying War against them, or in adhering to their Enemies, giving them Aid and Comfort. No Person shall be convicted of Treason unless on the Testimony of two Witnesses to the same overt Act, or on Confession in open Court.

The Congress shall have Power to declare the Punishment of Treason, but no Attainder of Treason shall work Corruption of Blood, or Forfeiture except during the Life of the Person attainted.

ARTICLE IV

SECTION 1 Full Faith and Credit shall be given in each State to the public Acts, Records, and judicial Proceedings of every other State. And the Congress may by general Laws prescribe the Manner in which such Acts, Records and Proceedings shall be proved, and the Effect thereof.

SECTION 2 The Citizens of each State shall be entitled to all Privileges and Immunities of Citizens in the several States.

A Person charged in any State with Treason, Felony, or other Crime, who shall flee from Justice, and be found in another State, shall on Demand of the executive Authority of the State from which he fled, be delivered up, to be removed to the State having Jurisdiction of the Crime.

No Person held to Service or Labour in one State under the Laws thereof, escaping into another, shall, in Consequence of any Law or Regulation therein, be discharged from such Service or Labour, but shall be delivered up on Claim of the Party to whom such Service or Labour may be due.

SECTION 3 New States may be admitted by the Congress into this Union; but no new State shall be formed or erected within the Jurisdiction of any other State; nor any State be formed by the Junction of two or more States, or Parts of States, without the Consent of the Legislatures of the States concerned as well as of the Congress.

The Congress shall have Power to dispose of and make all needful Rules and Regulations respecting the Territory or other Property belonging to the United States; and nothing in this Constitution shall be so construed as to Prejudice any Claims of the United States, or of any particular State.

SECTION 4 The United States shall guarantee to every State in this Union a Republican Form of Government, and shall protect each of them against Invasion, and on Application of the Legislature, or of the Executive (when the Legislature cannot be convened) against domestic Violence.

ARTICLE V

The Congress, whenever two thirds of both Houses shall deem it necessary, shall propose Amendments to this Constitution, or, on the Application of the Legislatures of two thirds of the several States, shall call a Convention for proposing Amendments, which, in either Case, shall be valid to all Intents and Purposes, as Part of this Constitution, when ratified by the Legislatures of three fourths of the several States, or by Conventions in three fourths thereof, as the one or the other Mode of Ratification may be proposed by the Congress; Provided that no Amendment which may be made prior to the Year One thousand eight hundred and eight shall in any Manner affect the first and fourth Clauses in the Ninth Section of the first Article; and that no State, without its Consent, shall be deprived of its equal Suffrage in the Senate.

ARTICLE VI

All Debts contracted and Engagements entered into, before the Adoption of this Constitution, shall be as valid against the United States under this Constitution, as under the Confederation.

This Constitution, and the laws of the United States which shall be made in Pursuance thereof; and all Treaties made, or which shall be made, under the Authority of the United States, shall be the supreme Law of the Land; and the Judges in every State shall be bound thereby, any Thing in the Constitution or Laws of any State to the Contrary notwithstanding.

The Senators and Representatives before mentioned, and the Members of the several State Legislatures, and all executive and judicial Officers, both of the United States and of the several States, shall be bound by Oath or Affirmation, to support this Constitution; but no religious Test shall ever be required as a Qualification to any Office or public Trust under the United States.

ARTICLE VII

The Ratification of the Conventions of nine States, shall be sufficient for the Establishment of this Constitution between the States so ratifying the Same.

Done in Convention by the Unanimous Consent of the States present the Seventeenth Day of September in the Year of our Lord one thousand seven hundred and Eighty seven and of the Independence of the United States of America the Twelfth. In witness whereof we have hereunto subscribed our Names,

Go. WASHINGTON
Presid't. and deputy from Virginia

Attest
WILLIAM JACKSON
Secretary

DELAWARE
Geo. Read
Gunning Bedford jun
John Dickinson
Richard Basset
Jaco. Broom

MASSACHUSETTS
Nathaniel Gorham
Rufus King

CONNECTICUT
Wm. Saml. Johnson
Roger Sherman

NEW YORK
Alexander Hamilton

NEW JERSEY
Wh. Livingston
David Brearley
Wm. Paterson
Jona. Dayton

PENNSYLVANIA
B. Franklin
Thomas Mifflin
Robt. Morris
Geo. Clymer
Thos. FitzSimons
Jared Ingersoll
James Wilson
Gouv. Morris

NEW HAMPSHIRE
John Langdon
Nicholas Gilman

MARYLAND
James McHenry
Dan of St. Thos. Jenifer
Danl. Carroll

VIRGINIA
John Blair
James Madison, Jr.

NORTH CAROLINA
Wm. Blount
Richd. Dobbs Spaight
Hu. Williamson

SOUTH CAROLINA
J. Rutledge
Charles Cotesworth Pinckney
Charles Pinckney
Pierce Butler

GEORGIA
William Few
Abr. Baldwin

Articles in addition to, and amendment of the Constitution of the United tates of America, proposed by Congress and ratified by the Legislatures of the several states, pursuant to the Fifth Article of the original Constitution.

(The first ten amendments were passed by Congress on September 25, 1789, and were ratified on December 15, 1791.)

AMENDMENT I

Congress shall make no law respecting an establishment of religion, or prohibiting the free exercise thereof; or abridging the freedom of speech, or of the press; or the right of the people peaceably to assemble, and to petition the Government for a redress of grievances.

AMENDMENT II

A well regulated Militia, being necessary to the security of a free State, the right of the people to keep and bear Arms, shall not be infringed.

AMENDMENT III

No Soldier shall, in time of peace be quartered in any house, without the consent of the Owner, nor in time of war, but in a manner to be prescribed by law.

AMENDMENT IV

The right of the people to be secure in their persons, houses, papers, and effects, against unreasonable searches and seizures, shall not be violated, and no warrants shall issue, but upon probable cause, supported by Oath or affirmation, and particularly describing the place to be searched, and the persons or things to be seized.

AMENDMENT V

No person shall be held to answer for a capital, or otherwise infamous crime, unless on a presentment or indictment of a Grand Jury, except in cases arising in the land or naval forces, or in the Militia, when in actual service in time of War or public danger; nor shall any person be subject for the same offence to be twice put in jeopardy of life or limb; nor shall be compelled in any criminal case to be a witness against himself, nor be deprived of life, liberty, or property, without due process of law; nor shall private property be taken for public use, without just compensation.

AMENDMENT VI

In all criminal prosecutions, the accused shall enjoy the right to a speedy and public trial, by an impartial jury of the State and district wherein the crime shall have been committed, which district shall have been previously ascertained by law, and to be informed of the nature and cause of the accusation; to be confronted with the witnesses against him; to have compulsory process for obtaining witnesses in his favor, and to have the Assistance of Counsel for his defence.

AMENDMENT VII

In Suits at common law, where the value in controversy shall exceed twenty dollars, the right of trial by jury shall be preserved, and no fact tried by a jury, shall be otherwise re-examined in any Court of the United States, than according to the rules of the common law.

AMENDMENT VIII

Excessive bail shall not be required, nor excessive fines imposed, nor cruel and unusual punishments inflicted.

AMENDMENT IX

The enumeration in the Constitution, of certain rights, shall not be construed to deny or disparage others retained by the people.

AMENDMENT X

The powers not delegated to the United States by the Constitution, nor prohibited by it to the States, are reserved to the States respectively, or to the people.

AMENDMENT XI

(Ratified on February 7, 1795)

The Judicial power of the United States shall not be construed to extend to any suit in law or equity, commenced or prosecuted against one of the United States by Citizens of another State, or by Citizens or Subjects of any Foreign State.

AMENDMENT XII

(Ratified on June 15, 1804)

The Electors shall meet in their respective states, and vote by ballot for President and Vice-President, one of whom, at least, shall not be an inhabitant of the same state with themselves; they shall name in their ballots the person voted for as President, and in distinct ballots the person voted for as Vice-President, and they shall make distinct lists of all persons voted for as President, and of all persons voted for as Vice-President, and of the number of votes for each, which lists they shall sign and certify, and transmit sealed to the seat of the government of the United States, directed to the President of the Senate;—The President of the Senate shall, in the presence of the Senate and House of Representatives, open all the certificates and the votes shall then be counted;—The person having the greatest number of votes for President, shall be the President, if such number be a majority of the whole number of Electors appointed; and if no person have such majority; then from the persons having the highest numbers not exceeding three on the list of those voted for as President, the House of Representatives shall choose immediately, by ballot, the President. But in choosing the President, the votes shall be taken by states, the representation from each state having one vote; a quorum for this purpose shall consist of a member or members from two-thirds of the states, and a majority of all the states shall be necessary to a choice. And if the House of Representatives shall not choose a President whenever the right of choice shall devolve upon them, before the fourth day of March next following, then the Vice-President shall act as President, as in the case of the death or other constitutional disability of the President.—The person having the greatest number of votes as Vice-President, shall be the Vice-President, if such number be a majority of the whole number of Electors appointed, and if no person have a majority, then from the two highest numbers on the list, the Senate shall choose the Vice-President; a quorum for the purpose shall consist of two-thirds of the whole number of Senators, and a majority of the whole number shall be necessary to a choice. But no person constitutionally ineligible to the office of President shall be eligible to that of Vice-President of the United States.

AMENDMENT XIII

(Ratified on December 6, 1865)

SECTION 1 Neither slavery nor involuntary servitude, except as a punishment for crime whereof the party shall have been duly convicted, shall exist within the United States, or any place subject to their jurisdiction.

SECTION 2 Congress shall have power to enforce this article by appropriate legislation.

AMENDMENT XIV

(Ratified on July 9, 1868)

SECTION 1 All persons born or naturalized in the United States, and subject to the jurisdiction thereof, are citizens of the United States and of the State wherein they reside. No State shall make or enforce any law which shall abridge the privileges or immunities of citizens of the United States; nor shall any State deprive any person of life, liberty, or property, without due process of law; nor deny to any person within its jurisdiction the equal protection of the laws.

SECTION 2 Representatives shall be apportioned among the several States according to their respective numbers, counting the whole number of persons in each State, excluding Indians not taxed. But when the right to vote at any election for the choice of electors for President and Vice President of the United States, Representatives in Congress, the Executive and Judicial officers of a State, or the members of the Legislature thereof, is denied to any of the male inhabitants of such State, being twenty-one years of age, and citizens of the United States, or in any way abridged, except for participation in rebellion, or other crime, the basis of representation therein shall be reduced in the proportion which the number of such male citizens shall bear to the whole number of male citizens twenty-one years of age in such State.

SECTION 3 No person shall be a Senator or Representative in Congress, or elector of President and Vice President, or hold any office, civil or military, under the United States, or under any State, who, having previously taken an oath, as a member of Congress, or as an officer of the United States, or as a member of any State legislature, or as an executive or judicial officer of any State, to support the Constitution of the United States, shall have engaged in insurrection or rebellion against the same, or given aid or comfort to the enemies thereof. But Congress may by a vote of two-thirds of each House, remove such diability.

SECTION 4 The validity of the public debt of the United States, authorized by law, including debts incurred for payment of pensions and bounties for services in suppressing insurrection or rebellion, shall not be questioned. But neither the United States nor any State shall assume or pay any debt or obligation incurred in aid of insurrection or rebellion against the United States, or any claim for the loss or emancipation of any slave, but all such debts, obligations and claims shall be held illegal and void.

SECTION 5 The Congress shall have power to enforce, by appropriate legislation, the provisions of this article.

AMENDMENT XV

(Ratified on February 3, 1870)

SECTION 1 The right of citizens of the United States to vote shall not be denied or abridged by the United States or by any State on account of race, color, or previous condition of servitude.

SECTION 2 The Congress shall have power to enforce this article by appropriate legislation.

AMENDMENT XVI

(Ratified on February 3, 1913)

The Congress shall have power to lay and collect taxes on incomes, from whatever source derived, without apportionment among the several States, and without regard to any census or enumeration.

AMENDMENT XVII

(Ratified on April 8, 1913)

The Senate of the United States shall be composed of two Senators from each State, elected by the people thereof, for six years; and each Senator shall have one vote. The electors in each State shall have the qualifications requisite for electors of the most numerous branch of the State legislatures.

When vacancies happen in the representation of any State in the Senate, the executive authority of such State shall issue writs of election to fill such vacancies: Provided, That the legislature of any State may empower the executive thereof to make temporary appointments until the people fill the vacancies by election as the legislature may direct.

This amendment shall not be so construed as to affect the election or term of any Senator chosen before it becomes valid as part of the Constitution.

AMENDMENT XVIII

(Ratified on January 16, 1919)

SECTION 1 After one year from the ratification of this article the manufacture, sale, or transportation of intoxicating liquors within, the importation thereof into, or the exportation thereof from the United States and all territory subject to the jurisdiction thereof for beverage purposes is hereby prohibited.

SECTION 2 The Congress and the several States shall have concurrent power to enforce this article by appropriate legislation.

SECTION 3 This article shall be inoperative unless it shall have been ratified as an amendment to the Constitution by the legislatures of the several States, as provided in the Constitution, within seven years from the date of the submission hereof to the States by the Congress.

AMENDMENT XIX

(Ratified on August 18, 1920)

The right of citizens of the United States to vote shall not be denied or abridged by the United States or by any State on account of sex.

Congress shall have power to enforce this article by appropriate legislation.

AMENDMENT XX

(Ratified on February 6, 1933)

SECTION 1 The terms of the President and Vice President shall end at noon on the 20th day of January, and the terms of Senators and Representatives at noon on the 3d day of January, of the years in which such terms would have ended if this article had not been ratified; and the terms of their successors shall then begin.

SECTION 2 The Congress shall assemble at least once in every year, and such meeting shall begin at noon on the 3d day of January, unless they shall by law appoint a different day.

SECTION 3 If, at the time fixed for the beginning of the term of the President, the President elect shall have died, the Vice President elect shall become President. If a President shall not have been chosen before the time fixed for the beginning of his term, or if the President elect shall have failed to qualify, then the Vice President elect shall act as President until a President shall have qualified; and the Congress may by law provide for the case wherein neither a President elect nor a Vice President elect shall have qualified, declaring who shall then act as President, or the manner in which one who is to act shall be selected, and such person shall act accordingly until a President or Vice President shall have qualified.

SECTION 4 The Congress may by law provide for the case of the death of any of the persons from whom the House of Representatives may choose a President whenever the rights of choice shall have devolved upon them, and for the case of the death of any of the persons from whom the Senate may choose a Vice President whenever the right of choice shall have devolved upon them.

SECTION 5 Sections 1 and 2 shall take effect on the 15th day of October following the ratification of this article.

SECTION 6 This article shall be inoperative unless it shall have been ratified as an amendment to the Constitution by the legislatures of three-fourths of the several States within seven years from the date of its submission.

AMENDMENT XXI

(Ratified on December 5, 1933)

SECTION 1 The eighteenth article of amendment to the Constitution of the United States is hereby repealed.

SECTION 2 The transportation or importation into any State, Territory, or possession of the United States for delivery or use therein of intoxicating liquors, in violation of the laws thereof, is hereby prohibited.

SECTION 3 This article shall be inoperative unless it shall have been ratified as an amendment to the Constitution by conventions in the several States, as provided in the Constitution, within seven years from the date of the submission hereof to the States by the Congress.

AMENDMENT XXII

(Ratified on February 27, 1951)

No person shall be elected to the office of the President more than twice, and no person who has held the office of President, or acted as President, for more than two years of a term to which some other person was elected President shall be elected to the office of the President more than once. But this Article shall not apply to any person holding the office of President when this Article was proposed by the Congress, and shall not prevent any person who may be holding the office of President, or acting as President, during the term within which this Article becomes operative from holding the office of President or acting as President during the remainder of such term.

AMENDMENT XXIII

(Ratified on March 29, 1961)

SECTION 1 The District constituting the seat of Government of the United States shall appoint in such manner as the Congress may direct:

A number of electors of President and Vice President equal to the whole number of Senators and Representatives in Congress to which the District would be entitled if it were a State, but in no event more than the least populous State; they shall be in addition to those appointed by the States, but they shall be considered, for the purposes of the election of President and Vice President, to be electors appointed by a State; and they shall meet in the District and perform such duties as provided by the twelfth article of amendment.

SECTION 2 The Congress shall have power to enforce this article by appropriate legislation.

AMENDMENT XXIV

(Ratified on January 23, 1964)

SECTION 1 The right of citizens of the United States to vote in any primary or other election for President or Vice President, for electors for President or Vice President, or for Senator or Representative in Congress, shall not be denied or abridged by the United States or any State by reason of failure to pay any poll tax or other tax.

SECTION 2 The Congress shall have power to enforce this article by appropriate legislation.

AMENDMENT XXV

(Ratified on February 10, 1967)

SECTION 1 In case of the removal of the President from office or of his death or resignation, the Vice President shall become President.

SECTION 2 Whenever there is a vacancy in the office of the Vice President, the President shall nominate a Vice President who shall take office upon confirmation by a majority vote of both Houses of Congress.

SECTION 3 Whenever the President transmits to the President pro tempore of the Senate and the Speaker of the House of Representatives his written declaration that he is unable to discharge the powers and duties of his office, and until he transmits to them a written declaration to the contrary, such powers and duties shall be discharged by the Vice President as Acting President.

SECTION 4 Whenever the Vice President and a majority of either the principal officers of the executive departments or of such other body as Congress may by law provide, transmit to the President pro tempore of the Senate and the Speaker of the House of Representatives their written declaration that the President is unable to discharge the powers and duties of his office, the Vice President shall immediately assume the powers and duties of the office as Acting President.

Thereafter, when the President transmits to the President pro tempore of the Senate and the Speaker of the House of Representatives his written declaration that no inability exists, he shall resume the powers and duties of his office unless the Vice President and a majority of either the principal officers of the executive department or of such other body as Congress may by law provide, transmit within four days to the President pro tempore of the Senate and the Speaker of the House of Representatives their written declaration that the President is unable to discharge the powers and duties of his office. Thereupon Congress shall decide the issue, assembling within forty-eight hours for that purpose if not in session. If the Congress, within twenty-one days after receipt of the latter written declaration, or, if Congress is not in session, within twenty-one days after Congress is required to assemble, determines by two-thirds vote of both Houses that the President is unable to discharge the powers and duties of his office, the Vice President shall continue to discharge the same as Acting President; otherwise, the President shall resume the powers and duties of his office.

AMENDMENT XXVI

(Ratified on July 1, 1971)

SECTION 1 The right of citizens of the United States, who are eighteen years of age or older, to vote shall not be denied or abridged by the United States or by any State on account of age.

SECTION 2 The Congress shall have power to enforce this article by appropriate legislation.

AMENDMENT XXVII

(Ratified on May 7, 1992)

No law varying the compensation for the services of Senators and Representatives shall take effect until an election of Representatives shall have intervened.

Glossary

acquittal A finding after trial of not guilty.

actual possession A condition in which a person has exclusive control over an object.

actus reus The behavior that must be committed to meet the definition of a crime.

administrative regulations Rules applied to organizations that are designed to protect public health, safety, and welfare in the marketplace.

aggravated assault A thrust against another person with the intention to cause serious bodily harm or death.

anomie A "normlessness" or lack of attachment felt by some people toward their society.

appeal A review of lower court decisions by a higher court to look for errors of law or procedure.

appellate jurisdiction The jurisdiction of courts that review specific legal issues raised in trial courts.

arraignment A hearing where the defendant is informed of the charges and of his or her rights, enters a plea.

arrest Process of taking a suspect into custody for the purpose of prosecution.

arson Burning property of another without the lawful consent of the owner.

assigned counsel A private attorney appointed by the court on a case-by-case basis from a list of available attorneys.

Auburn system A philosophy of imprisonment that emphasized labor and meditation. Offenders worked every day, but they did so in complete silence.

authentic justice Approach to criminal justice holding that sanctions should be more closely related to crime and that offenders should be punished in ways that neutralize their gain.

authoritarianism A tendency to favor blind obedience to authority.

bail A form of pretrial release where the court holds money or property to ensure that the arrestee will appear for trial.

balance between just punishment and public safety The proper consideration of necessary punishment of the offender to express public disapproval of law violation, and corrective treatment necessary to prevent repeated offenses.

battered woman syndrome An ongoing pattern of severe physical abuse that constitutes a continual threat of harm.

bench trial A trial in which the judge determines guilt or innocence.

Bill of Rights The first ten amendments to the Constitution–details many of the requirements for adjudication, such as arrests, warrants, searches, trials, lawyers, punishment, and other important aspects of criminal procedure.

biological determinism Positivists who see the roots of criminal behavior in biological attributes.

blocked opportunity Theory that crime results from lack of access to legitimate means for achieving goals.

booking A procedure in which an official record of the arrest is made.

bribery Voluntary giving or receiving anything of value with the intent of influencing the action of a public official.

burglary Unlawful entry into a building in order to commit a crime while inside.

case law Judicial application and interpretation of law as it applies in a given case.

case mortality Case attrition, in which arrests do not result in convictions for various reasons.

caseloads The large numbers of cases to be adjudicated in the courts.

civil law Formal rules that regulate disputes between private parties.

classical school A perspective in criminology that sees crime as resulting from the conscious exercise of an individual's free will.

clearance rate The proportion of open crime cases that are solved through the arrest of a suspect by police.

cognitive theory View that behavior results from habits of thought and interpretations of reality.

common law The body of unrecorded decisions made by English judges in the Middle Ages, reflecting the values, customs, and beliefs of the period.

community corrections Sanctions that are *alternatives to incarceration* in jail or prison (such as monetary penalties, probation, intensive supervision, and home confinement with electronic monitoring), or supervision in the community *after a sentence of incarceration* has been served (such as parole, work release, furloughs, and halfway houses).

community courts Decentralized courts that respond to neighborhood conditions using citizen advisory committees, volunteers, and teen courts.

community justice Corrections integrated with prevention efforts, wherein the justice system enhances community life, and communities partner effectively with the criminal justice system to share responsibility for social control.

community policing A service-oriented style of law enforcement that focuses on disorder in the community, crime prevention, and fear reduction (as opposed to the traditional focus on serious street crimes).

community prosecution A program in which prosecutors intervene in all disorderly behavior that affects the quality of life in a neighborhood.

commutation A modification or reduction of a sentence imposed on an offender.

computer crime Crimes in which computers are used as the *instrument* of the offense, and crimes in which computers are the *object* of the offense.

conflict view The view that an act becomes a crime only when it serves the interests of those in positions of power.

consensual model Prison management approach that maintains order by agreement between inmates and staff on the validity of rules.

consensus view The view that law reflects society's consensus regarding behavior that is harmful enough to warrant government intervention.

conspiracy Agreement between two or more persons to commit a crime or to carry out a legal act in an illegal manner.

constable A citizen in charge of weapons and equipment for one hundred families in his geographic area. In England constables were appointed by a local nobleman beginning around the year 900.

constitutions The fundamental principles of a society that guide the enactment of specific laws and the application of those laws by courts.

constructive possession A condition in which a person has the opportunity to exercise control over an object.

continuance A court-authorized postponement of a case to allow the prosecution or defense more time to prepare its case.

contract attorney programs Programs in which private attorneys, firms, or local bar associations provide legal representation to indigent defendants for a specific period contracted with the county.

control model Prison management approach characterized by strict enforcement of prison rules and few privileges for prisoners.

conviction A finding of guilt beyond a reasonable doubt.

corporal punishment Physical punishment short of the death penalty.

corporate crimes Dangerous or unjust actions in the conduct of business prompted by the desire for profits. Same as *regulatory offenses.*

corpus delicti Proof of an act and that the act resulted from the illegal actions of the defendant; also called proving the crime.

correctional institutions Medium security federal correctional institutions.

corruption A term referring to bribery or extortion, through misuse of official position, either for personal gain or through threats of harm or legal action to force payment.

courtroom work group The prosecutors, defense counsel, judges, and other courtroom personnel who represent distinct interests but share the goal of shepherding large numbers of cases through the adjudication process.

crime Form of conduct that society prohibits in order to maintain order.

crime commissions Early twentieth-century crime commissions included the Chicago Crime Commission (1919), the National Crime Commission (1925), and the Wickersham Commission (1931). These commissions focused on the improved operation of the criminal justice system as the best way to reduce crime.

crime control model The perspective that views the repression of criminal conduct as the most important function to be performed by the criminal justice system, through speed, efficiency, and finality in criminal justice processing.

crime profiling Analysis of criminal incidents to isolate the precise characteristics of offenders, victims, and situations in order to better understand and prevent crime.

crime rates The number of crimes committed divided by the population at risk. This provides an indication of the risk of victimization per capita.

crime scene profiles Examination of the circumstances surrounding criminal incidents in a search for patterns associated with criminal offending.

crime syndicate A system of loosely structured relationships among groups and individuals involved in organized crime.

crimes against persons Violent crimes involving the use of physical force.

crimes against property Crimes in which property is taken unlawfully and misused.

crimes against public administration Attempts to impede government processes through bribery, obstruction of justice, official misconduct, or perjury.

crimes against public order Acts that disrupt the peace in a civil society.

crimes of fraud Embezzlement, extortion, forgery, and fraud.

criminal (penal) code A compilation of all the criminal laws of a jurisdiction.

criminal homicide Murder or manslaughter.

criminal justice The management of police, courts, and corrections, and the study of the causes of and treatment for crime.

criminal justice system The more than 50,000 government agencies in the United States that deal with aspects of crime, including criminal law enforcement, the courts, and corrections.

criminal law A code that categorizes all crimes and punishments by type; formal rules designed to maintain social control.

criminal liability Establishing the presence of the elements of a crime in a given case, thereby subjecting the accused person to criminal penalties.

criminal subcultures Different forms of deviance that result when youths cease to adhere to middle-class standards and become part of the adult *criminal, conflict,* or *retreatist* subculture.

criminalization The legislative decision to make a behavior a crime.

criminologists Those who study the causes of crime and the treatment of offenders.

cruel and unusual punishment A portion of the Eighth Amendment prohibiting criminal penalties that violate "evolving standards of decency that mark the progress of a maturing society."

cynicism A belief that human conduct is motivated entirely by self-interest. A cynical person attributes all actions to selfish motives and has a pessimistic outlook on human behavior.

deadly force The use of lethal force by police against a suspect.

decriminalization The legislative decision to change a crime into a noncriminal act.

defense attorneys Attorneys who represent the legal rights of the accused in criminal or civil proceedings.

delinquency A criminal act committed by a person under the age of majority.

detention center A short-term secure facility that holds juveniles awaiting adjudication, disposition, or placement in an institution.

determinate sentencing A sentencing system that permits judges to impose fixed sentences that cannot be altered by a parole board.

deterrence Prevention of crime through the example of offenders being punished.

deviance Violation of a social norm.

deviant police subculture hypothesis The view that some police departments have groups of officers who place loyalty to each other above obedience to the law.

differential association Theory that a person becomes criminal or delinquent when he or she associates more with people who condone violation of the law than with people who do not.

discovery The process that entitles a suspect to review certain information gathered by the prosecutor.

dispute resolution A method of handling complaints outside the judicial process through a mediator appointed by the court.

district attorneys The name for city and county prosecutors in many jurisdictions.

diversion programs Alternatives to the formal criminal justice process that are implemented after charging but prior to adjudication; they attempt to achieve a noncriminal disposition of the case.

dogmatism An attitude characterized by tenacious adherence to one's opinions even though they may be unwarranted and based on insufficiently examined premises.

double jeopardy A constitutional provision that a person cannot be criminally prosecuted twice for the same offense.

Drug Use Forecasting Program in many major U.S. cities in which police take urine specimens from a sample of arrestees to determine what proportion of those arrested have already used drugs.

due process The use of accuracy, fairness, and reliability in criminal procedure to protect individual rights.

due process (constitutional) A legal protection included in the U.S. Constitution that guarantees all citizens the right to be adjudicated under established law and legal procedures.

due process model The perspective that considers preservation of individual liberties to be the most important function of the criminal justice system, through accuracy, fairness, and reliability in criminal procedure.

duress A defense in which a person claims to have engaged in criminal conduct because of a threat of immediate and serious bodily harm by another person.

effective counsel Competent representation by an attorney. It is ineffective assistance of counsel when unprofessional errors would have changed the outcome of the case.

electronic monitoring Surveillance of offenders in the community by means of electronic devices such as radio and telephone transmitters.

embezzlement The purposeful misappropriation of property entrusted to one's care, custody, or control to which one is not entitled.

entrapment A defense designed to prevent the government from manufacturing crime by setting traps for unwary citizens.

ethical view The perspective that sees crime as a moral failure in decision making.

exclusionary rule A legal principle that holds that illegally seized evidence must be excluded from use in trials.

excuse defenses Defenses that claim that criminal conduct should be excused because the defendant cannot be held rsponsible for it. Insanity and duress are examples.

expanding the net A potential result of punishment and control by distance, subjecting more offenders to stringent forms of surveillance who previously were dealt with less severely through traditional probation or other sanctions.

expert witness A person called to testify because of his or her special expertise in an area at issue in a legal proceeding.

extortion Purposely obtaining property from another person without consent through wrongful use of force or fear or under the guise of official authority.

FBI's Crime Index Tally of detailed reports of eight types of offenses: criminal homicide, forcible rape, robbery, aggravated assault, burglary, larceny, motor vehicle theft, and arson.

federal law enforcement Seventeen different agencies that investigate violations of federal law. Unlike state police agencies, few federal agencies engage in patrol work; most perform exclusively investigative functions.

felonies Serious crimes that are punishable by incarceration for more than one year.

felony drug courts Courts that handle only drug offenses and attempt to correct underlying causes of the illegal conduct.

Fifth Amendment The amendment to the Consitition that includes protection against self-incrimination.

"fleeing felon" rule The now obsolete common-law rule that police can use deadly force against any felon who flees the scene of a crime.

forgery Falsely making or altering an official document with the intent to defraud.

Fourth Amendment Amendment to the Constitution that prohibits searches without probable cause.

fraud Purposely obtaining the property of another person through deception.

frisk A patting down of the outer clothing of a suspect based on reasonable suspicion, designed to protect a police officer from attack with a weapon while an inquiry is made.

furloughs Unsupervised leaves from prison that are granted for only a few hours to permit an eligible inmate to be present at a relative's funeral, visit loved ones, go to a job interview, or otherwise attend to personal or family matters.

Gallup poll on crime Survey of a representative sample of the American public which found that crime surpassed education and economic issues as the most pressing local problem.

gender issues Issues that center on the fact that women offenders have different problems and in different proportions than men. For example, nearly half of women inmates have been sexually abused in the past versus only 12 percent of men.

general defenses Justifications or excuses for criminal conduct that are applicable to all criminal offenses.

general jurisdiction The jurisdiction of courts where most trials for felonies occur, as well as trials in major civil cases.

genetic risk assessment Technique that builds upon the discoveries in the area of DNA and genetic mapping, where genetic predispositions toward certain behaviors can be anticipated and prevented.

genocide Intentionally destroying an ethnic, racial, national, or religious group in a systematic manner.

good faith exception A rule stating that evidence seized with a defective warrant, not based on probable cause, is admissible in court if the police acted in good faith in presenting the evidence and the error was made by the judge.

good-time credits Small reductions in the time to be served, awarded to inmates for each day on which they obey prison rules.

grand jury A group of citizens who hear the evidence presented by a prosecutor to determine whether probable cause exists to hold a person for trial.

gross negligence Failure to perceive a substantial and unjustifiable risk when such failure is a gross deviation from the standard of care a reasonable person would observe.

group home Long-term nonsecure facilities that allow juveniles to attend school and employment in the community.

guideline sentences Sentences developed by examining the averages of past sentences imposed on various combinations of offenders and offenses and designed to achieve proportionality and uniformity without mandating specific sentences for certain crimes or offenders.

gun control Regulation of gun manufacturers, buyers, and sellers in an effort to minimize gun-related crime.

habitual offender laws Laws that subject multiple offenders to periods of incarceration ranging up to life imprisonment, on the grounds that they must be physically separated from society in order to protect society from their criminal conduct.

halfway houses Residential centers for ex-offenders in the community. Most halfway house residents are parolees or similar inmates near the end of their sentence.

hate crimes Offenses motivated by prejudice, usually against a particular race, religion, or sexual orientation.

High/Scope Perry Preschool Project, The A developmental program emphasizing intellectual and social development through active learning designed for children of low socioeconomic status and low IQ who are at high risk for failure in school.

hijacking The unauthorized seizure of a land vehicle, aircraft, or other conveyance while it is in transit.

house arrest A condition of probation or parole in which offenders are not permitted to leave their residences for purposes other than work, school, treatment, or other approved reasons.

identity fraud Manufacture and use of false identification and credit cards based on personal information stolen without the victim's knowledge.

ignorance of law A defense in which a defendant claims that a law is not widely known and that the person could not have been expected to be aware of it.

incapacitation Prevention of further criminal behavior by physically restraining the offender from engaging in future misconduct (usually through incarceration).

incarceration Segregation of offenders from the rest of the community in jails or prisons to rehabilitate, incapacitate, or punish them and to deter others from committing similar crimes.

Incredible Years training series A program offering behavior intervention techniques to assist parents and teachers living and working with children ages two to ten.

indeterminate sentencing A system of sentencing that empowers the judge to set a maximum sentence (up to the limit set by the legislature), and sometimes a minimum sentence, for the offender to serve in prison.

Index crimes The eight offenses tracked by the FBI's Crime Index.

indictment A formal accusation of a crime based on the vote of a grand jury.

information A formal accusation of a crime filed by a prosecutor based on the findings of a preliminary hearing.

injected or surgical implants An alternative to electronic bracelets that cannot be tampered with or defeated effectively, and that can be monitored via global positioning satellites (GPS).

insanity defense A claim that the defendant was not sane under law at the time of the act.

intensive supervision Probation or parole for which jurisdictions maintain small caseloads, make frequent contact with offenders under supervision, and require special conditions such as random drug tests, curfews, restitution to victims, electronic monitoring, or house arrest.

intention Conscious purposiveness in conduct; a factor in the determination of criminal responsibility.

intermediate sanctions Sentences designed to provide more rigorous supervision than normal probation, yet something less expensive than incarceration.

Interpol The International Criminal Police Organization composed of 177 member nations. It assists member law enforcement agencies requiring information about crimes or criminals of a transnational nature.

intimate partner violence Physical assaults between current or former spouses, boyfriends, or girlfriends.

jails Facilities operated by counties and municipalities to hold two main categories of inmates: those awaiting trial and those serving sentences of one year or less.

judge A person who objectively assesses the strength of a case, rules on issues of law and procedure, and in many cases determines the disposition of a case.

judicial review The U.S. Supreme Court's authority to review the constitutionality of acts of Congress.

jurisdiction The authority of a state, county, or city to apply its own laws within its own territory.

jury nullification Acquittal of a defendant despite facts that show guilt.

jury trial A trial in which the jury determines guilt or innocence.

justice The title of the judges of an appellate court.

justice of the peace An office established by Edward II in 1326 to assist the sheriff in enforcing the law. Eventually the role of the justice of the peace shifted to adjudication, while the sheriffs retained their local peacekeeping function.

justification defenses Defenses that admit to the criminal conduct, but claim it was justified by overwhelming circumstances, such as self-defense.

labeling theory View that adjudicating a juvenile as a delinquent encourages future delinquency through a negative public identity or changed self- image.

larceny Taking property of another person with the intent of depriving the owner.

Law Enforcement Assistance Administration (LEAA) Established in 1968, the LEAA was set up within the U.S. Department of Justice to allocate money to improve the efficiency and effectiveness of the criminal justice system. Between 1968 and 1977 the LEAA spent more than $6 billion on crime control programs and college education for police officers.

legalization Legislative decision to remove a prohibited behavior from the criminal law.

limited jurisdiction The jurisdiction of courts that have narrow legal authority over specific types of matters (e.g., surrogate court, tax court).

local jails Facilities used to detain adults awaiting trial and offenders serving sentences of one year or less.

local police The police departments of municipalities; local law enforcement also includes county sheriffs and special police agencies such as park, airport, transit, and university police.

mala in se Acts considered evil in themselves (e.g., assault and theft).

mala prohibita Acts considered undesirable although not inherently evil (e.g., drug use).

malfeasance A form of police corruption involving commission of an illegal act.

mandatory sentences Fixed sentences for offenders convicted of certain types of crimes such as gun-related crimes, drug offenses, and drunk-driving offenses.

manslaughter A mitigated murder: causing a death recklessly, or intentionally under extenuating circumstances.

maximum security Prisons usually with a wall surrounding the entire facility that house dangerous felons (about 26 percent of all inmates are incarcerated in such institutions).

maxing out Release from incarceration after the offender has served the entire sentence without ever being granted parole or accumulating enough good-time credits to justify early release.

media portrayals Public perceptions of crime and its victims are based largely on media images which focus on atypical sensational incidents.

mediation A process providing a forum in which the offender and the victim meet in a neutral setting where they can ask questions, communicate feelings of anger or remorse, and discuss ways in which the balance of justice can be restored in a fair and equitable manner; this may involve an apology, restitution, community service, or other alternative.

medium security Prisons that have some facilities outside the main enclosure and are surrounded by two rows of chain-link fence, topped with barbed wire (half of all inmates are serving time in these institutions).

mens rea The "guilty mind" or conscious decision to commit a criminal act.

mental health courts Specialized courts that focus on treatment and rehabilitation of mentally ill offenders who land in the criminal justice system.

merit selection A method for selecting judges that involves a combination of appointment and election.

metropolitan correctional centers (detention centers) Federal jail facilities for pretrial detention and for those serving short sentences.

minimum security Prison facilities that usually have no fences but have locking outside doors and electronic surveillance devices around the perimeter of the institution (about 23 percent of all inmates are in these institutions).

***Miranda* warning** A five-point warning derived from the case of *Miranda v. Arizona.* Its purpose is to provide fair notice to crime suspects of their basic constitutional rights.

misdemeanors Less serious crimes that are punishable by imprisonment for one year or less.

misfeasance A form of police corruption involving failure to perform a legal duty in a proper manner.

Missouri's parallel universe An effort by Missouri corrections to prepare inmates for release by engaging them in full-time work activities that imitate the outside world.

mistake of fact A defense in which a person claims that honest ignorance rules out the presence of a "guilty mind."

mistrial A trial that has been declared invalid because of a substantial error in law or procedure.

money laundering A method of "washing" illegally obtained money (e.g., from drugs or gambling proceeds) by making it appear as if the money were earned legally as part of a legitimate business.

multijurisdictional task forces Multiagency efforts to combat multijurisdictional crimes allowing for pooling of evidence, personnel, and expertise and to reduce unnecessary duplication of effort.

murder All intentional killings, as well as deaths that occur in the course of dangerous felonies.

mutual pledge system A system of community self-responsibility that existed in Britain during the Middle Ages, in which residents were held responsible for the conduct of their neighbors.

National Crime Victimization Survey (NCVS) A representative sample of the U.S. population is surveyed annually to determine the extent of victimization and the extent to which these incidents were reported to police.

National Incident-Based Reporting System Data collection program designed to gather information on victims, perpetrators, and circumstances of crime.

National Longitudinal Survey of Youth Self-report study investigating the extent of delinquency among young people.

National Violence Against Women (NVAW) Survey Interviews a national sample of 16,000 men and women regarding the circumstances of crimes against women.

necessarily included offenses ("Lesser" included offenses); offenses that are, by definition, included in a charge as part of another (more serious) offense.

necessity A defense in which a person claims to have engaged in otherwise criminal behavior because of the forces of nature.

negligence Failure to be aware of a substantial and unjustifiable risk.

net widening Process by which more offenders end up being placed under supervision of the criminal justice system even though the intent of a program was to divert offenders out of the system.

nolle prosequi A decision by a prosecutor not to press charges; also known as nol. pros.

nonfeasance A form of police corruption involving failure to perform a legal duty.

norms Social expectations about what constitutes appropriate behavior under different circumstances.

obstruction of justice Intentionally preventing a public servant from lawfully performing an official function.

offender accountability An approach to illegal behavior that makes offenders aware of the damage, loss, or injury they cause and their responsibility for it.

offender profiles Examination of offender backgrounds (e.g., physical and social characteristics, prior history, and method of conduct) to look for common patterns.

offenses against morality Acts considered undesirable, such as adultery and fornication, prostitution, and gambling.

official misconduct The unauthorized exercise of an official function by a public official with intent to benefit or injure another.

ordinances Laws that apply to a specific county, city, or town.

organized crime A continuing criminal enterprise that rationally works to profit from illicit activities that are often in great public demand. Its continuing existence is maintained through the use of force, threats, monopoly control, and/or the corruption of public officials.

overcriminalization Blurring the distinction between crime and merely inappropriate or offensive behaviors.

pardon A reprieve from a governor or from the president that excuses a convicted offender and allows release from prison without any supervision.

parens patriae (the state acts as a parent) The view that juvenile law violations are a sign that parents cannot or will not take care of their child adequately and that it is up to the state to step in and act in his or her best interests, thus preventing future misbehavior.

parole A phase of the criminal justice system in which an offender completes the end of a prison sentence under supervision in the community.

parole release Prisoner release decided by a parole board consisting of corrections officials and/or political appointees who evaluate the inmate's record and his or her behavior in prison to determine whether the inmate will be released to serve the remainder of the sentence under community supervision.

penitentiaries Maximum security federal correctional institutions.

Pennsylvania system A philosophy of imprisonment that promoted repentance through solitary confinement and prevented offenders from being corrupted by mixing with other offenders.

perjury Making a false statement under oath in an official proceeding.

personal risk An individual's risk of being a victim of crime; determined through calculation of crime rates in relation to population.

plea A statement of innocence or guilt.

plea bargaining An agreement by a prosecutor to press a less serious charge, drop some charges, or recommend a less severe sentence if the defendant agrees to plead guilty.

police brutality Use of excessive physical force by police in carrying out their duties.

police corruption Illegal acts or omissions of acts by police officers who, by virtue of their official position, receive (or intend to receive) any gain for themselves or others.

police discretion The ability to choose between arrest and nonarrest solely on the basis of the officer's judgment.

police pursuits Police chases of suspects immediately after a crime has been committed.

police stress Emotional pressure that is produced by the nature of police work such as public apathy, exposure to criminals, and injury to fellow officers.

policing Enforcing the law by apprehending violators and thereby protecting citizens. Crime prevention and social services such as education of the public are more recent emphases in law enforcement.

political crimes Acts viewed as a threat to the government.

positivism The perspective in criminology that sees human behavior as determined by internal and external influences, such as biological, psychological, and/or social factors.

precedents Previous court decisions that are followed in current cases to ensure consistency in the application of the law.

predispositional model The view that the attitudes and values of police officers are developed prior to entry into the law enforcement profession.

presentence investigation An investigation by the probation department that seeks information regarding the offender's personal and social background, criminal record, and any other information that may help the judge match the sentence to the offender.

presentence report A report conducted by a probation officer into an offender's background to assist the judge in determining an appropriate sentence.

pretrial intervention (PTI) A type of diversion program in which a prosecutor suspends prosecution of a case pending the fulfillment of special conditions by the defendant. If these conditions are met, the case is dismissed.

pretrial settlement conference A meeting of the prosecutor, defendant, counsel, and judge to discuss a plea before a trial is held. No plea negotiations can take place outside this setting.

preventive police The first organized police department in London, established in 1829. The popular English name for police officers, "bobbies," comes from Sir Robert Peel, a founder of the Metropolitan Police.

prisonsers with mental health problems More than half of offenders in prisons, jails, and on probation were identified as mentally ill.

private security Law enforcement agencies that protect private property and are paid by private individuals and corporations.

probable cause A reasonable link between a specific person and a particular crime; the legal threshold required before police can arrest or search an individual.

probation A system under which a person convicted of a crime serves a sentence in the community under the supervision of a probation officer.

procedural law The rules for adjudication of individuals suspected of violating the law.

professionalization Those changes in police organization, administration, and technology aimed at improving the efficiency of the police in the deterrence and apprehension of criminals.

progressivism Early twentieth-century era in policing that focused on efficiency, professionalism, and improved technology.

prosecutors Elected or appointed officials who represent the community in bringing charges against an accused person.

psychoanalytic theory Freudian theory that sees behavior as resulting from the interaction of the three components of the personality: id, ego, and superego.

public defenders Salaried attorneys paid by the government to represent indigents charged with crimes.

public safety exception Police may omit the *Miranda* warning prior to questioning a suspect when public safety is jeopardized.

punishment and control by distance A corrections approach that includes electronic monitoring, probation kiosks, and camera and satellite surveillance to partially restrict offenders' freedom of movement and to deprive them of some portion of their liberty.

racial profiling Alleged practice whereby police stop and search minorities for minor violations significantly more often than whites.

racketeering An ongoing criminal enterprise that is maintained through a pattern of criminal activity.

ranch, forestry camp, or farm A long-term nonsecure setting for adjudicated juveniles.

rape Sexual intercourse without effective consent.

rational choice theories Theories that examine how circumstances affect criminal thinking to explain why offenders commit crimes in some situations but not in others.

reasonable suspicion A situation in which a police officer has good reason to believe that criminal activity may be occurring; this permits a brief investigative inquiry of the suspect.

reasonableness standard A standard under which persons are culpable for their actions if they understand the consequences of those actions. Young children and the mentally ill are generally not held culpable owing to their inability to reason effectively.

reception/diagnostic center A short-term facility that screens sentenced juveniles for assignment to an appropriate level of custody.

recidivism Repeat offenses by an offender.

recklessness Conscious disregard of a substantial and unjustifiable risk.

reformatory movement Late nineteenth-century trend toward use of incarceration to reform through education.

regulatory offenses Activities of a business or corporation that are viewed as attempts to circumvent regulations designed to ensure fairness and safety in the conduct of business; include administrative, environmental, labor, and manufacturing violations as well as unfair trade practices.

rehabilitation The view that sees criminal behavior as stemming from social or psychological shortcomings; the purpose of sentencing is to correct or treat these shortcomings in order to prevent future crimes.

responsibility model Prison management approach that gives inmates more autonomy; staff guides prisoners' decision making rather than making all decisions for them.

restitution A form of restorative justice that usually takes the form of money, but it can also include returning property or performing services for the victim.

restorative justice Criminal justice process that focuses on sanctions directed primarily at repairing the injury to the victim rather than focusing on the adversarial relationship between the government and the offender.

retribution Punishment applied simply in proportion to the seriousness of the offense.

retributive model of justice Traditional approach to criminal justice that emphasizes the role of adversarial proceedings and the government in punishing offenders for their past acts as retribution and deterrence.

right to counsel A Sixth Amendment protection that guarantees suspects the right to representation by an attorney when their liberty is in jeopardy.

risk assessment Classifying and evaluating offenders based on their characteristics, crimes, and backgrounds to determine the likelihood of reoffending.

robbery Theft from a person using threats or force.

routine activities theory The theory that sees criminal events as the result of a combination of a motivated offender, a suitable target, and the absence of a capable guardian to intervene.

sanctions Ways to punish or place restrictions on offenders.

scapegoating Unfairly blaming and punishing a person or group for crimes.

search An exploratory inspection of a person or property based on probable cause of law violation.

seizure Confiscation of property occurring when there is some meaningful interference with the individual's possession of property.

selective enforcement An unwritten policy in which police are not required to fully enforce all laws as written.

selective incapacitation Identification of potential high-rate offenders for incarceration for longer periods as a means of reducing crime.

sentencing A judge's decision as to what is to be the most appropriate punishment, given the type of crime and offender, and within a specified range established by law.

sexual assault Forced sex, whether vaginal, anal, or oral.

shelter A short-term nonsecure facility that operates like a detention center but within a physically unrestricted environment.

shire reeve An official appointed by the British Crown who was responsible for overseeing the constables and several hundred families in a given area (called a "shire"). The modern word *sheriff* is derived from this term.

shock incarceration Short-term military-style "boot camps" designed primarily for nonviolent young offenders and featuring a military atmosphere and strict discipline.

simple assault A thrust against another person with the intention of injuring that person.

social bond Individual's attachment to society, including attachment to others, commitment to conventional activities, involvement in those activities, and belief in widely shared moral values.

socialization model The view that holds that police officers learn their attitudes and values from socializing experiences such as education and experience on the job.

Speedy Trial Act Legislation requiring that all criminal cases be brought to trial within one hundred days.

state police Enforcement agencies primarily engaged in highway patrol activities. About half of state police agencies also have the authority to conduct investigative work.

status offenses Undesirable behaviors that are unlawful only for juveniles, including habitual truancy, curfew violations, repeated running away, and ungovernability or incorrigibility in failing to respond to the reasonable requests of parents.

statutes Specific laws passed by legislatures that prohibit or mandate certain acts.

statutory rape Nonforcible sexual intercourse with a minor.

structural/conflict view The perspective that sees the criminal law as reflecting the will of those in power, and behaviors that threaten the interests of the powerful are punished most severely.

study release A program similar to work release, in which an inmate attends school by day and returns to jail or prison at night.

substantive criminal law Law defining the specific behaviors prohibited under the criminal law.

summons A written notice to appear in court.

surety Bail posted by a bondsman on behalf of an arrestee.

suspended sentence A delayed imposition of a prison sentence that requires the offender to fulfill special conditions such as alcohol, drug, or gambling treatment or payment of restitution.

synnomie The sharing of values to the point of harmonious accommodation of divergent views.

technocorrections The use of technology to monitor offenders and to prevent future crimes.

terrorism Offenses designed to intimidate or coerce a government or civilians in furtherance of political or social objectives.

therapeutic community model Prison drug treatment approach based on the notion that a person's attitudes, values, and self-esteem must change together with the targeted drug use behavior in order to create lasting change.

"three strikes" laws Laws under which conviction for a third felony results in an extended sentence, up to life imprisonment.

trafficking in humans The smuggling of women and children from their home countries, usually for purposes of sexual exploitation.

training school A long-term secure facility for adjudicated juveniles.

transnational crime Offenses in which the planning and execution of the crime involve more than one country.

transnational law enforcement International agreements and law enforcement efforts that attempt to serve the interests of all nations in the face of the growth of international travel, the transnational nature of the Internet, and the threat of international organized crime and terrorism.

trial jury A group of citizens (usually twelve) who decide on the guilt or innocence of a defendant.

truth in sentencing A sentencing provision that requires offenders to serve the bulk of their sentence (usually 85 percent) before they can be released.

U.S. courts of appeals Intermediate federal appellate courts.

U.S. district courts Federal trial courts of general jurisdiction.

U.S. magistrates Judges appointed by U.S. district court judges to conduct pretrial hearings and trials for minor civil and criminal offenses in federal court.

U.S. Supreme Court The highest court in the United States, which hears final appeals in cases involving federal law, suits between states, and interpretations of the U.S. Constitution.

Uniform Crime Reports (UCR) An annual compilation by the FBI of all crimes reported to the police in the United States.

universality of crime There is no society that has not reported problems with crime and what to do with offenders, but there is considerable variation among crime rates in different societies.

victim impact statements Statements by victims to the judge before sentencing about how the crime has harmed them.

victim profiles Examination of a large number of similar criminal incidents to find patterns in the types of persons who are victimized under certain circumstances.

Victim's Bill of Rights Legal changes that formally recognize the role and rights of victims in the justice process.

victimless crimes Offenses in which the "offender" and the "victim" are the same individual or in which the behavior is consensual.

vigilantism Seeking justice through lawless violence.

virtual prison An offender monitoring system in which the offender wears an ankle bracelet and a wireless tracking device that is monitored using Global Positioning Satellites (GPS) and the cellular network.

war crimes Violations of law committed in excess of the brutality of the war itself.

warrant A sworn statement by police that attests to the existence of probable cause in a given case; it is signed by a judge who agrees with the officers' assessment of the facts.

watch and ward system A system established in England in 1285 to aid constables in their law enforcement efforts. Men from each town were required to take turns standing watch at night. Crime suspects were turned over to the constable.

Weed and Seed Federal programs that combine enforcement with community services in an effort to reduce crime in targeted neighborhoods.

white-collar crimes Crimes of fraud, crimes against public administration, and regulatory offenses that are usually carried out during the course of a legitimate occupation.

work release Program that permits eligible inmates to work during the day at regular jobs in the outside world, returning to the jail or prison at night.

writ of certiorari A legal order from the U.S. Supreme Court stating that a lower court must forward the record of a particular case for review.

Name Index

Subject Index

Credits

Chapter 1 p. 0: Joel Gordon Photography; p. 3: ANA/The Image Works; p. 4: AP Images/Bill Janscha/; p. 6: Jana Birchum/The Image Works; p. 7: Ed Kashi/CORBIS; p. 11: Jack Carey/Alamy Images; p. 14: Ron Jaffe/CBS-TV/The Kobal Collection/Picture Desk, Inc.; p. 15: Brown Brothers; p. 17: North Wind Picture Archives.

Chapter 2 p. 23: AP Images/Gerald Herbert; p. 29: Marty Heitner/The Image Works; p. 30: Corbis Royalty Free; p, 32: AP Images/Jay Drowns; p. 34: Fran May/Taxi/Getty Images; p. 36: David Young-Wolff/PhotoEdit Inc.; p. 39: Content Mine International/Alamy Images; p. 41: Corbis Royalty Free; p. 46: Photodisc/Getty Images.

Chapter 3 p. 54: Joshua Lott/Bloomberg News /Landov; p. 59: ArenaPal/Topham/The Image Works; p. 61: Syracuse Newspapers/David Lassman/The Image Works; p. 62: AP Images/Reed Saxon; p. 63: Brian Palmer/Corbis/Sygma; p. 70: Kim Kulish/CORBIS; p. 72: Spencer Grant/PhotoEdit Inc.; p. 73: Syracuse Newspapers/Dennis Nett/The Image Works; p. 74: Jerry/Express News/Corbis/Sygma.

Chapter 4 p. 78: Bill Greenblatt/UPI/Newscom; p. 82: Ian Thraves/Alamy Images; p. 83: DAYTONA BEACH NEWS JRNL/Corbis/Sygma; p. 90: Columbia/Marvel/Kobel Collection/The Picture Desk; p. 92: Rhoda Sidney/Stock Boston.

Chapter 5 p. 97: Joos Mind/Taxi/Getty Images; p. 101: Joel Gordon Photography; p. 102: Sonda Dawes/The Image Works; p. 104: The Image Works/Mary Evans Picture Library Ltd; p. 105: North Wind Picture Archives; p. 106: North Wind Picture Archives; p. 108: 20th Century Fox TV/David E. Kelly/Picture Desk, Inc./Kobal Collection; p. 110: Roy Morsch/CORBIS; p. 113: Larry Rubenstein/Corbis/Bettmann; p. 114: AP Images/Mark Hertzberg; p. 115: Melanie Stetson Freeman/The Christian Science Monitor/ Getty Images; p. 120: David McNew/Getty Images; p. 121: Dave Porter/Alamy Images; p. 122: Steve Liss/Corbis/Sygma.

Chapter 6 p. 128: Monika Graff/The Image Works; p. 131: Matthew Cavanaugh/epa/CORBIS; p. 135: Mikael Karlsson/ Arresting Images; p. 137: Michael Newman/PhotoEdit Inc.; p. 139: AP Images/Lisa Poole; p. 141: Syracuse Newspapers/Carl J. Single/The Image Works; p. 143, left: Joel Gordon Photography; p. 143, right: Larry Mulvehill/The Image Works; p. 146: PhotoFest.

Chapter 7 p. 151: Mark Richards/PhotoEdit Inc.; p. 154: Paul J. Richards/Getty Images, Inc.—Agence France Presse; p. 157: Al Campanie/Syracuse Newspapers/The Image Works; p. 159: Carlos Barria/Reuters/Coris; p. 162: Arthur Turner/Alamy Images; p. 163: Joel Gordon Photography; p. 164: Carlos Cazalis/Getty Images, Inc.—Agence France Presse; p. 168: Universal TV/Kobal Collection/The Picture Desk; p. 169: Mikael Karlsson/Arresting Images; p. 170: Mikael Karlsson/Arresting Images.

Chapter 8 p. 178: Dwayne Newton/PhotoEdit Inc.; p. 183, top: PhotoFest; p. 183, bottom: Corbis/Bettmann; p. 185: NMPFT/ Daily Herald Archive/SSPL/The Image Works; p. 187: David Fenton/Getty Images; p. 192: Kari Marttila/Alamy Images; p. 193: Ramin Talaie/CORBIS; p. 196: Dung Vo Trung/Corbis/Sygma; p. 197: Ed Kashi/CORBIS; p. 199: Najlah Feanny/Corbis/Sygma; p. 200: Ken Stewart/Newscom; p. 204: Michael Newman/ PhotoEdit Inc.; p. 205: CBS-TV/The Kobal Collection/Picture Desk, Inc.; p. 208: Frank Ordo-ez/Syracuse Newspapers/The Image Works.

Chapter 9 p. 218: AP Images/Tammy McKinley; p. 221: Jeff Greenberg/Alamy Images; p. 223: Jeff Greenberg/The Image Works; p. 225: Mikael Karlsson/Arresting Images; p. 227: Dylan Martinez/Reuters/Corbis; p. 229: Mitch Wojnarowicz/Amsterdam Recorder/The Image Works; p. 232: Brand X Pictures/Alamy Royalty Free Images; p. 236: Mitch Wojnarowicz/The Image Works; p. 237: Lucy Nicholson/Getty Images, Inc.—Agence France Presse; p. 241: COLUMBIA TRI STAR/The Kobal Collection/Picture Desk, Inc.; p. 243: Stephen Argicola/The Image Works; p. 245: AP Images/Justin Sullivan; p. 247: REED SAXON/Getty Images, Inc.—Agence France Presse.

Chapter 10 p. 257: AP Images/Susan Walsh; p. 267: Bob Daemmrich/PhotoEdit Inc.; p. 269: Joel Gordon Photography; p. 271: Bob Daemmrich/The Image Works; p. 273: Comstock Images/Alamy Royalty Free Images; p. 277: COURT TV STILLS; p. 281: Michael Newman/PhotoEdit Inc.

Chapter 11 p. 288: AP Images/Stephen J. Carrera; p. 291: Corbis/Bettmann; p. 296: Corbis Sygma; p. 298: Michael Newman/PhotoEdit Inc.; p. 301: Douglas C. Pizac-Pool/Getty Images; p. 306: Michelle Bridwell/PhotoEdit Inc.; p. 308: Steve Earley/CORBIS; p. 309: Rick Maiman/Corbis Sygma.

Chapter 12 p. 317: Alcorn Jim/Corbis/Sygma; p. 321: Wilfredo Lee/Reuters/Corbis; p. 323: AP Images/Al Golub; p. 324: Michael Newman/PhotoEdit Inc.; p. 326: A. Ramey/PhotoEdit Inc.; p. 327: Spencer Grant/PhotoEdit Inc.; p. 334: Mikael Karlsson/Alamy Images; p. 337: Anrew Lichtenstein/Corbis Sygma; p. 338: WORKING TITLE/HAVOC/DEMMIE TODD/The Kobal Collection/Picture Desk, Inc.; p. 345: Paul Buck/Getty Images, Inc.—Agence France Presse; p. 347: AP Images/Ron Heflin.

Chapter 13 p. 356: Valentine Richmond History Center; p. 359: MPI/Getty Images; p. 360: AP Images/Rich Pedroncelli; p. 364: Joel Gordon Photography; p. 366: Peter Chen/Syracuse Newspapers/The Image Works; p. 367: A. Ramey/PhotoEdit Inc.; p. 371: Thinkstock/Alamy Royalty Free Images; p. 373: CASTLE ROCK ENTERTAINMENT/The Kobal Collection/Picture Desk, Inc.; p. 374: Mikael Karlsson/Arresting Images; p. 377: Sean Cayton/The Image Works; p. 380: A. Ramey/PhotoEdit Inc.; p. 381: AP Images/Joe Jines; p. 383: A. Ramey/Stock Boston.

Chapter 14 p. 390: A. Ramey/PhotoEdit Inc.; p. 393: Joel Gordon Photography; p. 396: Bob Daemmrich/The Image Works; p. 399: Bob Daemmrich/The Image Works; p. 401: David McNew/ Getty Images; p. 402: TOUCHSTONE/DAVID LEE/The Kobal Collection/Picture Desk, Inc.; p. 404: Najlah Feanny/Corbis/SABA Press Photos, Inc.; p. 406: Bob Daemmrich/The Image Works; p. 409: Mark Richards/PhotoEdit Inc.; p. 411: Journal Courier/The Image Works; p. 416: Joel Gordon Photography; p. 417: Joel Gordon Photography.

Chapter 15 p. 426: AP Images/Raleigh News & Observer; p. 429: Ian Cook/Time Life Pictures/Getty Images; p. 430: Ellen B. Senisi/The Image Works; p. 433: KTRK-TV VIA CNN/Getty Images, Inc.—Agence France Presse; p. 435: Joel Gordon Photography; p. 438: Joel Gordon Photography; p. 439: The Everett Collection; p. 441: Courtesy of The Incredible Years, www.incredibleyears.com.

Chapter 16 p. 448: Joel Gordon Photography; **p.** 455: Stephen Frisch/Stock Boston; p. 457: Jeff Greenberg/The Image Works; p. 459: Comstock Royalty Free; p. 461: AP Images/Jeff Kowalsky; p. 462: David Hoffman Photo Library/Alamy Images; p. 463: Richard Hutchings/PhotoEdit Inc.; p. 466: Michael Newman/ PhotoEdit Inc.; p. 468: Joel Gordon Photography; p. 469: AP Images/Craig Schreiner; p. 471: Hussein Akhtar/Corbis Sygma; p. 476: Joel Gordon Photography.

Chapter 17 p. 484: AP Images/Pat Sullivan; p. 488: Tony Freeman/PhotoEdit Inc.; p. 490: AP Images/Khue Bui; p. 492: Gabe Palmer/CORBIS; p. 493: Touchstone Pictures/David James/PhotoFest; p. 495: Comstock Premium/Alamy Royalty Free Images; p. 498: Dennis Brack/Bloomberg News/Landov LLC; p. 500: Corbis/Bettmann; p. 504: Stephen Morton/Bloomberg News/Landov LLC; p. 505: Vern Fisher/Sipa; p. 506: Bob Daemmrich/The Image Works; p. 512: YURI GRIPAS/ Reuters/Corbis; p. 513: Karen Bleier/Getty Images, Inc.—Agence France Presse.

Chapter 18 p. 518: AP Images; p. 520: AP Images/David Guttenfelder; p. 522: AP Images/Ryan Remiorz; p. 525: Corbis Royalty Free; p. 526: UNIVERSAL/Jonathan Olley/The Kobal Collection/Picture Desk, Inc.; p. 527: STR/Getty Images, Inc.— Agence France Presse; p. 529: AP Images/Sayyid Azim; p. 530: Richard Wareham Fotografie/Alamy Images; p. 534: LIONS GATE/ The Kobal Collection/Picture Desk, Inc.; p. 535: JUAN VRIJDAG/ Getty Images, Inc.—Agence France Presse; p. 537: Jeff Hutchens/Getty Images.